Canadian POLITICS

Canadian POLITICS

CRITICAL APPROACHES

3rd EDITION

Rand Dyck
Laurentian University

Nelson
Thomson Learning

Australia • Canada • Denmark • Japan • Mexico • New Zealand • Philippines
Puerto Rico • Singapore • South Africa • Spain • United Kingdom • United States

1120 Birchmount Road
Scarborough, Ontario M1K 5G4
www.nelson.com
www.thomson.com

Statistics Canada information is used with the permission of the Minister of Industry, as Minister responsible for Statistics Canada. Information on the availability of the wide range of data from Statistics Canada can be obtained from Statistics Canada's Regional offices, its World Wide Web site at http://www.statcan.ca, and its toll-free access number 1-800-263-1136.

Canadian Cataloguing in Publication Data

Dyck, Rand, 1943–
      Canadian politics : critical approaches

3rd ed.
Includes bibliographical references and index.
ISBN 0-17-616792-7

1. Canada – Politics and government.   I. Title.

JL75.D93 2000   320.971   C99-932556-6

Editorial Director	Evelyn Veitch
Acquisitions Editor	Nicole Gnutzman
Marketing Manager	Don Thompson
Project Editor	Jenny Anttila
Production Editor	Bob Kohlmeier
Copy Editor	Jim Leahy
Proofreader	Sarah Weber
Production Coordinator	Hedy Later
Art Direction	Suzanne Peden
Cover Design	Liz Harasymczuk
Cover Image	Masterfile
Composition Analyst	Elaine Andrews
Printer	Webcom

Printed and bound in Canada

   2   3   4   03 02 01 00

To the memory of Jackie

Brief Contents

Preface   xxi

PART 1   INTRODUCTION
Chapter 1   Approaching the Study of Politics   3
Chapter 2   The Historical Context and Institutional Foundations   23

PART 2   THE SOCIETAL CONTEXT
Chapter 3   Regional Economic Cleavages   39
Chapter 4   Canada's Aboriginal Peoples   63
Chapter 5   The French–English Cleavage and the Quebec Question   83
Chapter 6   Other Ethnic Groups and Multiculturalism   105
Chapter 7   Gender and Politics   119
Chapter 8   Class Cleavages   139
Chapter 9   The United States and the Global Environment   167

PART 3   LINKING PEOPLE TO GOVERNMENT
Chapter 10   The Canadian Political Culture   199
Chapter 11   Political Socialization, the Mass Media, and Public Opinion Polls   229
Chapter 12   Elections and the Electoral System   257
Chapter 13   Political Parties and the Party System   283
Chapter 14   Parties, Voting, and the Election Campaign   319
Chapter 15   Pressure Groups and Lobbying   341

PART 4   THE CONSTITUTIONAL CONTEXT
Chapter 16   The Canadian Constitution and Constitutional Change   373
Chapter 17   The Provinces and the Federal System   399
Chapter 18   The Charter of Rights and Freedoms   429

PART 5   GOVERNING
Chapter 19   Governing: The Policymaking Process and Policy Instruments   459
Chapter 20   The Executive: Crown, Prime Minister, and Cabinet   475
Chapter 21   The Bureaucracy   511
Chapter 22   Parliament   545
Chapter 23   The Judiciary   585

PART 6   CONCLUSION
Chapter 24   Conclusion   611
Glossary   619
Appendixes   643
Index   661

Contents

Preface   xxi

PART 1   INTRODUCTION   1
Chapter 1   **Approaching the Study of Politics**   3
The Political System   3
Approaches to the Study of Politics   9
The Pluralist Approach   10
The Public Choice Approach   12
Class Analysis   14
The State-Centred Approach   16
An Amalgam Model   18
Discussion Questions   20
Notes   21
Further Reading   22

Chapter 2   **The Historical Context and Institutional Foundations**   23
Early Settlement and Political Institutions   23
The Road to Confederation   25
Fusing the British Parliamentary System with American Federalism   26
Principles of the Canadian Constitution   31
The Road to Canadian Sovereignty   32
Conclusion   34
Discussion Questions   35
Notes   35
Further Reading   36

PART 2   THE SOCIETAL CONTEXT   37
Chapter 3   **Regional Economic Cleavages**   39
Distance and Division   39
Physiographic Regions   39
Transportation and Communications Systems   41
Population Distribution   44
Provinces and Territories   46
Regional Economic Differences   47
The Atlantic Provinces   48
Quebec   49
Ontario   49
The Prairie Provinces   49
British Columbia   50
The North   50
Regional Demands   51
Regional Economic Conflicts   51

Ownership of Natural Resources   51
Tariffs   52
Transportation   52
Banking   52
Taxation and Regulation of Natural Resources   53
Metropolitan Exploitation of the Hinterland   53
The Atlantic Provinces   54
Routine Regional Conflicts   55
Regional Economic Disparities   56
Equalization Payments   56
Regional Economic Development Programs   58
Conclusion   59
Discussion Questions   61
Notes   61
Further Reading   62

Chapter 4   Canada's Aboriginal Peoples   63
Historical Evolution   63
Aboriginal Demographic Profile Today   66
Aboriginal Political Issues since 1970   68
Land Issues   69
Governance Issues   73
Conclusion   79
Discussion Questions   80
Notes   80
Further Reading   81

Chapter 5   The French–English Cleavage and the Quebec Question   83
Historical Overview of French–English Relations   83
Pre-Confederation Developments   83
Post-Confederation Ethnic/Linguistic Conflicts   85
The French–English Demographic Profile in Canada Today   87
The Quiet Revolution: Quebec in the 1960s   88
Changes in Quebec   88
Federal Responses   89
The Separatist Option   91
Quebec in the 1970s, 1980s, and 1990s   91
The 1970s   91
The 1980s   92
The 1990s   93
French–English Relations in the Other Provinces   94
New Brunswick   95
Ontario   95
Manitoba   96
Other Provinces and Territories   96
French–English Relations in the New Millennium   97
Conclusion   98
Discussion Questions   100
Notes   100
Further Reading   102

Chapter 6   Other Ethnic Groups and Multiculturalism   105
Canadian Immigration Patterns   105
A Profile of Ethnic Minorities in Canada Today   108
Discrimination against Immigrants   109
Multiculturalism and Equity   110
Reaction against Multiculturalism and Immigration   113
Conclusion   115
Discussion Questions   117
Notes   117
Further Reading   118

Chapter 7   Gender and Politics   119
Evolution of Women's Rights to 1970   119
The Women's Movement after 1970   123
Representation in Politics and Government   *123*
Employment Issues   *125*
Constitutional, Legal, and Aboriginal Women's Issues   *128*
Reproduction, Sexuality, Health, and Violence Issues   *129*
The Feminization of Poverty, and Child Care   *130*
Women's Centres and Women's Groups   *130*
Other Gender Issues   131
Conclusion   133
Discussion Questions   134
Notes   134
Further Reading   136

Chapter 8   Class Cleavages   139
Defining Class   139
The Upper Class   141
Identifying the Corporate Elite   *141*
Demands of the Corporate Elite   *145*
The Middle Class   147
The Working Class   149
The Poor   153
The Rise of the Social Safety Net   155
The Demise of Social Programs   157
Class-Consciousness in Canada   159
Conclusion   160
Discussion Questions   161
Notes   161
Further Reading   164

Chapter 9   The United States and the Global Environment   167
The Global Setting   168
Foreign Governments   *168*
International Organizations   *168*
International Agreements   *170*
Transnational Corporations and Globalization   *171*
Global Influences in Defence and Foreign Policy   173
Defence Policy   *173*
Foreign Policy   *174*

Global Economic Influences on Canada 175
Foreign Investment 175
Trade 179
The Environment 182
Energy 183
Bond-Rating and Lending Agencies 183
Trade Unions 184
Global Influences on Canadian Culture 184
Broadcasting 184
Magazines 187
Film and Video 187
Publishing 188
Sound Recordings 189
Other 189
Global Influences on Other Aspects of Canadian Political Life 190
Conclusion 191
Discussion Questions 192
Notes 192
Further Reading 194

PART 3   LINKING PEOPLE TO GOVERNMENT   197
Chapter 10   The Canadian Political Culture   199
The Traditional Canadian Political Culture 200
Democracy 200
Distinguishing between Canadian and American Values 203
Other Basic Values 209
Canada's Changing Political Culture 211
"Limited Identities": Subcultures in Canada 213
Regional and Provincial Subcultures 213
Ethnic Subcultures 215
Class Subcultures 215
Other Subcultures 216
Political Participation 216
Electoral Participation 216
Nonelectoral Participation 219
Conclusion 221
Discussion Questions 223
Notes 223
Further Reading 226

**Chapter 11   Political Socialization, the Mass Media, and
Public Opinion Polls   229**
Political Socialization 230
The Family 230
The School 230
Peers 231
The Mass Media 232
Other Agents of Political Socialization 233
The Mass Media 234
Newspapers 235

Radio	*236*
Television	*236*
The Media and the Public	*239*
The Media and the Politicians	*241*
The Changing Media World	*243*
Public Opinion Polls	245
Measuring Public Opinion	*245*
Impact of Polls on the Public	*246*
Impact of Polls on the Authorities	*247*
Conclusion	248
Discussion Questions	250
Notes	251
Further Reading	254
Chapter 12 Elections and the Electoral System	**257**
The Redistribution Process	257
Distribution of Seats among Provinces	*257*
Drawing Constituency Boundaries	*258*
The Official Election Machinery	261
Setting the Date	*261*
Election Officials	*262*
The Voters' List	*262*
Nomination	*262*
Election Day	*263*
The Ballot	*263*
The Franchise	*264*
Evaluating the Electoral System	265
Discrepancies between Seats and Votes: National Level	*265*
Discrepancies between Seats and Votes: By Province	*267*
Remedies	*269*
Financing Elections	270
Pre-1974	*270*
The Legislation of 1974	*271*
The Results of the 1974 Legislation	*271*
Third-Party Advertising	*275*
The Royal Commission on Electoral Reform and Party Financing	*277*
A New Canada Elections Act	*278*
Conclusion	279
Discussion Questions	280
Notes	280
Further Reading	282
Chapter 13 Political Parties and the Party System	**283**
Historical Evolution of Canadian Parties	284
The First Party System, 1867–1921	*284*
The Second Party System, 1921–1957	*286*
The Third Party System, 1957–1993	*287*
The Fourth Party System, 1993–	*289*
Interpretations of the Canadian Party System	290
The Broker System	*290*

Class-Based Parties 291
One-Party Dominance 293
The Decline of Parties 293
Minor Parties 294
Party Organization 295
Party Membership 297
Party Leadership 298
Party Policymaking 301
General Structures and Operations 302
Party Ideology 306
Conclusion 311
Discussion Questions 312
Notes 313
Further Reading 315

Chapter 14 Parties, Voting, and the Election Campaign 319
The National Party Campaign 320
Party Headquarters and Pre-Writ Preparations 320
Election Strategy 322
Election Platform 323
The Leader's Tour 325
Media News Coverage 325
National Media Advertising 326
The Leaders' Debates 327
The Local Candidate Campaign 329
Nomination 329
The Local Campaign 329
Electoral Behaviour and Party Support 331
Conclusion 336
Discussion Questions 337
Notes 337
Further Reading 339

Chapter 15   Pressure Groups and Lobbying   341
The Array of Canadian Interest Groups 342
Business Groups 344
Nonbusiness Groups 346
Other Categorizations of Pressure Groups 346
Pressure Group Structures 349
Targets and Methods of Pressure Group Activity 350
The Bureaucracy 350
The Prime Minister and Cabinet 353
Parliament 354
Other Targets 355
Group Resources and Determinants of Success 357
Lobbying in Canada 359
Emergence of Modern Lobbying 359
Legalizing Lobbying: The Registration System 360
Lobbying Today 362
Defects in the System 364

Conclusion 365
Discussion Questions 366
Notes 367
Further Reading 369

PART 4   THE CONSTITUTIONAL CONTEXT   **371**
Chapter 16   **The Canadian Constitution and Constitutional Change**   **373**
Components of the Canadian Constitution 373
The Constitution Act, 1867 374
Amendments to the Constitution Act, 1867 375
British Statutes and Orders-in-Council 375
Organic Canadian Statutes 376
Constitution Act, 1982 376
Other Canadian Statutes 377
Judicial Decisions 377
Constitutional Conventions 378
The Quest for Constitutional Change 378
A Domestic Constitutional Amending Formula 379
A Constitutional Charter of Rights 381
The Quiet Revolution in Quebec 381
The Victoria Charter 381
The Constitution Act, 1982 383
The Meech Lake Accord 384
The Charlottetown Accord 387
The 1992 Referendum 389
Post-Charlottetown Constitutional Developments 391
Conclusion 393
Discussion Questions 394
Notes 395
Further Reading 396

Chapter 17   **The Provinces and the Federal System**   **399**
The Provincial Political Systems 400
The Confederation Settlement 402
Evolution of Canadian Federalism 404
Division of Powers 404
Federal–Provincial Finance 408
Federal Controls 415
Phases of Canadian Federalism 416
Canadian Federalism since 1984 420
The Social Union 421
Conclusion 422
Discussion Questions 424
Notes 425
Further Reading 427

Chapter 18   **The Charter of Rights and Freedoms**   **429**
Defining and Protecting Rights and Freedoms 429
En Route to the Charter 430
The Charter of Rights and Freedoms 432

The Reasonable Limits Clause 433
Fundamental Freedoms 434
Democratic Rights 436
Mobility Rights 437
Legal Rights 437
Equality Rights 440
Official Languages of Canada 441
Minority-Language Education Rights 442
Enforcement 442
General Provisions 442
Application of the Charter 443
The Notwithstanding Clause 443
Implications of Constitutionalizing the Charter of Rights 445
Conclusion 448
Discussion Questions 449
Notes 450
Further Reading 454

PART 5 GOVERNING 457
Chapter 19 **Governing: The Policymaking Process
and Policy Instruments** 459
Government in the New Millennium 459
The Policymaking Process 461
Initiation 461
Priority-Setting 463
Policy Formulation 463
Legitimation 464
Implementation 464
Interpretation 464
Policy Communities Revisited 465
Policy Instruments 467
Privatization of Conflict 467
Symbolic Response 467
Exhortation 467
Tax Expenditures 468
Public Expenditures 468
Regulation 468
Taxation 469
Public Ownership 469
State of Emergency 470
Conclusion 470
Discussion Questions 472
Notes 472
Further Reading 473

Chapter 20 **The Executive: Crown, Prime Minister, and Cabinet** 475
The Crown 475
The Governor General 476
Sources of the Crown's Powers 477
Discretionary Powers of the Crown 478

Other Functions of the Crown   479
Advantages and Disadvantages of the Monarchy   480
The Prime Minister and Cabinet   481
Powers of the Prime Minister and Cabinet   481
The Prime Minister   483
Composition of the Cabinet   488
Operation of the Cabinet   492
Central Agencies   497
The Memorandum to Cabinet and Expenditure Management System   500
Conclusion   503
Discussion Questions   504
Notes   505
Further Reading   508

Chapter 21   The Bureaucracy   **511**
Functions and Powers of the Bureaucracy   511
Government Departments   513
Number, Structure, and Size   513
Relations with Other Departments and Central Agencies   519
The Merit Principle and a Representative Bureaucracy   520
Political Activity   523
Collective Bargaining   523
The Estimates System   524
Departmental Interaction with Provinces and Pressure Groups   525
Crown Corporations   526
Administrative Agencies and Regulatory Tribunals   529
Controlling the Bureaucracy   532
Prime Minister, Ministers, and Cabinet   533
Bureaucrats Controlling Bureaucrats   533
House of Commons   533
The Judiciary   534
Ombudsmen   534
The Information Commissioner   534
Dysfunctions and Reform of the Bureaucracy   535
Dysfunctions of the Bureaucracy   535
Reform of the Bureaucracy: The New Public Management   536
Conclusion   539
Discussion Questions   540
Notes   541
Further Reading   543

Chapter 22   Parliament   **545**
Functions and Powers of the House of Commons   546
Composition of the House of Commons   547
The Parliamentary Timetable   548
The Typical Session   548
The Typical Week   549
Party Discipline   552
Caucus Meetings   555
Stages and Kinds of Legislation   555

Organization and Officers of the Commons   558
The Speaker   558
House Leaders, Party Whips, and Clerk   560
Voting   560
Speeches   561
The Committee System   561
Members' Services   563
Roles of Members of Parliament   565
The Government–Opposition Balance   566
Minority Government   567
Reform of the House of Commons   568
Purposes and Powers of the Senate   569
Composition of the Senate   570
Operation of the Senate   571
Senate Reform   576
Conclusion   578
Discussion Questions   579
Notes   580
Further Reading   582

Chapter 23   The Judiciary   **585**
The Function of Adjudication   585
Access to and Costs of Justice   587
Categories of Laws   588
Structure of the Courts   589
Provincial Courts   591
The Superior Trial Court   591
Provincial Courts of Appeal   592
The Federal Court of Canada   592
The Supreme Court of Canada   593
The Appointment of Judges   596
Retirement, Removal, and Independence of Judges   600
Conclusion   602
Discussion Questions   604
Notes   604
Further Reading   606

PART 6   CONCLUSION   **609**
Chapter 24   Conclusion   **611**
Critical, Realistic Reforms   612
Reducing the Incidence of Partisanship, Patronage, and Corruption   612
Loosening Party Discipline in the House of Commons   613
Supplying the Need for Stronger Politicians   614
Reforming the Electoral System   614
Reforming the Senate   615
Restricting Corporate Funding of Political Parties   615
Strengthening Political Parties   615
*Strengthening the Lobbyists Registration and
Access to Information Acts*   616
Improving Mass Media Coverage of Politics   616

Reversing Prime Ministerial Government   617
Notes   617

Glossary   619
Appendix A   Constitution Act, 1867 (excerpts)   643
Appendix B   Constitution Act, 1982, Schedule B   649
Index   661

Preface

This book presents the reality of Canadian government and politics in a concise but comprehensive manner. In its aim to be comprehensive, it includes all the traditional aspects of the subject—Parliament, Cabinet, federalism, elections, political parties, pressure groups, political culture, and so on—as well as those of more recent origin or interest, such as the mass media and public opinion polls, the judiciary, and the Charter of Rights and Freedoms. At the same time, the object is to present a lean account of the subject and to avoid unnecessary tangents or detail.

This text differs from its competitors in two principal ways. First, it gives greater emphasis to the societal setting of the political system, with chapters on regional economic cleavages, Aboriginal peoples, the French–English cleavage, other ethnic groups, gender, class, and the global environment. Second, it provides four analytical models with which to view the subject matter: the pluralist, public choice, class analysis, and state-centred approaches. The text refers to these four approaches wherever appropriate, and sets up an amalgamated analytical framework in which they all play a part. That framework takes from public choice theory the constant priority of those in power to enhance their chances of re-election; from class analysis, the inequality of political influence and the pervasive influence of capitalist values; from pluralism, the predominant influence, in a contest of floating coalitions of groups and interests, of business pressure groups; and from the state-centred model, the persistent influence of the bureaucracy.

As the troubled Canadian political system enters the new millennium, no text could be completely satisfied with the status quo. This book therefore points out aspects of the political and governmental operations of the country that are not working as well as they might, and suggests possible reforms and alternative arrangements, sometimes drawing on the experiences of other countries. Without being rigidly ideological, the book is a critical account, and seeks to make informed critics of its readers.

The preparation of this third edition gave me the opportunity to renew the acquaintance of many of those who assisted me in writing the earlier editions as well as to talk to a number of new sources of vital information. At the governmental level, this included officials in many government departments and agencies, especially from the Finance Department, Elections Canada, Statistics Canada, and Indian Affairs. Most federal government departments and agencies now have impressive and very helpful websites, which are easily accessed. Individuals who were particularly valuable included James Ross Hurley, John Walsh, and David Elder of the Privy Council Office; Claude Emery and James R. Robertson of the Library of Parliament; Aurèle Gervais, Peter Julian, Steve Coupland, and Nicole Mutter of the Liberal, NDP, PC, and Reform parties respectively; Ray Bonin, MP; and Gordon Quaiattini of Moorcroft Quaiattini Inc. Among the many research organizations and interest groups that gave me assistance, the Canadian Council on Social Development stood out. Here at Laurentian University, I acknowledge my indebtedness to my friends and colleagues Brian MacLean, Claude Vincent, Richard Théoret, Keith Sinclair, Osvaldo Croci, Bob Segsworth, Nicole Gagnier, the staff of the library, as well as Paul Seccaspina of Oracle Research.

The book is immensely better from having been vetted, in now three editions, by a variety of academics contacted by Nelson Thomson Learning. For this particular edition, John Carson, University of Toronto at Mississauga (Erindale); Christopher Dunn, Memorial University of Newfoundland; Avigail Eisenberg, University of British Columbia; Brenda O'Neill, University of Manitoba; Allan Tupper, University of Alberta; and particularly Jim Silver of the University of Winnipeg provided a large number of useful suggestions, although I do not hold them responsible for the results. The book is made much more readable too for its having been punctuated with creative and generous additions from Canada's leading cartoonists.

It is always a pleasure to deal with the people at Nelson. This edition was guided to publication by the talents and dedication of Nicole Gnutzman, Jenny Anttila, Bob Kohlmeier, Sue Peden, Elaine Andrews, and Joanne Sutherland.

As usual, my wife, Joan, provided the most supportive home environment that it is possible to imagine.

I thank all of these people most profoundly.

PART 1

Introduction

The introductory part of the book consists of two chapters. The first provides a general framework on which the rest of the book is built, and outlines a number of different approaches to the study of politics. These approaches reveal that the subject matter of political science is not all cut-and-dried factual material and that the same topic can be viewed from different perspectives. The second chapter explores the historical context of Canadian politics and sketches its institutional foundations. In particular, it deals with the aspects of the British and U.S. models that Canada chose as the basis for its own and establishes the institutional differences between the Canadian and U.S. systems of government.

Chapter 1

Approaching THE STUDY OF *politics*

Where does one start in the study of Canadian politics? How can the material be organized? How much of the material is of a factual nature, and how much is a matter of opinion? What different perspectives can be adopted in this study? These are the central questions addressed in this introductory chapter.

THE POLITICAL SYSTEM

Perhaps it is best to begin with the 30 million individuals who inhabit the territory called Canada. All of these individuals have an array of needs that they attempt to satisfy, ranging from water and food through security and friendship to self-esteem and self-fulfillment. These needs have been ranked by the psychologist Abraham Maslow into a hierarchy, some being more basic than others.[1] Political science sometimes lumps such needs together with interests, preferences, opinions, motivations, expectations, and beliefs, and calls them "wants." It is quite obvious that most of us spend much of our time trying to satisfy such needs or wants.

Most of us do so, in the first instance, by our own efforts, in pairs, in families, in organizations of all kinds, at work and at play, and do not automatically call for government support. At some point, however, we may begin to feel that the satisfaction of these needs or wants is beyond such personal, interpersonal, family, or group capacity, and come to the conclusion that the government should step in to help us. When we express the opinion that the government should take some action, we are converting a want into a "demand" and crossing the threshold between the **private** and **public sectors**.

We are thus introduced to the concept of **government**, which can be defined as the set of institutions that make and enforce collective, public decisions for a society. We must also deal with the concept of **power**, which is often defined in political science as the ability of one actor to impose its will on another, whether through force of personality or material inducement. Government, backed up by armed forces, police, and punishments, if necessary, possesses a particular kind of power called **coercion**. That is, the government has the ability to impose its will on us by means of sanctions or penalties. Indeed, as a general rule, *only* the government is allowed to use force or coercive power in society. But if we (or our ancestors) had a hand in the creation of such a government apparatus, as well as in the selection of the current governors, then we have in a sense agreed to be bound by its decisions, and we have cloaked it with "legitimacy." Such legitimate power is often called "authority," and a synonym for government is "the authorities." To some extent, we obey the government because of the threat or expectation of penalties if we do not, but we also obey because we accept government decisions to be binding on us and necessary for the general good. Think of stopping at a red light as an example.

Coming back to the definition of demands, therefore, we can say that a *demand* is the expression of opinion that some authoritative action be taken. What governments do is make and execute decisions for a society or formulate and enforce social or public policies.

Who are these authorities? As can be seen in the diagram of the political system in Figure 1.1, we usually divide them into four branches of government: the legislature, the executive, the bureaucracy, and the judiciary. The authoritative decision that a demand seeks can sometimes be made by a single branch of government. If the demand requires the adoption of a private bill—a company seeking incorporation, for example—then action of the legislative branch will be necessary. If an individual desires a patronage appointment or if a corporation wants a large monetary grant, then the political executive or Cabinet can respond to such entreaties. If the demand is for the provision of routine government services, such as disability benefits under the Canada Pension Plan, or for changes in technical regulations, then bureaucratic action will probably suffice. Finally, if the demand can only be settled by judicial interpretation or adjudication, then it should be addressed to the courts.

In many instances, however, the demand will require combined actions of any two of the executive, legislative, and bureaucratic branches, or even all three working together, such as in the formulation, passage, and implementation of a new law. The courts normally stand somewhat apart from the other three organs of government, operating on the principle of the

Figure 1.1   A Model of the Political System

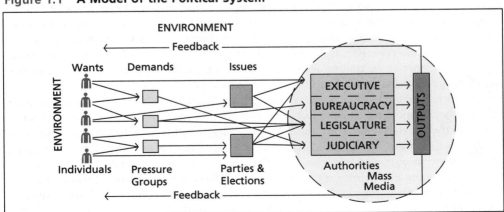

independence of the judiciary. Judicial decisions usually follow authoritative actions in other branches of government, such as when the Supreme Court threw out the abortion provisions of the Criminal Code. But they may also lead to subsequent legislative action, as when the government enacted an amendment to overturn a Supreme Court decision that had permitted an extreme state of intoxication to serve as an excuse for committing a sexual assault.

Authoritative decisions take many forms—laws, regulations, appointments, grants, contracts, services, and judgments—and are collectively referred to as the "outputs" of the political system. Authoritative decisions are also made in the provinces and in an assortment of regional and local councils and boards, and often require the agreement of two or more levels of government. Federal and provincial outputs can sometimes be in conflict, such as when the two levels pursue different spending strategies in dealing with government deficits during a recession.

Having encountered demands and authorities as two main parts of the political system, we must now discover how demands are transmitted from individuals to the government, as indicated in the model of the political system. This can be done on a personal basis, by means of a letter, fax, telephone call, e-mail, or face-to-face encounter. Sometimes such directly transmitted demands will achieve their desired result, but very often they will not. When they do not, it may be time to consider some kind of group action. Canadian society is replete with groups and social movements, and it is quite likely that a group already exists to articulate the concern that an individual decides to transmit. If such a group does not already exist, it may be worthwhile to create one since, as a general rule, the authorities are more likely to respond to a demand coming from a group than one from a single individual. Such groups are usually called *interest groups* or *pressure groups* and constitute an important part of Canadian political activity. The Canadian Chamber of Commerce and the Canadian Labour Congress are two prominent examples. Corporations and other institutions also make demands, either individually or in groups.

A special kind of group that is even more overtly political is the *political party*, and this instrument can also be used to transmit demands to the authorities. People join a political party or support it financially, and try to get it to recognize their concerns in its platform or policies. If the party forms the government (as the Liberals generally do), it can incorporate the demand into its decisions and government policy; if the party is in opposition (as is usually the case with the Conservatives and NDP), it may be able to bring the problem to national attention via the mass media. Parties are particularly responsive to such demands during an election campaign, seeking to attract the support of large numbers of individuals and groups by promising them the action they seek. Those dissatisfied with the manner in which existing parties are responding to their demands can create new parties, such as the Reform Party and the Bloc Québécois.

Another means of transmitting the demand to the authorities is, as suggested above, through the mass media of communication. The media are usually eager to publicize controversial issues and often delight in pointing out problems that the government has failed to resolve. The media give attention to individual and interest group concerns on a regular basis, cover political party activities, and are especially active in election campaigns. But the media are much more important than that. In providing the electorate with most of its information about politics and government, they shape the whole nature and quality of political discourse in Canada.

We have assumed thus far that any and all demands expressed actually reach the authorities. In fact, however, relatively few have any impact. Those that do not concern very many people or demands for action that is contrary to the values of the authorities of the day may be ignored. Governments have historically been much more sensitive to the views of the business community, for example, than to the concerns of Aboriginal peoples. Since the number of demands under serious consideration at any given time is such a small proportion of the total number being made, it is sometimes useful to distinguish between demands and "issues," the latter including only those that the authorities have taken under serious consideration or that have "registered."

The authorities are thus bombarded by demands, no matter what means are used to transmit them. What is more striking than the vast quantity of demands, however, is that there is usually intense conflict among them. The essence of politics and government, therefore, lies not only in making and executing decisions for society, but in having to choose among competing demands, in trying to resolve conflict, or in making social choices in the midst of social conflict. **Politics**, therefore, is said to originate in conflict, and is often defined as the struggle for power and the management of conflict. Here let us say it is activity in which conflicting interests struggle for advantage. It should also be added that the authorities can make their own demands, which may carry more weight than those arising from the wider society.

Demands are only one of two kinds of "inputs" in the system. The other is the concept of "support." This is not as concrete a phenomenon, but it is fairly evident as well. Support can be defined as a positive orientation toward something; as used in this context, three different parts of the system can be objects of support. First, one can support the government of the day, that is, the party and Cabinet that currently occupy the authoritative political positions (for example, the Chrétien Liberal government). Second, one can support the whole decision-making apparatus, or the constitutional principles and arrangements according to which decisions are being made. In this case, one might not support the government of the day, but still feel positively about the whole decision-making process. Most Canadians fall into this category most of the time. Third, one can support the political community called Canada. Again, one can do so without supporting the current government, or even without supporting the institutions it occupies. For example, an Albertan obsessed with Senate reform to articulate regional interests in federal institutions might support the political community without supporting the existing policymaking structures. On the other hand, a Quebec separatist would not support the political community of Canada.

Support is a more passive concept than demands, and usually exists in the realm of feelings and orientations rather than in action. Of course, action is involved in voting for one party or another on election day—in demonstrating support for the incumbent government or an opposition party. The act of voting is also a subtle indication of support for the decision-making structure and for the political community. But apart from voting (or standing at attention for the national anthem), support is mostly demonstrable in terms of such feelings as trust, efficacy, pride, and patriotism.

Whatever the type of output, it usually sparks a reaction in the rest of the system. This leads us to the concept of "feedback," that is, a communication of the outputs back into the system, in response to which the pattern of demands and support is altered. If an output satisfies a particular demand, then that demand will no longer have to be articulated. Think of the federal Official Languages Act silencing the demands for bilingualism. But the bilingualism issue also shows that the satisfaction of one demand may lead those involved to expect even more along

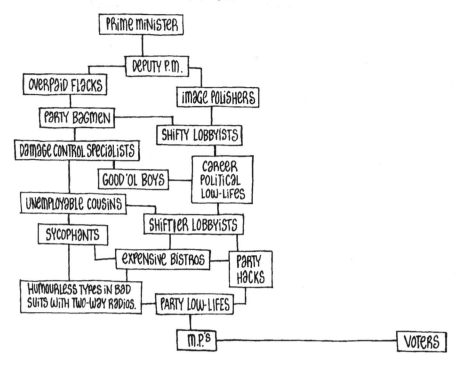

CANADA'S POLITICAL SYSTEM:

By Adrian Raeside (Victoria Times-Colonist). *Used with permission.*

the same lines: French-language services at the *provincial* as well as the *federal* level. On the other hand, a backlash may result: the Official Languages Act also promoted the articulation of contrary demands—protection for unilingual public servants, for example. Similarly, outputs affect support. Gratitude for the satisfaction of a demand will likely lead to increased levels of support, as shown by the relationship between the Mulroney government's Free Trade Agreement and the business community. On the other hand, those opposed to such an output will probably have less confidence in the authorities and the system, and their level of support will decline. The authorities will then respond in one way or another to this new pattern of demands and support, in the second stage of the feedback process.

By now we have established that the political system is a dynamic, circular, never-ending process in which the authorities react to demands and support, convert some of the demands into outputs, and then respond in turn to whatever changes in the pattern of inputs have resulted from the feedback from such outputs. Individuals and groups raise conflicting demands, but because there is a consensus on the legitimacy of the government, people generally abide by its authoritative decisions, even when they disagree with them. It is sometimes said, therefore, that politics and government are characterized by both conflict and consensus.

While the conflict is more evident, it normally operates within an underlying consensus about the decision-making apparatus and about remaining together as part of a united political community. Moreover, the authorities usually seek to develop some kind of consensus out of the conflicting demands.

One more part that must be added to the model we are constructing is the "environment" of the political system. This is an even more abstract concept than those encountered thus far, and can be defined as everything surrounding the political system. If the political system within a society is made up of all those actions and interactions concerned with the making of public policy, there also exist within the same society a geographic system (physical and human), an economic system, a social system, and perhaps many others. These other systems constitute the internal environment of the Canadian political system.

Most of these systems are characterized by internal divisions, and from these divisions springs the concept of "cleavages." A cleavage in political science terms is a deep, persistent division in society that has significant implications for the political system. The cleavages in Canadian society that most readily come to mind are between the geographic regions, between English, French, Aboriginal, and other ethnic and linguistic groups, and between various socioeconomic classes, as well as those related to gender, religion, and age. The relative importance and nature of these cleavages change over time.[2] While such cleavages are part of the environment of the political system, they can also be seen as the source of many of the demands expressed. In other words, demands can be said to originate from cleavages in the internal environment.

But there is also an external or global environment consisting of a huge number of international, multinational, transnational, and supranational factors, such as other states, international organizations, transnational corporations, and nongovernmental organizations (NGOs). In fact, in this age of **globalization**, such actors in the external environment increasingly serve both as the source of demands on national political systems and as constraints on domestic policymaking.

The model of the political system just described and illustrated in Figure 1.1 is designed to provide a framework for the study of government and politics in Canada. It is a simplified version of systems analysis, largely the work of Canadian political scientist David Easton,[3] which many of his colleagues find useful for organizing and explaining political phenomena.

Systems theory is closely related to a line of analysis called structural functionalism.[4] This approach begins with the identification of the "functions" that are or must be performed in any political system and then searches for the "structures" that perform them. Gabriel Almond postulated that seven basic functions are performed in any political system: interest articulation, interest aggregation, political socialization and recruitment, political communication, rule making, rule application, and rule adjudication. The last three of these generally correspond to the traditional functions of government as performed by the legislature, executive, and judiciary, but it may be useful to express such functions in less specific terms. Interest articulation consists essentially of making demands, while interest aggregation refers to the process of combining, consolidating, and narrowing the demands that are being expressed into manageable proportions or issues. Political socialization is the process of acquiring, teaching, or inculcating political values, attitudes, and opinions, a function that every political system finds necessary for its continued operation; political recruitment is the process of selecting political leaders, another obvious necessity. Political communication is a more general function of transmitting information among the various participants within the political system and between the system and its environment. Such a simple version of structural functionalism will be useful here in order to identify the structures that perform these basic functions. Once such structures have been discovered, however, it may well be found that they perform other functions as well. Since the political system and structural functionalism are straightforward and widely utilized approaches in political science, they are used together to provide a subtle framework for this book.

· ·

ALMOND'S SEVEN FUNCTIONS PERFORMED IN THE POLITICAL SYSTEM

1. Political socialization and recruitment
2. Interest articulation
3. Interest aggregation
4. Political communication
5. Rule making
6. Rule application
7. Rule adjudication

· ·

APPROACHES TO THE STUDY OF POLITICS

The political system and structural functionalism do not exhaust the possible analytical models that can be applied to Canadian politics. Any one of a number of other theoretical approaches can be used alongside them. Such models and approaches provide a guide in selecting significant and relevant facts, as well as in putting the facts together in a meaningful way. They direct our attention to different aspects of social reality and emphasize different relationships within the same population and territory. Before getting into the substance of our subject, therefore, we will outline four other approaches that political scientists have found useful and that will illuminate aspects of the Canadian political system from time to time in the remainder of the book: the pluralist, public choice, class analysis, and state-centred approaches.[5] They focus on such crucial questions as how widely power and influence are shared, which political actors in society are most important, which government institutions are most powerful, and how politicians seek and maintain power.

As seen in Figure 1.2, the four approaches can be divided into two groups, one emphasizing elites and the other incorporating the influence of the masses. The pluralist and public choice approaches contend that power is derived from the population at large, while the class and state-centred approaches argue that power is concentrated in the corporate and state elites, respectively, an "elite" being defined as a small group with a disproportionate amount of power. Figure 1.3 shows that the approaches can also be divided between those that are society-centred and those that focus on the autonomy of the state. The pluralist, public choice, and class approaches maintain that the authorities respond to various demands emanating from societal forces, while the state-centred approach is based on the assumption that those in government do what *they* think is best.

. . . .

Figure 1.2 **Mass and Elite Approaches**

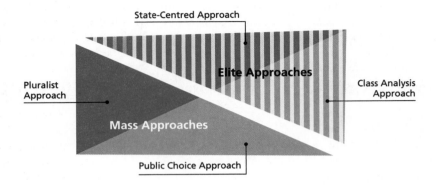

Figure 1.3 **Society-Centred and State-Centred Approaches**

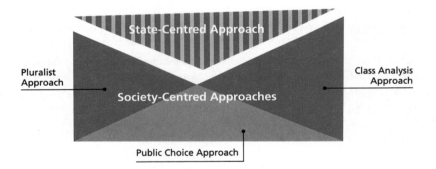

The Pluralist Approach

Pluralism is the analytical framework closest to the democratic ideal. It postulates that power is widely dispersed among many interests in society rather than tightly controlled by one or more groups or elites, and that the political system is characterized by much openness or "slack." In particular, pluralism suggests that individuals can make use of many different resources in their political participation; that those sharing a demand are free to join together to seek a governmental response; that such group action is the norm of political activity; and that the authorities are open to pressure from a wide variety of such interests. Pluralism does not necessarily expect everyone to be equally interested and involved, or everyone or all groups to be equally influential; indeed, it makes much of most individuals' political "inertia." But the theory argues that the authorities can be moved by the articulation of demands by different groups in different policy areas, and that the policies adopted are usually the result of compromises among competing group demands. The term "brokerage politics" is sometimes used in this connection because in a pluralist system the authorities engage in wheeling and dealing with the various groups in an effort to keep them all content. Pioneers of the pluralist approach include Robert Dahl, particularly in his book *Pluralist Democracy in the United States*. Many accounts of Canadian politics assume a basic pluralist perspective, even if they do not say so.

While pluralism assumes that group action is more common and effective than individual political activity, a more explicit "group" approach can also be identified. It puts particular stress on the role of pressure groups in both the making and execution of public policy. Political scientists are generally agreed that as society becomes increasingly specialized, the number of groups gets more numerous, and as political issues become more complex, political parties and politicians may be less and less capable of dealing with them. In these ways, at least, the significance of pressure groups increases, and no one doubts their contemporary importance. Paul Pross has explicitly emphasized the group approach in his work on Canadian politics, such as *Group Politics and Public Policy*. Business-oriented groups in particular have attracted much scholarly attention in recent years.[6]

In point form, the pluralist approach can be summarized as follows:

1. Power is widely dispersed in the political system and not monopolized by any state or corporate elite.
2. Individuals are free to employ a variety of resources at their disposal and to organize whatever groups they wish in order to back their demands to the authorities.
3. The authorities make decisions that are basically compromises among the various competing interests that articulate their demands.
4. Different policy areas are characterized by different individuals and groups making demands on different authorities.
5. Pressure group activity is increasingly replacing individual and party activity in the political system.

An overview of the evidence supporting this approach suggests that Canada has always been a pluralistic society, given its regional, provincial, ethnic, class, religious, gender, age, and other divisions. But in the new millennium, it will be even more pluralistic, especially in terms of ethnic diversity. Pluralism is also of growing relevance because various groups and interests are becoming more self-conscious and self-confident. Women, French-Canadians, Aboriginals, "other ethnic" groups, and non-Christian religious groups are challenging the elitism of the past. Whether elected or appointed, all the institutions of government are characterized by a new pluralism. Such interests, in the form of various subcultures, are part of the very political culture of the country and are even succeeding in changing provisions in the Constitution to protect themselves.

Certain aspects of the Canadian political system are particularly appropriate to pluralism. The broker system used by political parties as they design their election platforms is certainly one; so are the efforts of those who seek to strengthen the provinces in the operation of Canadian federalism. The limitation of authority that is provided when political institutions have checks on each other is a hallmark of this approach, and in that sense, federal–provincial conflict and the power of the courts to overrule both federal and provincial governments by means of the Charter of Rights and Freedoms are relevant. On the other hand, the original centralized framework of Canadian federalism has proved to be inappropriate in such a pluralistic society, and rigid party discipline in the House of Commons has sometimes been identified as dysfunctional.

Most Canadians have been true to the pluralist model in that they usually do not take advantage of opportunities to be active political participants, although their desire to be heard is probably increasing, and all kinds of organizations are asking for their views in public opinion polls. At least in the past, focusing on groups rather than on individuals provided greater resonance for the pluralist approach in this country. Canada has hundreds of interest groups, and many are active in the political process, but there are great disparities in the influence or resources among such pressure groups. Only a handful of groups speak for the poor and the working class, and the middle class has no collective voice. Every imaginable business interest has organized a pressure group, however, and several peak business associations are better endowed than national political parties. If pluralism means that much government activity is a response to the influence of pressure groups and that they are displacing parties in many respects, then it is certainly correct, as it is in emphasizing that government decisions are made in a diversity of specialized policy communities.

The Public Choice Approach

The public choice approach also begins with the assumption that Canada is a democracy. It postulates that rational, self-interested voters support the party whose policies are of greatest utility to themselves, and that politicians seeking re-election adopt policies that will most likely keep them in power. This approach emphasizes bargaining between politicians and voters and takes its inspiration from the economic system, its pioneer being Anthony Downs in his book *An Economic Theory of Democracy*.[7]

At first sight, in a democracy, the largest groups are most influential because they represent the greatest numbers of voters. This is only true, however, if the members of such groups are conscious of their common interests. Furthermore, since the authorities do not have to worry about the support of their committed voters, and since they are unlikely to win over those who are hostile, the usual recipe for political success is to concentrate on marginal, undecided voters or voters in strategically located constituencies, rather than on the will of the electorate as a whole.

Public choice theory argues that politicians will do almost anything to keep themselves in power. They take credit for popular policies or the strength of the economy, but blame others (international forces, provincial governments, the courts, and so on) for unpopular policies or economic decline. They give popular policies maximum publicity, but try to conceal those that are bound to be unpopular; they exaggerate the benefits of their policies and understate the costs. They take disagreeable decisions early in their term and unveil popular programs just before the next election. It would take an alert, informed, and skeptical electorate, therefore, to be able to see through the authorities' attempts to manipulate the "public choice." Public choice theory goes too far if it expects that individuals in the political marketplace are always as rational and well informed as they may be in their economic transactions.

The public choice approach can be summarized as follows:

1. Politics is a bargaining process in which both politicians and voters act in a rational, self-interested fashion, the politicians making promises in return for votes.
2. Politicians and parties generally adopt policies that will get themselves elected, and, other things being equal, they respond to those interests representing the largest number of votes.
3. Since it is a waste of effort to appeal to committed supporters or opponents, politicians concentrate on marginal, undecided, or strategically located voters.
4. Politicians try to maximize publicity of their successes and minimize their failures, take credit for good things and blame others for the bad, and manipulate the timing of positive and negative decisions.
5. A similar rational, self-serving bargaining process goes on at other points in the political system, such as between politicians and the bureaucracy, the authorities and pressure groups, and the authorities and the media.

In practice, the public choice approach can be seen at many points in the Canadian political system, especially in the relationship between politicians and voters in the formulation of election platforms and in the citizen's decision of how to vote. The operation of the House of Commons is also central to this approach because observing the partisan exchanges in that chamber helps voters make up their minds about which party will best satisfy their demands. Public choice is also relevant to the operations of the Cabinet as that body calculates which interests it will have to placate in order to ensure re-election. In this calculation, the role of public opinion polls is crucial, as governments, parties, the media, and other organizations seek to identify the basic concerns of different groups within the electorate. Governments rarely do what is in the long-term interest of the country if it conflicts with short-term electoral advantage.

The public choice approach gives particular attention to marginal voters. For a long time, the party preferences of a majority of Quebeckers (Liberal) and Westerners (Conservative) could be taken for granted so that parties focused their campaigns in Ontario, which had the largest number of flexible voters. Since 1984, Quebec has also provided a great pool of marginal voters, such that most parties have put new emphasis on that region in their campaigns. The threat of separation has only heightened the attention that parties and politicians pay to that province. The West has also become open to parties other than the Conservatives since 1993.

The public choice approach is confirmed on a daily basis when it emphasizes the ways in which the authorities portray their performance in the most favourable light, such as in timing, packaging, exaggerating benefits, and downplaying costs. When it comes to manipulating their message, however, the level of sophistication of the authorities far exceeds that of the average voter, and the public choice model probably overstates the extent to which voters are rational and well informed. The lack of class consciousness among all but the upper classes and the delayed political consciousness of women and certain other groups in society all attest to the skill of authorities and parties in persuading voters to support platforms that were not truly in their own interests.

By Dusan Petricic (The Toronto Star). *Reproduced with permission.*

Class Analysis

A third approach to the study of Canadian government and politics emphasizes socioeconomic classes or class analysis.[8] This approach is sometimes called neo-Marxism because to some extent it is based on the writings of Karl Marx. It is neither possible nor appropriate to deal with that analysis in any depth here, but the demise of Marxist-Leninism as a state-sponsored ideology in Eastern Europe does not necessarily make this critique obsolete. Suffice it to say that in Marxist eyes political activity is determined by economic relationships, particularly in the production process. In a capitalist system, Marx saw these relationships primarily in terms of a class struggle between the "proletariat" (the working class) and the "bourgeoisie" (the capitalist class). He emphasized that the latter would exploit the former until the proletariat engaged in an eventual revolution. Many modern observers see much truth in what Marx wrote over 100 years ago, but most would modify his analysis to some extent in the light of subsequent developments, which is why "class analysis" is a preferable label.

In this approach, the political elite normally takes orders from the capitalist elite, and the state is an instrument of bourgeois domination. Capitalism generally prefers to minimize the role of the state in order to allow "free market forces" to have full play, and capitalist forces have been influential in reducing the size of the state in recent years. Nevertheless, class analysts point out that the bourgeoisie will tolerate collective, public activity to some extent, but only to further its own interests in the accumulation of capital. Public policies advocated by the capitalist elite include, for example, the assumption by the public purse of many of the costs of capitalist development, called social capital, such as education, health care, electricity, and transportation. While a degree of fragmentation may exist within the bourgeoisie, such as between manufacturers and resource industries, this approach sees the state pursuing policies that seek to create or maintain the conditions in which capitalists can maximize their wealth, in what is called the "accumulation" function. Given today's universal franchise, however, most modern, democratic governments find it politically advantageous to disguise much of this activity on behalf of capital, and other classes *can* influence events if they act as a class.

Many political observers who do not necessarily claim the validity of a class analysis would nevertheless agree that the state gives priority to the demands of big business.[9] In part this is because the bourgeoisie provides personnel for public offices, organizes powerful pressure groups, finances political parties, and generally shapes societal values. Another reason for the predominance of the corporate elite is that the state depends on the capitalist system for the provision of jobs, economic growth, and a portion of tax revenues.

Class analysis recognizes that modern society is composed of more than just the bourgeoisie and the proletariat, and generally inserts between them the traditional "petite bourgeoisie" (farmers, small-business people, and self-employed professionals) and the "new middle class" (civil servants, teachers, and other salaried professionals). The increasing size of this latter group as well as the enfranchisement of the working class give both groups considerable significance today. Class analysts refer to the use of the state to benefit the middle or working classes as "legitimation." They still emphasize, however, that by humanizing and legitimizing the capitalist system and by disguising support for it, the bourgeoisie is able to continue its pursuit of the basic accumulation function.

If legitimation is not effective in facilitating capital accumulation, the government may have to resort to a third function, that of coercion. This involves adopting penalizing policies or measures to impose order, such as legislation to end strikes, or the intervention of the police to quell demonstrations. Coercion is more often imposed on labour, students, and other subordinate groups than on those with greater political and economic clout.[10]

Another central theme of class analysis is the influence of the external environment of the political system. The role of transnational corporations as sources of investment in Canada and the policies of dominant capitalist countries, especially the United States, are particularly important in this regard. So too are the actions of such organizations as the International Monetary Fund and the World Bank.

The class analysis literature in Canadian politics and economics is voluminous. Indeed, the whole political economy school of scholarship that goes back many decades and emphasizes the connection between politics and economics has been taken over by such writers. A list of such sources is contained at the end of Chapter 8, but two recent books in this field are Wallace Clement's *Understanding Canada: Building on the New Canadian Political Economy* and Tony Clarke's *Silent Coup: Confronting the Big Business Takeover of Canada*; the journal *Studies in Political Economy* and the publications of the Canadian Centre for Policy Alternatives are in the same tradition.

The class analysis approach can be summarized as follows:

1. The corporate elite or bourgeoisie not only controls the private sector of the economy, but also largely determines the shape of public policies that are designed to facilitate their accumulation of wealth.

2. This predominant influence is the result of the bourgeoisie's providing personnel for public offices and funds for political parties, shaping societal values, and organizing pressure groups; it also results from the dependence of the state on the capitalist system for the provision of jobs and economic growth.

3. The petite bourgeoisie, the new middle class, and even the working class must be accommodated to some extent by public policies that legitimate the capitalist system, and they can influence events if they act as a class.

4. If these classes are not satisfied by legitimation, the government may have to resort to coercion.

5. Especially in an era of globalization, modern states must also contend with powerful transnational corporations and international agreements that states have signed on their behalf.

Class analysts ironically find practical confirmation of their approach in the widespread definition of politics by the media, politicians, pressure groups, and other participants and observers in terms of regionalism, ethnicity, and gender, rather than class. Such definitions serve the interests of these apologists of capitalism—to disguise the underlying class conflict—as does the obsession with government deficits and debts at the expense of essential public services to the have-not segments of society. The Liberal and Conservative parties are heavily financed by major corporations, and reward such contributions in their general policies as well as in specific favours once in power. The most prominent pressure groups are those representing big business, while individual companies also lobby for government handouts. Individuals frequently serve as Cabinet ministers between stints in the corporate sector, and many senators represent corporate interests in their parliamentary work. Large corporations control most of the media and influence public opinion with carefully selected images that portray the ease and desirability of material success.

Class analysts point out that a close scrutiny of policy instruments reveals how the authorities choose more intrusive instruments and apply them more coercively when dealing with the working class (or with students at the 1997 APEC summit in Vancouver) than with the corporate elite. They demonstrate how governments disguise their routine servitude to the corporate sector with occasional legitimating measures for the working class. "Snitch lines" send welfare recipients to jail while corporate income tax evasion is rampant. And they remind us of incidents in which the full force of the law has been brought down on strikers or demonstrators, but not on corporate executives who allow pollution of the environment or who make employees work in hazardous conditions. As critical as they are of politicians' actions, such analysts are even more suspicious of the courts. Given the expense and elitist personnel involved, they do not expect judicially imposed limitations on the other branches of government to benefit the working classes. Moreover, class analysts are critical of U.S. transnationals operating in Canada and of efforts by the United States government to have Canada follow its lead. On the world stage, class analysts often support nongovernmental organizations (NGOs) as an antidote to transnational corporations.

The State-Centred Approach

Public choice theory, class analysis, and pluralism all see the state as responding to societal forces. The state-centred approach, on the other hand, views the state—those individuals endowed with the authority to formulate and implement public policies—as basically automomous from the rest of society. Public policies are made by the authorities without much reference to the demands flowing in from the public, and often despite them.[11] Since the authorities try to direct the development of society, the French word *dirigiste* is sometimes used to describe their activity. The executive and bureaucracy do what they think is best for the country or act in pursuit of their own preferences and priorities, regardless of anyone else's interests or opinions. Such state actors seek to enhance their autonomy by generating internally the information needed to pursue their objectives, and by maximizing their jurisdiction, discretionary power, and fiscal resources. It is possible to single out either the political executive or the bureaucracy in this approach, or to see them as acting together in making such decisions. Individually or in tandem, they try to persuade the public of their wisdom, or, failing that, resort to coercion, the main point being that government operations are quite divorced from public input. The originator of this approach was Eric Nordlinger, who wrote in his book *On the Anatomy of the Democratic State* that "the preferences of the state are at least as important as those of civil society in accounting for what the democratic state does and does not do."[12]

While the political executive (the prime minister and Cabinet in Canada) have the right to make major governmental decisions, subject to some kind of accountability to Parliament, some theorists prefer to emphasize the influence of the bureaucracy within the apparatus of the state.[13] They see the bureaucracy as the most important part of the policymaking process because neither legislators nor Cabinet ministers can possibly understand the details of complex modern issues, and are therefore content to be advised by their experts. Politicians may still have a role to play in identifying problems and determining priorities, but once that is done, they are in the hands of their advisers in finding ways to proceed.

It should be added that the state, as large as it is, is not without internal conflicts, and in order to maximize their influence and protect themselves, state forces are often wiser to develop functional links with certain private interests, especially pressure groups, than to try to act in total isolation. Thus, in a combination of state-centred and pluralist approaches, the concept of "policy communities" is often useful.[14] The state is composed of a conglomeration of specialized policy processes, each of which nurtures support from the most relevant interest in society.

The following points summarize the state-centred approach:

1. The state is largely autonomous from societal forces.
2. The authorities decide what is good for society and design policies to fulfill their vision of the public interest.
3. The politicians rely heavily on the bureaucracy for advice.
4. The authorities seek to enhance their autonomy by the internal generation of information and by maximizing their discretion, jurisdiction, and financial resources.
5. If necessary, the authorities resort to the manipulation of information or coercion in order to persuade the public of their wisdom, or seek the support of the most relevant societal interest.

A variant of the state-centred approach is that of institutionalism or neo-institutionalism. This approach essentially argues that the institutions that make up the state should be the principal focus of attention in political science. Like the state-centred approach, institutionalism downplays the importance of societal forces, and contends that institutions affect societal forces as much as the reverse. Institutionalism is particularly relevant to Canada because so much of our political debate is about governmental institutions, and because many societal forces—French, English, Aboriginal, and so on—are actually in conflict over institutional change. Institutionalism has always been an integral part of the political science discipline in this country, but neo-institutionalism is a reaction to an emphasis on broader social, cultural, and economic forces in recent years. In the book *Parameters of Power*, Keith Archer et al. argue that institutions help determine who has standing in the political process, structure the interactions of the players, are often the very things at stake in politics, and shape the interests at play in the political system. Institutionalism therefore seeks to discover each institution's basic principles and then to examine any contestation among such principles.[15]

The state-centred approach is anchored in the traditional Canadian political culture—in the values of deference to authority, elitism, and collectivism—and, at least in the past, Canadians have generally welcomed state intervention and trusted the authorities who intervened. Politicians and bureaucrats naturally took advantage of this invitation to function in such an autonomous fashion. This approach is related to the low level of political participation in Canada, to the minimal effort of most political parties to develop policy within their own ranks, and to the consequent lack of policy differences among the parties in election campaigns. Governing parties have changed policy directions so frequently after achieving power that to do so no longer causes particular criticism.

The state is not equally autonomous from societal forces in all policy areas. Foreign policy is one traditionally autonomous field because relatively few citizens feel deeply about it; in the past, the Constitution and federalism were other such state-centred sectors. Pierre Trudeau's policy of official bilingualism and Brian Mulroney's policies of privatization, deregulation, and deficit reduction were all imposed from the top rather than being demanded by the grassroots at the time. So, too, were the Goods and Services Tax (GST) and the Canada–U.S. Free Trade Agreement. These latter cases are good examples of what the authorities do when they encounter public criticism of state-centred policies: they resort to public relations campaigns and manipulation of public opinion via the media at public expense.

Other state-centred policies bear the mark of bureaucratic inspiration, although the bureaucracy contributes a great deal even to those that do originate with the political executive. In this advisory capacity, the bureaucracy does not always act in its own interest alone; sometimes bureaucrats promote policies that they genuinely believe are in the public interest. Cases of government (both politicians and bureaucrats) actually creating advocacy organizations to demand or support what the authorities themselves want to do have also been documented.[16]

An Amalgam Model

This book suggests that each of the approaches outlined above offers useful perspectives that enhance our understanding of Canadian government and politics. Accordingly, the approaches have been applied to the subject matter of each chapter wherever relevant. It should be added that these approaches do not necessarily constitute competitive explanations, and in fact often overlap. They point to the multidimensional character of politics, and are useful whenever they add insight to the explanation of aspects of the political system.

While the book takes the position that the Canadian political system is too variable and complex to be explained in any single, simple fashion, we can in fact extract and combine aspects of these four approaches in order to construct a coherent, general framework. The predominant influence of business pressure groups can be taken from pluralism and put together with the government's attempt to present itself to the electorate in the most favourable light from public choice theory, the pervasive influence of capitalist values from class analysis, and the persistent influence of the bureaucracy from the state-centred approach. The exercise of extracting and combining these aspects of the four approaches is demonstrated in Figure 1.4.

Canadian politics is characterized by a tremendous amount of pressure group activity, and conflicting group demands regularly confront the authorities. From among this plethora of group demands, however, the authorities most frequently single out business groups for special treatment. Business groups and individual corporations know where and how to apply pressure and have the resources to hire professional lobbyists to make their case. Since the authorities share many of their values and social background characteristics, the meeting of such forces is normally quite congenial.

While public choice theory may generally overrate the rationality of the average voter, it is quite correct in emphasizing the extent to which the authorities use public funds and the media to manage and manipulate messages to the electorate so as to portray their performance

Figure 1.4   A General Framework from the Four Approaches

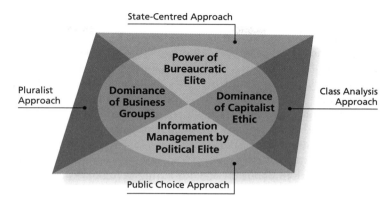

most favourably and therefore obtain re-election. If it must make unpopular decisions from time to time, the government will give careful attention to their timing and packaging, and try to find some other target on which it can pin the blame.

If there is one value that pervades Canadian policymaking more than any other, it is undoubtedly the capitalist ethic: allowing the economic elite to maximize its accumulation of wealth. Government policy can foster capital accumulation in many ways, such as with tax breaks, government grants and loans, lack of regulation, and impediments to unionization. This objective, of course, is often disguised as contributing to economic growth and the creation of employment and is diluted by a certain amount of taxation and regulation. It is also accompanied by the provision of social services and a limited degree of income redistribution. Now that all adults have the vote, the authorities must promise enough to the middle and lower classes to get themselves re-elected. But such promises are regularly unfulfilled, and those legitimation measures that are adopted are often overblown. Thus, while in the perspective of this book it is too extreme to say that accumulation and coercion tempered by legitimation explain everything political, the value that governments put on accumulation does explain a great deal of Canadian political activity.

Finally, while some authoritative decisions are taken by the political executive (and others by the courts), the bureaucracy advises on almost all prime ministerial, Cabinet, and ministerial decisions and then makes many others on its own. The decisions that governments are called on to make nowadays are so numerous and so technical that ministers have neither the time nor the expertise to get personally involved in more than a fraction of them. The rest get delegated to the bureaucrats, who often pursue their own conception of the public interest.

It is not the intention of this discussion to claim that individual and nonbusiness-group demands are never satisfied, that the public is totally at the mercy of the government's manipulative media management, that the authorities are never moved by values other than capital accumulation, or that the bureaucracy is the only branch of government that matters. But in an effort to portray a coherent and realistic picture of the national political system, it must be said that Canada does have a political elite that listens primarily to business groups, whose concern with re-election leads it to manage the message that the electorate receives about its performance, that is imbued with capitalist values, and that is guided to a large extent by the bureaucracy. The amalgam model explains more about Canadian government and politics than any other.

Two variations on the amalgam model should also be mentioned. The first is the concept of **elite accommodation**.[17] This refers to the interaction of various elites, either within government circles or in both the public and private sectors, in order to work out policies in their own mutual interests. Although they are seriously divided in some ways, the elites of various ethnic, regional, and other groupings have certain background characteristics and values in common that enable them to come to agreement. Specific individuals have often come to know each other before occupying elite positions or have shared educational and social institutions and experiences in their youth. It is sometimes argued that the mass members of any group have such confidence in their own group leaders that they will abide by whatever decisions have been arrived at in the interaction of their group leaders with other elites. It is even hypothesized that elite accommodation is a means of contributing to national unity in a country like Canada, which is characterized by so many cleavages. In other words, the mass members of various ethnic, religious, regional, or class groupings may find themselves in conflict with the mass members of other groups, but if their leaders can arrive at compromises with the leaders of other groups, the mass members will accept them.[18] The foremost advocate of elite accommodation, Robert Presthus, applies it primarily to interaction among the political, bureaucratic, and economic elites, an approach that is quite compatible with what is outlined above.

Another variation on the amalgam approach is that of the **embedded state**.[19] This is the idea that while the political and bureaucratic elites can sometimes function quite independently of societal forces, the state is so embedded in society that they cannot operate with total autonomy. Instead, because of this fusion of state and society or web of state–society interdependence, they interact with whatever societal elites are most relevant to their operations. In a sense, this is a variation on pluralism, with close interaction between specialized governmental elites and the pressure groups who constitute their principal clienteles.

....
DISCUSSION QUESTIONS

1. Does the use of theories, perspectives, approaches, and models add to the study of the "facts" of the political system? Why or why not?

2. Give examples from Canadian politics that support the pluralist approach.

3. What pressure groups are you aware of or do you belong to?

4. Do you agree that business groups have more influence than others? Why or why not?

5. What examples from Canadian politics support the public choice approach?

6. Give examples from Canadian politics that support class analysis.

7. Can you think of examples from Canadian politics that support the state-centred approach?

8. Do you agree that the bureaucracy is the most significant part of the government apparatus? Why or why not?

····································

NOTES

1. In *Canada: A Socio-Political Report* (Toronto: McGraw-Hill Ryerson, 1974), ch. 1, Ronald Manzer has linked these needs to the traditional political science concerns about security, liberty, equality, and fraternity.

2. For example, language is now more divisive than religion, but this was not always the case, and the class cleavage may have changed to some extent from a conflict over material issues to quality-of-life issues. It is also popular nowadays to talk about the politics of recognition or the politics of identity. On post-materialism, see Neil Nevitte, *The Decline of Deference: Canadian Value Change in Cross-National Perspective* (Peterborough: Broadview Press, 1996), p. 12.

3. David Easton, *A Systems Analysis of Political Life* (New York: John Wiley & Sons, 1965).

4. Gabriel Almond, "A Developmental Approach to Political Systems," *World Politics* 17, no. 2 (January 1965), pp. 183–214.

5. Other books to outline similar approaches are Stephen Brooks, *Public Policy in Canada: An Introduction*, 3rd ed. (Toronto: McClelland and Stewart, 1998); Stephen Brooks and Andrew Stritch, *Business and Government in Canada* (Scarborough: Prentice-Hall Canada, 1991); and Kenneth Kernaghan and David Siegel, *Public Administration in Canada* (Scarborough: Nelson Canada, 2nd ed., 1991; 3rd ed., 1995; 4th ed., 1999).

6. Brooks and Stritch, *Business and Government in Canada*; William Coleman, *Business and Politics* (Montreal: McGill–Queen's University Press, 1988); and W.T. Stanbury, *Business–Government Relations in Canada* (Toronto: Methuen, 1986). Pluralism and the group approach are increasingly viewed in combination with the state-centred approach in terms of "policy communities." See William Coleman and Grace Skogstad, eds., *Policy Communities and Public Policy in Canada* (Mississauga: Copp Clark Pitman, 1991).

7. Canadian applications include D.G. Hartle, *A Theory of the Expenditure Budgetary Process* (Toronto: University of Toronto Press, 1976); M.J. Trebilcock et al., *The Choice of Governing Instrument* (Ottawa: Economic Council of Canada, 1982); M.J. Trebilcock, *The Prospects for Reinventing Government* (Toronto: C.D. Howe Institute, 1994); Stanbury, *Business–Government Relations in Canada*, ch. 4; Mark Sproule-Jones, "Institutions, Constitutions, and Public Policies: A Public Choice Overview," in Michael Atkinson and Marsha Chandler, eds., *The Politics of Canadian Public Policy* (Toronto: University of Toronto Press, 1983); and Réjean Landry, "Biases in the Supply of Public Policies to Organized Interests," in Coleman and Skogstad, eds., *Policy Communities and Public Policy in Canada*. See also Thomas Flanagan's *Game Theory and Canadian Politics* (Toronto: University of Toronto Press, 1998).

8. Leo Panitch, "Elites, Classes, and Power in Canada," in Michael S. Whittington and Glen Williams, eds., *Canadian Politics in the 1990s*, 4th ed. (Scarborough: Nelson Canada, 1995); Tony Clarke, *Silent Coup: Confronting the Big Business Takeover of Canada* (Toronto: Lorimer, 1997).

9. Coleman, *Business and Politics*; Brooks and Stritch, *Business and Government in Canada*; and Robert Dahl and Charles Lindblom, *Politics, Economics and Welfare* (Chicago: University of Chicago Press, 1976).

10. Nicolas Baxter-Moore, "Policy Implementation and the Role of the State: A Revised Approach to the Study of Policy Instruments," in Robert Jackson et al., eds., *Contemporary Canadian Politics* (Scarborough: Prentice-Hall Canada, 1987).

11. Paul Sniderman et al., *The Clash of Rights: Liberty, Equality, and Legitimacy in Pluralist Democracy* (New Haven: Yale University Press, 1996) expected to find a large gap between the values of the elite and the mass, but found a remarkable similarity!

12. Canadian applications include Elizabeth Riddell-Dixon, "State Autonomy and Canadian Foreign Policy: The Case of Deep Seabed Mining," *Canadian Journal of Political Science* (June 1988), pp. 297–317; Leslie Pal, "Relative Autonomy Revisited: The Origins of Canadian Unemployment Insurance," *Canadian Journal of Political Science* (March 1986), pp. 71–102; Leslie Pal, *State, Class and Bureaucracy: Canadian Unemployment Insurance and Public Policy* (Montreal: McGill–Queen's University Press, 1987); K.R. Nossal, *The Politics of Canadian Foreign Policy*, 2nd ed. (Scarborough: Prentice-Hall Canada, 1989); and R. Brian Howe and David Johnson, "Variations in Enforcing Equality: A Study of Provincial Human Rights Funding," *Canadian Public Administration* (Summer 1995).

13. Kernaghan and Siegel, *Public Administration in Canada*.

14. Pross, *Group Politics and Public Policy* (Toronto: Oxford University Press, 1986); Coleman and Skogstad, *Policy Communities and Public Policy in Canada*.

15. Keith Archer et al., *Parameters of Power: Canada's Political Institutions* (Scarborough: Nelson Canada, 1995; 2nd ed., 1999).

16. Leslie Pal, *Interests of State: The Politics of Language, Multiculturalism, and Feminism in Canada* (Montreal: McGill–Queen's University Press, 1993).

17. Robert Presthus, *Elite Accommodation in Canada* (Toronto: Macmillan, 1973).

18. This phenomenon is close to the concept of "consociationalism." See Kenneth McRae, ed., *Consociational Democracy* (Toronto: McClelland and Stewart, 1974).

19. Alan C. Cairns, "The Embedded State: State–Society Relations in Canada," in Keith Banting, ed., *State and Society: Canada in Comparative Perspective*, vol. 31 of the Research Studies for the Royal Commission on the Economic Union and Development Prospects for Canada (Toronto, 1986) and reprinted in Alan C. Cairns, *Reconfigurations: Canadian Citizenship and Constitutional Change* (Toronto: McClelland and Stewart, 1995).

....

FURTHER READING

Archer, Keith, et al. *Parameters of Power: Canada's Political Institutions*. Scarborough: Nelson Canada, 1995; 2nd ed., 1999.

Brooks, Stephen. *Public Policy in Canada: An Introduction*, 3rd ed. Toronto: Oxford University Press, 1998.

Brooks, Stephen, and Andrew Stritch. *Business and Government in Canada*. Scarborough: Prentice-Hall Canada, 1991.

Clarke, Tony. *Silent Coup: Confronting the Big Business Takeover of Canada*. Toronto: Lorimer, 1997.

Clement, Wallace. *The Canadian Corporate Elite*. Toronto: McClelland and Stewart, 1975.

Clement, Wallace, ed. *Understanding Canada: Building on the New Canadian Political Economy*. Montreal: McGill–Queen's University Press, 1997.

Coleman, William. *Business and Politics*. Montreal: McGill–Queen's University Press, 1988.

Coleman, William, and Grace Skogstad. *Policy Communities and Public Policy in Canada*. Mississauga: Copp Clark Pitman, 1991.

Easton, David. *A Systems Analysis of Political Life*. New York: John Wiley & Sons, 1965.

McMenemy, John. *The Language of Canadian Politics: A Guide to Important Terms and Concepts*. Rev. ed. Waterloo: Wilfrid Laurier University Press, 1995.

Nevitte, Neil. *The Decline of Deference: Canadian Value Change in Cross-National Perspective*. Peterborough: Broadview Press, 1996.

Pal, Leslie. *Interests of State: The Politics of Language, Multiculturalism, and Feminism in Canada*. Montreal: McGill–Queen's University Press, 1993.

Panitch, Leo. *The Canadian State*. Toronto: University of Toronto Press, 1977.

———. "Elites, Classes, and Power in Canada." In Michael S. Whittington and Glen Williams, eds., *Canadian Politics in the 1990s*, 4th ed. Scarborough: Nelson Canada, 1995.

Presthus, Robert. *Elite Accommodation in Canada*. Toronto: Macmillan, 1973.

Pross, Paul. *Group Politics and Public Policy*. Toronto: Oxford University Press, 1986.

Sniderman, Paul M., et al. *The Clash of Rights: Liberty, Equality, and Legitimacy in Pluralist Democracy*. New Haven: Yale University Press, 1996.

Stanbury, W.T. *Business–Government Relations in Canada*. Toronto: Methuen, 1986.

Trebilcock, Michael J. *The Prospects for Reinventing Government*. Toronto: C.D. Howe Institute, 1994.

Chapter 2

The Historical Context
AND INSTITUTIONAL
foundations

How much violence occurred in Canada's constitutional development? How did the new British conquerors treat the almost completely French colony of Quebec? How much of the new government structure in 1867 was based on that of Britain, and how much on that of the United States? What were the key points in the move toward democracy and the achievement of Canadian sovereignty?

This chapter sketches the historical context within which the Canadian political system operates and outlines the basic institutional foundations of that system. It surveys the institutions established in the colonial period, focuses on the great fusion in 1867 of the British parliamentary system with a variation on American federalism, enumerates the main principles of the Canadian **Constitution**, and discusses the evolution of Canada from a British colony to a sovereign state.

EARLY SETTLEMENT AND POLITICAL INSTITUTIONS

The territory that is now called Canada was first occupied by self-governing Aboriginal peoples. France and Britain colonized parts of this territory in the 1500s and 1600s and periodically fought over them and others for nearly 200 years. The British Hudson's Bay Company took possession of Rupert's Land around Hudson Bay, and Britain took control of Nova Scotia and Newfoundland by the 1713 Treaty of Utrecht. Then, after the 1759 Battle of the Plains of Abraham, which was part of the Seven Years' War between these traditional European rivals, Quebec, Prince Edward Island, Cape Breton, and New Brunswick all became British colonies by the 1763 Treaty of Paris. This reduced France's North American holdings to the islands of St. Pierre and Miquelon. Interaction between the new British power and the Aboriginal peoples is discussed in Chapter 4.

The Royal Proclamation of 1763, the first distinctively Canadian constitutional document, created the colony of Quebec,[1] and purported to protect the interests of Aboriginal peoples. As far as ex-Europeans were concerned, Quebec was largely made up of French-speaking farmers, clergy, and seigneurs, but the British-appointed government was English-speaking, and the nonagricultural economy increasingly came under British control. On the other hand, British governors resisted the idea of imposing the English language and Protestant religion on such a homogeneous French-Catholic population.

In 1774, the **Quebec Act** provided for a new set of government institutions. It established a council in the colony, but no assembly. Roman Catholics were allowed freedom of religion and could be appointed to the council, while the colony combined British criminal law with French civil law. Meanwhile, the first elected assembly in the "Canadian" part of British North America was summoned in Nova Scotia in 1758, followed by Prince Edward Island in 1773.

At this point, the residents of the thirteen "American" colonies revolted against British rule. French Canadians essentially remained neutral in this dispute, and because little anti-British sentiment existed in the "Canadian" colonies, thousands of ex-Americans loyal to Britain—the United Empire Loyalists—migrated to "Canada." This migration led to the severing of New Brunswick from Nova Scotia in 1784, together with the creation of its own assembly. Then, in response to pressure from those Loyalists who migrated to Quebec and who were already accustomed to operating with an elected assembly, Britain passed the **Constitutional Act of 1791**. This gesture also served to reward the loyalty of the French for not joining in the American Revolution. The act divided the colony into two—Upper and Lower Canada—each with a governor, an appointed executive council, an appointed legislative council, and a locally elected assembly. In the case of Lower Canada, the appointed councils were primarily composed of anglophones, and the assembly, of francophones. In Upper Canada, which was almost exclusively English, the Constitutional Act provided for British, rather than French, civil law. The executive council gradually evolved into the Cabinet, while the legislative council was the forerunner of the Senate. Thus, by 1791, all the colonies had achieved **representative government**, that is, a set of political institutions including an elected legislative assembly.

Subsequent discord in the Canadian colonies was not so much between them and Britain as between the local assembly and the executive, composed of the governor and his appointed advisory executive council. The elected assembly represented the people and could articulate

··

Figure 2.1   Evolution of Canadian Pre-Confederation Political Institutions

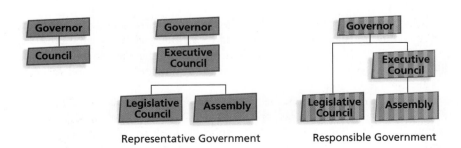

Representative Government   Responsible Government

their views but had no real power over the appointed councils. This situation was complicated by the cultural division in Lower Canada, where Lord Durham found "two nations warring in the bosom of a single state."[2] Reformers demanded **responsible government**, in which advisers to the governor would reflect the views of the elected assembly. That would mean that the members of the executive council came from the assembly and had its support. This presented a problem in the colonies, however, because on many subjects Britain wanted the governor to do its will, not that of the local assembly. This problem eventually erupted into the rebellions of 1837 in both Upper and Lower Canada, led by William Lyon Mackenzie and Louis-Joseph Papineau respectively, and forced the British government to appoint Lord Durham to investigate the situation.

The 1839 **Durham Report** provided a blueprint for solving the problems of assembly–executive relations, recommending that the principle of responsible government be implemented with respect to local affairs, so that the executive branch would govern only as long as it retained the confidence of the assembly. Durham outlined a division of powers between local and imperial authorities such that in local matters the governor would follow the advice of colonial authorities, but in matters of imperial concern he would act as an agent of the British government. Responsible government came to Nova Scotia, New Brunswick, and the colony of Canada in 1848, and three years later to Prince Edward Island. Thus, by 1851, all these pre-Confederation British colonies operated on the basis that the Cabinet or executive council had to resign if it lost the confidence of the elected legislative assembly. British Columbia would acquire responsible government when it joined Confederation, as would the other provinces as they were created.

Durham also recommended that Upper and Lower Canada be united into a single colony of Canada, partly as one last attempt to submerge and assimilate the French. The colonies were amalgamated by the 1840 **Act of Union**, but English did not remain the sole language of government operations for long. When it became clear that assimilation of the French Canadians would not be achieved, French was also recognized as an official language of the legislature. Moreover, most governments of the period were headed by one English and one French leader.

. . . .

THE ROAD TO CONFEDERATION

Shortly after achieving responsible government, the individual British North American colonies began to think of uniting with each other. The colonies were driven to consider uniting due to economic, political, and military factors.[3] Because the British had discontinued colonial trading preferences, and because a reciprocity treaty with the United States had expired, the colonies hoped to establish a new, large free trade area among themselves. Confederation offered the hope of economic prosperity; this large internal market would be enhanced by a railway link between the Maritimes and central Canada, which in turn would provide the latter with a winter Atlantic port. The future prospect of annexing and developing the West was also seen as a source of economic prosperity.

Meanwhile, the colony of Canada had experienced political deadlock between its two parts, then called Canada East (Quebec) and Canada West (Ontario), as well as between the French and English component groups. Public decisions had to be made in one large, combined set of governmental institutions, yet the needs and demands of the two parts were often quite different. This led to the practice of requiring a "double majority" (a majority of members from each part of the colony) for the passage of bills. Confederation would allow greater autonomy to the two parts because it would entail a central government to deal with problems that all the colonies had in common, but would also provide for provincial governments to handle distinctive internal matters on their own. Such a two-tier structure also appealed to the Maritime provinces, which did not feel like turning all decisions over to a distant central government.

The individual colonies also felt vulnerable in a military sense. The United States had a powerful army on their doorstep, and prominent Americans could be heard advocating the takeover of the existing colonies and/or the vast territories to the west. Moreover, the British government no longer seemed interested in providing military protection to the colonies. By joining together, the colonies would make American military aggression more difficult and provide a stronger force to resist its appetite for the "Canadian" West.

Confederation was thus precipitated by economic, political, and military problems and seemed to most colonial leaders to be a means of solving them. But it also held out the hope that the new country would one day become a prosperous, transcontinental nation similar to its southern neighbour.

In the 1860s, Nova Scotia, New Brunswick, and Prince Edward Island began to consider forming a Maritime union, and called the Charlottetown Conference of 1864 for this purpose. When delegates from the colony of Canada arrived, however, the idea of a larger union was put up for debate. Discussions continued at the Quebec Conference later that year, and the essentials of the Confederation scheme were agreed on. The London Conference of 1866 fine-tuned the agreement, leaving Prince Edward Island (and Newfoundland) temporarily on the sidelines. The four provinces—Nova Scotia, New Brunswick, Quebec, and Ontario— were officially united on July 1, 1867, by the **British North America Act**, later renamed the **Constitution Act, 1867.**

. . . .

FUSING THE BRITISH PARLIAMENTARY SYSTEM WITH AMERICAN FEDERALISM

Canadian confederation was the first attempt to fuse the principles of the British parliamentary system with those of federalism, although Australia would make a similar move shortly afterwards. Since the United States was the leading federal state of the day, and the one closest to Canada, the federal aspects of the new Constitution were directly related to those next door.

Within the new central government (often called the "federal government," only to make things more confusing), and within each of the governments of the new provinces, the British parliamentary system provided the institutional foundations. This system is based on the periodic popular election of the members of the House of Commons. Parliament also has a second or "upper" chamber, which in Britain was the hereditary House of Lords. Canada lacked the historic landed nobility found in Britain, however, so it was decided that the members of the Canadian Senate would be appointed by the prime minister. The third part of British Parliament is the monarch or the Crown, and approval of all three parts is necessary for the passage of legislation and certain other authoritative decisions. Canada would, of course, continue to be a monarchy, and automatically shared the widely esteemed British monarch of the day, Queen Victoria. On a practical daily basis, however, the governor general would exercise the functions of the Crown.

Although the British system is called parliamentary government, and although it is said that it operates on the principle of the **supremacy of Parliament**, such labels and descriptions are somewhat misleading. The core of the parliamentary system, even in 1867, was the prime minister and the Cabinet. While they must be members of Parliament, they are such an important part of Parliament that they often relegate both the monarch and other members of the House of Commons and Senate (or House of Lords) to a position of insignificance. To the prime minister and Cabinet are conferred the powers to lead the country and make the most important decisions in the political system. But the principle of responsible government holds that they retain their position and their powers only as long as they are supported by a majority in Parliament. If the House of Commons declares a lack of confidence in the prime minister and Cabinet, they must either resign and make way for another group to take their place, or else call an election, the latter option being most common. Because the prime minister and Cabinet ministers have seats in the legislative branch, mostly the House of Commons, the system is often termed a "fusion of powers"—that is, it involves a combination of legislative and executive powers.

In the British parliamentary system, then, the prime minister and Cabinet ministers, who have seats in Parliament, are given the power to introduce most legislation and the right to control most of the time of the legislature. They also have the exclusive power to introduce legislation of a financial nature—laws to either raise or spend money. They have wide powers of appointment, to draft subordinate legislation under the authority of laws, in international affairs, and essentially all powers necessary to provide effective political leadership for the country. The parliamentary system is executive-dominated, and because the British Parliament operates in the Palace of Westminster, this system is sometimes called the **Westminster model**. Other members of Parliament (MPs) may criticize and propose amendments, the monarch (or governor general) may advise and warn, but the prime minister and Cabinet almost always get their way. This is because a majority of the members of Parliament normally belong to the same political party as the prime minister and Cabinet, and together they constitute a **majority government**. Even more in Canada than contemporary Britain, the prime minister and Cabinet impose rigid party discipline on their MPs to support their every move.

Two art students use a sunny afternoon to do some homework in London's flowered Parliament Square. In the background is St. Stephen's Tower, which houses the bell known as Big Ben over the Houses of Parliament. (Max Nash/Canapress)

It should be added that while government was small and simple at the time of Confederation, it has gradually developed another important branch: the bureaucracy or public service. The bureaucracy essentially advises the prime minister and Cabinet on their decisions and then carries out whatever government programs have been authorized. The current Canadian bureaucracy consists of nearly half a million public servants.

The significance of the Senate has declined since Confederation because arriving there by appointment rather than election diminishes its members' legitimacy in a democratic age. The powers of the Senate have remained virtually equal to those of the House of Commons (unlike those of the British House of Lords, which have been curtailed), but senators have rarely felt it proper to exercise them. Moreover, independent behaviour has usually been discouraged by the fact that the party with a majority in the Senate has usually been the same one as has a majority in the Commons. If for any reason the Senate should ultimately defeat a government bill, it does not affect the constitutional standing of the prime minister and Cabinet. The principle of responsible government in the Westminster model, whether in Britain or Canada, does not apply to upper chambers. The model outlined above is also operational in each of the provinces, except that they now all possess one-chamber, or unicameral, legislatures.

The British parliamentary system also incorporates the principle of **judicial independence**. Although courts are established by acts of Parliament and judges are appointed by the prime minister and Cabinet or attorney general, the whole judicial system is then expected to operate independently of the executive and legislative branches of government. In the case of Britain itself, the judges have considerable discretion in interpreting laws, but lack the power of **judicial review**, that is, the power to declare them invalid. The Canadian judiciary soon appropriated to itself the power to invalidate laws that violated the federal–provincial division of powers, but were otherwise quite restrained.

The British parliamentary system is distinct in many ways from the U.S. presidental-congressional system. There, the president and the two houses of the legislature are independently elected, and no one is permitted to sit in more than one branch of government. The "separation of powers" means that executive, legislative, and judicial powers are distributed to three separate branches of government: president, Congress, and the courts, respectively.

. . . .

Figure 2.2   An Outline of Canadian Political Institutions

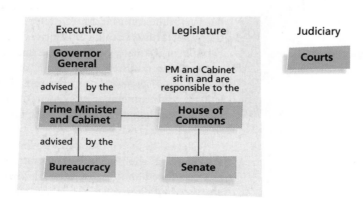

Moreover, the U.S. system is also characterized by "checks and balances" designed to ensure that the actions of any one branch of government are subject to veto by another. Members of the House of Representatives and the Senate have much more legislative power than their counterparts in the British parliamentary system in terms of both initiating bills and amending or vetoing those emanating from the president. Party discipline is also much looser, so that even if a majority of the members of Congress belong to the same party as the president, there is no guarantee that the president's initiatives will be passed. The Supreme Court also has the power of judicial review and can overturn any legislation it feels is in violation of the Constitution. Apart from the name of the upper chamber, the Senate, the Fathers of Canadian Confederation adopted virtually nothing from the U.S. system with respect to the internal operation of the federal and provincial governments.

On the other hand, the Fathers were dealing with a large piece of territory, one they hoped would soon become larger, someday equalling or exceeding that of the United States. They came from colonies that had separate identities and a previous semi-autonomous existence. In this respect, the model of American federalism could not help but influence the design of the new country they were establishing. It would have to be a **federation** of some kind, with a division of powers between the central and provincial governments.

Confederation was to a large extent the work of John A. Macdonald, who went on to become the first Canadian prime minister. Macdonald preferred a unitary state or legislative union in which the new central government would have almost all the powers and the provinces would be little more than municipalities. But Quebec and the Maritimes were not prepared to join such a system. Quebec in particular demanded an autonomous provincial government so that its linguistic and cultural concerns, such as education and civil law, would be placed in the hands of a French-speaking majority. The Maritimes, too, insisted on provincial governments because they did not want to lose their previously established identities, they had little in the way of municipal government to handle local problems, and they were far removed from the new capital in Ottawa. Hence, the logical compromise was a system that contained a central government to deal with common purposes and provincial governments to look after local concerns. Although this principle was essentially that of American federalism, it was also consistent with the existing British colonial tradition of having two levels of government (Britain and local), and the Fathers of Confederation were accustomed to such divided jurisdiction.

Macdonald accepted a federal form of government, then, to allow the former colonies to retain some of their political and economic independence, but he intended the new country to be a highly centralized federation. He felt that its economic and defensive objectives required a strong central government, a conviction reinforced by the conclusion held by most of the participants that the American Civil War (which had just ended as they began their deliberations) had been the result of too much power at the state level. Some historians have added that most of the Fathers of Confederation had links to banks and to railway and manufacturing companies, which looked upon the confederation project primarily as a source of profit. By controlling the development of the country at the centre, they would be free to exploit the hinterland.[4]

Federalism can be defined as a division of powers between central and regional governments such that neither is subordinate to the other. The Confederation settlement was not entirely consistent with this modern definition of federalism because in certain respects the provinces were made subordinate to the central government. Some observers thus prefer to label the arrangement at its creation as "quasi-federal."[5] Ironically, however, the Fathers used the word "confederation," which in political science indicates a loose, decentralized federation, the opposite of what Macdonald intended. In the U.S. federal system, for example, the central government was given only certain delegated powers, while the residual powers remained at the level of the states. Macdonald was determined to reverse this pattern; he essentially gave the provinces 16 enumerated powers and left the residual powers at the centre. He was also careful to give Ottawa unlimited powers of taxation, the broadest powers to regulate trade and commerce, and power over such other important fields as defence and the criminal law.

Besides dividing powers between the two levels of government, constitutional architects in both the United States and Canada had to decide how the provinces or states would be represented at the national level. In both cases, democracy required that the lower house of the legislature be based on the principle of representation by population, so that the most populous provinces or states would have the largest number of members in that chamber. To counterbalance this, and to protect the interests of the smaller states, the United States decided that each state, regardless of population, would have two senators at the national level. Some Fathers of Confederation preferred this idea, but others wanted representation by population in both houses of Parliament. The Canadian compromise was to base the Senate on the principle of equal *regional* representation rather than equal *provincial* representation.

Since Canadian politicians were already familiar with divided authority, it might seem that a fusion of the British parliamentary system and American federalism was not such a constitutional innovation. The colonial division of powers was a somewhat different kind, however, and more importantly, the whole ethos underlying the Canadian and U.S. systems was different. In the British parliamentary system, everything is designed to *facilitate* government action by concentrating power in the hands of the executive, whether in terms of its relationship with other institutions of government such as Parliament or the courts, or with territorial units such as local governments. In the American system, everything is designed to *inhibit* government action by preventing the concentration of power in the hands of any authority. Institutions of the national government—president, House of Representatives, Senate, and Supreme Court—should be able to veto each other, and they should collectively be kept in line by a division of powers that gives most authority to the states. It is largely because the British system is designed to facilitate government action and because the American system is designed to inhibit it that the fusion of the two systems in Canadian Confederation was such a distinctive phenomenon. John A. Macdonald saw the contradiction and therefore tried to establish a federal system that was much more centralized than that next door.

The only major change since the institutional structure was established in Canada in 1867 was the adoption of the **Charter of Rights and Freedoms** in 1982. It added to the scope of judicial review with respect to the federal–provincial division of powers by importing American-style judicial activism in the area of protecting individual rights and freedoms. Henceforth, the courts could disallow federal or provincial legislation that violated the Constitution either in terms of the division of powers or the Charter of Rights.

PRINCIPLES OF THE CANADIAN CONSTITUTION

The preceding discussion has identified three basic principles of the Canadian Constitution: responsible government, which is the essence of the British parliamentary system; federalism; and judicial review, especially since 1982. At least three other fundamental principles are also embedded in the Canadian Constitution: constitutional monarchy, the rule of law, and democracy.[6]

PRINCIPLES OF THE CANADIAN CONSTITUTION

- Responsible government
- Federalism
- Judicial review
- Constitutional monarchy
- Rule of law
- Democracy

In terms of its head of state, Canada is a **constitutional monarchy**. This is not a principle that attracts much attention, largely because the monarch herself lives in another country and because her actual power, as well as that of her Canadian representative, the governor general, is not extensive. Nevertheless, as outlined in Chapter 20, the monarchical system underlies a great deal of the operation of government in Canada, largely in the form of the Crown.[7] The Crown can be defined as the sum total of residual or discretionary powers still left in the hands of the monarch. The term constitutional monarchy basically means that the monarch reigns according to the Constitution and that the Constitution has put most of the powers of government into someone else's hands. Almost all of the powers once exercised by the monarch have been whittled away either by legislation or by constitutional convention.

The **rule of law** is another constitutional principle inherited from Great Britain that rests largely on convention and judicial precedent. In essence, it means that all government action must be based on law and that governments and government officials must obey the law. In other words, the law is supreme, and no one, including the lawmakers, is above it.[8] Courts in Canada as well as Britain have had occasion to overturn government decisions and actions that were not based on law.[9]

Finally, Canada is a **democracy**. This term, which is related to responsible government, constitutional monarchy, and the rule of law, will be analyzed more fully in Chapter 10. In Canadian terms, democracy has four components: popular sovereignty, meaning that the people ultimately rule, primarily through periodic elections; political equality, meaning that everyone has one vote on election day; political freedom, meaning that during and between elections people are free to organize and advocate for political purposes; and majority rule, meaning that except in defined situations designed to protect minority rights, the will of the majority prevails.

Make Chart

THE ROAD TO CANADIAN SOVEREIGNTY

Having outlined the development of the basic institutions and the fundamental constitutional principles of the Canadian political system, let us trace the evolution of Canada from British colony to sovereign state. Contrary to popular belief, the British North America (BNA) Act of 1867 (that is, the Constitution Act, 1867) did not directly advance the cause of Canadian independence. That act simply divided the powers that were already being exercised in Canada between a new central government and the provincial governments. British control still existed in many forms: British appointment of the governor general; the power of the governor general to reserve Canadian legislation for the approval of the British Cabinet; the power of the British government to disallow Canadian legislation; the power of the British Parliament to amend the BNA Act; the arbitrary extension to Canada of imperial legislation; the paramountcy of any British legislation in conflict with Canadian statutes; Canadian incapacity to pass legislation with extra-territorial effect; the authority of the Judicial Committee of the Privy Council as Canada's final court of appeal; and British control of Canadian foreign and trade policy. The act of confederation made Canada a more respectable and viable entity and ultimately strengthened its case for greater autonomy, but it did not fundamentally alter the British–Canadian relationship.

Canada had succeeded in claiming the right to control its own tariffs even before Confederation, and between 1867 and 1914 it became increasingly autonomous in making commercial treaties with other countries. The same was true in terms of political treaties, although progress in this area came more slowly. One modest advance was the inclusion of Prime Minister Macdonald as a member of the British team that negotiated the 1871 Treaty of Washington. Relations with Britain were handled through the governor general, the Colonial Office, the Canadian High Commissioner in London after 1879, and in periodic Imperial Conferences after 1887.

By the turn of the century Canadian autonomy had progressed to the point that when Prime Minister Wilfrid Laurier sent an official contingent to the South African (Boer) War, it was done more in response to Canadian public opinion than to British pressure. In the Alaska Boundary dispute of 1903, however, the British representative on the Anglo-Canadian half of the judicial tribunal voted with the three American representatives to award the United States a long strip of the northern British Columbia coastline. In defending Canadian interests, Britain was apparently not prepared to jeopardize its relations with the United States.

The ultimate independence of Canada and of several other British colonies is usually attributed to developments connected to the First World War. Although Canada was automatically at war in 1914 as a result of British action, the Canadian government did determine the extent of its own commitments. A series of conferences of Dominion prime ministers called the Imperial War Cabinet began in 1917, as Canada and the other dominions—Australia, New Zealand, and South Africa—demanded a role in policymaking in return for their wartime contributions. Prime Minister Robert Borden and his counterparts took part in the Paris Peace Conference and signed the peace treaties, and the dominions became individual members of the League of Nations. Thus, by 1919, Canada had gained new international status as a result of both accomplishments on the battlefield and subsequent demands for recognition at the conference table.

Postwar attempts to forge a unified Empire foreign policy broke down as various dominions sought to flex their fledgling muscles, and Prime Minister Mackenzie King insisted that Britain not co-sign the 1923 Halibut Treaty with the United States. Based on the Balfour Report, the Imperial Conference of 1926 ended with a proclamation of the complete equality in status of the United Kingdom and the dominions in internal, international, and imperial affairs. They were described in the proclamation as "autonomous Communities within the British Empire, equal in status, in no way subordinate one to another in any aspect of their domestic or external affairs, though united by a common allegiance to the Crown, and freely associated as members of the British Commonwealth of Nations."

Besides giving Canada complete autonomy in all policy fields, the 1926 declaration had implications for the position of the governor general. This official would no longer be an agent of the British government, but rather only a representative of the Crown. Disallowance of Canadian legislation by the British Cabinet and reservation of Canadian legislation by the governor general would now be obsolete. These arrangements were refined at another conference in 1930 and then constitutionalized in the **Statute of Westminster** of 1931. That statute provided that the Colonial Laws Validity Act (under which Dominion statutes were void if they conflicted with statutes of the Imperial Parliament) was no longer to apply to the dominions, that in the future no Dominion statute was to be declared void because it was repugnant to the law of the United Kingdom, and that no act of the Imperial Parliament was to extend to a Dominion unless the latter had requested and consented to its enactment. The Statute also declared that a Dominion Parliament had the power to enact laws having extra-territorial operation.[10]

The drive to loosen links with Britain was thus largely engineered by prime ministers Laurier, Borden, and King, without much apparent public pressure. Reducing British control would automatically increase the power of the Canadian state that these politicians controlled. O.D. Skelton, the trusted adviser of Liberal prime ministers in the early years of the 20th century, has also been identified as a leading advocate of breaking the British bonds in behind-the-scenes discussions with Laurier and King.[11]

After 1931, therefore, Canada was completely independent of Britain, but a number of anomalies somewhat disguised this fact. First, Canada continued to share a head of state with Britain, although from the Canadian perspective, that person was King or Queen of Canada. Even though the Canadian government now had the power to select the governor general, prime ministers continued to make British appointments (aristocrats, diplomats, and war heroes) until 1952. Of more importance, since Canada had not been able to decide how to amend the BNA Act within Canada, such amendments still had to be passed by the British Parliament, albeit only at Canadian request. In 1949 a procedure was developed to make constitutional amendments in Canada if they affected only the federal government, but it was not until 1982 that a comprehensive domestic formula for making constitutional amendments was agreed to. Also of great significance, the **Judicial Committee of the Privy Council (JCPC)** remained Canada's final court of appeal in criminal cases until 1933 and in all other cases, notably constitutional, until 1949. Other British legacies included the fact that, until 1965, the Union Jack and the Red Ensign, combining a smaller Union Jack in the corner with a Canadian crest, continued to serve as Canadian flags. In 1967 the government recognized "O Canada" rather than "God Save the Queen" as the Canadian national anthem, but it was not until 1980 that the former was designated officially.

Once Canada made an autonomous decision to take part, the Second World War saw the Canadian armed forces integrated with the Allied powers. Afterwards, however, British–Canadian ties declined as Canada's population became more diversified in its ethnic origins, as Britain occupied a diminished role in world affairs, and as both Britain and Canada drew closer and closer to the United States.[12] While the definitive break occurred between 1914 and 1940, perhaps the final realization did not dawn until the Suez Crisis of 1956, when Canada refused to support British action. The question of British and French bombardment of Egypt in defence of the Suez Canal in 1956 represented the first major international incident in which Canada found itself at odds with Britain.

As we enter the new millennium, Canada continues to share the Queen with Britain and several other countries and is part of the Commonwealth; nationals of both Canada and Britain have invested in each other's economies; the Canadian parliamentary and legal systems are based on those of Britain; a majority of Canadians speak a variant of the English language; and many are still linked to Britain by family ties. Otherwise, however, both Canada and Britain see each other as just another friendly, foreign country, with minimal influence and no control.

. . . .

CONCLUSION

This chapter has shown how Canada developed from a British colony to a sovereign state. It also traced the evolution of government institutions along the way, focusing primarily on the foundations established in 1867. Those foundations consisted of the grafting of the British parliamentary and American federal systems, although certain aspects of the latter were deliberately avoided. The discussion has also revealed the fact that the question of French–English relations has been integral to Canadian constitutional development from the very beginning.

(SC) The critical approaches outlined in Chapter 1 are of limited application to the evolution of Canadian constitutional development. But since that evolution has usually resulted from the decisions of a small political elite sitting around a table, whether this elite was British (1763–1864), colonial (1864–1867), Canadian (1980–1982), or some combination thereof (1926–1931), the state-centred approach is most appropriate. Canada became more democratic within its own government structures and more autonomous from Britain in a gradual progression of statist decisions without a great deal of input from society as a whole.

P In some cases, however, such as in the establishment of colonial assemblies and then in the recognition of responsible government, such authorities were forced to respond to public pressure. It was only in the 1837 rebellions in both Upper and Lower Canada that such pressure took on violent proportions, and only for a short period of time. Thus, the pluralist approach would emphasize that if and when the public articulated its demands for constitutional change, whether peacefully or violently, the authorities eventually responded.

Ⓒ It could also be said that constitutional developments reflected more than a mere desire for more democracy or more autonomy from Britain. Class analysts, for example, can identify the economic elites that had a hand in guiding constitutional developments, especially the decision to embark on Confederation in 1867. It served the profit-making purposes of the corporate elite to construct railways to outlying colonies if they would join the Confederation scheme. Many businessmen beyond railway promoters also felt that Confederation with a strong central government would be conducive to maximizing their profits.

DISCUSSION QUESTIONS

1. After the Conquest, how would you characterize the British treatment of French Canadians? Explain.

2. Why did French Canadians remain loyal to Britain during the American Revolution?

3. How did the United Empire Loyalists change the face of Canada?

4. What aspects of the French–English political relationship were established before or at Confederation?

5. What is meant by the "Westminster model," and how does it differ from the U.S. system of government?

6. What aspects of American federalism did Canada adopt, and what aspects did it reject?

7. Is there an inherent contradiction between the British parliamentary system and the American federal system? Explain.

8. How do the critical approaches outlined in Chapter 1 enhance our understanding of Canada's constitutional evolution and its institutional foundations?

NOTES

1. Some of the key sources on Canada's constitutional evolution are W.P.M. Kennedy, ed., *Documents of the Canadian Constitution, 1759–1915* (Toronto: Oxford University Press, 1918); R. MacGregor Dawson, *The Government of Canada*, 5th ed., revised by Norman Ward (Toronto: University of Toronto Press, 1970); and Bayard Reesor, *The Canadian Constitution in Historical Perspective* (Scarborough: Prentice-Hall Canada, 1992).

2. Lord Durham, *Report of the Affairs of British North America*, ed. Gerald M. Craig (Toronto: McClelland and Stewart, 1963).

3. P.B. Waite, *The Confederation Debates in the Province of Canada/1865* (Toronto: McClelland and Stewart, 1963); P.B. Waite, *The Life and Times of Confederation, 1864–1867*, 2nd ed. (Toronto: University of Toronto Press, 1962); and Donald Creighton, *The Road to Confederation* (Toronto: Macmillan, 1964).

4. Stanley B. Ryerson, *Unequal Union: Confederation and the Roots of Conflict in the Canadas, 1815–1873*, 2nd ed. (Toronto: Progress Books, 1973).

5. K.C. Wheare, *Federal Government*, 4th ed. (London: Oxford University Press, 1963).

6. Reesor, *The Canadian Constitution in Historical Perspective*, ch. 4.

7. David E. Smith, *The Invisible Crown* (Toronto: University of Toronto Press, 1996).

8. Reesor, *The Canadian Constitution in Historical Perspective*, pp. 66–71.

9. The most famous case is probably *Roncarelli v. Duplessis*, in which the courts found the premier of Quebec personally guilty of cancelling Roncarelli's liquor licence merely because he had provided bail for Jehovah's Witnesses.

10. Dawson, *The Government of Canada*, p. 54. See also his *The Development of Dominion Status, 1900–1936* (London: F. Cass, 1955), and *Constitutional Issues in Canada, 1900–1931* (London: Oxford University Press, 1933).

11. Many observers and historians saw the King and St. Laurent governments as the villains in the Americanization of Canada after the Second World War, although J.L. Granatstein argues that British weakness was of greater significance in this regard than any deliberate Canadian government objective. See Donald Creighton, *Canada's First Century* (Toronto: Macmillan, 1970); George Grant, *Lament for a Nation: The Defeat of Canadian Nationalism* (Toronto: McClelland and Stewart, 1965); and J.L. Granatstein, *How Britain's Weakness Forced Canada into the Arms of the United States* (Toronto: University of Toronto Press, 1989).

12. John Hilliker, *Canada's Department of External Affairs: The Early Years, 1909–1926* (Montreal: McGill–Queen's University Press, 1990).

FURTHER READING

Creighton, Donald. *The Road to Confederation*. Toronto: Macmillan, 1964.

———. *Canada's First Century*. Toronto: Macmillan, 1970.

Dawson, R. MacGregor. *The Government of Canada*, 5th ed. revised by Norman Ward. Toronto: University of Toronto Press, 1970.

Durham, Lord. *Report of the Affairs of British North America*, ed. Gerald M. Craig. Toronto: McClelland and Stewart, 1963.

Granatstein, J.L. *How Britain's Weakness Forced Canada into the Arms of the United States*. Toronto: University of Toronto Press, 1989.

Hilliker, John. *Canada's Department of External Affairs: The Early Years, 1909–1926*. Montreal: McGill–Queen's University Press, 1990.

Kennedy, W.P.M., ed. *Documents of the Canadian Constitution, 1759–1915*. Toronto: Oxford University Press, 1918.

Reesor, Bayard. *The Canadian Constitution in Historical Perspective*. Scarborough: Prentice-Hall Canada, 1992.

Ryerson, Stanley B. *Unequal Union: Confederation and the Roots of Conflict in the Canadas, 1815–1873*, 2nd ed. Toronto: Progress Books, 1973.

Smith, David E. *The Invisible Crown*. Toronto: University of Toronto Press, 1996.

Waite. P.B. *The Life and Times of Confederation, 1864–1867*, 2nd ed. Toronto: University of Toronto Press, 1962.

———. *The Confederation Debates in the Province of Canada/1865*. Toronto: McClelland and Stewart, 1963.

PART 2

The Societal Context

The next seven chapters deal with the main elements of the societal or socioeconomic context of the Canadian political system. It is widely held that the aspects of Canadian society most relevant to politics are its regional economic, ethnic, and class features, primarily because they represent deep, persistent divisions called cleavages. Many of the demands with which the authorities have to contend and many of the interests that the authorities represent originate from such cleavages.

Regionalism and conflicting regional economic claims have been a constant of Canadian politics since the beginning and continue to be animating agents. The ethnic/linguistic/cultural policy field was traditionally dominated by the French–English question, but recent political developments justify separate chapters on Aboriginal peoples and other ethnic groups and multiculturalism. The claims of the Native, French, English, and new Canadian communities have been legitimated in policy, law, and the Constitution, such as in the recognition of Aboriginal rights, official bilingualism, and multiculturalism, but the achievement of such recognition did not end ethnic conflict. That is partly because of the contrasting perceptions that each group has of its own history and current status. The class factor is not as obvious to many observers as some of the other cleavages, but it has probably become more evident as governments have curtailed social programs. It is now also common to point to the increasing importance of gender in the political system, justifying a separate chapter on that question.

Issues relating to ethnicity, gender, and sexual orientation are commonly referred to today as the politics of "identity" or the politics of "recognition," and some observers argue that they have become more important than traditional cleavages. Since other cleavages such as religion and age do not achieve the same political salience as those identified above, they are mentioned only in passing.

Although the conflicting demands within these cleavages are isolated into separate chapters for the sake of clarity, in real life the cleavages actually interact with each other. Sometimes these factors reinforce each other (poor immigrant women; rich Anglo businessmen), but at other times they cut across each other. In any case, the different socioeconomic groups all compete for the attention of governments. For example, in his book The Pursuit of Division, Martin Loney argues that feminists and multicultural advocates have dominated the attention of governments over the past few decades at the expense of the poor.

If the factors mentioned constitute the principal components of the internal environment of the Canadian political system, they must be accompanied by a discussion of the external or global environment. The world has become a "global village," and international, multinational, transnational, and supranational factors are important elements of any national political system. This is especially true of Canada, which has always been open to such external influences.

Chapter 3

Regional ECONOMIC *cleavages*

Manitoba was up in arms that the maintenance contract for the CF-18 military aircraft went to Quebec. Alberta was enraged at the 1980 National Energy Program. Quebec complained that the 1999 federal budget gave too much money to Ontario. The Atlantic groundfish industry has collapsed, the Saskatchewan wheat industry has fallen on hard times, and both regions demand federal assistance. Ontario argues that its residents pay too much into the Employment Insurance fund, such that their contributions are drained off to other parts of the country.

Regional economic cleavages are a basic fact of Canadian life. Many government decisions are direct responses to such cleavages, and most policies at least have to take them into account. Regions usually have some concrete, physical foundation, and are more powerful when they correspond to explicit political divisions. But to some extent regions are also a state of mind. In any case, regional economic cleavages can be most usefully discussed in terms of distance and division, regional economic differences, regional economic conflicts, and regional economic disparities. These topics thus constitute the four parts of this chapter in its examination of the geography and economy of Canada.

....

DISTANCE AND DIVISION
Physiographic Regions

In terms of size, Canada's 9 922 000 km^2 pale beside Russia's 17 075 000 km^2, but exceed China's 9 597 000 km^2 and the United States's 9 363 000 km^2. From east to west Canada is 5050 km long, and from southern to northern tip it stretches 4600 km. The territory involved is vast, even the part below the 60th parallel, which has traditionally been of most interest to politicians because it is more densely populated and is organized into provinces. Prime Minister Mackenzie King once remarked that if some countries had too much history, Canada had too much geography.[1] In fact, St. John's, Newfoundland, is closer to London, England, than to Victoria, BC, and many Canadians feel closer to adjacent U.S. states than to other Canadian regions. Such tremendous distances have always had a crucial influence on the Canadian political system, both in generating regional economic demands and influencing patterns of support.

Distance would be difficult enough to cope with even if the territory involved was one level, undifferentiated plain, but the problem is immensely complicated by divisions caused by physical barriers. Canada is usually divided into five basic physiographic regions, as shown in Figure 3.1. The Atlantic provinces are in the rocky Appalachian region, while British Columbia and the Yukon are composed of the even more mountainous Western Cordillera. Extending in a great sweep around Hudson Bay is the rugged Canadian or Precambrian Shield. It encompasses most of Quebec and Ontario and northern parts of the Prairies, and melds into Arctic tundra above the 60th parallel. This leaves only two level plains regions: the Interior Plains of the Prairie provinces, and the Great Lakes–St. Lawrence Lowlands of southern Ontario and Quebec. In other words, the vast territory is divided into five main regions by natural barriers running in a north–south direction. It is often simpler to travel southward to the United States than to cross the barriers into another part of Canada.

One aspect of Canadian geography that counterbalances these north–south forces is the river and lake system. In this respect, the central historical role of the St. Lawrence River and the Great Lakes has often been noted.[2] Since this natural east–west flow was enhanced by the construction of the St. Lawrence Seaway, ships have been able to go halfway across the country, a fact that improves Canada's capacity to engage in international trade.

Figure 3.1   Canada's Physiographic Regions

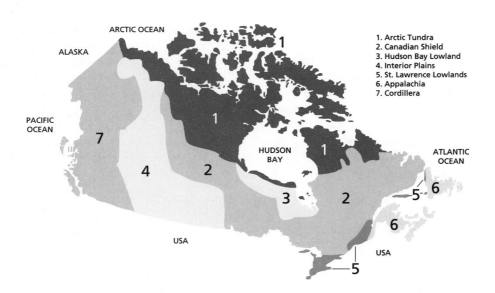

1. Arctic Tundra
2. Canadian Shield
3. Hudson Bay Lowland
4. Interior Plains
5. St. Lawrence Lowlands
6. Appalachia
7. Cordillera

Transportation and Communications Systems

Apart from the Great Lakes–St. Lawrence water route, transportation and communications systems in Canada had to be constructed across the natural barriers. The establishment of each of these great transportation and communications projects dominated successive eras in Canadian politics, and even upon their completion demands continued to be expressed with respect to viability, maintenance, rates, and service.

Railways were the stuff of Canadian politics throughout the 19th and early 20th centuries. In particular, they formed a crucial part of the Confederation Settlement of the 1860s and 1870s. The Maritimes agreed to enter Confederation only if they were linked to central Canada by the Intercolonial Railway, and British Columbia was persuaded to join in 1871 with the promise of a transcontinental rail link within ten years.[3] Political scandal involving railways then led to the defeat of Sir John A. Macdonald in 1872, but after his re-election in 1878 the construction of the Canadian Pacific Railway (CPR) to Vancouver became one of his lasting monuments. Macdonald brought the project to completion in 1885, only four years behind schedule.[4] Although it was a private company, the CPR received enormous government assistance in the form of cash and land grants that later became prime real estate in the centre of many Canadian cities. While the building of the CPR was one of the great heroic events in Canadian history, it was also a classic example of the state's being used for the advantage of private capital.[5]

Since the CPR served the southern part of Western Canada, demands immediately arose for other, more northerly routes. This was especially so because the Prairies chafed under the CPR monopoly clause that, in the absence of competition, allowed it to charge high rates. Indeed, freight rates have been a constant complaint of Western Canadians since the day the CPR was completed. Eventually other railways were built, but even with government assistance they went into receivership, and in the 1919–23 period they were bailed out by the federal government in the creation of the Canadian National (CN) system. Thus, the establishment of CN as a Crown corporation was a benefit to bankrupt capitalist interests.

When both CP and CN wanted out of the passenger side of the railroad business, a separate Crown corporation, VIA Rail, was created in 1977–78. Although politicians made initial promises about improving Canada's rail passenger service, the system was starved for funds and steadily declined until, because of large annual subsidies, the Mulroney government discontinued half the routes in 1990. Train enthusiasts howled in protest and argued that the extent of government subsidization of highway, marine, and air transport should be taken into consideration when railway deficits were discussed. Nevertheless, rationalization of the country's railway system continued to be a major issue throughout the 1990s, and the Chrétien government privatized Canadian National by selling shares to the public.

The early 20th century was almost as obsessed with automobiles as the previous era was with railways. Since roads are primarily a provincial responsibility, however, their political significance was and continues to be greatest at that level. The federal government was mainly called on to ensure that a decent highway extended across the whole country for commercial, recreational, and symbolic purposes. Thus, in 1949, the federal government signed the Trans-Canada Highway agreement with the provinces under which Ottawa paid one-half the cost of bringing a transcontinental highway up to a national standard. It was eventually completed in 1962, but not before some provinces demanded more than 50 percent, and Newfoundland in particular managed to secure some 90 percent, of the funding from the federal government. Prince Edward Island later gained a "fixed link" to the mainland with the construction of the Confederation Bridge to replace the ferry service. Most provinces continue to demand that Ottawa help them finance the upgrading of their portion of the highway, and it is estimated that needed upgrades to the Canadian highway network in general would cost billions of dollars.

Given the distances involved, it is not surprising that demands also arose for a coordinated nationwide airline service, passenger as well as cargo. Then transport minister C.D. Howe negotiated a deal to create Trans-Canada Airlines (now Air Canada) as a joint private–public corporation, but when the private backers withdrew at the last minute, TCA was created in 1937 as a Crown corporation. Air Canada was later one of the Mulroney government's first candidates for privatization. Official thinking in the late 1980s was that the country was now well served by a variety of private carriers and that the government airline no longer served a **public policy purpose**. With the sale of major airports and related assets in the 1990s (the privatization of the Toronto Pearson Airport by the Mulroney government being especially controversial), the federal government substantially evacuated the transportation industry, a field in which it was historically very active. This followed a deregulation of the whole transportation system, although the industry is still subject to some regulation by the Canadian Transportation Agency. Demands from one region or another are constantly on the agenda of that agency too.

....

MAJOR TRANSPORTATION AND COMMUNICATIONS LINKS AND AGENCIES

- Canadian Pacific
- Canadian National
- VIA Rail
- Canadian Transportation Agency
- Trans-Canada Pipeline
- Canadian Radio-television and Telecommunications Commission (CRTC)
- Canadian Broadcasting Corporation (CBC)
- National Film Board
- Telesat
- Teleglobe

Oil and natural gas pipelines, a newer means of transportation, have figured prominently in Canadian politics since 1950. Sometimes the desire of Western provinces to sell petroleum coincided with that of Eastern Canadians' wish to buy it, but at other times interregional conflicts arose with respect to pricing, exportation, and importation of these resources. Although privately owned, pipelines have sought considerable government support in one form or another. The construction of the main natural gas line to Eastern Canada, the Trans-Canada Pipeline, was probably the most controversial issue on the Canadian political agenda in the mid-1950s and had a major role to play in the defeat of the St. Laurent government in 1957. Another controversial pipeline will bring offshore natural gas from the Sable Island field to Nova Scotia, New Brunswick, and beyond.

Transportation presents special challenges in the North. Roads and railways were virtually nonexistent there until the Diefenbaker government sponsored its "Roads to Resources" program, and the Yellowknife region of the Northwest Territories became linked to Edmonton. The Alaska Highway, which passes through the Yukon on its way from British Columbia, has been a crucial part of that territory's development. Various pipeline proposals have also been significant to the North. The proposed Mackenzie Valley Gas Pipeline of the 1970s and the Berger Commission, which was appointed to assess it, had a major effect on northern and southern attitudes alike. Berger recommended that the pipeline be put on hold for ten years while Native land claims were settled, as well as for environmental reasons. Few such pipelines have yet been constructed in the North, although that is more a matter of economics than of concern about Aboriginals or the environment, and the issue is likely to be revisited.

As far as communications are concerned, telegraph, telephone, radio, and television usually developed first in the private sector. But because some of these systems were natural monopolies or because of the limited number of frequencies available, they soon led to government regulation, now primarily done by the **Canadian Radio-television and Telecommunications Commission (CRTC)**. That agency issues radio and television licences and Canadian content regulations and reviews telephone rates. In most of these sectors demands also arose for public ownership, such as in the Prairie provinces' telephone systems and in the **Canadian Broadcasting Corporation (CBC)**. Amid great controversy, CBC radio began in 1932 in response to pressure for more Canadian content and more enlightened programming than was usually provided on local private stations, many of which carried U.S. programs. It became operational in English and French with its own stations as well as affiliated private stations in 1936. The same motives led to the establishment of the National Film Board (NFB), in 1939, and of CBC television in 1952. In 1977, the CBC also began to televise proceedings of the House of Commons on a second channel, now called CPAC and operated by the cable companies, and in 1989 it established an English-language all-news channel, Newsworld. Meanwhile, certain provinces also became involved in educational television, and many new privately owned stations and networks appeared. Great competition exists among them for government assistance, the best channels and frequencies, and other preferential treatment by the CRTC. To supplement the country's terrestrial microwave system, the government took the initiative in 1969 to launch Telesat, a joint public–private supplier of domestic communications satellite services. Intercontinental communications via submarine cables and satellites are handled by Teleglobe Canada, which was a Crown corporation until the Mulroney government privatized it in 1987.

Thus, in the field of transportation and communications, demands to overcome distances and divisions have been dominant features of Canadian politics. Governments have primarily responded with assistance to private corporations, the establishment of Crown corporations, and the creation of regulatory agencies. In order to create and hold together a nation, Canadians built east–west institutions that ran counter to the natural north–south geographic features of the continent and the perpetual pull of the United States. In the neoconservative 1980s and cash-starved 1990s, however, both the Mulroney and Chrétien governments privatized a number of government operations in this field, reduced support for others, especially the CBC, and generally deregulated the transportation industry. Governments started to dismantle these east–west links, as well as to sign north–south trade deals, leading many to question the continued existence of Canada as an independent nation-state. Symbolically, both CP Rail and the newly privatized CN Rail sold off track in Canada and laid off hundreds of employees but became major players in the United States.

Population Distribution

Geographic barriers are only one complication to the distances that characterize Canada; the distribution of population is another, for the people are not spread uniformly throughout this gigantic territory. It is commonly emphasized that the overall density of the Canadian population is one of the lowest in the world, some 3.0 people per km². But it is really more significant that there is no permanent settlement in nearly 90 percent of the country and that 72 percent of the population is huddled within 150 km of the U.S. border.[6]

Provincial population disparities affect the allocation of seats in the House of Commons—indeed the whole power structure in Ottawa—and the calculation of federal transfer payments. The population of the various provinces can be seen in Table 3.1.

Geographers frequently speak of the core, "heartland," or "metropolis" on the one hand, and the "periphery" or "hinterland" on the other, concepts that can be usefully applied to political science. The Toronto–Ottawa–Montreal triangle obviously constitutes the core of Canada, and Ontario and Quebec combined contain 62 percent of its people. While central Canada constitutes the political core of the country, it is also the economic heartland, containing the largest concentration of corporate head offices, especially in the Toronto area. Moreover, it is the communications and cultural core, containing the headquarters of French and English CBC, CTV, Global, and private French television, many other Canadian cultural

TABLE 3.1   **Population of Provinces and Territories**

	1996 Census		July 1999	
Ontario	10 753 573	(37.3%)	11 560 899	(37.8%)
Quebec	7 138 795	(24.7%)	7 363 262	(24.1%)
British Columbia	3 724 500	(12.9%)	4 029 253	(13.2%)
Alberta	2 696 826	(9.3%)	2 968 992	(9.7%)
Manitoba	1 113 898	(3.9%)	1 143 391	(3.7%)
Saskatchewan	990 237	(3.4%)	1 028 137	(3.4%)
Nova Scotia	909 282	(3.2%)	940 825	(3.1%)
New Brunswick	783 133	(2.7%)	754 741	(2.5%)
Newfoundland	551 792	(1.9%)	541 164	(1.8%)
Prince Edward Island	134 557	(0.5%)	137 796	(0.5%)
Northwest Territories	64 402	(0.2%)	41 668	(0.1%)
Yukon	30 766	(0.1%)	30 688	(0.1%)
Nunavut	—	—	27 146	(0.1%)
Canada	28 846 761		30 567 962	

Adapted from "INFOMAT: A Weekly Review," Catalogue No. 11-002, April 18, 1997; and the CANSIM database, Matrix No. 6367-6379.

institutions, and most of the Canadian computer industry. The rest of the country, the hinterland or periphery, with its smaller population base, regularly complains that it is overlooked by both public and private decision makers. It is not surprising that many Westerners advocate a reformed Senate that would be based on equal representation for each province, while Quebec is extremely sensitive to its proportion of the total Canadian population, which by 1995 had fallen below a symbolic 25 percent.

The distribution of the Canadian population is even more complicated. In addition to this national core–periphery system, a series of regional core–periphery systems exists across the country. Several metropolitan centres dominate their own regional hinterlands: Vancouver in British Columbia; Edmonton and Calgary in Alberta; Regina and Saskatoon in Saskatchewan; Winnipeg in Manitoba; Toronto in Ontario; Montreal in Quebec; and Halifax and to a lesser extent St. John's in Atlantic Canada. The same could be said of Whitehorse in the Yukon and Yellowknife in the Northwest Territories. The interior of BC and northern Ontario are two examples of regions within a province that feel isolated from and exploited by their own economic cores, Vancouver and Toronto respectively.

Such regional cores are heavily urbanized, and are termed "census metropolitan areas" (CMAs) by Statistics Canada. The 25 largest metropolitan centres in Canada (see Table 3.2) constituted 62.1 percent of the total population in 1996. More than one politician has calculated that the support of only these highly urbanized areas would be enough to form a government. Overall, Statistics Canada categorized 77.9 percent of the population as urban in 1996.

TABLE 3.2   **Population of Census Metropolitan Areas, 1996**

Toronto	4 263 757	Victoria	304 287
Montreal	3 326 510	Windsor	278 685
Vancouver	1 831 665	Oshawa	268 773
Ottawa-Hull	1 010 498	Saskatoon	219 056
Edmonton	862 597	Regina	193 652
Calgary	821 628	St. John's	174 051
Quebec City	671 889	Sudbury	160 488
Winnipeg	667 209	Chicoutimi	160 454
Hamilton	624 360	Sherbrooke	147 384
London	398 616	Trois-Rivières	139 956
Kitchener	382 940	Saint John	125 705
St. Catharines	372 406	Thunder Bay	125 562
Halifax	332 518		

Adapted from Population and Dwelling Counts, *Catalogue No. 93-357.*

Provinces and Territories

In speaking of regionalism in Canada, then, we begin with great distances complicated by geographic barriers and concentrations of population that cause variations in political and economic power. In addition, it was partly because of such distances and divisions that provinces and territories were created. Whether originally separate colonies of Britain or later carved out of the Western territories, the provinces were granted considerable power by the Constitution. The political-legal-constitutional basis of such units is quite different from the natural, physiographic basis of regions, and the fit between regionalism and provincialism is not perfect. Feelings of regionalism can exist within a province, such as in the northern parts of many provinces; regional sentiment can cut across provinces, as in the case of people in northwestern Ontario feeling psychologically closer to Manitoba than to southern Ontario; and provinces can be lumped together into regions, such as the Maritimes or the Prairies. Nevertheless, the connection between regionalism and provincialism is a compelling relationship. In discussing the question of regionalism, the 1979 Task Force on Canadian Unity had this to say:

> Regional communities require an institutional framework if they are to become viable units which can express themselves and organize their collective life in an effective manner. For that reason, it seems to us that the provinces and the northern territories are the basic building blocks of Canadian society and the logical units on which to focus a discussion of Canadian regionalism, even though they may not be the most "natural" regions from an economic point of view.[7]

The creation of provinces and territories has two primary effects as far as regional economic demands are concerned. On the one hand, if a region is identified with a political unit, that unit can become a persuasive transmitter of regional demands to Ottawa. Regional demands articulated by a provincial premier or territorial government are harder to ignore than those that come from less authoritative sources. In fact, to politicize such regional demands in this way may well serve to magnify them, since premiers and bureaucrats can use such diversity to justify an increase in their power. On the other hand, provinces and territories may be able to facilitate the decision-making process by handling local problems that are not controversial at the provincial or territorial level but that would cause great difficulty in Ottawa. The basic quest in the establishment of a federal system of government is to find the most appropriate division of powers and responsibilities between the national and provincial levels. This issue, the degree of centralization and decentralization in Canada, has never been settled to everyone's satisfaction, as was demonstrated by the debate over the Meech Lake and Charlottetown Accords from 1987 to 1992 and subsequent constitutional questions that threaten the continued existence of the country. Canadians still raise demands about the design of the federal system as well as about policies within it.

In the 1990s, Quebec came closer than ever to separating from the rest of Canada. If it were to leave with its existing borders intact (a somewhat debatable issue), Quebec would take almost one-quarter of the Canadian population with it, about 16 percent of its territory, and about 25 percent of Canada's gross domestic product. Among many other complications, from a strictly geographic point of view, the separation of Quebec would raise the question of continuing transportation links between Atlantic Canada and Ontario, border-crossing impediments, and jurisdiction over the St. Lawrence Seaway.[8]

In terms of distance, natural barriers, population distribution, and political divisions, then, it is most common to speak of the following principal Canadian regions: Ontario, Quebec, the Prairies, the Atlantic region, British Columbia, and the North. Ontario and Quebec qualify as separate regions because of their size and provincial status. The Prairie provinces and the Atlantic provinces are sufficiently small and similar in character to be grouped together for many purposes as two regional units. British Columbia's claim to regional status is less well established, but it has gained increasing recognition because of its size and its geographic division and distinctiveness from the Prairie provinces. Newfoundland often makes a claim for similar status at the eastern end of the country, but primarily because of its much smaller size, it is usually lumped with the three Maritime provinces to form the Atlantic region. The North has traditionally been ignored, but is increasingly regarded as a separate region worthy of mention. On the other hand, to those on the periphery, Ontario and Quebec seem to constitute a single central core.

REGIONAL ECONOMIC DIFFERENCES

Having identified the regions of Canada, we may now proceed to examine their economies. Such a discussion, utilizing the distinctions among primary, secondary, and tertiary sectors, reveals striking regional economic differences that serve to reinforce their geographic distinctiveness and create another pattern of demands on the Canadian political system.[9]

Regional economic differences begin with primary industries, that is, the natural resource and energy base of the various provinces. The importance of natural resources to the national economy has been a central tenet of Canadian political economy for generations; it is usually termed the **staples theory** and is identified with the famous economic historian Harold Innis.[10] It postulates that Canadian economic development has relied on a succession of resource exports—furs, fish, timber, wheat, minerals, and energy—rather than manufacturing; Canadians are mere "hewers of wood and drawers of water." The staples theory also includes the notions of dependence on one or more foreign industrial centres and of an economy that remains underdeveloped and that is subject to the rise and fall of international markets. In international trade, Canada continues to this day to rely primarily on exports of natural resources. Sometimes an element of interregional exploitation is involved as well, especially in the relationship between inner and outer Canada.

To economists, secondary industry consists of manufacturing, construction, and utilities. Manufacturing includes the initial processing and refining of primary products as well as the making of finished goods, and generally produces more revenue and more jobs than primary industry, is less seasonal, and commands higher wages. Many observers have criticized the economic policy of almost all Canadian governments for having fostered the exploitation and exportation of raw natural resources rather than having developed an industrial policy that would give priority to manufacturing. They also blame the banks for preferring resource companies and foreign-owned manufacturers in their lending policies.[11] Furthermore, the fact that both governments and corporations in Canada spend so little money on "research and development" (R&D) does not augur well for the future when "high tech" and productivity will be so important.

Economists then put transportation and communications, trade, finance, insurance and real estate, private services, and public administration into the tertiary or services category.

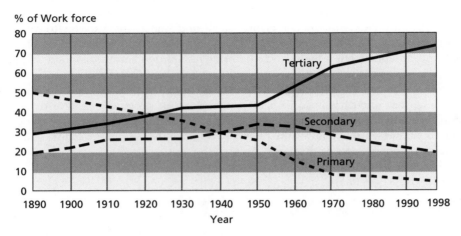

Figure 3.2   Employment in Canada by Sector

Source: Stephen Brooks and Andrew Stritch, Business and Government in Canada *(Scarborough: Prentice-Hall Canada, 1991), p. 96; Statistics Canada,* Labour Force Update *(Spring 1999), Cat. No. 71-005-XPB. Brooks and Stritch reprinted with permission of Pearson Education Canada Inc.*

While the Canadian economy was never strong on manufacturing, much political attention in this "postindustrial" era is focused on the services sector. Figure 3.2 demonstrates the contemporary importance of the tertiary sector in outlining the trends in the Canadian labour force among the three divisions of the economy.

The Atlantic Provinces[12]

The Atlantic provinces have a distinctive and heavy reliance on fishing, which has rarely been a very prosperous industry. In the 1990s, however, the Atlantic fishery was in deeper trouble than ever before, primarily due to a dramatic reduction in groundfish stocks, especially cod, and an oversupply of fishers, plant workers, and trawlers. The three Maritime provinces have a substantial agricultural base, which has provided prosperity for a few large firms but generally poor returns for most farmers. New Brunswick, Newfoundland, and Nova Scotia also engage in forestry and mining, while Newfoundland possesses great quantities of hydroelectric power in Labrador. None of these resources has led to much general prosperity in any of the Atlantic provinces, however, and most of the larger projects have been developed by central Canadian or foreign firms. Some processing and refining of natural resources takes place in the region, but among other factors, the small local market and the distance from major population centres have left the region in a state of underdevelopment. Led by New Brunswick, a new emphasis on communications technology has revitalized the Atlantic provinces' economies to some extent, for in the modern technological world, physical distance is not the hindrance it was in the past. Newfoundland's offshore petroleum is finally flowing, and two other promising developments are the proposed Voisey's Bay nickel mine in Labrador and the Sable Island natural gas field off Nova Scotia.

Quebec

The Quebec economy is more diversified than that of the Atlantic region and somewhat more prosperous. Quebec's primary industries include farming in the St. Lawrence Lowlands, along with mining and forestry in the Canadian Shield. That shield is also traversed by numerous powerful rivers, making hydroelectricity Quebec's most valuable resource. Huge dams have been built on many of its rivers, including the controversial James Bay hydroelectric project. Hydro is the basis of Quebec's aluminum industry, for example, as well as of much other secondary industry. Quebec also stands out in the production of pulp and paper, especially newsprint. In addition, Quebec is much stronger than the Atlantic region in the more sophisticated aspects of manufacturing. Thus, in addition to the refining and processing of metals, oil, and the production of textiles, food and beverages, and chemicals, Quebec produces clothing, aeronautics, electronics, pharmaceuticals, and transportation equipment. It also houses a large financial sector. The fact that economic power in Quebec used to rest largely in English-Canadian and foreign hands fuelled the nationalist debate in that province. But since 1960 a major transformation has occurred, and both the public and francophone private sectors in Quebec have repatriated a great deal of industrial ownership. One means of doing so was the Caisse de Dépôt et Placement, which invested Quebec Pension Plan premiums in domestic firms.

Ontario

Ontario has always had the strongest and most diversified economy of any region. The province has an abundance of natural resources, including a great expanse of prime agricultural land in the Great Lakes Lowlands, and vast stretches of trees and almost every conceivable mineral in the Canadian Shield. The province also contains several powerful rivers for the production of hydroelectricity, although it is increasingly dependent on nuclear power in this regard. Ontario's early development of hydroelectricity and of a steel industry gave it a head start over other regions. A skilled labour force, a large domestic market, proximity to the United States, and the advantage of federal tariff and banking policies also helped to make it the manufacturing heartland of the country. It now produces over half of the Canadian total, including automobiles, electronic products, machinery, and publishing, in addition to steel, food and beverages, smelting and refining, metal fabrication, and pulp and paper, although many of these industries were hit hard by the 1990–92 recession. In addition, Ontario leads the country in the tertiary sector, such as finance, trade, and services, and the seats of the two largest governments in the country, in Ottawa and Toronto, also provide considerable employment, although less than in the past.

The Prairie Provinces

The Prairie provinces are historically associated with agriculture, especially wheat, other grain, and livestock, and this industry continues to be very important. Saskatchewan in particular suffered from a dramatic decline in the grain industry in the 1980s, however, and poor weather, high costs, and soft international markets continue to plague Canada's farmers. The high value of primary industry in the Prairies is largely due, therefore, to Alberta's oil and natural gas production, and Alberta has thus become the richest part of the country by many measures.

Petroleum is also of increasing significance in Saskatchewan, in concert with that province's other mineral resources, potash and uranium. In addition, Alberta possesses large amounts of coal, and Manitoba, of nickel, copper, and zinc. Forestry has been an important industry in Manitoba and more recently in Alberta, while Manitoba's hydroelectricity complements the petroleum of the other two Prairie provinces. Thus, while the Prairies can be compared to the Atlantic region to some extent in their relatively heavy dependence on primary industry, a contrast is readily apparent: resource extraction on the Prairies is usually a more profitable venture. The Prairies are also engaged in a certain amount of manufacturing, including food and beverages, transportation equipment, machinery, metal fabrication, chemicals, petrochemicals, and fertilizer. With the new wealth of the Western provinces, especially since 1960, the finance, trade, and service industries have expanded rapidly, and the Prairies are less dependent on Ontario in this respect than they used to be.

British Columbia

Mountainous British Columbia is the leading forestry province and also specializes in mining, including natural gas, copper, and coal. Several fertile river and lake valleys provide for farming, and, being a coastal province, BC also possesses a significant fishing industry. The mountains are the source of several large rivers that have been dammed for the production of hydroelectricity, and, as in Quebec, the abundant electricity is used to produce aluminum as well as being exported. Manufacturing is primarily related to the forestry, mining, and agricultural bases of the BC economy: assorted wood products such as shakes and shingles and pulp and paper; food and beverages; and the processing and refining of metals, petroleum, chemicals, and coal. Asian immigration has expanded the services sector, especially finance, but BC's heavy dependence on resource exports entails periodic economic downturns.

The North

The North, now divided into the three territories of the Yukon, Northwest Territories, and **Nunavut,** has very limited agriculture and forestry, given its frigid climate, short growing season, and lack of soil. Mining has inspired many southerners to venture north over the years, especially in the gold rushes of the 1890s in Dawson City, and the 1930s in Yellowknife. Other isolated mineral deposits have been found, but most proceeded with artificially high levels of government support, and many have since been abandoned. The prospects of oil and natural gas are more promising, especially in the Mackenzie River delta and the Beaufort Sea. Government policy has encouraged northern petroleum exploration at public expense, but it awaits full-scale development. The unstable world price, the uncertain supply in southern Canada and the United States, the outstanding Aboriginal land claims, and the cost and difficulty of transporting the petroleum southward have all combined to limit such a flow. Northern Natives used to be self-sufficient in hunting, fishing, and trapping, activities that continue to occupy them to some extent, while tourism is on the increase. In general, however, the inhospitable climate, the isolation, the small and transient labour force, and the poor transportation facilities conspire to retard economic development of the region. But positive recent signs include settlement of many Native land claims, the discovery of diamonds, and the creation of the eastern territory of Nunavut in 1999. Increased autonomy from Ottawa should better allow the territories to respond to local needs.

Regional Demands

Since most natural resources fall within provincial jurisdiction, demands arising from the primary sector are often first addressed to the respective provincial government. So are the environmental concerns that economic development often engenders. Every primary industry has also sought federal government support of one kind or another over the years, however, and most other regional economic demands are primarily directed to Ottawa. In response, its policy outputs have often benefited a certain industry throughout the country. At other times, its support of one region has also been in the national interest, such as in the creation of the **Canadian Wheat Board** to help Prairie farmers export more grain. Because these farmers could then pay higher federal taxes and buy more goods produced in other provinces, such a policy generally made the whole country more prosperous. Similarly, if Ottawa protects or promotes the Atlantic fishing industry, the rest of the country will pay less in employment insurance and equalization payments to that region.

Thus, as a result of regional economic differences, the national government regularly faces demands to assist a single industry or the economy of a single province or region. Many such demands have elicited a positive response, especially when the case was desperate, popular, or articulated by the right interest. Such outputs do not necessarily involve conflict between one region and another, and sometimes benefit them all.

REGIONAL ECONOMIC CONFLICTS

More often than not, however, demands from one region *do* conflict with those from another. The most pervasive expression of such regional economic conflict has undoubtedly been between the Prairie and Ontario regions. Since Ontario's regional interests have historically been persuasive with the federal government, the analysis is usually put in terms of the central core versus the periphery of the country, especially the West,[13] and involve five principal complaints.

Ownership of Natural Resources

The problem of natural resource ownership began in 1870 with the creation of the province of Manitoba. While the Eastern provinces and British Columbia always had jurisdiction over their own natural resources, Ottawa decided to retain such control in the case of Manitoba, and when Saskatchewan and Alberta were created in 1905, these provinces were placed in the same subordinate position. The logic of prime ministers Macdonald in 1870 and Wilfrid Laurier in 1905 was that the federal government (i.e., central Canada) should control such resources in the national interest, allowing Ottawa to guide the development of the West. The Prairie provinces fought vehemently against this discrimination, and were finally successful in gaining control of their natural resources in 1930.

Tariffs

In the second place, the West complained for generations that Canadian **tariff** policy was designed in the interest of Ontario (and to a lesser extent Quebec) at the expense of the Prairies. This was because as early as the 1879 **National Policy**, Macdonald saw the tariff as a means of promoting and protecting the industrial heartland of central Canada. Adding a tariff (an import tax) to the price of imported manufactured goods would raise their price above that of goods manufactured in Canada, even if foreign production costs were lower, and allow domestic goods to be sold more cheaply than imports. In practice, it was largely foreign firms that established themselves in central Canada behind this tariff wall, but the tariff at least had the beneficial effect of creating jobs in Canada rather than in Britain or the United States. Ontario thus gained employment in producing tractors for Western Canada, for example, but Western Canadians felt that this was contrary to their interests because, in the absence of such a tariff, they would have been able to buy a cheaper tractor from the United States. Furthermore, when Canada resorted to tariff protection of its manufacturing industry, other countries were likely to respond by restricting their imports of Canadian grain. The West demanded lower tariffs at every opportunity, and especially in the 1920s sent its own farmer representatives to the House of Commons to fight on this front. Tariffs among all countries have gradually come down since 1945, but the issue took on a new life in the 1980s with the Western demand for a free trade agreement between Canada and the United States. Thus, the controversial Free Trade Agreement between the two countries, which took effect in 1989, can be seen as a response to 110 years of Western discontent with the tariff aspect of the National Policy.[14]

Transportation

Another aspect of Macdonald's National Policy that displeased the West was transportation and especially railways. In choosing to live so far from the central core of the country, Westerners expected to pay additional transportation costs, although many demanded that railway freight rates be subsidized by Ottawa. Indeed, the Crow's Nest Pass Act (or **Crow rate**) of 1897 was an attempt to do just that, and provided a low rate for transporting Prairie grain to eastern ports. After successfully fighting to retain the Crow rate in the 1920s, many Westerners were greatly upset by the Trudeau government's increase in these rates, as well as by the Chrétien government's decision in 1995 to abolish the Crow rate entirely. But a more legitimate complaint was about peculiar inequities within the freight rate structure, including higher rates for finished goods than for raw materials (which discouraged manufacturing in the West), discrimination against short hauls, and deviations from the principle of distance determining price.

Banking

The West also protested against national banking policy. In contrast to community-based unit banks as in the United States, Canada deliberately developed a centralized branch banking system. This policy was in part an attempt to construct a sound, stable banking community that would avoid frequent local collapses, but the lack of competition it involved was also favoured by the established banking interests themselves, providing more evidence of corporate pressure on government policy. The result was a handful of large national banks, usually with headquarters in Montreal or Toronto, and with local branches spread across the country. From a hinterland perspective, money deposited in the local branch of a national bank would not remain in the community to be lent out for local purposes, but was sent to headquarters in central Canada to be used in the economic development of Ontario or Quebec. Moreover, decisions to make large loans were centralized at the head office, so that Western entrepreneurs would have to travel east in order to borrow substantial sums. This was another reason for the farmers' revolt of the 1920s, and displeasure with the Canadian banking system had much to do with the rise of the Social Credit Party in Alberta in the 1930s. For many decades Ottawa refused to make any changes to this policy, but in the 1970s, when the West became stronger in spite of it, the federal government finally responded. On the one hand, Ottawa eased restrictions on chartering regional banks, and several new Western banks were established. On the other hand, the existing national banks saw the merit of decentralizing decision making within their own operations, so that larger decisions could be made on location. Unfortunately, several of these new Western financial institutions faltered in the 1980s, largely because of a downturn in the Western region's economy that Westerners blamed on Trudeau's National Energy Program.

Taxation and Regulation of Natural Resources

By that time, the original conflict over natural resources had re-emerged, especially with respect to petroleum pricing. National energy policy in the 1950s and 1960s had actually favoured the West, for Alberta was guaranteed a market for its oil and natural gas as far east as Ontario. But the West overlooked that fact after the OPEC (Organization of Petroleum Exporting Countries) cartel agreed on an artificial rise in the international price of oil in 1973. At this point, federal policy began to favour the consumer/manufacturing interest of central Canada at the expense of the producer interest of the West. The height of the regional economic conflict occurred in 1980 with the Trudeau government's **National Energy Program (NEP)**, which imposed new federal taxes, retained a larger share of petroleum revenues for Ottawa, kept the national price below the world level, encouraged frontier—largely offshore—development, and promoted Canadianization of the industry, all objectives inimical to most Westerners. Eventually a partial compromise between central and Western interests was reached in 1981, and the Mulroney government later scrapped the NEP entirely. Nevertheless, the NEP had a profound effect on the Western Canadian psyche, especially when combined with the West's simultaneous opposition to Ottawa's constitutional initiatives and bilingualism policy.

Metropolitan Exploitation of the Hinterland

These four policy areas—tariffs, transportation, banking, and resources—represent the most serious regional economic conflicts in Canadian history, but they can be seen in a broader context. The metropolitan–hinterland thesis suggests that the West was created as a colony of central Canada and was intended to be held in a subordinate and dependent relationship.[15] Western feeling about its situation was captured in a famous cartoon in the Grain Growers' Guide as early as 1915, and while it is depicted in agricultural terms, the image provided in

Figure 3.3   **The Canadian Economy as Seen by Many Westerners**

"The Milch Cow," by Arch. Dale *(1882–1962), from the* Grain Growers Guide *(December 15, 1915). Reproduced courtesy of the Glenbow Archives, Calgary, Canada (NA-3055-24).*

Figure 3.3 is still appropriate some 85 years later. Dissatisfaction with both the Liberal and Conservative parties' focus on Quebec issues in the 1980s and early 1990s led to deep feelings of **Western alienation** and then to the formation of the Reform Party, whose initial slogan was "The West Wants In." Although it broadened its focus by the time of the 1993 federal election, the Reform Party won the majority of seats west of Ontario, and almost all of them in British Columbia and Alberta, and repeated this feat in 1997.

The Atlantic Provinces

Many of the Western economic conflicts with central Canada have been echoed by the Atlantic provinces. This was especially true of post-Confederation tariff policy, which also appeared to do the Maritimes more harm than good. Nova Scotia and New Brunswick entered Confederation in 1867 as proud and prosperous colonies, and while changes in marine technology (from wooden sailing ships to steel steamships) were probably the principal factor responsible, their economies quickly declined. Whatever the reason, Maritimers preferred to blame federal economic policy for much of their difficulty. The Atlantic provinces shared the West's concerns about federal freight rates, although they received subsidization in this area, too, and they opposed federal resource policy in the 1980s, prompting them to fight for provincial ownership of offshore petroleum. They differed from the West to some extent on the Canada–U.S. Free Trade Agreement, fearing that it would eliminate many of their subsidy programs. They also complained of an insufficiently aggressive federal government when it came to protecting Atlantic fish stocks from foreign overfishing. Another common complaint of the Atlantic and Western regions is that the federal government does most of its purchasing or procuring in central Canada. While the economic complaints of the two outlying regions have thus generally coincided, they have occasionally been at odds, such as in the relative decline of Maritime representation in federal political institutions as the West's population expanded.

Routine Regional Conflicts

Smaller-scale regional economic disputes are also a routine, if not daily, occurrence in Canadian politics. Attempts to support the steel plant in Sydney, Nova Scotia, arouse opposition in Sault Ste. Marie, Ontario; awarding the CF-18 maintenance contract to Canadair of Montreal infuriates supporters of Bristol Aerospace of Winnipeg (and further reinforces Western alienation);[16] extending drug patent protection for multinational pharmaceutical firms in Quebec offends Canadian generic drug producers in Ontario; promoting frontier petroleum exploration (including federal assistance to Newfoundland's Hibernia project) upsets conventional oil and gas producers in Alberta; assisting foreign automobile plants in Ontario raises the ire of Quebec; and the attempt to fight inflation in Toronto with high interest rates angers those in almost every other part of the country who wish to see such rates lowered.

The list of regional economic conflicts is almost endless, and most readers can probably add their own examples. Even subsidizing Western grain farmers or Atlantic fishers, which could be seen to be of indirect benefit to central Canada, is increasingly opposed by those in Ontario who feel that they are paying most of the cost. Besides these regional economic conflicts that engaged the attention of Ottawa, interprovincial conflicts may also develop. The most serious of these was probably the fight between Quebec and Newfoundland over the Churchill Falls hydroelectric project in Labrador. Ontario also insists that its residents

Standing tall above the calm waters of Trinity Bay, Hibernia's 600 000-tonne drilling structure began its 500-kilometre journey to the Grand Banks in May 1997. (Jonathan Hayward/Canapress)

be allowed to work in the construction industry in Quebec, the subject of a prolonged interprovincial battle.

REGIONAL ECONOMIC DISPARITIES

Conflicts between regions are exacerbated in Canada because of regional economic inequalities or disparities. As mentioned, some have-not regions blame federal economic policies for their fate. Even if this charge has some truth to it, no observer can overlook other factors: Canada's primary resources are not evenly distributed and the regions have different sizes and populations and are at variable distances from key export markets.

Among the available measures of regional economic disparity are provincial gross domestic product (GDP) (the total value of all goods and services produced), per capita personal income, per capita provincial fiscal capacity, and provincial unemployment rates. These measures are shown in Table 3.3.

The table generally indicates three categories of provinces: three rich ones (Ontario, Alberta, and British Columbia); four poor ones (the Atlantic provinces); and three intermediate provinces (Quebec, Manitoba, and Saskatchewan). Quebec has a larger economy than any province other than Ontario, of course, but this figure is not so impressive when expressed on a per capita basis. Per capita income statistics show that the average Ontarian received about $6000 more than the average Newfoundlander, with the other provinces arrayed in between. It is also true as a general rule that the provinces with the highest unemployment rates have the highest provincial taxes, while Alberta's petroleum revenue allows it to get by without a provincial sales tax at all. Needless to say, provinces and regions select whichever figures put them in the worst possible light when they demand that Ottawa do something to reduce such disparities.

In addition to developing national social programs and assisting various industries in a uniform national policy, successive governments have focused on two principal means to deal with the specific question of regional economic disparities. One is to give federal funding to have-not provincial governments and the other is to engage in regional economic development programs.

Equalization Payments[17]

In 1957 Ottawa finally responded to repeated provincial demands and began to make **equalization payments**. These annual cash grants to the have-not provinces are designed to allow them to raise their services to an acceptable national level but can be spent for any purpose. In other words, they are unconditional grants, with no strings attached. The formula according to which provincial eligibility is calculated is extremely complex, now taking into account some 33 sources of provincial income, and designed to equalize the per capita yield of such provincial revenues across the country. The normal pattern has been for seven provinces to qualify (all except Ontario, Alberta, and British Columbia), but the formula had to be changed in 1981 in order to exclude Ontario, at its own request. The equalization formula used to be renegotiated every five years at federal–provincial conferences, but in recent times Ottawa has altered the formula unilaterally. Nevertheless, as Table 3.4 reveals, the sums involved are astounding—over $9 billion annually.

TABLE 3.3   **Provincial Gross Domestic Product, Per Capita Personal Income, Per Capita Provincial Fiscal Capacity, and Provincial Unemployment Rate**

	Gross Domestic Product 1997	Est. 1999 Per Capita Income	Per Capita Prov. Fiscal Capacity 1998	Unemployment Rate 1998
	($ millions)			(percent)
Newfoundland	10 880	19 523	3 688	17.9
Prince Edward Island	2 943	19 739	3 951	13.9
Nova Scotia	20 322	20 922	4 164	10.7
New Brunswick	17 061	20 397	4 108	12.1
Quebec	185 366	22 949	4 894	10.4
Ontario	347 149	25 788	5 754	7.2
Manitoba	29 246	23 415	4 480	5.7
Saskatchewan	28 260	21 581	5 035	5.9
Alberta	101 069	25 127	7 314	5.7
British Columbia	109 347	24 920	5 865	8.9
Canada	—	24 267	5 431	8.3

Sources: Adapted from "Provincial Gross Domestic Product by Industry", Catalogue No. 15-203; and <www.statcan.ca>.

Equalization payments were entrenched in the Constitution in 1982, so that while the federal government may change the formula at any time, it cannot withdraw from its responsibility in this regard. Section 36 reads as follows:

Parliament and the government of Canada are committed to the principle of making equalization payments to ensure that provincial governments have sufficient revenues to provide reasonably comparable levels of public services at reasonably comparable levels of taxation.

Many find it puzzling that Quebec should qualify as a have-not province and, indeed, that when its revenue shortfall is multiplied by its large population, it should receive almost as much in equalization payments as all the other have-not provinces combined. The explanation seems to rest with the following facts: Quebec has less natural resource wealth than is commonly assumed, its industry was historically small-scale, business profits were often taken out of the province and sent to corporate headquarters elsewhere, its steel industry was slow to get started, and it did not enjoy Ontario's proximity to the U.S. automobile industry. Moreover, until 1960 its labour force was not well trained and the Roman Catholic Church in the province discouraged entrepreneurial activity among its deferential flock. Whatever

TABLE 3.4   **Equalization Payments, 1999–2000 (Dollars)**

Quebec	4 464 000 000	Manitoba	929 000 000
Nova Scotia	1 239 000 000	Saskatchewan	377 000 000
New Brunswick	1 054 000 000	PEI	222 000 000
Newfoundland	1 003 000 000	Total	9 288 000 000

Source: Department of Finance, Major Federal Transfers to Provinces, 1999 Budget. *Reproduced with the permission of the Minister of Public Works and Government Services Canada, 2000.*

the reasons, Quebec does well by these federal payments, to which people in all provinces contribute via their federal taxes.

Many attempts have been made to identify the overall "winners" and "losers" of Confederation, that is, which provinces have a net gain or loss when all their federal taxes and benefits have been totalled. This debate has been particularly centred on Quebec, but the results of federalist and sovereignist studies have often been contradictory. Two University of Calgary economists concluded, for example, that between 1961 and 1992 Quebec received $168 billion more in federal spending than it contributed in tax and other revenues to Ottawa, and it is still commonly assumed that Quebec receives a net $4 billion annually. On a per capita basis, at least, there is no question that the Atlantic provinces are the largest beneficiaries.[18]

Regional Economic Development Programs

The second means of reducing regional economic disparities is to establish federal **regional economic development programs**.[19] Among the early versions of such policy were the Prairie Farm Rehabilitation Administration (PFRA) of 1935; the Maritime Farm Rehabilitation Act of 1948; the Agricultural Rehabilitation and Development Act of 1961, renamed the Agricultural and Rural Development Act (ARDA) in 1966; the Atlantic Development Board of 1962–63; the Area Development Agency of 1963; and the Fund for Rural Economic Development (FRED) of 1966. These payments and programs culminated in the establishment of the Department of Regional Economic Expansion (DREE) in 1969, which was later renamed the Department of Regional Industrial Expansion (DRIE) and has undergone many changes of organization and emphasis since. The basic thrust of this program was to designate those parts of the country that needed economic assistance (essentially the whole country except Ontario's Golden Horseshoe, that is, Toronto and westward around the head of Lake Ontario), and then to provide grants to firms that would locate or expand existing operations in such areas. An element of federal–provincial cooperation was usually involved, primarily through economic and regional development agreements. Even before the 1994 national infrastructure program, some grants also went to provinces or municipalities in order to provide the basic infrastructure that might attract industry, such as highways, water and sewage systems, and industrial parks.

In 1987 another reorganization created several separate regional economic development agencies, which now consist of the **Atlantic Canada Opportunities Agency (ACOA)**, Federal Economic Development in Northern Ontario (FedNor), Western Economic Diversification Canada (WD), and the Canada Economic Development Office for Quebec Regions (CED). What remained of DRIE became the Department of Industry, Science and Technology, later Industry Canada, and these agencies continue to be attached to that department. The 1995 budget reduced funding for these agencies and directed them to focus their assistance on small and medium-sized enterprises, to make more extensive use of loans instead of grants, to establish investment pools run jointly with private-sector lending institutions, and to work with the provinces to reduce overlap and duplication in assistance to business.

The frequent reorganization of economic development programs is probably an indication of their recognized deficiencies. Many cases could be documented of corporations receiving money without being in need of it, or taking the money and not living up to their commitments to create jobs. On the other hand, some positive results have also occurred. In any case, federal politicians face a never-ending stream of appeals from have-not communities, have-not provinces, and companies in difficulty (as well as have-provinces and companies not in difficulty) to use the federal power of the purse to make their lives a little easier. In an era of fiscal restraint, however, such appeals increasingly fall on deaf ears.

CONCLUSION

The Canadian physical environment is primarily characterized by regionalism, and many demands stemming from such regions can be identified. Some demands seek improved transportation and communications links to bind the country more closely together. Others desire increased provincial or territorial autonomy in order to deal locally with their distinctive problems. A third category of demands concerns federal assistance to one region or another at no expense to other regions, while a fourth involves federal policy that does result from conflicting regional demands. Finally, regional economic disparities lead have-not regions and provinces to demand further assistance from Ottawa. While such patterns of regional and provincial demands are a constant of Canadian politics, their intensity in the 1990s, especially in the case of Quebec, reached levels that threatened the continued integrity of the political system. This was at the very time that the federal government's financial situation led it to cut spending and privatize Crown corporations designed to hold the country together.

P Of the approaches outlined in Chapter 1, pluralism is most relevant here. In the first place, pluralists point to the obvious geographic and economic diversities in Canada, and argue that national policies must allow for regional variations. They point out that it was this diversity that led to the initial creation of the provinces and the federal system. Power has been dispersed to the provincial political units because many of the diversities can be better accommodated at that level. Secondly, pluralists cite the interplay of many such forces at the national level, and claim that a plethora of examples can be found to demonstrate that government policies have stemmed from vociferously articulated regional economic demands. However much one region or another feels neglected from time to time, government decisions are usually compromises among various competing interests.

PC The other three approaches generally take the opposite point of view—that is, that in the interplay of regional forces, Ontario has usually dominated. Public choice theory, for example, emphasizes the voting power of central Canada in the design of most government policies in this field. Moreover, during the Pearson and Trudeau eras, when Quebec could be counted on to vote Liberal and the West went predominantly Conservative, elections were essentially fought out in Ontario, the province with not only the largest electorate but also the greatest number of *marginal* voters. This partly explains the thrust of Trudeau's constitutional and energy policies—especially the National Energy Program—which were strongly supported in Ontario but raised great anguish in the West.

SC The state-centred approach comes to much the same conclusion but for different reasons. It concentrates on the predominance of people from central Canada in such authoritative positions as the Cabinet and bureaucracy, and the ability of these authorities to operate autonomously, without public pressure. If 60 percent of members of Parliament and Cabinet ministers come from Ontario and Quebec, it is only to be expected that many federal policies will benefit the central part of the country. If the bureaucratic elite has similar geographic origins, this tendency will only be reinforced. In some periods in Canadian history, Western or Atlantic regional demands were more satisfactorily addressed, usually when powerful regional ministers or strong provincial premiers engaged in a process of elite accommodation. But in the case of the 1980 National Energy Program, a combination of an unrepresentative Cabinet and an autonomous bureaucracy produced a policy to which the West reacted with hostility.[20] Partly in response to the NEP, Senate reform became a key point in constitutional discussions because the outlying provinces saw equal and effective provincial representation in that body as their only counterweight at the federal level to the predominance of central Canada in the House of Commons and Cabinet.

© Class analysts also see a centralist thrust to most federal policies, but one that primarily facilitates the accumulation of capital among central Canadian corporations. Early railway policy, national tariff and banking policies, the bailout of the predecessors of CN, legislative support of private pipelines, corporate grants under DREE and DRIE, the reliance on natural resource exploitation, reluctance to develop a Canadian industrial policy, and the attempted privatization of the Pearson Airport were all designed to benefit capitalist interests, most of which were headquartered in central Canada. Some such analysts argue that parties have encouraged voters to think of Canadian politics in terms of conflict that "revolves around the allocation of power and resources across geographic units rather than, for example, among social classes."[21] In this perception, regions are less significant than classes and have been used to distract Canadians from class cleavages.

DISCUSSION QUESTIONS

1. Are the traditional demands and/or complaints of each region in Canadian federal politics justified?

2. To what extent is the Reform Party a product of Western alienation?

3. To what extent can federal policies be taken to help one region without upsetting another?

4. Is decentralization of the federal system an answer to conflicting regional demands? Why or why not?

5. To what extent are regional disparities a result of natural endowments of provinces and regions?

6. What can be done to lessen the problem of regional economic disparities?

7. How can each of the four critical approaches enhance our understanding of regional economic politics in Canada?

NOTES

1. House of Commons, *Debates*, June 19, 1936.
2. Donald Creighton, *The Empire of the St. Lawrence* (Toronto: Macmillan, 1956).
3. Railways figured in Confederation deals as recently as 1949, when Newfoundland joined Canada.
4. The whole romantic story is told in Pierre Berton, *The National Dream* and *The Last Spike* (Toronto: McClelland and Stewart, 1970 and 1971).
5. For an analysis along these lines, see Robert Chodos, *The CPR: A Century of Corporate Welfare* (Toronto: Lorimer, 1973).
6. Statistics Canada, *Canada's Population from Ocean to Ocean* (cat. no. 98-120, January 1989), p. 16.
7. Task Force on Canadian Unity, *A Future Together* (Ottawa: Supply and Services, 1979), pp. 26–27. The "provincialism" of this report was rejected by its government sponsor (Prime Minister Trudeau), but it may have inspired his successors.
8. Several recent books speculate on this question. From a specifically geographic point of view, see Scott Reid, *Canada Remapped* (Vancouver: Pulp Press, 1992).
9. Stephen Brooks and Andrew Stritch, *Business and Government in Canada* (Scarborough: Prentice-Hall Canada, 1991), ch. 4.
10. Wallace Clement and Daniel Drache, *A Practical Guide to Canadian Political Economy* (Toronto: Lorimer, 1978), pp. 9–14; *New Practical Guide to Canadian Political Economy* (Toronto: Lorimer, 1985).
11. Ibid., pp. 32–35, where R.T. Naylor's perspective on the role of the banks is briefly summarized.
12. One convenient source on the economic bases of the provinces is Rand Dyck, *Provincial Politics in Canada*, 3rd ed. (Scarborough: Prentice-Hall, 1996).
13. David Kilgour, *Uneasy Patriots: Western Canadians in Confederation* (Edmonton: Lone Pine Publishers, 1988), and *Inside Outer Canada* (Edmonton: Lone Pine, 1990); Don Braid and Sydney Sharpe, *Breakup: Why the West Feels Left Out of Canada* (Toronto: Key Porter Books, 1990); and Roger Gibbins, Keith Archer, and Stan Drabek, eds., *Canadian Political Life: An Alberta Perspective* (Dubuque, IA: Kendall Hunt, 1990).
14. By this time many large central Canadian corporations also saw advantages for themselves in such a policy.
15. Donald Smiley, *The Federal Condition in Canada* (Toronto: McGraw-Hill Ryerson, 1987), p. 159.

16. Robert Campbell and Leslie Pal, *The Real Worlds of Canadian Politics* (Peterborough: Broadview Press, 1989).

17. Robin W. Boadway and Paul A.R. Hobson, *Equalization* (Montreal: McGill–Queen's University Press, 1998).

18. Robert Mansell and Ronald Schlenker, "The Provincial Distribution of Federal Fiscal Balances," *Canadian Business Economics* (Winter 1995), pp. 3–22, which also showed that Alberta lost $139 billion while Ontario lost $45 billion. See also a study by the Fraser Institute, *Government Spending Facts* (Vancouver, 1990); Phil Hartling, *Federal Expenditures as a Tool for Regional Development* (Halifax: Council of Maritime Premiers, 1990); and Statistics Canada, Provincial Accounts. A fuller account of federal–provincial finance is contained in Chapter 17.

19. Anthony Careless, *Initiative and Response: The Adaptation of Canadian Federalism to Regional Economic Development* (Montreal: McGill–Queen's University Press, 1977); Economic Council of Canada, *Living Together: A Study of Regional Disparities* (Ottawa, 1977); and Donald J. Savoie, *Federal–Provincial Collaboration: The Canada–New Brunswick General Development Agreement* (Montreal: McGill–Queen's University Press, 1981).

20. Peter Foster, *The Sorcerer's Apprentices: Canada's Super-Bureaucrats and the Energy Mess* (Don Mills: Collins, 1982).

21. Janine Brodie, "The Concept of Region in Canadian Politics," in David Shugarman and Reg Whitaker, eds., *Federalism and Political Community* (Peterborough: Broadview Press, 1989), p. 36, and *The Political Economy of Canadian Regionalism* (Toronto: Harcourt, Brace, Jovanovich, 1990).

FURTHER READING

Alberta Report (weekly newsmagazine).

Berger, Thomas. *Northern Frontier, Northern Homeland: The Report of the Mackenzie Valley Pipeline Inquiry.* Ottawa: Supply and Services Canada, 1977, republished by Douglas and McIntyre, Vancouver, 1988.

Braid, Don, and Sydney Sharpe. *Breakup: Why the West Feels Left Out of Canada.* Toronto: Key Porter Books, 1990.

Brodie, Janine. *The Political Economy of Canadian Regionalism.* Toronto: Harcourt, Brace, Jovanovich, 1990.

Canada. Task Force on Canadian Unity. *A Future Together.* Ottawa: Supply and Services, 1979.

Clement, Wallace, and Daniel Drache. *The New Practical Guide to Canadian Political Economy.* Toronto: Lorimer, 1985.

Dyck, Rand. *Provincial Politics in Canada,* 3rd ed. Scarborough: Prentice-Hall Canada, 1996.

Gibbins, Roger. *Conflict and Unity,* 3rd ed. Scarborough: Nelson Canada, 1994.

Gibbins, Roger, Keith Archer, and Stan Drabek, eds. *Canadian Political Life: An Alberta Perspective.* Dubuque, IA: Kendall Hunt, 1990.

Kilgour, David. *Uneasy Patriots: Western Canadians in Confederation.* Edmonton: Lone Pine Publishers, 1988.

———. *Inside Outer Canada.* Edmonton: Lone Pine Publishers, 1990.

Reid, Scott. *Canada Remapped.* Vancouver: Pulp Press, 1992.

Savoie, Donald J. *The Canadian Economy: A Regional Perspective.* Toronto: Carswell, 1986.

———. *Regional Economic Development: Canada's Search for Solutions,* 2nd ed. Toronto: University of Toronto Press, 1992.

Tomblin, Stephen. *Ottawa and the Outer Provinces.* Halifax: Lorimer, 1995.

Western Economic Opportunities Conference. *Documents and Verbatim Record.* Calgary, July 1973.

Chapter 4

Canada's *ABORIGINAL peoples*

Should Aboriginal peoples be allowed to hunt and fish at will? How can their land claims be dealt with fairly? How can the lives of urban Aboriginals be improved? Should Canada proceed with constitutional reform on other issues before it resolves Aboriginal concerns? While the way in which they have been governed over the past 150 years is obviously a failure, is Aboriginal self-government a realistic alternative? What does it mean? In short, how can the claims of Canada's Aboriginal peoples be addressed after 29 million "immigrants" have taken possession of most of the inhabitable land and completely changed the country's way of life? Aboriginal issues have attracted widespread interest even among non-Aboriginals in recent years, but opinion is divided on how to deal with them.

This chapter will examine the historical evolution of Canada's Aboriginal peoples, detail their demographic profile today, and outline the principal political issues they have raised, especially with respect to land and governance. These issues are so unprecedented in official Canadian political experience that they are not easily understood. Much hope was placed in the recommendations of the Royal Commission on Aboriginal Peoples, and while concrete action has been taking place at an unprecedented rate in recent years, there is still a long way to go.

HISTORICAL EVOLUTION

Native or Aboriginal peoples have inhabited Canada for perhaps as long as 40 000 years, most experts linking their origins to Asia. They are an extremely varied group. Those who settled in the southern part of what is now Canada, as well as those in the Yukon and Mackenzie Valley of the north, are officially termed "North American Indians," but, given the erroneous origin of the label, they prefer to be called "First Nations" peoples. Those located in the eastern Arctic and northern islands used to be called Eskimo and are now referred to as "Inuit." Before Europeans came to the continent, most Aboriginals functioned as nomadic hunters, but some were more permanent fishermen, carvers, or farmers. They were self-sufficient and self-governing. Practising their own forms of government for thousands of years, they generally made decisions on the basis of consensus rather than by voting, and in many cases women (sometimes called clan mothers) and elders played a significant role. In their close attachment to the land, they did not think in terms of private ownership; instead, they believed in the shared use of land and saw themselves as trustees of the land for future generations.

It was the fur trade more than anything that led to the invasion by Europeans and to wars between the British and the French in North America. The fur trade was devastating for the Aboriginal peoples, totally disrupting their way of life and introducing new diseases such as smallpox that severely reduced their population.

In the **Royal Proclamation of 1763**, which divided up the territory acquired by Britain, Indian rights were clearly defined, however much they have since been ignored.[1] In a large area called Indian Territory, the purchase or settlement of land was forbidden without Crown approval, that is, without a treaty between the Crown and the Aboriginal people concerned. This is sometimes called the principle of "voluntary cession." Shortly afterwards, the Crown concluded land-cession agreements with Indians in what is now southern Ontario in order to provide for the United Empire Loyalists moving in from the United States. Indians originally received a lump-sum payment and, later, annuities.

From about 1830 onward the system changed, and the Crown set aside reserves in exchange for the cession of Indian land, in addition to providing benefits such as the right to hunt and fish on unoccupied Crown land. The first major treaties of this kind were the Robinson Treaties of 1850 in northern Ontario and the Douglas Treaties on Vancouver Island.

The 1867 Constitution Act gave jurisdiction over Indians and lands reserved for the Indians to the federal government. Parliament soon passed the **Indian Act**, which was consolidated in 1876 and provided for federal government control of almost every aspect of Indian life. The Indian Act aimed at assimilating Aboriginals into the new white majority, and represented a colonialism—the exploitation, domination, and subjugation of a people by an imperial power—as obnoxious as European countries practised anywhere else in the world. One of the provisions of the Indian Act allowed for "enfranchisement," which encouraged Indians to give up their Indian status. Thus began the distinction between **status Indians**, those registered with the federal government according to the terms of the Indian Act, and nonstatus Indians, those not so registered.

Meanwhile, the treaty-making process continued apace, with treaties numbered 1 to 11 covering most of northern Ontario and the Prairie provinces, and parts of British Columbia, the Yukon, and the Mackenzie Valley of the Northwest Territories. These treaties were primarily designed to clear Aboriginal title so that the transcontinental railway could be built and western immigrant settlement could begin. Such treaties contained an extinguishment clause, such that Aboriginal rights were given up in exchange for treaty rights. In return for surrendering title to the lands involved, Indians received tracts of land for reserves as well as other benefits such as small annuities, gratuities, schools, hunting and fishing rights, agricultural implements, cattle, and ammunition. In retrospect, almost everyone agrees that the Natives were taken advantage of in these negotiations and that the land given them for reserves was usually small, remote, and lacking in resources.[2] Nevertheless, Aboriginals guard their treaty rights religiously because they have little else, and those Indians in much of British Columbia and the Arctic with whom no treaties were signed at all were even worse off. Figure 4.1 is a map of the historic Indian treaties.

By this time another identifiable group existed besides status, nonstatus, treaty, and non-treaty Indians. These were the Métis, essentially the descendants of white fur traders and Indian

Figure 4.1   Historic Indian Treaties

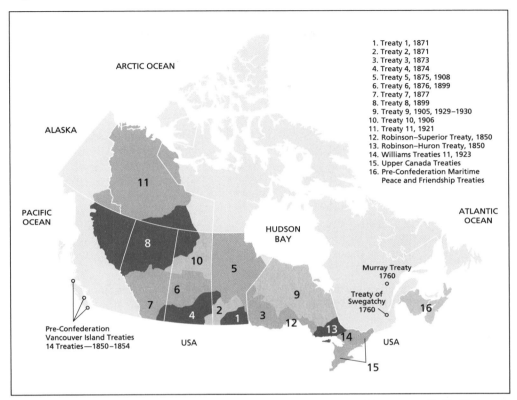

Source: Indian and Northern Affairs Canada, 1998. Reproduced with the permission of the Minister of Public Works and Government Services Canada, 2000.

women. Found largely on the Prairies, the Métis combined nomadic hunting with farming. They were not covered by the Indian Act or by treaties, and were therefore left to the mercy of new white settlers and provincial and territorial governments. It is not surprising, therefore, that Louis Riel took up their cause in 1885 in the second Riel Rebellion in Saskatchewan. After having been crushed, they remained in an even weaker position to fend for themselves.

The one group of Aboriginals left untouched by government, although not by fur traders, missionaries, and other whites, was the Eskimo or Inuit who inhabited the Northwest Territories, the coast of northern Labrador, and about 25 percent of northern Quebec. A 1939 Supreme Court ruling declared that the Eskimo came within the meaning of Indians in the 1867 Constitution Act (though not under the Indian Act), but it was not until the 1950s that the federal government began to deliver health and educational services to them and later to relocate them into about 40 (now 53) permanent settlements, largely on the coast of the Arctic mainland, Hudson Bay, and northern Quebec.[3] This disruption of their traditional lifestyle based on hunting and trapping caused them to depend increasingly on social assistance and intermittent wages.

....

ABORIGINAL DEMOGRAPHIC PROFILE TODAY

Partly because there is such diversity among Aboriginal Canadians and partly because they were not always easy to find, census and other demographic statistics in this area are not considered as definitive as for other groups. On the basis of the 1996 census, Canada contained 799 010 Aboriginals, based on identity, and about 1.1 million Aboriginals, based on ancestry. These figures respectively represent 2.8 percent and 3.7 percent of the total population. Many reported multiple ancestries, almost all of them in combination with non-Aboriginal origins. The Department of Indian Affairs and Northern Development collects its own statistics, which are likely to be more accurate. They are provided in Table 4.1, which indicates a 1998 total of 1 356 285 Aboriginals, or 4.4 percent of the total population.

Whichever figures are used, Canadian Aboriginals break down into three official categories: North American Indians (75–80 percent), Métis (15–20 percent), and Inuit (4–5 percent). Aboriginal Canadians are not spread uniformly across the country, their concentrations being higher in the western part of the country.

Besides these legal distinctions, there are 11 major Aboriginal linguistic families, the largest being Cree, Inuktitut (the language of the Inuit), and Ojibway, but more than 50 Aboriginal languages exist. About one-quarter of the Aboriginal population have an Aboriginal language

TABLE 4.1   Distribution of Aboriginal Canadians by Category and by Location, 1998

	Registered Indians	Non-Status Indians	Métis	Inuit	Total Population	Percentage of Provincial/ Territorial Population
Atlantic Provinces	25 469	28 500	3 900	9 000	66 869	1.8
Quebec	62 405	86 800	19 000	10 200	178 405	2.4
Ontario	149 829	162 800	26 000	6 300	344 929	3.0
Manitoba	102 651	12 000	45 600	900	161 151	14.1
Saskatchewan	103 041	10 000	33 100	600	146 741	14.3
Alberta	83 418	46 800	57 900	3 400	191 518	6.6
British Columbia	110 228	76 300	22 400	2 300	211 228	5.3
Yukon	7 630	1 200	400	200	9 430	29.8
Northwest Territories	14 814	700	3 800	26 700	46 014	67.8
TOTAL	659 485	425 100	212 100	59 600	1 356 285	4.5

Source: Statistics from Population Projections of Registered Indians, 1996–2021, *Information Analysis Section, Indian and Northern Affairs Canada (1999);* Projections of Populations with Aboriginal Ancestry, Canada, Provinces/Regions and Territories, 1991–2016, *Statistics Canada, 1995, Catalogue No. 91-5390XPE; and* Population Projections for Canada, Provinces and Territories, 1993–2016, *Statistics Canada, 1994, Catalogue No. 91-520. Reproduced with the permission of the Minister of Public Works and Government Services Canada, 2000.*

as mother tongue, largely confined to the Inuit and those who live on reserves, but only 15 percent actually speak an Aboriginal language at home. About 68 percent of Aboriginals reported English as mother tongue in 1996, while 6 percent reported French.

About 60 percent of status Indians live on reserves, of which there are about 2370, with an average size of about 1160 hectares. They are distributed among some 600 bands or **First Nations**, with an average population of about 650 persons. Among off-reserve, urban areas, Regina, Saskatoon, Winnipeg, and Edmonton have the highest concentrations of such groups, although large numbers also reside in Vancouver, Calgary, and Toronto.

These basic statistics present only part of the picture. At least of equal significance are the distressing statistics on Aboriginal poverty.[4] Many reserve families have incomes far below the poverty line, and apart from a few Aboriginal urban professionals, the same is true for most of those who live off-reserve. Related to this level of poverty are alarming rates of Aboriginal alcoholism, violence, suicide, mortality, low educational attainment, and unemployment. The suicide rate among Native youth is at least five times the national average, and Aboriginal Canadians are much more likely to be murdered or die from accidents, poisoning, or violence. The overall life expectancy of Aboriginal Canadians is seven years shorter than that of non-Natives, which is due to poor health services and housing on reserves. Twice as many Native infants die before they are one year old. Diabetes, tuberculosis, pneumonia, and other respiratory diseases are common on reserves, as are gastroenteritis, rheumatic fever, ear infections, meningitis, hepatitis, intestinal infections, skin diseases, and disorders of the nervous system. Housing is often sadly deficient, being overcrowded and lacking in running water, indoor toilets, and central heating. While the government is anxious to point out that considerable improvement has been recorded in on-reserve living conditions since 1960, it acknowledges that 50 percent of dwellings on First Nations reserves still require renovation or replacement.[5] Moreover, the Aboriginal population is younger than the non-Aboriginal counterpart, and is growing twice as fast because of high birth and fertility rates.

In essence, the typical Native scenario runs as follows: having been stripped of their land, original livelihood, and culture, and having been placed on unproductive reserves, many Indians find themselves with little to do. The resulting poverty, unemployment, idleness, and reliance on welfare often leads them to seek solace in alcohol and drugs. Many Natives also resort to family and other violence, which in turn brings them into trouble with the law. Not being able to pay their fines, and subject to discrimination at the hands of the police, the courts, and other aspects of the justice system, they then go to jail, where they become even more alienated, depressed, and abused.

Aboriginal Canadians have suffered from untold discrimination and indignity at every turn. Reflecting a colonial mentality, the Indian Act treated them like children and required non-Native bureaucratic approval for almost any band decision. In the past, Indian babies were frequently removed from the reserves to be adopted by non-Native parents, and until the 1970s, Indian children were forced to go to residential schools, where they were punished, sometimes to the point of assault, for speaking their Native language or engaging in Native cultural and spiritual traditions.[6] Native languages and cultures were systematically discouraged, and traditional forms of government and medicine outlawed. Indians living on reserves did not even have the right to vote in federal elections until 1960, and between 1927 and 1951, the Indian Act made it an offence for a First Nation to hire a lawyer to bring a claim against Canada without government consent. As in the case of French Canadians, this protracted attempt to assimilate Aboriginals was a dismal failure.

Part of the reason for so little progress in improving the condition of Aboriginal life in Canada is the relatively small number of people involved and hence the invisibility of the problem. The dispersion of Aboriginal peoples has also made it difficult for them to get elected to federal or provincial governments and has recently generated demands for guaranteed Aboriginal seats in Canadian legislatures. Another reason is the negative stereotype among non-Natives and the mistaken belief that Aboriginals have brought all these difficulties upon themselves.[7]

······································

ABORIGINAL POLITICAL ISSUES SINCE 1970

For a variety of reasons, Canada's Native peoples and their problems became a major concern of Canadian politics in the 1990s and beyond. In part they were insulted by the terms of the 1963 Royal Commission on Bilingualism and Biculturalism, which spoke of English and French as being Canada's two "founding races." They were also offended by the 1969 Trudeau–Chrétien **White Paper on Indians**, which called for their complete integration, if not assimilation, into the wider Canadian society. The paper reflected Trudeau's obsession with individual rights and his blindness to the concept of collective or group consciousness, just as did his attitude toward Quebec. More than any other single factor, the White Paper was the spark that ignited the Aboriginal movement in Canada. More positive influences were the sympathetic Berger Inquiry into the proposed Mackenzie Valley gas pipeline,[8] as well as the increased awareness of Aboriginal issues worldwide. Now that most European colonies around the world had been liberated, partly through the efforts of the United Nations, many observers came to see that indigenous peoples in the new world had also been victims of colonialism. If it was unrealistic for them to pursue self-determination via majority control of an independent country (as in South Africa, for example), the Aboriginals in Canada would at least insist on ensuring their survival and development as distinct nations and restructuring the Canadian political system so that they would have control over their own affairs.[9]

Aboriginal people organized and took initiative, learning from the civil rights movement and the new left of the 1960s and anti-colonial Third World liberation movements. They began to fight back, as had colonized Third World peoples. The incidence of sit-ins, roadblocks and other blockades, rallies, court cases, hunger strikes, and international protests increased. Indeed, at the 1989 annual meeting of the **Assembly of First Nations**, a mutual defence pact based on the NATO agreement was signed to the effect that bands would support each other and send reinforcements when requested. Then, in 1990, two incidents helped place Aboriginal concerns in the public consciousness: Native MLA Elijah Harper was instrumental in defeating the Meech Lake Accord, and the Mohawks of Oka, Quebec, took the law into their own hands to protect what they considered to be their land from the expansion of a non-Aboriginal golf course.

Since 1970, then, the crowded Canadian political agenda has had to find room for a variety of Aboriginal issues, which are made all the more complex because of the diversity within the Aboriginal community. These issues include Aboriginal self-government, land claims, social conditions, economic development, Aboriginal languages, Aboriginal women, educational issues, and justice. For the purposes of this text, the issues can be discussed under the broad headings of land issues and governance issues. Although it is easier to visualize

Aboriginal self-government when it is based on a specific piece of territory, the issues of land claims and governance have often proceeded somewhat independently of each other.

Land Issues

In most of the country, North American Indians signed treaties with the Crown under which they ceded the land to the government in return for protected reserves. But, especially in British Columbia and the North, few such treaties were signed, leaving North American Indians and Inuit in these regions without a land base. The Métis have never possessed any land, with the result that only about one-third of Aboriginal peoples have a land base on which to rely. This gives rise to the issue of **Aboriginal title**, that is, a claim to the land on the basis of traditional occupancy and use rather than treaty. The existence of such Aboriginal title was first recognized in the *Calder* case in 1973 in connection with the Nisga'a band in British Columbia, but the Supreme Court of Canada was split on the question of whether such title had been subsequently extinguished. In response, the government of Canada announced its intention to negotiate Aboriginal title but only where treaties did not exist, and only six at a time. This policy was not satisfactory, because even where treaties were signed, Indians are increasingly challenging their terms and implementation. Moreover, some Métis have also raised the land issue, so the federal government eventually removed earlier restrictions. A great variety of Aboriginal land claims have therefore been launched in the past 25 years. They fall into two categories: **comprehensive claims** based on Aboriginal title (that is, traditional use and occupancy of land) that have not been dealt with by treaty or other legal means, and **specific claims** arising from alleged nonfulfillment of Indian treaties and other lawful obligations.

NORTHERN LAND CLAIMS

Such claims have moved relatively faster in the North than in the south, since north of the 60th parallel the federal government is in charge of the land as well as of Aboriginals. In fact, agreement in principle has been achieved in three comprehensive land claims in the North: the Council of Yukon First Nations (later broken down into four smaller parts), the Inuvialuit, and the Tungavik Federation of Nunavut. The Dene-Métis claim in the western Arctic was approved in principle but then rejected, and has subsequently been divided into smaller claims, with success reported in the case of the Gwich'in and Sahtu Dene and Métis. Besides providing land and money, such comprehensive claims clarify Native hunting, fishing, and trapping rights and clear obstacles to future economic development.[10] It should be noted, however, that the rights of current property owners have been protected and that in many cases the specific land boundaries have yet to be designated. In 1993 the federal government announced that it would no longer require blanket extinguishment clauses as a condition for settling comprehensive land claims.

. . . .

Figure 4.2   Nunavut Territory

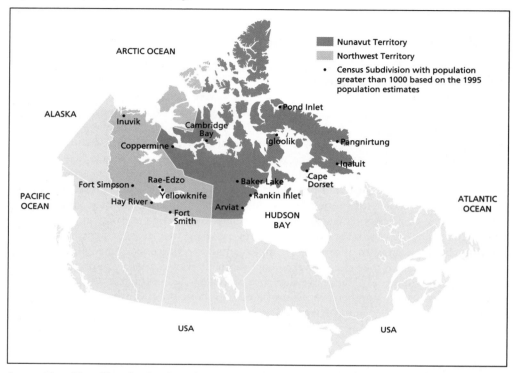

Source: Adapted from "Canadian Social Trends", Catalogue No. 11-008, Spring 1997, Number 44, page 17.

SOUTHERN LAND CLAIMS

In the south, where Ottawa has responsibility for "Indians and lands reserved for the Indians" but where the provinces have jurisdiction over public lands, land claims have moved more slowly. Aboriginals have generally found provincial governments even less sympathetic to their issues than Ottawa, and conflict has often developed between Indian bands and natural resource companies as well as with other non-Aboriginals who now live on the land in question. Ottawa insists that provinces be party to such settlements and contribute to their costs, arguing that it is in the provinces' interests to establish certainty of title to lands and resources. Thus far, relatively few comprehensive land claim successes can be reported below the 60th parallel.

The main provincial comprehensive land claim settlement was the 1975 **James Bay and Northern Quebec Agreement** between the Cree and Inuit and the government of Quebec, supplemented by several subsequent agreements. The James Bay Agreement gave the Natives exclusive use of 13 700 km² of land and an additional 450 000 km² of exclusive hunting, fishing, and trapping rights, along with $225 million in cash in return for allowing Quebec to construct a giant hydro development project in the area. While the deal was unprecedented and widely heralded in many quarters, one terrible side effect was the mercury poisoning of fish, due to an unanticipated chemical reaction between water and rock in the flooded land, and of the Natives who ate them. This problem and the growing perception that the deal may have been less generous to the Native community than originally thought made the Cree of Quebec hesitant to agree to the second, "Great Whale," phase of the James Bay project.

Other comprehensive claims negotiations in eastern Canada are proceeding with the Conseil des Atikamekw et des Montagnais and the Innu Nation. The Labrador Inuit Association reached a land claims agreement with Ottawa and the Newfoundland government in 1998 that gives the Inuit 15 800 km² of land and $255 million. This agreement was particularly interesting in light of the discovery and purchase by Inco Limited of a large nickel deposit at Voisey's Bay, Labrador.

Since the province of British Columbia contains a large proportion of North American Indians and few treaties, the land claims issue has been particularly significant there. The provincial government was reluctant to begin such negotiations, however, and the BC Supreme Court was not much help. When the Wet'suwet'en and Gitksan appealed the *Delgamuukw* case to the Supreme Court of Canada in 1997, however, that court was more sympathetic. It ordered that in such cases, various kinds of oral history evidence be admissible. The Supreme Court of Canada also provided its first comprehensive statement on Aboriginal title: A group must establish its exclusive occupation of the land in question prior to the time when the Crown asserted sovereignty. While the Supreme Court of Canada allowed for Crown infringement on Aboriginal title for valid legislative objectives, it specified that the groups with Aboriginal title need to be involved in the decision-making process around such a proposed infringement. As for the specific case itself, the Supreme Court of Canada ordered a retrial to be conducted with these new guidelines, which should have implications for Aboriginal title and land claims negotiations in other provinces as well.[11]

As mentioned, the neighbouring Nisga'a tribe in northwest BC, which has been seeking recognition of their Aboriginal title for over 100 years, took their claim to court in the 1973 *Calder* case, and has been negotiating with Ottawa ever since. Once the province entered the negotiations in 1990, however, prospects of a settlement improved. In 1992, the governments of Canada and British Columbia signed a B.C. Treaty Commission Agreement with the First Nations of that province, and negotiations began. The Nisga'a served as pioneers again when they finally signed the first modern-day treaty with Ottawa and the BC government in August 1998. The Nisga'a gained 1930 km² of land, $190 million in cash, and self-government powers akin to municipal governments in return for giving up the right to future land claims and Native tax-exempt status. It was a complex document including sections on forestry, mining, wildlife and the environment, public access, the administration of justice, finance, taxation, and many more. The treaty was subsequently ratified by the Nisga'a people in a referendum, and also required the approval of the federal and BC legislatures. While opposed by a minority of Nisga'a, some surrounding Aboriginals, and some in other provinces who felt that they had given up too much, the treaty's most vociferous opposition arose in the provincial legislature, where a demand for a provincial referendum was loudly voiced. If it succeeds in obtaining official approval, and even more, if it acquires popular support, the Nisga'a treaty may well serve as a model for treaties with other Aboriginal groups.

Specific land claims result from alleged breaches of the government's legal obligations and dissatisfaction with treaties—especially the fact that bands did not receive the full amount of land that the treaties promised. Such claims have arisen in most of the provinces, but until recently Ottawa was not keen to hear them. Between 1973 and 1998, Canada settled 207 specific claims, although not always to First Nations' satisfaction, with well over 100 still in negotiation. The greatest progress has been reported in Saskatchewan.

OTHER LAND ISSUES

Another dimension of land issues concerns what Aboriginals are allowed by treaties to do on public lands. Aboriginal treaty rights, especially hunting and fishing rights, frequently conflict with provincial law. Some progress has been made on this front, especially in two Supreme Court of Canada decisions in 1990. The Court ruled that a 1760 Huron treaty was valid, and its provision that Indians be allowed "the free exercise of their Religion [and] their Customs" prevented Quebec from prosecuting Hurons for practising Native customs and fishing in provincial parks. The Court also gave Indians new hope in a BC decision that stated that section 35(1) of the Charter of Rights affords Aboriginal people constitutional protection against provincial legislative power and that the clause should be given a generous, liberal interpretation. In this case the Court said that the Aboriginals' right to fish could override provincial regulations regarding the size of a net.[12] The Supreme Court went considerably further in the 1999 *Donald Marshall* case. It ruled that the treaty rights of the Mi'kmaq in Atlantic Canada allowed them to make a "moderate livelihood." Subject to government regulations with respect to conservation, they could catch lobster or eels during the period when the fishing season was closed to non-Aboriginals.[13] In Saskatchewan, Manitoba, and Ontario, landmark court decisions have held that even the provinces' Métis have hunting and fishing rights under the Constitution no different from the rights of status Indians.

The Innu of Labrador protested for several years against low-level NATO military training flights around Canadian Forces Base Goose Bay, which they claimed were a hazard to human health and the environment. Both federal and Newfoundland governments rejected their arguments, however, and encouraged even more countries to take advantage of the location. Meanwhile, the government of Newfoundland moved the Mushuau Innu community of Davis Inlet to an island off the Labrador coast, where they developed even worse social and health problems—including severe solvent abuse among children—and had even fewer economic opportunities than before. Later, Ottawa intervened to relocate them on the Labrador mainland. Ottawa and Newfoundland also signed a self-government framework agreement and land claims agreement with the Innu of Labrador, although the youth suicide rate remained alarming.

Yet another aspect of the land question arose in the conflict at Oka, Quebec, in the summer of 1990, the most serious conflict between Indians and authorities of modern times.[14] The municipal council's decision to expand a golf course on land claimed by resident Mohawks as sacred ground (a claim of traditional occupancy but not guaranteed by treaty) led to an armed standoff between Mohawk warriors and the Quebec provincial police in which one police officer was killed. The Mohawks were supported by the nearby Kahnawake reserve, which also set up barriers and blockaded the Mercier Bridge to Montreal. The Canadian Armed Forces were later brought in, and Aboriginal demonstrations took place across the country. While some local non-Aboriginal residents stoned vehicles carrying Mohawk families, most Canadians hoped that the incident would speed up the process of settling hundreds of outstanding Aboriginal land claims before any worse violence occurred. Unfortunately, violence did erupt again—in a land dispute at Ipperwash, Ontario, in 1995, in which a police officer killed an unarmed demonstrator, Dudley George.

Governance Issues[15]

Aboriginal Canadians have long demanded improvements in government health, social, housing, and educational services, and some minor improvements have been made over the years. Natives began to feel, however, that they were too constrained by the Indian Act and that Native problems required Native solutions. They were tired of living at the mercy of politicians and bureaucrats, a fact highlighted by the Mulroney government's reduction in Native postsecondary education support in 1989 and cuts to Native newspapers, broadcasting, organizations, and subsidized housing in 1990.[16] Yet most Aboriginals did not want to gut the Indian Act and existing government programs until they had something better to put in their place.

The first positive official response to Aboriginal discontent was the Hawthorn Report of 1966, *Survey of the Contemporary Indians of Canada*. It took the position that Aboriginal Canadians needed a greater degree of local autonomy and deserved a higher level of government services to compensate for everything that had happened in the past. Because non-Aboriginal Canadians had built a prosperous society on the lands and resources originally owned by Aboriginals, the latter should be considered "citizens plus." Nothing much came of this report at the time, and indeed, the next initiative, the 1969 White Paper, took the opposite approach—that Aboriginal Canadians should be treated exactly as other Canadians, and that even the Indian Act should be repealed. As mentioned above, it was the angry Aboriginal response to the White Paper that finally sparked the beginning of changes in the issue of governance.

Aboriginal Canadians argued that they should be able to choose their own decision-making processes, for they could hardly be expected to support the apparatus that created their current problems. Before the passage of the Indian Act, they had sophisticated and distinctive forms of government and many wanted to return to such traditional ways, feeling that the system of elected band councils was an alien imposition. Going well beyond such decision-making machinery, they also wanted **Aboriginal self-government**. Natives want to control their own affairs, but the specific structures of such proposed self-government are not clear-cut. Some advocates would accept a kind of super-municipality, but others have more ambitious plans that would be harder to fit into the Canadian constitutional framework. For the moment, the demand is for a "two-track" approach: constitutional recognition of the *inherent* right of Aboriginal self-government stemming from their unique history as Canada's original inhabitants, plus concurrent progress toward greater community-based control at the local level. In this way, an array of self-government arrangements and institutional models can be developed within the existing constitutional setup. Self-government would also help them take action to preserve Aboriginal languages, which are in danger of becoming extinct.

THE CONSTITUTION ACT, 1982, TO MEECH LAKE

The first improvement in the constitutional recognition of Aboriginal rights occurred after widespread protests in connection with the constitutional negotiations in 1981–82. The Constitution Act, 1982, ultimately contained two clauses of interest here. Section 25 guaranteed that the Charter would not be construed so as to abrogate or derogate from any Aboriginal, treaty, or other rights or freedoms pertaining to the Aboriginal peoples of Canada, including any rights recognized by the Royal Proclamation of 1763, and any rights or freedoms "that now exist by way of land claims agreements or may be so acquired." Section 35 recognized and affirmed the existing Aboriginal and treaty rights of the Aboriginal peoples of Canada, including the Indian, Inuit, and Métis peoples. To conform with the equality rights clause in the Charter, the Indian Act was amended to remove the clause that had previously taken away Indian status from Aboriginal women who married white men but granted such status to white women who married Indian men. Bill C-31 (1985) led to the reinstatement of nearly 100 000 Aboriginal women and their children, but since bands were allowed to control their own membership, a high proportion of those reinstated in status have had difficulty in returning to the reserve.

Based in part on the recommendations of the 1983 Penner Report (Report of the Special Committee of the House of Commons on Indian Self-Government), section 35 of the 1982 Constitution Act was temporarily amended to provide for a series of federal–provincial first ministers' conferences on Aboriginal rights between 1983 and 1987. Prime ministers Trudeau and Mulroney, in turn, tried unsuccessfully to get provincial premiers and Native leaders to agree to the terms of a constitutional amendment recognizing the principle of Aboriginal self-government. Several premiers insisted that the concept be clarified before they would agree even in principle, while Aboriginal leaders wanted the principle recognized as an inherent right. At the 1987 conference, Georges Erasmus, national Chief of the Assembly of First Nations, spoke as follows:

> Nothing short of Aboriginal self-government will achieve our aspirations for survival as distinct peoples. Attempts by governments at integration and assimilation over the years have failed and we have rejected them. We must be able to control our lives on our own lands and using our own resources.[17]

Although the constitutional talks broke down, two pieces of legislation were passed to provide for self-government in specific localities. The 1984 Cree-Naskapi (of Quebec) Act set in place self-government arrangements for the Indians of Quebec who were parties to the James Bay land claim agreement, and the 1986 Sechelt Indian Band Self-Government Act allowed the Sechelt band in British Columbia to assume control over their lands, resources, health and social services, education, and local taxation in what is usually called the "municipal model." (The Sechelt later signed a land claim agreement-in-principle that will lead to the second modern-day treaty). Given the absence of constitutional advance, however, Canadian Natives were understandably opposed to the Meech Lake Accord, which addressed Quebec's constitutional demands but completely overlooked their own. Even supporters of the accord found it hard to blame Elijah Harper for withholding unanimous consent when it came before the Manitoba legislature for approval.

THE CHARLOTTETOWN ACCORD

Harper's stand, together with the Oka affair, precipitated a dramatic breakthrough of constitutional concern with Aboriginal issues and participation of Native leaders in constitutional negotiations. For the first time, Aboriginal leaders were given the same status as premiers in

By Adrian Raeside (Victoria Times-Colonist). *Used with permission.*

the talks leading up to the 1992 Charlottetown Accord, and that document addressed Aboriginal concerns in a more extensive and satisfactory way than it did the demands of Quebec.

The Charlottetown Accord would have recognized the inherent right of Aboriginal peoples to self-government and acknowledged that such First Nations governments constituted a third order of government in Canada, analogous to the provinces. The document provided for self-government agreements to be negotiated among the three levels of government, with access to the courts to enforce such rights delayed for a five-year period. Federal and provincial laws would remain in place until superseded by Aboriginal laws, but the latter would have to be consistent with the preservation of peace, order, and good government in Canada. In addition to provisions for Aboriginal self-government, Native peoples were to have a new role of one kind or another in the House of Commons, Senate, Supreme Court, first ministers' conferences, and the constitutional amending formula. Despite the enormous leap in official thinking that this section of the accord represented, a majority of Aboriginal voters opposed it in the referendum. Some found the provisions lacking in detail, and many Aboriginal women felt that their individual (Charter) rights were being sacrificed for new group rights. In any case, a majority of non-Aboriginals also rejected it on other grounds.

POST-1992 PROGRESS

Since 1992, activity in the area of Aboriginal governance has been limited to legislative and administrative changes such as experiments in delegating federal or provincial government powers to First Nations communities.[18] One interesting initiative was the experimental dismantling in Manitoba of the Department of Indian Affairs as it affected First Nations. A framework agreement to this effect was signed in December 1994 by the Minister of Indian Affairs and the Grand Chief of the Assembly of Manitoba Chiefs. The department would essentially withdraw from exercising its functions at the request of local First Nations governments. In mid-1995, the minister announced that Ottawa was launching new negotiations to give Indians in all provinces much wider powers, and outlined how the government would implement the inherent right of Aboriginal self-government, acknowledging that in the Chrétien government's view, the principle was already contained in section 35 of the Constitution Act, 1982. According to the August 1995 ministerial statement, the principles of Aboriginal self-government are as follows:

- The inherent right is an existing Aboriginal right recognized and affirmed under the Canadian Constitution.
- Self-government will be exercised within the existing Canadian Constitution. [It] does not mean sovereignty in the international sense. Aboriginal peoples will continue to be citizens of Canada and the province or territory where they live ...
- The Canadian Charter of Rights and Freedoms will apply fully to Aboriginal governments. ... The current provisions of the Charter that respect the unique Aboriginal and treaty rights of Aboriginal peoples will continue to apply.
- All federal funding for self-government will come from the reallocation of existing resources.
- Where all parties agree, rights in self-government agreements may be protected in new treaties under Section 35 of the Constitution Act, 1982. They may also be protected through additions to existing treaties, or as part of comprehensive land claims agreements.
- Federal, provincial, territorial and Aboriginal laws must work in harmony. Certain laws of overriding federal and provincial importance, such as the Criminal Code, will prevail.
- The interests of all Canadians will be taken in account as agreements are negotiated.

In its report, a year later, the **Royal Commission on Aboriginal Peoples** identified four "touchstones" as a framework for its recommendations. These were a new relationship between Aboriginal and non-Aboriginal people based on equality, respect, and reconciliation; self-determination for Aboriginal peoples within Canada through self-government, that is, the right to control their collective futures; economic self-sufficiency for Aboriginal peoples, including breaking the cycle of poverty and dependency on government transfers and creating meaningful employment opportunities; and personal and collective healing for Aboriginal peoples and communities, to remedy the effects of decades of mistreatment and neglect. The commission endorsed Aboriginal self-government in its widest sense and the basic separation of Aboriginal and non-Aboriginal societies. Among other things, it proposed a division between "core" areas, where Aboriginal governments would be free to exercise authority and legislate on their own initiative, and "peripheral" areas, which would require self-government treaties or agreements with other governments. It also proposed an Aboriginal Parliament, dual Canadian–Aboriginal citizenship, an independent lands and treaties tribunal, an Aboriginal development bank, an action plan on health and social conditions, and an Aboriginal-controlled education system.[19]

The Chrétien government seemed reluctant to rush into the implementation of the Royal Commission's more exotic recommendations, preferring the course on which it had previously embarked. In 1997, the government issued a general response called *Gathering Strength— Canada's Aboriginal Action Plan*. It began with a Statement of Reconciliation, apologizing for past wrongs, especially the horrors of the residential school system. Next, in a Statement of Renewal, the document adapted the Royal Commission's four touchstones to the following basic principles: renewing the partnerships, strengthening Aboriginal governance, developing a new fiscal relationship, and supporting strong communities, people, and economies.

Whether or not the 1995 and 1997 federal declarations amounted to anything close to inherent Aboriginal self-government, considerable progress continues to be made on the community-based track of the concept. Aboriginal people now control over 80 percent of DIAND's program funding, and Aboriginal authorities increasingly deliver such services as education, language and culture, police services, health care and social services, housing, property rights, and adoption and child welfare. In this vein, Ottawa signed an agreement in 1997 with the Mi'kmaq chiefs in Nova Scotia, transferring education authority to First Nations' control. Some 80 First Nations are negotiating legislated self-government agreements. Meanwhile, the United Church of Canada also issued a full and formal apology for the abuse that Aboriginal children endured in church-run residential schools, although a number of lawsuits against various churches and the government on this issue have been launched.

In the Northwest Territories, a 1992 plebiscite ratified the boundary divisions for the creation, in 1999, of a new territory called **Nunavut**, an area inhabited almost solely by Inuit. It has all the government institutions associated with a province or territory while being characterized by a form of Aboriginal self-government. In addition, several Yukon First Nations have signed final land claim and self-government agreements with the federal and territorial governments, while other agreements are at various stages of negotiation. They require that each First Nation have a constitution and a citizenship code; they also outline how First Nations powers relate to territorial and federal powers.[20]

Prime Minister Brian Mulroney signs the Nunavut Land Claim Agreement with Paul Quassa, president of the Tungavik Federation of Nunavut in Iqaluit, NWT, May 25, 1993. (Fred Chartrand/ Canapress)

THE ABORIGINAL JUSTICE QUESTION

Because of the high proportion of Aboriginals in Canada's correctional system, one important aspect of self-government is the concept of an autonomous or parallel Aboriginal justice system. In such a system, Native cases would be diverted from the regular judicial process to allow convictions and sentences to be based on Aboriginal values and community traditions. Support for this concept has come from the Canadian Bar Association and the Law Reform Commission of Canada, as well as from many provincial inquiries into the treatment of Natives in the regular judicial system—especially the Donald Marshall Inquiry in Nova Scotia and the Aboriginal Justice Inquiry in Manitoba. Marshall was a Nova Scotia Mi'kmaq imprisoned for over ten years for a crime he did not commit. The Manitoba inquiry centred on the rape and murder of Helen Betty Osborne, an Indian girl in The Pas, and on the shooting of an Aboriginal leader by a Winnipeg police officer. Both of these inquiries, as well as those in other provinces, documented incidents of the brutalization of Aboriginal peoples by the criminal justice system.

While governments have generally ruled out a wholesale parallel Aboriginal justice system, several provinces have allowed experimental judicial processes involving Aboriginal input. More Aboriginals have been hired as police officers; some reserves have their own Aboriginal police forces and justices of the peace; and a few even maintain their own correctional facilities. Increasingly, judges dealing with Aboriginal defendants are following Native traditions (or consulting with Native elders) in imposing their sentences, such as restitution and banishment. Perhaps with the high rate of Aboriginal incarceration in mind, the federal Parliament amended the Criminal Code in 1995 to read: "All available sanctions other than imprisonment that are reasonable in the circumstances should be considered for all offenders, with particular attention to the circumstances of Aboriginal offenders." The Supreme Court brought this clause to the attention of other judges in the 1999 *Gladue* case, and it was then applied by the BC Court of Appeal in the *Armbruster* case.[21]

OTHER ABORIGINAL ISSUES

Many other Aboriginal political issues have arisen in recent years. One is the extent to which Indians have a right to operate gambling facilities on their reserves, now that casinos have become a leading source of revenue for both Indian bands and provincial governments. Another is the question of tax exemption. In 1995, the federal government began to enforce its Indian Remission Order so that status Indians who earn employment income for duties performed off-reserve would have to pay income tax. A third issue is cigarette and other smuggling based on Indian reserves that straddle the Canada–U.S. border, especially in Quebec. Rather than deal with the problem head-on, given the risk of armed violence, Ottawa and Quebec decided to reduce their respective cigarette taxes so that the profitability of smuggling would be reduced, and many other provinces were forced to follow suit. The fate of Aboriginals in a separate Quebec has also been widely discussed in recent years.

Land claim settlements and Aboriginal self-government are not likely to affect the fate of the many Aboriginals who have left the reserve to live in urban centres. The rates of poverty, unemployment, violence, and substance abuse among urban Aboriginals are probably as high as those among Indians living on reserves. Aboriginal women in particular are concerned about issues of day-to-day survival in a harsh urban environment, such as housing, education, and the future of their children. Aboriginals are disproportionately represented among the inner-city poor all across the country, and this aspect of Aboriginal politics is likely to assume increasing importance in the future.[22]

Two of the traditional weaknesses of the Aboriginal cause have been a general attitude of passivity and a lack of effective organization of Native groups. Recent years, however, have witnessed the emergence of strong and vocal pressure groups, such as the Assembly of First Nations (status Indians), the Native Council of Canada (nonstatus Indians), the Métis National Council, and the Inuit Tapirisat. Many other Aboriginal groups exist at the provincial or territorial level, such as the Council of Yukon First Nations and the Native Women's Association.

CONCLUSION

The multidimensional Aboriginal problem in Canada will be hard to solve, but the Canadian public is finally listening. If the Nisga'a Treaty is used as a basis for other land claims/self-government agreements, it will establish certain government structures and practices that have never been seen in Canada before. Some non-Natives hold Aboriginal peoples responsible for most of their own problems, resent the fact that in certain respects Aboriginals are already treated more generously than other groups in society, and oppose such new solutions. Other non-Aboriginals support efforts to improve the conditions of Aboriginal life and welcome such solutions, arguing that government policies and corporate practices rather than the Natives themselves are to blame for the plight of Aboriginals in this country.

Most thoughtful observers want to improve existing government programs; enlarge and strengthen reserves, attempting to make them more economically viable; respect treaty rights; recognize land claims (as long as they do not interfere with non-Native economic development); move toward the principle and practice of Aboriginal self-government; and treat Native peoples more fairly in the justice system. Although progress so far has been slight, a new generation of well-educated, articulate, and insistent Aboriginal leaders has arrived on the scene.[23] In the early years of the new millennium, the public should expect almost daily announcements of tentative or final land claims agreements, self-government agreements, and judicial decisions relating to Aboriginal rights.

P The Aboriginal question confirms many of the tenets of the pluralist approach. Because their organizations were historically weak if not nonexistent, Aboriginals did not even try to exert any influence on the authorities. But in recent years, they have converted this inertia into activism, and their organizations have functioned as effective pressure groups. Indeed, in an almost corporatist manner, Aboriginal leaders have been integrated into the policymaking process since 1992, and the delegation of powers of self-government (and recognition of the inherent right to self-government) goes well beyond the pluralist–corporatist concept of delegating self-regulating powers to professional groups.

SC The state-centred approach is also particularly appropriate to this question. At first, almost every decision with respect to Canadian Aboriginals was made by the bureaucrats in the Department of Indian Affairs. In most cases, what the politicians and bureaucrats thought was in the interests of the Aboriginal peoples clearly was not. The relocation of the

Inuit to the high Arctic was one of many such authoritative fiascoes. The relocation of the Innu of Davis Inlet is a more recent manifestation of the same approach, and the paternalistic attitude of the Clyde Wells government in Newfoundland is evidence that some political authorities continue to treat Aboriginals like children.

©   Class analysts would fault large corporations as well as government elites for the sorry state of Aboriginal life in Canada. The corporate elite did its best to preserve the most productive land for itself, even to the point of denying Native peoples reserve land in British Columbia and the North. Corporations have frequently challenged Aboriginal rights when valuable supplies of trees, minerals, petroleum, or fish were found on reserve land or on land or water that Indians had claimed as theirs by Aboriginal title. Confrontations between forestry companies and Aboriginals have occurred at Temagami in Ontario, Clayoquot Sound in British Columbia, and in New Brunswick, and vehement right-wing opposition broke out to the Nisga'a treaty in BC.

DISCUSSION QUESTIONS

1. What are the causes of the generally poor condition of Aboriginal life in Canada?

2. What are the principal Aboriginal demands on the political agenda, and how far can or should the government go to address them?

3. What can be done to make First Nations reserves more economically viable?

4. What is meant by Aboriginal self-government? How far should it go?

5. How would an Aboriginal justice system interact with Canada's traditional justice system?

6. What can be done to improve the living conditions of urban Aboriginals?

7. How do the critical approaches outlined in Chapter 1 enhance our understanding of Aboriginal political issues?

NOTES

1. The Royal Proclamation was a strong statement on Indian rights, and today's Aboriginal Canadians point to the significance of its inclusion in the 1982 Charter of Rights. It can be found, among other places, in Michael Asch, *Home and Native Land: Aboriginal Rights and the Canadian Constitution* (Toronto: Methuen, 1984). See Darlene Johnston, *The Taking of Indian Lands: Consent or Coercion?* (Saskatoon: University of Saskatchewan Native Law Centre, 1989).

2. Thomas R. Berger, *A Long and Terrible Shadow: White Values, Native Rights in the Americas* (Vancouver: Douglas & McIntyre, 1991).

3. A subsequent and controversial relocation occurred in 1953–55. See Royal Commission on Aboriginal Peoples, *The High Arctic Relocation* (Ottawa: Supply and Services Canada, 1994, cat. no. Z1-1991/1-41-3-1E).

4. Peter R. Oberle, *The Incidence of Family Poverty on Canadian Indian Reserves* (Ottawa: Indian and Northern Affairs Canada, 1993).

5. Minister of Indian Affairs and Northern Development, *Gathering Strength—Canada's Aboriginal Action Plan* (Ottawa, 1997), p. 23; Geoffrey York, *The Dispossessed: Life and Death in Native Canada*

(Toronto: Lester & Orpen Dennys, 1989); Pauline Comeau and Aldo Santin, *The First Canadians* (Toronto: Lorimer, 1990); Ellen Bobet, "Indian Mortality," *Canadian Social Trends* (Statistics Canada, Winter 1989); and a series in *The Globe and Mail* by Thomas Walkom in April 1990.

6. John Milloy, *"A National Crime": The Canadian Government and the Residential School System, 1879 to 1986* (Winnipeg: University of Manitoba Press, 1998).

7. Grand Chief of the Assembly of First Nations, Phil Fontaine, responds to non-Aboriginal charges about the corruption and nepotism practised by some chiefs by reminding us that most of the members of the former non-Aboriginal Grant Devine government in Saskatchewan have been convicted of corruption.

8. Thomas Berger, *Northern Frontier, Northern Homeland: The Report of the Mackenzie Valley Inquiry* (Ottawa: Supply and Services Canada, 1977, republished by Douglas & McIntyre, Vancouver, 1988).

9. Asch, *Home and Native Land*, pp. 32–37, and Michael Asch, ed., *Aboriginal and Treaty Rights in Canada: Essays on Law, Equality and Respect for Difference* (Vancouver: UBC Press, 1997).

10. The Inuvialuit agreed to 91 000 km^2 and subsurface rights in the western Arctic Islands as early as 1984. The Yukon Indians agreed to 41 439 km^2 and $248 million in 1990. The Dene-Métis claim in the western Arctic, which includes title to 180 000 km^2 of land and subsurface mineral rights to 10 000 km^2, along with $500 million, was approved in principle but then rejected. In agreeing to the creation of Nunavut, the Inuit of the eastern Arctic received title to 350 000 km^2 and $580 million in compensation for renouncing all other land claims.

11. *Delgamuukw v. British Columbia*, [1997] 3 S.C.R. 1010; *Calder v. Attorney General of B.C.*, [1973] S.C.R. 313; *Guerin v. The Queen*, [1984] 2 S.C.R. 335; and *Ontario (Attorney General) v. Bear Island Foundation*, [1991] 2 S.C.R. 570; Mary C. Hurley, "Aboriginal Title: The Supreme Court of Canada Decision in *Delgamuukw v. British Columbia*," Library of Parliament Background Paper no. BP-459E, October 1998.

12. *R. v. Sioui*, [1990] 1 S.C.R. 1025; *R. v. Sparrow*, [1990] 1 S.C.R. 1075.

13. *R. v. Marshall*, [1999] S.C.R. (September 17, 1999).

14. Geoffrey York and Loreen Pindera, *People of the Pines: The Warriors and the Legacy of Oka* (Toronto: Little Brown, 1991); Craig MacLaine and Michael Baxendale, *This Land Is Our Land* (Toronto: Optimum, 1990); and Robert Campbell and Leslie Pal, *The Real Worlds of Canadian Politics*, 2nd ed. (Peterborough: Broadview Press, 1991), ch. 4.

15. Bruce Clark, *Native Liberty, Crown Sovereignty: The Existing Aboriginal Right to Self-Government in Canada* (Montreal: McGill–Queen's University Press, 1990).

16. Murray Angus, *"And the Last Shall Be First": Native Policy in an Era of Cutbacks* (Toronto: NC Press, 1991).

17. Georges Erasmus, "Opening Remarks," First Ministers' Conference on Aboriginal Constitutional Affairs, Ottawa, March 26, 1987. See also Frank Cassidy, ed., *Aboriginal Self-Government* (Halifax: Institute for Research on Public Policy, 1991).

18. Audrey Doerr, "Building New Orders of Government—The Future of Aboriginal Self-Government," *Canadian Public Administration* 40, no. 2 (Summer 1997).

19. Royal Commission on Aboriginal Peoples, *Report of the Royal Commission on Aboriginal Peoples*, cat. no. Z1-1991/1-1E (Ottawa: Supply and Services, 1996).

20. Michael S. Whittington, "Aboriginal Self-Government in Canada," in Michael S. Whittington and Glen Williams, eds., *Canadian Politics in the 1990s*, 4th ed. (Scarborough: Nelson Canada, 1995).

21. *R. v. Gladue*, [1999] 1 S.C.R. 688; *R. v. Armbruster*, (1999) BC Court of Appeal.

22. Law Commission of Canada, *Urban Aboriginal Governance in Canada: Re-fashioning the Dialogue*, cat. no. JL 2-5-/1999E (Ottawa).

23. Kathy Brock, "Consensual Politics: Political Leadership in the Aboriginal Community," in Maureen Mancuso et al., eds., *Leaders and Leadership in Canada* (Toronto: Oxford University Press, 1994).

••••••••••••••••••••••••••••••••

FURTHER READING

Alfred, Taiaiake. *Peace, Power, Righteousness: An Indigenous Manifesto*. Toronto: Oxford University Press, 1999.

Angus, Murray. *"And the Last Shall Be First": Native Policy in an Era of Cutbacks*. Toronto: NC Press, 1991.

Asch, Michael. *Home and Native Land: Aboriginal Rights and the Canadian Constitution*. Toronto: Methuen, 1984.

Asch, Michael, ed. *Aboriginal and Treaty Rights in Canada: Essays on Law, Equality and Respect for Difference*. Vancouver: UBC Press, 1997.

Berger, Thomas. *Northern Frontier, Northern Homeland: The Report of the Mackenzie Valley Pipeline Inquiry*. Ottawa: Supply and Services Canada, 1977, republished by Douglas & McIntyre, Vancouver, 1988.

————. *A Long and Terrible Shadow: White Values, Native Rights in the Americas*. Vancouver: Douglas & McIntyre, 1991.

Boldt, Menno. *Surviving as Indians: The Challenge of Self-Government*. Toronto: University of Toronto Press, 1993.

Campbell, Robert, and Leslie Pal. *The Real Worlds of Canadian Politics*, 2nd ed. Peterborough: Broadview Press, 1991.

Canada. Royal Commission on Aboriginal Peoples. *Report of the Royal Commission on Aboriginal Peoples*. Ottawa: Supply and Services, 1996.

Cassidy, Frank, ed. *Aboriginal Self-Government*. Halifax: Institute for Research on Public Policy, 1991.

Clark, Bruce. *Native Liberty, Crown Sovereignty: The Existing Aboriginal Right to Self-Government in Canada*. Montreal: McGill–Queen's University Press, 1990.

Elliott, J.L., and Augie Fleras. *The "Nations Within": Aboriginal State Relations in Canada, the United States and New Zealand*. Toronto: Oxford University Press, 1992.

Engelstad, Diane, and John Bird, eds. *Nation to Nation: Aboriginal Sovereignty and the Future of Canada*. Concord, ON: Anansi, 1992.

Frideres, James S. *Aboriginal Peoples in Canada: Contemporary Conflicts*, 5th ed. Scarborough: Prentice-Hall Allyn & Bacon Canada, 1998.

Long, J. Anthony, Menno Bolt, and Leroy Little Bear. *Governments in Conflict? Provinces and Indian Nations in Canada*. Toronto: University of Toronto Press, 1988.

Long, David, and Olive Dickason. *Visions of the Heart: Canadian Aboriginal Issues*. Toronto: Harcourt Brace, 1996.

MacLaine, Craig, and Michael Baxendale. *This Land Is Our Land*. Toronto: Optimum, 1990.

Mawhiney, Anne-Marie. *Towards Aboriginal Self-Government: Relations between Status Indian Peoples and the Government of Canada, 1969–1984*. New York: Garland, 1994.

McKee, Christopher. *Treaty Talks in British Columbia: Negotiating a Mutually Beneficial Future*. Vancouver: UBC Press, 1996.

Mercredi, Ovide. *In the Rapids: Navigating the Future of First Nations*. Toronto: Viking, 1993.

Milloy, John. *"A National Crime": The Canadian Government and the Residential School System, 1879 to 1986*. Winnipeg: University of Manitoba Press, 1998.

Morrison, Andrea. *Justice for Natives: Searching for Common Ground*. Montreal: McGill–Queen's University Press, 1997.

Morse, B. *Aboriginal Peoples and the Law: Indian, Métis and Inuit Rights in Canada*. Don Mills: Oxford, 1984.

Smith, Dan. *The Seventh Fire: The Struggle for Aboriginal Government*. Toronto: Key Porter, 1993.

York, Geoffrey. *The Dispossessed: Life and Death in Native Canada*. Toronto: Lester & Orpen Dennys, 1989.

York, Geoffrey, and Loreen Pindera. *People of the Pines: The Warriors and the Legacy of Oka*. Toronto: Little, Brown, 1991.

Chapter 5

The French–English
CLEAVAGE AND THE
Quebec question

Both world wars were marked by French–English conscription crises in Canada. In the late 1960s, the Trudeau regime enacted the controversial Official Languages Act and made the federal government officially bilingual. Quebec introduced a French-only sign law and demanded constitutional recognition as a distinct society. The increasing unilingualism of Quebec and the expansion of bilingualism in the rest of the country seemed unfair to many Canadians. Bilingual air traffic control was a heated issue throughout the post-1960 period.[1] The "rest of Canada" generally felt that Ottawa was giving preferential treatment to Quebec in government policy and spending in order to persuade it to stay within Confederation, a feeling that played a part in the rise of the Reform Party in the 1990s.

The French–English cleavage is at least as problematic as the regional economic one in Canadian politics, and the two reinforce each other in the question of Quebec's place in Confederation. Among all the ethnic/linguistic/cultural issues in Canadian politics, the English–French cleavage has always had the greatest significance, primarily reflecting the numbers of people involved, the historical dimensions of the question, and the territorial base of Canada's francophones in Quebec.

This chapter begins with an examination of French–English relations up to 1960, followed by a numerical profile of the French–English linguistic picture in Canada today.[2] It then discusses the Quiet Revolution in Quebec, developments in the relationship between Quebec and the rest of Canada to the start of the new millennium, and French–English relations in the other provinces, ending with a note of speculation on the future. The constitutional implications of the cleavage are further examined in Chapter 16.

HISTORICAL OVERVIEW OF FRENCH–ENGLISH RELATIONS
Pre-Confederation Developments

Almost every Canadian political decision since 1759 has reflected the French–English divisions to some extent, and the tensions that currently threaten the continued existence of the country can probably best be understood in historical context. As outlined in Chapter 2, the French first colonized what is now the province of Quebec, but when the British defeated them on the Plains of Abraham, many changes occurred in the colony. Except for the clergy and the seigneurs, the French elite retreated to France, leaving the British to take control of the economy. The British also formed the government, and the conquerors assumed that the population would soon become "English."

Certain things did not change, however. The people continued to speak French and attend the Roman Catholic Church, which became a highly influential and autonomous organization. It would probably have been impossible to transform Quebec into an Anglo-Protestant colony—at least without a great deal of coercion and/or immigration—and the British soon exhibited a policy of tolerance and accommodation. By the time of the Quebec Act of 1774, the British recognized the inevitable, and guaranteed the French their religious rights and their own system of civil law.

As "English" immigrants moved into what is now Ontario in the 1780s, especially the United Empire Loyalists from the new United States, it became logical to divide the colony into two: Lower Canada (Quebec) would be essentially French-Catholic, and Upper Canada (Ontario) would be Anglo-Protestant. This separation was recognized in the Constitutional Act of 1791.

Difficulties between the popular assembly and the appointed executive and legislative councils became increasingly serious after 1800, culminating in the armed revolts in both colonies in 1837. The battle for democracy in Lower Canada was complicated by the ethnic factor, as French Canadians were predominant in the assembly alone. Lord Durham felt that the ethnic problem could only be solved by another attempt to assimilate the French. Hence, he recommended that the two colonies be reunited into the colony of Canada in which English would be the official language and the anglophone population of the rapidly expanding western portion (Ontario) would soon outnumber the French.

This final attempt at assimilation was to no avail. In recognition of its failure, the French language was increasingly used along with English in the government, cabinets were usually alliances between English and French leaders, and the legislature operated on the informal principle of the double majority—legislation had to have the approval of a majority of representatives from both sections of the colony.

Given this historical evolution, the logic of Confederation and the cultural guarantees of section 133 of the Constitution Act, 1867, are perfectly understandable. Both French and English could be used in all aspects of the federal Parliament, and laws were passed in both languages. Both languages could also be used in whatever federal courts were later established. The francophone minorities in Ontario, Nova Scotia, and New Brunswick were inarticulate and ignored, even though the Acadian minority in New Brunswick constituted 16 percent of the provincial population. However, the anglophone minority in Quebec, at 20 percent and centred in Montreal, was well organized and in control of the economy of the province. This ensured that English could be used along with French in the legislature and courts of Quebec. None of these constitutional provisions was particularly controversial in 1867, and protection of the Protestant school system in Quebec and the Roman Catholic system in Ontario attracted greater interest. No constitutional right was granted to **minority-language schools**: religious rights were seen in educational terms; language rights only applied in legislatures and courts.

• •

OFFICIAL BILINGUALISM IN THE CONSTITUTION ACT, 1867

- Federal Parliament, proceedings and laws
- Federal courts
- Quebec parliament, proceedings and laws
- Quebec courts

Post-Confederation Ethnic/Linguistic Conflicts

THE RIEL REBELLIONS

Although the two language groups have been regularly accommodated in government circles since 1867, five serious linguistic conflicts erupted from the time of Confederation to the Second World War. The first Riel Rebellion precipitated the creation of the province of Manitoba in 1870, as the French-Catholic Métis Louis Riel led the fight for provincial status. During that uprising, and in a situation of uncertain government authority, an Ontario Orangeman was executed by a Métis court-martial. Riel maintained a fairly low profile afterward, but in 1885 he re-emerged in what is now Saskatchewan to lead the second Riel Rebellion on behalf of western Natives and Métis who had been treated shamefully by the government. After quelling the rebellion, the federal government charged Riel with treason and found him guilty in a famous trial in Regina. Ethnic and religious tensions across the country rose to a fever pitch, for while English Protestants regarded Riel as a murderer, traitor, and madman, French Catholics believed he was a patriot and a saint. To Prime Minister John A. Macdonald fell the unenviable decision of whether to let Riel hang or to use the executive power of mercy to spare him. Caught in the middle of this heated confrontation, Macdonald followed the will of the majority and had Riel hanged. This exacerbated the level of French-Catholic outrage across the country, especially in Quebec. As a result, Honoré Mercier and his Parti National were elected in that province in 1886, and the close attachment of the people of Quebec to Macdonald's Conservative Party was permanently damaged. Moreover, Mercier argued that the Riel affair had demonstrated the lack of French-Canadian influence in Ottawa, leading him to demand greater provincial autonomy for Quebec.

BILINGUALISM IN MANITOBA

The second linguistic conflict occurred in Manitoba in 1890. Since the small settlement was about equally divided between French and English, Riel insisted that the 1870 Manitoba Act follow the Quebec precedent of giving the two languages official status in the new province's legislature and courts. (Because the province was equally divided between Protestants and Roman Catholics, the separate school system was also guaranteed.) After its creation, however, Manitoba attracted thousands of English-speaking immigrants and others who chose to identify with the anglophone community. Hence, in 1890, the anglophone majority passed the Official Language Act (later declared unconstitutional), which removed the official status of French in the province's legislature and courts. To solidify its control of the province, the same group abolished the separate school system, both moves leading to French-Catholic opposition within Manitoba and beyond.[3]

BILINGUALISM IN ONTARIO: REGULATION 17

The third main linguistic conflict concerned minority French-language education rights. Although minority-language schools had not been constitutionally guaranteed, the Protestant schools in Quebec, mostly in Montreal, naturally operated in English, and it was only logical that French-language schools be established in francophone parts of New Brunswick and Ontario. In 1913 the Whitney government issued Regulation 17, which virtually abolished the use of French in the Ontario school system; English was to become the sole language of instruction after the third year, and the study of French as a subject was limited to one hour a day. Whitney claimed that he was doing Franco-Ontarian citizens a favour by forcing them to learn English in an English-speaking province, but Franco-Ontarians denounced the regulation and challenged it in court. The 1917 *Mackell* case confirmed, however, that constitutional protection in educational matters applied only to religious minorities, not linguistic ones.[4]

THE FIRST CONSCRIPTION CRISIS

The Regulation 17 incident in Ontario had its greatest implications in Quebec during the **conscription crisis** of the First World War, the fourth major French–English confrontation. As a British colony, Canada was automatically at war, but could determine its own degree of involvement. Despite small standing armed forces, the Conservative government of Robert Borden made excessive commitments. Appeals for volunteers had promising results initially, but as reinforcements were needed later in the war, few recruits came forward. The government therefore decided to resort to conscription—compulsory military service—in 1917. Borden knew that French Canada generally felt indifferent to the conflict and that conscription would divide the country along linguistic lines. Having few French Canadians in his Cabinet to start with, the prime minister appealed to Liberal leader Wilfrid Laurier to join him in a coalition government. Laurier refused the offer, although most of the English-speaking Liberal MPs did join in a **Union Government** in 1917, and the subsequent enforcement of conscription entailed considerable violence. A conscription-inspired riot in Quebec City in the spring of 1918, which the federal government sought to quell by sending in the army, left four people dead and many others injured. This confrontation destroyed what little French-Canadian support remained for the Conservative Party after the execution of Louis Riel.

THE SECOND CONSCRIPTION CRISIS

Ontario repealed Regulation 17 in 1927 and French–English tensions returned to a normal, controllable level until they were inflamed by the fifth ethnic conflict, another conscription crisis during the Second World War. In 1939, the Liberal Prime Minister Mackenzie King was in power with a strong contingent of ministers and MPs from Quebec. Although still closely allied with Britain, Canada entered the war as an independent country, and its leader was extremely cautious in determining its degree of involvement. King knew that conscription would be resisted in French Canada, so he was even more reluctant than Borden to adopt it. After first promising not to impose conscription, he held a national plebiscite to let himself off the hook. While 80 percent of voters outside Quebec agreed to release King from his promise, Quebec voted 73 percent against. On the basis of the slogan "conscription if necessary, but not necessarily conscription," King managed to postpone the adoption of compulsory military service until almost the end of the war. Given the sensitivity with which conscription was imposed on this occasion, King is credited by most observers with having skilfully kept the country together in the circumstances.

....

THE FRENCH–ENGLISH DEMOGRAPHIC PROFILE IN CANADA TODAY

The distribution of French and English communities within and outside Quebec today is shown in Table 5.1. Although Statistics Canada gathers figures on ethnic origin, mother tongue, and language spoken at home, it is difficult to use statistics on ethnic origin because so many Canadians are now an ethnic mixture and because an increasing number prefer to call themselves "Canadians." It is more reliable to use figures for mother tongue, even though this does not exactly measure the same thing as ethnic origin. Employing mother-tongue figures, then, we label the groups anglophone, francophone, and allophone, the last being those with a mother tongue other than English or French.

According to the 1996 census, the number of people in Canada as a whole having English as their mother tongue was 17 072 000, or 59.8 percent of the population, while the number having French as their mother tongue was 6 712 000, or 23.5 percent. Both of these groups increased over the 1986–96 period in absolute numbers, but their percentage of the total dropped, primarily because of the high immigration of those having other linguistic backgrounds.

The Quebec population is made up of 5 741 000 francophones and 622 000 anglophones, or 81.5 percent and 8.8 percent respectively. There are close to one million francophones living outside Quebec, but 85.5 percent of all francophones in Canada live in Quebec. Thus, while Quebec is predominantly French and Canada outside Quebec is predominantly English,

TABLE 5.1 Mother Tongue, Home Language, and Bilingualism in Quebec, in Canada Outside Quebec, and in Canada as a Whole (Percentages)

	Mother Tongue			*Home Language*			*Bilingualism* Anglo- Franco- Allo-			
	English	*French*	*Other*	*English*	*French*	*Other*	*phones*	*phones*	*phones*	*Total*
Quebec	8.8	81.5	9.7	10.8	82.8	6.4	61.7	33.7	46.7	37.8
Canada outside Quebec	76.6	4.5	18.7	86.3	2.9	10.9	6.9	83.8	5.3	9.8
Canada	59.8	23.5	16.6	67.6	22.6	9.8	8.8	40.8	11.2	17.0

Source: Adapted from 1996 Census of Canada data.

it is not strictly accurate to equate French Canada with Quebec or English Canada with the rest of the country.

Statistics on bilingualism reveal that 17 percent of the total population could carry on a conversation in both official languages, including 8.8 percent of anglophones and 40.8 percent of francophones. The table also shows that linguistic minorities—francophones outside Quebec and anglophones and allophones inside Quebec—are most likely to speak both English and French. On the other hand, only about one-third of francophones in Quebec and only 6.9 percent of anglophones outside Quebec are bilingual. Nevertheless, the rate of official bilingualism rose by almost 1 percent between 1986 and 1996, no doubt primarily due to French and English immersion and second-language programs in provincial school systems.

....

THE QUIET REVOLUTION: QUEBEC IN THE 1960S
Changes in Quebec

Until 1960, Quebec was basically a traditional, conservative, rural, poorly educated, patronage-oriented society, heavily influenced by the Roman Catholic Church. Dominated by the authoritarian Premier Maurice Duplessis from 1935 to his death in 1959, the inward-looking population was taught that only he could protect them from evil external influences such as Ottawa. Duplessis governed with three main allies: the Church, which he empowered to oversee social policy; the farmers, who were overrepresented in the legislature; and American capital, which was encouraged to enter the province and create jobs for those who were no longer needed on the farm. He was unconcerned about working conditions in these new resource and manufacturing operations or the fact that since the companies were foreign owned, employees had to master English in order to get promoted.

The Quebec of the past 40 years, however, is quite a different province and society from that which existed before 1960. After that date, the province underwent a **Quiet Revolution**, consisting of a dramatic change of values and attitudes, especially toward the state, a new collective self-confidence, and a new brand of nationalism. It was a time of urbanization, democratization, modernization, secularization, and bureaucratization, and rather than a nationalism of inward-looking survival, it became one of expansion and growth, outward looking and aggressive. These features of the new Quebec had many implications for French–English relations in both the Quebec and Canadian political systems.

The government of Jean Lesage (1960–66) took over many of the functions previously administered by the Church.[5] The most important of these was education, which was radically modernized. Health and welfare programs were also made public rather than charitable responsibilities. With the nationalization of private power companies, Hydro-Québec became a huge Crown corporation supplying all the electricity in the province. Lesage also reformed almost every piece of legislation on the books, especially labour and electoral laws, added reams of new ones, and created many government agencies.

All these new and expanded public responsibilities required substantial additional revenues, and Lesage put immense pressure on Ottawa to increase federal–provincial grants, to allow Quebec to opt out of the conditions attached to them, and to give the province a greater share of joint taxation. In areas of provincial jurisdiction, Quebec began to move toward distinctive programs, designing its own pension plan, which was then used as a model for the Canada Pension Plan. As time went on, the province began to demand an ever larger jurisdiction, including international francophone links, leading to perpetual federal–provincial discord. As far as the Quebec private sector was concerned, francophones had lower incomes and lower-status jobs than anglophones, but the Lesage government did little of substance to rectify this situation, probably for fear of driving out Anglo-Canadian and foreign investment.

Much of the analysis of the Quiet Revolution centres on the concept of the **new middle class**—civil servants, teachers, professors, and other salaried professionals. Since upward mobility was still difficult in the English-dominated private sector, this new class used Quebec nationalism in order to further its own aspirations in the expansion of the Quebec state.[6] They sponsored an enormous increase in provincial government programs and agencies.

By the mid-1960s, however, future prime minister Pierre Elliott Trudeau had established a constituency of federally oriented Quebec francophones who promoted an alternative or contrary set of demands. One of their priorities was that French be used as a language equal to English in the corridors of power in Ottawa. Since the federal Parliament and courts were already theoretically bilingual, the main gap in official bilingualism at the national level was in the executive branch, where English was the working language of the public service, at least at policymaking levels. Such federally oriented Quebec francophones were also concerned about the fate of francophone minorities in the other provinces. The new self-confidence of the Québécois inspired these dwindling minorities to greater self-assertiveness.

Federal Responses

Although the British North America Act of 1867 guaranteed the use of either English or French in the federal Parliament and courts, the extent of official bilingualism in Ottawa was minimal before 1960. It was not until 1927 that postage stamps became bilingual; in 1934 bilingual bank notes were introduced, and in 1945 bilingual federal family allowance cheques were provided in Quebec.[7]

During the early 1960s, the federal government grappled somewhat haphazardly with Quebec's new demands. The Diefenbaker government (1957–63) introduced simultaneous English/French interpretation into Parliament, began printing all federal government cheques in a bilingual format, and appointed a French-Canadian governor general. Immediately after taking office, the Pearson government (1963–68) established the **Royal Commission on Bilingualism and Biculturalism**

> to inquire into and report upon the existing state of bilingualism and biculturalism in Canada and to recommend what steps should be taken to develop the Canadian Confederation on the basis of an equal partnership between the two founding races.

Even before the commission reported, however, Pearson felt obliged to act on Quebec's demands. He gave Quebec and the other provinces more federal funds and taxation power, removed conditions from many shared-cost programs, and permitted Quebec to make international arrangements with France.

In response to the demands of francophones who did not focus on Quebec, Pearson and Trudeau introduced an Official Languages bill to make the Canadian public service bilingual, much to the consternation of those unilingual public servants who were now pressured to learn French. Parliament passed the **Official Languages Act** in 1969, and since that time Canada has been officially and effectively bilingual in its federal institutions. Ottawa also began to support French immersion educational programs as well as to assist francophone minorities in other provinces.

••••••••••••••••••••••••••••••••••••

PRINCIPAL PROVISIONS OF THE OFFICIAL LANGUAGES ACT

- Canada is a country with two official languages, English and French, and both languages have equal status, rights, and privileges in federal government institutions.
- Canadians have the right to full and equal access to Parliament and to the laws and courts and the right to be served by and communicate with the institutions of the federal government in either English or French from any head office, in the national capital region, and in any federal government office across the country or abroad where there is significant demand.
- Canadians employed by the federal government have the right to work in the official language of their choice wherever practicable, and both English- and French-speaking Canadians are ensured of equitable opportunities for employment and advancement in federal institutions so that the federal public service is representative of the two official language groups.
- The Canadian government is committed to support the vitality of English- and French-speaking minority communities, especially by encouraging and assisting the provinces and territories to provide minority and second-language education.

The question of French–English relations, or "national unity," was the principal political issue throughout the Trudeau era (1968–79, 1980–84). At that point it became clear that two models existed to deal with the problem. The first—the territorial principle—would recognize Quebec as the homeland of French Canada and give that province powers and resources to protect and promote its linguistic and cultural distinctiveness. Quebec would essentially be "French" and the rest of Canada primarily "English."[8] The second option—the personality principle—would treat Quebec as "une province comme les autres" and promote bilingualism at the federal level and in the other provinces so that each person could use either language anywhere in the country.

English Canadians had difficulty accepting these demands, which seemed excessive and contradictory: making Quebec more French and more autonomous at the same time as promoting French in Ottawa and the other provinces. They did not understand that the two demands came largely from two different groups of francophones, with contrary conceptions of French Canada. Trudeau fought against recognition of Quebec as the homeland of French Canada and opposed giving that province special recognition or power. He argued that any kind of special status would be the first step toward separation; he feared that a nationalistic French Quebec would be inward-looking and intolerant; and he felt that francophone Quebeckers would have more opportunity if they followed his example, became bilingual, and participated in the life of a larger country. Part of Trudeau's popularity in English Canada stemmed from the perception that he was "anti-Quebec," but he was passionately "pro-French" in promoting bilingualism in Ottawa and across the country.

The Separatist Option

During the 1960s, advocates of Quebec separatism began to emerge. Because of their conviction that the normal political process was not responding quickly enough to the demands of the Quiet Revolution, one wing of the separatist movement, the **Front de Libération du Québec (FLQ)** resorted to violence, including periodic bombings that killed 2 people and injured at least 27. In October 1970, two small cells of the FLQ kidnapped a British diplomat and abducted and murdered Quebec cabinet minister Pierre Laporte. Trudeau invoked the coercive **War Measures Act**, giving the police and armed forces special powers to quell the violence, and over 400 innocent, peaceful separatist supporters were arrested in the process. By crushing the FLQ, by giving French Canadians more clout in Ottawa, and by guaranteeing pan-Canadian bilingualism in the Constitution in 1982, Trudeau hoped to undercut any Quebec demand for special status or separatism.

QUEBEC IN THE 1970S, 1980S, AND 1990S
The 1970s

In spite of the fact that a centralist Trudeau government was in power, the first Robert Bourassa government in Quebec (1970–76) gained a degree of autonomy from Ottawa in the fields of family allowances and immigration. It also passed **Bill 22** to give primacy to the French language in many spheres in the province, such as in the operations and documents of public and para-public authorities. As far as education was concerned, immigrant children who did not already have a "sufficient knowledge" of English were obliged to go to French-language schools. This was an attempt to have such children join the majority French linguistic group in the province rather than become "English," as so many previous immigrants had done. Relying on immigration to bolster the francophone segment of the population became a vital issue after the French-Canadian birthrate plummeted in the 1960s. Bill 22 also aimed at the francization of the private sector by pressuring companies to use French as the language of internal corporate operations. The more Quebec moved in the direction of French unilingualism, the more English Canada resisted Trudeau's national policy of bilingualism, and the larger grew the number of anglophones who left Quebec.

The Parti Québécois (PQ) was elected to office in 1976 under René Lévesque with an even more nationalistic program.[9] Faced with a hostile Trudeau government in Ottawa, the PQ made few gains in provincial autonomy. But it did pass **Bill 101**, the Charter of the French Language, which extended Bill 22 by making French the predominant language in the province. It generally turned the persuasive and optional aspects of Bill 22 into coercive and mandatory ones, and English Quebeckers and English Canadians generally were strongly opposed to many aspects of Bill 101. It made French the only official language of the legislature (although laws continued to be translated unofficially into English); only individuals (not corporations) could use English in Quebec courts; the only children who could go to English schools in the province were those whose parents had done so; and all commercial signs had to be in French only.[10] All four of these clauses were subsequently ruled unconstitutional by the courts, but in other ways Bill 101 still stands, and French continues to be the official language of the province.

By *Adrian Raeside* (Victoria Times-Colonist). *Used with permission.*

The 1980s

In 1980 the PQ government held a **referendum** on the question of pursuing a more independent relationship with Canada called **sovereignty association**. Many federal politicians, including Trudeau and Justice minister Jean Chrétien, and several provincial premiers encouraged Quebeckers to defeat the PQ proposal, promising them "renewed federalism" if they did so.[11] When sovereignty association was turned down by a vote of 60 percent to 40 percent, new federal–provincial constitutional negotiations began, culminating in the Constitution Act, 1982. Ironically, even though the whole effort was supposed to appeal to the residents of that province, Quebec alone objected to the act. That was because it reflected the Trudeau vision of a bilingual Canada rather than recognizing the distinctive French character of Quebec. Nevertheless, it became law in all parts of the country. As far as language was concerned, the act reinforced official bilingualism at the federal level and in New Brunswick, and guaranteed minority official-language education in the provinces where numbers warranted. Many Quebeckers never forgave Trudeau and Chrétien for adopting such a significant constitutional document without Quebec's consent.

The second Bourassa government, elected in 1985, was first able to convince the more receptive Mulroney government to allow Quebec to play a fuller part in the **Francophonie**, the international French-speaking community. Then, in 1988, the Supreme Court of Canada declared the sign provision of Bill 101 to be unconstitutional as a violation of freedom of expression, even "commercial expression."[12] Bourassa responded by using the "notwithstanding clause" in the federal and Quebec charters of rights to pass **Bill 178**, which provided for French-only outdoor signs but allowed some bilingual signs indoors. Violating a constitutional right and giving preference to French collective rights over (English) individual rights produced a vehement reaction among English Quebeckers and an anti-Quebec, anti-French response in the rest of the country. On the other hand, it should be noted that in 1983 some aspects of Bill 101 were voluntarily relaxed, and in 1986 Quebec ensured the provision of social and health services in English to its anglophone minority. Moreover, when the five-year limit on Bill 178 ran out in 1993, Bourassa replaced it with **Bill 86**, which allowed bilingual signs outside as well as inside stores, as long as the French lettering was predominant.

The main item on the Bourassa–Mulroney agenda was the **Meech Lake Accord**, which was designed to bring Quebec back of its own free will into the Canadian constitutional fold. The **distinct-society clause** in the accord provided for the recognition of Quebec as a distinct society within Canada, provincial nomination of senators and Supreme Court judges, provincial vetoes on a wider range of constitutional amendments, constitutionalization of Quebec's rights in immigration, and provincial opting-out, with compensation, of federal programs set up within their jurisdiction. In many respects Meech Lake reflected the approach of the 1979 Task Force on Canadian Unity, which had been promptly shelved when its recommendations were contrary to Trudeau's vision of Canada. English-Canadian reaction against Meech Lake stiffened after Bill 178, and in the end, the Newfoundland and Manitoba legislatures failed to approve it before the deadline. Many Quebeckers felt betrayed again, Quebec began a much more aggressive campaign to wrest powers from Ottawa, and several Quebec members of Parliament quit the Conservative and Liberal parties to sit as Quebec *indépendantistes* in the Bloc Québécois led by Lucien Bouchard.

The 1990s

After intense post-Meech discussions taking the form of the all-party **Bélanger–Campeau Committee** and the Quebec Liberal Party's **Allaire Report**, the Quebec legislature decided that a referendum on **sovereignty** would be held in the province in 1992. Those opposed to independence hoped that the rest of Canada would offer Quebec a model of a new federation before that time so that the voters would have an acceptable federalist option. Such a vision was embodied in the **Charlottetown Accord**. If ratified, Quebec would essentially have achieved fulfillment of its Meech Lake demands, including recognition as a distinct society within Canada based on its French-language majority, unique culture, and civil law tradition. All provinces would have received increased power over immigration, an enlarged veto over constitutional amendments, and compensation when opting out of national programs. Quebec and the other provinces would have secured some nine powers in addition to immigration if they chose to use them, but this fell far short of the Allaire Report's demands. In the end, 56.7 percent of Quebeckers voted against the accord, just slightly more than did so in the rest of Canada.

After the disheartening, if not traumatic, experience of the Charlottetown Accord, all federal parties decided to put constitutional issues on the back burner, especially the Chrétien Liberals, elected a year later. In 1994, however, the Parti Québécois was re-elected in Quebec under Jacques Parizeau. As in 1976, the PQ argued that it was "safe" to elect it to government, because sovereignty would be decided in a separate, subsequent referendum. For the next two years the Parizeau government kept adjusting its concept of sovereignty and delaying the date of the vote until it thought it had a version that would be accepted by the Quebec public.

The referendum on Quebec sovereignty was held in October 1995. While the PQ government proposed a kind of sovereignty that retained significant links to the rest of Canada, its proposal was turned down by a vote of 50.6 percent to 49.4 percent. Such a close result was not particularly comforting to those who wanted to keep the country together, especially when the charismatic Lucien Bouchard succeeded Jacques Parizeau as Quebec premier and promised another referendum within a few years' time.

After governing for three years, Bouchard called an election for November 1998. During the campaign, he announced that there would be another referendum on sovereignty, but only when "winning conditions" existed. While the PQ won the election in terms of seats, it actually polled 1 percent less of the popular vote than the Liberals, now led by Jean Charest. Although Bouchard clearly won a majority of the francophone vote, it was not the degree of popular support that he anticipated, and the election result diluted his enthusiasm for another referendum in the near future.

FRENCH–ENGLISH RELATIONS IN THE OTHER PROVINCES

The distribution of French and English communities in the various provinces in 1996 is shown in Table 5.2. In absolute numbers, francophone minorities, defined by mother tongue, were located primarily in Ontario (500 000) and New Brunswick (242 000); between them, these two provinces contained over three-quarters of francophones outside Quebec. As percentages, the francophone minorities were largest in New Brunswick (33.2 percent), Ontario (4.7 percent), Manitoba (4.5 percent), Prince Edward Island (4.3 percent), and Nova Scotia (4.0 percent).

The Quebec government and most Quebeckers have been more concerned about internal linguistic matters than about what happens to French minorities in other provinces. Nevertheless, the Quiet Revolution led francophones outside Quebec to seek to preserve their language and culture. Often under pressure from Prime Minister Trudeau, some provincial premiers hoped that by extending rights or services to their francophone minorities, they would help to forestall separatism in Quebec. Thus, considerable improvement has been made in minority francophone rights in many provinces since 1965.[13] As mentioned, all provinces were bound by the Constitution Act, 1982, to provide education in the minority official language where numbers warranted. In addition, the Supreme Court ruled that francophone parents must have some control over their children's French-language education.[14] Amendments to the Criminal Code in 1978 and 1988 forced all provinces to provide for criminal trials in French by 1990, if demanded by the accused.

Much has been written about the Trudeau government's creation of minority official-language education rights across the country. It has been widely said that this was the real reason he pushed the concept of a Charter of Rights and Freedoms. Moreover, Ottawa helped to create the demand for French-language schools in the nine anglophone provinces. The federal government sought to create advocacy organizations that would promote its own agenda[15] and then pressured such official-language minority groups to demand and establish French-language schools and gave the provinces the money to finance them. All this was designed to undercut Quebec's claim that it was the homeland of French Canada, and was a classic case of a government's not waiting for societal forces to demand what it wanted to do.

TABLE 5.2 **English and French Mother Tongue and Home Language, by Province, 1996 (Percentages)**

	Mother Tongue		Home Language	
	English	French	English	French
Newfoundland	98.5	0.5	99.2	0.2
Prince Edward Island	94.1	4.3	97.2	2.3
Nova Scotia	93.2	4.0	96.3	2.3
New Brunswick	65.3	33.2	68.9	30.5
Quebec	8.8	81.5	10.8	82.8
Ontario	73.1	4.7	83.6	2.9
Manitoba	74.7	4.5	88.3	2.1
Saskatchewan	84.4	2.0	94.6	0.6
Alberta	81.5	2.1	91.1	0.7
British Columbia	76.1	1.5	86.5	0.5
Yukon	86.8	3.8	95.4	1.8
Northwest Territories	56.7	2.2	68.8	1.0
TOTAL	59.8	23.5	67.6	22.6

Source: Adapted from 1996 Census of Canada data. Multiple answers have been distributed equally between the languages indicated.

New Brunswick

New Brunswick implemented its own Official Languages Act in 1969, which was constitutionalized at provincial request in 1982.[16] New Brunswick also improved the Acadian educational system at all levels and provided provincial government services in both languages. Under the Richard Hatfield government, it embarked on a policy of cultural equality based on a "separate but equal" strategy rather than individual or institutional bilingualism, with parallel unilingual school boards and other public bodies (Bill 88). The adoption of official bilingualism in New Brunswick was facilitated by all-party support, but many years later, in 1991, the anti-bilingual Confederation of Regions (COR) Party elected several members to the provincial legislature. Faced with this threat, New Brunswick constitutionalized Bill 88 in 1993 to further protect the right of English and French linguistic communities in the province to distinct cultural and educational institutions.[17]

Ontario

Ontario began to provide French-language secondary schools in 1968, and later established the right of every Franco-Ontarian to go to a French-language school, whether or not warranted by numbers. Ontario then guaranteed French trials in the provincial courts and gradually extended French-language provincial services. In 1986, under premier David Peterson, the province passed Bill 8, which became effective in 1989 and provided for the translation of laws as well as for provincial government services in French in 22 designated regions of the province. Meanwhile, simultaneous French–English interpretation in the legislature began in 1987, and Franco-Ontarians were granted the right to have French-language schools run by trustees elected by the francophone population. As in New Brunswick, the considerable voting power of the Franco-Ontarian community encouraged all parties to support such initiatives, but the combination of Quebec's Bill 178 and Ontario's Bill 8 was too much for some Ontarians to bear. COR did well in parts of the province in the 1988 federal election and some 70 municipalities symbolically declared themselves officially unilingual in 1989–90.

Manitoba

Manitoba moved very slowly on French-language initiatives, but was pushed by a series of Supreme Court of Canada decisions beginning in 1979. The 1890 Official Language Act was declared unconstitutional (a violation of the 1870 Manitoba Act), all laws had to be passed in both languages, trials had to be available in French, and most government documents had to be bilingual.[18] In the 1981–88 period the NDP government tried to implement the Supreme Court decisions as well as to expand French-language services, while the opposition Conservatives inflamed the issue with an all-out attack. Once in office, however, the Filmon PC government continued the NDP approach, and the Supreme Court refined the guidelines on which government documents had to be translated.

Other Provinces and Territories

Given their small francophone minorities, Saskatchewan and Alberta took very little action on French-language issues. Indeed, even asking a question in French in the Alberta legislature created quite a controversy. In the 1988 *Mercure* case, however, the Supreme Court of Canada ruled that Saskatchewan (and by implication, Alberta) was bound by an 1886 territorial statute to pass laws in both French and English and to provide for court cases in French.[19] The Court allowed the province to opt out of these requirements, however, by repealing the territorial law by means of a single bilingual provincial statute. Both provinces proceeded to do so, but did allow French to be spoken in their legislatures and courts. With federal arm-twisting and financial incentives, Saskatchewan also began to translate some of its English-only laws into French. Meanwhile, under federal government pressure, both the Yukon and Northwest Territories granted French official status, but advances for francophone minorities in other provinces have been minimal.

Linguistic minorities at the provincial level find it necessary to organize in order to pursue their objectives. Such groups include the Association canadienne-française de l'Ontario (ACFO), the Société franco-manitobaine, and the Société des acadiens du Nouveau-Brunswick. These provincial French groups have also joined together in the Fédération des communautés francophones et acadienne du Canada. Meanwhile, the English minority in Quebec has also formed its own increasingly militant pressure group, Alliance Quebec.

By Malcolm Mayes (Edmonton Journal). *Reproduced with permission.*

FRENCH–ENGLISH RELATIONS IN THE NEW MILLENNIUM

Given that francophones constitute nearly 25 percent of the Canadian electorate, given their historic constitutional rights, given their geographic concentration in Quebec and majority control of such a large province, and given their modern-day self-consciousness and self-confidence, the French fact in Canada cannot be ignored. If English Canada wants Quebec to remain part of the country, it cannot go back to the easy days of pre-1960 unilingualism and federal government centralization.

As outlined earlier, two basic approaches to accommodating this French presence persist. Given that 86 percent of the French are located in Quebec and that 82 percent of Quebeckers are French-speaking, the first is to recognize that Quebec is the heartland of French Canada; in short, French Canada equals Quebec. This approach would give that province special recognition and responsibility to protect itself in the North American English linguistic environment. Whether or not it is justified, Quebec has a "siege mentality" with respect to its language and culture, and language has replaced the Church as the focus of French-Canadian identity. The Quebec corporate elite is now a francophone group, and they, along with the new middle class in the Quebec public sector, see themselves benefiting from increased provincial autonomy.

The second approach is to promote the bilingual character of the whole country and most or all of the provinces—that is, the idealistic Trudeau vision that contends that French Canada does not equal Quebec. As mentioned above, over 4.8 million Canadians, or 17 percent of the population, claimed that they could speak both official languages. The official bilingualism rate in Quebec was 37.8 percent, and in New Brunswick, 32.6 percent. While most of these are people of French origin, the policy of official bilingualism is also supported by politically active social, economic, and cultural elites, including "new anglophone bilinguals who have invested heavily in their own bilingualism or that of their children."[20] Given the tiny proportion of residents who speak French in many provinces and in the North, however, and given the hostility to the imposition of bilingualism in many parts of the country (as evidenced by the popularity of the Reform Party), it appears that the limits of national bilingualism have been reached.

There is, however, a synthesis lying between these extremes. As advocated by Bourassa and Mulroney (and possibly after 1995 by Chrétien), it sees Quebec as a distinct French society with significant powers within Canada, but the country as a whole retains a bilingual character. It is the option long supported by a majority of Quebeckers, who reject both the separatist and Trudeau positions and want to remain in Canada—but in a Canada that recognizes their distinctiveness. Many observers feel that the only hope of keeping the country intact in a recognizable form is to find a formula along these lines that would be supported by a majority of Canadians both inside and outside Quebec.

In the early 1990s, however, especially in the wake of the Bill 178 controversy, many detected a visible decline in the will of both French and English to live together. Quebeckers felt increasingly self-confident about going it alone, and many English Canadians invited them to do so. The death of the Meech Lake Accord in 1990 caused many Quebeckers to feel rejected by English Canada, and support for the existing political community and partnership fell to a new low on both sides. Quebec awaited the response of the rest of Canada after its Allaire Report proposed that Ottawa turn almost all its powers over to the province in a relationship not far removed from sovereignty association. English-Canadian public opinion generally hoped that Quebec would remain in Canada, but it was not prepared to grant that province much in the way of special powers or to eviscerate the federal government in appeasement. A whole array of books began to be written about a Canada without Quebec, although a few people wrote more hopefully about a reconciliation.[21]

The results of the 1995 Quebec referendum on sovereignty were not encouraging. While a slim overall majority of Quebeckers voted No, nearly 60 percent of francophones in Quebec favoured the PQ proposal. Many of these did not necessarily support an independent Quebec, but had not heard an encouraging response from the rest of Canada. The Chrétien government responded in a variety of ways, both encouraging Quebec to stay and raising fears about its fate if it left, and even a Supreme Court decision on the legality of a unilateral declaration of Quebec independence was a mixed blessing. Meanwhile, the nine "anglo" provincial premiers penned the **Calgary Declaration** in 1997, trying to reconcile the "unique character of Quebec" with the equality of all the provinces.

A more encouraging development was the result of the Quebec provincial election in late 1998. While the Parti Québécois was re-elected, it was not by the margin most observers anticipated. Thus, it was not the first of the "winning conditions" that Premier Bouchard looked forward to along the road to another referendum on sovereignty within his second mandate. Complacent policymakers in Ottawa breathed a sigh of relief, but the situation nevertheless remained volatile.

CONCLUSION

The ethnic cleavages that are such a prominent feature of the Canadian political system are based in part on the number and variety of groups involved, but also on the contrasting perceptions each group has of its own history and current status. The French remember when they were the dominant group in the country and are acutely conscious of their current minority status. They desperately want to preserve their language and culture against the pervasive forces of Anglo-American television and other media. The French of Quebec want to enlarge their capacity to govern themselves, and those outside Quebec want to maximize opportunities to use their own language. English-speaking Canadians, on the other hand, are still by far the largest single group in the land, and resent the number of jobs, mostly in the public sector, that now require fluency in English and French. They also tend to support the idea of provincial equality and are skeptical about distinct status for Quebec.

P Of the approaches outlined in Chapter 1, pluralism is probably most relevant to the discussion of the French–English cleavage. In the first place, the French–English relationship in Canadian society is the very essence of pluralism; it is a basic fact of Canadian political life and animates much of the political activity in the country. The fundamental coexistence of two dominant ethnic groups establishes an underlying pluralism and also provides the foundation for most of the other pluralistic aspects of Canadian government and society. Secondly, the pluralist approach is clearly correct in anticipating regular bargaining between such groups in the policymaking process and in not expecting that the groups will always operate on a level playing field. In this case, however, such political interaction has not always required the involvement of organized pressure groups.

SC The state-centred approach begins with the fact that the British and French "charter groups" have historically dominated positions of political power, although the British usually prevailed over the French.[22] Apart from two prime ministers, French Canadians generally occupied minor positions in the federal Cabinet until 1968, when Pierre Trudeau drew his principal ministers from Quebec. A similar imbalance existed until recently in the public service, but under the Official Languages Act, hiring and promotion preferences have given the French language and francophone public servants a more equitable, if not superior, position. The state-centred approach takes the perspective that many policies in this field reflect the interests or prejudices of the political elite rather than the demands articulated by the wider society. In particular, Trudeau's imposition of official bilingualism was carried out despite the opposition of a majority of the anglophone population and the indifference of a majority of francophones in Quebec. Moreover, his *dirigiste* approach is evident in his creation and financing of official-language minority advocacy groups throughout the country, his determination to guarantee their rights in the Charter, and his funding of whatever official bilingualism he could persuade provincial governments to offer.

PC In terms of the public choice approach, French Canadians constitute about 25 percent of the electorate, which should be sufficient to demand much attention. On the other hand, Quebec voted Liberal so often that it did not figure prominently in any party's electoral calculations between 1896 and 1960. The neglect of bilingualism at the federal level was one result, although the delayed implementation of conscription in the Second World War is an indication that French Canada could not be completely taken for granted. After the Quiet Revolution, when their demands increased and were backed by the threat of separation, and especially after 1984 when their voting preferences became more volatile,

Quebec francophones became the most courted group in the country. Every party except Reform tried to bid for their votes.

Ⓒ Class analysts are interested in socioeconomic rather than ethnic cleavages, but find certain links between the two.[23] They are particularly interested in the relationship between class and ethnicity in Quebec. In the pre-1960 period the titans of big business in Quebec reflected the dominance of British, Anglo-Canadian, and Anglo-American backgrounds. They took little interest in promoting francophone concerns and made English the language of business. Premier Maurice Duplessis welcomed "English" capital into Quebec and did not object to exploitation of French-speaking workers. Then, in the Quiet Revolution, a new middle class of francophone Quebeckers made itself felt in the province's public sector and passed laws to improve the lot of francophones in the private sector as well. These developments fostered the emergence of a new entrepreneurial class in the province, and the economic elite in Quebec today is francophone in character. Class analysts also cite the use of the War Measures Act in 1970 as an unnecessary resort to coercion by the state. They argue that ethnic politics are a reflection of underlying economic, class-based forces. They also suggest that the capitalist-controlled political elite has chosen to emphasize the ethnic factor in Canadian politics in order to distract the population from any consciousness of class divisions. Capitalist forces did not want English and French working people across the country to realize how much they had in common.

DISCUSSION QUESTIONS

1. How would you characterize the interaction between the English majority and the French minority in Canadian history?

2. What are their respective visions of their place in Confederation?

3. Should the French minorities outside Quebec have the same rights and services as the English minority in Quebec? Explain.

4. Is the territorial or the personality principle a more realistic basis for language policy in Canada? Explain.

5. Why do most Quebeckers insist on constitutional recognition that Quebec is a distinct society within Canada? What additional powers do they seek?

6. What is likely to happen to official bilingualism if Quebec ever separates?

7. How do the various critical approaches outlined in Chapter 1 help us to understand the French–English cleavage in Canada?

NOTES

1. Sandford Borins, *The Language of the Skies: The Bilingual Air Traffic Control Conflict in Canada* (Montreal: McGill–Queen's University Press, 1983).

2. Although the label "English" is sometimes used in this chapter to refer to language, as opposed to ethnic origin, special mention should be made of the Scots, who historically controlled the fur trade,

the banks and other financial institutions, the major universities, and much of the government. Many prime ministers, for example, were of Scottish background. See Pierre Berton, *Why We Act Like Canadians* (Toronto: McClelland and Stewart, 1982), pp. 77–78.

3. *A.G. Manitoba v. Forest*, [1979] 2 S.C.R. 1032. Canada's involvement in the British Boer War also complicated French–English relations to a limited extent.

4. *Ontario Roman Catholic Separate School Trustees v. Mackell*, [1917] A.C. 62.

5. Dale Thomson, *Jean Lesage and the Quiet Revolution* (Toronto: Macmillan, 1984).

6. Kenneth McRoberts, *Quebec: Social Change and Political Crisis*, 3rd ed. (Toronto: McClelland and Stewart, 1993).

7. Office of the Commissioner of Official Languages, *Our Two Official Languages over Time*, rev. and updated ed. (Ottawa, 1996).

8. Kenneth McRoberts, "Making Canada Bilingual: Illusions and Delusions of Federal Language Policy," in David Shugarman and Reg Whitaker, eds., *Federalism and Political Community* (Peterborough: Broadview Press, 1989), and Kenneth McRoberts, *Misconceiving Canada: The Struggle for National Unity* (Toronto: Oxford University Press, 1997). See also Guy Laforest, *Trudeau and the End of a Canadian Dream* (Montreal: McGill–Queen's University Press, 1995).

9. Graham Fraser, *René Lévesque and the Parti Québécois in Power* (Toronto: Macmillan, 1984); Joseph Carens, *Is Quebec Nationalism Just?* (Montreal: McGill–Queen's University Press, 1995). For France's role in the whole saga, see J.F. Bosher, *The Gaullist Attack on Canada, 1967–1997* (Montreal: McGill–Queen's University Press, 1998).

10. William Coleman, "From Bill 22 to Bill 101: The Politics of Language under the Parti Québécois," *Canadian Journal of Political Science* (September 1981), pp. 459–85.

11. Gertrude John Robinson, *Constructing the Quebec Referendum: French and English Media Voices* (Toronto: University of Toronto Press, 1998).

12. *Ford v. Quebec (Attorney General)*, [1988] 2 S.C.R. 712. Marcel Fournier et al., *Quebec Society: Critical Issues* (Scarborough: Prentice Hall Canada, 1997).

13. C. Michael MacMillan, *The Practice of Language Rights in Canada* (Toronto: University of Toronto Press, 1998).

14. *Mahe v. Alberta*, [1990] 1 S.C.R. 342.

15. Leslie Pal, *Interests of State: The Politics of Language, Multiculturalism, and Feminism in Canada* (Montreal: McGill–Queen's University Press, 1993).

16. New Brunswick court cases include *Jones v. A.G. New Brunswick*, [1975] 2 S.C.R. 182 and *Société des Acadiens v. Association of Parents*, [1986] 1 S.C.R. 549.

17. James Ross Hurley, *Amending Canada's Constitution: History, Processes, Problems and Prospects* (Ottawa: Supply and Services, 1996).

18. Manitoba cases include *A.G. Manitoba v. Forest*, [1979] 2 S.C.R. 1032; *Reference re Manitoba Language Rights*, [1985] 1 S.C.R. 721; *Order re Manitoba Language Rights*, [1985] 2 S.C.R. 347; *Bilodeau v. Attorney General Manitoba*, [1986] 1 S.C.R. 449; and *Reference re Manitoba Language Rights*, [1992] 1 S.C.R. 212. Parallel Quebec cases include *Attorney General of Quebec v. Blaikie*, [1979] 2 S.C.R. 1016, and *MacDonald v. City of Montreal*, [1986] 1 S.C.R. 460.

19. *Mercure v. Attorney General Saskatchewan*, [1988] 1 S.C.R. 234.

20. McRoberts, "Making Canada Bilingual," p. 90.

21. David J. Bercuson and Barry Cooper, *Deconfederation: Canada without Quebec* (Toronto: Key Porter, 1991); Alan Freeman and Patrick Grady, *Dividing the House: Planning for a Canada without Quebec* (Toronto: HarperCollins, 1995); Gordon Gibson, *Plan B: The Future of the Rest of Canada* (Vancouver: Fraser Institute, 1994); Daniel Drache and R. Perin, *Negotiating with a Sovereign Quebec* (Toronto: Lorimer, 1992); Phillip Resnick, *Toward a Canada–Quebec Union* (Montreal: McGill–Queen's University Press, 1991); Jeremy Webber, *Reimagining Canada: Language, Culture, Community, and the Canadian Constitution* (Montreal: McGill–Queen's University Press, 1994); Roger Gibbins and Guy Laforest, *Beyond the Impasse: Toward Reconciliation* (Montreal: Institute for Research on Public Policy, 1998); J.E. Trent, R.A. Young, and Guy Lachapelle, eds., *Québec-Canada: What Is the Path Ahead?* (Ottawa: University of Ottawa Press, 1996); David Thomas, *Whistling Past the Graveyard: Constitutional Abeyances, Quebec, and the Future of Canada* (Toronto: Oxford University Press, 1997); Marcel Côté and David Johnston, *If Québec Goes ... The Real Cost of Separation* (Toronto: Stoddart, 1995); R.A. Young, *The Secession of Quebec and the Future of Canada*, rev. and

expanded ed. (Montreal: McGill–Queen's University Press, 1998); and R.A. Young, *The Struggle for Quebec* (Montreal: McGill–Queen's University Press, 1999).

22. John Porter, *The Vertical Mosaic* (Toronto: University of Toronto Press, 1965); Rick Helmes-Hayes and James Curtis, eds., *The Vertical Mosaic Revisited* (Toronto: University of Toronto Press, 1998).

23. Janine Brodie and Jane Jenson, *Challenge, Crisis and Change: Politics and Class in Canada Revisited*, 2nd ed. (Ottawa: Carleton University Press, 1990).

· ·

FURTHER READING

Borins, Sandford F. *The Language of the Skies: The Bilingual Air Traffic Control Conflict in Canada*. Montreal: McGill–Queen's University Press, 1983.

Bothwell, Robert. *Canada and Quebec: One Country, Two Histories*, rev. ed. Vancouver: University of British Columbia Press, 1998.

Canada. Royal Commission on Bilingualism and Biculturalism. *Report*. Ottawa: Queen's Printer, 1967.

Carens, Joseph. *Is Quebec Nationalism Just?* Montreal: McGill–Queen's University Press, 1995.

Coleman, William. "From Bill 22 to Bill 101: The Politics of Language under the Parti Québécois." *Canadian Journal of Political Science* (September 1981), pp. 459–85.

———. *The Independence Movement in Quebec 1945–1980*. Toronto: University of Toronto Press, 1985.

Cook, Ramsay. *Canada, Quebec and the Uses of Nationalism*. Toronto: McClelland and Stewart, 1995.

Côté, Marcel, and David Johnston. *If Québec Goes … The Real Cost of Separation*. Toronto: Stoddart, 1995.

Fournier, Marcel, et al. *Quebec Society: Critical Issues*. Scarborough: Prentice Hall Canada, 1997.

Fraser, Graham. *René Lévesque and the Parti Québécois in Power*. Toronto: Macmillan, 1984.

Gagnon, Alain-G. *Quebec: State and Society*, 2nd ed. Toronto: Nelson Canada, 1993.

Gibbins, Roger. *Conflict and Unity*, 3rd ed. Scarborough: Nelson Canada, 1994.

Gibbins, Roger, and Guy Laforest. *Beyond the Impasse: Toward Reconciliation*. Montreal: Institute for Research on Public Policy, 1998.

Joy, Richard. *Canada's Official Languages*. Toronto: University of Toronto Press, 1992.

Laforest, Guy. *Trudeau and the End of a Canadian Dream*. Montreal: McGill–Queen's University Press, 1995.

MacMillan, C. Michael. *The Practice of Language Rights in Canada*. Toronto: University of Toronto Press, 1998.

McRoberts, Kenneth. "Making Canada Bilingual: Illusions and Delusions of Federal Language Policy." In David Shugarman and Reg Whitaker, eds., *Federalism and Political Community*. Peterborough: Broadview Press, 1989.

———. *Quebec: Social Change and Political Crisis*, 3rd ed. Toronto: McClelland and Stewart, 1993.

———. *Misconceiving Canada: The Struggle for National Unity*. Toronto: Oxford University Press, 1997.

Pal, Leslie. *Interests of State: The Politics of Language, Multiculturalism, and Feminism in Canada*. Montreal: McGill–Queen's University Press, 1993.

Resnick, Philip. *Thinking English Canada*. Toronto: Stoddart, 1994.

Robinson, Gertrude Joch. *Constructing the Quebec Referendum: French and English Media Voices*. Toronto: University of Toronto Press, 1998.

Thomas, David. *Whistling Past the Graveyard: Constitutional Abeyances, Quebec, and the Future of Canada*. Toronto: Oxford University Press, 1997.

Thomson, Dale. *Jean Lesage and the Quiet Revolution*. Toronto: Macmillan, 1984.

Trent, J.E., R.A. Young, and Guy Lachapelle, eds. *Québec-Canada: What Is the Path Ahead?* Ottawa: University of Ottawa Press, 1996.

Webber, Jeremy. *Reimagining Canada: Language, Culture, Community, and the Canadian Constitution*. Montreal: McGill–Queen's University Press, 1994.

Young, Robert A. *The Secession of Quebec and the Future of Canada*, rev. and expanded ed. Montreal: McGill–Queen's University Press, 1998.

———. *The Struggle for Quebec*. Montreal: McGill–Queen's University Press, 1999.

Chapter 6

Other Ethnic GROUPS AND *multiculturalism*

With high immigration rates from the Third World, the number of Canadians who belong to visible minorities increases daily. Many established Canadians welcome this development and cherish this diversity, but this multicoloured tapestry is not to everyone's taste. Employment equity and affirmative action programs designed to assist visible minorities have generated much controversy. Meanwhile, the members of many ethnic groups that arrived generations ago either ease into a pattern of "Canadianized" assimilation or attempt to keep their languages and cultures alive. While the Liberal Party is sometimes accused of entrenching multiculturalism in the Constitution in order to attract immigrant votes, the Reform Party opposes public funding of multiculturalism and high levels of immigration.

It is obvious that the growing number and visibility of other ethnic groups in Canadian society increasingly vie with Aboriginal and French–English issues on the political agenda. The three principal topics that arise in this area are immigration policy, preserving and promoting the identity of ethnic groups (or multiculturalism), and ensuring that individuals belonging to such groups are treated equitably in law and society. This chapter begins with an examination of Canadian immigration patterns and a profile of ethnic minorities in Canada today. It then discusses the historic pattern of discrimination that new Canadians experienced and their demands for equality. The next part deals with responses to such demands in the 1970s and 1980s, especially their success in achieving the policy of multiculturalism and in overcoming inequities. The chapter ends with an account of recent opposition to large-scale immigration, publicly funded multiculturalism, and employment equity.

CANADIAN IMMIGRATION PATTERNS

Following the Aboriginals, the French, and the British, people from many other lands began to immigrate to Canada. By 1867, a sizable German contingent had already arrived, and, shortly afterwards, the wide open spaces of northern Ontario, the Prairies, and British Columbia attracted large numbers of immigrants from continental Europe as well as from Britain and the United States. Railway construction and western settlement were two key objectives of the Macdonald government's 1879 National Policy (incorporating the 1872 Dominion Lands Act), and the first dramatic surge of immigrants arrived during the 1880s. These included Danes, Dutch, Icelanders, Poles, Ukrainians, Finns, Norwegians, and Swedes. In British Columbia, between 1881 and 1884, nearly 16 000 Chinese were brought in as contract labourers to work on the CPR. Nova Scotia and Ontario also received a substantial number of Blacks who were escaping from slavery in the United States.

Between 1910 and 1913, the largest number of immigrants in the country's history arrived in Canada—1 400 000 over four years! The prosperous 1920s were another active decade, but immigration declined significantly during the Depression and the Second World War. After the war, another huge wave of immigrants came to Canada, largely from southern Europe. They were supplemented by postwar refugees from around the world, one of the largest groups being from Hungary after its 1956 revolution. Table 6.1 indicates the fluctuation in numbers of immigrants arriving in Canada, by decade; when the figures are complete, they will show the 1990s to be the biggest decade in Canadian immigration history, with well over 2 million immigrants.

Overall, Britain was the leading source of immigrants between 1900 and 1965. During that time, immigration policy favoured British, American, and European newcomers, since they were considered to be well educated and skilled, and, being predominantly Caucasian, better able to assimilate. After the Immigration Act was significantly amended in 1967, Canadian immigration patterns changed radically, as Table 6.2 demonstrates. In 1957, over 90 percent of the immigrants were from Britain or continental Europe, a figure that fell to 18 percent in 1997. In contrast, Asian immigrants accounted for less than 2 percent of total immigrants in 1957, up to 54 percent in 1997.

Table 6.3 reveals the individual countries from which most immigrants came in the 1994–97 period. It shows the huge exodus from Hong Kong prior to the transfer of that colony

TABLE 6.1 **Immigrant Arrivals in Canada, by Decade**

1861–1871	183 000	1931–1941	150 000
1871–1881	353 000	1941–1951	548 000
1881–1891	824 000	1951–1961	1 543 000
1891–1901	828 000	1961–1971	1 429 000
1901–1911	1 759 000	1971–1981	1 447 000
1911–1921	1 612 000	1981–1991	1 374 000
1921–1931	1 203 000		

Source: Employment and Immigration Canada, "Immigration Statistics," 1992, Cat. No. MP22-1/1992. Reproduced with the permission of the Minister of Public Works and Government Services Canada, 2000.

TABLE 6.2 Principal Sources of Immigrants to Canada, Selected Years (Percentages)

	Britain	*Europe*	*Asia*
1957	38.6	52.6	1.3
1967	28.0	43.8	9.3
1977	15.7	19.8	21.0
1987	5.6	19.1	44.3
1997	2.2	15.7	54.2

Source: Employment and Immigration Canada, "Immigration Statistics," Annual, and Citizenship and Immigration, "Facts and Figures, 1997: Immigration Overview," Cat. No. MP43-333/1998/E. Reproduced with the permission of the Minister of Public Works and Government Services Canada, 2000.

from Britain to China, along with large numbers from other Asian countries, principally India, the Philippines, China, Taiwan, and Sri Lanka. The modest numbers from the United Kingdom and the United States pale in comparison. After 1997, China became the top source of Canadian immigrants.

TABLE 6.3 Top 11 Source Countries, 1994–1997

Hong Kong	127 866
India	74 222
China	61 784
Philippines	58 038
Taiwan	41 586
Sri Lanka	26 778
Pakistan	26 699
United Kingdom	22 348
Bosnia-Hercegovina	20 105
Iran	19 625
United States	17 570

Source: Citizenship and Immigration Canada. Reproduced with the permission of the Minister of Public Works and Government Services Canada, 2000.

....

A PROFILE OF ETHNIC MINORITIES IN CANADA TODAY

The census regularly asks respondents to state their ethnic origin, but these statistics are increasingly difficult to interpret because, as mentioned in Chapter 5, so many Canadians now have multiple ethnic origins and because a large proportion simply answer "Canadian." Statistics on ethnic origin seem to indicate, however, that apart from "Canadian," the largest ethnic origins are as follows: English, French, Scottish, Irish, German, Aboriginal, Italian, Ukrainian, Chinese, Dutch, Polish, and South Asian, in approximately that order.

Ethnic groups can be further classified as **visible minorities**, defined in the Employment Equity Act as "persons, other than Aboriginal peoples, who are non-Caucasian in race or non-white in colour," and "invisible" minorities—mostly those with European origins. Some public policies such as multiculturalism apply to both groups, while others, such as employment equity, apply only to visible minorities.

The proportion of those who report origins other than British, French, or Canadian is much higher west of Quebec than in the eastern half of the country. Recent immigration patterns have changed the face of Canada, especially that of its three largest cities, Toronto, Montreal, and Vancouver. The 1996 census probably provides better statistics on this subject than ever before, as seen in Table 6.4.

Table 6.4 establishes that nearly three-quarters of the visible minorities in Canada reside in the three largest cities. Examined in another way, 31.6 percent of the Toronto population is made up of visible minorities, as is 31.1 percent of the Vancouver population. It should be

TABLE 6.4   **Visible Minorities, by Location, 1996**

	Toronto	*Vancouver*	*Montreal*	*Other*	*Total*
Chinese	335 185	279 040	46 115	199 810	860 150
South Asian	329 840	120 140	46 165	174 440	670 585
Black	274 935	16 400	122 320	160 205	573 860
Arab/West Asian	72 160	18 155	73 950	80 400	244 665
Filipino	99 110	40 710	14 385	79 995	234 200
Latin American	61 655	13 830	46 700	54 790	176 975
Southeast Asian	46 510	20 370	37 600	68 285	172 765
Japanese	17 050	21 880	2 315	26 890	68 135
Korean	28 555	17 080	3 500	15 700	64 835
Other	73 090	16 985	8 360	32 880	131 315
TOTAL	1 338 090	564 590	401 410	893 395	3 197 485
Percentage	41.8	17.7	12.6	27.9	

Source: Adapted from 1996 Census of Canada data.

added that Calgary and Edmonton have sizable Chinese and South Asian communities, while the largest visible minority in Ottawa-Hull and Halifax is Black, and in Winnipeg, Filipino. While 29 percent of the visible minorities were born in Canada, the three provinces of Ontario, British Columbia, and Quebec had the highest share of immigrant visible minorities. Indeed, one-quarter of the visible minorities were immigrants who had arrived between 1991 and 1996.

DISCRIMINATION AGAINST IMMIGRANTS

Many immigrants settled in ethnic communities and started their own social and cultural organizations such as clubs, choirs, folk dance troupes, and newspapers. Many families spoke the ethnic language at home, but the children generally became proficient in English at school, and the second generation often assimilated into the Anglo-Canadian way of life, as intended. Such ethnic groups maintained a low public profile and made few demands. Once arrived, they were largely ignored by federal and provincial governments, although the occasional privilege was granted, such as promises to Mennonites and Hutterites of exemption from military service. In Manitoba between 1896 and 1916 it was legal to establish bilingual English and other-language schools in areas of concentrated ethnic settlement.

It was not always the case, however, that immigrants were ignored: sometimes they were subject to deliberate discrimination, such as in the Immigration Act and during the First and Second World Wars. Immigrants have also faced a number of legal barriers that made it difficult for them to play an active part in mainstream politics, government, and in society in general. These barriers included discrimination in voting rights, employment, media depictions, and political participation. Over and above legalized discrimination, most people who belong to visible minorities (as well as Aboriginals) have faced racial animosity, at least including abusive comments on a regular basis.[1]

As noted above, for 100 years Canadian immigration policy gave preference to Caucasians. As time went on, however, Canada moved further and further from its British origins, and a growing number of Canadians began to realize the bias in the country's immigration policy. International and domestic pressure thus forced the Pearson government to revise the **Immigration Act** in 1967 to remove its preference for Anglo-Europeans. The great bulk of immigrants in recent years have been visible minorities, although some observers have noted that immigration policy is designed to skim the cream of the crop from Third World countries, to attract doctors, other professionals, and entrepreneurs.

The worst case of federal government mistreatment of visible minorities (other than Aboriginals) was that of Japanese Canadians in the Second World War. When Japan entered the war, Canadian citizens of Japanese origin were automatically suspected of being loyal to Japan, a suspicion without any foundation. Canadian citizens of Japanese background were uprooted from the west coast, interned in "relocation centres," and had their property confiscated. At the end of the war, about 4000 were deported.[2]

Because the federal franchise was sometimes based on provincial franchises, the bias against Asians in British Columbia carried over to federal elections. At the federal level, itself, Canadian citizens who came from countries with which Canada was at war (principally Germany and Austria) had their right to vote taken away in 1917. Then, until after the

Second World War, Canadians of Chinese, Japanese, and East Indian descent had no vote unless they had served in the armed forces. On the other hand, until 1975, British subjects resident in Canada could vote in federal elections even without becoming Canadian citizens.

Untold cases of discrimination against both visible and invisible ethnic minorities in the area of employment have occurred throughout Canadian history. Blacks and Asians probably suffered most, but so did Caucasians with accents and Canadian citizens who had come from countries with which Canada was at war. Such discrimination extended to government employment and was sometimes even authorized by law. In British Columbia, provincial labour laws in the early part of this century prohibited the employment of Asians in order to preserve jobs for whites.

Canadians of "other ethnic origins" are also sensitive to the way in which the media have portrayed them. In many cases, the complaint is that they are not portrayed at all, and that the media present a picture of a homogeneous white Canadian society. This is changing, however, as television stations now hire a large number of visible-minority anchors and reporters.

A final barrier to the equality of those of other ethnic origins has been discrimination within political parties. They were generally not welcomed into mainstream parties, and when they did find entry, they were usually given only subordinate roles. They had a hard time winning party nominations, unless it was in hopeless or clear-cut "ethnic" constituencies. It was not until the Diefenbaker era, around 1960, that Canadians of Ukrainian background started to make inroads into the Conservative Party. Visible minorities progressed much more slowly, being most welcome in the Liberal Party in recent years.

MULTICULTURALISM AND EQUITY

It has already been noted that changes to the Immigration Act in 1967 altered the ethnic composition of the Canadian population. This increase in the numbers of people of other ethnic origin gave them more leverage to demand improvements in their status as citizens. Changes in the 1970s and 1980s were largely positive for such groups and started with the adoption of the policy of multiculturalism.

The original mandate of the 1963 Royal Commission on Bilingualism and Biculturalism was to concentrate on the English and French languages and cultures and to make recommendations in the wake of the Quiet Revolution in Quebec. By that time, however, the number of people in the country belonging to "other" ethnic groups was sufficient to force a change in the commission's terms of reference. Largely due to pressure from Ukrainian Canadians, the Royal Commission was also asked to examine "the contribution made by other ethnic groups to the cultural enrichment of Canada and the measures which should be taken to safeguard that contribution." The term "multiculturalism" came into use at about this time, and the Commission recommended that increased government attention be given to other ethnic groups including public funding in certain areas. With this encouragement, such groups began to demand public financial assistance as well as verbal and moral support.

In 1971, partly due to the Royal Commission recommendations, group pressure, and politicians hoping to win votes, the Trudeau government announced a new official policy of multiculturalism within a bilingual framework. **Multiculturalism** is the official recognition of the diverse cultures in a plural society; it involves encouraging immigrants to retain their lin-

The Dionysos Greek Dancers perform a traditional dance at Heritage Days in Edmonton. (Bruce Edwards/ Canapress)

guistic heritages and ethnic cultures instead of abandoning them and assimilating with the dominant group. The government felt that it was "overdue for the people of Canada to become more aware of the rich tradition of the many cultures"[3] in the country. It argued that the Canadian identity would not be undermined by multiculturalism; indeed, cultural pluralism was the very essence of the Canadian identity. Such diversity makes Canada a more interesting place to live in terms of foods, restaurants, languages, and cultures. In providing links to virtually every other country in the world, this array of ethnic groups also enhances Canada's international image and influence.

Ottawa established a number of new programs to implement the multicultural policy and a government department to administer them. To some people of such ethnic origins, however, the policy did not provide for complete ethnic equality because the policy of official bilingualism preserved the historic dominance of the British and French groups. Others saw multiculturalism more as a symbolic than substantive policy, one that was primarily aimed at preserving ethnic folklore. Some Quebeckers viewed multiculturalism as an attempt to diminish their claim of being a distinct society within Canada.

BASIC OBJECTIVES OF MULTICULTURALISM POLICY

- To assist cultural groups to retain and foster their identity.
- To assist cultural groups to overcome barriers to their full participation in Canadian society.
- To promote creative exchanges among all Canadian cultural groups.
- To assist immigrants in acquiring at least one official language.[4]

One of the fascinating aspects of multiculturalism policy was the role of the Citizenship Branch of the Secretary of State Department in funding multicultural advocacy groups in order to demand services, legislation, recognition, and rights from the government. This was done at the direction of the Trudeau Liberal government and served to help it implement its campaign commitments and advance its own vision of the country.[5] Besides its financial support of individual ethnic groups and their diverse projects, the government established the Canadian Consultative Council on Multiculturalism in 1973, which was later renamed the Canadian Ethnocultural Council.

Once in place, the policy of multiculturalism legitimized demands for many other changes both in terms of promoting ethnic identities and removing barriers to equity. The next stage was the government's creation of the Canadian Human Rights Commission in 1978. Most provinces already had such bodies to deal with complaints of discrimination in the private sector and to promote anti-discrimination educational programs, but the new commission closed certain loopholes within federal jurisdiction.

Another advance was the Charter of Rights and Freedoms in 1982, which provided constitutional protection against discrimination by federal and provincial governments in the equality rights clause, section 15. Moreover, the Charter endorsed affirmative action programs to overcome past discrimination. After intense pressure from various ethnic groups, an additional section was added to the Charter to the effect that it would be interpreted "in a manner consistent with the preservation and enhancement of the multicultural heritage of Canadians" (section 27).

The Multiculturalism ministry that began to take form in the 1970s gradually increased in status, and 1988 saw the passage of a new Canadian Multiculturalism Act. The act gave multiculturalism a stronger legal base by consolidating existing policies and practices into legislation, provided a more detailed policy statement on multiculturalism, and created the Canadian Multicultural Advisory Committee. In 1991 the Mulroney government created a new Department of Multiculturalism and Citizenship.

As part of a massive reorganization of government departments and functions in 1993, immigration was lumped under Public Security, giving the impression that immigration had become a problem of national security. Immigration was later resurrected as a separate ministry, combined with Citizenship, but at the same time, multiculturalism became part of the Canadian Heritage Department, which reduced it in status, although it shared a junior minister with Status of Women Canada.

In 1986 the federal **Employment Equity** Act designated visible minorities, women, people with disabilities, and Aboriginals as groups that could benefit from affirmative action programs with respect to hiring in the public service. While those not included complained about reverse discrimination, some ethnic leaders criticized the lack of specific goals and timetables in the legislation.[6]

The treatment of Japanese Canadians during the Second World War nagged at the Canadian conscience for nearly 45 years until the Mulroney government announced a settlement package in the 1988 **Japanese Redress Agreement**, which provided, among other things, $21 000 for each of the surviving internees. This led to demands from other ethnic groups that they be similarly compensated for wartime discrimination in Canada.

Some provinces also demonstrate support for the concept of multiculturalism. Ontario, for example, instituted a heritage language policy in its school system. Then, in 1993 it passed what was called the strongest employment equity legislation in the country, but the law did not survive the new provincial PC government elected in 1995. In Quebec, on the other hand, while French-speaking immigrants are welcomed in order to bolster the francophone population, other immigrants are required to attend the French-language school system and are otherwise encouraged to assimilate into the majority French culture.

On the partisan front, the Liberal Party in particular began to welcome those of other ethnic origins into its ranks. Such groups were naturally inclined toward the Liberal Party anyway, seeing that it had usually been in power when they arrived in the country, and that it was the party that initiated the policy of multiculturalism. On the other hand, the practice in many large cities of packing Liberal Party nomination and leadership delegate selection meetings with "instant Liberals" from various ethnic groups—primarily Sikh, Italian, Greek, Portuguese, Croatian, Korean, Macedonian, and Chinese—has come under attack. While this practice has the advantage of integrating these immigrants into the Canadian political process and of giving them political influence they had previously lacked, it sometimes provokes animosity between two or more such groups and alienates those who have been members and worked hard for the party for many years. Such conflict also provides much fodder for the media. *The Globe and Mail* revealed in October 1996, for example, that then Defence minister David Collenette had hired a number of consultants at public expense to advise him on the views of various ethnic groups in his constituency.

Taking their cue from Aboriginal, francophone, and anglophone minority groups, nearly every other ethnic group has established a national organization to promote its culture and to function as a pressure group from time to time. Examples include the Italian National Congress, the German Canadian Congress, and the National Association of Japanese Canadians. As noted above, many such groups were actively encouraged to organize by the government itself, and they were to find common ground in the Canadian Ethnocultural Council. That group also receives considerable government funding, a fact that some critics feel was responsible for its low-key opposition to the Charlottetown Accord, which did not advance the multiculturalism cause.[7] The council now consists of a coalition of 37 national ethnic organizations representing over 100 groups.[8] Beyond domestic matters, ethnic groups have also demonstrated occasional influence on Canadian foreign policy.

REACTION AGAINST MULTICULTURALISM AND IMMIGRATION

If the responses to demands from the multicultural community were largely positive in the 1970s and 1980s, such was not entirely the case in the 1990s. Opposition surfaced toward immigration in general, visible-minority immigration in particular, as well as multiculturalism, employment equity, and other related policies and practices.[9]

This opposition was partly a response to the recession of the early 1990s and the

By *Adrian Raeside* (Victoria Times-Colonist).
Used with permission.

continuing high unemployment rate afterwards. Most economists agree that immigration has little effect on the unemployment rate, that immigration causes as many jobs to be created as immigrants actually fill. Moreover, with a low birth rate and an aging population, Canada needs a relatively high annual intake of immigrants for economic reasons alone. Such views, however, were widely rejected by voters in the 1990s, who saw recent immigrants taking jobs away from long-time residents. As for the source of immigrants, while the level of Canadian acceptance and tolerance of nontraditional immigrants is high, it is not unlimited. The Reform Party was the first to break rank with an all-party consensus on these issues, calling for a severe cut in annual immigration levels and a greater emphasis on skills. Other parties resisted to some extent, but the Chrétien government did reduce the target from 250 000 to about 200 000 in 1994 and imposed a $975 right-of-landing fee. It also announced that it would withdraw from the direct delivery of immigrant integration services and indicated that beginning in 1996, the balance between economic, family and other immigrant components would place greater emphasis on attracting those with the capacity to settle quickly and contribute to Canada's economy. The government flew several trial balloons with respect to immigration reform in the post-1996 period, but backed off any significant action before the beginning of the new century. It did decide to move away from an emphasis on occupation, trade, or training, as such, in favour of overall education and skill levels that could be useful in a variety of jobs. It also hoped to force entrepreneurial immigrants to bring better English- or French-language skills with them (along with their money) and to actually reside in Canada instead of just investing and then leaving again. The government also revamped the troubled Immigration and Refugee Board.

In 1995, after a number of crimes were committed by immigrants who had been ordered deported but who had remained in the country, that board lost its jurisdiction over appeals on humanitarian grounds by criminals declared a danger to the public. This did not satisfy critics, however, who complained about the numerous illegal immigrants and bogus refugee claimants who continued to make a new home in Canada.

The policy of official multiculturalism was also under increasing attack. In an era of government fiscal restraint, more and more Canadians were reluctant to provide public funding for multicultural purposes, a sentiment first given official voice by the Spicer Commission in 1991.[10] Some members of the multicultural community even spoke out against the policy, especially Toronto MP John Nunziata and writer Neil Bissoondath. They maintained that official multiculturalism is divisive, that it ghettoizes visible minorities, fosters racial animosity, and detracts from national unity.[11] They argued that multiculturalism emphasizes our differences rather than our similarities as Canadians. A 1995 survey found that only 20 percent of respondents agreed with the statement that "the government should provide funding to ethnic groups so they can protect their traditions and language," while 66 percent disagreed. Critics argue that with the new concern to balance the government's books, it is hardly appropriate for it to foster the maintenance of foreign traditions while starving national cultural institutions. The money would be better spent teaching immigrants about basic Canadian values.

Others have attacked multiculturalism from a different angle. For example, in refuting the claim of systemic prejudice and discrimination against visible minorities, Martin Loney argues that the people at a real disadvantage in Canadian society are the poor—of every ethnic origin. The money provided for public subsidization of multiculturalism, Loney states, would be better spent on those who truly need it.[12]

The 1990 decision of the RCMP to allow Sikh mounties to wear turbans as a religious symbol produced considerable opposition. So did the wearing of turbans in the halls of the Royal Canadian Legion. On the other hand, the House of Commons lost no time in waiving a similar rule when the first turbaned Sikh MP was elected in 1993.

Since most newcomers to Canada settle in Toronto, Montreal, and Vancouver, an increase in racial tensions in these three cities has become apparent. Relations between the Black community and the Montreal and Toronto police forces have been strained, while ethnic gangs and inter-ethnic gang wars are becoming more common.

The framers of the Charlottetown Accord wrote that "Canadians are committed to racial and ethnic equality in a society that includes citizens from many lands who have contributed, and continue to contribute, to the building of a strong Canada that reflects its cultural and racial diversity." They thought multicultural leaders would be happy, but some complained that this clause was only a statement of equality, building on section 15 of the Charter, and not an enhancement of the principle of multiculturalism, as contained in section 27. In other words, for some multicultural advocates, guaranteeing *equity* is not enough; they also want government to go further to protect and promote *identity*.[13] Even though Toronto, for example, has six ethnic radio stations, two closed-circuit audio services, an ethnic television station, three ethnic specialty services, and another six channels accessible with special receiving equipment, ethnic groups continue to put pressure on the Canadian Radio-television and Telecommunications Commission to provide for more.

CONCLUSION

Given the current low birth rate, immigration is necessary for Canada's economic expansion. Increasingly coming from Third World countries, immigrants to this country will be demanding their share of political influence as well as more government support in their quest for equity and identity. When unemployment is high and balanced budgets are a priority, however, some Canadians are likely to be resistant to visible-minority immigration and publicly financed multiculturalism programs. Moreover, increased racial problems can be anticipated over the next decades, particularly in Canada's largest metropolitan centres.

P Ethnic diversity is the essence of the pluralism approach. Combined with the diversity of the Aboriginal, British, and French elements of the population, the influx of other ethnic groups makes Canada one of the most heterogeneous societies in the world. Even before the official policy of multiculturalism was enunciated, many Canadians of all origins celebrated this diversity as a key component of the Canadian national identity: a cultural mosaic in contrast to the American melting pot. The pluralist approach therefore relates to the interaction of many ethnic pressure groups as they seek to promote increased immigration (especially from their home country), good relations between Canada and the country of origin, multiculturalism, employment equity, constitutional status, and changes in traditional Canadian ways. Pluralism also allows for considerable slack in the system, a gap that was eventually filled by organized ethnic groups as their members grew in numbers and self-confidence and as they worked with relevant government officials and agencies in a specialized and tightly knit policy community, as well as becoming active within political party organizations.

PC The public choice approach is also relevant to developments in multiculturalism in the last 30 years. When ethnic groups began to form significant numbers of voters, the Liberal Party could adopt policies fostering higher levels of immigration as well as multiculturalism. It promised even more in return for votes and participation, especially at its nomination meetings. The Mulroney Conservatives did exactly the same in the 1984–93 period. In the 1990s, however, parties had to be more circumspect. The Liberals tried to retain the support of the ethnic community with high immigration levels but, for a variety of reasons outlined above, faced the opposition of certain other voters, diluting the government's enthusiasm for both immigration and state-supported multiculturalism. That politicians abandoned the multicultural constituency to some extent reflects the fact that it was weakened by geographical dispersion and internal diversity.

SC The state-centred approach is most applicable to the pre-1970 period, in which politicians and bureaucrats formulated policies in this field isolated from societal pressures. Until recently, the state elite contained very few people of non-British or non-French origin, and most were not only insensitive to ethnic concerns, but were actually determined to keep the country as white as possible.[14] John Porter found such a "vertical mosaic" in the political elite as well as in all the other societal elites he studied.[15] Cabinets and bureaucracies in Ottawa, Ontario, Manitoba, Saskatchewan, and British Columbia have reflected more varied hues in recent years, but policy changes are probably more related to voting power and public opinion than to actual changes within the state elite.

In another sense, the state-centred approach was particularly relevant to the Trudeau era. Around the time that the policy of official multiculturalism was adopted, the government sought to create multicultural advocacy organizations that would promote its own agenda. The politicians and bureaucrats justified their actions by arguing that such interests were inherently difficult to organize on their own. Fledgling ethnic groups (which just happened to represent large numbers of new voters) therefore required government support.[16]

© Class analysts emphasize the class nature of ethnicity in Canada; for them, ethnic inequalities are merely an aspect of economic and class inequalities in society and result from the capitalist pursuit of profit. Domestic and multinational companies often exploited immigrant labour—for example, indentured Chinese immigrants who built the CPR, workers in the garment trade in Toronto or Montreal, or seasonal agricultural workers. Individual affluent Canadian families may also have taken advantage of foreign domestics. Supported by such corporations and other wealthy interests, traditional political parties tried to co-opt ethnic leaders and disguise the real interests of ethnic groups by promising recognition of their cultural identities rather than genuine economic equality. On the other hand, many ethnic leaders preferred this kind of recognition.[17] Class analysts also point out that one influential group of immigrants—recent arrivals from Hong Kong—have demonstrated considerable influence only because of their vast quantities of capital.[18]

DISCUSSION QUESTIONS

1. What annual levels of immigration are appropriate as we begin the new millennium? Does the state of the economy matter?

2. What kinds of immigrants should Canada seek out?

3. Should the government redress discriminatory policies of the past? Explain.

4. To what extent should immigrants be encouraged to retain their languages, cultures, and customs? Should such retention be supported by the public purse?

5. To what extent should established Canadian practices and customs be modified in order to accommodate recent immigrants?

6. How do each of the critical approaches discussed in Chapter 1 enhance our understanding of politics in this field?

NOTES

1. For example, John Marlyn, *Under the Ribs of Death* (Toronto: McClelland and Stewart, 1957, 1964).
2. Ann Gomer Sunahara, *The Politics of Racism: The Uprooting of Japanese Canadians during the Second World War* (Toronto: Lorimer, 1981).
3. Prime Minister's Statement in the House of Commons, October 8, 1971; Andrew Cardozo and Louis Musto, eds., *The Battle over Multiculturalism: Does It Help or Hinder Canadian Unity?* (Ottawa: PSI Publishing, 1997).
4. Marc Leman, "Canadian Multiculturalism" (Ottawa: Library of Parliament Research Branch, 1995), p. 4.
5. Leslie Pal, *Interests of State: The Politics of Language, Multiculturalism, and Feminism in Canada* (Montreal: McGill–Queen's University Press, 1993).
6. Daiva Stasiulis, "Deep Diversity: Race and Ethnicity in Canadian Politics," in M.S. Whittington and G. Williams, eds., *Canadian Politics in the 1990s*, 4th ed. (Scarborough: Nelson Canada, 1995), p. 209.
7. Yasmeen Abu-Laban, "The Politics of Race and Ethnicity: Multiculturalism as a Contested Arena," in James P. Bickerton and Alain-G. Gagnon, eds., *Canadian Politics*, 2nd ed. (Peterborough: Broadview Press, 1994), p. 255.
8. Leman, "Canadian Multiculturalism," p. 5.
9. Jean Leonard Elliott and Augie Fleras, *Multiculturalism in Canada: The Challenge of Diversity* (Scarborough: Nelson Canada, 1991), and *Unequal Relations: An Introduction to Race and Ethnic Dynamics in Canada* (Scarborough: Prentice-Hall Canada, 1991).
10. Citizens' Forum on Canada's Future, *Report to the People and Government of Canada* (Ottawa: Supply and Services, 1991).
11. Neil Bissoondath, *Selling Illusions: The Cult of Multiculturalism in Canada* (Toronto: Penguin, 1994), and "A Question of Belonging: Multiculturalism and Citizenship," in William Kaplan, ed., *Belonging: The Meaning and Future of Canadian Citizenship* (Montreal: McGill–Queen's University Press, 1993); John Nunziata, "Multiculturalism Policy Feeds Discrimination," *The Toronto Star*, October 31, 1989.
12. Martin Loney, *The Pursuit of Division: Race, Gender, and Preferential Hiring in Canada* (Montreal: McGill–Queen's University Press, 1998).
13. Abu-Laban, "The Politics of Race and Ethnicity," p. 251.
14. Stasiulis, "Deep Diversity," pp. 196–98.
15. John Porter, *The Vertical Mosaic* (Toronto: University of Toronto Press, 1965); Rick Helmes-Hayes and James Curtis, eds., *The Vertical Mosaic Revisited* (Toronto: University of Toronto Press, 1998).
16. Pal, *Interests of State*.

17. Karl Peter, "The Myth of Multiculturalism and Other Political Fables," in Jorgen Dahlie and Tissa Fernando, eds., *Ethnicity, Power and Politics in Canada* (Toronto: Methuen, 1981); Kogila Moodley, "Canadian Multiculturalism as Ideology," *Ethnic and Racial Studies* (July 1983); Loney, *The Pursuit of Division.*
18. Stasiulis, "Deep Diversity," pp. 209–12.

. . . .
FURTHER READING

Abu-Laban, Yasmeen. "The Politics of Race and Ethnicity: Multiculturalism as a Contested Arena." In James P. Bickerton and Alan-G. Gagnon, eds., *Canadian Politics*, 2nd ed. Peterborough: Broadview Press, 1994.

Abu-Laban, Yasmeen, and Daiva Stasiulis, "Ethnic Pluralism under Siege: Popular and Partisan Opposition to Multiculturalism." *Canadian Public Policy* (December 1992).

Anderson, Christopher G., and Jerome H. Black, "Navigating a New Course: Liberal Immigration and Refugee Policy in the 1990s." In Leslie A. Pal, ed., *How Ottawa Spends, 1998–99.* Toronto: Oxford University Press, 1998.

Bissoondath, Neil, "A Question of Belonging: Multiculturalism and Citizenship." In William Kaplan, ed., *Belonging: The Meaning and Future of Canadian Citizenship.* Montreal: McGill–Queen's University Press, 1993.

———. *Selling Illusions: The Cult of Multiculturalism in Canada.* Toronto: Penguin, 1994.

Cardozo, Andrew, and Louis Musto, eds. *The Battle over Multiculturalism: Does It Help or Hinder Canadian Unity?* Ottawa: PSI Publishing, 1997.

Driedger, Leo. *Multi-Ethnic Canada: Identities and Inequalities.* Toronto: Oxford University Press, 1996.

Elliott, Jean Leonard, and Augie Fleras. *Multiculturalism in Canada: The Challenge of Diversity.* Scarborough: Nelson Canada, 1991.

———. *Unequal Relations: An Introduction to Race and Ethnic Dynamics in Canada.* Scarborough: Prentice-Hall Canada, 1991.

Kelley, Ninette, and Michael Trebilcock. *The Making of the Mosaic: A History of Canadian Immigration Policy.* Toronto: University of Toronto Press, 1998.

Loney, Martin. *The Pursuit of Division: Race, Gender, and Preferential Hiring in Canada.* Montreal: McGill–Queen's University Press, 1998.

Megyery, Kathy, ed. *Ethnocultural Groups and Visible Minorities in Canadian Politics: The Question of Access.* Toronto: Dundurn Press, 1991.

Multiculturalism and Citizenship Canada. *Multiculturalism … Being Canadian.* Ottawa: Supply and Services Canada, 1987.

Pal, Leslie. *Interests of State: The Politics of Language, Multiculturalism, and Feminism in Canada.* Montreal: McGill–Queen's University Press, 1993.

Palmer, Howard. "Mosaic versus Melting Pot? Immigration and Ethnicity in Canada and the United States." In Eli Mandel and David Taras, eds. *A Passion for Identity.* Toronto: Methuen, 1987.

Stasiulis, Daiva. "Deep Diversity: Race and Ethnicity in Canadian Politics." In M.S. Whittington and G. Williams, eds. *Canadian Politics in the 1990s*, 4th ed. Scarborough: Nelson Canada, 1995.

Sunahara, Ann Gomer. *The Politics of Racism: The Uprooting of Japanese Canadians during the Second World War.* Toronto: Lorimer, 1981.

Troper, Harold, and Morton Weinfeld. *Ethnicity, Politics and Public Policy.* Toronto: University of Toronto Press, 1999.

Young, Margaret. *Canada's Immigration Program.* Library of Parliament. Background Paper BP-190E, October 1998.

Chapter 7

Gender
AND
politics

Feminists seek gender equality—employment equity, pay equity, equity in law, equity in the various institutions of government, and equity in the family setting. Not all women are agreed on all these demands, however, and while a large proportion of men support most of them, many young men feel that employment equity makes it even more difficult for them to find a job. Sexual harassment and assault have become major societal concerns; so have abortion, divorce, child care, and many issues related to reproduction. Gender issues have created considerable political controversy and are of increasing significance as women take a more equal part in the economic and political systems. Beyond the equality of women are other gender-related issues, specifically concerning the gay, lesbian, and bisexual communities.

This chapter begins by outlining the historical evolution of women's rights in Canada. It then examines the women's movement today, which has brought a whole new set of demands onto the political agenda. After discussing the contemporary manifestations of such issues, the chapter concludes with an overview of gay and lesbian concerns.

EVOLUTION OF WOMEN'S RIGHTS TO 1970

Men and male-oriented issues virtually monopolized Canadian politics before 1900. In those early years, when all women were expected to marry and then became chattels of their husbands, they first had to fight for educational and occupational rights, such as admission to universities and to the medical and legal professions.[1] This battle was led by the first prominent feminist, Dr. Emily Stowe, who in 1880 was the first female to practise medicine in Canada. The first female lawyer was admitted to the bar in 1897. Women later demanded the right to make contracts and to own property, and increasingly began to work in factories and offices, to become teachers and nurses, and to make major contributions "on the farm." At the turn of the century, farm women in particular became active in reform organizations of many kinds, pressing for the prohibition of alcohol and the establishment of new public health facilities, better housing, and improved working conditions for women and children.

As influential as women were in promoting these causes, many began to feel that their impact would always be limited until they could vote. Thus, in what is sometimes called the "first wave" of the women's movement, women demanded the franchise, a demand that did not necessarily pit all women against all men, but still aroused great hostility. It was a conflict between those who saw women primarily as wives and mothers, whose influence could be best exercised within the home, and those who felt that women should be treated as equals of men in the wider society.

After the outbreak of the First World War, proponents of female suffrage had an additional argument—that women should be rewarded for their contribution to the war effort. Thus, after the vociferous efforts of some of the most articulate women of the day, Manitoba, Alberta, and Saskatchewan extended the right to vote to women in 1916; Ontario and British Columbia followed suit a year later; and all the other provinces except Quebec followed shortly afterward. The first women legislators in the British Commonwealth, Louise McKinney and Roberta Macadams Price, were elected in Alberta in 1917; they were replaced in 1921 by Nellie McClung and Irene Parlby. Mary Ellen Smith was elected to the BC legislature in 1918 and became the first Canadian female cabinet minister in 1921.

At the federal level, the Borden government deliberately manipulated the franchise for the 1917 election, in part by giving the vote to women in the armed services (mostly nurses) and by allowing soldiers fighting abroad to appoint their nearest female relative at home—women who would likely support the war effort—to cast their vote by proxy. A year later the vote was extended to all women, and they had their first chance to exercise this new right in the 1921 election.

Many reforms in social legislation took place immediately after the enfranchisement of women. These included mothers' allowances, child welfare acts, prohibition of child labour, and an increase in the age for compulsory schooling and at which marriage could be solemnized within the province. At the federal level, the divorce law was amended to establish "equality of cause" between wife and husband, and the Old Age Pensions Act was passed.[2] These reforms and other advances were only achieved after constant pressure: organizing women's groups, writing leaflets, plays, and letters to the editor, engaging in demonstrations and debates, and lobbying politicians. Yet, while the right to vote entailed the right to hold office (except in New Brunswick until 1934), very few women were actually elected.

In 1921 Agnes Macphail was the first woman elected to the House of Commons. In 1935 a second woman was elected. Macphail stayed on until 1940 and then became the first woman elected to the Ontario legislature in 1943. A vigorous, articulate, and witty MP and MPP, Macphail promoted radical and progressive causes of many kinds, but she could only do so much by herself to advance women's issues in such an entrenched male bastion.[3] The five most eastern provinces were slower to elect women, as Table 7.1 indicates. It was not until 1940 that Quebec women were enfranchised, largely as a result of the determined leadership of Thérèse Casgrain and after 13 previous bills to this effect were defeated. Even worse, the legal status of married women under the Quebec Civil Code was such that until 1955 a woman could not seek a separation on the grounds of her husband's adultery, and until 1964 had no right to carry on a trade without her husband's consent.[4]

The number of women who won seats in the House of Commons before 1970 was minuscule, as Table 7.2 demonstrates. Indeed, many of the pre-1970 female MPs were the widows or daughters of male members of Parliament. Female political participation was inhibited by many factors. First, both sexes were traditionally socialized into the view that politics was a

TABLE 7.1   Women's Franchise and First Woman Elected

	Franchise	*First Woman Elected*
Canada	1917/18	1921
Manitoba	1916	1920
Alberta	1916	1917
Saskatchewan	1916	1919
B.C.	1917	1918
Ontario	1917	1943
Nova Scotia	1918	1960
New Brunswick	1919	1967
P.E.I.	1922	1970
Newfoundland	1925	1975
Quebec	1940	1961

Source: Penney Kome, Women of Influence *(Toronto: University of Toronto Press, 1985); T.H. Qualter,* The Electoral Process in Canada *(Toronto: McGraw-Hill Ryerson, 1970). Reproduced with permission.*

masculine pursuit and that women should remain in the home. Such socialization patterns even affected those women who were not wives, mothers, and homemakers. Second, most women were constrained by the responsibilities of homemaking and child-rearing. Such roles had little prestige and prevented women from accumulating the money, contacts, and experience that political careers usually require. The long hours and unpredictable schedules of politicians conflicted with most women's family commitments and prevented them from being away from home for any length of time. Such factors at least delayed a woman's entry into active politics. Third, political parties discouraged female candidacies, however much they needed women at the constituency level to raise money and stuff envelopes. Most parties set up a separate women's auxiliary organization rather than encourage their participation in the mainstream of the party. When consciousness of the lack of female candidates increased, women were nominated more frequently, but usually as sacrificial lambs against a strong male incumbent. This was especially evident in the two major parties, and led to the "law" that the closer a party is to power, the less likely it is to nominate women candidates.[5]

Until the late 1920s, no women had been appointed to the other house of Parliament, the Senate. When an enterprising group of Western women took this issue to court, the Supreme Court of Canada ruled in 1928 that women were not eligible for appointment to the Senate. In 1929 this decision was appealed to the Judicial Committee of the Privy Council, which in the **Persons case** overruled the Supreme Court and declared women to be "qualified persons" within the meaning of section 24 of the 1867 Constitution Act and eligible to sit in the Senate. The women's movement continues to celebrate this decision in the form of the "Person's Day Breakfast." Prime Minister Mackenzie King immediately appointed Cairine

TABLE 7.2   Number of Women Elected in Federal Elections, 1921–1968

Election	Women	Election	Women
1921	1	1953	4
1925	1	1957	2
1926	1	1958	2
1930	1	1962	4
1935	2	1963	4
1940	1	1965	3
1945	1	1968	1
1949	0		

Source: Penney Kome, Women of Influence. *Reproduced with permission.*

Wilson to the Senate, but even here progress was slow. The second woman was not appointed until 1935, and 18 years would pass before three more received the call.

It was not until 1957 that the first woman, Ellen Fairclough, was appointed to the federal Cabinet, by John Diefenbaker; she was followed by Judy LaMarsh in 1963. The advance of women to the Cabinet at the provincial level was also very slow: BC and Alberta, 1921; Quebec, 1962; Manitoba, 1966; and New Brunswick, 1970.

Because other cleavages overshadowed the gender cleavage for the first 100 years after Confederation,

farm women, working women, French-Canadian women, Protestant women, western women, [and] city women had quite different collective identities following from the ways in which class, religion and place entwined in Canadian politics. There was no single identity, nor was there a single women's politics.[6]

Nevertheless, gradual improvements continued to be made in federal and provincial programs and legislation. The federal Family Allowances Act of 1944, for example, provided a small monthly payment to each Canadian mother to help care for her children, and often represented the only independent income the woman possessed. In 1952 Ontario passed the first equal pay legislation, to be followed by federal legislation two years later. After the invention of the birth control pill in 1960, amendments to the Criminal Code in 1969 made it legal to advertise birth control devices in Canada, and a new Divorce Act made it easier for people to get out of an unfulfilling marriage.

....

THE WOMEN'S MOVEMENT AFTER 1970

Around 1970 attitudes toward women and their role in society had changed sufficiently that it was now possible to speak of the **women's movement** and the word "feminist" became a common term. Such terms are used to describe those who seek to establish complete gender equality, to free men and women from restrictive gender roles, and to end the subordination of women. However, even within the women's movement a variety of perspectives exists, including socialist feminists, Marxist feminists, radical feminists, and liberal feminists. There was even a call to "reinvent" the discipline of political science along feminist lines.[7]

This "second wave" of the women's movement coincided with the **Royal Commission on the Status of Women**, appointed in 1967 and reporting in 1970. It "provided a solid statistical base and a framework for most of the feminist action that followed during the 1970s,"[8] and made 167 recommendations, not all of which have been implemented even 30 years later. Since that time gender issues have become an important, daily factor in Canadian politics, and pioneered at the federal level in 1971, most governments now designate a minister responsible for women's issues. In 1972 the federal government established the Office of Employment Opportunity, followed by the Canadian Advisory Council on the Status of Women in 1973; the first federal–provincial conference on women's issues convened in 1982, and in 1995, Ottawa issued the Federal Plan for Gender Equality. This plan committed the government to apply gender-based analysis in the development of legislation, policies, and programs. A major part of the government department Status of Women Canada is the Women's Program, which supports the work of some 300 women's organizations and other groups toward achieving women's full participation in Canadian society.

Representation in Politics and Government

In the post-1970 era, women's participation in politics and government increased substantially. Table 7.3 shows the increase in the number and proportion of women in the House of Commons in this period. Many of the factors that inhibited women from becoming politicians before 1970 are still present, although in recent years some parties have created special funds to support female candidates.

At the Cabinet level, Jeanne Sauvé was appointed in 1972, Monique Bégin and Iona Campagnolo in 1976, and Flora MacDonald in 1979, but by the 1980s, one or two token female ministers were clearly insufficient. Brian Mulroney usually had six women in his cabinets after 1984. The rest of the provinces eventually appointed women ministers: Ontario and Prince Edward Island in 1972, Newfoundland in 1979, Saskatchewan in 1982, and Nova Scotia in 1985. Bob Rae came close to gender equality in his 1990 Ontario NDP cabinet: 11 women out of 26.

In the post-1970 period Canada finally saw women elected as political party leaders. Alexa McDonough (NDP) led the way in Nova Scotia in 1980, to be followed by Sharon Carstairs (Liberal, Manitoba), Elizabeth Weir and Barbara Baird-Filliter (NDP and PC respectively, New Brunswick), Lynda Haverstock (Liberal, Saskatchewan), Lyn McLeod (Liberal, Ontario), Rita Johnston (Social Credit, BC), Catherine Callbeck (Liberal, PEI), Pam Barrett (NDP, Alberta), and Nancy MacBeth (Liberal, Alberta). After Rosemary Brown made a

TABLE 7.3   **Representation of Women in the House of Commons,
1970–1997**

Election	Number Elected	Proportion of MPs (percent)
1972	4	2
1974	9	3
1979	11	4
1980	14	5
1984	27	10
1988	39	13
1993	53	18
1997	62	21

Source: Status of Women Canada, "Towards Equality for Women—A Canadian Chronology," 1994, updated by author. Reproduced with the permission of the Minister of Public Works and Government Services Canada, 2000.

serious stab at the NDP national leadership in 1975 and Flora Macdonald for the PCs in 1976, it remained for Audrey McLaughlin to make history when she was elected leader of the federal New Democratic Party in 1989, the first woman to lead a major national party. Alexa McDonough succeeded her in 1995.

Two of these provincial leaders even served as premier. Rita Johnston inherited the BC premiership from her disgraced predecessor, Bill Vander Zalm, while Catherine Callbeck was the first woman to be elected to premiership in 1993. Somewhat similarly to Johnston, Kim Campbell took over the federal PC leadership and prime ministership in 1993, only to lose the subsequent election to Jean Chrétien, at least partly because of the faults of her male predecessor.

Jeanne Sauvé pioneered women's political participation in several fields: she was the third federal woman Cabinet minister, the first woman Speaker of the House of Commons, and the first woman governor general (1984), followed by Adrienne Clarkson in 1999. Meanwhile, Bertha Wilson became the first woman to sit on the Supreme Court of Canada in 1982. Between 1989 and 1990, and from mid-1999 onward, there were three women out of nine judges on the Supreme Court, but the number fell back to two between 1990 and 1999. Women judges have also been appointed at an ever-increasing rate in other courts, and in 1999, 20 percent of federally appointed judges were women (199 out of 992).

Within the federal bureaucracy, the first women joined the RCMP in 1974, and the first woman deputy minister (Sylvia Ostry) was appointed in 1975; in the 1980s, women became eligible for full combat roles in the armed forces, and the first woman general was named in 1988. In 1993, Jocelyne Bourgon became the first woman to hold the top public service position in Ottawa, Secretary to the Cabinet and Clerk of the Privy Council.

Employment Issues

Since about 70 percent of women of working age are now in the labour force (up from 50 percent in 1980), and since women constitute about 46 percent of the labour force, one major feminist concern is employment.[9] Women have traditionally been paid less than men, underrepresented in managerial positions, and discouraged from undertaking nontraditional occupations. In 1985, full-time female workers earned on average 65.5 percent of what men earned, leading to demands for "equal pay for work of equal value" or **pay equity**. The first jurisdictions to pass pay equity legislation were the federal government, Manitoba, Ontario, and Quebec, and by 1996, women's full-time earnings had risen to an average of 73 percent of men's.[10] On the other hand, while Ontario's Pay Equity Act was considered the most successful of its kind, it was not enthusiastically embraced by the Mike Harris government after 1995. Then the federal government got itself embroiled in a mammoth and protracted pay equity dispute with its own clerical staff, most of whom were female, which it finally settled in late 1999 for $3.6 billion. Moreover, companies within federal jurisdiction, such as Bell Canada, refused to respond to pay equity demands of their employees until ordered to do so by the courts.

Beyond pay equity is the broader subject of **employment equity**, that is, the elimination of discrimination in hiring and promoting, which is sometimes combined with **affirmative action** programs to give preference to women and other groups in order to make up for past inequities. In 1980 the federal bureaucracy established a pilot project with respect to affirmative action in the hiring of women, and in 1983 this was made mandatory in all federal government departments. The 1984 Royal Commission Report, *Equality in Employment*, written by Rosalie Abella, became the foundation of the 1986 Employment Equity Act. It extended employment equity requirements to all Crown corporations, all federally regulated companies with over 100 employees, and other large companies in receipt of major government contracts. Despite these measures and the Public Service Reform Act of 1992, women occupied only 23 percent of executive jobs and made up only 16 percent of those earning $100 000 or more annual salaries in 1997, while they constituted just under 50 percent of the federal government work force.[11] Ontario passed an even more extensive Employment Equity Act in 1993, which was the subject of much controversy in the 1995 provincial election campaign and was quickly repealed by the Harris government.

Because most businesses see employment equity as a drain on their bottom line, they oppose the idea in the private sector. Indeed, the area in which women are most severely underrepresented is at the top of private corporations. A 1999 survey of the top 500 industrial companies in Canada found only 13 women who held the position of chief executive officer, and among 560 companies, only 7.5 percent of the members of boards of directors were women.[12] The three most prominent female CEOs at the end of the 1990s were Maureen Kempston Darkes at General Motors of Canada, Bobbie Gaunt at Ford Canada, and Heather Reisman of Indigo Books & Music.

In the 1996 census, the ten most common jobs for women were retail salespersons, secretaries, cashiers, registered nurses, accounting clerks, elementary school teachers, food servers, general office clerks, babysitters, and receptionists. In these fields, pay is generally low and opportunities are relatively few. On the other hand, it should not be overlooked that women have made gains in several professional occupations. In 1991, women accounted for 27 percent of all doctors, dentists, and other health-diagnosing and -treating professionals, and 56 percent of pharmacists; at the time of the 1996 census, women constituted 30 percent of all medical doctors in Canada. Figure 7.1 compares the percentages of women in selected occupations between 1982 and 1993.

Women make up about 70 percent of the part-time work force, sometimes by choice, but often by necessity, and part-time workers generally have few benefits and little job security. In this era of global restructuring, companies are turning even more to part-time, contract workers, and women are expected to suffer the most from such developments. Figure 7.2 compares the numbers of men and women who worked part-time in 1993 and outlines the major reasons for seeking such work.

The value of work performed by women without pay is of increasing concern to many observers but has been difficult to estimate. Economists point out that while women who work for pay contribute to government revenues by paying income taxes, women who work in the home without remuneration generally carry out a variety of functions, such as caring for the young and the elderly, that reduces the demand for public services. Unpaid work in the home makes a major contribution to the economy that does not show up in traditional statistics: according to one estimate, in 1992 its value was nearly $300 billion, or 41 percent of the gross domestic product.[13]

The 1992 study found that women performed two-thirds of unpaid work, such as household maintenance, caregiving, and volunteer work, which was worth some $16 580 per year

Figure 7.1   Women as a Percentage of People Employed in Selected Occupations

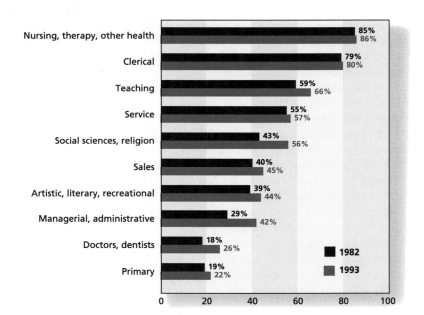

Source: Adapted from Canadian Social Trends (Spring 1995), Statistics Canada, Cat. No. 11-008.

Figure 7.2 Part-Time Workers, 1993

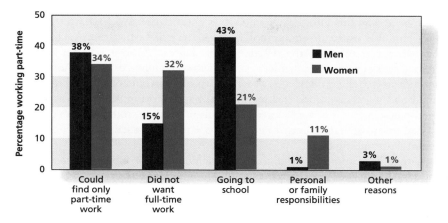

Source: Adapted from "Women, Men and Work," Statistics Canada, Cat. No. 71-220.

on an individual basis. On average, women spent approximately 29 hours per week on housework, almost double that of men. The results of the attempt by the 1996 census to measure unpaid work by full-time paid workers are shown in Figure 7.3 and confirm that in addition to engaging in unpaid work in higher proportions than men, women also devoted longer hours to these activities.

Figure 7.3 Proportion of Time Spent on Unpaid Housework and Unpaid Child Care by Full-Time Paid Workers, 1996

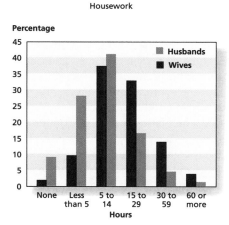

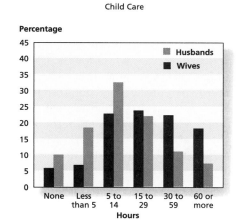

Source: Adapted from 1996 Census of Canada data.

Constitutional, Legal, and Aboriginal Women's Issues

A third category of post-1970 women's issues is related to the Constitution and the law. The first major issue was the question of equality rights in the 1982 Charter of Rights and Freedoms. This was especially important because the courts had made a mockery of the gender equality provision in the 1960 Bill of Rights. As the Charter emerged from federal–provincial negotiations, gender equality was to be lumped into section 15 with such other factors as race, religion, and age, which governments would be allowed to override with the notwithstanding clause. Such treatment at the hands of 11 male first ministers galvanized the women's movement as never before; as a result of pressure from women's groups, section 28 was added to the final document to give gender equality a place of its own and protection from the notwithstanding clause.[14]

Women thus became part of the coalition including other Charter-based rights-bearers who used the Charter to advance their cause.[15] There followed a series of feminist challenges to laws that women felt discriminated against them. Women achieved the right to maternity leave under the Unemployment Insurance Act. Although they lost their first challenge in the so-called "rape-shield" case (hoping to restrict questions about past sexual history put to defendants in a case of sexual assault), the courts agreed that "no means no" with respect to a woman's consent to sexual relations. A later case did protect a complainant's confidential counselling records. Battered wives have been excused for murdering their offending husbands; gender discrimination in private employers' disability plans has been removed; and physical requirements that discriminate against women must be proven necessary for a job. The government itself encouraged such legal activity with the **Court Challenges Program** under which it subsidized the Legal Education and Action Fund (LEAF) in making such challenges. This was a continuation of Ottawa's attempt to strengthen the women's movement by funding advocacy groups.[16] When the Mulroney government cancelled the Court Challenges Program in 1992, women protested, and it was reinstated by the Chrétien government.

On the other hand, the Supreme Court did not advance the cause of women in decisions dealing with such issues as the deduction of child-care expenses from a self-employed woman's income tax (the 1993 *Symes* case) and the taxation of support payments while men who made such payments deducted them from their income tax (the 1995 *Thibaudeau* case). In both of these decisions the female justices on the court dissented. In order to reverse the effect of the *Thibaudeau* case, the federal government amended the Income Tax Act so that child support payments would no longer be deductible from the donor's income tax and so that recipients of such payments would no longer need to declare them as taxable income. The Supreme Court has made some interesting decisions regarding the entitlements of women (and their children) upon divorce, and one author contends that men actually made greater use of the equality provisions in section 15 than women, especially in child-custody cases.[17]

On the constitutional front, in the 1987–90 period, the **National Action Committee on the Status of Women (NAC)** and certain subsidiary groups actively opposed the Meech Lake Accord. Having become part of the constitutional policy community in 1982, they demanded participation in any subsequent constitutional decisions and were concerned that the accord, drawn up by 11 men, had nothing to say about women's rights. Certain anglophone women were afraid that their constitutional gains of 1982 might be diluted in Quebec by the accord's "distinct society" clause for that province. Interestingly enough, their concerns were not shared by most Quebec feminists. The NAC was also unhappy with the Charlottetown

Accord, for even though it did reiterate the equality of men and women in the Canada clause, it was articulated in weaker language than that of other rights. Like Aboriginals, official francophone minorities, people with disabilities, and other groups that had achieved constitutional standing in 1982, women's groups were not satisfied with subsequent constitutional documents unless their status was further reinforced.[18]

Another long-standing legal issue was that of the equality of Aboriginal women relative to Aboriginal men. A provision in the Indian Act denied Indian status to Native women who married white men, but no such loss was involved when an Indian man married a white woman. After the *Lavell* case upheld this clause in the Indian Act, much pressure was brought to bear on the government, and in 1985 the provision was repealed. The Indian Act was amended to restore Indian status and the right to be considered for band membership to Indian women (and their children) who had lost such status through intermarriage. Their fate continued to rest, however, with the band membership. A year before, the Constitution itself was amended to recognize and affirm that Aboriginal and treaty rights were guaranteed equally to male and female persons.

Reproduction, Sexuality, Health, and Violence Issues

One of the main feminist rallying cries of the post-1970 period is that women must be able to control what happens to their own bodies. Many women's organizations supported Dr. Henry Morgentaler in his long fight (including several court cases, clinic raids, and jail terms) to reform the Criminal Code's provisions on abortion.[19] Although amendments were made in 1968, feminists did not regard these as sufficient, and the Supreme Court of Canada threw out the abortion law in the famous 1988 *Morgentaler* case. The Court also dismissed the *Borowski* case on fetal rights as well as the case against Chantal Daigle on father's rights.[20] The prospect of having no law at all restricting abortion was appealing to most feminists, but a sizable proportion of public opinion disagreed; in 1990 the Mulroney government introduced a compromise abortion law, which was defeated in the Senate. The Mulroney government also appointed a Royal Commission on New Reproductive Technologies, which was plagued by internal disputes and whose 1993 report endorsed a cautious approach to this controversial subject.

Prostitution, pornography, sexual stereotyping, sexual harassment, and sexual assault are other major areas of concern to women's groups, although feminists are not totally united on the first two.[21] While they universally oppose practices that exploit or demean women, some women defend the "freedom of expression" argument in discussions of pornography, and some, the "right to work" defence of prostitution. The courts have also become engaged in these issues and ruled, in 1990, for example, that the existing law against soliciting was valid as a "reasonable limit" on freedom of speech.

Women have repeatedly protested, with only limited results, sex-role stereotyping in educational materials and in the media, where women are portrayed in traditional roles or as sexual objects.

Also of concern are the courts' treatment of sexual assault cases, sexual harassment in the workplace, and violence against women. In one study, one-half of all Canadian women reported that they had experienced at least one incident of violence by a male since the age of 16, and nearly 40 percent, one incident of sexual assault.[22] The federal government embarked on an initiative to combat family violence between 1988 and 1995 that, among other things, contributed to the creation of shelters for battered women and that was supplemented by some provinces.[23]

While Canadian women clearly live longer than men (the average life expectancy of women being 81.4 years compared with 75.7 years for men), women are concerned about their own particular health issues. Probably the main concern is breast cancer, which one in nine women is expected to develop. Pressure has mounted on governments to take more initiative in this area, and some have responded. Occupational health problems are also of increasing concern.

The Feminization of Poverty, and Child Care

Chapter 8 will reveal the large extent to which Canada has experienced the **feminization of poverty**. As pointed out there, no less than 60 percent of sole-support mothers raise their children below the poverty line. With or without a partner, large numbers of women with pre-school children find it necessary to work outside the home to support themselves and their families.[24] This was the case even after the Child Tax Credit was added to the income tax system in 1978 to replace the Family Allowance for low-income families. Such programs as pay equity, employment equity, higher minimum wages, increased unionization, and improved job training and literacy programs will help decrease the incidence of women living in poverty.

One of the major unresolved "women's issues" today is that of daycare for children. Federal support for daycare used to be available under the Canada Assistance Plan for those in need, and was supplemented by provincial and/or municipal programs. The level of funding, however, is inadequate for low-income women, and many middle-income women find it difficult to find, let alone finance, daycare for their children. The Mulroney government introduced legislation for a national daycare program in 1988, but when the bill failed to pass before the election, it fell victim to the budgetary restraints of 1989–92. Provincial programs in this area vary considerably, with only Quebec approaching an adequate standard. In 1995, there were 360 000 licensed full-time child-care spaces available, while some 1.3 million children under the age of 6 had mothers in the paid labour force.

Women's Centres and Women's Groups

Many women's centres were established across the country in the 1980s, financed by federal and/or provincial governments. While such centres primarily served as support and referral agencies for battered wives and others seeking help, they also promoted a variety of other women's causes such as abortion law reform. The Mulroney government cut the budget for such centres in 1989 and 1990, but then restored some of the funding after a vehement protest.

The National Council of Women of Canada (NCWC) was created in 1893 and still represents 750 000 women in autonomous provincial, regional, and municipal councils. The Voice of Women (VOW) was formed in 1960 around peace issues. The Canadian Advisory Council on the Status of Women (CACSW) was set up by the government in 1973 in response to the Royal Commission on the Status of Women. It is made up of government appointees who advise the responsible minister on women's concerns.

The number of women's groups has increased remarkably in recent years. The foremost women's pressure group today is the National Action Committee on the Status of Women (NAC). It was established in 1972, largely in response to government inaction on the Status of Women report. It functions as an umbrella lobbying group for over 650 local and national member groups representing over three million women. An indication of its importance and of politicians' consciousness of the female vote was the separate televised leaders' debate held on women's issues in 1984 and sponsored by NAC.[25]

Less sympathetic to the NAC and affiliated groups than the Trudeau regime, the Mulroney government refused to attend NAC's annual meeting in 1989 and 1990, anticipating criticism of its cutbacks, and even began to fund the rival organization, REAL Women. REAL (Realistic, Equal, Active for Life) Women was founded in 1984 and opposes all feminist demands. The Catholic Women's League and various anti-abortion ("pro-life") groups have also played a major role on the abortion issue from the anti-feminist point of view. Thus, women themselves are divided on some or all of the issues raised, and this division gives male politicians and bureaucrats an excellent excuse to take no action. When Ottawa changed the method of distributing grant money to women's groups to a project-by-project basis in 1998–99, NAC complained that the Chrétien government was treating it even more disrespectfully than the Conservatives had done.

OTHER GENDER ISSUES

A variety of political issues related to homosexuality have arisen in recent years, and these also figure prominently at the beginning of the new millennium.[26] In most cases, politicians are reluctant to deal with demands coming from the gay, lesbian, and bisexual communities, forcing these groups to take their concerns directly to the courts.

By Brian Gable (The Globe and Mail). *Reprinted with permission from* The Globe and Mail.

One of the first demands in this area was for protection from individual discrimination in human rights codes, essentially to prevent discrimination in the private sector, such as in hiring or accommodation. Quebec was the first province to enact legislation prohibiting discrimination on the grounds of **sexual orientation**. The federal government was among the laggards in this area, not adding such a clause to the federal Human Rights Act until 1996. When the Charter of Rights was adopted in 1982, section 15 prohibited discrimination by government or in law on the basis of sex. Although sexual orientation was not explicitly included, the Supreme Court of Canada ruled unanimously in the 1995 *Egan* case that the clause did indeed include sexual orientation. However, the court was split on whether such discrimination was involved in the case before them, which concerned the payment of the federal spouses' pension to same-sex couples. The deciding judge in the case ruled that denial of pension rights constituted a reasonable limit on such discrimination, so that the specific claimants actually lost. In 1998, the Supreme Court reaffirmed that the Charter included sexual orientation, ruling in the *Vriend* case that this ground be added to the Alberta Individual Rights Protection Act.[27] Thus, by the late 1990s, whether by legislation or court decision, sexual orientation had been added to all the human rights codes in Canada. Meanwhile, in 1995, Justice Minister Allan Rock ran into considerable difficulty in introducing a bill designed to increase sentences for those convicted of committing hate crimes, including crimes against homosexuals. Despite opposition within the Liberal caucus, the bill was eventually passed.

The next phase of the battle for equality in this area centred on gay and lesbian couples. In 1998, the Ontario Court of Appeal recognized same-sex survivor pension benefits in the *Rosenberg* case, and many employers in both the public and private sectors have extended employee benefits (health, dental, and retirement plans, and so on) to same-sex couples. In mid-1999, the Supreme Court outlawed the clause in the Ontario Family Law Act that restricted financial support to opposite-sex spouses after separation from their partner.[28] Henceforth, a same-sex spouse could apply for such support just as in any common-law relationship. About the same time, the federal government passed pension legislation that granted survivor benefits to the gay and lesbian partners of its own employees and also withdrew objections to gay and lesbians receiving survivor benefits under the Canada Pension Plan. Other successes have been achieved in such areas as the adoption by one partner of a same-sex couple of the other's biological child, and the power to make medical decisions on behalf of an incapacitated same-sex partner, with Ontario and British Columbia leading the way.[29]

In late 1998, a homosexual rights group, the Foundation of Equal Families, launched a massive lawsuit against Ottawa, seeking changes to 58 federal statutes on the basis that they now violated the sexual orientation provision of section 15 of the Charter. While the group said that it was tired of waiting for the politicians to act, it also indicated that it would be happy to abandon the case if the government introduced such amendments on its own. In this vein, the province of Quebec passed an omnibus bill in 1999 that changed 28 provincial laws and 11 regulations to eliminate discrimination on the grounds of sexual orientation and excluded only marriage and adoption. The House of Commons passed a Reform Party motion that upheld the definition of marriage as a union between a man and a woman, but one day later an Angus Reid poll indicated that 53 percent of Canadians agreed that if same-sex couples wanted to marry, they should be allowed to do so. In the wake of the *M. v H.* decision, Ontario unenthusiastically amended 67 pieces of legislation, but its use of the label "same-sex partner" rather than "spouse" did not impress the gay and lesbian community.

CONCLUSION

Although women's issues have been on the political agenda at least since the turn of the century, today's politicians must pay much more attention to gender questions than ever before. Increased participation by women in the work force and in society in general has created dramatic changes in the political system. This chapter has shown that, although the record is mixed in the post-1970 period, women have made immense progress overall. By the start of the new millennium, the main obstacles to further progress included the fiscal restraint practised by all governments and a certain amount of backlash against employment equity programs. The increasing number and proportion of women in influential positions should, however, guarantee that advances will continue. At the same time, the gay and lesbian communities have recently experienced more advances than setbacks in their struggle for equality. Most of their successes have so far been achieved in the courts.

P The pluralist approach emphasizes the vast increase in the number of women's groups in recent years and their increasing influence on public policymaking. Once again, organization and mobilization have effects on public policy. To some extent this influence has been achieved within narrow status-of-women policy communities. Women's groups have also become part of the rough and tumble of constitutional politics, and have played a significant part in some of the bargains adopted. This pluralism of Canadian society is enhanced by the increasing acceptance of the alternative lifestyles represented by the gay and lesbian communities, but as mentioned above, gay and lesbian groups have not had as much success within the political system as within the legal system.

SC The state-centred approach explains the period of inaction on women's issues (1920–70) by the fact that women were largely excluded from the Cabinet and bureaucracy. Some have argued that when governments finally decided to act in this field, it was bureaucrats in status-of-women agencies who set the government agenda, bypassing women's groups and failing to reflect their predominant concerns.[30] Somewhat contrary to this perspective is that of Leslie Pal, who emphasizes the close links between the bureaucratic agencies established in this field and the women's groups that the government was itself helping to support financially.[31]

Women are still seriously underrepresented in all organs of government as well as in Parliament, but the proportion of women elected to Parliament increases with every federal election and their one-third contingent on the Supreme Court is not likely to be reduced. Women can be appointed to some of these positions to increase their numbers, but greater female representation in the corridors of power will also require political parties and voters to elect more women to Parliament. Women are slowly rising to the top of some other institutions in society and are increasingly able to engage in processes of elite accommodation, but they remain almost invisible in the ranks of the influential corporate elite.

© Many radical, socialist, and neo-Marxist feminists take the view that women will never achieve full equality and emancipation in a capitalist system, which they claim depends on the exploitation of women. Some also point to the coercive aspect of the pre-1990 abortion laws, which were designed and passed primarily by men. Socialist feminists argue that "class and gender interact in the present system to produce women's inequality, and that significant transformations in both are necessary for women's emancipation."[32] A quite different class-based analysis of feminism is offered by Martin Loney, who argues that the feminist movement has usurped the struggle for equality by concentrating only on women, and left behind the traditional concerns of the working class: poverty, inequality of opportunity, and social marginalization of men, women and children alike.[33]

PC Public choice theory focuses on the number of women voters, past voting restrictions, and the degree of gender consciousness among women voters. Women did not even have a vote for the first 50 years of Confederation, for example, and for a long time after that they seemed less concerned with gender than with other issues—ethnicity, region, and class. Since 1970, more women are conscious about "women's issues," and governments are paying more attention to them. But while women make up one-half of the electorate, they are not united on such issues, and this provides a good excuse for governments not to take action, such as the Mulroney government's abandonment of its promised national daycare program.

DISCUSSION QUESTIONS

1. Are you personally affected by the gender cleavages discussed in this chapter? If so, how?

2. How do you explain the lull in women's political activities after they obtained the vote?

3. How do you explain the increase in women's collective self-consciousness over the past 30 years?

4. Do women party leaders have a more difficult time getting their parties elected than male leaders? Explain.

5. To what extent should the private sector adopt employment equity programs?

6. How far should governments go in providing public daycare programs?

7. How far should legislation go in recognizing same-sex relationships?

8. How do each of the critical approaches outlined in Chapter 1 enhance our understanding of gender politics in Canada?

NOTES

1. Early developments are outlined in a 1993 Status of Women Canada publication called *Toward Equality for Women—A Canadian Chronology*. Other books on the subject include Jean Cochrane, *Women in Canadian Politics* (Toronto: Fitzhenry & Whiteside, 1977); Penney Kome, *Women of*

Influence (Toronto: University of Toronto Press, 1985); Janine Brodie, *Women and Politics in Canada* (Toronto: McGraw-Hill Ryerson, 1985); Linda Kealey and Joan Sangster, eds., *Beyond the Vote: Canadian Women and Politics* (Toronto: University of Toronto Press, 1989); and Sandra Burt et al., eds., *Changing Patterns: Women in Canada* (Toronto: McClelland and Stewart, 1988).

2. Royal Commission on the Status of Women, *Report* (Ottawa: 1970), p. 338.
3. Doris Pennington, *Agnes Macphail, Reformer: Canada's First Female M.P.* (Toronto: Simon & Pierre, 1989); Terry Crowley, *Agnes Macphail and the Politics of Equality* (Toronto: Lorimer, 1990).
4. Micheline D. Johnson, "History of the Status of Women in the Province of Quebec," Background study for the Royal Commission on the Status of Women (Ottawa, 1968), p. 49.
5. Janine Brodie, *Women and Politics in Canada* (Toronto: McGraw-Hill Ryerson, 1985), and "Women and Political Leadership: A Case for Affirmative Action," in Maureen Mancuso et al., eds., *Leaders and Leadership in Canada* (Toronto: Oxford University Press, 1994); Heather MacIvor, *Women and Politics in Canada* (Peterborough: Broadview, 1996).
6. Jane Jenson, "Wearing Your Adjectives Proudly: Citizenship and Gender in Turn-of-the Century Canada," *Canadian Political Science Association* (May 1990), p. 12.
7. Jill Vickers, *Reinventing Political Science: A Feminist Approach* (Halifax: Fernwood Publishing, 1997); Sandra Burt, "Rethinking Canadian Politics: The Impact of Gender," in Michael S. Whittington and Glen Williams, eds., *Canadian Politics in the 1990s*, 4th ed. (Scarborough: Nelson Canada, 1995).
8. Kome, *Women of Influence*, p. 86.
9. Unless otherwise noted, the statistics in this section come from the 1996 census. See also Statistics Canada, *Women in Canada: A Statistical Report*, 3rd ed., cat. no. 89-503E (Ottawa, 1995).
10. Statistics Canada, *The Daily*, March 23, 1998, and *Earnings of Men and Women*, cat. no. 13-217 (1996). According to Statistics Canada, single full-time female workers earned 93 percent of the earnings of single men. Not everyone is satisfied with these two measurements, however; Economic Gender Equality Indicators, a report of a project commissioned by federal and provincial ministers responsible for the Status of Women, points out that if part-time workers are included (more of whom are women), the total earnings gap between women and men is approximately 50 percent (cat. no. SW21-17/1997E). Similar feminist perspectives on female employment can be found in Status of Women Canada, Economic Equality Workshop 1993, Summary of Proceedings, and Status of Women Canada, *Finding Data on Women: A Guide to Major Sources at Statistics* Canada, cat. no. SW21-22/1998E (Ottawa, 1998).
11. Treasury Board, *Employment Equity in the Public Service, Annual Report 1996–97* (Ottawa: Supply and Services, 1997).
12. *Catalyst*, as reported in *The Globe and Mail*, January 28, 1999.
13. William Chandler, "The Value of Household Work in Canada, 1992," National Income and Expenditure Accounts, Fourth Quarter 1993, cat. no. 13-001, vol. 41, no. 4, based on the 1992 General Social Survey.
14. See Penney Kome, *The Taking of Twenty-Eight* (Toronto: Women's Educational Press, 1983), and *Women of Influence*, ch. 10.
15. Alan Cairns, *Disruptions: Constitutional Struggles, from the Charter to Meech Lake* (Toronto: McClelland and Stewart, 1991); Rainer Knopff and F.L. Morton, *Charter Politics* (Toronto: Nelson Canada, 1992).
16. Leslie Pal, *Interests of State: The Politics of Language, Multiculturalism and Feminism in Canada* (Montreal: McGill–Queen's University Press, 1993).
17. Burt, "Rethinking Canadian Politics."
18. Cairns, *Disruptions*.
19. Robert Campbell and Leslie Pal, *The Real Worlds of Canadian Politics*, 2nd ed. (Peterborough: Broadview Press, 1991); Janine Brodie et al., *The Politics of Abortion* (Toronto: Oxford University Press, 1992).
20. *R. v. Morgentaler*, [1988] 1 S.C.R. 30; *Borowski v. Canada (Attorney General)*, [1989] 1 S.C.R. 342; *Tremblay v. Daigle*, [1989] 2 S.C.R. 530.
21. The 1989 first edition of Campbell and Pal's *The Real Worlds of Canadian Politics* contains a chapter on the pornography debate; see also MacIvor, *Women and Politics in Canada*.
22. Holly Johnson, *Dangerous Domains: Violence Against Women in Canada* (Scarborough: Nelson Canada, 1996), based on Statistics Canada, *The Violence Against Women Survey, 1993*.

23. See articles on wife assault and shelters for abused women in Statistics Canada, *Canadian Social Trends* (Autumn 1994).
24. National Council of Welfare, *Poverty Profile 1994*; David Ross and Richard Shillington, *The Canadian Fact Book on Poverty—1994* (Ottawa: Canadian Council on Social Development, 1994).
25. Jill Vickers et al., *Politics as If Women Mattered: A Political Analysis of the National Action Committee on the Status of Women* (Toronto: University of Toronto Press, 1993).
26. Didi Herman, *Rights of Passage: Struggles for Lesbian and Gay Legal Equality* (Toronto: University of Toronto Press, 1994); Miriam Smith, *Lesbian and Gay Rights in Canada: Social Movements and Equality-Seeking, 1971–1995* (Toronto: University of Toronto Press, 1999).
27. *Egan v. Canada*, [1995] 2 S.C.R. 513; *Vriend v. Alberta*, [1998] 1 S.C.R. 493.
28. *M. v. H.*, [May 20, 1999].
29. Mary C. Hurley, "Sexual Orientation and Legal Rights," *Library of Parliament Current Issue Review* 92-1E (October 1998); website of EGALE (Equality for Gays and Lesbians): http://www.egale.ca.
30. Burt, "Rethinking Canadian Politics," pp. 182–83.
31. Pal, *Interests of State*.
32. Burt, "Rethinking Canadian Politics," p. 187.
33. Martin Loney, *The Pursuit of Division: Race, Gender, and Preferential Hiring in Canada* (Montreal: McGill–Queen's University Press, 1998).

FURTHER READING

Andrew, Caroline, and Sanda Rodgers, eds. *Women and the Canadian State*. Montreal: McGill–Queen's University Press, 1997.

Bashevkin, Sylvia. *Toeing the Lines*. Toronto: University of Toronto Press, 1985; 2nd ed., 1992.

———. *Women on the Defensive*. Toronto: University of Toronto Press, 1998.

Bégin, Monique, et al. *Some of Us: Women in Canadian Power and Politics*. Mississauga: Random House, 1991.

Best, Pamela. "Women, Men & Work." *Canadian Social Trends*. Ottawa: Statistics Canada, Spring 1995.

Brodie, Janine. *Women and Politics in Canada*. Toronto: McGraw-Hill Ryerson, 1985.

Brodie, Janine, et al. *The Politics of Abortion*. Toronto: Oxford University Press, 1992.

Burt, Sandra. "Rethinking Canadian Politics: The Impact of Gender." In Michael S. Whittington and Glen Williams, eds., *Canadian Politics in the 1990s*, 4th ed. Scarborough: Nelson Canada, 1995.

Burt, Sandra, et al., eds. *Changing Patterns: Women in Canada*. Toronto: McClelland and Stewart, 1988; 2nd ed., 1993.

Campbell, Robert, and Leslie Pal. *The Real Worlds of Canadian Politics*. Peterborough: Broadview Press, 1989; 2nd ed., 1991.

Cleverdon, Catherine L. *The Woman Suffrage Movement in Canada*. Toronto: University of Toronto Press, 1974.

Crowley, Terry. *Agnes Macphail and the Politics of Equality*. Toronto: Lorimer, 1990.

Dobrowolsky, Alexandra. *The Politics of Pragmatism: Women, Representation, and Constitutionalism in Canada*. Toronto: Oxford University Press, 1999.

Gingras, François-Pierre, ed. *Gender and Politics in Contemporary Canada*. Toronto: Oxford University Press, 1995.

Herman, Didi. *Rights of Passage: Struggles for Lesbian and Gay Legal Equality*. Toronto: University of Toronto Press, 1994.

Hurley, Mary C. "Sexual Orientation and Legal Rights," *Library of Parliament Current Issue Review*, 92-1E, October 1998.

Johnson, Holly. *Dangerous Domains: Violence Against Women in Canada*. Scarborough: Nelson Canada, 1996.

Kealey, Linda, and Joan Sangster, eds. *Beyond the Vote: Canadian Women and Politics*. Toronto: University of Toronto Press, 1989.

Kome, Penney. *The Taking of Twenty-Eight*. Toronto: Women's Educational Press, 1983.

———. *Women of Influence*. Toronto: Doubleday Canada, 1985.

Loney, Martin. *The Pursuit of Division: Race, Gender and Preferential Hiring in Canada*. Montreal: McGill–Queen's University Press, 1998.

MacIvor, Heather. *Women and Politics in Canada*. Peterborough: Broadview, 1996.

Pal, Leslie. *Interests of State: The Politics of Language, Multiculturalism and Feminism in Canada*. Montreal: McGill–Queen's University Press, 1993.

Pennington, Doris. *Agnes Macphail, Reformer: Canada's First Female M.P.* Toronto: Simon & Pierre, 1989.

Report of the Royal Commission on the Status of Women. Ottawa: Information Canada, 1970.

Sharpe, Sydney. *The Gilded Ghetto: Women and Political Power in Canada*. Toronto: HarperCollins, 1994.

Smith, Miriam. *Lesbian and Gay Rights in Canada: Social Movements and Equality-Seeking, 1971–1995*. Toronto: University of Toronto Press, 1999.

Status of Women Canada. *Economic Gender Equality Indicators*. Cat. no. SW21-17/1997E. Ottawa, 1997.

Tremblay, Manon, and Caroline Andrew, eds. *Women and Political Representation in Canada*. Ottawa: University of Ottawa Press, 1998.

Vickers, Jill. *Reinventing Political Science: A Feminist Approach*. Halifax: Fernwood Publishing, 1997.

Vickers, Jill, et al. *Politics as If Women Mattered: A Political Analysis of the National Action Committee on the Status of Women*. Toronto: University of Toronto Press, 1993.

Chapter 8

Class
CLEAVAGES

A few Canadian families are among the richest people in the world, while an increasing number of others line up at soup kitchens and food banks because they cannot afford to buy food. Obsessed with their deficits and debts, federal and provincial governments have usually blamed their fiscal woes on the costs of social programs, and have cut back sharply on social assistance. No adult can make ends meet on the minimum wage, but small businesses claim they will go bankrupt if it is raised. Canadian history is replete with examples of workers being fired for trying to form unions and of being clubbed by police when they went on strike.[1] By almost any measure, the rich are getting richer and the poor are getting poorer.

The concept of class is not as clear-cut as that of region or ethnicity, and Canadians are generally more conscious of regional and ethnic cleavages. Nevertheless, class is an important generator of political activity in most countries, and Canada has its deep-seated class cleavages as well. A discussion of class cleavages in Canada must therefore not only clarify the concept, but also explain why it is not a more significant factor in Canadian politics. This chapter will begin by discussing various definitions of class, then examine the political role of the upper, middle, and working classes, and of the poor. It concludes with a discussion of the social safety net—its rise and demise—and the question of Canadian class-consciousness.

DEFINING CLASS

When dealing with the concept of class, it is customary to start with Karl Marx, who predicted that every capitalist economy would produce a class system consisting primarily of the **bourgeoisie**, the owners of the means of production, and the **proletariat**, the workers. The proletariat would sell their labour for a price; the bourgeoisie would pay them as little as possible (and less than they were worth), thereby accumulating profit or surplus value. While religion and the prospect of a pleasant after-life might keep them content for a while, the workers would eventually come to resent their low wages and exploitation, and finally engage in a violent revolt.

Capitalist societies have not evolved exactly as Marx predicted, and today's neo-Marxists, while adhering to the essence of their mentor, usually make certain alterations in his analysis. Marx did provide for a small **petite bourgeoisie** of farmers, small-business people, and self-employed professionals, but this class has become more significant than he expected. Furthermore, the **new middle class** of civil servants, teachers, nurses, and other salaried professionals was almost unforeseen in the mid-1800s, and it has become another large and important force. Thus, as mentioned in Chapter 1, those who analyze politics in terms of class speak of the bourgeoisie (the economic elite), the petite bourgeoisie (the old middle class), the new middle class, and the proletariat (the "working class"). As well, they often identify "fractions" within each class.

On the other hand, those social scientists who are not neo-Marxists commonly divide individuals and families into the upper, middle, and working classes, based on such interrelated factors as income, occupation, and education. With these measures, the divisions between the classes are less clear-cut than in the neo-Marxist analysis. Dennis Forcese, for example, defines classes as "aggregates of persons distinguished principally by wealth and income."[2] Although such inequalities both produce and result from inequalities in other characteristics such as education and occupation, income is the simplest measure to use.

One means of measuring income inequality is to divide the population into five groups of equal numbers, or quintiles, ranging from highest to lowest income and to indicate the share of total income received by each group. Table 8.1 presents such proportions for the year 1996; it also shows that before transfers and taxes the highest 20 percent gained about 50 percent of the income and the lowest 20 percent had virtually no income. Transfers provide almost all the income of the lowest quintile, and taxes take a little away from the rich to redistribute to the poor. Even after taxes and transfers, however, the highest 20 percent of the population received over 40 percent of the total income, while the lowest 20 percent received just 5.6 percent. These figures are remarkably constant over time.

Another problem in analyzing social class is the distinction between "objective" and "subjective" class. Objective class refers to the class into which analysts place a person, according to criteria such as type of work or level of income, while subjective class means the class to which people think or feel they belong, even if it contradicts objective standards. Many people who consider themselves to be middle class would be categorized as working class by social scientists, and Marx himself foresaw the phenomenon of "false consciousness."

TABLE 8.1   **Income Shares of Quintiles before and after Transfers and Taxes, 1996 (Percentages)**

	Income before Transfers and Taxes	Total Money Income after Transfers	Income after Taxes and Transfers
Lowest quintile	0.7	4.6	5.6
Second quintile	7.3	10.0	11.3
Middle quintile	15.9	16.3	17.1
Fourth quintile	26.3	24.7	24.6
Highest quintile	49.8	44.5	41.5

Source: Adapted from Statistics Canada, Income after Tax, Distributions by Size in Canada, 1996, Catalogue No. 13-210.

Somewhat similarly, people may see themselves as working class but adopt a deferential attitude toward their "betters."

A qualification that should be added relates to the changing nature of class. Some analysts contend that those born after 1945 have distinctive "postmaterialist" orientations that are less concerned with traditional class polarization than with "quality of life" and "lifestyle" questions such as environmental, women's, identity, and minority issues.[3]

Relying on neo-Marxist and other class-based analyses, Table 8.2 divides the Canadian population into classes and attempts to estimate the approximate number and percentage of voters (that is, people over 18 years of age) in each class. These objective figures are obviously not as definitive as those on region, ethnicity, or gender, and must also be hedged by considerations of subjective class.[4]

TABLE 8.2   **The Class Structure in Canadian Society**

	Voters	*Percentage of Electorate*
Upper class	500 000	2.5
Middle class	3 000 000	15.0
Petite bourgeoisie	1 500 000	7.5
New middle class	1 500 000	7.5
Working class	13 500 000	67.5
Unionized	4 500 000	22.5
Not unionized	9 000 000	45.0
Poor	3 000 000	15.0
Working	1 500 000	7.5
Welfare	1 500 000	7.5

Source: Devised by author.

THE UPPER CLASS
Identifying the Corporate Elite

It is not difficult to identify those who compose the upper class. Canada possesses many fabulously rich entrepreneurs and some of the wealthiest families in the world. In 1999, *Canadian Business* magazine produced a list of the 100 richest Canadians, and the top 30 of the **corporate elite** are included together with their estimated fortunes in Table 8.3.[5]

Other analysts sometimes have slightly different numbers or rankings, but Ken Thomson and the Irving family are always at the top of the heap. Thomson used to be the main

TABLE 8.3   **The 30 Richest Canadians, 1999**

Ken Thomson	$20.97 billion
Arthur, James, and John Irving	6.67 billion
Galen Weston	5.37 billion
Charles Bronfman	5.34 billion
Jeff Skoll	4.8 billion
Bombardier family	3.42 billion
Jimmy Pattison	2.2 billion
Mannix family	2.15 billion
Ted Rogers	2.06 billion
Terry Matthews	1.95 billion
Bernard Sherman	1.83 billion
Paul Desmarais	1.74 billion
Izzy Asper	1.57 billion
Leslie Dan	1.56 billion
Michael DeGroote	1.45 billion
Saputo family	1.32 billion
André Chagnon	1.21 billion
David Azrieli	1.14 billion
Jean Coutu	1.09 billion
Charles Sirois	1.08 billion
Wallace McCain	1.08 billion
Harrison McCain	1.04 billion
Saul Feldberg	1 billion
Kruger family	950 million
Reichmann family	895 million
Richardson family	860 million
Robert Miller	855 million
Lawrence Tanenbaum	835 million
Ron Joyce	810 million
Vittorio De Zen	780 million

Source: Canadian Business, *July 30/August 13, 1999.*

proprietor of Canadian newspapers, but, having sold many of them, he now concentrates on the information and publishing fields. The Irving family owns most of New Brunswick, including large tracts of woodlands, pulp mills, all the English-language daily newspapers in the province, oil refineries, gas stations, shipbuilding, trucking, bus lines, railways, and potato operations. Having sold E.B. Eddy Paper Co., Galen Weston concentrates on Loblaws, in addition to many other food enterprises including Weston, Zehrs, Neilson Cadbury Canada, and the upper-class clothing store, Holt Renfrew. Seagrams is the largest asset of the "Montreal" Bronfmans, Charles, Edgar Sr. and Edgar Jr., who now live in New York; in 1995 they took over MCA Universal Studios in Hollywood and later PolyGram. Jeff Skoll, a young newcomer to the list, is co-founder of the California Internet auction company eBay Inc.

Another category of wealthy Canadians are the corporate chief executive officers (CEOs) who do not actually own their own firms, as do those mentioned above. Many of the most highly paid CEOs in 1998, however, were also owners; Table 8.4 includes the exorbitant value of salary, bonus, incentives, shares, and other benefits for one year alone.

Sometimes another distinction is made between the "indigenous elite" and the "comprador elite," the latter being made up of the executives of branches of foreign-owned firms[6] (see also Chapter 9). The comprador elite take orders from the corporate headquarters abroad, a good example being Brian Mulroney when he was president of the Iron Ore Company of Canada, in which Hanna Mining of Cleveland had a controlling interest. On the other hand, many Canadian firms have now become multinationals. Thomson, Irving, Weston, the Bronfmans, and the McCains are among those that have many foreign assets, as do such companies as Northern Telecom and the Laurentian Group.

The individuals and families of great wealth and/or income identified above and many others of slightly inferior stature own or control many of the large corporations operating in Canada. Some individuals and families own hundreds of firms, the families of great wealth are frequently joint owners of corporations, and the extent of intercorporate connections is high.[7] In recent years, many have been more concerned to take over competitors (often reducing the labour force in the process) rather than to create any new wealth or jobs in the country.

A final point here concerns the vital part that Canadian banks play in the operations of the corporate elite. They do so because much corporate activity is financed by large bank loans. Thus, many of the individuals named above sit on the boards of directors of major Canadian banks, where their presence assures their company or companies of preferential banking treatment.[8] Indeed, a whole theory has been advanced regarding the manner in which the banks have directed the development of the Canadian economy. They have contributed to the widespread foreign ownership in Canada because of their preference for financing foreign branch plants in Canada rather than domestic manufacturers; they have exacerbated regional disparities in their preference for central Canadian clients; and they have encouraged a resource-based economy by preferring export-oriented resource companies to manufacturing.[9]

Most members of the corporate elite inherited a good deal of their wealth; such a transfer is facilitated by the lack of a wealth or inheritance tax in Canada. As far as the other aspects of their social background are concerned, John Porter found a near Anglo-Protestant monopoly in the 1960s, as did Wallace Clement in the 1970s, but this is beginning to change. Several of the largest corporate families are of Jewish background, and French Canadians are increasingly prominent in such circles, now including Paul Desmarais (originally from Sudbury) and his sons, Claude Castonguay (Laurentian Group), the Bombardier family, André Chagnon (Groupe Vidéotron), Jean Coutu (pharmacies), Charles Sirois (Teleglobe), Pierre-Karl Péladeau (Quebecor), and Bernard Lemaire (Cascades paper). Those of other ethnic backgrounds are also joining the corporate elite, such as Vic De Zen (Royal plastics), the Bata family (shoes), Frank Stronach (Magna), the Ghermezian brothers (the West Edmonton Mall), and Li Ka-shing (Husky Oil). While Toronto remains the financial capital of the country, the economic elite is also increasingly diverse in terms of geography, with a new Western flavour.

TABLE 8.4   Highly Paid Chief Executive Officers, 1998 (Dollars)

Peter Munk	Barrick Gold	38 918 951
Richard Currie	Loblaws	34 122 152
Frank Stronach	Magna International	26 154 250
Frank Hasenfratz	Linamar Corp.	21 397 831
Galen Weston	George Weston	15 226 858
Gerald Schwartz	Onex Corp.	11 697 375
Ivan Fecan	Baton Broadcasting	8 950 417
Charles Baillie	Toronto-Dominion Bank	8 505 447
Bradley Wechsler	IMAX	8 478 766
Richard Gelfond	IMAX	8 478 766
Ronald Southern	ATCO Ltd.	8 343 612
Paul Desmarais Jr.	Power Corp.	7 134 888
J.R. Shaw	Shaw Communications	6 680 553
John Lacey	Western Int'l Communications	6 134 400
Edgar Bronfman Jr.	Seagram Co.	6 005 395
Lawrence Bloomberg	First Marathon	4 875 000
Matthew Barrett	Bank of Montreal	4 560 261
Richard Harrington	Thomson Corp.	4 451 003
Peter Godsoe	Bank of Nova Scotia	4 448 076
John Roth	Northern Telecom	4 038 932
Steven Hudson	Newcourt Credit Group	3 973 680
Archibald McLean	Maple Leaf Foods	3 471 866
Brian Levitt	Imasco Ltd.	3 393 847
André Desmarais	Power Corp.	3 295 470
James Bullock	Laidlaw Inc.	2 853 331

Source: The Globe and Mail, *April 26, 1999. Reprinted with permission from* The Globe and Mail.

Demands of the Corporate Elite

The social homogeneity of the members of the corporate elite may have started to change, but the upper class is no less unified in its basic values. One value that still characterizes the members of this group is the desire to maximize their ownership and control of the private sector and to press the public sector to adopt such policies as will allow them to go about their business of "accumulation."

It is not difficult, therefore, to draw the general lines of the public policy demands of the economic elite. Essentially, they want to be left alone: cut government spending on social programs so that their taxes can be minimized, and get rid of annual government deficits and reduce the accumulated national debt. If taxes are necessary, do not levy estate or wealth taxes. Avoid corporate and progressive individual taxes as much as possible, and provide generous loopholes, write-offs, and tax shelters.[10] Minimize government regulation, labour legislation, and environmental protection, as well as anti-combines laws and other restrictions on corporate takeovers. As Peter Newman says, "what unites [the capitalist elite] is common resentment of the multiplying intrusions of politicians and bureaucrats into the once-sacrosanct ground of Canadian capitalism."[11]

Governments have normally responded positively to such demands. Under the Mulroney government, for example, the progressive nature of the personal income tax was reduced when ten tax brackets were reduced to three, and a $500 000 lifetime capital gains tax exemption was introduced, although this was subsequently lowered to $100 000. Brian Mulroney's finance minister Michael Wilson allowed the corporate elite to continue to deduct 80 percent of the cost of business meals and entertainment, causing the government to lose about $1 billion in tax revenues every year.[12] Other losses to the treasury occur because investors can deduct interest paid on loans used to buy shares, and because only 80 percent of dividends from Canadian corporations are taxable. Wilson completed his tax reform package with the Goods and Services Tax (GST), which most observers believed would benefit the rich by shifting the burden from income to sales taxes. Liberal finance minister Paul Martin reduced the entertainment deduction to 50 percent and discontinued the $100 000 capital gains exemption, but capital gains are still taxed at a lower rate than other forms of income. At the same time, he slashed federal contributions to provincial social programs, discussed in more detail later in this chapter. When the Chrétien Cabinet overturned a CRTC decision and gave Paul Desmarais' Power Corp. subsidiary Power DirecTV a share of the direct-to-home satellite TV market, many observers raised their eyebrows, given the close connection between Power Corp. and the federal Liberal government. Even worse, the Liberals allowed the Bronfman family to transfer $2 billion in Seagram shares to the United States, averting about $700 million in capital gains taxation in the process.

As is argued in Chapter 22, the Senate, especially its influential Banking Committee, often functions as a lobby for big business within the apparatus of government.[13] Big business has also found an ally in the judicial system, as time and again the courts have extended to corporations aspects of the Charter of Rights and Freedoms that were intended to protect individuals.

In her book *Behind Closed Doors*, Linda McQuaig shows how the rich use their political influence to obtain tax breaks that are paid for by those with lesser incomes. While Canada's personal and corporate income tax system is riddled with loopholes, it is one of the few countries in the world without a tax on wealth or inheritance. Figure 8.1 reveals how federal and provincial governments have greatly increased their reliance on personal income taxes over

....

Figure 8.1 **Comparison of Federal and Provincial Revenues Derived from Personal and Corporate Income Taxes, 1985–1995**

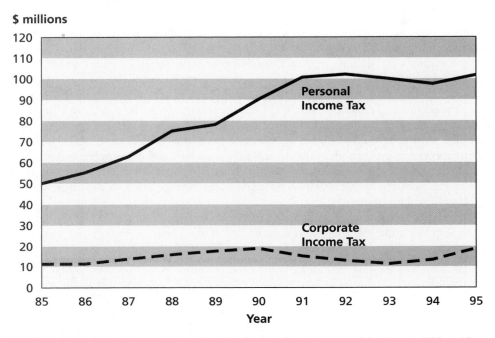

Source: Devised by author, based on figures from Canadian Tax Foundation, Finances of the Nation, *1997, p. A3.*

the post-1985 period while keeping corporate income taxes stable. Indeed, personal income taxes increased from 10.4 per cent of GDP in 1980 to 14.9 percent in 1996, while corporate income taxes declined from 3.9 percent of GDP to 2.7 percent. Moreover, Canadian anti-combines laws are laughable and represent one of the few fields where American regulation of the private sector is more stringent. There is also evidence of widespread illegal insider trading on Canadian stock markets.

Three principal exceptions to this pressure to minimize the role of government must be noted. First, while the economic elite demands that government minimize spending on others, it often expects sizable chunks of public funds for itself. The new "acquisitors," for example, have "exploited to [the] utmost the Canadian tradition of government subsidies in everything from offshore oil to horror films."[14] This tradition goes back as far as the turn of the century when railway companies were given generous amounts of public funds and public lands; it has continued in a wide range of fields at the federal level ever since, especially in terms of regional economic development, and is carried on in give-aways to resource companies at the provincial level. The extent of actual government contributions to business was first made common knowledge by David Lewis, then leader of the New Democratic Party (NDP), in the 1972 election campaign and in his book, *Louder Voices: Corporate Welfare Bums.*[15] Very often, as subsequent NDP leaders have reiterated, the public money involved takes the form of capital cost allowances, deferred taxes, or "tax expenditures" (taxes foregone by the government), which are essentially the same thing as a cash grant.

A second exception to the general pattern of corporate demands is the rare occasion on which the economic elite has actually favoured new social programs. Motives here include increasing the purchasing power of the poor and working class, reducing the amounts that companies themselves have to pay in employee benefits, improving their corporate image, and ensuring the basic stability of society so that the upper classes do not have to worry about violent protests from the poor or unemployed. Alvin Finkel writes of the reform measures adopted in the Depression of the 1930s: "The actions taken were those that businessmen-politicians and other pro-capitalist politicians believed would placate working-class and farmer demands while being assured at the same time that business power within the overall system would be preserved."[16]

In the third place, business leaders sometimes favour an expansion of government activity, usually in the provision of basic utilities or infrastructure, that will decrease their costs or increase their profits. For example, businessmen in Ontario shortly after 1900 encouraged the provincial government to create a Crown corporation to provide a cheap, reliable supply of electricity, and resource companies have often demanded that governments build roads and railways to save them the trouble.

As noted in Chapter 1, the Canadian state gives priority to big-business demands because it depends on the private sector to a large extent to create jobs. Beyond that, politicians respond to the demands of the economic elite for three main reasons. First, corporate executives and politicians often come from the same ranks, including prime ministers and ministers of finance. Brian Mulroney, Michael Wilson, John Turner, and Paul Martin are good examples. Second, companies have many avenues of influence available: making a direct, personal pitch, using professional lobby firms to help them make contact with public decision makers for a fee, and taking advantage of their membership in pressure groups.

Among the hundreds of business pressure groups in existence, the **Business Council on National Issues (BCNI)** is probably the most powerful, representing as it does the chief executive officers of the 150 largest firms in the country. Its executive director, Tom d'Aquino, is a household name in Ottawa.[17] Third, throughout their history both the Conservative and Liberal parties have largely been financed by large corporate contributions. This has changed somewhat in recent years (see Chapter 12), but a link between corporate contributions and general public policy, if not to specific corporate favours, is not difficult to establish. In addition, in the 1988 election, Canadians witnessed an unprecedented parallel campaign in which the country's major corporations spent millions of dollars on top of their party donations to persuade Canadian voters of the merits of free trade. In short, even an admirer of the corporate elite like Peter Newman could write that "the combined power exercised by ... the new Canadian Establishment has seldom been exceeded in any nation that dares call itself a functioning democracy."[18]

THE MIDDLE CLASS

As outlined earlier, the traditional middle class, or "petite bourgeoisie," consisted of farmers, small-business people, and self-employed professionals, including doctors and lawyers. This group could also be called the upper middle class. The "new middle class" consists of civil servants, teachers, and other salaried professionals such as nurses, social workers, librarians, engineers, accountants, and the like. Neo-Marxists generally emphasize the ownership or control of the means of production, but as Leo Panitch says, this century has seen the development of a stratum of employees without such ownership or control but who "nevertheless dispose of labour in terms of managing, supervising, and controlling the labour of others."[19]

To some extent, these two fractions of the middle class have considerably different economic interests and therefore different political demands. First, the members of the petite bourgeoisie are usually much wealthier than those of the new middle class and have many more tax breaks. Second, the petite bourgeoisie is made up of the self-employed and/or employers, while the new middle class is mostly composed of those who work for someone else. The new middle class largely works in the public sector, either directly for governments or in para-governmental institutions such as schools, universities, and hospitals. In the third place, this public-sector branch of the new middle class is increasingly organized into unions, such as government employee unions and nurses', teachers', and professors' associations. The petite bourgeoisie, on the other hand, normally abhors unions almost as much as does the economic elite. Moreover, while it is common for members of the working class to think of themselves subjectively as middle class, the opposite may be true in the case of nurses and teachers who are in the process of being "proletarianized." The combination of managerial changes to the way in which work is done and severe funding cuts of the last 15 years has led rapidly growing numbers in these two professions to think of themselves and to act as members of the working class.[20]

While the middle class is therefore far from being a unified force, its members are normally well educated, and most are economically comfortable since they receive above-average levels of income. They own their homes and cars, and usually have assorted other material possessions. The middle class has benefited in recent years from structural changes in the economy; indeed, the categories of management, administration, and health are among the few that have grown in both number of jobs and proportion of total income.

Unlike the upper class, members of the middle class may not be sufficiently affluent to finance their own educational and medical needs, and usually demand and benefit from government programs in these fields. In addition, while not all members of the middle class can take advantage of the clauses written into the tax laws to benefit the wealthy,[21] they do enjoy such tax shelters as RRSPs and certain investment incentives (see Figure 8.2). But the middle class pays a disproportionate amount of the taxes to finance government programs of all kinds. A study of federal tax changes between 1984 and 1988, for example, showed that while those earning under $13 000 and those over $117 000 gained, the hardest hit were middle-class families making between $29 000 and $43 000.[22] Thus it is on the "middle middle" and especially "lower middle" classes that the federal and provincial personal tax increases in recent years have fallen most heavily.

Many groups within the middle class are organized by profession, primarily at the provincial level. But there is no umbrella pressure group that transmits the class's demands collectively to the authorities. Some—especially those who are unionized—have been attracted by NDP promises to shift the tax burden to the corporate sector and upper classes, but most continue to support the Liberal and Conservative parties because of their lack of sympathy with the NDP's links to industrial labour unions. To some extent, therefore, even the new middle class confirms Marx's contention that the petite bourgeoisie functioned primarily as an ally of the economic elite.

Figure 8.2   Distribution of RRSP Tax Breaks by Income

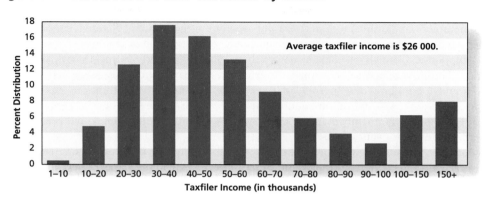

Source: Canadian Council on Social Development, Insight *(April 1995). Used with permission.*

THE WORKING CLASS

The working class is generally identified with manual or routine as opposed to intellectual work. Its members normally lack postsecondary education, but they are often qualified in a trade. They usually, but not always, receive less income than those in the middle class and are more frequently unionized. The typical member of the working class is engaged in resource exploitation, assembly line production, secretarial and clerical work, sales, and a variety of crafts and trades. (That portion of the working class living below the poverty line is discussed below in the section "The Poor.") While Marx categorized farmers as part of the petite bourgeoisie because of their ownership of land, most Canadian farmers have had to struggle for their existence. These less affluent farmers have sometimes cooperated with organized labour to support such organizations as the Cooperative Commonwealth Federation (CCF) and NDP.

The difference in economic status between unionized and nonunionized members of the working class is often profound, and the issue of unionization is a significant one for many of its members. Karl Marx's predictions of a violent proletarian revolt were dealt a blow when the Macdonald government legalized trade unions in Canada in 1890 and when the franchise was extended to the working class. Since then, the courts have decided that labour legislation falls primarily within provincial jurisdiction, and the impediments to unionization have varied across the country. Many provincial governments as well as many companies have been viciously hostile toward the formation of unions, and Canada has experienced a large number of violent strikes. Among the key labour struggles in Canadian history were the 1919 Winnipeg General Strike, the 1937 General Motors Strike in Oshawa, the 1945 Ford Strike in Windsor, the 1949 Asbestos Strike in Quebec, and the woodworkers strike in Newfoundland in 1959.[23] Labour legislation also deals with conciliation, mediation, arbitration, picketing, labour standards, occupational health and safety standards, and compensation for injury on the job. All of these usually provide minimal protection for the working class, as governments claim to be responding to labour demands but still seek to avoid offending their own corporate supporters.

Others things being equal, it is in the interests of members of the working class to belong to a union: unionized employees almost always have higher wages (sometimes higher than the middle class), adequate benefits, better working conditions, and more protection against arbitrary treatment and dismissal than those who do not engage in such collective bargaining. In other words, a union and the collective agreement bring the rule of law into the workplace. The Economic Council of Canada reported in 1989 that nearly 80 percent of unionized workers had private pension coverage, for example, compared with only 30 percent of those who were not unionized.[24] In spite of these facts, the rate of unionization among "paid workers" is very low. Total union membership in 1998 was 3 906 400, or 33.1 percent of the 11 801 200 potential members in the country. This overall rate has ranged between 31 and 35 percent for over twenty years.[25]

Moreover, the number of blue-collar jobs is declining in such areas as resource industries, construction, and manufacturing where unionization was most common. New jobs in the "postindustrial" society are largely found in services, especially in the private sector, and are traditionally part-time, poorly paid, and nonunionized. Between 1981 and 1998, the proportion of jobs in goods-producing industries fell from 34 to 26 percent, while that in the services sector increased from 66 to 74 percent.[26] Lacking a union, and given the nature of their job, those in sales and services occupations are not as likely to be class-conscious or to develop social democratic values as those who produce goods. The proportion of unionized workers in different sectors is shown in Table 8.5.

The composition of the unionized work force is changing in other ways as well. Once composed primarily of private-sector, male, manual workers, public-sector workers now constitute slightly over 50 percent of the union movement, and women now constitute over 43 percent of union members.[27] Public-sector unions make up three of the seven largest unions in the country, which are as follows: the Canadian Union of Public Employees (CUPE), 389 800; National Union of Provincial Government Employees, 309 000; Canadian Auto Workers (CAW), 222 500; United Food and Commercial Workers, 200 000; United Steelworkers, 180 000; the Communication, Energy, and Paperworkers (CEP), 144 300; and the Public Service Alliance (PSAC), 142 300.

The 1980s and 1990s were not good years for the working class. High unemployment diminished the bargaining power of Canadian workers and forced them to concentrate on matters of job security rather than remuneration. On the other hand, high interest rates in the early part of this period strengthened the resolve of employers to reduce costs in areas such as wages paid to employees. Tax changes only exacerbated the situation, as did the recession of the early 1990s and government restraint programs across the country. The forces of globalization and international trade agreements led multilateral corporations to close many large operations in Canada in order to take advantage of lower wages, unregulated working conditions, and an absence of environmental standards in other countries. A dramatic Canadian example was Maple Leaf Foods, which threatened to close down its plants unless workers took a pay cut. In Edmonton, 750 workers thus lost their jobs, while in Burlington, 900 accepted a contract that cut their wages by up to 40 percent.[28] As one study pointed out, "the proliferation of non-standard work arrangements, such as part-time work, subcontracting, home work, self-employment and overtime, has produced a more precarious job market for modest-income families."[29]

The foremost concern of the working class is thus the level of unemployment in the country. Although the official rate fell marginally toward the turn of the new century, regis-

TABLE 8.5   **Union Members as a Percentage of Paid Workers, by Industry, 1998**

Agriculture	4.8
Other primary	29.3
Manufacturing	35.0
Construction	31.8
Utilities	70.7
Goods-producing sector	34.1
Trade	14.2
Transportation & warehousing	47.1
Finance, insurance, real estate & leasing	10.0
Professional, scientific & technical services	6.3
Management, administrative & other support	14.6
Educational services	73.2
Health care & social assistance	55.9
Information, culture & recreation	30.2
Accommodation & food services	8.5
Other services	11.4
Public administration	69.7
Services-producing sector	32.8

Source: Adapted from "The Labour Force Survey," Catalogue No. 7100003.

tering an annual 8.3 percent in 1998, most observers believe that the real unemployment rate is much higher, perhaps double. This is because the official rate does not include those who are too discouraged to seek work, the underemployed, and those working part-time who prefer to work full-time.

High unemployment levels also led the working class to focus their demands on the Unemployment Insurance program. This program was introduced in 1941 to tide workers over between jobs, but given the high national unemployment rates in the years since, especially in certain regions, UI was used much more heavily than was originally anticipated. With such large numbers of workers drawing on the fund, it has become both a vital source of individual and regional income and the subject of almost daily political controversy. Made more generous in 1971, unemployment insurance has been regularly restricted ever since, involving lower average payments, a shorter maximum duration of benefits, and a dramatic reduction in the percentage of the unemployed qualifying for benefits. The program's name was changed to "Employment Insurance" in 1996.[30] In 1989, 74 percent of those unemployed qualified for unemployment insurance, whereas in 1997, only 36 percent did. The decline, shown dramatically in Figure 8.3, hit women much harder than men. With thousands of unemployed workers eliminated from the EI program, it is no wonder that the fund accumulated an annual surplus of some $6 or $7 billion and a cumulative surplus of some $20 billion by 1999, which the Chrétien government lumped into general revenues, allowing them to claim that they had balanced the budget. Political embarrassment led them to soften restrictions somewhat in mid-1999.

The **Canadian Labour Congress (CLC)** is the lobbying body for over two million workers. The CLC has the largest actual membership of any pressure group in the country and therefore represents the greatest number of voters. Its influence is diminished, however, by its divergent values and its outsider status, as well as by the fact that not all unions belong to it. Whether it increased or decreased its influence by affiliating with the NDP in 1961 is still an open question. Many unions have not joined any central organization, and others have formed such rival groups as the Confédération des syndicats nationaux (CSN, with 242 830 members). The historic factionalism within the Canadian union movement has not helped the cause of the working class.[31] Thus, out of a potential 11.8 million paid workers, only 3.9 million have joined a union, and only 2.3 million have affiliated with the largest central labour organization in the country.

Figure 8.3 **Percent of Unemployed Receiving Unemployment Insurance, 1989–1997**

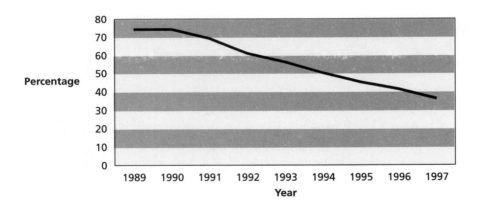

Source: Canadian Labour Congress, based on data compiled from Statistics Canada from the monthly Employment Insurance System data file provided by Human Resources Development Canada. Reproduced with permission.

····································

THE POOR[32]

The poor can be defined as those living below the **poverty line**. Although different organizations use slightly different definitions of poverty, the most common is the "low-income cut-off" of Statistics Canada. It is calculated as follows: any individual or family that spends more than 54.7 percent of their income on food, clothing, and shelter is considered to be living in poverty.[33] Statistics Canada strenuously argues that the low-income cut-off is a bureaucratic term, not a poverty line, but it is widely accepted as such.

Using this measure, the proportion of the population living in poverty declined from 25 percent in 1969 to 16.6 percent in 1986, but increased again since the mid-1980s to 17.9 percent in 1996. Table 8.6 shows the number of people below the poverty line, indicating that the absolute number of poor Canadians has increased along with population growth. It should be emphasized, however, that there is also a large group of near-poor that exists just above the arbitrary poverty line, and that many below it are *far* below it. The average income deficiency among those living in poverty was an almost constant $7000 throughout this period, but the aggregate income deficiency rose from $14 billion to over $19 billion. This is the amount of money it would take to bring these people up to the poverty line. The actual number of people collecting social assistance was over 2.5 million in 1998, down from over 3 million in 1994–95, but this decrease was partly due to stricter eligibility rules.

Much could be said about each of the various categories of people living in poverty, such as women, Aboriginals, people with disabilities, and the elderly. The aspect of poverty that is

---

TABLE 8.6   **Number of Canadians below the Poverty Line, 1980–1996**

Year	Canadians Living in Poverty	Year	Canadians Living in Poverty
1980	3 871 000	1990	4 179 000
1981	3 910 000	1991	4 543 000
1982	4 265 000	1992	4 757 000
1983	4 653 000	1993	5 143 000
1984	4 737 000	1994	4 941 000
1985	4 494 000	1995	5 205 000
1986	4 254 000	1996	5 294 000
1987	4 253 000		
1988	4 040 000		
1989	3 770 000		

Source: Adapted from Statistics Canada, Income Distributions by Size, *Catalogue No. 13-207.*

probably most heartbreaking, however, is that 30 percent of the poor people in Canada are children; in other words, over 20 percent of children live in poverty.[34] The child mortality rate is twice as high among families at the lowest income level than at the highest, and in 1986 the high-school drop-out rate among children from poor families was 2.2 times the rate of others. This tie between low income and low education is self-perpetuating, and ways must be found to encourage the children of poor families to pursue their education. The *Canadian Poverty Fact Book—1989* asserts that "the educational opportunities of children, whether at the primary, secondary or post-secondary level, must not be limited by the economic circumstances of their parents."[35] It also documents how children from low-income families stand out from their better-off peers: "They are less healthy, have less access to skill-building activities, have more destructive habits and behaviours, live more stressful lives, and are subject to more humiliation. In short, they have less stable and less secure existences and as a result they are likely to be less secure as adults."[36]

Although the House of Commons passed a resolution in 1989 to seek the goal of eliminating child poverty in Canada by the year 2000, the number of children living in poverty actually increased by 50 percent. While more than half of these poor children live in two-parent families, over 40 percent of the children below the poverty line live with lone-parent mothers, and over 60 percent of families headed by a lone-parent mother live in poverty. In terms of depth of poverty, lone-parent mothers with children are also further below the poverty line than other groups; hence the expression, the **feminization of poverty**.

Many poor people work full-time (27 percent of family heads and 19 percent of unattached individuals), and others part-time (40 percent and 54 percent, respectively), so that the poor can be about equally divided between those who work and those who are unemployed or unemployable.[37] Although part-time work is increasingly the norm in Canadian society today, it has many drawbacks.

The working poor try to scrape by on the minimum wage or have more than one low-paying job. Because the minimum wage is even lower than welfare benefits (both being below the poverty line), many working poor choose to go on welfare because they are often better off that way. Rather than raise the minimum wage, however, many provincial governments actually reduced welfare benefits in the 1990s. Even the combined incomes of two family members earning the minimum wage would not raise them above the poverty line.[38] As with the working class above the poverty line, employment insurance is of vital importance to the working poor.[39] In the sweeping changes brought to the program by both the Mulroney and Chrétien governments discussed above, the lowest-income groups were the biggest losers.

When their EI runs out, the working poor become the welfare poor. Welfare benefits vary considerably from province to province; they are not generous, contrary to the impression of many who have not had to rely on them; and studies repeatedly show that the incidence of welfare fraud is minimal. One of the chronic concerns about the welfare system across the country has been its disincentive effect for the welfare poor to seek employment. Earned income is usually deducted from welfare benefits, so that it is often not worth the effort to find a job.

The poor are generally unorganized and collectively inarticulate in the political system. They lack the skills to organize effectively as pressure groups primarily because they do not have the education, money, and time to develop such skills. On the other hand, three main pressure groups attempt to include the voice of the poor in the political process. The first is the Canadian Council on Social Development (CCSD), which represents middle-class, bureaucratic, and even some corporate concern with the state of social policy in the country.

By Denny Pritchard. Reproduced with permission.

It has often provided the blueprint for social reform, even if it did not have the power to ensure that its recommendations were followed, and is an important source of data on social programs. Because the CCSD does not actually represent the poor as such, the government sponsored the creation of the National Council of Welfare (NCW) in 1969 as an advisory group speaking on behalf of welfare clients themselves. Its members include welfare recipients, public housing tenants, and other low-income citizens as well as those involved in providing services to the poor. It also produces studies of the poverty problem and other social issues; even though it is funded by the government, the NCW is usually more critical and radical than the CCSD. The third pressure group, the National Anti-Poverty Organization (NAPO), was formed in 1971. It is an umbrella organization of some 700 local and provincial poverty groups across the country, representing over five million Canadians living below the poverty line. Considering its lack of resources, it is surprisingly effective in articulating its point of view.

THE RISE OF THE SOCIAL SAFETY NET[40]

Reflecting the influence of the affluent economic elite, the North American predilection to abide by private market forces, and the assumption that jurisdiction over such matters rested primarily with the provinces, the federal government was slow to get involved in the provision of health and social service programs. By the early 1980s, however, Canada had become a "welfare state" in which federal, provincial, and municipal governments were engaged in a wide range of programs that contributed to a **social safety net** protecting the weakest members of society, especially those unable or not expected to earn a living on their own. The principal federal measures can be divided into five basic fields—those relating to the young, the elderly, people with disabilities, the unemployed, and health insurance. These programs, together with their dates of adoption, are listed below.

- Old Age Pensions (1927)
- Blind Persons' Allowances (1937)
- Unemployment Insurance (1941)
- Family Allowances (1944)
- Old Age Security (1951)
- Disabled Persons' Allowances (1954)
- Unemployment Assistance (1956)
- Hospital Insurance (1957)
- Canada Pension Plan (1965)
- Canada Assistance Plan (1966)
- Guaranteed Income Supplement (1966)
- Medical Insurance (1968)
- U.I. Amendments (1971)
- Spouse's Allowances (1975)
- Child Tax Credit (1978)
- Canada Child Tax Credit (1993)
- National Child Tax Benefit (1997)

Of these programs, only the **Canada Assistance Plan (CAP)**, the Guaranteed Income Supplement, the Spouse's Allowance, and the Canada Child Tax Credit (now the National Child Tax Benefit) were specifically designed to help the poor. Unemployment Insurance, the Canada and Quebec Pension Plans, and health programs provide income or health insurance regardless of income, and the Old Age Security and the discontinued Family Allowances were originally universal programs. Nevertheless, in a relative sense, they all benefit the poor more than the affluent. Table 8.1 showed that without taxation and a redistribution of income via social programs, the lowest quintile would have virtually no income. Using deciles instead of quintiles, the Centre for Social Justice shows that in terms of market income alone, the richest 10 percent of Canadian families made 314 times more than the poorest 10 percent of families.[41]

Almost all of these measures faced much upper-class and corporate opposition before being adopted. Virtually all were passed when a Liberal government was in office, although it should be added that the first unemployment insurance legislation was introduced by the Conservative R.B. Bennett but thrown out by the courts, and the Diefenbaker government made incremental improvements to earlier Liberal measures.[42] In the cases of hospital and medical insurance, the CCF pioneered the measures at the provincial level in Saskatchewan, and in several instances the Liberals introduced the federal programs when they were in a minority position in Parliament and depended on CCF or NDP support. The trade union movement, churches, and other progressive organizations like the Canadian Council on Social Development were also responsible for popularizing such programs and pressing the government to implement them.

Other aspects of the social security net include special federal programs for war veterans and Aboriginals, and training schemes for the unemployed. Many provincial services supplement those outlined above. Primitive provincial welfare programs before the turn of the century gave way to mothers' allowances and family benefits after 1900, while child welfare programs, residential services, hospitals, workers' compensation, and student assistance can be found in every province. Some provinces provide supplementary family allowances and assistance to the elderly; some include dental, drug, optical, and paramedical services under medicare; and most provide a variety of other public health, crisis intervention, rehabilitation, and information and referral services. Some of these programs are partially funded through federal–provincial shared-cost programs. Thus, in spite of the resistance of the upper classes and the economic elite, the lot of the working class and poor in Canada could be and has been worse.

THE DEMISE OF SOCIAL PROGRAMS

In fact, it has become worse since the middle of the 1980s. Both federal and provincial governments in the 1990s were obsessed with their accumulated debts and current budgetary deficits, which they, along with business interests and conservative think-tanks, blamed on over-spending on social programs. Although social programs loom large in both federal and provincial government budgets, Canada actually stands near the bottom of OECD countries in the proportion of gross domestic product spent on social programs, as seen in Table 8.7. In another measure, although the United Nations has repeatedly ranked Canada first in terms of its Human Development Index, we fell to tenth place in its Human Poverty Index.

TABLE 8.7   Gross Public Social Expenditure as a Percentage of GDP, OECD Countries, 1995

Sweden	35.2
Finland	32.4
Denmark	32.2
France	30.1
Germany	27.9
Netherlands	27.8
Norway	27.6
Italy	23.7
United Kingdom	22.9
Spain	21.6
Canada	**18.2**
United States	15.8
Australia	15.7
Japan	13.8

Source: Economic, Labour and Social Affairs Division, OECD. Reproduced with permission.

It is possible, therefore, that debts and deficits have been caused by under-taxation rather than by over-spending; indeed, on a comparative basis, Canada derives less tax revenue from corporations than most of its major allies. As noted earlier, Canada is also one of the few major Western industrialized countries without a tax on inheritance or wealth.[43] Linda McQuaig's book *Shooting the Hippo* also blames the Bank of Canada's policy on maintaining high interest rates and a high Canadian dollar for promoting unemployment (and therefore social spending) and high payments on existing government debts.[44]

Those in power from the mid-1980s onward agreed that social spending had to be chopped. By means of the "clawback," the Mulroney government effectively removed the universal aspect of old age security but without redistributing such savings to the poor. In 1990 it reneged on its Canada Assistance Plan commitments with respect to providing half the costs of provincial and municipal social assistance in the three most prosperous provinces. In 1993, Ottawa reduced unemployment insurance entitlements to 57 percent of normal wages to a maximum of $425 a week, and replaced the Family Allowance Program with the refundable Child Tax Benefit. The latter move was designed to have a greater redistributive impact. The only social program the Mulroney government actually improved on was the Spouse's Allowance, in 1985.

Many observers saw Mulroney's package of economic policies—the Canada–U.S. Free Trade Agreement, privatization, deregulation, tax reform including the GST, reductions in transfers to the provinces, and the many cutbacks in social programs—as an integrated strategy. While the government claimed that these measures were introduced either to improve the economy or to cut the deficit, they had the collective effect of making the rich richer and reducing the standard of living of the poor and the working class. Several provinces, led by Alberta and Ontario, made their own massive cuts in social spending and would have done so regardless of reductions in federal transfers.[45]

When the Chrétien Liberals were elected in 1993, any plan to reform social programs was hijacked by Paul Martin's 1995 budget. Martin cut transfers to the provinces far beyond anything attempted by the Mulroney government, especially in health, postsecondary education, and welfare: a decrease of $7 billion over the 1996–98 period. Besides lumping the three programs together under the label **Canada Health and Social Transfer (CHST)**, Ottawa repealed the Canada Assistance Plan, and removed the conditions under which provinces received such funding. This meant that welfare would now have to fight it out with health and postsecondary education within provincial budgetary processes, and provincial governments could restrict social assistance eligibility and promote "workfare" schemes at will. In other words, although less was heard about it, the welfare sector bore the brunt of federal cutbacks even more than the health and education sectors.

The main cutbacks to social programs at both the federal and provincial levels in the 1985–2000 period can be listed as follows:[46]

- Reduced welfare benefits in all provinces (21.6% in Ontario in December 1995) as well as cuts to supplementary benefits.
- Cuts to services for people with disabilities—eligibility rules, home care, attendant care, and special transportation needs.
- Social housing programs abandoned by the federal government and most provinces.
- Severe federal cutbacks to unemployment insurance.
- Repeal of the Canada Assistance Plan, reducing federal contributions to provincial welfare programs and removing federal standards.

- Federal and provincial cuts to health care.
- Introduction of provincial workfare schemes for those collecting social assistance (and in Ontario, legislation prohibiting such participants from collective bargaining or going on strike).
- Alarming increases in homelessness, especially in large cities.
- Increased reliance on food banks, from 75 in 1984 to 625 in 1998.
- Dramatic increases in university tuition fees in most provinces.

All of these government cuts to social programs and the resulting deterioration in the way of life of millions of Canadians led to increasing protests in the late 1990s. The Canadian Council on Social Development, the National Council of Welfare, the National Anti-Poverty Organization, the Caledon Institute, the Canadian Labour Congress, and many other groups demanded recognition of "social condition"—that is, level of income—in federal and provincial human rights codes as an additional ground upon which to prohibit discrimination.

Even the United Nations scolded Canadian governments for what had transpired. Its Committee on Economic, Social and Cultural Rights criticized Canada in 1998 for its departure from the UN Covenant on these matters, especially given Canada's high ranking on the Human Development Index and its obvious capacity to achieve a high level of respect for all UN Covenant rights. It slammed Ottawa and the provinces for having adopted the policies listed above "which exacerbated poverty and homelessness among vulnerable groups during a time of strong economic growth and increasing affluence."

....

CLASS-CONSCIOUSNESS IN CANADA

Although the decline in Canadian social programs came under attack both within and beyond our borders, the perennial question of the relative lack of **class-consciousness** among the working and poor classes in Canada deserves some comment. Those who defend the lack of such consciousness argue that other social divisions take precedence in Canada, that the system permits social mobility, that most people feel themselves to be middle class, that material benefits are widely shared, and that the political system has accommodated working-class interests along with those of other groups. Those who decry the lack of working-class class-consciousness argue that the upper classes, the petite bourgeoisie, and even the new middle class have defined what is politically relevant in society in regional, ethnic, and religious terms.[47] When politicians and political parties appeal to members of the working class as Albertans, French Canadians, or Protestants rather than as workers, the latter develop a perverted view of who is an enemy or a friend. Members of one union can be persuaded that they should be hostile to the demands of another, or that they should support coercive back-to-work legislation to end another union's strike. They can also be collectively hoodwinked into thinking that their wage demands fuel inflation and must be curtailed by programs of wage and price controls. Mass media ownership by the corporate elite also has much to do with subjective social class. The poor, lacking in resources and having often given up, could hardly be expected to mount the kind of political organization that could challenge the defenders of the status quo. In discussing the "myth of classlessness," Allahar and Côté pin the blame for this self-delusion on the predominant liberal ideology, which explains social inequalities as stemming from varied individual effort and not from structured class relations.[48]

....

CONCLUSION

Whatever conception of class one wishes to employ, the existence of different classes in Canadian society cannot be denied. In this chapter, it was useful to divide the population into four classes: upper, middle, working, and poor. If such class cleavages do not usually result in political action, it must be that many Canadians are unaware of them, consider them acceptable, or feel powerless to change them.

Ⓒ Of the approaches outlined in Chapter 1, class analysis is obviously the one most concerned with class cleavages. The corporate elite has adopted a very effective strategy of placing on the national agenda, and making dominant, certain overarching themes: first, free trade, then, the deficit, and more recently, tax cuts. Each of these has as its inevitable product the reduction of the size and role of the state. The class approach is also concerned with the lack of class-consciousness among the working class and the poor. Given such a weak sense of class-consciousness in the two lower classes, how do class analysts explain the social security safety net? They argue that some such measures directly benefit the corporate sector, and the rest serve to legitimate the capitalist system and ensure social peace.[49] After the vote was extended to the working class, some minimal response had to be made to address its political demands, but not so much as to interrupt the accumulation activity of the bourgeoisie.

PC Public choice theory requires that voters be rational, self-interested, and conscious of their group position, something that many Canadian workers apparently are not. In spite of their numbers, such workers therefore rarely constitute a strategic group at election time. Politicians often promise programs of interest to the working class but do not fulfill them; sometimes they even completely reverse their electoral commitments, as in the case of Trudeau's flip-flop on wage and price controls in 1974. Once the Chrétien Liberals were elected in 1993, they dragged their feet in implementing their Red Book commitments with respect to job creation and social programs. On rare occasions, however, politicians strike a bargain with the working class in which the former promise social programs in return for votes.

SC State-centred theorists argue that because of the divisions within the working class and their low level of class-consciousness, politicians and bureaucrats can ignore their demands more easily than in the case of regional economic and ethnic demands. Moreover, since very few working-class politicians have ever been elected in Canada and most bureaucrats are of middle-class background, policies have been designed in the interests of those in power. Rodney Haddow has gone further to synthesize the class-based and state-centred approaches in his study of poverty reform in Canada. He shows that the bureaucrats in the influential Finance department look at every issue through the eyes of big business, acting as an agent of capitalist class interests in the halls of power.[50] It should also be noted, however, that some bureaucrats take a wider view of the national interest. Those public servants in departments oriented toward lower classes, such as health, welfare, labour, and human resources, along with their provincial counterparts, have been known to join organizations like the CCSD and do what they can to persuade the politicians to adopt their recommendations.[51] On the other hand, they generally do not feel capable of initiating such policies on their own.[52]

P Finally, pluralists emphasize the role of the one main working-class pressure group, the Canadian Labour Congress, and other groups speaking for the lower classes. When faced with the resources available to business pressure groups, however, this is a lopsided contest. Like the other segments of society, the labour movement has its own elite—the leaders of the largest unions in the country. But John Porter found that the composition of the labour elite was quite different from others. Lacking socioeconomic credentials, the labour elite has minimal links to the other elites, whether in terms of marriage, friendship, school ties, or politics.[53] What is even more striking is the absence of any group that could be said to represent the middle class. If policy is arrived at through pressure group interaction, it is the middle class whose unarticulated interests are ignored.

DISCUSSION QUESTIONS

1. To what class do you and your family belong? Assess your family's class-consciousness.

2. What is the best way to define and distinguish among social classes?

3. Why do so many Canadians conceive of Canada as a middle-class nation?

4. Do you feel that the economic elite owe their wealth and power primarily to their own honest, individual efforts or to inheritance, exploitative forms of profit-making, and manipulation of the political system? Explain.

5. Given that unions are generally the best way of improving the lot of the working class, why are they not more popular among members of that class?

6. How do you explain the existence of the social safety net, given the lack of political power of the poor and working class?

7. What would you do to eliminate child poverty?

8. How do each of the approaches outlined in Chapter 1 add to our understanding of class politics in Canada?

NOTES

1. Irving Abella, ed., *On Strike* (Toronto: James Lewis & Samuel, 1974).
2. Dennis Forcese, *The Canadian Class Structure* (Toronto: McGraw-Hill Ryerson, 1975), p. 14; 4th ed., 1997). Other basic books on class include Alfred A. Hunter, *Class Tells: On Social Inequality in Canada* (Toronto: Butterworths, 1981 and subsequent editions); Henry Veltmeyer, *Canadian Class Structure* (Toronto: Garamond Press, 1986); and James Laxer, *The Undeclared War: Class Conflict in the Age of Cyber Capitalism* (Toronto: Penguin Books, 1998).
3. Neil Nevitte, Herman Bakvis, and Roger Gibbins, "The Ideological Contours of 'New Politics' in Canada: Policy, Mobilization and Partisan Support," *Canadian Journal of Political Science* (September 1989), pp. 475–503; Neil Nevitte, *The Decline of Deference: Canadian Value Change in Cross-National Perspective* (Peterborough: Broadview Press, 1996).

4. Henry Veltmeyer's *Canadian Class Structure* (Toronto: Garamond Press, 1986) is the only attempt by a Canadian sociologist that I could find to estimate the actual number of people in each class. He does so for those in the labour force, and I have generally based Table 8.2 on his figures. But since I am more interested in numbers of *voters* in each class, I had to add spouses, children over 18, and retirees to his figures. I did so by applying an arbitrary factor of 0.5 to the number in each class in the labour force. Union membership in Canada is about 4 million, of whom I arbitrarily placed 1 million in the middle class (unionized teachers, civil servants, etc.). Paid workers number about 11 million, of whom I placed the 1 million mentioned above into the middle class, 1 million as working poor, and the other 9 million as working class. Statistics show about 5 million below the poverty line, but about one-third of these are nonvoting children.

5. Peter C. Newman, *The Canadian Establishment*, vol. 2: *The Acquisitors* (Toronto: McClelland and Stewart, 1990); *Titans: How the New Canadian Establishment Seized Power* (Toronto: Penguin Books, 1998); Diane Francis, *Controlling Interest: Who Owns Canada?* (Toronto: Macmillan, 1986); Tony Clarke, *Silent Coup: Confronting the Big Business Takeover of Canada* (Toronto: Lorimer, 1997); Anton L. Allahar and James E. Côté, *Richer and Poorer: The Structure of Inequality in Canada* (Toronto: Lorimer, 1998); Stephen McBride and John Shields, *Dismantling a Nation: The Transition to Corporate Rule in Canada* (Halifax: Fernwood Publishing, 1997); and the Westhawk Group, *Gross Income: Disclosing Executive Pay in Canada* (Toronto: McGilligan Books, 1997).

6. Wallace Clement, *The Canadian Corporate Elite* (Toronto: McClelland and Stewart, 1975), and his *Continental Corporate Power* (Toronto: McClelland and Stewart, 1977).

7. Clarke, *Silent Coup*; Allahar and Côté, *Richer and Poorer*; Laxer, *The Undeclared War*; Statistics Canada, *Inter-Corporate Ownership 1998*, cat. no. 61-517-XPB (June 1998).

8. Stephen Brooks and Andrew Stritch, *Business and Government in Canada* (Scarborough: Prentice-Hall Canada, 1991), pp. 143–53.

9. R.T. Naylor, *The History of Canadian Business* (Toronto: Lorimer, 1975).

10. Linda McQuaig details "how the rich won control of Canada's tax system ... and ended up richer" in *Behind Closed Doors* (Toronto: Penguin, 1987). See also her *The Quick and the Dead* (Toronto: Penguin, 1991).

11. Newman, *The Acquisitors*, p. 569.

12. *The Toronto Star*, March 20, 1990, p. A23.

13. Colin Campbell, *The Canadian Senate: A Lobby from Within* (Toronto: Macmillan, 1978); John McMenemy, "The Senate as an Instrument of Business and Party," in Paul Fox and Graham White, eds., *Politics: Canada*, 7th ed. (Toronto: McGraw-Hill Ryerson, 1991).

14. Newman, *The Acquisitors*, p. 13.

15. David Lewis, *Louder Voices: Corporate Welfare Bums* (Toronto: James Lewis & Samuel, 1972); R. Chodos and R. Murphy, eds., *Let Us Prey* (Toronto: Lorimer, 1974); Ontario Coalition for Social Justice, *Unfair $hares: Corporations and Taxation in Canada* (March 1998).

16. Alvin Finkel, *Business and Social Reform in the Thirties* (Toronto: Lorimer, 1979), p. 176.

17. Newman, *Titans*, in which Tom d'Aquino boasts of determining the government's whole agenda.

18. Newman, *The Acquisitors*, p. 578.

19. Leo Panitch, "Elites, Classes, and Power," in Michael S. Whittington and Glen Williams, eds., *Canadian Politics in the 1990s*, 4th ed. (Scarborough: Nelson Canada, 1995), p. 168.

20. I owe this observation (as well as many other improvements to the book) to Prof. Jim Silver of the University of Winnipeg.

21. McQuaig, *Behind Closed Doors*.

22. Allan Maslove, *Tax Reform in Canada: The Process and Impact* (Halifax: Institute for Research on Public Policy, 1989).

23. Abella, *On Strike*; Walter Stewart, *Strike!* (Toronto: McClelland and Stewart, 1977), ch. 4.

24. Economic Council of Canada, *Legacies, Twenty-Sixth Annual Review*, 1989, p. 45.

25. Statistics Canada, *The Labour Force Survey*. An alternative source is Statistics Canada, *CALURA, Part II—Labour Unions*.

26. Economic Council of Canada, *Legacies*, p. 41; Statistics Canada, *Labour Force Survey, 1998*.

27. Statistics Canada, *Labour Force Survey, 1998*; *Unionization in Canada: A Retrospective (1995)*, cat. no. 75-001-SPE (Summer 1999).

28. Centre for Social Justice, *The Growing Gap* (Toronto: 1998), p. 13, quoting *The Toronto Star*, March 21, 1998.

29. Clarence Lochhead and Vivian Shalla, "Delivering the Goods: Income Distribution and the Precarious Middle Class," *Perception* 20, no. 1 (Canadian Council on Social Development, 1996); see also Laxer, *The Undeclared War*.

30. Z. Lin, "Employment Insurance in Canada: Recent Trends and Policy Changes," *Canadian Economic Observer* (July 1998).

31. Gad Horowitz, *Canadian Labour in Politics* (Toronto: University of Toronto Press, 1968).

32. The field of social policy analysis is now blessed with a multitude of organizations that provide data relevant here. These include the Canadian Council on Social Development, the National Council of Welfare, the Caledon Institute of Social Policy, the National Anti-Poverty Organization, the Centre for Social Justice, the Ontario Coalition for Social Justice, the Canadian Labour Congress, and the Canadian Centre for Policy Alternatives.

33. These are post-transfer but pre-tax figures on household income. Although the Statistics Canada low-income cutoffs are fairly conservative and could hardly be accused of over-estimating the degree of poverty in the country, Human Resources Canada has recently come up with its own alternative measure of poverty, which it calls a "Market Basket Measure."

34. Canadian Council on Social Development, *The Progress of Canada's Children, 1997*.

35. Canadian Council on Social Development, *The Canadian Poverty Fact Book—1989*, p. 93.

36. Ibid., 1994, p. 2.

37. National Council of Welfare, *Poverty Profile 1993* (Ottawa: Supply and Services, 1995), p. 57.

38. Ibid., 1989, p. 91. As of January, 1999, here are the provincial minimum wage levels, together with the year of their most recent revision: Alberta, $5.90 (1999); BC, $7.15 (1998); Manitoba, $6.00 (1999); New Brunswick, $5.50 (1996); Newfoundland, $5.25 (1997); Nova Scotia, $5.50 (1997); Ontario, $6.85 (1995); PEI, $5.40 (1997); Quebec, $6.90 (1998); Saskatchewan, $6.00 (1999). The federal government used to set a minimum wage for workers in federal jurisdiction, which was once thought to be a model for the provinces to follow, but it now merely defers to the rate in each province. Figures courtesy of the Canadian Council on Social Development, based on Human Resources Development Canada, Labour Program.

39. It was implemented shortly after the Depression, when unemployed men were placed in labour camps. When they began a trek from BC to Ottawa, they were blocked by police in the Regina Riot of July 1, 1935.

40. Denis Guest, *The Emergence of Social Security in Canada* (Vancouver: UBC Press, 1980; 3rd ed., 1998); Jacqueline S. Ismael, ed., *Canadian Social Welfare Policy: Federal and Provincial Dimensions* (Montreal: McGill–Queen's University Press, 1985).

41. Centre for Social Justice, *The Growing Gap*.

42. P.E. Bryden, *Planners and Politicians: Liberal Politics and Social Policy 1957–1968* (Montreal: McGill–Queen's University Press, 1997).

43. Roger S. Smith, *Personal Wealth Taxation* (Toronto: Canadian Tax Foundation, 1993), p. iii.

44. Linda McQuaig, *Shooting the Hippo: Death by Deficit and Other Canadian Myths* (Toronto: Viking, 1995).

45. Walter Stewart, *Dismantling the State* (Toronto: Stoddart, 1998); Don Waterfall, *Dismantling Leviathan: Cutting Government Down to Size* (Toronto: Dundurn Press, 1995); Stephen McBride and John Shields, *Dismantling a Nation* (Halifax: Fernwood Publishing, 1993 and 1997).

46. See, for example, three National Council of Welfare publications: *A Blueprint for Social Security Reform* (Autumn 1994); *The Canada Assistance Plan: No Time For Cuts* (Winter 1991); and *Funding Health and Higher Education: Danger Looming* (Spring 1991); the Caledon Institute of Social Policy, "Green Light, Red Flat: Caledon Statement on the Social Security Review," 1994; Steven Langdon et al., *In the Public Interest: The Value of Public Services* (Prescott: Voyageur Publishing, 1995); NAPO, *Poverty and the Canadian Welfare State: A Report Card* (June 1998); NAPO, *Submission to the United Nations Committee on Economic, Social and Cultural Rights*, November 17, 1998; Ken Battle, "Persistent Poverty," Caledon Institute, December 1997; and the Centre for Social Justice, *The Growing Gap*. It is hard to know the effects of the new National Child Benefit. See Douglas Durst, ed., *Canada's National Child Benefit: Phoenix or Fizzle?* (Halifax: Fernwood Publishing, 1999).

47. Janine Brodie and Jane Jenson, *Crisis, Challenge and Change: Party and Class in Canada Revisited* (Ottawa: Carleton University Press, 1988).

48. Allahar and Côté, *Richer and Poorer*, pp. 24–26; Alan Frizzell and Jon H. Pammett, eds., *Social Inequality in Canada* (Ottawa: Carleton University Press, 1997).

49. Finkel, *Business and Social Reform in the Thirties*.

50. Rodney Haddow, *Poverty Reform in Canada 1958–1978: State and Class Influences on Policy Making* (Montreal: McGill–Queen's University Press, 1993; Rianne Mahon, "Canadian Public Policy: The Unequal Structure of Representation," in Leo Panitch, ed., *The Canadian State: Political Economy and Political Power* (Toronto: University of Toronto Press, 1977).

51. Richard Splane, "Social Policy-Making in the Government of Canada: Reflections of a Reformist Bureaucrat," in S.A. Yelaja, ed., *Canadian Social Policy* (Waterloo: Wilfrid Laurier University Press, 1978).

52. Rand Dyck, "The Canada Assistance Plan: The Ultimate in Cooperative Federalism," *Canadian Public Administration* (Winter 1976), pp. 587–602. Carl Cuneo and Leslie Pal engaged in an interesting intellectual dialogue on the question of the significance of class in the bureaucracy in the March 1986 issue of the *Canadian Journal of Political Science*, pp. 71–102.

53. John Porter, *The Vertical Mosaic* (Toronto: University of Toronto Press, 1965), chs. XI and XVII; Rick Helmes-Hayes and James Curtis, eds., *The Vertical Mosaic Revisited*. Toronto: University of Toronto Press, 1998.

FURTHER READING

Abella, Irving, ed. *On Strike*. Toronto: James Lewis & Samuel, 1974.

Allahar, Anton L., and James E. Côté. *Richer and Poorer: The Structure of Inequality in Canada*. Toronto: Lorimer, 1998.

Brodie, Janine, and Jane Jenson. *Crisis, Challenge and Change: Party and Class in Canada Revisited*. Ottawa: Carleton University Press, 1988.

Brooks, Stephen, and Andrew Stritch. *Business and Government in Canada*. Scarborough: Prentice-Hall Canada, 1991.

Bryden, P.E. *Planners and Politicians: Liberal Politics and Social Policy 1957–1968*. Montreal: McGill–Queen's University Press, 1997.

Centre for Social Justice. *The Growing Gap*. Toronto, 1998.

Clarke, Tony. *Silent Coup: Confronting the Big Business Takeover of Canada*. Toronto: Lorimer, 1997.

Clement, Wallace. *The Canadian Corporate Elite*. Toronto: McClelland and Stewart, 1975.

Coleman, William. *Business and Politics: A Study of Collective Action*. Montreal: McGill–Queen's University Press, 1988.

Durst, Douglas, ed. *Canada's National Child Benefit: Phoenix or Fizzle?* Halifax: Fernwood Publishing, 1999.

Economic Council of Canada. *Legacies, 1989 Annual Review*. Ottawa: Supply and Services, 1989.

Forcese, Dennis. *The Canadian Class Structure*. Toronto: McGraw-Hill Ryerson, 1975; 4th ed., 1997.

Frizzell, Alan, and Jon H. Pammett, eds. *Social Inequality in Canada*. Ottawa: Carleton University Press, 1997.

Guest, Denis. *The Emergence of Social Security in Canada*. Vancouver: University of British Columbia Press, 1980; 3rd ed., 1998.

Haddow, Rodney S. *Poverty Reform in Canada 1958–1978: State and Class Influences on Policy Making*. Montreal: McGill–Queen's University Press, 1993.

Helms-Hayes, Rick, and James Curtis, eds. *The Vertical Mosaic Revisited*. Toronto: University of Toronto Press, 1998.

Langdon, Steven, et al. *In the Public Interest: The Value of Public Services* (Prescott: Voyageur Publishing, 1995).

Laxer, James. *The Undeclared War: Class Conflict in the Age of Cyber Capitalism*. Toronto: Penguin Books, 1998.

Lewis, David. *Louder Voices: The Corporate Welfare Bums*. Toronto: James Lewis & Samuel, 1972.

McBride, Stephen, and John Shields. *Dismantling a Nation: The Transition to Corporate Rule in Canada*, 2nd ed. Halifax: Fernwood Publishing, 1997.

McQuaig, Linda. *Behind Closed Doors*. Toronto: Penguin, 1987.

———. *The Quick and the Dead*. Toronto: Penguin, 1991.

———. *Shooting the Hippo: Death by Deficit and Other Canadian Myths*. Toronto: Viking, 1995.

National Council of Welfare. *Poverty Profile 1993*. Ottawa, 1995.

Newman, Peter C. *Titans: How the New Canadian Establishment Seized Power*. Toronto: Penguin Books, 1998.

Palmer, Bryan. *Working-Class Experience: The Rise and Reconstitution of Canadian Labour, 1800–1980*. Toronto: Butterworth, 1983.

Panitch, Leo, ed. *The Canadian State: Political Economy and Political Power*. Toronto: University of Toronto Press, 1977.

Porter, John. *The Vertical Mosaic*. Toronto: University of Toronto Press, 1965.

Ross, David, and Richard Shillington. *The Canadian Fact Book on Poverty—1994*. Ottawa: Canadian Council on Social Development, 1994.

Stewart, Walter. *Strike!* Toronto: McClelland and Stewart, 1977.

———. *Dismantling the State*. Toronto: Stoddart, 1998.

Veltmeyer, Henry. *Canadian Class Structure*. Toronto: Garamond Press, 1986.

West Hawk Group. *Gross Income: Disclosing Executive Pay in Canada*. Toronto: McGilligan Books, 1997.

Chapter 9
The United States and
THE GLOBAL
environment

The Canadian armed forces have participated in the Gulf War and many United Nations and/or NATO peacekeeping operations. The United States is a major market for Quebec electricity and Alberta petroleum. European and U.S. agricultural subsidies (and the Canadian weather) have nearly destroyed the Canadian grain industry. Canadians watch far more American television than their own, and the United States does not understand why Canada wants to protect its own magazines. Many companies operating in Canada have closed as a result of the combined forces of global restructuring, the early 1990s recession, and the **Canada–U.S. Free Trade Agreement**.

Canada obviously does not exist in a vacuum; instead, it is linked to the rest of the world by all sorts of political, economic, defensive, cultural, demographic, and individual ties. These links constitute the global environment of the Canadian political system; they have an ever-increasing impact upon it, causing Canadian governments more and more difficulty in pursuing their own policy preferences.

The country started as a combination of French and British colonies, with all basic decisions being made abroad. As Canada emerged into a sovereign state, however, the world was becoming increasingly interdependent, so that even though the country gained the legal powers to make decisions for itself, it faced a multitude of external influences. Given its location next to the most powerful country on earth, Canada was particularly susceptible to influence from the United States in the second half of the 20th century and onward into the 21st.

This chapter details Canada's slow but steady absorption into the U.S. sphere of influence. It discusses the demands and pressures that the United States makes on the Canadian political system, the effects of the U.S. presence on Canadian values and opinions, and the policies that have been adopted to both foster and resist such absorption. This influence can be seen most clearly in the areas of defence and foreign policy, economics, and culture. But as if this were not enough, the Canadian political system is increasingly subject to a variety of other international, multinational, and supranational pressures, many of which can be subsumed under the heading of **globalization**. Thus, in the new millennium, Canada will have to contend with many external influences beyond those of the United States.

The chapter begins with a discussion of this wider context. In particular, it introduces the foreign governments, international organizations, international agreements, and transnational corporations that constitute our principal external links.

THE GLOBAL SETTING

Foreign Governments

Foreign governments take decisions every day, in both foreign and domestic policy, that can have some effect on Canada. Sometimes this impact is deliberate, but often it is unintentional. Of course, it is the responsibility of our foreign affairs officials (and in really crucial situations, the minister of Foreign Affairs, the minister of Finance, or even the prime minister) to put pressure on such governments so that their decisions are not harmful to Canada. By far the most likely foreign government policies to have an impact on Canada are those of the United States, and these will be detailed below under the headings of Defence Policy, Foreign Policy, the Economy, and Culture.

An unending list of other countries' policies could also be provided, of which a few examples will have to suffice. Looking at Canada's second largest trading partner, the European Union, one dispute concerned the EU regulation banning the import of furs from animals caught using leg-hold traps. Another was the EU rejection of our lumber exports because of its concern about Canadian forestry practices, as well as the EU requirement that all softwood lumber imports from Canada be treated to kill the pinewood nematode beetle. There were also disagreements over the labelling of champagne and scallops exported from Canada. On the other hand, Canada had long complained about a number of European countries that over-fished within Canadian territorial waters. This issue came to a head in 1995 when Canadian authorities seized a Spanish vessel off the coast of Newfoundland because of the excessive quantity of turbot on board. European agricultural subsidies are also a source of great distress to Canadian policymakers. On a different plane, the Canadian government (and Canadian public) are regularly solicited for financial and other assistance in the wake of natural disasters in one country or another. One example was the 1998 call from Honduras and Nicaragua after the destruction of Hurricane Mitch in that region; in 1999, it was an earthquake in Turkey.

International Organizations

Canada has joined a multitude of international organizations with the aim of taking advantage of opportunities to influence other countries' policies, to expand our external trade, and to promote joint objectives with other states. Nevertheless, such membership often entails obligations and responsibilities that influence Canadian domestic or foreign policies. A list of the principal international organizations to which Canada belongs follows, but a few examples of how such organizations have an impact on Canadian policies should be mentioned. Belonging to the United Nations, perhaps especially when Canada also sits on the Security Council, gives a middle-ranking country such as this a platform to promote its altruistic as well as its self-interested objectives. But the UN also makes claims on Canada, such as to pay our regular share of its budget and to answer the call (and pay the bill) whenever it decides to set up a peacekeeping force in far-flung trouble spots around the world. The United Nations has also criticized several domestic Canadian policies, including Quebec language legislation and federal and provincial laws on labour, Aboriginals, and women. As mentioned in Chapter 8, the UN Economic, Social and Cultural Affairs Committee raked Canada over the coals in 1998 for the deterioration of its social programs. Although the United Nations has few coercive resources to apply to governments that break their commitments to its covenants, the organization wields considerable prestige, and its moral suasion is sometimes enough to make governments change their domestic policies.

··

LEADING INTERNATIONAL ORGANIZATIONS TO WHICH CANADA BELONGS

- The United Nations
- The World Trade Organization
- NATO
- NORAD
- The International Monetary Fund and the World Bank
- The Organisation for Economic Co-operation and Development (OECD)
- The Commonwealth
- La Francophonie
- The Organization of American States
- The G7 and G8
- Asia–Pacific Economic Cooperation Council (APEC)

The **World Trade Organization (WTO)** (successor to the General Agreement on Tariffs and Trade) can actually order its members to change their trading practices. For example, in the Uruguay Round of GATT talks, Canada agreed to abandon its historic use of marketing boards. Then, in response to American complaints regarding split-run magazines, the WTO ordered Canada to discontinue a federal excise tax and postal subsidies to protect domestic magazines. It has also ruled on such issues as the EU ban on Canadian beef, Canadian and Brazilian subsidies to their aerospace industries, and what it deemed to be export subsidies to Canadian dairy products. Canada even expected to lose cases dealing with drug patent policy and the 1965 Canada–U.S. Auto Pact. The WTO has thus become a huge impediment to the pursuit of Canadian government policies, that is, Canadian **sovereignty**, in a wide range of sensitive fields.

The WTO is not alone. The International Monetary Fund puts pressure on member countries with respect to the size of national deficits, advising the Canadian government in 1991 not to raise public servants' salaries and in 1999 to cut income taxes and the debt. When the leaders of the Asia-Pacific Economic Cooperation (APEC) summit met in Vancouver in 1997, the treatment of those who were protesting the ruthless dictators among them became a leading domestic political issue in Canada. International organizations to which Canada does not belong can also take decisions that have a major influence on domestic policies. The Organization of Petroleum Exporting Countries (OPEC) raised the international price of oil in the early 1970s with dramatic implications for Canadian petroleum policies.

Standing from left, Mexican President Carlos Salinas de Gortari, U.S. President George Bush, and Prime Minister Brian Mulroney are all smiles as their respective trade representatives, Jaime Serra Puche, Carla Hills, and Michael Wilson, initial the North American Free Trade Agreement in San Antonio, 1992. (Pat Sullivan/Canapress)

International Agreements

Beyond the obligations and covenants of such international organizations as mentioned above, Canada often signs international agreements with one or more foreign government. Once again, such agreements usually present both opportunities and obligations and provide a certain amount of constraint on subsequent domestic policymaking. Of all such agreements signed by Canada over the years, the Canada–U.S. Free Trade Agreement and the North American Free Trade Agreement stand out.

THE CANADA–U.S. FREE TRADE AGREEMENT

The 1989 Free Trade Agreement (FTA) between Canada and the United States was probably the most significant that this country ever signed. It is a wide-ranging pact that covers almost every aspect of the bilateral relationship.[1] The agreement removed almost all barriers to the cross-border flow of goods and services between the two countries. Each could henceforth send its products to the other without tariffs, quotas, or other impediments, but each continued to apply its own tariffs to imports from other countries. Goods had to be at least 50 percent domestically produced in order to qualify, and most services were also included. Specific provisions related to agriculture, energy, automobiles, investment, financial services, the entry of businesspersons, and the procurement clause, which provided that every government contract over $25 000 had to be open to bids from either country. For any future conflicts in trade between the two countries, a complex **dispute-settlement mechanism** involving binational panels and binding arbitration was set up. If either country refused to abide by the final decision of the arbitrators, however, the other could retaliate ("countervail"), as before.

When it is said that "either country could send its goods and services across the border without impediment," what is meant is that in general neither government could regulate, restrict, or tax such goods and services as they crossed the border. This is because for most purposes the two countries were to be seen as a single market in which corporations based in either were to be treated equally.[2] In other words, free trade deals are primarily about reducing the role of government and turning more powers over to corporations in the marketplace. It is a tremendous concession to corporations for governments to voluntarily abandon their powers in this way.

NAFTA

The ink was hardly dry on the Canada–U.S. Free Trade Agreement when the Mulroney government began talks with the United States and Mexico about a **North American Free Trade**

Agreement (NAFTA). This agreement essentially extended the FTA to Mexico, and most provisions in the two agreements were identical. (Thus, the expression NAFTA is now commonly used to include both agreements.) Canada entered the agreement mainly to prevent the other partners from endangering its position, although some corporations saw it as a means of enhancing the efficiency of their operations. Much like its predecessor, the major components of NAFTA included agriculture, the auto industry, business and professional services, energy, financial services, investment, telecommunications, textiles and apparel, and transportation.[3]

Opponents feared that companies would move from Canada to Mexico because of the low wages and environmental standards in that country; they also complained that Mexico was able to negotiate stronger clauses on energy and culture than had Canada under the FTA. While the Canadian government claimed that certain domestic services and industries were either protected or not affected by NAFTA (culture, water, environmental, health, safety and labour standards, and social programs), critics noted that the protective wording in these fields was weak.[4] Despite pre-election fanfare, the Chrétien government was content with minor changes in the pact once in power. It established the office of the environmental arm of the agreement in Montreal. Not long afterwards, Canada signed a separate free trade deal with Chile, while talks continued toward establishing a Free Trade Area of the Americas, encompassing the 34 countries of the whole hemisphere, by 2005. In the wake of these agreements came the "Open Skies" agreement with the United States in 1995. It essentially deregulated the cross-border airline industry, giving U.S. and Canadian companies equal access to routes between the two countries.

Transnational Corporations and Globalization

The pressures exerted by a foreign government are often made on behalf of corporations with head offices in that country, and international agreements are often about removing government controls on corporate behaviour. This sometimes makes it difficult to distinguish

By Adrian Raeside (Victoria Times-Colonist). Used with permission.

between pressures exerted by foreign governments as opposed to those of **transnational corporations**, but here we will try to focus on corporations themselves. Transnational corporations have always made demands on domestic political systems wherever they established themselves, but traditionally these did not differ in kind from those of companies headquartered in that country. Globalization is changing the nature of corporate behaviour, however, whether in the economic or political spheres. It is commonly characterized by the lowering of tariffs and creation of larger free trading areas and by the increasing mobility of capital and worldwide corporate competition. Such "economic forces have pushed the issue of market liberalization to the forefront" and capital's perception "that there is too much government hindering the globalization process ... had led to an assault on the powers of the nation-state."[5] The world is increasingly one integrated global economic unit in which national boundaries are much less significant than in the past.

The globalization that has characterized corporate behaviour in recent years has meant that more companies are outgrowing their domestic state, that they are introducing new forms of technology at an incredible rate, that they are merging and taking each other over, and that they are opening or closing operations strictly on the basis of economic efficiency and without regard to traditional location. Corporate money, banking, finance, and investment flow between countries almost at will. Such globalization has had many implications for the Canadian economy, mostly as the result of transnational corporations closing their manufacturing plants in this country. The main political implication of globalization is that it is increasingly difficult for national or provincial governments to maintain distinctive labour, tax, or environmental laws because such companies regularly threaten to move to other jurisdictions that they find more congenial.

• •

PRINCIPAL CHARACTERISTICS OF GLOBALIZATION

- Comprehensive free trade agreements
- Removal of state controls on corporate behaviour
- Cross-border capital flows
- World-wide corporate competition
- Mega-mergers of largest transnational corporations
- Massive diffusion of technological change and corporate specialization
- Closure of transnational plants in developed countries and migration to the Third World

While NAFTA and the WTO have already placed many impediments on member states to confine the scope of their policymaking, one effort that would have gone considerably further was the **Multilateral Agreement on Investment (MAI)**. This proposal was discussed among the highly industrialized OECD countries. To its supporters, the MAI was merely an international investment agreement that would set rules for the operation of the global economy so that Canadian companies investing abroad could expect fair treatment and vice versa. But its opponents saw it as a comprehensive charter of rights for transnational corporations "restricting what governments can do to regulate foreign investment and corporate behaviour, and creating new rights for corporations to challenge government decisions."[6] Critics argued that governments would be hobbled in their objectives of taxing, regulating, and setting standards and that Canada would no longer be able to give preference to its own people via tax breaks, subsidies, grants, or other support to promote employment, research and development, or Canadian content. Although the Canadian government was intimately involved in these negotiations, it maintained that it intended to hold out for a whole list of exemptions. In a remarkable effort of multinational grassroots organization (perhaps an example of the more positive side of globalization), including the Council of Canadians, the OECD was persuaded to abandon the project, but it will likely be picked up by the WTO before long.

....

GLOBAL INFLUENCES IN DEFENCE AND FOREIGN POLICY
Defence Policy

Shortly after Confederation, Britain withdrew its garrisons from Canada and left the colony to fend for itself militarily. Neither that nor Canada's colonial status stopped Britain from expecting Canadian assistance in the Boer War around the turn of the century and much greater military support in the First World War, however irrelevant these wars were to Canada.

Canada's first military engagement after achieving full autonomy was the Second World War. The United States did not enter the war until the end of 1941, although for two years it cheered on the Allied forces from the sidelines. In 1940, Canada and the United States signed the Ogdensburg Agreement, which set up the Canada–United States Permanent Joint Board on Defence to study the common defence problems of the two countries and make recommendations to their governments. In 1941, the Hyde Park Declaration extended the planning of continental defence to cover the production of war materials.

After the war, the United States became increasingly obsessed with containing Soviet communism and in 1949 persuaded Canada and most Western European countries to form a new military alliance, the North Atlantic Treaty Organization (NATO). Commitments to NATO required a great increase in the size of the Canadian armed forces. U.S. attention was then drawn to the confrontation between North and South Korea. The UN military intervention in the Korean War was effectively a U.S. effort, to which Canada made a significant military contribution and lost 1550 lives.

The next phase of the North Americanization of Canadian defence was a series of radar lines built across northern Canada in the 1950s to intercept anticipated Soviet bombers. One of these, the Distant Early Warning (DEW) Line, was installed and staffed by the United States. These arrangements logically led to the North American Aerospace Defence Command (NORAD) of 1958. This agreement provided for a joint Canada–U.S. air defence system with headquarters in Colorado; an American was commander-in-chief and a Canadian was second in command. A Defence Production Sharing Program was established in 1959, the same year in which the Diefenbaker government cancelled the legendary Canadian airplane, the Avro Arrow. The advisability of this cancellation continues to be debated, but it meant the continued reliance on foreign-produced aircraft for Canadian air defence.[7]

Diefenbaker also encountered two serious missile crises in the 1957–63 period. When U.S. President John Kennedy used the establishment of Soviet missile bases in Cuba as an excuse to announce a naval blockade of that country, the Canadian Cabinet waited three days before putting its armed forces in a state of highest alert. Since the Americans expected this would be done automatically, the Cuban missile crisis soured relations between the two leaders, and this state was further compounded by American annoyance at Canada's stand with respect to BOMARC missiles. These had been established by the United States at two bases in Canada as part of the NORAD Agreement and were intended to be armed with nuclear warheads. Some Cabinet ministers wished to take possession of the warheads as planned, but others argued that to place the warheads on Canadian soil would appear to proliferate the nuclear arms race. The Canadian–American defence relationship became a prominent issue in the 1962 and 1963 election campaigns. The Diefenbaker government eventually fell apart over the issue in 1963: it was defeated on a nonconfidence motion, and the Liberals won the resulting election under Lester Pearson. The new prime minister had the warheads installed as part of Canada's international commitments, but they were ultimately removed in 1971.

Pearson's successor, Pierre Trudeau, cut defence spending, and in a new emphasis on protecting domestic sovereignty, he halved Canada's NATO contingent in 1969. Nevertheless, Canada repeatedly renewed the NORAD Agreement and eventually bought another foreign plane, the F-18, to replace its archaic military aircraft. The most prominent new issue had to do with allowing the United States to test yet another new weapon, the Cruise missile, over Canadian territory because of the resemblance of its terrain to that of the Soviet Union. In spite of considerable popular protest, the Trudeau government allowed the tests to take place starting in 1983, as did succeeding governments.[8]

The Mulroney government promised to make defence a much higher priority than during the Trudeau years, and published a hawkish white paper on the subject in 1987. Partly due to public opposition, and partly to budgetary considerations, the paper was not implemented, a decision that was vindicated when the Cold War effectively ended a year or so later. On the other hand, when Iraq invaded Kuwait in 1990, Canada readily agreed to participate in the U.S.-led Gulf War coalition, which was, like the Korean affair, theoretically a United Nations operation, and then in the various phases of the Balkan war. Even though the Cold War was over, the Chrétien government renewed the NORAD agreement in 1996 and soon felt United States pressure to agree to a new continental missile defence system.

Thus it is clear that before 1931 Britain continued to influence Canadian military operations, and that from 1945 to 1991 the United States exerted significant pressure on Canadian defence policy. Even though Canada did not always respond as energetically as the United States wished, such external demands influenced Canadian political outcomes, particularly helping to defeat the Diefenbaker government. Some Canadians were satisfied with the arrangement because the country was protected by the U.S. military arsenal and had to pay relatively little for its own defence. Others did not like the U.S. pressure and the loss of control of a vital aspect of public policy.

Foreign Policy

To the extent that foreign policy can be distinguished from defence policy, the degree of U.S. influence in this field has also been a controversial question.[9] Canada sees itself as a "middle power" that has staked out an independent position on recognizing and/or trading with countries such as China, Cuba, and the Soviet Union. While Canada did not become directly involved in the Vietnam War, many Canadians would have preferred a foreign policy more critical of many U.S. military or diplomatic initiatives around the world, such as in Latin

America, Korea, and Nicaragua. Nevertheless, the Canadian government was quick to respond to U.S. demands to contribute to its military efforts in the Gulf War and its peacekeeping mission to intervene in the fighting among warlords in Somalia, both ostensibly in the name of the United Nations. Throughout the 1990s, the United States threatened to retaliate against Canada because of its trade with Cuba, especially by means of the Helms-Burton Act.

In response to broader international pressure, Canada made a major contribution in the Bosnian civil war, as well as trying to end the tribal warfare in Rwanda. Such humanitarian interventions sparked debate within Canada, other countries, and the United Nations over the kind of rapid-reaction force most appropriate. Canada had an impressive record as an international peacekeeper, having participated in some 63 such exercises, but the behaviour of the Airborne Regiment in Somalia somewhat sullied this reputation. Nevertheless, Canada continues to contribute to some 15 peacekeeping operations around the world, including NATO's stabilization force in Bosnia-Herzegovina.

As we enter the new millennium, Canada has undertaken a number of new initiatives that have wide support around the world but often not as much next door. Canada was a leader in the campaign to ban anti-personnel landmines, which culminated in an anti-landmines treaty signed in Ottawa in 1997. This country was also at the forefront of the effort to establish an International Criminal Court, building on its active participation in prosecuting former Yugoslavian war criminals before the UN International Criminal Tribunal. Foreign Affairs Minister Lloyd Axworthy put these and other initiatives (cross-border problems with illicit drugs, weapons, terrorism, refugees, and the environment) in the context of a move from concentrating on "state security" to "human security" and from peacekeeping to peacebuilding.[10]

GLOBAL ECONOMIC INFLUENCES ON CANADA

The U.S. economic influence on Canada is even more pervasive than its impact on defence and foreign policy. This influence is felt in almost every aspect of Canadian life, including investment, trade, environment, energy, government borrowing, and labour unions. Much of this pressure pre-dated the Canada–U.S. Free Trade and the North American Free Trade agreements, whose effects go far beyond trade, but those two treaties only exacerbated it. In many ways, Canada constitutes a zone within the American economy rather than a distinctive national economy,[11] although in other ways Canada is increasingly under a broader range of external economic influences.

Foreign Investment

In the "British period" of Canadian history, a great deal of investment in Canada came from Britain. Some of this foreign capital was in the form of British companies operating in Canada such as the Hudson's Bay Co., but to a large extent it took the form of Canadian borrowing in the London bond market in what is called "portfolio investment" or "debt securities." Interest had to be paid on such loans, but ownership remained largely in Canadian hands.

When Canada entered the "American period" of its history, the source of foreign investment largely shifted from Britain to the United States and the form of investment switched from loans to "direct" or "equity" investment, that is, control through the ownership of shares. Thus, to a large extent the Canadian economy has come to consist of branch plants of U.S. parent corporations. These companies typically operate in many other countries, too, and therefore gain the label of "multinational" or transnational corporations. Table 9.1 indicates the shift from British to U.S. investment in Canada between 1900 and 1967.

This pattern of economic development was fostered in the first instance by the National Policy of 1879, which put a tariff on imported manufactured goods. Rather than export to Canada from the United States and pay the tariff, American companies set up branch plants within Canada behind the tariff wall. This was advantageous for the creation of employment in Canada and contributed to the general prosperity of the country. Partly because U.S. entrepreneurs were more inclined to take risks than Canadians and partly because Canadian banks were more willing to lend money to established foreign companies, the degree of foreign ownership continued to increase.

It was not only U.S. manufacturers that attracted favourable consideration from Canadian banks; so too did foreign companies that sought to exploit Canadian natural resources. "A large proportion of the investment in resource exploitation reflected the needs of the United States investors for raw materials for their processing and manufacturing plants in the United States." This integration often had the practical impact "of reducing the likelihood of further processing activity of Canadian natural resources in Canada."[12] Thus, along with many aspects of manufacturing, the mining, forestry, and petroleum industries came to be characterized by a high degree of foreign, mostly U.S., ownership. In fact, the **Gray Report** of 1972 (*Foreign Direct Investment in Canada*) began with these words: "The degree of foreign ownership and control of economic activity is already substantially higher in Canada than in any other industrialized country and is continuing to increase."[13]

The ten largest multinationals operating in Canada in 1999 are identified in Table 9.2. Other familiar corporate names that are foreign-owned include Mitsui & Co., A & P, Mobil Oil, Costco., Ultramar, Weyerhaeuser, DuPont, General Electric, McDonald's, Toyota, Pratt & Whitney, Mitsubishi, Chevron, John Deere, Hewlett-Packard, Husky Oil, Nabisco, Nestlé, Kraft, Dow Chemical, and Pepsi-Cola. In total, 30 of the top 100 companies in Canada in terms of 1999 revenue were foreign-owned.

TABLE 9.1　**Percentage of British, U.S., and Other Foreign Investments in Canada, 1900–1967**

	1900	1914	1930	1939	1946	1950	1960	1967
U.S.	13.6	23.0	61.2	60.0	71.8	75.5	75.2	80.7
U.K.	85.2	72.4	36.3	35.8	23.2	20.1	15.1	10.3
Other	1.1	4.6	2.4	4.1	4.9	4.2	9.6	8.9

Source: Privy Council Office, Foreign Direct Investment in Canada, *p. 15. Reproduced with the permission of the Minister of Public Works and Government Services Canada, 2000.*

TABLE 9.2   **The Ten Largest Multinational Corporations in Canada, 1999**

General Motors of Canada Ltd. (U.S.)	Sears Canada Inc. (U.S.)
Ford Motor Co. of Canada Ltd. (U.S.)	Honda Canada Inc. (Japan)
Chrysler Canada Ltd. (U.S.)	Canada Safeway Ltd. (U.S.)
IBM Canada Ltd. (U.S.)	Shell Canada Ltd. (Netherlands)
Imperial Oil Ltd. (U.S.)	Cargill Ltd. (U.S.)

Source: The Financial Post 500, *Summer 1999. Reproduced with permission.*

Most advocates of the capitalist system such as "free market" economists are enthusiastic boosters of unlimited foreign investment, and it is now the policy of the Canadian government to seek such investment at every opportunity. Such advocates claim that maximum efficiency results from capital being able to flow wherever it will yield the greatest returns. In this case, defenders of foreign investment argue that Canada still needs foreign capital and that such investment creates jobs, which in turn raise the Canadian standard of living. They also say that Canadians are too timid to take advantage of risky investment opportunities in their own country and that efficiency is enhanced when multinationals transfer "state-of-the-art" technology as well as well-trained managers and management techniques to their branch plants.

Others take the view that these advantages are short-term or short-sighted.[14] In the first place, more capital may eventually flow out of the country in interest and dividends than was originally brought in. Second, multinationals are likely to purchase supplies and component parts from the parent company or parent country, rather than buying them and creating employment in Canada. Third, such plants usually remain small and inefficient ("truncated") because they are designed to serve only the Canadian market rather than being encouraged to compete in export markets with the parent plant or branches set up in other countries. Critics also claim that a branch plant economy suffers because most of its research and development (R&D) is done in the parent plant. This limits the number of interesting and challenging jobs in science, engineering, and technology located in Canada. As convenient as it is to import such technology, this process hinders Canadian innovative efforts to develop distinctive export products, for almost all studies indicate that R&D and the resulting increase in productivity are the secrets of future economic success.

Critics of the situation also worry that decisions of multinational corporations, while based on the same profit motive as those of domestic firms, are less likely to conform to the Canadian national interest. If layoffs or shutdowns are necessary, for example, these are usually slated for branch plants first, and such a high degree of U.S. ownership perpetuates the resource-export orientation of the Canadian economy. The ultimate symbolic disadvantage of foreign-owned companies is that they may occasionally choose or be required to conform to the laws of the country in which their parent is located rather than those of Canada. The extension of U.S. laws to branch plants located in Canada is called **extraterritoriality**, and has regularly occurred, especially in the case of the Trading with the Enemy Act. When such branch plants in Canada have tried to do business with countries on the U.S. "enemy list," they have been told that they must follow U.S. law, thus reducing production and job opportunities in Canada.

More recent statistics on the state of foreign investment in various Canadian industries are shown in Table 9.3. The proportion of foreign control declined between 1971 and 1984 but has increased ever since. In 1996, as measured by operating revenues, foreigners controlled over 50 percent of three industries: chemicals, chemical products (pharmaceuticals) and textiles, transportation equipment (automobiles), and electrical and electronic products. Not surprisingly, the United States is the parental home of 53.6 percent of the 12 725 foreign-owned corporations in Canada. The low value of the Canadian dollar made Canadian firms ripe for sale to foreigners, recent examples being the Weyerhaeuser takeover of MacMillan Bloedel in the forestry industry, the CIT Group purchase of Newcourt Credit, and the sale of fibre-optics maker JDS Fitel to Uniphase Corp.

The policies that Canadian governments have adopted to counter this threat of U.S. or other foreign ownership and control of the Canadian economy can be divided into four main categories. First, Crown corporations have been established, partly to ensure that the company involved remains in Canadian hands. The Bank of Canada, Atomic Energy of Canada Ltd., and Petro-Canada were federal outputs developed in response to demands that a Canadian presence in strategic industries be retained.

Second, while leaving other corporations to function privately, the federal government often created regulatory agencies. The principal government response to the Gray Report was

TABLE 9.3   **Foreign-Controlled Shares of Various Canadian Industries, 1996 (Percentage)**

Wood and paper	28.9
Energy	35.9
Chemicals, chemical products, textiles	64.4
Metallic minerals and metal products	29.4
Machinery and equipment	37.0
Transportation equipment	57.8
Electrical and electronic products	56.4
Construction and real estate	10.4
Communications	16.5
Services	13.3
Consumer goods and services	23.2
Finance and insurance industries	27.0
All industries	31.1

Source: Adapted from Statistics Canada, CALURA—Part I—Corporations, 1996, Catalogue No. 61-220.

the creation of the **Foreign Investment Review Agency (FIRA)**. FIRA "screened" foreign takeovers of larger Canadian companies and new ventures by foreign firms in Canada in much the same way as took place in other countries, approving the deal if it involved "significant benefit to Canada." Although the Cabinet rarely disallowed any such initiatives and imposed minimal conditions, and although the agency had no jurisdiction at all over the expansion of existing foreign interests already in Canada and was not taken seriously by Canadian nationalists, FIRA became a major irritant to the United States. The first act of the less nationalistic Mulroney government in 1984 therefore was to replace FIRA with Investment Canada. In its recast form, the agency had the opposite objective of attracting increased foreign investment to Canada. Then, in the Canada–U.S. Free Trade Agreement, Investment Canada was restricted to screening acquisitions of firms with a value over $150 million and could not impose any performance requirements. The 25 percent ceiling on foreign ownership of Canadian banks was eliminated for U.S. investors, and the latter would now be able to start new operations in Canada without restriction. The National Energy Board, the Atomic Energy Control Board, and the Canadian Transportation Authority were other regulatory agencies designed to protect the Canadian national interest in important respects.

In the third place, ownership restrictions and tax incentives were introduced. Maximum foreign ownership limits exist in certain fields such as broadcasting, financial institutions, newspapers and publishing, and, before the Free Trade Agreement, banking. Incentives to Canadian ownership were exemplified by the National Energy Program of 1980. Its incentive (largely tax write-offs) was sufficient to persuade the Reichmann brothers to buy Gulf Canada from its American owners. Finally, the government established funding agencies such as the Business Development Bank of Canada, whose mandate is to encourage Canadian entrepreneurship when the commercial banks are not interested.

Many of these policies were half-hearted and others were later diluted under U.S. pressure. Many were weakened or withdrawn by the Mulroney government, both to increase foreign investment and to remove irritants in the Canada–U.S. relationship. Although the degree of foreign investment has increased considerably since the mid-1980s, hardly anyone is concerned in this era of globalization. A few economic nationalists regard the situation as more critical than ever, especially in the light of the Free Trade Agreement, but most observers remain indifferent or take the opposite side of this issue, seeing foreign investment as the source of badly needed jobs. Perhaps of greater current concern is the tendency of Canadian companies to move some of their head-office functions to the United States, as in the case of Seagram, Nortel Networks, and Nova Chemicals.

Trade

External trade constitutes over 30 percent of Canada's national income and provides about three million jobs. At the same time as they try to maximize their exports, all countries seek to protect their domestic industry from foreign competition through the imposition of tariffs, quotas, customs duties, and the like. In 1947, however, Canada was among the signatories of the General Agreement on Tariffs and Trade (GATT) under which countries pledged to remove such trade restrictions on a multinational basis. GATT allows its members to go even further with bilateral agreements, as Canada and the United States did in defence production arrangements.

Canadian exports to the United States exceeded those to the United Kingdom after 1921 and edged up to over 81 percent by 1997. Imports from the United States constituted nearly 50 percent of the Canadian total from the start and rose to 76 percent in 1997, as indicated in Table 9.4. Because of geographic proximity, it is only logical that Canada and the United States be closely linked by trade. It is even more likely because of their complementary resources and industries—the abundance of primary resources in Canada and the amount of manufacturing in the United States. Indeed, provinces trade more with neighbouring states than with each other, although much of this trade is of an intrafirm character rather than truly international.

Given the degree to which Canadian prosperity depends on export trade, it is advantageous to have ready access to the U.S. market; it is also convenient to have such a close supply of goods that are not produced in Canada. On the other hand, to have put so many eggs in one basket means that in times of U.S. recession, demand for Canadian goods falls off and the Canadian economy takes a nose-dive too; and in prosperous periods, U.S. inflation also tends to increase prices in Canada. Furthermore, protectionist pressure in the United States for new or increased tariffs or quotas against Canadian exports can have a devastating effect on certain industries. Canada often has a positive balance with the United States in merchandise trade, but this is somewhat artificial, given the extent of imported parts within the exported goods; moreover, the nonmerchandise sector, which includes travel, services, and outflowing profits and dividends, usually results in an overall Canadian deficit in the total trade between the two countries.

Canadian policymakers had been concerned for some time that the country was dangerously dependent on the U.S. economy while being left out of the various regional trading blocks being formed, especially the EEC (now the European Union). The Diefenbaker and Trudeau governments tried unsuccessfully to diversify the Canadian export market to Britain

TABLE 9.4 Canadian Exports to and Imports from the United States, Selected Years, 1886–1997 (Balance of Payments Basis, Percentage)

	Exports to U.S.	*Imports from U.S.*
1886	44	44
1911	38	61
1921	46	69
1951	59	69
1967	64	72
1977	70	70
1986	78	69
1993	80	73
1997	81	76

Source: Adapted from Statistics Canada, Canada Year Book, Catalogue No. 11-402; and the Statistics Canada website <www.statcan.ca>, Imports and Exports of Goods on a Balance-of-Payments Basis (after 1991).

and Europe respectively, while the Pearson government signed the sectoral **Auto Pact** with the United States to guarantee a balanced exchange of automobiles and parts. Trudeau also sought to negotiate other sectoral free trade deals with the United States, but the latter was not interested. In fact, a protectionist mood descended on the U.S. Congress in the early 1980s, and new barriers to many Canadian exports were imposed: on shakes and shingles, softwood lumber, potash, potatoes, fish, and specialty steel.

Modern pressure for a free trade agreement with the United States came largely from the corporate sector, led by the Business Council on National issues, and especially Western Canadian resource producers, whose spokesman was former Alberta premier Peter Lougheed. The issue was also popularized by the right-wing think tank, the C.D. Howe Institute, and by a Senate committee report. Brian Mulroney was apparently converted when U.S. protectionist measures began to be felt in Canada and when the Trudeau-appointed Macdonald Royal Commission on the Economic Union and Development Prospects for Canada recommended that the country take such a "leap of faith." Mulroney found an advocate of free trade in the White House, so he and Ronald Reagan set the negotiations in motion. After many ups and downs, the Canada–U.S. Free Trade Agreement was finalized in October 1987, and took effect January 1, 1989.[15]

Those Canadians who favoured the agreement argued that in the absence of the deal the United States would have continued to apply a series of protectionist measures, threatening more jobs.[16] Canadian firms would now have access to the huge unprotected U.S. market, allowing them to expand and create employment. Supporters of the FTA admitted that many Canadian firms would go under and thousands of Canadian jobs would be lost because of the competition from larger American companies, but they claimed that such competition would force Canadian corporations to become stronger, more specialized and efficient, and more capable of functioning in the global economy. Defenders also hailed the likelihood of increased U.S. investment in Canada, as well as higher levels of investment from other countries wishing to take advantage of Canadian access to the U.S. market. Many asked whether any practical alternative existed.

While the Conservative government found supporters of the Free Trade Agreement among big business, Western resource industries, and the province of Quebec, the federal Liberal and New Democratic parties opposed it, along with the province of Ontario, organized labour, and nationalist groups.[17] Opponents argued that the deal would lead to a loss of jobs rather than an increase, because the Canadian market would be inundated by U.S. exports and small Canadian firms would not be able to compete. Massive layoffs and shutdowns were predicted, particularly in such industries as processed food, electrical goods, textiles, clothing, and footwear, industries where the labour force was largely female. Jobs would also be lost because U.S. branch plants would close, supplying the Canadian market instead from the parent plant south of the border, and some Canadian firms would move to the United States to take advantage of backward labour and environmental laws in certain states. It was clearly designed, they said, to enshrine neoconservative values and corporate rights and prevent the recurrence of such economic nationalistic measures as FIRA and the National Energy Program.[18] Nationalists also argued that the United States was a faltering industrial giant, with its large government and foreign trade deficits, and was not a reliable market. They felt that for reasons outlined throughout this chapter, the existing degree of integration of the two countries' economies was already detrimental to Canadian interests. Many were dissatisfied with the dispute-settlement mechanism, which would not ultimately prevent some of the incidents that inspired the deal in the first place.

Many opponents worried that the final definition of "unfair subsidy" would endanger agricultural marketing boards, regional development programs, and the Canadian social safety net. They expected pressure for policy harmonization in every field: taxation, pollution control and product standards, and social programs. Opponents also saw threats to basic Canadian values, in which there would be pressure for less government, less caring and equality, more social Darwinism ("survival of the fittest"), and more obsession with profits. Finally, they felt that the Free Trade Agreement would reduce Canadian flexibility of action on the world stage and limit its ability to pursue an independent Canadian foreign policy.

The results have been mixed. On the one hand, trade between Canada and the United States has boomed in both directions; on the other, thousands of Canadian manufacturing jobs have disappeared. Some of the broader fears may have been overblown, and where they have been realized, it is sometimes impossible to separate the effects of the Free Trade Agreement from those of technological change, globalization, the low value of the Canadian dollar, worldwide neoconservative forces, and the early 1990s recession. The number of conflicts has been large, however, and some of the same issues that precipitated the Free Trade Agreement have continued to be problematic, especially Canadian exports of softwood lumber, the agricultural sector, and cultural industries. Specific areas of dispute include uranium, beer, magnesium, steel, swine, wheat, sugar, peanut butter, tobacco, milk, meat, paper, salmon and herring, poultry products, magazine publishing, and country-music television. Angry American farmers have blockaded the border in protest against agricultural imports from Canada, and other specific problems will be mentioned below. As far as the FTA leading to even further integration is concerned, in 1999 the continentalist C.D. Howe Institute predictably urged Canada to adopt the U.S. dollar as its currency.

In 1997, the European Union (EU) collectively constituted Canada's second-largest export market at 5.5 percent, and Japan was third at 4.0 percent. Similarly, on the import side, the collective EU was our second-largest supplier, at 8.7 percent, and Japan was third at 3.1 percent. Before the signing of NAFTA, Canadian trade with Mexico was negligible.

The Environment

Canadians have seriously damaged their own environment over the years, but the situation has been aggravated by proximity to the United States and by some of its even less restrictive anti-pollution laws. The largest transboundary environmental issue is that of acid rain. Canadian research generally shows that about 50 percent of the acid rain falling north of the Canada–U.S. border is caused by U.S. sources. The primary cause is sulphur dioxide emitted from coal-burning hydroelectric plants in the Ohio Valley. These emissions flow northward and fall into Canadian lakes and rivers, killing plant and animal life, as well as damaging trees, cars, and buildings. Thus, after pressing the issue for many years, Canada welcomed the U.S. Clean Air Act of 1990 as a major forward step in controlling North American air pollution.

The pollution of the Great Lakes is the other serious bilateral environmental problem. Here again, most of the responsibility rests with the chemicals discharged from the larger proportion of factories and waste dumps situated on the U.S. shores of the lakes. Phosphorus levels were reduced in the 1970s, but the Great Lakes are still in a critical state because of toxic pollution. The two countries try to improve the situation through the Boundary Waters Treaty.

Because of the peculiarities of the boundary between British Columbia and Alaska, Canada and the United States have had continuing differences over west coast salmon. A boundary dispute was settled in 1984, but especially after 1995, a conflict erupted over conservation. Canadian salmon fishers voluntarily reduced their catch because of dwindling stocks, but neither U.S. fishers nor the U.S. government were prepared to follow suit. Other recent environmental irritants between the two countries are the Libby Dam and the Arctic National Wildlife Refuge.

As far away as Canada is, fishing also constituted a long-standing environmental issue with European countries on the Atlantic coast. A number of them historically hauled huge quantities of fish from the Grand Banks just outside Canadian territorial waters. They even defied multinational agreements to abide by annual quotas until, at least in the case of cod, there were too few fish left for either Europeans or Canadians to catch.

Energy

In the energy sector, the voracious U.S. industrial complex usually wants to import Canadian electric power and petroleum. Governments in Quebec, New Brunswick, Manitoba, and BC have been eager to export electricity, and those of Alberta, Saskatchewan, and BC, to supply oil and/or natural gas. The federal government has normally approved these sales with little hesitation, although the **National Energy Board** is charged to ensure that long-term Canadian needs will not be compromised in the process. Native and environmental groups in some provinces have not been so favourably disposed to the hydro or nuclear plants necessary to produce the electricity, however, and Canadian nationalists worry about the future supply of petroleum for domestic purposes. Part of the controversy surrounding the Trans-Canada Pipeline project in 1956 derived from the involvement of U.S. firms and from the fact that the pipeline would serve the eastern United States as well as eastern Canada.

The degree of U.S. ownership of the Canadian petroleum industry also caused considerable conflict between the two countries. The **National Energy Program (NEP)** of 1980 set a target of 50 percent Canadian ownership of the oil and gas industry by 1990 and gave certain preferences to Petro-Canada and private Canadian firms. U.S. petroleum companies in Canada protested, and their government pressured Canada to remove these incentives to Canadianization. The Trudeau government made minor concessions, and the Mulroney Cabinet dismantled the NEP entirely and began to privatize Petro-Canada.

The energy provisions of the Canada–U.S. Trade Agreement alarmed many Canadians. It created a North American energy pool in which prices could not be discriminatory (that is, Canada had to sell oil, gas, or electricity to the United States at the Canadian domestic price), and if cutbacks were ever necessary, domestic sales had to be reduced by the same proportion as exports. On this point the agreement went beyond existing GATT requirements.[19]

Bond-Rating and Lending Agencies

In making public policy decisions, federal and provincial governments in Canada must often defer to the dictates of bond-rating and lending agencies. This is because such agencies assign credit ratings, which in turn determine the interest rates at which governments borrow money to finance their deficits. Here it is important to note that Canadian federal and provincial governments do much of their borrowing in the United States and in European countries, and it is often these bond-rating and lending agencies that tell them how much they can spend.

Especially in the era of rampant budget deficits, premiers and prime ministers made regular forays to Wall Street to try to persuade such agencies that government finances were sound.

Trade Unions

Historically, Canadian trade unions have been closely allied with those in the United States. Many unions in Canada, such as the United Steelworkers of America and the United Auto Workers, were part of "international unions" that had their headquarters in the United States. The Canadian union movement justified the relationship by arguing that as long as it had to bargain with multinational corporations, it needed the support of international unions, especially their larger strike funds. Membership in international unions peaked in 1965 at 67 percent of all union members in Canada. Since then, many of those involved in organized labour have felt uncomfortable with these arrangements. In recent years, therefore, a nationalist trend has been apparent in the Canadian labour movement, and several unions have either cut their ties with the international headquarters or defected to a different union. Bob White's creation of an autonomous Canadian Auto Workers union is the most striking example, but even some that remain part of international unions have successfully demanded greater autonomy than before. Thus, in 1998, 1 177 000 or only 30 percent of Canadian union members belonged to international unions.[20] The largest remaining international unions in Canada are the United Food and Commercial Workers, the Steelworkers, and the Teamsters.

GLOBAL INFLUENCES ON CANADIAN CULTURE[21]

Broadcasting

Television is the most significant cultural institution of the second half of the 20th century, whether used for entertainment, information, or advertising. The average Canadian watches about 22.8 hours of television per week, 60 percent of it foreign programming (mostly American in the case of anglophones).[22] Broken down by language group, anglophones watch 70 percent foreign programs while francophones watch only 33.5 percent. If a Canadian wanted to watch U.S. television 24 hours a day, it would be quite possible to do so. Much of the population lives close enough to the U.S. border to receive U.S. channels through the air; failing that, Canadian stations broadcast a large proportion of U.S. programming. Then, about 75 percent of Canadian households have purchased cable television, which normally offers them all the U.S. networks as well as additional Canadian channels. Beyond cable, many Canadians have pay television, which extends the U.S. content, for example, to U.S. movies and "superstations." Finally, satellite dishes can pick up even more U.S. channels, and pizza-sized dishes bring direct-to-home satellite transmission.

Canadians watch their own news, public affairs, and sports programs quite conscientiously, but otherwise prefer U.S. programs. Indeed, U.S. public television stations near the border depend on Canadians to contribute funds to their operations. Canadian television has a higher reputation abroad than it does at home, and those few Canadian series that are produced are readily sold to foreign networks.

Figure 9.1 **Market Share of Content by Origin in the Cultural Industries of Canada**

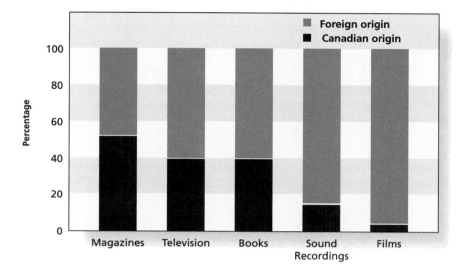

Source: Based on figures from Canadian Heritage website: http://www.pch.ca.

There are two main reasons why Canadian television networks broadcast so much U.S. programming. First, it is much cheaper to buy a U.S. show or series than to produce a Canadian one, costing about $100 000 and $1 million per hour respectively. Second, U.S. programs generally attract a larger audience, so that they command higher advertising rates than do Canadian ones. If profit is the name of the game (or minimizing its deficit in the case of the publicly owned CBC), then the best way to play is to provide U.S. fare.

By way of protecting and promoting Canadian culture in the broadcasting field, the Crown corporation, the **Canadian Broadcasting Corporation (CBC)**, in its radio and television networks, and Radio-Canada, its French-language equivalent, is a crucial agent of Canadian cultural expression. The origins of the CBC in the mid-1930s were discussed in Chapter 3; today, CBC radio is commercial-free, has virtually 100 percent Canadian content, and can be heard in almost every part of the country. Programs like "This Morning," "As It Happens," and "Cross-Country Checkup" are widely regarded as crucial links in keeping the country together. CBC television is less successful, mainly because the television medium is so expensive. The Mulroney government slashed millions of dollars from the CBC's budget after 1984, making the corporation's task even harder. The 1991 Task Force on the Economic Status of Canadian Television, like many similar earlier reports, lamented the fact that government budget cuts for the CBC forced it to rely more and more on advertising revenue, reducing the income potential of private television broadcasters and causing the CBC to deviate from the high-quality cultural programming that Canadians rightfully expect from their public broadcaster.[23]

All such reports have said that the CBC should receive adequate, ongoing, multi-year, and stable public funding to enable it to fulfill its mandate,[24] but the Chrétien government cut its budget even further. In spite of such cuts and severe layoffs, the CBC decided in 1995 to remove all foreign programs in prime time.

A second main pillar of the broadcasting industry is the regulatory agency, the **Canadian Radio-television and Telecommunications Commission (CRTC)**.[25] This agency issues broadcasting licences and Canadian-content regulations, which are more stringent for the CBC than for private stations and networks. The CRTC currently requires all television stations to provide at least 60 percent Canadian content over the year, although in prime time, private broadcasters can go as low as 50 percent; the Canadian content rules for specialty and pay-TV channels range between 30 and 60 percent.

The CRTC, under strong industry and popular pressure to allow more U.S. outlets in Canada, approved cable and pay television, which diluted the audiences of Canadian channels. Canadians must buy cable TV in order to obtain the parliamentary channel and the CBC all-news channel, Newsworld. When the United States protested the substitution of an American country-music channel in favour of a Canadian channel, the compromise arrived at was to allow the American channel to buy a portion of the Canadian one. Also in 1995, the CRTC authorized direct-to-home (DTH) satellite services, the so-called "death stars." Many nationalists accuse the CRTC of selling out to Canadian cable and satellite companies in their saturation of the Canadian television audience with U.S. fare, and fear for the future of Canadian content when the largely American 500-channel universe is beamed directly into Canadian homes.

By *Adrian Raeside* (Victoria Times-Colonist). *Used with permission.*

Magazines

Magazines are perhaps the second most important vehicle of popular culture, and this Canadian industry is also permeated by U.S. content. The 1995 Task Force on the Canadian Magazine Industry spoke of the "massive penetration of the Canadian market by foreign magazines," and added that "the United States is a daily presence in the life of every Canadian, through television programming, sports and film. It is reasonable to expect that the content of American magazines will be of interest to Canadians."[26]

While Canadian magazines lead foreign magazines in terms of subscriptions in Canada, foreign magazines account for the great bulk of English-language newsstand sales. Overall, Canadian magazines have increased from 23 percent in 1959 to about 50 percent of the total circulation today, but as with television, the picture is much more positive on the French side than the English. The 1995 task force emphasized the significance of such circulation figures as follows: "The larger the circulation, the more advertising a magazine can attract; the greater the advertising revenue, the more it can afford to spend on editorial content; and the more it spends, the more likely it will be attractive to readers, with the result that circulation will grow."[27]

When it comes to protecting Canadian magazines, the main protective device has related to the deduction of advertising expenses. Since 1965, Canadian firms could only deduct magazine advertising expenses from their income tax if those advertisements were placed in magazines published in Canada. A major controversy occurred when these measures were introduced, especially because the Pearson government tried to include the "Canadian" or **split-run** editions of *Time* and *Reader's Digest* in the legislation. Such editions added a minute amount of Canadian content to the American edition so as to masquerade as Canadian magazines, and then sold advertising to Canadian firms. The U.S. government threatened to withhold its assent to the Auto Pact, forcing Canada to exempt these two magazines until the Trudeau government finally removed the concession in calmer circumstances in 1976. *Time* continued to produce a "Canadian" edition with minimal Canadian content, but advertisers could not deduct their advertising costs. In the 1990s, however, *Sports Illustrated* started to produce a so-called Canadian split-run edition that challenged the law because such editions could now be physically printed in Canada via satellite. As mentioned above, the World Trade Organization ordered Canada to abandon a federal excise tax and postal subsidies that had been introduced to protect its domestic magazines, and Ottawa responded in 1998 by introducing legislation to effectively ban split run magazines. When the U.S. threatened to launch an all-out trade war over the issue on behalf of the publisher, Time-Warner, Canada retreated. In the end, it allowed foreign magazines sold in Canada to carry up to 18 percent of Canadian ads without any Canadian content; to exceed the 18 percent threshold, they would have to include at least 50 percent Canadian editorial content; and the limit on foreign ownership of a Canadian magazine was raised from 25 to 49 percent. In the wake of this capitulation, observers expected several U.S. magazines to establish "Canadian" editions, contributing to the demise of a number of genuinely Canadian magazines.

Film and Video

The Canadian film industry is even weaker than television or magazines, and the average Canadian moviegoer has rarely if ever seen a Canadian feature film. Canadian films have achieved a respectable reputation abroad, but do not achieve a comparable domestic box office success as those of other countries in their domestic market. Less than 5 percent of the screen time in Canadian movie theatres is devoted to Canadian films (and most of that is in the sophisticated Toronto and Montreal markets), a figure that remains depressingly static.[28] U.S. movie producers make many feature films in Canada every year, taking advantage of its scenic locations, its technical expertise, and the low Canadian dollar, but these are always disguised as U.S. movies by the time they hit the screen.

The problem has many causes, including the fact that the two companies that virtually monopolize the large urban cinema markets, Famous Players and Cineplex-Odeon, are fully or partly American owned, and that the film distribution system is U.S.-controlled. Other factors are the undeniable Canadian fascination with Hollywood, the small Canadian market, and a shortage of funds. Canadian feature films are dramatically underfunded in both production and marketing. The average Hollywood film has a production budget of over $50 million and a marketing budget of over $25 million, whereas the average Canadian feature film has a budget of under $5 million, of which only about $250 000 is earmarked for marketing. Canadian productions do slightly better in the home video market, but Canadian titles make up less than 5 percent of the inventory of retail video stores.

A number of instruments have been adopted to promote the Canadian film industry. First, another Crown corporation, the National Film Board (NFB), has an illustrious history, making impressive Canadian films and winning many international awards. The NFB had 53 original productions and 64 original co-productions in 1997–98. It suffers from two serious disadvantages, however: insufficient funding to make feature films, with the result that it has concentrated on documentaries and short films; and no effective mechanism for making its films available to the general public. Since the NFB made few feature films, the government established a funding agency in this field, Telefilm Canada. It provides about $40 million annually for the development, production, distribution, and marketing of Canadian feature films, and few if any would be made without it. It also administers $15 million from the Canada Television and Cable Production Fund. An assortment of tax credits is also available, while ministers of communications have repeatedly tried to reform the film distribution system so that theatres would screen more Canadian feature films. They have had limited success, however, because the system was controlled in the United States, and for a time U.S. president Ronald Reagan, a former actor, would not relent. In 1999, the government endorsed a proposal to set up a $150 million feature-film fund, mostly by pooling existing resources and by eliminating a tax break for Hollywood films shot in Canada.

Publishing

When it comes to books, the Canadian market is again dominated by U.S. content; it is estimated that 60 to 70 percent of the Canadian book market consists of imported books. Of books published in Canada in 1996–97, Canadian publishing firms outnumbered foreign firms 301 to 20, but the Canadian firms had just slightly more than half the sales.[29] Both kinds of companies also sell foreign titles in Canada to supplement their Canadian offerings. Canadian firms such as Nelson Thomson Learning, the publisher of this book, and McClelland and Stewart produce a much larger number of new titles in Canada than such branch-plant firms as McGraw-Hill Ryerson, which do publish Canadian books but put greater efforts into distributing their U.S. titles. Books are like television shows: they are cheaper to import than to make domestically. The problem is aggravated by the lack of effort to sell Canadian books at Canadian bookstores, although the situation may be changing with the advent of new mega-bookstores in many cities. Paperback books at newsstands, drug stores, and supermarkets come almost entirely from the United States because the publishers-distributors who control the supply are U.S.-owned companies.

In the publishing field, the so-called "Baie Comeau" policy provides that when the parent publisher of a Canadian subsidiary is taken over by another foreign firm, the Canadian branch is supposed to be sold to a Canadian buyer, although this has not always happened. For example, a British firm, Pearson Education, was allowed to buy Prentice Hall Canada. The Canadian Heritage Department also administers the Book Publishing Industry Development Program.

Sound Recordings

Sound recording is another vulnerable industry. In 1992–93, some 15 foreign-controlled record companies had 84.6 percent of sales in Canada, even though 172 Canadian-controlled companies were also in business. More significantly, sales with Canadian content or by Canadian artists constituted only about 14.5 percent of total sales in 1995–96, and as for new releases, 828 (or 12.4 percent) contained Canadian content or were by Canadian artists, compared with 5827 that did not.[30] The CRTC requires that AM and FM radio stations play 35 percent Canadian music, a regulation that was generally seen as the catalyst for the explosion of the Canadian music industry over the past 25 years.

Other

The Canadian newspaper and radio industries are much more autonomous. Firms in these industries are required by law to remain in Canadian hands, and several aggressive Canadian chains are alive and well in both industries. Nevertheless, the influence of the United States can be detected in these industries, too: the ready availability in some centres of such U.S. papers as *USA Today* and U.S. radio stations; the reliance on U.S. newsgathering agencies abroad, such as American Press reports; the dependence on U.S. sources for comics, crossword puzzles, commentators, and personal advice programs and columns; and the tendency to include a large proportion of news coverage of U.S. events.

Other cultural fields could be mentioned—theatre and art—as well as the wider realm of education (including universities), but the basic situation there is much the same: most aspects of Canadian culture are heavily influenced by U.S. institutions and values, and most Canadians accept this state of affairs without complaint. To a large extent the Canadian presence in such industries is the result of demands made by the nationalist minority for protection from U.S. domination and for promotion of Canadian content, a concern first given official expression in the **Massey Royal Commission** Report on National Development in the Arts, Letters, and Sciences in 1951.

That commission recommended that public financial assistance be provided to the arts, and in response, the Canada Council (now the **Canada Council on the Arts**) was set up in 1957. It gives life-saving grants to hundreds of individual writers, artists, musicians, and play-wrights as well as to almost every orchestra, theatre centre, art gallery, and ballet and opera company in the country. The Social Sciences and Humanities Research Council of Canada (SSHRCC) has taken over the subsidization of academic research and writing. Other than the measures mentioned above, Canada has imposed ownership restrictions in several areas of the cultural field, and Canadian immigration regulations require that before hiring a non-Canadian, employers must demonstrate that no qualified Canadian is available. This applies in particular to university professors and the heads of cultural institutions such as the Stratford Festival and the Art Gallery of Ontario.

GLOBAL INFLUENCES ON OTHER ASPECTS OF CANADIAN POLITICAL LIFE

Defence, foreign policy, economics, and culture may stand out, but even before the free trade agreements, American influence was also established in practically every other aspect of Canadian life. Many of these have been or will be noted in other chapters of this book, but a brief catalogue can be included here. In areas sometimes far removed from politics are the links of many religious organizations and fraternal groups like the Kiwanis and Masons, which also have their headquarters in the United States. No one can deny the integration of Canadian and American professional sport, including the loss of the Canadian orientation of the National Hockey League. The future of the remaining Canadian franchises in the NHL may well depend on governments being prepared to offer them subsidies of some kind.[31] A major area of scientific activity in Canada has been the development and refinement of the "Canadarm," this country's contribution to the U.S. space program. How predictable that the division of Spar Aerospace that produced this symbol of Canadian expertise was sold to U.S. interests in 1999!

In the semi-political realm, many social and political protest movements, including farmer and women's movements and anti-poverty and Aboriginal groups, have spilled over the border to some extent, although in some cases the external influences go well beyond the United States. While Canadians generally consider themselves ahead of Americans in social policy, the U.S. New Deal in the 1930s and the U.S. War on Poverty in the 1960s inspired pallid replicas in Canada. Similarly, while most Canadians cherish their universal health care system, increasing problems have led some observers to look to the American system for answers.

In the political system, American influences (as well as those from other countries) can be seen in the changing nature of Canadian political values (less deference, demands for more popular participation) and in party ideologies (the shift to the right). Party leadership conventions have long been considered to be an adaptation of those in the United States, and many would regard the whole Reform Party phenomenon as a U.S. transplant. Certainly its proposed Triple-E Senate is based precisely on the equivalent American chamber. The Canadian lobbying industry increasingly resembles that across the border, and the adoption of the Charter of Rights and Freedoms has had the tendency to legalize and therefore Americanize the operation of the whole political system.[32]

·····································

CONCLUSION

Canada follows U.S. examples because of tradition, adoration, convenience, or economics; because the U.S. presence makes it necessary; and because of explicit U.S. government or corporate pressure. Most observers expect that, directly or indirectly, the free trade agreements will increase such U.S. influence on almost all aspects of Canadian policy. Thus, during the 20th century, Canada went from being a British colony to a colony of the United States, or from colony to nation to colony.[33] The Mulroney government was particularly cooperative with the United States, while the Chrétien regime saw itself as friendly but more businesslike, ready to pursue Canadian interests where they differed from those of the United States. Furthermore, as political, economic, and environmental developments become common global problems, Canada must increasingly respond to transnational and supranational demands. As insistent as demands may be from forces in the domestic Canadian society, Canadian politicians must also pay greater attention to their global surroundings.

(SC) It is often contended in political science that a country's foreign policy is more state-centred than its domestic policy—that politicians and bureaucrats operate with greater autonomy in international affairs.[34] In Canada's case, the continentalism of postwar economic policies was largely the work of the American-born minister of trade and commerce, C.D. Howe, and others in the political and bureaucratic elites that shared his assumptions.[35] A more nationalistic elite briefly held sway in the late 1960s and 1970s, including Walter Gordon and Herb Gray. The concept of free trade emerged after Mulroney's election in 1984 even though it had not been mentioned during that election campaign and had not been preceded by widespread public demands.

© The class-based approach also has much to say about the external environment.[36] Indeed, a large part of the capitalist domination of Canadian government and society consists of multinational firms. Class analysts are foremost among those who criticize the extent to which the Canadian government has supported, and Canadian companies have been part of, the U.S. military–industrial complex. Multinational corporate links shape Canadian economic policy in many ways, including the reliance on resource exports, the weakness in manufacturing, and the virtual absence of research and development. Class-based analysis cites Brian Mulroney as an excellent example of the comprador elite, claiming that his upbringing in a U.S. company town in Quebec and his later stint as president of a U.S. subsidiary in that province left him with a markedly deferential approach to Canada–U.S. relations.[37] Class analysts further decry the influx of foreign investment, the limited effort to diversify trade patterns, the international environmental devastation, and the limited control over national energy resources. As far as "free" trade is concerned, it was primarily the corporate sector that pressed for such deals because they would tie the hands of the state and make the corporations more free from government encroachment. Many U.S. subsidiaries supported the Canadian Alliance for Trade and Job Opportunities, the ad hoc corporate group that pushed for free trade before and during the 1988 election campaign. Representatives of Canadian industry—both foreign and domestic—were part of the FTA negotiating process through Sectoral Advisory Groups on

International Trade, but the Canadian Labour Congress was not involved. In addition, class analysts abhor the anticipated exploitation of Mexican labour under NAFTA, and are profoundly concerned about U.S. corporate influence on Canadian culture.

The other approaches outlined in Chapter 1 are less concerned about the external environment. Public choice theory might note that the 1988 election was almost a single-issue election and that different regional voting patterns emerged depending on whether voters felt that free trade was in their own interest. Finally, the pluralist approach would concede that domestic groups can rarely persuade the government to stand up to the bullying tactics of the United States or multilateral organizations and agreements primarily designed in its interests, such as the WTO. Nevertheless, it may be worth the effort: an international grassroots campaign (partly dependent on the Internet) and including the Council of Canadians stood up to the multinationals and stopped or at least stalled the adoption of the Multilateral Agreement on Investment.

DISCUSSION QUESTIONS

1. Is globalization just another name for giving multinational corporations free rein to maximize their profits? Explain.

2. How much scope does globalization leave to nation-states to make distinctive domestic policies?

3. How much scope does Canada have to develop an independent foreign policy?

4. What are the advantages and disadvantages of foreign investment in Canada? Of the other economic relationships between the two countries?

5. What are the advantages and disadvantages of the Canada–U.S. Free Trade Agreement? What alternatives were available in the increasing regionalization of world trading patterns?

6. What are the advantages and disadvantages of the close cultural relationship between Canada and the United States?

7. How do the various critical approaches outlined in Chapter 1 add to our understanding of global influences on the Canadian political system?

NOTES

1. Bruce Doern and Brian Tomlin, *Faith and Fear: The Free Trade Story* (Toronto: Stoddart, 1991); Stephen Brooks and Andrew Stritch, *Business and Government in Canada* (Scarborough: Prentice-Hall Canada, 1991), ch. 13; Robert Campbell and Leslie Pal, *The Real Worlds of Canadian Politics*, 2nd ed. (Peterborough: Broadview Press, 1991).

2. Andrew Jackson and Bob Baldwin, *The Lessons of Free Trade: A View from Canadian Labour* (Ottawa: Canadian Labour Congress, 1997); Duncan Cameron and Mel Watkins, *Canada under Free Trade* (Toronto: Lorimer, 1993).

3. Government of Canada, *The North American Free Trade Agreement at a Glance*, cat. no. E74-56/1-1993E; Jeffrey M. Ayres, *Defying Conventional Wisdom: Political Movements and Popular Contention against North American Free Trade* (Toronto: University of Toronto Press, 1998).

4. Andrew Jackson and Matthew Sanger, eds., *Dismantling Democracy: The Multilateral Agreement on Investment and Its Impact* (Toronto: Lorimer, 1998); John Dillon, *Challenging "Free Trade" in Canada: The Real Story* (Ottawa: Ecumenical Coalition for Economic Justice, 1996; distributed by the Canadian Labour Congress).

5. Stephen McBride and John Shields, *Dismantling a Nation: Canada and the New World Order* (Halifax: Fernwood Publishing, 1993), p. 20; William Watson, *Globalization and the Meaning of Canadian Life* (Toronto: University of Toronto Press, 1998); Linda McQuaig, *The Cult of Impotence: Selling the Myth of Powerlessness in the Global Economy* (Toronto: Viking, 1998).

6. Jackson and Sanger, *Dismantling Democracy*.

7. Knowlton Nash, *Kennedy and Diefenbaker* (Toronto: McClelland and Stewart, 1990); H.B. Robinson, *Diefenbaker's World* (Toronto: University of Toronto Press, 1989).

8. J.L. Granatstein and Robert Bothwell, *Pirouette: Pierre Trudeau and Canadian Foreign Policy* (Toronto: University of Toronto Press, 1990).

9. Canada, *Foreign Direct Investment in Canada* (Ottawa: Supply and Services, 1972), ch. 19; K.R. Nossal, *The Politics of Canadian Foreign Policy*, 3rd ed. (Scarborough: Prentice-Hall Allyn Bacon Canada, 1997); David Dewitt and John Kirton, *Canada as a Principal Power* (Toronto: Wiley, 1983); Costas Melakopides, *Pragmatic Idealism: Canadian Foreign Policy, 1945–1995* (Montreal: McGill–Queen's University Press, 1998); Andrew F. Cooper, *Canadian Foreign Policy: Old Habits and New Directions* (Scarborough: Prentice Hall Allyn Bacon Canada, 1997); Maxwell A. Cameron et al., *To Walk Without Fear: The Global Movement to Ban Landmines* (Toronto: Oxford University Press, 1998); and the annual series *Canada among Nations* produced since 1984 by the Carleton University (Norman Paterson) School of International Affairs.

10. Department of Foreign Affairs and International Trade website: http://www.dfait-maeci.gc.ca.

11. Glen Williams, "Regions within Region: Continentalism Ascendant," in M.S. Whittington and G. Williams, eds., *Canadian Politics in the 1990s*, 4th ed. (Scarborough: Nelson Canada, 1995).

12. *Foreign Direct Investment in Canada*, p. 14.

13. Ibid., p. 5.

14. Kari Levitt, *Silent Surrender: The Multinational Corporation in Canada* (Toronto: Macmillan, 1970).

15. Doern and Tomlin, *Faith and Fear*; Michael Hart, *Decision at Midnight: Inside the Canada–U.S. Free Trade Negotiations* (Vancouver: University of British Columbia Press, 1995).

16. John Crispo, ed., *Free Trade: The Real Story* (Toronto: Gage, 1988).

17. John W. Warnock, *Free Trade and the New Right Agenda* (Vancouver: New Star Books, 1988), pp. 116–17; Williams, "Regions within Region."

18. Duncan Cameron, ed., *The Free Trade Deal* (Toronto: Lorimer, 1988); Warnock, *Free Trade and the New Right Agenda*; Maude Barlow, *Parcel of Rogues* (Toronto: Key Porter Books, 1991); Mel Hurtig, *The Betrayal of Canada* (Toronto: Stoddart, 1991); and Cameron and Watkins, eds., *Canada under Free Trade*.

19. Brooks and Stritch, *Business and Government in Canada*, p. 396.

20. Human Resources Development Canada, *Directory of Labour Organization in Canada, 1998*, cat. no. L2-2/1998.

21. Michael Dorland, ed., *The Cultural Industries in Canada* (Toronto: Lorimer, 1996); Tom Henighan, *Ideas of North: A Guide to Canadian Arts and Culture* (Vancouver: Raincoast Books, 1997); Statistics Canada, *Canada's Culture, Heritage and Identity: A Statistical Perspective*, cat. no. 87-211, 1997, and *Focus on Culture*, cat. no. 87-004-XPB; Canadian Heritage website, *Recent Cultural Statistics*, 1997: http://www.pch.gc.ca.

22. Statistics Canada, *Canada's Culture, Heritage and Identity*.

23. Department of Communications, *Report of the Task Force on the Economic Status of Canadian Television* (Ottawa, 1991), p. 9.

24. Ibid., p. 169.

25. Herschel Hardin, *Closed Circuits* (Vancouver: Douglas & McIntyre, 1985); Marc Raboy, *Missed Opportunities: The Story of Canada's Broadcasting Policy* (Montreal: McGill–Queen's University Press, 1990); the *Report of the Task Force on Broadcasting Policy* (Ottawa: Supply and Services, 1986); and Dorland, ed., *The Cultural Industries in Canada*.

26. Task Force on the Canadian Magazine Industry, *A Question of Balance* (Ottawa, 1994), p. 40.

27. Ibid., p. 40.

28. Canadian Heritage, *A Review of Canadian Feature Film Policy*, February 1998; *The Film and Video Industry in Canada: An Overview*, April 1997; and *A Guide to Federal Programs for the Film and Video Sector*, September 1998. See also *The Canadian Film and Television Production Industry: A 1998 Profile* published by the CFTP Association, February 1998.

29. Canadian Heritage, *The Canadian Book Publishing Industry*, November 1998. The percentage of non-Canadian books bought in Canada, as shown in Figure 9.1, is 60 percent, but Victor Rabinovitch, former assistant deputy minister, Canadian Heritage, cites 70 percent in "The Social and Economic Rationales for Canada's Domestic Cultural Policies," in Dennis Browne, ed., *The Culture/Trade Quandary: Canada's Policy Options* (Ottawa: Centre for Trade Policy and Law, 1998), p. 30.

30. Statistics Canada, *Sound Recording 1992–93*, cat. no. 87-202 (July 1994); *Canada's Culture, Heritage and Identity: A Statistical Perspective*, cat. no. 87-211-XPB (December 1997); Ernst & Young, *Report Submitted to the Task Force on the Future of the Canadian Music Industry, Final Report*, March 1995.

31. Jim Silver, *Thin Ice: Politics and the Demise of an NHL Franchise* (Halifax: Fernwood Publishing, 1996).

32. S.M. Crean, "Reading between the Lies: Culture and the Free Trade Agreement," in Cameron, ed., *The Free Trade Deal*; David J. Elkins, *Beyond Sovereignty: Territory and Political Economy in the Twenty-First Century* (Toronto: University of Toronto Press, 1995); David Thomas, ed., *Canada and the United States: Differences That Count* (Peterborough: Broadview Press, 1993); Dorland, *The Cultural Industries in Canada*.

33. Donald Creighton, *Canada's First Century* (Toronto: Macmillan, 1970); George Grant, *Lament for a Nation: The Defeat of Canadian Nationalism* (Toronto: McClelland and Stewart, 1965); and Robert Chodos et al., *The Unmaking of Canada: The Hidden Theme in Canadian History since 1945* (Toronto: Lorimer, 1991). Northrop Frye notes that Canada passed from a pre-national to a post-national phase without ever having become a nation, in his Conclusion to Carl F. Klinck, ed., *The Literary History of Canada: Canadian Literature in English* (Toronto: University of Toronto Press, 1976).

34. Tom Keating, "The State, the Public and the Making of Canadian Foreign Policy," in Robert Jackson et al., eds., *Contemporary Canadian Politics: Readings and Notes* (Scarborough: Prentice-Hall Canada, 1987); Elizabeth Riddell-Dixon, "State Autonomy and Canadian Foreign Policy: The Case of Deep Seabed Mining," *Canadian Journal of Political Science* (June 1988), pp. 297–317.

35. Williams, "Regions within Region."

36. Wallace Clement, *Continental Corporate Power* (Toronto: McClelland and Stewart, 1977); Gordon Laxer, *Open for Business: The Roots of Foreign Ownership in Canada* (Don Mills: Oxford University Press, 1989); and Levitt, *Silent Surrender*.

37. As a boy, Mulroney ingratiated himself with the U.S. owner of the Tribune company, Col. Robert McCormick, and sang for him whenever he came to town. See John Sawatsky, *Mulroney: The Politics of Ambition* (Toronto: Macfarlane Walter & Ross, 1991), p. 13.

FURTHER READING

Ayres. Jeffrey M. *Defying Conventional Wisdom: Political Movements and Popular Contention against North American Free Trade.* Toronto: University of Toronto Press, 1998.

Barlow, Maude. *Parcel of Rogues.* Toronto: Key Porter Books, 1991.

Barlow, Maude, and Bruce Campbell. *Take Back the Nation.* Toronto: Key Porter Books, 1991.

Cameron, Duncan, and Mel Watkins, eds. *Canada under Free Trade.* Toronto: Lorimer, 1993.

Cameron, Maxwell A., et al. *To Walk without Fear: The Global Movement to Ban Landmines.* Toronto: Oxford University Press, 1998.

Campbell, Robert, and Leslie Pal. *The Real Worlds of Canadian Politics*, 2nd ed. Peterborough: Broadview Press, 1991.

Canada among Nations. Annual. Toronto: Lorimer until 1998; then Oxford University Press.

Chodos, Robert, et al. *The Unmaking of Canada: The Hidden Theme in Canadian History since 1945.* Toronto: Lorimer, 1991.

Chodos, Robert, et al. *Canada and the Global Economy.* Halifax: Lorimer, 1995.

Clement, Wallace. *Continental Corporate Power*. Toronto: McClelland and Stewart, 1977.

Cooper, Andrew F. *Canadian Foreign Policy: Old Habits and New Directions*. Scarborough: Prentice Hall Allyn Bacon Canada, 1997.

Dewitt, David, and John Kirton. *Canada as a Principal Power*. Toronto: Wiley, 1983.

Doern, Bruce, and Brian Tomlin. *Faith and Fear: The Free Trade Story*. Toronto: Stoddart, 1991.

Dorland, Michael, ed. *The Cultural Industries in Canada*. Toronto: Lorimer, 1996.

Elkins, David J. *Beyond Sovereignty: Territory and Political Economy in the Twenty-First Century*. Toronto: University of Toronto Press, 1995.

Flaherty, David, and Frank E. Manning, eds. *The Beaver Bites Back? American Popular Culture in Canada*. Montreal: McGill–Queen's University Press, 1993.

Foreign Direct Investment in Canada (Gray Report). Ottawa: Supply and Services, 1972.

Granatstein, J.L., and Norman Hillmer. *For Better or Worse: Canada and the United States in the 1990s*. Mississauga: Copp Clark Pitman, 1991.

Hardin, Herschel. *Closed Circuits*. Vancouver: Douglas & McIntyre, 1985.

Hart, Michael. *Decision at Midnight: Inside the Canada–U.S. Free Trade Negotiations*. Vancouver: University of British Columbia Press, 1995.

Henighan, Tom. *Ideas of North: A Guide to Canadian Arts and Culture*. Vancouver: Raincoast Books, 1997.

Jackson, Andrew, and Matthew Sanger. *Dismantling Democracy: The Multilateral Agreement on Investment and Its Impact*. Toronto: Lorimer, 1998.

Johnson, Andrew F., and Andrew Stritch, eds. *Canadian Public Policy: Globalization and Political Parties*. Toronto., Copp Clark Ltd., 1997.

McBride, Stephen, and John Shields. *Dismantling a Nation: Canada and the New World Order*. Halifax: Fernwood Publishing, 1993; 2nd ed., 1997.

McDonald, Marci. *Yankee Doodle Dandy*. Toronto: Stoddart, 1995.

McQuaig, Linda. *The Cult of Impotence: Selling the Myth of Powerlessness in the Global Economy*. Toronto: Viking, 1998.

Melakopides, Costas. *Pragmatic Idealism: Canadian Foreign Policy, 1945–1995*. Montreal: McGill–Queen's University Press, 1998.

Nossal, K.R. *The Politics of Canadian Foreign Policy*, 2nd ed. Scarborough: Prentice-Hall Canada, 1989; 3rd ed., 1997.

Raboy, Marc. *Missed Opportunities: The Story of Canada's Broadcasting Policy*. Montreal: McGill–Queen's University Press, 1990.

Report of the Royal Commission on the Economic Union and Development Prospects for Canada. Ottawa: Supply and Services, 1984.

Silver, Jim. *Thin Ice: Politics and the Demise of an NHL Franchise*. Halifax: Fernwood Publishing, 1996.

Thomas, David, ed. *Canada and the United States: Differences That Count*. Peterborough: Broadview Press, 1993.

Warnock, John W. *Free Trade and the New Right Agenda*. Vancouver: New Star Books, 1988.

Watson, William. *Globalization and the Meaning of Canadian Life*. Toronto: University of Toronto Press, 1998.

Williams, Glen. *Not for Export: The International Competitiveness of Canadian Manufacturing*, 3rd ed. Toronto: McClelland and Stewart, 1994

PART 3

Linking People to Government

Having examined the societal environment of the Canadian political system, we are ready to explore Canadian politics as such. The three traditional elements of Canadian politics are the electoral system, political parties, and pressure groups, each of which, along with voting and the election campaign, is discussed in its own chapter in the following section. But the context of values, attitudes, opinions (and how they are acquired), and patterns of political participation in which these three familiar institutions operate must also be examined. Moreover, no one can deny the ubiquitous importance of the mass media and public opinion polls as links between people and government today. Thus, we begin with chapters on the Canadian political culture, and political socialization, the mass media, and public opinion polls.

Chapter 10

The Canadian POLITICAL culture

Most Canadians think they live in the best country on earth, but they do not get overly excited by national symbols like the flag or "O Canada." Others would prefer to live in an independent Quebec and some would not object to becoming part of the United States. Canadians have historically looked upon the state as a benevolent force, although recent surveys indicate widespread disrespect for all institutions in society, including government. The Meech Lake Accord was drawn up behind closed doors, and Canadians have since demanded more meaningful participation in the country's constitutional affairs. On the other hand, the voter turnout rate in elections appears to be on the decline.

All these phenomena and countless others are encompassed in the concept of **political culture**, which can be defined as the sum total of the politically relevant values, beliefs, attitudes, and orientations in a society. Vague and elusive as these values and attitudes may be, they are thought by most political scientists to influence what is done within a political system, and the discipline therefore does its best to identify them.

Political culture includes feelings people have toward the overall political community of Canada—reactions to national symbols (flag, anthem, Constitution) and feelings of patriotism, nationalism, and pride, including the question of how people feel toward their province as opposed to the whole country. A second aspect of political culture involves beliefs regarding the role of the state—how large a part Canadians want government to play in their lives and the kinds of policies it should adopt. Another variable consists of orientations to the decision-making apparatus. Are people aware of it, and to what extent do they want to control it? How do Canadians feel, in general, about the police, the bureaucracy, the courts, and the politicians? Do citizens trust them? Alternatively, do people feel that their participation in the political system can make any difference? And to what extent do they participate? Patterns of actual participation can also be considered part of political culture.

Given the breadth of the political culture concept, political scientists use two principal methods of identifying its ingredients, both of which we will rely on here.[1] One is to survey individual Canadians and ask them about their attitudes and values. If and when such values and attitudes are widely shared, they can be said to constitute the collective political culture. A second approach is to develop an understanding of the political culture from observing the operation of the political system and society more generally. This can be achieved, for example, from a reading of history and literature and from a study of government decisions and political institutions.

This chapter will focus on the Canadian commitment to democracy, distinguish between Canadian and U.S. political values, attempt to identify other aspects of the Canadian national identity, discuss the concept of subcultures or "limited identities," and examine patterns of Canadian political participation. While political culture is usually considered to be fairly stable, it will also be necessary to sketch how in the Canadian case it seems to be changing.

THE TRADITIONAL CANADIAN POLITICAL CULTURE
Democracy

The first conclusion that emerges from a quest for Canadian political values is that almost all Canadians believe in **democracy**. The preamble to the Canadian Charter of Rights and Freedoms acknowledges democracy to be a foremost value in the country when it speaks of Canada as a "free and democratic society," but the Charter is not particularly enlightening about what this means. Definitions of democracy in the modern Western world usually include the elements of popular sovereignty, political equality, political freedom, and majority rule.[2]

POPULAR SOVEREIGNTY

Popular sovereignty means that the people have the final say, which in large, modern political systems usually takes the form of elections at certain specified intervals. At the federal and provincial levels in Canada, the Constitution requires that elections be held at least every five years, and tradition usually reduces this interval to four. For most Canadians, this is a sufficient opportunity for the exercise of popular sovereignty, although few would be content with anything less. Some states have a tradition of plebiscites or referendums, but these devices are largely foreign to the Canadian mentality. Although their incidence is slightly higher at the provincial and municipal levels, only three national plebiscites or referendums have occurred since 1867: 1898 on the prohibition of liquor sales; 1942 on conscription; and 1992 on the Charlottetown Accord. At least in the past, Canadians cherished representative democracy in which elected officials and appointed authorities made decisions on their behalf.

Popular sovereignty is thus normally exercised in periodic elections, which are, more than anything, mere opportunities to select those who will be responsible for making the big political decisions over the next four years or so on behalf of the whole population. As pointed out in Chapter 14, specific policy mandates are rare. Needless to say, it is an element of the law-abiding nature of most Canadians that everyone recognize the legitimacy of the election results and accept this expression of the popular will, however misguided it might sometimes seem. While Canadians allow many public officials like judges to be appointed, a consensus now exists that the Senate should become an elected body.

POLITICAL EQUALITY

Given the significance of elections as the means of implementing the principle of popular sovereignty, a second aspect of democracy is that everyone is equal on election day. In essence, this means that every person has one vote and no more than one vote, as provided by the Canada Elections Act and Charter of Rights and Freedoms. It is only in relatively recent times, however, that Canada has met this ideal, and at one time or another in the past several groups were excluded: those without property, women, and various ethnic groups, including Aboriginal Canadians.

The principle of one person–one vote is a minimal expression of **political equality**. A major deviation from the ideal occurs if constituencies are not divided among provinces on the basis of "representation by population." Chapter 12 reveals significant deviations in this respect. Another discrepancy occurs if constituencies are not of equal population size within a province, which is also a considerable problem because of Canada's huge uninhabited spaces. These are issues that concern political scientists more than the general public, but are of increasing interest to the courts as well.

It should also be said that even if every vote carried exactly equal weight, there remains considerable room for inequality in the electoral system. Political parties in Canada are to a large extent privately financed, and it may well be that those who contribute money to a party or candidate expect something in return. Thus, those who have the resources to help finance elections are likely to have more influence than those who merely vote. Beyond election day itself, tremendous inequalities in political influence begin to emerge, such as in pressure group and lobbying activity. Such nonelectoral inequalities, however, are beyond the scope of political equality as a bare ingredient of the definition of democracy.

POLITICAL FREEDOM

Just as the 1982 Charter of Rights and Freedoms enhanced protection of aspects of popular sovereignty and political equality, it also provided an explicit constitutional statement of **political freedom** in Canada, as discussed in detail in Chapter 18. According to section 2 of the Charter,

Everyone has the following fundamental freedoms:

(a) freedom of conscience and religion;
(b) freedom of thought, belief, opinion and expression, including freedom of the press and other media of communication;
(c) freedom of peaceful assembly; and
(d) freedom of association.

It is a mistake to think that the Charter created these political freedoms. Instead, what it basically provided was a new means of enforcing them—using the courts to invalidate legislation that infringed them rather than having to persuade politicians to do so. It is therefore interesting to note the extent to which they were respected or violated before its adoption.

That political freedoms were a long-standing part of the Canadian political culture, recognized by government authorities as well as by the general public, can be seen in the relatively small number of cases where they were seriously infringed (leaving aside government treatment of Aboriginals, which went well beyond denying them political freedom). Three of these cases occurred at the federal level.[3] The first interference with freedom of speech or assembly had to do with section 98 of the Criminal Code prohibiting "unlawful associations." It was introduced after the 1919 Winnipeg General Strike and not repealed until 1936. The language of section 98 was sufficiently wide "to encompass the extravagant rhetoric of a trade-union meeting," and was used by the police to spy on unions, socialist and social democratic organizations, and ethnic groups. The Communist Party was a particular target, and many party members were imprisoned or deported. The second case involved the incarceration and/or deportation of Canadians of Japanese extraction during the Second World War, depriving this group of personal liberty, property, and livelihood, as well as freedom of expression. The third example, the invocation of the War Measures Act in 1970, outlawed support for the FLQ, but was used to imprison over 400 nonviolent Quebec separatists who had no connection to that organization.

The use of such measures on even three occasions raises the question of how committed the political authorities were to the principle of political freedom. Furthermore, the overwhelming popular support given to the implementation of such measures indicates a rather superficial commitment to political freedom on the part of the population at large.[4] This relates to the strong Canadian feeling of deference to authority, which is discussed below. While Canadians normally believe in political freedom, therefore, they seem prepared to let the authorities restrain such individual or group liberty at the least threat of violence.

Violations of political freedom have been more common at the provincial level, especially during the authoritarian regime of Maurice Duplessis in Quebec and with the peculiarities of the Aberhart government in Alberta, also discussed in Chapter 18. The commitment to political freedom of more recent provincial authorities was brought into question when in 1981–82 certain premiers insisted that the "notwithstanding" clause be inserted into the Charter of Rights and Freedoms. Federal and provincial governments are both allowed to override the political freedoms guaranteed in the Charter merely by admitting that intention. On the other hand, some premiers felt that the traditional means of protecting civil liberties was superior to turning the function over to the courts. In the first 20 years after adoption of the Charter, the Quebec sign law provided the most controversial exercise of the notwithstanding clause, which is an indication that the authorities are either committed to political freedoms or else that they believe their electorates would not tolerate infringements.

MAJORITY RULE

The Canadian conception of democracy also incorporates the notion of **majority rule**—that is, in case of dispute, the larger number takes precedence over the smaller number. This principle is generally accepted in elections and in legislatures that result from elections. On the other hand, it is sometimes felt necessary to protect certain minorities from the actions of the majority, so that specific minority rights are given constitutional protection. The Constitution Act, 1867, recognized Roman Catholic and Protestant minority education rights, as well as French and English minority language rights in the federal and Quebec legislatures and courts. Extension of these rights to Manitoba and their subsequent removal and resurrection were discussed in Chapter 5.

Over the past generation, Canada has extended minority rights in the Constitution to a considerable degree. The 1982 Charter of Rights guaranteed French and English language rights in all parts of the federal and New Brunswick governments, as well as French and English minority-language education rights in parts of all provinces where numbers warrant. The Charter also introduced the concept of constitutional equality rights for women (not actually a minority), and prohibited federal or provincial discrimination against minorities. The fact that the notwithstanding clause can be used to override minority rights other than those dealing with language or gender indicates that certain rights were considered to be more sacred than others and that majority rule can still apply in certain cases. But women and Charter-based minorities—official language, other ethnic, and Aboriginal minorities—have all used their new constitutional status to protect and promote their own interests.

Thus it is safe to say that almost every Canadian would claim democracy to be a fundamental political value of the country and would support the four main ingredients identified. Canadian governments, both before and after 1982, have probably had as respectable records in refraining from the violation of democratic principles as any in the world. Nevertheless, given the fact that popular sovereignty is only exercised every four years or so, and given the limited scope of political equality, the apparent ease with which governments can violate fundamental freedoms, and the tension between majority rule and minority rights, the extent to which democracy is indeed a fundamental Canadian value should not be overstated.

Distinguishing between Canadian and American Values

Once beyond the consensus on democracy, it is difficult to find widespread agreement on other Canadian political values. One approach that bears promise, however, is to contrast widely held Canadian values with those of the United States. Of course, Canadian and American values are very much alike, and not all residents are conscious of them, whether similar or different. But a rich academic literature exists on this subject, the key proponent of this approach being the American sociologist Seymour Martin Lipset, who consolidated his thoughts on the subject

By Brian Gable (The Globe and Mail). *Reprinted with permission from* The Globe and Mail.

in his book *Continental Divide*. In Lipset's analysis, these differences have their foundation in the revolutionary origins of the United States and the "counter-revolutionary" (i.e., reaction against that revolution) origins of Canada. Lipset's analysis ties in well with another widely accepted view of Canadian values, often called the Hartz-Horowitz or "fragment" theory.[5]

Many have made the point that while the American Declaration of Independence lists the objectives of "life, liberty and the pursuit of happiness," Canada's 1867 Constitution Act talks about "peace, order and good government." Lipset goes on from this point to outline his basic distinction as follows: "Canada has been and is a more class-aware, elitist, law-abiding, statist, collectivity-oriented, and particularistic (group-oriented) society than the United States.[6] Among Canadian commentators on the subject, Pierre Berton has noted that Canadians are law-abiding, peaceful, orderly, deferential toward authority, cautious, elitist, moralistic, tolerant, diffident, and unemotional.[7] For example, when former U.S. President George Bush spoke of wanting to make the United States into a "kinder, gentler" society, many observers immediately thought of Canada. This approach leads us to identify five basic Canadian values that can be distinguished from those in the United States.

BALANCE BETWEEN INDIVIDUALISM AND COLLECTIVISM

If there is a value other than democracy to which most Canadians adhere, it is probably that of **individualism**, liberalism, or capitalism, often expressed as the sanctity of private enterprise or individual economic freedom. The general principle is widely shared that everyone should be free to go about their business as they choose and that those with the greatest talent or who work the hardest should reap the benefits of their abilities and/or labour. In Paul Sniderman's survey, for example, 65 percent of Canadians believed that people who have made a lot of money were "willing to work and take advantage of the opportunities all of us have,"[8] while 13 percent felt that they have usually done so at the expense of others. The extent of commitment to individualism can be best gauged, however, in comparison with the United States.

While both countries have "mixed economies" today—that is, a combination of private enterprise and government involvement—the United States remains the world's last stronghold of liberalism or individualism with a relatively smaller public sector than other modern states. This is only to be expected, given its revolutionary origins—revolting against an oppressive foreign government—and its self-proclaimed role in recent times as the leader of the "free world" and capitalist forces. Canada, on the other hand, has been less hostile toward public intervention and more inclined to rely on government. This is partly because of the geographic environment of the Canadian political system, and the U.S. threat, as seen in Chapters 3 and 9, but it also stems from the basic Canadian value of **collectivism** or community, a value derived in the first instance from the French feudal system and the arrival of the United Empire Loyalists. Both founding groups (to say nothing of a similar value shared by Aboriginal Canadians) saw society not as a mass of grasping, ambitious individuals, but as an organic community in which all people—high and low—had their place and did their respective part to contribute to the welfare of the whole. In Sniderman's survey, 58 percent of Canadians agreed with the statement that "I am glad that I have a government that looks after me in so many ways," while 32 percent disagreed; 25 percent of Americans, compared with 50 percent of Canadians, agreed that "the government should see to it that everyone has a job and a standard of living."[9]

The balance between capitalism and collectivism in Canada can be seen in Table 10.1, which measures the degree of government intervention in the economy. It shows, for example, that the public-sector share of the Canadian gross domestic product is now about 46 percent in terms of expenditures and about 43 percent in terms of revenue. This is still relatively low in global terms, but Canada is in an almost exactly intermediate position relative to the other Western democracies. The table indicates that Canada occupies a similar ranking

TABLE 10.1   **Government Employment as Percentage of Total Labour Force, Tax Receipts as Percentage of GDP, and Government Expenditure and Revenue as Percentage of GDP, 1995**

Govt. Employment as % of Total Labour Force		Tax Receipts as % of GDP		Govt. Expenditure & Revenue as % of GDP		
					Rev.	Exp.
Sweden	31.2	Denmark	51.3	Sweden	57.5	63.8
Norway	30.8	Sweden	49.7	Denmark	58.1	59.6
Denmark	30.7	Belgium	46.5	Finland	52.8	55.9
Finland	25.2	Finland	46.5	Belgium	49.8	51.7
France	24.9	France	44.5	France	48.2	51.6
Austria	22.8	Luxembourg	44.0	Switzerland	53.8	47.7
New Zealand	22.1	Netherlands	44.0	Netherlands	49.3	50.0
Iceland	19.9	Austria	42.4	Luxembourg	52.9	45.0
Canada	**19.6**	Norway	41.5	Greece	45.0	52.1
Belgium	19.0	Greece	41.4	Austria	47.4	48.6
Italy	16.1	Italy	41.3	Norway	50.9	45.8
Australia	16.0	Germany	39.2	Italy	44.5	49.5
Spain	15.7	New Zealand	38.2	Germany	45.9	46.6
Germany	15.4	**Canada**	**37.2**	**Canada**	**42.7**	**45.8**
Portugal	15.3	UK	35.3	Portugal	39.8	42.5
UK	14.1	Spain	34.0	UK	37.2	42.3
Switzerland	14.0	Switzerland	33.9	Spain	37.9	41.2
United States	13.4	Portugal	33.8	Ireland	36.3	36.9
Ireland	13.4	Ireland	33.8	Iceland	36.0	35.1
Luxembourg	12.0	Japan	28.5	Australia	34.9	35.6
Netherlands	11.9	United States	27.9	United States	32.1	34.3
Japan	6.0			Japan	32.0	28.5

Source: OECD in Figures, © OECD, 1998. *Reproduced by the permission of the OECD.*

with respect to government employment as a percentage of total labour force (19.6 percent) and total tax receipts as a percentage of GDP (37.2 percent). This complements an observation made in Table 8.7 in Chapter 8 with respect to government social expenditures as a percentage of gross domestic product.

Thus, while Canadians might instinctively claim a commitment to capitalism and might still be less reliant on the state than many other countries, it would be more accurate to say that the accumulation of public demands has given Canada an economy almost evenly divided between private and public sectors.

Canada is generally less collectivist than Western Europe, and while the difference between the two North American countries should not be overstated, much concrete evidence of a significant variation exists. The extent of federal and provincial Crown corporations, including broadcasting, transportation, electricity and other resources, is unheard of south of the border; the Canadian public health insurance system stands out in great contrast to that of the United States; the Canadian social security system is considered more adequate; and taxes are generally higher in order to finance such collective activity. In just about every policy field, in fact, the extent of government intervention is greater in Canada than in the United States—labour legislation, agricultural marketing boards, and environmental regulation being further examples.[10] Two other differences between the two countries are that individual property rights, so valued in the United States, are not guaranteed in the Canadian Constitution and that while private American individuals and corporations are generous philanthropists, Canadians prefer to have charitable causes funded by the government.[11]

PARTICULARISM AND TOLERANCE

A second difference in the basic values of the two countries has to do with the distinction between "universalism" and **particularism**, leading many to argue that pluralism is a more appropriate description of Canada than the United States. This distinction is commonly expressed in terms of the melting pot and the mosaic: immigrants to the United States are urged to become "unhyphenated" Americans, whereas Canada encourages the retention of cultural particularisms. Sometimes this Canadian heterogeneity is simply called tolerance, and sometimes it is linked to the recognition of group rights as opposed to individual rights. The distinctiveness of the French-Canadian Roman Catholic community was the original basis of this value, but it has now spread to policies of multiculturalism and recognition of other group rights even in the Constitution.

As noted in Chapter 6, multiculturalism means encouraging the retention of ethnic cultures rather than trying to assimilate all newcomers into some kind of homogeneous Canadianism. This official policy is seen as a means of enriching and enlivening the country, encouraging new Canadians to feel at home, promoting tolerance and minimizing discrimination, and perhaps enhancing Canada's contribution to world harmony. Lipset notes, however, that an ethnic revival has occurred in many countries, including the United States, and even there the ideal of the melting pot is being replaced by that of the mosaic. He is not the only one to suggest that the two countries no longer present sharp contrasts in this respect.[12]

Particularism might be extended to women in the sense that they, like minorities, generally benefit from more advanced legislation in Canada than in the United States. It could also be seen in terms of acknowledging the existence of social classes. Americans have even less class-consciousness than Canadians, being imbued with the belief that through hard work anyone can make it to the top, and even more Americans than Canadians feel that they belong to the middle class. All of this affects the tolerance of unions, which is greater in Canada, because middle-class America sees no need for them. Particularism also has a territorial dimension—the fact that Canadian provinces are stronger than the American states. Decentralization in Canada is accompanied by stronger regional or provincial loyalties and identities, due again to the example set by Quebec. Finally, American universalism can also be seen in its foreign policy, which would brook no compromise with "evil empires," whereas Canada has often played a useful negotiating role on the international scene because of the lessons of compromise and tolerance learned at home.[13]

DEFERENCE TO AUTHORITY

Another fundamental difference between Canadian and American values is the much greater **deference to authority** in Canadian society.[14] Canadians demonstrate greater respect toward the law, judges, police, religious leaders, and many others with "legitimate power." Peace, order, and good government rather than individual liberty is the Canadian ideal, and many observers have noted that Canada is probably the only country where a police officer, the Mountie, is a national symbol—certainly a contrast to the U.S. hero, Horatio Alger, the self-made man. Unlike Americans, Canadians are not instinctively suspicious of the state; indeed, Canadians have not seen the government in terms of an alien imposition, but as the authorized agent to respond to their individual and collective demands. Such respect for authority and trust in government goes so far as to permit much greater government secrecy in Canada than in the United States, to be less concerned about the admissibility of evidence obtained illegally by the Crown,[15] and even to allow the RCMP to engage in a wide range of illegal activities such as opening mail and breaking into and burning buildings.[16] To recognize the pervasive presence of the state is to acknowledge, perhaps unconsciously, the significance of the bureaucracy.[17]

Deference is related to other values already mentioned. Americans are the epitome of the "Protestant ethic," that is, members of Protestant sects that emphasize hard work in this life as the key to entering the next. But in their frenzy to get ahead at all costs, individualistic, competitive, and achievement-oriented Americans may find it necessary to bend or break the law. Canadians, less obsessed with material success, are more likely to obey a law even if they do not like it. Crime rates are considerably lower in Canada, gun control laws are stronger, and the drug problem is less severe. Furthermore, the United States has many more lawyers per capita, and Americans are more litigious by nature, having a much greater propensity to take disputes to court.

Deference to authority comes in part from the monarchical and feudal traditions, which contain the idea of an organic community made up of people of different status. These values were reinforced by the two dominant churches in Canadian history, Roman Catholic and Anglican, which recognize priests, bishops, archbishops (as well as cardinals and popes in the former case) in a great hierarchy between ordinary mortals and God. Americans, on the other hand, exalting the sovereignty of "We, the People," revolted against the monarchical system and, when it came to religion, turned to anti-elitist, Protestant sects where power resided in the local congregation. Respect for authority and the law is also related to the settlement of the western frontier. In the Canadian West, the law and enforcement of the law by the RCMP preceded settlement, whereas in the violent American frontier, settlers arrived ahead of the law. This state of affairs not only provided Canada with a more peaceful settlement of its frontier (and, believe it or not, better treatment of its Aboriginals), but reinforced the previously established respect for law and order.

EGALITARIANISM

In his more recent work, Lipset argues that in some ways Canada is more egalitarian than the United States.[18] One striking example is in the constitutional equality of women. In the United States the proposed Equal Rights Amendment did not pass, whereas at about the same time, Canada adopted a strong guarantee of gender equality (including affirmative action) in the 1982 Canadian Charter of Rights and Freedoms. Somewhat similarly, the health and welfare programs that flow from Canadian collectivism ensure a greater degree of equality for the poor and working classes. Canada extends this redistributive egalitarianism to have-not regions as well as have-not individuals through equalization payments and regional economic development programs. Even in the realm of higher education, Canada now appears to be more egalitarian than the United States, as seen in Figure 10.1. The subtle differences in the public's commitment to equality in the two countries are revealed the following measures in Sniderman's study: 47 percent of Americans but only 31 percent of Canadians agreed that "we have gone too far in pushing equal rights in this country," and 7 percent of Americans but 12 percent of Canadians agreed that "in a fair economic system, all people should earn about the same."[19]

Figure 10.1   **Ten OECD Countries with the Highest Percentage of Young Adults Enrolled* in University, 1988**

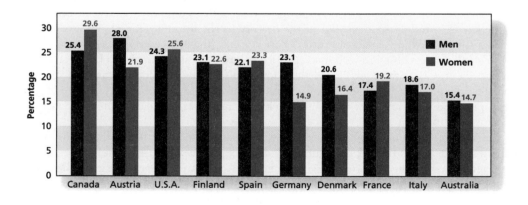

Source: *Adapted from Statistics Canada,* Canadian Social Trends, *Catalogue No. 11-008 (Autumn 1993).*
*Full-time and part-time enrollment converted to full-time equivalents. Population is those of theoretical university enrollment age (18–25 in Canada).

Canadian **egalitarianism** is related to the comparative strength of class-consciousness, trade unions, and social democratic parties in the two countries. It can also be seen in a strong cooperative movement, stretching from Prairie grain elevators to Quebec's caisses populaires to the Antigonish movement in the Maritimes. Perhaps it also results from the feeling of noblesse oblige among those in the upper echelons of the hierarchy, the feudal concept that the lord was responsible for the well-being of his serfs. In any case, Lipset argues that Canadians are more committed to "redistributive egalitarianism, while Americans place more emphasis on meritocratic competition and equality of opportunity." He also admits that the United States has a greater hierarchy of educational institutions than is found in Canada.[20]

CAUTION, DIFFIDENCE, DEPENDENCE, AND NONVIOLENCE

The fifth value difference to emerge from the Lipset analysis relates to Canadian caution and diffidence, sometimes called a national inferiority complex. It includes our historical dependence on other countries, the lack of will to be truly exceptional or to stand out from the crowd, or the absence of a spirit of innovation and risk taking.[21] Canadians delight in the security of savings and understatement. Of course there have been many Canadian "winners" in all walks of life, in whose accomplishments Canadians vicariously share: Margaret Atwood, Glenn Gould, Wayne Gretzky, Karen Kain, Donovan Bailey, Céline Dion, and Bryan Adams, for example, in addition to Nobel Prize winners Frederick Banting, Lester Pearson, John Polanyi, and those who have been lost to other countries such as Joni Mitchell and John Kenneth Galbraith. But Canadians sometimes take satisfaction in being "beautiful losers"; they are obsessed with "survival" rather than success; they are especially good at deprecating themselves, and almost always think things American are superior. As Pierre Berton says, they are prudent and cautious, sober and solemn, and introverted, uncertain, and always questioning themselves. Most Canadians take quiet satisfaction in their accomplishments—a 1995 survey showed that 89 percent of Canadians felt proud when they saw the Canadian flag or heard the national anthem—but they are embarrassed to proclaim it aloud.[22] Above all, as Constable Benton Fraser demonstrates on the TV series *Due South*, Canadians are polite![23]

Although Canada made major contributions to two world wars, Canadians are not a warlike people.[24] They abhor violence at home and abroad; they have no enemies, and their military establishment is minimal. Instead, they have tried to be peacemakers and peacekeepers in international relations, putting special emphasis on the United Nations (another collective authority), trying to reduce the militancy of the foreign policy of the United States in quiet, backroom diplomacy, and helping to remove the causes of war through assistance to the Third World.

Other Basic Values

At least in the past, four additional national characteristics based on geography, ethnicity, and political institutions have also been considered part of the basic Canadian political value structure. Some of these were identified as basic constitutional principles in Chapter 2.

First, Canadians are a northern people, attached to the land.[25] To a large extent they enjoy the wilderness, relish four distinct seasons, including the cold, and are immensely proud of the beauty and variety of their natural surroundings, whether it is the Rocky Mountains, the Prairie wheatfields, the rugged Canadian Shield, or picturesque Atlantic fishing villages.[26]

Second, Canada is an officially bilingual country. French and English have been recognized as official languages, at least at the federal level, and since 1970 or so have become well established in national institutions. Governors general, prime ministers, ministers, Supreme Court judges, members of Parliament, and senior bureaucrats are increasingly expected to be able to function in both languages, and for those who arrive at such high office without such capability, second-language training is available at public expense. Federal publications, signs, services, and ceremonies all reflect this policy, and while many oppose it, others see it as a key feature distinguishing Canada from the United States.[27] The companion policy of official multiculturalism has already been covered in terms of particularism and tolerance.

Third, Canada is a federation, with a division of powers between two levels of government such that neither is subordinate to the other. This characteristic of government was adapted from the United States, but Canadian federalism has developed its own unique features, as seen in Chapter 17, especially an extremely decentralized character. This has resulted from Quebec's promotion of provincial autonomy, with the governments of the other large, wealthy provinces following suit.

Canada's adoption of the British parliamentary system is a fourth prominent national characteristic. Both federal and provincial governments operate with a strong executive, a relatively weak legislative branch, and, until 1982, a judiciary that had very limited powers of judicial review. The recent addition to the Constitution of a Charter of Rights and Freedoms granting authority to the courts to invalidate legislation conflicting with the Charter is a U.S. anomaly grafted onto the British institutional trunk. Other than the Charter and the French civil code used in Quebec, the whole Canadian legal system is based on that of Britain, including the British common law.

One place to look for basic Canadian political values would be in the Constitution. Unfortunately, the Canadian Constitution has never included a statement of basic values beyond that of "peace, order and good government," but the **Canada Clause** in the Charlottetown Accord made such an attempt, which more or less confirms the values identified above. These fundamental characteristics include:

- Democracy
- Parliamentary system of government
- Federal system of government
- Aboriginal peoples constitute one of three orders of government
- Quebec constitutes a distinct society within Canada
- Official bilingualism (including official language minorities)
- Racial, ethnic, and cultural equality and diversity
- Individual and collective human rights and freedoms
- Equality of men and women
- Equality of the provinces, but recognition of diversity

When pollster Allan Gregg asked ordinary Canadians in 1995 what they thought was distinctive about Canada and Canadians, he received much the same results as discussed above: nonviolence, tolerance of minorities, humane treatment of the poor and disadvantaged, official bilingualism, history and climate, and reluctance to boast.[28] In short, Canadians have traditionally seen themselves inhabiting a sprawling, decentralized country of great natural beauty and variety; they are an officially bilingual and multicultural society characterized by severe regional and ethnic strains; and their political system fuses the British parliamentary system with American federalism. Canadians have a restrained commitment to democracy, combined with deferential and elitist traits, and prefer a strong government. This reflects the strength of social democratic sentiments and has resulted in redistributive egalitarianism. Moreover, in an international reflection of its domestic character, Canada is a peaceful, constructive member of the world community.

CANADA'S CHANGING POLITICAL CULTURE

As Canada approached the new millennium, many aspects of this traditional value structure seemed to be changing. Different concepts of democracy emerged, the distinction between Canadian and American values appeared to decline, and some of the other values identified above had diminishing support. Much of this transformation can be attributed to the presence of the United States, directly or indirectly; some of it is part of a worldwide change in political values; and some is not so easily explained.[29]

As far as democracy is concerned, the 1990s saw an upsurge in interest in the means of more direct popular participation. The most common prescription in this regard is the **referendum**, in which legislators would be guided or bound by frequent referrals to the electorate as a whole. Quebec has used this device twice on the question of sovereignty; certain other provinces now require it for approval of constitutional amendments; and some have prescribed its use for other issues such as significant tax increases. Many observers believe that since the Charlottetown Accord was put to a popular vote in 1992 any other major constitutional changes will require a national referendum as well, even though this is not mandated by the constitutional amending formula.

Direct participation also includes the concept of the **initiative**, in which legislators respond to demands expressed by voters in the form of a petition, although this device has not made much headway. The third aspect of this "new democracy" is the **recall**, in which a certain proportion of electors in a constituency sign a petition forcing their member of Parliament to resign. This device seems to be gaining popularity, although at the time of writing, it has been legislated only in BC.

Another aspect of dissatisfaction with the traditional notion of democracy is the now commonly advanced idea that elected members of Parliament should vote on certain issues in accordance with the views of their constituents rather than follow the party line. Even assuming that it would be technically possible to discover the majority opinion in a legislator's constituency, however, this argument has not yet been advanced with sufficient strength to transform existing practices. This stance does not always influence the legislative behaviour of even Reform Party MPs, but individual defections from the party line, including the Liberal case, were more common after 1993 than ever before.

Several of the Canadian values described above emanate from British, United Empire Loyalist, or French feudal origins and may lose their salience as these influences fade into the past or are diluted by immigration from other parts of the world. The distinctions between Canadian and American values are also threatened in at least three ways by the influence of the United States on Canada. First, given the extent of U.S. control over Canada and Canadian exposure to the United States, values implicit in that country's popular culture, as transmitted by television, movies, books, magazines and music, in business, and the military, are likely to have some impact on those north of the border. It is debatable whether distinctive Canadian values can withstand the homogenizing force of modern technology, especially that originating from the south.[30] Second, nationalists see all these influences increasing under the Free Trade Agreement and NAFTA, and fear that the distinctiveness of Canadian values will suffer as a result. Third, some observers such as Lipset feel that the adoption of a U.S.-style Charter of Rights and Freedoms will have a profound effect on diminishing distinctive Canadian values. The Charter places the power of the state under judicial restraint and "makes Canada a more individualistic and litigious culture."[31]

In a country that articulates its basic values so diffidently to start with, these powerful threats are not to be taken lightly. The situation is only exacerbated when a major party leader, Preston Manning, takes much of his script from south of the border. There are several recent indications that support for collectivism and feelings of deference in Canada are already on the decline, one of which was the refusal to endorse the Charlottetown Accord, a product of the political elite.[32] Although it cannot be blamed entirely on Americans, the obsession with government debts and deficits at both federal and provincial levels has seriously eroded social programs and many other public interventions into the private sector. Privatization of Crown corporations and deregulation have become rampant. Canadians have also developed an increasingly negative attitude toward politicians, as seen in Table 10.2.

Even the other distinctive Canadian values mentioned have recently been challenged.[33] Some commentators contend that Canadians have not really valued the land, but rather raped it; that bilingualism is not so much a source of pride as of discord; that Canadians do not show much tolerance toward racial minorities now that such groups are increasingly numerous and visible; that the Trudeau and Mulroney governments destroyed much of Canadians' respect for and trust in government authority; and that the ubiquitous neoconservative ideology weakened the public sector and rendered impotent the collectivist, social democratic streak of the Canadian character. As far as equality is concerned, Canadians still appear to treasure equal access to health care and perhaps public schools, but they show little concern when politicians reduce redistributive social programs. A study by the Canadian Policy Research Networks, for example, found a new emphasis on self-reliance and fiscal responsibility: "The strong sense of collective responsibility is now balanced by recognition that families and individuals must take more responsibility for themselves and their kind."[34]

TABLE 10.2	"Most Politicians Can Be Trusted to Do What Is Best for the Country"[35] (Percentages)		
	Fall 1984	*Winter 1988*	*Winter 1993*
Agree	24.7	22.6	11.7
Depends	44.6	38.4	46.3
Disagree	30.3	38.6	41.3

Source: Decima Quarterly (Reports 19, 36, 56). Research, courtesy of the Centre for the Study of Democracy, Queen's University. The author has collapsed 11 categories into 3.

In his immersion in the study of Canadian values, Environics pollster Michael Adams asserts that "the stereotype of Canadians as respectful and reserved, and not that imaginative, is fast losing its validity.... The status associated with once-cherished institutions ... has gone into steep decline. Established authority has had its legitimacy questioned in every sphere." Canadians have rejected the power of traditional institutional authorities, and with that rejection comes a decline in civility and reluctance to break the rules.[36]

An even more comprehensive study to come to similar conclusions about the changing nature of the Canadian political culture is Neil Nevitte's book *The Decline of Deference*. He relies on the 1981 and 1990 World Values Surveys, which polled citizens of all the advanced industrial countries. Although the book does not necessarily deny the validity of the traditional Canadian political culture sketched above, practically every item in his study now contradicts those observations. His foremost figure is that those Canadians expressing a "high degree" of confidence in government institutions fell from 36.9 percent in 1981 to 29.4 percent in 1990, and was lower than in most of the comparable countries. He presents much corroborating evidence from the same surveys—rising interest in politics, falling confidence in nongovernmental institutions, rising potential for protest, falling general deference—and then argues that it is not American influence that has been the culprit: all advanced industrial states experienced similar value transformations over that decade.[37]

· ·
'LIMITED IDENTITIES': SUBCULTURES IN CANADA

Even before recent changes in basic Canadian political values, the latter were submerged to some extent by regional, provincial, ethnic, and class variations. For generations, political scientists and historians in Canada have debated whether a pan-Canadian political culture really existed, or whether it made more sense to emphasize regional, provincial, ethnic, and class **subcultures** or **limited identities**.[38] Subcultures are distinctive collections of values, beliefs, attitudes, and orientations held by smaller groups within the society. Given the strong influences of region, ethnicity, and class in Canada society, it is not surprising that smaller clusters of values and attitudes based on these three factors would constitute subcultures, supplementing whatever pan-Canadian values can be identified. In his study of the Canadian political culture, David Bell emphasizes that language and cultural divisions, regionalism, and class cleavages (as well as the omnipresence of the United States) are more than supplementary; they are dominant characteristics of the Canadian political culture and the "roots of disunity," retarding the development of more uniform values.[39]

Regional and Provincial Subcultures

Regional or provincial identities and loyalties, variations in attachment to national political values, variations in such attitudes as political efficacy and trust in government, and differences in party systems, political participation, and voting behaviour are all evidence of regional or provincial political subcultures.[40] Many of these subjects will be examined later, but a general description of each subculture can be provided now.

Canadians are frequently polled as to their respective federal and provincial loyalties. Table 10.3 indicates the results on this subject of a 1994 *Maclean's*/Decima poll. The figures can be taken to mean that Ontarians have the least defined concept of a provincial identity in Canada, and see themselves as Canadians who happen to be situated in Ontario. Quebeckers and Newfoundlanders have the strongest sense of being a "distinct society." The proud sense of history felt by the Maritime provinces is still evident, although it is restrained by a modern feeling of dependence on Ottawa and the rest of the country.

The survey indicates that Westerners are quite centrally oriented, in spite of the fact that Alberta and British Columbia have increasingly strong self-images and that residents harbour feelings of **Western alienation**. Such alienation was defined in 1980 as follows:

> A regionally distinct political culture through and within which are expressed economic discontent, the rejection of a semi-colonial status within the Canadian state, antipathy towards Quebec and French-Canadian influence within the national government, the irritation of the West's partisan weakness within a succession of Liberal national governments, and the demand from provincial political elites for greater jurisdictional autonomy.[41]

Westerners also provide restrained support for the democratic principle of majority rule, which to them means that national policies are designed in the interests of central Canada. Many Westerners also reject the existing decision-making structure in which the Senate does not give them sufficient voting strength to overcome Ontario's influence in other branches of government.

Nelson Wiseman advises us, however, that each of the three Prairie provinces has a somewhat distinctive political culture, largely based on different patterns of settlement. Manitoba

TABLE 10.3   **Federal and Provincial Orientations of Canadians: "Do You Think of Yourself as a Canadian First or as a Citizen of Your Province?" (Percentages)**

	Canadian	Provincial
Newfoundland	39	57
Prince Edward Island	50	44
Nova Scotia	69	27
New Brunswick	64	26
Quebec	45	49
Ontario	90	9
Manitoba	77	11
Saskatchewan	82	7
Alberta	74	16
British Columbia	76	17
All Canada	72	22

Source: Maclean's, January 3, 1994. Used with permission.

was historically dominated by ex-Ontario liberals and developed a "liberal" political culture; Saskatchewan became the home of a large contingent from the British working class, giving it a left-wing populist political culture; and Alberta was populated with ex-Americans—religious, radical, populist, individualistic, and often preoccupied with monetary theories—who provided the base for a right-wing, populist, plebiscitarian political culture.[42]

Ethnic Subcultures

French Canada provides the best example of both an ethnic subculture within Canada and the fact that values and attitudes can change over time. In the pre-1960 period, Quebec was extremely conservative in its attitudes and values, was heavily influenced by the Roman Catholic Church, had a low general level of education, and was less committed to the value of democracy than the rest of the country.[43] It was very inward-looking and obsessed with survival and with being left alone. Quebec remains a distinct ethnic subculture today, but its values have changed. It is still concerned with the preservation of the French language and culture but no longer looks to the Church as a means of doing so. The Quebec provincial government has become the primary engine of French-Canadian "national" survival, and Quebeckers have become profoundly democratic. They now believe strongly in majority rule (at least within the province) and in political equality, for example, in regulating election contributions. French Canadians have become politically sophisticated, their culture has flourished, their attitudes have become more "progressive" than those of other Canadians on such issues as daycare, abortion, common-law marriages, and homosexuality, and they are becoming increasingly aggressive economically. A new francophone entrepreneurial elite is even confident of taking on the Americans under free trade. Somewhat similarly to the Prairie provinces, then, the distinctive provincial and ethnic subcultures for francophone Quebeckers coincide.[44] According to a July 1995 *Maclean's* survey, however, 75 percent of Quebeckers reported feeling pride when they saw the Canadian flag or heard the national anthem.

New multicultural and Aboriginal subcultures are also increasingly evident in Canada. Both groups have been passive until recently, neither articulating their demands strongly nor even participating actively as political candidates or voters. At the beginning of the 1990s, however, both subcultures suddenly became more self-confident and aggressive, demanding their place as party delegates, candidates, or participants in constitutional negotiations. Aboriginals have a distinct conception of their place in Canadian society and want to govern themselves, while the multicultural community wants to be a full participant in the overall political system.

Class Subcultures

Within the general Canadian political culture, different classes exhibit somewhat distinctive values, attitudes, and orientations, even where the individuals involved are lacking in class-consciousness. Attitudes of trust in government and feelings of political efficacy naturally decline from upper- to middle- to working-class groups, and are lowest among the poor. It is also likely that the upper classes are less committed to communitarian and egalitarian values than the working classes, and are more attached to elitism and hierarchy. In short, the upper classes have a political subculture distinguished by feelings of self-confidence, trust, and participation and by demands for the retention of the status quo; the working classes have a political subculture characterized by alienation, lack of participation, and by demands for substantial economic reform. Most of the poor have dropped out of the political system entirely, evidence of a truly distinctive subculture.[45]

Other Subcultures

In recent years, it has become trendy to argue that the subcultures identified above are becoming less distinct and are being supplanted by others. David Foot, in his book *Boom, Bust and Echo*, argues that the population can most meaningfully be divided into groups based on date of birth, giving him the Baby Boomers (1947–66), the Baby Busters (1967–79), and the Baby Boom Echo (1980–95).[46] One does not have to agree with him completely to acknowledge that as the baby boom cohort ages, it will be making new demands on government. Nevitte divides the population into two main groups: those born before 1945 with their "materialist" orientations, and those born after 1945, the "postmaterialist" generation. He finds that this dividing line explains a great deal about differences in Canadian values.[47] Michael Adams argues that all demographic criteria are increasingly irrelevant, and he therefore divides the population into 12 categories based on values, age, and lifestyle.[48] Whatever the merits of these new approaches, their groupings have yet to gain as much recognition as the subcultures identified above.

....

POLITICAL PARTICIPATION

Since many of the basic political values relate directly or indirectly to citizen participation in the political system, patterns of political participation can also be considered an aspect of political culture. Political participation consists of "those voluntary activities by citizens that are intended to influence the selection of government leaders or the decisions they make."[49] Numerous avenues of political participation exist, but actual participation takes effort, which not everyone is willing to exert, and which is partly related to the possession of **political efficacy**—a sense of political competence and a feeling that one can have some impact on the system. In a 1993 survey, for example, two-thirds of respondents complained that politics was too complicated for them to understand, that people like themselves had no say about what government did, and that government did not care about their opinions.[50] Participation also depends on the possession of such resources as time, money, and information. In the Canadian case, the opportunities for participation far exceed actual levels of involvement.

Electoral Participation

Voting on election day is a crucial aspect of democracy, as previously defined, and is the most common form of political participation in Canada. The voter turnout rate is also one of the few forms of participation that can be regularly and reliably measured. The overall average national turnout rate since 1900 has been about 73 percent, or nearly three-quarters of those eligible to vote. The rate by province for each federal election between 1984 and 1997 is provided in Table 10.4. The 1993 rate appears to be lower than normal, perhaps due to the fact that a year-old voters' list—from the 1992 referendum—was used. The number who voted is accurate, but the list of eligible voters was inflated because (1) an estimated 205 000 people on the 1992 list had died and (2) an estimated 1 617 384 people on the 1992 list had moved without asking to be deleted but had their names added under their new address. Thus, if these 1 822 384 people are subtracted from the 19 906 796 names of eligible voters in 1993, the real number would be 18 984 412, and the real turnout rate would be 73.0 percent—exactly the modern-day average. Unfortunately, the "official" rate of 70 percent gains credibility and appears to be part of a trend when the turnout rate fell to 67 percent in 1997. Table 10.4 also indicates the average turnout rate in provincial elections over the 1974–1998 period.

Prince Edward Island normally leads the nation at both federal and provincial levels, with an average turnout in recent federal elections of nearly 80 percent and an even higher provincial rate, suggesting that in the small confines of that province, politics has a higher salience in residents' lives than elsewhere. Quebec, Saskatchewan, and New Brunswick also have relatively high turnout rates at both levels, although Saskatchewan took a nosedive in recent years. Ontario has an average federal turnout but a low provincial rate; Newfoundland, on the

TABLE 10.4 **Percentage Voter Turnout, by Province, in Federal Elections, 1984–1997, and Average Voter Turnout in Provincial Elections, 1974–1998**

	Federal Elections					**Provincial Elections**
					Ave-rage	*Average Turnout 1974–98*
	1984	**1988**	**1993**	**1997**		
Newfoundland	65.5	67.1	55.1	55.2	60.7	77.6
Prince Edward Island	84.6	84.6	73.2	72.8	78.8	83.6
Nova Scotia	75.4	74.8	64.7	69.4	71.1	74.1
New Brunswick	77.3	75.9	69.6	73.4	74.1	79.0
Quebec	76.2	75.2	77.1	73.3	75.5	80.7
Ontario	75.8	74.6	67.7	65.6	70.9	63.4
Manitoba	73.2	74.7	68.7	63.2	70.0	72.3
Saskatchewan	77.9	77.8	69.4	65.3	72.6	78.8
Alberta	69.1	75.0	65.2	58.5	67.0	57.1
British Columbia	77.6	78.7	67.8	65.6	72.4	72.9
NWT	67.9	70.8	62.9	58.9	65.1	—
Yukon	77.9	78.4	70.4	69.8	74.1	—
Average	75.3	75.3	69.6	67.0	71.8	

Source: Data compiled from Thirty-Sixth General Election 1997: Official Voting Results: Synopsis. Reproduced with the permission of the Minister of Public Works and Government Services Canada, 2000. Full responsibility for calculations and for conclusions drawn rests with the author. Provincial results also calculated by author.

other hand, has an average provincial turnout but the lowest turnout rate in federal elections. Albertans turn out even less for provincial than federal elections; Alberta is the only case of a provincial election in which less than 50 percent of voters turned out at the polls, although this is common in municipal elections throughout the country.

To some extent, these figures reflect varying degrees of interest in politics and loosely parallel the pattern of federal loyalties in Table 10.3 on the subject of regional subcultures. But these figures are also influenced by such factors as the degree of party competition within the province. The 25 to 30 percent who do not vote are generally alienated from or uninformed about the political system; they are primarily made up of the poor and working classes.

The federal turnout rate for the 1980s falls between the extremes of other countries, as revealed in Table 10.5. Canada is well above the United States in voter turnout, about the same as Britain, and behind many other states.

Within the 70 to 75 percent who do vote, we can distinguish among degrees of knowledge and involvement. As Chapter 14 indicates, the level of information of the typical voter should not be overestimated, and many who vote have paid little or no attention to the campaign. While 80 percent claim to have exposed themselves to television or newspaper coverage of the election campaign, only 20 percent follow politics closely on a daily basis between elections.

A study of the 1984 election found that as a national average, voters could name 3.3 provincial premiers (out of ten) and 36 percent could define the concepts of left and right and place the NDP as the furthest left of the three main parties. The level of factual and conceptual knowledge increased with level of education and reading about politics in newspapers and magazines; significant regional variations were also evident, but viewing political programs on television was of negligible impact.[51]

Beyond those who cast an "informed vote," a smaller proportion of the electorate becomes actively involved in the election campaign. A small number attend all-candidates meetings;

TABLE 10.5 **Percentage Voter Turnout Rates in Eighteen Countries, 1980s**

Australia	94.3	Greece	82.0
Belgium	93.8	Ireland	74.2
Austria	91.5	United Kingdom	74.0
New Zealand	90.5	Spain	73.4
Italy	89.8	**Canada**	**73.3**
Sweden	89.1	Japan	71.4
France	86.2	India	62.0
Denmark	86.1	United States	54.3
Netherlands	83.4	Switzerland	47.5

Source: *Privy Council Office, Royal Commission on Electoral Reform and Party Financing, vol. I, pp. 52–53. Reproduced with the permission of the Minister of Public Works and Government Services Canada, 2000.*

TABLE 10.6   **Numbers of Individuals Making Financial Contributions to National Parties and Local Candidates, 1993 and 1997 Elections**

	1993		1997	
	Parties	*Candidates*	*Parties*	*Candidates*
PC	44 728	25 460	23 352	20 353
Liberal	41 058	32 907	34 429	21 906
NDP	65 301	12 367	50 434	15 119
Reform	49 488	25 211	75 587	20 624
Bloc	29 084*	26 337	18 885	13 215
TOTAL	229 659	122 282	202 687	91 217

Sources: Report of the Chief Electoral Officer Respecting Election Expenses, 1993, *and Elections Canada,* Registered Political Parties' Fiscal Period Returns for 1997, *calculations by author. Reproduced with the permission of the Minister of Public Works and Government Services Canada, 2000. Full responsibility for calculations and for conclusions drawn rests with the author.*
*Bloc figures include nonelection year 1994.

some work as deputy returning officers and poll clerks; some join a political party and vote at its local nomination meeting; some contribute money to political parties; some contribute time to a local candidate to do mailing, telephoning, or door-to-door canvassing; and a small number in each constituency become totally preoccupied with the local campaign. Members of this last group, including candidates themselves, are sometimes called "gladiators" as distinct from the great bulk of the population who are primarily "spectators."[52]

Table 10.6 indicates the number of individuals who contributed money to the five main parties and their local candidates in 1993 and 1997. Since some individuals made contributions to both parties and candidates, there is a certain amount of double-counting, and probably no more than 250 000 out of an electorate of 19 million, or slightly more than 1 percent, made financial contributions. This contrasts with the 13 percent who claim that they often or sometimes give money.[53]

Nonelectoral Participation

The political participation of most Canadians peaks at election time, but many avenues are open between elections in which to make demands, demonstrate support, or otherwise become involved in the political process. Most Canadian political parties do not maintain reliable lists of party members, but Ken Carty estimates this figure to be about 2.7 percent of the population.[54] It is known that many people sign up before or during the campaign and then let their membership lapse.

Another means of political participation is to join a voluntary group, an action that at least 50 percent of Canadians claim to do.[55] As seen in Chapter 15, any group, whatever its primary orientation, can become a pressure group, so that membership in any group is potentially political. Even if the group itself takes a political turn, however, passive members rarely do more than send the occasional preprinted postcard to their MP or the prime minister. On the other hand, active executive and staff members of such groups may become highly involved in political campaigns. Even more initiative is required to *form* such a group, usually to protest against some political decision or lack of action at the municipal, provincial, or federal level.

Such group participation usually involves communicating with the authorities in routine ways, but occasionally it takes the form of peaceful demonstrations (locally or on Parliament Hill); sit-ins and other types of civil disobedience; and the rare case of violent protest. As noted above, Canadians are generally a peaceful lot, and instances of political violence are uncommon. The main historical incidents of violence were the two Riel Rebellions of 1870 and 1885, the conscription riots in Quebec City in 1918, the Winnipeg General Strike of 1919, the Regina Riot of 1935, various FLQ incidents of the 1960s culminating in the FLQ crisis of 1970, and the Mohawks' armed standoff at Oka in 1990.[56]

TABLE 10.7	Percentage Level of Participation in Selected Political Activities, 1993, by Occupation, Income, and Education				
	Discuss Politics	*Party Work*	*Sign Petition*	*March/ Rally*	*Sit-in*
Occupation					
Blue collar	75	4	71	26	9
White collar	89	6	76	26	7
Professional/managerial	86	9	78	37	10
Income					
Under $20 000	70	5	54	21	7
$20 000–39 999	80	5	69	24	8
$40 000–59 999	82	7	77	30	9
$60 000–69 999	87	9	76	27	10
$70 000 & over	87	12	79	30	7
Education					
Elementary or less	68	9	34	14	5
Some secondary	75	4	57	18	6
Complete secondary	82	8	69	19	6
Some university	82	7	78	32	10
University degree	86	7	86	45	13

Source: Mishler and Clarke, "Political Participation in Canada," p. 137.

Canadians can also participate politically between elections as individuals—writing, faxing, or e-mailing letters to MPs or the prime minister, writing letters to the editors of newspapers, calling radio or television phone-in shows, signing petitions, or telephoning or meeting an MP. As with so many other aspects of political participation, however, it is difficult to obtain solid data on the degree of this category of individual involvement. One survey has reported the figures to be about 20 percent,[57] but in general, few people take the initiative to do any of these things.

One interesting question is the relationship between degree of participation and social status. Table 10.7 indicates five forms of participation broken down by level of income and education and occupational status. The table demonstrates that the degree of involvement increases with level of income and education, and from blue-collar to white-collar to professional and managerial occupations. Possession of money provides the resources that facilitate high levels of participation. Such a pattern even exists for political protests, for students involved in such activities tend to be sons and daughters of the upper or upper-middle class.[58]

···

CONCLUSION

Although the values and attitudes that constitute the political culture of any society are difficult to establish, certain Canadian political values can be identified, the foremost being a rudimentary belief in democracy. In many cases, it helps to see Canadian values in contrast to those of the United States. Canada has a more even balance between individualism and collectivism; it gives greater weight to particularism, tolerance, and deference to authority; it is also more egalitarian, cautious, diffident, and dependent. To some extent, however, these differences between Canadian and American values are in decline. Efforts to define pan-Canadian values, attitudes, and identities are also complicated by the existence of regional, ethnic, and class political subcultures. As for political participation in Canada, it "bears little similarity to the classical democratic ideal of widespread citizen involvement in all aspects of the political process."[59] Whether it is the low level of public information and participation that requires a reliance on elitist representative government to make public decisions, or the nature of representative government that encourages such low popular involvement is not entirely clear.[60]

(SC) The limited nature of Canadian democracy, combined with Canadian deference to authority, means that political authorities have considerable autonomy in making their decisions, as the state-centred approach suggests. It would be too much to claim that the state is completely autonomous from the rest of society and from demands flowing from the public, but it now becomes clear why state authorities have, to a large extent, been able to pursue their own conception of the national interest. Canadians are also respectful of those in positions of authority in other segments of society, and this chapter has identified the various regional/provincial, ethnic, and class subcultures whose leaders come together in a process of elite accommodation. They devise compromise arrangements with which to satisfy the mass members of these groups. On the other hand, such state-centred dominance appears to be increasingly challenged by a demand for more popular input.

In terms of participation, the authorities choose the most convenient date for the election and the message to be conveyed, and, content in the knowledge that few people know what is going on and even fewer can be bothered to do anything about it, carry on with their own agenda. Politicians may encourage popular participation when it serves their own purposes, but bureaucrats are notoriously suspicious of public involvement. Even if the public is now demanding more meaningful participation, they are not turning out in any greater numbers on election day.

P Pluralists centre on the "limited identities" that characterize Canadians and the many subcultures that exist in the country, each one providing a shading to the national values identified. They also focus on the values of particularism and tolerance. Rather than emphasize the elite interaction that emanates from such subcultures, however, pluralists note that most of these interests are organized into pressure groups and that public policies are the outcome of a broader interplay among such groups. Pluralism emphasizes that individuals are free to join or form any group, and while over half of Canadian adults do so, the passivity of most members comes as no surprise.

PC This chapter also demonstrates that relatively few citizens either are well informed or participate beyond voting, surely a smaller number than the public choice approach would have anticipated. Whether such behaviour is based on a rational understanding that greater effort would not be worthwhile or on simple apathy and laziness, it is clear that the "public choice" is often not a well-informed one.

C Class analysts are generally critical of the Canadian values and attitudes identified in this chapter. In particular, they emphasize the narrow conception of democracy held by most Canadians, deriding the notion of one person–one vote as a genuine measure of political equality, the view that political freedom is meaningful in the absence of economic and social freedom, and the claim that an election every four years is an effective implementation of popular sovereignty. They also contend that the capitalist ethic is still predominant among the political and economic elite and that much of the government intervention that has occurred has been welcomed rather than opposed by the bourgeoisie. They put little stock in such "tory" ideas as trusting a concerned and paternalistic political or economic elite to advance the position of the working class. Such analysts emphasize class subcultures and view regional and ethnic subcultures largely in class terms. They argue, too, that Canadians have not respected their heritage of natural resources, that federalism has impaired Ottawa's capacity to ensure greater economic equality in the country, and that the state has not been strong in improving the conditions of the working class.

As for participation, class analysts claim that the bourgeoisie encourages the masses to vote, but only to choose between parties equally committed to the capitalist system. If political violence occurs, such as in the Winnipeg General Strike, the Regina Riot, or the Oka incident, the authorities move the police in quickly to quell it, frequently exacerbating the situation with such coercive measures.

···

DISCUSSION QUESTIONS

1. Do you believe that periodic elections are a sufficient means of exercising the principle of popular sovereignty, and that the principle of one person–one vote is a sufficient mark of political equality? Explain your answer.

2. How deep is the Canadian commitment to political freedom? What situations do you think justify government restriction of such freedom?

3. What kinds of minority rights should be protected in the Constitution, and in what circumstances should Canada follow the principle of majority rule?

4. To what extent do you agree with the Lipset analysis of the differences between Canadian and American values? To what extent has the traditional Canadian political culture been transformed in recent years?

5. Do you think it is more productive to speak of the national Canadian political culture or only of various subcultures? Is the national political culture more than just a sum of the subcultures?

6. How do you account for the fairly consistent voter turnout in Canadian elections?

7. What forms of political participation have you engaged in? Why haven't you and/or other Canadians participated more?

8. How high a level of political information and political participation does a democracy require?

9. How do the critical approaches outlined in Chapter 1 enhance our understanding of the Canadian political culture?

···

NOTES

1. See, for example, David V.J. Bell, "Political Culture in Canada," in Michael S. Whittington and Glen Williams, eds., *Canadian Politics in the 1990s*, 4th ed. (Scarborough: Nelson Canada, 1995). The evidence from the two methods sometimes conflicts, as will be discussed at some length below.
2. Henry B. Mayo, *An Introduction to Democratic Theory* (New York: Oxford University Press, 1960), ch. 4; Don Carmichael et al., *Democracy and Rights in Canada* (Toronto: Harcourt Brace Jovanovich, Canada, 1991).
3. Thomas R. Berger, *Fragile Freedoms* (Toronto: Clarke, Irwin & Co., rev. and updated, 1982).
4. Paul M. Sniderman et al., *The Clash of Rights: Liberty, Equality, and Legitimacy in Pluralist Democracy* (New Haven: Yale University Press, 1996).
5. Seymour Martin Lipset, *Continental Divide* (New York: Routledge, 1990). The Hartz, McRae, Horowitz, and Christian and Campbell "fragment theory," is also discussed in terms of party ideology in Chapter 13 of this book.
6. Ibid., p. 8.
7. Pierre Berton, *Why We Act Like Canadians* (Toronto: McClelland and Stewart, 1982).
8. Sniderman, *The Clash of Rights*, p. 91.
9. Ibid., pp. 99 and 123.
10. Lipset argues that the United States has more government regulation and uses Sylvia Ostry's "Government Intervention: Canada and the United States Compared," *Policy Options* (March 1980), pp. 26–31, to support his argument. Ostry, however, refers specifically to consumer and anti-trust

regulation. See also David Thomas, ed., *Canada and the United States: Differences That Count* (Peterborough: Broadview Press, 1993).

11. Allan Gregg and Michael Posner, *The Big Picture: What Canadians Think about Almost Everything* (Toronto: Macfarlane Walter & Ross, 1990), pp. 11–13, 29.

12. Lipset, *Continental Divide*, ch. 10; Howard Palmer, "Mosaic versus Melting Pot? Immigration and Ethnicity in Canada and the United States," in Eli Mandel and David Taras, eds., *A Passion for Identity* (Toronto: Methuen, 1987).

13. Given evidence of intolerance at home, this self-defined Canadian international image is a touch moralistic and in part provides an alternative role to that of a U.S. toady!

14. Edgar Friedenberg, *Deference to Authority* (White Plains, NY: M.E. Sharpe, 1980); Judy M. Torrance, *Public Violence in Canada* (Montreal: McGill–Queen's University Press, 1986).

15. Section 24(2) of the Charter allows the admissibility of tainted evidence if it does not detract from the "repute" of the Court!

16. Sniderman, *The Clash of Rights*, p. 27.

17. Dominique Clift, *The Secret Kingdom: Interpretations of the Canadian Character* (Toronto: McClelland and Stewart, 1989), p. 153.

18. Lipset, *Continental Divide*, p. 156.

19. Sniderman, *The Clash of Rights*, ch. 4.

20. Apart from all the methodological problems in *Maclean's* magazine's annual ranking of Canadian universities, the author wishes to point out that the whole operation is essentially American-inspired and irrelevant to Canada. All Canadian universities are respectable, and the qualitative differences between them are minimal, unlike the situation in the United States.

21. Margaret Atwood, *Survival* (Toronto: Anansi, 1972); W.L. Morton, *The Canadian Identity* (Toronto: University of Toronto Press, 1961); Clift, *The Secret Kingdom*, p. 227.

22. Lipset, *Continental Divide*, ch. 4; *Maclean's*, July 1, 1995, p. 15; Michael Adams says that Canadians fear "committing an unforgivable act of hubris" if they praised their country, *Sex in the Snow: Canadian Social Values at the End of the Millennium* (Toronto: Penguin Books, 1998), p. xxi.

23. According to Walter Stefaniuk, *You Asked Us … About Canada* (Toronto: Doubleday Canada, 1996), the Canadian habit of frequently adding "eh?" to a spoken sentence is a "politeness marker," designed to include the listener in the conversation, p. 1.

24. While almost all recent U.S. presidents had distinguished military records, few Canadian prime ministers had any at all. John Diefenbaker and Lester Pearson were invalided home in the First World War after being hit, respectively, by an entrenching tool and a London bus, while Pierre Trudeau avoided military service in the Second World War, motorcycling through the Quebec woods in a Nazi uniform! On the other hand, Canada has more cenotaphs than the United States, and Canadian seniors make greater use of military titles.

25. Morton, *The Canadian Identity*, and articles by Carl Berger and Cole Harris in Peter Russell, ed., *Nationalism in Canada* (Toronto: McGraw-Hill, 1966).

26. Not all foreigners were equally impressed: one unkind Englishman said that "Canada is Montreal and Vancouver with bugger all in between," and Voltaire referred to Canada disparagingly as "quelques arpents de neige."

27. Gregg and Posner, *The Big Picture*, p. 23. The Spanish fact is increasingly unavoidable in the United States.

28. *Maclean's*, July 1, 1995, p. 15.

29. Neil Nevitte, *The Decline of Deference: Canadian Value Change in Cross-National Perspective* (Peterborough: Broadview Press, 1996), argues that the change in Canadian values is consistent with changes in other advanced industrial states and is not the result of American influence.

30. The Massey Commission asked this question just at the dawn of the television age. See Clift, *The Secret Kingdom*, p. 142, and George Grant, *Technology and Empire* (Toronto: Anansi, 1969).

31. Lipset, *Continental Divide*, p. 225.

32. Nevitte, *The Decline of Deference*; Gregg and Posner, *The Big Picture*, pp. 11–13, 54–6, 65–8, 204–5; Alan Frizzell et al., *The Canadian General Election of 1988* (Ottawa: Carleton University Press, 1989), pp. 105, 112; and Peter C. Newman, *The Canadian Revolution 1985–1995: From Deference to Defiance* (Toronto: Viking, 1995).

33. For example, William Thorsell, "Let Us Compare Methodologies," *The Globe and Mail Report on Business*, May 1990. He challenges the myths of monarchy, linguistic duality, mixed economy, helpful fixer in international affairs, and kinder, gentler nation, adding that many Canadians are even questioning the ideal of democracy. See also Michael Valpy, "The Myth of Canadian Compassion," in *Family Security in Insecure Times* (Ottawa: Canadian Council on Social Development, 1993).

34. Suzanne Peters, *Exploring Canadian Values: Foundations for Well-Being, and A Synthesis Report* (Canadian Policy Research Networks Inc., 1995), p. vi.

35. The question in full: "I'd like you to tell me how you personally feel about this statement by giving me a number between plus or minus 5, where +5 means you totally agree with the statement and –5 means you totally disagree with the statement. Many people's opinions fall somewhere between these two points depending on how they feel about the statement. The statement is: Most politicians can be trusted to do what is best for the country."

36. Adams, *Sex in the Snow*, pp. xxv, 7, 16–17.

37. Nevitte's effort is impressive and convincing, as far as it goes. Although he is quite convinced of his thesis, even he says "it might be that survey data are just not adequate to the task or that the WVS simply do not ask the right questions.... Are the indicators adequate? Do they really measure what they are supposed to measure?" (pp. 299–300). This author is struck by the paradox that Canadian respondents told Nevitte of their high and increasing interest in politics, for example, though the voter turnout rate seems to be declining at both federal and provincial levels. There is little doubt about the direction in which Canadian values have shifted over the past 20 years or so, but when observers rely on survey data alone to make their judgments, the findings are probably exaggerated. What respondents tell an interviewer is not always identical to how they actually behave or what they actually believe.

38. J.M.S. Careless, "Limited Identities," *Canadian Historical Review* (March 1969), pp. 1–10.

39. David V.J. Bell, *The Roots of Disunity: A Study of Canadian Political Culture*, rev. ed. (Toronto: Oxford University Press, 1992).

40. Richard Simeon and David Elkins, "Regional Political Cultures in Canada," *Canadian Journal of Political Science* (September 1974), pp. 397–437, along with their book, *Small Worlds* (Toronto: Methuen, 1980); John Wilson, "The Canadian Political Cultures: Towards a Redefinition of the Nature of the Canadian Political System," *Canadian Journal of Political Science* (September 1974), pp. 438–83; and Nelson Wiseman, "The Use, Misuse, and Abuse of the National Election Studies," *Journal of Canadian Studies* (Spring 1986), pp. 21–35.

41. Roger Gibbins, *Prairie Politics and Society* (Toronto: Butterworths, 1980), p. 191; Roger Gibbins and Sonia Arrison, *Western Visions: Perspectives on the West in Canada* (Peterborough: Broadview Press, 1995).

42. Nelson Wiseman, "The Pattern of Prairie Politics," *Queen's Quarterly* 88, no. 2 (Summer 1981); "Provincial Political Cultures," in Christopher Dunn, ed., *Provinces: Canadian Provincial Politics* (Peterborough: Broadview Press, 1996).

43. Pierre Elliott Trudeau, "Some Obstacles to Democracy in Quebec," in *Federalism and the French Canadians* (Toronto: Macmillan, 1968).

44. Michael Ornstein, Michael Stevenson, and Paul Williams, "Region, Class and Political Culture in Canada: Is There an English-Canadian Subculture?" *Canadian Journal of Political Science* (June 1980). See Philip Resnick, *Thinking English Canada* (Toronto: Stoddart, 1995), and Kenneth McRoberts, ed., *Beyond Quebec: Taking Stock of Canada* (Montreal: McGill–Queen's University Press, 1995).

45. Ornstein, Stevenson and Williams, "Region, Class and Political Culture in Canada."

46. David Foot, *Boom, Bust and Echo: How to Profit from the Coming Demographic Shift* (Toronto: Macfarlane Walter & Ross, 1996).

47. Nevitte, *The Decline of Deference*.

48. Adams, *Sex in the Snow*, pp. xx, 10.

49. William Mishler and Harold D. Clarke, "Political Participation in Canada," in Michael S. Whittington and Glen Williams, eds., *Canadian Politics in the 1990s*, 4th ed. (Scarborough: Nelson Canada, 1995), p. 130.

50. Ibid., p. 134.

51. Ronald D. Lambert et al., "The Social Sources of Political Knowledge," *Canadian Journal of Political Science* (June 1988), pp. 359–74.

52. Lester Milbraith, *Political Participation* (Chicago: Rand McNally, 1965), and Richard Van Loon, "Political Participation in Canada," *Canadian Journal of Political Science* (September 1970), pp. 376–99.

53. Mishler and Clarke, "Political Participation in Canada"; W.T. Stanbury, "Financing Federal Political Parties in Canada, 1974–1986," in Alain Gagnon and Brian Tanguay, eds., *Canadian Parties in Transition* (Scarborough: Nelson Canada, 1989).

54. R. Kenneth Carty, *Canadian Political Parties in the Constituencies*, Royal Commission on Electoral Reform and Party Financing Research Studies, vol. 23, cat. no. 21-1989/2-41-23E.

55. Statistics Canada, *Caring Canadians, Involved Canadians*, cat. no. 71-542-XPE, August 1998.

56. Torrance, *Public Violence in Canada*.

57. Mishler and Clarke, "Political Participation in Canada," p. 134.

58. Ibid., pp. 139–40.

59. William Mishler, *Political Participation in Canada: Prospects for Democratic Citizenship* (Toronto: Macmillan, 1979), p. 36.

60. Jon Pammett, "Political Education and Democratic Participation," in Pammett and Jean-Luc Pépin, eds., *Political Education in Canada* (Halifax: Institute for Research on Public Policy, 1988), p. 210.

••••••••••••••••••••••••••••••••

FURTHER READING

Adams, Michael. *Sex in the Snow: Canadian Social Values at the End of the Millennium*. Toronto: Penguin Books, 1998.

Ajzenstat, Janet, and Peter J. Smith, eds. *Canada's Origins: Liberal, Tory or Republican?* Montreal: McGill–Queen's University Press, 1995.

Bashevkin, Sylvia. *True Patriot Love: The Politics of Canadian Nationalism*. Don Mills: Oxford University Press, 1991.

Bell, David. *The Roots of Disunity: A Look at Canadian Political Culture*, rev. ed., Toronto: McClelland and Stewart, Oxford University Press, 1992.

———. "Political Culture in Canada." In Michael S. Whittington and Glen Williams, eds., *Canadian Politics in the 1990s*, 4th ed. Scarborough: Nelson Canada, 1995.

Berger, Thomas R. *Fragile Freedoms*. Toronto: Clarke, Irwin, rev. and updated, 1982.

Berton, Pierre. *Why We Act Like Canadians*. Toronto: McClelland and Stewart, 1982.

Careless, J.M.S. "Limited Identities." *Canadian Historical Review* (March 1969), pp. 1–10.

Foot, David K. *Boom, Bust and Echo: How to Profit from the Coming Demographic Shift*. Toronto: Macfarlane Walter & Ross, 1996.

Friedenberg, Edgar J. *Deference to Authority*. White Plains, NY: M.E. Sharpe, 1980.

Gregg, Allan, and Michael Posner. *The Big Picture: What Canadians Think about Almost Everything*. Toronto: Macfarlane Walter & Ross, 1990.

Hardin, Herschel. *A Nation Unaware*. Vancouver: J.J. Douglas Ltd., 1974.

Lipset, Seymour Martin. *Continental Divide*. New York: Routledge, 1990.

Mishler, William. *Political Participation in Canada: Prospects for Democratic Citizenship*. Toronto: Macmillan, 1979.

Mishler, William, and Harold Clarke. "Political Participation in Canada." In Michael S. Whittington and Glen Williams, eds., *Canadian Politics in the 1990s*, 4th ed. Scarborough: Nelson Canada, 1995.

Morton, W.L. *The Canadian Identity*. Toronto: University of Toronto Press, 1961.

Nevitte, Neil. *The Decline of Deference: Canadian Value Change in Cross-National Perspective*. Peterborough: Broadview Press, 1996.

Nevitte, Neil, and Roger Gibbins. *New Elites in Old States: Ideologies in the Anglo-American Democracies*. Toronto: Oxford University Press, 1991.

Newman, Peter C. *The Canadian Revolution 1985–1995: From Deference to Defiance*. Toronto: Viking, 1995.

Ostry, Sylvia. "Government Intervention: Canada and the United States Compared." *Policy Options* (March 1980), pp. 26–31.

Pocklington, T.C., ed. *Liberal Democracy in Canada and the United States*. Toronto: Holt, Rinehart and Winston, 1985.

Resnick, Philip. *Thinking English Canada*. Toronto: Stoddart, 1994.

Thomas, David, ed. *Canada and the United States: Differences That Count*. Peterborough: Broadview Press, 1993.

Torrance, Judy M. *Public Violence in Canada*. Montreal: McGill–Queen's University Press, 1986.

Trudeau, Pierre. *Federalism and the French Canadians*. Toronto: Macmillan, 1968.

Verney, Douglas V. *Three Civilizations, Two Cultures, One State: Canada's Political Traditions*. Durham, NC: Duke University Press, 1986.

Wiseman, Nelson. "The Pattern of Prairie Politics." *Queen's Quarterly* 88, no. 2 (Summer 1981).

———. "Provincial Political Cultures." In Christopher Dunn, ed., *Provinces: Canadian Provincial Politics*. Peterborough: Broadview Press, 1996.

Chapter 11

Political Socialization, THE MASS MEDIA, and Public Opinion Polls

Surveys indicate that many adults cannot identify their member of Parliament and that more children can name American political officeholders than Canadian ones. The latter fact is often blamed on the inadequacies of the educational system or related to the high proportion of U.S. television to which Canadians are exposed. Given their reliance on the mass media as the source of their political information, another concern of many Canadians is the high proportion of daily newspapers owned by one man, Conrad Black. During election campaigns parties spend millions of dollars on media advertising and public opinion polls.

It is now commonly observed that the mass media and public opinion polls are two of the most important elements in the political system. The mass media—principally television, newspapers, and radio—are the primary source of most Canadians' knowledge and opinion about topical political issues and current personalities.[1] The older medium of magazines and the newer Internet could also be mentioned. Another important link between people and government is the public opinion poll, as parties, pressure groups, governments, and the media themselves seek to discover Canadians' opinions on every conceivable matter.

In terms of the seven functions outlined in Chapter 1, the mass media and public opinion polls predominate in performing the function of "political communication" between the public and government and among different branches of government. In addition, few of the other political functions could be performed without at least partial dependence on the media. This is especially true of **political socialization**, but it also holds for interest articulation and aggregation, political recruitment, rule making, rule application, and rule adjudication.

This chapter begins by outlining the various agents of political socialization, a principal one being the mass media. It then surveys the state of the media in Canada, including the question of ownership. It examines the relationship between the media and the public and between the media and the politicians, and concludes with a discussion of the role of public opinion polls.

····························

POLITICAL SOCIALIZATION

Political socialization is the process by which individuals acquire their political values, attitudes, information, and opinions. Looked at in another way, it is the process by which society passes on its basic values or political culture from one generation to another. Political socialization is sometimes called political learning or education.

The process of political socialization consists in part of direct, individual observation of political phenomena but is mostly performed by intermediaries or agents of socialization. It is relatively easy to identify the main agents of political socialization in Canada but much more difficult to evaluate their relative impact. We begin with the four traditional agents—family, school, peers, and the media, family and peers sometimes being called "private" agents, and schools and media labelled "public" agents—and then examine other such influences.

The Family

The portrait of a "family" in Canada today is more varied than in the past, but the family remains the basic cell of Canadian society. Despite many modern pressures—the increasing incidence of mothers working outside the home, the high divorce rate, and competing influences such as peers and the media—parents, step-parents, or sometimes grandparents are the first major influence on a child's attitudes and values. At the very least, families provide children with certain circumstances of birth, especially their regional and ethnic origins and their social class, all of which are bound to have some effect on their political attitudes and behaviour.[2] Next, most children absorb attitudes and values, some of which are of political significance, in a kind of osmosis from their family's talk and behaviour. Parents' casual comments about politics, politicians, parties, and police are good examples. In the third place, some parents deliberately try to indoctrinate their children with certain political values, such as supporting a particular political party or developing a sense of political efficacy.

It seems, however, that what children pick up unconsciously and unintentionally is just as significant as what parents try to teach. For example, if parents talk about politics in the home, with or without attempting to guide their children's orientations, their children will remain more politically interested later in life. If parents have a moderate or strong identification with a particular political party, children usually begin with the same party preference, whether or not parents insist on it, although they may change parties later as their experience grows and as they encounter other influences. Since the degree of party identification in Canada is relatively weak, as seen in Chapter 14, the influence of parents in this respect should not be overestimated.[3] Nor should the more general political impact of the family in modern times, for political socialization is a process that continues throughout one's life.

The School

The school is the second main agent of political socialization. Although Canada has ten distinctive provincial educational systems, the decline of the family's influence and the greater use of child-care centres and kindergarten have probably increased the importance of the "school." Like the family, it is an early enough influence that it is likely to shape basic lifelong values. All school systems in Canada and elsewhere deliberately attempt to inculcate certain basic values and attitudes, including some of a political nature, such as a feeling of affection or support for the country, the governmental apparatus, the head of state, the police, the flag, and the national anthem. Some, even in Canada, go beyond this to dwell on the virtues of capitalism, cooperation, or other ideological, moral, religious, or political values.

Given the diversity of Canadian society, many questions arise about the role of the school in the political socialization process. Since the provinces have jurisdiction over education, do they deliberately contribute to distinctive provincial political cultures at the expense of overall country? The radically different accounts of certain historical events found in French and English textbooks, such as whether Louis Riel was a traitor or a hero, are often cited as examples of the biased role of formal education in this process.[4] One point is clear: the forces of dualism, regionalism, and continentalism in Canadian society make it difficult for the school system to develop any pan-Canadian sense of national identity.[5]

Every educational system must also decide to what extent it should promote satisfaction with and support for existing political arrangements as opposed to advocating reform. Perhaps the best prescription on this point was articulated by A.B. Hodgetts, who wrote that the school should seek to produce an intelligent, knowledgeable affection for one's country along with a critically responsible interest in it.[6] Most observers feel, however, that the current state of Canadian political education is deficient and that students are not exposed to enough direct teaching about politics. When it comes to current events, for example, even high-school students usually demonstrate a deplorable lack of recognition of such figures as provincial premiers and federal Cabinet ministers and a lack of knowledge about which political parties form federal and provincial governments.[7]

Such gaps in political information reinforce the view that modern students are free spirits who do not always pay much attention to what teachers, textbooks, or school systems are trying to convey. That is why the school's second type of influence may be of equal or greater importance. Just as happens in the family setting, students develop attitudes, values, and skills from the school in an informal and unintentional manner. Such unconscious transmissions occur in teachers' remarks beyond the formal curriculum, in class discussions and excursions, and in extracurricular activities. The authority structure of the classroom or school can also be a factor. An authoritarian teacher or principal would likely promote different attitudes toward participation and dissent than would be acquired in a more democratic setting.

Peers

Peers are the third main agent of political socialization. Peers are simply friends, acquaintances, associates, cohorts, fellow students, workers, homemakers, and members of teams and clubs. The concept of "peer pressure" is probably most familiar at the adolescent level and is not usually concerned with political values, attitudes, and opinions; but we are all susceptible to peer influence at any stage of our lives. Wherever and whenever two or more people communicate, political issues of one kind or another may arise, and one person can influence the other. At this stage, given the likelihood that basic values have already been established, it is attitudes and opinions that are most open to persuasion. In any larger group setting, including peer-group discussions that turn to politics, one person often becomes dominant, because of that person's knowledge, position, or strength of character.

An excellent example of the use of peer-group leaders occurs during election campaigns when the Canadian Labour Congress tries to persuade its members to vote for the New Democratic Party. Given the leadership status of union stewards, it is expected that they will be successful in their effort to "talk up" the NDP at coffee or lunch breaks. Since all union members are probably affected by government in a similar way, this a natural setting in which certain attitudes or opinions can be changed. Even in peer groups, therefore, the influence can be deliberate or indirect.

The Mass Media

The mass media are the fourth main agent of socialization. They are more often instruments of entertainment than enlightenment, however, and personal interaction with family members, teachers, or peers normally carries greater impact than passive, impersonal exposure to the media. Moreover, while the first three agents are likely to influence lifelong values and attitudes, the media primarily transmit opinions on topical issues and personalities. Such short-term stimuli are, however, becoming increasingly important in determining how people vote.

Once again, media influence can be divided into that which is unconscious and that which is deliberate. In their editorials, newspapers explicitly attempt to influence opinions, while on the other pages of the paper, Canadians generally expect news coverage to be as unbiased and factual as possible. Whether newspapers can keep such a fine line between subjective editorials and objective reporting is an interesting question, and some have detected bias in the headlines, positioning, pictures, and selection of items to be included or excluded in various newspapers. For example, readers sometimes claim to find a pro-Conservative slant in the

Federal Transportation Minister David Collenette is scrummed by the media about the failed ONEX bid for Air Canada at a transportation systems show in Toronto in November 1999. (Frank Gunn/Canapress)

news coverage of *The Globe and Mail*, a Liberal slant in *The Toronto Star*, and a Reform Party slant in the *National Post*. Television does not usually have editorials, as such, but it actually has greater possibilities for presenting biased news coverage than do newspapers. This and other aspects of the media are analyzed in detail below.

Other Agents of Political Socialization

The family, school, peers, and media are probably the main agents of political socialization in Canada, but certainly not the only ones. Political parties, churches, groups of various kinds, corporations, think tanks, and the government itself are secondary influences on political attitudes, values, information, and opinions.

Political parties practise the art of persuasion and seek to influence opinions and party preferences on a daily basis. Those who already identify with a particular party find that the simplest means of forming an opinion on any issue is to take their cue from the party leader. The more one identifies with a party or leader, the greater the propensity to defer to the partisan perspective expressed, and the less one is inclined to make the effort to research the issue for oneself.

Like political parties, individual corporations are in the business of persuasion, trying to sell their own goods and services. Sometimes, however, companies will also try to influence political attitudes and opinions, an effort that is called **advocacy advertising**. Many such corporations were involved in the free trade debate, especially during the 1988 election campaign, expressing their support through "speeches, debates, letters, advertisements, information sessions with employees, and inserts in newspapers."[8] Others have used the media to try to influence Canadians' opinions on tax changes, nuclear energy, the National Energy Program, and drug patents. Sometimes employers also try to influence the opinions or voting preferences of their own employees with internal memos about how different parties or policies would affect the firm.

While the power of religion in Canadian society is generally declining, churches have often influenced the political values, attitudes, and opinions of their members in the past, and their role in this connection remains significant. The classic case was the Roman Catholic Church in Quebec before 1960, when it had a close relationship with political authorities and did not hesitate to tell its members how to behave politically. That church continues to take a strong stand across the country on the abortion issue, but it is not the only religious denomination involved in the abortion debate. Most churches also articulate positions on other political issues from time to time, whether it be poverty, foreign policy, foreign aid, or capital punishment.[9]

Over half of the population belongs to a group of some kind, and although the orientation of such groups is primarily nonpolitical, all have the potential to influence their members' political views. Some, such as the Canadian Labour Congress, the Catholic Women's League, or the Canadian Medical Association, are quite determined to do so, as well as to extend their influence beyond their own members to the public at large. Others such as the Boy Scouts or Girl Guides try to instill in children an informed affection for the country. Some groups only get involved in political indoctrination on rare occasions when the interests of the group are threatened by government action, such as the funeral directors' association fighting against the Goods and Services Tax. As with parties and churches, taking one's opinions from the urging of a group one belongs to or respects will obviate the need to make further individual effort to understand the issue.

Many interest groups are sources of useful information about public policy, and it is therefore sometimes difficult to separate them from "think tanks" whose main purpose is to provide analyses of such policies. Canada now possesses a considerable number of the latter, and their studies often influence politicians, bureaucrats, or the public at large. Many are on the "right" side of the political spectrum, for example, the Fraser Institute, the C.D. Howe Institute, the Canada West Foundation, and the Donner Canadian Foundation. In addition to such groups as the Caledon Institute and Centre for Social Justice and others that were mentioned in Chapter 8 that specialize in social policy, those on the "left" include the Canadian Centre for Policy Alternatives and the Council of Canadians.[10]

Finally, the government itself is often engaged in efforts to influence public views and behaviour. Sometimes this is done for what are widely recognized as legitimate purposes, such as encouraging physical fitness and discouraging smoking, impaired driving, racial discrimination, wife battery, and the use of drugs. Sometimes it is done for broadly acceptable political purposes, such as promoting vacations in Canada, the purchase of Canadian-made goods, or national unity. Governments are also expected to inform the public about new laws, regulations, and programs, through pamphlets and the mass media, but it is a fine line between simple information and extolling the virtues of such initiatives for partisan purposes. The Mulroney government, for example, spent large sums of public funds flaunting the merits of the Free Trade Agreement and the Goods and Services Tax in advertising campaigns that most observers felt were excessive and self-serving. In the latter case, the Speaker declared such advertising to be an affront to the House of Commons, as it took place even before debate there had concluded. Governments often use public funds for "public education" purposes just before or during an election campaign, as they circumvent, at public expense, the spending ceilings of federal or provincial electoral laws. The Harris government in Ontario set new precedents in this regard in 1998–99.

How Canadians individually and collectively acquire their political values, attitudes, and opinions is a complicated question. The whole process is so haphazard and complex and the stimuli in each person's own environment are so diverse that no deliberate effort is guaranteed to be successful. Instead, Canadians acquire many of their political values, attitudes, and opinions in a totally unconscious way. Moreover, many Canadians are only semi-socialized: they simply do not have many political values, attitudes, and opinions or much political information. The general level of political awareness is not high, which in turn is reflected in patterns of political participation, as noted in Chapter 10.

THE MASS MEDIA

In surveying the state of the newspaper, radio, and television industries in Canada today, we should first note that the privately owned media exist primarily to make a profit, and that whatever political functions they serve are incidental. Peter Trueman makes the point, for example, that major television newscasts in Canada are broadcast late at night so as not to deprive the networks of prime-time advertising revenues generated by larger audiences earlier in the evening.[11]

Newspapers

Just over five million copies of Canadian newspapers are published daily.[12] The Canadian newspaper industry has been characterized by concentrated chain ownership for decades, but the number of chains is becoming smaller, their size is becoming larger, and some of the key players have changed. By 1999, Conrad Black owned 57 of 104 daily newspapers in Canada, including the new *National Post*, either in his Hollinger or Southam companies. These holdings represented about 41 percent of the total daily circulation. By buying the Sun newspaper group in 1998, Quebecor became the second-largest chain, with 15 papers and 22 percent of the total circulation. *The Toronto Star* became a chain when it acquired 4 other southern Ontario newspapers, with a 14 percent share of the total circulation. Ken Thomson, who had long been the owner of the largest chain in Canada, sold most of his holdings to Black, so that he was left with *The Globe and Mail* and 8 smaller papers and a 11 percent share of the national circulation. The Desmarais family owns 4 papers in Quebec, as does the Irving family in New Brunswick, leaving 10 papers as independents or members of tiny chains. Thus some of the wealthiest men in Canada control the country's newspaper industry. In provincial terms, Black has a monopoly in Newfoundland and PEI, along with an overwhelming dominance in Saskatchewan, Nova Scotia, and BC, while Irving has a monopoly of English-language newspapers in New Brunswick.

Concentrated ownership of Canadian newspapers has always caused considerable concern in some quarters. Many fear that the owner of several papers will gain an unhealthy degree of influence over public opinion by establishing a common point of view for all papers in the chain. This anxiety deepened when there appeared to be collusion between the Southam and Thomson chains when Thomson closed the *Ottawa Journal* on the very same day in 1980 that Southam shut the *Winnipeg Tribune*, leaving each in a monopoly position. These actions prompted an investigation under the Combines Act, and charges of collusion were laid. Nothing demonstrates the weakness of Canadian competition laws as much as the acquittal of Thomson and Southam chains on these charges.[13] An earlier case against Irving's monopoly in New Brunswick met the same fate in the courts.

The incident also led the Trudeau government to appoint the **Kent Royal Commission on Newspapers**, which called for some divestment of current ownership as well as rigid control of future concentrations. Tom Kent also expressed concern in his report with the degree to which newspapers were involved in the ownership of radio and television stations, cable TV, and magazines, and recommended restrictions in multimedia holdings. He also sought to ensure that individual newspaper editors had complete autonomy, so that they could not be told how to do their job by a common corporate owner.

The government's initial response to these recommendations consisted of introducing a bill to restrict any further concentration of media ownership in Canada, but not to disturb the status quo. Later, however, responding to strong corporate pressure, it abandoned the bill and took no action at all. It should be added that the Royal Commission did not actually find much evidence that any central owner had imposed a common editorial policy or standardized news coverage on all the newspapers; the most undesirable result was a reduction in the diversity of perspectives on national politics.[14] While chain ownership has some advantages, the possibility of owners intervening in such undesirable ways continues to exist.

Conrad Black's dominant position in the Canadian newspaper industry has created more alarm than that of Ken Thomson or any predecessor, for a number of reasons beyond the fact that his control is even more extensive. One is that Black is much more ideological than other owners—"an ardent and passionate political warrior."[15] His political views are more right-wing than those of other owners and he is more active in imposing his ideological vision on the country. Whether or not he dictates editorial policy to his many editors, he hires those who agree with him and packs his chain with right-wing columnists, including his wife, Barbara Amiel, and Diane Francis, and Andrew Coyne. He is also accused of axing a large number of jobs whenever he buys a newspaper, of neglecting local coverage, and of filling the paper with cheap wire copy. He and his defenders claim, on the other hand, that without his enthusiasm for newspapers and his efficiency moves, many newspapers would have gone under.

Radio

The radio and television industries are distinct from newspapers in two respects: the degree of government regulation involved and the public ownership of English CBC and French Radio-Canada networks.

Canadians listen to about 21 hours of radio per week on average, and about 10 percent of this is on the **Canadian Broadcasting Corporation (CBC)**. The CBC operates two radio networks in each of English and French, Radio One and Two in English (35 and 10 stations respectively) and Première Chaîne and Chaîne culturelle in French (19 and 7 stations, respectively). Through several hundred transmitter stations, coverage is almost nationwide. In addition, it operates northern services and Radio-Canada International, and has three affiliated private radio stations. CBC radio has a sophisticated audience and plays a major role in transmitting information and opinion in its extended newscasts and in such programs as *This Morning, As It Happens*, and *Cross-Country Check-Up*.

Apart from CBC/Radio-Canada, the Canadian radio industry consists of nearly 500 local AM and FM stations, which put varying degrees of effort into news-gathering and public affairs programming. These stations used to be independently owned, but are increasingly characterized by chain ownership, just as in the newspaper industry. Ownership changes quite frequently, but by 1994 over half of the radio market in Canada was controlled by the ten leading firms. Like newspapers, radio stations must be Canadian-owned, but the limited Canadian content on private radio stations has become a problem. Since they mainly transmit music, the CRTC has issued Canadian-content rules, now 35 percent, as noted in Chapter 9.

Television

In 1997, the average Canadian watched 22.7 hours of television per week, more in French Quebec and among women, those over 60 years of age, and those with lower incomes, and less in Alberta and among men, those under 18, and those with higher incomes. Of the television Canadians watched, 28.7 percent was drama, 23.6 percent news and public affairs, 12.8 percent comedy, 10.2 percent variety and games, and 8.3 percent sports. Viewers consumed 79 percent of this fare from Canadian stations and 21 percent from foreign stations.

As with radio, the CBC attracts about 10 percent of the television audience. The publicly owned CBC/Radio-Canada television network has 22 stations across the country, 14 English and 8 French. English production is centred in Toronto and French production in Montreal. These are supplemented by agreements with 19 English and 5 French privately owned affiliated stations, which agree to telecast a certain amount of CBC programming. This usually includes national news and public affairs, but not always drama or more sophisticated cultural programs.

The CBC also established its Newsworld channel in 1989 and its French equivalent, RDI, set up in 1995. These all-news channels cover many political events live and more extensively than regular CBC, with which they work closely, and provide much regional coverage, documentaries, and in-depth interview programming. Newsworld is only available on cable, but while its audience is small, most members of the political elite tune in regularly. There is also Newsworld International, and while the CBC used to operate the national parliamentary channel on cable, it is now called the Cable Public Affairs Channel and is run by the cable companies. In some provinces another channel carries provincial legislative proceedings, and several provinces have educational television channels.

CBC television has a strong commitment to Canadian programming, but suffers from a chronic shortage of funds. After severe bloodletting under the Mulroney government and the appointment of hostile members to its board of directors, the CBC had reason to expect better treatment under the Chrétien regime. Instead, that government slashed the CBC budget even further, precipitating the resignation of the corporation's president. Ironically enough, the Liberals then replaced him with former Tory Communications minister Perrin Beatty, who proceeded with additional cuts until he departed five years later.

On the private side of television, the CTV network consists of 25 stations centred in CFTO in Toronto. CTV reaches 97 percent of English-language television households; it also operates a news channel and has interests in six other specialty channels. The Toronto-based CanWest Global system, owned by Izzy Asper of Winnipeg, now considers itself to be the third national English-language network. Most major cities also have one or more unaffiliated, independent private English stations. On the French side, the TVA network is centred in Télé-Métropole in Montreal and consists of nine other private stations, while Quatre Saisons is a second private French network with seven stations.

About 75 percent of Canadian homes subscribe to cable television, more than in any other country. Cable stations receive television signals from large satellite dishes and transmit them by means of cables to individual subscribers. To some extent the CRTC regulates which channels they carry, but in general, cable television is designed to bring the major U.S. networks into almost every Canadian home. This gives most Canadians two chances to view popular U.S. shows—either on the originating network or on CBC, CTV, or Global, which bid for such programs. The Canadian cable industry is dominated by the giants of Canadian television and radio: Rogers Communications (29 percent), Shaw Cablesystems and Vidéotron (19 percent each), Cogeco Inc. (9 percent), Moffat Communications (4 percent), and Fundy Cablevision (2 percent). The variety of other channels on cable television, some of them of Canadian origin, is constantly increasing, but for some channels the subscriber must pay an additional fee. As mentioned in Chapter 9, popular and industry pressure forced the CRTC to allow such a wide range of U.S. channels to be available on Canadian cable and pay television. In 1994, the CRTC approved ten new "specialty services," Canadian or American, including "pay-per-view," and a year later authorized the first direct-to-home (DTH) satellite service. All of this and an increasing number of specialty, pay, and pay-per-view channels since (now reaching 60 to 70 channels in some urban markets) has served to dilute the audience of the conventional Canadian television stations.

One of the main concerns about the Canadian television industry is the preponderance of American content. Requiring Canadian television stations to be domestically owned or to telecast 50 percent or more Canadian content is virtually meaningless when almost all residents are within reach, directly or via cable, of a large assortment of U.S. television channels. On this point, Fletcher talks of "American images crowding out Canadian ones,"[16] and Ed Black writes of the problem of trying to serve a small population in two language groups "who live in tempting, embarrassing, and almost smothering proximity to [ten times as many] Americans who speak the language of Canada's majority ... They also have the world's most penetrating and effective system for transmitting ideas en masse."[17] Trueman adds:

> I have felt for years that the greatest threat to Canada's integrity as a nation is not the crisis in Quebec ... but American television ... Think of the overwhelming preponderance of American programming, which in an unobtrusive way pumps us full of American values, American hopes, American history, even American patterns of speech.[18]

While the CBC has recently gone to an almost all-Canadian format in prime-time hours, the private stations and networks realize that profits can generally be maximized by telecasting as much U.S. programming as the CRTC will allow. The most popular television shows among Canadian anglophones are all American, but one should not underestimate the attraction of Canadian national newscasts, *Hockey Night in Canada*, *The Royal Canadian Air Farce*, *This Hour Has 22 Minutes*, *Canada AM*, *The Morning News*, *The Fifth Estate*, *Marketplace*, *Téléjournal*, *Le Point*, and *W5*.

Figure 11.1 illustrates the percentage of time spent watching Canadian-content programs. The overall average is 40 percent, but this varies from 66.5 percent among francophones to

Figure 11.1   Percentage of Time Spent Watching Canadian-Content Programs, Anglophones and Francophones, 1997

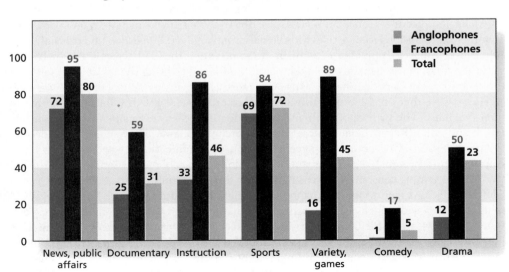

Source: Adapted from Statistics Canada, Television Viewing Bank, Catalogue No. 87F006XPE.

30 percent for anglophones. In every category, francophones watch more Canadian content than anglophones, although the latter do watch more Canadian than foreign coverage in two main categories: news and public affairs and sports. What is probably most troubling is the low proportion of Canadian content in the drama category, especially on the anglophone side.

Many media analysts decry the small amount of Canadian content available and/or viewed by Canadian television watchers. In this sensitive situation, it is almost unbelievable that the CRTC would fail to enforce the Canadian-content commitments, especially in the drama category, made by the CTV and Global networks, that it would continue to license numerous new American cable channels, and that successive federal governments would slash the budget of the main alternative, the CBC.[19]

The Media and the Public
PUBLIC PERCEPTIONS OF THE MEDIA

The influence of the mass media in the political system is profound and appears to be constantly increasing.[20] Most of the information Canadians receive about the political process comes from television, newspapers, or radio rather than from direct observation or other sources such as books or magazines, except perhaps for *Maclean's*. Some recipients may be able to separate this information from whatever commentary or biases accompany it, but many are also swayed by the particular perspective that the media give to the data they present. When asked about their preferred medium for political information, a majority of people choose television, with newspapers second, and radio third. Those who prefer television feel it is most fair and believable for all kinds of information, and most complete, except perhaps for business and economic news.[21]

Three different theories have arisen regarding the role of the media in influencing the public.[22] The first assumed that the media had a direct and crucial impact on virtually every individual in the community in terms of providing and interpreting information. When survey research showed this theory to be faulty, a second emerged to replace it. This was that the media primarily influence opinion leaders—those people who pay close attention to political developments and who then transmit this information and opinion to those around them in peer-group situations. There is probably much truth to this theory, but the current perspective on the role of the media is that their most important effect on the general public is in the realm of setting the political agenda for the country.[23] In other words, the media tell people what to think about, what the important issues are, and which political personalities are significant. They help to define what is political. This is a function the media share with political parties, and while parties may be more important as initiators of issues, these will not likely remain on the agenda without media attention.

The **parliamentary press gallery** is a key player in developing a consensus about what these issues are.[24] In part, this reflects the influence of the daily Question Period in the House of Commons, which provides gallery reporters with short, superficial, and controversial issues that are well suited to media, especially television, coverage. In addition to their representatives in the press gallery, all media outlets receive wire services. The most important is Canadian Press, an agency collectively owned by member newspapers, which hires several CP reporters in Ottawa and wires their stories to all outlets. Stories originating in other cities by reporters of individual papers are sent to Canadian Press, rewritten, and wired to all other members. Canadian Press also has an electronic outlet, Broadcast News (BN).

THE REALITY OF DIFFERENT MEDIA COVERAGE

Public perception of the merits of the different media are somewhat distressing to those who know their real advantages and disadvantages. Because of cost and time constraints, television is restricted in the number of items it can cover in any newscast and must present a shorter and more superficial account of political events than either radio or newspapers. It cannot present the whole story or very many stories, and such editing necessarily involves selection or bias on someone's part. Everyone is familiar with the 60- to 90-second "news clip" with a 10-second "sound bite" of the actual voice of political leaders, in which how something is said is usually more important than what is said. Recent research indicates that the length of the sound bite is even decreasing, and "Canadians are rarely exposed to their leaders for anything longer than the time it takes for them to blurt out 8 or 10 words."[25] The transcript of a 30-minute newscast would make up about one-third of a single newspaper page.[26]

Moreover, because it is a visual medium, television must aim to show colourful, dramatic, emotional, conflictual, or entertaining pictures. Riots, demonstrations, and political conventions usually make good television, but the daily routine of politics does not lend itself as well to compelling visual coverage. Witness the efforts taken by politicians and the media to find contrived and engaging settings in which to stage political happenings, make announcements, or tape interviews. From Question Period to election campaigns, political events are now designed to appeal to television's definition of the news.[27] Television portrays images and impressions and is therefore much better at dealing with political leaders and personalities than with issues. When John Turner issued a 40-point policy manifesto just before the 1988 election, for example, "the electronic media ... could not cope with such a cornucopia of ideas that had not been pre-digested into a simple theme wrapped around a few easily grasped issues."[28]

These characteristics make television more open to distortion and exploitation, with the result that it may be the least believable and most biased of the three media.[29] Television meets the needs of the average citizen with a short attention span who is looking for visual stimulation and who does not wish to invest too much effort in understanding the political system. Ed Black writes that television has replaced religion as the new "opiate of the masses."[30]

This situation is exacerbated by the increasing tendency of political parties and politicians to gear their activities to the demands of television. Press conferences are now dominated by television lights and cameras; leaders' tours during election campaigns are "photo opportunities"; party conventions and leaders' debates are scheduled for maximum air time; and governments convey public information via catchy, superficial television commercials rather than in detailed newspaper advertisements or pamphlets. In addition, in preparing for elections, parties put greater effort into designing television commercials and trying them out before focus groups than in devising solutions to the country's problems; the televised leaders' debate has become the single most important event in an election campaign; and elections often turn more on leader images than issues, policies, local candidates, or other leading figures in the party. The appearance, style, and general image of the party leader, including his or her ability to perform on television, have become of crucial importance.[31] This increasing emphasis on appearance, largely because of television, is often said to trivialize politics.

Newspapers generally offer more comprehensive coverage of political events, presenting both greater factual information and a wider range of interpretation. While the "average" Canadian relies on television for political information, those with political influence, whether in government, parties, pressure groups, or peer-group situations, depend on newspapers. Those who prefer newspapers over television have higher educations, higher incomes, and are better informed. Furthermore, the broadcast media and opposition parties tend to take their cues from newspapers. In short, "the major daily newspapers remain the primary source of public affairs information not only for top decision-makers but also for the most politically attentive segment of the population at all levels, though television news has also become an important source."[32]

It should be added that the degree of political participation increases sharply with a person's level of newspaper consumption. In other words, those who make the effort to increase their political information by reading a newspaper are not only better informed but are also most likely to go on to engage in some form of political participation, as shown in Table 11.1.

Among newspapers, *The Globe and Mail* is read by nearly three-quarters of Canada's top-level decision makers across the country and more than 90 percent of media executives; it thus tends to set the agenda for other news organizations, including the Canadian Press.[33] The independent but financially troubled *Le Devoir* occupies a somewhat similar position in French Canada. It is likely that few beyond the political elite read or are influenced by the editorials in such newspapers, however, and there is little evidence that editorial endorsement has much impact on the outcome of elections.[34]

TABLE 11.1 **Extent of Political Participation by Level of Newspaper Consumption (Percentages)**

Activity	Low	Medium	High
Voting	79	84	90
Campaigning	22	38	55
Contacting MPs	17	18	34
Community action	12	19	27

Source: William Mishler, Political Participation in Canada, p. 73.

The Media and the Politicians

Politicians need publicity and therefore have a great interest in how the media cover their behaviour. Even though they and their bureaucratic advisers have their own direct sources, these authorities also depend on the media to provide information they need about what is happening at home and abroad. The media, in turn, rely on the authorities for most of their information. A number of issues arise from this mutually dependent relationship.

POLITICIANS AND MEDIA OWNERS

In the newspaper era, when papers were individually owned by their editor, newspaper owners were generally on friendly terms with politicians, and regular confidential consultations took place. Several editors, including Joseph Howe and George Brown, were politicians themselves, and one politician, Henri Bourassa, founded a newspaper, *Le Devoir*. Most papers had a partisan perspective that was evident in their news columns and editorials. However, such factors as chain ownership, the quest for a mass audience, and the public expectation that partisanship be restricted to the editorial page have changed the relationship between politicians and media owners. Indeed, to a large extent, the party press has been replaced by the critical press.[35] Some newspapers do retain partisan views, as mentioned above, and the new *National Post* seems to be a throwback to an earlier era. Content analysis of the 1984 and 1988 election campaigns revealed that some papers treated the leader of their choice more favourably than the others, but that in terms of overall space (or time) the major newspapers along with the three English-language television networks gave almost equal attention to the three main party leaders.[36] It has also been observed that French-Canadian journalists are allowed greater personal opinion in their reports, positive or negative, than in English Canada.[37]

POLITICIANS AND JOURNALISTS

A second issue is the relationship between working journalists and politicians. Both groups are essentially engaged in the same business, one needing publicity and the other, information. In principle, reporters should maintain enough distance from politicians in order to cover them objectively; on the other hand, it is often necessary to cultivate close relations in order to get the kind of information the media seek. Allan Fotheringham writes that "the narrowest line in journalism is the line between exploiting your sources (without ever destroying them) and being captured by them."[38] Journalists also worry that a critical account of a politician on one occasion may jeopardize a good story the next time around. Furthermore, since politicians often confidentially seek out the opinions of reporters, the latter sometimes have to agonize over whether to reveal information that was given to them "off the record," that is, in the expectation that it will not be used. There is also the question of whether the media should transmit information that they are not supposed to have, such as when Global Television came into advance possession of a summary of the 1988 budget.

Another problem the media have to face is how much privacy to leave politicians. When do a politician's personal habits begin to interfere with his or her public functions, and when should they be revealed?[39]

These issues also relate to the complex legal question of libel, often defined as "a false statement about a person that is to his or her discredit."[40] In general, the media in Canada are cautious in what they write or broadcast, and the politicians are fairly thick-skinned, so that court cases involving libel are relatively rare. Three celebrated exceptions involved a CBC television show portraying former Alberta Premier Peter Lougheed in an unflattering light in negotiations over the tar sands project; a *Victoria Times* cartoon featuring Bill Vander Zalm, then the BC welfare minister, plucking the wings off a fly representing welfare recipients; and accounts in the *Ottawa Citizen* of Mulroney Defence minister Robert Coates's night-time activities on an official trip to Germany.[41] Less serious instances of media bias or error are supposed to be handled by the CRTC, individual companies' "ombudsmen," or voluntary press councils.

NEWS MANAGEMENT

"News leaks" are yet another issue in the relations between media and politicians. When governments do not know what course to follow, they sometimes leak a proposal to the media as a "trial balloon," hoping for guidance from the kind of reaction received. Ed Black points out that this practice is necessary because today's politicians usually have little time to respond to problems and little chance to sit back and give them comprehensive consideration.[42]

Leaks are part of a broader problem of **news management** and manipulation, which appears to be increasingly common.[43] This relates especially to the timing and selective distribution of information; exaggerating the positive while keeping secret or past deadline time that which is negative; giving preference to friendly reporters over others; making prime ministerial requests for network television time for less than important announcements; or outright lying. News management also involves putting the best face on an unpopular government action or a politician's performance by having a partisan official tell the media how successful it actually was, in the hope that the media will transmit this evaluation to their audience. Those involved in such efforts are often called "media handlers" or **spin doctors**, because they try to put the best face, or "spin," on any event. As noted in Chapter 20, memoranda to Cabinet proposing new government action must be accompanied by a communications strategy.[44]

An even more serious aspect of news management is censorship via the Official Secrets Act or the now repealed War Measures Act. In 1970, for example, the media were prohibited from transmitting any stories that supported the FLQ. Short of actual censorship is the highly secretive tradition of Canadian governments. In 1982, however, the Access to Information Act made it somewhat easier for the media as well as other interested parties to obtain access to government information.

The ultimate problem in media–government relations is political interference with the "freedom of the press," or as the Charter of Rights puts it, "freedom of the press and other media of communication." This is one of the sacred principles of democracy as discussed in Chapter 10. The most blatant examples of such political interference have occurred at the provincial level. In Quebec, Maurice Duplessis kept the press under control by awarding advertising and printing contracts to newspaper owners and financial gifts to members of the press gallery.[45] In Alberta, the Social Credit government in the 1930s deliberately tried to force newspapers to retract any criticisms of the government. Occasional attempts have been made by various Prime Ministers' Offices over the years to have the CBC take a certain perspective on a vital national issue. Much has been written—both claiming and refuting bias—about the CBC's coverage of the Meech Lake Accord. Government pressure was also suspected in 1966 when the CBC cancelled the highly popular but critical public affairs program "This Hour Has Seven Days"; in connection with the 1992 CBC series "The Valour and the Horror;" and in the suspension of CBC reporter Terry Milewski, who covered the 1998 APEC summit.[46] On the French side, the Trudeau government accused the Radio-Canada network of being riddled with separatists who gave a biased interpretation of federal–provincial relations. Although there was probably some truth to the charge, it smacked of political interference.

The Changing Media World

Probably few aspects of the political system are in such a state of rapid change as the mass media. David Taras has summarized the changes as a convergence of technologies, of corporations, of news and entertainment, and of cultures.[47] The first involves the merging of television, telephone, satellite, cable, and computer. The convergence of corporations is rampant at the start of the new millennium, whether in Canada or on a global scale, whether in the media industry or beyond. Apart from Conrad Black's newspaper empire, the most relevant media conglomerations have taken place in the United States, but that does not mean they are irrelevant to Canada: Disney/ABC; Westinghouse/CBS; General Electric/NBC; Rupert Murdoch/20th Century Fox/Fox Broadcasting; Viacom/Paramount Studios/Blockbuster Video; Time-Warner/Turner Broadcasting; Seagrams/Universal Studios/PolyGram; and Sony/Columbia Pictures/Cineplex-Odeon. The convergence of news and entertainment relates primarily to making television news more entertaining, and the convergence of cultures refers to the expansion of American popular culture around the world.

Few if any of these changes are positive for the vital place of the media in the Canadian political system. Reliance on television, with its convergence of news and entertainment, rather than newspapers provides a more superficial understanding of political developments. Since reliance on television in Canada usually means exposure to American television, this tendency detracts from public knowledge in a second way (the convergence of cultures). The increased concentration of ownership of newspapers, radio, and television (the convergence of corporations) is not a healthy development in any democracy that values the maximum diversity of opinions. Such ownership only enhances the predominance of right-wing opinion already amply supplied by radio talk-show hosts, think tanks, columnists, and pundits. On the other hand, the opposite trend toward a fragmentation of audiences allows individuals to ignore broader public questions as they expose themselves to media coverage of only a few personal interests. The political impact of the Internet in this situation is not yet entirely clear. While it is a liberating force that permits people to gain information, connect with others having similar concerns, and provide direct feedback to government, it can also be used for antisocial purposes.

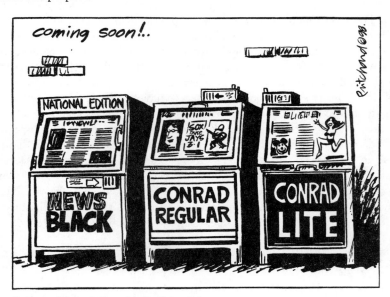

By Denny Pritchard. Reproduced with permission.

PUBLIC OPINION POLLS

Opinions are more specific, numerous, and changeable than values and attitudes. While very unstable, opinions about topical issues and current personalities often affect the political behaviour of individuals, especially in voting, and polls of the public's opinions frequently influence the actions of government.

Measuring Public Opinion

The phrase **public opinion** is sometimes used to imply that all members of the public hold a unanimous, informed view on a particular issue. In actuality, many opinions are held on any issue, and each issue only interests a certain segment of the population. Furthermore, most political opinions are not well informed. They are based on little information, they are simplifications of complex issues, and they are often internally contradictory. Indeed, it is often the case that people form their opinions first and then look for information to confirm them; at the very least, they "seek out information that conforms to their predispositions ... and avoid or reinterpret any contrary and non-supportive messages."[48]

Given this great conglomeration of viewpoints, public opinion is very difficult to gauge. Haphazard methods such as reading editorials or letters to the editor or listening to open-line programs are obviously unreliable, but so are many amateur public opinion surveys. On the other hand, professional polling agencies claim to be able to select a representative sample of people, ask carefully worded questions, and report with a high degree of accuracy the opinions of the whole population. Such polls have assumed an immense importance in contemporary Canadian politics: "No political party plans campaign strategy without them, no government is prepared to risk major policy initiatives without gauging public opinion, and for major news organizations they are an indispensable reporting tool, both between and during elections."[49]

Beyond the now-common procedure for conducting a public opinion poll, two special techniques deserve mention. The first is "tracking," which entails telephoning samples of 100 to 500 people nightly during an election campaign in order to see how day-to-day developments are affecting them. The second is the "focus group," in which a small number of people are gathered together behind a one-way mirror with a group leader who encourages them to voice their "gut" reaction to various leaders, issues, and slogans.

Who are these professional pollsters?[50] Although the Canadian branch of the Gallup Poll has operated in Canada since 1941, political and governmental polling did not begin in earnest until about 1960. After hiring U.S. polling companies for a while, the Liberals chose Martin Goldfarb as their official party pollster. He worked closely with long-time Liberal strategist, Senator Keith Davey. Goldfarb also had corporate clients and did frequent and lucrative work for many government departments throughout the Pearson and Trudeau regimes. Like the Liberals, the Conservatives originally employed U.S. pollsters, but in the late 1970s, Allan Gregg and his Decima Research became the official party pollster. Like Goldfarb, Gregg had a corporate clientele and did polling for government departments when his party was in power. After the disastrous PC showing in the 1993 election, in which he was chief strategist as well as pollster, Gregg sold Decima Research to the lobby firm Hill and Knowlton.

By this time many other public opinion polling companies came to play a part, often being hired by media outlets, political parties, governments, or government departments. Some of the leading firms at the turn of the new century are listed below. All of them also do much nonpolitical polling, and many of them have become Canadian multinationals. A number of lobbying firms, especially Earnscliffe Strategy Group and Hill and Knowlton also do polling as part of their comprehensive consulting work.

··

LEADING PUBLIC OPINION POLLING FIRMS

- Angus Reid Group
- Environics Research Group
- POLLARA
- Ekos Research Associates
- Goldfarb Consultants
- Decima Research
- ComQUEST Research
- Compas Inc.
- Léger & Léger

After the 1993 election campaign, only the Liberal Party could afford to employ a resident professional pollster—Michael Marzolini, now of POLLARA. He does considerable government polling as well, but unlike Goldfarb and Gregg before him, must share this political work with competitors.[51]

These professional polling companies all have slightly different methodologies and are never hesitant to criticize each other, especially when the results of one survey differ from those of another. Exactly how accurate are they? The only way a survey's accuracy can be tested is through a comparison of its results immediately before an election with the electoral outcome itself. The immediate pre-election findings of most professional agencies have usually been within the range of accuracy that the survey claimed, typically that the results were accurate within plus or minus 4 percent 19 times out of 20, but exceptional inaccurate predictions do occur.

When two or more firms are seeking the same information but produce different results, doubts naturally arise about their methodology. The way a question is worded, the optional responses available, the sequence of the questions, the degree to which respondents are telling the truth, and many other variables can influence the result and account for such differences. Timing is also an important consideration, for results can sometimes be out of date by the time they are tabulated and reported.

Impact of Polls on the Public

One main issue that arises in the discussion of polls and pollsters is whether their pre-election predictions influence the actual election results. This question cannot be answered categorically, but it is unlikely that their direct effect is that great. First, most voters do not pay much attention to the poll results; second, not everyone believes them; and third, it is not important to everyone to vote for the winning side, even if this is clear in advance. While some voters may want to jump on the victorious bandwagon—**bandwagon effect**—at least a few are likely to switch to the predicted loser—"the underdog effect"—either out of sympathy or to try to prevent an overwhelming victory for the prospective winner.[52]

On the other hand, polls may have a significant indirect effect on the election results. The media are as obsessed with the polls as the politicians are, and the survey results may well cause the media to concentrate on those parties and politicians who are in the lead or ignore those who are trailing. Furthermore, polls have a considerable effect on party morale. A positive poll usually generates greater enthusiasm and effort, better candidates, and larger financial contributions, while a negative poll saps the spirit of leaders, candidates, and footsoldiers alike. Both of these results undoubtedly affect the subtle "momentum" of the campaign.

Another issue can be addressed more categorically: polls definitely detract from the discussion of real issues in the election campaign.[53] The media are fascinated by polls primarily because they are good for business, and, given the media's ability to influence the political agenda even during election campaigns, they emphasize the **horse-race effect** of the contest. They tend to spend more time on trying to determine who is ahead than on comparative analysis of party platforms, asking leaders to comment on the latest poll results, for example, rather than how the party would deal with a particular public problem. Now that the media actually hire or even own polling firms, survey results are becoming major news items in themselves. Polls sometimes also affect the voter turnout rate, by generating feelings of complacency or hopelessness.

Many political losers have blamed their fate on the public opinion polls and some have called for the prohibition of polls during part or all of the campaign. Such bans do exist in many countries.[54] Whatever their faults, however, polls enliven the campaign and increase the information available, and many argue that to prohibit their publication in the media would not prevent parties, candidates, and others from conducting their own surveys. The main effect of a publication ban would be to give certain crucial information to those who could afford to conduct a survey and to deny it to the general public, a highly undemocratic suggestion.[55]

One of the amendments to the Canada Elections Act made in the wake of the Royal Commission on Electoral Reform was to prohibit, in the final three days of the campaign, the broadcast, publication, or dissemination of the results of new or scientifically conducted opinion surveys that would identify a political party or candidate. This restriction was soon challenged by the Thomson and Southam newspaper chains as a violation of freedom of the press, and their challenge was upheld by the Supreme Court of Canada.[56]

Impact of Polls on the Authorities

Another main question in the study of public opinion is the relationship between polls and the response of the authorities.[57] For nearly 100 years after Confederation, governments had to act in the absence of a reliable survey, but it now seems that they are reluctant to make any decision until it can be based on a poll. Since opinion is likely to be considerably divided, however, polls do not always provide clear-cut guidance.

Even when public opinion is clearly in favour of a certain course of government action, the authorities may decide otherwise. This may be the consequence of the politicians' own convictions, the recommendations of the public service, the pressure of interest groups and lobbyists, or the rigidity of party discipline. Indeed, some hold the view that even in a democracy, politicians are not obliged to *follow* public opinion; they may also *lead* it.[58] This is especially the case, now that we realize how uninformed, superficial, and changeable most public opinions really are. While politicians and bureaucrats may be accused of acting in their own self-interest if they do not follow a clear-cut preference among the public, they may actually be relying on a deeper understanding of the issue, the greater information at their disposal, a more sophisticated analysis of its implications, a concern for minority rights, or a less prejudicial attitude. Capital punishment has been an issue on which public opinion was quite clear, for example, but one on which the authorities repeatedly went their own way. Should Parliament reinstate capital punishment in response to overwhelming popular opinion based on a mistaken impression about rising crime rates, a desire for retribution, and an assumption of deterrence? Most political issues are even more complicated than capital punishment, and on most, public opinion is much more divided; thus the correlation between public opinion and public policy is not as strong as might be expected.

Most governments nowadays spend huge sums of public funds on surveying public attitudes on various issues. In his book *Margin of Error*, Hoy reveals just how many public policies were adopted over the years and how many election dates were set on the basis of polls. He also shows how important they were in the 1988 election campaign. First, the Conservatives used many publicly funded polls to determine their election platform. Second, the Liberals surveyed public opinion in Quebec to see if a Senate veto of the Free Trade Agreement would detract from their support in that province. Third, the NDP avoided the free trade issue (and left the Liberals to capitalize on it) because party polling indicated that the NDP lacked public credibility on economic issues.[59] Indeed, the NDP used focus groups as early as 1984 to find that the phrase "ordinary Canadians" was preferable to "working Canadians" in its advertising.[60] When even the NDP starts to base its strategy on focus groups and public opinion polls, it is hard to overstate their current significance.

CONCLUSION

Students of political science and other readers of this book quite likely belong to the small proportion of the population for whom politics is a central concern and who are well informed about the subject. Such readers must be careful not to assume that the rest of the population is similarly inclined. In any case, this chapter has demonstrated the enormous significance of the media, especially television and mass circulation newspapers, and documented the increasing use in all branches of politics of public opinion polls and polling firms. Individually and combined, the electronic media and public opinion polls have completely transformed Canadian politics in the past 50 years.

Ⓒ Of the approaches outlined in Chapter 1, class analysts have the most to say about the subject matter of this chapter. They emphasize the deliberate attempt of the bourgeoisie to socialize the masses into an acceptance of the status quo. They argue that the public agents of socialization, the school and the media, transmit messages to serve the interests of the economic elite, the school through elite control of the political system, and the media through outright elite ownership. Traditional political parties and pressure groups join in to help define politics in nonclass terms so that the lower classes are socialized into supporting a system that does not operate in their interests.[61] Socialization, in such observers' terms, is indoctrination into the virtues of capitalism.

Class analysts also have much to say about the political role of the media. First, there is nothing as elitist in Canadian society as the ownership of newspapers and private radio and television stations, and such owners have been known to issue orders regarding coverage of political events. Second, the media elite also includes a small number of influential journalists and columnists from whom most of their colleagues take their lead. The media and political elites share socioeconomic characteristics and meet at social gatherings.[62] Third, even when owners do not deliberately interfere in the editorial operations of their companies, the media transmit role models and images of an elite version of reality. As Fletcher says, "the media tend to reinforce the dominant institutional and cultural patterns of authority. By setting the limits for public debate, the media generally exclude serious challenges to the status quo."[63] Ed Black adds that the public generally acquiesces in decision making by the elites so long as their decisions do not stray very far beyond society's broad set of fundamental values, and even those values are subject to some manipulation.[64] Some class analysts go further and argue that the media promote consumerism, the myth of "middle classness," and private ownership of property, and are "a powerful ideological weapon for holding the mass of people in voluntary submission to capitalism."[65]

The economic and political elites can use their control over the mass media to legitimate their power and reduce the extent to which they need to rely on coercion. Portraying protesters, radicals, and union leaders among others in an unfavourable light and trivializing political discourse will help enormously to maintain the status quo. While the public is easily convinced of the dangers of public control of the media, it does not seem to be concerned about problems resulting from concentrated private ownership. It is even more difficult for the general public to see how state intervention, for example, regulating ownership, could protect the principle of freedom of the press.[66]

Wallace Clement and others point to the extent to which the richest and most powerful families in Canada either made their fortunes in the media business or else control media outlets alongside other interests.[67] They say, along with the Kent Report, that "freedom of the press is not a property right of owners."[68] The costs of establishing a new media outlet of any kind are prohibitive except to the most wealthy individuals in the land, and this pattern of ownership allows them to shield their economic operations from media scrutiny. Moreover, among the leading business pressure groups are the Canadian Association of Broadcasters (CAB), representing private radio and television companies, and the Canadian Newspaper Association. Through pressure on the CRTC and successive governments, the CAB has ensured its members a highly profitable position in the Canadian broadcasting system, while nothing so demonstrates the political dominance of the economic elite as the quick abandonment of the Kent Report due to pressure from the newspaper industry.

Class analysts also point out the corporate connections between media outlets and public opinion polls. Only affluent interests can afford to conduct a proper national poll, and to the extent that they can keep it secret, they enhance their control over the masses.

P ⌐ In contrast, the pluralist approach emphasizes the multitude of media outlets in the country, including the increasing number of cable television channels and the creation of several new morning tabloid newspapers. There are many sources of information to choose from and considerable competition between and among them, although only a few large cities enjoy competitive daily newspapers. Pluralists also claim that the frequent revelations of the views of the public in the form of public opinion polls is a sign of the openness of government and society.

PC ⌐ Public choice theorists have identified a "media game" between the media and the politicians corresponding to the rational, self-seeking relationship between politicians and voters.[69] In this case, the two parties are engaged in an exchange in which each needs the other in order to maximize its self-interest. As for public opinion polls, the public choice approach is probably most relevant because polls are a principal means for the authorities to identify what the public wants from the government. In this view, the authorities detect what policies would get them the most votes and then promise such policies in the election campaign. As Taras writes, "polling tells the parties where the swing votes are—in which regions and among which income, ethnic, and age groups—and the messages that are most likely to move those votes."[70]

SC ⌐ State-centred theorists begin by pointing out how the state can use the school system to encourage each new generation to feel satisfied with the status quo or helpless to change it. The authorities also engage in massive publicly financed advertising campaigns to persuade the electorate of the wisdom of their actions. The prime minister attempts to influence public opinion through press conferences and special televised statements, for example, and the bureaucrats use the media to foster favourable publicity about their program needs, especially when fighting for additional resources or against stringent cutbacks. Perhaps the main method of manipulation used by the bureaucracy, however, is not so much in what information is disseminated, as in that which is withheld. The state-centred approach also points out that the amount of money spent by governments and even bureaucrats to do their own polling is quite staggering.

DISCUSSION QUESTIONS

1. Think about the relative importance of the agents of political socialization in your own life. Can you decipher your own socialization process?

2. Does the fact that media companies have an impact on public opinion mean that concentrated ownership should be more restricted than in other industries?

3. What are the advantages and disadvantages of obtaining information from each of television, radio, and newspapers?

4. Should the publication of public opinion polls be prohibited at some stage of an election campaign? Explain.

5. How seriously should the authorities take the results of public opinion polls? Is the government justified in taking so many public opinion polls at public expense? Explain.

6. How do the various critical approaches outlined in Chapter 1 add to our understanding of political socialization and the role of the mass media and public opinion polls in the Canadian political system?

····································

NOTES

1. Edwin R. Black, *Politics and the News: The Political Functions of the Mass Media* (Toronto: Butterworths, 1982), pp. 6–7, points out that this is "secondhand or vicarious experience," as opposed to gaining information and opinions from real, personal experience.
2. Ronald Landes, "Political Education and Political Socialization," in Jon Pammett and Jean-Luc Pépin, eds., *Political Education in Canada* (Halifax: Institute for Research on Public Policy, 1988), p. 17.
3. Jon Pammett, "The Development of Political Orientations in Canadian School Children," *Canadian Journal of Political Science* (March 1971), pp. 132–40.
4. Marcel Trudel and Genevieve Jain, *Canadian History Textbooks: A Comparative Study* (Ottawa: Royal Commission on Bilingualism and Biculturalism, 1970).
5. Landes, "Political Education and Political Socialization," p. 17.
6. A.B. Hodgetts, *What Culture? What Heritage?* (Toronto: Ontario Institute for Studies in Education, 1968), p. 76.
7. John Ricker and Alan Skeoch, "The Contribution of Ontario's Schools to Political Education," in Pammett and Pépin, *Political Education in Canada*, p. 70.
8. Alan Frizzell et al., *The Canadian General Election of 1988* (Ottawa: Carleton University Press), p. 69.
9. The Canadian Conference of Catholic Bishops has extended traditional Catholic concerns and made passionate appeals on poverty, unemployment, housing, and other class issues.
10. David Taras, *Power and Betrayal in the Canadian Media* (Peterborough: Broadview Press, 1999), ch. 8.
11. Peter Trueman, *Smoke and Mirrors: The Inside Story of Television News in Canada* (Toronto: McClelland and Stewart, 1980), p. 188.
12. The volatility in this industry is such that specific ownership figures might become out of date at any time.
13. Stephen Brooks and Andrew Stritch, *Business and Government in Canada* (Scarborough: Prentice-Hall Canada, 1991). The mutually advantageous simultaneous closings were deemed by the courts to be a coincidence and a normal part of doing business.
14. Frederick J. Fletcher, *The Newspaper and Public Affairs* (Ottawa: Royal Commission on Newspapers, 1981), pp. 29, 35, 87. The main exception was Paul Desmarais, who insisted that his newspapers in Quebec not support the "Yes" position in the 1980 Quebec referendum. See also the main Royal Commission Report, pp. 163–67; and David Taras, *The Newsmakers* (Scarborough: Nelson Canada, 1990), pp. 8–17.
15. James Winter, *Democracy's Oxygen: How Corporations Control the News* (Montreal: Black Rose, 1997); Maude Barlow and James Winter, *The Big Black Book: The Essential Views of Conrad and Barbara Amiel Black* (Toronto: Stoddart, 1997); John Miller, *Yesterday's News: Why Canada's Daily Newspapers Are Failing Us* (Halifax: Fernwood Publishing, 1998).
16. Frederick J. Fletcher and Daphne Gottlieb Taras, "Images and Issues: The Mass Media and Politics in Canada," in Michael S. Whittington and Glen Williams, eds., *Canadian Politics in the 1990s*, 3rd ed. (Scarborough: Nelson Canada, 1990), p. 229.
17. Black, *Politics and the News*, p. 80.
18. Trueman, *Smoke and Mirrors*, p. 161.
19. This point was also made in Chapter 9. Herschel Hardin, *Closed Circuits* (Vancouver: Douglas & McIntyre, 1985); Marc Raboy, *Missed Opportunities: The Story of Canada's Broadcasting Policy* (Montreal: McGill–Queen's University Press, 1990; and Taras, *Power and Betrayal*.

20. The general thrust of David Taras in *The Newsmakers*. See Chapter 11 of his book for a discussion of how the media are performing functions previously the domain of political parties.
21. Environics Media Study (Environics Research Group, December 1986), cited by Peter Desbarats, *Guide to Canadian News Media*, 2nd ed. (Toronto: Harcourt Brace Jovanovich, 1990), p. 28; see also its 1991 Media Study.
22. John McMenemy, "Getting to Know the Parties by the Company We Keep: Local Sources of Party Imagery," in Alain Gagnon and Brian Tanguay, *Canadian Parties in Transition* (Scarborough: Nelson Canada, 1989), pp. 309–10.
23. Taras, *The Newsmakers*, pp. 30–31; Walter C. Soderlund et al., "Regional and Linguistic Agenda Setting," in *Canadian Journal of Political Science* (December 1980), pp. 347–56; Walter C. Soderlund et al., *Media and Elections in Canada* (Toronto: Holt, Rinehart and Winston, 1984); Fletcher, *The Newspaper and Public Affairs*, p. 16; Fletcher and Taras, "Images and Issues: The Mass Media and Politics in Canada," p. 222; Black, *Politics and the* News, p. 183; Desbarats, *Guide to Canadian News Media*, p. 149; and Arthur Siegel, *Politics and the Media in Canada* (Toronto: McGraw-Hill Ryerson, 1983), p. 14.
24. Taras, *The Newsmakers*, ch. 3; and Allan Levine, *Scrum Wars: The Prime Ministers and the Media* (Toronto: Dundurn Press, 1993).
25. Taras, *Power and Betrayal*, p. 208.
26. Taras, *The Newsmakers*, p. 102.
27. For example, in the GST debate, Jean Chrétien and his Liberal colleagues from the House of Commons marched to the doors of the Senate, and the senators "invited" television cameras onto the floor to substitute for the lack of coverage of the Senate debate on television. The Oka standoff involved concerted attempts by both sides to control the TV coverage.
28. Alan Frizzell et al., *The Canadian General Election of 1988* (Ottawa: Carleton University Press, 1989), p. 33.
29. Taras, *The Newsmakers*, ch. 4.
30. Black, *Politics and the News*, p. 90; Knowlton Nash, *Trivia Pursuit: How Showbiz Values Are Corrupting the News* (Toronto: McClelland and Stewart, 1998).
31. Taras, *The Newsmakers*, ch. 5; Howard K. Penniman, ed., *Canada at the Polls, 1984* (Durham, NC: Duke University Press, 1988), pp. 184 and 201; and Levine, *Scrum Wars*.
32. Fletcher, *The Newspaper and Public Affairs*, p. 23.
33. Ibid., p. 30; Taras, *The Newsmakers*, pp. 87–89. It is not yet clear to what extent the *National Post* has cut into this dominance.
34. Fletcher, *The Newspaper and Public Affairs*, p. 11.
35. In contrast to Pierre Trudeau, who characteristically held the media in contempt while on occasion manipulating them masterfully (notably in the 1968 election and the 1970 October Crisis), Brian Mulroney, a media and telephone junkie, telephoned editors on occasion to canvass their opinion, but with no comparable mastery. Michel Gratton, *So, What Are the Boys Saying? An Inside Look at Brian Mulroney in Power* (Toronto: McGraw-Hill Ryerson, 1987); and Taras, *The Newsmakers*, pp. 139–40. Jean Chrétien is related to Paul Desmarais through the marriage of their children. Allan Fotheringham claims that until his retirement in 1988, editor Beland Honderich ran *The Toronto Star* with an iron hand and manipulated the news in favour of his own political predilections. See *Birds of a Feather: The Press and the Politicians* (Toronto: Key Porter Books, 1990), pp. 73, 94–95. *The Globe and Mail* found it necessary to reprint a collage of its pro–free trade editorials on the page opposite shortly before the 1988 election.
36. Frizzell et al., *The Canadian General Election of 1988*, p. 84; and *The Canadian General Election of 1984* (Ottawa: Carleton University Press, 1985), pp. 60–68; R.H. Wagenberg et al., "Campaigns, Images and Polls: Mass Media Coverage of the 1984 Canadian Election," *Canadian Journal of Political Science* (March 1988), pp. 117–29.
37. Taras, *The Newsmakers*, pp. 76–79.
38. Fotheringham, *Birds of a Feather*, pp. 33, 139.
39. Ibid., p. 249.
40. Siegel, *Politics and the Media in Canada*, p. 80.
41. Ibid., pp. 79–82; Wilfred H. Kesterton, *The Law and the Press in Canada* (Toronto: McClelland and Stewart, 1976); The Royal Commission on Newspapers, pp. 47–53; and Desbarats, *Guide to Canadian News Media*, p. 157.

42. Black, *Politics and the News*, p. 12; Taras, *The Newsmakers*, p. 234.

43. See books by such press secretaries as Patrick Gossage, *Close to the Charisma: My Years between the Press and Pierre Elliott Trudeau* (Toronto: McClelland and Stewart, 1986), and Michel Gratton, *So, What Are the Boys Saying?* as well as Taras, *The Newsmakers*, pp. 125–130, 158, 172.

44. See also Taras, *Power and Betrayal*, p. 52

45. Pierre Laporte, *The True Face of Duplessis* (Montreal: Harvest House, 1960).

46. David Taras, "Television and Public Policy: The CBC's Coverage of the Meech Lake Accord," *Canadian Public Policy* (September 1989), pp. 322–34; Elly Alboim, "Inside the News Story: Meech Lake as Viewed by an Ottawa Bureau Chief," in Roger Gibbins et al., eds., *Meech Lake and Canada: Perspectives from the West* (Edmonton: Academic Printing and Publishing, 1988); and John Meisel, "Mirror? Searchlight? Interloper?—The Media and Meech," in David Smith, Peter MacKinnon, and John Courtney, eds., *After Meech Lake: Lessons for the Future* (Saskatoon: Fifth House Publishers, 1991); Desbarats, *Guide to Canadian News Media*, p. 41; Taras, *Power and Betrayal*, ch. 6.

47. Taras, *Power and Betrayal*.

48. Black, *Politics and the News*, p. 168.

49. Frizzell et al., *The Canadian Federal Election of 1988*, p. 91.

50. I am indebted to Paul Seccaspina of Oracle Research in Sudbury for assistance on this subject. See Professional Marketing Research Society, *Directory of Canadian Marketing Research Organizations*, and *National Membership Directory*, both published annually. That organization has also published *Rules of Conduct and Good Practice*, and *A History of Marketing Research in Canada* (1985).

51. Jenefer Curtis, "Captain Crunch," *Saturday Night*, September 1998.

52. John Turner's election in Vancouver Quadra in 1984 is often cited as an example of the underdog effect, given that all polls in the constituency indicated that he would lose.

53. Taras, *The Newsmakers*, p. 187, 192–94; Desbarats, *Guide to Canadian News Media*, p. 138.

54. Claire Hoy, *Margin of Error* (Toronto: Key Porter Books, 1989), pp. 219–20; and Taras, *The Newsmakers*, p. 193.

55. Hoy, *Margin of Error*, p. 228. Hoy discusses the government's first poll on the conscription issue in 1942, which it wanted to keep secret, p. 14. See also Paul Fox, "The Danger Is Private Polling," in Paul Fox and Graham White, eds., *Politics: Canada*, 6th ed. (Toronto: McGraw-Hill Ryerson, 1987).

56. *Thomson Newspaper Co. v. Canada (Attorney General)*, [1998] 1 S.C.R. 877.

57. Richard Johnston, *Public Opinion and Public Policy in Canada* (Toronto: University of Toronto Press, 1986).

58. Hoy writes that in one view "the essence of parliamentary democracy is that we elect politicians to lead, to take risks, to stand for something more than the latest popular sentiment or the collective public wisdom, which may be based more on short-term emotion or outright ignorance than on anything else," *Margin of Error*, p. 7.

59. Hoy, *Margin of Error*, pp. 1–5. In 1984, the NDP fired one pollster and hired an American replacement, Vic Fingerhut, over the issue of trying to change the negative public perception of its economic policies. See Penniman, ed., *Canada at the Polls, 1984*, p. 129.

60. Penniman, ed., *Canada at the Polls, 1984*, p. 131.

61. Janine Brodie and Jane Jenson, *Crisis, Challenge and Change: Party and Class in Canada Revisited* (Ottawa: Carleton University Press, 1988).

62. Fotheringham describes one such event, a Barbara Frum party, in *Birds of a Feather*, pp. 146–50.

63. Fletcher and Taras, "Images and Issues," pp. 233–34.

64. Black, *Politics and the News*, pp. 188–89.

65. Fletcher and Taras, "Images and Issues," p. 223; Black, *Politics and the News*, pp. 43–44; John Porter, *The Vertical Mosaic* (Toronto: University of Toronto Press, 1965), ch. XV; and Ted Magder, "Taking Culture Seriously: A Political Economy of Communications," in Wallace Clement and Glen Williams, eds., *The New Canadian Political Economy* (Montreal: McGill–Queen's University Press, 1989). The "right-wing shift" at *The Globe and Mail* in 1989 could also be mentioned.

66. Desbarats, *Guide to Canadian News Media*, p. 69.

67. Wallace Clement, *The Canadian Corporate Elite* (Toronto: McClelland and Stewart, 1975), pp. 270–86.

68. Royal Commission on Newspapers, p. 1.

69. M.J. Trebilcock et al., *The Choice of Governing Instrument* (Ottawa: Supply and Services, 1982), and W.T. Stanbury, *Business–Government Relations in Canada* (Toronto: Methuen, 1986), pp. 147–48 and ch. 11.
70. Taras, *The Newsmakers*, p. 186.

....

FURTHER READING

Barlow, Maude, and James Winter. *The Big Black Book: The Essential Views of Conrad and Barbara Amiel Black.* Toronto: Stoddart, 1997.

Bird, Roger, ed. *Documents of Canadian Broadcasting.* Ottawa: Carleton University Press, 1988.

Black, E.R. *Politics and the News: The Political Functions of the Mass Media.* Toronto: Butterworths, 1982.

Comber, Mary Anne, and Robert S. Mayne. *The Newsmongers: How the Media Distort the Political News.* Toronto: McClelland and Stewart, 1986.

Desbarats, Peter. *Guide to Canadian News Media*, 2nd ed. Toronto: Harcourt Brace Jovanovich, 1990.

Fletcher, Frederick J. *The Newspaper and Public Affairs.* Ottawa: Royal Commission on Newspapers, 1981.

Fletcher, Frederick J., and Daphne Gottlieb Taras. "Images and Issues: The Mass Media and Politics in Canada." In Michael S. Whittington and Glen Williams, eds., *Canadian Politics in the 1990s.* Scarborough: Nelson Canada, 3rd ed., 1990; 4th ed., 1995.

Fotheringham, Allan. *Birds of a Feather: The Press and the Politicians.* Toronto: Key Porter Books, 1990.

Fox, Bill. *Spin Wars.* Toronto: Key Porter Books, 1999.

Fox, Paul. "The Danger Is Private Polling." In Paul Fox and Graham White, eds., *Politics: Canada*, 6th ed. Toronto: McGraw-Hill Ryerson, 1987.

Frizzell, Alan, et al. *The Canadian General Election of 1984.* Ottawa: Carleton University Press, 1985.

———. *The Canadian General Election of 1988.* Ottawa: Carleton University Press, 1989.

———. *The Canadian General Election of 1993.* Ottawa: Carleton University Press, 1994.

———. *The Canadian General Election of 1997.* Toronto: Dundurn Press, 1997.

Hodgetts, A.B. *What Culture? What Heritage? A Study of Civil Education in Canada.* Toronto: Ontario Institute for Studies in Education, 1968.

Holmes, Helen, and David Taras, eds. *In the Public Interest: Mass Media and Democracy in Canada.* Toronto: Holt, Rinehart and Winston, 1992.

Hoy, Claire. *Margin of Error.* Toronto: Key Porter Books, 1989.

Magder, Ted. "Taking Culture Seriously: A Political Economy of Communications." In Wallace Clement and Glen Williams, eds., *The New Canadian Political Economy.* Montreal: McGill–Queen's University Press, 1989.

Miller, John. *Yesterday's News: How Canada's Daily Newspapers Are Failing Us.* Halifax: Fernwood Publishing, 1998.

Nash, Knowlton. *The Microphone Wars: A History of Triumph and Betrayal at the CBC.* Toronto: McClelland and Stewart, 1994.

———. *Trivia Pursuit: How Showbiz Values Are Corrupting the News.* Toronto: McClelland and Stewart, 1998.

Pammett, Jon, and Jean-Luc Pépin, eds. *Political Education in Canada.* Halifax: Institute for Research on Public Publicy, 1988.

Royal Commission on Newspapers. Ottawa: Supply and Services, 1981. See also its background research studies.

Sawatsky, John. *The Insiders: Government, Business and the Lobbyists*. Toronto: McClelland and Stewart, 1987.

Taras, David. *The Newsmakers*. Scarborough: Nelson Canada, 1990.

————. *Power and Betrayal in the Canadian Media*. Peterborough: Broadview Press, 1999.

Trueman, Peter. *Smoke and Mirrors: The Inside Story of Television News in Canada*. Toronto: McClelland and Stewart, 1980.

Winter, James. *Democracy's Oxygen: How Corporations Control the News*. Montreal: Black Rose, 1997.

Chapter 12

Elections and the
ELECTORAL
system

If elections are a crucial component in the definition of a democracy, it is important that they be conducted in the fairest possible way. Everyone should be able to vote, every vote should be equal on election day, and every province should be fairly represented in the House of Commons. This chapter will show whether the Canadian electoral system comes close to these ideals. While the electoral system usually produces a majority of seats for the winning party without a majority of the votes cast, governing parties regularly claim a mandate to implement their election platform. Opposition parties, on the other hand, are usually short-changed in the number of seats they obtain. In other words, the Canadian electoral system does not award seats in proportion to a party's popular vote. Even greater controversy surrounds the question of party and election finance, as some parties grossly outspend others.

This chapter examines the formal, legal, and official aspects of the electoral system, and has four parts: redistribution, or determining the number of seats each province is entitled to and drawing the electoral map; the official organization of elections; an evaluation of the electoral system and suggestions for reform; and party and election finance. The actual electoral contest between political parties and the questions of electoral behaviour and party support are discussed in Chapter 14.

THE REDISTRIBUTION PROCESS

Redistribution is the process of dividing the country into electoral districts or constituencies. It involves two stages: first, deciding how many seats in the House of Commons to allot to each province and territory and, second, actually drawing constituency boundaries within them.

Distribution of Seats among Provinces

The Constitution Act of 1867 requires that the readjustment process be repeated after each decennial census, for example, 1981, 1991, and 2001. Given the federal character of Canada with its strong provincial loyalties, the search for a fair means of distributing seats in the House of Commons among the provinces has been a long and unsatisfactory one. Four different formulas have been used over the years, but none has ever commanded unanimous support.[1] The formula used following the 1991 census and the one that resulted in the current 301 seats in the House of Commons after the 1997 election was adopted by means of the Representation Act, 1985. It involves the four following steps.

1. Starting with 282 seats, two seats are allocated to the Northwest Territories and one to the Yukon, leaving 279 seats.

2. The total population of the ten provinces is divided by 279 to obtain the electoral quota or quotient.

3. This electoral quota is divided into the population of each province to obtain the number of seats each is entitled to.

4. If these provincial seat allocations result in any province having fewer seats than it has senators, then (under the "senatorial clause") it obtains such additional seats as to equal its number of senators; if the allocations result in any province having fewer seats than it had in 1976, then (under the "grandfather clause") such additional seats are also added.

Table 12.1 illustrates how such calculations were made. As mentioned, regardless of current population, each province is guaranteed at least as many members of Parliament as it has senators, and at least as many seats as it had in 1976. These two clauses have the effect of overrepresenting all provinces except Ontario, British Columbia, and Alberta. In the mid-1990s, Ontario gained four seats and BC, two, but these two provinces and Alberta still have fewer seats than their populations justify. The 301 seats are currently divided as follows:

Ontario	103	New Brunswick	10
Quebec	75	Newfoundland	7
British Columbia	34	Prince Edward Island	4
Alberta	26	Northwest Territories	1
Manitoba	14	Nunavut	1
Saskatchewan	14	Yukon	1
Nova Scotia	11		

Drawing Constituency Boundaries

The second phase of the redistribution process, drawing constituency boundaries within each province, was historically the prerogative of the politicians. They regularly engaged in the process of **gerrymandering**, that is, manipulating constituency boundaries so as to ensure as far as possible the re-election of the members of the government party.[2] In the absence of any written rules, some constituencies had huge populations while others were extremely small. The Electoral Boundaries Readjustment Act of 1964 established a new system, however, so that beginning with the post-1961 redistribution, this task has been performed by independent commissions. An electoral boundaries commission is appointed for each province, chaired by a judge designated by the chief justice of the province. The other two members of each commission

TABLE 12.1   Redistribution Formula Using the 1991 Census Figures

Province or Territory	Number of Seats Established in 1976 and Constituting 33rd Parliament[1]	Calculations					Electoral Quotient
		Population 1991	National Quotient[2]	Rounded Result	Special Clauses[3]	Total	
Newfoundland	7	568 474	97 532	6	1	7	81 211
Prince Edward Island	4	129 765	97 532	1	3	4	32 441
Nova Scotia	11	899 942	97 532	9	2	11	81 813
New Brunswick	10	723 900	97 532	7	3	10	72 390
Quebec	75	6 895 963	97 532	71	4	75	91 946
Ontario	95	10 084 885	97 532	103	—	103	97 912
Manitoba	14	1 091 942	97 532	11	3	14	77 996
Saskatchewan	14	988 928	97 532	10	4	14	70 638
Alberta	21	2 545 553	97 532	26	—	26	97 906
British Columbia	28	3 282 061	97 532	34	—	34	96 531
Northwest Territories[4]	2	57 649	—	—	—	2	—
Yukon Territory	1	27 797	—	—	—	1	—
TOTAL	282	27 296 859				301	

Source: Elections Canada, Representation in the Federal Parliament, *Cat. No. SE 3-25/1993, 1993. Reproduced with the permission of the Minister of Public Works and Government Services Canada, 2000.*
[1] *Assign two seats to the Northwest Territories and one to the Yukon Territory (three seats).*
[2] *Use 279 seats and population of provinces to establish national quotient (27 211 413 + 279 = 97 532).*
[3] *Add seats to provinces pursuant to "Senatorial Clause" guarantee in the Constitution and new "Grandfather Clause" (based on 33rd Parliament).*

are appointed by the Speaker of the House of Commons, typically including an academic and the provincial chief electoral officer or some other nonpartisan legislative official. All commissions draw extensively on the support and assistance of the chief electoral officer's staff, and digital computerized technology now simplifies the task of drawing electoral maps.

The commissions swing into action as soon as the provincial population figures are available from the census. Theirs is a very delicate task of trying to arrive at a design that will provide constituencies of approximately equal population size throughout the province while also accounting for geographic characteristics, communities of interest, and other peculiarities. The most difficult problem is in dealing with sparsely populated rural or northern regions at the same time as concentrated urban centres. In recognition of this problem, the commissions in the 1960s and 1970s were allowed to deviate from the average population figure to a maximum tolerance of plus or minus 25 percent, but in the 1980s and 1990s, the law allowed them to exceed this limit "in circumstances viewed by the commission as being extraordinary" in order to arrive at a manageable geographic size for all districts. They must also consider the "community of interest or community of identity in or the historical pattern of an electoral district." Thus rural and northern constituencies tend to be under the provincial quotient and southern, urban ones slightly over it. In the 1995 operation, only two constituencies out of 301 exceeded the 25 percent limit (one in Newfoundland and one in Quebec), and 80 percent were within plus or minus 12.5 percent of the provincial quotient.[3] The Royal Commission on Electoral Reform and Party Financing recommended a tolerance of 15 percent, but a 1999 court decision affecting the Northwest Territories alone was satisfied with plus or minus 25 percent.

The publication of the map of proposed electoral boundaries is followed by a period of public hearings, which are normally held at several different locations in the province. During these hearings interested individuals, municipalities, groups, and MPs appear to express their views on the proposals. Then, within a year of the population data's becoming available, the commissions must complete their reports. They are sent through the chief electoral officer to the Speaker of the House of Commons, who must ensure that they are tabled and referred to the appropriate Commons committee. Written objections, signed by at least ten MPs, may be filed with this committee, which has 30 days while the House is sitting to discuss and raise objections to the report. The committee's proceedings are sent back to the electoral boundaries commissions, which have the authority to alter their report or leave it as is. Thus, it is the independent commissions and not the politicians who have the final say.[4] Because of the time needed by the chief electoral officer, returning officers, and political parties to make adjustments in their operations, the new boundaries cannot be used at an election until at least one year after the date that the representation order encompassing the new boundaries is proclaimed. This is why the 1997 election was the first to be held on the basis of the 1991 census.

The effect of the provisions of both aspects of the redistribution process is to undermine the basic democratic principle of political equality or "one person, one vote." Since it takes fewer votes in smaller provinces and in rural parts of all provinces to elect a member of Parliament, such votes are worth more than those in large provinces or in urban areas. John Courtney points out that the degree of intraprovincial similarity in constituency size is increasing, but that there is a widening disparity between the size of constituencies in different provinces.[5] In general, however, Canadians accept this deviation from the principle of representation by population or political equality out of charity, ignorance, or recognition of the fact that the Canadian population is peculiarly distributed. On the other hand, the democratic rights provision of the Charter of Rights and Freedoms opens up the possibility of a legal challenge on this subject. As mentioned in Chapter 18, several provincial redistribution schemes have been so challenged.[6]

The processes outlined above did not unfold as they were supposed to after the 1991 census. The electoral boundaries commissions drew new maps, which were ready shortly after the 1993 election, but many newly elected MPs were not happy with the results. A government bill would have abolished the boundaries commissions and suspended the Electoral Boundaries Readjustment Act for up to two years, possibly pre-empting a redistribution before the 1997 election. The Tory majority in the Senate was unhappy with this abuse of power by the Liberal majority in the Commons, however, and effectively killed the bill.[7]

THE OFFICIAL ELECTION MACHINERY
Setting the Date

The prime minister normally has the prerogative to call the election within a five-year period from the previous electoral contest. Largely based on the government party's standings in the public opinion polls, the election is typically called about four years after the previous campaign. The average time between elections since 1867 has been about 41 months, reflecting the shorter tenure of minority governments. Going into the fifth year, especially to the five-year limit, is usually seen as a sign of political weakness, and most governments waiting that long have been defeated. The governor general must approve the prime minister's request to dissolve Parliament in order to call an election, but this is normally automatic. Only once in Canadian history (1926), in rather peculiar circumstances, did a governor general refuse such a request, as discussed in Chapter 20. The defeat of a government in a nonconfidence vote in the House of Commons is the alternative precipitator of an election, in which case the prime minister's leeway is limited to choosing the exact date.

Public opinion polls can be wrong, of course, or public opinion can change between the calling of the election and the actual voting day, so that the apparent advantage for the party in power in choosing the election date is not absolute, as John Turner discovered in 1984 when an 11-point lead in June dissolved into a 22-point lag by September. Many such reversals during the campaign period have also occurred at the provincial level, and Chapter 14 discusses the highly volatile nature of Canadian party preferences. Nevertheless, because of the potential unfairness of the existing system and because the uncertainty of the date causes inconvenience to many of those involved, some observers would prefer to establish fixed election dates. New Zealand has demonstrated that this can be done within the British parliamentary system.

By Paul Lachine. Reproduced with permission.

Election Officials

The **chief electoral officer** is responsible for the overall administration of the election and must function with absolute impartiality. This post is therefore filled by a resolution of the whole House of Commons, rather than by a regular public servant hired by the government. On the other hand, returning officers, who organize the election in each of the 301 electoral districts (also called constituencies or ridings), are chosen by the Cabinet, and are usually partisan appointees. Ironically, once appointed, they are expected to function in a completely nonpartisan fashion. Before the election call, each returning officer will have divided the constituency into polling divisions (or polls) of about 350 voters each, and a typical urban constituency will have about 200 polls. Because such preparations must be made beforehand, returning officers work part-time between elections and full-time during the campaign. They usually serve until a different party comes to power and replaces them with its own supporters. Many informed observers believe that this peculiar and paradoxical situation should be changed.[8]

The Voters' List

In Canadian federal elections, the **voters' list** has historically been compiled from scratch after the election writ is issued. This was done by means of a door-to-door enumeration in which the returning officer appointed two enumerators to collect the names of eligible voters in each polling division. It was largely because of this lengthy process that Canadian election campaigns used to be at least 47 days long.

The 1993 reforms permitted the use of electoral lists prepared within the previous 12 months to substitute for a full-fledged enumeration. Since the 1992 referendum was held almost exactly a year before the 1993 election, there was no 1993 enumeration except in Quebec (which had held its own simultaneous referendum). This incident had implications for the voter turnout rate, as mentioned in Chapter 10.

Reforms introduced in 1996 provided for a permanent Register of Electors, the base of which was compiled in one last door-to-door enumeration in April 1997 (except in Alberta and Prince Edward Island, which used the most recent provincial voters' list). Henceforth, that register will be automatically updated from such sources as income tax, citizenship and immigration, driver's licence, and vital statistics files. With such a permanent voters' list, it was possible to reduce the length of the 1997 election period to 36 days. In any case, a ballot can also be issued to a qualified person whose name is not on the voters' list.

Nomination

About 95 percent of candidates are nominated at a meeting of a political party, but they must then submit formal **nomination** papers endorsed by 100 people on the local voters' list accompanied by a $1000 deposit. Candidates receive one-half of this amount back if and when they file their financial statement, and those who received at least 15 percent of the vote are also reimbursed the other $500. Official candidates of registered parties must obtain the party leader's endorsement in order to use the party name on the ballot. This requirement was mainly adopted to pre-empt the possibility of local conflicts over who was the legitimate standard-bearer of the party, but it effectively gives the leader a veto over nominations—with many implications. In 1974, for example, Robert Stanfield denied the party label to Leonard Jones, who was nominated as the Conservative candidate in Moncton, because of Jones's outspoken opposition to official bilingualism, and Brian Mulroney refused to endorse discredited ex–Cabinet minister Sinclair Stevens in 1988. When a number of Liberal backbenchers voted against government bills in mid-1995, Prime Minister Chrétien warned them that he might not sign their nomination papers in the next election, although only John Nunziata ultimately met this fate, and then ran successfully as an Independent.

Election Day

After nomination day, the returning officer arranges for the ballots to be printed and then allows people to vote in advance polls or by special ballot.[9] Recent reforms made voting much more convenient for those not at home on election day, including members of the armed forces and federal and provincial government officials posted outside the country; those absent from the country for less than five years who intend to return; and those who are unable to vote at the advance poll because they are temporarily out of the country. By this time, the returning officer is also busy hiring and training deputy returning officers and poll clerks to look after each polling station on election day and finding appropriate polling stations, typically in schools, church basements, or community centres.

Canadian federal elections are held on Mondays, and the polls used to be open from 9 a.m. to 8 p.m. local time. The 1993 reforms scrapped the clause whereby, if the Monday in question was a statutory holiday the election would be held on the next day. Because voters in the western part of the country complained that the winner was often decided even before their votes had been counted, the Royal Commission on Electoral Reform and Party Financing proposed a system of staggered hours for different time zones. This recommendation was implemented for the 1997 election and meant that the polls closed at approximately the same time all across the country, and ballots were counted and results announced more or less simultaneously. As before, however, broadcasters were not allowed to report results from other regions until the polls closed in their own time zone. Voters are entitled to three consecutive hours off work in which to cast their ballot, and since 1993, the sale of liquor is no longer prohibited during polling hours. Other recommendations of the Royal Commission that made the system more user-friendly include the provision that polling stations must have level access, the establishment of mobile polls for the elderly or disabled, and the appointment of an interpreter and the use of a template for the visually impaired.

Voters mark their X in private on the ballot provided, and when the polls close the deputy returning officer and poll clerk count them, usually in the company of scrutineers from the various candidates who are allowed to challenge unorthodox markings on ballots and generally keep the whole process honest. Results are announced an hour or so after the polls close and the candidate with the most votes, the **first-past-the-post**, is declared elected. This means that the winner usually does not actually have a majority of the votes cast, only a plurality.

The Ballot

The secret ballot was introduced into federal elections in 1874, so that in the first two elections after Confederation, people voted orally and were subject to bribery or intimidation, including

Montrealers living in the Westmount–St-Louis riding cast their advance vote in Westmount in 1998. Unseasonably fine weather and the chance to avoid the November 30 rush drove voters to cast their ballots in unexpectedly large numbers, catching scrutineers understaffed and causing delays. (Robert Galbraith/Canapress)

the threat of physical assault if they voted the wrong way! Moreover, before 1874 Canada had "nonsimultaneous" elections in which different constituencies voted on different days. This practice allowed the government to call the election in its safest seats first, and then, having won them, hope that other constituencies would jump on the bandwagon.

The candidates are listed in alphabetical order on the ballot, and, since 1970, the ballot contains their party affiliation, if any. The chief electoral officer keeps a registry of political parties, and only registered parties (those that run at least 50 candidates) are allowed to use the party label on the ballot. Such parties must also register their national and constituency official agents and auditors for the purposes of keeping track of the party's and candidates' finances. Twelve parties were registered for the 1988 election, 14 for 1993, and 10 for 1997.[10]

The Franchise[11]

The extension of the **franchise** beyond males with substantial property was mentioned in passing in Chapters 4 to 8. This evolution in Canada was complicated by the use of different provincial franchises in federal elections between 1867 and 1885 and between 1898 and 1917. The federal franchise between 1885 and 1898 required that males be property owners, but this qualification was gradually eliminated in most provinces about 1900. In 1917 the franchise was manipulated so as to maximize support for the incumbent government. The vote was extended to women serving in the war as well as to female relatives of men overseas, but denied to Canadian citizens who had come from "enemy alien" countries. In 1918 all women were granted the vote, and since 1920 a uniform federal franchise has existed. The only exception was that Canadians of Asian ancestry (especially those from Japan, China, and India) living in British Columbia were denied the right to vote in federal elections because the federal law disqualified anyone who for reasons of race was denied the vote under provincial electoral statutes. All such restrictions were removed by 1948. The vote was extended to the Inuit in 1953 and to Indians living on reserves in 1960. The voting age was reduced from 21 to 18 in 1970, and British subjects who were not Canadian citizens lost their vote in 1975.

By that time, the **Canada Elections Act** disqualified only the following individuals from voting: the chief and assistant chief electoral officers, returning officers (except in the case of a tie), federally appointed judges, prison inmates, those deprived of their liberty by reason of mental disease, and those convicted of corrupt or illegal electoral practices. In the course of the 1988 campaign, however, three of these disqualifications were challenged in the courts in terms of the Canadian Charter of Rights and Freedoms, which guarantees the vote to every Canadian citizen. In the case of judges and those in mental institutions, the provisions of the act were declared unconstitutional and the disqualifications removed. The courts made a number of contradictory decisions on whether prison inmates should be able to vote, and the 1993 amendments gave the vote to inmates serving sentences of less than two years. In 1996, however, long-term prisoners were successful in persuading the courts to remove the two-year restriction.[12]

The other principal ingredients of the 1993 reforms were as follows: electors may now place their own ballots in the ballot box; candidates and canvassers are authorized to enter any apartment building; and financial contributions are prohibited from outside the country.

EVALUATING THE ELECTORAL SYSTEM

In each constituency, the candidate with the most votes wins, even if this is less than 50 percent. Among the advantages of this electoral system are its simplicity, its quick calculation of results, and its provision of a clear-cut representative for each constituency. When all the local results are cumulated nationally, however, the proportion of seats a party wins does not necessarily bear much relationship to its overall share of the **popular vote**. Take as an extreme, hypothetical example a two-person race in each constituency in which the Liberal candidate beat the Conservative candidate by one vote in every case: the Liberal Party would then win 100 percent of the seats from just over 50 percent of the vote, and the Conservative Party would have 0 percent of the seats from just under 50 percent of the vote. In fact, this example is not so hypothetical: in the New Brunswick election of 1987, the Liberals won 100 percent of the seats with about 60 percent of the popular vote. Many political scientists and other observers are therefore concerned that such overall disparities can occur between percentage of seats won and percentage of popular vote.

Discrepancies between Seats and Votes: National Level

The actual disparities can be analyzed for both the national and provincial levels.[13] Overall, in 23 elections since 1921, the party with the largest popular vote won more seats than it deserved on 22 occasions, while the second party was usually somewhat underrepresented. When it comes to minor parties, those with concentrated regional support were often overrepresented, while those with broad national ("diffuse") support usually lost out. The CCF/NDP, for example, regularly received only about half as many seats as its popular vote merited.

Some observers credit this electoral system with producing a majority government—the leading party obtaining more than 50 percent of the seats—even though a party rarely wins over 50 percent of the popular vote. In only three federal elections between 1921 and 1997 (1940, 1958, and 1984) did the winning party obtain at least 50 percent of the vote, and this automatically produced a majority government. On eight other occasions, a minority government resulted. But on the other 12 occasions out of 23, this electoral system manufactured a majority government in terms of seats, even though the leading party did not win a majority of the vote. Thus, this "first-past-the-post" system does have a tendency to produce a majority government, but, at the same time, it weakens the opposition. Moreover, on three occasions (1957, 1962, and 1979) the party with the second-largest popular vote ended up with more seats than the party that came first, and therefore went on to form the government, as happened in the Quebec provincial election of 1998 and twice in Saskatchewan.

TABLE 12.2 Comparison of Percentage of Popular Vote and Percentage of Seats by Party for Federal Elections, 1921–1997

	Liberal		Conservative		CCF/NDP	
	% Vote	% Seats	% Vote	% Seats	% Vote	% Seats
1921	41	49	30	21	—	—
1925	40	40	46	47	—	—
1926	46	52	45	37	—	—
1930	45	37	49	56	—	—
1935	45	71	30	16	9	3
1940	52	74	31	16	9	3
1945	41	51	27	27	16	11
1949	49	74	30	16	13	5
1953	49	64	31	19	11	9
1957	41	40	39	42	11	9
1958	34	18	54	79	10	3
1962	37	38	37	44	14	7
1963	42	49	33	36	13	6
1965	40	49	33	36	18	8
1968	45	58	31	27	17	8
1972	38	41	35	40	18	12
1974	43	53	36	36	16	6
1979	40	40	36	48	18	9
1980	44	52	33	37	20	11
1984	28	14	50	75	19	11
1988	32	28	43	57	20	15

		Liberal	PC	NDP	Reform	BQ
1993	% Vote	41.3	16.0	6.9	18.7	13.5
	% Seats	60.0	0.7	3.1	17.6	18.3
1997	% Vote	38.5	18.8	11.0	19.4	10.7
	% Seats	51.5	6.6	7.0	19.9	14.6

Source: Reports of the Chief Electoral Officer, *adapted by author. Material used with permission of the Chief Electoral Officer of Canada, 1999. Full responsibility for calculations and for conclusions drawn rests with the author.*

In the 1993 context, the Liberals and Bloc were overrepresented, but Reform, the NDP, and especially the PCs, deserved more seats in terms of their popular vote. Reform deserved to be the official opposition in the sense that it received more votes than the Bloc; the NDP deserved party status because 7 percent of the vote would theoretically produce about 20 seats; and the Conservatives ran a close third to Reform in popular vote and more than doubled the vote of the NDP but suffered from ridicule of its two-member caucus. The 1997 election also gave the Liberals a majority of seats that they did not deserve, gave the regionally concentrated Bloc more seats than it merited, and continued to underrepresent the more nationally based PCs and NDP.

Discrepancies between Seats and Votes: By Province

Another set of disparities between popular vote and seat figures exists on a province-by-province basis. In this case, Alan Cairns was particularly struck by the disparity between the Conservative vote and seats in Quebec (1896–1984) and between the Liberal vote and seats in Western Canada (since 1957). Table 12.2 shows the distribution of seats won per province in 1997 and Table 12.3, the provincial breakdown of the seats–votes ratio for 1997.

Cairns observed that such disparities affect parties in three principal ways: image, strategy, and policy. Each party's image is largely derived from the attention given to its number of elected members in the House of Commons rather than from its popular vote. Thus, when the Conservatives had virtually no members from Quebec before 1984, they gained a non-French or anti-French image, even though they usually obtained at least 13 percent of the popular vote in that province. Similarly, the Liberals acquired an image of an anti-Western

TABLE 12.2   Results of 1997 Election—Seats Won by Party by Province

	Liberal	Reform	Bloc	PC	NDP	Ind.	Total
Newfoundland	4	0	0	3	0	0	7
Prince Edward Island	4	0	0	0	0	0	4
Nova Scotia	0	0	0	5	6	0	11
New Brunswick	3	0	0	5	2	0	10
Quebec	26	0	44	5	0	0	75
Ontario	101	0	0	1	0	1	103
Manitoba	6	3	0	1	4	0	14
Saskatchewan	1	8	0	0	5	0	14
Alberta	2	24	0	0	0	0	26
British Columbia	6	25	0	0	3	0	34
Northwest Territories	2	0	0	0	0	0	2
Yukon	0	0	0	0	1	0	1
TOTAL	155	60	44	20	21	1	301

Source: Report of the Chief Electoral Officer. Reproduced with the permission of the Minister of Public Works and Government Services Canada, 2000.

TABLE 12.3   Comparison of Percentage of Seats and Votes in 1997 Election by Province

	Liberal		Reform		Bloc		PC		NDP	
	%V	%S	%V	%S	%V	%S	%V	%S	%V	%S
Newfoundland	38	57	3	0	0	0	37	43	25	0
PEI	45	100	2	0	0	0	38	0	15	0
Nova Scotia	28	0	10	0	0	0	31	45	30	55
New Brunswick	33	30	13	0	0	0	35	50	18	20
Quebec	37	35	0	0	38	59	22	7	2	0
Ontario	50	98	19	0	0	0	19	1	11	0
Manitoba	34	43	24	21	0	0	18	7	23	29
Saskatchewan	25	7	36	57	0	0	8	0	31	36
Alberta	24	8	55	92	0	0	14	0	6	0
BC	29	18	43	74	0	0	6	0	18	9
NWT	43	100	12	0	0	0	17	0	21	0
Yukon	22	0	25	0	0	0	14	0	29	100
TOTAL	38.5	51.5	19.4	19.9	10.7	14.6	18.8	6.6	11.0	7.0

Source: Report of the Chief Electoral Officer, *adapted by author. Reproduced with the permission of the Minister of Public Works and Government Services Canada, 2000.*

party after 1957 because they rarely elected members west of Ontario, even though they normally received over 20 percent of the Western vote. Historians and political scientists have even contributed to a misinterpretation of Canada's past by concentrating on seats rather than votes, such as in exaggerating the Liberal sweep in Quebec in 1896 (53 percent of the vote, 75 percent of the seats) and the national Liberal victory in 1935 (45 percent of the vote, 71 percent of the seats), and giving the NDP the image of a minor party because, as mentioned, it elected only about half as many members as its popular vote actually justified. In the 1997 context, on a provincial basis, Reform won 19 percent of the votes in Ontario but its Western seats (as well as the style of most of its members) contributed to a Western image. The Conservatives and NDP deserved to win seats in provinces where they were shut out, and the Bloc did not merit its image of being so popular in Quebec.

As far as strategy is concerned, when Conservatives despaired of electing members from Quebec and felt they could form a government without much representation from that province, they ignored it, especially in 1957.[14] The Liberals often felt that campaigning in the West was a waste of time and money and therefore concentrated their effort elsewhere. These strategies are not good for keeping the country together, one of the functions that political parties and elections are supposed to perform.

Finally, since the elected members of the party have a major role to play in the development of party policy, Conservative policy did not reflect the concerns of French Canada when the party lacked francophone and Quebec MPs, just as Liberal policy tended to ignore Western concerns because there were so few Liberals elected from Western Canada. This is especially serious for the party that forms the government, when it has few or no MPs from a province or region to put into the Cabinet. Between 1962 and 1984, either Quebec or the West was effectively left out of national decision making at the Cabinet level. Residents of such provinces or regions understandably feel that national policy does not reflect their interests and turn to provincial governments to defend these interests or start to think in separatist terms.

Remedies

Since Cairns first brought these problems to scholarly attention, reform of the electoral system has been frequently discussed. The extreme remedy would be a system of "proportional representation" in which constituencies would be eliminated and each party would receive as many seats in each province as its popular vote there dictated. Most observers feel, however, that Canadians do not want to part with local constituency representation. William Irvine proposed a system somewhat akin to that in Germany in which about half of the MPs would be elected from constituencies, as they are now. The others, called "provincial MPs," would be designated on the basis of popular vote by party in each province to bring each party's proportion of popular vote and percentage of seats into line, both in individual provinces and in the country as a whole. Irvine hoped to overcome the lack of representation of important segments of opinion in party caucuses and the Cabinet, as well as to avoid the sense of regional–ethnic alienation that stems from this situation.[15] On the other hand, his system would rarely produce a majority of seats for any party as long as at least three serious contenders existed, let alone five!

That is why several authorities have suggested a smaller number of provincial MPs, say 50 or 60, who would overcome the worst problems of the existing system but still make majority government possible.[16] This system would start with the regularly elected constituency MPs who are necessary to ensure the representation of all parts of Canada. But some 50 supplementary MPs would be added, to be distributed on the basis of popular vote by party by province. They would correct the greatest discrepancies between the proportion of seats and votes, which in the pre-1984 period would mean rewarding the Liberals for their 20+ percent of the vote in the Western provinces and the Conservatives for their 13+ percent of the popular vote in Quebec. For the party in power, such supplementary MPs could provide provincial representation in the Cabinet; for opposition parties, they would speak up for their provinces in the caucus and in Parliament, improving the party's image and policies. Representing an entire province, it is not likely that such provincial MPs would be underemployed, and they would probably soon shed the status of "second-class" representatives. They could be drawn from the party's candidates in each province that were most narrowly defeated in the general election, and would seek re-election in a specific constituency the next time around.

Reform along these lines was first officially endorsed by the Pépin–Roberts Task Force on Canadian Unity in 1979, and the idea appealed to both Pierre Trudeau and Ed Broadbent as party leaders at the time. But while it would benefit all four federalist parties in some ways, and perhaps the unity of the nation as a whole, its implementation appears unlikely. Some parties and politicians are concerned that it would benefit others more than themselves, while many are worried about the prevalence of minority or coalition governments. Some feel it would give party organizers too much power in choosing and ranking candidates, and others argue that parties should have to fight for victory solely in individual constituencies.

This idea was given added legitimacy when a similar scheme was proposed in 1998 by the Jenkins Commission on Voting Systems in Great Britain. The Jenkins report recommended that Britain retain the single-member constituency system (with the modification of a preferential ballot) but "top up" the constituency MPs with additional members (15 to 20 percent) who would render a closer relationship between a party's vote and seats.

FINANCING ELECTIONS[17]
Pre-1974

Before 1974, Canada had no effective laws with respect to party and election finance, and numerous irregularities and outright scandals occurred. The Liberal and Conservative parties relied almost completely on contributions from big business at the national level, which usually produced a surplus to be distributed to candidates' campaigns as well, and candidates were otherwise dependent on donations from local small firms. Both parties had fundraisers (sometimes called "bagmen")—often senators who could exploit their corporate connections and make use of their abundant spare time—assisted by corporate volunteers. Business also made contributions in kind, such as various skilled human resources. Corporate contributions were supplemented by fundraising dinners, but party leaders themselves occasionally had to come to the party's rescue. This was especially the case in the Depression elections of 1930 and 1935, when the Conservatives were led by a multimillionaire R.B. Bennett. The CCF/NDP depended primarily on individual membership fees supplemented by union contributions, but in this case the flow of funds was reversed, and the local candidates had to help finance the central campaign. Overall, the Liberals and Conservatives raised and spent far more than the CCF/NDP, at both the national and local levels.

The secrecy surrounding party and election finance before 1974 makes it difficult to know exactly how many irregularities and scandals actually took place. The first to come to light was the **Pacific scandal** of 1872, in which a group of businessmen eager to obtain the contract to build the CPR donated some $350 000 to John A. Macdonald's election campaign. When the scandal was revealed, Macdonald's government was defeated in the House of Commons, precipitating another election, which he lost. The second major scandal that came to public attention was the Beauharnois Scandal of 1930, in which a similar group gave $600 000 to the Liberal Party in hopes of obtaining the contract to build the Beauharnois Dam on the St. Lawrence River. By the time the deal was publicly exposed, the Liberal Party was in opposition, and its leader, Mackenzie King, rather incredulously denied any knowledge of such a large contribution.[18] In the 1960s, the Rivard scandal involved drug trafficker Lucien Rivard, who had been a regular contributor to the Liberal Party. He apparently felt that such donations, in addition to his attempted bribery of a government lawyer in a bail proceeding, should get him out of jail. These schemes did not work, but another, throwing a hose over the prison wall and escaping, turned out quite well!

This and other small-scale scandals in the 1960s, together with increasing public expectations of political morality, caused the Pearson government to appoint a commission on the subject of party and election finance in 1964. But when its recommendations were published two years later, no action was taken. It required the heightened sense of public outrage at political immorality in the United States (the Watergate scandal), along with opposition pressure in the minority government period of 1972–74, to produce legislation more or less as recommended in 1966. Amendments to the Canada Elections Act were passed in 1974 but did not take effect until the election of 1979.

The Legislation of 1974

The legislation had five basic provisions. First, while no limit was placed on the size of contributions, a ceiling was imposed on both national party spending and on candidate expenditures.[19] Next, the disclosure provision required that the names of those contributing over $100 be filed with the chief electoral officer and such records be open to public inspection. A tax credit provision was added so that contributors with taxable incomes would receive a 75 percent income tax credit for contributions up to $100, a 50 percent tax credit for contributions between $100 and $550, and a 33 percent credit for contributions over $550, to a maximum tax credit of $500. Finally, candidates who received at least 15 percent of the vote would have a portion of their expenses subsidized by the public purse, the original formula being replaced by a flat 50 percent rate in amendments made in 1983. The same amendments altered the broadcasting provisions of the act, and instead of subsidizing parties for 50 percent of their broadcasting costs, parties would henceforth pay full price for such commercials and be subsidized for 22.5 percent of their total national expenditures if they spent at least 10 percent of their maximum. This threshold was reduced from 10 to 2 percent in 1997 (or 5 percent of the votes cast in constituencies in which it ran candidates), but even so, only the five largest parties qualified.

The objectives of the legislation were thus to increase the equity, openness, and participatory nature of the electoral system. Equity would be enhanced in limiting candidate and national party spending, as well as by the public subsidy provision; the disclosure clause would make it difficult in the future for large, secret contributions to be made in return for some favourable government decision; and the tax credit would encourage individual contributions and reduce Liberal and Conservative dependence on corporations.

The Results of the 1974 Legislation

The figures in Tables 12.4 to 12.9 from the 1997 election reveal a great deal of change in Canadian election finance since 1974. For all the difficulties and loopholes remaining in the act, it has produced a more honest and somewhat more equitable system.[20] At the same time, the need of political parties for more money to use mass marketing techniques in their electoral campaigns has driven them to become more reliant on subsidization by the state.

Tables 12.4 and 12.5 present the picture of a typical constituency contested by the four main federalist parties. The ceiling on candidate spending was about $63 500, and the Liberal and Reform candidates spent about 75 percent of this maximum. Since they both received over 15 percent of the vote, they also benefited from the public reimbursement of about 50 percent of their expenditures. All four parties relied heavily on individual contributions, while the Liberal candidate in particular was inundated with corporate contributions, and the NDP candidate received some financial support from trade unions. The Liberal and Reform candidates also received major sums from their party organization, such that the Liberals racked up an apparent surplus of almost $40 000.

TABLE 12.4 Financial Statistics, Main Candidates in a Typical Constituency (Brant, Ontario), 1997 Election (Dollars)

	Ceiling	Expenditures	Contributions	Reimbursement	Apparent Surplus (Debt)
Liberal	63 488	48 429	62 557	25 525	39 653
Reform	63 488	43 602	28 090	23 838	8 326
PC	63 488	16 505	20 568	0	4 063
NDP	63 488	22 749	17 833	0	(4 916)

Sources (Tables 12.4–12.9): Chief Electoral Officer, Contributions and Expenses of Registered Political Parties and Candidates, 1997 (website: http://www.elections.ca), and Registered Political Parties' Fiscal Period Returns for 1997, adapted by author. Reproduced with the permission of the Minister of Public Works and Government Services Canada, 2000. Full responsibility for calculations and for conclusions drawn rests with the author.

Tables 12.6 and 12.7 combine contributions to candidates within the campaign period with contributions to parties throughout the whole 1997 election year. These tables do not include all contributions, only those from the three sources listed—individuals, corporations, and unions. They show that while Reform, PC, NDP, and Bloc candidates relied on individual contributions more than corporate ones, Liberal candidates received more in corporate than individual donations, and NDP candidates received almost as much in union as individual contributions. At the national party level, the Liberals and PCs both received more from corporations than from individuals; Reform continued to rely mainly on individuals, and the NDP received twice as much in individual contributions as from unions. In the combination of candidate and party contributions, corporate contributions greatly exceeded individual contributions in the Liberal case; the two were almost equal in the PC case; in Reform, individual contributions exceeded corporate; and in the NDP, individual donations exceeded those of

TABLE 12.5 Individual, Corporate, Union, and Other Contributions to Main Candidates in a Typical Constituency, 1997 Election (Brant, Ontario) (Dollars)

	Individual	Corporate	Union	Party/Political Organization	Total
Liberal	117 (20 693)	38 (26 674)	0 (0)	15 216	62 557
Reform	88 (10 323)	5 (1 375)	0 (0)	16 392	28 090
PC	72 (13 518)	20 (7 050)	0 (0)	0	20 568
NDP	71 (9 756)	0 (0)	5 (5 897)	2 180	17 833

TABLE 12.6 Number of Individual, Corporate, and Union Contributions to Candidates and Parties, 1997 Election

	Liberal	Reform	PC	NDP	Bloc
Candidates					
Individual	21 906	20 624	20 353	15 119	13 215
Corporate	10 315	3 225	7 157	520	85
Union	51	1	4	1 483	1
Parties					
Individual	34 429	75 587	23 352	50 434	18 885
Corporate	7 527	1 259	3 235	597	0
Union	16	0	0	273	0
Total					
Individual	56 335	96 211	43 705	65 553	32 100
Corporate	17 842	4 484	10 392	1 117	85
Union	67	1	4	1 756	1

TABLE 12.7 Value of Individual, Corporate, and Union Contributions to Candidates and Parties, 1997 Election (Dollars)

	Liberal	Reform	PC	NDP	Bloc
Candidates					
Individual	3 998 645	3 052 119	3 291 423	1 660 536	1 854 835
Corporate	4 782 303	1 184 903	2 529 675	154 213	30 553
Union	48 708	1 000	6 116	1 558 728	450
Parties					
Individual	5 701 064	5 538 165	4 545 316	5 125 038	1 960 630
Corporate	11 229 938	1 910 961	6 435 732	269 847	0
Union	15 704	0	0	2 749 574	0
Total					
Individual	9 699 709	8 590 284	7 836 739	6 785 574	3 815 465
Corporate	16 012 241	3 095 864	8 965 407	424 060	30 553
Union	64 412	1 000	6 116	4 308 302	450

unions. The Bloc relied almost exclusively on individual contributions, reflecting its connections in Quebec, where at the provincial level, only individual contributions are allowed.

The national spending ceiling for parties running 301 candidates was $11 358 749. Table 12.8 shows that the Liberals and PCs came close to this ceiling, while the NDP spent about half as much as allowed. Reform and Bloc had lower ceilings because they ran fewer candidates, but both were considerably below them. If the expenditures of all candidates of each party are combined, the approximate averages are as follows: Bloc, $50 000; Liberal, $46 000; PC and Reform, $29 000; and NDP, $17 000. Adding national and candidate spending, the Liberals stood at $25 million, the PCs at $19 million, Reform and the NDP at about $11 million each, and the Bloc at $5 million. These figures indicate larger residual disparities than most observers expected.

Table 12.9 indicates that the five main parties each received a public reimbursement of approximately 22.5 percent of its national expenditures. It also shows that 292 of 301 Liberal candidates and 70 out of 75 Bloc candidates gained at least 15 percent of the vote in their constituencies and therefore a public reimbursement of about 50 percent of their expenses. About two-thirds of PC and Reform candidates similarly qualified, but only 87 out of 301 New Democrats did so. In total, parties and candidates received some $24 million from the public purse.

TABLE 12.8 **Total Election Expenses of Five Main Parties, 1997 Election (Dollars)**

	Candidates	*National*	*Total*
Liberal	13 863 889	11 247 141	25 111 030
PC	8 801 230	10 288 333	19 089 563
Reform	6 724 593	4 921 733	11 646 326
NDP	5 278 489	5 976 724	11 255 213
BQ	3 751 205	1 629 497	5 380 702

TABLE 12.9 **Public Subsidies to Parties and Candidates, 1997 Election**

	National Party	*Candidates*	*No. of Subsidized Candidates*	*Total*
Liberal	$2 520 844	$6 638 324	292	$9 159 168
PC	$2 179 906	$ 3 584 504	189	$5 764 410
Reform	$1 107 390	$2 926 913	161	$4 034 303
NDP	$1 344 763	$1 500 639	87	$2 845 402
BQ	$366 637	$1 838 451	70	$2 205 088

How do political parties obtain such funds? Liberal, PC, and Reform parties tend to use well-connected supporters within the corporate elite to volunteer their time in soliciting funds from other members of the corporate elite. Senators are often useful in performing this function. All parties are now also adept at direct-mail techniques. After obtaining lists of people (from magazines, professional organizations, or any other likely source), they mail out hundreds or thousands of computer-generated letters soliciting contributions (highlighting the tax credit available).[21] Sometimes parties confer special benefits on those giving over a certain sum. The Liberals and Conservatives especially also raise huge amounts of money at dinners ($100/plate, $500/plate etc.) at which the party leader or other luminaries speak.

For a time, especially using direct-mail techniques, the Liberals and Conservatives both received about half their contributions from individuals, although the Liberals have since regressed. Table 12.10 shows that some of the largest corporations in the country gave the Liberal and Conservative parties contributions of $50 000 or more during 1997, but these figures are only slightly higher than their routine, annual contributions. By 1997, most large national corporations also included the Reform Party in their thoughts (somewhat contradicting its populist image), although usually at a lower rate.

In contrast, the NDP received only two corporate contributions and one individual contribution of over $10 000, but gained a small number of large union donations, as seen in Table 12.11. In total, these pale in comparison with the corporate contributions to the Liberal and Conservative parties, and a problem of inequity on both the contributions and expenditure sides of the equation remains. In order to render the contest more equitable, some provinces in their own elections have imposed a limit on the size of contributions instead of, or in addition to, a limit on candidate and party spending. On the other hand, the NDP erased its 1997 election debt by 1999, at which time the Liberals were still over $2 million in debt, the PCs had a $10 million debt, offset by a $4 million trust fund, and Reform had accumulated a bank balance of over $1 million.

Third-Party Advertising

Another major problem in the realm of election finance is **third-party advertising**, that is, spending by groups other than candidates and political parties. The 1974 act had prohibited advocacy group spending during an election campaign that favoured or opposed a party or candidate, but exempted such spending that was related to an issue. The 1983 amendment removed that exemption and prohibited any election expense that was not channelled through a party or candidate campaign. It was argued that the only way party and candidate spending ceilings could be effective was if any spending on their behalf was included in the parties' budgets, such as in the case of Canadian Labour Congress spending to promote the NDP. But in the 1980s more and more groups began to advertise for or against various parties or candidates without having these expenses included in the parties' budgets. While such advertising was clearly a violation of the spirit of the act as well as its specific terms, the **National Citizens' Coalition (NCC)** challenged sections 70 and 72 of the act in the Alberta Court of Queen's Bench in 1984. That decision ruled the clauses unconstitutional as a violation of the freedom-of-expression provisions of the Charter of Rights and Freedoms. Technically the ruling applied only to federal elections in Alberta, but when the government did not appeal the ruling, the chief electoral officer decided not to prosecute any violations of these sections anywhere in Canada.

TABLE 12.10 Largest Contributions to Liberal, Conservative, and Reform Parties, 1997 Election (Dollars)

	Liberal	*Conservative*	*Reform*
Bank of Montreal	100 575	96 679	51 520
ScotiaMcLeod Inc.	118 995	107 377	10 000
Nesbitt Burns	120 767	84 859	210
CIBC Wood Gundy	116 499	94 094	11 000
Bank of Nova Scotia	112 677	73 127	39 520
TD Bank	105 851	77 738	41 520
Rogers Communications etc.	91 692	155 227	10 000
CNR	99 568	87 860	70 000
Royal Bank	95 417	94 706	41 780
RBC Dominion Securities	99 453	90 318	13 200
Banque Nationale	82 103	50 000	25 000
CIBC	84 136	79 054	43 250
Northern Telecom	98 885	75 000	25 000
KPMG Peat Marwick Thorne	61 701	35 228	1 520
Bombardier	86 069	37 090	0
BCE	79 007	54 646	10 000
Midland Walwyn	78 606	88 477	21 520
TD Securities	80 356	81 026	41 520
Canadian Pacific	52 645	53 177	30 680
Southam Inc.	65 572	10 471	10 000
Anthony Fell	51 000	50 423	0
Power Corp.	31 000	67 090	0
Molson	62 682	36 254	21 520
SNC Lavalin Inc.	51 345	25 000	0
Brazeau River Investments	50 000	50 000	0

Source: Elections Canada, Registered Political Parties' Fiscal Period Returns for 1997. Reproduced with the permission of the Minister of Public Works and Government Services Canada, 2000. Full responsibility for calculations and for conclusions drawn rests with the author. [22]

Third-party advertising increased enormously in the 1988 election campaign, especially in the case of the pro–free trade group, the Canadian Alliance for Trade and Job Opportunities. Receiving corporate contributions of as much as $250 000 from such companies as Canadian Pacific, Alcan Aluminum, and Shell; $200 000 from each of Noranda, Imperial Oil, and the Royal Bank; and at least $100 000 from each of Sun Life, Manufacturers' Life, Northern

TABLE 12.11   **Largest NDP Contributions, 1997 Election (Dollars)**

CLC	600 914
Canadian Auto Workers	252 056
USWA National Headquarters	173 850
CEP National Headquarters	136 445
CUPE	87 260
UFCW National Headquarters	69 999
USWA District #6	58 893
Canadian Machinists	50 500
SEIU	50 000
Ontario Federation of Labour	49 559
UFCW Canadian Council	48 815

Source: Elections Canada, Registered Political Parties' Fiscal Period Returns for 1997. *Reproduced with the permission of the Minister of Public Works and Government Services Canada, 2000. Full responsibility for calculations and for conclusions drawn rests with the author.*

Telecom, IBM, INCO, Olympia & York, and Texaco, the group collected and spent over $5 million.[23] With only one political party in favour of free trade, namely the Conservatives, any advertising that promoted the Free Trade Agreement also promoted the Conservative Party. Thus the Conservatives benefited from some $5 million in advertising by advocacy groups on top of its own national budget of nearly $8 million, with the same large corporations contributing to both causes. Such third-party advertising made a mockery of party spending ceilings and is widely thought to have helped the Conservatives achieve re-election by turning the momentum of the campaign back in their favour during the last two weeks, especially in Ontario.

The Royal Commission on Electoral Reform and Party Financing

In response to widespread public criticism of this problem and the retiring chief electoral officer's repeated recommendations for change in this and other aspects of the Canada Elections Act, the Mulroney government appointed a **Royal Commission on Electoral Reform and Party Financing** shortly after the 1988 election. It was headed by the former president of Provigo Inc., Pierre Lortie. That commission identified several other concerns, held public hearings across the country, and commissioned extensive academic research. The Royal Commission recommended that spending during the election period by individuals or organizations other than candidates and political parties be restricted to $1000. The commission argued that to limit paid advertising of such advocacy groups during the 30- to 40-day period every four years was a "reasonable limit" on freedom of expression and would stand up to judicial scrutiny.

This limit was legislated prior to the 1997 election, in a diluted form (only applying to advertising expenses of advocacy that promoted a candidate or party, and excluding that which promoted an issue). But it was immediately challenged by the NCC, and Alberta courts once again found that it violated the Charter. In a later decision regarding the Quebec referendum law, however, the Supreme Court of Canada indicated that it would probably uphold the federal limit, if the case were ever appealed.[24]

Among other issues that the commission considered were whether a ceiling should be put on political contributions and whether such contributions should be limited to individuals, using the Quebec model of "financement populaire," rather than being made by corporations, unions, or other groups. It rejected such changes, but it did recommend extending the spending limit and tax credit provisions of the law to nomination meetings and leadership conventions. To restrict the expenditures of those seeking a party nomination was considered advantageous to potential women candidates in particular. The issue of regulating the financing of leadership campaigns arose when Jean Chrétien and Paul Martin each spent over $2 million in seeking the Liberal Party leadership in 1990, while Sheila Copps could not raise $1 million and Lloyd Axworthy declined to run for financial reasons. The Royal Commission also recommended the creation of a number of Aboriginal constituencies and rewards for parties that elected a significant proportion of women MPs. As mentioned, a number of relatively minor amendments were enacted just before the 1993 election, but nothing has come of the commission's wider recommendations.

A New Canada Elections Act

In June 1999, a new Canada Elections Act (Bill C-83) was introduced. If passed, this massive document would replace the old act and address many of the issues and problems that have been identified above. If passed unamended, some of the highlights of the new act would be as follows:

- Third-party spending would be limited to $150 000, of which no more than $3000 could be spent in each electoral district on advertising for or against candidates.
- A candidate's nomination deposit would be refunded in full if reporting requirements were met, rather than being partially based on the number of votes received.
- The threshold for disclosure of donor names would be increased to $200 from $100, but disclosure of addresses as well as names would be required.
- Donors would be eligible for a tax credit of 75 percent for the first $200 contribution rather than the first $100
- Election advertising and publication or broadcast of new survey results would be prohibited on election day.
- Media outlets would have to reveal the methodology of survey results broadcast or published.
- Returning officers would receive the right to vote, and in case of a tie, a by-election would be held in the constituency.

The proposals took into account a 1999 Ontario court decision in response to the Communist Party of Canada challenge to certain provisions of the existing act. While the new bill was consistent with that and various other recent court decisions, traditional opponents like the National Citizens' Coalition and the Canadian Newspapers Association immediately threatened to fight it.

....

CONCLUSION

If elections are crucial to the operation of Canadian democracy, it is unfortunate that the electoral system is so flawed. The principle of representation by population is widely breached, and while the actual operation of the system on election day is now basically satisfactory, parties are not awarded seats in proportion to their popular support, and the financing of elections is defective in many ways. The Royal Commission on Electoral Reform and Party Financing made many worthy recommendations for improvement, but only technical, administrative changes have been made.

Ⓒ Of the approaches outlined in Chapter 1, class analysts make many points, especially with respect to party and electoral finance. They emphasize that corporate contributions are made for a reason, and they have little difficulty in finding the quid pro quo: governments give corporations tax concessions of all kinds, loans, grants, and contracts; preferential legislation and regulations; government deficit reduction; and free trade. While in office, the Conservatives in particular extracted donations from individuals within corporate management, the small-business community, and the self-employed upper middle class, and then adopted policies of interest to these groups.

PC The public choice model is interested in the mechanics of the electoral system insofar as they determine which groups within the electorate must be accommodated by political parties in order to achieve victory. An electoral system that overrepresents some interests and underrepresents others will affect the promises political parties make. Moreover, if the relationship between seats and votes is skewed, public choice theorists note that certain interests can be ignored. The way in which the mechanics of the electoral system traditionally gave the Liberals more seats than they deserved in Quebec and fewer in Western Canada (with the reverse for the Conservatives) meant that both parties put greatest effort into Ontario, which is where such effort would pay them dividends. In any case, no party that wants to form the government can ignore the fact that Ontario contains over one-third of the constituencies. Public choice also has things to say about how parties, once in office, can get around those planks of their election platforms that they never intended to implement.

P Pluralists note that in the redistribution process it is often more important for a constituency to reflect a distinct "community of interest" than to have a number of voters exactly equal to that in other ridings. The elimination of restrictions to the franchise and the judicial elimination of restrictions on third-party advertising are also likely to increase the diversity of viewpoints expressed and members elected.

(SC) State-centred theorists and neo-institutionalists emphasize how the mechanics of the electoral system can affect the results and how most of these mechanics are beyond the interest or comprehension of the general electorate. Such concerns include the way in which the redistribution process is handled, the discrepancies between votes and seats, and the rules with respect to party and election finance. One of the most blatant is how established parties have rigged the rules to favour themselves in the distribution of broadcast time and in the subsidies for party advertising, as mentioned in Chapter 14.

DISCUSSION QUESTIONS

1. Given the peculiar distribution of the Canadian population, to what extent should we adhere to the principle of "representation by population"?

2. Should the party leader have a veto on local nominations? Why or why not?

3. Should the electoral system be reformed to bring about a closer relationship between percentage of votes and percentage of seats for each party? If so, how?

4. What changes should be made to the law governing party and election finance?

5. What are the arguments on each side of the debate over third-party advertising?

6. How do each of the critical approaches outlined in Chapter 1 enhance our understanding of the Canadian electoral system?

NOTES

1. From 1867 to 1915, the basic procedure was to obtain a quota by giving Quebec 65 seats and dividing Quebec's population by 65. This quota would then be divided into each other province's population to determine its number of seats. The only exception was the "one-twentieth rule," under which no province could lose seats unless its share of the national population had decreased by at least one-twentieth between the last two censuses. In 1915 a second exception was added, the "senatorial clause," under which no province could have fewer seats in the House of Commons than it had in the Senate. The second formula was adopted in 1946. It provided for 255 (later 263) seats divided among the provinces in proportion to their share of the total population of the country. But after 1951 a "15 percent clause" was added, providing that no province could lose more than 15 percent of the number of seats to which it had been entitled at the last readjustment. The third formula, called the "amalgam" formula, was adopted in 1974 and guaranteed that no province could lose seats at all. Quebec was again used as the basic yardstick, and the other provinces were divided into large, intermediate, or small categories, with different calculations for each.

2. For Sir John A. Macdonald's efforts, see R.M. Dawson, "The Gerrymander of 1881," *Canadian Journal of Economics and Political Science* (May 1935), pp. 197–221.

3. Louis Massicotte, "Electoral Reform in the Charter Era," in Alan Frizzell and Jon H. Pammett, eds., *The Canadian General Election of 1997* (Toronto: Dundurn Press, 1997), p. 178.

4. Jean-Marc Hamel argued that politicians should have only one chance to influence the commissions—at the stage of public hearings—not a second chance in parliamentary committees. *Report of the Chief Electoral Officer of Canada* (Ottawa: Supply and Services, 1989), p. 15. For revelations of other partisan influence, see *Maclean's* (January 25, 1988), p. 14.

5. John C. Courtney, "Parliament and Representation: The Unfinished Agenda of Electoral Redistributions," *Canadian Journal of Political Science* (December 1988), pp. 675–90; and Andrew

Sancton, "Eroding Representation-by-Population in the Canadian House of Commons: The Representation Act, 1985," *Canadian Journal of Political Science* (September 1990), pp. 441–57.

6. See Chapter 18; John C. Courtney et al., eds., *Drawing Boundaries: Legislatures, Courts and Electoral Values* (Saskatoon: Fifth House Publishers, 1992).

7. Massicotte, "Electoral Reform in the Charter Era."

8. *Report of the Chief Electoral Officer of Canada*, p. 46.

9. Advance polls are held on the tenth, ninth, and seventh days before election day. Proxy voting is permitted in the case of illness and physical incapacity, and for students and people in various mobile occupations; after completing the proper forms, they can appoint another qualified elector to vote in their place. Members of the Canadian public service and armed forces stationed overseas, along with their qualified spouses and dependents, can also vote by mail, as can anyone who will be unable to vote at an advance poll or on polling day.

10. Progressive Conservative, Liberal, NDP, Reform, Bloc Québécois, Canadian Action, Green, Christian Heritage, Marxist-Leninist, and Natural Law parties.

11. Elections Canada, *A History of the Vote in Canada* (Ottawa: Public Works and Government Services, 1997); T.H. Qualter, *The Election Process in Canada* (Toronto: McGraw-Hill Ryerson, 1970).

12. Chief Electoral Officer, *Towards the 35th General Election* (Ottawa: 1994), cat. no. SE 1-5/1993; Massicotte, "Electoral Reform in the Charter Era"; *Sauvé v. Canada (A.G.)*, [1993] 2 S.C.R. 438; *Sauvé v. Canada (Chief Electoral Officer)*, [1996] 1 F.C. 857.

13. Alan C. Cairns, "The Electoral System and the Party System in Canada," *Canadian Journal of Political Science* (March 1968), pp. 55–80.

14. John Meisel, *The Canadian General Election of 1957* (Toronto: University of Toronto Press, 1962).

15. William Irvine, *Does Canada Need a New Electoral System?* (Kingston: Institute of Intergovernmental Relations, Queen's University, 1979).

16. Ibid., ch. 5. The most comprehensive recent analysis is Henry Milner, ed., *Making Every Vote Count: Reassessing Canada's Electoral System* (Peterborough: Broadview Press, 1999).

17. K.Z. Paltiel, *Political Party Financing in Canada* (Toronto: McGraw-Hill Ryerson, 1970); Paltiel, "The 1984 Federal General Election and Developments in Canadian Party Finance," in Penniman, *Canada at the Polls, 1984* (Durham, NC: Duke University Press, 1988); Paltiel, "Political Marketing, Party Finance and the Decline of Canadian Parties," in Alain Gagnon and Brian Tanguay, eds., *Canadian Parties in Transition* (Scarborough: Nelson Canada, 1989); W.T. Stanbury, "Financing Federal Political Parties in Canada, 1974–1986," in Gagnon and Tanguay, eds., *Canadian Parties in Transition*; Stanbury, *Business–Government Relations in Canada* (Toronto: Methuen, 1986), ch. 10; Joseph and Peter Wearing, "Mother's Milk Revisited: The Effect of Foreign Ownership on Political Contributions," *Canadian Journal of Political Science* (March 1990), pp. 115–23; and Stephen Brooks and Andrew Stritch, *Business and Government in Canada* (Scarborough: Prentice-Hall Canada, 1991), ch. 9.

18. T.D. Regehr, *The Beauharnois Scandal* (Toronto: University of Toronto Press, 1990).

19. The national party ceiling was based on 30 cents per name on the national voters' list, while the candidate ceiling was based on one dollar per voter for the first 15 000 names on the local voters' list, 50 cents for each of the next 10 000 names on the list, and 25 cents for each of the names beyond the first 25 000. In subsequent elections an inflation factor was applied to these amounts. Paltiel, "The 1984 Federal General Election."

20. Stanbury, "Financing Federal Political Parties."

21. Paltiel, "The 1984 Federal General Election," pp. 139–40.

22. Other contributions over $50 000: Liberal: CND Management Corp, $75 000; Merrill Lynch, $54 814; PC: Virtual Pizza, $147 700; Michael Meighen, $101 568; Lawrence & Co., $100 000; 2866-5594 Quebec Inc., $99 054; Drake Goodwin Corp., $98 034; 611897 Alberta Ltd. $50 000; Grant Forest Products, $50 000; and Ronald V. Joyce, $50 000. The largest Reform contribution was from Ken Kalopsis, at $47 075, while the NDP's largest individual and corporate contributors were Mary Norris, $24 357; Osler Hoskin & Harcourt, $17 500; and Canada Trustco Mortgage Co., $11 500.

23. *The Toronto Star*, December 9, 1989, p. C1.

24. Massicotte, "Election Reform in the Charter Era"; *National Citizens' Coalition Inc. v. A.G. Canada*, [1984] 11 D.L.R. (4th) 481; *Somerville v. Canada (A.G.)*, [1996] 136 D.L.R. (4th) 205 (Alta C.A.); *Libman v. Quebec (Attorney General)*, [1997] 3 S.C.R. 569.

FURTHER READING

Cairns, Alan C. "The Electoral System and the Party System in Canada." *Canadian Journal of Political Science* (March 1968), pp. 55–80.

Courtney, John C. "Parliament and Representation: The Unfinished Agenda of Electoral Redistributions." *Canadian Journal of Political Science* (December 1988), pp. 675–90.

Courtney, John C., et al., eds. *Drawing Boundaries: Legislatures, Courts and Electoral Values*. Saskatoon: Fifth House Publishers, 1992.

Elections Canada. *Canada's Electoral System*.

———. *A History of the Vote in Canada*. Cat. no. SE3-36-1997E. Ottawa: Public Works and Government Services Canada, 1997.

———. *Reports of the Chief Electoral Officer of Canada* (for each federal election).

———. *Representation in the Federal Parliament*.

———. *Report of the Chief Electoral Officer Respecting Election Expenses*.

———. *Annual Reports of the Chief Electoral Officer*.

Irvine, William. *Does Canada Need a New Electoral System?* Kingston: Institute of Intergovernmental Relations, Queen's University, 1979.

Johnston, J. Paul, and Harvey Pasis. *Representation and Electoral Systems*. Scarborough: Prentice-Hall Canada, 1990.

Milner, Henry, ed. *Making Every Vote Count: Reassessing Canada's Electoral System*. Peterborough: Broadview Press, 1999.

Paltiel, K.Z. *Political Party Financing in Canada*. Toronto: McGraw-Hill Ryerson, 1970.

Qualter, T.H. *The Election Process in Canada*. Toronto: McGraw-Hill Ryerson, 1970.

Royal Commission on Electoral Reform and Party Financing. *Reforming Electoral Democracy*. 4 vols. Ottawa: Supply and Services, 1992.

Sancton, Andrew. "Eroding 'Rep-by-Pop' in the Canadian House of Commons: The Representation Act, 1985." *Canadian Political Science Association* (June 1989), pp. 441–51.

Stanbury, W.T. *Business–Government Relations in Canada*. Toronto: Methuen, 1986.

Chapter 13

Political Parties AND THE Party System

Political parties are integral to the operation of almost every aspect of a modern political system, but Canadians are generally more attuned to their faults than to their virtues. For most of the post-1867 period, the Liberal and (Progressive) Conservative parties dominated the Canadian political scene, although the latter was reduced to minor party status in the 1990s. The New Democratic Party has been a stable contender since 1961, while various smaller parties—the Progressives, CCF, Social Credit, Créditistes, and Union Nationale—have come and gone, some of them forming governments at the provincial level. In the 1990s, the Bloc Québécois (BQ) and the Reform Party joined the fray, and after the Liberal resurgence in the 1993 and 1997 elections, the NDP, PCs, and Reform all sought to become the alternative government.

A **political party** can be defined as an organized group that nominates candidates and contests elections in order to influence the personnel and policy of government. While some parties operate for long periods of time in the political wilderness and may be able to exert a certain amount of influence without being in power, every party ultimately hopes to form the government and make policy and personnel decisions on its own. More subtle differences between parties and other groups in society can also be noted. Whereas most other groups possess a fairly narrow focus and articulate a single interest, political parties are usually broader in scope and seek to aggregate, combine, consolidate, or appeal to many different interests or demands. In the process, parties reduce these interests and demands to a manageable quantity called "issues." In addition, while other groups provide "functional" representation—economic, occupational, cultural, religious—political parties are closely tied to the formal institutions of government, including the electoral system and Parliament, all of which are based on territorial representation.

Another function of political parties is to recruit decision makers, primarily by means of the electoral system. They usually choose as candidates people who have been party members for some time and who have been "groomed" or trained. The government party also appoints certain political officeholders, often from the ranks of its own supporters, a practice referred to as **political patronage**. In addition to recruitment, parties engage in political socialization and citizen education as they point out their own strengths and their opponents' weaknesses in the daily partisan battle in Parliament as well as on the election trail.

Parties are also integrally involved in the rule-making function, as they organize the legislative and executive operations of government. The formal and informal procedures of the House of Commons and Senate are completely imbued with partisan considerations, especially in the party discipline they display, while the Canadian Cabinet tradition is that all ministers are drawn from a single party so that they will be able to come to agreement more easily on government policy.

Beyond the list of functions mentioned in Chapter 1, parties may be engaged in formulating public policy. In theory, at least, each party develops a distinctive election platform; the successful party then proceeds to implement it, while the opposition parties continue to provide clear-cut policy alternatives. In reality, the policymaking role of political parties is often minimal, parties do not always provide policy alternatives to the electorate, and governments frequently ignore their election platforms in office, while obtaining their policy ideas from other sources.

This chapter is divided into four main sections: the historical evolution of Canadian political parties; interpretations of the Canadian party system; party organization; and party ideology. Party and electoral finance were examined in Chapter 12, and the role of parties in the electoral campaign, including electoral behaviour and party support, is discussed in Chapter 14.

HISTORICAL EVOLUTION OF CANADIAN PARTIES

At this point, a brief discussion of the historical evolution of the Canadian political party system may be useful. Ken Carty suggests dividing this evolution into four parts, or four party systems; these can be distinguished by the number of parties in contention and their different approaches to seeking election, and can be structured around lists of prime ministers, their parties, and their dates of office.[1]

John A. Macdonald, the founder of the Conservative Party, served as prime minister for 19 years. (William Topley/National Archives of Canada/PA-027013)

The First Party System, 1867–1921

Until 1921, the Conservative and Liberal parties monopolized Canadian politics. David E. Smith points out that successful party leaders such as John A. Macdonald and Wilfrid Laurier sponsored great national projects on the one hand while being masters of detailed constituency and patronage politics on the other.[2]

The Conservative Party is usually said to have had its beginnings in 1854 when John A. Macdonald formed a coalition of four pre-Confederation groupings: Tories and Moderates from Upper Canada (Ontario), along with English businessmen and French Conservatives from Lower Canada (Quebec). Party lines for individual politicians were quite flexible in those days, and many MPs were called "ministerialists" because of their promise to support the ministry of the day in return for

Sir Wilfrid Laurier, Canada's first French-Canadian prime minister, pronounced some 93 years ago that the 20th century would belong to Canada. (Photographer unknown/Canapress)

government favours. Alliances among groups were also unstable, but Macdonald's coalition gradually melded into an organized political party. The two main groups left out of this coalition—the French radicals in Quebec and the Clear Grits from Upper Canada—periodically joined forces in the pre-Confederation era, but it was not until much later that they became the nucleus around which an organized Liberal party took form. After Macdonald was disgraced by the Pacific scandal, the Liberals took office between 1873 and 1878 under Alexander Mackenzie, but his government reflected this early lack of cohesion. Macdonald returned to power in 1878 and the Conservatives demonstrated increasing party unity as time went on. After the execution of Louis Riel, however, French-Canadian support started to fall away from the Conservative Party, helped by the fact that an attractive French Canadian, Wilfrid Laurier, became leader of the Liberal Party shortly afterwards. Macdonald died in 1891, and his party experienced a period of great instability as it went through four leaders in the subsequent five years. Thus, with the government party in decline and the Liberals finally showing the marks of a well-organized national party, it is not surprising that Laurier won the watershed election of 1896.[3] At that time Canada moved from a situation of Conservative **one-party dominance** to a classic **two-party system** in which Liberals and Conservatives competed on equal terms.

TABLE 13.1   Prime Ministers, 1867–1921

John A. Macdonald	Conservative	1867–1873
Alexander Mackenzie	Liberal	1873–1878
John A. Macdonald	Conservative	1878–1891
John Abbott	Conservative	1891–1892
John Thompson	Conservative	1892–1894
Mackenzie Bowell	Conservative	1894–1896
Charles Tupper	Conservative	1896
Wilfrid Laurier	Liberal	1896–1911
Robert Borden	Conservative	1911–1920
Arthur Meighen	Conservative	1920–1921

Laurier governed quite successfully until he was beaten in 1911, when the two main issues were reciprocity (free trade with the United States) and the naval question (whether Canada should establish its own navy or contribute to that of Britain). Robert Borden's Conservatives took over and were soon confronted with the monumental task of managing Canada's war effort. In 1917, after three years of war, Borden concluded that conscription would have to be adopted, but conscious of French-Canadian opposition, he proposed a coalition government with Laurier, who still led the Liberals in opposition. Most English-speaking MPs agreed to join the Conservatives in a **Union Government** in 1917, but Laurier and the French-Canadian Liberals remained in opposition, leaving that party badly split. With conscription, the Conservatives almost totally alienated French Canada, at the same time as the policies of both Conservative and Liberal parties upset the farming community in English Canada, notably the West. Thus, while Mackenzie King succeeded Laurier as Liberal leader in 1919 and skilfully pursued party reconciliation, Arthur Meighen inherited an unpopular Conservative Party in 1920 when he took over from Borden.

The Second Party System, 1921–1957

The 1921 election marked the end of the two-party system in Canada; from that point onward, there were always other parties in contention, leading to the label **two-plus** or **two-and-a-half party system**. Moreover, in this period dominated by Mackenzie King and Louis St. Laurent, the Liberal government was characterized by decentralized ministerial accommodation in which strong regional–ethnic Cabinet ministers exercised a great deal of individual power and then spoke for their regions in the development of a national consensus.

In 1921, farmers entered the contest with their own Progressive candidates and elected more members than the Conservatives,[4] while two Labour members were also successful. Farmers were particularly unhappy with conscription, tariff, and agricultural and transportation policies, as well as prevailing political practices such as party patronage and rigid party discipline in the House of Commons. Nevertheless, Mackenzie King led his Liberals to victory in 1921, in 1925, and again in 1926 (after a brief Conservative interruption caused by the King–Byng dispute discussed in Chapter 20), and by the late 1920s most of the Progressive MPs either had become Liberals or had been defeated. A few of the more radical farmers joined with the Labour members to form the Ginger Group in Parliament, while the Liberals were defeated in 1930, primarily because of the onset of the Depression.

TABLE 13.2   Prime Ministers, 1921–1957

Mackenzie King	Liberal	1921–1926
Arthur Meighen	Conservative	1926
Mackenzie King	Liberal	1926–1930
R.B. Bennett	Conservative	1930–1935
Mackenzie King	Liberal	1935–1948
Louis St. Laurent	Liberal	1948–1957

By this time the Conservatives were led by R.B. Bennett. Although he exercised vigorous leadership and even departed from orthodox Conservative policy to some extent, Bennett did not know how to cope with the unemployment, poverty, and general devastation the Depression wrought. Along with almost every other government in office during this period, Bennett's Conservatives were defeated in 1935, and Mackenzie King's Liberals returned to power.

Besides contributing to this change of government, the Depression was the catalyst for the creation of several new political parties. The Cooperative Commonwealth Federation (CCF) was formed in Calgary in 1932, an amalgam of the parliamentary Ginger Group, the intellectual League for Social Reconstruction, largely centred in Toronto and Montreal, and various farmer and labour groups and scattered socialist and farmer–labour parties, primarily from the West. In 1933 the party adopted its radical platform, the Regina Manifesto, at its meeting in that city, and chose Labour member of Parliament J.S. Woodsworth as its leader. The party elected several MPs in 1935 and took office in Saskatchewan in 1944 under T.C. (Tommy) Douglas.[5]

The Social Credit Party was born in Alberta in 1935 around the charismatic evangelist William Aberhart. The party was originally concerned with the reform of the banking system as a means of dealing with the Depression, but abandoned this platform when it proved to be both unworkable and unconstitutional. After Alberta became prosperous with the discovery of oil in the 1940s, Social Credit transformed itself into an orthodox conservative party under E.C. Manning. The party remained in power in Alberta for 36 years, came to power in British Columbia in 1952, and also elected several Western MPs.[6]

In Quebec, a group of disgruntled progressive Liberals defected from their provincial party in 1935 to join forces with the chronically unsuccessful provincial Conservative Party in the new Union Nationale. The leader, Maurice Duplessis, quickly discarded the comprehensive reform program on which the party was elected a year later and became ultra-conservative. Despite this shift in emphasis, the Union Nationale remained in power in Quebec until 1960 with only a four-year interruption between 1940 and 1944.[7]

None of these developments impeded the Liberal Party at the federal level; it continued to elect majority governments from 1935 to 1948 under Mackenzie King and then, until 1957, under his successor, Louis St. Laurent. King's conciliatory skills were severely tested during the Second World War (1939–45), but his government avoided a serious second conscription crisis. He also presided over the initiation of the Canadian welfare state. The St. Laurent period was one of great prosperity, largely financed by a tremendous inflow of American investment.[8]

The Conservative Party floundered for 20 years after 1935, having previously alienated French Canada, and having been blamed, however unfairly, for the Depression. It changed leaders repeatedly, changed party policy to some extent, and changed the party name to Progressive Conservative in 1942, all to no avail.

The Third Party System, 1957–1993

The Liberal dominance was at least temporarily halted in the 1957 election. The next 35 years was a period of alternating minority and majority governments, Progressive Conservative and Liberal, and David Smith contends that at least the Diefenbaker and Trudeau eras were marked by a more pan-Canadian approach, as each leader had a vision of the national interest that he sought to impose. In this period as well, television linked individual voters to these leaders without the need for regional or ethnic intermediaries. Some of these characteristics might also be applied to the Mulroney era.

The political climate was suddenly transformed with the choice of John Diefenbaker as Conservative party leader in 1956, partly due to the public's increasing resentment of Liberal complacency and arrogance, as demonstrated in the infamous **pipeline debate**. Diefenbaker led the Conservatives to a surprising minority government victory in 1957 and then to a record majority in 1958. His decline was almost as rapid as his ascent, however, as his government fell apart over defence policy. The party was reduced to a minority government position again in 1962, and defeated a year later, after which it engaged in a long period of bitter in-fighting over the leadership question.[9]

During the Diefenbaker period, significant developments in two minor parties took place. The CCF, which had seen its federal fortunes decline throughout the 1950s, decided to combine its efforts with those of the new national labour organization, the Canadian Labour Congress. The result was the creation of the New Democratic Party (NDP) in 1961. T.C. Douglas was persuaded to leave the premiership of Saskatchewan to become the first national NDP leader.[10] Then, out of the blue, a group of Social Credit or Créditiste MPs was elected from Quebec in 1962, just when the Western wing of the party was starting to decline.[11]

Lester Pearson's Liberals were elected in 1963 and re-elected in 1965, but the success of the Créditiste group in Quebec, NDP support in other parts of the country, and the continuing appeal of John Diefenbaker, especially in the West, denied Pearson a majority government. Nonetheless, in spite of his minority government status, Pearson tackled many controversial issues, particularly the new nationalism in Quebec, the Canada Pension Plan, medicare, and a new flag. One opposition party or another supported each of Pearson's measures so that he was able to continue in office until he retired.[12]

In 1968, the Liberals gained a majority government under their new leader Pierre Elliott Trudeau, but just narrowly defeated Robert Stanfield's Conservatives in 1972. In the resulting minority government, the Liberals worked closely with the NDP under David Lewis, but this

TABLE 13.3	**Prime Ministers, 1957–1993**		
John Diefenbaker	Progressive Conservative	1957–1963
Lester B. Pearson	Liberal	1963–1968
Pierre Elliott Trudeau	Liberal	1968–1979
Joe Clark	Progressive Conservative	1979–1980
Pierre Elliott Trudeau	Liberal	1980–1984
John Turner	Liberal	1984
Brian Mulroney	Progressive Conservative	1984–1993
Kim Campbell	Progressive Conservative	1993

support was withdrawn two years later. With Trudeau ridiculing Stanfield's proposal for **wage and price controls**, the Liberals were returned with a majority in 1974, only to turn around and implement such a policy themselves. By 1979, the Liberals had apparently accumulated other faults as well, for they were defeated by the Conservatives, now led by Joe Clark. Nine months later, the Clark government fell with parliamentary rejection of its budget, and Trudeau hastily withdrew his resignation as Liberal leader to lead his party back to power in early 1980.[13]

The separatist Parti Québecois formed the government of Quebec between 1976 and 1984 under René Lévesque. After persuading Quebeckers to give Canada one last chance in their 1980 referendum, Trudeau patriated the Constitution, together with a Charter of Rights and Freedoms, and enacted the controversial National Energy Program.[14] He resigned in 1984, turning the reins over to John Turner, who was pitted against the new Conservative leader, Brian Mulroney. In the 1984 election, the Conservatives won a landslide victory, including a startling majority of the seats in Quebec.[15] After the negotiation of the Canada–U.S. Free Trade Agreement and the Meech Lake Accord, Mulroney led his party to a second successive majority government in 1988, only to see Meech Lake fail to acquire the unanimous approval of new provincial governments in 1990.[16] The 1980s might be termed the decade of the **three-party system**, for, between elections at least, the NDP became entrenched as a third national party.

The Fourth Party System, 1993–

The 1993 and 1997 elections saw two of the traditional Canadian political parties, the Progressive Conservatives and NDP, supplanted by two new parties, the Bloc Québecois and Reform. With five parties in the picture, Canada began to take on the appearance of a **multi-party system.**

The Liberal Party's obsession with Quebec was the main reason that the West preferred the Conservatives after 1957. When Westerners perceived that federal Conservatives were likewise concerned primarily with holding on to their unprecedented Quebec support after 1984, however, several new parties emerged in the West. The most enduring was the Reform Party headed by Preston Manning, son of the former Social Credit premier of Alberta. Then, with the collapse of the Meech Lake Accord, sovereigntist sentiment increased in Quebec, and several Conservative and Liberal MPs defected to form a new federal separatist party, the Bloc Québecois. Thus, five parties of considerable strength contested the 1993 federal election, and produced a highly unusual result: the Liberals did well across the country, the Bloc Québecois displaced the Conservatives in Quebec, and the Reform Party displaced the Conservatives in the West. The PCs held on to 16 percent of the popular vote but retained only two seats, and the NDP did badly everywhere. Given that a minimum of 12 seats is required for official party standing in the House of Commons, only three parties came back as recognized parties, two of them new, and it seemed that a real and regionalized multi-party system had developed.[17] The 1997 election returned five official but highly regionalized parties, at least in terms of seats won.

The whole evolution of the Canadian party system, together with sub-eras, can be summarized as in Table 13.4.

TABLE 13.4   **Evolution of Canadian Party System by Era**

Era	Major Parties	Minor Parties	Label
1867–1896	Conservative	Liberal	One-party dominance
1896–1921	Liberal, Conservative		Two-party system
1921–1935	Liberal, Conservative	Progressive	Two-plus party system
1935–1957	Liberal	Conservative, CCF, Social Credit	One-party dominance
1957–1980	Liberal, Conservative	CCF/NDP, Social Credit	Two-plus party system
1980–1993	Liberal, Conservative, NDP		Three-party system
1993–	Liberal	Reform, NDP Conservative, Bloc Québécois	Multi-party system

INTERPRETATIONS OF THE CANADIAN PARTY SYSTEM

Faced with the rather unusual party system—or succession of party systems—just outlined, several political scientists have proposed theories or interpretations in order to explain them.

The Broker System

The most traditional explanation is the **broker or brokerage** theory.[18] The essence of this interpretation is that, given the multiple cleavages in Canadian society and the function of parties to aggregate interests, political parties in Canada should be conciliators, mediators, or brokers among the cleavages already identified—that is, regions, ethnic and linguistic groups, genders, classes, religions, and ages. The theory suggests that maximizing their appeal to all such groups is not only the best way for parties to gain power, but, in the fragmented Canadian society, is also necessary in order to keep the country together. Thus, in their search for power, parties should act as agents of national integration and attempt to reconcile as many divergent interests as possible.

The interests to which parties give most attention are presumably those of greatest concern to the voters. In the past, religion was often prominent, while gender and age are emerging as increasingly important in the future. Throughout most of Canadian history, however, the two overriding cleavages that have concerned people as well as parties have been those of region and ethnicity. While the class cleavage is the central focus of politics in most countries, it has usually attracted little attention in Canada, and the broker theory emphasizes the middle-class–consciousness of most Canadians. The broker theory can thus be seen to argue that the Liberal and Conservative parties have no central ideological interests and merely promise to satisfy the most important interests felt by the voters at any point in time. Alternatively, they can be said to disguise their real ideological interests—protecting the capitalist system—by emphasizing ethnic and regional concerns instead of class interests.[19] In any case, ideological differences between these two parties are not profound. Defenders of the broker system argue that parties should not foment artificial class conflicts and ideological differences in a country that is already seriously divided; they should bring people together rather than drive them apart.

However appealing the broker system may be, its implications should not be overlooked. By concentrating on regional and ethnic cleavages, parties minimize the role of ideology in Canadian politics. Parties are opportunistic and pragmatic rather than offering the electorate a choice of principled, distinctive programs. Parties do not generate innovative policy approaches, but are content instead to respond to public opinion polls and interest group demands. What parties offer to the electorate in the place of alternative solutions to national problems are alternative slogans and leaders, the latter increasing in significance in a television age.

Class-Based Parties

A second perspective on the Canadian party system, and a reaction to the broker approach, is the concept of a **class-based party** system.[20] Like the broker model, the class-based theory is partly an explanation of the existing system, but when it comes to prescribing an ideal situation, it rejects the status quo. Class-based analysts expect that in the pre-democratic period in a country such as Canada two parties will develop, both of which defend the capitalist system.

When the vote is extended to the working class, however, a new working-class party will emerge that either joins the competition or displaces one of the existing parties, generally forcing politics to take on an ideological and class-based character. This evolution clearly occurred in Britain, for example, and can also be seen to some extent in the United States.

In late-19th-century Canada, when the Liberal Party began to challenge the Conservatives, they both defended capitalism and differentiated themselves on ethnic and religious grounds, as well as on minor policy differences such as the tariff. When the vote was extended to the working class at the turn of the century, some isolated labour, socialist, and communist political activity occurred, and by 1920 new class-based farmer and labour parties existed. But the newly enfranchised working class did not manage to create a successful class-based party, as the Liberals and Conservatives did everything in their power to discourage such a development, using both seductive and coercive techniques.

Mackenzie King introduced policy innovations to attract farmer and labour voters and co-opted leaders

Mackenzie King, the longest-serving prime minister, thwarted class politics with his successful pursuit of brokerage politics. (Photographer unknown/National Archives of Canada/C-027645)

of both farmer and labour movements into the Liberal Cabinet, while the Conservatives used force to quell the 1919 Winnipeg General Strike and the 1935 On-to-Ottawa Trek of the unemployed.[21] Eventually, the farmers' intense interest in politics declined, and the working class continued to support the two old-line parties on ethnic/religious and regional grounds, rendered content by the occasional piece of social legislation.

The Depression represented the collapse of the capitalist system and, as might have been expected, gave rise to new ideologically based parties. Of these, the CCF became the most sustained working-class party, but most members of that class continued to support the two traditional parties. Although unionization expanded significantly in the 1940s, the CCF's success was impeded by the Liberal Party's exploitation of divisions within the working class,[22] and by extremist anti-CCF propaganda sponsored by the business community. The CCF achieved its highest popular standing in the 1943–45 period, after which Liberal welfare initiatives helped to draw off working-class support. As mentioned, this decline led to the creation of the NDP in 1961 as a marriage of the CCF and the CLC, but even with the NDP's organic link to the labour movement, most working-class Canadians continued to vote Liberal or Conservative (and later, Bloc Québécois and Reform).

The lack of class-consciousness among the Canadian working class has been noted earlier, in Chapter 8.[23] A major reason for its absence is that the Liberals and Conservatives were firmly entrenched when the franchise was extended to the working class and had already defined politics around social differences other than class. These two parties either appealed to one or more ethnic/religious and regional groups or else developed pan-Canadian appeals that diverted attention from class-based issues. These parties persuaded most voters that they belonged to the middle class and gave them the impression of inclusion and social mobility.

Janine Brodie and Jane Jenson make the point that class-consciousness requires prior ideological and organizational activity by groups such as unions, farmers, cooperatives, and other reformers. They demonstrate that classes as active and self-conscious social actors have to be created, and that class-based organizations must precede the expectation of class-based voting.[24] The attempts by farmers and unions to redefine Canadian politics in class terms were repelled by the traditional parties, their leaders were co-opted by the Liberal Party, and both organizations were internally divided. Moreover, many Canadian affiliates of American unions were encouraged to remain aloof from partisan politics.

Advocates of a class-based party system point out that the existing system is partially class-based—the upper and middle classes are conscious of their class position and vote accordingly; it is just that the working class does not vote appropriately. They claim that a class-based system would provide ideological alternatives in elections that would make them more meaningful, and would more likely than at present offer innovative solutions to national problems. Moreover, the broker system, with its emphasis on multiple cleavages, is dangerously destabilizing, for if the Liberals and Conservatives are unsuccessful as brokers, one or more ethnic–regional units can threaten to separate. In such circumstances, class could be the integrating ingredient: "A nation like Canada, which is in danger of falling apart on ethnic-regional lines, may be held together by a politics which unites the people of various regions and ethnic groups around the two poles of left and right."[25] Canadians would ideally be united by their common class position into two or three national class-based parties. Finally, it is said that class-based politics and parties are already the norm in Western Canadian provincial politics, so that this theory is quite a realistic proposition after all.

One-Party Dominance

The one-party-dominance thesis is a third general theory regarding Canadian parties. H.G. Thorburn maintains, for example, that instead of looking at the Canadian party system as being historically made up of two major parties, it has really been dominated by one—the Liberals—since about 1900.[26] The Liberals are the "government party," power-oriented rather than issue-oriented, attracting "winners" and "successes" as supporters and candidates, and maintaining themselves in office with the help of public service expertise, public opinion polls, and the chance to choose election day. The Conservatives can be seen as the "opposition party," ordinarily having to settle for the role of critics (from within the range of ideological conformity) but being elected to office only on those rare occasions when the people get thoroughly fed up with the Liberals. With their divisiveness, "opposition mentality," and lack of preparedness to govern, however, the Conservatives do not remain in power very long. Finally, the NDP can be termed the "innovative party," never really having a chance to govern nationally, but being responsible for introducing new ideas from beyond the range of current ideological conformity, both at the federal and provincial levels. For a time in the 1980s, some observers thought that Thorburn's designations might be out-of-date, but sure enough, the Liberals returned to power in 1993. Since that time, however, it could be argued that the Reform Party has functioned as the principal party of innovation, this time from the right.

The Decline of Parties

A final interpretation, coming from John Meisel, emphasizes the decline of political parties.[27] He suggests a number of reasons why the traditional functions of parties have been taken over by other institutions. A decline in ideological differences among the parties has resulted in their being less capable of offering innovative solutions to national problems. People prefer to participate directly in specialized voluntary associations rather than take their concerns to an omnibus political party, with the result that the number and strength of interest groups has greatly increased. Such issue-oriented individuals anticipate more prompt and effective satisfaction of their demands by participating in group action, quite possibly by interacting with the bureaucracy, than by going through traditional political party channels.

The quantity and complexity of information with which governments have to deal has come to mean that generalist politicians can no longer cope with it, leaving them increasingly dependent on the bureaucracy. This culminates in a situation in which interest groups confer with the bureaucrats and work out policies that the politicians can neither understand nor alter, further reducing the role of political parties in the policymaking process. Federal–provincial conferences and committees of all kinds have become the forum in which many public policies are ironed out, and once certain political and bureaucratic compromises have been made, there is little that other politicians or parties can do about them.

Meisel also notes that parties now gear most of their activity to the demands of the media, and to the extent that elections are dominated by leader images and leader debates, the need for traditional party organizations diminishes. Similarly, public opinion polls provide better feedback to politicians than their traditional discussion with party activists. Investigative journalism has reduced the role of the opposition in Parliament; direct-mail appeals have replaced traditional forms of party fundraising; and modern transnational corporations are beyond the control of any party or government. Other recent developments that have contributed to the decline of parties are the increasing power of the prime minister, the influence of election strategists and other specialist advisers, and the new role of the courts and the Charter of Rights and Freedoms.

Meisel's critique of Canadian political parties has inspired other commentary that either defends them or suggests that rather than declining, they are in a state of transition.[28] Defenders of parties admit that certain traditional functions are being performed by interest groups, the media, public opinion polls, and the bureaucracy, but argue that others are simply being carried out by parties in different ways. Whether one prefers "decline" or "transition," Meisel makes many valid points.

Minor Parties

So much for theories that account for the overall party system in Canada. But because Canada has had more minor parties than any other similar political system, political scientists have also developed several theories to account specifically for them. Essentially, they can all be explained by the fact that at one time or another, ethnic, regional, or class grievances have gone unsatisfied by the broker parties. Moreover, new minor parties are only to be expected when individual voter identification with existing parties is generally so weak, and when ideological stagnation and opportunism characterize the broker system. In particular, if the working class never managed to establish a major party in Canada, it is not surprising that several minor working-class parties would be created.

The principal factors responsible for the rise of the various minor parties in Canada involve region (including institutional malfunction), ethnicity, class or ideology, a poor economy, and charismatic leadership, as seen in Table 13.5 below.

TABLE 13.5   Factors Involved in the Rise of Minor Parties

	Region	Ethnicity	Class/ Ideology	Economy	Leader
Progressives	*		*	*	
CCF			*	*	
Social Credit	*		*	*	*
Reconstruction			*	*	
Bloc Populaire	*	*			
NDP			*		
Créditistes	*	*	*	*	*
Libertarian			*		
Christian Heritage			*		
Green			*		
Confederation of Regions	*	*			
Reform	*	*	*		
Bloc Québécois	*	*			*

On a more theoretical note, it has also been argued that the rigid party discipline enforced in the Canadian Parliament has encouraged the development of minor protest parties.[29] When certain interests felt frustrated by the requirement of toeing the party line in Ottawa, they turned to form minor parties, usually at the provincial level, to vent their grievances. Some have gone so far as to suggest that the parliamentary system, with its rigid party discipline, is unsuitable for such a diverse country. S.M. Lipset applies his theory primarily to the Progressives and Social Credit, but it could equally apply to the Reform Party and perhaps to the Bloc Québécois.

Maurice Pinard's theory relates the rise of minor parties to a situation of one-party dominance when dissatisfaction with the traditional party eventually sets in.[30] In these circumstances, voters see little use in supporting the weak existing opposition party and turn instead to a new minor party, especially if it is headed by a strong, populist, charismatic leader. Pinard applies this hypothesis primarily to the strange eruption of Créditiste support in Quebec in 1962, when, as a result of a downturn in the economy, many Quebeckers grew tired of supporting the Liberals, but preferred the fiery Réal Caouette to the traditional Conservative alternative.

Another prominent theory relating to minor parties is that of C.B. Macpherson in his explanation of the series of one-party-dominant eras in Alberta provincial politics. He labels this system, which included the nontraditional United Farmers and Social Credit, as a "quasi-party" system.[31] Macpherson applies a kind of Marxist theory to explain the situation by arguing that the province was characterized by a homogeneity of class interests—the predominance of small, independent producers—so that little internal class conflict could be detected. Instead, the whole Alberta society was held in a quasi-colonial relationship by Eastern Canada. The feeling of being exploited by the privileged classes in the East led Albertans to unite behind a dominant provincial party. Macpherson has been faulted for exaggerating the extent of one-party dominance in the province as well as overstating the proportion of farmers, but Albertans continued to act as if they were a homogeneous society exploited by the East for decades after he identified this phenomenon.

The rise of the CCF in Saskatchewan has also attracted specific explanations, including the collectivist streak in the Canadian political culture, which seems particularly strong in that province. Disagreeable weather, social isolation, and corporate and federal government exploitation all encouraged cooperative behaviour and organizations that eventually became transformed into a political party, the Cooperative Commonwealth Federation.[32]

····································

PARTY ORGANIZATION

A political party has been defined as an organized group, but the structure of such a group requires clarification. Several different components of each party can be identified: the **parliamentary party** or **party caucus**, that is, the party's elected representatives in Parliament; the **extra-parliamentary party** organization made up of party activists and executive members; the party headquarters, bureaucracy, or staff; and ordinary party members.

When it comes to comparing party organizations, it is useful to apply two theoretical models, those of the **mass party** and the **cadre party**. These two models can be differentiated in five main ways—membership, leadership, finance, policymaking, and general structures and operations—as shown below.

Distinguishing between Mass and Cadre Parties

	Mass Party	Cadre Party
Membership	Has or aspires to have a large membership that possesses considerable power over the parliamentary wing, executive members, and party staffers.	Dominated by a small local or national elite; content with small membership; denies membership effective power.
Leadership	Chooses its leader at a convention or by giving every member a vote, and maintains some kind of control over the leader afterward.	Allows the parliamentary party to select the leader, who then operates without any formal accountability.
Finance	Financed by membership fees and other small contributions from its members.	Depends on a relatively small number of large contributions, usually corporate.
Policymaking	Allows the membership to have a meaningful say in determining party policy.	Permits the parliamentary party, especially the leader and/or Cabinet, to formulate party policy.
General Structures & Operations	Operates democratically, according to a written constitution, and throughout the year.	Run by an elite, pays little attention to its constitution, and barely exists except at election time.

While real-life parties should not be expected to fall perfectly into either of these theoretical categories and while every party may bear characteristics of both mass and cadre models, these ideal types are useful in comparing the main Canadian parties. The discussion of party and election finance in Chapter 12 showed that the Liberal and Conservative parties began as cadre parties dependent on large corporate contributions and then moved to an intermediate position in which they now receive up to half of their revenues from individual donations. The CCF/NDP, on the other hand, was always essentially a mass party with respect to party finance, which is more or less the case with the Reform and BQ parties, too, although Reform started to solicit large corporate contributions in 1997.

Before examining the other four aspects of party organization in detail, it is appropriate to outline the main aspects of party reorganization in the lead-up to the new millennium.[33] After the decimation of the PC party in the 1993 election, it engaged in a massive overhaul. Jean Charest's three-step "3R" plan to restore the PCs as a relevant political force consisted of restructuring the party, rebuilding its policy platform, and returning to government (election preparedness). He then appointed a national restructuring committee, which engaged in extensive consultation with party activists across the country. At the national meeting of the party in April 1995, the party adopted a new constitution, a new executive structure, a new policymaking process, a new national membership program, a new statement of party aims and principles, and provision for the direct election of the next leader. The party regained official status in the 1997 election, but shortly afterwards lost its leader to the Quebec Liberals. That required the party to operationalize its new leadership selection process earlier than planned, and against a backdrop of Reform leader Preston Manning's call for the two right-wing parties to unite.

If the PC constitution had not been seriously re-examined since 1956, this was almost as true in the case of the equally weakened post-1993 NDP. It therefore engaged in a similar renewal process, with the results ratified at its October 1995 convention. The party reconfigured its structures, policymaking process, and leadership selection process. In addition, the NDP reassessed its links with labour and other social movements and the federal–provincial relationship within the party, and adoped a new mission statement and set of principles. The NDP also regained official status in 1997, which immensely improved its financial status.

The victorious party in 1993 and 1997, the Liberals, had less necessity to reorganize in the 1990s. Instead, they continued to hold their biennial conventions, fine-tune their constitution, provide policy ideas to the government, and generally retain their unchallenged one-party dominance. Meanwhile, the Reform Party replaced the Bloc as official opposition in 1997, after which, as noted, Preston Manning devoted much attention to trying to establish a "united alternative" to the "government party." The first step in such a project was a conference in Ottawa in February 1999; those in attendance, largely Reform party members, voted to launch such a new party, a decision supported by 60.5 percent of the approximately 50 percent of the Reform members who voted in a subsequent intra-party referendum.

Party Membership

A significant difference among the parties can be seen in their provisions for membership. The NDP aspires to a large membership, and local activists often operate an annual, year-round membership and renewal drive. New members must take an oath that they support the party's principles, and only those who have been members for at least 30 days and who live in the constituency are allowed to vote at nomination meetings. Constituency association representation at party conventions is based on the size of the local membership, and the party is unique in having affiliated members, that is, members of unions that have voted to affiliate with the party. Like the NDP, the Reform Party has a 30-day membership qualification period, and convention (called "assembly") representation is based on the number of local members.

Although they may also conduct membership drives for a few weeks a year, the Liberals are normally more casual about the annual renewal of party memberships. For the most part their members sign up in connection with the meeting to nominate a candidate for the next election or to choose delegates to a national convention. The Liberals have a national rule requiring that a person must be a member for at least 90 days before being allowed to vote for the party leadership, but rules for nomination meetings are determined at the provincial level. Even with such restrictions, it is typical for aspiring Liberal candidates or delegates to sign up large numbers of new members (often from ethnic groups in urban centres) just before the deadline.

The PCs adopted new national membership rules in 1995 such that a person must be a member for at least 14 days before being allowed to vote at nomination or delegate-selection meetings. PC party headquarters now engages in an annual national membership drive in which renewal notices are sent out by Ottawa. All parties have difficulty collecting complete current lists of their members at provincial or national headquarters. The Liberals and NDP maintain a list of contributors at the national level, but leave provincial sections to keep track of actual members. On the other hand, Reform and, since 1995, the PCs have a list of party members in their head offices. Whether a party has a list of members or contributors or both, it can use the list repeatedly during the year for fundraising purposes.

Party Leadership

There is probably less distinction among the parties when it comes to the question of leadership. The Liberals relied on the Parliamentary party to select its leaders before 1919 and the Conservatives did so until 1927, but both then moved to choose their leaders at national delegate conventions.[34] While leadership conventions are a more democratic means of choosing the party leader, the preference of party delegates does not always correspond to that of the parliamentary party, sometimes contributing to considerable friction between the new leader and the caucus. The dates and winners of party leadership contests are contained in Table 13.6.

It can be seen that the Liberals have alternated anglophone and francophone leaders, partly by accident and partly by design. The Conservatives never had a francophone leader before

TABLE 13.6   **Dates of Election of Major Party Leaders**

Liberal	Conservative	CCF/NDP
1919 Mackenzie King	1927 R.B. Bennett	1932 J.S. Woodsworth
1948 Louis St. Laurent	1938 Robert Manion	1942 M.J. Coldwell
1958 Lester B. Pearson	1942 John Bracken	1960 Hazen Argue
1968 Pierre E. Trudeau	1948 George Drew	1961 T.C. Douglas
1984 John Turner	1956 John Diefenbaker	1971 David Lewis
1990 Jean Chrétien	1967 Robert Stanfield	1975 Ed Broadbent
	1976 Joe Clark	1989 Audrey McLaughlin
	1983 Brian Mulroney	1995 Alexa McDonough
	1993 Kim Campbell	
	1995 Jean Charest	
	1998 Joe Clark	

		Bloc Québécois
		1990 Lucien Bouchard
Reform		
1991 Preston Manning		1997 Gilles Duceppe

Jean Charest, Brian Mulroney being the first bilingual Quebecker to hold the post in that party. Most Liberal leaders have been Roman Catholics (King and Pearson excepted), while most PC leaders have been Protestants (with the exception of Clark, Mulroney, and Charest). All Liberal leaders have come from Ontario or Quebec, while the origin of most Conservative leaders was outside central Canada. Lawyers represent the most common occupational background (St. Laurent, Diefenbaker, Stanfield, Trudeau, Lewis, Turner, Mulroney, Charest, and Chrétien). Audrey McLaughlin was the first female national party leader in Canadian history, although Rosemary Brown (NDP), Flora MacDonald (PC), and Sheila Copps (Liberal) gave male contenders a run for their money in 1975, 1976, and 1990 respectively.

With the exception of Brian Mulroney and Preston Manning, all of the leaders have had some experience in the House of Commons or in provincial legislatures (Bracken, Drew, Stanfield, and McDonough), Douglas having been both a premier and an MP. What is quite striking in many cases, however, is the brevity of this parliamentary experience. Most were relatively inexperienced in politics when they were chosen, and the Liberals' tendency to co-opt an extra-parliamentary notable for their leader has often been noted. Especially in a television age, a fresh face may be just as important as legislative experience in order to obtain the job, although it might not be so useful afterwards. Alternatively, in the case of Turner and Chrétien, a period out of the Commons' spotlight was apparently considered advantageous by the delegates who chose them. Joe Clark is the only person to be elected leader on two widely separated occasions.

An even more democratic procedure than the leadership convention has been utilized in recent years, that is, to allow every card-carrying member of the party to cast a vote for the leadership. Such a procedure avoids much of the cost of holding a national convention; it eliminates the unholy fight among various candidates for delegates at the constituency level; it ensures that the decision is not left to the more affluent members of the party who can afford the travel costs; and it removes the circus atmosphere of the convention. The Parti Québécois was the first Canadian party to move to a "one member–one vote" leadership selection process, and many other provincial party leaders have now been elected on this basis. It has become popular to issue party members a PIN (personal identification number) and have them telephone in their choice rather than vote by ballot at the local level. Such procedures have potential problems of their own, however, including technological breakdowns, an unrepresentative electorate, and the involvement of voters who have no knowledge of the candidates or who actually support other parties. Many partisans also feel that the loss of the publicity value of a nationally televised convention is too high a cost, and suggest that by imposing spending limits on candidates and subsidizing delegates' expenses, some of the worst features of conventions can be avoided.

Despite the advantages of a full-fledged convention, all parties have been influenced by the pressure for more popular participation in the leadership selection process. While Preston Manning was elected at Reform's founding convention, the Reform constitution provided that all members of the party would vote in any subsequent leadership contest. Similarly, when the NDP replaced Audrey McLaughlin in 1995, it wished to give each grassroots member of the party a direct vote but still retain the drama of a convention. It sought to do so by providing for regional "primaries" in which all members could vote and that would determine which candidates would appear on the ballot at the actual delegate convention. After choosing Jean Chrétien in the traditional way in 1990, the Liberal Party adopted a new system in 1992 modelled on their provincial counterparts in Ontario, which combines giving every member a vote with also having a leadership convention. Every party member votes on the leadership candidates, as well as for delegates, and the latter are elected in proportion to the popular vote received by each leadership candidate at the local level.

When Kim Campbell resigned as PC leader after the 1993 election, the national executive appointed Jean Charest as interim leader, to be confirmed by a vote at the next general meeting of the party. At the same time that it did so, the party adopted a new constitution that provided for the next leader to be chosen by a vote of all party members. When Charest was persuaded to lead the Quebec Liberals, the PC Party put its new leadership selection process into play in 1998. It gave each member of the party a vote, but weighted these votes so that each constituency had equal power, regardless of the size of its membership. Constituencies varied in size from about 60 to 1200 members, for a total eligible electorate of about 90 000. Members voted at a central location within their constituency, but in certain cases there had to be more than one site, and in really remote places, members voted by phone. Joe Clark came close to winning a majority on the first ballot, and won easily on a second vote three weeks later, with about 50 000 PC members voting at least once. The PCs did not derive much free media coverage from the exercise, partly because they were the "fifth" party in the House of Commons, but it was all they could afford and had the advantage of forcing the party to engage in a good deal of local logistical organization.

Most parties also have **leadership review** mechanisms in their constitutions, although these vary in detail. The NDP opens nominations for the position of leader at their national convention every two years, so that, at least in theory, the leader can be immediately replaced. However, in the absence of a concrete challenger, no vote is needed.

A leadership review provision ("Are you in favour of holding a leadership convention?") was not added to the PC constitution until 1974, as a result of the civil war within the party over John Diefenbaker's leadership between 1962 and 1967. In 1977, with Joe Clark at the helm, 93 percent rejected the idea of a leadership convention, and in 1981, 66 percent did so. Two years later, an almost identical 67 percent again opposed a leadership convention, but Clark decided to resign and call a leadership convention anyway. Running to succeed himself, he was defeated by Brian Mulroney. At the same time, the leadership review mechanism had caused so much turmoil in the party that it was changed so now the question is only put at the first convention following an election that the party loses.

Seeking to avoid the Conservatives' difficulty, the Liberals added a leadership review clause in 1966 to the effect that at the first convention after each election (win or lose), delegates vote on whether they want a leadership convention to be called. Whether it was Pierre Trudeau, John Turner, or Jean Chrétien, the party has always solidly backed its leader. The Reform Party asks the question at every biennial national party assembly: "Do you want a leadership vote to be called?" and Preston Manning has never been seriously challenged.

By Malcolm Mayes (Edmonton Journal). *Reproduced with permission.*

Party Policymaking

All political parties have difficulty designing their policymaking process. On the one hand, they want to give ordinary party members an opportunity to contribute to party policy (a mass characteristic), but at the same time, no party establishment wants to be saddled with unrealistic policy commitments (a cadre notion). Thus, they all struggle to combine these two forces in the most appropriate way.

Liberal and Conservative national conventions or general meetings usually include a policy session and sometimes focus primarily on policy. But even if specific resolutions are debated and passed, which is not always the case, party leaders retain the right to determine official party policy. While parliamentary leaders may be influenced by such discussions to some extent, they are in no way bound by the policy resolutions of the party organization.

The Liberal Party did not even hold a national convention between 1919 and 1948, and instead mainly relied on the public service for policy advice. When the Liberals found themselves in opposition after 1957, however, and cut off from the public service, Lester Pearson was forced to turn to the party organization to help develop new policy proposals. A "thinkers' conference" held in Kingston in 1960 was followed by a national party policy rally in 1961, and once in power after 1963, the Pearson government quickly implemented most of the policies that had been adopted. Under Pierre Trudeau, the party held several more party policy conferences, but in contrast to Pearson, Trudeau did not pay much attention to the results.[35] Jean Chrétien tried to replicate the early 1960s experience with a policy conference in Aylmer in 1991, followed by the biennial party convention a year later, which debated such policy ideas. The Red Book used as the party platform in the 1993 election drew substantially upon these two party meetings. With resolutions emanating from provincial sections, the four party commissions (youth, women, Aboriginal, and seniors), the national executive, and the caucus, the party continued to hold a day of policy workshops at its subsequent biennial conventions, culminating in a half-day of discussion of the most important policy resolutions in the plenary session.

The Conservatives discussed policy to some extent at their many leadership conventions. But after the 1956 convention, Diefenbaker attempted to destroy all evidence of its policy proposals and governed for five years without any policy guidance from the party. When Robert Stanfield became leader in 1967, he was anxious to develop a stronger policy orientation, organizing a thinkers' conference in 1969, encouraging policy discussions at the grassroots level of the party, and then calling a national policy conference in 1971. Although he retained the right to make the final decisions, Stanfield took the results quite seriously, and possibly because he was able to use this party-generated policy in the 1972 election campaign, the Conservatives made major gains. Still finding themselves in opposition, however, both Stanfield and the party lost enthusiasm for policy. Joe Clark (1976–83) was not guided by the party very much in some of his policies, and Brian Mulroney relied primarily on the public service, Royal Commissions, backroom advisers, and public opinion polls for his policies, although he held an unmemorable party policy conference in 1991. Recognizing past deficiencies, and as part of its rebuilding process after 1993, Jean Charest led the party to design a new policymaking process combining greater membership input with expert advice. The party moved from "principles to policy to platform" with a major policy convention in August 1996 that determined the main lines of its 1997 election platform.

The NDP has always claimed to be particularly distinctive in the realm of party policymaking. It has regular policy sessions every two years, which are indeed the predominant item on the convention agenda. Grassroots constituency associations are invited to submit resolutions in advance, and, most important, resolutions passed by the convention are considered to be official and binding on the leader and the parliamentary party. Giving such power to the rank-and-file membership, however, sometimes hobbled the leadership with policies that were embarrassing, unworkable, or at odds with its own views; there was often no connection between the hordes of resolutions passed; and occasionally problems erupted between the parliamentary caucus and the party organization. The party executive and council were thus allowed to submit resolutions of their own, and the council, which is subject to greater leadership manipulation than the convention, was given authority to "flesh out" the meaning of policies adopted. The post-1993 NDP was not so sure that its traditional policymaking system was adequate, however, and revamped it in 1995. Instead of passing random policy resolutions at whim, riding associations would be primarily expected to respond to policy papers prepared by the policy review committee and Social Democratic Forum—two groups within the party with considerable policy resources and expertise. If the NDP policymaking process is now less distinctive from other parties, this party still gives greater priority to policy debate and takes more seriously the resolutions passed.

As for the Reform Party, a certain tension exists in its policymaking process between its populist intentions and the leadership group around Preston Manning. It adopted a full-scale platform at its founding convention but established an elaborate policymaking process in which policy resolutions could originate at the constituency level, from caucus, from party task forces, and from the executive council. Such resolutions were collated by the resolutions committee, and an "exposure draft" sent out to constituency associations for prioritization. The top 40 were then put on the agenda of the next national assembly. Changes to party policy had to be approved by a majority of votes cast as well as a majority in a majority of provinces. In keeping with its populist approach, the executive council of the party could conduct an informal poll of the membership on an issue as well as hold a formal referendum.

General Structures and Operations
CONVENTIONS

All parties have constitutions that outline their objectives, structures, and procedures. In theory, at least, the ultimate authority in each party is the party convention, which all parties now hold quite regularly at an average of about two-year intervals (Liberal: 1996, 1998, 2000; NDP: 1995, 1997, 1999; Reform: 1996, 1998, 2000; PC: 1995, 1999). The convention agenda normally includes the election of the party executive, constitutional amendments, policy discussions, and instruction in local election organization, but such conventions also serve important social and morale-building purposes. In the Liberal and Conservative parties, each constituency association is entitled to an equal number of delegates, while in the NDP and Reform, representation is based on the size of the local membership. All parties include certain ex-officio delegates such as MPs, and in some cases MPPs, MLAs, and nominated or recently defeated candidates. In the NDP, affiliated labour unions also send delegates. The array of women's, youth, campus, Aboriginal, ethnic, and other associated groups is too complicated to fathom here, but party conventions are not very representative of the electorate.

Even at the level of party activists, most are of middle-class background. While women have traditionally done much menial work in these parties without being allowed to be part of the elite, most parties have deliberately boosted the effective participation of women within their ranks in recent years. Ethnic minorities have also begun to demand a more meaningful role.

PARTY EXECUTIVE

Each party has a national executive, including a president, vice-presidents, treasurer, and so on, and each establishes a number of executive committees or special-interest commissions. These officials usually perform such duties on a part-time basis, although it is helpful for the president to be close to Ottawa and readily available for meetings, campaign organization, and other functions. Both the Liberals and Conservatives have sometimes elected a senator as party president since such a person has considerable free time and is on the public payroll, saving the party the cost of a presidential salary. The party president usually has the confidence of the leader, and the contest for the presidency is sometimes a surrogate vote on the leadership. Dalton Camp was probably the most famous party president in Canadian history because of his feat in using that position to engineer the leadership convention that toppled John Diefenbaker. The Liberals and Conservatives have a two-tier executive structure, Reform has only one, and the NDP has three, the third being a council that meets twice a year as a sort of mini-convention and is the governing body of the party between conventions.

PARTY HEADQUARTERS

Three parties maintain headquarters in Ottawa, which are staffed by permanent party employees. This office is headed by the national director in the Liberal and Conservative cases, and the Federal Secretary in the NDP. These chief executive officers usually maintain close relations with the leader and caucus, and in the case of the Liberals, who are usually in power, the Prime Minister's Office. In each case, the size of the party staff varies considerably, depending on party finances and the imminence of an election. The PC and NDP offices were

---

National Structures of the Four Main Canadian Parties (approximate size)

Liberal	*NDP*
Management Committee (16)	Officers (6)
National Executive (50)	Executive (25)
	Council (102)
PC	*Reform*
Management Committee (20)	Executive Council (33)
National Council (350)	

dramatically scaled down after the 1993 election, the latter having to sell its building and move into smaller rented space. In 1999, the Liberals maintained a staff of about 25, some of whom worked in the Federal Liberal Agency, the fundraising branch of the office. The PC office, including the PC Fund, employed 18 people, with three additional organizers out in the field, while the NDP had grown back to 12. The role of party headquarters during election campaigns is outlined in Chapter 14. Between elections, headquarters performs a variety of functions such as collecting money, ensuring local organizations are alive and well, arranging for speakers to local annual meetings, planning conventions, publishing newsletters, conducting surveys, and researching policy.

The Reform Party maintains a research and communications office in Ottawa, which, dealing largely with parliamentary work, is mostly funded by the public purse, while the official national office of the party is in Calgary, with a staff of about 20 headed by an executive director. This separation of the parliamentary and extra-parliamentary offices is consistent with its populist intentions and image, but creates certain difficulties in coordination and communication. The party tries to overcome such problems with semi-annual joint caucus–executive meetings, quarterly strategic retreats (usually in Calgary), a weekly teleconference between officials in the two locations, and busy telephone and fax lines.

FEDERAL–PROVINCIAL PARTY LINKS

The federal nature of Canada and the existence of two levels of government at which political parties seek to influence policy and personnel raise the question of the relationship between national and provincial party organizations.[36] To oversimplify the situation, the Conservative Party could be said to have a "confederal" character—that is, the federal and provincial PC parties are essentially independent of each other. There is virtually no formal organizational or financial link between the two wings of the party, and the provincial wing is weak to nonexistent in BC, Saskatchewan, and Quebec. Thus, federal and provincial party memberships are separate, and a complete set of federal riding associations and executives co-exists with provincial party organizations at the grassroots level, although it is largely the same people who are members of both.

By contrast, the NDP could be called an "integrated" party because, with the exception of Quebec, one joins the NDP at the provincial level and automatically becomes a member of the national party, almost as if it were an afterthought. Only in areas of its strongest support does the party maintain full-fledged separate federal and provincial constituency associations; provincial offices of the party theoretically serve the needs of both federal and provincial parties; and a provincial convention also deals with federal matters from its own perspective. To help overcome the inevitable provincial orientation of this combined operation and to combat the dormancy of the federal party at the provincial and constituency levels between federal elections, the party created a Council of Federal Ridings in each province, but this experiment had mixed results. Federal organizers work out of provincial offices in the preelection period and the provincial party headquarters devotes its full attention to the federal election campaign once it is called. The two levels of the party are integrated financially, such that the provincial parties must contribute 15 percent of their annual revenues to the federal party. In turn, the latter reimburses each section for 15 percent of the direct-mail proceeds it raises in their province. In Quebec, however, the federal party operates independently of any provincial party of the same name. The 1995 Renewal Convention sought to give the federal party more of a stand-alone presence, such that revenue sharing is less important, and 75 percent of the federal council is elected at the federal convention of the party rather than at provincial conventions.

The Liberal Party is characterized by two different federal–provincial relationships. In Quebec, Ontario, Alberta, and British Columbia, the party is split into federal and provincial wings, each of which has separate finances, memberships, constituency associations, executives, conventions, and offices. The other provinces and territories have a joint Liberal Party, although, as in the case of the NDP, such an integrated relationship gives the party a provincial orientation. It is possible to join the federal party directly, but it is more common to join the provincial party and become an automatic member of the federal organization. Whether separate or joint, federal party headquarters pays each provincial party organization $4000 annually per "unheld" federal riding to be used to advance the interests of the federal party. There are also joint dinners and other fundraising events where proceeds are shared.

The Bloc Québécois has no provincial counterpart, as such, but the Parti Québécois more or less fulfills that function. Because of leadership frictions and slightly different versions of sovereignty, the two parties are not necessarily as intimate as outsiders assume, but after the 1995 Quebec referendum, Bloc leader Lucien Bouchard moved back to Quebec to take over the PQ leadership.

Meanwhile, Preston Manning wanted to concentrate all of Reform's attention at the national level, and persuaded his members to back his objection to any provincial party branches. That did not completely end the discussion, however, for federal Reform members in provinces like Alberta and Ontario were often found to be active in the provincial PC party. Moreover, a provincial party in British Columbia had previously adopted the "Reform Party" label and continued to operate with a platform similar to Manning's, but without organic links to his federal party.

THE IRON LAW OF OLIGARCHY

To return to the concepts of mass and cadre parties, the relationships among the party membership, the executive, the parliamentary caucus, and the party leadership must be examined. As noted earlier, in a mass party, the membership, executive, and conventions have real power, whereas a cadre party is controlled by the leader and parliamentary wing. But political theorist Robert Michels claims that a tendency toward elitism is inevitable within all political parties, and formulated his famous **iron law of oligarchy**.[37] Even in parties that seek or profess to belong to the mass category, a small elite invariably develops, such that rank-and-file party members have little real power.

One tendency is for party leaders, whether or not in government, to create a small coterie of advisers, who cut the leader off from party influence. This was particularly so in the Liberal Party during the tenure of Pierre Elliott Trudeau.[38] As party leader, Trudeau virtually ignored the party organization, paying little attention to its policy-generation efforts, its increasing debt, and its cynical electoral strategies, but did participate in its unsavoury patronage practices. In fact, he left almost all party and electoral matters in the hands of Jim Coutts in the Prime Minister's Office and Senator Keith Davey, neither of whom held any official position in the Liberal Party. Their style of operation and their ignoring the party organization led to initiatives to allow the party organization to take back control of the party policy, platform, appointments, and electoral strategy. The party's constitution was amended in 1992 to solidify these changes, and the party organization was more satisfied with its relationship with Chrétien's PMO.

A second common development is that the parliamentary wing of the party claims precedence over the party organization. In terms of policy, for example, when a party has official status in the House of Commons, it is entitled to hire a substantial number of research assistants, the lack of which between 1993 and 1997 significantly crippled the PC and New Democratic parties. In every such party, even in opposition, the complement of publicly paid staff supporting the leader, caucus, and individual MPs clearly outnumbers the staff at party headquarters and may prescribe different policy approaches than come out of party policy discussions. Moreover, when a party forms the government, it has the entire public service to advise it, and may find that the world looks somewhat different from the position of public responsibility than from the Opposition benches. Caucus members are usually more concerned about getting re-elected than ordinary policy-oriented party members, and may thus seek to tone down certain ideas emanating from the grassroots of the party.

In the third place, even though the party organization has periodic elections, a small group of executive members often seek re-election for many terms and effectively maintain control. They use their experience, their access to party information, their connections, their control of party funds, and their influence over party policy to do so. Member apathy is also a factor, for the great bulk of party members are inactive and quite happy to have a handful of activists take charge.

Thus, we can conclude that the Liberals and Conservatives started out as cadre parties in the areas of membership, leadership, finance, policymaking, and general structures and operations but have moved some distance in the direction of the mass party model. The NDP is therefore less distinctive than it once was, but continues to be significantly closer to the mass party model than its two traditional rivals. In some respects, Reform and the Bloc also approximate the mass party model, although both have had dominant leaders (Lucien Bouchard and Preston Manning) who ensured that the membership did not get out of control.

....

PARTY IDEOLOGY

Discussions of party ideology might be a relatively straightforward task in some political systems, but they are not so in Canada. Parties often play down their ideological differences in the search for votes, their positions change over time, and they are all internally divided to some extent. Moreover, it is difficult to know where to find evidence of party ideology and how to measure it, possible sources being election rhetoric, party policy resolutions, policies adopted when in office, government spending patterns, or surveys of the attitudes of party activists.

When the Liberals and Conservatives were the two dominant parties, most discussions of party ideology focused on whether there were any differences between them. Some observers concluded that no basic ideological differences existed;[39] either they were both pure broker parties with no ideology, responding pragmatically and opportunistically to public opinion polls in the pursuit of power, or else they were equally committed to the capitalist system but prepared to remedy its worst faults in order to maintain popular support. A second interpretation was that while no fundamental ideological differences existed between them, they maintained certain consistent policy differences.[40] Historians generally observed, for example, that the Liberals were more continentalist or U.S.-oriented, while the Conservatives favoured the British connection; that the Liberals were more sympathetic to the concerns of Quebec and French Canada, while the Conservatives (at least after 1957) were more in tune with Western Canada; that the Liberals favoured lower tariffs than the Conservatives; and that the Liberals advocated provincial rights, while the Conservatives preferred a strong central government. In recent times, however, it appears that many of these stands have been reversed, and voters must be forgiven if they were suspicious about how deeply held such differences were.

A more comprehensive and theoretical perspective that includes the NDP and Reform parties is that genuine ideological differences do exist in Canada, and that such ideologies as **liberalism, conservatism**, and **democratic socialism** can be found to differentiate these four parties to some extent. The ideological continuum can be sketched in diagrammatic form as in Figure 13.1. This perspective is based on the writing of Louis Hartz, Kenneth MacRae, Gad Horowitz, and William Christian and Colin Campbell, among others, and is sometimes called the "fragment theory."[41] It suggests that the basic ideology in Canada is liberalism, but that traces of socialism and conservatism also exist, and that each of the ideologies is more or less represented by a corresponding party. Liberalism seeks to liberate the individual and maximize each individual's freedom and potential, something that almost all Canadians would support. Differences emerge, however, about who should be liberated, about what the inhibiting agent is, and about how to go about such liberation. Such differences primarily focus on the role of the state.

Democratic socialism seeks to liberate the individual from the inequalities and exploitation of the capitalist system; it believes in equality of condition, not merely equality of opportunity; and it prescribes a large element of state action or collectivism in order to achieve such liberation and equality. These views are generally referred to as being on the **left**. In particular, democratic socialism emphasizes government planning, regulation, ownership of some of the major industries of the country, progressive taxation, and redistribution of income via

Figure 13.1   The Ideological Continuum in Canada

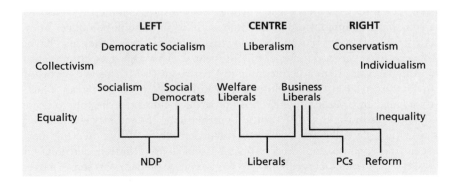

social programs. Democratic socialists are sometimes subdivided between "socialists" and "social democrats," depending on the extent to which they wish the state to intervene and the extent of equality they wish to effect. The early CCF was certainly more socialistic than the current New Democratic Party, with the latter's majority being of the social democratic persuasion. The CCF/NDP take credit for introducing public hospital and medical insurance when they formed the government of Saskatchewan, pressing for other social welfare programs, advocating a more progressive taxation system, creating a variety of Crown corporations in the provinces where they held power, and supporting the creation of several such government bodies in Ottawa.

Liberalism, too, has a dual personality and can be subdivided into "welfare" and "business" variants. Business liberals believe that the state inhibits individual self-fulfillment and that its role should be minimized so that individualism can prevail. Welfare liberals, on the other hand, take the view that the state can be a positive agent in liberating individuals from the constraints of other forces including the private-enterprise economy. Welfare liberals therefore stand for a combination of individualism and collectivism and a combination of equality and inequality, which they usually label "equality of opportunity." In terms of the diagram, then, the Liberal Party is composed of business and welfare liberals, leaving it in the centre of the Canadian ideological continuum. While Liberals obviously hold private market forces in greater esteem than does the NDP, Liberal governments introduced old age pensions, family allowances, and many other social welfare programs over the years. Historians generally point out that the Liberal Party made an ideological shift about 1919 from a business–liberal to a welfare–liberal orientation, although some observers see a shift backward after 1993.

Conservatism also has two variants. On the one hand, conservatives seek to liberate the individual from the restrictions of the state. Reducing the role of the state to a minimum and allowing capitalistic market forces to determine the distribution of power and wealth is often labelled "individualism." If this results in inequalities or elitism, conservatives are generally unconcerned; that is how it should be, because inequalities are both natural and deserved— some people are better and some work harder than others. These attitudes are labelled as being on the **right**, and these conservatives can also be called "business liberals." Historically, those who took a more extreme position on this issue than their counterparts in the Liberal Party were found primarily in the Conservative Party, and an even more extreme faction became the core of the Reform Party.

But a second wing of the Progressive Conservative Party is the progressive element, people who are sometimes called **red tories**. These Conservatives combine beliefs in privilege and collectivism, seeing society as an organic whole, emphasizing community values as well as **individualism**, and standing for order, tradition, stability, and noblesse oblige. They believe in hierarchy, in which everyone should occupy his or her place, but they also have a paternalistic concern with the condition of all the people. This aspect of conservatism is not unique to Canada, being found quite commonly in Britain and the rest of Europe; it stands out only in contrast to a lack of such sentiment within American conservatism. Thus, the ideology of the Canadian Conservative Party is not as clear-cut as the diagram indicates and is at least as divided as in the other two parties. Furthermore, the red tory element overlaps to some extent with welfare liberalism and even social democracy. While the Mulroney government pursued a fairly consistent business–liberal agenda—privatization, deregulation, deficit reduction, and cutting of social programs—its Conservative predecessors sometimes exhibited a strong red tory touch, such as in the creation of the RCMP, CBC, CNR, and the National

Energy Board, in the Bennett New Deal, and in the Stanfield proposal for wage and price controls. An alternative diagram, Figure 13.2, clarifies the position of the red tory influence in the Conservative Party. It also indicates why it is sometimes difficult to distinguish among social democrats, welfare liberals, and red tories, and why some New Democrats feel closer to some Conservatives than to certain Liberals.[42]

If liberalism in the United States lacks the collectivist touch, how does one explain its presence in three of the four Canadian party ideologies? One explanation focuses on the United Empire Loyalists, who removed most of the collectivist tendencies from the U.S. political culture when they migrated to Canada and left behind almost undiluted business liberalism. The United Empire Loyalists rendered ideological diversity legitimate in Canada and because of their early predominance, made collectivism a respectable and important element in the Canadian political culture. In fact, they added to the collectivist approach already found in the feudal background of French Canada, that is, the ideas of hierarchy, order, stability, and community. Collectivism was reinforced by subsequent waves of British immigration, whose intellectual baggage included both red tory and socialist views, along with the influence of the Social Gospel movement.[43] Such collectivist tendencies were discussed in Chapter 10.

There is so much overlap in the ideological orientation of the Liberal and Conservative parties in particular that it is sometimes difficult to detect the distinctions made above, and political scientists often ask the question: "Does party matter?"[44] Indeed, from about 1945 to 1980 or so the Liberal and Conservative parties shared a basic ideological approach that emphasized economic growth based on foreign investment, expanding the welfare state, and engaging in a certain amount of macroeconomic government regulation called Keynesian economics.[45] As time went on, however, this consensus broke down. Thus, especially after the Conservatives took office in 1984, policy and ideological differences between the two parties were much more obvious, with the Mulroney government pursuing a business–liberal or **neoconservative** agenda in which renewed reliance was placed on market forces, and the extent of government intervention was actually reduced. In other words, conservatism up to this

....

Figure 13.2 **Canadian Party Ideology**

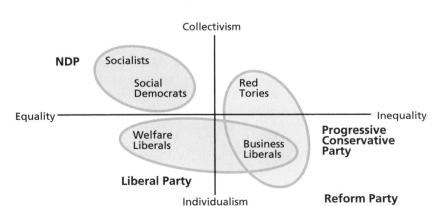

point had upheld the status quo and simply opposed further change, but the new neoconservatism wanted to turn the clock back and "dismantle the state" to some degree.[46]

Indeed, over the past 15 years, the whole ideological spectrum shifted to the right. For the first time in Canadian history, social programs are being cut back rather than expanded; Crown corporations are being privatized rather than created; regulations are being repealed rather than promulgated; public debts and deficits are being reduced rather than increased; and public servants are being fired rather than being hired. The phenomenon goes beyond one or two parties; it is happening around the world, and in Canada it has affected governing parties of all ideological persuasions in the 1990s: the NDP, especially in Saskatchewan; the Parti Québécois; and Liberal governments in several provinces and in Ottawa. In 1999, federal NDP leader Alexa McDonough encouraged the party to debate the merits of adopting a more centrist position akin to many social democratic party governments in Europe.[47]

The Reform Party was very much part of this shift to the right, and exerted great influence at both federal and provincial levels even though it did not form the government. The other leaders of this right-wing crusade, Conservative premiers Ralph Klein in Alberta and Mike Harris in Ontario, followed the Reform program to a tee. Reform believed in downsizing the role of government, reducing taxes and regulation, privatizing Crown corporations, discontinuing many government programs, cutting back on social programs, laying off public servants, and eliminating the deficit and repaying the debt. This was all consistent with a belief in individualism, which is unconcerned about whether it leads to socioeconomic inequalities. (Ironically, the Reform Party is a strong believer in treating everyone, including provinces, equally in law.) What distinguished Reform from other Canadian parties was a complete absence of the collectivist value. In this respect, it was almost a clone of the U.S. Republican Party, with which it maintained contact.[48]

It should be added that the Reform Party had two other main concerns. First, it believed in populism; that is, it is against elitism and professes to value the wisdom of ordinary people. To some extent this is also an Americanism as opposed to the traditional Canadian belief in British parliamentary democracy. The second was a territorial focus—that the West was getting shortchanged within Confederation.

The other new party, the Bloc Québécois, had one main objective: Quebec sovereignty. The question of nationalism generally overwhelms the left–right ideological approach in Quebec, but in some respects nationalism can be provided for within the format presented earlier. Nationalism is a kind of collectivism that usually involves a large role for the state, and at the pan-Canadian level—trying to make Canada more independent of Britain or the United States—has been a consistent mark of left-wing parties such as the NDP, as well as of red tories and left-wing Liberals. Although it is also possible for right-wingers to be nationalistic, the PQ has usually been placed on the left side of the continuum, somewhere between the Liberals and the NDP. The BQ, being made up of people who were previously members of a variety of other parties, does not have a comprehensive program apart from Quebec sovereignty and therefore no clear-cut left–right ideological stance. Nevertheless, since its creation, it has usually adopted a slightly left-wing approach when required to take a stand on other issues.

To return to the shift to the right, the NDP is generally occupying the previous position of the Liberal Party. The Chrétien government pursued the same kind of leaner government that it previously condemned under Mulroney, and Finance minister Paul Martin was forced to rationalize his dismemberment of the welfare state, which was largely the creation of his father Paul Martin, Sr., a Liberal Cabinet minister from the 1940s to the 1960s. As a result, a crush occurred on the right-wing side of the spectrum. The Conservative Party found it difficult to identify its own ideological space between the Chrétien Liberals and Manning's Reform Party. The PCs claimed to be more understanding of Quebec than Reform, of course, and therefore to be a "national" party; but it was hard to carve out a niche just slightly to the left of Reform, especially when so many provincial Conservatives were voting for that other federal party, and when Conservative governments in Alberta and Ontario were implementing Reform policies. It seemed logical to Preston Manning to engineer some kind of merger of right-wing forces in the country, but many observers believed that there was more of an ideological divide between the two parties than met the eye. Tory leader Joe Clark declined the invitation, and a PC convention in 1999 supported his position.[49]

CONCLUSION

However much Canadians tire of their endless bickering and lack of inspiration, political parties perform several crucial functions in the political system. In particular, they sort out the political issues, and in trying to bridge some of the many Canadian cleavages, make the political system more manageable. Many political observers are concerned about the danger of major political parties being outflanked by single-issue groups, whether as advocacy groups during and between election campaigns or as single-interest parties, in the representation of political interests and as the focus of political activity.[50] Such scholars argue that steps must be taken to strengthen mainline parties so that they can overcome their current lack of organizational depth and enhance their capacity to perform their representational and policymaking functions. Perhaps Canadians expect too much of their parties and place upon them too much of the burden of keeping the country together. Perhaps parties do not perform their functions well and are also dysfunctional in some respects. Perhaps their functions and methods of operation are in a state of change. But they must not be allowed to deteriorate further.

PC Since parties are so central to the operation of the political system, all of the approaches outlined in Chapter 1 have something to say about them. Parties are one of the main objects of the public choice approach, for example, and the efforts of political parties to bargain promises for votes can be seen in the attempt to develop attractive election platforms and in party policymaking processes. Politicians make such promises as will lead to their election, while rational, self-interested voters support the party whose policies are of greatest utility to themselves.[51] At least in the Liberal and Conservative parties, such promises and policies are not seriously limited by ideological consistency. As noted in Chapter 14, however, the alleged quid pro quo takes place in an environment of vague proposals, slogans, and leader images as far as the parties are concerned, and prejudices, ignorance, and family traditions on the part of many voters.

 The pluralist model is particularly applicable to the broker system. In a country with many cleavages, it is not only desirable but necessary that political parties seek to accommodate the demands of all major groups. Unlike class analysts, pluralists do not see class divisions as taking priority over ethnic, religious, regional, or other concerns. They also note the increased role of women and new ethnic groups in party operations.

Ⓒ   Class analysts' concern with corporate contributions to the Liberal and Conservative parties was addressed in Chapter 12. Here this approach can be seen in its critique of the broker system and in its alternative prescription for a class-based party system. In such analysts' eyes, the Liberal and Conservative parties (at least) are apologists for the capitalist system but have deliberately defined Canadian politics in terms of region and ethnicity in order to disguise their true motives. Both parties are so intermeshed with the capitalist system that any apparent choice they provide to the electorate is purely illusory. Other elite theorists observe that party activists overrepresent "elite" characteristics in society in terms of ethnicity and gender, and emphasize the inevitable tendency toward oligarchy within all political parties, such that rank-and-file members have little real power.

ⓈⒸ   The state-centred approach is not overly interested in political parties and argues that it is largely irrelevant which party forms the government because the subsequent "government policy" is developed within the Cabinet and bureaucracy. Such policy is more related to social and economic conditions and to the authorities' priorities than to election promises or party platforms. When parties neglect to develop policy within their ranks and fail to provide distinctive election platforms, they serve to confirm this contention. Even if they do put effort into the generation of party policy and even if they do propose specific policy positions in the campaign, government policies are rarely enacted without some evidence of bureaucratic modification. On the other hand, when a party comes to power fully committed to a new approach, the results are obvious. A Pearsonian commitment to social welfare programs, a Trudeauesque obsession with linguistic rights, or a Mulroneyite determination for free trade and deficit reduction (to say nothing of distinctive NDP, Social Credit, or Conservative approaches at the provincial level) all demonstrate that the state apparatus is not immune from party and societal influences.

DISCUSSION QUESTIONS

1. Why are political parties so prominent at the federal and provincial levels of government in Canada and so insignificant at the municipal level in most cases?

2. What historical events, political personalities, or other factors have been determining influences in the evolution of the Canadian party system?

3. Given the negative implications of the broker system (such as the emphasis on leadership and the lack of clear-cut policy alternatives in many cases), do you feel it would be advantageous to move to a class-based system? Why or why not?

4. Do you agree with the class-based theorists that the Liberals and Conservatives have defined Canadian politics in brokerage terms in order to disguise their own class-based interests?

5. What is the best method of choosing party leaders and the best approach to leadership accountability?

6. Is it possible in this complex, technological, information-driven age for ordinary party members to make useful suggestions for national policies, or is it inevitable that the policymaking function will be turned over to party leaders and their advisers, bureaucrats, and pressure groups?

7. Are the NDP and Reform parties closer to the mass party model than the Liberals and Conservatives?

8. Is there a distinctive ideological base for the major parties in Canada? Is there at least a distinctive, consistent approach to policy questions?

9. How do each of the critical approaches outlined in Chapter 1 enhance our understanding of Canadian parties and the party system?

NOTES

1. R.K. Carty, "Three Party Systems: An Interpretation of the Development of National Politics," in Hugh G. Thorburn, ed., *Party Politics in Canada*, 7th ed. (Scarborough: Prentice Hall Canada, 1996).
2. David E. Smith, "Canadian Political Parties and National Integration," in Alain Gagnon and Brian Tanguay, eds., *Canadian Parties in Transition* (Scarborough: Nelson Canada, 1989). Carty and Smith divide the periods in the same way but use different criteria.
3. J. Murray Beck, *Pendulum of Power* (Scarborough: Prentice-Hall Canada, 1968).
4. Ibid.; W.L. Morton, *The Progressive Party in Canada* (Toronto: University of Toronto Press, 1950).
5. Walter Young, *Anatomy of a Party: The National CCF 1932–1961* (Toronto: University of Toronto Press, 1969); Walter Young, *Democracy and Discontent* (Toronto: Ryerson Press, 1969); and S.M. Lipset, *Agrarian Socialism: The Cooperative Commonwealth Federation in Saskatchewan* (Los Angeles: University of California Press, 1950).
6. Alvin Finkel, *The Social Credit Phenomenon in Alberta* (Toronto: University of Toronto Press, 1989).
7. H.F. Quinn, *The Union Nationale* (Toronto: University of Toronto Press, 1963).
8. Reginald Whitaker, *The Government Party: Organizing and Financing the Liberal Party of Canada 1930–58* (Toronto: University of Toronto Press, 1977).
9. J.L. Granatstein, *The Politics of Survival: The Conservative Party of Canada, 1939–1945* (Toronto: University of Toronto Press, 1967), and George Perlin, *The Tory Syndrome: Leadership Politics in the Progressive Conservative Party* (Montreal: McGill–Queen's University Press, 1980).
10. Lynn McDonald, *The Party That Changed Canada: The New Democratic Party, Then and Now* (Toronto: McClelland and Stewart, 1987); Desmond Morton, *The New Democrats 1961–1986: The Politics of Change* (Toronto: Copp Clark Pitman, 1986); and Alan Whitehorn, *Canadian Socialism: Essays on the CCF and the NDP* (Toronto: Oxford University Press, 1992).
11. Maurice Pinard, *The Rise of a Third Party: A Study in Crisis Politics* (Scarborough: Prentice-Hall Canada, 1971), and Michael Stein, *The Dynamics of Right-Wing Protest: A Political Analysis of Social Credit in Quebec* (Toronto: University of Toronto Press, 1973).
12. Peter C. Newman, *The Distemper of Our Times* (Toronto: McClelland and Stewart, 1968).
13. Jeffrey Simpson, *Discipline of Power: The Conservative Interlude and the Liberal Restoration* (Toronto: Personal Library, 1980).
14. Christina McCall-Newman, *Grits: An Intimate Portrait of the Liberal Party* (Toronto: Macmillan, 1982), and Stephen Clarkson and Christina McCall, *Trudeau and Our Times*, 2 vols. (Toronto: McClelland and Stewart, 1990 and 1994).
15. Barry Kay et al., "The Character of Electoral Change: A Preliminary Report from the 1984 National Election Study," in Joseph Wearing, ed., *The Ballot and Its Message: Voting in Canada* (Toronto: Copp Clark Pitman, 1991).

16. Graham Fraser, *Playing for Keeps* (Toronto: McClelland and Stewart, 1989).

17. Alan Cairns, "An Election to Be Remembered: Canada 1993," *Canadian Public Policy* (September, 1994), and Alan Frizzell et al., *The Canadian General Election of 1993* (Ottawa: Carleton University Press, 1994).

18. H.G. Thorburn, "Interpretations of the Canadian Party System," in H.G. Thorburn, ed., *Party Politics in Canada*, 6th ed. (Scarborough: Prentice-Hall Canada, 1991); R.M. Dawson, *The Government of Canada*, 4th ed. (Toronto: University of Toronto Press, 1963), ch. 21; J.A. Corry and J.E. Hodgetts, *Democratic Government and Politics*, 3rd rev. ed. (Toronto: University of Toronto Press, 1959), ch. VIII; and Paul Fox, "Middle-of-the Road Parties Are the Canadian Tradition," in his *Politics: Canada*, 6th ed. (Toronto: McGraw-Hill Ryerson, 1987).

19. Conrad Winn and John McMenemy, *Political Parties in Canada* (Toronto: McGraw-Hill Ryerson, 1976), pp. 19–26.

20. Janine Brodie and Jane Jenson, *Crisis, Challenge and Change: Party and Class in Canada Revisited* (Ottawa: Carleton University Press, 1988); Charles Taylor, *The Pattern of Politics* (Toronto: McClelland and Stewart, 1970), and Gad Horowitz, "Toward the Democratic Class Struggle," in Trevor Lloyd and Jack McLeod, eds., *Agenda 1970* (Toronto: University of Toronto Press, 1968).

21. On seduction, see Whitaker, *The Government Party*, e.g., the co-opting of Saskatchewan farm leader C.A. Dunning and Humphrey Mitchell from the labour movement; on coercion, see Judy Torrance, *Public Violence in Canada* (Montreal: McGill–Queen's University Press, 1986).

22. The Liberals actually welcomed communist support if such working-class divisions would weaken the CCF. Gad Horowitz, *Canadian Labour in Politics* (Toronto: University of Toronto Press, 1968).

23. Jon Pammett, "Class Voting and Class Consciousness in Canada," *Canadian Review of Sociology and Anthropology* 24, no. 2 (1987), pp. 269–90; Keith Archer, "The Failure of the New Democratic Party: Unions, Unionists, and Politics in Canada," *Canadian Journal of Political Science* (June 1985), pp. 353–66; Michael Ornstein et al., "Region, Class and Political Culture in Canada," *Canadian Journal of Political Science* (June 1980), pp. 227–71; and Elisabeth Gidengil, "Class and Region in Canadian Voting: A Dependency Interpretation," *Canadian Journal of Political Science* (September 1989), pp. 563–87.

24. Brodie and Jenson, *Crisis, Challenge and Change*; Gagnon and Tanguay, eds., *Canadian Parties in Transition*.

25. Horowitz, "Toward the Democratic Class Struggle," p. 254.

26. Thorburn, "Interpretations of the Canadian Party System"; Whitaker, *The Government Party*; and Perlin, *The Tory Syndrome*.

27. John Meisel, "Decline of Party in Canada," in H.G. Thorburn, ed., *Party Politics in Canada*, 5th ed., (Scarborough: Prentice-Hall Canada, 1985), and John Meisel, "The Dysfunctions of Canadian Parties: An Exploratory Mapping," in Thorburn, ed., *Party Politics in Canada*, 6th ed.

28. Gagnon and Tanguay, eds., *Canadian Parties in Transition*.

29. S.M. Lipset, "Democracy in Alberta," *Canadian Forum* (November/December 1954); and Roger Gibbins, *Regionalism: Territorial Politics in Canada and the United States* (Toronto: Butterworths, 1982), ch. 5.

30. Maurice Pinard, *The Rise of a Third Party*; "Third Parties in Canada Revisited," *Canadian Journal of Political Science* (September 1973), pp. 439–60.

31. C.B. Macpherson, *Democracy in Alberta: Social Credit and the Party System* (Toronto: University of Toronto Press, 1953).

32. J.F. Conway, "Explaining the Roots of Canada's Third Parties," *Canadian Journal of Political Science* (1978), pp. 99–124.

33. Much of the material in this section is based on party constitutions and interviews with leading party officials. Many of the observations on the NDP are confirmed in Keith Archer and Alan Whitehorn, *Political Activists: The NDP in Convention* (Toronto: Oxford University Press, 1997).

34. John C. Courtney, *The Selection of National Party Leaders* (Toronto: Macmillan, 1973); John C. Courtney, *Do Conventions Matter? Choosing National Party Leaders in Canada* (Montreal: McGill–Queen's University Press, 1995); Heather MacIvor, "The Leadership Convention: An Institution under Stress," and Alan Whitehorn and Keith Archer, "Party Activists and Political Leadership: A Case Study of the NDP," in Maureen Mancuso et al., eds., *Leaders and Leadership in Canada* (Toronto: Oxford University Press, 1994).

35. Joseph Wearing, "Can an Old Dog Teach Itself New Tricks? The Liberal Party Attempts Reform," in Gagnon and Tanguay, eds., *Canadian Parties in Transition*.

36. Donald Smiley, *Canada in Question: Federalism in the Eighties*, 3rd ed. (Toronto: McGraw-Hill Ryerson, 1980), and Rand Dyck, "Relations between Federal and Provincial Parties," in Gagnon and Tanguay, eds., *Canadian Parties in Transition*.

37. Robert Michels, *Political Parties* (New York: Free Press, 1966).

38. Wearing, "Can an Old Dog Teach Itself New Tricks?"

39. Winn and McMenemy, *Political Parties in Canada*, pp. 4–5.

40. Dawson, *The Government of Canada*, pp. 466–72, and J.R. Mallory, *The Structure of Canadian Government* (Toronto: Macmillan, 1971), p. 197.

41. Louis Hartz, *The Founding of New Societies* (New York: Harcourt, Brace and World, 1964); Gad Horowitz, "Conservatism, Liberalism and Socialism in Canada: An Interpretation," *Canadian Journal of Economics and Political Science* (May 1966), pp. 143–71; Horowitz, "Notes on 'Conservatism, Liberalism and Socialism in Canada,'" *Canadian Journal of Political Science* (June 1978), pp. 383–99; and William Christian and Colin Campbell, *Political Parties and Ideologies in Canada*, 3rd ed. (Toronto: McGraw-Hill Ryerson, 1990), and *Parties, Leaders, and Ideologies in Canada* (Toronto: McGraw-Hill Ryerson, 1996). The anticipated ideological distinction among the three traditional parties was confirmed with respect to the treatment of public-sector employees in André Blais et al., *Governments, Parties and Public Sector Employees* (Montreal: McGill–Queen's University Press, 1997), as well as in Archer and Whitehorn, *Political Activists*, and in Paul M. Sniderman et al., *The Clash of Rights: Liberty, Equality, and Legitimacy in Pluralist Democracy* (New Haven: Yale University Press, 1996).

42. Neil Nevitte, Herman Bakvis, and Roger Gibbins, "The Ideological Contours of 'New Politics' in Canada: Policy, Mobilization and Partisan Support," *Canadian Journal of Political Science* (September 1989), pp. 475–503.

43. Horowitz, "Conservatism, Liberalism and Socialism in Canada."

44. James McAllister, "Do Parties Make a Difference?" in Gagnon and Tanguay, eds., *Canadian Parties in Transition*; Winn and McMenemy, *Political Parties in Canada*.

45. Duncan Cameron, "Political Discourse in the Eighties," in Gagnon and Tanguay, eds., *Canadian Parties in Transition*.

46. Walter Stewart, *Dismantling the State* (Toronto: Stoddart, 1998), and Stephen McBride and John Shields, *Dismantling a Nation: The Transition to Corporate Rule in Canada* (Halifax: Fernwood Publishing, 1997).

47. On this subject, see Anthony Westell, *Reinventing Canada* (Toronto: Dundurn Press, 1994), and Christopher Dunn, *Canadian Political Debates: Opposing Views on Issues That Divide Canadians* (Toronto: McClelland and Stewart, 1995), Part Six.

48. Brooke Jeffrey, *Hard Right Turn: The New Face of Neo-Conservatism in Canada* (Toronto: HarperCollins, 1999), and Trevor Harrison, *Of Passionate Intensity: Right-Wing Populism and the Reform Party of Canada* (Toronto: University of Toronto Press, 1995).

49. Neil Nevitte et al., *Unsteady State: The 1997 Canadian Federal Election* (Toronto: Oxford University Press, 1999).

50. Pierre Lortie, "The Challenge of Electoral Reform: Combining Innovation with Continuity," Royal Commission on Electoral Reform and Party Financing, Winnipeg, November 26, 1990.

51. W.T. Stanbury, *Business–Government Relations in Canada* (Toronto: Methuen, 1986), ch. 4.

FURTHER READING

General

Azoulay, Dan. *Canadian Political Parties: Historical Readings*. Toronto: Irwin Publishing, 1999.

Brodie, Janine, and Jane Jenson. *Crisis, Challenge and Change: Party and Class in Canada Revisited*. Ottawa: Carleton University Press, 1988.

Campbell, Colin, and William Christian. *Parties, Leaders, and Ideologies in Canada*. Toronto: McGraw-Hill Ryerson, 1996.

Carrigan, D.O. *Canadian Party Platforms: 1867–1968.* Toronto: Copp-Clark, 1968.

Carty, R. Kenneth. *Canadian Political Party Systems.* Peterborough: Broadview Press, 1992.

Christian, William, and Colin Campbell. *Political Parties and Ideologies in Canada.* 3rd ed. Toronto: McGraw-Hill Ryerson, 1990.

Courtney, John C. *Do Conventions Matter? Choosing National Party Leaders in Canada.* Montreal: McGill–Queen's University Press, 1995.

Courtney, John C. *The Selection of National Party Leaders.* Toronto: Macmillan, 1973.

Forbes, H.D., ed. *Canadian Political Thought.* Toronto: Oxford University Press, 1985.

Horowitz, Gad. "Conservatism, Liberalism and Socialism in Canada: An Interpretation." *Canadian Journal of Political Science* (May 1966), pp. 143–71.

Nevitte, Neil, et al. *Unsteady State: The 1997 Canadian Federal Election.* Toronto: Oxford University Press, 2000.

Perlin, George. *Party Democracy in Canada.* Scarborough: Prentice-Hall Canada, 1988.

Simpson, Jeffrey. *Spoils of Power: The Politics of Patronage.* Toronto: Collins, 1988.

Tanguay, A.B., and A.-G. Gagnon, eds. *Canadian Parties in Transition,* 2nd ed. Scarborough: Nelson Canada, 1996.

Thorburn, H.G. *Party Politics in Canada.* Scarborough: Prentice-Hall Canada, 7 editions, incl. 1994.

Wearing, Joseph. *Strained Relations: Canadian Parties and Voters.* Toronto: McClelland and Stewart, 1988.

Liberal Party

Goldfarb, Martin, and Thomas Axworthy. *Marching to a Different Drummer.* Toronto: Stoddart, 1988.

Greenspon, Edward, and Anthony Wilson-Smith. *Double Vision: The Inside Story of the Liberals in Power.* Toronto: Doubleday, 1996.

McCall-Newman, Christina. *Grits: An Intimate Portrait of the Liberal Party.* Toronto: Macmillan, 1982.

Wearing, Joseph. *The L-Shaped Party: The Liberal Party of Canada 1958–1980.* Toronto: McGraw-Hill Ryerson, 1981.

Whitaker, Reginald. *The Government Party: Organizing and Financing the Liberal Party of Canada 1930–58.* Toronto: University of Toronto Press, 1977.

Conservative Party

English, John. *The Decline of Politics: The Conservatives and the Party System 1901–20.* Toronto: University of Toronto Press, 1977.

Granatstein, J.L. *The Politics of Survival: The Conservative Party of Canada, 1939–1945.* Toronto: University of Toronto Press, 1967.

Martin, Patrick, Allan Gregg, and George Perlin. *Contenders: The Tory Quest for Power.* Scarborough: Prentice-Hall Canada, 1983.

McLaughlin, David. *Poisoned Chalice: The Last Campaign of the Progressive Conservative Party?* Toronto: Dundurn Press, 1994.

Perlin, George. *The Tory Syndrome: Leadership Politics in the Progressive Conservative Party.* Montreal: McGill–Queen's University Press, 1980.

Simpson, Jeffrey. *Discipline of Power: The Conservative Interlude and the Liberal Restoration.* Toronto: Personal Library, 1980.

Taylor, Charles. *Radical Tories.* Toronto: House of Anansi, 1982.

CCF/NDP

Archer, Keith, and Alan Whitehorn. *Political Activists: The NDP in Convention.* Toronto: Oxford University Press, 1997.

Avakumovic, Ivan. *Socialism in Canada.* Toronto: McClelland and Stewart, 1978.

Lipset, S.M. *Agrarian Socialism: The Cooperative Commonwealth Federation in Saskatchewan.* Los Angeles: University of California Press, 1950.

McDonald, Lynn. *The Party That Changed Canada: The New Democratic Party, Then and Now.* Toronto: McClelland and Stewart, 1987.

McLeod, Ian. *Under Siege: The Federal NDP in the Nineties.* Toronto: Lorimer, 1994.

Morton, Desmond. *The New Democrats 1961–1986: The Politics of Change.* Toronto: Copp Clark Pitman, 1986.

Whitehorn, Alan. *Canadian Socialism: Essays on the CCF and the NDP.* Toronto: Oxford University Press, 1992.

Young, Walter. *Anatomy of a Party: The National CCF 1932–1961.* Toronto: University of Toronto Press, 1969.

Social Credit

Finkel, Alvin. *The Social Credit Phenomenon in Alberta.* Toronto: University of Toronto Press, 1989.

Irving, J.A. *The Social Credit Movement in Alberta.* Toronto: University of Toronto Press, 1959.

Macpherson, C.B. *Democracy in Alberta: Social Credit and the Party System.* Toronto: University of Toronto Press, 1953.

Pinard, Maurice. *The Rise of a Third Party: A Study in Crisis Politics.* Scarborough: Prentice-Hall Canada, 1971.

Stein, Michael. *The Dynamics of Right-Wing Protest: A Political Analysis of Social Credit in Quebec.* Toronto: University of Toronto Press, 1973.

Reform Party

Dobbin, Murray. *Preston Manning and the Reform Party.* Toronto: Lorimer, 1991.

Flanagan, Tom. *Waiting for the Wave.* Toronto: Stoddart, 1995.

Jeffrey, Brooke. *Hard Right Turn: The New Face of Neo-Conservatism in Canada.* Toronto: HarperCollins, 1999.

Harrison, Trevor. *Of Passionate Intensity: Right-Wing Populism and the Reform Party of Canada.* Toronto: University of Toronto Press, 1995.

Manning, Preston. *The New Canada.* Toronto: Macmillan, 1992.

Sharpe, Sydney, and Donald Braid. *Storming Babylon: Preston Manning and the Rise of the Reform Party.* Toronto: Key Porter Books, 1992.

Chapter 14

Parties, Voting, and THE ELECTION campaign

Why were Jean Chrétien's Liberals re-elected by such a narrow margin in 1997? Why were the election results so regionalized? How were the local campaigns of candidates organized? How seriously should we take the Liberals' election manifesto, "Red Book II"? How much do party standings in the public opinion polls change during the course of the campaign? To what extent does media coverage of the campaign and the leaders' debate influence the results?

Elections are not only the most colourful and exciting element in the Canadian political system; they are also in many ways the most important. Certain elections are great landmarks in a country's history and often change its course. Almost all the daily efforts of parties and politicians are ultimately geared toward maximizing their support in the next electoral contest. The election campaign constitutes the area in which political parties, the mass media, public opinion polls, and political participation all come together to play their most extensive role.

The primary function of elections is to allow the mass of citizens to choose their parliamentary representatives and, indirectly, their governmental leaders. In structural-functional terms, elections serve to recruit many of those who subsequently perform the rule-making function. Besides recruiting political leaders, elections serve to inform the public, which is part of the political socialization function. Moreover, both political parties and pressure groups take advantage of elections to articulate certain interests, and most parties aggregate interests in trying to put forward a comprehensive, attractive election platform. Elections also serve the political communication function of transmitting information among the various participants within the system and between the system and its environment.

Beyond the functions as outlined by Almond in Chapter 1, elections serve a legitimation function. That is, by exercising their franchise, voters legitimize the power of those elected by agreeing to be bound by their decisions. This activity presumably also generates popular support for the political system as a whole. Elections similarly help to integrate the system by putting everyone in it through a common national experience. To the extent that policy concerns are central to the campaign, elections may also provide policy guidelines for the authorities and a feeling of political efficacy for the voters.

The official side of the electoral system having been examined in Chapter 12, this chapter explores the more colourful side of the campaign—that dominated by political parties, candidates, the media, and public opinion polls. The chapter has three main parts: the national party campaign; the local candidate campaign; and electoral behaviour and party support.[1]

THE NATIONAL PARTY CAMPAIGN
Party Headquarters and Pre-Writ Preparations

At the national level, political parties usually start thinking about the next election some two years before they expect it to be called, and start planning in earnest about a year ahead. This planning entails setting up a national campaign committee, which ponders such matters as strategy, policy, image, and budget. Most federal parties also have campaign committees in each province, with varying degrees of centralization or decentralization of authority. Parties usually hire extra organizers in the pre-election period and deploy them to reactivate local associations. Funds permitting, party headquarters also conducts public opinion polls throughout the inter-election period in order to see how the voters perceive the various leaders, parties, and issues. For the party in power such polls are central to deciding when to call the election in the first place. Even though the governing party conceals the chosen date, obvious election preparation encourages the other parties to get into the act, such that an unstoppable momentum usually develops.

Despite the fact that the governing party has the right to choose election day, neither the Conservatives in 1993 nor the Liberals in 1997 were particularly well prepared for the elections they instigated. In choosing the June 2, 1997, election date, for example, Liberal strategists were somewhat concerned that only three and a half years had elapsed since the last contest. Nevertheless, Michael Marzolini's POLLARA polling indicated that the party was well ahead of its rivals, the Liberals would have the advantage of being best prepared for the short 36-day election period, and they could claim that they had implemented most of their 1993 platform. As nominations and other preparatory electoral organizational work proceeded, the government made a number of pre-election announcements that should have increased its lead.[2] In addition, to ward off a charge of being insensitive to the serious flooding that had suddenly taken place in Manitoba, the party flew Prime Minister Jean Chrétien to that province the day before he called the election, but unfavourable television coverage of his visit betrayed the opportunism of the effort. Moreover, when Chrétien announced the election on April 27, he had trouble explaining to the media why he had done so.

Another party activity that begins before the calling of the election is the search for good candidates. This is essentially a task of the local party organizations, and headquarters rarely imposes a candidate on an unwilling constituency association. However, the leader, regional lieutenants, and party organizers are always on the lookout for new blood, and head office may try to parachute a few "star" candidates into safe seats. The Liberals, Conservatives, and NDP all ran a full slate of candidates up to and including the 1997 elections, so where local organizations were weak, the national party sometimes had to take the initiative to find a candidate for them. In order to ensure a minimum number of candidates of Cabinet calibre, to guarantee enough female and multicultural candidates, and to avoid controversial local choices, Chrétien had the party give him, as leader, the power to appoint candidates in certain cases. His exercise of this discretion was more frequent and controversial in 1993 than in 1997.

By *Dan Murphy* (Vancouver Province). *Reproduced with permission.*

The NDP hoped to achieve gender parity in its 1993 and 1997 candidates, but was later content with having nearly 50 percent women *or* visible minorities. Even so, this entailed considerable and often difficult negotiation between headquarters and riding associations. In total in 1997, 408 out of 1672 candidates, or 24.4 percent, were women. The percentage of women candidates in the five main parties was as follows: NDP 35.5, Liberal 27.9, Bloc 21.3, PC 18.6, and Reform 10.1.[3] To offset the image of its parliamentary representation, the Reform Party's headquarters was more concerned to encourage the nomination of young and multicultural candidates.

National fundraising is another activity that goes on between elections, although it intensifies immediately before and during the election period. This topic was discussed in Chapter 12. Despite the state of financial crisis that hit the PCs and NDP after the 1993 election, all parties were in relatively good financial shape going into 1997.

Once the election is called, party headquarters continues to perform such pre-writ activities as polling, fundraising, and candidate recruitment. Either before or immediately after the election call, headquarters is also engaged in holding campaign colleges, schools, and seminars for candidates, campaign managers, and other local campaign officials. Headquarters will also design logos, other artwork, and as the campaign progresses, one or more leaflets that candidates can order or adapt for their own local purposes. In some cases, nowadays, it even produces videos. Another headquarters activity is the preparation of draft "issue letters" and fact sheets for candidates to use, either in promoting their own party's platform or in attacking that of others. During the campaign, headquarters normally communicates with candidate campaigns on a daily basis, via fax or e-mail, in efforts to bolster morale, ensure uniformity of presentation, and alert the candidates to a change in course.

Election Strategy

Election strategy involves deciding which groups within the electorate are to be targeted; whether to emphasize leader or issues, and, if the latter, which issues; and whether to mount an offensive or defensive campaign. In 1997, for example, a weakness of all parties except Reform was that they deviated from their own game plan and priorities to defend themselves against criticism from opponents. Strategists determine the itinerary of the leader's tour, the content and range of the party's advertising, and where extra organizational efforts will be concentrated. During the campaign, the national campaign committee discusses such things as "modification to the leader's tour, daily tracking of polling results, focus group findings, ongoing testing of campaign slogans and phrasing, the final changes of the ads and when to replace one round of ads with subsequent ones, and preparations for the leaders' debates."[4]

The Liberals basically hoped to get the 1997 election over with while they were still ahead in the polls. They had a nationally respected leader, a popular Finance minister, and a successful performance in reducing the government deficit, and expected to take advantage of Bloc Québécois divisions in Quebec. To the extent that they had any strategy beyond such opportunism, they failed to transmit it to the media, the public, or even their own local activists.[5] Most of the key Liberal strategists worked in the Prime Minister's Office, except for John Rae, seconded from Power Corp. in Montreal. They were divided on the fundamental question of whether the party should emphasize its record of deficit reduction or propose new programs, and this indecision was reflected in the early stages of the campaign. The Liberals were then thrown off track when Preston Manning acquired an advance copy of their election platform and leaked it two days early. In the end, the Liberals did not succeed in exploiting the divisions within the Bloc Québécois; they even alienated many Quebec voters when Chrétien finally revealed that in his opinion separation would require a majority of more than 50 percent in a referendum. If this pronouncement was intended to bolster the party's Western flank, it did not succeed. They lost ground everywhere during the campaign and their ultimate 37.9 percent of the vote gave them a majority of only five seats.

The Conservatives planned to exploit the popularity of their attractive, popular, and fluently bilingual leader, Jean Charest, but beyond that, the party was divided on election strategy, image, and policy.[6] Charest espoused "distinct society" status for Quebec, for example, but was reluctant to say so west of Ontario. The PCs criticized the Liberal record on unemployment and tried to make the case that their promised tax cuts would lead to increased jobs, as Mike Harris claimed had happened in Ontario. Indeed, the party targeted former Tory supporters in that province in particular, and hoped that the Ontario premier would endorse them, which he never did.

With the federal deficit virtually eliminated, the Reform Party had to find another focus for the 1997 campaign.[7] Based on the successful Mike Harris strategy of releasing his election platform (the Common Sense Revolution) a year ahead of time, Reform produced its own platform in October 1996. By the spring of 1997, however, a hard line on Quebec seemed to be the best way to consolidate its support in the West. Instead of the regular polling done by some of the other parties, Reform relied on one large poll conducted by André Turcotte of ATRS in April 1997. Preston Manning continued to argue against any kind of distinct or special status for Quebec—that all provinces were equal—but that Quebec would benefit from Reform policy of devolving federal powers to *all* provinces. This emphasis, together with its serendipitous leaking of the Liberal platform, gave Reform control of the election agenda to a large extent, and it often received top billing on nightly television newscasts. On the other hand, its anti-Quebec message was not much help in the objective of making inroads into Ontario; voters in that province preferred a more moderate approach to the question of national unity.

By instinct, the NDP preferred to talk about government involvement in job creation, trying to appeal to supporters who had drifted away to the Liberals in 1993.[8] This approach was mainly popular in Atlantic Canada, with high unemployment exacerbated in this period by the decline of the fishing industry. The Liberals had also alienated that region by putting deficit reduction ahead of social programs. With affection for the NDP leader, Alexa McDonough, because of her Atlantic origins, this region responded with an unprecedented degree of support, as did women generally. But the NDP message was so different from that of other parties that it was not taken seriously by most of the media and commentators.[9] On the other hand, the NDP hoped to avoid the national unity question, fearing that it would lose Western votes to Reform if that party was successful in making it an election issue. Although not as affluent as the Liberals, the NDP hired ComQuest to do its polling, and also relied to a limited extent on small focus groups. The NDP originally targeted about 50 potentially winnable ridings, but reduced this by half as the campaign progressed.

When Lucien Bouchard moved to Quebec to become premier in 1996, he was succeeded as Bloc Québécois leader by Michel Gauthier. Gauthier never achieved a comfortable command of the party, however, and was replaced by Gilles Duceppe after a divisive leadership race only a month before the election call.[10] These developments encouraged the Liberals to expect gains in Quebec at the Bloc's expense. Shortly after the campaign started, the BQ faced another problem: former Quebec premier Jacques Parizeau's newly published memoirs claimed that, contrary to what the party had said during the 1995 referendum campaign, he would have made a unilateral declaration of independence if the referendum result had been successful. This incident cast a pall of dishonesty over the whole independence movement. But while Quebec nationalists temporarily moved toward Jean Charest's PC camp, given his position on "distinct society" and his performance in the debates, they later went back to voting for the Bloc after Reform's anti-Quebec television commercial made them feel more defensive. The Bloc successfully argued that it was still needed to speak up for Quebec in Ottawa.

Election Platform

One of the Liberals' great assets in the 1993 campaign was their "Red Book," *Creating Opportunity: The Liberal Plan for Canada*. To some extent the Red Book was based on a thinkers' conference in 1991 and policy debates at a party convention in 1992. Chrétien claimed that, if elected, he would adhere to every word, and it provided a tremendous prop for a leader who was otherwise not policy-oriented in his public appearances.[11] The Liberals claimed by 1996 that they had implemented 78 percent of their promises, although conspicuously unfulfilled

NDP leader Alexa McDonough (centre) raises her arms in celebration with local candidates while on a campaign stop in Toronto in 1997. (Frank Gunn/Canapress)

was their promise which, however worded, was widely understood to mean that they would get rid of the GST. The Liberals put much effort into developing another comprehensive 102-page platform in 1997, often referred to as "Red Book II." It was primarily based on *A Record of Achievement: A Report on the Liberal Government's Thirty-Six Months in Office*, together with the 1997 budget, but as a pale imitation of the original, it attracted virtually no attention.[12]

The Conservatives turned to the architects of the 1995 Mike Harris victory in Ontario, indeed two of the authors of the Common Sense Revolution document, to prepare their election platform.[13] This 61-page booklet, based on the Winnipeg policy resolutions of 1996 and party research, was released in mid-March of 1997. Inspired by Harris, its centrepiece was a 10 percent reduction in the federal income tax, even though polling generally indicated that instead of a tax cut, Canadians preferred to put excess government revenues toward deficit elimination and increased spending on health care.

As it had done in 1993, the 1997 NDP election platform committee combed through party convention resolutions to develop a coherent and appealing platform, which again emphasized government involvement in the creation of jobs. It ended up with a 53-page document, *A Framework for Canada's Future*, the draft of which was presented to the federal party convention in Regina just prior to the election call.[14]

The Reform Party had passed a variety of planks at its various assemblies, and these formed the basis for its 1997 election platform. The 24-page document was called *Fresh Start for Canadians*, and was issued a year in advance.[15] Since deficit reduction had been appropriated by the Liberals since 1993 and was no longer much of an issue, Reform turned to the place of Quebec in Confederation as its main focus, along with tax cuts, family values, criminal justice, and reducing the size of government.

Even though the Bloc Québécois had a single overriding objective, to remove Quebec from Canada, it drafted a 122-page election platform and later issued a 35-page summary, both of which barely referred to Quebec sovereignty.[16]

The Leader's Tour

The leader's tour consists of each party leader crisscrossing the country many times over the 36-day campaign period. Almost like a royal tour, party "advance men" go ahead of the leader to make sure that every detail is in place. The leader is then accompanied by a horde of strategists and support staff, as well as by reporters who pay to travel aboard the party-chartered plane or bus. All this effort is expended not only to attract attention in the areas visited, but also to generate national media coverage. Since this kind of coverage is free, in contrast to paid advertising, it is eagerly sought, and parties spare no trouble or expense to obtain it. Frizzell and Westell write that parties

> should arrange events every day so that the TV crews, pressed by deadlines and demands from home stations for footage, will have little option but to picture the leader in a favourable setting ... [and] ensure that in every speech or statement there is a phrase that sums up the message in a couple of seconds.[17]

An innovation in 1997 was that instead of each network placing a complete crew of its own on each of the leader's tours, the five major television networks—CBC, CTV, Global, Radio-Canada, and TVA—pooled their resources and personnel on the party leaders' campaign planes and buses.

Media News Coverage

Parties hope that the leader's tour will garner them one story every day on the national television news and in daily newspapers. Such was generally the case when there were only three national parties in the race, but with five party leaders to cover in 1993 and 1997, networks sometimes grouped different campaigns together so that each party did not get an individual item on the national news every night. This also reduced the length of leaders' sound bites.[18]

In previous elections, television and newspapers gave virtually equal time or space to the various party leaders, although the kind of treatment was not always so equitable. But a study of media coverage in 1997 found wide disparities between the CBC National news and the front page of *The Globe and Mail*. The former had relatively equitable coverage of the five parties (Liberal 16.3 percent, Reform 14.7 percent, Bloc 11.8 percent, PC 9.5 percent, and NDP 8.3 percent), but while the Liberals gained the largest amount of coverage, 62 percent of it was deemed unfavourable, compared with only 14 percent that was favourable. As for the front page of *The Globe and Mail*, the Liberals received almost as much coverage as the four other parties combined, but 55 percent of it was unfavourable, compared with only 15 percent that was favourable.[19]

In addition to such regular news coverage, another innovation of 1997 was CBC Newsworld's provision of 15 minutes of television time per day (Monday to Friday) for each party. The first five minutes could be used for a statement from the party leader or other spokesperson, followed by a ten-minute question period. The Cable Public Affairs Channel (CPAC) also tried to be helpful to voters in various ways, such as in giving viewers a feel for the logistics of a local campaign.

National Media Advertising

Each party turns its national paid media advertising over to one or more advertising agencies along with at least some indication of the party's campaign strategy. As noted in Chapter 11, the most important part of the media campaign is television, and most parties spend huge amounts of money on the production of television commercials alone.

The purchase of broadcast time is regulated by the Elections Act, and cannot start until a week after the election call. Representatives of registered parties meet with the Broadcasting Arbitrator before the election to try to agree on an allocation of broadcasting time. If they cannot agree, the arbitrator makes the allocation within the guidelines of the act. It requires each broadcaster to make available, for purchase by registered political parties, six and one-half hours of prime time during the campaign. Such an allocation among parties is primarily based on the number of seats held in the House of Commons and on popular vote received in the previous election. No party can receive more than one-half of the total time, but candidates are allowed to purchase time for their own use outside these hours allotted to parties. Having been awarded over twice as much time as the Liberals and three times as much as the NDP in 1988, the Conservatives were allowed to saturate the airwaves in the last week of the campaign. In addition to purchasable time, parties are awarded free radio and television time in the same proportions.

Many observers, including supporters of minor parties, considered this distribution of paid and free broadcasting time to be extremely unfair, and the Royal Commission on Electoral Reform recommended a more equitable system. Part of the problem is that it is not known until midway through the campaign which parties would be able to nominate at least 50 candidates and therefore become registered. In 1992, the Reform Party went to court and successfully challenged its original allotment of 11 minutes for the forthcoming election. Since the Broadcasting Arbitrator himself was still dissatisfied with the distribution in 1997, he used his discretion to allot one-third of the time equally among all the registered parties, which significantly increased the time of smaller parties. The results are shown in Table 14.1, which omits parties that ultimately failed to qualify, that is, were unable to nominate 50 candidates.

When the Reform Party case went to the Alberta Court of Appeal in 1995, that court struck down the clause that prevented a party from purchasing more than their allocated time on any station. Thus, in 1997, parties were free to purchase more time than allocated to them under the act, providing stations were willing to sell them such time and subject to the overall limits on each party's election expenses. The official allocation therefore became most significant as the basis for the distribution of free time for each party. Another court case had effectively removed the blackout rules that prohibited candidate advertising on election day and the day before, although the decision left intact the prohibition on party advertising during the last 48 hours.[20]

One of the most memorable, if short-lived, negative commercials was that run by the Tories in 1993. It featured Jean Chrétien's face (the left side slightly paralyzed from a childhood disease) with such voice-over comments as "I personally would be very embarrassed if he were to become prime minister of Canada" and "Is this a prime minister?" After an instantaneous public uproar, Kim Campbell had it removed.[21] An almost equally striking commercial in the 1997 campaign was sponsored by the Reform Party. It showed a red, slashed circle stamped over the faces of Jean Chrétien, Jean Charest, Gilles Duceppe, and Lucien Bouchard, and essentially said, "We've had enough political leaders from Quebec." Above all, this com-

TABLE 14.1   **Allocation of Broadcast Time, 1997 Election (in Minutes)**

Liberal Party	118
Reform Party	51
Bloc Québécois	43
Progressive Conservative Party	34
NDP	26
Natural Law Party	17
Green Party	13
Christian Heritage Party	13
Marxist-Leninist Party	12
Canadian Action Party	6

Source: Report of the Broadcasting Arbitrator, *included in the* Report of the Chief Electoral Officer *for the 1997 election. Reproduced with the permission of the Minister of Public Works and Government Services Canada, 2000.*

mercial was designed to undercut Jean Charest after his "victories" in the leaders' debates. Apart from other parties' "attack" ads against the Reform Party in Western Canada, the 1997 commercials were rather bland, especially those of the Liberal Party. The fact that the PCs used 15 national television commercials in contrast to eight or nine in the case of the other parties has been cited as a sign of the Tories' inability to find the right package.[22] Being a national party, the Liberals had to buy television commercial time in all parts of the country, whereas the other parties, especially Reform and the Bloc, could save money by buying on a regional basis. The Reform Party left radio and print advertising for candidates to do on their own, while the NDP used radio commercials effectively in Nova Scotia.

The Leaders' Debates

Another main aspect of the national campaign is the televised leaders' debate.[23] These have been held in 1968, 1979, 1984, 1988, 1993, and 1997 (that is, every election since 1968 except 1972, 1974, and 1980), and are probably here to stay. Debates tend to benefit the opposition and minor party leaders who might otherwise have difficulty obtaining coverage, but it would be virtually impossible for the incumbent prime minister to refuse such a debate anymore. Originally a by-product of the influence of American presidential politics, the debates have become crucial aspects of the campaign because of the combined importance of leaders and television.

The leaders' debates are not mentioned in either the Canada Elections Act or the television broadcasting regulations, and the consortium of television stations that carry them essentially set the rules. The recommendation of the Royal Commission on Electoral Reform and Party Financing that the debates become obligatory and regulated has not been implemented. The debates have to fit into the television networks' schedules and are held when least advertising revenue would be lost. In 1993, with a large number of parties in the race, the consortium agreed that only five parties would take part: those that were represented in Parliament and that had had a consistent impact in public debates and public opinion. Mel Hurtig, leader of the new National Party of Canada, went to court to try to force his way into the debate, but did not succeed. The 1997 debates also consisted of the leaders of the five largest parties.

Although they are carefully trained and briefed (speechwriters prepare opening and closing statements and one-liners), the leaders are in a much less controlled setting than they are used to. The debates are one of the few opportunities for the public to see them functioning on their own. The 1984 and 1988 debates each featured a dramatic one-on-one exchange between Brian Mulroney and John Turner that was also endlessly replayed afterward. The 1993 and 1997 leaders' debates were less dramatic than in the two previous cases, partly because with five leaders involved, there was less opportunity for one-on-one confrontations. Two hours long, divided into four segments, the 1997 debates featured questions asked by members of the studio audience as well as selected journalists. Since 1984, there have been separate French and English debates on successive nights, making it immensely beneficial for a party leader to be bilingual. Alexa McDonough was not overly active in the French debate in 1997, and Preston Manning was a virtual bystander. In 1997, Chrétien tried to act subdued and prime ministerial, and was obviously more comfortable in French than in English, while Manning's practice of asking questions of the other leaders had the effect of reducing his own air time.[24]

As noted, each party immediately sends forth its "spin doctors" to persuade reporters that its leader won, but whether the public makes up its own mind on the winner or awaits the verdict of media commentators is not entirely certain. Each leader's performance is judged in relation to the others, as well as relative to the media's expectations. As an example of pack journalism at its height,[25] it was widely felt that Jean Charest "won" both the English and French debates in 1997. About two-thirds of the electorate watched at least one debate in both 1984 and 1988, about 55 percent in 1993, and about 50 percent in 1997.[26] Although the size of the audience appears to be declining, those who watch the debates tend to be well-

By Graham Harrop (The Globe and Mail). *Reproduced with permission.*

informed, peer-group opinion leaders who may well influence others who failed to tune in themselves. Partly because of the large size of the audience and partly because sound bites may be replayed afterwards, the debates "dominate journalistic commentary for at least several days." On the other hand, the debates should not be overemphasized, because "they can also be rapidly overtaken by other campaign events."[27] In fact, the most memorable aspect of the 1997 debates was that the moderator of the French debate collapsed just as Chrétien was to answer a question on what majority he would accept on a vote for Quebec independence, and the debate had to be adjourned and resumed some days later.

THE LOCAL CANDIDATE CAMPAIGN
Nomination

With a permanent voters' list now in place, local constituency associations no longer get to provide the returning officer with a list of names of party supporters who wish to be enumerators, so each party's first priority is the **nomination** of its candidate. In the case of incumbents, ambitious newcomers, and those who anticipate the date of the next election, the nomination meeting is often held before the election is called. This allows many preparations, such as the production of lawn signs, to be made ahead of time so that the campaign can get off to a strong and early start.

Given the explicit recruitment function of elections, it turns out that parties have nominated, and voters supported, a set of candidates quite unrepresentative of the general population. Nominated candidates overrepresent all the "elite" variables in Canadian society—class (upper-middle), ethnicity (anglophone), religion (prestige Protestant and Roman Catholic), and gender (male). Historically, the largest single category of candidates has been lawyers, although other professionals and businesspeople of the same socioeconomic status are now common as well. Parties usually nominate francophones in French-Canadian constituencies, but not many non-British or non-French candidates appeared until recently. Besides the working class, women have been the most underrepresented of any demographic group, although the number of women candidates has increased significantly in the past few elections.

Because of its tendency to attract a certain number of racists and other undesirables, prospective Reform Party candidates must complete a form detailing their background, and the local nomination and selection committee screens potential candidates and undertakes background checks. If an "undesirable" person still manages to get nominated, the leadership may have to expel a candidate, as it did in one case in 1993.

The Local Campaign

Once the nomination has taken place, a campaign committee headed by the campaign manager is established (see Figure 14.1). In most campaigns the other key official is the canvass organizer, who sets up the door-to-door "foot canvass" to distribute literature and/or the telephone canvass. Whether canvassers contact voters on the doorstep or on the phone, the object

....

Figure 14.1   Structure of a Typical Local Campaign Committee

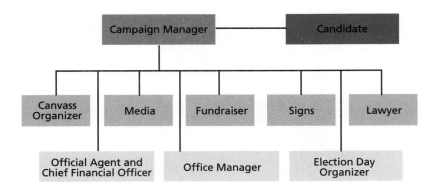

is only secondarily to spread the party's message. Canvassers primarily hope to discover the party or candidate preferences of prospective voters and to seek out their own supporters. Armed with a voters' list, they will put a positive, negative, or other distinguishing mark beside the names of all voters contacted. To cover an entire constituency in this fashion, especially if it is done two or three times as is often attempted by the NDP, requires a veritable army of volunteers and an elaborate hierarchical organization.[28] Since the campaign will need volunteers for many other tasks, and since few people relish door-to-door canvassing, the canvass organizer will probably not have enough workers and therefore have to concentrate efforts in priority polls. If money is more plentiful than personnel, the local campaign may rely instead on media advertising, but as at the national level, the increasing fragmentation of the television audience raises doubts about whether this is a good investment.

In recent elections, some constituency associations have done their own local polling, and since a permanent voters' list makes it easier to find voters' phone numbers and addresses, parties are employing even more sophisticated techniques. Rather than just identifying supporters and opponents, for example, parties use massive phone banks to find out which issues concern individual voters, especially marginal ones, and to follow up with a customized letter or even candidate visit to address such issues. The Conservatives were the first party to become expert at computer-assisted mail and telephone campaigning directed at members of key groups in targeted constituencies.[29] Short videos are also supplementing the distribution of printed leaflets. In the past, much of this work was voluntary, but paid staff are increasingly engaged, sometimes consisting of "volunteers" paid by a business or union. The local campaign is thus a complex operation requiring more and more sophistication, staffing, and funding.

Since this book would like to encourage people to be more active in, as well as better informed about, the Canadian political system, it assures its readers that they would be welcomed with open arms if they went to the local headquarters of the candidate of their choice and volunteered their services. They might be asked to canvass or to put up signs, or their computer skills might be used in some way. In time, with more experience, they might be invited to be part of the campaign committee.

All this activity culminates on election day, when the organization tries to have party scrutineers placed in all the polls. Ideally, an inside scrutineer in each poll keeps track of which people on the list have cast their ballot, while an outside scrutineer periodically collects this information and then heads out to encourage all those previously identified as party supporters to get out to vote.

....

ELECTORAL BEHAVIOUR AND PARTY SUPPORT

Research by political scientists into electoral behaviour has shattered many myths. These include the myth of the rational, well-informed voter, the myth of the voter securely attached to a single party, the myth of the voter who weighs party positions on various issues before deciding how to cast his or her ballot, the myth that the voter identifies with the ideological position of a particular party, and the myth that most voters make up their minds long before the election is called.

Given the fact that the Liberals were so regularly victorious in Canadian federal elections between 1935 and 1984 and again in 1993 and 1997, it is tempting to believe that a large proportion of voters have a strong identification with the Liberal Party and that any result other than a Liberal triumph is unlikely. Research shows, however, that more and more voters have no enduring party identification. Some of these flexible electors possess a superficial party preference but constitute a large pool of voters ready to be moved by the particular issues, candidates, and leaders in the campaign.[30] The overall aggregate stability, therefore, masked "the potential for significant variation in electoral outcomes,"[31] as became evident in the 1984 Conservative landslide. Other factors that add flexibility to the system are the group that votes in one election but not the next, as well as the newly eligible voters in each election, who generally seem to favour the incumbent government.[32] Table 14.2 summarizes the lack of consistency among the electorate between the 1993 and 1997 elections. Only 42 percent of 1997 voters supported the same party as in 1993, but this was a marked increase from about 30 percent in 1988 and 1993.

TABLE 14.2 **1997 Voter Preference Compared with 1993 (Percentages)**

Voted same party	42
Switched parties	18
Previous voters not voting	7
Previous nonvoters voting*	14
Not voting either time	9
Newly eligible voters	10

Source: Published with permission, from The Canadian General Election of 1997 *(Toronto: Dundurn, 1997), by Jon Pammett and Alan Frizzell.*
*Includes those who did not remember whether or how they had voted in 1993.

In most other Western democracies the degree of voter identification with a specific party is much higher, and the flexibility of the Canadian electorate demands explanation. Jon Pammett accounts for this phenomenon as follows:

> The most basic [factor] is that Canadian political culture is relatively apolitical. While Canadians are moderately interested in politics, this interest does not translate for most into substantial political involvement. The amount of detailed political information possessed by the average Canadian is low. Studies of children's political learning, or socialization, show a relatively weak transference of preference for a political party from parent to child ... because these feelings may not be strongly or persistently held in the adult "socializer.[33]

Another factor is that a large proportion of voters feel negatively about almost everything associated with the political system and switch from party to party for negative rather than positive reasons.

Table 14.3 indicates the extent and direction of vote switching between 1993 and 1997. The Reform Party and the Bloc managed to hang on to about 80 percent of their previous supporters, while the three older parties had lower retention rates. The barely successful Liberals retained only 63 percent, while losing 11 percent of their 1993 vote to the PCs, 7 percent to the NDP, and 8 percent to Reform.

The voting decision is an extremely complex and subtle one that is not easily explained. Nevertheless, voters are often asked what factor was most influential in helping them make up their mind—party, leader, issues, or local candidate. It is clear that the party is the most important determinant, while the relative importance of issues and leaders varies from one election to another, and the local candidate is not normally a crucial factor. In the leader-dominated elections of 1958 and 1968, for example, the whole country voted positively for

TABLE 14.3   **Where the 1993 Vote Went in 1997 (Percentages)**

	1993 Behaviour							
1997	**LIB**	**PC**	**NDP**	**REF**	**BQ**	**OTH**	*Did not vote*	*Not eligible*
LIB	63	15	13	8	2	19	26	24
PC	11	51	4	2	7	10	11	16
NDP	7	5	59	9	2	7	6	6
REF	8	20	9	80	2	8	10	10
BQ	1	1	—	—	78	3	7	11
OTH	1	—	2	2	—	15	2	3
Did not vote	9	8	13	6	10	38	38	31

Source: Published with permission, from The Canadian General Election of 1997 *(Toronto: Dundurn, 1997), by Jon Pammett and Alan Frizzell.*

John Diefenbaker and Pierre Trudeau respectively, and in 1984, Quebeckers in particular were moved to vote for Brian Mulroney. In 1979 and 1980, on the other hand, voters felt negatively about Joe Clark and Pierre Trudeau, so that issues became more important. In 1988, the free trade question along with the lack of enthusiasm for all three leaders gave the election a much stronger issue orientation than usual. The significance of the leader has declined in recent years; as Pammett puts it, "despite the fact that popular commentary is fond of debating the effects of the leaders' appearance, dress, hairstyles or speaking styles on the public, the bulk of the population does not rate these things highly when it comes to making up their minds."[34] The 1993 and 1997 campaigns did not feature a single dominant issue or popular leaders, in which case the importance of the party as a whole was more evident. This is revealed in Table 14.4, which provides responses to an open-ended question on this subject in 1993.

Voters will often say that they were moved by the issues, but except for the one-issue BQ supporters, many have trouble identifying the issues that supposedly influenced them, or can only identify very general topics.[35] In 1997, 30 percent could not identify any important election issue, and 40 percent of these issue-less voters chose the Liberals. Pammett concludes that "the combination of the increase in nonvoting with the lack of issue identification [is] potentially ... worrisome for the health of Canadian democracy."[36]

In short, as Lawrence Leduc writes, "the Canadian electorate continues to be one with relatively weak long-term attachments to political parties, low ideological commitment, and high responsiveness to short-term forces such as leaders, issues, or political events."[37] Such flexibility means that about half of the electorate makes up its mind during the course of the campaign, that elections remain highly unpredictable, and that there are few **safe seats**. As a result, the turnover rate in the Canadian House of Commons exceeds that of almost all other countries.

These revelations also cast doubt on the question of whether elections provide a policy mandate for the successful party—hence the concept of the **absent mandate**. First, Canadian parties rarely present a comprehensive election platform. Next, government parties do not seem to feel bound by the specific policies they proposed in the campaign, such as the Liberal opposition to wage and price controls in 1974 and to the GST in 1993. In the third place, the limited role that issues play in the campaign seriously detracts from the claim of any gov-

TABLE 14.4	Reasons for Voting (Open-Ended Question), 1993 (Percentages)				
	Liberals	*PC*	*NDP*	*Reform*	*Bloc*
Issues	27	20	24	26	51
Leadership	14	10	5	6	12
Local candidate	7	20	21	2	5
Party	52	50	50	68	33

Source: Published with permission, from The Canadian General Election of 1993 *(Toronto: Dundurn, 1993), by Jon Pammett and Alan Frizzell.*

ernment that it has a mandate to pursue a particular policy. For example, free trade was never mentioned in the 1984 campaign and the GST was almost totally overlooked in 1988. Fourth, even on the rare occasion that a single issue figures prominently, the winning party almost never obtains a majority of the total votes cast, and certainly not a majority in all regions of the country, "so a national mandate is absent."[38] The free trade issue in 1988 provided the closest thing to a policy mandate for any Canadian government in recent times, yet the Conservatives received only 43 percent of the overall popular vote and less than 40 percent in six provinces and territories.[39] The Liberals made much of their Red Book during and immediately after the 1993 campaign, but as time went on, they strayed further and further from it.

The other aspect of electoral behaviour that has attracted much attention from political scientists is the relationship between voters' regional, ethnic, and class background and their party preference.[40] This relates to the cleavages discussed in Chapters 3 to 8. At least until the 1984 federal election, certain patterns of socioeconomic support for the three main parties could be identified. First, there were wide variations in regional support. The Liberals dominated Quebec, and the Conservatives excelled in the West, especially Alberta. While these respective patterns were not quite as dramatic in terms of popular vote as in the proportion of seats won, they were still significant. Liberal support in Quebec had been virtually unchanged since 1900, but the Conservative popularity in the West was primarily a legacy of John Diefenbaker in the 1950s and 1960s. Such party strongholds resulted in the situation that election campaigns were most heatedly contested in Ontario, which could swing either way.

A second marked pattern in Canadian voting behaviour was religion. Roman Catholics were strongly inclined to vote Liberal, whether they were French, English, or of other ethnic background, and regardless of where they lived in the country. This situation was especially striking when one considers that no serious religious issues had divided the parties in Canadian federal politics for generations.[41]

Ethnicity was another significant factor in Canadian electoral behaviour. The historic French-Canadian preference for the Liberal Party is well known and existed outside as well as within Quebec. Among those of non-British and non-French origins, the Liberals also did best, especially among post–Second World War immigrants (largely of Mediterranean and Indian subcontinental origins), who apparently reacted with gratitude to the fact that the Liberal Party was in office when they arrived.

A final demographic factor is social class, the expectation being that upper-class citizens would vote Conservative, the middle class would support the Liberals, and the working and poorer classes would vote NDP. In most Western democracies such a pattern is quite significant, but it is not borne out well in Canada.[42] The Liberal Party usually attracted nearly the same degree of support from all classes except farmers, who voted distinctively Conservative. As indicated in Chapter 8, only a small proportion of the working class vote for working-class parties. The NDP, for example, normally gets relatively more support from skilled and unskilled labour than from other groups, but it does not get as much from either group as does each of the other parties.

The low level of **class-consciousness** in Canada is quite striking. When voters were asked in 1979 if they thought of themselves as belonging to a social class, only 42 percent said yes, 25 percent identifying with the middle class and 10 percent with the working class. When forced to choose a class, 54 percent selected the middle class, compared with 33 percent for the working class, but three-fifths of this 33 percent reported themselves to be quite satisfied with their material standard of living. This leaves only about 13 percent who could be called a militant, dissatisfied core of the working class. Chapter 8 indicated that about two-thirds of voters could actually be said to belong to the working class, but without greater working-class–consciousness, class-based voting can hardly be expected. In 1979, the NDP received the support of 11 percent of those not belonging to unions, 21 percent of union members, and 30 percent of those belonging to unions affiliated to the party.[43]

The 1984 and 1988 elections ran counter to generations of traditional voting patterns, especially with Quebec French-Canadian Roman Catholics preferring the Conservatives over the Liberals. The 1993 election then saw the West abandon the Conservatives for Reform, and Quebec switch to the Bloc Québécois. Thus, such socioeconomic patterns of party support as were once evident seem to have vanished.

In 1997, even more than in 1993, regional patterns of party support predominated.[44] Table 14.5 indicates how the Liberal vote was centred in Ontario, moderated in Atlantic Canada, and weak in the West. The PC vote declined from Atlantic to Quebec to Ontario to the West. The NDP was strongest in Atlantic Canada and the West. If these regional variations characterized the so-called "national" parties, it was all the more evident in Bloc and Reform support. Michael Marzolini shows that while voters in all regions thought that the Liberals were the best party for the country, only in Ontario were the Liberals considered best for their region. Responding to regional interests, regional issues, and regional leaders (native sons and daughters, especially McDonough and Manning), most people voted for the party that they considered best for their region.[45]

Surveys also indicated slight variations in party support by age, gender, education, and income. In a nutshell, Bloc voters tended to be young and male, with lower incomes and levels of education. Reform supporters were disproportionately older males with relatively low levels of education but high incomes. The NDP scored highest among female, well-educated, and older voters with lower incomes. The Liberals and Conservatives were virtually indistinguishable and did not stand out in any of these respects.[46]

TABLE 14.5   Popular Vote by Party and by Region, 1997 (Percentages)

	Atlantic	*Quebec*	*Ontario*	*West*
Liberal	33	37	50	28
PC	34	22	19	10
Reform	9	—	19	42
NDP	24	2	11	17
BQ	—	38	—	—

Source: Calculations by author from Chief Electoral Officer Report of 1997 Election. Reproduced with the permission of the Minister of Public Works and Government Services Canada, 2000.

....

CONCLUSION

While public opinion polls are increasingly common, elections remain the definitive measure of the public will. As such, elections leave much to be desired, because they rarely produce a victorious party with a specific policy mandate. Parties may offer only vague slogans like "national unity"; elections frequently turn on leader or party images; successful parties often renege on their policy promises once in office; and a large proportion of voters pay little attention to the campaign. As defective as elections are, however, caution should be exercised before jumping on populist bandwagons like holding frequent referendums on specific issues. In many cases, the electorate—having less incentive to be accommodating—takes policy positions that are more extreme and emotional and less well informed than those of political parties. Referendums are at odds with the virtues of representative democracy and may endanger the rights of certain ethnic, linguistic, religious, ideological, or other minorities.

PC Of the approaches outlined in Chapter 1, the public choice model is, at least at first sight, the one most relevant to elections. Extensive public opinion polling by political parties confirms the claims of this approach that parties make calculated promises in order to get elected, concentrating on strategically located groups. Parties tend to ignore their committed supporters as well as those who are hostile, and then, within a certain ideological range, promise whatever their polls tell them will maximize their electoral success. Nevertheless, the preceding account of voting behaviour puts into question some of the other claims of the public choice approach, at least with respect to its assumption of rational and well-informed voters. The average person spends more time researching the purchase of a television set or perusing the weekly supermarket fliers than in comparing party platforms. The successful party also emerges with a less specific policy mandate than the public choice model suggests.

© Class analysts add that the bargains struck between parties and voters during the campaign may not be honoured afterwards. Promises made to middle-income voters and the working class—for example, that social programs are a "sacred trust" or that wage controls will not be adopted—are often broken by the victorious party in record time. To a large extent, as discussed in Chapter 12, class analysts attribute this to the issue of party finance. That is, once in office, parties do what their financial supporters or such corporate-funded bodies as the Business Council on National Issues or the C.D. Howe Institute want them to do, which is often at odds with their promises. Class analysts add that parties nominate and voters support a set of candidates who bear little resemblance to the general population, over-representing all the "elite" variables in Canadian society.

P Pluralists emphasize the necessity of designing a party's election platform so that it appeals to many groups in society—all major ethnic categories, industries, regions, genders, and classes. Such platforms are usually classic brokerage documents. Election manifestos are increasingly based on what public opinion polls indicate the public wants or is willing to accept. Pluralists also point to the socioeconomic group preferences that have been evident in elections and the extent to which each party appeals to a coalition of certain groups. In addition, they note the increasing involvement of pressure groups in the election campaign.

(SC) Even this most "popular" aspect of the political system reveals the extent to which the state is relatively autonomous from the rest of society, as state-centred theorists contend. This is primarily because the focus of election campaigns is not usually on policy. If voters are uninformed about issues, if they make their decision on the basis of leader or party images, or local candidate preferences, and if parties present only vague policy directions that few politicians or voters take seriously in any case, post-election policy innovation will stall or be dominated by the prime minister, Cabinet, and bureaucracy. If the authorities decide to adopt policies that were not mentioned in the campaign or to leave unfulfilled promises that were made, they merely resort to publicly paid advertising campaigns to demonstrate the necessity of the statist decision.

DISCUSSION QUESTIONS

1. Can anything be done to give more emphasis to the substance of each party's campaign (platform) and less to its presentation (personality, image, and advertising)?

2. Is the distribution of media time during election campaigns fair? If not, how could it be improved?

3. Is it fair to exclude minor party leaders from the leaders' debates?

4. Why is Canadian party identification lower than that in other Western industrialized countries?

5. How rational and well informed is the average voter?

6. If you voted recently, explain how you came to your decision.

7. How do each of the approaches outlined in Chapter 1 enhance our understanding of the material in this chapter?

NOTES

1. Alan Frizzell and Anthony Westell, eds., *The Canadian General Election of 1984* (Ottawa: Carleton University Press, 1985); Alan Frizzell, Jon H. Pammett, and Anthony Westell, eds., *The Canadian General Election of 1988* (Ottawa: Carleton University Press, 1989); Alan Frizzell, Jon H. Pammett, and Anthony Westell, eds., *The Canadian General Election of 1993* (Ottawa: Carleton University Press, 1994); and Alan Frizzell and Jon H. Pammett, eds., *The Canadian General Election of 1997* (Toronto: Dundurn Press, 1997).

2. Edward Greenspon, "Following the Trail of Campaign '97," in Frizzell and Pammett, eds., *The Canadian General Election of 1997* (hereinafter referred to as *1997*), p. 22.

3. Chief Electoral Officer, *Thirty-Sixth General Election 1997, Official Voting Results, Synopsis* (Ottawa, 1997), pp. 9–10.

4. Alan Whitehorn, "Alexa McDonough and the Atlantic Breakthrough for the New Democratic Party," in Frizzell and Pammett, eds., *1997*, p. 94.

5. Stephen Clarkson, "Securing Their Future Together: The Liberals in Action," in Frizzell and Pammett, eds., *1997*, p. 54.

6. Peter Woolstencroft, "On the Ropes Again? The Campaign of the Progressive Conservative Party in the 1997 Federal Election," in Frizzell and Pammett, eds., *1997*, pp. 72–73.

7. Anthony Westell, "Setting the Stage," in Frizzell and Pammett, eds., *1997*, p. 17.

8. Whitehorn, "Alexa McDonough," in Frizzell and Pammett, eds., *1997*, p. 96.

9. Greenspon, "Following the Trail," in Frizzell and Pammett, eds., *1997*, p. 29.

10. André Bernard, "The Bloc Québécois," in Frizzell and Pammett, eds., *1997*, pp. 135–36.

11. Stephen Clarkson, "Yesterday's Man and His Blue Grits: Backward into the Future," in Frizzell et al., eds., *The Canadian General Election of 1993*, p. 33.

12. Clarkson, "Securing Their Future Together," in Frizzell and Pammett, eds., *1997*, pp. 44–46.

13. Woolstencroft, "On the Ropes Again?" in Frizzell and Pammett, eds., *1997*, pp. 78–79.

14. Whitehorn, "Alexa McDonough," in Frizzell and Pammett, eds., *1997*, p. 94.

15. Faron Ellis and Keith Archer, "Reform at the Crossroads," in Frizzell and Pammett, eds., *1997*, p. 118.

16. Bernard, "The Bloc Québécois," in Frizzell and Pammett, eds., *1997*, p. 143.

17. Frizzell and Westell, in Frizzell, Pammett, and Westell, eds., *The Canadian General Election of 1988*, p. 75; David Taras, *The Newsmakers* (Scarborough: Nelson Canada, 1990), pp. 154–67.

18. Christopher Dornan, "The Television Coverage: A History of the Election in 65 Seconds," in Frizzell and Pammett, eds., *1997*, p. 165.

19. Clarkson, "Securing Their Future Together," in Frizzell and Pammett, eds., *1997*, p. 51.

20. *Reform Party of Canada et al. v. Canada (Attorney General)*, Alberta Court of Appeal, March 10, 1995; *Somerville v. Canada (Attorney General)*, Alberta Court of Appeal, June 5, 1996.

21. Peter Woolstencroft, "'Doing Politics Differently': The Conservative Party and the Campaign of 1993," in Frizzell et al., eds., *1993*, p. 20; Lionel Lumb, "The Television of Inclusion," in Frizzell et al., eds., *1993*, p. 122; Walter I. Romanow et al., *Television Advertising in Canadian Elections: The Attack Mode, 1993* (Waterloo: Wilfrid Laurier University Press, 1999).

22. Woolstencroft, "On the Ropes Again?" in Frizzell and Pammett, eds., *1997*, p. 86.

23. Lawrence LeDuc, "The Leaders' Debates: (... And the Winner Is ...)," in Frizzell and Pammett, eds., *1997*; Lawrence LeDuc and Richard Price, "Great Debates: The Televised Leadership Debates of 1979," *Canadian Journal of Political Science* (March 1985); David Lanoue, "Debates That Mattered: Voters' Reaction to the 1984 Canadian Leadership Debates," *Canadian Journal of Political Science* (March 1991); and Taras, *The Newsmakers*, pp. 167–75.

24. LeDuc, "The Leaders' Debates," in Frizzell and Pammett, eds., *1997*, p. 126.

25. Greenspon, "Following the Trail," in Frizzell and Pammett, eds., *1997*, p. 30.

26. LeDuc, "The Leaders' Debates," in Frizzell and Pammett, eds., *1997*, p. 212.

27. Ibid., pp. 207–8.

28. Jerome H. Black, "Revisiting the Effects of Canvassing on Voting Behaviour," *Canadian Journal of Political Science* (June 1984); Tom Brook, *Getting Elected in Canada* (Stratford: Mercury Press, 1991); and Lynda Erickson and R.K. Carty, "Parties and Candidate Selection in the 1988 Canadian General Election," *Canadian Journal of Political Science* (June 1991), pp. 331–49.

29. George Perlin, "Opportunity Regained: The Tory Victory in 1984," in Howard R. Penniman, ed., *Canada at the Polls, 1984* (Durham, NC: Duke University Press, 1988), p. 85.

30. Lawrence LeDuc, "The Flexible Canadian Electorate," in Penniman, ed., *Canada at the Polls, 1984*, p. 40.

31. Harold D. Clarke et al., *Political Choice in Canada* (Toronto: McGraw-Hill Ryerson, 1980), p. 204; Frizzell et al., eds., *1988*, p. 109.

32. A point made repeatedly in Pammett's work.

33. Jon H. Pammett, "Elections," in M.S. Whittington and G. Williams, eds., *Canadian Politics in the 1990s*, 4th ed. (Scarborough: Nelson Canada, 1995), p. 242.

34. Pammett, "The Voters Decide," in Frizzell and Pammett, eds., *1997*, p. 234.

35. Typically, about 30 percent cannot name a single issue. Pammett explains that to affect an election outcome, an issue must meet three conditions: it must be salient, skewed, and linked to one party. These conditions further reduce the possibility that issues will affect the outcome. "Elections," in Whittington and Williams, eds., *Canadian Politics in the 1990s*, 3rd ed., p. 279.

36. Pammett, "The Voters Decide," in Frizzell and Pammett, eds., *1997*, p. 236.

37. LeDuc, "The Flexible Canadian Electorate," in Penniman, ed., *Canada at the Polls, 1984*, p. 51; LeDuc, "The Changeable Canadian Voter," in Frizzell et al., *1988*.

38. Harold D. Clarke et al., *Absent Mandate* (Toronto: Gage, 1984), p. 182.

39. Surveys indicated that only about one-half of the voters claimed to make up their mind primarily on the basis of the free trade issue, some on each side. Frizzell et al., eds., *1988*, p. 124; and Richard Johnston et al., "Free Trade and the Dynamics of the 1988 Canadian Election," in Joseph Wearing, ed., *The Ballot and Its Message* (Toronto: Copp Clark Pitman, 1991).

40. Elisabeth Gidengil, "Canada Votes: A Quarter Century of Canadian Election Studies," *Canadian Journal of Political Science* (June 1992). The definitive book on the 1997 election, *Unsteady State: The 1997 Canadian Federal Election* (Toronto: Oxford University Press, 2000), by Neil Nevitte and associates, came out just as this book went to press.

41. Richard Johnston, "The Reproduction of the Religious Cleavage in Canadian Elections," *Canadian Journal of Political Science* (March 1985), pp. 99–117; William Irvine, "Explaining the Religious Basis of the Canadian Partisan Identity: Success on the Third Try," *Canadian Journal of Political Science* (September 1974), pp. 560–63.

42. Jon Pammett, "Class Voting and Class Consciousness in Canada," *Canadian Review of Sociology and Anthropology* 24, no. 2 (1987), pp. 269–90; Keith Archer, "The Failure of the New Democratic Party: Unions, Unionists, and Politics in Canada," *Canadian Journal of Political Science* (June 1985), pp. 353–66; Elisabeth Gidengil, "Class and Region in Canadian Voting: A Dependency Interpretation," *Canadian Journal of Political Science* (September 1989), pp. 563–87; Ronald D. Lambert et al., "Social Class and Voting," in James Curtis et al., eds., *Social Inequality in Canada* (Scarborough: Prentice-Hall Canada, 1988); and Keith Archer, *Political Choice and Electoral Consequences* (Montreal: McGill–Queen's University Press, 1990).

43. Pammett, "Class Voting and Class Consciousness in Canada," and Keith Archer, "The Failure of the New Democratic Party: Unions, Unionists, and Politics in Canada," pp. 353–66.

44. Elisabeth Gidengil et al., "Making Sense of Regional Voting in the 1997 Canadian Federal Election: Liberal and Reform Support Outside Quebec," *Canadian Journal of Political Science* (June 1999).

45. Michael Marzolini, "The Regionalization of Canadian Electoral Politics," in Frizzell and Pammett, eds., *1997*, pp. 194–96; 304.

46. Pammett, "The Voters Decide," in Frizzell and Pammett, eds., *1997*, pp. 244–46.

··································

FURTHER READING

Archer, Keith. "The Failure of the New Democratic Party: Unions, Unionists, and Politics in Canada." *Canadian Journal of Political Science* (June 1985), pp. 353–66.

———. *Political Choices and Electoral Consequences*. Montreal: McGill–Queen's University Press, 1990.

Bashevkin, Sylvia, ed. *Canadian Political Behaviour*. Toronto: Methuen, 1985.

Brodie, Janine, and Jane Jenson. *Crisis, Challenge and Change: Party and Class in Canada Revisited*. Ottawa: Carleton University Press, 1988.

Caplan, Gerald, Michael Kirby, and Hugh Segal. *Election: The Issues, the Strategies, the Aftermath*. Scarborough: Prentice-Hall Canada, 1989.

Clarke, Harold D., et al. *Political Choice in Canada*. Toronto: McGraw-Hill Ryerson, 1980.

———. *Absent Mandate*. Toronto: Gage, 1984.

———. *Absent Mandate: Interpreting Change in Canadian Elections*, 2nd ed. Toronto: Gage, 1991.

———. *Absent Mandate: Canadian Electoral Politics in an Era of Restructuring*, 3rd ed. Toronto: Gage, 1996.

Fraser, Graham. *Playing for Keeps: The Making of the Prime Minister, 1988*. Toronto: McClelland and Stewart, 1989.

Frizzell, Alan, and Jon H. Pammett, eds. *The Canadian General Election of 1997*. Toronto: Dundurn Press, 1997.

Frizzell, Alan, and Anthony Westell, eds. *The Canadian General Election of 1984*. Ottawa: Carleton University Press, 1985.

Frizzell, Alan, Jon H. Pammett, and Anthony Westell, eds. *The Canadian General Election of 1988*. Ottawa: Carleton University Press, 1989.

———. *The Canadian General Election of 1993*. Ottawa: Carleton University Press, 1994.

Gidengil, Elisabeth. "Canada Votes: A Quarter Century of Canadian Election Studies." *Canadian Journal of Political Science* (June 1992).

Johnston, Richard, et al. *Letting the People Decide: Dynamics of a Canadian Election*. Montreal: McGill–Queen's University Press, 1992.

McLaughlin, David. *Poisoned Chalice: The Last Campaign of the Progressive Conservative Party?* Toronto: Dundurn Press, 1994.

Nevitte, Neil, et al. *Unsteady State: The 1997 Canadian Federal Election*. Toronto: Oxford University Press, 2000.

Pammett, Jon. "Class Voting and Class Consciousness in Canada." *Canadian Review of Sociology and Anthropology* 24, no. 2 (1987), pp. 269–90.

———. "Elections." In Michael S. Whittington and Glen Williams, eds., *Canadian Politics in the 1990s*, 4th ed. Scarborough: Nelson Canada, 1995.

Penniman, Howard R., ed. *Canada at the Polls, 1984*. Durham, NC: Duke University Press, 1988.

Romanow, Walter I., et al., *Television Advertising in Canadian Elections: The Attack Mode, 1993*. Waterloo: Wilfrid Laurier University Press, 1999.

Taras, David. *The Newsmakers*. Scarborough: Nelson Canada, 1990.

Wearing, Joseph, ed. *The Ballot and Its Message*. Toronto: Copp Clark Pitman, 1991.

Chapter 15

Pressure GROUPS AND lobbying

The Non-Smokers' Rights Association fights against the advertising of cigarettes, while the Canadian Tobacco Manufacturers' Council strives to maintain sponsorship of athletic and cultural events. The four large business pressure groups applaud the government's balanced-budget doctrine and reliance on market forces, while the Canadian Labour Congress protests against free trade, cutbacks to unemployment insurance, and back-to-work legislation. The Canadian Federation of Students and the Canadian Association of University Teachers abhor the cuts that Ottawa (and the provinces in turn) have made in transfer payments to postsecondary education, and try to generate public concern about the impact of persistent underfunding and skyrocketing tuition costs. The Canadian Association of Chiefs of Police and other police organizations called for and defended the gun registration law, Bill C-68, while the gun lobby continued to oppose it long after it was passed.

Pressure groups or interest groups such as these develop in almost every political system when individuals with common concerns band together in order to strengthen their cause. A **pressure group or interest group** can therefore be defined as any group that seeks to influence government policy without contesting elections, that is, without putting forward its own candidates. Although the terms are basically interchangeable, it could be said that an interest group *becomes* a pressure group when it actively pursues an objective with government. Alternatively, they have been defined as "organizations whose members act together to influence public policy in order to promote their common interest."[1] Most such groups originally form for nonpolitical purposes and retain nonpolitical functions, but almost inevitably get drawn into political activity from time to time because of the pervasiveness of government.

The term **lobbying** is generally used to refer to any organized attempt to influence the authorities, an activity that is most commonly undertaken by pressure groups but could of course be done by individuals, companies, or other political actors. Increasingly, however, pressure groups have been joined by professional lobbying firms in this activity.

In the traditional discussion of functions performed in the political system, pressure groups are assigned the primary task of interest articulation. They normally have a narrow focus and are organized around a single, central interest that they try to impress upon those in authority. National pressure groups often experience internal regional, provincial, ethnic, and/or class tensions that must be bridged in constructing the message that they wish to articulate, so that such groups also play a limited part in the aggregation of interests. Because it is sometimes difficult to distinguish between interest articulation and interest aggregation, Paul Pross speaks of the "interest promotion" function of such groups.[2]

The party and electoral systems were originally assumed to be the principal means of accommodating various interests within the Canadian political system. Individuals would take their concerns to parties; parties would respond to any interest that appeared to be important; and regional, ethnic, religious, economic, professional, and other interests could be encompassed within the territorial representation provided by the electoral system. As society became more complex, however, Canadians increasingly demonstrated a preference to form or join more specialized, functional groups rather than rely exclusively on the territorial representation of parties and elections. Thus, in the promotion of interests, pressure groups provide a supplementary kind of functional representation, especially between elections.[3]

Besides interest articulation and aggregation, pressure groups engage in political communication. They transmit demands from the people to the authorities, as well as disseminate information in the other direction. In addition, groups may assist in the communication between different parts of government or between federal and provincial levels of government. They frequently communicate among themselves and build temporary alliances or coalitions around common problems.

Pressure groups are also involved in the rule-making function. The enhanced complexity of society has meant that public issues now require reliance on information that is so technical and voluminous that politicians and parties, lacking both time and expertise, cannot handle it well. Consequently, pressure groups regularly interact with the bureaucracy to work out technical arrangements to their mutual satisfaction, and present these proposals to the politicians and parties as a fait accompli. Pressure groups are also increasingly involved in the rule-application function, that is, in the administration of government programs and even in regulation.

Pross goes beyond the functions listed in Chapter 1 by adding that of legitimation. When groups participate peacefully and cooperatively, they demonstrate support for the political system and confer legitimacy upon both it and those with whom they are interacting. Governments encourage groups to lend them such legitimacy and support by welcoming their advances, by "drawing them into a privileged advisory position," and sometimes by helping to create them. By keeping the authorities abreast of current demands and societal changes, pressure groups promote "general political stability."[4] If they can successfully achieve accommodations across regional and ethnic cleavages, they also become important unifying agents in Canadian society.

Having established their functions, this chapter proceeds to identify some of the leading Canadian pressure groups, to outline their targets and methods, to assess their resources, and to reveal the activity of professional lobbying firms.

....

THE ARRAY OF CANADIAN INTEREST GROUPS

The number of interest groups operating in Canada is in the thousands, so not all can be identified here. Instead, only some of the largest, most influential, or more interesting will be mentioned. Such a selective list can be seen in Table 15.1.

TABLE 15.1   Leading National Canadian Pressure Groups[5]

Business
Alliance of Manufacturers & Exporters Canada
Canadian Chamber of Commerce
Business Council on National Issues
Canadian Federation of Independent Business
Retail Council of Canada
Canadian Bankers' Association
Automotive Industries Association of Canada
Canadian Association of Broadcasters
Canadian Construction Association
Canadian Life & Health Insurance Association
Mining Association of Canada
Canada's Research-Based Pharmaceutical Companies
Canadian Pulp and Paper Association
Canadian Tobacco Manufacturers' Council

Agriculture
Canadian Federation of Agriculture
National Farmers Union

Labour
Canadian Labour Congress

Professions
Canadian Bar Association
Canadian Medical Association
Canadian Nurses' Association
Canadian Association of University Teachers
Canadian Association of Chiefs of Police
Canadian Teachers' Federation
Canadian Federation of Students

Ethnic
Fédération des communautés francophones et acadienne du Canada
Assembly of First Nations
Canadian Ethnocultural Council
National Congress of Italian Canadians
National Association of Japanese Canadians

continued

Table 15.1 (*continued*)

Religious
Canadian Council of Churches
Canadian Conference of Catholic Bishops
United Church of Canada
Canadian Jewish Congress

Causes
Council of Canadians
John Howard Society
Canadian Civil Liberties Association
National Action Committee on the Status of Women
Canadian Council on Social Development
National Council of Welfare
Greenpeace Canada
Mothers Against Drunk Driving
Non-Smokers' Rights Association
National Anti-Poverty Organization

Other
Royal Canadian Legion
Consumers' Association of Canada
Federation of Canadian Municipalities

Business Groups[6]

In the case of business, nothing prevents individual companies from lobbying on their own behalf for grants, subsidies, tariff changes, loan guarantees, tax write-offs, government contracts, or policy changes, and many firms do so on a regular basis. In addition, it is evident from Table 15.1 that despite their supposed or real competition, the private firms within almost every industry have organized a common pressure group to promote the interests of the industry as a whole. Thus, to a large exent, the "system of business interest associations in Canada is highly fragmented, consisting of many small, narrowly focused organizations."[7] William Coleman counted about 600 business groups that were active in Canadian federal politics, about 40 percent of which were in the manufacturing sector. He summarizes the business pressure group scene as follows:

> a relatively small number of associations with members that are generally large firms, operating in large oligopolistic sectors. These associations spend in excess of $1 million annually, employ a minimum of 10 to 15 people, are institutionally bilingual, and have an officer, if not their head office, in Ottawa. Associations in this category are visible to the attentive public; their leaders are quoted frequently in the business press and move freely in government circles.... The several roles they play gives them a system of

comprehensive political contacts, ranging from lower and middle technical levels of the bureaucracy to senior officials, MPs, and Cabinet ministers.[8]

Superimposed upon these industrial groupings are such "peak" organizations as the **Alliance of Manufacturers and Exporters Canada (AMEC)**, the **Canadian Chamber of Commerce (CCC)**, the **Business Council on National Issues (BCNI)**, and the **Canadian Federation of Independent Business (CFIB)**. The Alliance of Manufacturers and Exporters Canada, a recent merger of the Canadian Manufacturers' and Canadian Exporters' Associations, can be seen as an aggregative organization, an umbrella under which many separate manufacturing and other exporting groups gather. The Canadian Chamber of Commerce, formed in 1925, calls itself Canada's "largest business organization," representing over 170 000 business members. Its goal is to foster and improve the economic climate in Canada so that all businesses can continue to grow and prosper. Like the other three peak business groups, it engaged in a long and ultimately successful public education campaign about the dangers of the government deficit. The Canadian Federation of Independent Business was founded in 1971 by John Bullock, and represents some 93 000 small and medium enterprises. Often active on tax policies and labour laws, it promotes entrepreneurship, small business, and free enterprise,. The Business Council on National Issues, led by Tom d'Aquino, was formed in 1976 and represents the chief executive officers of 150 of the largest firms in the country, which together have some 1.3 million employees. The BCNI sees itself as the "senior voice of Canadian business," and gives automatic membership on its board of directors to the heads of the CCC, AMEC, and the Conseil du Patronat du Québec. The organization was particularly influential with the Mulroney Conservative government; it fought hard for the Canada–U.S. Free Trade Agreement, and, having been successful in that enterprise, then sought, in its own words, "to broaden public understanding of the need for more responsible fiscal policies." While Canada thus lacks a single peak voice for the business community as a whole, that community may be even more influential for being represented by at least four national organizations.

On the agricultural side of business, nearly 100 active associations vie for influence, the two broadest being the Canadian Federation of Agriculture (CFA), tending to represent the more affluent farmers, and the National Farmers Union (NFU), speaking for those who are

By Denny Pritchard. Reproduced with permission.

not doing so well.[9] The CFA was formed in 1935 and now represents 19 provincial farm and national or regional commodity organizations. Other specific commodity groups exist outside the aegis of the CFA, such as the Canadian Cattlemen's Association.

Nonbusiness Groups

The **Canadian Labour Congress (CLC)** functions more satisfactorily as a common voice for organized labour, but only 59 percent of Canadian union members actually belong to unions affiliated with the CLC. About 6 percent belong to the Quebec-based Conseil des Syndicats Nationaux (CSN), while unions representing the other 35 percent have not joined any central labour organization. The CLC maintains a link to the New Democratic Party, as do many of its individual unions, which is unique among Canadian pressure groups.

Many of the ethnic groups in Canada have their own organization, such as the National Congress of Italian Canadians, the German Canadian Congress, the National Association of Japanese Canadians, the Chinese Canadian National Council, and the National Association of Canadians of Origins in India. Most of these have been brought together, with government support, in the peak organization, the Canadian Ethnocultural Council. The largest of several Aboriginal groups is the **Assembly of First Nations**. The English and French, on the other hand, are only organized where they are minorities—the anglophone Alliance Quebec and the Fédération des communautés francophones et acadienne, which incorporates provincial units such as the Association canadienne-française de l'Ontario (ACFO). Most of the religious denominations in Canada function as pressure groups from time to time, with the Canadian Conference of Catholic Bishops, the United Church of Canada, and the Canadian Jewish Congress probably being most influential. The Roman Catholic Church is now a member of the umbrella Christian group, the Canadian Council of Churches.

Most professions have organizations that speak for their members on relevant issues, the Canadian Medical and Bar Associations being two of the oldest and most important. The CMA was formed in 1867 and has about 42 000 members. In addition to serving the needs of its own members, the CMA advises the government on other health matters in the broader public interest. The Canadian Bar Association, incorporated in 1921, has a membership of over 35 000, which represents approximately two-thirds of all practising lawyers. Besides promoting the interests of the legal profession, as such, the CBA is uniquely involved in the legislative process, since it has expertise in every aspect of the law.

The Royal Canadian Legion is by far the largest veterans' organization, going back to 1926 and representing about 500 000 members who served in Canada's armed forces or who are associated with those who did. Besides working for better pensions and other benefits for its own members and a strong military establishment, the Legion is prominently involved in public service and charitable work.

Other Categorizations of Pressure Groups

However much any of the above-mentioned groups claim to be pursuing the public interest, they can be generally categorized as "self-interested" groups because their principal concern is to improve their own economic position. The true "public interest" group exists to promote causes that it sees as beneficial to society as a whole and that do not directly benefit its own members: the John Howard Society (improving prison conditions and the lot of ex-inmates), the Canadian Council on Social Development (promoting better social policy), the Canadian Civil Liberties Association (protecting civil liberties from government infringement), and a variety of environmental groups, among others.

With the exception of some of the public interest and ethnic groups, those named above and many others are called **institutionalized pressure groups** because they are permanent, well-established, formal organizations. Almost all maintain a head office in Ottawa with a full-time staff, a sizable budget, and a reasonably stable membership. Most have developed continuous links with the authorities and represent their members' interests on a daily basis, year after year.

These characteristics are not possessed by all pressure groups, however, and other labels have been attached to them. Some groups spring up spontaneously around a specific issue, and once the issue is resolved, they fade away. Such **issue-oriented groups** lack the institutionalized groups' permanence, office, staff, budget, membership, and access to the authorities. Instead, they more likely resort to attracting public attention to their cause through media coverage of such actions as demonstrations. Since issue-oriented groups usually disappear when the issue has been resolved, they are not as familiar as institutionalized groups, but several famous examples can be cited. In the early 1970s the Stop Spadina group opposed extension of the Spadina Expressway in Toronto and the People or Planes group fought the proposed Pickering airport east of that city; later, "Bread Not Circuses" opposed Toronto's bid to host the 1996 Olympic Games. Somewhat similar was the group called Thin Ice, which was successful in the bitterly fought campaign to prevent the spending of vast amounts of public funds to keep the NHL's Winnipeg Jets in Winnipeg.[10] Other recent cases include Rural Dignity, a spontaneous national group that sprang up to fight against the deterioration of rural and small-town life in general, and of its mail service in particular, and the Foundation for Equal Families, fighting for same-sex amendments to 58 federal statutes. Proposed reform of the Divorce Act, especially with respect to custody matters, spawned a variety of fathers' rights and even grandparents' rights groups. If their issue is not resolved, or if they anticipate further challenges, such groups may become a more permanent fixture, gradually evolving from an issue-oriented group to the institutionalized category.

Political scientists often find it useful to distinguish between pressure groups and **social movements**. Many of the issue-oriented groups referred to are, in fact, part of larger, unstructured social movements, of which the environmental, women's, peace, human rights, and consumers' movements have been most prominent. Other examples include the Aboriginal, gay and lesbian, and animal rights movements. A social movement has been defined as an informal network of organizations and individuals who on the basis of a collective identity and shared values engage in political and/or cultural struggle intended to expand the boundaries of the existing system and undertake collective action designed to affect both state and society.[11] They begin at the margins of the political system, possessing an alternate vision of "the good life," and usually consist of coalitions of small, local groups that have not (yet) hardened into a cohesive national pressure group.[12] The umbrella women's group, the National Action Committee on the Status of Women (NAC), is a coalition of some 650 member groups, while the Canadian Environmental Network contains over 2000 groups. Such movements run into much bureaucratic and political party resistance, and often do not achieve immediate success. In the long run, however, they widen the scope of public discourse, and parties and other mainstream political institutions eventually respond. Take recent improvements in legislation with respect to women and the environment, for example, and changes in public attitudes toward war, Aboriginals, homosexuals, and the treatment of animals.

The Council of Canadians (C of C) is a kind of citizens' movement that provides a critical voice on key national issues such as safeguarding social programs, promoting economic justice, renewing democracy, asserting Canadian sovereignty, preserving the environment, and promoting alternatives to corporate-style free trade. The C of C has been active on such issues as free trade, seniors' benefits, drug testing, the use of growth hormones in cattle, and the sale of Canadian water. In turn, it was a key part of the Action Canada Network, a coalition of some 50 groups including farmers, nurses, teachers, environmentalists, unions, artists, anti-poverty advocates, women, and churches that was active in the 1980s. The C of C and its partners put much effort into stopping the Multilateral Agreement on Investment (MAI), working successfully with similar grassroots groups around the world. The Internet facilitates both national and international grassroots political campaigns, and such international social movements and networks are often seen as one of the few counterweights to corporate globalization in the modern world.[13] To some extent the Action Canada Network was replaced from the mid-1990s onward by the Alternative Federal Budget (AFB) movement. This involves many organizations, including the CLC, the CFS, NAC, NAPO, NFU, unions, and environmental groups, which hammer out a detailed and sophisticated alternative federal budget each year. With extensive nationwide grassroots input and published by the Canadian Centre for Policy Alternatives, the annual AFBs are meant to show that, despite globalization and fiscal pressures, there *are* alternatives, contrary to what governments have said.

Other categorizations are also sometimes useful in discussing pressure groups. Most groups are "autonomous" in the sense that they develop without government initiative, although they may later seek government financial support. The creation of "reverse" groups, on the other hand, involves politicians or bureaucrats. This may be for either personal gain or in the hope of promoting a certain public policy objective. In the late 1960s, for example, the federal government began to fund anti-poverty, women's, minority official language, Aboriginal, and other ethnic groups,[14] and by 1987 it was handing out $185 million to interest groups in grants of over $50 000 (and much more in smaller grants). At that point, however, the Mulroney government began to cut back on grants to Aboriginal, women's, poor, and disabled

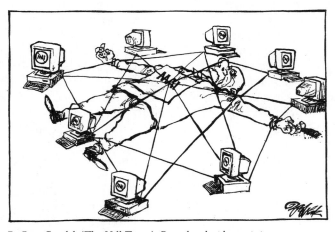

By Peter Zazulak (The Hill Times). *Reproduced with permission.*

people's groups, both for fiscal and ideological reasons, something the Trudeau government had also done on occasion when a particular group became too critical of the hand that fed it. Such grant reductions demonstrate a lack of political sincerity as well as the dangers involved in a group's becoming too critical and too dependent.[15]

A distinction can also be made between "active" groups, which have a formal organization and a name, and "categoric" groups, which are simply a number of unorganized individuals who share a common characteristic. Categoric groups are potential pressure groups, since an issue could come along that would bring them to life, but if their numbers are sufficient, the authorities will pay attention to them even in their latent state.

Pressure Group Structures

A word should be added about the structure of pressure groups. Issue-oriented groups may burst forth anywhere an issue arises—at the federal, provincial, or municipal level. Institutionalized groups, on the other hand, tend to be organized wherever government decisions regularly affect them. The federal nature of the country means that authoritative decisions are made at two (or even three) levels of government, and most institutionalized groups parallel the federal structure of government.[16] They find it advantageous to be organized at both levels because, as discussed in Chapter 17, the division of powers between the federal and provincial governments is so blurred. The Canadian Medical Association is composed of ten autonomous provincial divisions (such as the Manitoba Medical Association), the Canadian Chamber of Commerce has strong provincial branches (such as the Ontario Chamber of Commerce), and so does the Canadian Labour Congress (the Nova Scotia Federation of Labour). The CCC and CLC in particular also maintain municipal organizations—local chambers of commerce or boards of trade in every sizable community, and 121 local labour councils across the country.

Many pressure groups, including teachers, nurses, students, and professors, are actually more strongly organized at the provincial level than in Ottawa. This is because they are more affected by decisions of provincial governments than by federal ones. Some, such as the medical and legal professions, are even delegated powers by provincial governments to regulate themselves.

By increasing the number of decision-making centres in the political system, federalism generally makes it easier for groups to block government action, but harder to initiate new programs. Sometimes the national organization requests assistance from the provincial wings in dealing with an issue in Ottawa, while at other times a provincial unit seeks support from the national organization. For example, the insurance industry and the medical profession first fought against medicare in Saskatchewan when it was introduced there, then transferred the fight to Ottawa to oppose a national program, and finally went back to individual provinces to try to persuade them stay out of the national scheme.[17] At other times, certain groups use their closer relations with provincial governments to transform the provinces into allies in the group's attempt to pressure Ottawa, such as in the insurance industry's opposition to the Canada Pension Plan, the mining industry's fight against federal tax reform, or the petroleum industry's campaign against the National Energy Program.[18]

It should be added in this connection that many national groups are beset by regional and linguistic problems, and that the Quebec wing of many national organizations has a distinct status of one kind or another. Other groups seem to handle the cleavages fairly well, having a regular provincial branch in Quebec, attempting to operate on a bilingual basis at the national level, and striving to reconcile regional–ethnic differences within the organization.

....

TARGETS AND METHODS OF PRESSURE GROUP ACTIVITY

Besides being affected by the federal system, Canadian interest groups are very much influenced in their operations by the fact that they exist in a parliamentary system. This, despite the name, places most of the decision-making power in the hands of the bureaucracy, the prime minister, and the Cabinet. Pressure groups that understand this basic truth direct most of their attention to these executive branches of government.

In this connection, the concept of **policy communities** (or policy networks) should be mentioned.[19] This concept is based on the premise that each field of public policy is discrete and specialized, with its own constellation of participants. Each policy community consists of a grouping of government agencies, pressure groups, corporations, institutions, media people, and individuals including academics who have an interest in that particular policy field and attempt to influence it. Paul Pross argues that every policy community is divided into two parts. The first, the "sub-government," includes a "lead government agency," other policy-making agencies, and a small group of interests with the right to be consulted on a daily basis; the second, the "attentive public," is composed of the other actors mentioned. In either case, these actors initially attempt to establish their legitimacy with the lead agency, and if they achieve such recognition and status, they may be appointed to advisory committees and be made part of the agency's information flow. Pross cites the examples of the Canadian Bankers' Association and the Canadian Tax Foundation as groups that have achieved such legitimacy, as opposed to the National Farmers Union, which has not.

Once such groups are given the privilege of consultation and access to strategic information, they normally behave quite cooperatively, and the whole policy community becomes cohesive and mutually supportive. All the actors involved, including the lead agency, prefer to keep the issues that concern them within the community, and have a strong incentive to resolve any problems there rather than open the issues up to Cabinet discussion or, even worse, public debate and confrontation. More will be said about such policy communities in Chapter 19, but for now it is sufficient to emphasize the specialized nature of different policy fields, the varied configurations of actors they contain, and the increasing reliance of governments on partnerships in the private sector. Figure 15.1 provides a diagram of a typical policy community.

The Bureaucracy

As will be discussed in Chapter 21, the bureaucracy advises the prime minister and Cabinet on almost all of their decisions; it drafts legislation and regulations according to the Cabinet's general instructions; it proposes budgets and spends government money; and it implements policies and programs once they have been given Cabinet and/or legislative approval. All of these areas hold considerable scope for bureaucratic discretion, and Pross speaks of "bureaucratic pluralism," in which various government agencies and departments gain considerable autonomy.[20]

Figure 15.1   The Policy Community

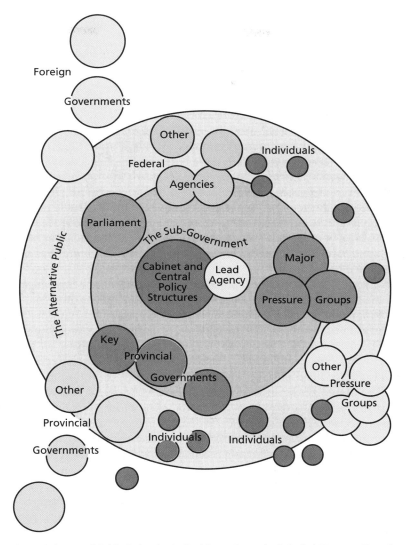

Source: From Group Politics and Public Policy by A. Paul Pross. Copyright © Oxford University Press Canada 1986. Reprinted by permission of Oxford University Press Canada.

It is for this reason that institutionalized groups in particular direct their messages at the bureaucratic target more than at any other institution of government.[21] Many pressure group demands involve technical matters that only the bureaucracy understands and that it may be able to satisfy without reference to the politicians. Although bureaucrats may initially consider meeting pressure groups as a waste of precious time and be suspicious of their motives,[22] such groups try to cultivate close relationships with the senior public servants so that they feel comfortable in contacting these officials on an informal, direct, day-to-day basis. This contact can take the form of telephone calls, meetings, letters, e-mails, faxes, and business lunches. If a first-name relationship emerges, so much the better.[23] The Canadian Construction Association, for example, has an annual meeting with a large number of deputy ministers and other senior government officials.

A close relationship often develops between a pressure group and its most relevant government department. This relationship may, however, be a reciprocal one, as desirable for the public service as it is for the group. In return for the various ways in which the bureaucracy can respond to group demands, the group may possess information that the department needs or desires in order to understand certain situations with which it is trying to deal. As issues become too complex for politicians—ministers or MPs—to understand, and larger numbers of issues, constituents, and obligations eat up their time, legislation is increasingly drafted in skeletal form with the specifics delegated to the bureaucracy to be added later in the form of regulations or "delegated legislation." Bureaucrats regularly consult pressure groups as they draft such legislation, design new programs, and draw up regulations. As president of the Canadian Tobacco Manufacturers' Association, for example, Bill Neville managed to dilute the original regulations dealing with the anti-smoking message that the Health Department imposed on packages of cigarettes.[24] The group may also be a valuable ally in persuading other bureaucratic agencies or Cabinet to do what the department wants, and in various "output" functions described below.

Thus, what is called a **clientele relationship** sometimes develops between such groups as the Royal Canadian Legion and the Department of Veterans' Affairs, between the Canadian Federation of Agriculture and the Department of Agriculture and Agri-food, between the Canadian Medical Association and the Department of Health, between the petroleum and mining associations and the Department of Natural Resources, and between business organizations and the departments of Finance and Industry. The relations between such an agency or department and its allied pressure groups may become so close that it is difficult to tell them apart. The agency or department almost becomes an extension of the pressure group, making policy in the interest of the group and promoting within the higher councils of government the interests they both represent. The minister, deputy minister, and department of Finance speak for the business community, while the minister, deputy minister, and department of Agriculture speak for the farming community, and so on.

Although pressure groups are usually seen in terms of their "input" function—making demands or "policy advocacy"—they may also perform various "policy participation" or "output" functions. A group may be better equipped to inform its specialized membership or audience about new laws, regulations, or programs than a department that is restricted to the conventional media or other regular channels of communication. Ethnic groups, for example, can help the Immigration Department in the dissemination of information about policy changes to a specialized audience. In addition, the cooperation of the group might be indispensable to the successful execution of a program, such as the role of the medical profession in the administration of medicare. In some cases, as noted, certain groups are even delegated powers of self-regulation, especially the medical and legal professions at the provincial level. As government coped with decreasing funds in the 1990s, they often sought private-sector partnerships as a way of offloading services, improving service delivery, and encouraging civic engagement.[25]

Besides such direct, personal, informal contact, interest groups interact with the bureaucracy through numerous permanent and ad hoc advisory committees. Most departments set up several advisory committees and offer representation on them to the pressure groups most affected. The Canadian Bar Association sits on liaison committees, for example, with the Supreme, Federal, and Tax Courts of Canada, the Canadian Construction Association is represented on the Canadian Labour Force Development Board, and the Canadian Bankers' Association represented the banks on numerous Y2K committees and task forces set up by the Bank of Canada. The National Council of Welfare is a classic "reverse" group that was not only created by government to serve as an advisory committee directly representing poor people, but was even given a home and staff within the building housing the Welfare Department.

In addition, public servants themselves may be members of interest groups. For example, bureaucrats in welfare departments often belong to the Canadian Council on Social Development, a situation that naturally assists the group in maximizing its influence; medical bureaucrats may belong to the Canadian Medical Association, and legal bureaucrats to the Canadian Bar Association. In fact, considerable movement of personnel takes place between interest groups and the higher levels of the public service; officials often move from pressure group jobs to the bureaucracy or vice versa.

The Prime Minister and Cabinet

The prime minister and Cabinet form the second branch of government that pressure groups frequently try to influence. This is because they make the major governmental decisions in a parliamentary system, as discussed in Chapter 20. Since many decisions are made by individual ministers or Cabinet committees, it is probably most productive to submit single-issue representations to individual ministers, who indeed spend much of their time in meetings with such groups.[26] If a minister stays in one position long enough, a pressure group may be able to construct a more personal, informal relationship, as did the Canadian Federation of Agriculture with Jimmy Gardiner, who served as minister of Agriculture from 1935 to 1957.[27] The practice of shuffling ministers from one department to another every couple of years decreases the likelihood of developing such intimacy. The social scene in Ottawa should also be mentioned, for parties and receptions provide excellent opportunities for Cabinet ministers, deputy ministers, and established pressure group representatives (especially corporate) to meet and mingle.

Occasionally ministers are themselves members of the interest group, in which case this interlocking membership is probably an advantage to the group. Less institutionalized groups, on the other hand, may have to forgo such close relationships with Cabinet ministers in favour of letters, faxes, or other means of more formal or mass communication.

The concept of **elite accommodation**[28] is particularly relevant to this process. It claims that most public decisions in Canada emerge from the interaction of three agents: the Cabinet, the senior public service, and pressure groups, especially in the business field. The individuals who occupy the top positions in these sectors are elites both in the sense of being small numbers of people with disproportionate amounts of power (compared with ordinary citizens) and in the sense of their exclusive socioeconomic backgrounds, coming from families of higher social class, higher incomes, and higher educations. Robert Presthus thus postulates that the common backgrounds and values of political, bureaucratic, and corporate leaders help to facilitate agreement among them. Commanding the heights of these sectors of society, they easily accommodate each other in the working out of public policies. Lobbyists from professional lobbying firms also fit perfectly into this arrangement.

Corporatism, on the other hand, is a concept that includes labour in the equation. Corporatism conceives of society as being divided into a relatively few functional sectors, such as business, labour, farmers, and professions, and prescribes some type of formal, functional representation in the making of general policies for society as a whole, especially in the interaction of large national groups like business, labour, and government. Corporatism is sometimes identified with the powers of self-regulation that are delegated to professional organizations, and Canadian farmers have sometimes argued that each sector of society should be self-governing and that functional representation should replace territorial representation in Parliament. But in the sense of multilateral negotiation among conflicting social interests in which the state is a major party, corporatism is much more prevalent in other countries than in Canada. That is largely because Canada does not have a single, authoritative peak organization that speaks for either business or labour, because labour is generally not given the same kind of attention that it is accorded elsewhere, and because of greater hostility between labour and business. The closest Canadian approximation to corporatism involved tripartite (business, labour, and government) schemes tried in the 1970s to develop general economic policies.[29] Elite accommodation is generally a more accurate depiction of the Canadian scene than corporatism, therefore, largely because the former virtually eliminates the labour component.

Parliament

The third main branch of the government is the legislature or Parliament, but as will be discussed in Chapter 22, it largely legitimizes decisions previously taken by the executive. That being the case, the House of Commons is not as often the target of interest group activity, but it does remain the object of considerable attention. One of the main reasons that a bill is usually sent to a legislative committee during its passage is to allow interest groups to make representations on it, and such committee scrutiny of bills may carry on for weeks. Especially in a majority government situation, however, ministers have traditionally been reluctant to accept amendments proposed at the legislative stage, so that groups were better advised to make their case at the executive level before the bill was made public. It has even been said that the sight of a pressure group at the legislative level in Canada is a sign that the group already failed at the level of the bureaucracy and the Cabinet.

Nevertheless, groups also converge on MPs in their offices or inundate them with letters, telegrams, or postcards from group members. For example, while not diminishing its influence at the levels of Cabinet and bureaucracy, the Canadian Chamber of Commerce is particularly adept at applying pressure on MPs through its base in almost every constituency across the country. Groups also meet with chairs of Commons standing committees, individual party caucuses, or caucus committees. Certain MPs may already belong to the interest group or may be persuaded to join, in which case they can be expected to speak on behalf of the group on a committee or in the Commons, in another aspect of interlocking membership between groups and authorities. Many pressure group–inspired amendments to legislation have been accepted in recent years, perhaps most notably the changes made to the Charter of Rights before its final adoption in the early 1980s as a result of pressure from women's, Aboriginal, disability, and ethnic groups. The Standing Committee on Finance, with its pre-budget hearings, is now integrated into the expenditure management system, and listens to established groups on an annual basis.

The upper chamber of Parliament, the Senate, is involved in a somewhat different dimension. Because so many senators have close corporate connections and function regularly as lobbyists for big business, the Senate has been called a "lobby from within."[30] During passage in that chamber, much legislation is considered by the Senate Committee on Banking, Trade and Commerce, most of whose members hold directorships in Canadian banks and other large corporations. Such holdings have not deterred committee members from active consideration of questions relating to financial institutions in what many observers see as a classic case of conflict of interest.

Other Targets

Interest groups have many targets beyond these three main branches of government. If they can find a legal or constitutional angle to their demand, for example, such groups may take cases to the courts. Corporations have sometimes challenged federal or provincial legislation in the courts as a violation of the division of powers; francophone groups have used the courts to uphold constitutionally guaranteed minority language rights when politicians were reluctant to do so; and Aboriginal groups are increasingly using the courts to uphold or broaden the meaning of treaty and Aboriginal rights. The Charter of Rights and Freedoms provides added potential for targeting the courts by actually inviting individuals and groups to challenge federal or provincial legislation they consider to be discriminatory. For example, the Canadian Federation of Students planned to go to court to challenge the Bankruptcy and Insolvency Act on the grounds that it discriminated against students on the basis of age, a violation of section 15 of the Charter, and same-sex groups made major advances in the courts at the end of the century.[31]

As mentioned, only the Canadian Labour Congress has seen fit to attach itself formally to a political party. This strategy may have reduced the group's impact on Liberal and Conservative governments as it awaited an NDP victory, however, and other groups remain scrupulously nonpartisan so that they can exert equal influence on whichever party is in power. Another target of pressure group activity is the Royal Commission. These elaborate investigations of public problems normally invite pressure groups and experts to submit briefs in public hearings in order to supplement whatever original research the commission itself undertakes, as well as to generate support for its recommendations. Sometimes a pressure group is actually represented on the commission itself, as in the case of the Canadian Medical Association and the Hall Royal Commission on Medical Services in the 1960s.

Besides their direct representations to government, pressure groups increasingly try to influence public opinion in the hope that the authorities will respond to a clear message from the public. In what is called "advocacy advertising," corporations and groups use media advertising in an attempt to sway public opinion to their point of view.[32] In 1991, for example, both the Pharmaceutical Manufacturers Association of Canada (now Canada's Research-Based Pharmaceutical Companies) and the rival Canadian Drug Manufacturers' Association took out media advertisements to make their case on the question of patent protection for new pharmaceuticals.

Many pressure groups increase their public profile once an election has been called. This phenomenon, discussed in Chapter 12, is usually called "third-party" or advocacy advertising. Pressure groups often seek the response of parties and candidates to questions of concern to the group. They then indicate their support or opposition in media advertising, which is contrary

A kilometre-long convoy of tractors, combines, and pickup trucks rumbles down a highway near Edmonton, August 1999. Farmers who participated in the cavalcade said they wanted people to recognize how drought, plummeting grain prices, and soaring costs are crippling their businesses. (Ed Kaiser/Canapress)

to the spirit of expenditure ceilings in the Canada Elections Act. Groups on either side of the abortion debate and the National Citizens' Coalition are regular examples, while the Canadian Alliance for Jobs and Trade Prospects and its anti–free trade counterpart, the Pro-Canada Network, were particularly visible in 1988. National or local pressure groups sometimes target particular politicians, especially ministers, for defeat.

Such coalitions are an increasingly prominent part of the political system. The Council of Canadians helped to found the Action Canada Network, the Canadian Environmental Network is another active coalition, and many of the business groups mentioned have joined a coalition calling on government to revamp its cost-recovery policies. The Canadian Federation of Students and the Canadian Association of University Teachers have both joined the Public Education Network, among others.

If all else fails, the group may resort to demonstrations, protest marches, tractor parades, sit-ins, and road and bridge blockades. Some of these are peaceful and legal, such as the orderly demonstrations that are an almost daily occurrence on Parliament Hill and that frequently greet prime ministers on their travels. The Canadian Federation of Students organized the pan-Canadian Days of Action in October 1998, featuring protest marches, rallies, sit-ins, and informational pickets. But the frustration of Aboriginal, environmentalist (e.g., Greenpeace), and other radical or issue-oriented groups increasingly takes the form of civil disobedience. The armed standoff at Oka, Quebec, in 1990 was one of the rare occasions in which a group resorted to violence.

Pressure groups are not restricted to one target and method, of course, and groups may use a variety of methods directed at a number of different targets. The Canadian Labour Congress, for example, was so distraught over the wage and price control program in 1975 that beyond its direct daily contact with government officials, its annual brief to the Cabinet, and its affiliation with the NDP, it challenged the legislation in the Supreme Court and organized a national day of protest. Five years later, the CLC held one of the largest demonstrations in Canadian history on Parliament Hill. After a few tense moments, it ended peacefully, much to the relief of the anxious House of Commons security guards.

GROUP RESOURCES AND DETERMINANTS OF SUCCESS

The fact that an institutionalized group like the CLC could fight an issue on so many fronts and still lose leads to the question: Why are groups sometimes successful and sometimes not? A variety of factors are involved in accounting for such success and failure, including the following:

- members
- cohesion
- money
- information
- leadership and prestige
- tenor of message
- financial position of government
- absence of oppostion

The size of the group is probably most important; since membership numbers represent votes, the authorities feel comfortable ignoring very small groups because the electoral consequences would be minimal. In this respect, the National Action Committee on the Status of Women and the Canadian Labour Congress, with over three million and over two million members respectively, should be regularly successful in having the authorities respond to their demands because they are the largest pressure groups in Canada. However, it should be noted that in both cases this membership is indirect, since members first belong to a group or a union that is itself attached to the national body.

The fact that the CLC is not usually very influential points to the importance not just of a large membership, but of the cohesiveness of the organization. First of all, as mentioned, only about one-third of paid workers belong to unions and less than 60 percent of Canadian union members belong to the CLC, so that the labour movement as a whole is not very cohesive. But even among those who are members of the CLC, unity, commitment, and militancy are notoriously lacking. In addition to the weak sense of class-consciousness in Canada, there is a lack of union-consciousness, an unwillingness of one union to support another. The CLC's ultimate threat to Liberal or Conservative governments is that the more unhappy the group is, the more likely its members are to vote NDP. But even on those occasions when the CLC "declared war" on the government, the bulk of its members continued to vote for the old-line parties. Liberal and Conservative governments apparently feel that the CLC is so incapable of mobilizing its members behind the demands issued by its leadership that it can often be ignored. The Canadian Federation of Students could also benefit from greater cohesion.

The CLC and CFS contrast with such other groups as the Royal Canadian Legion or the Canadian Chamber of Commerce in this respect. Both of these, and many others, are able to mobilize their members to inundate the authorities with demands for concerted action. The CCC, for example, issues periodic action calls that tell its members to "use the facts and arguments outlined in this bulletin [to] deliver the message in your own words on your own letterhead to your Member of Parliament by letter, phone, fax or in person. Send a copy of your message directly to the Minister of Finance and the Prime Minister."[33]

As in other aspects of politics and life in general, money is an important resource. In the case of pressure groups, money can buy staff, offices, organization, expertise, publicity, and other useful weapons with which to get the group's message across. The four peak business groups, especially the Business Council on National Issues, are very well endowed financially, giving them the capacity both to generate the information to strengthen their case and to transmit it to relevant targets.

In fact, except for those representing big business or highly paid professions, most groups struggle with their finances. Typical of medium-sized interest groups, the Canadian Association of University Teachers has a budget of about $3.3 million, and the Canadian Construction Association of about $2 million. On rare occasions, on the other hand, the very poverty of the group may actually be an asset in seeking government assistance: it sometimes strengthens the case for public support.

Information is a fourth crucial resource in pressure group politics. Especially at the bureaucratic level, where much of this politics takes place, any vital information that is lacking as the public service drafts technical laws and regulations will be eagerly accepted. Even at the political level, the group may be able to present data and alternative analyses of policy that will lead ministers to rethink their proposals. Closely associated with information is the professional expertise of the pressure group's staff, and in this connection, the large business groups are able to produce mounds of well-researched and glossy documents. The Canadian Bar Association makes frequent representations to parliamentary committees, royal commissions, and government departments, and because of its expertise in both the substance of many issues and in the drafting of legislation, is often asked for advice. The CBA and Canadian Chamber of Commerce are among many groups that constantly monitor federal political issues and the passage of legislation and keep their members informed via monthly newsletters.

The quality of group leadership and the prestige of the group are other important factors. In recent years, for example, even the Canadian Labour Congress has quite deliberately sought to choose "smooth," articulate, attractive leaders to make its case. When dealing with a Liberal or Conservative government, however, organized labour probably does not rival doctors, lawyers, or businesspeople as far as prestige is concerned.

The tenor of the group's message is also important. If a basic correspondence exists between the demands of the group and the government's stated objectives or the prevailing values of society in general, the pressure group will have greater success than if there is a vast gap in ideological perspective. Contrast the BCNI, which was widely seen as actually *setting* the agenda of the business-oriented Mulroney government,[34] with the CLC, which was virtually ignored. Similarly, the minister responsible for the Status of Women in that Cabinet repeatedly refused to meet the National Action Committee on the Status of Women because of its intense criticism. At the same time, the government cut NAC's grant and gave the first federal grant to its rival, REAL Women (Realistic, Equal, Active for Life). Canadian banks are used to getting their way with government, but it was largely because of the negativity of public opinion that the government rejected the bank mergers in 1998–99.[35]

Related to ideology is the sharing of a professional orientation between group leaders and authorities, especially in the bureaucracy. Many examples could be given of the success of a group because its officials shared the professional norms of the relevant public servants in their reciprocal, clientele relationship. A government or societal guilty conscience can sometimes also be helpful, such as in the provision of grants to Aboriginal, Japanese-Canadian, or anti-poverty groups.

Since many pressure group demands relate to the spending of public money, the financial position of the government will often influence a group's success, as the Canadian Federation of Students could attest. In the prosperous and free-spending 1960s and 1970s, for example, requests for funds were more likely to be fulfilled than in the 1980s, the 1990s, and in the early years of the new century, which constituted an era of government restraint.

Finally, a group will be more influential if it has no organized opposition. One of the reasons for the success of the Canadian Medical Association over the years, for example, was that it had medical politics almost all to itself.[36] Contrast that situation with the evenly divided forces on either side of the abortion or tobacco advertising debates. Somewhat similarly, the Canadian Federation of Students finds its message diluted and contradicted by minor rival groups. Alternatively, success can be influenced by whether or not a rival group expresses more or less the same point of view, such as in the competition between the Canadian Federation of Agriculture and the National Farmers Union.

LOBBYING IN CANADA

The tendency of the rich and powerful, including big business, to benefit from pressure group politics and elite accommodation can only be enhanced by recent developments in the practice of lobbying in Canada. If lobbying is the activity of trying to influence the authorities, it is, of course, a perfectly legitimate activity for anyone to undertake in a democracy. Traditionally, individuals, companies, unions, and pressure groups of all kinds have done their own lobbying, but in recent years Canada has seen the mushrooming of professional lobbying—consultant or government relations firms that lobby on behalf of an individual, company, or pressure group in return for a fee.

Emergence of Modern Lobbying

Those engaged in the new lobbying industry justify their existence largely in terms of the increasing size and complexity of government. The federal government grew enormously in the 1960s and 1970s, and the policymaking process was restructured so that corporations and interest groups could no longer find their way around Ottawa.[37] That the hostile budgets of 1980 (National Energy Program) and 1981 (corporate tax reform) caught the business community by surprise also contributed to the development of means through which the corporate sector could make its voice heard more effectively.

The early 1980s was a period in which new means of influence were being sought, and an expansion of lobbying firms appeared to take place about the time the Mulroney government was elected in 1984. Many of the leading figures in the initial establishment of professional lobby firms, such as Gerald and Fred Doucet, Gary Ouellet, Patrick MacAdam, Frank Moores, Bill Fox, Bill Neville, and David Angus, were cronies of the prime minister.[38] Certain leading legal firms also set up lobbying operations.

Given that the bureaucracy can satisfy many of the corporations' needs, many bureaucrats left to join or form lobbying firms in order to capitalize on their inside knowledge and connections. Federal conflict-of-interest guidelines preclude senior government employees from dealing with their former departments for one year after their departure from public employment, but these rules were sometimes broken, and, in any case, many critics doubt that it is sufficient time in which to be away.

Legalizing Lobbying: The Registration System

After the emergence of such professional lobbying firms, a consensus developed among politicians that legislation, registration, and regulation were necessary. The registration idea was part of the Conservatives' ethics package unveiled after its early troubled record of Cabinet resignations due to conflicts of interest and numerous legal charges against Tory backbenchers.[39] The legislation might never have come to pass without the consensus and determination of three key backbenchers—Albert Cooper (PC), Don Boudria (Liberal), and John Rodriguez (NDP)[40]—but the government diluted their original draft.

According to the 1989 **Lobbyists Registration Act**, a lobbyist is an individual

who, for payment, on behalf of any person or organization ... undertakes to arrange a meeting with a public office holder or to communicate with a public office holder in an attempt to influence

(a) the development of a legislative proposal ...
(b) the introduction, passage, defeat or amendment of any bill or resolution ...
(c) the making or amending of any regulation ...
(d) the development or amendment of any policy or program ...
(e) the awarding of any monetary grant or contribution or other financial benefit ... or
(f) the awarding of any contract.

The legislation acknowledged that lobbying public officeholders was a legitimate activity, but required lobbyists to register because it was desirable that officials and the public knew who was attempting to influence government and because paid lobbyists should not impede free and open access to government. It excluded representations made to parliamentary committees or other cases where the representations were a matter of public record; oral or written submissions made to a public officeholder by an individual on behalf of any person or organization with respect to the enforcement, interpretation, or application of existing acts or regulations; and submissions made in direct response to a written request for advice or comment from a public officeholder. Otherwise, lobbyists had to file a return including the name and address of the lobbyist and the lobbying firm, the name and address of the client, and the subject matter of the solicitation.

The law divided lobbyists into two categories: those who worked for a client for a fee were classified as "Tier I" lobbyists, while "Tier II" lobbyists included those who engaged in traditional pressure group or corporate lobbying—that is, "in-house" employees whose duties involved communicating with public officeholders on behalf of the organization that employs them. Both types of lobbyists had to register their activities in the Registry of Lobbyists.

Many critics felt that the legislation was very weak and contrasted it with the U.S. law on this subject, which was adopted in 1946.[41] Some lobbyists did not register, and even when they did, the disclosure provisions in the Canadian law were quite minimal. In their report, lobbyists merely had to record which of 52 general categories of subject matter (agriculture, energy, etc.) was involved and which of seven general categories of objects (legislation, contract, etc.) they were trying to influence. The law did not require revelation of the specific object of the representations, and was almost totally lacking in an effective enforcement mechanism.

The whole procedure provided a lucrative living to those who could claim to be intimates of ministers or ministries, and favoured those who could afford to hire such professional lobbyists. In what John Sawatsky calls "one of the most odious lobby campaigns in the history of Canada," the fight of the Pharmaceutical Manufacturers Association of Canada to extend drug patent protection, "Gerry Doucet handled the PMAC file in GCI's (Government Consultants International) office; his brother Fred handled the issue in the Prime Minister's Office."[42] In the Mulroney era, ministers were allowed to set up large offices full of personal or partisan assistants headed by a chief of staff with which to provide stronger direction to the bureaucracy. As a result, lobbyists' efforts were often focused on ministers' offices, and even though most firms took on lobbyists with Liberal connections too, Tory partisan links were particularly important. Partly because of the newness of the phenomenon, much of the early lobbying was a fairly crude process of selling access to ministers and their staff.

A parliamentary committee reviewed the Lobbyists Registration Act in 1993 and made many recommendations to strengthen the act. These recommendations were not implemented before the PCs were defeated, but the Liberal Party promised in the Red Book to take such action. Not surprisingly, the lobbyists lobbied ferociously against greater transparency in their operations, and the amendments that were finally adopted in 1995 were a pale imitation of what had been recommended by the committee and promised during the election campaign. The information now required for the registration of each lobbying undertaking includes the following:

- name and business address of the lobbyist and name and address of the lobbying firm
- name and business address of the client and anyone who controls the client's activities
- if the client is a corporation, the name and business address of the parent corporation and those subsidiaries that directly benefit from the lobbying activity
- if the client is a coalition, the name and business address of each corporation or organization that is a member of the coalition
- subject matters, including the specific legislative proposal, bill, resolution, regulation, policy, program, grant, contribution, financial benefit, or contract sought
- name of each department or other governmental institution lobbied
- source and amount of any government funding provided to the client
- whether payment is contingent on the success of the lobbying
- communication techniques used, including grassroots lobbying, i.e., appeals to the public through the mass media or direct communication that seek to persuade members of the public to communicate directly with and apply pressure on the public officeholder.[43]

Rather than do away with the distinction between Tier I and Tier II lobbyists, the new act recognizes three categories: Tier I (consultant lobbyists who lobby for clients), and two types of Tier II (in-house) lobbyists—"corporate" and "organization"—that is, employees of corporations or interest group organizations for whom lobbying is a significant part of their duties. Otherwise, the new legislation is somewhat more rigorous in what has to be reported. Rather than explain just the general object of lobbying, lobbyists must identify the specific legislative proposal, bill, resolution, regulation, policy, program, or contract in question as well as the name of each department or other governmental institution lobbied. Coalitions and grassroots lobbying efforts have to be registered for the first time, and if contingency fees are involved, this must be disclosed, as must the source and amount of any government funding of the client. As for enforcement, the registrar can audit information contained in any return or other document submitted and issue interpretative bulletins and advisory opinions, while the six-month limitation of proceedings on contraventions is extended to two years. The ethics counsellor previously appointed by the Liberal government to administer the Conflict of Interest Code for ministers, parliamentary secretaries, and senior government officials was required to work with interested parties to develop a code of conduct for lobbyists. Lobbyists have a legal obligation to comply with the code, which took effect in March 1997. The ethics counsellor can investigate and publicly report on breaches of the code and the fees, disbursements, and expenses paid to a lobbyist relating to any lobbying activity.[44]

Lobbying Today

In the Chrétien government, ministers were forced to get by with a small number of partisan assistants, and the bureaucracy was allowed to operate with greater independence. Hence, the focus of lobbyists' efforts switched to some extent from ministers' offices to the level of the senior bureaucracy. Having Liberal connections was still important for lobbyists, however, because a knowledge of Cabinet thinking helped them influence decisions actually taken by the bureaucracy. Another distinctive mark of the Chrétien government was its massive consultation program; it sought the views of the stakeholders involved in so many issues that it almost overwhelmed both traditional pressure groups and Tier I lobbyists.

Not just because of the change of government, lobbying became more sophisticated with time. Instead of (or in addition to) promising access to ministers, lobbyists had to be better informed. They now promise to be able to tell their clients what the government is thinking and where it is going and to provide strategic advice on how and whom to lobby.

With massive layoffs in the public service, the government cannot always engage in as much policy analysis as before, and does not always know what it needs. Especially in the procurement field, therefore, it is more likely to seek out private-sector expertise and ask what is actually available before determining what it needs. A typical lobby firm nowadays claims to "work closely with senior business leaders and government decision makers, understanding the needs of both and crafting strategic, proactive government relations programs that achieve results; brokering the solutions that bring the private and public sectors together meeting the fundamental needs of both; understanding the dynamics at play in the political system, how priorities and initiatives are established and how decisions are made." It promises "the ability to communicate across government with bureaucratic and political decision makers regardless of partisan persuasion; offers strategic assistance on procurement, privatization, and commercialization projects and on the building and management of coalitions; and monitors and analyzes the legislative process."

In arranging for a client's visit, lobbyists will typically communicate with ministers and their offices, telling them what to expect from the representation and how they can avoid any trouble. The lobbyist may occasionally accompany or even speak for the client, but usually not. Instead, the lobbyist acts as a mediator between the public official and the client, calling the official back after the meeting and perhaps arranging another. If the client's issue is not on the minister's agenda, the lobbyist will approach the relevant public servant lower down in the hierarchy.

Since the reports of the Lobbyists Registration Branch are still not particularly revealing, it is fortunate that a private company, Advocacy Research Centre (ARC), fills the gap with a biweekly edition of the *Lobby Monitor*. This publication reveals the major lobbying efforts currently in progress, the techniques being used, and the people involved. The same company publishes an annual edition of *The Federal Lobbyists*, which gives a complete listing of lobbyist registrations for the year. Armed with these sources, the public can obtain a better understanding of the lobbying process, since the *Lobby Monitor* in particular is an investigative (though not critical) effort that reveals much more than is required under the law.

According to the 1999 edition of *The Federal Lobbyists* (based on registrations under the act), there were nearly 2500 registered lobbyists in existence, about 600 of them consultant lobbyists (Tier I), 400 of them lobbyists on corporations' own payrolls, and 1500 of them lobbyists working for nonprofit interest group organizations.[45] Since the work of Tier II lobbyists is not particularly controversial, it is more interesting to focus on those belonging to Tier I— those working for professional consultant or government relations lobbying firms.

In 1999, 325 such lobbying firms existed. Over three-quarters were one-person operations; 18 percent had two to five persons on staff; three percent had six to ten, and only 1 percent employed over ten lobbyists. A handful of lobbyists had individual firms as well as being part of a larger operation. A majority had only one client; 20 percent had two to five clients, 9 percent had six to ten, and only 8 percent had over ten clients. A single client will often entail multiple registrations, since each lobbying effort has to be individually acknowledged. Table 15.2 reveals the number of registrations and the number of registered lobbyists of the largest consultant lobbyist firms.[46]

TABLE 15.2 Largest Consultant Lobbying Firms, 1999

	Registrations	*Lobbyists*
Capital Hill Group	97	7
GPC Government Policy Consultants	74	28
Hill & Knowlton Canada	44	17
Global Public Affairs	44	7
Association House	34	14
Earnscliffe Strategy Group	31	3
Industry Government Relations Group	30	6
Grey, Clark, Shih & Associates	27	4
Gowlings	23	15
Public Perspectives	22	3
SAMCI (Susan Murray)	20	9
CFN Consultants	20	9
C.G. Management & Communications	19	5
Hession, Neville & Associates	19	4
Summa Strategies	14	6

Source: John A. Chenier and Scott R. Duncan, eds., The Federal Lobbyists, 1999, p. 198. Used with permission.

As indicated above, corporations make the greatest use of consultant lobbyists, but many corporations are clients of more than one professional lobby firm. Eurocopter Canada hired ten consultant lobbyists from five different firms. Besides corporations, a number of governments use the services of such lobbyists—the provinces of Alberta, Saskatchewan, and Newfoundland, and such foreign countries as Hong Kong, Gabon, and Zambia. At least two federal Crown corporations—Atomic Energy of Canada and VIA Rail—also found it advisable to employ lobbyists, as did many provincial Crown corporations. Moreover, a number of trade unions, several First Nations, and the universities of Guelph and Saskatchewan were also lobbyist clients. Among the coalitions registered in 1999 were those on Biomedical and Health Research and Demutualizing Insurance Companies.

Finally, it should be noted that some corporations and pressure groups have in-house lobbyists (Tier II) but also make use of professional lobby firms (Tier I) to supplement their efforts, while others rely exclusively on one category or the other. For example, Air Canada registered 12 corporate and 2 consultant lobbyists, while Canadian Airlines International had only 6 corporate lobbyists, although both companies increased their artillery during the 1999 airline restructuring battle. Chrysler had 2 corporate lobbyists, compared with 8 at Ford and 15 at GM, while the latter two each hired 1 consultant lobbyist. As for pressure groups, Canada's Research-Based Pharmaceutical Companies had 8 organizational lobbyists and 7 consultant lobbyists and the Canadian Bankers' Association had 24 organizational and 6 consultant lobbyists.

Many traditional pressure groups engage professional lobbyists to supplement their supplications to government because Tier I lobbyists tend to be better strategists and can be used to build coalitions and share expenses on matters in which such cooperation is advantageous. On the other hand, several pressure groups, including the Canadian Federation of Students, the Canadian Association of University Teachers, and the Business Council on National Issues, use only organizational lobbyists.

Defects in the System

While the revised law was a slight improvement on the original, it remained highly defective. "By leaving vague the definitions of lobbying, and by excluding any lobbying associated with a consultative exercise, the government ... left much room for those sincerely wishing to avoid disclosing their activities or their aims to do so."[47] It did not require lobbyists to disclose positions currently or recently held in national political parties, ministers' offices, or the federal public service; it did not actually prohibit the use of contingency fees; and it did not require disclosure of the global cost of each lobbying campaign. It was not only lobbyists themselves who fought against a stronger law; it was also in the interests of bureaucrats and ministers that the lobbying activity be kept behind closed doors.

The point at which lobbyists must register is when they communicate with a public official on behalf of a client. If they work under a general retainer, monitoring federal government activities and/or providing strategic advice on how or whom to lobby, they can charge for their services but do not have to register. Hence, much of the work of legal firms in this area is not registered. As mentioned, submissions with respect to the enforcement, interpretation, or application of a law or regulation by a public official are also exempt. Moreover, the enforcement of the Lobbyists Registration Act itself is still defective. It was not until 1999 that the RCMP looked into its first potential violation of the act in connection with a Liberal activist close to the prime minister who did not register as a lobbyist but allegedly met civil servants on behalf of a Shawinigan hotel owner who received a $100 000 government cheque to expand his operation.

Although a small number of trade unions and First Nations have employed lobbyists, it is generally true that the only actors who can afford the services of consultant lobbyists are corporations or business pressure groups. That partisan ties continue to play a significant part in the lobbying process makes the system doubly objectionable. Moreover, the very invention of consultant lobbyists gives many individuals, companies, and traditional pressure groups the impression that they must hire someone to do their bidding for them, rather than take their demands directly to the relevant authorities free of charge. In some cases, they have come to feel that they have lost their democratic right to approach their own government and even their member of Parliament.

CONCLUSION

This discussion confirms the contention that pressure groups and lobbying are becoming increasingly important in the Canadian political system. The number and activity of such groups has grown over time, and however much they are an unintended appendage to the system, modern government could simply not do without them. Much has been said in academic circles in recent years about how pressure groups are displacing political parties, and a comparison of the budgets and staff of the leading parties and pressure groups only confirms the disparities in their resources. But because most lobbying takes place in the private offices of bureaucrats and ministers, parties and elections continue to be more visible to the general public. While media, opposition party, and academic exposure and the ARC publications make pressure groups more noticeable all the time, the Lobbyists Registration Act needs to be further strengthened in order to put pressure groups and lobbyists in proper perspective.

P Of the approaches outlined in Chapter 1, pluralism is at first sight most relevant to the subject of pressure groups. It argues that public policy emerges from the competiton and accommodation among organized groups. Pluralists argue that all interests in society are free to organize and participate in the group competition, as the array of pressure groups mentioned in this chapter at least partly confirms. They contend that the political system is not tightly controlled by any elite, business or otherwise; it contains much "slack," which any interest can fill by merely getting organized. Each policy field has its own specialized audience and participants, so that different groups are influential in different areas. Pluralists would endorse public financial assistance to those interests that are truly lacking in organizational resources and would advise issue-oriented groups to seek cheap media publicity if they do not have well-established links to the authorities or the capacity to impress them in the usual behind-the-scenes way.

SC Given the frequency and intensity with which the authorities are approached by pressure groups and other lobbyists, it would take a resolute government indeed to ignore such group reaction, as is argued by the state-centred approach. In discussing the autonomy of the state, therefore, the concept of policy communities and the close relationship between a government department and a principal client group commend themselves. As Coleman and Skogstad write, "sectoral state actors appear more able to control the policy agenda ... when they enjoy the support of well organized client interests. Close state–societal relations may augment the state's ability to proceed with its state–societal agenda."[48] The concept of policy communities, therefore, combines the pluralist and state-centred approaches. It also bears a certain resemblance to elite accommodation, which was discussed earlier in the chapter.

(C) Class analysts refute the pluralist claim that with a little effort any interest can organize itself into a group; doing so is beyond the capacity of many individuals and interests. Such analysts are among those most alarmed at the disparity in resources and consequent influence between affluent business groups and hard-pressed labour, farmer, consumer, Aboriginal, women's, and anti-poverty groups. Many "have-not" groups depend heavily on government support for their very existence but then find it cut just when they are beginning to make themselves heard. Moreover, class analysts add, nearly half the population does not belong to any pressure group, the poorest and weakest part at that. Furthermore, businesses can lobby as individual firms, in functional pressure groups, or in peak business groups, so that they have more approaches from which to choose. The recent advent of expensive professional lobby firms, which only the corporate sector can afford, merely heightens the disparities between business and other groups.

Class analysts and others contend that the predominance of business groups is not only a matter of material resources; it also flows naturally from the marriage of a capitalist economy with a democracy and reflects the dominant ideology of the two parties that have alternated in government. Leo Panitch writes that "it is not that political and bureaucratic officials decide to favour capitalist interests in case after case; it is rather that it rarely even occurs to them that they might do other than favour such interests."[49] In the same vein, Ralph Miliband says that "it is easier for ministers to ditch their stocks and shares when appointed to public office than it is to ditch their basic sympathies and predispositions toward the business world."[50] Moreover, the state is dependent on businesses and business groups for the performance of the economy, so that the government takes seriously any promise to create jobs or any threat to contract employment.[51] In his book, *Titans*, Peter C. Newman argues that the Business Council on National Issues under President Tom d'Aquino set the agenda for all recent Canadian governments. First, it was free trade, then deficit reduction, and after that, tax cuts, each of them reducing the size and role of the state. The BCNI and its allies like the C.D. Howe Institute only lost out on the Multilateral Agreement on Investment (MAI). "The regimes of Brian Mulroney and Jean Chrétien came to agree that what was good for the BCNI was good for Canada," and Tom d'Aquino emerged as "the most powerful influence on public policy formation in Canadian history."[52]

....

DISCUSSION QUESTIONS

1. Are you a member of any groups that at least occasionally try to influence government policy? Are you familiar with any local issue-oriented groups or social movements?

2. Why do business groups have more influence than other kinds of groups? Do they have too much?

3. How could the unorganized be helped to organize and how could weak groups be strengthened in order to offset the influence of business?

4. In what sense do pressure groups act as integrating agents in society? On balance, are they more divisive or integrative?

5. What factors led to the growth in the professional lobbying industry in Canada in recent years?

6. How could the Lobbyists Registration Act be strengthened to keep lobbying completely above-board?

7. How do each of the approaches outlined in Chapter 1 enhance our understanding of pressure groups and lobbying?

....

NOTES

1. Paul Pross, *Group Politics and Public Policy* (Toronto: Oxford University Press, 1986).
2. Ibid., p. 87.
3. Ibid., esp. ch. 11.
4. Ibid., pp. 92–93.
5. Many groups are sloppy in their use of an apostrophe in their name. I have tried to be faithful to their desires, even when it was grammatically incorrect! *Associations Canada: The Directory of Associations in Canada* (Toronto: IHS/Micromedia, 1998) is an excellent source.
6. William D. Coleman, *Business and Politics: A Study of Collective Action* (Montreal: McGill–Queen's University Press, 1988); Stephen Brooks and Andrew Stritch, *Business and Government in Canada* (Scarborough: Prentice-Hall Canada, 1991), ch. 7; and W.T. Stanbury, *Business–Government Relations in Canada* (Toronto: Methuen, 1986), esp. ch. 7.
7. Coleman, *Business and Politics*, p. 6.
8. Ibid., p. 45. In 1994 he counted over 600. See "One Step Ahead: Business in the Policy Process in Canada," in Mark Charlton and Paul Barker, eds., *Crosscurrents: Contemporary Political Issues*, 2nd ed. (Scarborough: Nelson Canada, 1994).
9. Grace Skogstad, *The Politics of Agricultural Policy-Making in Canada* (Toronto: University of Toronto Press, 1987); and Helen Jones Dawson, "An Interest Group: The Canadian Federation of Agriculture," *Canadian Public Administration* (June 1960), pp. 134–49; Coleman, *Business and Politics*, ch. 6.
10. Jim Silver, *Thin Ice: Money, Politics and the Demise of an NHL Franchise* (Halifax: Fernwood Publishing, 1996).
11. Susan Phillips, "New Social Movements in Canadian Politics: On Fighting and Starting Fires," in James P. Bickerton and Alain-G. Gagnon, eds., *Canadian Politics*, 2nd ed. (Peterborough: Broadview Press, 1994); William K. Carroll, ed., *Organizing Dissent: Contemporary Social Movements in Theory and Practice*, 2nd ed. (Toronto: Garamond Press, 1997); and Jill Vickers, *Reinventing Political Science: A Feminist Approach* (Halifax: Fernwood Publishing, 1997).
12. Claude Galipeau, "Political Parties, Interest Groups, and New Social Movements," in Alain Gagnon and Brian Tanguay, eds., *Canadian Parties in Transition* (Scarborough: Nelson Canada, 1989).
13. Jeffrey M. Ayres, *Defying Conventional Wisdom: Political Movements and Popular Contention against North American Free Trade* (Toronto: University of Toronto Press, 1998); R.S. Ratner, "Many Davids, One Golilath," in Carroll, ed., *Organizing Dissent*.
14. Leslie Pal, *Interests of State: The Politics of Language, Multiculturalism, and Feminism in Canada* (Montreal: McGill–Queen's University Press, 1993).
15. See William Coleman and Grace Skogstad, eds., *Policy Communities and Public Policy in Canada* (Mississauga: Copp Clark Pitman, 1990), esp. chs. 1, 2, 7, 8, 9.
16. H.G. Thorburn, *Interest Groups in the Canadian Federal System* (Toronto: University of Toronto Press, 1985).

17. Malcolm Taylor, *Health Insurance and Canadian Public Policy* (Montreal: McGill–Queen's University Press, 1978).

18. M.W. Bucovetsky, "The Mining Industry and the Great Tax Reform Debate," in Paul Pross, ed., *Pressure Group Behaviour in Canadian Politics* (Toronto: McGraw-Hill Ryerson, 1975); Glyn Berry, "The Oil Lobby and the Energy Crisis," *Canadian Public Administration* (Winter 1974), pp. 600–35; and Glen Toner and Bruce Doern, "The Two Energy Crises and Canadian Oil and Gas Interest Groups," *Canadian Journal of Political Science* (September 1986), pp. 467–93.

19. Pross, *Group Politics and Public Policy*, ch. 6; Coleman, *Business and Politics*, ch. 4; Leslie A. Pal, *Beyond Policy Analysis: Public Issue Management in Turbulent Times* (Scarborough: ITP Nelson, 1997), ch. 6.

20. Paul Pross, "Parliamentary Influence and the Diffusion of Power," *Canadian Journal of Political Science* (June 1985), pp. 235–66.

21. In its advice to lobbyists, Corpus Information Services, *The Government Relations Handbook* (Don Mills: Southam, 1989), p. 1-1, suggests that contacts be made from the director level up.

22. Ibid., p. 1-2.

23. Pross, *Group Politics and Public Policy*; Brooks and Stritch, *Business and Government in Canada*, ch. 7.; Coleman, *Business and Politics*; and Stanbury, *Business–Government Relations in Canada*, ch. 7.

24. Brooks and Stritch, *Business and Government in Canada*, pp. 237–38.

25. Leslie Seidel, *Rethinking the Delivery of Public Services to Citizens* (Montreal: Institute for Research on Public Policy, 1995); Coleman, *Business and Politics*, ch. 3.

26. Pross, "Parliamentary Influence and the Diffusion of Power."

27. Dawson, "An Interest Group: The Canadian Federation of Agriculture."

28. Robert Presthus, *Elite Accommodation in Canada* (Toronto: Macmillan, 1973).

29. Stephen McBride, "Public Policy as a Determinant of Interest Group Behaviour: The Canadian Labour Congress' Corporatist Initiative, 1976–1978," *Canadian Journal of Political Science* (September 1983), pp. 501–17; the fragmented nature of both business and labour in Canada is emphasized in Michael Howlett and M. Ramesh, *The Political Economy of Canada: An Introduction* (Toronto: McClelland and Stewart, 1992).

30. Colin Campbell, *The Canadian Senate: A Lobby from Within* (Toronto: Methuen, 1983), and John McMenemy, "The Senate as an Instrument of Business and Party," in Paul Fox and Graham White, eds., *Politics: Canada*, 7th ed. (Toronto: McGraw-Hill Ryerson, 1991).

31. Miriam Smith, *Lesbian and Gay Rights in Canada: Social Movements and Equality-Seeking, 1971–1995* (Toronto: University of Toronto Press, 1999).

32. Brooks and Stritch, *Business and Government in Canada*, pp. 260–64, and Stanbury, *Business–Government Relations in Canada*, ch. 12.

33. The Canadian Chamber of Commerce, "Action Call," 1990.

34. Peter C. Newman, *Titans: How the New Canadian Establishment Seized Power* (Toronto: Penguin, 1998), pp. 154–62.

35. John A. Chenier and Scott R. Duncan, eds., *The Federal Lobbyists, 1999* (Ottawa: ARC Publications, 1999), pp. 225–29.

36. Malcolm Taylor, "The Role of the Medical Profession in the Formulation of Public Policy," *Canadian Journal of Economics and Political Science* (February, 1960), pp. 108–27.

37. Peter Aucoin, "Organizational Change in the Machinery of Canadian Government: From Rational Management to Brokerage Politics," *Canadian Journal of Political Science* (March 1986), pp. 3–27.

38. Brooks and Stritch, *Business and Government in Canada*, ch. 4.

39. Ian Greene, "Conflict of Interest and the Canadian Constitution: An Analysis of Conflict of Interest Rules for Canadian Cabinet Ministers," *Canadian Journal of Political Science* (June 1990), pp. 233–56.

40. John Sawatsky, *The Insiders: Government, Business, and the Lobbyists* (Toronto: McClelland and Stewart, 1987), ch. 20.

41. Brooks and Stritch, *Business and Government in Canada*, p. 240; and Sawatsky, *The Insiders*, Epilogue.

42. John Sawatsky, *The Insiders*, pp. 315–16.

43. Lobbyists Registration Branch website, "A Guide to Registration": http://www.strategis.ic.gc.ca.

44. Ibid.

45. Chenier and Duncan, *The Federal Lobbyists, 1999*.

46. Ibid.

47. John A. Chenier, ed., *The Federal Lobbyists, 1995* (Ottawa: ARC Publications, 1995), p. ii.

48. Coleman and Skogstad, *Policy Communities and Public Policy in Canada*, p. 6.
49. Leo Panitch, ed., *The Canadian State: Political Economy and Political Power* (Toronto: University of Toronto Press, 1977), p. 14.
50. Ralph Miliband, *The State in Capitalist Society* (London: Quartet Books, 1973), p. 55.
51. Brooks and Stritch, *Business and Government in Canada*, ch. 1, and Coleman, *Business and Politics*, ch. 1.
52. Newman, *Titans*, pp. 154–62.

....

FURTHER READING

Associations Canada. *The Directory of Associations in Canada, 1998/99*. Toronto: IHS/Micromedia, 1999.

Ayers, Jeffrey M. *Defying Conventional Wisdom: Political Movements and Popular Contention against North American Free Trade*. Toronto: University of Toronto Press, 1998.

Brooks, Stephen. "Too Close for Comfort? Lobbying and Political Parties." In A. Brian Tanguay and Alain-G. Gagnon, eds., *Canadian Parties in Transition*, 2nd ed. Scarborough: Nelson Canada, 1996.

Campbell, Colin. *The Canadian Senate: A Lobby from Within*. Toronto: Macmillan, 1978.

Carroll, William K., ed. *Organizing Dissent: Contemporary Social Movements in Theory and Practice*, 2nd ed. Toronto: Garamond Press, 1997.

Chenier, John A., ed. *The Federal Lobbyists 1995*. Ottawa: ARC Publications, 1995.

Chenier, John A., and Scott R. Duncan, eds. *The Federal Lobbyists, 1999*. Ottawa: ARC Publications 1999.

Coleman, William. *Business and Politics*. Montreal: McGill–Queen's University Press, 1988.

Coleman, William, and Grace Skogstad. *Policy Communities and Public Policy in Canada*. Mississauga: Copp Clark Pitman, 1990.

Howlett, Michael, and M. Ramesh. *The Political Economy of Canada: An Introduction*. Toronto: McClelland and Stewart, 1992.

The Lobby Monitor. Ottawa: ARC Publications, biweekly.

McBride, Stephen. "Public Policy as a Determinant of Interest Group Behaviour: The Canadian Labour Congress' Corporatist Initiative, 1976–1978." *Canadian Journal of Political Science* (September 1983), pp. 501–17.

Newman, Peter C. *Titans: How the New Canadian Establishment Seized Power*. Toronto: Penguin, 1998.

Pal, Leslie A. *Interests of State: The Politics of Language, Multiculturalism, and Feminism in Canada*. Montreal: McGill–Queen's University Press, 1993.

———. *Beyond Policy Analysis: Public Issue Management in Turbulent Times*. Scarborough: ITP Nelson, 1997.

Phillips, Susan D. "New Social Movements in Canadian Politics: On Fighting and Starting Fires." In James P. Bickerton and Alain-G. Gagnon, eds., *Canadian Politics*, 2nd ed. Peterborough: Broadview Press, 1994.

———. "Competing, Connecting, and Complementing: Parties, Interest Groups, and New Social Movements." In A. Brian Tanguay and Alain-G. Gagnon, eds., *Canadian Parties in Transition*, 2nd ed. Scarborough: Nelson Canada, 1996.

Presthus, Robert. *Elite Accommodation in Canadian Politics*. Toronto: Macmillan, 1973.

Pross, Paul, ed. *Pressure Group Behaviour in Canadian Politics*. Toronto: McGraw-Hill Ryerson, 1975.

———. *Group Politics and Public Policy*. Toronto: Oxford University Press, 1986.

Sawatsky, John. *The Insiders: Power, Money and Secrets in Ottawa*. Toronto: McClelland and Stewart, 1987.

Silver, Jim. *Thin Ice: Money, Politics and the Demise of an NHL Franchise*. Halifax: Fernwood Publishing, 1996.

Smith, Miriam. *Lesbian and Gay Rights in Canada: Social Movements and Equality-Seeking, 1971–1995*. Toronto: University of Toronto Press, 1999.

Stanbury, W.T. *Business–Government Relations in Canada*. Toronto: Methuen, 1986.

Taylor, Malcolm. *Health Insurance and Canadian Public Policy*. Montreal: McGill–Queen's University Press, 1978.

PART 4

The Constitutional Context

The constitutional context of Canadian government and politics forms the framework of the "government" part of the political system and is analyzed in the three following chapters. Chapter 16 outlines the ingredients of the Canadian Constitution and the succession of attempts to make major changes to it. One of the most important aspects of the Constitution is the relationship between the federal and provincial governments. Thus, Chapter 17 examines all aspects of Canadian federalism. The other central aspect of the Constitution since 1982 is the Charter of Rights and Freedoms. How it has been interpreted and how it has affected the operation of the Canadian political system are discussed in Chapter 18.

Chapter 16

The Canadian Constitution
AND CONSTITUTIONAL
change

What is the Canadian Constitution? What formula should be used to amend it? Should the distribution of powers between Ottawa and the provinces be altered? Should Quebec be given constitutional recognition as a distinct society? Should the Constitution be given a new, inspiring preamble? These and related constitutional questions have obsessed Canadian policymakers and scholars for many years, yet many remain unresolved. Canada has gone through several attempts at constitutional review since 1960, but most of the issues involved spilled over into the new millennium.

The Canadian Constitution would be easier to comprehend if it consisted of a single piece of paper by that name. In the absence of such a document, we can define a **constitution** as "the whole body of fundamental rules and principles according to which a state is governed." To be more specific, the Constitution provides for the basic institutions of government and the relations between them, the relations between national and provincial governments, and the relations between governments and citizens.[1] Such a comprehensive definition suggests that the final product will not be neat and tidy, and that some of its ingredients may not be written down at all. In structural-functional terms, the Constitution outlines how the rule-making, rule-application, and rule-adjudication functions will be performed and by what political structures.

This chapter begins by examining the ingredients of the Canadian Constitution and then considers successive attempts at constitutional change. These include the search for a domestic amending formula, the quest for a constitutional Charter of Rights, and the pressures for constitutional change arising from the Quiet Revolution in Quebec: the 1971 Victoria Charter, the Constitution Act, 1982, the 1987 Meech Lake Accord, and the 1992 Charlottetown Accord, all attempting to resolve the "Quebec problem."

COMPONENTS OF THE CANADIAN CONSTITUTION

In the search for the components that fit the definition of a constitution provided above, it will be seen that the Canadian Constitution is a great hodge-podge. Some parts of it are written and other parts are unwritten. The principal components of the Canadian Constitution are as follows: the Constitution Act, 1867; the amendments to the Constitution Act, 1867; British statutes and orders-in-council; organic Canadian statutes; the Constitution Act, 1982; judicial decisions; and Constitutional conventions.

The Constitution Act, 1867

We turn first to the formal, legal documents, the most important of which is the **British North America (BNA) Act**, 1867, which in 1982 was officially renamed the **Constitution Act, 1867**.[2] This was the law passed by the British Parliament that joined Nova Scotia, New Brunswick, Ontario, and Quebec together as the new Dominion of Canada, as mentioned in Chapter 2. The act contained many components that would be expected in a constitution, providing much of the basic machinery and institutions of government and establishing a federal system.

The act lacks an inspirational introduction, and its preamble is seriously out of date. It merely states that the four original provinces have expressed their desire "to be federally united with a constitution similar in principle to that of the United Kingdom." Many of the subsequent 147 clauses are also obsolete, and several have actually been repealed.

Part III deals with the executive power, and section 9 declares that the executive authority over Canada is vested in the Queen. Subsequent clauses refer to the governor general and to the Canadian Privy Council, which is "to aid and advise in the Government of Canada." Section 13 observes that the governor in council refers to the governor general acting by and with the advice of the Canadian Privy Council. Note that the prime minister and Cabinet are not explicitly mentioned.

Part IV establishes the legislative power, the Senate and House of Commons. The Senate (sections 21–36) is based on the principle of equal regional representation, and the act details the qualifications for appointment. Section 26 allows for the appointment of four or eight extra senators, the power used by Prime Minister Brian Mulroney in 1990 to get the Goods and Services Tax passed. Sections 37 to 57 deal with the House of Commons. Many of these provisions have been superseded by other legislation, but sections 53 and 54 require that money bills originate in the House of Commons, and within it, from members of the executive branch.

Part V concerns the constitutions of the provinces, including the position of lieutenant governor. Since the 1867 act created the provinces of Ontario and Quebec, sections 69 to 87 establish their legislatures, whereas the legislatures of Nova Scotia and New Brunswick continued in their pre-Confederation form.

Part VI, the "Distribution of Legislative Powers" between the central and provincial governments, is probably the most important part of the document. This includes section 91, the federal powers; section 92, provincial powers; section 93, education; and section 95, concurrent powers.

Part VII is concerned with the judiciary. It is a short section that, in section 96, allows the governor general to appoint superior, district, and county judges. It also provides for judges' retirement and removal, and allows Parliament to set up a general court of appeal. Note that the 1867 act does not explicitly establish the Supreme Court of Canada.

Part VIII deals with the division of provincial revenues, debts, assets, and taxation at the time of Confederation. It makes clear that the provinces have possession of their own lands, mines, and minerals. Part IX is a miscellaneous collection, including section 132, the treaty power, and section 133, regarding the use of the English and French languages. The last section provides for the admission of other colonies.

The Constitution Act, 1867, was thus very brief on the executive and judicial branches of government. It included virtually nothing about limiting the powers of government in relation to the people. The act also lacked any mention of the means to amend it, but since it was a statute of the British Parliament, most formal changes to the act have been made by the British Parliament at Canadian request.

Amendments to the Constitution Act, 1867

Formal amendments to the 1867 act are indeed the second ingredient of the Canadian Constitution. Some of these are more important than others, and some did not have to be made in London, so that the exact number of such amendments is not easy to determine. The Constitution Act, 1982, sought to make a definitive list, however, and Schedule I to that act lists 17 amendments to the 1867 act made by the British Parliament and another eight made by the Canadian Parliament that are still operative. The former were often termed "British North America Acts" of whatever year in which they were passed, but in 1982, they were mostly renamed "Constitution Act" of the appropriate year. The most important of the 17 British amendments to the 1867 act are as follows:

- Constitution Act, 1907—established a new regime of federal–provincial grants
- Constitution Act, 1915—established a new distribution of Senate seats
- Constitution Act, 1930—transferred ownership of natural resources to Western provinces
- Constitution Act, 1940—added unemployment insurance to the list of federal powers
- Newfoundland Act, 1949—joined that province to Canada
- Constitution Act, 1951—allowed Ottawa to legislate with respect to old age pensions
- Constitution Act, 1960—made it mandatory for provincial superior court judges to retire at age 75
- Constitution Act, 1964—extended federal power in the field of old age pensions

British Statutes and Orders-in-Council

The third major component of the Canadian Constitution is a collection of British statutes and orders-in-council. Chief among these is the Statute of Westminster, 1931, which declared Canada to be totally independent of Britain. The Northwest Territories, British Columbia, and Prince Edward Island were British colonies added to Canada by means of British orders-in-council, that is, decisions of the British Cabinet. These, along with the 1949 amendment that added Newfoundland, completed the territorial dimensions of what we now know as Canada and are included in the Constitution for that reason. The four British orders-in-council in question are as follows:

- Rupert's Land and North-Western Territory Order, 1870—transferred Hudson's Bay Company lands to Canada
- British Columbia Terms of Union, 1871—joined that province to Canada

- Prince Edward Island Terms of Union, 1873—joined that province to Canada
- Adjacent Territories Order, 1880—added Arctic Islands to Canada

Organic Canadian Statutes

If the British order-in-council that transferred the Northwest Territories to Canada is considered part of the Canadian Constitution, so are the Canadian statutes that carved provinces out of those territories: the Manitoba Act of 1870 and the Saskatchewan and Alberta Acts of 1905. Although it may seem strange to consider ordinary Canadian statutes as part of the Constitution, those of such constitutional significance can be distinguished from others by calling them "organic."

Constitution Act, 1982

Although the Constitution Act, 1982, was in a sense the last amendment to the 1867 Constitution Act to be passed by the British Parliament, it is worthy of separate mention. While Canada was completely self-governing after 1931, many amendments to the 1867 act still had to be made by the British Parliament because no formula had been developed to do so in Canada. The Constitution Act, 1982, contained such a domestic constitution-amending formula, and the **Canada Act** passed by the British Parliament at the same time finally terminated all British authority over Canada.[3] It thus provided Canada at long last with a domestic constitutional amending formula (outlined below). As noted in Chapter 20, however, the constitutional documents of 1982 did not alter the position of the monarchy in Canada. The same person continues to be recognized as Queen of Canada as is claimed by several other countries, including Britain.

Queen Elizabeth signs Canada's constitutional proclamation in Ottawa on April 17, 1982, as Prime Minister Pierre Trudeau looks on. (Ron Poling/Canapress)

The second main aspect of the Constitution Act, 1982, was the Charter of Rights and Freedoms. The Charter guaranteed fundamental, democratic, legal, egalitarian, and linguistic rights and freedoms against government intrusion. In other words, the Charter of Rights and Freedoms imposed formal new limitations on the government in interaction with its citizens. In addition, it changed the manner in which such civil liberties were protected, now relying more on judicial interpretation than parliamentary restraint. The Charter is examined in depth in Chapter 18.

The 1982 act also contained statements on equalization payments to have-not provinces, multiculturalism, and Aboriginal rights. As far as the division of powers was concerned, a new section 92A was added that clarified and extended provincial powers over natural resources.

According to the Constitution Act, 1982, the Constitution of Canada consists of the British statutes and orders-in-council and Canadian statutes mentioned above. These 26 formal, legal documents make up the Constitution in the narrow sense of being subject to the constitutional amending formula adopted in 1982. Important as they are, these documents are silent on so many vital aspects of the fundamental rules and principles according to which Canada is governed that they cannot possibly constitute the entirety of the Canadian Constitution. Most authorities would therefore cast a much wider net in selecting the ingredients of the Constitution in its broader sense.

Other Canadian Statutes

The next ingredient that most authorities would include are certain other organic or fundamental Canadian statutes. For example, many aspects of the Supreme Court are provided for only in the **Supreme Court Act**, an ordinary law that fleshes out the provisions of the 1867 act with respect to the judicial branch of government, along with the Federal Court Act. It could be argued that certain other important Canadian statutes should also be included, such as the Parliament of Canada Act, the Bill of Rights, the Canada Elections Act, the Citizenship Act, the Emergencies Act, the Canadian Human Rights Act, the Yukon Act, and the Nunavut Act. Where to stop in formulating such a list is not clear.

Judicial Decisions

Judicial decisions that have clarified or altered provisions of the 1867 act or other parts of the Constitution must also be included. The largest body of such decisions are the judgments of the British **Judicial Committee of the Privy Council (JCPC)**, Canada's final court of appeal until 1949, which significantly affected the division of powers between the federal and provincial governments. As discussed in Chapter 17 on Canadian federalism, it was John A. Macdonald's intention to create a strong central government, but the Judicial Committee interpreted the 1867 act in such a way as to minimize federal powers and maximize those of the provinces. The court decisions that effected such a wholesale transformation of the federal nature of the country have to be considered part of the Constitution alongside the actual provisions of the original act.

A number of earlier court decisions also imposed restrictions on government power vis-à-vis its citizens—that is, in the area of rights and freedoms—and many such decisions have been made since the Charter of Rights was adopted in 1982. These "rights and freedoms" decisions are part of the Constitution along with the "division of powers" decisions mentioned.

Constitutional Conventions

Thus far, all the ingredients listed can actually be found in written form, however difficult it would be to collect them all together. The final component of the Constitution, on the other hand, has never been confined to writing. It consists of **constitutional conventions**, that is, unwritten rules of constitutional behaviour that are considered to be binding by and upon those who operate the Constitution, but that are not enforceable by the courts.[4] Conventions develop from traditions, and through constant recognition and observance become as established, rigid, and sacrosanct as if they were written down. Many of these informal rules have been inherited from Britain, some have been modified in the Canadian environment, and others are unique to Canada. Some conventions are more important than others, and some may be recognized by judges even if they cannot be enforced by the courts. But, as in Britain, conventions are no less real for remaining in an unwritten form. Many of them relate to the executive branch of government, which is given slight attention in the 1867 act. The dominant position of the prime minister and Cabinet, the subordinate place of the governor general, and the principle of responsible government (i.e., that the Cabinet must resign or call an election if it loses the confidence of the House of Commons) are three of many conventions that are part of the Constitution. Such conventions will be discussed at relevant points in subsequent chapters.[5]

The Constitution of Canada, therefore, is a rather complex phenomenon. It has two central documents—the Constitution Act, 1867, with its amendments, and the Constitution Act, 1982; it contains other written documents including other British statutes and orders-in-council, Canadian statutes, and British and Canadian court decisions; and, in its unwritten part, it incorporates a whole series of constitutional conventions that fill in gaps or alter the way in which written provisions are implemented. Many observers would prefer a neater Constitution; some want it to be updated; and others would like it to be more inspirational so that it could function more satisfactorily as a symbol of unity. Thus far, however, attempts to recast the Canadian Constitution in any of these ways have foundered.

THE QUEST FOR CONSTITUTIONAL CHANGE

In the early years of Confederation, one principal concern for constitutional change involved completing the territorial integrity of Canada with the eventual creation of ten provinces and now three territories. Another early constitutional issue was achieving autonomy from Britain by means of the Statute of Westminster, along with the abolition of court appeals to the Judicial Committee of the Privy Council. Two other persistent constitutional questions also arose prior to 1960: the search for a formula by which the 1867 act and the Constitution generally could be formally amended in Canada, and the proposal that rights and freedoms or civil liberties be given constitutional protection. These two issues then became enmeshed in constitutional issues inspired by the Quiet Revolution in Quebec, leading to the 1970 Victoria Charter, the Constitution Act, 1982, the 1987 Meech Lake Accord, and the 1992 Charlottetown Accord.

A Domestic Constitutional Amending Formula

As the final thrust toward full Canadian independence took place after the Balfour Declaration of 1926, it became clear that Canadians would have to find a way to amend the 1867 act in Canada. For over 50 years federal and provincial governments wrestled with the problem without being able to agree on an acceptable balance between rigidity and flexibility.

Attempts to find a domestic **constitutional amending formula** began in 1927, but since no success was achieved before 1931, the Statute of Westminster contained a clause allowing the British Parliament to amend the 1867 act at Canadian request. Further attempts were made in 1935–36, and in 1949 a partial domestic amending formula was adopted that became the BNA Act Amendment (#1) of 1949. That act added a clause to section 91 to the effect that in matters of concern to the national government alone, the federal Parliament could make constitutional amendments in Canada, without reference either to the provinces or to Britain. However, five exceptions remained, the most important being that any amendment affecting the provinces would still have to be made by the British Parliament. The basic question was whether such amendments should first require the unanimous approval of the provincial governments (as demanded by Quebec in order to protect its rights and powers) or whether the prior approval of a lesser number of provinces would be sufficient. In the absence of a resolution of this problem, a constitutional convention developed such that the federal government would not request an amendment to the federal–provincial division of powers without the unanimous consent of the provinces. Thus, in the case of the transfer of unemployment insurance from provincial to federal jurisdiction in 1940, the designation of pensions and supplementary benefits as concurrent powers in 1951 and 1964 respectively, and the imposition of a retirement age of 75 years for judges in 1960, Ottawa did not request British action until it had obtained the agreement of all the provinces.[6]

Further attempts to find a complete domestic formula were made around 1950 and 1960, and federal–provincial agreement was reached on the Fulton–Favreau formula in 1964. It provided that unanimous federal and provincial consent be required for changes to the division of powers (ss. 91, 92, and 93) and language provisions (s. 133), but on other matters affecting the whole country, the agreement of the federal government plus two-thirds of the provinces representing at least 50 percent of the population would be sufficient. After having agreed to this formula, the Jean Lesage government of Quebec rescinded its approval—ironically now fearing that the unanimity requirement would prevent making certain changes that Quebec wanted—and the formula died.

As discussed above, a domestic constitutional amending formula was finally adopted as part of the Constitution Act, 1982. Part V of the act actually provided for five such formulas, depending on the subject matter of the amendment: unanimous consent of federal and provincial legislatures; consent of Parliament and seven provincial legislatures representing 50 percent of the population; consent of Parliament and one or more provinces affected; consent of Parliament alone; consent of a provincial legislature alone.

First, as set out in section 41, unanimous federal and provincial consent was required to amend any of the following items:

(a) the office of the Queen, the Governor General and the Lieutenant Governor of a province;

(b) the right of a province to a number of members in the House of Commons not less than [its] number of Senators ...;

(c)   the use of the English or the French language [at the federal level];

(d)   the composition of the Supreme Court of Canada; and

(e)   changes to this list of subjects requiring unanimous consent.

Second, for other matters affecting both levels of government, the 1982 document required the approval of the federal Parliament and the legislatures of two-thirds of the provinces representing at least 50 percent of the Canadian population. However, no amendment that reduced provincial powers, rights, or privileges could affect a province that did not agree to it. This clause effectively meant that if seven provinces (representing at least 50 percent of the population) wished to transfer one of their powers to a willing federal government but the three other provinces did not, the change would only affect the seven that agreed to it. The document went on to say that if such an amendment related to education or culture, Canada would provide compensation to any province to which the amendment did not apply. Thus, if nine provinces and the federal government agreed to transfer education from provincial to federal jurisdiction, Ottawa would pay compensation to the province that continued to operate its own education system.

For greater clarity, section 42 listed certain subjects to which the two-thirds and 50 percent formula applied, but on which the opting-out of dissenting provinces was inappropriate. These include:

(a)   the principle of proportionate representation of the provinces in the House of Commons ...;

(b)   the powers of the Senate and the method of selecting Senators;

(c)   the number of members by which a province is entitled to be represented in the Senate and the residence qualifications of Senators;

(d)   the Supreme Court of Canada [other than its composition];

(e)   the extension of existing provinces into the territories; and

(f)   the establishment of new provinces.

In the third place, constitutional matters that applied to one or more but not all provinces, including boundary alterations and changes to the use of the English or French languages within a province, could be amended with the approval of the federal Parliament and the legislative assembly of each province to which the amendment applied. Fourth, those provisions relating to the executive government of Canada or the Senate and House of Commons could be amended by the federal Parliament alone. This clause allowed the partial amending formula adopted in 1949 to be repealed. Finally, each province could amend its own constitution in matters not affecting any other jurisdiction (or the position of lieutenant governor), as had been recognized as early as 1867.

In general, the rigidity and opting-out provisions of the 1982 amending formula were considered a victory for the provinces, and a trade-off for accepting the federal government's Charter of Rights.[7] The formula required that the federal Parliament and provincial *legislatures* approve such amendments, not just *cabinets*, as had often sufficed in the past. This innovation had later implications for the Meech Lake Accord, for while it was initially adopted by all ten provincial *premiers*, it ran into trouble when it came before certain provincial *legislatures*. Thus, the 1982 amending formula was not a simple one and was not designed to approve amendments easily. It did, however, put an end to requests to the British Parliament to make Canadian constitutional amendments.

A Constitutional Charter of Rights

Given the lack of a constitutional charter of rights in Britain and that country's generally impressive record of protecting civil liberties, based on parliamentary restraint, the common law, public opinion, and political culture, Canadians were not originally concerned about the absence of a bill of rights in their Constitution. After federal mistreatment of Japanese Canadians in the Second World War, however, and after provincial discrimination against Asians (BC), Jehovah's Witnesses and political dissidents (Quebec), and violations of freedom of the press (Alberta), some Canadians began to advocate a constitutional bill of rights along the lines of that of the United States. One person who felt very strongly about this question was John Diefenbaker, and when he became prime minister he had Parliament pass a Bill of Rights in 1960. The bill had major structural weaknesses, however. Such deficiencies led many observers to recommend constitutionalizing the bill, which was part of the rationale for the Charter of Rights and Freedoms, another part of the Constitution Act, 1982, discussed in detail in Chapter 18.

The Quiet Revolution in Quebec

The unresolved issues of a domestic amending formula and a constitutional charter of rights then became part of the third main thrust of constitutional change, that which emanated from the **Quiet Revolution** in Quebec. This was primarily related to Quebec's place in the Canadian federation as well as to the general division of powers between the two levels of government. Such demands have been the essence of Canadian politics for the past 40 years[8] and threaten the continued existence of the country as we know it. Table 16.1 lists the significant constitutional developments over the period 1960–2000.

The Victoria Charter

As noted in Chapters 5 and 17, many of Quebec's demands could be and were addressed by bureaucratic, legislative, and judicial decisions, at the federal level, in Quebec, or in other provinces, and did not require formal constitutional changes. By the end of the 1960s, however, the government of Quebec was demanding changes of a constitutional nature, demands often echoed by certain other provinces. Following the initiative of Ontario premier John Robarts's Confederation of Tomorrow Conference in 1967, a series of federal–provincial conferences over the 1968–1971 period led to agreement on the Victoria Charter in June 1971.

The **Victoria Charter** contained a constitutional amending formula and a constitutionalized bill of rights, provided for provincial consultation on Supreme Court appointments, guaranteed equalization payments to redress regional disparities, and represented some progress on changes to language rights and to the federal–provincial division of powers. But, after endorsing the document in Victoria, the Bourassa government later responded to nationalist public opinion in the province and vetoed the package because Quebec had not received sufficient additional powers in the field of social policy.

TABLE 16.1 **Constitutional Developments, 1960–2000**

1. Quiet Revolution, 1960–1966
2. John Robarts's Confederation of Tomorrow Conference, 1967
3. Federal–provincial constitutional conferences, 1968–1971
4. Victoria Charter, June 1971
5. Trudeau's proposal for patriation & amending formula, 1975
6. Trudeau's revival of Victoria Charter proposal, 1976
7. Election of Parti Québécois, 1976
8. Trudeau's Bill C-60, Phase I, 1978
9. Federal–provincial conferences, October 1978 and February 1979
10. Task Force on Canadian Unity, January 1979
11. René Lévesque's sovereignty-association proposal, November 1979
12. Quebec referendum, May 1980
13. Federal–provincial constitutional conferences, June and September 1980
14. Federal unilateral package, October 1980
15. Supreme Court decision on unilateral package, September 1981
16. Federal–provincial conference, November 1981
17. Proclamation of Constitution Act, 1982, April 17, 1982
18. Bourassa government's five demands, 1985
19. Meech Lake conferences, April and June 1987
20. Legislative ratification of Meech Lake Accord, 1987–1990
21. Federal–Provincial Conference on Meech Lake Accord, May 1990
22. Death of Meech Lake Accord, June 1990
23. Allaire and Bélanger–Campeau Reports, 1991
24. Citizens' Forum, November 1990–June 1991
25. Beaudoin-Edwards Committee on amending formula, June 1991
26. New federal constitutional reform package, September 1991
27. Dobbie-Beaudoin Committee, February 1992
28. Federal–provincial–Aboriginal negotiations, April–August 1992
29. Charlottetown Accord, August 1992
30. National referendum, October 26, 1992
31. Election of PQ government in Quebec, 1994
32. Quebec vote on sovereignty, October 30, 1995
33. Calgary Declaration, September 1997
34. Supreme Court decision on unilateral declaration of independence, August 1998
35. Social Union Agreement, 1999

The Constitution Act, 1982

The 1970s and early 1980s thus saw a tug-of-war between Ottawa and Quebec, with the other provinces arrayed in between, over the amending formula, the Charter of Rights, the Supreme Court, the Senate, language rights, and the division of powers. As noted in Chapter 5, the Trudeau strategy continued to be based on the extension of French-language services from coast to coast to coast in order to undermine Quebec's claim to be linguistically distinctive and therefore to require additional powers.[9] Increasingly, he had to fight the other provinces, too, as most of them also demanded greater decentralization.

After the collapse of the Victoria Charter, Trudeau tried a number of devices to pre-empt the election of a separatist government in Quebec and, after its success in 1976, to convince Quebeckers to follow his lead: proposals for patriation with an amending formula in 1975–76 and for institutional reform in 1978. The Pépin–Robarts Task Force on Canadian Unity might have been a fruitful basis on which to approach the problem, but because its recommendations differed from Trudeau's own principles of centralization and national bilingualism, he immediately dismissed them. In May 1980, four years after its election, the Parti Québécois government asked the people of Quebec for a mandate to negotiate **sovereignty association** with the federal government—that is, Quebec would be a sovereign state, but with continued economic links to the rest of Canada. Trudeau and other federal ministers entered the referendum campaign, promising that if Quebeckers turned down the PQ plan, Ottawa would initiate a process of constitutional renewal. When Quebec rejected Lévesque's proposal by a margin of 60 percent to 40 percent, Trudeau immediately embarked on a new round of federal–provincial constitutional discussions.

By October of that year, however, Trudeau abruptly gave up on trying to come to federal–provincial agreement and issued his own package of constitutional reform proposals, which he intended to have adopted by the British Parliament without provincial consent. This package was particularly provocative to the Quebec government and a large proportion of Quebeckers because it reflected Trudeau's version of a centralized, bilingual country, rather than the kind of constitutional reform—a distinct status and increased powers for Quebec—that they assumed he had promised in the referendum debate. Upset at both the substantive and the procedural aspects of the Trudeau initiative, several other provinces also challenged it in the courts. The provinces claimed that Trudeau's unilateral action in securing significant constitutional amendments was a violation of constitutional convention. In one of its most famous decisions, the Supreme Court of Canada ruled that nothing in *law* prevented the federal government from unilaterally requesting that such an amendment be made by Britain. On the other hand, unilateral federal action would violate the constitutional *convention* that provincial consent should be secured beforehand. In a rare example of judicial recognition of conventions, the Court went on to interpret the convention as requiring a "substantial degree of provincial consent" but not necessarily unanimity. A majority of the Court argued that the federal nature of Canada would be greatly changed if Ottawa could unilaterally alter the powers of the provincial governments in this way.[10] This decision prompted Trudeau to sit down with the premiers again, and in October 1981 they came up with compromises on all sides in the package that became the Constitution Act, 1982. Ironically, Quebec, which had been the inspiration of it all, was the one dissenter.[11]

The act itself had already been extensively discussed. It contained a domestic constitutional amending formula and a Charter of Rights. It also included the constitutional entrenchment of equalization payments to have-not provinces and an amendment to the division of powers that enhanced provincial control over natural resources. The Charter essentially constitutionalized the federal and New Brunswick Official Languages Acts to guarantee the rights of official-language minorities to government services, trials, and so on. It also established the rights of official-language minorities to schools in their own language wherever numbers warranted. The clear objective of these provisions was to entrench official bilingualism across the country to the extent that Prime Minister Trudeau could persuade provincial premiers to do so. On the other hand, the Constitution Act, 1982, did not respond to any of the demands for constitutional change emanating from Quebec. It is not surprising that Quebec Premier René Lévesque refused to sign it, but it is doubtful that a federalist premier of that province would have reacted much differently. Nevertheless, Quebec was legally bound by the document in almost all respects. This imposition created much hostility within Quebec toward Trudeau, his Justice Minister Jean Chrétien, the other provinces, and the Charter itself.

The Meech Lake Accord

Although the 1982 act was operative in Quebec, Brian Mulroney was determined that Quebec should symbolically rejoin the Canadian constitutional family "with honour and enthusiasm." He therefore asked the new federalist Quebec premier, Robert Bourassa, to outline his conditions for such a reunion. The Quebec government proceeded to make five demands: constitutional recognition of Quebec as a "distinct society" within Canada; a veto on constitutional amendments; increased jurisdiction over immigration; participation in Supreme Court appointments; and financial compensation when Quebec opted out of national programs set up by Ottawa within provincial jurisdiction.

After considerable preparation, Mulroney called the premiers together at Meech Lake in April 1987 and with surprising speed they agreed to a document that addressed Quebec's

By André-Philippe Côté (Le Soleil). *Reproduced with permission.*

demands and became known as the **Meech Lake Accord**. The prime minister secured unanimous provincial consent by extending to the other provinces most of the same rights as were demanded by Quebec. The document also contained clauses that constitutionalized the Supreme Court of Canada, provided for provincial participation in Senate appointments, and guaranteed annual first ministers' conferences on the Constitution and on the economy.[12]

Despite the relative ease with which it was drafted, the Meech Lake Accord generated much controversy. On the negative side, many critics did not approve of the designation of Quebec as a distinct society within Canada, and especially objected to the phrase that it was the role of the government and legislature of Quebec to "preserve and promote" that distinctiveness. No one was sure what implications the **distinct-society clause** would have for the federal–provincial division of powers, leaving it for judicial clarification on an issue-by-issue basis. Some felt that in a federation all provinces had to have exactly equal status, and many argued that, armed with the distinct-society clause, Quebec would immediately begin to challenge federal powers in a variety of fields. Others worried about the status of the English and Aboriginal minorities within Quebec, as well as the francophone minorities in other provinces, and some women's groups argued that the distinct-society clause might be used to override the gender equality provisions of section 28 of the Charter of Rights and Freedoms.

A second objection to the accord was that it enlarged the list of subjects that required unanimous provincial consent in the constitutional amending formula, especially the list contained in section 42, such as changes to most aspects of the Senate and the creation of new provinces. Many critics felt that Senate reform and the transformation of the Northern territories into provinces would be virtually impossible if such amendments required agreement of all ten provinces instead of only seven.

Objections to Quebec's expanded role in immigration and to provincial involvement in the nomination of judges to the Supreme Court of Canada were also raised by those opposed to increases in provincial power. But these concerns were not expressed as vehemently as those relating to the provisions allowing provinces to opt out of national programs within provincial jurisdiction and be compensated by Ottawa. Fears were expressed that satisfactory new national social programs (such as daycare or a guaranteed annual income) would never materialize because provinces would be compensated for programs that merely met national *objectives*, not national *standards*. Apart from criticizing what was in the accord, many opponents faulted it for what was left out. The North was not allowed to nominate senators or Supreme Court judges; Aboriginal rights were not strengthened; and multiculturalism was ignored.

Others condemned the process through which the accord had emerged—a behind-the-scenes gathering of (male) first ministers. In the post-Charter era, individual Canadians in all parts of the country insisted on being part of the constitutional amendment process; moreover, the primacy of Quebec's concerns was rejected by those given constitutional standing by the Charter—women, Aboriginals, and multicultural and other minorities.[13] The public now demanded more meaningful participation in the process of constitutional change.

The leading opponents of Meech Lake were former prime minister Pierre Trudeau, whose vision of a centralized, bilingual federation was at odds with the document, and Clyde Wells, elected as premier of Newfoundland in April 1989, two years after the accord had been drafted. The federal Liberal and New Democratic parties were both split on the accord, but generally managed to agree on a number of proposed amendments to address the concerns of various disenchanted groups: Aboriginals, the North, linguistic minorities, women, and those concerned about multiculturalism and the opting-out provisions. The federal government took the position, however, that no changes could be made because they might destroy the fragility of the compromises contained in the accord.

Those who defended Meech Lake argued that it would symbolically bring Quebec back into the constitutional fold and would overcome the isolation and betrayal that many residents of that province felt after 1982. They called this the "Quebec round," and argued that Aboriginal, Northern, Western, and other concerns would be next on the constitutional agenda. Rather than promote incremental separatism, they felt that the accord would give Quebec the flexibility to remain satisfied within Confederation. Supporters contended that in demographic, linguistic, and cultural terms, the distinctiveness of Quebec society could not be denied. Those who felt that Trudeau's concept of official bilingualism was unrealistic for certain parts of the country thought that the accord, in noting that French-speaking Canadians are centred in Quebec, might lessen linguistic tensions and the pressure for bilingualism.

Many political scientists and others had long argued that the provinces should have a say in the appointment of senators and Supreme Court judges. In the former case, this was because the Senate was intended to represent the provinces within Ottawa's decision-making structure; in the latter, because the Supreme Court rules on federal–provincial disputes. Many true federalists also contended that Ottawa should not be able to invade provincial jurisdiction with its spending power and set up national programs without provincial consent, as had often happened in the past. In addition, many felt that Quebec had a legitimate interest in immigration, given its low birth rate and its isolation in an English-speaking North American environment.

Supporters pointed out that multicultural and Aboriginal rights in Quebec were protected against the distinct-society clause, and that most Quebec women did not feel threatened by it. Defenders of Meech Lake also welcomed the constitutionalization of the Supreme Court.

According to the constitutional amending formula adopted in 1982, the accord then had to be approved by the federal and all provincial legislatures within three years, that is, before June 23, 1990.[14] In most cases such legislative approval came rather easily, but governments changed in New Brunswick and Manitoba before the accord could be ratified by the legislatures of those two provinces, and their new governments had reservations about the accord. Both provinces set up legislative committees that held extensive public hearings and delayed ratification. In the case of Manitoba, the new Gary Filmon government was in a minority position, while the new Wells government in Newfoundland later rescinded the legislative approval that that province had previously given to the accord.

Thus, with three provinces left to ratify the accord, Prime Minister Mulroney convened a first ministers' conference in Ottawa in May 1990. After a week of protracted, behind-the-scenes negotiations, the participants emerged with a modest companion resolution, adopted to the satisfaction of Manitoba and New Brunswick. Still with his substantive and procedural reservations, Clyde Wells would only agree to put it before the Newfoundland legislature, not to endorse it. Amid a bitter public exchange between Wells and the federal government, the Newfoundland legislature did not vote on the accord a second time before the deadline. Meanwhile, the accord also ran into difficulty in the Manitoba legislature, where Aboriginal MLA Elijah Harper delayed passage beyond the deadline because of the absence of any advance for Native peoples.

The Charlottetown Accord

With the death of the Meech Lake Accord, many observers felt that Quebec was destined to leave Confederation, given that the demands incorporated in the accord were the province's basic minimum. Sure enough, nationalist and separatist sentiment in Quebec mushroomed over the next year or so as the Quebec Liberals and Parti Québécois issued new constitutional proposals. The Liberal position first appeared as the **Allaire Report,** which called for a highly decentralized federation in which Quebec and the other provinces would have almost all powers, including 22 new ones. According to the report, Quebec would insist on exercising its full sovereignty in the areas of jurisdiction already exclusive to it according to the present Constitution, notably social affairs, urban affairs, culture, education, housing, recreation, family policy, manpower policy, natural resources, health, and tourism. It would do the same in other fields that it somewhat dubiously claimed were currently either shared with Ottawa or not mentioned in the Constitution, such as agriculture, unemployment insurance, communications, regional development, energy, environment, language, research and development, and public security. Ottawa and Quebec would share jurisdiction over Aboriginal affairs, revenue and taxation, immigration, financial institutions, justice, fisheries, foreign policy, post office, telecommunications and transportation, and the federal government would have exclusive power over only defence, customs and excise, and management of the national debt.

Representing both major parties as well as other interests in the province, Quebec's **Bélanger–Campeau Committee** report argued that unless a satisfactory proposal for a new constitutional arrangement was forthcoming from the rest of Canada, Quebec should separate. It therefore recommended that a referendum on Quebec sovereignty be held in June or October 1992 and that if the referendum was positive, Quebec would acquire the status of a sovereign state within one year of the date it was held. Bélanger–Campeau anticipated that in the interim, the rest of Canada would offer Quebec some kind of new partnership, perhaps along the lines of the Allaire Report, so that Quebeckers would essentially have two alternatives before them when they cast their vote.

The Mulroney government responded in November 1990 with the appointment of the Citizens' Forum on Canada's Future headed by CRTC Chair Keith Spicer. Responding to the criticism that the public had been shut out of the Meech Lake negotiations, the **Citizens' Forum** encouraged ordinary Canadians to discuss constitutional issues and transmit their views to the committee. Although many were growing weary of the subject by this time, a large proportion of Canadians engaged in angry exchanges, the Constitution becoming a lightning rod for every conceivable grievance in the country. After listening to some 400 000 Canadians over an eight-month period, the forum's June 1991 report supported recognition of Quebec's distinctiveness (even if the anglophone public did not agree), Aboriginal self-government, and settlement of Native land claims. On the other hand, the forum suggested that official bilingualism was a divisive issue and government funding for multiculturalism should be cut.

Meanwhile, in response to another problem central to the defeat of Meech Lake, the federal government set up a joint House of Commons–Senate Committee to study the constitutional amending formula. This Beaudoin-Edwards Committee also reported in June 1991 and endorsed a change in the formula that would restrict the requirement for unanimous provincial consent and replace it with regional vetoes, as well as allow national referendums on a new Constitution.

The prime minister also appointed Joe Clark as the Minister Responsible for Constitutional Affairs and set up a special Cabinet committee on Canadian Unity and Constitutional Negotiations. The committee agreed on a 28-point package of constitutional proposals in September 1991 called *Shaping Canada's Future Together*. Yet another joint Commons–Senate committee was set up to gather public reaction to the package and other reports on the subject. The government decided to supplement its hearings with a series of specialized public forums on specific constitutional issues, and the Dobbie-Beaudoin Committee on the Renewal of Canada issued its report in February 1992.

Meanwhile, Joe Clark was persuaded to try to develop a collective federal–provincial–territorial–Aboriginal response to offer to Quebec before the fall. After several rounds of negotiations, Clark, the nine premiers, and the territorial and Aboriginal leaders all agreed on a comprehensive constitutional proposal in July. Quebec Premier Bourassa considered that it was promising enough to return to the bargaining table for the first time since the demise of the Meech Lake Accord, and a full-fledged constitutional conference took place in Ottawa in mid-August. After nearly a week of hard bargaining, the leaders unanimously signed a new constitutional accord upon which they put the final touches in Charlottetown a week later. It had four main parts:[15] the Canada clause, a Triple-E Senate, Aboriginal self-government, and changes to the division of powers.

THE CANADA CLAUSE

The 1992 **Charlottetown Accord** began with a new **Canada Clause** that would recognize Quebec as a distinct society within Canada as well as enumerate the other fundamental values and characteristics of the country: democracy, the rule of law, a parliamentary and federal system, the Aboriginal peoples of Canada and their enhanced rights, official-language minorities, cultural and racial diversity, individual and collective rights, gender equality, and the equality and diversity of the provinces.

THE TRIPLE-E SENATE

A new **Triple-E Senate** would give each province 6 representatives and each territory 1, for a total of 62. It would be popularly elected, except that Quebec members would be chosen by the National Assembly. The institution would have a veto over federal laws that taxed natural resources but virtually no power over government money bills. For other legislation a defeat in the Senate would trigger a joint sitting of both houses in which MPs would outnumber senators by 337 to 62. Defeat of a government bill in the Senate would not be considered a vote of nonconfidence, but bills dealing with the French language and culture would have to be approved by a majority of francophone members. To enhance their independence, senators would not be eligible to sit in the Cabinet, but they would have the power to ratify or veto key government appointments.

To compensate Ontario and Quebec for their loss of 18 senators, these two provinces would each be given 18 additional seats in the House of Commons. In an effort to maintain the general principle of representation by population, British Columbia would gain four MPs and Alberta two, and it was agreed that a supplementary redistribution of Commons seats would be held after the 1996 census to reflect BC's rapidly increasing population. Quebec was also guaranteed a mimimum of 25 percent of the Commons seats.

ABORIGINAL SELF-GOVERNMENT

Native peoples would have their inherent right to **Aboriginal self-government** enshrined in the Constitution, but with no access to the courts to enforce it for five years. Aboriginal governments would constitute a third order of government, analogous to Ottawa and the provinces. Federal and provincial governments committed themselves to negotiate Aboriginal self-government agreements and their laws would continue to apply until displaced. New Aboriginal laws could not be inconsistent with laws essential to the preservation of peace, order, and good government in Canada and would also have to comply with the Charter of Rights and Freedoms, subject to the use of the notwithstanding clause. The accord would entrench treaty rights in the Constitution but not result in any new land rights. Sections 25 and 35 of the 1982 Constitution Act were strengthened, and Métis rights, especially in Alberta, were also given recognition.

THE DIVISION OF POWERS

The fourth main issue was the federal–provincial division of powers. As in the Meech Lake Accord, provinces could opt out of new national shared-cost programs set up within provincial jurisdiction and receive federal financial compensation if the programs met national objectives. In addition, Ottawa offered to withdraw from six fields at provincial request: forestry, mining, tourism, recreation, housing, and municipal and urban affairs, again with financial compensation. Culture and labour market training would essentially become provincial powers, and the two levels would share jurisdiction in immigration, telecommunications, and regional development. Thus, beyond the immigration power in Meech Lake, provinces would now have full or partial power over ten additional fields of public policy. In return for this increased decentralization of powers, Ottawa hoped to strengthen the economic union by eliminating interprovincial trade barriers, but had to settle for agreement in principle, with the issue to be negotiated later.

OTHER

Provisions of Meech Lake with respect to the Supreme Court of Canada were included in the accord, along with those concerning an annual meeting of first ministers, and changes in the constitutional amending formula, except that the creation of new provinces would no longer require unanimous consent, a part of Meech Lake that had been heavily criticized. Ontario premier Bob Rae was successful in having a social charter added to the document to guarantee rights to health care, social services, and education, workers' rights, and protection for the environment. The guarantee of equalization payments was strengthened, and the federal reservation, disallowance, and declaratory powers were essentially removed.

The 1992 Referendum

The accord would be of no effect until ratified by Parliament and the ten provincial legislatures. Before ratification, however, the federal government announced that a national **referendum** would be held on the new constitutional deal on October 26, the same date selected by Quebec for its constitutional referendum, now on the Charlottetown Accord rather than sovereignty. The decision to hold such a referendum was based on three main considerations: Alberta and BC laws required a referendum on constitutional amendments, so that three provinces would be voting on the accord in any case; Meech Lake had been criticized for lack of public input; and public approval would lend legitimacy to the agreement and spur the 11 legislatures into speedy affirmative action.

On a national basis the referendum result was 55 percent no and 45 percent yes. As shown in Table 16.2, majorities voted no in Quebec, Nova Scotia, the four Western provinces, and the Yukon. Even though the referendum was not legally binding, there was no point in bringing the constitutional package before legislatures for ratification: the Charlottetown Accord was dead.

Public opinion polls showed that rather than base their decision on the contents of the accord as such, many people who voted no did so to vent their anger and frustration with Prime Minister Mulroney, the premiers, and politicians and governments in general.[16] Such was the problem of holding the vote during a period of severe recession and at a time when respect for incumbent politicians was at an all-time low. Voters were not in a generous frame of mind, and rather than seeing it as a multi-sided compromise, they generally felt that the accord gave too much to others and not enough to themselves. Thus, the negative vote in Quebec was largely based on the view that the accord did not give Quebec sufficient new powers, but many outside Quebec argued that that province got too much. Many Westerners did not see the proposed reforms to the Senate as sufficient protection of their interests in Ottawa, and many Aboriginal Canadians were dissatisfied with the provisions on Native self-

TABLE 16.2   Results of the National Referendum on the Charlottetown Accord (Percentages)

Newfoundland	63.2	36.8
Prince Edward Island	73.9	26.1
Nova Scotia	48.8	51.2
New Brunswick	61.8	38.2
Quebec	43.3	56.7
Ontario	50.1	49.9
Manitoba	38.4	61.6
Saskatchewan	44.7	55.3
Alberta	39.8	60.2
British Columbia	31.7	68.3
Northwest Territories	61.3	38.7
Yukon	43.7	56.3
TOTAL	45.0	55.0

Source: Chief Electoral Officer of Canada, Referendum 92: Official Voting Results *(Ottawa, 1992), p. 4. Reproduced with the permission of the Minister of Public Works and Government Services Canada, 2000. Quebec data: Directeur général des élections du Québec, Rapport des résultats officiels du scrutin— Référendum du 26 Octobre 1992, Sainte-Foy, 1992, p. 49. Reproduced with permission.*

government. Indeed, while the accord was primarily designed to address the constitutional insecurity of Quebec, Aboriginal Canadians, and Western and smaller provinces, a majority in all three groups believed that their elites had not bargained hard enough.

Post-Charlottetown Constitutional Developments

One year later, in 1993, the Chrétien Liberals were elected on the promise that they would concentrate on improving the economy and put constitutional issues aside.[17] On the other hand, the Parti Québécois returned to power in Quebec in 1994 on the exact opposite platform—that it would move quickly to take Quebec outside Confederation. When the polls showed that Premier Jacques Parizeau could not achieve a majority of Quebec voters on the question of his choice—complete independence—he succumbed to the pressure of public opinion and from Bloc leader Lucien Bouchard and agreed to an extensive list of continuing links to Canada.[18] This seriously diluted proposal was ratified in an agreement between the PQ, the BQ, and Mario Dumont's small party, Action démocratique du Québec, and the legislature passed a bill setting the referendum date for October 30, 1995. The convoluted question put to the people of Quebec was as follows: "Do you agree that Quebec should become sovereign, after having made a formal offer to Canada for a new economic and political partnership, within the scope of the bill respecting the future of Quebec and of the agreement signed on June 12, 1995?"

The bill in question would allow a sovereign Quebec to use the Canadian dollar as its currency and its residents to retain concurrent Canadian citizenship. It anticipated the adoption of a new Quebec constitution and retention of Quebec's existing boundaries. The government of Quebec was then to propose a treaty of economic and political partnership with the rest of Canada. The treaty would set up a joint Council (executive), Secretariat (bureaucracy), Assembly (legislature), and Tribunal (court); establish rules for the division of assets and debt; and provide for the free movement of goods, individuals, services, and capital. If agreement with the rest of Canada on such a treaty was not achieved within a year, Quebec would unilaterally declare its sovereignty and expect recognition by other states, anticipating continued membership in the North American Free Trade Agreement. Premier Parizeau virtually vacated the leadership of the "Yes" campaign when it became obvious that the cause had a chance only if the much more popular Bouchard became its effective leader.

The federal government stuck to its position that if Quebeckers could be persuaded that "Yes" meant actual separation, a majority would vote "No." Ottawa thus made no counteroffers until polls showed that such a strategy was seriously flawed and could lead to defeat. In the final week of the campaign, Prime Minister Chrétien promised change—constitutional, if necessary, but not necessarily constitutional—if Quebeckers voted "No." The three principal changes he alluded to were some kind of recognition of Quebec as a distinct society, some kind of veto over constitutional amendments, and some kind of decentralization of powers from Ottawa. The other dramatic development of the last few days was a gigantic "No" rally in Montreal, made up primarily of Canadians from coast to coast who "invaded" the city in order to tell Quebeckers how much the rest of Canada wanted them to stay.

The result of the referendum could not have been closer: 50.6 percent voted "No," while 49.4 percent voted "Yes." The turnout rate was a record 92 percent. Considerable controversy surrounded the high number of rejected ballots (most of them favouring the "No" side), but it was clear that nearly 60 percent of the francophones in the province had voted "Yes." Close but still defeated, Parizeau promptly resigned the premiership in favour of Bouchard.

After the suspenseful Quebec referendum results, Prime Minister Chrétien had Parliament pass a resolution recognizing Quebec as a distinct society within Canada. He also promised that regardless of the official constitutional amending formula, no constitutional amendments would be passed without the approval of each region of the country (including Quebec), and that labour-market training would be transferred from federal to provincial jurisdiction. Such measures were part of "Plan A" or the "carrot" approach to being nice to Quebec.[19] The government also pursued the "stick" approach or "Plan B," the principal part of which was to refer a hypothetical question to the Supreme Court of Canada, asking it to rule on the legality of a unilateral declaration of independence by Quebec.

In September 1997, nine provincial premiers (excluding Lucien Bouchard) gathered in Calgary to see if it would be productive to talk about the Constitution again before Quebec's next election. The premiers' declaration tried to reconcile the "unique character of Quebec society" with the equality of all the provinces. While substituting "unique" for "distinct" and emphasizing provincial equality might attract some support in English Canada, it was less certain that the **Calgary Declaration** would appeal to most Quebeckers. The following are the main points of the declaration:

1. All Canadians are equal and have rights protected by law.
2. All provinces, while diverse in their characteristics, have equality of status.
3. Canada is graced by a diversity, tolerance, compassion and an equality of opportunity that is without rival in the world.
4. Canada's gift of diversity includes Aboriginal peoples and cultures, the vitality of the English and French languages and a multicultural citizenry drawn from all parts of the world.
5. In Canada's federal system, where respect for diversity and equality underlies unity, the unique character of Quebec society, including its French-speaking majority, its culture and its tradition of civil law, is fundamental to the well-being of Canada. Consequently, the legislature and government of Quebec have a role to protect and develop the unique character of Quebec society within Canada.
6. If any future constitutional amendment confers powers on one province, these powers must be available to all provinces.
7. Canada is a federal system where federal, provincial, and territorial governments work in partnership while respecting each other's jurisdictions. Canadians want their governments to work cooperatively and with flexibility to ensure the efficiency ... of the federation. Canadians want their governments to work together particularly in the delivery of their social programs. Provinces and territories renew their commitment to work in partnership with the government of Canada to best serve the needs of Canadians.

In August 1998, the Supreme Court delivered its decision on the legality of Quebec separation.[20] It answered the specific questions in the negative: "secession of a province 'under the Constitution' could not be achieved unilaterally"; furthermore, international law does not give Quebec the right to unilateral secession from Canada because "Quebec does not meet the threshold of a colonial people or an oppressed people, nor can it be suggested that Quebecers have been denied meaningful access to government to pursue their political, economic, cultural and social development."

While that part of the judgment pleased federalists, the Court did not stop there. It went on to say that "the continued existence and operation of the Canadian constitutional order could not be indifferent to a clear expression of a clear majority of Quebecers that they no longer wish to remain in Canada." In other words, "a clear majority vote in Quebec on a clear question in favour of secession would confer democratic legitimacy on the secession initiative which all of the other participants in Confederation would have to recognize."

The Court added that "although there is no right, under the Constitution or at international law, to unilateral secession, the possibility of an unconstitutional declaration of secession leading to a *de facto* secession is not ruled out. The ultimate success of such a secession would be dependent on recognition by the international community."

Then, Bouchard called an election for November 30, 1998. Although he won the largest number of seats, Jean Charest's Liberals actually collected a greater number of votes. This lukewarm public endorsement forced Bouchard to postpone plans for yet another referendum on some variation of Quebec sovereignty. On the other hand, Ottawa and the provinces came to an agreement on the "social union," discussed in more detail in Chapter 17, but as in the case of the Constitution Act, 1982, Quebec did not agree. All of these developments left the constitutional crisis hanging.[21]

Meanwhile, a number of constitutional amendments of less national significance were passed, all of them using that part of the amending formula involving the federal Parliament and the single province affected.[22] In 1987, a constitutional amendment added Pentecostals to the list of religious denominations that had a right to operate their own schools in Newfoundland; in 1993, an amendment strengthened the principle of French–English dualism in the public institutions of New Brunswick; and in 1994, once the Confederation Bridge replaced the ferry service to New Brunswick, an amendment removed the requirement that Ottawa provide a steamship service to Prince Edward Island. In 1996, a further amendment regarding education in Newfoundland reduced the role of the churches in the school system, while another in 1998 in Quebec permitted a change in the structure of school boards in the province from a religious to a linguistic basis.

··

CONCLUSION

Canada has one of the oldest constitutions in the world. Although it has been altered incrementally over its 135-year existence by formal amendments, judicial interpretation, and conventions, its basic provisions remain intact. Since the Quiet Revolution, the issue of constitutional amendment has never been far from the top of the Canadian political agenda, and at the dawn of the new millennium, the country continued to face a constitutional crisis that threatened to split it apart.

 Of the approaches outlined in Chapter 1, the state-centred theory is most relevant to the Constitution and constitutional change. These questions have historically been the preserve of federal and provincial political and bureaucratic elites. Before 1982, constitutional accommodations could be made among first ministers and their advisers at federal–provincial conferences and only needed to be ratified by federal and provincial cabinets. After 1982, legislative approval was also required, but that did not necessarily involve the wider society. Elite theorists would add to the picture a small number of representatives from the intellectual elite—constitutional law professors, political scientists, historians, economists, and journalists.

P Pluralists, on the other hand, point to the increasing public interest in such matters. They emphasize that several elite-designed proposals have foundered once exposed to public opinion: the Fulton–Favreau formula and the Victoria Charter in Quebec, and Meech Lake in other parts of the country. The public now demands more meaningful participation in the process of constitutional change. This participation was provided for in the public hearings of legislative committees on Meech Lake and the subsequent Citizens' Forum, but some pluralist critics go further and advocate the convening of constituent assemblies on the subject. When three provinces decided to hold a referendum on the Charlottetown Accord, a national referendum was held, and it is commonly thought that if the issue is revisited, a referendum will be required again even though it is not required by the constitutional amending formula.

C Class analysts see the Constitution as legitimizing arrangements for the capitalist elite to control the political system. They also consider constitutional issues as a device used by politicians to distract the public from the real issues of unemployment, the exploitation of workers, and the unfair distribution of wealth. They think of what might have happened if all the effort that went into constitutional discussions could have been directed toward pressing social issues. Many class analysts would also argue that the decentralized thrust of most of the recent constitutional initiatives is consistent with and has the same effect as the drive for free trade, the elimination of the deficit, and the emerging campaign for tax cuts: they all are intended to weaken the central state. Moreover, they are being pushed by many of the same people, especially the C.D. Howe Institute and the Business Council on National Issues. A specific and dramatic case of the latter's influence in even this field can be found by comparing a BCNI constitutional proposal that preceded it to the nearly identical Calgary Declaration.[23]

....

DISCUSSION QUESTIONS

1. Would it be possible or advisable to incorporate all ingredients of the Canadian Constitution into a single document? Why or why not?

2. Is the 1982 constitutional amending formula too rigid? If so, how should it be changed?

3. What is your assessment of the key provisions of the Meech Lake and Charlottetown Accords?

4. To what extent should politicians be guided by popular referendums on constitutional matters?

5. What are the advantages and disadvantages of Canadians attempting to address all their constitutional problems simultaneously?

6. To what extent can Canadians resolve their "constitutional" problems in nonconstitutional ways?

7. How do each of the critical approaches outlined in Chapter 1 help us to understand the Canadian Constitution and constitutional change?

NOTES

1. Alan C. Cairns has defined the Constitution in similar terms as follows: "[It] is the body of understandings defining the basic institutions of government and the relations between them, plus the relationships between governments in the federal system, and between the citizens and those governments." See *Constitution, Government, and Society in Canada* (Toronto: McClelland and Stewart, 1988), p. 31.

2. The act has not been included in this book in its entirety, but the crucial sections are reproduced in Appendix A. See Bernard Funston, *Consolidated Canadian Constitutional Documents* (Toronto: Carswell, 1994; Bernard Funston and Eugene Meehan, *Canada's Constitutional Law in a Nutshell*, 2nd ed. (Toronto: Carswell, 1998); and Bayard Reesor, *The Canadian Constitution in Historical Perspective* (Scarborough: Prentice-Hall Canada, 1992).

3. Theoretically, the Constitution Act, 1982, is an appendix to the Canada Act, and the Charter of Rights and Freedoms is part of the Constitution Act.

4. Many definitions of conventions exist and are discussed by Andrew Heard in *Canadian Constitutional Conventions* (Toronto: Oxford University Press, 1991). My definition is an amalgam of those he cites.

5. Even a legal text such as *Constitutional Law of Canada*, 2nd ed., by Peter Hogg (Toronto: Carswell, 1985; Student Edition 1999) includes conventions as part of the Constitution. The question of judicial recognition of such conventions is addressed below.

6. On about ten other occasions constitutional amendments were made without prior consultation with the provinces because Ottawa considered they were of exclusive federal concern. These included repeated redistributions of seats in the House of Commons and the entry of Newfoundland into Confederation. See Guy Favreau, *The Amendment of the Constitution of Canada* (Ottawa: Queen's Printer, 1965), and Paul Gérin-Lajoie, *Constitutional Amendment in Canada* (Toronto: University of Toronto Press, 1950).

7. Alan C. Cairns, *Constitution, Government and Society in Canada*.

8. Edward McWhinney, *Quebec and the Constitution 1960–1978* (University of Toronto Press, 1979); Edward McWhinney, *Canada and the Constitution 1979–1982* (University of Toronto Press, 1982); and Peter Russell, *Constitutional Odyssey* (Toronto: University of Toronto Press, 1992).

9. Kenneth McRoberts, *Misconceiving Canada: The Struggle for National Unity* (Toronto: Oxford University Press, 1997); Ian Greene, *The Charter of Rights* (Toronto: Lorimer, 1989), pp. 37–38; and Michael Mandel, *The Charter of Rights and the Legalization of Politics in Canada* (Toronto: Wall and Thompson, 1989; rev. ed. 1994), pp. 17, 20, 22, and 111.

10. *Reference re Amendment of the Constitution of Canada*, [1981] 125 DLR (3rd) 1. See Heard, *Canadian Constitutional Conventions*, and Mandel, *The Charter of Rights*, pp. 22, 24–34, 111. In another political decision, the Court decided that Quebec had never had a veto on constitutional amendments: *Re: Objection to a Resolution to Amend the Constitution*, [1982] 2 S.C.R. 793. See Marc Gold, "The Mask of Objectivity: Politics and Rhetoric in the Supreme Court of Canada," *The Supreme Court Law Review* 7 (1985).

11. Keith Banting and Richard Simeon, eds., *And No One Cheered: Federalism, Democracy and the Constitution Act* (Toronto: Methuen, 1983); Roy Romanow, J. Whyte, and H. Leeson, *Canada … Notwithstanding: The Making of the Constitution 1976–1982* (Toronto: Methuen, 1984); and Ross

Sheppard and M. Valpy, *The National Deal: The Fight for a Canadian Constitution* (Toronto: Macmillan, 1984).

12. Michael Behiels, ed., *The Meech Lake Primer: Conflicting Views of the 1987 Constitutional Accord* (Ottawa: University of Ottawa Press, 1989); *Canadian Public Policy* (September 1988); Roger Gibbins, ed., *Meech Lake and Canada: Perspectives from the West* (Edmonton: Academic Printing and Publishing, 1988); Peter Hogg, *Meech Lake Constitutional Accord Annotated* (Toronto: Carswell, 1988); Bryan Schwartz, *Fathoming Meech Lake* (Winnipeg: Legal Research Institute, University of Manitoba, 1987); K.E. Swinton and C.J. Rogerson, *Competing Constitutional Visions: The Meech Lake Accord* (Toronto: Carswell, 1988); and David Milne, *The Canadian Constitution* (Toronto: Lorimer, 1991).

13. Alan C. Cairns, *Constitution, Government, and Society in Canada*, and *Disruptions: Constitutional Struggles, from the Charter to Meech Lake* (Toronto: McClelland and Stewart, 1991).

14. The former Cabinet secretary and clerk of the Privy Council, Gordon Robertson, argued strenuously that no such deadline existed, but to no avail.

15. Alan C. Cairns, *Reconfigurations: Canadian Citizenship and Constitutional Change* (Toronto: McClelland and Stewart, 1995); Curtis Cook, ed., *Constitutional Predicament: Canada after the Referendum of 1992* (Montreal: McGill–Queen's University Press, 1994); Kenneth McRoberts and Patrick Monahan, eds., *The Charlottetown Accord, the Referendum and the Future of Canada* (Toronto: University of Toronto Press, 1993); Peter Russell, *Constitutional Odyssey*, 2nd ed. (Toronto: University of Toronto Press, 1993); Patrick C. Fafard and Douglas M. Brown, *Canada: The State of the Federation 1996* (Kingston: Institute of Intergovernmental Affairs, 1996); and F. Leslie Seidel, *Seeking a New Canadian Partnership: Asymmetrical and Confederal Options* (Montreal: Institute for Research on Public Policy, 1994).

16. Richard Johnston et al., *The Challenge of Direct Democracy: The 1992 Canadian Referendum* (Montreal: McGill-Queen's University Press, 1996).

17. Harvey Lazar, ed., *Canada: The State of the Federation 1997: Non-Constitutional Renewal* (Kingston: Institute of Intergovernmental Relations, 1997); Fafard and Brown, *Canada: The State of the Federation 1996*. The advisability of making another attempt at "megaconstitutional change" is debated by Kathy Brock and Michael Lusztig in Mark Charlton and Paul Barkers, eds., *Crosscurrents: Contemporary Political Issues*, 3rd ed. (Scarborough: ITP Nelson, 1998), ch. 6.

18. Réjean Pelletier, "From Jacques Parizeau to Lucien Bouchard: A New Vision? Yes, But ..." in Lazar, *Canada: The State of the Federation 1997*.

19. Robert Howse, "Searching for Plan A: National Unity and the Chrétien Government's New Federalism," in Lazar, *Canada: The State of the Federation 1997*; Gordon Gibson, *Plan B: The Future of the Rest of Canada* (Vancouver: Fraser Institute, 1994).

20. *Reference re Secession of Quebec*, [1998] 2 S.C.R. 217; David Schneiderman, ed., *The Quebec Decision: The Supreme Court Case and Commentary* (Toronto: Lorimer, 1999).

21. Robert A. Young, *The Struggle for Quebec: From Referendum to Referendum?* (Montreal: McGill–Queen's University Press, 1999).

22. J.R. Hurley, *Amending Canada's Constitution: History, Processes, Problems and Prospects* (Ottawa: Minister of Supply and Services Canada, 1996).

23. Paula Mallea, "Brief to the Manitoba Legislative Task Force on Canadian Unity," Brandon, January 15, 1998 (Winnipeg: Canadian Centre for Policy Alternatives—Manitoba, 1998). I am indebted to Jim Silver for this information.

FURTHER READING

Banting, Keith, and Richard Simeon, eds. *And No One Cheered: Federalism, Democracy and the Constitution Act*. Toronto: Methuen, 1983.

Behiels, Michael, ed. *The Meech Lake Primer: Conflicting Views of the 1987 Constitutional Accord*. Ottawa: University of Ottawa Press, 1989.

Cairns, Alan C. *Constitution, Government and Society in Canada*. Toronto: McClelland and Stewart, 1988.

————. *Disruptions: Constitutional Struggles, from the Charter to Meech Lake*. Toronto: McClelland and Stewart, 1991.

————. *Reconfigurations: Canadian Citizenship and Constitutional Change*. Toronto: McClelland and Stewart, 1995.

Cohen, Andrew. *A Deal Undone: The Making and Breaking of the Meech Lake Accord*. Vancouver: Douglas & McIntyre, 1990.

Cook, Curtis, ed. *Constitutional Predicament: Canada after the Referendum of 1992*. Montreal: McGill–Queen's University Press, 1994.

Favreau, Guy. *The Amendment of the Constitution of Canada*. Ottawa: Queen's Printer, 1965.

Funston, Bernard. *Consolidated Canadian Constitutional Documents*. Toronto: Carswell, 1994.

Funston, Bernard, and Eugene Meehan. *Canada's Constitutional Law in a Nutshell*, 2nd ed. Toronto: Carswell, 1998.

Gérin-Lajoie, Paul. *Constitutional Amendment in Canada*. Toronto: University of Toronto Press, 1950.

Gibbins, Roger, ed. *Meech Lake and Canada: Perspectives from the West*. Edmonton: Academic Printing and Publishing, 1988.

Heard, Andrew. *Canadian Constitutional Conventions*. Toronto: Oxford University Press, 1991.

Hogg, Peter. *Canada Act Annotated*. Toronto: Carswell, 1982.

————. *Meech Lake Constitutional Accord Annotated*. Toronto: Carswell, 1988.

————. *Constitutional Law of Canada*, 2nd ed. Toronto: Carswell, 1985; Student Edition, 1999.

Hurley, J.R. *Amending Canada's Constitution: History, Processes, Problems and Prospects*. Ottawa: Minister of Supply and Services Canada, 1996.

Johnston, Richard, et al. *The Challenge of Direct Democracy: The 1992 Canadian Referendum*. Montreal: McGill–Queen's University Press, 1996.

Lazar, Harvey, ed. *Canada: The State of the Federation 1997: Non-Constitutional Renewal*. Kingston, Institute of Intergovernmental Relations, 1997.

Lazar, Harvey, and Tom McIntosh, eds. *Canada: The State of the Federation 1998: How Canadians Connect*. Kingston: Institute of Intergovernmental Relations, 1998.

McRoberts, Kenneth. *Misconceiving Canada: The Struggle for National Unity*. Toronto: Oxford University Press, 1997.

McRoberts, Kenneth, and Patrick Monahan, eds. *The Charlottetown Accord, the Referendum and the Future of Canada*. Toronto: University of Toronto Press, 1993.

McWhinney, Edward. *Quebec and the Constitution 1960–1978*. Toronto: University of Toronto Press, 1979.

————. *Canada and the Constitution 1979–82: Patriation and the Charter of Rights*. Toronto: University of Toronto Press, 1982.

Mandel, Michael. *The Charter of Rights and the Legalization of Politics in Canada*. Toronto: Wall and Thompson, 1989; rev. ed., 1994.

Milne, David. *The Canadian Constitution*. Toronto: Lorimer, 1991.

Monahan, Patrick J. *Meech Lake: The Inside Story*. Toronto: University of Toronto Press, 1991.

————. *Constitutional Law*. Toronto: Irwin Law, 1997.

Parti Québécois. *Quebec in a New World*. Toronto: Lorimer, 1994.

Reesor, Bayard. *The Canadian Constitution in Historical Perspective*. Scarborough: Prentice-Hall Canada, 1992.

Romanow, Roy, J. Whyte, and H. Leeson. *Canada ... Notwithstanding: The Making of the Constitution 1976–1982*. Toronto: Methuen, 1984.

Russell, Peter. *Constitutional Odyssey*, 2nd. ed. Toronto: University of Toronto Press, 1993.

Schneiderman, David, ed. *The Quebec Decision: The Supreme Court Case and Commentary*. Toronto: Lorimer, 1999.

Seidel, F. Leslie. *Seeking a New Canadian Partnership: Asymmetrical and Confederal Options.* Montreal: Institute for Research on Public Policy, 1994.

Swinton, K.E., and C.J. Rogerson. *Competing Constitutional Visions: The Meech Lake Accord.* Toronto: Carswell, 1988.

Task Force on Canadian Unity. Hull: Canadian Government Publishing Centre, 1979.

Thomas, David. *Whistling Past the Graveyard: Constitutional Abeyances, Quebec, and the Future of Canada.* Toronto: Oxford University Press, 1997.

Young, Robert A. *The Struggle for Quebec: From Referendum to Referendum?* Montreal: McGill–Queen's University Press, 1999.

Chapter 17
The Provinces
AND THE FEDERAL
system

Liberal Prime Minister Mackenzie King once said that he would not give "one red cent" to a Tory provincial government. Provincial party leaders often centre entire election campaigns on complaints about Ottawa, and federal–provincial squabbles are a daily occurrence in Canadian political life, such as a nasty fight in 1999 between the federal and BC governments over a torpedo test range off Vancouver Island. The courts threw out federal legislation that aimed at alleviating the Depression, ruling that only the provinces could pass such laws. In the postwar period, Ottawa introduced a multitude of national programs within provincial jurisdiction—especially postsecondary education, health insurance, and social assistance—and through financial inducements persuaded the provinces to join them. The federal government now pays over $30 billion a year to provincial governments, but throughout the 1990s cut back on such transfers to considerable provincial and public complaint. Then, in 1999, nine provinces and Ottawa signed a widely heralded "social union" agreement.

The federal character of Canada is designated in the Canadian Constitution and its impact is seen in almost every aspect of governance and society. The federal system is closely related to regional economic cleavages, is important for ethnic cleavages, influences the Canadian political culture, and affects the operation of the electoral system, political parties, and pressure groups. Federalism also has a major impact on the institutions of the national government.

In a formal sense, **federalism** can be defined as a division of powers between central and regional governments such that neither is subordinate to the other. This definition distinguishes the relationship between national and provincial governments from that between provincial and municipal governments, for in the latter case the municipalities are clearly subordinate entities while in the former, provinces are "coordinate" or equal in status to the central government. This equality of status is provided for in the constitutional division of powers between the two levels of government, which is found primarily in sections 91 and 92 of the Constitution Act, 1867. Other aspects of federalism are also important, however, such as federal–provincial financial relations (taxing and spending) and joint policymaking mechanisms. Moreover, the institutions of federalism are embedded in a "federal society" that supports such a two-tier structure of government.

....

Figure 17.1   **Map of the Provinces and Capitals**

This chapter begins by sketching the political systems of the provinces and outlining the federal system in Canada at its creation; it then traces the evolution of the federal system, especially through changes in the division of powers and federal–provincial financial relationships. In the following section this evolution is depicted in chronological phases, as the federal system veered between centralization and decentralization. The chapter concludes with a discussion of Canadian federalism today, including the "social union" agreement.

....

THE PROVINCIAL POLITICAL SYSTEMS

Canada is composed of ten provinces and three territories. The provinces are autonomous within the powers given them by the Constitution, but the powers of the territories—increasingly similar to those of the provinces—could theoretically be revoked. This leaves the territories constitutionally subordinate to the federal government.

Each of the provinces has considerable political and economic significance in its own right, and can be considered a separate political system.[1] Each one has a full complement of governmental institutions, which are subject to societal demands in much the same way as this book earlier outlined at the federal level. Each province also has a somewhat distinctive political culture, party system, and array of pressure groups. In sketching a quick picture of these provincial political systems, it will be seen that their operations bear a striking resemblance to those at the federal level.

Each province is theoretically headed by the lieutenant governor, who is appointed by the federal prime minister and who represents the Queen. The lieutenant governors function as the monarch and governor general do, primarily performing ceremonial and social functions. Apart from an emergency situation, they are no longer expected to exercise personal discretion in the operation of government. The effective head of the provincial government is the premier, the equivalent of the prime minister, along with the cabinet; they are officially called the Executive Council. The provincial cabinet typically sets priorities, decides how much money to raise and spend, and how to do so, determines policies, gives direction for the preparation of legislation, oversees departmental administration, and makes order-in-council appointments. Premiers usually select their ministers from the elected members of the legislature and try to balance various interests; the size of the provincial cabinet varies in proportion to the size of the province and averages about 18 ministers.

Provincial cabinets now operate with formal procedures and a cabinet committee system, usually dominated by the committees concerned with social and economic development. A cabinet secretariat has emerged to provide policy, procedural, and secretarial assistance to the premier, the cabinet, and cabinet committees.[2] While ministers are said to be individually responsible for their departments and collectively responsible for government policy, determined premiers can make their presence felt throughout the provincial government's operations in an even more effective way than is possible for the prime minister in Ottawa.

The provincial legislatures are the elected representatives of the people, usually chosen at four-year intervals. These representatives are termed MLAs in seven provinces, MPPs in Ontario, MHAs in Newfoundland, and MNAs in Quebec. Each provincial legislature has only one chamber, divided between government and opposition members. With the expansion of provincial government activity over the past 30 or 40 years, legislative sessions became longer, committee work became more extensive, members of the legislature were deluged with constituents' problems with the provincial bureaucracy, and the position increasingly became a full-time job. When in session, each provincial legislature has a daily oral question period that provides the focus for most mass media coverage. Provincial legislatures have become busy and often exciting forums, and private members can now do a better job than in the past in the areas of criticizing, questioning, and informing the cabinet. Nevertheless, premiers and cabinets continue to make the crucial decisions, and legislators are not much closer to being involved directly in the decision-making process.

Given the expansion of provincial governments, at least until 1990 or so, provincial politicians are increasingly dependent on the bureaucracy or public service to advise them on their decisions and the implementation of their programs. In addition to providing services, enforcing rules, collecting taxes, and engaging in other administrative activities, the public service must draft regulations which contain the detailed substance of the law in question. This may involve consultation with relevant pressure groups. Thus, the modern provincial bureaucracy is no mere neutral agent in providing advice; it is a power to be reckoned with in its own right.

The most important provincial responsibilities in Canada tend to be health and education, meaning that these departments are usually the largest in terms of budgets and personnel. Finance departments are also significant at this level of government, as are such central agencies as cabinet secretariats and treasury or management boards. In addition, each province has an array of semi-independent agencies, boards, commissions, and Crown corporations, operating outside the ordinary departmental structure. These typically include a public hydro commission, a public utilities commission, a human rights commission, a workers' compensation board, a labour relations board, and a liquor commission, although provinces have engaged in widespread privatization programs over the past 15 years.

While provincial cabinets, legislatures, and bureaucracies may regularly interact with their federal counterparts, they do so on a basis of autonomy and equality. On the other hand, the federal and provincial judicial systems in Canada are officially integrated, as noted in Chapter 23. Each province establishes its own hierarchy of courts, at the base of which are "provincial courts" whose judges are appointed by the provincial cabinets. Above this level, the judges are appointed by Ottawa. The element of integration can also be seen in the passage of criminal laws by Ottawa, by its dependence on the provinces for enforcement, and in appeals from provincial courts of appeal to the Supreme Court of Canada. The latter includes appeals of reference cases that provincial cabinets can refer to their own supreme court.

Every province also establishes a municipal level of government, typically including cities, towns, villages, townships, and rural municipalities. The province determines the structures, responsibilities, and financial powers of these local governments. They are usually responsible for services to property such as streets, sidewalks, water, sewers, garbage and police and fire protection, recreation, and libraries. As for the provision of services to people such as health, welfare, and housing, these responsibilities may be largely delegated to municipalities, retained by the province, or shared. In most provinces, a second local authority, the school board, is elected separately from the municipal council, but a recent trend has seen such school boards lose much of their power to the provincial department of education or even the cabinet.

Many observers have noted that especially since about 1970, Canada has seen a phenomenon of **province-building**, as provincial governments expanded their operations in both absolute terms and relative to Ottawa. Even if both levels have slimmed down considerably in recent years, the operation of provincial (and municipal) governments is of tremendous significance. Table 17.1 compares employment and expenditure figures for these various levels for 1996–97.

TABLE 17.1   **Federal, Provincial, and Municipal Employment and Expenditure, 1996–1997**

	Employment	*Expenditure*
Federal	361 397	$167 293 500 000
Provincial	1 328 675	$176 726 700 000
Municipal	905 486	$39 252 200 000

Source: Canadian Tax Foundation, Finances of the Nation, 1998. Used with permission.

THE CONFEDERATION SETTLEMENT

The fundamentals of Canadian federalism, often called the **Confederation Settlement**,[3] were incorporated into the 1867 British North America Act, which in 1982 was renamed the Constitution Act, 1867. As noted in Chapter 2, the principal architect of Confederation was

Sir John A. Macdonald, who intended the new country to be a highly centralized federation. In many ways, in fact, the Confederation Settlement was not consistent with the modern definition of federalism because in certain respects the provinces were made subordinate to the central government.[4]

The Confederation Settlement consisted of five principal components: first, the division of powers between the central and provincial governments; second, the division of financial resources; third, federal controls imposed upon the provinces; fourth, provincial representation in the central institutions; and fifth, certain cultural guarantees.

As far as the **division of powers** between the central and provincial governments was concerned, the Fathers of Confederation gave the provinces 16 specific **enumerated powers** in section 92 (e.g., hospitals and municipal institutions) and then left everything else—the **residual powers**—to Ottawa, in section 91. For greater certainty, however, they also included 29 enumerations of federal powers such as trade and commerce and national defence. Two **concurrent powers**—agriculture and immigration—were listed in section 95, and the treaty power in section 132 provided the federal government with the power to implement Empire treaties, regardless of their subject matter.

In the division of financial resources, federal dominance was even more apparent. The Fathers gave Ottawa the power to levy any mode or system of taxation, which included both **direct taxes** and **indirect taxes**. Since the only tax widely used at the time was the customs duty, an indirect tax, provincial power over direct taxation was not considered to be very significant. Instead, the provinces were expected to raise their revenues from the sale of shop, saloon, tavern, and auctioneer licences, as well as to rely on federal subsidies. The federal government was to pay each province an annual per capita grant of 80 cents plus a small subsidy to support its government and legislature. The federal government also assisted the provinces by assuming their pre-Confederation debts. It should be added that the provinces were authorized to raise revenues from their natural resources, but this source was not taken very seriously at the time because few such resources (except trees) had yet been discovered.

In the third place, in a clear departure from what is now regarded as the federal principle, Ottawa was given several means of controlling the provinces. The lieutenant governor, a federal appointee, was permitted by section 90 to reserve provincial legislation for the consideration of the federal Cabinet—the power of **reservation**—which could then approve or reject it. Even if the lieutenant governor gave assent to a piece of provincial legislation, however, the federal Cabinet could subsequently disallow it—the power of **disallowance**. Then, under section 92(10)(c), the federal government could declare any local work or undertaking to be for the general advantage of Canada and thus place it within federal jurisdiction—the **declaratory power**.

Given the highly centralized nature of the division of powers, the limited financial resources of the provinces, and the federal controls, it is clear that the Confederation Settlement of 1867 placed the provinces in a subordinate position, somewhat akin to municipalities, rather than giving them the equal or coordinate status provided for in the modern definition of federalism.

In the light of the federal government's dominant position, it is not surprising that the smaller provinces were concerned with their representation in Ottawa. The fourth aspect of the Confederation Settlement, therefore, was agreement on provincial representation in the House of Commons and the Senate, a question of much more concern at the time than the division of powers. The great compromise that allowed Confederation to go forward was that the provinces would be represented according to population in the Commons but that regional equality would prevail in the Senate. Thus each of the three original regions—the Maritimes, Quebec, and Ontario—was to receive 24 senators, appeasing smaller provinces that could be easily out-voted in the lower chamber.

Such concern about provincial representation *within* the institutions of the national government has come to be called "intrastate federalism" as opposed to an emphasis on relations *between* federal and provincial governments, or what is sometimes termed "interstate federalism."[5] Beyond the House of Commons and the Senate, interests of the various provinces can be represented within the Cabinet and, perhaps less explicitly, within the bureaucracy and Supreme Court, an issue that arises in the discussion of these institutions in the next part of the book. To some extent, federal–provincial (or interstate) tensions can be reduced if "intrastate" mechanisms are working effectively so that the people of all provinces feel adequately represented within the national government's policymaking process. But rigid party discipline and representation by population in the House of Commons and unilateral federal appointment of senators and Supreme Court judges may diminish such confidence, and as a result, provincial premiers often come to be the principal articulators of provincial interests.

Confederation was more than just a union of provinces; it was also a uniting of two cultural groups, English and French. (Nobody gave Aboriginals much thought at the time.) Thus, the fifth aspect of the Confederation Settlement might be called cultural guarantees. Considering the anxiety of French Canadians about the preservation of their language and culture, these guarantees were surprisingly minor. Section 133 of the 1867 act made French and English official languages in the federal Parliament and federal courts as well as in the Quebec legislature and Quebec courts—but nowhere else. At the time, religion was probably of greater concern than language, so existing separate school systems in the provinces (especially Ontario and Quebec) were guaranteed by allowing the federal government to step in to restore them, if necessary, according to section 93. French Canada was also protected by giving power over property and civil rights to the provinces so that Quebec could maintain certain cultural particularisms, including its civil law system.

Since the evolution of French-language rights is discussed in Chapter 5 and since the question of representation is addressed in Chapter 22, this chapter will proceed to track the development of the Confederation Settlement in its other three aspects, the division of powers, financial resources, and federal controls.

EVOLUTION OF CANADIAN FEDERALISM

In a discussion of the evolution of Canadian federalism, a key concern will be to explain how the very centralized federation created in 1867 became the highly decentralized Canada of today. In all three areas—the division of powers, financial resources, and federal controls—this trend is apparent.

Division of Powers

The evolution of the division of powers between federal and provincial governments can be examined in two respects: formal constitutional amendments that altered the division of powers, and judicial decisions that interpreted sections 91, 92, and 132 of the Constitution Act of 1867. It will be seen that the latter development was by far the more important.

CONSTITUTIONAL AMENDMENTS

Since 1867, only five formal constitutional amendments have been adopted that directly affected the division of powers. First, in 1940, unemployment insurance was added to the list of federal powers in section 91 after the courts had earlier declared it to belong to the provinces. Second, in 1951, old age pensions were made a concurrent power, allowing the federal government into this area as well. In the third place, in 1964, federal jurisdiction in the pensions field was enlarged to include widows' and survivors' benefits and disability pensions. Fourth, in 1949, the federal Parliament was allowed to amend the Constitution unilaterally in areas of purely federal concern, a power previously held by Britain. (This amendment was repealed in 1982 with the adoption of a more general amending formula). Finally, in 1982, the new section 92A increased provincial jurisdiction over natural resources, while the Charter of Rights and Freedoms generally reduced the powers of both levels of government. Thus, in the first three cases, the net result was a slight increase in federal powers, but, as pointed out in Chapter 16, this increase was accomplished with the unanimous consent of the provinces. Some provinces complained about the 1949 amendment, but it did not directly affect their powers. The 1982 natural resources amendment was the only formal constitutional amendment that in any way increased provincial powers at the expense of Ottawa.

JUDICIAL INTERPRETATION

Judicial interpretation of the federal and provincial powers in the 1867 act is a much more complicated subject. Before 1949, the **Judicial Committee of the Privy Council (JCPC)** in London was Canada's final court of appeal, and most constitutional decisions were rendered by that body. There is no doubt that its decisions had a major impact in transforming the nature of Canadian federalism from a centralized to a decentralized system, whether it acted out of ignorance or by deliberate design. The JCPC decisions can be examined primarily in terms of the Peace, Order, and Good Government clause, the Trade and Commerce power, and the Treaty power.

Section 91 of the 1867 act has two parts. First, the **Peace, Order, and Good Government clause** says that all powers not given to the provinces in section 92 are left with the federal government. This is also known as "POGG" or the residual clause, and reads as follows:

> It shall be lawful for the Queen, by and with the Advice and Consent of the Senate and House of Commons, to make laws for the Peace, Order, and good Government of Canada, in relation to all matters not coming within the Classes of Subjects by this Act assigned exclusively to the Legislatures of the Provinces; and for greater Certainty, but not so as to restrict the Generality of the foregoing Terms of this Section, it is hereby declared that (notwithstanding anything in this Act) the exclusive Legislative Authority of the Parliament of Canada extends to all Matters coming within the Classes of Subjects next hereinafter enumerated.

Then, for greater certainty, a list of 29 examples of federal powers is included, a clause that was logically unnecessary and eventually became counterproductive. In a nutshell, in the course of its judgments, the Judicial Committee drove a wedge between these two parts of section 91, decided that the 29 enumerations were the *real* federal powers rather than just examples, and ignored the Peace, Order, and Good Government clause except in time of national emergency.

How it managed to transform the residual clause into an emergency power is very difficult to fathom and is the subject of much scholarly discussion and whole books and courses on Canadian constitutional law. On the other hand, the JCPC gave an extremely broad interpretation to section 92(13), property and civil rights in the province, finding that almost any matter that was the subject of a federal–provincial constitutional dispute could be incorporated within this provincial power. That is why so little was left over for the federal residual clause. The full text of sections 91 and 92 is included in Appendix A.

Let us briefly summarize the leading POGG cases to see how this strange development took place.[6] In *Russell v. the Queen*, 1882, the federal Temperance Act was challenged. This law provided the means by which the people of a local community could vote to outlaw the sale of alcohol. The JCPC ruled that the regulation of liquor was not mentioned explicitly in sections 91 and 92, and that while it affected property and civil rights (Mr. Russell's tavern and his right to operate it), the main purpose of the act was the promotion of public order and safety throughout the Dominion. Thus the federal act was a valid exercise of the Peace, Order, and Good Government power. However, in an 1883 case, *Hodge v. the Queen*, the Judicial Committee ruled that there was a double aspect to the regulation of liquor— "subjects which in one aspect and for one purpose fall within s. 92, may in another aspect and for another purpose fall within s. 91." This decision opened the door for provincial action in the liquor field as well. Then, in the Local Prohibition case of 1896, the JCPC said that the Peace, Order, and Good Government clause was merely supplementary to the enumerations in section 91, and that POGG would come into play only if a subject could not be found in the list of enumerations in either section 91 or 92, and if the subject had attained such dimensions as to affect the body politic of the country as a whole. From this point, at which the POGG clause was divorced from the rest of section 91 and at which the list of enumerations effectively became *the* federal powers, matters in dispute were increasingly found to fit into property and civil rights in the provinces.

POGG was then transformed into an **emergency clause** in a series of cases in the 1920s. In the *Board of Commerce* case, 1922, the Privy Council said that the regulation of prices and profiteering would normally fall within section 92(13), and only in special circumstances such as war or famine could such matters become of national importance. In the *Fort Frances* case, 1924, federal regulation of the price and supply of newsprint was upheld because it had been done in wartime, an emergency that justified federal action in a field that would ordinarily be provincial. Finally, in the 1925 *Toronto Electric Commissioners v. Snider* case, federal legislation to deal with serious strikes was ruled unconstitutional since labour–management relations were normally matters of property and civil rights in the province, and could only be the subject of federal action in an emergency. Faced with the disparity between this line of interpretation (that POGG was only an emergency clause), and that used in the *Russell* case (that POGG was a simple residual clause), the JCPC resorted to a reinterpretation of the earlier case: the evil of drunkenness at the time of the *Russell* case must have amounted to a national emergency!

A series of "New Deal" cases followed in the 1930s in which federal laws in the fields of unemployment insurance, labour standards, and the marketing of farm products were ruled invalid since the legislation was intended to be permanent rather than deal only with the temporary emergency of the Depression. These highly controversial decisions rendered Ottawa impotent in dealing with the human devastation wrought by the Depression. Strangely enough, however, when the *Russell* case was duplicated in the 1946 Canada Temperance

Federation case, the JCPC disavowed the emergency doctrine and reverted to the simple residual basis of POGG.

When appeals to the Privy Council were abolished in 1949, all eyes were on the Supreme Court to see which line of interpretation it would take with respect to POGG—emergency power or residual clause? The record has been unclear, but in general the federal level has won more cases than it did before 1949. Perhaps this reflects the Supreme Court's better understanding of the Canadian situation, or its reaction to the excessive provincial orientation of the JCPC. Some of these federal victories have been based on POGG as a simple residual clause (with an issue having national but not emergency dimensions), such as the *Johannesson* case, which reaffirmed federal control over aviation and airports, the BC and Newfoundland off-shore minerals cases, which gave Ottawa jurisdiction over the area beyond the BC and Newfoundland coasts, and *Munro v. National Capital Commission*, which permitted federal regulation of property in the National Capital Region. But in the leading decision, the Anti-Inflation Act reference of 1976, the Court was badly split. The majority of judges that upheld it did so for different reasons: some adhered to the emergency doctrine, while others were prepared to accept a broader interpretation of POGG. Later environmental cases such as *The Queen v. Crown Zellerbach Canada Ltd.* in 1988 and the *Oldman River* decision in 1992 have strengthened federal jurisdiction over pollution control with extra-provincial implications. Ottawa's control over telephones and telecommunications has also been enhanced.[7] Even if a recent pro-Ottawa stance can be detected, however, the net effect of judicial interpretation of the Peace, Order, and Good Government clause since 1867 is to have greatly increased provincial powers at federal expense.

A similar fate awaited the federal **Trade and Commerce clause**, section 91(2). The Fathers of Confederation deliberately expressed this clause in wide, general, unlimited terms, "the regulation of trade and commerce," but as early as the *Parsons* case, 1881, the JCPC basically restricted federal power to international and interprovincial trade. Besides drawing this unanticipated but rigid line between interprovincial trade (federal) and intraprovincial trade (provincial), the courts created a no man's land wherever the two kinds of trade were unavoidably combined. The general result of this line of interpretation was to enhance the provincial power over property and civil rights, and to downgrade the federal commerce power. Since 1949, the Supreme Court has rendered more realistic judgments in this area, recognizing the complexity of the situation and often favouring the federal side.

The **Treaty power**, section 132, effectively says that in cases of Empire treaties, the division of powers becomes inoperative and the federal government can implement them regardless of subject matter. Such was the decision of the *Aeronautics* case of 1932; the *Radio* case of the same year applied this rule to non-Empire treaties as well. However, in the 1937 *Labour Conventions* case, the JCPC reversed itself and said that Ottawa could only implement treaties the subject matter of which was within federal jurisdiction. In this particular case, the subject matter fell instead into property and civil rights.

The combined effect of the judicial interpretation of the Peace, Order, and Good Government, Trade and Commerce, and the Treaty powers has been to reduce significantly the intended dominance of the federal government, and to increase substantially the scope of provincial powers, especially with the broad interpretation given to property and civil rights. This influence has been very controversial in political, judicial, and academic circles because it was clearly contrary to John A. Macdonald's conception of Canadian federalism and because it did not permit Ottawa to take many initiatives desired by centralist advocates.[8]

Some observers give the JCPC the benefit of the doubt and think it operated in ignorance; others feel that it chose to adopt a narrow, literal line of interpretation, rather than the "aspect doctrine," a competing legal approach. Still other commentators argue that the British judges deliberately imposed their own decentralized conception of federalism on Canada or supported the provinces out of personal conservative ideological motives. The JCPC could only deal with the cases brought before it, of course, so that the decentralized results of its interpretation also depended on a greater number of challenges to federal than provincial laws. Several such cases were initiated by corporations that expected to be given a freer hand in their pursuit of profits if power remained at the provincial level. Other cases were started by provincial premiers with the support of their cabinets and advisers, which followed naturally from the legitimation in a federal constitution of subnational elites.

On the other hand, many observers contend that the Judicial Committee's line of interpretation was consistent with the increasing size and distances that characterized the country as time went on, as well as with societal forces and public orientations, at least outside Ontario. They argue that Canada has a federal, decentralized, diversified *society*, and the provincial bias pervading so many of the JCPC's decisions was "in fundamental harmony with the regional pluralism" of that society. However desirable centralization may have seemed at the outset, it was inappropriate in the long run "for the regional diversities of a land of vast extent and a large, geographically concentrated, minority culture."[9] Most French-Canadian observers, for example, were quite happy with the line of interpretation taken by the JCPC. Thus, Alan Cairns finds it impossible "to believe that a few elderly men in London deciding two or three constitutional cases a year precipitated, sustained, and caused the development of Canada in a federalist direction the country would otherwise not have taken."[10] Moreover, he observes,

> the discovery and amplification of an emergency power in Section 91 may have done an injustice to the intentions of Macdonald for the residual power, but it did allow Canada to conduct herself virtually as a unitary state in the two world wars in which centralized government authority was both required and supported.[11]

Federal–Provincial Finance[12]

In the Confederation Settlement, the federal government was given the power to levy any kind of tax, while the provinces were restricted to direct taxation.[13] Ottawa assumed provincial debts (also paying debt allowances to those provinces with smaller debts) and paid unconditional grants to the provinces based on 80 cents per capita and in support of governments and legislatures. While the intention was thus to create a highly centralized federation, the financial factor also ultimately contributed to the increased power of the provinces. This situation came about because the provinces successfully lobbied for larger federal grants, mostly unconditional in nature, than were set out in 1867; because the provinces levied direct taxes, such as income taxes, which they were not expected to use; and because some provincial revenues, such as those from natural resources, turned out to be more significant than anticipated.

Provincial revenues proved to be inadequate from the beginning, and special grants and arrangements had to be made immediately. A wholesale change in the grant system followed in 1907. By this time, too, the provinces had begun to levy their own direct personal and corporate income taxes, a situation complicated by the federal entry into the same fields during the First World War. About the same time, the **conditional grant** made its appearance. This was a grant paid by the federal government to the provinces in an area of provincial jurisdiction but for which provincial revenues were deemed to be inadequate. The provinces usually had to match the federal share of 50 percent, as well as adhere to whatever conditions or standards Ottawa imposed. The most important conditional grant in the early years was the old age pension, which started in 1927.

With both levels of government taxing the same personal and corporate incomes, but in a totally uncoordinated fashion, and with the two levels increasingly intertwined in conditional grant programs, the federal–provincial financial situation became very complicated. This muddied state of affairs worsened with the advent of the Depression, when even fewer funds were available to go around. The result was the appointment of the **Rowell–Sirois Commission**, officially the Royal Commission on Dominion–Provincial Relations, in 1937. Its 1940 report recommended that the costly responsibility for unemployment insurance be transferred to the federal government, that Ottawa again assume provincial debts, and that the provinces give up the fields of personal and corporate income taxes and succession duties to the federal government. In return, the federal level should pay the provinces an annual unconditional grant based on need. The first recommendation was quickly implemented, as was a temporary Wartime Taxation Agreement, but the report's other suggestions were shelved.

Before 1940, therefore, the two levels of government were relatively independent on both the taxation and expenditure sides of public finance. Since the Second World War, on the other hand, they have become intimately intertwined, and Ottawa has taken the lead (sometimes with provincial encouragement) in coordinating the various ingredients of the federal–provincial financial relationship. The complicated federal–provincial financial situation since 1940 might be simplified somewhat by taking three aspects separately: taxation agreements, conditional and block grants, and equalization payments.

FEDERAL–PROVINCIAL TAXATION AGREEMENTS

Since 1942 the taxation side has been characterized by a series of five-year federal–provincial agreements. The name and terms of the **taxation agreements** have changed over the years— tax rental, tax sharing, tax collection, and so on—but the basic objective has been the same: to effect a degree of coordination in the field of federal–provincial taxation. The main taxes in question were personal and corporate income taxes and succession duties, although succession duties or estate taxes are no longer applied in any province. Since 1962 the provincial portion of personal income tax has been allowed to vary, and today, while the federal tax is standard across the country (except for Quebec), the provincial portion varies widely.

Table 17.2 indicates how much of an individual's personal income tax is extracted by each province as a percentage of his or her basic federal tax. Except for Quebec, all personal income taxes are collected by Ottawa in the first instance, after which the provincial portion is transferred back. Quebec collects its own personal income tax, so that its residents complete two separate income tax forms. The federal income tax return in Quebec reflects the fact that that province receives a "tax abatement" of 16.5 personal income tax points to cover the financing of those conditional grant programs from which it has opted out, a tax abatement being a transfer of "tax room" from the federal to the provincial level. All provinces

TABLE 17.2 **Provincial Personal Income Rates, 1999, as Percentage of Basic Federal Tax**

Newfoundland	69.0
New Brunswick	60.0
Prince Edward Island	58.5
Nova Scotia	57.5
Manitoba	48.5
British Columbia	49.5
Saskatchewan	48.0
Alberta	44.0
Ontario	39.5

Source: Ernst & Young, LLP. Used with permission.

except Ontario, Quebec, and Alberta also have tax collection arrangements with Ottawa with respect to provincial corporate income taxes. Alberta served notice in its 1999 budget, however, that it planned to disengage its provincial income tax from the federal tax because it believed in a completely different tax structure.

CONDITIONAL AND BLOCK GRANTS

The Rowell–Sirois Report frowned on shared-cost programs, preferring that each level of government operate independently. Nevertheless, joint programs expanded considerably after 1940, as pressure from the CCF, industrial unions, and other newly articulated interests on the left forced federal and provincial governments into the joint development of a welfare state. The most important shared-cost social programs were postsecondary education (1952), hospital insurance (1957), the **Canada Assistance Plan (CAP)** (1966), and medical insurance (1968). Health insurance later replaced the two earlier measures in this field.

Federal grants for postsecondary education have always been of a **block grant** variety, that is, a sum of money given to each province for the operating costs of postsecondary educational institutions but without any detailed conditions or strings attached. Between 1967 and 1977 they were based on a formula of providing 50 percent of such expenditures.

The other major **shared-cost programs** originally fell into the conditional grant category. The usual pattern here was that after it had laid down certain conditions, the federal government paid approximately 50 percent of the cost of each program. In the case of hospital insurance, for example, Ottawa would pay half the cost of provincial programs that provided their residents with basic hospital care without charge. The provinces could finance their half of the program costs from premiums or general tax revenues. Medical insurance was an extension of the prior program to cover basic doctors' services. Ottawa would fund half of any provincial health care program that was comprehensive (covering all necessary health services provided by hospitals and medical practitioners), universal (covering the whole population), portable (covering the costs of provincial residents while temporarily absent from the province), accessible (not impeding or precluding reasonable access to services by extra charges), and publicly administered. Under the Canada Assistance Plan, Ottawa similarly provided half the funding for almost any provincial or municipal program that provided social assistance and welfare services based on need.

Most of these programs fell constitutionally within provincial jurisdiction, but Ottawa always maintained that its **spending power** allowed it to make payments to individuals, institutions, and other governments in fields over which Parliament did not necessarily have the power to regulate. The federal government even claimed that it could attach conditions to such spending and has often done so. The constitutional status of this argument has been addressed by the courts in several cases.[14]

While a combination of provincial pressure and federal political and bureaucratic expansionism inspired most of these programs, the provinces often criticized the federal conditions attached as being out of place in areas of provincial jurisdiction. Quebec in particular took this point of view in the early 1960s. The Pearson government responded in 1965 with the Established Programs (Interim Arrangements) Act, which allowed provinces to opt out of certain conditional grant programs and continue to receive federal funding as long as they maintained an equivalent program. Then, in the 1970s, Ottawa became upset at the rapidly escalating costs of many of these programs, along with its commitment to finance 50 percent of whatever the provinces spent on them. In 1977 the federal government therefore transferred health insurance from the conditional to the block grant category, under the **Established Programs Financing Act**. Ottawa removed the detailed conditions attached to the health insurance programs, as many provinces wished, but in return, the federal government no longer felt obliged to pay 50 percent of the provincial program costs. The federal grants now took the form of tax transfers as well as cash, and henceforth, Ottawa would only

By Brian Gable (Globe and Mail). *Reprinted with permission from* The Globe and Mail.

increase its funding of such programs by a certain annual percentage, which would not necessarily cover one-half of their overall costs. The tax transfers represent federal tax revenue forgone as a result of a coordinated reduction of federal taxes and an increase in provincial taxes such that the position of the taxpayer is left unchanged. Removing the conditions from health insurance grants, however, led to problems with hospital user fees, doctors' double-billing, and the provinces' use of health care funds for other purposes. Federal and public displeasure at these developments led Ottawa to pass the **Canada Health Act** in 1984, to much provincial condemnation. This law penalized provinces that did not meet its five conditions (comprehensiveness, universality, portability, accessibility, and public administration) and that permitted user fees and double-billing in the health field.

Especially after 1982, the federal share of such programs fell below 50 percent, and the 1990s saw a progression of freezes and cuts in such funding. The Canada Assistance Plan remained a conditional grant program, with Ottawa continuing its 50 percent contribution until the Mulroney government put a ceiling on its CAP contributions to the three richest provinces in the early 1990s. This discrimination remained intact until 1999.

The 1995 federal budget brought in by Finance Minister Paul Martin inaugurated a major transformation of federal–provincial transfer payments. Established Program Funding (post-secondary education and health insurance) and the Canada Assistance Plan (social assistance and welfare services) were combined into one block grant, beginning in 1996–97, called the **Canada Health and Social Transfer (CHST)**. It would be a combination of cash payments and tax points, but would represent a significant reduction in previous amounts and Ottawa's expenditures would no longer be driven by provincial costs. As a block grant, the CHST would not contain the conditions of CAP—the only condition on welfare transfers was that provinces not impose a minimum residency requirement. Ottawa felt that it could not retain previous conditions when it was reducing its contributions, and was particularly loath to provoke the PQ government of Quebec immediately before the 1995 referendum.

All the federal off-loading, including the CHST and the shift to tax points, had serious consequences for many social programs, especially in have-not provinces. Because the latter do not have a strong tax base, they benefit more from the transfer of dollars than of tax points. This and other developments in fiscal federalism have thus constituted some of the ways in which the "redistributive state" has been eroded. Moreover, few social reformers trusted provincial governments to spend the smaller amounts on social programs. On the other hand, the federal Liberal government announced that it would continue to enforce the principles of the Canada Health Act, and fought with Alberta over the funding of private health clinics that charged "facility fees."

EQUALIZATION PAYMENTS

The third aspect of federal–provincial finance consists of **equalization payments**.[15] Picking up on the Rowell–Sirois Report's recommendation, but not until 1957, the federal government began to pay unconditional grants to have-not provinces based on provincial need, so that all could offer a relatively equal standard of services. The basic idea behind equalization payments was to bring the have-not provinces up to the national average tax yield per capita. At first only 3 provincial taxes were considered in the equalization formula, but the number has increased to 33—including almost every conceivable source of provincial revenue. Typically,

Ontario, British Columbia, and Alberta have been above the national average and have not received equalization payments, but Alberta petroleum revenues raised the national average so high that Ontario began to qualify in 1980, and an adjustment to the formula had to be made to remove natural resource revenue. Such revenues were later added back, but Alberta was removed along with the Atlantic provinces in the calculation of the national average. The current formula uses as a base the average of per capita revenue of five representative provinces (Quebec, Ontario, Manitoba, Saskatchewan, and British Columbia). Any province whose total per capita revenue is below this average receives a payment based on the per capita shortfall multiplied by the province's population. Equalization payments were not touched by the federal reforms of 1995.

Combining these three (or, after 1996–97, two) major federal contributions to the provinces, Table 17.3 shows that in 1993–94 Ottawa paid the provinces some $8.0 billion in equalization payments and over $28 billion in health and postsecondary education block grants and conditional CAP grants, for a total of $36.2 billion. These transfers fell to $34 billion in 1997–1998 but then rose again to over their 1993–1994 level by 1999–2000, and were scheduled to increase to over $40 billion by 2001–2002. Even so, these figures do not include smaller conditional and unconditional federal grants. In contrast, unadjusted for inflation, the federal grant of 80 cents per capita in 1867 would amount to about $24 million today!

OTHER PROVINCIAL REVENUES

The provinces have discovered and levied over 30 forms of direct taxation that were unanticipated in 1867.[16] The enormous natural resource revenues that some provinces receive on top of direct taxation and federal contributions are also significant. Over and above the revenue that is collected in the form of corporate income taxes, provinces obtain specific natural resource revenues from forests, including taxes on logging operations; leases and rentals of Crown lands; and royalties, rentals, and stumpage fees from timber and forest management. They also obtain revenues from mines, including taxes on mining operations, acreage taxes, licence and permit fees, rentals and lease payments, and royalties on mineral production. In addition, the petroleum-producing provinces collect revenue from oil and gas, including proceeds from the sale of Crown oil and gas leases, taxes on oil and gas production, royalties, freehold taxes, lease rentals, and fees and permits.[17] The balance between federal transfers and the provinces own revenue sources, including natural resources, can be seen in Table 17.4.

Thus, the combination of unanticipated federal grants, direct taxes, and natural resource revenues has contributed significantly to the enhanced status of the provinces in the Canadian federal system. It should be added that pressure for decentralization and for turning taxation power over to the provinces comes from those provinces that have substantial personal and corporate incomes to tax. The Atlantic provinces and Manitoba sometimes fight against decentralization because they would not benefit if their taxation powers were expanded while Ottawa's were lessened. They want to keep Ottawa strong so that it can redistribute revenues at least by means of equalization payments.[18] It should also be repeated that the two levels of government began by operating more or less independently of each other, taxing and spending in different areas, with federal grants being unconditional in nature. Now, the federal and provincial governments are closely intertwined by taxation agreements on the revenue side and by conditional and block grant programs in terms of expenditures.

TABLE 17.3   Federal Transfers to Provinces and Territories, 1993–2004 ($ millions)

	1993–1994	*1997–1998*	*1999–2000*	*2003–2004*
Newfoundland				
CHST*	608	510	511	515
Equalization	900	1 088	1 003	1 108
Total**	1 427	1 495	1 416	1 518
Prince Edward Island				
CHST	135	117	127	138
Equalization	175	233	222	258
Total	294	328	327	369
Nova Scotia				
CHST	946	816	877	939
Equalization	889	1 301	1 239	1 473
Total	1 758	2 003	2 002	2 275
New Brunswick				
CHST	760	647	700	746
Equalization	835	1 093	1 054	1 202
Total	1 519	1 633	1 648	1 823
Quebec				
CHST	7 967	6 895	7 035	7 392
Equalization	3 878	4 820	4 464	5 365
Total	11 508	11 233	11 020	12 148
Ontario				
CHST	10 320	9 253	10 600	11 991
Equalization	0	0	0	0
Total	10 320	9 253	10 600	11 991
Manitoba				
CHST	1 133	975	1 063	1 145
Equalization	901	1 016	929	1 008
Total	1 951	1 919	1 924	2 068
Saskatchewan				
CHST	969	850	946	1 018
Equalization	486	117	377	477
Total	1 349	854	1 210	1 362

continued

Table 17.3 *(continued)*

	1993–1994	1997–1998	1999–2000	2003–2004
Alberta				
CHST	2 583	2 236	2 669	3 023
Equalization	0	0	0	0
Total	2 583	2 236	2 669	3 023
British Columbia				
CHST	3 461	3 275	3 765	4 352
Equalization	0	0	0	0
Total	3 461	3 275	3 765	4 352
TOTAL				
CHST	28 882	25 574	28 293	31 261
Equalization	8 063	9 670	9 288	10 892
Total	36 171	34 229	36 580	40 929

Source: 1999 Federal Budget. Reproduced with the permission of the Minister of Public Works and Government Services Canada, 2000.
*CHST replaced Established Program Financing (EPF) and Canada Assistance Plan (CAP) after 1995.
**Equalization associated with tax point transfers under CHST appears in both the Equalization and CHST figures, so totals are adjusted to avoid double counting.

Federal Controls

As mentioned, the 1867 Constitution Act contained three specific federal controls over the provinces: reservation, disallowance, and the declaratory power. The decline in the use of these powers has also increased the stature of the provinces. In the first 30 years after Confederation all three controls were actively used, and this had the effect of keeping the provinces subordinate to Ottawa.[19] Their use has gradually declined since then, the two major exceptions being the combatting of anti-Asian legislation in BC around 1900, and the outlawing of Social Credit legislation in Alberta in the 1930s. Overall, reservation has been used 70 times, but on 14 occasions the federal government assented to the provincial legislation that the lieutenant governor had reserved, and it was last exercised in 1961. The federal Cabinet used its disallowance power 112 times, most recently in 1943. The declaratory power has been used 470 times, mostly to put local railroads into federal jurisdiction in the early years, but not since 1961. It is now a convention of the Constitution, superseding the written words of the 1867 act, that Ottawa not use these federal controls,[20] and the Charlottetown Accord would have removed them. As these were the federal powers that originally precluded Canada from being classified as a true federation, their disuse has meant that the provinces have shrugged off their subordinate status. Canada is now a genuine federation, and a highly decentralized one at that.

TABLE 17.4   **Estimated Federal Transfers and Provinces' Own Revenues, 1996–1997**

	Federal Transfers ($ millions)	Provinces' Own Revenues ($ millions)	Total Provincial Revenues ($ millions)	Percent of Total Provincial Revenues Derived from Ottawa
Newfoundland	1 559.4	2 187.8	3 747.2	41.6
PEI	291.3	549.4	840.7	34.6
Nova Scotia	1 900.2	3 099.4	4 999.6	38.0
New Brunswick	1 515.4	3 383.8	4 899.2	30.9
Quebec	7 577.3	35 837.9	43 415.2	17.5
Ontario	6 300.3	49 192.8	55 493.1	11.4
Manitoba	1 821.7	5 324.6	7 146.3	25.5
Saskatchewan	827.2	5 380.4	6 207.6	13.3
Alberta	1 394.6	16 123.8	17 518.4	8.0
BC	2 049.4	22 346.6	24 396.0	8.4
NWT	1 067.1	287.8	1 354.9	78.8
Yukon	362.2	112.6	474.8	76.3
TOTAL	26 666.1	143 826.9	170 493.0	15.6

Source: Canadian Tax Foundation, Finances of the Nation, 1998. Used with permission.

PHASES OF CANADIAN FEDERALISM

Putting these three aspects of the Confederation settlement together and examining their simultaneous operation, we can now divide the years since 1867 into a number of eras of Canadian federalism,[21] as illustrated in Figure 17.2. These divisions demonstrate pendulum-like swings between centralization and decentralization and show that the evolution from a centralized to a decentralized federal system has not been a unilinear process.

The period 1867–96 can be classified as **quasi-federalism,** in which the provinces were subordinate to Ottawa. The courts gave the intended broad interpretation to federal powers, especially Peace, Order, and Good Government; the federal level was still predominant in finance; and John A. Macdonald made widespread use of the federal controls of reservation, disallowance, and the declaratory power.

The period 1896–1914 can be termed one of **classical federalism**. During these years the two levels were equal in status but independent. By now, the courts generally favoured the

Figure 17.2   **Centralization and Decentralization in Canadian Federalism**

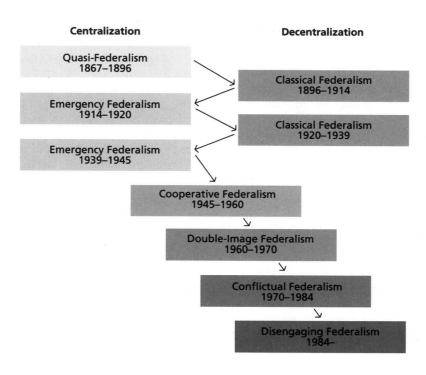

provinces, the provinces had more money to spend, and the federal government made little use of its controls, so that the provinces were no longer subordinate. This was also the period before taxation agreements and conditional grants; that is, there was little connection between federal and provincial operations—they were independent.

Classical federalism was displaced by **emergency federalism** during the war years, 1914–20. In this era the courts permitted the federal government virtually unlimited powers under the emergency doctrine and the War Measures Act. The federal government also increased its financial resources in this period with the imposition of personal and corporate income taxes. Ironically, in this most centralized phase of Canadian federalism—more centralized even than in the first 30 years—the use of the federal controls was unnecessary because of the courts' emergency interpretation of Peace, Order, and Good Government.

Between the wars, from 1920 to 1939, Canada reverted to another period of classical federalism. In these years, again, the two levels of government were equal in status (neither subordinate to the other) and operated more or less independently. Only a handful of conditional grants, for example, were developed during this time.

During the Second World War, from 1939 to 1945, Canada entered another period of emergency federalism. Once again, the courts allowed Ottawa to operate almost like a unitary government under the emergency interpretation of POGG and the War Measures Act. Public finance was also highly centralized with the development of the Wartime Taxation Agreements, under which the federal government took complete control over personal and corporate income taxes and succession duties. As in the First World War, any additional use of the federal controls was unnecessary.

The postwar world brought with it a completely new phase: **cooperative federalism**. The essence of this concept is that while neither level is subordinate to the other (the same as in classical federalism), they are closely intertwined, rather than operating independently. Here the crucial variable is financial relations. As noted in that connection earlier, the post-1945 period has been marked by federal–provincial taxation agreements on the revenue side and a host of shared-cost programs in terms of expenditures.

Cooperative federalism results from several developments.[22] First, federal and provincial objectives must often be harmonized if public policy is to be effective, such as in the case of countercyclical fiscal policy. Second, public pressure forces the federal government to establish minimum standards throughout the country in certain public services within provincial jurisdiction such as health care. In the third place, the two levels of government compete for tax revenues and end up needing to coordinate these efforts to some extent, at least for the convenience of taxpayers. Fourth, given a generally vague division of powers, federal and provincial ministers and bureaucrats all seek to maximize their jurisdiction and eventually overlap with the other level of government.

Cooperative federalism is made operational by hundreds of **federal–provincial conferences** at all levels—first ministers, departmental ministers, deputy ministers, and even lesser officials, who engage in almost continuous consultation, coordination, and cooperation. Cooperative federalism can be conducted on a multilateral basis, involving the federal government and several or all provinces, or, alternatively, on a bilateral basis in which Ottawa interacts with individual provinces. Since the ministers and bureaucrats involved are all part of the executive branch of government, cooperative federalism is sometimes called **executive federalism**. Two main implications of executive federalism are that legislatures, political parties, and the public at large are not given much role to play in decisions that emerge from the secrecy of such meetings, and that federal–provincial conflicts are worked out in conferences rather than referred to the courts.

Executive federalism can therefore be defined as "relations between elected and appointed officials of the two levels of government." When it is practised at the level of first ministers, it is often called "federal–provincial summitry." The **first ministers' conference**, that is, a federal–provincial conference of premiers and the prime minister, is nowhere provided for in the written Constitution and rests on a conventional base.[23] Nevertheless, since 1945 this institution has made many significant Canadian policy decisions, especially with respect to constitutional issues, shared-cost programs, and taxation and fiscal arrangements.[24] Some of these had to be ratified later by federal and provincial legislatures, but legislative approval was usually a formality. Such agreements could rarely be altered in any legislature because they would then have to be changed in all 11.

Successful federal–provincial summitry depends on the mutual respect of its participants and a willingness to engage in negotiation. Hence, this form of executive federalism was practised more successfully by Lester Pearson (1963–68) and in the first term of the Mulroney government (1984–88) than by Pierre Trudeau (1968–84) or in the second Mulroney term (1988–92). First ministers' meetings generally declined in frequency and moved from the Government Conference Centre to the comfort and privacy of the prime minister's residence in the Chrétien period. On an individual basis, premiers were among the few people who had ready access to the prime minister.[25]

Executive federalism conducted at the level of departmental ministers and leading bureaucrats is sometimes labelled "functional" or "bureaucratic" federalism. This form of executive federalism is frequently more successful than federal–provincial summitry, partly because the officials involved often share certain professional norms, and once they reach a consensus, these experts may be able to "sell" it to their departmental ministers. Functional federalism works best with **departmental Cabinets** in which individual federal and provincial ministers and deputy ministers have considerable autonomy so that they can interact productively with their counterparts at the other level of government. Such interaction was therefore hampered by the trend between the mid-1960s and 1993 toward **institutionalized Cabinets** in which decisions were made in Cabinet committees and under the guidance of powerful central agencies such as finance departments, treasury boards, and Cabinet offices, as discussed in Chapter 20.[26]

Canadian federalism between 1945 and 1960 may have been "cooperative" in the sense that the two levels of government were closely intertwined, but it continued to be highly centralized in the postwar period. The ministers and bureaucrats in Ottawa who had almost single-handedly run the country during the Second World War were reluctant to shed their enormous power. Moreover, they had discovered **Keynesian economics**, which prescribed a leading role for the central government in guiding the economy.[27]

The Diefenbaker government after 1957 was more sensitive to provincial demands, and the whole picture was increasingly complicated from about 1960 onward by the Quiet Revolution in Quebec. Thus, for about a decade, Canada experienced cooperative federalism with a French (or bilingual) twist, which has been called "double-image federalism."[28] This period still witnessed an intertwined, nonsubordinate relationship between the two levels of government, but cooperation was sometimes harder to come by, with Quebec regularly rejecting federal initiatives. Moreover, for the first time since 1890 or so, language and culture became important again in a constitutional sense. An extension of official bilingualism and the concept of opting-out were hallmarks of this phase of Canadian federalism, which saw a significant degree of decentralization take place.

Then, between about 1970 and 1984, federal–provincial relations became less cooperative, and the period might best be described as one of **conflictual federalism**. Quebec and the other provinces were more aggressive than ever, but the Trudeau government was not prepared for any further decentralization. Thus, the taxation agreements were now accompanied by more provincial unhappiness, and block funding replaced conditional grants in important areas, leaving the two levels less intertwined than before. Moreover, especially at the level of first ministers, federal–provincial conferences frequently failed to come to any agreement, and Ottawa often chose to act unilaterally. Issues in this period were also considered too serious to leave to bureaucrats alone. Another factor involved after 1970 was the attempt at both levels to engage in more rational decision making, so that departmental ministers and their officials no longer operated with the same autonomy. Besides politicians displacing bureaucrats in this phase, federal–provincial conflicts were more frequently referred to the courts, resulting in a renewed emphasis on the division of powers.

The Trudeau era was characterized by years of federal–provincial discord over resource and energy policies, especially the National Energy Program, federal–Newfoundland conflict over offshore oil, and federal–Saskatchewan conflict over the regulation and taxation of that province's oil and potash industries. When these disputes coincided with Trudeau's unilateral attempt to amend the Constitution and to entrench official bilingualism as a national policy, many Western Canadians began to re-examine their place in the federation. Some of the heat was reduced when Trudeau conceded the new section 92A, which recognized enhanced provincial jurisdiction over natural resources, in order to secure federal NDP support for the 1982 constitutional package and as a peace offering to the West.

CANADIAN FEDERALISM SINCE 1984

When Brian Mulroney came to power in 1984, he was determined to improve federal–provincial relations and embark on another period of decentralized, Pearsonian cooperative federalism. During his first term many would say he succeeded, for much of the federal–provincial animosity of the Trudeau years seemed to dissipate. Western and Eastern concerns about energy resources were respectively resolved to a large extent in the 1985 Western and Atlantic Accords. The highlight of the Mulroney approach, of course, was the 1987 Meech Lake Accord, which was designed to bring Quebec symbolically into the new constitutional framework and which would have generally increased provincial powers at Ottawa's expense.[29] Trudeau was the leading dissenter, feeling that Mulroney had given too much away.

During its second term, however, the Mulroney government increasingly aroused provincial anger, especially as it became obsessed with deficit reduction and cut back on grants to the provinces. The Mulroney government also enforced the Liberals' Canada Health Act, which imposed penalties on provinces that allowed doctors to extra-bill or permitted hospitals to charge user fees. Ontario, Alberta, and BC objected to the 1990 policy of reducing their grants under the Canada Assistance Plan, and several provinces, especially Ontario, were opposed to the Canada–U.S. and North American Free Trade Agreements. But the major federal–provincial dispute of the Mulroney years concerned the Goods and Services Tax (GST), although to some extent it was just "good politics" for provincial premiers to jump on the anti-GST bandwagon because of widespread popular opposition. At first, only Quebec agreed to partial integration of its sales taxes with the new federal tax, even though many mutual advantages would have accrued to other provinces had they done so.

The Chrétien Liberals began by appointing a specific minister to be in charge of federal–provincial relations. The new government was initially popular with provincial governments in offering funds under the national infrastructure program, and was somewhat successful in negotiating a reduction in barriers that provinces imposed to the free movement of people, goods, services, and capital across the country. This was called the **Agreement on Internal Trade** and came into effect in July 1995. While it has substantial exceptions and lacks an effective enforcement mechanism, it has enhanced economic integration within Canada.[30] The Chrétien government had no initial success in implementing their promise to replace the GST, however, only managing to persuade three Atlantic provinces to harmonize their retail sales taxes with the federal tax. Moreover, Ottawa made the provinces angry with reductions in their transfers from 1995 to 1999. The principal complaints included severe reductions in health, postsecondary education, and welfare transfers, although provinces also joined in to protest the cuts to almost every other aspect of federal government operations, such as a wide range of transportation subsidies. At the same time, most provinces supported the principle of reducing government deficits, and seven were pleased that Ottawa did not cut equalization payments.[31]

In the wake of the defeat of the Charlottetown Accord and then the 1995 Quebec referendum, Ottawa decided to cede Quebec's foremost demand—provincial control over labour market training. Rather than risk embarking on a form of asymmetrical federalism, however, the Chrétien government offered to transfer this responsibility to all provinces via bilateral and slightly different federal–provincial deals. Then, the 1997 federal budget replaced the Child Tax Benefit with a new integrated National Child Benefit system developed through federal–provincial cooperation and supported by all ten provinces. Under the new scheme, Ottawa provides income support for all low-income families with children via the income tax system. While provinces can thereby reduce provincial welfare benefits by equivalent amounts, they must reinvest the savings in earning supplements and other benefits for working-poor families.[32] Whether or not this new system had much effect on reducing the child poverty rate, it was a model of federal–provincial cooperation. The federal government also considerably withdrew from the forestry, mining, and energy fields, to focus on research in these areas; some provinces eliminated overseas offices and worked out of federal posts abroad instead; and the two levels of government pooled their resources in the realm of tourism.[33]

THE SOCIAL UNION

Despite several significant federal–provincial agreements over the post-1995 period—agreements whose effects were usually both decentralizing and disengaging—many issues (the Canada Health Act, for one) remained unresolved, and federal and provincial governments continued to crave some authoritative rules for their ongoing relationship. The Social Union is a term acquired by this search for a definitive framework on which to construct or modify federal, provincial, or joint social programs.

Among the concerns of the federal government were provinces not spending federal funds for the purposes intended (including violations of the Canada Health Act), and continuing barriers to social mobility from province to province despite the Agreement on Internal Trade. Perhaps most of all, Ottawa demanded the right to use its spending power to make transfers to individuals, such as the Millennium Scholarships, which Quebec in particular opposed.

The provinces, on the other hand, wanted to end unilateral federal changes in jointly funded programs (such as the Canada Health and Social Transfer cutbacks of 1995–99); they sought to ensure that any joint program offered to one province would be available to all; they insisted that Ottawa obtain provincial consent before establishing new joint social programs; and they at least expected to be consulted on programs in which Ottawa made direct transfers to individuals.

After many difficult negotiating sessions at the ministerial level, an agreement was finalized among the premiers and Prime Minister Chrétien (with Quebec dissenting) in February 1999 called the **Social Union Framework**. Such congeniality was encouraged by the simultaneous delivery of a multi-billion–dollar increase in federal transfers to the provinces in the 1999 budget. The key points in the Social Union Framework are as follows:

- Mobility within Canada—Governments will eliminate residency-based policies or practices that constrain access to social programs and are committed to the mutual recognition of occupational qualifications for access to employment opportunities.
- Public accountability and transparency—Each government agrees to use funds transferred from another order of government for the purposes agreed upon and pass on increases to its residents.

- Reciprocal notice and consultation—Governments agree to give one another advance notice before implementing a major change in a social policy or program that would substantially affect another government.
- Equitable treatment—For any new Canada-wide social initiatives, arrangements made with one province (territory) will be made available to all.
- Funding predictability—The federal government will consult with provincial and territorial governments at least one year prior to renewal or significant funding changes in existing social transfers.
- New Canada-wide initiatives—The federal government will not introduce new social programs that are funded through intergovernmental transfers without the agreement of a majority of provincial governments.
- Direct federal spending—When the federal government introduces new Canada-wide social programs funded through direct transfers to individuals, it will, prior to implementation, give at least three months notice and offer to consult.[34]

The framework contained a large quantity of goodwill verbiage that did not really alter the existing operation of federal–provincial relations. The two most significant points were that the federal government agreed not to introduce new social programs involving transfers of money to the *provinces* without the support of a majority of provinces, and that Ottawa retained the right to use its spending power to make transfers directly to *people*. While it was unfortunate that the PQ government of Lucien Bouchard refused to sign the document, and while some centralist commentators thought Ottawa gave too much away, the Social Union Framework was consistent with the principles of modern federalism as well as with the thrust of Canadian thinking on the subject over the preceding 15 years. Especially in the second term of the Chrétien government, but perhaps ever since 1984, that thrust might be termed collaborative but **disengaging federalism**.[35]

CONCLUSION

Federalism in Canada both is based on and intensifies regional, economic, and ethnic cleavages. In the beginning, the Canadian federal system was highly centralized, but this original design was soon found to be inappropriate for the society in which it operated. When the cleavages became difficult to overcome, and as "province-builders" competed with "nation-builders," Canada gradually became a very decentralized federation. Both in the courts and in negotiations with Ottawa, the provinces successfully fought for more powers and more financial resources. While federalism often seems to be an unending source of intergovernmental discord, as well as a convenient excuse at both levels of government for not responding to demands, the maze of cooperative federal–provincial interaction should not be ignored.

(SC) As in the case of the Constitution, the state-centred approach is most relevant to the Canadian federal system. It maintains that federal and provincial governments act in their own interests or in accordance with their own conception of the public interest, without much regard for the wishes of the general public. Ministers and bureaucrats usually want to maximize their own power and responsibility, so that both levels of government have expanded operations to the point of considerable overlap. Federal authorities argue for federal jurisdiction, revenue, conditions, standards, and controls, while provincial authorities fight for maximum provincial revenue, flexibility, and freedom.

Some state-centred theorists contend that much of the federal–provincial discord is an artificial competition among federal and provincial politicians and bureaucrats, rather than a real fight reflecting public opinion. Provincial governments demand powers, money, and constitutional vetoes in the name of their residents, but the residents themselves may be indifferent as to whether they are taxed, regulated, or provided for by federal or provincial governments. The cooperative mechanisms of executive federalism and the central role of the public service in bureaucratic federalism can also be seen as evidence of the state-centred approach, for the public can do little but accept whatever arrangements are worked out among federal and provincial bureaucrats and then sold to their ministers. The federal–provincial conference is one of the prime venues in which elite accommodation takes place. If provincial electorates have confidence in their own political leaders, the voters will accept whatever promises are negotiated between the two sets of elites as they grapple with the problems of overlapping jurisdiction.

The centralist and decentralist swings, which have been identified above, are sometimes analyzed in terms of the concepts of nation-building as opposed to province-building. The overarching concern of the national political elite—prime ministers, federal cabinets, and leading bureaucrats—has been to construct a strong central government. But the creation of provinces produced counterbalancing provincial political elites—premiers, provincial cabinets, and bureaucrats—who were more interested in building strong provinces. Province-building is usually related to post–Second World War increases in provincial revenues and in the size of provincial bureaucracies, the creation of provincial Crown corporations and central planning agencies, and a willingness and capacity of provincial governments to intervene in the process of industrial development and diversification. In short, province-building means that the provincial state plays a significant role within the confines of the provincial society. Strong provincial governments want more powers, autonomy, and money, which explains much of the pressure for decentralization in the Canadian federal system since 1960 or so.

Nation-building and province-building are not confined to government elites. In each case, they have been supported by certain societal forces. At the national level, these include elements of the business community (banking, transportation, communications, manufacturing) and by most of the anglophone intellectual elite. Provincial political elites also had support within their societies, primarily including natural resource companies, professionals, and others concerned with property.

P Pluralists note that provincial political and bureaucratic elites genuinely represent diversified provincial societies and that it was in response to the scattered and diverse population with its different interests and regional loyalties that a federation was originally established. Pluralist theorists are among those who contend that the Judicial Committee of the Privy Council was farsighted in interpreting the division of powers in a decentralist direction; contrary to the intentions of John A. Macdonald, its decisions were entirely consistent with the "federal society" into which Canada evolved. Federalism allows provincial governments to take action in the interests of their own cultural majorities or distinctive industries that would generate much controversy at the national level. It permits experimentation in social policies, such that those that prove successful at the provincial level (e.g., medicare) can later be adopted in other provinces and/or at the national level.[36] Federalism also maximizes the number of organized groups that can make their voices heard, some at the national level and others in the provinces.

(C) Most class analysts decry decentralization of the federal system for its stifling of creative, national programs.[37] They would prefer new and stronger national social programs and labour and environmental standards, which are not possible because of broad provincial jurisdiction. Generally speaking, class analysts assume that the federal government is more likely than the provinces to produce "progressive" policies. They want a strong and redistributive central state with high and uniform national standards and are suspicious of what provincial governments would do with federal health or welfare grants without conditions attached. While arguing for greater centralization, class analysts point out how frequently private corporate interests have taken the opposite position. The corporate elite has often used its influence with friendly provincial governments to frustrate national initiatives and has challenged the federal government in court in order to enhance provincial jurisdiction in places where it has been more influential at that level.[38] More generally, business wants a relatively weak, nonredistributive federal government, and to some extent class analysts might go so far as to say that constitutional debates and seemingly obscure skirmishes over the details of fiscal federalism have been a veil behind which a struggle has been waged over the size and character of the central state. Corporate preference for decentralization is not absolute, however; it depends on what actions provincial governments try to take. In Saskatchewan in the 1970s, mining and petroleum companies challenged the constitutionality of provincial NDP legislation they opposed, and in Alberta in the 1930s and 1940s, the banks took oppressive Social Credit banking legislation to the courts.

PC Finally, public choice theorists see Ottawa's relations with the provinces in electoral terms. If Ontario and Quebec have the largest number of marginal seats at stake, for example, federal authorities will be most responsive to the demands articulated by their governments. This can be seen in the case of the National Energy Program (supported by Ontario) or in awarding Quebec instead of Manitoba the CF-18 maintenance contract. On the other hand, it is often productive for provincial governments to base their election campaigns on opposition to Ottawa.

DISCUSSION QUESTIONS

1. Are you a centralist or a decentralist? Why? What are the advantages and disadvantages of centralization and decentralization in Canadian federalism?

2. Why has Ontario usually preferred a highly centralized federal system? Do the residents of other provinces want a decentralized federal system or is it just the politicians and bureaucrats in such provinces who do?

3. Is it possible to have a clear-cut division of powers between federal and provincial governments in a modern era of such extensive government activity?

4. Should the federal government be able to spend money for any purpose, even within provincial jurisdiction? Should it be able to set conditions on provincial medicare programs? What do you think of the new Social Union agreement?

5. Should federal grants to the provinces take the form of conditional, block, or unconditional grants? Why?

6. What are the advantages and disadvantages of executive federalism?

7. How have the weaknesses of intrastate federalism contributed to the importance of interstate federalism?

8. How do each of the approaches outlined in Chapter 1 enhance our understanding of Canadian federalism?

NOTES

1. Rand Dyck, *Provincial Politics in Canada: Towards the Turn of the Century*, 3rd ed. (Scarborough: Prentice-Hall Canada, 1996).
2. *Decision-Making Processes and Central Agencies in Canada: Federal, Provincial and Territorial Practices* (Ottawa: Privy Council Office, 1998).
3. Donald Smiley, *The Canadian Political Nationality* (Toronto: Methuen, 1967).
4. K.C. Wheare, *Federal Government*, 4th ed. (London: Oxford University Press, 1963).
5. D.V. Smiley and R.L. Watts, *Intrastate Federalism in Canada* (Toronto: University of Toronto Press, 1985).
6. Peter Russell et al., *Federalism and the Charter* (Ottawa: Carleton University Press, 1989); Peter Hogg, *Constitutional Law of Canada*, 2nd ed. (Toronto: Carswell, 1985; Student Edition 1999); Patrick J. Monahan, *Constitutional Law* (Toronto: Irwin Law, 1998); Bernard Funston, *Consolidated Canadian Constitutional Documents* (Toronto: Carswell, 1994); and Bernard Funston and Eugene Meehan, *Canada's Constitutional Law in a Nutshell*, 2nd ed. (Toronto: Carswell, 1998).
7. *R. v. Crown Zellerbach Canada Ltd.*, [1988] 1 S.C.R. 401; *Alberta Government Telephones v. Canada (Canadian Radio-television and Telecommunications Commission)*, [1989] 2 S.C.R. 225; *Friends of the Oldman River Society v. Canada (Minister of Transport)*, [1992] 1 S.C.R. 3; *Ontario Hydro v. Ontario (Labour Relations Board)*, [1993] 3 S.C.R. 327; and *Téléphone Guèvremont Inc. v. Quebec (Régis des télécommunications)*, [1994] 1 S.C.R. 878.
8. V.C. MacDonald, "Judicial Interpretation of the Canadian Constitution," *University of Toronto Law Journal* 1 (1935–36), pp. 260–85, and the *O'Connor Report*, Senate of Canada, 1939. It is ironic that judicial interpretation contributed to decentralizing a centralized Canadian federation but centralized a decentralized federation in the United States. See Roger Gibbins, *Regionalism* (Toronto: Butterworths, 1982), ch. 4.
9. Alan C. Cairns, "The Governments and Societies of Canadian Federalism," *Canadian Journal of Political Science* (December 1977), pp. 695–725.
10. Alan C. Cairns, "The Judicial Committee and Its Critics," *Canadian Journal of Political Science* (September 1971), pp. 301–45, and reprinted in Cairns, *Constitution, Government and Society in Canada* (Toronto: McClelland and Stewart, 1988).
11. Cairns, *Constitution, Government, and Society in Canada*, p. 63.
12. Canadian Tax Foundation, *Finances of the Nation* (Toronto: Annual); David B. Perry, *Financing the Canadian Federation, 1867–1995: Setting the Stage for Change* (Toronto: Canadian Tax Foundation, 1997); Robin W. Boadway and Paul A.R. Hobson, *Intergovernmental Fiscal Relations in Canada* (Toronto: Canadian Tax Foundation, 1993).
13. The distinction is usually expressed as follows: direct taxes are derived from the very people who are intended to pay them, while indirect taxes are extracted from one person in the expectation that they will be passed on to someone else.

14. *Reference re Canada Assistance Plan (B.C.)*, [1991] 2 S.C.R. 525; *Finlay v. Canada (Minister of Finance)*, [1993] 1 S.C.R. 1080; Keith Banting, *The Welfare State and Canadian Federalism* (Kingston: McGill–Queen's University Press, 1982), pp. 52–54; Canada, *Federal–Provincial Grants and the Spending Power of Parliament: Working Paper on the Constitution* (Ottawa: Queen's Printer, 1970); D.V. Smiley and R.M. Burns, "Canadian Federalism and the Spending Power: Is Constitutional Restriction Necessary?" *Canadian Tax Journal* 17 (1969), pp. 468–82; and Andrew Petter, "Federalism and the Myth of the Federal Spending Power," *Canadian Bar Review* (September 1989), pp. 448–79.

15. T.J. Courchene, *Equalization Payments: Past, Present and Future* (Toronto: Ontario Economic Council, 1984); Robin W. Boadway and Paul A.R. Hobson, *Equalization* (Kingston: McGill–Queen's University Press, 1998).

16. G.V. La Forest, *The Allocation of Taxing Powers under the Canadian Constitution*, 2nd ed. (Toronto: Canadian Tax Foundation, 1981).

17. Canadian Tax Foundation, *Provincial and Municipal Finances, 1989*, p. 12:1.

18. Jim Silver, "Constitutional Change, Ideological Conflict and the Redistributive State," in James McCrorie and Martha MacDonald, eds., *The Constitutional Future of the Prairie and Atlantic Regions of Canada* (Regina: Canadian Plains Research Center, 1992), pp. 231–72.

19. G.V. La Forest, *Disallowance and Reservation of Provincial Legislation* (Ottawa: Queen's Printer, 1965).

20. Andrew Heard, *Canadian Constitutional Conventions* (Toronto: Oxford University Press, 1991).

21. This discussion is loosely based on J.R. Mallory, "The Five Faces of Canadian Federalism," in P.-A. Crépeau and C.B. Macpherson, eds., *The Future of Canadian Federalism* (Toronto: University of Toronto Press, 1965).

22. Donald Smiley, *Canada in Question: Federalism in the Seventies* (Toronto: McGraw-Hill Ryerson, 1972), p. 56.

23. Heard, *Canadian Constitutional Conventions*, pp. 110–16.

24. Richard Simeon, *Federal–Provincial Diplomacy* (Toronto: University of Toronto Press, 1972).

25. Donald J. Savoie, *Governing from the Centre: The Concentration of Power in Canadian Politics* (Toronto: University of Toronto Press, 1999).

26. J. Stefan Dupré, "Reflections on the Workability of Executive Federalism," in Richard Simeon, ed., *Intergovernmental Relations* (Toronto: University of Toronto Press, 1985), and D.V. Smiley, *The Federal Condition in Canada* (Toronto: McGraw-Hill Ryerson, 1987), pp. 87–89.

27. J.L. Granatstein, *The Ottawa Men: The Civil Service Mandarins 1935–1957* (Toronto: Oxford University Press, 1982).

28. Mallory, "The Five Faces of Canadian Federalism."

29. The Meech Lake Accord is discussed in Chapter 16.

30. Robert H. Knox, "Economic Integration in Canada through the Agreement on Internal Trade," in Harvey Lazar, ed., *Canada: The State of the Federation 1997: Non-Constitutional Renewal* (Kingston: Institute of Intergovernmental Relations, Queen's University, 1997).

31. Among the best sources on this subject are the reviews published annually since 1980 by the Queen's University Institute of Intergovernmental Relations. See also Martin Westmacott and Hugh Mellon, eds., *Challenges to Canadian Federalism* (Scarborough: Prentice-Hall Canada, 1998).

32. Ken Battle, "The 1997 Budget and the Child Benefits Package," in Thomas J. Courchene and Thomas A. Wilson, *The 1997 Federal Budget: Retrospect and Prospect* (Kingston: John Deutsch Institute for the Study of Economic Policy, 1997), and Douglas Durst, ed., *Canada's National Child Benefit: Phoenix of Fizzle?* (Halifax: Fernwood Publishing, 1999).

33. Jocelyne Bourgon, *Fourth Annual Report to the Prime Minister on the Public Service of Canada* (Ottawa, 1997). The merits of national as opposed to federal standards are debated by Roger Gibbins and Ronald Manzer in Mark Charlton and Paul Barker, eds., *Crosscurrents: Contemporary Political Issues*, 3rd ed. (Scarborough: ITP Nelson, 1998), ch. 7.

34. Intergovernmental Affairs website, "A Framework to Improve the Social Union for Canadians," February 4, 1999: http://www.pco-bcp.gc.ca/aia.

35. Lazar, ed., *Canada: The State of the Federation 1997: Non-Constitutional Renewal*; Lazar and Tom McIntosh, eds., *Canada: The State of the Federation 1998/99: How Canadians Connect* (Kingston: Institute of Intergovernmental Relations, Queen's University, 1999); and Robert A. Young, ed., *Stretching the Federation: The Art of State in Canada* (Montreal: McGill–Queen's University Press, 1999).

36. Ironically, it was the later foe of decentralization, Pierre Trudeau, who told the socialist academic community in 1961 that they should not be so obsessed with centralization; that progressive social policies could sometimes be pioneered more successfully at the provincial level. "The Practice and Theory of Federalism," in Michael Oliver, ed., *Social Purpose for Canada* (Toronto: University of Toronto Press, 1961).
37. See, for example, John Porter, *The Vertical Mosaic* (Toronto: University of Toronto Press, 1965).
38. J.R. Mallory, *Social Credit and the Federal Power in Canada* (Toronto: University of Toronto Press, 1954); Silver, "Constitutional Change, Ideological Conflict and the Redistributive State."

....

FURTHER READING

Banting, Keith. *The Welfare State and Canadian Federalism.* Kingston: McGill–Queen's University Press, 1982; 2nd ed., 1987.

Cairns, Alan C. *Constitution, Government, and Society in Canada.* Toronto: McClelland and Stewart, 1988.

Canadian Tax Foundation. *Finances of the Nation.* Toronto, annual (under various authors).

Funston, Bernard. *Consolidated Canadian Constitutional Documents.* Toronto: Carswell, 1994.

Funston, Bernard, and Eugene Meehan. *Canada's Constitutional Law in a Nutshell.* 2nd ed. Toronto: Carswell, 1998.

Heard, Andrew. *Canadian Constitutional Conventions.* Toronto: Oxford University Press, 1991.

Hogg, Peter. *Constitutional Law of Canada,* 2nd ed. Toronto: Carswell, 1985; Student Edition, 1999.

Institute of Intergovernmental Relations, Queen's University. *Canada: The State of the Federation,* annual (under the name of various editors).

LaSelva, Samuel. *The Moral Foundations of Canadian Federalism: Paradoxes, Achievements, and Tragedies of Nationhood.* Montreal: McGill–Queen's University Press, 1997.

Mallory, J.R. "The Five Faces of Canadian Federalism." In P.-A. Crépeau and C.B. Macpherson, eds., *The Future of Canadian Federalism.* Toronto: University of Toronto Press, 1965.

Perry, David B. *Financing the Canadian Federation, 1867–1995: Setting the Stage for Change.* Toronto: Canadian Tax Foundation, 1997.

Petter, Andrew. "Federalism and the Myth of the Federal Spending Power." *Canadian Bar Review* (September 1989), pp. 448–79.

Privy Council Office. *Federal–Provincial Programs and Activities: A Descriptive Inventory, 1994–1995.* Ottawa: Supply and Services, 1995.

Rocher, François, and Miriam Smith, eds. *New Trends in Canadian Federalism.* Peterborough: Broadview, 1995.

Russell, Peter, et al. *Federalism and the Charter.* Ottawa: Carleton University Press, 1989.

Silver, Jim. "Constitutional Change, Ideological Conflict and the Redistributive State." In James McCrorie and Martha MacDonald, eds., *The Constitutional Future of the Prairie and Atlantic Regions of Canada.* Regina: Canadian Plains Research Center, 1992.

Simeon, Richard. *The Political Economy of Canadian Federalism: 1940–1984.* Toronto: University of Toronto Press, 1985.

Smiley, D.V. *The Canadian Political Nationality.* Toronto: Methuen, 1967.

———. *The Federal Condition in Canada.* Toronto: McGraw-Hill Ryerson, 1987.

Smiley, D.V., and R.L. Watts. *Intrastate Federalism in Canada.* Toronto: University of Toronto Press, 1985.

Stevenson, Garth. *Unfulfilled Union,* 3rd ed. Toronto: Gage, 1989.

Swinton, Katherine. *The Supreme Court and Canadian Federalism: The Laskin–Dickson Years.* Toronto: Carswell, 1990.

Trudeau, Pierre Elliott. "The Practice and Theory of Federalism." In Michael Oliver, ed., *Social Purpose for Canada.* Toronto: University of Toronto Press, 1961.

Westmacott, Martin, and Hugh Mellon, eds. *Challenges to Canadian Federalism*. Scarborough: Prentice-Hall Canada, 1998.

Wheare, K.C. *Federal Government*, 4th ed. London: Oxford University Press, 1963.

Young, Robert A., ed. *Stretching the Federation: The Art of State in Canada*. Montreal: McGill–Queen's University Press, 1999.

Chapter 18

The
CHARTER OF RIGHTS
and freedoms

Does freedom of expression prohibit restrictions on pornography and prostitution? Is restriction of Sunday shopping a violation of freedom of religion? Does a person have the right to counsel when stopped by a police officer to take a breath test? Does freedom of association guarantee the right to strike? Should terminally ill people be allowed to end their own lives? Should tobacco companies be allowed to advertise cigarettes? Should police officers be able to enter dwellings without a search warrant? In the case of sexual relations, does "no" mean "no"? When should legislatures overrule judicial decisions?

Civil liberties consist of rights and freedoms that individuals enjoy beyond the reach of the government or the state. Such rights and freedoms are an integral part of a democratic political system and represent territory into which the government is not allowed to enter as it makes and enforces public policy for a society. They have recently been entrenched in the Canadian Constitution in the form of the Charter of Rights and Freedoms, and it is increasingly the task of the judiciary to determine if and when governments have encroached upon them.

This chapter begins by defining such rights and freedoms and discussing the means of protecting them in Canada before 1982. The central part of the chapter examines the provisions of the Charter of Rights and Freedoms and the principal court cases that interpreted each clause up to the turn of the new century. It concludes by discussing the implications of the Charter for the overall political system.

DEFINING AND PROTECTING RIGHTS AND FREEDOMS

Rights and freedoms are commonly classified into four categories.[1] The first relates to political liberty, including the fundamental freedoms of speech, press, assembly, and religion. The second, legal rights, includes the procedural rights of a person suspected or accused of committing a crime, a liberty encompassing that person's right to legal counsel, a presumption of innocence, bail, and a fair trial. The third aspect of such rights and freedoms involves equality rights, that is, freedom from discrimination on such bases as gender, race, religion, or age.

Canadians almost universally support these three categories of rights and freedoms, and they are therefore embedded and expanded on in the Charter. The fourth category, economic rights, is more controversial. While the right to own property, for example, is widely adhered to and recognized in law as well as in the Bill of Rights, it has not been enshrined in the Charter.[2]

Political systems that value such rights and freedoms have adopted two principal methods to protect them. The British approach is to make Parliament supreme, but on the presumption that neither the legislature nor the executive would infringe civil liberties because both are held in check by public opinion, tradition, the political culture, and self-restraint. Such rights and freedoms are so deeply ingrained in the values of the people and politicians alike that the latter would never think of infringing them, even though, in theory, Parliament could do so. While the courts cannot overturn legislation in Britain—that is, they do not have the power of **judicial review**—they have wide **judicial discretion** in the interpretation of laws, and many civil libertarian values have been introduced into the law as canons of interpretation.[3] Thus, even in the British system, judicial precedents accumulated into the common law offer some protection against arbitrary government action. So does the basic constitutional principle, the **rule of law**, which requires that every official act be based on law. In typical British manner, then, the fact that they were not written down did not mean that civil liberties did not exist.

The American approach, derived in reaction to an imperial government that *did* encroach on colonial liberties, is to provide for a written statement of civil liberties (usually called "civil rights") in the Constitution or in a constitutional Bill of Rights. Then, if legislation is passed or the executive takes action that is felt to violate a person's rights, such acts can be challenged in the courts. It is up to the courts to determine whether the government has infringed civil rights as defined in the Constitution. The courts thus have the power of judicial review and can overturn offensive legislation or executive acts.

Before we explore the role of judicial review in greater detail, it should be added that while bills and charters of rights restrict the actions of governments, they do not extend in most cases to private, interpersonal relationships. Prohibitions against private discrimination, such as in employment and accommodation, are instead generally covered by human rights codes. Each province has such a code, as does the federal government, and they are enforced by human rights commissions through investigation, conciliation, and, if necessary, adjudication of disputes.[4]

EN ROUTE TO THE CHARTER

A discussion of protecting rights and freedoms in Canada can be divided into three eras. In the first, Canada inherited the British system based on parliamentary restraint within parliamentary supremacy, but the Canadian situation was complicated by the adoption of federalism. Hence, Canada possessed two supreme legislatures, one in Ottawa and another in the provinces, each operating within its own constitutional jurisdiction. Federalism allowed the courts to engage in judicial review in the sense of invalidating federal or provincial legislation that violated the division of powers. In so doing, federalism opened the door to judicial review in the protection of rights and freedoms. That is, if the courts could show that either level of government infringed civil liberties in the process of exceeding its jurisdiction in terms of the division of powers, then the courts could strike down the law.

Thus, even before the adoption of a constitutional bill or charter of rights, the Canadian courts were able to intervene to a limited extent to overturn legislation that violated such rights. The simultaneous violation of the division of powers and civil liberties most often took place at the provincial level, where the courts found provincial legislation infringing federal power in the realm of criminal law.

Because a division of powers case would still allow the other level of government to pass legislation offensive to rights and freedoms, the courts sometimes supplemented this ground for their decisions by citing the preamble to the 1867 Constitution Act. It speaks of Canada's desire to have "a constitution similar in principle to that of Great Britain." Since Britain recognized civil liberties (albeit without judicial review), Canadians should enjoy them too. This interpretation, sometimes called an **implied bill of rights**, would have allowed the courts to go beyond the division of powers in striking down legislation that violated rights and freedoms, but it was rarely and inconsistently applied.[5]

Three principal cases of judicial protection of such rights and freedoms arose in the period before 1960. First, freedom of the press was at issue in the 1938 *Alberta Press Bill* case. Among other things, Alberta legislation allowed the government to order newspapers to reveal the sources of unfavourable comment and gave it the right to respond to criticism. The courts found this legislation invalid because it was an infringement of the federal criminal law power.[6] In 1953, the freedom of religion of Jehovah's Witnesses in Quebec was at stake, this time in requiring them to obtain permission from the chief of police before they could distribute their literature on the sidewalk. Once again the federal criminal law power and the preamble proved to be useful in overturning a provincial law.[7] In 1957 the Supreme Court disposed of Premier Maurice Duplessis's **Padlock Law** on the same grounds. This law had given the premier and attorney general the power to padlock any building that Duplessis considered was being used for the propagation of communism and bolshevism, but left these terms undefined and was used against opposition groups of any kind.[8]

Another means of protecting rights and freedoms even in the pre-1960 period was to find executive actions to be contrary to the rule of law. This ground was used successfully on three occasions with respect to police and government treatment of Jehovah's Witnesses in the Duplessis period in Quebec. In the most famous case, the court found the premier himself had acted contrary to the rule of law: that is, he took action based not on law but on his dislike of Jehovah's Witnesses when he personally cancelled Roncarelli's liquor licence.[9]

Violations of civil liberties that did not also violate the division of powers gave the courts little discretion. For example, in a 1903 case that concerned denial of the vote to Asians in British Columbia provincial elections, the courts ruled that such electoral matters were entirely within the jurisdiction of provincial politicians.[10] Neither did Canadian Blacks find any satisfaction in the courts when they challenged discriminatory practices.[11] While the federal government was generally more sensitive to rights and freedoms than the provinces, its record was not unblemished, especially in the case of Aboriginals, the Winnipeg General Strike, and its treatment of citizens of certain ethnic groups during the two world wars. Ottawa's internment of Canadian citizens of Japanese extraction during the Second World War proved both that the federal government was not above reproach and that the courts could do nothing about it.[12]

The fact that both federal and provincial politicians would stoop to such violations of civil liberties and the realization that the courts could not be counted on to invalidate them unless they also contained a division of powers problem persuaded John Diefenbaker to enact the

A March 1973 photo of John Diefenbaker, the architect of the Canadian Bill of Rights, 1960. (Fred Chartrand/Canapress)

Canadian Bill of Rights in 1960.[13] This document inaugurated the second era in the protection of rights and freedoms in Canada. The bill's apparent aim was to allow the courts to invalidate legislation that they found to conflict with the Bill of Rights, but if so, this aim was not clearly articulated. The courts were never completely certain if they had been given this power or not. Other serious gaps in the bill were that it only applied to the federal government, not to the provinces; that it allowed legislation to be passed that overrode the bill, as long as this was acknowledged (a notwithstanding clause); that as an ordinary piece of legislation, the bill could be amended in the routine way; and that it was superseded by the War Measures Act, at the very time when it might be needed most.

Not surprisingly, the courts made limited use of the Bill of Rights. Only once, in the *Drybones* case of 1970, did they decide that a clause of an act violated the Bill of Rights and was therefore inoperative.[14] The bill was more useful in clarifying legal rights and was referred to in several cases to fill in gaps in such definitions as what was meant by the "right to counsel," the "right to an interpreter," and the "right to a fair hearing."[15]

Several other cases arose regarding violations of rights and freedoms within federal jurisdiction, but in each case the Court found a way around applying the Bill of Rights.[16] At the same time, provinces occasionally violated civil liberties in the post-1960 period, but the Bill of Rights was of even less assistance in these cases.[17]

THE CHARTER OF RIGHTS AND FREEDOMS

Recognizing the limitations and ambiguities of the Canadian Bill of Rights, and wanting to incorporate new kinds of rights into the Constitution, several politicians, most notably Pierre Trudeau, attempted to improve it. Ironically, in the midst of this quest, Trudeau invoked the War Measures Act in 1970 and used it to encroach upon the freedom of speech of innocent, nonviolent Quebec separatists. Finally, in 1982, with the adoption of the Canadian **Charter of Rights and Freedoms,** he accomplished his objective. The Charter essentially replaced the Bill of Rights, using much of its language in the sections on fundamental freedoms and legal rights, but going beyond it to include democratic, linguistic, mobility, egalitarian, and limited Aboriginal rights.

Not only did Trudeau want to remedy the deficiencies in the Bill of Rights; he was also determined to protect official minority language rights across the country in an effort to undercut Quebec's claim that it represented French Canada. Moreover, Trudeau hoped to counter centrifugal forces throughout the land and pressures for general decentralization to the provinces by creating an instrument that the courts could use to cut down self-serving provincial laws. As a new national symbol, the Charter would also serve to increase the allegiance of all citizens to the national government.

The Charter is generally a much stronger document than its predecessor. Besides being broader in scope, the Charter applies equally to both federal and provincial governments, and being entrenched into the Constitution, it is difficult to amend. It states very clearly that the courts are to invalidate any legislation that they feel conflicts with the provisions of the Charter.

On the other hand, the rights articulated in the Charter are not absolute. In the first place, section 1 indicates that such rights are subject to "such reasonable limits, defined by law, as can be demonstrably justified in a free and democratic society." The courts are thus allowed to find that, while a piece of legislation does violate certain rights, it is still acceptable according to their definition of reasonable limits. Second, in the areas of fundamental freedoms, legal rights, and equality rights, either level of government is allowed to pass legislation contrary to the Charter by means of the notwithstanding clause, section 33. Governments were not expected to acknowledge in advance that legislation was contrary to the Charter, so the notwithstanding clause would normally come into play when legislation was introduced to override a judicial decision regarding a Charter right. Such a bill can only be exempted from the provisions of the Charter for a five-year period, after which it becomes inoperative if not repassed for another five years.

The Charter of Rights and Freedoms has profoundly affected the operation of the Canadian political system. Let us now examine the provisions of the Charter and see how they have been interpreted by the courts, especially the Supreme Court of Canada. The following discussion only sketches the broad lines of Charter interpretation during its first 18 years of operation, and is not intended to be a definitive statement of the law.[18]

The Reasonable Limits Clause

Section 1 is often called the "reasonable limits" clause and reads as follows:

> The Canadian Charter of Rights and Freedoms guarantees the rights and freedoms set out in it subject only to such reasonable limits prescribed by law as can be demonstrably justified in a free and democratic society.

The Supreme Court has made extensive use of section 1, upholding many laws that it considered to be in violation of Charter rights but that were saved by being reasonable limits upon them. At the very least, restrictions on Charter rights must be "prescribed by law." For example, after striking down Ontario's first film censorship law because the statute did not stipulate any standards for cutting or banning films, the Supreme Court approved a revised statute in which the criteria were more clearly articulated in the law. In other words, film censorship is a reasonable limit on freedom of expression as long as the criteria of the censors were "prescribed by law."[19]

As for restrictions that can be "demonstrably justified in a free and democratic society," the Court developed guidelines in the *Oakes* case, which have come to be called the **Oakes test**.[20] First, the objective of the government in limiting a right must be pressing and substantial; second, the means must be proportional to that objective. Three criteria are attached to this second point: the limit must be rationally connected to the government objective; it should impair the right as little as is necessary in order to achieve the objective; and the costs of the impairment to the right must be proportional to their benefits. The Oakes test has been applied in subsequent interpretations of the **reasonable limits clause** in a large proportion of Charter cases.

Fundamental Freedoms

Section 2 lists the following **fundamental freedoms**:

- (a) freedom of conscience and religion;
- (b) freedom of thought, belief, opinion and expression, including freedom of the press and other media of communication;
- (c) freedom of peaceful assembly; and
- (d) freedom of association.

FREEDOM OF RELIGION

With respect to freedom of religion, the Supreme Court invalidated the Lord's Day Act as an infringement of freedom of religion because its restrictions on Sunday activities were clearly related to the Christian sabbath and discriminated against other religions. On the other hand, the Court upheld the Ontario Retail Business Holidays Act, designed to preserve Sunday as a day of rest but on a secular rather than a religious foundation. A number of cases have taken the view that a child welfare authority may approve of a blood transfusion for a child despite the parents' religious beliefs to the contrary. Public schools may no longer hold a compulsory and exclusively Christian school prayer or religious studies classes. And, while Ontario's publicly funded Roman Catholic separate school system has been upheld as a pre-Charter constitutional right, public funding for other private religious schools is not guaranteed.[21]

FREEDOM OF EXPRESSION

With respect to freedom of expression, a wide range of issues has been brought before the courts. Perhaps most controversial was the Supreme Court's rejection of the French-only sign provision of Quebec's Bill 101, which was held to be a violation of Quebec's own Charter of Rights as well. The Court decided that freedom of expression not only included the freedom to express ideas, but also the freedom to choose the language in which to express them. Moreover, the concept of freedom of expression incorporated "commercial expression." In this case, the Court hinted that it would be a reasonable limit on freedom of commercial expression in Quebec if the law were amended to provide for the *predominant* rather than the *exclusive* use of French on commercial signs.[22] Freedom of commercial expression was also involved in Quebec's successful effort to restrict advertising aimed at children. But the Supreme Court disallowed the federal prohibition of cigarette advertising; the Court ruled that a *partial* ban would be more acceptable, and the government amended the legislation accordingly.[23]

In cases involving anti-Semitic denials of the Holocaust, the Court threw out the Criminal Code provision prohibiting the spreading of false news, but a majority turned around and concluded that the section prohibiting the dissemination of hate literature was a reasonable limit on freedom of expression.[24] The question of hatred on the Internet is even more difficult to address.

By Susan Dewar (Ottawa Sun). *Reproduced with permission.*

Several freedom of expression cases have involved the labour movement. The Court ruled that freedom of expression includes the freedom of trade unions to engage in picketing, even secondary picketing, and that the right to distribute leaflets regarding a labour dispute is even more extensive. On the other hand, it is a reasonable limit on that right to prohibit the picketing of courthouses by court employees, even during a legal strike.[25]

Other cases have arisen in connection with election campaigns. Attaching posters on public property including utility poles was protected by freedom of expression, and paying a portion of the campaign expenses of candidates and parties from the public purse does not infringe a taxpayer's right to freedom of expression. On the other hand, limits on third-party advertising during election campaigns have thus far been invalidated, as was the provision in the Canada Elections Act prohibiting the publication of public opinion polls during the final three days of a federal election campaign. Federal legislation prohibiting public servants from engaging in electoral work for a political party or candidate was found to be invalid, but the more balanced Ontario legislation on the subject was upheld.[26]

Freedom of expression encompasses freedom of the press, and several cases have dealt with this issue. The Court found it a reasonable limit that the Criminal Code prohibits the publication of the name of the victim of sexual assault if the victim so requests. Compelling journalists to reveal their sources of information, prohibiting the CBC from showing the mini-series *The Boys of St. Vincent*, restricting media coverage of the Paul Bernardo case before his trial, and clearing the court in the case where public knowledge would further victimize the victim of sexual assault are other issues that have been addressed by judicial decisions. The Nova Scotia legislature was even allowed to limit media access to its proceedings.[27]

Obscenity also falls into this category, where one main case stands out, *R. v. Butler*. The Court divided pornography into different categories, saying that portrayals of sex with violence and sex that is degrading or dehumanizing can be restricted by the authorities, but that a portrayal of explicit sex that is neither violent nor degrading is generally acceptable unless it depicts children. Parliament strengthened the provisions dealing with child pornography in 1993, and in a later case, an artist's depiction of children in various sexual activities was deemed to be art rather than pornography. As in the case of hatred, the problem of pornography on the Internet has not been solved. As for prostitution, the Supreme Court upheld the prohibition on communicating for the purposes of sidewalk solicitation, Chief Justice Brian Dickson feeling that this was a reasonable limit on freedom of expression.[28] Interestingly, the two women on the Court dissented, finding that the Code infringed both freedom of expression and freedom of association, and was not just a reasonable limit on them.

FREEDOM OF PEACEFUL ASSEMBLY AND ASSOCIATION

In another controversial decision, the Supreme Court ruled that freedom of association does not guarantee the right of trade unions to strike. Thus freedom of association does not prevent federal or provincial legislatures from passing back-to-work legislation or otherwise interfering in the collective bargaining process. Justices Dickson and Wilson dissented on this decision, arguing that the freedom to belong to a union is of little value if the union cannot engage in a strike as a last resort. Labour was happier with the ultimate disposition of the *Lavigne* case in which the Court rejected Mr. Lavigne's objection to part of his union dues going to support causes with which he did not agree.[29]

Democratic Rights

Under **democratic rights** in sections 3 to 5, the Charter guarantees that every citizen of Canada has the right to vote in federal and provincial elections; that no Parliament can continue for more than five years from the previous election, except in time of real or apprehended war, invasion, or insurrection; and that each Parliament must sit at least once every year. Section 3 has been cited in several cases dealing with federal and provincial electoral laws that deny the vote to certain categories of people. At the national level, it was used in the course of the 1988 election to invalidate provisions in the Canada Elections Act that denied the vote to federally appointed judges and patients in mental institutions. Many similar cases have arisen in connection with provincial electoral laws, especially relating to prisoners, persons on parole, and those remanded but not yet charged. In 1993 the Supreme Court agreed with the Federal Court of Canada that denying prisoners the right to vote violated section 3, but in the meantime, the law had been amended to allow those serving less than two years to vote. When this law was challenged, in turn, all prisoners were awarded the vote in federal elections.[30]

Another interesting application of section 3 arose in cases involving the drawing of provincial constituency boundaries, especially in BC and Saskatchewan. Indeed, the courts surprised many observers by ruling that such a matter came within the scope of section 3 at all. In the 1989 *Dixon* case in British Columbia, the electoral map was disallowed because constituency boundaries did not approach "equality of voting power" and such disparities could not be justified on any other grounds. In Saskatchewan, the Court of Appeal invalidated that province's electoral map in 1991 primarily because of disparities between the size of urban and rural ridings, but a quick appeal to a divided Supreme Court of Canada re-established it. Even though the electoral map systematically overrepresented rural voters, a majority of the Court decided that they would not insist on greater equality in the size of constituencies because "effective representation" had been achieved. Other cases have not gone as far as the Supreme Court of Canada, but the PEI electoral map was disallowed by the courts of that province, while the Alberta map was upheld.[31]

Mobility Rights

Under section 6, **mobility rights**, every citizen of Canada has the right to enter, remain in, and leave Canada, and every citizen or permanent resident has the right to take up residence and pursue the gaining of a livelihood in any province. On the other hand, laws providing for reasonable residency requirements for receiving public services are acceptable, as are laws that give preference to local residents if the unemployment rate in that province is higher than the national rate. Mobility rights were included in the Charter because of Pierre Trudeau's concern that some provinces were restricting the entry of residents of other provinces, as in the case of cross-border employment. Mobility rights have not featured frequently in judicial interpretation, but have arisen in unanticipated ways. It is often professionals—usually lawyers—denied permission to practise in a particular province who have tried to use mobility rights to their advantage. They have generally been unsuccessful because the Court has said that section 6 does not guarantee the "right to work." But while it has upheld the right of each province to establish its own professional qualifications, these cannot be based on provincial boundaries. On the other hand, PEI legislation that taxed nonresidents at a higher level than residents did not violate section 6.[32]

Legal Rights

Legal rights are contained in sections 7 to 14. In section 7, everyone has the right to life, liberty, and security of the person and the right not to be deprived thereof except in accordance with the principles of fundamental justice. "Security of the person" was used as the main basis for throwing out the abortion provision of the Criminal Code in the famous *Morgentaler* case in 1988. A majority of the Court ruled that that law, with all its arbitrary and bureaucratic procedures, violated the security of the person of the woman concerned, and constituted a "profound interference with a woman's body." Having invalidated the abortion law in the *Morgentaler* case, the Court declined to rule in the absence of any legislation in the *Borowski* case on whether the "right to life" included fetal rights. But in the *Daigle* case, the Court found no fetal right to life in the Quebec Charter of Rights, the Canadian Criminal Code, or the common law, and ruled that the "father" has no right to prevent an abortion. Similarly, in the 1999 *Dobson* case, the Court ruled that a woman could not be sued for having harmed her fetus during pregnancy.[33] Sue Rodriguez, dying of Lou Gehrig's disease, was not able to persuade the Court that security of the person provided her with the right to an assisted suicide—only a minority of judges agreed with her.[34]

Security of the person was also involved in the *Operation Dismantle* case. The Supreme Court ruled that the causal link between American Cruise missile testing in Canada and the threat to the security of the person because of the potential escalation of the international arms race was uncertain, speculative, and hypothetical.[35]

By *Steve Nease* (Oakville Beaver). *Reproduced with permission.*

"Security of the person" and "fundamental justice" combined in the *Singh* case to require the Immigration Department to provide an oral hearing for refugee claimants when their life could be in danger if deported. Fundamental justice necessitated giving such claimants an opportunity to state their case and to know the case against them. This case was the cause of much of the subsequent backlog in the Immigration Department. Fundamental justice was also violated, the Court ruled, in connection with the B.C. Motor Vehicle Act, under which a person's driving privileges could be suspended without his or her knowledge; then, driving in this state of ignorance, the person could be imprisoned when caught.[36]

Fundamental justice is often linked to the presumption of innocence in section 11(d). For example, in the *Daviault* case, the Supreme Court allowed an extreme state of drunkenness to be used as a rare defence in a rape case; otherwise, it ruled, the accused's right to fundamental justice and presumption of innocence would have been violated. The government quickly amended the law to prevent a recurrence of this interpretation. In the *Seaboyer* case, the Court invalidated the rape-shield law that prohibited the use of evidence of the complainant's previous sexual activity. But Parliament proceeded to amend the Criminal Code, primarily by tightening up the concept of consent (no means no). Then, in a case that attracted much public attention in early 1999, the Supreme Court overturned the acquittal of an Alberta man who had conducted a job interview in a trailer with a young woman wearing shorts and a T-shirt. Although the woman said "no" three times to his sexual advances, the Alberta courts considered his actions "less criminal than hormonal," and were roundly criticized by the Supreme Court for dealing in "inappropriate myths and stereotypes."[37] Parliament has also amended the Criminal Code to overcome Supreme Court rulings with respect to innocence on account of mental disorder and the production of medical records in sexual assault proceedings, while the Court partially reversed the *Seaboyer* decision with respect to the complainant's confidential counselling records.

Section 8 establishes the right to be secure against unreasonable search and seizure. In dismissing the charge of collusion between the Southam and Thomson newspaper chains, the Court extended this right to corporations and decided that a reasonable search by the police or other government authorities had to be authorized by statute and conducted after a search warrant was issued by an impartial arbiter (almost exclusively a judge) who had reasonable and probable grounds to believe that an offence had been committed and that the evidence was located in the place to be searched. This decision did nothing to remedy the feebleness of the Combines Investigation Act, now the Competition Act. Many cases in this realm have arisen with respect to drug seizures, with the general rule being that a search will not be wrongful if authorized by law, if the law itself is reasonable, and if the search is conducted in a reasonable manner. Similarly, a police officer's demand to see a person's driver's licence and insurance card during a spot check is not an unreasonable search, and male prisoners can be frisked by female guards. But taking blood samples without legal authorization and strip searches at Canadian border points without the opportunity to contact counsel were outlawed.[38]

In at least two cases with respect to section 8, Parliament passed legislation to counter the effect of Supreme Court decisions. To offset the *Feeney* decision, an amendment to the Criminal Code made it easier to obtain a warrant before entering a dwelling house in order to make an arrest of a fleeing suspect. Another amendment facilitated the obtaining of bodily substances such as hair samples for forensic DNA analysis after the decision in the *Stillman* case that such was not provided for. Then, in the 1999 *Godoy* case, the Supreme Court ruled that police officers responding to a 911 call had the right to enter a dwelling house in order to ascertain the health and safety of the caller.[39]

Section 9 grants the right not to be arbitrarily detained or imprisoned, and section 10 reads that on arrest or detention, everyone has the right to be informed promptly of the reasons therefor and the right to contact a lawyer without delay and to be informed of that right. A huge number of Charter cases have arisen in this connection; for example, the Court has ruled that random police spot checks are a reasonable limit on the right not to be arbitrarily detained and that roadside breath tests do not include the right to retain counsel. However, if a person fails that test and is asked to accompany the police officer to a police station, the individual has a right to retain counsel before the police station breathalyzer test. In the *Clarkson* case, an intoxicated woman who voluntarily waived her right to counsel and then proceeded to confess to the murder of her husband was acquitted because she was not aware of the consequences of not having counsel present, and the double-murder confessions of a man with an IQ of less than 80 were not admitted as evidence because he did not understand his rights. The Court has ruled that a person has the right to be told of his or her right not only to a lawyer but also to legal aid, and must have a reasonable opportunity to exercise these rights. In a 1995 case, for example, a man convicted of rape and murder was granted a new trial because he had been subjected to an "intensive and manipulative interrogation by police" during which his repeated requests to consult a lawyer were ignored.[40]

Section 11 includes a variety of rights available to a person charged with an offence. "To be tried within a reasonable time" has been extremely controversial after the *Askov* decision, which found that a delay of almost two years between a preliminary hearing and a trial had been excessive. The lower courts took this to mean that everyone had a right to a trial within six to eight months of being charged, and some 34 500 cases were stayed, dismissed, or withdrawn in Ontario alone. The Supreme Court then took the unprecedented initiative to point out in a speech by one of its members that this was not what the *Askov* decision intended.[41]

Persons charged cannot be compelled to testify against themselves, cannot be denied reasonable bail without just cause, and are presumed innocent until proven guilty according to law in a fair and public hearing by an independent and impartial tribunal. The "impartial tribunal" was addressed in the *Valente* case, cited again in Chapter 23. In this connection, the Supreme Court also found that before 1992, the Crown had an unfair advantage in naming stand-by prospective jurors and in having a greater number of peremptory challenges in the jury selection process. The presumption of innocence was addressed in the *Oakes* case. Under the "reverse onus" clause of the Narcotics Control Act, a person proved to be in possession of a narcotic was also presumed to be guilty of trafficking and it was up to the person charged with possession to prove his or her innocence on the trafficking charge. Although many observers find this to be a perfectly acceptable requirement when large quantities of drugs are involved, the *Oakes* case invalidated this clause as an unreasonable limit on the presumption of innocence. On the other hand, a person occupying the driver's seat of a vehicle is presumed to have "care and control" of the vehicle unless he or she can prove otherwise. Thus, even if the vehicle is not in motion, an intoxicated person in the driver's seat can be convicted of impaired driving. The Court has also ruled that indiscreet remarks by politicians about a case before the courts, however regrettable, cannot be used as a defence to throw the case out. Persons charged are guaranteed trial by jury where the maximum punishment for the offence is imprisonment for five years or more, and, whether finally acquitted of the offence or found guilty and punished, cannot to be tried for it again.[42]

Everyone has the right not to be subjected to any cruel and unusual treatment or punishment. In this connection, the Court ruled that a minimum sentence of seven years for illegally importing any quantity of narcotic into Canada was excessive. Indeterminate sentences for dangerous offenders have, however, been upheld, as was the extradition of fugitives to countries where the death sentence might be imposed.[43]

The final clause of section 11 provides that a party or witness in any proceedings who does not understand or speak the language in which the proceedings are conducted or who is deaf has the right to the assistance of an interpreter.

Equality Rights

Equality rights are contained in section 15, which reads as follows:

(1)   Every individual is equal before and under the law and has the right to the equal protection and equal benefit of the law without discrimination and, in particular, without discrimination based on race, national or ethnic origin, colour, religion, sex, age or mental or physical disability.

(2)   Subsection (1) does not preclude any law, program or activity that has as its object the amelioration of conditions of disadvantaged individuals or groups including those that are disadvantaged because of race, national or ethnic origin, colour, religion, sex, age or mental or physical disability.

In the *Andrews* case the Supreme Court laid down a two-step process for interpreting equality rights.[44] The Court first determines if the case in question involves an inequality in law or treatment in terms of the personal characteristics listed in section 15 (or of others analogous to them), and then whether there has been a discrimination, that is, a harmful or prejudicial effect. In other words, inequalities and distinctions are permitted if no negative discrimination or disadvantage—social, political, or legal—is involved. According to Ian Greene, the Court made it clear that "it intends to interpret section 15 to help clearly disadvantaged groups in society," although it may have backtracked to some extent in more recent cases.[45]

The Court overturned the 1978 Bill of Rights decision that allowed the Unemployment Insurance Commission to discriminate against pregnant women because they were pregnant, not because they were women. In addition, it agreed that provincial human rights codes must not prevent girls from playing on boys' athletic teams. In the 1995 *Egan* case, the Supreme Court ruled unanimously that the Charter prohibited discrimination on the basis of sexual orientation, even though this ground was not explicitly listed in section 15, but a majority then found that the case in question (old age spousal benefits for a same-sex couple) was subject to reasonable limits. Indeed, the courts have found a close link between section 15 and section 1 of the Charter, and reasonable limits has been used to justify certain other kinds of discrimination. In the case of mandatory retirement, for example, the Court ruled that while such a policy was a violation of equality rights and did involve discrimination, it was reasonable for laws to require retirement at age 65. Then, in the more aggressive *Vriend* decision, the Court reaffirmed that the Charter included sexual orientation and ordered Alberta to add it to its Individual Rights Protection Act.

Same-sex benefits received a major boost in the 1999 M. *v.* H. case, in which the Ontario Family Law Act was found to be a violation of section 15 when it only provided for support for an opposite-sex spouse. The Court no longer felt that such distinctions were saved by the reasonable limits clause.[46] Besides sexual orientation, the Supreme Court has recognized citizenship and marital status as analogous grounds to the rights enumerated in section 15. On the other hand, subsection (2), which permits **affirmative action** programs that give preference to those who have been discriminated against in the past, has not been actively used.

Official Languages of Canada

Sections 16 to 22 of the Charter constitutionalize the federal and New Brunswick official-languages acts and reaffirm the limited official bilingualism of Quebec and Manitoba. These sections guarantee that certain government agencies will operate on a bilingual basis, as discussed in Chapter 5. Although judicial interpretation of linguistic rights has been extensive, it related almost exclusively to the original provisions of the 1867 Constitution Act as well as the 1870 Manitoba Act rather than to the 1982 Charter. The extension of official bilingualism in the federal and New Brunswick official-languages acts was ruled valid; several aspects of Quebec's Bill 101 were invalidated because they conflicted with section 133 of the 1867 act; the 1890 Official Language Act of Manitoba, which removed French as an official language in the province, was considered a violation of the Manitoba Act; and the Supreme Court then required Manitoba to translate all its laws into French.[47] As noted above, the unilingual sign provisions of Bill 101 were challenged in terms of freedom of expression rather than on the basis of sections 16 to 23. A new section 16.1 was added to the Charter in 1993 to reinforce the equality of the two official languages in New Brunswick.

Pierre Trudeau promoted minority-language education rights as the central element of the Charter of Rights and Freedoms. (Photographer unknown/Canapress)

Minority-Language Education Rights

Section 23 deals with constitutional **minority-language education rights**, and some would argue that they were the only part of the Charter with which Pierre Trudeau was truly concerned.[48] Section 23 has come before the courts in two main contexts. First, the Supreme Court struck down the provision in Bill 101 that allowed only the children of parents who were themselves products of the English school system in Quebec to go to that system, essentially those who were already there (the "Quebec clause"). Indeed, section 23 (the "Canada clause") was deliberately drafted so that it would conflict with this clause, in order that Canadian citizens who moved to Quebec could also send their children to the English schools. Section 23 limits such access in all provinces to areas "where numbers warrant." The Supreme Court has decided not only what number of francophone students warrant a French-language school, for example, but also that it must have a "distinct physical setting" and that French-language parents must have a say in the "management and control" of it.[49]

Enforcement

Section 24 makes clear, where the Bill of Rights did not, that the courts have the power to interpret the Charter and to invalidate laws that conflict with it. It also moves in the American direction with regard to the admissibility of evidence. The Charter does not actually bar illegally obtained evidence, as in the United States; the admission of such evidence is acceptable as long as it does not bring the administration of justice into disrepute. The Supreme Court laid the basis for interpreting this section in the *Collins* case.[50] First, evidence should be excluded if it would prejudice the fairness of the trial, and second, the more seriously the obtaining of the evidence violates the Charter, the more compelling is the need to exclude it. In the third place, however, if to exclude the evidence would bring the judicial system into disrepute, the evidence should not be excluded. Such questionable evidence usually related to a violation of the right to counsel or to an unreasonable search or seizure.

General Provisions

Sections 25 through 30 relate to specific groups in society, and were discussed in relevant chapters earlier in the book. Section 25 says that the rights and freedoms in the Charter shall not be construed so as to abrogate or derogate from any Aboriginal, treaty, or other rights or freedoms that pertain to the Aboriginal peoples of Canada including any rights or freedoms that have been recognized by the Royal Proclamation of October 7, 1763, and any rights or freedoms that may be acquired by the Aboriginal peoples of Canada by way of land claims settlement. A more positive Aboriginal clause in the Constitution Act, 1982, is section 35, which is not actually part of the Charter itself. The potential of the 1982 document to advance Aboriginal rights has never been clear, but encouraging signs emerged from the *Sparrow* and *Marshall* cases. In acquitting an Indian from the offence of using a bigger fishing net than authorized by law, the Supreme Court asserted that governments must bear the burden of proving laws are necessary if they have a negative effect on any Aboriginal right. On the other hand, the Supreme Court invented a "reasonable limits" clause for section 35 that was not really there. In another early case on the subject of treaty rights, the Court ruled that an ancient treaty-based fishing right took precedence over a Quebec law that prohibited fishing in provincial parks. Then, as mentioned in Chapter 4, the *Delgamuukw* case provided a comprehensive statement on Aboriginal title and opened the door to accepting oral history evidence for purposes of such land claims.[51]

Section 27 asserts that the Charter shall be interpreted in a manner consistent with the preservation and enhancement of the multicultural heritage of Canadians, and section 28 reads that notwithstanding anything in the Charter, the rights and freedoms referred to in it are guaranteed equally to male and female persons. The women's movement considered the addition of section 28 essential so that governments would not be able to use the notwithstanding clause (section 33) to override the gender equality provision of section 15. According to section 29, nothing in the Charter abrogates or derogates from any rights or privileges guaranteed by or under the Constitution of Canada in respect of denominational, separate, or dissentient schools. This clause protects section 93 of the 1867 Constitution Act, which guaranteed existing Protestant and Roman Catholic separate schools. Although section 93 clearly discriminates against other religions, the drafters of the Charter did not want to take responsibility for altering rights established in the original Constitution.[52]

Application of the Charter

Section 32 clarifies that the Charter applies to the Parliament and government of Canada, including the Yukon and Northwest Territories (and now Nunavut), and to the legislature and government of each province. By implication, it also applies to the municipal level of government. Thus all legislation in Canada must be consistent with the Charter, as must all actions of government executives—ministers, public servants, police officers, and so on. It is not intended to apply to the private sector, but certain institutions occupy an ambiguous position. While the courts interpret the Charter, for example, it is not certain whether their own actions are governed by it.[53] The Charter has been applied to law societies because they have been delegated governmental powers, and to community colleges, but more autonomous semi-public institutions such as hospitals and universities are exempt.[54] As mentioned earlier, federal and provincial human rights codes rather than the Charter regulate certain aspects of the private sector. But since such codes take the form of laws, they must also remain consistent with the Charter.[55]

The Notwithstanding Clause

Section 33 is the famous **notwithstanding clause**. Parliament or legislatures may exempt laws from three parts of the Charter—fundamental freedoms (section 2), legal rights (sections 7–14), and equality rights (section 15)—but not from democratic rights, mobility rights, or linguistic rights. This provision was a compromise between provincial premiers, who wanted the clause to apply to the whole Charter, and Pierre Trudeau, who was adamant that it could not be used to circumvent the three sections about which he cared most. For the sections it covers, a federal or provincial legislature merely has to expressly declare in a statute that the act or a provision thereof shall operate notwithstanding a specific provision of the Charter. If such action is taken, however, it is only good for five years, after which it lapses or must be re-enacted.

Despite the number of times the Supreme Court has invalidated federal or provincial legislation since 1982, governments have rarely re-enacted such provisions under section 33. Over the first 18 years, it was used only in Saskatchewan and Quebec. The government of Grant Devine used section 33 even before a court interpretation of its back-to-work legislation to settle a public service strike in 1986, and before the Alberta Labour reference made such use of the notwithstanding clause unnecessary. During the first Parti Québécois period in Quebec, up to 1985, the notwithstanding clause was routinely applied, as a matter of principle, to all new legislation passed in that province as well as to all pre-1982 laws. The Liberal government of Robert Bourassa discontinued that practice, but used the notwithstanding clause to get around the Supreme Court decision with respect to bilingual signs in the province. As mentioned, when the Supreme Court ruled that French-only store signs violated their owners' freedom of expression, Bourassa invoked section 33 (and the equivalent clause in the Quebec Charter of Rights) and then passed what he considered to be a compromise law that allowed certain English signs inside the store.

This incident in particular, together with a general public adoration of the Charter and a distrust of politicians who sought to find ways around it, gave the notwithstanding clause a negative reception in most of English Canada. Since 1988, politicians have rarely even contemplated its use. As noted, Quebec has its own reasons to dislike the Charter, but Alberta otherwise provides the main locus of anti-Charter sentiment, and a number of incidents arose in that province that caused some residents to request the use of section 33. One was to prevent the victims of a sterilization program (from an earlier period in the province's history) from appealing for compensation; another was when the Supreme Court of Canada ruled that sexual orientation had to be added to the Alberta Individual Rights Protection Act. A similarly sensitive situation would arise if the Supreme Court interpreted sexual orientation in such a way as to legalize homosexual marriages. The Alberta-based Reform Party also asked the federal government to use the notwithstanding clause to overturn a lower BC court decision justifying the possession of child pornography as an element of freedom of expression. None of these requests succeeded.[56]

Nevertheless, section 33 is often defended as a general principle: it allows democratically elected legislators to have the final say. It also takes pressure off judges to solve political crises because they know that politicians can, if necessary, override their strictly legal decisions.[57] While reflecting the fact that it was born of political compromise, the notwithstanding clause in the Charter leaves Canadians with a strange system under which the courts can overrule the legislatures but the legislatures can overrule the courts. Rank Canadian political compromise that it is, this system of protecting civil liberties may turn out to be superior to either total legislative supremacy or exclusive judicial review. Some observers advocate the abolition of the notwithstanding clause, but others (including the author), not wanting to entrust their fate entirely either to legislatures or to courts, prefer the checks and balances that they provide to each other.

By *Brian Gable* (The Globe and Mail). *Reprinted with permission from* The Globe and Mail.

IMPLICATIONS OF CONSTITUTIONALIZING THE CHARTER OF RIGHTS

After nearly 20 years of experience, the Charter of Rights and Freedoms continues to attract both passionate support and opposition. Supporters and opponents alike agree, however, that the Charter has significantly changed the operation of the Canadian political system. The courts have become involved in almost all of the most difficult political issues that have arisen over the past 18 years: Aboriginal rights, abortion, assisted suicide, French-only signs, gender equality, impaired driving, mandatory retirement, minority-language schools, official bilingualism, political rights of public servants, pornography, prostitution, redistribution of constituency boundaries, the right to strike, same-sex spousal benefits, separate schools, sexual assault, sexual orientation, Sunday shopping, testing the Cruise missile, and tobacco advertising. Such cases have enmeshed the courts in considerable political controversy and, as Russell says, the Charter has "judicialized politics and politicized the judiciary."[58]

The first major implication of constitutionalizing the Charter, therefore, was to increase the role of the courts in the political process at the expense of the elected politicians. Adopted at a time when politicians were generally regarded with considerable cynicism and disrespect, the Charter was embraced by the Canadian public as a welcome addition to the Constitution. Oblivious to the strengths and weaknesses of rights protection before 1982, a vast majority had more faith in judges than in parliamentarians and believed that their rights would be better protected that way.

Many scholars, as well as other observers and practitioners, take the opposite point of view, the most scathing attack on the "legalization of politics" in Canada having been made by law professor Michael Mandel. He mounts five main arguments. First, an enormous "leeway" exists within which the courts make highly political decisions, but judges disguise their work through legal interpretations and abstract principles that are unintelligible to the general public. Mandel challenges the generally accepted view that while politicians make popular, political, self-serving decisions, judges' decisions are impartial, objective, technical, rational, and in the public interest. Marc Gold supports Mandel in this view in writing that "judicial rhetoric functions both to obscure the true basis for the decision reached and to sensitize the audience into accepting the result as both legitimate and appropriate."[59] Especially given the reasonable limits clause, almost every Charter case could have been decided differently, and the content of Canadians' rights has "depended to a large extent upon which judges happened to sit on the panels that heard the cases." Canadian scholars are thus beginning to examine the records of individual Supreme Court judges and to categorize them ideologically.[60] The Supreme Court itself has made some very political moves, and members of the Court make little effort to divorce themselves from the hurly-burly of daily political developments in Ottawa.[61]

Mandel's second argument is that while the Charter has been sold as enhancing democracy and the power of the people, it has really reduced the degree of popular control over government by transferring power from representative, accountable legislatures and politicians to unrepresentative, unaccountable, and unrestrained judges, courts, and an elitist legal profession. "It is both simpler and cheaper to get to see your MP than to get to see a judge."[62]

In the third place, legalized politics enhances individual and corporate rights against the collective welfare of the community (as in the tobacco advertising decision) and is therefore part of the wider Americanization of Canada. The adoption of individualistic American values in the Charter, as opposed to traditional Canadian collectivism, is strengthened by the tendency of the courts to cite American precedents when making their decisions.[63]

Mandel's fourth point is that legalized politics is conservative, class-based politics that defends existing social arrangements and undermines popular movements. For a variety of reasons including the cost of litigation, the background and attitudes of judges, the biases in the law and the Charter, the socially disadvantaged and labour unions were better off without it. "The Charter is capable of opposing every kind of discrimination but class discrimination." Joel Bakan adds that the Charter is "Just Words," and that its principles have failed to promote social justice because it is interpreted by such a conservative institution.[64]

Finally, Mandel argues that Canadians have come to attribute such significance to Charter rights that we are in danger of forgetting the much more important social rights about which it is silent. Is the right to have one's child educated in a certain language more important than to educate children at public expense? Is the distribution of trade union funds more important than the basic right of collective bargaining with the possibility of a strike? Is the right of a doctor to work in a hospital after 65 years of age more important than a basic right to public health services? In making these points, Mandel at least offers a reminder to question the face value of court decisions, to refrain from glorifying the Charter, judges, lawyers, and courts, and to remember traditional ways of making public decisions.

While Mandel and others are obviously correct in noting the increase in judicial power at the expense of politicians, it should be added that the courts have been relatively, and increasingly, deferential to existing laws. For example, between 1996 and 1998, the Supreme Court struck down only 12 laws in 76 Charter cases.[65] Despite all the criticism of its decisions, the Supreme Court of Canada has found that most of the challenged laws were *not* violations of the Charter, and in a high proportion of other cases it invoked the reasonable limits clause to allow laws to stand even though they violated one Charter right or another. When governments chose to defend existing laws, they were usually successful, and without too much effort, they have been able to "Charterproof" new ones.[66] Moreover, the new political role of the courts is sometimes exploited by the politicians. The latter are "often quite relieved to have controversial and unpredictable issues transformed into 'nonpartisan' questions about rights and about the correct interpretation of the Constitution so they can be taken off their hands and resolved in the courts."[67] On the other hand, after the *Morgentaler* decision, the Mulroney government pressured the Supreme Court to delay the *Borowski* hearing until after new abortion legislation had been passed by Parliament. According to Greene, this "was obviously a strategy to keep the abortion issue out of the public spotlight until after the imminent federal election."[68]

A second main implication of the Charter is that public consciousness of the policymaking role of the courts has created greater interest in the quality of judicial appointments. In some ways this is advantageous, for that quality has not been overly impressive in the past. On the other hand, to begin selecting judges on the basis of their ideological orientations would be another regrettable element in the Americanization of the Canadian system. Several observers have recommended screening Supreme Court and other judicial nominees by a parliamentary committee, but others argue that that would create more problems than it solves.[69]

A third implication of the adoption of the Charter, as Peter Russell, Mandel, and others have pointed out, is that minority groups increasingly bypass the usual political processes—legislatures, cabinets, and bureaucracies—and take their demands directly to the courts instead.[70] To some extent this has happened when such groups were unable to accomplish their goals through traditional political activity, in which case this alternative avenue is advantageous. After all, it can be argued, democracy is more than majority rule; it is also about individual rights, which in some cases might be better protected by courts than by legislatures.[71] However, groups may simply believe it is less trouble to go to court rather than to engage in the struggle of mobilizing popular support for their cause. Few observers, even in the legal profession, would welcome a general transformation of all political activity into legal activity with the attendant loss of political and organizational skills that traditionally characterize a democracy. Seymour Martin Lipset fears that the Charter will remove one of the last traits that distinguish Canadians from Americans by increasing the litigious character of citizen–state relations and bring about a "rights-centred" political culture.[72]

In the fourth place, the Charter has had an effect on the federal–provincial relationship. In its first ten years of operation, the Supreme Court invalidated more substantive provincial statutes than federal ones, many involving minority-language rights, and often in Quebec. In this and other policy fields, Morton and Knopff argued that the Charter has "transferred authority ... out of provincial legislatures and into the federal courts." Indeed, they coined the term "court party" to describe the link between "Charter groups" such as official-language minorities, feminists, civil libertarians, Aboriginals, visible minorities, people with disabilities, and gay men and lesbians, and the ascendancy of judicial power in Canadian politics. They argued that "Ottawa has been able to forge a strategic alliance with select, non–territorial-based interest groups and with sympathetic federally-appointed judges" at the expense of the provinces.[73] If this is true, the Charter was working even better than Trudeau anticipated! But after 1992, the Supreme Court nullified fewer provincial statutes on the basis of the Charter, and it appeared that the Court had become both more deferential to legislatures in general and more willing to accommodate provincial policy diversities.

If Morton and Knopff are correct in their identification of interests that have most frequently turned to the courts rather than the politicians, have these same groups benefited most from this profound change in the political system? Undoubtedly official-language minorities are among the biggest winners, but Mandel is not the only one to hold that business has also been a major beneficiary. The editors of *Charting the Consequences: The Impact of Charter Rights on Canadian Law and Politics* remind us that many Charter rights have been extended to corporations, that businesses have used the Charter "to challenge all variety of legislative measures," and that corporations gained at the expense of labour from court interpretation of Freedom of Association in the context of strikes.[74] As for such social movements as those regarding women, Aboriginals, and gays and lesbians, the record is not as clear as Morton and Knopff imply. All such groups have experienced wins and losses, while the Charter has caused internal divisions over whether to pursue a legal or political strategy, and these groups' "agendas have had to conform to a more liberal, individualistic path than they might otherwise have chosen to follow."[75]

CONCLUSION

The protection of civil liberties in Canada has always occupied an intermediate position between the parliamentary sovereignty of Britain and the judicial review of the United States. The adoption of the Charter of Rights and Freedoms moved the country considerably closer to the U.S. model. As time goes on, its unconscious influence on the Canadian political culture and the use of U.S. precedents by the Supreme Court of Canada will probably enhance this southward pull. On the other hand, the reasonable limits and notwithstanding clauses in the Charter are unique Canadian responses to the question.

P Of the approaches outlined in Chapter 1, pluralism is most relevant to the addition of the Charter of Rights in the protection of civil liberties in Canada. In emphasizing individualist values and lauding the Charter in protecting them, pluralists draw their inspiration from the ideology of liberalism as articulated by such philosophers as John Locke and John Stuart Mill. Liberalism emphasizes the basic rationality of all people and advocates equality and liberty as embodied in the fundamental freedoms—of speech, press, religion, and association—and in the rule of law. Pluralists thus point out how often very ordinary people have gained from Charter restraints on police and from such decisions as the right to be informed of the right to legal aid. Pluralists expect that equality rights together with affirmative action programs will help to remove various kinds of discrimination. They also observe that judicial decisions have been ideologically balanced, citing the *Lavigne* case, which ultimately ended in a pro-labour decision even if many previous ones were anti-labour. Rather than be concerned that the legalization of politics has discouraged groups and popular movements from engaging in traditional political organization, pluralists welcome an additional means by which such demands can be advanced, and point to special programs to fund certain kinds of Charter challenges.

Ⓒ Class analysts have a less positive view of the Charter, which follows the general line of argument made by Mandel above. Charter rights have often been used to benefit corporations rather than individuals, such as in the *Big M Drug Mart*, tobacco advertising, and *Southam* cases. The stringent search requirements laid down in the latter case constituted another blow to the already weak laws restricting corporate collusion in Canada.[76] On the other hand, the Court denied unions a constitutional right to strike, and showed more sympathy to nonunionized workers (in the *Edwards* case) than to organized workers because the former were much less of "a threat to the social status quo."[77] Mandel cites the *Singh* and *Morgentaler* cases as two of the few where the socially disadvantaged appeared to have benefited from a Charter decision, but he reminds us to look at subsequent attempts by governments to dilute these victories through legislation and regulation. Moreover, the costs of taking cases to the courts are generally prohibitive except to wealthy individuals and corporations, and in 1992 the Mulroney government cancelled the Court Challenges Program that had funded many Charter cases, although the Liberals later resurrected it. Mandel also stresses the Charter's preference for individualism over collectivism, adding that it "unites people against the state but the result is to leave them at the mercy of private power."[78]

Class analysts also emphasize the elitist background of judges and question whether they can make fair decisions for the ordinary mortals who appear in court. For example, Andrew Petter writes,

> there is nothing about the Canadian judiciary to suggest that they possess the experience, the training or the disposition to comprehend the social impact of claims made to them under the Charter, let alone to resolve those claims in ways that promote, or even protect, the interests of lower income Canadians.[79]

ⓈⒸ In one sense, a Charter of Rights or other means of restraining government action is contrary to the view of state-centred theorists. The *Singh* decision, for example, necessitated a complete overhaul of the refugee admission system, and the *Askov* decision created chaos in the Ontario court system. On the other hand, state-centred theorists emphasize the frequency with which the Supreme Court has used the "reasonable limits" clause to justify state infringement of Charter rights, such as on film censorship, soliciting, Holocaust deniers, and some kinds of picketing. In addition, they point out that the Charter has been used far more often to restrict individual police actions than to overturn major government policies, such as in Operation Dismantle.

DISCUSSION QUESTIONS

1. What are the advantages and disadvantages of the "reasonable limits" clause in the Charter?

2. What are the advantages and disadvantages of the "notwithstanding" clause in the Charter?

3. Are Canadian fundamental freedoms and other democratic values better protected since 1982? Why or why not?

4. Is the Charter biased in favour of individuals accused of breaking the law? Why or why not?

5. Does legalized Charter politics inherently favour business interests and discriminate against the socially disadvantaged?

6. Does the Charter discourage traditional political activity?

7. How do each of the approaches outlined in Chapter 1 contribute to our understanding of the Charter of Rights and Freedoms and its effects on the Canadian political system?

NOTES

1. For example, Peter Hogg, *Constitutional Law of Canada*, 2nd ed. (Toronto: Carswell, 1985), ch. 28; Student Edition, 1999.
2. Alexander Alvaro, "Why Property Rights Were Excluded from the Canadian Charter of Rights and Freedoms," *Canadian Journal of Political Science* (June 1991), pp. 309–29.
3. While the British courts do not have such power, the European Court of Justice, part of the European Union, can make nonbinding decisions on whether British acts violate civil liberties. Moreover, the European Convention has now been incorporated into the British Human Rights Bill. Although the British courts do not have the explicit right to strike down public law that they deem to be in conflict with the European Convention, the bill virtually obliges the government to rewrite statutes in response to criticism by the courts.
4. On the other hand, the Supreme Court has occasionally found violations of Charter rights within provincial human rights codes, and, unless protected by the reasonable limits clause, has expunged them.
5. It was first articulated in the *Alberta Press Bill* case and used as a supplementary argument to criminal law in several cases, but never on its own.
6. *Reference re Alberta Statutes*, [1938] S.C.R. 100.
7. *Saumer v. City of Quebec*, [1953] S.C.R. 299.
8. *Switzman v. Elbling and Attorney-General of Quebec*, [1957] S.C.R. 285.
9. *Roncarelli v. Duplessis*, [1959] S.C.R. 121. In *Chaput v. Romain*, [1955] S.C.R. 834, police had broken up a private meeting of Jehovah's Witnesses, and in *Lamb v. Benoit*, [1959] S.C.R. 321, the police arrested Jehovah's Witnesses for distributing their literature. In all three cases, action of the authorities was ruled contrary to the rule of law.
10. *Cunningham v. Tomey Homma*, [1903] A.C. 151. On the other hand, the federal power over naturalization and aliens had allowed the Court to overturn an earlier anti-Asian law in BC in *Union Colliery Co. of B.C. Ltd. v. Bryden*, [1899] A.C. 580.
11. Ian Greene, *The Charter of Rights* (Toronto: Lorimer, 1989), p. 18.
12. Thomas Berger, *Fragile Freedoms*, rev. ed. (Toronto: Clarke Irwin, 1982). Greene also refers to the secret trials held in connection with the Gouzenko spy affair in 1945, in *The Charter of Rights*, p. 21.
13. Walter Tarnopolsky, *The Canadian Bill of Rights*, 2nd rev. ed. (Toronto: McClelland and Stewart, 1975). Saskatchewan had an earlier provincial Bill of Rights, while Alberta and Quebec each passed one later. These provincial bills of rights could not be constitutionally entrenched any more than the federal one was.
14. *R. v. Drybones*, [1970] S.C.R. 282. The Indian Act created a liquor offence that had harsher penalties for Indians than the equivalent offence for non-Indians.
15. These respective cases are *Brownridge v. The Queen*, [1972] S.C.R. 926; *A.-G. Ont. v. Reale*, [1975] 2 S.C.R. 624; and *Lowry and Lepper v. The Queen*, [1974] 26 D.L.R. (3rd) 224.
16. *Robertson and Rosetanni v. The Queen*, [1963] S.C.R. 651 (upholding the regulation of operating hours of a bowling alley based on the Lord's Day Act); *A.G. Can. v. Lavell and Isaac v. Bédard*, [1974] S.C.R. 1349 (upholding a distinction in the Indian Act between men and women marrying whites); *Hogan v. The Queen*, [1975] 2 S.C.R. 574 (denying the right to counsel before taking a breathalyzer test, after the *Brownridge* case had upheld such a right).

17. *Oil, Chemical and Atomic Workers International Union v. Imperial Oil Ltd. and A.-G. B.C.*, [1963] S.C.R. 584 (denying unions the right to contribute to the NDP via a checkoff procedure); *Walter v. A.-G. Alta.*, [1969] S.C.R. 383 (upholding Alberta legislation restricting the settlement of Hutterites); *Morgan v. A.-G. P.E.I.*, [1976] 2 S.C.R. 349 (upholding PEI legislation restricting the ownership of land in the province to PEI residents); *A.-G. Can. and Dupond v. Montreal*, [1978] 2 S.C.R. 770 (upholding a Montreal bylaw prohibiting parades and public gatherings); and *Nova Scotia Board of Censors v. McNeil*, [1978] 2 S.C.R. 662 (upholding provincial film censorship boards).

18. Gérald A. Beaudoin and Errol Mendes, *The Canadian Charter of Rights and Freedoms*, 3rd ed. (Scarborough: Carswell, 1996); Eugene Meehan et al. *The 1999 Annotated Canadian Charter of Rights and Freedoms* (Scarborough: Carswell, 1998); and Robert J. Sharpe and Katherine E. Swinton, *The Charter of Rights and Freedoms* (Toronto: Irwin Law, 1998).

19. *Re Ontario Film and Video Appreciation Society and Ontario Board of Censors*, [1984] 45 O.R. (2d) 80.

20. *R. v. Oakes*, [1986] 1 S.C.R. 103; Janet Hiebert, *Limiting Rights: The Dilemma of Judicial Review* (Montreal: McGill–Queen's University Press, 1996).

21. *R. v. Big M Drug Mart Ltd.*, [1985] 1 S.C.R. 295. Of course, Big M itself had no religion, but "worshipped only the Almighty Dollar." Michael Mandel, *The Charter of Rights and the Legalization of Politics in Canada*, rev. ed. (Toronto: Wall & Thompson, 1994), p. 316. *R. v. Edwards Books and Art Ltd.*, [1986] 2 S.C.R. 713. Chief Justice Dickson's famous passage about a restful, recreational Sunday is located on p. 770. *Zylberberg et al. v. The Director of Education of the Sudbury Board of Education* (1988), 65 O.R. 641 (Ont. C.A.); *Alder v. Ontario*, [1996] 3 S.C.R. 609; *Re Davis* (1982), Can. Charter of Rights Ann. 9.1-1 (Alta. Prov. Ct.—Fam. Div.).

22. *Ford v. Quebec (Attorney General)*, [1988] 2 S.C.R. 712; *Devine v. Quebec (Attorney General)*, [1988] 2 S.C.R. 790.

23. *Irwin Toy Ltd. v. Quebec (Attorney General)*, [1989] 1 S.C.R. 927; *RJR-MacDonald Inc. v. Canada (Attorney General)*, [1995] 3 S.C.R. 199.

24. *R. v. Keegstra*, [1990] 3 S.C.R. 697; *R. v. Zundel*, [1992] S.C.R. 731; Mandel, *The Charter of Rights*, rev. ed., pp. 369–76.

25. *RWDSU v. Dolphin Delivery Ltd.*, [1986] 2 S.C.R. 573; *B.C.G.E.U. v. British Columbia (Attorney General)*, [1988] 2 S.C.R. 214; Mandel, *The Charter of Rights*, rev. ed., ch. 5.

26. *Osborne v. Canada (Treasury Board)*, [1991] 2 S.C.R. 69; *Thomson Newspapers Co. v. Canada (Attorney General)*, [1998] 1 S.C.R. 877.

27. *Her Majesty the Queen v. Canadian Newspapers*, [1988] 2 S.C.R. 122; *Canadian Broadcasting Corp. v. New Brunswick (Attorney General)*, [1996] 3 S.C.R. 480; *Dagenais v. Canadian Broadcasting Corp.*, [1994] 3 S.C.R. 835; and *New Brunswick Broadcasting Co. v. Nova Scotia (Speaker of the House of Assembly)*, [1993] 1 S.C.R. 319; Kristen Douglas and Mollie Dunsmuir, *Charter of Rights and Freedoms: Fundamental Freedoms* (Ottawa: Parliamentary Research Branch, Current Issue Review, 84-16E, 1998).

28. *R. v. Butler*, [1992] 1 S.C.R. 452; *R. v. Skinner*, [1990] 1 S.C.R. 1235; James R. Robertson, *Prostitution* (Ottawa: Parliamentary Research Branch, Current Issue Review 82-2E, 1998); Robertson, *Pornography* (Ottawa: Parliamentary Research Branch, Current Issue Review 84-3E, 1998).

29. *Reference re Public Service Employee Relations Act, Labour Relations Act, and Police Officers Collective Bargaining Act of Alberta*, [1987] 1 S.C.R. 313. Two other simultaneous cases made up the "labour trilogy": *Public Service Alliance of Canada v. The Queen*, [1987] 1 S.C.R. 424, and *Saskatchewan v. Retail, Wholesale and Department Store Union*, [1987] 1 S.C.R. 460. According to Mandel, however, Dickson "always had section 1 in the back of his mind," *The Charter of Rights*, rev. ed., p. 270. *Lavigne v. Ontario Public Service Employees Union*, [1991] 81 D.L.R. (4th) 545 (S.C.C.); Joel Bakan, *Just Words: Constitutional Rights and Social Wrongs* (Toronto: University of Toronto Press, 1997).

30. *Canadian Disability Rights Council v. Canada*, [1988] 21 F.T.R. 268 (T.D.); *Belczowski v. Canada*, [1993] 2 S.C.R. 438; *Sauvé v. Canada (Chief Electoral Officer)*, [1996] 1 F.C. 857.

31. *Dixon v. British Columbia (Attorney General)*, [1989] 59 D.L.R. (4th) 247 (B.C.S.C.); *Reference re Provincial Electoral Boundaries (Sask.)*, [1991] 2 S.C.R. 158.

32. *Law Society of Upper Canada v. Skapinker*, [1984] 1 S.C.R. 357; *Black v. Law Society of Alberta*, [1989] 1 S.C.R. 591; *Basile v. Attorney-General of Nova Scotia*, [1984] 11 D.L.R. (4th) 219 (N.S.C.A.).

33. *R. v. Morgentaler*, [1988] 1 S.C.R. 30; *Borowski v. Canada (Attorney General)*, [1989] 1 S.C.R. 342; Mandel, *The Charter of Rights*, rev. ed., pp. 405–33; Mollie Dunsmuir, *Abortion: Constitutional and*

Legal Developments (Ottawa: Parliamentary Research Branch, Current Issue Review 89-10E, 1998); *Dobson (Litigation Guardian of) v. Dobson*, [1999] S.C.R. (July 9, 1999).

34. *Rodriguez v. British Columbia (Attorney General)*, [1993] 3 S.C.R. 519; Mollie Dunsmuir et al., *Euthanasia and Assisted Suicide* (Ottawa: Parliamentary Research Branch, Current Issue Review 91-9E, 1998).

35. *Operation Dismantle Inc. v. The Queen*, [1985] 1 S.C.R. 441; Mandel, *The Charter of Rights*, rev. ed., pp. 74–81.

36. *Singh v. Minister of Employment and Immigration*, [1985] 1 S.C.R. 177; *Re B.C. Motor Vehicle Act*, [1985] 2 S.C.R. 486; *R. v. Beare*, [1988] 2 S.C.R. 387; *R. v. Higgins*, [1988] 2 S.C.R. 387.

37. *R. v. Daviault*, [1994] 3 S.C.R. 63; *R. v. Seaboyer*, [1991] 2 S.C.R. 577; and *R. v. Ewanchuk*, [1999] 1 S.C.R. 330; Marilyn Pilon, *Life, Liberty and Security of the Person under the Charter* (Ottawa: Parliamentary Research Branch, Current Issue Review, 91-6E, 1998).

38. *Hunter v. Southam Inc.*, [1984] 2 S.C.R. 145; *R. v. Dyment*, [1988] 2 S.C.R. 417; *R. v. Simmons*, [1988] 2 S.C.R. 495; *R. v. Hufsky*, [1988] 1 S.C.R. 621; *R. v. Thomson*, [1988] 1 S.C.R. 640; *R. v. Ladouceur*, [1990] 1 S.C.R. 957; *Weatherall v. Canada (Attorney General)*, [1993] 2 S.C.R. 872.

39. *R. v. Feeney*, [1997] 2 S.C.R. 13; *R. v. Stillman*, [1997] 1 S.C.R. 607; *R. v. Godoy*, [1999] 1 S.C.R 311.

40. *R. v. Therens*, [1985] 1 S.C.R. 613; *R. v. Thomsen*, [1988] 1 S.C.R. 640; *Clarkson v. The Queen*, [1986] 1 S.C.R. 383; *R. v. Manninen*, [1987] 1 S.C.R. 1233; *R. v. Brydges*, [1990] 1 S.C.R. 190; *R. v. Burlingham*, [1995] 2 S.C.R. 206; *R. v. Evans*, [1991] 1 S.C.R. 869.

41. *R. v. Askov*, [1990] 2 S.C.R. 1199; *R. v. Rahey*, [1987] 1 S.C.R. 588.

42. *R. v. Oakes*, [1986] 1 S.C.R. 103; *R. v. Whyte*, [1988] 2 S.C.R. 3; *R. v. Holmes*, [1988] 1 S.C.R. 914; *R. v. Vermette*, [1988] 1 S.C.R. 985.

43. *R. v. Smith (Edward Dewey)*, [1987] 1 S.C.R. 1045; *R. v. Lyons*, [1987] 2 S.C.R. 309; *R. v. Milne*, [1987] 2 S.C.R. 512; *Kindler v. Canada (Minister of Justice)*, [1991] 2 S.C.R. 779.

44. *Andrews v. Law Society of British Columbia*, [1989] 1 S.C.R. 143; *R. v. Turpin*, [1989] 1 S.C.R. 1296; Mandel, *The Charter of Rights*, rev. ed., pp. 337–53; David Schneiderman and Kate Sutherland, eds., *Charting the Consequences: The Impact of Charter Rights on Canadian Law and Politics* (Toronto: University of Toronto Press, 1997), chs. 6, 7, 8, and 9; Bakan, *Just Words*.

45. Greene, *The Charter of Rights*, p. 172; Mary C. Hurley, *Charter Equality Rights: Interpretation of Section 15 in Supreme Court of Canada Decisions* (Ottawa: Parliamentary Research Branch, Background Paper BP-402E, 1998).

46. The Bill of Rights case was *Bliss v. A.-G. Can.*, [1979] S.C.R. 183; the Charter case that overturned it was *Brooks v. Canada Safeway Ltd.*, [1989] 1 S.C.R. 1219; the Supreme Court refused to review the Ontario Court of Appeal ruling in the *Blainey* case, which found that this was not a case of reasonable limits; *Egan v. Canada*, [1995] 2 S.C.R. 513; *McKinney v. University of Guelph*, [1990] 3 S.C.R. 229, where the Court said it would defer to legislatures in the area of mandatory retirement; *Vriend v. Alberta*, [1998] 1 S.C.R. 493; and *M v. H.*, [1999] S.C.R. (May 20, 1999).

47. *Jones v. A.G. New Brunswick*, [1975] 2 S.C.R. 182; *Attorney General of Quebec v. Blaikie*, [1979] 2 S.C.R. 1016; *A.G. Manitoba v. Forest*, [1979] 2 S.C.R. 1032; *Reference re Manitoba Language Rights*, [1985] 1 S.C.R. 721; *Order re Manitoba Language Rights*, [1985] 2 S.C.R. 347; *Bilodeau v. Attorney General Manitoba*, [1986] 1 S.C.R. 449; *Reference re Manitoba Language Rights*, [1992] 1 S.C.R. 272; Mandel, *The Charter of Rights*, rev. ed., ch. 3.

48. Kenneth McRoberts, *Misconceiving Canada: The Struggle for National Unity* (Toronto: Oxford University Press, 1997).

49. *Attorney General of Quebec v. Quebec Association of Protestant School Boards*, [1984] 2 S.C.R. 66; *Mahe v. Alberta*, [1990] 1 S.C.R. 342.

50. *R. v. Collins*, [1987] 1 S.C.R. 265.

51. *R. v. Sparrow*, [1990] 1 S.C.R. 1075; *R. v. Sioui*, [1990] 1 S.C.R. 1025; *Delgamuukw v. British Columbia*, [1997] 3 S.C.R. 1010; *Ontario (Attorney General) v. Bear Island Foundation*, [1991] 2 S.C.R. 570; *R. v. Marshall*, [1999] S.C.R. (September 17, 1999); Mandel, *The Charter of Rights*, rev. ed., pp. 353–69; Schneiderman and Sutherland, *Charting the Consequences*, ch. 5.

52. *Reference re Bill 30, An Act to Amend the Education Act (Ont.)*, [1987] 1 S.C.R. 1148. The Ontario Court of Appeal made greater use of this section than did the Supreme Court of Canada.

53. *RWDSU v. Dolphin Delivery Ltd.*, [1986] 2 S.C.R. 573; Mandel, *The Charter of Rights*, rev. ed., p. 283.

54. *McKinney v. University of Guelph*. But the *Lavigne* case treated community colleges as part of government; *Lavigne v. Ontario Public Service Employees Union*, [1991] 2 S.C.R. 211.

55. The *Blainey* case found that a clause in the Ontario Human Rights Code allowed discrimination against women in sports organizations, and since this was inconsistent with the Charter, it was held to be of no force or effect and was later repealed. This case demonstrates how the Charter can indirectly affect the private sector, as does the *Vriend* case.

56. The distinctive Quebec and Alberta approaches to the Charter are discussed in Schneiderman and Sutherland, *Charting the Consequences*, chs. 1 and 2; Rainer Knopff and F.L. Morton, *Charter Politics* (Scarborough: Nelson Canada, 1992).

57. Greene, *The Charter of Rights*, p. 107; Mandel, *The Charter of Rights*, pp. 87–96; David Johansen and Philip Rosen, *The Notwithstanding Clause of the Charter* (Ottawa: Parliamentary Research Branch, 1997).

58. Peter Russell, "The Political Purposes of the Canadian Charter of Rights and Freedoms," *Canadian Bar Review* (March 1983).

59. Marc Gold, "The Mask of Objectivity: Politics and Rhetoric in the Supreme Court of Canada," *The Supreme Court Law Review* 7 (1985), p. 458.

60. Andrew Heard, "The Charter in the Supreme Court of Canada: The Importance of Which Judges Hear an Appeal," *Canadian Journal of Political Science* (June 1991).

61. The Court repeatedly linked Quebec and Manitoba language cases, for example, to balance pro-French with pro-English cases, and backtracked on language rights after the Parti Québécois was safely out of power. Even more political were the Court decisions that paved the way for the adoption of the Charter in the Patriation Reference of 1981 and the Quebec Veto Reference of 1982. Marc Gold writes, for example, that "however much a judicial opinion may reflect how the court actually reached its decision, it is clear that the opinion should be viewed primarily as a portrayal of how the court wanted itself to be viewed in reaching that decision," "The Mask of Objectivity," p. 457.

62. Mandel, *The Charter of Rights*, rev. ed., p. 69.

63. Christopher Manfredi, "The Use of United States Decisions by the Supreme Court of Canada under the Charter of Rights and Freedoms," *Canadian Journal of Political Science* (September 1990), pp. 499–518.

64. Mandel, *The Charter of Rights*, rev. ed., p. 440; Bakan, *Just Words*.

65. York University Centre for Public Law and Public Policy, 1999, posted on the Canada Watch website (www.yorku.ca/robarts); Patrick Monahan and Michael J. Bryant, "The Supreme Court of Canada's 1996 Constitutional Cases: The End of Charter Activism?" *Canada Watch*, April 1997.

66. Schneiderman and Sutherland, *Charting the Consequences*, pp. 344–45.

67. Andrew Heard, "The Charter in the Supreme Court of Canada: The Importance of Which Judges Hear an Appeal," *Canadian Journal of Political Science* (June 1991).

68. Greene, *The Charter of Rights*, p. 176.

69. Mark Charlton and Paul Barker, eds., *Crosscurrents: Contemporary Political Issues*, 3rd ed. (Scarborough: Nelson Canada, 1998), ch. 15; Jacob S. Ziegel, *Merit Selection and Democratization of Appointments to the Supreme Court of Canada* (Montreal: Institute for Research on Public Policy, 1999).

70. Russell, "The Political Purposes of the Canadian Charter of Rights and Freedoms"; Schneiderman and Sutherland, *Charting the Consequences*, chs. 6–9; Miriam Smith, *Lesbian and Gay Rights in Canada: Social Movements and Equality-Seeking, 1971–1995* (Toronto: University of Toronto Press, 1999).

71. Robert Martin and Philip L. Bryden debate whether the Charter is undemocratic in Charlton and Barker, eds., *Crosscurrents*, 3rd ed.

72. Seymour Martin Lipset, *Continental Divide* (New York: Routlege, 1990).

73. F.L. Morton and Rainer Knopff, "The Charter Revolution and the Court Party," *Osgoode Hall Law Journal* (Fall 1992); Knopff and Morton, *Charter Politics*.

74. Schneiderman and Sutherland, *Charting the Consequences*, p. 346; chs. 3 and 4.

75. Ibid., p. 344.

76. Ontario Attorney General Roy McMurtry, one of the authors of the Charter, actually foresaw this possibility and referred to it in an address to a group of corporate lawyers in which he emphasized the value of the Charter for big business. He is now Chief Justice of Ontario. See Mandel, *The Charter of Rights*, rev. ed., pp. 168–69.

77. Ibid., p. 229.
78. Ibid., p. 301.
79. Quoted in ibid., p. 43.

FURTHER READING

Alvaro, Alexander. "Why Property Rights Were Excluded from the Canadian Charter of Rights and Freedoms." *Canadian Journal of Political Science* (June 1991).

Bakan, Joel. *Just Words: Constitutional Rights and Social Wrongs.* Toronto: University of Toronto Press, 1997.

Beatty, David. *Putting the Charter to Work.* Montreal: McGill–Queen's University Press, 1987.

Beaudoin, Gérald A., and Errol Mendes. *The Canadian Charter of Rights and Freedoms,* 3rd ed. Scarborough: Carswell, 1996.

Berger, Thomas. *Fragile Freedoms,* rev. and updated. Toronto: Clarke Irwin, 1982.

Borovoy, Alan. *When Freedoms Collide: The Case for Our Civil Liberties.* Toronto: Lester & Orpen Dennys, 1988.

Gold, Marc. "The Mask of Objectivity: Politics and Rhetoric in the Supreme Court of Canada." *The Supreme Court Law Review* 7 (1985).

Greene, Ian. *The Charter of Rights.* Toronto: Lorimer, 1989.

Heard, Andrew. "The Charter in the Supreme Court of Canada: The Importance of Which Judges Hear an Appeal." *Canadian Journal of Political Science* (June 1991).

Hiebert, Janet. "Fair Elections and Freedom of Expression under the Charter." *Journal of Canadian Studies* (Winter, 1989–90).

———. "The Evolution of the Limitation Clause." *Osgoode Hall Law Journal* (Spring 1990).

———. *Limiting Rights: The Dilemma of Judicial Review.* Montreal: McGill–Queen's University Press, 1996.

Hogg, Peter W. *Constitutional Law of Canada,* 1999 Student Edition. Toronto: Carswell, 1999.

Knopff, Rainer, and F.L. Morton. *Charter Politics.* Scarborough: Nelson Canada, 1992.

Mandel, Michael. *The Charter of Rights and the Legalization of Politics in Canada.* Toronto: Wall and Thompson, 1989; rev. ed., 1994.

Manfredi, Christopher. "The Use of United States Decisions by the Supreme Court of Canada under the Charter of Rights and Freedoms." *Canadian Journal of Political Science* (September 1990).

———. *Judicial Power and the Charter.* Toronto: McClelland & Stewart, 1993.

Meehan, Eugene, et al. *The 1999 Annotated Canadian Charter of Rights and Freedoms.* Scarborough: Carswell, 1998.

Morton, F.L. "The Political Impact of the Canadian Charter of Rights and Freedoms." *Canadian Journal of Political Science* (March 1987).

Morton, F.L., Peter Russell, and Michael Withey. "Judging the Judges: The Supreme Court's First One Hundred Charter Decisions." In Paul Fox and Graham White, eds., *Politics: Canada,* 7th ed. Toronto: McGraw-Hill Ryerson, 1991.

Romanow, Roy. "Shortcomings and Dangers in the Charter." *Canadian Parliamentary Review* (Spring 1986).

Russell, Peter. "The Effect of a Charter of Rights on the Policy-Making Role of Canadian Courts." *Canadian Public Administration* (Spring 1982).

———. "The Political Purposes of the Canadian Charter of Rights and Freedoms." *Canadian Bar Review* (March 1983).

Russell, Peter, Rainer Knopff, and Ted Morton, eds. *Federalism and the Charter.* Ottawa: Carleton University Press, 1989.

Schmeiser, D.A. *Civil Liberties in Canada.* London: Oxford University Press, 1964.

Schneiderman, David, and Kate Sutherland, eds. *Charting the Consequences: The Impact of Charter Rights on Canadian Law and Politics.* Toronto: University of Toronto Press, 1997.

Sharpe, Robert J., and Katherine E. Swinton. *The Charter of Rights and Freedoms.* Toronto: Irwin Law, 1998.

Smith, Miriam. *Lesbian and Gay Rights in Canada: Social Movements and Equality-Seeking, 1971–1995.* Toronto: University of Toronto Press, 1999.

Tarnopolsky, Walter. *The Canadian Bill of Rights,* 2nd, rev. ed. Toronto: McClelland and Stewart, 1975.

Tarnopolsky, Walter, and G.A. Beaudoin, eds. *The Canadian Charter of Rights and Freedoms: Commentary.* Toronto: Carswell, 1982.

PART 5

Governing

Having examined the societal and constitutional contexts of the political system and the means of linking people to government, we now begin to focus on the authorities themselves or what might be termed "governing." This section, therefore, examines the individual institutions of government in detail. These institutions are the executive, including the Crown, the prime minister and the Cabinet; the bureaucracy; Parliament, including the House of Commons and the Senate; and the judiciary. Although in one sense, all these institutions make up the government of Canada, students of politics should be aware that the prime minister and Cabinet are often referred to as the "government of the day." And although the PM and Cabinet ministers have seats in

"Parliament," that term is distinguished from the government by referring to all members of the House of Commons and Senate. The functions and operations of each branch of government are outlined, as are the kinds of outputs or authoritative decisions that each can make. Initially, however, Chapter 19 briefly discusses government in the new millennium and puts these institutions into the context of the policymaking process. It thus provides an overview of how these institutions interact with each other in order to produce public policies. It also outlines the array of policy instruments from which the authorities choose.

Chapter 19

Governing: The Policymaking PROCESS AND POLICY instruments

To many citizens, Ottawa is one big blur; it is "the government." Some people with a little more sophistication disparage "the politicians," "the bureaucrats," or "the judges," but without much knowledge of who is really responsible for the decisions about which they are complaining. While the institutions of government interact in many and mysterious ways, it is the job of political science to distinguish one from the other and to analyze how they operate individually and collectively.

The discussion of the individual institutions of government that follows in subsequent chapters will be more meaningful if they are first put in the context of government in the new millennium and of the policymaking process. This chapter provides an overview of that process, indicating in a general way how the various institutions interact with each other in the making of public policy. This is followed by an elaboration of the concept of policy communities, which was first broached in Chapter 15. The chapter ends with an overview of policy instruments, that is, the various devices among which the authorities choose to give effect to their decisions.

GOVERNMENT IN THE NEW MILLENNIUM[1]

Government was defined in Chapter 1 as the set of institutions that make and execute collective public decisions for a society. That chapter explained how most Canadians initially try to satisfy their needs and wants without government intervention—that is, in the private sector—but may eventually call for some kind of collective, public-sector action.

Until about 100 years ago, the role of government in society was very limited. But over the first 85 or so years of the 20th century, government operations expanded enormously. Most Canadians saw the government as an extension of themselves, and as long as it did not unduly interfere with their own efforts to get ahead, they welcomed its expansion.

Since about 1985, however, politicians, bureaucrats, the media, commentators, think tanks, and many citizens in all Western industrialized countries have said that we have too much government: too much government expenditure, too much taxation, too much regulation, and too much government debt. Governments of all ideological persuasions were consumed with balancing their budgets and downsizing and restructuring their operations in what constituted a new relationship between governments, markets, and civil society. There was a general consensus that "government over the past forty years has grown too big, absorbs too many resources, and is a drag on both economic performance and civic independence."[2] In principle, it was probably a valuable exercise to force politicians and bureaucrats to re-examine everything government was doing to see if it was really necessary or whether it could be done better in other ways. Unfortunately, the reality was that the poorest segment of society bore the greatest burden of this downsizing of government, which had many painful and devastating effects.

Figure 19.1 illustrates the decline in federal departmental spending between 1994–95 and 1998–99, the period in which the largest cuts were made.

Figure 19.1   Departmental Spending, 1998–1999 Relative to 1994–1995

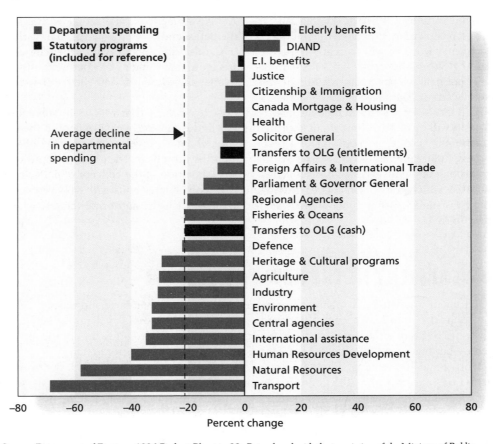

Source: Department of Finance, 1996 Budget Plan, *p. 38. Reproduced with the permission of the Minister of Public Works and Government Services Canada, 2000.*

At the start of the new century, the federal government's debt stood at $580 billion, while other governments' debts in Canada brought total public indebtedness to at least $750 billion. Some provinces have passed laws to prohibit adding to their debts, but it is unlikely that any governments will spend excessively in the future. For example, in order to cope with emergencies, most include contingency funds within their budgetary forecasts. Ottawa itself planned to spend about $160 billion per year, but over one-quarter of that was on interest on the previously accumulated debt. Although only 2.8 million people or roughly 20 percent of the labour force work in the public sector (including all levels of government), total government taxes are equivalent to about 37 percent of the gross domestic product (GDP), the total value of all production in the economy, and total government spending is about 44 percent of GDP, the difference now being made up by other government revenues.[3] Thus, even the downsized public sector is a force to be reckoned with. Now that governments are balancing their books on an annual basis, however, they began the new century in a more equable frame of mind, reacting prudently but positively to public needs that could not be met without their intervention.

THE POLICYMAKING PROCESS

Public policy can be defined as "a course of action or inaction chosen by public authorities to address a given problem or interrelated set of problems."[4] Leslie Pal adds that every policy has three key elements: the definition of the problem, the goals to be achieved, and the instruments chosen to address the problem and to achieve the goals.[5] In Chapter 1, a model of the whole political system was presented; it included such components as demands, support, outputs, feedback, the authorities, and the environment. Now imagine focusing in more detail on the authorities part of that model. The result would be an enlargement of that part of the system directly involved in the policymaking process and would look something like the model shown in Figure 19.2. Here, as in the model shown in Chapter 1, it should be emphasized that the process is circular, an ongoing process without a definable beginning or end, in which policies adopted at an earlier stage or in a different policy field or problems that develop in the implementation stage become the reasons behind the initiation of new demands on the state.

As the model suggests, the actual policymaking process can be divided into six phases: initiation, priority-setting, policy formulation, legitimation, implementation, and interpretation. Not all policies or decisions involve such an elaborate process including all the institutions of government; indeed, many can be made unilaterally by the prime minister, the Cabinet, a minister, the bureaucracy, or the courts. But the model shows the policymaking process in its broadest form, that is, a policy that requires the passage of a new law or an amendment to an existing law and that is later interpreted by the courts. Such a model does not necessarily imply that decision makers within each phase function with complete rationality; they may equally well act out of expediency or habit.

Initiation

The authorities are bombarded daily with hundreds of demands. These demands emanate from many different sources: the provinces, opposition parties, the media, pressure groups, lobbyists,

Figure 19.2   **The Canadian Policymaking Process**

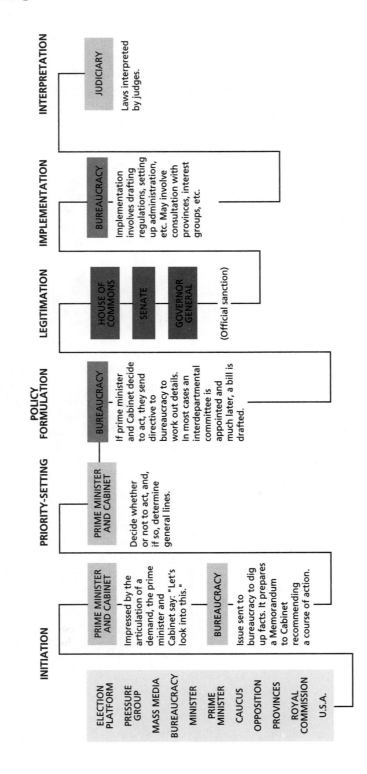

corporations, royal commissions, election promises, personal concerns of ministers or the prime minister, the government caucus, the bureaucracy, foreign countries (usually the United States), or other forces within the internal or external environments of the political system. The policymaking process is set in motion when the prime minister and Cabinet, frequently termed "the government," having been impressed with the articulation of a demand, decide to look into the matter further. On a smaller scale, a single minister may also make such a decision, although Donald J. Savoie tells us not to underestimate the extent to which ministers pursue initiatives recommended to them in "mandate letters" from the prime minister.[6] It is at this point that a "demand" is sometimes said to become an "issue." An issue, therefore, is a demand that has made it onto the public agenda and that is under serious consideration by the authorities. In such a case, the Cabinet ordinarily sends a directive to the bureaucracy that it wants more information on the matter.

Priority-Setting

The second phase of the policymaking process involves the prime minister and Cabinet again, this time in their priority-setting capacity. Responding to the Memorandum to Cabinet prepared by the public service and recommending a course of action, they decide which of the proposals they have selected for consideration are worthy of adoption. In other words, the prime minister and Cabinet (or on lesser issues an individual minister) must decide whether or not to take action on the issue, and if they decide to act, they must determine the general lines of the new initiative. At this point the Cabinet may also choose which policy instrument will be most appropriate to achieve their objective. Here a major constraint is the cost of the proposal, since almost all such proposals face fierce competition with others for the scarce financial resources available. If they are not sure about what course to follow, they may publish policy alternatives in "coloured papers" and make them available to the public. A "green paper," for example, consists of an early consideration of an issue, with little indication of the direction of government policy.[7]

Policy Formulation

The limited number of projects that have been given the green light by the Cabinet in the priority-setting phase then enter the policy formulation phase. Once it has approved a proposal in principle, the Cabinet usually sends another directive to the bureaucracy to work out the details. This is often a very time-consuming process that requires coordination among many federal government departments and may also involve consultation with provincial governments, interest groups, and others. Questions may be referred back to the Cabinet for further direction. At this stage on major, complex policy initiatives, the Cabinet sometimes issues a "white paper," which provides a clear indication of its intentions but still leaves room for public input with respect to details. Eventually another Memorandum to Cabinet is submitted, this one outlining the substance of policy.[8] If the proposal is approved and if it requires legislative action, the policy formulation stage culminates in a bill being drafted on the basis of the Memorandum to Cabinet. During this process, the minister will probably discuss the principles of the proposal with interested members of the government caucus.

Legitimation

The proposal then enters the legislative arena, that is, Parliament—the House of Commons and the Senate. The relevant minister may accept technical alterations to the bill as it proceeds through the House of Commons and the Senate, but the main intent or principle of the bill cannot be changed without going back for the Cabinet's approval. The legislative stage is referred to as legitimation because the bill is put under the scrutiny of all the democratically elected representatives of the people and made legitimate by their approval. The Cabinet and members of Parliament contribute political expertise to the process, but given the shortage of time and limited technical expertise characteristic of the legislative branch, most such bills are passed in "skeletal" form; that is, a statute usually contains only the general principles or objectives that the authorities wish to achieve, and the act delegates authority to the relevant minister, on the advice of the bureaucracy, to issue regulations to flesh it out later in the process. The legitimation stage ends with the token approval of the governor general, which is the sign that the policy has been officially sanctioned.

Implementation

Royal assent is by no means the end of the policymaking process. Few laws attain any significance just by sitting on the statute books; they must be implemented in order to be made effective. Implementation almost always involves the drafting of detailed **regulations** by the bureaucracy, to add meat to the skeleton of the statute. Even though they have the same legal standing as if they were part of the enabling statute itself, the regulations that a law authorizes the executive to make are given only slight scrutiny by either ministers or Parliament, and thus are almost the exclusive preserve of the bureaucracy. Implementation normally requires the setting up of new administrative machinery—new staff, new agencies, new field offices, and new operational manuals, among other things. It is therefore not surprising that most legislation does not automatically take effect upon royal assent; it is not "proclaimed" or made operational until the government is ready to implement it.

Interpretation

The policymaking process may well end, at least for the time being, with the implementation phase. But if new legislation is involved, it is often subject to judicial interpretation. Its constitutionality may even be challenged in the courts, especially if it appears to violate the Charter of Rights and Freedoms in any way. Thus, especially since 1982, it is appropriate to add a sixth phase to the policymaking process, that of judicial interpretation. Judges always had an impact on a law by means of how they interpreted it, but if a statute is actually challenged in the courts, the judiciary must decide whether its provisions are contrary to the Charter or to the division of powers between federal and provincial governments.

POLICY COMMUNITIES REVISITED

Although this section of the book focuses on the operation of the authoritative policymaking institutions, it must be emphasized that they operate within a never-ending "political" environment. Indeed, if various interests know that the authorities have a problem under active consideration, they usually step up their attempts to influence the course of authoritative decision making. Moreover, policymakers are finding it increasingly advantageous if not necessary to consult and even to develop partnerships with relevant organized interests.[9] It is in this context that the concept of **policy communities** should be mentioned again.[10]

While Figure 19.2 provides a framework in which to understand the policymaking process and the interaction of various government institutions in general, it must be emphasized that distinctive policy communities, participants, and processes are involved in different fields. Power is dispersed in many directions, and different politicians, bureaucrats, interest groups, and individuals participate in different sectors of public policy. The prime minister, Cabinet, and central policy structures are at the core of the whole process regardless of subject matter, but each policy community has its own "lead government agency," normally a department or section of a department of government: Health for health policy, Fisheries and Oceans for fisheries policy, and so on.

Each lead agency is surrounded by associated Crown corporations and regulatory agencies, such as the CBC and CRTC operating at arm's length from the Canadian Heritage department, or the Canadian Transportation Agency and VIA Rail, which are linked to Transport. Still within the "subgovernment" circle are the major pressure groups, lobbyists, and corporations, provincial governments, and parliamentary committees interested in respective policy fields. The wider "attentive public" consists of other pressure groups, other provincial governments, and other parliamentarians, corporations, and individuals interested in a particular policy field but who are not part of the inner circle.[11]

Thus, in the initiation stage of the policymaking process, demands primarily arise from the responsible minister, lead agency officials, associated government agencies, pressure groups, lobbyists, and corporations, and interested parliamentarians within each distinctive policy community. When a minister or the Cabinet seeks advice on whether or not to take action on a particular problem, they refer the problem to the lead agency in each field.

In the priority-setting phase, it may only take a single minister to make the decision to go forward. But on controversial issues or policies involving major expenditures, decisions are taken out of the specialized policy community and made subject to the critical review and/or veto of Cabinet committees or the Cabinet as a whole, acting on the advice of such central agencies as the Department of Finance, Treasury Board, or the Privy Council Office.

Once a policy initiative has survived the priority-setting barrier, however, the minister or Cabinet refers the matter back to the lead agency to coordinate the efforts involved in policy formulation. An interdepartmental committee representing every government agency with an interest in the policy is usually appointed at this stage, and, as mentioned, if pressure groups, lobbyists, and interested corporations are aware that a new policy is under consideration, they will do their best to get involved. Pressure groups, provincial governments, or other interested actors may be formally consulted in this phase of the process, especially because governments nowadays have fewer resources with which to analyze alternatives on their own, but in any case, the officials in the lead agency are sure to be conscious of the views of their "attentive public" and take its past representations and anticipated reaction into account. Moreover, before the minister or Cabinet gives final approval to a new policy or bill, these officials will likely have been subject to further pressure from within the policy community.

When legislation is required to implement the policy, the legitimation phase is dominated by those parliamentarians with a particular interest in the subject. This phase also attracts the attention of the major pressure groups, the key provincial governments, and the individuals within the general public who are part of the specialized policy community. If a bill goes to a parliamentary committee, for example, the committee is made up of interested MPs, before whom specialized bureaucrats, pressure groups, and other experts make representations.

Again at the next phase, the lead agency is primarily responsible for implementing the policy. But it often does so in close consultation with the pressure groups and provincial governments most intimately involved. They may be asked, for example, to comment on the first draft of the regulations. It is especially at this level that new partnerships are being formed between the lead agency and the most relevant private-sector actors. Reductions in government funding, for example, may leave departments little choice other than to bring such groups into the implementation process.

Finally, if the legislation is challenged in court, the challenger is usually a corporation, pressure group, provincial government, or individual member of the "attentive public" whose views are not consistent with the final version of the policy. The government defends its legislation on the advice of the lead agency and the Department of Justice.

This discussion thus indicates that while a fairly uniform process exists for the making of Canadian public policy, regardless of subject matter, the specific individuals, corporations, groups, and lead agencies involved vary to a large extent from one policy field to another. Such key players in each distinctive policy community are often referred to as **stakeholders**.

By Peter Zazulak (The Hill Times). *Reproduced with permission.*

POLICY INSTRUMENTS

Once the authorities take notice of a problem, they must choose the means of addressing the issue. The specific techniques or devices chosen are often called **policy instruments**. Except for an explicit decision *not* to act, such instruments constitute government intervention in the private sector of society and are commonly categorized according to the degree of intervention, intrusiveness, or coerciveness they represent.[12] Nicolas Baxter-Moore includes nine stages of intervention in his discussion of the subject, while other authorities present slightly different categorizations of such instruments. These nine policy instruments are outlined below.

Privatization of Conflict

The full range of policy instruments theoretically encompasses the decision to take no action at all. It is very common for the government to decide to leave the problem to be handled entirely by the forces of the private sector. Baxter-Moore refers to such public inaction as the "privatization of conflict" and points out that it can assume two forms: The government can either completely ignore the problem or explicitly decide to refer the question to some private-sector authority. An example of the latter would be the self-regulation of professional bodies such as medical and legal associations.[13] Due to the changed philosophy of government of the past 15 or 20 years, governments have made increasing use of this policy instrument. They have decided to ignore a greater proportion of demands than previously and even vacated many areas of former public activity in favour of leaving issues to be dealt with by private market forces.

Symbolic Response

The second policy instrument is the symbolic response. This can take the form of a statement of government concern, consultation with those raising the problem, passive dissemination of information, appointment of a task force or Royal Commission, or setting up of a new government department. All of these, at least in the short run, are substitutes for any substantive government action. It is commonly held, for example, that a Royal Commission is appointed to take the heat off the government in connection with some problematic situation in the hope that by the time the commission's report is published, the problem will have evaporated. Since this instrument is also consistent with the new philosophy of downsizing government, it is even more popular than before.

Exhortation

The third degree of intervention is often called exhortation. This instrument goes one step further than the symbolic response because in this case the government urges the public to change its behaviour in some way. Exhortation uses persuasion in an attempt to secure voluntary compliance with government objectives without recourse to threats or rewards. "Participaction" commercials are one example, while others are pleas to restrain wage demands or to conserve the use of water or electricity (without any accompanying rate increases or regulations), or promotion of "blue box" programs or the use of condoms. Because of its need to change public attitudes in order to accept major policy shifts, especially the FTA and GST in the 1980s, and to highlight equity and lifestyle policy concerns, the federal government became the country's largest advertiser. But in the new governance environment since then, information-based instruments have become even more important.[14]

Tax Expenditures

Tax expenditures are the fourth category of policy instrument. These consist of tax credits and tax deductions that individuals or companies can claim by spending money in certain ways: contributing to political parties, making certain kinds of investments, donating to charities, and so on. A catalogue of such tax concessions fills an annual government document 150 pages long![15] Tax expenditures do not actually involve taxing or spending by government; rather, they are tax-based incentives to use individual or corporate income in particular ways. While they cost the government money that it would otherwise receive in tax revenues, tax expenditures are widely used because they are basically invisible and do not attract much criticism; they neither *seem* to cost any money nor involve any sort of coercion. While tax expenditures are generally the most popular policy instrument of all, as corporations and individuals vigorously seek them out in order to reduce their taxes, it should be added that they do come at a cost. They result in less revenue for government to use for redistributive programs and/or higher taxes paid by those who are unaware of or do not qualify for such tax credits, especially lower-income individuals.

Public Expenditures

The fifth policy instrument, one that is much more obvious, is public expenditures. Unlike tax expenditures, public spending involves the actual disbursement of funds acquired and controlled by the state. The size of modern government budgets is an indication of how frequently the authorities have tried to solve problems by spending public money. The instrument of public expenditure has many subcategories; governments provide transfer payments to individuals, such as in employment insurance, old age security, and social assistance programs; the federal government advances money to the provinces for health care, postsecondary education, and many other purposes; governments subsidize farmers, fishers, painters, and orchestras, and give contracts, grants, loans, and loan guarantees to corporations. The "spending power" of the federal government—that is, its right to spend money for any purpose it chooses—was discussed in Chapter 17. The government also engages in public expenditure in the provision of public services—helping the unemployed fine jobs, defending the country, or engaging in research. In this age of retrenchment, of course, governments avoid this policy instrument, and have reduced their expenditures and services quite dramatically, as demonstrated in Figure 19.1.

Regulation

Government becomes more intrusive still when it chooses the instrument of regulation.[16] Almost every aspect of our lives is now regulated by government, although we may not always be aware of it. Minimum wage laws; highway speed limits; restaurant and elevator inspections;

gradations of eggs; building codes; consumer product safety; rent controls; pollution emissions; hunting, fishing, driver, and liquor licences; store hours; seat belts; Canadian content on radio and television; telephone rates; and bilingual labelling are examples that just scratch the surface.

Government regulation interferes with individual or corporate freedom more than any instrument listed previously and is therefore more frequently criticized. But such regulations were obviously considered necessary by one government or another in order to promote some greater public purpose, such as public health, safety, or order; Canadianization; bilingualism; or protection from corporate exploitation. Many of these regulatory functions have been delegated to semi-independent regulatory agencies such as the CRTC, marketing boards, provincial rent control tribunals, or liquor licensing boards rather than to regular government departments. Such agencies are discussed in more detail in Chapter 21. Ordinarily, governments with less money to spend rely more heavily on the instrument of regulation. But in the neoconservatism of recent Canadian politics, the corporate sector in particular has pressed for a pulling back of government in this area, too, resulting in a large amount of **deregulation**. International trade agreements have also constrained the use of regulatory instruments.[17]

Taxation

Taxation, the seventh type of policy instrument, is generally considered even more intrusive than regulation because, while it also has the effect of constraining behaviour, it actually takes something away from the individuals or corporations on whom it is imposed.[18] Previous chapters have provided some indication of the number and kinds of taxes levied by both federal and provincial governments. Personal and corporate income and general sales taxes are used by both levels of government, to say nothing of excise taxes; special taxes on alcohol, tobacco, amusement, and gasoline; natural resource levies; health insurance premiums; payroll taxes; and the property taxes used by municipal governments. Just as in the case of regulation, however, many people are not conscious of all the taxes they pay. Thus, the relative extent of the intrusiveness of taxation is somewhat subjective, depending on the awareness of and degree of constraint imposed by various taxes, as well as on the level of consciousness of and support for the public programs they are used to finance. The public became aroused over the very visible GST, for example, even though it largely replaced the invisible manufacturers' sales tax.

In the new governance environment, governments have primarily balanced their budgets by reducing expenditures rather than increasing their taxes, as outlined in Chapter 8. Indeed, as soon as a balanced budget is in sight, there are demands for tax cuts, and cuts rather than increases are now on the public agenda. On the other hand, "various charges and fees for special benefits and services are, if anything, growing in use."[19] Besides user fees imposed on many social services in recent years, tolls on certain highways are also becoming more common.

Public Ownership

The eighth policy instrument is **public ownership**, typically taking the form of a Crown corporation. Governments routinely regulate and tax private companies, of course, but to "nationalize" them—to take them into public ownership or to create Crown corporations—obviously represents a greater degree of government intervention. At both federal and provincial levels, the "collectivist" streak in the Canadian political culture has given rise to the existence of a large number of important state enterprises, including the Canadian Broadcasting Corporation, the Canada Mortgage and Housing Corporation, the Bank of Canada, the Farm Credit Corporation, Atomic Energy of Canada Ltd., the Cape Breton Development Corporation, and electric power corporations in most of the provinces. Governments usually resort to public enterprise only as a last resort, however, when taxation and regulation fail to meet their objectives.[20] In the wave of neoconservatism that swept the country in the late 1980s and 1990s, the Mulroney and Chrétien governments "privatized" several Crown corporations, including Air Canada and Canadian National, putting such organizations (back) into the private sector **(privatization)**. Several provincial governments also privatized some of their Crown corporations.

State of Emergency

Baxter-Moore completes his catalogue of policy instruments with the **state of emergency**. In a situation of natural disasters, domestic insurrection, or external military threat, governments can usually invoke emergency powers. These powers give special coercive functions to the police and/or military to assist the government in achieving its policy objectives. The use of the **War Measures Act** in the First and Second World Wars is the best Canadian example. Prime Minister Trudeau invoked the War Measures Act again in 1970 to deal with the FLQ crisis. Armed forces personnel suddenly appeared on the streets of Ottawa and Montreal, the police were given extraordinary powers, and certain civil liberties were suspended. Acknowledgment that the War Measures Act was inappropriate in these circumstances led to the creation of a less coercive Emergencies Act in 1988. Happily, the state of emergency is used less than any other policy instrument in Canada, although the armed forces have been called upon to help out in recent natural disasters such as severe flooding in Manitoba, the ice storm in central Canada and New Brunswick, and a heavy snowfall in Toronto.

··

CONCLUSION

This discussion of the policymaking process and policy instruments is of necessity superficial. It does, however, provide a framework on which to hang the remaining chapters of the book, which deal in greater detail with the individual institutions of government, and it introduces the reader to the range of devices available to a government in order to achieve its objectives.

PC In terms of the approaches outlined in Chapter 1, public choice theory argues that in the initiation and priority-setting phases the Cabinet will choose to look into and then act on those issues that provide benefits to marginal voters. In choosing policy instruments, the authorities will similarly be guided by the anticipated reaction of these same marginal groups.[21]

SC The state-centred approach contends that the policymaking process functions without significant input from society as a whole. The initiation phase is dominated by demands from politicians and bureaucrats themselves, and the authorities define as "issues" only those demands that are of interest to them. Most of the other phases of the policymaking process are carried out behind closed doors by bureaucrats and politicians, and when their actions are unveiled to the public in the legitimation phase, members of Parliament must toe the party line and are not allowed to respond to the demands of their constituencies. State-centred theorists also emphasize that the bureaucracy is present in more phases of the policymaking process than any other institution of government.

C The class analysis model assumes that whatever the formal phases of the policymaking process, the political system ultimately responds to the demands of the bourgeoisie or corporate elite. This school of analysis emphasizes the connections between the state and corporate elites and, while discovering much evidence of such linkage, adds that "the economically powerful have not had to seek political office directly [for] their interests are usually served by those who are already there."[22]

Class analysis finds that the political, bureaucratic, and corporate elites share many characteristics and values.[23] At least until recently, the Cabinet, higher public service, and pressure group leadership was made up of men who had family, corporate, educational, geographic, and/or social ties.[24] Even today, the *wife* of the president of the most powerful business group, the Business Council on National Issues, is the assistant deputy minister of the equally powerful department of Finance.

Class analysts also have the most to say about the choice of policy instruments. They divide policy outputs between those that facilitate the accumulation of capital for the bourgeoisie, those that encourage the legitimation of the capitalist system by promoting social harmony, and those that provide for coercion if accumulation is seriously threatened by proletarian elements. Such analysts also distinguish between the transparency, intrusiveness, and coerciveness of various policy instruments in terms of the classes to whom they are applied.[25] The state will often disguise its activities on behalf of capital accumulation, using less visible instruments, while it will employ more obvious instruments when it seeks to legitimize its rule. The state will use less intrusive instruments against dominant-class interests (e.g., tax expenditures) and more intrusive policies against subordinate classes or groups (e.g., taxation). On the other hand, it will respond to corporate demands for government assistance with public expenditures, while it will offer only symbolic responses to working-class demands. Finally, if the state must take action against dominant-class interests, it will not attach significant coercive penalties to such instruments, but it tends "to enforce all instruments more coercively when they are targeted at labour and other subordinate groups."[26] In this instance, the small fines handed out to corporate polluters can be contrasted with the "heavier financial penalties for unions involved in unofficial strikes ... and heavy police presence at sites of labour unrest."[27] Class analysts would take exception to the widespread consensus in recent years that "if possible, [government] policy should depend on market mechanisms and individual choice, and minimize spending and regulation."[28]

DISCUSSION QUESTIONS

1. How much has the environment of governance changed since 1985? Why?

2. Do all demands have an equal chance of coming to the attention of the prime minister and Cabinet? Explain.

3. To what extent do the social background characteristics of the prime minister and Cabinet ministers skew their choice of issues? To what extent are electoral considerations dominant in their choice?

4. Do you agree with the sequence of policy instruments outlined in the continuum of degree of government intrusiveness?

5. Do you agree with the class analysis view that the degree of intrusiveness and coerciveness of policy instruments varies according to the class that is subject to the intervention?

6. How do the other approaches outlined in Chapter 1 enhance our understanding of the subjects addressed in this chapter?

NOTES

1. John C. Strick, *The Public Sector in Canada: Programs, Finance and Policy* (Toronto: Thompson Books, 1999).
2. Leslie A. Pal, *Beyond Policy Analysis: Public Issue Management in Turbulent Times* (Scarborough: ITP Nelson, 1997), pp. 55–56.
3. Karin Treff and David B. Perry, *1998 Finances of the Nation* (Toronto: Canadian Tax Foundation, 1998).
4. Pal, *Beyond Policy Analysis*, p. 2.
5. Ibid., p. 5.
6. Donald J. Savoie, *Governing from the Centre: The Concentration of Power in Canadian Politics* (Toronto: University of Toronto Press, 1999), pp. 137–38, 324, 343.
7. Kenneth Kernaghan and David Siegel, *Public Administration in Canada: A Text*, 2nd ed. (Scarborough: Nelson Canada, 1991; 3rd ed., 1995), pp. 128–30.
8. Department of Justice, *The Federal Legislative Process in Canada* (Ottawa: Supply and Services, 1987).
9. Pal, *Beyond Policy Analysis*, ch. 6.
10. This concept, based on Paul Pross's *Group Politics and Public Policy* (Toronto: Oxford University Press, 1986), especially ch. 6, was first discussed in this book in Chapter 15. See also William Coleman and Grace Skogstad, *Policy Communities and Public Policy in Canada* (Mississauga: Copp Clark Pitman, 1990).
11. For a discussion of the social policy community, see A.R. Dobell and S.H. Mansbridge, *The Social Policy Process in Canada* (Montreal: Institute for Research on Public Policy, 1986). Coleman and Skogstad outline this policy community as well as several others.
12. Nicolas Baxter-Moore, "Policy Implementation and the Role of the State," in Robert Jackson et al., eds., *Contemporary Canadian Politics: Readings and Notes* (Scarborough: Prentice-Hall Canada, 1987).
13. Ibid., p. 340. This example was mentioned in Chapter 15 as one objective of professional pressure groups. Some authorities, however, prefer to put self-regulation in the regulation category.
14. Pal, *Beyond Policy Analysis*, p. 123.
15. Department of Finance, *Tax Expenditures*, cat. no. FI-27/1998E (Ottawa, 1998).
16. John C. Strick, *The Economics of Government Regulation: Theory and Canadian Practice*, 2nd ed. (Toronto: Thompson Books, 1993).

17. Pal, *Beyond Policy Analysis,* pp. 116–21.
18. There is some disagreement about these points in the literature; sometimes regulation is considered more intrusive than taxation, and at other times taxation is treated as a type of regulation.
19. Pal, *Beyond Policy Analysis,* p. 122.
20. Allan Tupper and Bruce Doern, *Public Corporations and Public Policy in Canada* (Montreal: Institute for Research on Public Policy, 1981).
21. See the more recent perspectives on this subject in M.J. Trebilcock, *The Prospects for Reinventing Government* (Toronto: C.D. Howe Institute, 1994).
22. Dennis Olsen, *The State Elite* (Toronto: McClelland and Stewart, 1980), p. 21; Wallace Clement, *The Canadian Corporate Elite: An Analysis of Economic Power* (Toronto: McClelland and Stewart, Carleton Library, 1975).
23. Clement, *The Canadian Corporate Elite,* p. 258; Robert Presthus, *Elite Accommodation in Canada* (Toronto: Macmillan, 1973); Rodney Haddow, *Poverty Reform in Canada 1958–1978: State and Class Influence on Policy Making* (Montreal: McGill–Queen's University Press, 1993).
24. See, for example, John Porter, *The Vertical Mosaic* (Toronto: University of Toronto Press, 1965); Rick Helmes-Hayes and James Curtis, eds., *The Vertical Mosaic Revisited* (Toronto: University of Toronto Press, 1998).
25. Baxter-Moore, "Policy Implementation and the Role of the State," pp. 346–48.
26. Ibid.
27. Ibid.
28. Pal, *Beyond Policy Analysis,* p. 128.

. . . .

FURTHER READING

Baxter-Moore, Nicolas. "Policy Implementation and the Role of the State: A Revised Approach to the Study of Policy Instruments." In Robert Jackson et al., eds., *Contemporary Canadian Politics: Readings and Notes.* Scarborough: Prentice-Hall Canada, 1987.

Brooks, Stephen. *Public Policy in Canada: An Introduction,* 2nd ed. Toronto: McClelland and Stewart, 1993; 3rd ed., 1998.

Department of Justice. *The Federal Legislative Process in Canada.* Ottawa: Supply and Services, 1987.

Dobell, A.R., and S.H. Mansbridge. *The Social Policy Process in Canada.* Montreal: Institute for Research on Public Policy, 1986.

Doern, G. Bruce, and Richard Phidd. *Canadian Public Policy: Ideas, Structure, Process,* 2nd ed. Toronto: Nelson Canada, 1992.

Haddow, Rodney. *Poverty Reform in Canada 1958–1978: State and Class Influence on Policy Making.* Montreal: McGill–Queen's University Press, 1993.

Helmes-Hayes, Rick, and James Curtis, eds. *The Vertical Mosaic Revisited.* Toronto: University of Toronto Press, 1998.

Kernaghan, Kenneth, and David Siegel. *Public Administration in Canada: A Text,* 3rd ed. Scarborough: Nelson Canada, 1995; 4th ed., 1999.

Olsen, Dennis. *The State Elite.* Toronto: McClelland and Stewart, 1980.

Pal, Leslie A. *Public Policy Analysis: An Introduction,* 2nd ed. Scarborough: Nelson Canada, 1992.

———. *Beyond Policy Analysis: Public Issue Management in Turbulent Times.* Scarborough: ITP Nelson, 1997.

Porter, John. *The Vertical Mosaic.* Toronto: University of Toronto Press, 1965.

Presthus, Robert. *Elite Accommodation in Canada.* Toronto: Macmillan, 1973.

Pross, Paul. *Group Politics and Public Policy.* Toronto: Oxford University Press, 1986.

Savoie, Donald J. *Governing from the Centre: The Concentration of Power in Canadian Politics.* Toronto: University of Toronto Press, 1999.

Stanbury, W.T. *Business–Government Relations in Canada.* Toronto: Methuen, 1986.

Strick, John C. *The Public Sector in Canada: Programs, Finance and Policy*. Toronto: Thompson Books, 1999.

Trebilcock, M.J. *The Prospects for Reinventing Government*. Toronto: C.D. Howe Institute, 1994.

Trebilcock, M.J., et al. *The Choice of Governing Instrument*. Ottawa: Economic Council of Canada, 1982.

Treff, Karin, and David B. Perry. *1998 Finances of the Nation*. Toronto: Canadian Tax Foundation, 1998.

Tupper, Allan, and Bruce Doern. *Public Corporations and Public Policy in Canada*. Montreal: Institute for Research on Public Policy, 1981.

Chapter 20

The Executive: Crown
PRIME MINISTER,
and cabinet

When the Queen visits Canada, she is often mistakenly referred to as Queen of England rather than Queen of Canada. Some Canadians are very attached to the monarchy, but others cannot understand what all the fuss is about. On the political front, few events in Ottawa match the suspense and speculation of the naming of a new Cabinet or a major Cabinet shuffle. Almost every member of Parliament aspires to become a Cabinet minister someday, and many ministers hope to become prime minister. These positions offer many perks and much prestige, the possibility of influencing the shape of public policy, and the opportunity to do favours for one's constituency, province, and friends.

As seen in Chapter 19, the prime minister and Cabinet are active in many phases of the Canadian policymaking process. Their decisions will sometimes be overturned by the courts and occasionally even by Parliament, and are usually based to a considerable extent on advice from the bureaucracy. But in the end, the prime minister and Cabinet do make and are responsible for making the biggest political decisions in the country. This chapter begins with a discussion of the Crown, including the monarch and governor general, and then examines the political executive, the prime minister and Cabinet.

THE CROWN

To classify Canada as a **constitutional monarchy** means that it is a democracy headed by a king or queen. In other words, the Queen is the Canadian head of state, but she reigns according to the Constitution. Canada is also said to have "dual executive"—the formal and largely symbolic executive powers are given to the Queen, but the effective executive is made up of the prime minister and Cabinet.

The concept of the **Crown** revolves around the head of state and can be defined as the collectivity of executive powers exercised by or in the name of the monarch. Although the Crown was not mentioned as performing any of the basic functions of government in Chapter 1, rule making, application, and adjudication are often performed in the name of the Queen or governor general.[1] On the other hand, the Crown does perform useful functions in the Canadian political system that are largely of a symbolic and ceremonial nature.

The Crown is not only the collectivity of executive powers; it also represents the entire state and embodies what belongs to the people collectively. This can be seen in Crown corporations (state-owned corporations) or Crown lands (state-owned lands). The Crown is also central to the legal system: Crown attorneys, those who prosecute crimes on behalf of society; court cases initiated in the name of the Queen referred to as *R.* (for *Regina*) *v. John Doe* or court cases against the government (*Smith v. The Queen*); branches of the judiciary called the Court of Queen's Bench; and lawyers awarded the title of Queen's Counsel (QC). The term "royal" is also widely used in Canada to refer to institutions that function for the advantage of all in the name of the Queen: the Royal Canadian Mint; royal commissions, which investigate problems for the general good; and the Royal Canadian Mounted Police, whose job is to capture violators of society's laws. Three important aspects of Parliament also reflect the existence of the monarchical system: Royal Assent, the speech from the throne, and Her Majesty's Loyal Opposition. "Loyal Opposition" demonstrates that criticism of the government has been legitimized and institutionalized in the name of the Queen.

The concept of the Crown is not widely understood by Canadians, and as David Smith writes, it is largely "invisible" to them. For example, since the Queen represents the whole state and its people, oaths of allegiance to the Queen are really pledges of support for the Canadian political system, and "God Save the Queen" really means "God help us to govern ourselves."[2] Putting the Queen's picture on stamps or coins, in classrooms or courtrooms, is not to glorify her personally, but to recognize her as a unifying symbol of the state. Similarly, in speaking of the powers of the Crown, it is best to see them as being in the possession of the Queen but exercised by the prime minister and Cabinet. The monarch "holds the powers on behalf of the people," as a custodian or trustee. She does not use them, but her presence keeps those who do wield them from becoming too powerful or irresponsible. It is an elegant fiction that the government of the day advises the Crown on the use of such powers. The Crown also "acts as the repository for the decorative and emotional functions which are inevitable in any state."[3] It is probably beneficial to divert favourable popular feelings to the harmless head of state because politicians might abuse such popularity. Another misconception is that the adoption of the Constitution Act, 1982, affected Canada's relationship with the Queen. That act allowed Canada to amend its own Constitution, but it left the Queen in place as the Canadian head of state.

The Governor General

The Queen of Canada, Elizabeth II, is also Queen of other countries, and normally resides in London, England. That means that she needs a local representative in Canada, the governor general, who may perform any of her functions and exercise any of her powers in her absence. Until 1926 the governor was a double agent: besides being the representative of the Queen, he was an agent of the British government, and as long as Canada was a British colony, the governor general exercised authority over Canada on behalf of the British Cabinet. Today, the governor general is only the personal representative of the Queen and has no connection whatsoever to the British government. The Canadian prime minister actually chooses the governor general, who serves a term of approximately five years. Surprisingly, even though the Canadian government has made the selection since 1926, it continued to appoint British governors general until 1952, when Vincent Massey became the first Canadian-born person to hold the post. Since then, as indicated in Table 20.1, Canada has alternated anglophone and francophone appointments.

TABLE 20.1 **Governors General since 1952**

Vincent Massey	1952–59
Georges Vanier	1959–67
Roland Michener	1967–74
Jules Léger	1974–79
Edward Schreyer	1979–84
Jeanne Sauvé	1984–90
Ramon Hnatyshyn	1990–95
Romeo Leblanc	1995–99
Adrienne Clarkson	1999–

Sources of the Crown's Powers

The Queen of Canada and governor general derive their powers, all of which are exercised according to firmly established constitutional conventions, from three main sources: the Constitution Act, 1867, the Letters Patent, and the royal prerogative. Section 9 of the 1867 act declared that the "Executive Government and Authority of and over Canada is ... vested in the Queen," and section 15 made her Commander-in-Chief of Canada's military forces. Among the powers given explicitly to the Queen was the one to appoint extra senators, as was done by Brian Mulroney in 1990, although this must be done on the recommendation of the governor general. The 1867 act gave the governor general the power to appoint other senators and judges, to appoint the Speaker of the Senate, to give royal assent to legislation, and to recommend money bills to the House of Commons. In addition, it referred to the governor's power to summon and dissolve Parliament. The governor in council, meaning the Cabinet operating in the name of the Crown, was given the power to appoint lieutenant governors and other officers. In fact, the act was somewhat sloppy in not carefully distinguishing between the governor general and the governor in council, which suggests that even as early as 1867 the governor was normally expected to act on the advice of the Cabinet.

The Letters Patent is an obscure document that creates the office of governor general and accords it additional authority.[4] The Letters Patent confer upon the governor general all powers of the monarchy with respect to Canada, including the title of Commander-in-Chief, the power to appoint and remove ministers and judges, to summon, prorogue, and dissolve Parliament, and the power of pardon.

The royal prerogative or **prerogative powers** involve the residual authority of the Crown, which remains from the days when the monarch was almost absolute. These are customary, unwritten powers, although some of them, such as the right to summon and dissolve Parliament, are mentioned in the Constitution Act, 1867, and in the Letters Patent. Being unwritten, the prerogative powers are vulnerable to parliamentary restriction. Many such powers have been taken away and given to the prime minister and Cabinet—such as the power to negotiate treaties, to declare war and peace, and to appoint ambassadors—and those that remain could be removed if Parliament chose to do so.

Discretionary Powers of the Crown

Despite the impressive theoretical list of powers possessed by the Queen and governor general, there is no doubt that in a democratic age almost all of them must be exercised on the advice of the government—the prime minister and Cabinet—of the day. It would be totally uncon-stitutional, for example, for the governor to refuse to give assent to any piece of legislation. The Queen retains a minimal right to decide on certain honours herself, primarily within Britain, but the governor general was stripped of this power in the early years of this century. Canada created its own set of honours in 1967, the Order of Canada, and while such honours are pre-sented by the governor general, they are decided upon by a nonpartisan committee consisting of the Chief Justice of Canada, the Clerk of the Privy Council, the Undersecretary of State, the Chair of the Canada Council of the Arts, the President of the Royal Society of Canada, and the President of the Association of Universities and Colleges of Canada.

The most important prerogative power of the governor general is the appointment of the prime minister, but this must be performed on the basis of constitutional convention. In ensuring that the office of prime minister is never vacant, the governor general normally relies on the operation of political parties and elections, and does not have far to look. On two occasions in the 1890s, however, the governor had to help find a person to be prime min-ister. This action was necessitated by the sudden death of John A. Macdonald in 1891 and then of John Thompson in 1894, for in both cases the Conservative Party did not possess an obvious successor. Political parties are better organized today, and prefer to choose their own leader. Thus, if the position should suddenly become vacant, such as through the death of the prime minister, the Cabinet and/or government caucus would usually name an acting leader pending a leadership convention.

The two most controversial acts of Canadian governors general took place in 1896 and 1926, when the men in question not only acted on their own initiative but refused the advice of the prime minister and Cabinet. The first concerned the question of making government appointments. Many appointments are officially authorized by the governor general, even though they are actually decided upon by the prime minister or Cabinet. But the Charles Tupper government chose to retain office after it lost the 1896 election (awaiting defeat in the House of Commons), and during that interim period presented a list of several recom-mended appointments to the governor general, which he refused to make. Lord Aberdeen felt that the newly elected Wilfrid Laurier, rather than the recently defeated Tupper, had the authority to make such appointments, and that he was actually upholding the Constitution by interceding.[5]

The second famous case of refusing government advice, the **King–Byng dispute**, had to do with the **dissolution of Parliament**. The governor general normally summons and dissolves Parliament on the advice of the prime minister, but in 1926 Lord Byng refused Mackenzie King's request to dissolve Parliament and call an election. In this case, the governor general was primarily influenced by the fact that a motion of censure against the government regarding a scandal in the Customs Department was under debate in the House of Commons. The request for a dissolution appeared to be an attempt to curtail debate and avoid defeat in the Commons. In addition, the opposition Conservatives actually had more seats than the governing Liberals (who had been kept in power with the support of the Progressives), and an election had been held only eight months before. Thus, it seemed logical to Lord Byng to try to avoid an election when an alternative government might be available. As in 1896, the governor general felt that he was upholding the Constitution against unscrupulous behaviour by the government rather than subverting the democratic will.

Most authorities agree that King's advice was inappropriate and that Byng was right in not automatically acceding to the advice.[6] On the other hand, many feel that Byng should not have refused until he had assured himself that another viable government could be found. When the Meighen government fell three days later and a dissolution was granted to King's successor, it appeared that the governor had acted in a partisan way. Byng's position was further weakened when the electorate returned King to office in the subsequent election. Although it should not be thought that the voters understood the subtleties of the situation or that they cast their ballots primarily on this issue, the impression that the election results repudiated the governor general's intervention has probably made subsequent governors more wary of using their prerogative powers.

The fourth potential prerogative power of the governor general is to dismiss a government. Constitutional convention allows a governor to do so if the government refuses to resign after an election defeat or refuses to resign or call an election after a clear vote of nonconfidence. This has never happened at the federal level in Canada, but the power was exercised as recently as 1975, amid great controversy, in Australia. Indeed, in the 1981–82 period in Canada, Governor General Edward Schreyer contemplated forcing an election (tantamount to dismissing a government) if the Trudeau government had not backed down from its threat to impose unilateral amendment of the Constitution and agreed to further negotiations with the provinces.

The great Canadian constitutional scholar Eugene Forsey staunchly defended Lord Byng's refusal in 1926, arguing that such intervention was valid as long as the governor general could find another government to take responsibility for his action. Indeed, Forsey found many other hypothetical situations in which he would approve of similar intervention.[7] Others find it impossible to specify the exact circumstances in which a governor general might refuse the advice of a prime minister. A third view is that in a democratic age, the governor general should leave even outrageous government behaviour to the will of the electorate. Everyone is agreed, however, that in normal circumstances governors general must act on the advice of the prime minister and Cabinet. Before they invoke such emergency powers, "they must be sure they have reached the danger point, and that their actions will stand up to the subsequent judgement of other institutions and the people."[8]

The governor general has been called an insurance policy against the unforeseeable,[9] or a "constitutional fire extinguisher" whose emergency powers can only be used "when normal controls cannot operate and a crisis gets out of hand."[10] Andrew Heard adds that "governors should intrude into the democratic process only to the minimum extent absolutely required for the basic functioning of Parliamentary government."[11] Since the governor general is to function as an impartial symbol of unity, any act that could remotely be interpreted as partisan must be avoided.

Other Functions of the Crown

Leaving aside these very rare occasions, the governor general primarily plays a ceremonial and symbolic role. The governor general presides over the opening of Parliament, reading the government's speech from the throne, lays a wreath at the national war memorial on

Remembrance Day, and leads Canada Day celebrations. The governor general is busy entertaining at Rideau Hall: visiting dignitaries must be wined and dined, honours and awards must be presented, and receptions of every kind must be held. Foreign diplomats present their credentials to, and take their leave of, the governor general acting as the Canadian head of state. Although extremely busy in Ottawa, the governor general is also expected to maintain a hectic travel schedule, promoting national unity, demonstrating moral leadership, encouraging good works as patron of many service organizations, and performing other ceremonial functions across the country. The Stanley and Grey Cups were both donated by governors general, and the Lady Byng trophy by Lord Byng's wife.

Between the drastic intervention of the emergency powers and the glamorous ceremonial activities lies the traditional advisory role of the monarch: the right to be consulted, the right to encourage, and the right to warn the prime minister in the secrecy of their regular meetings.[12] Prime ministers often find it helpful to confide certain problems that cannot be discussed with anyone else, and on which the governor general might be able to offer sage advice. Due to the limited term (normally about five years), the usefulness of the governor general to a Canadian prime minister cannot compare with the Queen's experience in advising a British prime minister in this respect, but many prime ministers have spoken warmly of these relationships.[13]

Advantages and Disadvantages of the Monarchy[14]

The fact that the Queen of Canada is neither a resident nor even a citizen of Canada has given

Queen Elizabeth II records her Commonwealth Day radio broadcast at Buckingham Palace in London, 1998. (Fiona Hanson/ Canapress)

rise to considerable dissatisfaction with the position in some quarters and raised the question of abolishing the monarchy. The Queen's position as Canadian head of state is left over from the time Canada was a British colony. Some Canadians feel that this is inconsistent with their country's independent status and find that her British background and residence seriously detract from her ability to perform one of her main functions— to serve as a symbol of Canadian national unity—especially as far as Canadians of non-British background are concerned. Some take the view that most of the ceremonial functions of the head of state are foreign, archaic, and too expensive, while other critics argue that the monarchical system brings with it a whole set of undemocratic values and attitudes, including hierarchy, elitism, and privilege.

Supporters of the monarchy point out that the Crown played a part in allowing French-speaking Canadians to retain rights and privileges after the Conquest,[15] and that the monarchy helps to legitimize the pluralism of society by attracting attention to groups and demands that might otherwise be overlooked. There are some worthy causes, the Aboriginal question being one, that can benefit considerably from the impartial prestige and media power of the monarchy. It is also argued that Canada benefits from the worldwide celebrity status of the Queen and her capacity for pomp and ceremony. Most people like a little celebrity and spectacle in their life, and a royal family is an appropriate group to provide it. Moreover, apart from paying the costs of a royal visit, Canada gets all the prestige of the monarchy free of charge. The monarchy also helps to distinguish Canada from the United States, and as head of the Commonwealth, the Queen provides a link between Canada and many other countries.

Supporters of the monarchy point out that the great advantage of dividing the head of state and head of government functions is to make the best use of the prime minister's time. The latter can concentrate on the serious business of governance, while the governor general or Queen tend to the ceremonial functions. It is difficult for a partisan prime minister to serve as a symbol of unity, but being above the partisan fray, it is theoretically possible for a governor general or Queen to do so.

Given the advantages and disadvantages of the monarchy, Canada has the choice of retaining the Queen as head of state or elevating the governor general to the position of a head of state, as several other former British colonies have done. Such a move would depart from historical tradition and cause some dislocation in renaming and reorienting all those public institutions that now bear the crown or royal label. On the other hand, as time diminishes Canada's historic ties to Britain and as immigration dilutes the proportion of the population with British connections, Canada will someday probably reconsider retaining the British royal family as its own. Canada could continue to be a leading member of the Commonwealth and to recognize the Queen as the head of that organization even if she were replaced by a ceremonial Canadian president or stand-alone governor general. A majority of Australians want such a republic but cannot decide how they would choose a new president.

....

THE PRIME MINISTER AND CABINET[16]

The prime minister and Cabinet are usually referred to as the "government" of the day, as in "the Chrétien government." Although the ministers are also members of Parliament, it is in their capacity as the **government** that they perform the rule-making function in the political system. Within their deliberations, individual ministers also engage in a certain amount of interest articulation, and most of their decisions involve high-level interest aggregation. This section of the chapter is largely concerned with how they carry out these functions. It begins by examining the powers of the political executive in Canada and then discusses the preeminent position of the prime minister. The composition and operation of the Cabinet, including Cabinet committees, are addressed in the following sections, after which an outline of Cabinet support agencies is provided, along with two examples of how the political executive functions as a whole.

Powers of the Prime Minister and Cabinet

Given the importance of the prime minister and Cabinet, it is ironic that they are not provided for in the written parts of the Constitution, their functions and powers resting instead on custom and convention.[17] What *is* provided for in the 1867 Constitution Act is a Privy Council to advise the governor general in the exercise of the powers of that office. As mentioned above, at other points the 1867 act refers to the governor in council, which essentially means the Cabinet functioning as the Privy Council. In fact, the Cabinet acts as a committee of the Privy Council, but rather than merely advising the governor general, it actually makes the decisions in question. With the rare exception of governors general intervening on their own discretion, the prime minister and Cabinet exercise whatever powers are given to the Queen or the governor general in the Constitution.

Thus, after an election, the governor general calls on the leader of the party with the most members elected to the House of Commons to become prime minister and to form a government. If there is any doubt about who won the election, an incumbent prime minister has the right to remain in office until defeated in the House of Commons, but the transfer of power usually takes place within a few weeks of the election and before Parliament meets. The prime minister assumes the title "Right Honourable"[18] and selects the Cabinet ministers, all of whom are sworn into the Privy Council. This allows them to use the title "Honourable" as well as the initials "PC" (Privy Councillor, not to be confused with Progressive Conservative) behind their name. Since these are lifelong appointments and titles, members of former Cabinets remain in the Privy Council, but only those in the Cabinet of the day are invited to Cabinet meetings, hence the concept of the Cabinet as a committee of the Privy Council. From time to time other prominent people are appointed to the Privy Council as an honour, but they are not invited to Cabinet meetings either.[19] The Privy Council normally consists of about 300 members, almost all of them current or former federal Cabinet ministers. The title President of the Privy Council can be assumed by the prime minister, but it is often bestowed upon another Cabinet minister such as the minister of Intergovernmental Affairs.

In normal circumstances, then, the prime minister and Cabinet exercise the powers of the Crown. These powers include the summoning and dissolving of Parliament, the pardoning power, and the appointment of senators, judges, and other officials, including royal commissions. The prime minister and Cabinet, rather than the governor general, really recommend money bills to Parliament, and all international acts and the general conduct of foreign relations are the prerogative of the Cabinet, including declaring war and peace, signing treaties, appointing ambassadors, and recognizing foreign governments. The Cabinet may feel it politically advantageous to have Parliament debate declarations of war and may need to submit legislation to Parliament to make treaties effective, but unlike the system in the United States, such international acts are essentially within the purview of the executive, not the legislature.

Exercising the powers of the Crown is only a small part of the reason that the prime minister and Cabinet are the centre of gravity in the Canadian political system, however. More important, they have the responsibility for providing political leadership and determining priorities for the country. That is, the prime minister and Cabinet decide which problems to deal with, establish the general thrust and direction of new policies, and determine the spending priorities of the government. As noted in Chapter 19, the Cabinet is bombarded by demands but chooses to look into only a few of them in the initiation phase of the policy-making process, and then gives the green light to even fewer, in the priority-setting phase. In the British and Canadian systems, the responsibility for initiating legislation rests primarily with the prime minister and Cabinet. As will be seen in Chapter 22, opportunities do exist for other members of Parliament to introduce bills, but most of the time of the House of Commons is set aside for government business. The **speech from the throne** provides the prime minister and Cabinet with an opportunity to outline their legislative program at the beginning of the session, while the Constitution requires that any bill to raise or spend money must also originate with the Cabinet. The Cabinet's virtual monopoly over the passage of legislation should ensure coordination among government policies, while its total monopoly over financial legislation is designed to guarantee a close relationship between policies adopted and the funds to make them effective. Such strong executive leadership, based on tradition, necessity, and the Constitution Act, has evolved over many centuries and has generally proven itself to be an effective way to run a country.

Beyond the powers of the Crown and this general leadership function, Cabinet power is also derived from specific acts of Parliament. Almost every law delegates to a minister or the governor in council the power to make decisions of one kind or another. Among other things, these include the quasi-legislative power to issue regulations under a law, sometimes called delegated or subordinate legislation. That is, on the advice of their bureaucrats, ministers are given the power to flesh out the bare bones of the statute with all sorts of detailed stipulations that Parliament did not have the time or expertise to discuss. The Cabinet is also given many quasi-judicial powers, such as hearing appeals from administrative agencies like the Canadian Radio-television and Telecommunications Commission (CRTC). It is also on the basis of such acts of Parliament that individual ministers are charged with supervising the administration of their departments. They provide direction and leadership, establish priorities, and transmit the prime minister's or their personal or party perspectives, all in an effort to ensure that public servants remain accountable to democratically elected leaders and public opinion. In addition, ministers are involved in Parliament, answering questions about the department's operations, defending departmental spending proposals, and piloting bills emanating from the department.

The principle of **ministerial responsibility**—each minister being held responsible to Parliament for everything that goes on in his or her department—was once thought to entail a minister's resignation over errors of public servants, even those that the minister knew nothing about.[20] In an age of big government, however, the principle has lost most of its meaning. Ministers can still be criticized for departmental failures, and are expected to correct them, but they rarely resign except for serious personal mistakes and conflicts of interest. Much depends on the personal ethical code of the minister to do the "proper thing,"[21] and the sanction for error rests more with the prime minister (demotion or forced resignation) than with Parliament.

The Prime Minister

The system of government that Canada inherited from Britain has traditionally been called **Cabinet government**, but such a label does not do justice to the modern pre-eminence of the prime minister. Most observers agree that Cabinet government has been transformed into a system of **prime ministerial government**,[22] and no one doubts that the prime minister has enormous power and should be singled out for special attention.

Prime ministers have always lent their name and style to the government, such as the "Trudeau Cabinet" or the "Mulroney government," and "the ebb and flow of the fortunes of the government are directly linked to their performance."[23] Donald J. Savoie demonstrates how this pre-eminence begins before the prime minister is even sworn into office. An elaborate transition planning process involving the entire deputy minister community and led by the Privy Council Office is designed to give the incoming PM all he or she needs to know about forming and operating a government, and many significant decisions are made in this transition period. Such a process has to have such a focus because at that point in time, the PM is the only known member of the incoming Cabinet.[24] The pre-eminence of the prime minister over Cabinet colleagues can subsequently be seen in ten of the PM's principal powers, rights, or responsibilities, some of which have always existed while others are of more recent origin. In many cases, these relate to the different arenas in which the prime minister must operate, such as Cabinet, Parliament, party, media, federal–provincial relations, international diplomacy, and the economy,[25] and can be enumerated as follows:

- Cabinet-maker
- Chair of Cabinet meetings
- Party leader
- Chief policymaker
- Leading player in the House of Commons
- Chief personnel manager
- Controller of government organization
- Adviser to governor general
- Chief diplomat
- Public persuader

First, the prime minister is the Cabinet-maker.[26] Prime ministers select their own ministers and, subject to certain conventions discussed below, decide what portfolios to assign them. Ministers are also issued with "mandate letters" that inform them of the PM's policy expectations in their portfolio.[27] Ministers thus owe allegiance to the prime minister, who can promote and demote them, ask for their resignation, and, if necessary, dismiss them. All of these possibilities tend to keep ministers submissive if and when there is any difference in their policy priorities. Prime ministers are usually reluctant to drop or demote ministers who have outlived their usefulness, although appointment to the Senate provides a valuable safety valve in this connection. Mackenzie King's skilled precipitation of the resignation of Defence minister J.L. Ralston in 1944 is the classic case of a prime minister acting as a ruthless butcher.[28]

The prime minister's chairmanship of Cabinet meetings is a second main source of power. To start with, the prime minister determines the agenda of such meetings. A former Cabinet secretary wrote, for example, that for any reason the prime minister deems sufficient the order of business may be altered, and an agenda already settled may be set aside in favour of other subjects of greater importance and urgency. The PM may suspend meetings, summon additional meetings, dispense with or extend the normal record kept by the secretary, or modify or set aside the normal rules of procedure.[29] In addition to the usual advantages of a meeting chair, the prime minister benefits from receiving a confidential memo prepared by the Privy Council Office that contains a summary of various ministers' views on each agenda item and suggestions on how to achieve the PM's own objectives. The PM is also advantaged by the peculiar way in which Cabinet decisions are arrived at. Rather than by motions and votes, the decision is reached when the PM summarizes the discussion and articulates the "consensus." If and when this bears little resemblance to the actual tenor of the meeting,[30] ministers who do not agree with this interpretation either keep quiet or resign. Even though many decisions are now made by Cabinet committees, the prime minister decides which committees will be struck, who will chair them, who will sit on them, and which matters will be sent to them, so that this delegation of power from the full Cabinet does not necessarily reduce the PM's control.

In the third place, the prime minister is the leader of the party. The PM's pre-eminence has probably increased over the years as political parties have become more cohesive and as election campaigns have come to focus on party leaders.[31] In fact, many ministers may have been elected on the leader's coattails. Some prime ministers, like Pierre Trudeau, may ignore and neglect the party between elections, but others, like Brian Mulroney, seemed to be more clearly in personal control of the party machine. As leader, the prime minister can control party organization, personnel, strategy, and policy.[32] Moreover, unlike other ministers, some of whom may have specialized constituencies of support within the party, the PM has been chosen by the party as a whole, and can usually count on a broad base of support.

Fourth, the prime minister could be called chief policymaker. It has already been shown how the PM has the first word on government policy, such as in deciding how seriously to take the party's election platform and in issuing mandate letters to new ministers. But he or she also has the last word, whether in personal interaction with individual ministers, within the Cabinet chamber, in Parliament, or in other forums such as the media. Modern government, of course, is too complex for political leaders to have an active role in formulating all policies, but the prime minister can pursue a number of personal priorities, as well as play a critical role in defining other problems.[33] In two extreme examples, R.B. Bennett delivered a startling series of radio broadcasts in 1935 that committed his Conservative Party to a wide-ranging, radical "new deal," and Pierre Trudeau returned from a meeting with West German Chancellor Helmut Schmidt in 1975 to announce a major restraint program without even consulting his minister of Finance.[34] In any case of real or apparent policy conflict between the party organization and the government, between two ministers, or between a minister and the prime minister, the PM rules.

In the fifth place, the prime minister is the central player in the House of Commons.[35] Some prime ministers have had greater control over the House and have been better performers there than others: Diefenbaker was always more comfortable in the Commons than Pearson, for example. Even since prime ministers have delegated direction of the business of the House to a government House leader, they are still expected to be there for the oral Question Period every day, in contrast to Britain, where the prime minister only appears twice a week, and in which they set the tone for the government as a whole.[36] On the other hand, on a day that they expect a particularly rough reception from the opposition, prime ministers can find some excuse to absent themselves from the House and leave their ministers to answer for some problem.

A sixth source of prime ministerial pre-eminence is an enormous power of appointment. Besides ministers, this includes the appointment of senators, Supreme Court judges, deputy ministers, and heads of a wide range of government agencies.[37] The appointment power can serve to keep those hopeful for appointment docile and supportive, as well as to impose the PM's ideological position on much of the government.

Given the extent and power of the bureaucracy today, the prime minister's control over government organization, the seventh power, is also significant. Subject to usually routine parliamentary approval, and on the advice of the Machinery of Government section of the PCO, the PM can decide to create new departments and set out their mandates. Prime ministers can also reorganize government departments, such as Trudeau's amalgamation of Trade and Commerce and External Affairs to give the latter a more commercial orientation. Today, it is more common to abolish departments or agencies that predecessors have established or to privatize Crown corporations.

In the eighth place, the prime minister personally advises the governor general on such matters as when to call the next election. This power is sometimes thought to be important in permitting prime ministers to get their own way in conflicts with ministers, government backbenchers, or the parliamentary opposition because none of these members want to risk their seats and the many benefits of public office.

Furthermore, in an era of summit diplomacy, the prime minister increasingly overshadows the minister of Foreign Affairs on the world stage.[38] The prime minister doubled as secretary of state for external affairs until 1946 and still functions as Canada's chief diplomat in annual bilateral meetings with the U.S. president, annual meetings of the Group of Seven leading industrial countries, Commonwealth conferences, meetings of the Francophonie and APEC, and occasional appearances at the United Nations.

The prime minister is also the chief "public relations officer" of the government or "public persuader."[39] Television has become the main instrument for transmitting the prime minister's message to his or her party, the government, and the public, and survival in the "battleground" of media relations "threatens to become the key determinant of prime ministerial success."[40] Trudeau and Mulroney used television to appeal to public opinion for support on such issues as wage and price controls or constitutional reform, for example, but the PM does not need to search out publicity or national media attention—it is always there.[41] A crucial position in the Prime Minister's Office is the press secretary, who organizes the prime minister's media appearances and often speaks on the PM's behalf.[42]

In order to perform these ten varied and significant functions, the prime minister must be adequately advised. It is not surprising, therefore, that both Trudeau and Mulroney substantially enlarged their two principal sources of advice, the Prime Minister's Office (PMO) and the Privy Council Office (PCO). These two agencies will be examined in detail below.

Given all these powers as well as a deferential majority in the House of Commons, the PM can usually succeed in terms of controlling the policy and personnel of government. Richard Crossman and others trace the historical evolution of the centre of power in the British parliamentary system from monarch to Parliament, from Parliament to Cabinet, from Cabinet to public service, and from public service to prime minister.[43] In many respects, in fact, the Canadian prime minister is more powerful than the American president, except of course in terms of international clout. In order to get his agenda adopted, the latter must bargain with Congress, in which party discipline is not strong, whereas prime ministers can normally count on a disciplined majority to back their measures. Indeed, the expansion of the PCO and PMO, the holding of prime ministerial news conferences, the making of televised addresses to the nation, luxurious travel arrangements, and other conspicuous trappings of power have led many observers to criticize the presidentialization of the office of prime minister.[44]

Others continue to emphasize the restraints on the power of the prime minister, such as financial constraints, opposition from the provinces, international influences, and the limits to which government policy of any kind can effect societal change.[45] The prime minister is often at the mercy of events, and despite trying to control them, they may cause the PM to fall in public support and in turn lose much of his or her overall influence. But within the operation of the government itself, the PM has few constraints other than lack of time.[46] Although opposition party leaders in Canada are vulnerable to attack from within their own ranks, even unpopular PMs have stayed on until they were ready to go. The main exception

By Andy Donato (Toronto Sun). *Reproduced with permission.*

was in 1896 when Mackenzie Bowell's Cabinet rebelled and forced him from office; in 1963, John Diefenbaker only survived a Cabinet revolt by appealing over the heads of the Cabinet to his supporters in the government caucus.[47] Generally speaking, then, prime ministers are almost as unmovable as American presidents, who have a fixed term of office.

Out of 20 prime ministers between 1867 and 2000, 8 held the position for two years or less, while 12 served at least a four-year term of office, as seen in Table 20.2. Of the 12 longest-serving PMs, 9 were lawyers, 7 were anglophone Protestants, 4 were francophone Catholics, and Brian Mulroney, a fluently bilingual anglophone Catholic. Robert Borden came from the Atlantic region, 5 hailed from Quebec, 4 from Ontario, and R.B. Bennett and John Diefenbaker spent their adult lives in the West. At least 2 (Bennett and Trudeau) were extremely wealthy, and several others (Chrétien, St. Laurent, Turner, Mulroney, and King)

TABLE 20.2   **Prime Ministers of Canada, Ranked by Tenure in Office**

Mackenzie King	21 yrs., 5 mos.	Alexander Mackenzie	4 yrs., 11 mos.
John A. Macdonald	19 yrs.	John Thompson	2 yrs.
Pierre Elliott Trudeau	15 yrs., 5 mos.	Arthur Meighen	1 yr., 8 mos.
Wilfrid Laurier	15 yrs., 3 mos.	John Abbott	1 yr., 5 mos.
Brian Mulroney	8 yrs., 9 mos., 1 wk.	Mackenzie Bowell	1 yr., 4 mos.
Robert L. Borden	8 yrs., 9 mos.	Joe Clark	9 mos.
Louis St. Laurent	8 yrs., 7 mos.	Kim Campbell	133 days
Jean Chrétien	6 yrs., 8 mos.*	John Turner	80 days
John Diefenbaker	5 yrs., 10 mos.	Charles Tupper	69 days
R.B. Bennett	5 yrs., 3 mos.		
Lester Pearson	5 yrs.		

As of July 2000.

had abundant corporate connections. Lester Pearson and Mackenzie King came from elitist academic–public-service backgrounds.

Composition of the Cabinet

In theory, all Cabinet ministers are equal, although in practice this is far from being the case. Pierre Trudeau periodically designated one minister as deputy prime minister; as deputy PM to Mulroney, Don Mazankowski exercised general administrative control of the government and a small deputy prime minister's office was created to support him. Mazankowski's appointment as deputy prime minister allowed Mulroney to travel, campaign, and think about the broader picture, but some observers began to wonder who was really running the country. Sheila Copps's appointment as Jean Chrétien's deputy prime minister in 1993 seemed to be of much less significance; in fact, both Paul Martin and Herb Gray appeared to have more power than she did, and Gray donned the deputy PM mantle in Chrétien's second term.

A forerunner to the deputy prime minister was the francophone "lieutenant" of various anglophone first ministers. Ernest Lapointe (1923–41) and Louis St. Laurent (1941–48), the Quebec lieutenants of Mackenzie King, were each given wide discretion to deal with issues from that province. Macdonald used George-Étienne Cartier in a similar role for a few years, and to some extent C.D. Howe was an anglophone lieutenant to Louis St. Laurent.[48]

Below the deputy PM are the regular departmental ministers, each normally in charge of a single department. An informal ranking of these departments may result in variations in influence among this group of ministers, with Finance, Foreign Affairs, Justice, Health, Treasury Board, Human Resources, and Transport usually being among the key portfolios. A handful of ministers will not have full-fledged departments to administer, but are attached to larger departments, and the current list is completed with the government leaders in the House of Commons and the Senate. PMs sometimes appoint junior ministers, variably called ministers without portfolio, ministers of state, or secretaries of state, and until Jean Chrétien, and unlike in Britain, the Canadian tradition was that all ministers, even these junior ones, were included in the Cabinet.

Since the Cabinet occupies such a central position in the Canadian policymaking process, every interest in the country would like to be represented around the Cabinet table.[49] This desire alone creates pressure to expand its size. In general, the Cabinet contained about 13 or 14 ministers before 1911, then rose to around 20 until about 1960, increased to the 30 mark under Trudeau, and to around 40 in the Mulroney period.[50] Chrétien reduced the size of his Cabinet to 23 in 1993, but it rose to 28 in his second term. His nine junior secretaries of state were part of the ministry, but not invited to Cabinet. The secretaries of state each had a small staff and operating budget and received 75 percent of a Cabinet minister's pay.

While the prime minister decides who will sit in the Cabinet, several conventions have come to constrain the PM's prerogatives in the selection of ministers.[51] In the first place, reflecting the fact that Canada is a democracy and that the ministers represent the people, all Cabinet ministers must have a seat in Parliament. Like in Britain, and unlike in the United States, ministers sit in the legislative branch of government at the same time as they form the executive.

A seat in Parliament would theoretically include a seat in the Senate. A number of senators sat in the early post-Confederation cabinets—indeed, senators Abbott and Bowell served briefly as prime minister in the 1890s—but the modern tradition is to include only one senator in the Cabinet. This senator usually serves as government leader in that chamber and has no departmental responsibilities. The Diefenbaker Cabinet functioned between 1958 and 1962 without a single senator, however, while Brian Mulroney gave Senator Lowell Murray important responsibilities as minister of Federal–Provincial Relations in the Meech Lake period.

Almost all ministers therefore have a seat in the House of Commons. It is possible for the prime minister to name someone to the Cabinet who has not won election to the Commons, but convention dictates that such a person run in a by-election as soon as possible in order to obtain a seat. This sometimes happens when a PM chooses to appoint someone of unusual qualifications from outside parliamentary life, rather than a sitting backbencher, a practice that does not reflect well on the party's parliamentary caucus and is usually resented by those who were passed over. In at least two cases such appointees lost the by-election in which they sought entry to the House and ultimately resigned from the Cabinet, confirming the view that it is impossible to sit in the Cabinet very long without a seat in Parliament.[52] Having been selected as Liberal leader in 1984 after an absence from politics, John Turner even served briefly as prime minister without a seat, but this was only temporarily legitimate.

A prime minister will usually feel compelled to appoint veteran MPs to the Cabinet, including those who served in previous Cabinets or those who ran for the party leadership. It is often thought safer to put leadership rivals into the Cabinet, subject to all its constraints, than to leave them to continue their campaigns outside. As a result of this necessity, able newcomers are often overlooked. The prime minister will also be concerned with the ideological slant of the Cabinet and either seek to balance various ideological factions within the party or else to ensure that a particular stream predominates.

The next constraint on the prime minister is the convention that each province be represented in the Cabinet. This flows from the fact that Canada is a federation and that the

Senate has never performed its intended role of representing provincial interests in Ottawa. Thus, with the occasional exception of Prince Edward Island, every province that has elected a member to the government side of the chamber has always been awarded a Cabinet position. In both the Trudeau and Clark governments, the prime minister chose to appoint senators to the Cabinet to represent provinces that had not elected any or enough government members (the three Western provinces in the former case and Quebec in the latter). That such a practice breaks the modern tradition of having only one senator in the Cabinet attests to the importance of provincial representation. The convention of provincial representation usually results in some ministers being appointed only because their province needs a Cabinet representative, rather than on their merits, leaving worthy MPs from other locations excluded because their region is already adequately represented. Where an inner Cabinet or Priorities and Planning Committee existed in the past, a similar concern occurred for provincial representation within that smaller group.

It is not only that residents of a province feel more secure if one of their number is in the Cabinet; it is also useful for the Cabinet itself to have such provincial representation.[53] In fact, ministers essentially wear two hats: they speak for their department as well as for their province. This arrangement is functional for patronage as well as policy purposes: those government appointments and contracts awarded on a partisan basis will be the responsibility of the relevant provincial minister, often called the "political minister" for that province. Two of the most famous cases of regional ministers were Allan MacEachen and Lloyd Axworthy, who succeeded in bringing public works of all kinds to eastern Nova Scotia and Winnipeg respectively.

Larger provinces are not content with a single minister, of course, and in a Cabinet of 30 or 40 members, Ontario and Quebec have sometimes exceeded 10 each. In such cases the ministers can be distributed so that each region within the province gains its own representative. Before 1984 Quebec was usually underrepresented in the Cabinet when the Conservatives were in power, largely because not many PC members were elected from that province, while the West was inadequately represented in the Pearson and Trudeau cabinets. In 1999, rather typically, Chrétien had 12 Ontario ministers, 7 from Quebec, 2 from BC, and 1 from every other province. Table 20.3 indicates the regional distribution of federal Cabinet ministers (including the prime minister) when each new government took office.[54]

The next convention of Canadian Cabinet-making is a recognition of the need for a balance of ethnic representatives. A proper balance of anglophone and francophone ministers—that is, about one-third francophone and two-thirds anglophone—may result almost automatically from the carefully constructed provincial representation. French Canadians were underrepresented even in Liberal governments before 1963, however, and often grossly underrepresented in Conservative cabinets. It was only in the Pearson, Trudeau, and Mulroney cabinets that francophone ministers achieved or exceeded the one-third benchmark. Those of other ethnic origins were not proportionately represented in Canadian cabinets until the Clark and Mulroney periods. Michael Starr, of Ukrainian background, was one of the first to be appointed, in 1957, but nontraditional representatives in recent years included Stanley Haidasz, Leonard Marchand, Norman Cafik, Lincoln Alexander, Don Mazankowski, Ray Hnatyshyn, Steve Paproski, Judy Erola, Charles Caccia, Otto Jelinek, Sergio Marchi, Alfonso Gagliano, Herb Dhaliwal, and Maria Minna.

As for other social divisions, the religion factor was much more important in the pre-1900 period than it is today. Some early prime ministers were careful to balance representation

TABLE 20.3   **Regional Distribution of Federal Cabinet Ministers at the Beginning of Each Ministry**

	Atlantic	Quebec	Ontario	West	Total
Macdonald (1867)	4	4	5	—	13
Mackenzie (1873)	5	3	6	—	14
Macdonald (1878)	5	4	4	1	14
Laurier (1896)	4	5	4	1	14
Borden (1911)	4	5	7	2	18
Borden (1917)	6	4	9	3	22
Meighen (1920)	5	3	6	3	17
King (1921)	4	6	6	3	19
Bennett (1930)	4	5	7	3	19
King (1935)	5	5	4	2	16
St. Laurent (1948)	4	6	7	3	20
Diefenbaker (1957)	8	3	6	4	21
Pearson (1963)	4	7	11	4	26
Trudeau (1968)	6	10	10	3	29
Clark (1979)	5	5	11	9	30
Trudeau (1980)	5	12	12	4	33
Turner (1984)	5	10	12	2	29
Mulroney (1984)	5	11	11	13	40
Chrétien (1993)	3	5	10	5	23

Source: W.A. Matheson, The Prime Minister and the Cabinet, *updated by author.*

among Protestant groups as well as between Protestants and Catholics. Ministers increasingly decline to declare a religious affiliation, however, and the Jewish community has usually claimed one or two spots since the initial appointment of Herb Gray in 1969. Prime ministers are now more concerned to appoint women to the Cabinet. As noted in Chapter 7, the Cabinet contained 1, 2, or 3 women between 1957 and 1984; 6 out of 40 in 1984, 4 out of 23 in 1993, and 7 out of 28 in 1999. Since it was difficult to include representatives of all expectant groups in his original Cabinet of only 23, Chrétien tried to appease others in the appointment of his secretaries of state: 3 women, 1 minister from PEI, 1 Aboriginal, and one Asian Canadian.

Matheson writes of a representative Cabinet as follows:

> Adherence to the representation principle first introduced by Sir John A. Macdonald in 1867 has brought together the elites from the various subcultures and provided them with a means whereby they can work together to stabilize the Canadian political system. Thus in the Canadian context the Cabinet has filled a dual role, for in addition to exercising the usual functions of executive leadership, the Cabinet has provided an

arena in which the elites may counter the dysfunctional and unstabilizing effects of cultural, regional, and religious fragmentation.[55]

Once the PM has chosen the people who will form the Cabinet, they must be assigned portfolios, that is, departmental responsibilities. Certain traditions surround this task, too, such as that Finance usually goes to an anglophone in whom the business community has confidence; Fisheries and Oceans is normally given to someone from Atlantic Canada (or BC); and Agriculture has traditionally (but not always) gone to a Westerner. Justice was historically awarded to a Quebecker, primarily because of the dual system of law in that province, and Public Works and the Post Office were also often claimed by ministers from Quebec. It was sometimes argued that francophone ministers preferred Cabinet posts that dispensed a great deal of patronage, while only anglophones were trusted with the big economic portfolios.[56] Whatever truth there might once have been in this portrait, it changed dramatically under Trudeau, as he appointed the first francophone ministers of Trade and Commerce and Finance.

It is not normally expected that ministers will be expert in the field to which they are appointed, partly because the electorate is not likely to furnish the prime minister with members of Parliament with such credentials. Indeed, an argument can be made that a semi-expert is more dangerous than a total amateur since the latter will have enough sense to listen to the real experts within the department, while the former might try to substitute his or her limited knowledge for theirs. Thus, apart from the minister of Justice's being a lawyer, there is no necessary relationship between ministers' training or pre-political occupation and their departmental assignment.

Parliamentary secretaries are not Cabinet ministers, although they have sometimes been seen as "ministers-in-waiting." They have been a permanent fixture on the political scene since 1943 and have been provided for in legislation since 1959. They are members of Parliament who "assist the minister in such manner as the minister directs," which most often takes the form of making speeches on behalf of the minister, receiving deputations, sitting in for the minister in House debates, whether of government or private members' bills or on adjournment, defending the department's estimates, and maintaining liaison with other MPs. The Chrétien regime included 26 parliamentary secretaries, but the position was not regarded as being a stepping stone to Cabinet because MPs in the position were rotated annually.

Operation of the Cabinet
CABINET SOLIDARITY, COLLECTIVE RESPONSIBILITY, AND SECRECY

The Cabinet has traditionally been seen as a collective decision-making body. Exceptions to this notion include the prime minister's making some decisions single-handedly, and decisions taken by Cabinet committees or by individual ministers. Regardless of which or how many ministers are involved in making such decisions, however, the Cabinet operates on the principle of **Cabinet solidarity**, which means that all ministers must publicly defend all Cabinet policies or else resign. The most extreme manifestation of Cabinet solidarity can be seen in terms of the annual **budget**, the most important government policy statement of the year. Only the Finance minister and PM know much about it until the budget is delivered in Parliament. Matheson writes:

This procedure is unfortunate, in that it prevents the experience of the Cabinet from being utilized in the preparation of the budget and makes a mockery of the idea of Cabinet responsibility, since ministers must assume responsibility for something they have had little or no voice in preparing. It also illustrates the great influence of the civil servants who advise the Minister of Finance on this matter.[57]

Ministerial resignations because of policy differences are very rare in Canada, perhaps only 28 since 1867,[58] which suggests that the thought of giving up the perks of office engenders considerable flexibility in ministers' principles. Cabinet solidarity has only been suspended in the case of parliamentary debates and votes on capital punishment and abortion.

Cabinet solidarity is related to the principle of **collective responsibility** to Parliament. Occasionally, a gaffe can be pinned on a single minister who is persuaded to resign, but if the government loses the confidence of the legislature, it cannot simply jettison the one minister most closely attached to the measure in question. It must collectively resign or call an election. More will be said on this point in Chapter 22.

Cabinet solidarity and collective responsibility are also linked to a third principle, that of **Cabinet secrecy** or confidentiality. Cabinet operations are shrouded in secrecy and ministers are not supposed to disclose information about its deliberations. Such confidentiality protects state secrets, protects the Cabinet against opposition and media exploitation of ministerial discord, and protects senior civil servants from identification and public criticism. Cabinet secrecy is also justified as the only way in which ministers can engage in no-holds-barred discussion of crucial issues and in which public servants can render impartial advice. Cabinet documents are not normally made public for 20 years, and, as a result, we do not know as much about how the Cabinet operates as about decision-making bodies that meet in public, a fact that particularly frustrates political scientists. On the other hand, clever ministers are conscious that information represents power and that a well-timed leak can sometimes benefit them when involved in a battle within Cabinet. Prime Minister Pearson had much difficulty with ministers who regularly leaked confidential Cabinet documents.

DEPARTMENTAL AND INSTITUTIONALIZED CABINETS

As mentioned, Cabinet-level decisions can be made by the prime minister alone, by the Cabinet collectively, by a Cabinet committee, or by a single minister. In this connection, Chapter 17 briefly referred to the distinction between a **departmental Cabinet** and an **institutionalized Cabinet**.[59] The former was characteristic of the Canadian Cabinet before 1960 or so, perhaps especially in the Mackenzie King and St. Laurent eras, in which ministers and departments were largely autonomous. Each developed its own policies and

Lester B. Pearson announces at an Ottawa press conference on December 14, 1967, that he has decided to resign as leader of the Liberal Party. (Peter Bregg/Canapress)

programs with little regard for central coordination and with only minimal prime ministerial interference.[60] Strong ministers could make many decisions and policies without consulting their colleagues, and such ministers tended to remain in charge of a single department for long periods of time (e.g., Jimmy Gardiner as minister of Agriculture for 22 years) rather than being shuffled on a regular basis. Such autonomous departmental ministers often doubled as strong regional ministers, who were also allowed to handle regional responsibilities on their own.[61] In addition, senior appointed officials usually served their careers within a single department and became "carriers of the interests, traditions, skills and memories of these particularized bureaucratic organizations."[62] At the same time, however, prime ministers could make certain decisions unilaterally, and some interfered in the operations of various departments more than others. R.B. Bennett and John Diefenbaker gained a reputation for excessive interference, for example, while Louis St. Laurent was said to give too much authority to individual ministers.[63]

Despite the assumption of collective Cabinet decision-making, the institutionalized or collegial Cabinet is really a product of the period after 1960 and the enormous expansion of government activity in the past 40 years. As society and its problems became more complex, individual ministers and departments could no longer make decisions and policies in isolation. The policies of one department almost inevitably affected those of another. More consultation and coordination were called for, with the result that ministerial collegiality replaced departmental autonomy. To some extent the need for policy coordination coincided with the view that Cabinet ministers should have greater control over the bureaucracy, while another stimulus was the development of techniques for more rational government decision-making. The Pearson era was transitional in this respect, and the institutionalized Cabinet became fully developed in the Trudeau period, more or less synonymous with his approach of increasing the rationality of government policymaking.[64]

In the new approach, the Priorities and Planning Committee of Cabinet established the overall priorities of the government. Too often in the past, it was argued, policymaking started at the bottom instead of at the top, no one had a view of the whole picture, and policymaking had been ad hoc and incremental. Then, the Prime Minister's Office and the Privy Council Office were expanded and strengthened so as to provide independent policy analysis to the prime minister and Cabinet. The Department of Finance and the Treasury Board also became more effective central agencies, advising the Cabinet on its financial decisions. When ministers presented their departmental proposals to Cabinet in the past, the bureaucratic initiatives were often rubber-stamped because neither prime minister nor Cabinet colleagues had the resources to challenge them. Trudeau wished to re-establish political direction to the public service.

Next, to avoid Cabinet overload and to enhance specialization within it, most of the Cabinet's work was done in committees. These included functional committees like that on social policy, and coordinating committees such as one on federal–provincial relations. Cabinet procedures were also rigidly adhered to, including agendas, advance notice of issues, and advance circulation of background documents.

In addition, new techniques of policy analysis, especially at the bureaucratic levels, provided ministers with a more rational basis for their decisions. Finally, the attempt to go beyond traditional departmental thinking on problems led to the setting up of new ministries of state and task forces, and public discussion of policy options was encouraged by means of publishing green papers and white papers on a subject before the Cabinet had made up its mind.

All of these measures tended to render Cabinet decisions more coordinated, organized, disciplined, political, and rational, hence the term "institutionalized Cabinet." Whatever the benefits of this approach, however, it also had negative implications. First, most ministers did not have the time or capacity to study all the background documents that were prepared for them. Second, departmental bureaucrats often became subordinate not to their ministers but to the new central agencies, the PCO, PMO, Treasury Board, and Department of Finance. Third, policies were often coordinated and analyzed to the point of paralysis.[65] They had to pass through so many time-consuming procedural barriers that they sometimes emerged irrelevant to the problem they were originally designed to address. Fourth, as was usually the case in previous governments, a small, informal group of trusted ministers and intimate advisers emerged as a "supergroup" who made key decisions regardless of the authorized channels.[66] Finally, since this decision-making model was generally replicated at the provincial level, it had particularly negative effects on federal–provincial relations.

Peter Aucoin has drawn an interesting contrast between the Trudeau and Mulroney approaches to political leadership. Trudeau's objective of "rational management" involved collegial argument such that Cabinet meetings were an intellectual exercise featuring an interplay of ideas. The prime minister, as political philosopher, had his own policy goals in certain fields, but otherwise set up a system of checks and balances from which the best argument would eventually triumph. At least in his first term, Mulroney's main objectives were consensus and compromise. Unlike Trudeau, he excelled at people management, and therefore preferred to deal with ministers on a one-by-one basis rather than collectively. Mulroney continued where John Turner left off in dismantling much of the "rational" policymaking machinery, both of them feeling that it was too elaborate, complex, and slow. They also argued that the responsibility of individual ministers should be restored, and being distrustful of the bureaucracy, Mulroney relied excessively on the PMO and ministers' offices, and underutilized the PCO.[67]

Jean Chrétien announced his intention to revert to the St. Laurent model of a departmental Cabinet in which individual ministers and departments were allowed to look after their own affairs. The maze of Cabinet committees was reduced, and departments were allowed more leeway in moving funds from one program to another as long as they did not exceed their overall allotment. Even in an era of government downsizing, however, the complexity of issues required such coordination and consultation that the 40-year-old model was no longer adequate. The Finance Department began to fill the gap, partly because the budget and the deficit were the driving forces of the day, but also because some kind of coordinating device was needed. Insiders report that the influence of other central agencies, especially the PCO, was also stronger than ever in the Chrétien government, so that, in fact, not much had changed.[68]

CABINET AND CABINET COMMITTEES

In addition to three Chrétien "Cabinet retreats" per year, the Cabinet as a whole normally meets for about three hours once a week.[69] An agenda is prepared by the PCO under the prime minister's supervision and circulated in advance. Ministers sit around the Cabinet table in order of precedence, while the Clerk of the Privy Council, two deputy clerks, and one or two note-takers sit along the wall. These officials are rarely asked to speak, but they may pass notes to the prime minister. The PCO will have prepared a briefing note for the PM for guidance in getting through the meeting successfully, but it is not always heavily relied upon.

The first item on the agenda is "General Discussion," which includes whatever is on the PM's mind. Federal–provincial relations in one form or another is usually included in this item. The second item is "Presentations," in which ministers may be invited to brief the Cabinet on various issues. The third item is a list of "Nominations" or government appointments to be confirmed. The fourth item is Cabinet committee decisions, attached to the agenda as appendices. In theory these can be challenged in the full Cabinet, since in most cases about half of the ministers did not sit on the committee that made the decision. But such challenges annoy the PM and are rarely made.

This description of Cabinet operations reveals that Cabinet is no longer a collective decision-making body.[70] That is partly because, since the mid-1960s, more and more Cabinet work has been done by Cabinet committees rather than by the full Cabinet.[71] Each committee also normally meets once a week, and ministers are likely to be members of one or two committees. Unlike Cabinet meetings as such, ministers may bring along advisers to Cabinet committees, so they are less reliant on their own personal resources.

Between the Pearson and Mulroney regimes, the Priorities and Planning Committee was clearly the most important Cabinet committee. Its special functions included setting priorities, allocating budgets, reviewing other committee decisions, making many important decisions itself, and supervising federal–provincial relations. Being chaired by the prime minister and containing the most important ministers (including the chairs of other Cabinet committees) also added to its significance. On the other hand, Joe Clark pioneered the two-tier Cabinet in Canada by explicitly naming an inner Cabinet instead of Priorities and Planning. In fact, that brief period saw another major departure from the usual collective decision-making process because the full Cabinet rarely met.

Prime Minister Kim Campbell answers questions at a news conference in Ottawa. (Chuck Mitchell/Canapress)

Kim Campbell reduced the number of Cabinet committees from 11 to 5, and in 1993, Chrétien established only 4 Cabinet committees: Economic Development Policy, Social Development Policy, Treasury Board, and the Special Committee of Council. In his second term, Chrétien renamed the two policy committees "Economic Union" and "Social Union." The first, chaired by Ralph Goodale, had 17 members, and the second, chaired by Anne McLellan, had 12, with four ministers sitting on both. The Treasury Board was chaired by the president of the Treasury Board, and the Finance minister served as vice-chair, with four other ministers also members and five alternates. The Special Committee of Council, chaired by Herb Gray, was a group of nine who handled routine legal matters.[72] Ad hoc committees were also used.

Cabinet committees function much like Cabinet as a whole. Working with the chairperson and the PM, the PCO will develop and distribute an agenda that is largely composed of Memorandums to Cabinet from various departments. Policy specialists within the PCO will have been involved in the preparation of a briefing note for the committee chair to reflect "the centre's" perspective of the issues in question. Much interdepartmental discussion and negotiation will have taken place in advance, but if the committee cannot come to a consensus, the Memorandum is returned for further work. If it is approved, it is attached to the agenda of the next meeting of Cabinet as a whole.

The Treasury Board, as the third Cabinet committee, operates somewhat differently. It has its own support agency, the Treasury Board Secretariat (TBS), and the Cabinet committee sits in judgment as TBS officials across the table present cases for the proposed expenditure of funds.

Central Agencies

In addition to regular departments that advise individual ministers, the subject of Chapter 21, four main agencies exist to support the prime minister and/or the Cabinet as a whole. These four **central agencies**, already mentioned in passing, are the Prime Minister's Office, the Privy Council Office, the Finance Department, and the Treasury Board.

THE PRIME MINISTER'S OFFICE

The **Prime Minister's Office (PMO)**, made up of temporary, partisan loyalists, was considerably expanded by both Trudeau and Mulroney. It deals with such matters as the prime minister's party relations, partisan appointments, correspondence, media relations, public appearances, travels, constituency matters, and speeches, and briefs the PM on legislative proceedings.[73] Most of all, it organizes the PM's hectic schedule of appointments and meetings. It monitors political developments, offers policy advice from a partisan point of view, and helps the PM handle crises.[74] When Brian Mulroney first came to office, he put all his closest advisers into the PMO and expanded its influence even beyond the level it enjoyed under Trudeau. However, after a series of political mistakes and the government's sharp decline in the polls, most of these original advisers were let go and a new chief of staff brought order to the operation. Ironically, Mulroney seconded a career public servant, Derek Burney, rather than a partisan friend to transform this partisan office. After the 1988 election, the PMO was less influential.

Jean Chrétien's PMO of about 90 bodies was headed by chief of staff Jean Pelletier. Its other principal officials were Eddie Goldenberg, senior policy adviser; Chaviva Hosek, policy and research director; and Peter Donolo (and later, Françoise Ducros), director of communications. As noted below, the PM meets daily with the head of the PMO to be briefed on developments from a partisan perspective.

THE PRIVY COUNCIL OFFICE

The **Privy Council Office (PCO)** has served several unique purposes since it was recognized as the Cabinet secretariat and since Cabinet meetings became more businesslike in 1940 due to the pressures of war.[75] Composed of senior public servants, unlike the partisans of the PMO, the PCO serves as the Prime Minister's public service department and secretariat to the Cabinet and its committees. Indeed, the head of the PCO, the **Clerk of the Privy Council and Secretary to the Cabinet** is the highest-ranking public servant of all, and the responsibilities of the office radiate from the Clerk's three primary functions: the Prime Minister's Deputy Minister, Secretary to the Cabinet, and Head of the Public Service.[76]

In the first place, the PCO provides logistical support for the Cabinet and ensures its smooth operation. This involves preparing agendas, organizing meetings, writing and distributing background material, taking and circulating minutes, and communicating Cabinet decisions. It performs the same services for Cabinet committees; in fact, a branch of the PCO serves as a secretariat for each Cabinet committee (except for Treasury Board, which is supported by the Treasury Board Secretariat), and provides advice to the chair of each committee on agenda items.

But this is much more than a mechanical, secretarial function: the PCO "plays a key role in the elaboration of government policy, supporting the Prime Minister in providing leadership and direction to the Government." In its policy coordination role, the PCO works closely with line departments, as well as with the other three principal central agencies "to ensure that new proposals are consistent with the Government's overall objectives and policies, and that all affected interests have been consulted."[77] Trudeau's original intention in expanding the Privy Council Office was to establish a source of policy advice for himself as prime minister, independent of regular departments, with which he could counter regular bureaucratic recommendations.

Next, the PCO provides advice on such matters as "the broad organization of government, the appointment of individuals to key positions, and the mandates of these senior office holders."[78] Much of the policy leadership and coordination mentioned above is operationalized through the Clerk's position as head of the public service. Responsible for the quality of expert, professional advice and service provided by the public service to the political executive, the Clerk advises on the machinery of government and the appointment, mandates, and promotion of deputy ministers. Moreover, since the Federal–Provincial Relations Office was reintegrated with the PCO in 1993, the latter provides leadership and coordination in all aspects of federal–provincial relations. A whole section of the Office serves the Minister of Intergovernmental Affairs. The PCO also supports the deputy prime minister if that minister has no other place to hang his or her hat.

The PCO under Jean Chrétien was originally headed by Jocelyne Bourgon, the first woman to occupy this prestigious post, and then by Mel Cappe. The office contained Deputy Secretaries of Operations and Plans and Consultation and a Deputy Minister of Intergovernmental Affairs. Others in the PCO were responsible for advising on Security and Intelligence, Priorities and Planning, Aboriginal Affairs, Constitutional Affairs, Foreign and Defence Policy, Economic and Regional Development Policy, Social Development, Machinery of Government, Senior Personnel Management, and Legislation and House Planning. Essentially, at least one "representative" from each department works in the PCO at any time, serving as liaison officers between their department and the PCO. After providing intelligence to the PCO while there, these officers go back to departments indoctrinated with central values. The PCO itself describes the process as follows: "When these officers leave the Privy Council Office, it is with a better appreciation of the workings of the central decision-making process and the vital interrelations that must be considered when developing programs or administering operations."[79]

The Clerk chairs a meeting of senior PCO officials every morning to identify issues to raise with the PM, and all officials of the PCO are expected to alert the Clerk about developments that come to their attention and that might interest the PM or about which the PM might be questioned if the House of Commons is in session. The Clerk and the Chief of Staff of the PMO then meet jointly with the prime minister to review problems and respectively render nonpartisan and partisan advice. The prime minister will be supported throughout the day with detailed strategy notes with regard to meetings, talking to important people in the office, or making critical telephone calls, all of which helps the PCO obtain the kind of results it considers best.

Thus it could be said that the Clerk of the Privy Council is the lynchpin of the government of Canada. This chapter has already established that the prime minister vastly outranks individual Cabinet ministers, and the Clerk, the closest adviser to the PM, has his or her "safe pair of hands"[80] on almost everything that really counts: drafting the speech from the throne, working with the Finance Department and the Treasury Board on the budget, organizing the machinery of government, writing mandate letters for ministers and deputy ministers, appointing and evaluating deputy ministers, chairing the coordinating committees of deputy ministers, keeping an eye on Memorandums to Cabinet, helping to strategize Cabinet and Cabinet committee meetings, and keeping track of federal–provincial relations. The prime minister may be the most important player in the actual making of government decisions, but the Clerk will be advising on almost every one.

THE FINANCE DEPARTMENT

The **Department of Finance** and the Treasury Board primarily supply financial advice to the Cabinet, and have historically exercised a cautioning, restraining influence on new program proposals.[81] The Finance Department is responsible for the government's overall revenue and expenditure situation (macroeconomic policy), including its accumulated debt and annual deficit (if any), and advises on allocations among departments. Under the powerful deputy minister, the department is also the chief adviser on taxation policy and on transfer payments to the provinces. While reporting directly to the minister of Finance and in that sense an ordinary department of government, Finance has a special responsibility of advising the Cabinet collectively on such matters, being incorporated into the process of developing Memorandums to Cabinet, as well as preparing the annual budget via the Expenditure Management System.

The Finance Department has always enjoyed considerable pre-eminence, but in an age of government restraint and retrenchment, its influence necessarily increases; especially in the first term of the Chrétien regime, that department really determined the government's agenda.[82] When Finance said that there was no more money available, for example, Red Book promises were ignored. To some extent it was the minister of Finance talking, but in large measure he was repeating what his senior officials told him to say.

THE TREASURY BOARD SECRETARIAT[83]

The **Treasury Board** is a committee of Cabinet chaired by the minister, called President of the Treasury Board, who is in turn in charge of a full-fledged government department, the **Treasury Board Secretariat**. This Secretariat, under the Secretary of the Treasury Board and Comptroller General, has the overall responsibility for controlling regular departmental spending, being involved in the detailed development of departmental budgets, the Estimates, and overseeing the actual expenditure of funds. The Treasury Board is also in charge of labour relations in the public service and issues policies on personnel, administration, and finance. Although its perspective is more detailed than that of Finance, the two agencies usually see things in a similar light, and Treasury Board's influence also increases when a government is obsessed with its deficit.

The Memorandum to Cabinet and Expenditure Management System

The most significant decisions taken by the Cabinet during any year are the adoption of new policies and the design of the annual budget. These two aspects of the decision-making system can be profitably examined in order to witness the interaction of all the elements previously discussed, namely prime minister, Cabinet, Cabinet committees, minister, departments, and central agencies. They take the form of Memorandums to Cabinet and the Expenditure Management System, respectively.

THE MEMORANDUM TO CABINET

A **Memorandum to Cabinet (MC)** is "the key instrument of written policy advice to Cabinet and, as the tool an individual Minister uses to obtain the support of Cabinet colleagues for a proposed course of action, it plays a pivotal role in the Cabinet decision-making process."[84] The MC starts in an individual department, which develops a policy proposal in consultation with other departments and agencies likely to have an interest, as well as with the PCO, Treasury Board Secretariat, and Finance. Once signed by a minister, the MC is sent to the PCO where it is printed, distributed, and placed on the agenda of the relevant Cabinet committee. It is the prime minister's prerogative to determine to which committee each MC is referred. The PCO secretariat prepares briefing notes for the committee chair that outline the gist of the issue, include Treasury Board and Finance Department comments, and offer suggestions as to how the chair might best conduct the Cabinet committee meeting.

In the committee, the sponsoring minister may make an oral presentation, occasionally involving audio-visual aids such as flip-charts and PowerPoint overheads called "decks." The Cabinet committee's report on the MC is called a Committee Report (CR) and is referred either to the full Cabinet for ratification or back to the sponsoring minister to be reworked. If the committee was unanimous, the CR is usually just appendixed to the agenda of the full Cabinet, and when ratified, an RD (Record of Decision) is issued and referred to the relevant department for action. If a full-scale Cabinet discussion is required, the PCO and PMO prepare briefings for the prime minister, which include advice on how best to approach the discussion in the meeting, such as where various ministers stand on the issue. Audio-visual presentations are occasionally used for the full Cabinet as well.

Each Memorandum to Cabinet contains a ministerial recommendation and an analysis. The former includes a one-sentence summation of the issue and the decision that the sponsoring minister seeks. If it involves the expenditure of funds or bureaucratic resources, it must contain information about costs, sources of funds, and person-years of work. For this reason, departments are advised to establish contact with both Finance and Treasury Board early in the drafting process and maintain contact with them throughout. The next section is the rationale, which may mention the key groups or interests affected. The problems and strategies section notes the positive or negative impacts on a province, region, or other sector of society. The section on political considerations describes consultations with caucus, past party commitments, and so on, while the section on departmental positions outlines the positions taken by concerned departments, for or against. The analysis section is supposed to provide ministers with an outline of the full range of realistic options, the advantages and disadvantages of each, and their financial and policy implications.

Each MC is accompanied by a communications plan that explains how the minister intends to present and explain a decision to the public. It normally assesses attention given to the issue in the House of Commons, in the media, in public opinion polls, and by lobbyists. It identifies the groups with an interest in the proposal, and explains how the department will deal with each one. In particular, it outlines the announcement-day media strategy, as well as follow-up activities to reinforce the message, including speaking tours.

THE EXPENDITURE MANAGEMENT SYSTEM

The government had a formalized system for determining its financial priorities and the distribution of funds long before 1979, but many observers considered it inadequate. New policies had been developed without much concern for their financial implications, and departmental budgeting had started from the bottom up. Thus it fell to Prime Minister Joe Clark to implement a more institutionalized procedure, the Program and Expenditure Management System (PEMS). The system evolved under successive regimes, and the new Liberal government reformed the expenditure management system once again in 1993, largely because of its commitment to reducing the deficit. The annual cycle of the new **Expenditure Management System (EMS)**, providing for input from departments, TBS, Commons committees, Cabinet committees, ministers, PCO, the Finance Department, the minister of Finance, and the prime minister, is best observed in Figure 20.1.[85]

The budget is the government's most important and most comprehensive policy statement of the year. Under Chrétien and Martin, it came "to dominate policy and decision making in Ottawa as never before."[86] Among other things, it is the "key document for decisions on funding major initiatives." While the diagram shows that many interests are given an opportunity to contribute to budget deliberations, especially government departments with their annual business plans, the truth is that its final form is largely the work of the minister of Finance, the PM, and the leading officials of the Treasury Board, Finance Department, and PCO. Both Chrétien and Martin were known "to introduce new measures and policies under the cover of budget secrecy and avoid debate in Cabinet." In Chrétien's case, the most prominent example was the Millennium Scholarship Fund.[87]

When Donald Savoie asserts that "Cabinet is no longer where the important decisions are made,"[88] he is in part stating a matter of fact that the full Cabinet does not really make decisions because they have already been made in Cabinet committees. But his theme is that ministers and Cabinet as a whole are increasingly subordinate to the prime minister, who can influence Cabinet committee as well as individual ministerial decisions in a variety of ways, as outlined above. The flow of government business is often from the centre to the departments, instead of from departments to the centre, and ministers have moved from being

....

Figure 20.1   The Expenditure Management System

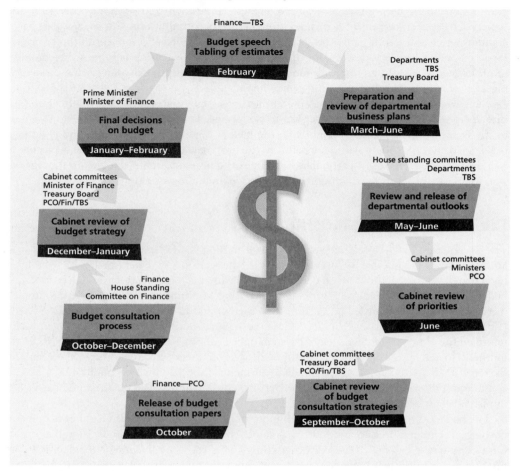

Source: Treasury Board of Canada Secretariat, The Expenditure Management System of the Government of Canada, 1995, Cat. No. BT22-37/1995. *Reproduced with the permission of the Minister of Public Works and Government Services Canada, 2000.*

sources of power to being mere advisers to the PM. With a few exceptions, they are not the most influential advisers either. In short,

> power in the federal government has shifted away from line ministers and their departments towards the centre, and also, within the centre itself, power has shifted to the prime minister and his senior advisers at both the political and public service levels and away from Cabinet and Cabinet committees.[89]

Savoie goes so far as to say that "Cabinet has now joined Parliament as an institution being bypassed."[90]

....

CONCLUSION

While it is anomalous for Canada to share its head of state with others, every country needs symbols of unity and colourful ceremonies. In this connection there are advantages in having a head of state separate from the head of government. In addition, the Crown helps to "keep the government honest." The governor general can intervene in rare emergency situations to ensure that the government of the day does not abuse its power. On a daily basis, however, the political executive is the most significant part of the policymaking process. Individuals want to be appointed to the Cabinet, and societal interests want to feel represented there. Given its importance, the composition of the Cabinet and the manner in which the political executive makes decisions are of great interest to political science. This chapter has shown how the executive decision-making process has changed over time, however, and how power has come to be concentrated in the hands of the prime minister and central government agencies.

(SC) Given the obvious power of the prime minister and Cabinet, the state-centred theory has much to say about the political executive. Most prime ministers, even Mackenzie King, had some personal conception of the public interest that they sought to pursue, but some were more courageous than others about imposing their own agenda in the absence of public support. In promoting their personal ideas, the prime minister and Cabinet must, of course, rely on advice from the bureaucracy. In fact, they often do little more than prioritize problems and then charge the public service with finding solutions to them. Trudeau's objective of rendering the whole decision-making process more rational reflected a dirigiste mentality—government directing society rather than responding to it. On the other hand, in emphasizing privatization, deregulation, and deficit reduction, Mulroney determined that government should not direct society to the same extent, ironically attempting to lead society to be less reliant on the state. For Chrétien, too, the priority was also to reduce the deficit and to render the government less capable of responding to societal demands.

(C) Class analysts claim that the prime minister and Cabinet either come from or respond to the whims of the bourgeoisie. Most Cabinet ministers have been lawyers or business-people and are largely from the petite bourgeoisie or upper middle class rather than the corporate elite. Nevertheless, the big-business connections of Cabinet ministers are quite striking.[91] At the time of Confederation, for example, many ministers were simultaneously directors of railway companies. During the Borden period, ministers were required to divorce themselves from their former business connections, but under King and St. Laurent some ministers maintained such relationships. It is only since about 1960 that ministers have been required to resign directorships and sever active business connections under various versions of conflict-of-interest guidelines. Most have done so, including such former businessmen as Walter Gordon, Robert Winters, Eric Kierans, James Richardson, John Crosbie, Michael Wilson, and Paul Martin, but Sinclair Stevens was forced to resign from the Mulroney Cabinet for not having separated his private and personal affairs.

Class analysts maintain that even if ministers are required to resign corporate positions and to put their investments into some kind of trust, their previous corporate connections will never be far from their mind. Moreover, ministers will be contemplating their post-political existence. Significant numbers of ex-ministers, including Brian Mulroney, have been appointed to corporate boards; many others assumed active executive positions in the business or lobbying communities; and John Turner and Jean Chrétien both worked among big businessmen during their brief respite from politics. Such evidence of the close connection between Cabinet members and the business community bolsters the class analysis critique, especially when only two prominent labour leaders, Humphrey Mitchell and Jean Marchand, have ever been named to the Cabinet. Class analysts such as John Porter found considerable intermarriage and other family connections among the political, bureaucratic, corporate, and intellectual elites.[92]

P Pluralists can hardly argue against the elitist nature of the Cabinet, but they emphasize the conventions of provincial and regional representation therein, and point out that the Cabinet is becoming more diverse in social background over time. Even one of his critics acknowledged that of all political leaders of his generation, Mackenzie King alone really understood that "the essential task of Canadian statesmanship is to discover the terms on which as many as possible of the significant interest groups of our country can be induced to work together in a common policy."[93]

PC Mackenzie King was also perhaps the ultimate practitioner of "public choice" politics. He carefully calculated the electoral consequences of every decision, took whatever decisions were necessary to retain power, and felt that political security usually lay in inaction rather than action.[94] Much evidence of bending to the public choice can also be found in the records of other prime ministers and cabinets, even those of Trudeau and Mulroney, who claimed to be unconcerned with the electoral consequences of their policies. Consistent with the public choice approach, every Cabinet document from both regimes contained a "communications strategy which spells out in considerable detail how policies should be sold."[95]

DISCUSSION QUESTIONS

1. Was Lord Byng justified in 1926 in refusing to grant Prime Minister Mackenzie King a dissolution of Parliament?

2. What are the advantages and disadvantages of recognizing the Queen as our head of state?

3. Do the prime minister and Cabinet, backed up by a majority in the House of Commons, have too much power in the Canadian system of government?

4. Do you think "Cabinet government" or "prime ministerial government" is a more accurate label for the Canadian system of government? Explain your answer.

5. Is the prime ministership becoming increasingly presidentialized? In the absence of the American system of checks and balances between president and Congress, what constraints must the prime minister live with?

6. What were the advantages and disadvantages of the Trudeau effort to make Cabinet decision making more rational?

7. How do each of the approaches outlined in Chapter 1 enhance our understanding of the material in this chapter?

....

NOTES

1. Indeed, David E. Smith, *The Invisible Crown* (Toronto: University of Toronto Press, 1995), writes that "the Crown is the organizing force behind the executive, legislature, administration, and judiciary in both the federal and province spheres of government ... [and] reaches into every area of government activity," p. x.

2. Frank McKinnon, *The Crown in Canada* (Calgary: McClelland and Stewart West, 1976), p. 13.

3. Ibid., p. 47.

4. For the new Letters Patent of 1947, see the *Canada Gazette*, Part I, October 11, 1947, pp. 3014–16. See also Andrew Heard, *Canadian Constitutional Conventions* (Toronto: Oxford University Press, 1991), p. 16.

5. J.T. Saywell, "The Crown and the Politicians: The Canadian Succession Question, 1891–1896," *Canadian Historical Review* (December 1956), pp. 309–37.

6. See, for example, MacKinnon, *The Crown in Canada*, pp. 127–132, and J.R. Mallory, *The Structure of Canadian Government*, rev. ed. (Toronto: Gage, 1984), pp. 51–57.

7. Eugene A. Forsey, *The Royal Power of Dissolution of Parliament in the British Commonwealth* (Toronto: Oxford University Press, 1943; reprinted 1968); "Appointment of Extra Senators under Section 26 of the British North America Act," *Canadian Journal of Economics and Political Science* (May 1946), pp. 159–67; and "Mr. King and Parliamentary Government," *Canadian Journal of Economics and Political Science* (November 1951), pp. 451–67.

8. MacKinnon, *The Crown in Canada*, p. 124.

9. Heard, *Canadian Constitutional Conventions*, p. 47.

10. Ibid., p. 123.

11. Ibid., p. 47.

12. Walter Bagehot, *The English Constitution* (London: Collins, 1963), first published in 1867.

13. See, for example, MacKinnon, *The Crown in Canada*, pp. 56, 101, 103, and Vincent Massey, *What's Past Is Prologue* (Toronto: Macmillan, 1963).

14. David E. Smith, *The Republican Option in Canada, Past and Present* (Toronto: University of Toronto Press, 1999), does not find a republican spirit in either Canada's past or present.

15. W.L. Morton, *The Canadian Identity* (Toronto: University of Toronto Press, 1961); Smith, *The Invisible Crown*.

16. Former premier of Saskatchewan Allan Blakeney, along with Sandford Borins, has written a comprehensive book on how to run a government: *Political Management in Canada: Conversations on Statecraft*, 2nd ed. (Toronto: University of Toronto Press, 1998).

17. Andrew Heard, *Canadian Constitutional Conventions* (Toronto: Oxford University Press, 1991), ch. 3.

18. This title was originally based on appointment to the British Privy Council, but Lester Pearson created "Right Honourable" as a Canadian title, which is bestowed upon the prime minister, governor general, and chief justice of the Supreme Court.

19. In a burst of generosity near the end of his term in 1992, Brian Mulroney appointed a number of prominent Canadians to the Privy Council, including his pal Conrad Black.

20. Kenneth Kernaghan and David Siegel, *Public Administration in Canada: A Text*, 2nd ed. (Scarborough: Nelson Canada, 1991), pp. 379–85.

21. Heard, *Canadian Constitutional Conventions*, pp. 52–56.

22. The concept was first popularized by Richard Crossman in Britain in his Introduction to Walter Bagehot, *The English Constitution* (London: Collins, 1963) and elaborated in *The Myths of Cabinet Government* (Cambridge, MA: Harvard University Press, 1972). See also Patrick Weller, *First among Equals: Prime Ministers in Westminster Systems* (London: Allen & Unwin, 1985). Donald J. Savoie,

Governing from the Centre: The Concentration of Power in Canadian Politics (Toronto: University of Toronto Press, 1999), has made the most definitive such argument in Canada.

23. Savoie, *Governing from the Centre*, p. 71.

24. Ibid., pp. 81–82.

25. Leslie Pal and David Taras, eds., *Prime Ministers and Premiers: Political Leadership and Public Policy in Canada* (Scarborough: Prentice-Hall Canada, 1988); and Peter Aucoin, "Prime Ministerial Leadership: Position, Power, and Politics," in Maureen Mancuso et al., *Leaders and Leadership in Canada* (Toronto: Oxford University Press, 1994).

26. W.A. Matheson, *The Prime Minister and the Cabinet* (Toronto: Methuen, 1976), ch. III, and R.M. Punnett, *The Prime Minister in Canadian Government and Politics* (Toronto: Macmillan, 1977), ch. 4.

27. Savoie, *Governing from the Centre*, pp. 137–39; 343.

28. R.M. Dawson, *The Conscription Crisis of 1944* (Toronto: University of Toronto Press, 1961). Other examples include Trudeau's dismissal of six ministers in 1974.

29. A.D.P. Heeney, "Cabinet Government in Canada: Developments in the Machinery of the Central Executive," *Canadian Journal of Economics and Political Science* (August 1946), pp. 282–301; Savoie, *Governing from the Centre*, p. 125.

30. Savoie, *Governing from the Centre*, p. 328.

31. Leslie Pal, "Prime Ministers and Their Parties: The Cauldron of Leadership," in Pal and Taras, *Prime Ministers and Premiers*.

32. Matheson, *The Prime Minister and the Cabinet*, pp. 127–28.

33. Leslie Pal, "Hands at the Helm? Leadership and Public Policy," in Pal and Taras, *Prime Ministers and Premiers*, p. 25; Savoie, *Governing from the Centre*, p. 316.

34. Christina McCall-Newman, *Grits* (Toronto: Macmillan, 1982), pp. 236–37; Richard Gwyn, *The Northern Magus* (Toronto: McClelland and Stewart, 1980), pp. 325–27; and Patrick Gossage, *Close to the Charisma* (Toronto: McClelland and Stewart, 1986), pp. 145–46.

35. Punnett, *The Prime Minister in Canadian Government and Politics*, ch. 6, and Matheson, *The Prime Minister and the Cabinet*, ch. IX.

36. Savoie, *Governing from the Centre*, p. 94.

37. In this connection, a 1935 minute of the Privy Council is often cited. It can be found in A.D.P. Heeney, "Cabinet Government in Canada," and in Thomas Hockin, ed., *Apex of Power*, 2nd ed. (Scarborough: Prentice-Hall Canada, 1977), pp. 29–30.

38. Kim Richard Nossal, "Political Leadership and Foreign Policy: Trudeau and Mulroney," in Pal and Taras, *Prime Ministers and Premiers*; Savoie, *Governing from the Centre*, pp. 134–37.

39. Frederick Fletcher, "The Prime Minister as Public Persuader," in Hockin, *Apex of Power*. See also Punnett, *The Prime Minister in Canadian Government and Politics*, p. 22.

40. David Taras, "Prime Ministers and the Media," in Pal and Taras, *Prime Ministers and Premiers*, p. 36.

41. Savoie, *Governing from the Centre*, p. 72. In fact, an obsession with media attacks on minor points often distracts PMs from more important aspects of their work.

42. Gossage, *Close to the Charisma*; and Michel Gratton, *So, What Are the Boys Saying?* (Toronto: McGraw-Hill Ryerson, 1987); Bill Fox, *Spinwars: Politics and New Media* (Toronto: Key Porter Books, 1999).

43. Fred Schindeler, "The Prime Minister and the Cabinet: History and Development," in Hockin, *Apex of Power*, p. 22.

44. Denis Smith, "President and Parliament: The Transformation of Parliamentary Government in Canada," in Hockin, *Apex of Power*, p. 315.

45. Hockin, "The Prime Minister and Political Leadership: An Introduction to Some Restraints and Imperatives," in *Apex of Power*. See also Punnett, *The Prime Minister in Canadian Government and Politics*, p. 157, Matheson, *The Prime Minister and the Cabinet*, pp. 170–76, and Pal and Taras, *Prime Ministers and Premiers*, pp. 102–3.

46. Savoie, *Governing from the Centre*, pp. 87–97, 108.

47. Peter C. Newman, *Renegade in Power* (Toronto: McClelland and Stewart, 1963).

48. F.W. Gibson, *Cabinet Formation and Bicultural Relations* (Ottawa: Queen's Printer, 1970), ch. VIII; John English, "The 'French Lieutenant' in Ottawa," in R.K. Carty and W.P. Ward, eds., *National Politics and Community in Canada* (Vancouver: University of British Columbia Press, 1986); and Matheson, *The Prime Minister and the Cabinet*, pp. 34–38.

49. Matheson, *The Prime Minister and the Cabinet*, chs. II and V.
50. Ibid., p. 32.
51. Heard, *Canadian Constitutional Conventions*.
52. General A.G.L. McNaughton served for over nine months as minister of Defence in 1944–45, suffering a by-election loss and a general election loss before finally resigning from the Cabinet. Pierre Juneau resigned as secretary of state when he failed to win a by-election in 1975.
53. Herman Bakvis, *Regional Ministers* (Toronto: University of Toronto Press, 1991). Bakvis has other interesting things to say about ministerial quality in "Cabinet Ministers: Leaders or Followers" in Maureen Mancuso et al., eds., *Leaders and Leadership in Canada* (Toronto: Oxford University Press, 1994).
54. This table does not include all ministers because cabinets were shuffled after being formed. Nevertheless, it provides just as accurate a presentation of provincial representationas the inclusion all ministers, because the latter figures would be skewed due to varied lengths of ministerial service.
55. Matheson, *The Prime Minister and the Cabinet*, pp. ix, 22–23.
56. On this subject, see the seven case studies in the study of the Royal Commission on Bilingualism and Biculturalism edited by Frederick W. Gibson, *Cabinet Formation and Bicultural Relations*. Gibson argues that francophones had no monopoly on the desire for patronage, p. 172.
57. Matheson, *The Prime Minister and the Cabinet*, pp. 90–91.
58. S.L. Sutherland, "Responsible Government and Ministerial Responsibility: Every Reform Is Its Own Problem," *Canadian Journal of Political Science* (March 1991), p. 101.
59. J. Stefan Dupré, "Reflections on the Workability of Executive Federalism," in Richard Simeon, ed., *Intergovernmental Relations* (Toronto: University of Toronto Press, 1985).
60. J.W. Pickersgill, *The Mackenzie King Record*, vol. 1 (Toronto: University of Toronto Press, 1960), p. 7.
61. Bakvis, *Regional Ministers*.
62. Donald Smiley, *The Federal Condition in Canada* (Toronto: McGraw-Hill Ryerson, 1987), p. 88.
63. Matheson, *The Prime Minister and the Cabinet*, p. 178.
64. G. Bruce Doern and Peter Aucoin, eds., *The Structures of Policy-Making in Canada* (Toronto: Macmillan, 1971) and *Public Policy in Canada* (Toronto: Macmillan, 1979); Colin Campbell and George Szablowski, *The Superbureaucrats* (Toronto: Macmillan, 1979); several articles in Hockin's *Apex of Power*; Peter Aucoin, "Organizational Change in the Machinery of Canadian Government: From Rational Management to Brokerage Politics," *Canadian Journal of Political Science* (March 1986), pp. 3–27; and Richard French, *How Ottawa Decides*, 2nd ed. (Toronto: Lorimer, 1984). Christopher Dunn and Paul Barker debate the merits of the institutionalized Cabinet in Mark Charlton and Paul Barker, eds., *Crosscurrents: Contemporary Political Issues*, 3rd ed. (Scarborough: ITP Nelson, 1998), ch. 12.
65. Peter Aucoin, "Organizational Change in the Machinery of Canadian Government."
66. Punnett, *The Prime Minister*, p. 110; Walter Stewart, *Shrug: Trudeau in Power* (Toronto: New Press, 1971), ch. 11.
67. Aucoin, "Organizational Change in the Machinery of Canadian Government."
68. Savoie, *Governing from the Centre*, p. 325. The "official" version is provided in Jocelyne Bourgon's *Third Annual Report to the Prime Minister on the Public Service of Canada* (Ottawa: Privy Council Office, 1995), p. 16.
69. This account is partly based on Savoie's *Governing from the Centre*.
70. Ibid., pp. 273, 360.
71. Earlier Cabinet committees were primarily used in the First and Second World Wars. See descriptions in Punnett, *The Prime Minister in Canadian Government and Politics*, pp. 72–74, and Matheson, *The Prime Minister and the Cabinet*, pp. 83–87.
72. PCO website: http://www.pco-bcp.gc.ca.
73. Marc Lalonde, "The Changing Role of the Prime Minister's Office," *Canadian Public Administration* (Winter 1971), pp. 509–37; Privy Council Office, *Decision-Making Processes and Central Agencies in Canada: Federal, Provincial and Territorial Practices* (Ottawa, 1998), pp. 2–3.
74. Savoie, *Governing from the Centre*, p. 99; Thomas Axworthy, "Of Secretaries to Princes," *Canadian Public Administration* (Summer 1988), pp. 247–64.
75. A.D.P. Heeney, *The Things That Are Caesar's* (Toronto: University of Toronto Press, 1972), ch. 6; and Gordon Robertson, "The Changing Role of the Privy Council Office," *Canadian Public Administration*

(Winter 1971), pp. 487–508. Mr. Robertson was Clerk of the Privy Council throughout much of the Pearson and Trudeau periods.

76. Privy Council Office, *The Role and Structure of the Privy Council Office* (Ottawa, 1999), p. 1.
77. PCO, *Decision-Making Processes and Central Agencies in Canada*, p. 4.
78. Ibid., p. 3.
79. Ibid.
80. Donald Savoie's description, *Governing from the Centre*, ch. 5.
81. Donald J. Savoie, *The Politics of Public Spending in Canada* (Toronto: University of Toronto Press, 1990), ch. 4.
82. Edward Greenspon and Anthony Wilson-Smith, *Double Vision: The Inside Story of the Liberals in Power* (Toronto: Doubleday Canada, 1996).
83. Savoie, *The Politics of Public Spending in Canada*, ch. 5.
84. This whole section is based on the Privy Council Office's document, *Memorandum to Cabinet*, a public document brought to my attention by James Hurley of the PCO and supplemented by a delightful interview.
85. Treasury Board, *The Expenditure Management System of the Government of Canada* (Ottawa: Supply and Services, 1995).
86. Savoie, *Governing from the Centre*, p. 189.
87. Ibid., pp. 189, 317.
88. Ibid., p. 260.
89. Ibid., pp. 7–8, 338.
90. Ibid., p. 362.
91. Matheson, *The Prime Minister and the Cabinet*, pp. 121–25.
92. John Porter, *The Vertical Mosaic* (Toronto: University of Toronto Press, 1965), ch. XVII.
93. F.H. Underhill, *In Search of Canadian Liberalism*, quoted in Hockin, *Apex of Power*, p. 290.
94. "Mackenzie King genuinely believed and frequently said that the real secret of political leadership was more in what was prevented than in what was accomplished." Pickersgill, *The Mackenzie King Record*, vol. 1, p. 10. This was obviously the strategy of Jean Chrétien as well.
95. David Taras, "Prime Ministers and the Media," in Pal and Taras, *Prime Ministers and Premiers*, p. 38.

FURTHER READING

Aucoin, Peter. "Organizational Change in the Machinery of Canadian Government: From Rational Management to Brokerage Politics." *Canadian Journal of Political Science* (March, 1986), pp. 3–27.

Bakvis, Herman. *Regional Ministers*. Toronto: University of Toronto Press, 1991.

Blakeney, Allan, and Sandford Borins. *Political Management in Canada: Conversations on Statecraft*, 2nd ed. Toronto: University of Toronto Press, 1998.

Dupré, J. Stefan. "Reflections on the Workability of Executive Federalism." In Richard Simeon, ed., *Intergovernmental Relations*. Toronto: University of Toronto Press, 1985.

English, John. "The French 'Lieutenant' in Ottawa." In R.K. Carty and W.P. Ward, eds., *National Politics and Community in Canada*. Vancouver: University of British Columbia Press, 1986.

Forsey, Eugene. *The Royal Power of Dissolution of Parliament in the British Commonwealth*. Toronto: Oxford University Press, 1943; reprinted 1968.

Gossage, Patrick. *Close to the Charisma*. Toronto: McClelland and Stewart, 1986.

Gratton, Michel. *So, What Are the Boys Saying?* Toronto: McGraw-Hill Ryerson, 1987.

Greenspon, Edward, and Anthony Wilson-Smith. *Double Vision: The Inside Story of the Liberals in Power*. Toronto: Doubleday Canada, 1996.

Heard, Andrew. *Canadian Constitutional Conventions*. Toronto: Oxford University Press, 1991.

Hockin, Thomas, ed. *Apex of Power*, 2nd ed. Scarborough: Prentice-Hall Canada, 1977.

Lalonde, Marc. "The Changing Role of the Prime Minister's Office." *Canadian Public Administration* (Winter 1971), pp. 509–37.

Mancuso, Maureen, et al., eds. *Leaders and Leadership in Canada*. Toronto: Oxford University Press, 1994.

Matheson, W.A. *The Prime Minister and the Cabinet*. Toronto: Methuen, 1976.

McKinnon, Frank. *The Crown in Canada*. Calgary: McClelland and Stewart West, 1976.

McWhinney, Edward. "Prerogative Powers of the Head of State" *Canadian Bar Review* (January 1957), pp. 92–96.

Pal, Leslie, and David Taras, eds. *Prime Ministers and Premiers: Political Leadership and Public Policy in Canada*. Scarborough: Prentice-Hall Canada, 1988.

Privy Council Office. *Decision-Making Processes and Central Agencies in Canada: Federal, Provincial and Territorial Practices*. Ottawa, 1998.

———. *The Role and Structure of the Privy Council Office*. Ottawa, 1999.

Punnett, R.M. *The Prime Minister in Canadian Government*. Toronto: Macmillan, 1977.

Robertson, Gordon. "The Changing Role of the Privy Council Office." *Canadian Public Administration* (Winter 1971), pp. 487–508.

Savoie, Donald J. *The Politics of Public Spending in Canada*. Toronto: University of Toronto Press, 1990.

———. *Governing from the Centre: The Concentration of Power in Canadian Politics*. Toronto: University of Toronto Press, 1999.

Saywell, J.T. "The Crown and the Politicians: The Canadian Succession Question 1891–1896." *Canadian Historical Review* (December 1956), pp. 309–37.

Smith, David E. *The Invisible Crown*. Toronto: University of Toronto Press, 1995.

———. *The Republican Option in Canada, Past and Present*. Toronto: University of Toronto Press, 1999.

Smith, Denis. "President and Parliament: The Transformation of Parliamentary Government in Canada," in Thomas Hockin, ed., *Apex of Power*, 2nd ed. Scarborough: Prentice-Hall Canada, 1977.

Chapter 21

The BUREAUCRACY

Federal public servants deliver the mail, issue old age security cheques and passports, process income tax and GST forms, admit immigrants, approve new drugs and search for illicit ones, engage in UN peacekeeping operations, guard penitentiaries, negotiate treaties with domestic Aboriginals as well as with foreign countries, and provide myriad other services that are often taken for granted by the general public. For the most part, the federal bureaucracy performs these functions in a more than satisfactory manner, but if any hitch occurs, Canadians are quick to condemn the "red tape" and "slow-moving bureaucrats" in Ottawa. Whether such faults are more characteristic of government than of large, private-sector corporations and whether the Chrétien government's downsizing of the bureaucracy will change its methods of operation for better or worse remain open questions.

Even though the bureaucracy, or public service, is generally not as visible as the other three branches of government, it is no less important. Most citizens encounter public servants in the provision of services, but the bureaucracy is probably even more significant in its advisory role. Modern government is so pervasive and complex that the prime minister and ministers hardly ever make a move without the advice of their permanent, expert staff. Most public servants work in various government departments, but these are supplemented by a vast array of Crown corporations and administrative agencies of many kinds. In fact, the bureaucracy has become so large and indispensable that many observers wonder whether it can be kept under political control.

This chapter begins by examining the functions and powers of the bureaucracy. It then deals in turn with the three main kinds of bureaucratic organization: the government department, the Crown corporation, and administrative agencies and regulatory tribunals. The chapter concludes with a discussion of controlling the bureaucracy and recent attempts to reform it.

FUNCTIONS AND POWERS OF THE BUREAUCRACY

The traditional function of the bureaucracy is that of rule application or policy implementation, that is, administering policies established by the prime minister, Cabinet, and legislature. While this is still an important part of its work, the bureaucracy is equally involved in the function of rule making. Besides advising the politicians in their capacity as rule makers, the bureaucracy is delegated wide "quasi-legislative" powers to make subordinate rules on its own. And while the courts are the foremost adjudicators of disputes in society, the bureaucracy has also encroached upon their territory in the rule adjudication function, such that many disputes are now resolved by "quasi-judicial" administrative tribunals. Less formally, the bureaucracy also engages in interest articulation, in the sense of various departments speaking up for their own concerns or helping to advance the demands of their principal clientele. Interdepartmental and central agencies are involved in interest aggregation, the bureaucracy recruits large numbers of significant political actors, and it has an important role in political communication, listening to the public and transmitting the government's response.

If the significance of the bureaucracy can be seen in its performance of all seven traditional functions in the political system, this can also be demonstrated by examining its presence in the model of the policymaking process presented in Chapter 19. First, it plays a crucial part in the initiation phase. The bureaucracy may be a source of demands, whether these are self-interested or on behalf of its clientele, since administrators of a program may be among the first to recognize its inadequacies. Even if a demand reaches the prime minister and Cabinet from other sources, once the politicians decide to look into an issue further, the public service will usually be asked to provide them with additional information and advice.

If the prime minister and Cabinet decide to take additional action at the priority-setting stage, the bureaucracy is then centrally involved in the policy formulation phase. With its concentration of technical information and experience, the public service spends a great deal of its time in formulating policies, since the details of such policies are usually beyond the grasp of the politicians.

In analyses of the role of the bureaucracy in policy formulation, several distinct subtheories arise, the first of which is the **rational choice** model. It suggests that once a problem has been identified, the bureaucrats will seek the most rational means to solve it. Public servants go through a rational procedure of setting their goal, developing a full range of possible solutions, gathering material on the pros and cons of each such alternative, and then making the most rational choice. Given the tremendous informational resources of the bureaucracy in modern government, it is sometimes assumed that such rational decisions are actually possible.

Other observers argue that the bureaucracy is more inclined toward **incrementalism**, claiming that bureaucrats are likely to make only marginal changes in existing policy at any one time. That is to say, the bureaucracy's analysis of options is not so comprehensive, and its decisions and recommendations are usually small-scale, incremental alterations to the status quo.

Once the policy, program, or law has received political authorization by Parliament in the legitimization phase, implementation is almost exclusively a bureaucratic responsibility. In today's complex society, the politicians are forced to leave wide discretionary powers to the public service to carry out their general, abstract goals.[1] A considerable lag often exists between the political approval of a law and its effective implementation, during which time the public service drafts regulations under the act, sets up new administrative machinery, and hires new personnel. Because of the time and informational constraints on Parliament, most bills are passed in rather general or skeletal form, and the real meat or substance of the law is expressed in the **regulations** issued under it. These are published under the authority of the minister or Cabinet in the *Canada Gazette*. The implementation of a law may thus see the bureaucracy making decisions that constitute quasi-legislative outputs that involve time-consuming negotiations with the provinces or with relevant interest groups.

Once the date set for the start of a new program arrives, it is the bureaucracy that actually provides the service, does the regulating, or performs whatever other rule application functions are involved. Implementation also requires disseminating information to the public about new policies or programs. Governments now spend great quantities of public funds advertising their programs on the grounds that this is essential if they are to be fully effective. A final aspect of implementation is program evaluation, that is, an assessment of the adequacies of a policy after a period of operation. Program evaluation is becoming a more regular and sophisticated addition to the field of policy analysis.

Given its role in almost all phases of the policymaking process, reference to "bureaucratic power" in political science or contentions that the bureaucracy is more powerful than the legislature or even the prime minister and Cabinet should not be surprising. It is more conventional to say that the prime minister and Cabinet make the most important decisions in the political system and that they theoretically control the bureaucracy. The bureaucrats *advise* on almost every decision, but the prime minister and ministers actually *make* the political decisions. Donald Savoie argues that career officials "respond whenever *clear* and *consistent* political direction is given."[2] But this is not to deny the extent of bureaucratic power in the modern state. Table 21.1 shows that the number of people involved in the federal public service is close to 350 000, and breaks this number down into its component parts. These figures exclude the federal courts, Parliament (governor general, House of Commons, and Senate), and the political staff of the prime minister and ministers. About 60 000 armed forces personnel are included in the work force of the Defence Department, while about 19 500 RCMP personnel are included in the agencies attached to the Solicitor General.

TABLE 21.1   **The Federal Public Service, as of 1998–1999**

Regular government departments	213 990
Crown corporations	74 504
Other government agencies	56 363
Agents of Parliament	2 042
TOTAL	346 899

Source: *Privy Council Office*, Portfolio Management, *January 1999; calculations by author. Reproduced with the permission of the Minister of Public Works and Government Services Canada, 2000.*

GOVERNMENT DEPARTMENTS
Number, Structure, and Size

Most Cabinet ministers oversee a family or portfolio of separate but related organizations including a government department, service agencies, Crown corporations, and regulatory tribunals.[3] Government **departments** are created and reorganized by Acts of Parliament, which also set out the responsibilities of each. But the prime minister and Cabinet can determine the internal structure of the department and even have the power to transfer responsibilities from one department to another.

A major consolidation of departments took place in 1993, reducing the overall number from 25 to 20. The following departments continued to operate much as before: Finance, Fisheries and Oceans, Indian and Northern Affairs, International Trade, Justice, and Transport. External Affairs became Foreign Affairs and Agriculture became Agriculture and Agri-Food. Industry incorporated Science, Small Business, and Consumer and Corporate Affairs; Public Works and Government Services were combined; and Natural Resources was formed from Forestry and Energy, Mines and Resources. The most significant changes were the creation of Human Resources Development, which incorporated Employment, Welfare, and Labour; and Canadian Heritage, made up of Secretary of State, Multiculturalism, and Communications. Under Kim Campbell, Immigration was lumped with the Solicitor General into Public Security, but Jean Chrétien re-established these two separate departments. Chapter 20 mentioned 28 ministers, leaving seven without full-fledged departments—the prime minister; deputy prime minister; government leaders in the House of Commons and Senate; Labour; Intergovernmental Affairs; and International Cooperation—while two ministers shared Foreign Affairs and International Trade. The largest departments in terms of personnel are National Defence, Revenue Canada, Human Resources Development, and Public Works and Government Services. Table 21.2 lists the government departments in the Chrétien era, together with the size of the department's personnel and that of administrative agencies and Crown corporations attached to the department.

The government department assumes a pyramidal shape, with the minister at its apex. Since ministers in this system (unlike in the United States) are chosen from among the politicians elected to Parliament, it is too much to hope that they will be experts in the work of the department or able managers. All that is expected is that they are individuals with intelligence, ideas, common sense, and an ability to relay government priorities and public opinion to departmental experts as well as to relate expert advice from the department to Parliament and the public. Ministers will naturally develop some expertise if they stay in one Cabinet position for any length of time, but nowadays they are usually shuffled to another department just as they are getting the hang of it. Jean Chrétien reverted to the earlier practice of leaving ministers in place if moves could be avoided.

Ministers are responsible for their department in the sense that they are expected to provide overall direction and to accept criticism for its faults. In other words, ministers take most of the credit or blame for what the department does, whether or not they know what is going on within it. As pointed out in Chapter 20, the principle of **ministerial responsibility** was once thought to mean that ministers had to resign for serious mistakes made by their public servants, even if unaware of them. Whether this theory was ever practised in Canada is questionable— there are no cases of such resignations since 1867—but certainly in this age of big government it is not a realistic proposition.[4] What does ministerial responsibility mean today? First, ministers occasionally resign over their personal mistakes, but not as routinely as in Britain. Second, they must take political responsibility and answer to Parliament for all the actions of their officials. The minister must explain and defend the actions of the department in Parliament, especially during Question Period, and when a bureaucratic error is made, the minister must apologize and promise to correct the mistake. Third, although ministers may discreetly discipline the offender, they should not violate the traditions of public-service anonymity.[5]

The more permanent head of the department is the **deputy minister**. Appointed by the prime minister (on the advice of the secretary to the Cabinet), "deputies" or "DMs" are usually career public servants. In other words, they are rarely patronage appointments. Deputy

TABLE 21.2   Government Departments in the Chrétien Era, Including Size of Work Force and Associated Agencies and Crown Corporations

	Department	Administrative Agencies	Crown Corporations	Total
Agriculture and Agri-Food	5 408	4 556	862	10 826
Canadian Heritage	4 615	2 099	9 440	16 154
Citizenship and Immigration	3 815	1 026		4 841
Environment	4 141	95		4 236
Finance	706	504	1 691	2 901
Fisheries and Oceans	8 569		32	8 601
Foreign Affairs and International Trade*	3 806	1 264	1 075	6 145
Health	5 969	129	13	6 111
Human Resources Devel.	20 074	108	87	20 269
Indian and Northern Affairs	3 254	6		3 260
Industry	4 892	9 666	1 208	15 766
Justice	2 254	248		2 502
National Defence	81 417	890		82 307
Natural Resources	3 671	716	6 023	10 410
Public Works and Government Services	11 557	60	47 529	59 146
Revenue	40 422			40 422
Solicitor General	210	34 147		34 357
Transport	4 480	257	6 544	11 281
Treasury Board	780			780
Veterans Affairs	3 235	105		3 340
(Prime Minister/PCO	715	487		1 202)
TOTAL	213 990	56 363	74 504	344 857

Source: Privy Council Office, Portfolio Management, January 1999; calculations by author. Reproduced with the permission of the Minister of Public Works and Government Services Canada, 2000.
*One department but two separate ministers.

ministers have two principal roles: they act as chief policy adviser to the minister and function as manager of the department; they, not the minister, run the department.[6] Such officials used to spend a lifetime working their way to the top of a single department and became great experts in its subject matter. Since the 1962 Glassco Report, which recommended the adoption of private-sector managerial techniques in the public sector, emphasis in the appointment of deputy ministers has switched from expertise in the subject matter of the department to managerial skills that can be applied in any administrative setting. In recent years they, too, have been frequently shuffled from one department to another. Even so, the deputy minister is usually there longer than the minister and is thus likely to develop greater knowledge of the department's work. Deputy ministers also interact regularly with DMs in other federal departments, provincial DMs in corresponding departments, and the heads of pressure groups particularly interested in the department's work.

The relationship between the minister and the deputy minister is of great interest and concern to political science and public administration.[7] In theory, the minister sets the priorities for the department, based to some extent on the party platform, the prime minister's objectives, and the minister's own projects. Whether in determining priorities or in implementing them, the DM ideally provides a number of options among which the minister can choose. The deputy should give the minister advice that is based not only on administrative, technical, and financial considerations, but that is also sensitive to the political context. Evidence exists that the reality of the relationship sometimes approaches this theoretical ideal. On the other hand, weak ministers may be mere puppets of their bureaucratic advisers, and even strong ministers may encounter bureaucratic resistance to new initiatives such as in being denied relevant information, having it delayed, or in having new policies implemented without enthusiasm.[8] In any case, ministers are busy doing other things and do not spend much time in their departmental offices. In most cases (Finance being an exception), the minister and deputy minister only see each other during a weekly briefing session.[9]

Besides their loyalty to their department, deputy ministers nowadays have strong links to the centre of government, especially the Privy Council Office. The Clerk of the Privy Council chairs weekly deputy minister breakfast meetings, monthly luncheons, semi-annual retreats, and several standing committees of deputy ministers; they have been appointed by the centre, their promotion prospects depend on the centre, and they spend a great deal of their time "managing sensitive files for the centre."[10] Through the Clerk, deputy ministers have a connection to the prime minister that increasingly approaches the importance of the relationship with their own minister.

It is not easy for a single, solitary, temporary, amateur minister to impose his or her will on the deputy minister and the hundreds or thousands of other expert, permanent public servants who have established departmental attitudes, values, policies, and procedures. The small personal staff that ministers are allowed to appoint may be of some assistance in this situation. On the other hand, the minister's staff is primarily engaged in promoting the image and reputation of the minister,[11] and doing favours for supporters and friends. While they may provide partisan policy advice, any effort to interfere in the administration of the department will be strongly resented by the deputy minister. In the Mulroney regime, ministers set up large offices headed by a powerful chief of staff whose authority rivalled that of the deputy minister and who was, among other things, the target of most lobbying efforts. As in other ways, Chrétien reverted to an earlier era by reducing the size and significance of ministerial offices and eliminating the chief of staff position. Ministers could hire a maximum of five officers and seven support staff, with a maximum salary budget of $550 000 and a maximum operating budget of $500 000. One sign of the lesser importance of such offices was that lobbyists transferred their attention to the bureaucracy.

It is sometimes suggested that Canada should move to the American practice of replacing the whole top level of bureaucrats when the government changes so that the leading officials in each department will be enthusiastically supportive of the new regime. To some extent this was the basis of the Mulroney experiment with powerful chiefs of staff. Given the minor ideological differences between the Canadian parties at the national level, however, few observers find this either necessary or desirable. Opposition parties often accuse the public service of becoming too sympathetic to a longstanding government party (e.g., in the 1935–57 and 1963–84 Liberal periods), but the Diefenbaker, Clark, and Mulroney cabinets did not rid themselves of more than one or two senior bureaucrats. At the provincial level, however, this issue has on occasion been a problem for social democratic governments.

Below the deputy minister, the department is typically divided into several branches each headed by an assistant deputy minister (ADM); these in turn are subdivided again and again. Figure 21.1 illustrates this hierarchical structure in the case of the Public Works and Government Services Department. Those divisions of a department that actually carry out services and interact with the public are said to be performing "line" functions. Except for the top managerial posts, most of the line positions in any department will be located in the "field"—in local offices in communities across the country. But every department will also have "staff" divisions that serve such internal needs as policy development and research, personnel, financial, information, and legal divisions. These positions are normally located in Ottawa along with the heads of the line divisions.

The hundreds or thousands of public servants in the department are ranged in descending levels of authority under the deputy minister and share four basic characteristics: they are expert, permanent, impartial, and anonymous. First, they are chosen on their merits—ability, knowledge, training, and/or experience—for the duties their position entails. Second, they are career public servants, who normally remain within the public service until retirement. Third, they are nonpartisan and expected to serve whichever party comes to power with equal loyalty and enthusiasm. Fourth, bureaucrats are not normally identified in public; instead, the minister speaks for the department and takes the public and parliamentary responsibility for its performance. Even when public servants brief the media about new policies, for example, they are only referred to as "officials of the department."

The federal public service is divided into six occupational categories, within which are a large number of more specific occupational groups. The six categories, with examples of groups they contain, are as follows: executive group (senior management); scientific and professional (statistics, auditing); administrative and foreign service (personnel administration, program administration); technical (drafting); administrative support (clerical and regulatory, secretarial, stenographic and typing); and operational (correctional, firefighter). The first four categories are called "officer" categories, generally requiring postsecondary education, while the last two are called "support." Recent university graduates are normally hired in the administrative and foreign service or scientific and professional groups, and work their way up from there. Within each group are many levels or steps—for example, within the clerk category are CR1, CR2, etc.—that determine one's salary level. It is an extremely complex operation to draw up a job description for over 200 000 positions and to evaluate and classify them for purposes of determining necessary qualifications and salary. At the end of the century, the whole public service was embroiled in designing a new classification plan called Universal Classification Standard (UCS), which was intended to simplify the service, reduce the number of different jobs, and render the standard gender-neutral. Each position would be based on four factors: skill, effort, responsibility, and working conditions.

Figure 21.1   Organizational Structure of Public Works and Government Services Canada, 1999

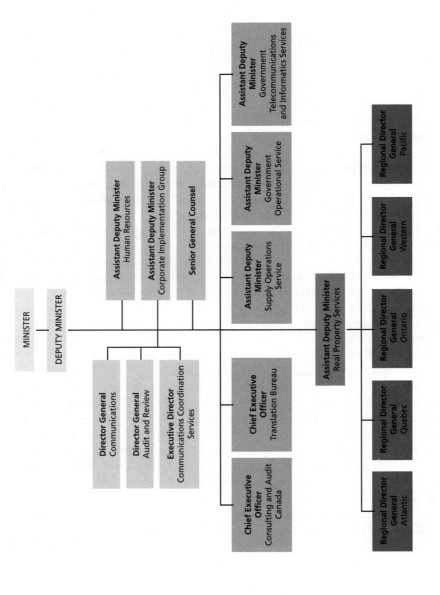

Source: Public Works and Government Services Canada, 1999–2000 Estimates, p. 58.

Some public servants spend much of their time applying for positions higher in the scale and going to interviews in the hope of promotion. In order to make the appointment and promotion processes as equitable as possible, notice of vacancies must be given, and after the interviews are conducted and decisions made, there is provision for appeal, meaning that the whole operation is characterized by long delays and procedural rigidities. As in any hiring situation, it is difficult to make the interview fair and to prevent favouritism from intruding. Those who do stay in their jobs are subject to annual performance evaluation by their superiors that may also result in the filing of grievances and appeals.

Relations with Other Departments and Central Agencies

The operation of a government department is complicated by the necessity of interacting with other departments as well as by the authority of various central bureaucratic agencies to intervene in its affairs. Since almost any law, policy, or program affects a variety of departments, many permanent and ad hoc interdepartmental committees exist. Among the permanent ones are two coordinating committees of deputy ministers, one on management and the other on policy. Beyond these, whenever a new policy is under active consideration, an ad hoc interdepartmental committee is appointed to look into it. Not only must the problem be examined from a number of departmental perspectives, but it is also subject to considerable bureaucratic "politics" and territorial claims. Ministers as well as deputy ministers constantly have to reconcile their departmental interests with the need to coordinate their activities with other departments, and generally cannot act unilaterally if such action would have any impact on other departments' programs or policies.[12]

The central agencies that complicate the life of a department include the Public Service Commission (PSC), the Treasury Board Secretariat, the Privy Council Office, the Department of Finance, and the Prime Minister's Office, most of which were mentioned in Chapter 20. The **Public Service Commission** is a three-member board headed by a chair of deputy minister status that safeguards the principles of competence, nonpartisanship, and representation, and that is theoretically in charge of all hiring, promotions, and dismissals. In practice, however, the PSC delegates much of its authority to individual departments. It is primarily concerned to police the merit system, preventing appointments and promotions from being made on partisan or discriminatory grounds, and is consequently involved in the appeal process (called recourse) when claims of discrimination of any kind are made. It considers several thousand appeals every year and offers staff development and training programs, including second-language training, to thousands more.

The **Treasury Board Secretariat** was discussed in Chapter 20, but its role merits re-emphasis, especially in personnel, financial, and expenditure management. The TBS essentially determines the terms and conditions of employment for the public service. It is in charge of the classification or reclassification of positions, and represents the employer in the collective bargaining process. On the financial management side, the TBS is responsible for the preparation of the Estimates, which normally involves cutting back on departmental spending proposals, especially when the government's priority is to reduce the deficit and balance the budget. It also establishes the policy framework in such areas as information technology, contracting, and accounting, oversees the actual expenditure of public funds, and tries to improve departmental management through such devices as program evaluation.[13] Along with the TBS, the Department of Finance is usually an opponent of new department spending programs and an advocate of retrenchment.

The Privy Council Office's relations with regular government departments have also been referred to above and are perhaps even more significant than those of the TBS. They primarily arise in connection with policy development and coordination, reallocation of programs between departments, the reorganization of departments, and senior management appointments. Although the deputy minister will probably have had a hand in the mandate letter given to the new minister of the department, these letters are ultimately drafted by the PCO with the approval of the PM. The PCO will also take a great interest in any new policy proposal emanating from the department, typically in a Memorandum to Cabinet. The Prime Minister's Office, on the other hand, does not interact frequently with departments except with respect to new policy initiatives or political problems (i.e., crises) engaging the prime minister.

The Merit Principle and a Representative Bureaucracy

For about 40 years after Confederation, the Canadian public service operated on the **spoils system**, under which the party that won an election could replace those holding civil service positions with its own friends and supporters. One of the main motives for entering the political arena in that era was to reward family and friends with **political patronage**—government jobs and contracts.[14] Such partisan, amateur personnel proved to be increasingly inadequate as government operations grew more complex after the turn of the century. Hence the passage of the Civil Service Amendment Act in 1908, which created the Civil Service Commission (predecessor to the Public Service Commission). It meant that public servants in Ottawa were hired on the **merit system**, and after the 1918 Civil Service Act, field positions were also to be based on merit. Politicians, however, were reluctant to give up their traditional right to reward their supporters with government jobs, and it is difficult to say exactly when the merit system was finally entrenched. The foundations of the modern merit system in Ottawa were laid in the 1930s by O.D. Skelton, especially at External Affairs, Clifford Clark in Finance, and Graham Towers at the Bank of Canada.[15]

If patronage was virtually eliminated in the public service, however, there remained considerable scope for partisan appointments in other areas, to say nothing of contracts for corporate friends. Senators, the boards of regulatory and other administrative agencies and Crown corporations, certain diplomatic posts, the PMO and ministers' offices, lieutenant governorships, citizenship court judgeships, and the real judgeships were all positions in which partisan appointments still prevailed. The Liberals accused Brian Mulroney of excessive patronage, but in fact the Chrétien government had an undeserved reputation for being more restrained. The Liberals did, however, wind up 73 agencies and restructure 47 others, eliminating some 665 patronage positions in the process,[16] not because of moral reservations but as an economic move.

Almost as soon as the merit system was fully effective, the call began to be made that the bureaucracy should be more representative of the society it serves. Given the power of the public service and the assumption that its recommendations and decisions would reflect the origins and pre–public service values of its members, many critics argued that the public service could only be responsive to all parts of society if it included a proportional representation of various groups in the population. The senior levels of the public service had always overrepresented males, anglophones, the middle and upper classes, the well educated, and Ontarians.[17] Thus it was claimed that policy recommendations and implementation reflected an insensitivity to women, francophones, and other ethnic groups, to the peculiarities of hinterland regions and provinces, and to the working class and the poor.

The first main concerns in this connection were the small number of francophones in the higher reaches of the bureaucracy and the virtual absence of the use of the French language at the policymaking levels. The passage of the **Official Languages Act** of 1969 essentially bilingualized the executive branch of government. It gave both English- and French-speaking citizens the right to deal with head offices of government departments in either official language, as well as with local offices where numbers warranted. It also expanded language training programs started by the Pearson government in 1964, made recruitment and promotion of francophones a higher priority, and designated certain positions as bilingual. The Treasury Board was given authority to oversee the whole language policy program, and the position of Commissioner of Official Languages was created to be responsible for assessing the implementation of the policy, dealing with complaints, and reporting back to Parliament. It was fortunate that the Quebec educational system had improved by this time so that the new policy involved little or no loss of quality in government appointments and promotions. It did, however, ignite a backlash against the preference given to French Canadians and to bilingualism. Nevertheless, the Official Languages Act was incorporated into the Charter of Rights and Freedoms in 1982.

As of March 31, 1998, 32 percent of public service positions (58 432) had been designated as bilingual, 57 percent (104 539) as English essential, 6 percent (11 803) as French essential, and 4 percent (7 965) as requiring either official language. It became increasingly indispensable for public service executives to become bilingual: in a policy adopted in May 1998, for example, new second-language proficiency requirements were imposed for those at or aspiring to the assistant deputy minister level.[18] Table 21.3 shows the language designation of actual public servants by category. The figures in the table bear a reasonably close approximation to census statistics (French mother tongue just under 25 percent), although francophones are overrepresented in the administrative and foreign service and administrative support categories.

Women also began to be targeted for increased representation in the higher levels of the public service in the 1960s and 1970s.[19] In addition, the pay equity program of the 1980s and 1990s was primarily designed to ensure that women received equal pay for doing work that had the same value as that done by men. It is not easy to compare the value of dissimilar jobs, but many occupational groups made up largely of women have had their salaries increased as a result. Unfortunately, the largest pay equity case did not go so smoothly. The government and the Public Service Alliance of Canada (PSAC) fought for years over a union demand for back pay for some 200 000 current and former secretaries and clerks, largely women. The government offered a $1.3 billion settlement, but the union sought an equity award in the $4 or $5 billion range. The union won at both the Canadian Human Rights Commission and the Federal Court of Canada, leading to a $3.6 billion negotiated settlement.

The next stage of making the public service more representative of society came in 1983, when an explicit affirmative action program was adopted for women, Aboriginals, and people with disabilities; two years later the list was expanded to include visible minorities. Once again, this did not necessarily result in a decline in the quality of appointments and promotions, but

TABLE 21.3   Language Designation of Public Servants by Category

	Anglophone		Francophone		Total
	#	%	#	%	#
Executive	2 043	74	778	26	2 761
Scientific & professional	16 762	76	5 293	24	22 055
Administrative & foreign service	47 417	69	21 304	31	68 721
Technical	12 411	76	3 919	24	16 330
Administrative support	32 978	66	16 989	34	49 967
Operational	18 875	76	5 960	24	24 835
Incomplete records	108	71	44	29	152
TOTAL	131 223	71	53 598	29	184 821

Source: Based upon figures extracted from Table 13 of The Annual Report to Parliament on Official Languages 1997–1998, Treasury Board of Canada Secretariat. Reproduced with the permission of the Minister of Public Works and Government Services Canada, 2000.

it sparked opposition from those who did not fall into the designated categories, such as able-bodied, anglophone, white, male university graduates. A new Employment Equity Act in 1995 required identification and elimination of employment barriers against persons in the four designated groups and the adoption of positive policies and practices that would ensure that such people achieved a degree of representation in each occupational group proportional to their numbers in the Canadian work force. Table 21.4 indicates the number and percentage of people in the four designated groups in each of the six main occupational categories.

While the achievement of greater equity in educational attainment and recent affirmative action programs will probably reduce some of the elitist aspects of bureaucratic activity in the future, it should be added that two significant variables have been largely overlooked. The first is the geographic origins of senior public servants. Local people are naturally hired in field offices across the country, including Atlantic Canada and the West, but little effort has been made to bring people from these regions to the policymaking levels of the bureaucracy in Ottawa. Such levels have been dominated by those from families of professional bureaucrats in the Ottawa area. The higher bureaucracy is even less representative of the population in terms of class. Senior bureaucrats often have more than one university degree, and most come from middle-class backgrounds.

This whole discussion of a **representative bureaucracy** assumes that public servants will retain the geographic, ethnic, linguistic, class, and gender biases of their origins. Instead, some observers argue, they may become imbued with the values and attitudes of their new workplace, and end up as part of the amorphous, self-serving, middle-class, central Canadian, bilingual, bureaucratic elite.[20]

TABLE 21.4   **Public Service by Employment Equity Groups**

	Women		Aboriginals		People with Disabilities		Visible Minorities		Total Employees
	#	%	#	%	#	%	#	%	#
Executive	803	25.1	58	1.8	93	2.9	91	2.8	3 203
Scientific/Professional	7 174	32.2	366	1.6	508	2.3	2 247	10.1	22 306
Admin. & Foreign Service	37 673	52.2	1 867	2.6	2 995	4.1	3 544	4.9	72 200
Technical	3 846	24.7	285	1.8	411	2.6	527	3.4	15 583
Admin. Support	38 328	84.0	1 514	3.3	2 339	5.1	2 401	5.3	45 634
Operational	2 977	14.2	680	3.3	597	2.9	450	2.2	20 905
TOTAL	90 801	50.5	4 770	2.7	6 943	3.9	9 260	5.1	179 831

Source: Treasury Board of Canada Secretariat, Employment Equity in the Public Service, *Annual Report 1997–1998. Reproduced with the permission of the Minister of Public Works and Government Services Canada, 2000.*

Political Activity

It is one thing to eliminate partisanship in appointments and promotions, but quite another to deny civil servants their basic democratic rights. Do these professional, permanent, impartial government employees have any political rights at all? The Public Service Employment Act of 1967 allowed most federal public servants to attend political meetings and make financial contributions to candidates or parties, and to take a leave of absence to stand for political office. But government employees were not permitted to work for or against a candidate or party in federal or provincial elections. When these restrictions were challenged in the Supreme Court, the Court ruled that they violated public servants' freedom of expression. They were "over-inclusive" and in many ways went "beyond what is necessary to achieve the objective of an impartial and loyal civil service."[21] A Quebec Superior Court decision later enhanced the political rights of RCMP officers. Except for deputy ministers, therefore, restrictions on political activity have largely been eliminated.

Collective Bargaining

Historically, public servants did not belong to unions and had little input into determining their level of salary or other terms and conditions of employment. Employee influence in these matters gradually increased over time until they were granted collective bargaining rights in 1967 by means of the Public Service Staff Relations Act and the Public Service Employment Act. The 70 or so occupational groups mentioned above essentially constitute bargaining units whose representatives engage in negotiations with the Treasury Board, which acts as the employer. Given so many separate collective agreements represented by some 16 different unions (the largest being the Public Service Alliance of Canada, which represents about 120 000 employees), the collective bargaining process in the federal public service is extremely complex. It is somewhat simplified by the signing of master agreements that include two or more bargaining units on certain issues, and the adoption of the Universal Classification Standard should simplify it further. When renegotiating their contract, the bargaining agent must specify in advance whether it wishes to have a possible impasse resolved by referral to binding arbitration or to a conciliation board, leading, if necessary, to a strike.

Certain subjects are recognized as rights of the employer and are not negotiable, and certain groups of public servants are excluded from the collective bargaining process. These include officers of Parliament, deputy ministers, casual and part-time employees, and personnel administrators. The Supreme Court has ruled that members of the RCMP can form employee associations but not formally unionize. Furthermore, some groups such as federal hospital workers and correctional officers, who are allowed to bargain, are not allowed to strike. Most bargaining units choose the conciliation–strike option, and public service strikes have most frequently occurred in the post office, which was transformed into a Crown corporation in 1981.

On several occasions, however, the government suspended collective bargaining on monetary matters and the right to strike.[22] The first was in connection with the wage control program of 1974; the second was with the similar "6 and 5" program in 1982; and the third was the severe limitation on public-service salary increases announced in the 1991 budget. This resulted in a 33-day strike by the PSAC involving about 70 000 workers. All collective agreements were extended for 24 months from their expiry date, with pay increases of 0 and 3 percent; the Conservatives then passed legislation in early 1993 to extend the agreements for two additional years with no pay increases. The Liberals extended the wage freeze until 1996–97 and froze increment increases as well, effectively suspending collective bargaining for most of the decade. It was only in 1998 that the government began negotiating small salary increases again, and a short strike of blue-collar and correctional officers occurred in early 1999.

The Estimates System

As noted at several points earlier in the book, the authorities spend a great deal of their time discussing the expenditure of public funds. Members of Parliament want money allocated to their constituencies, premiers and federal ministers press to get funds allocated to their provinces, and bureaucrats seek funding for their programs and departments. In addition, much of the pressure on the authorities from interest groups, lobbyists, and corporations consists of demands for federal funds. In earlier eras such spending was the prerogative of individual politicians or governing parties and was carried out on a patronage basis.[23] Nowadays, the spending process has been highly bureaucratized, and it is the function of the **Estimates** system to decide how such funds will be allocated in any fiscal year.

The role of the Cabinet in setting the overall parameters of the expenditure process was mentioned in Chapter 20. At that level various procedures under different names have been used by different governments over the years. Under the current Expenditure Management System, the Cabinet decides on the advice of the Finance Department, the Treasury Board, and the Privy Council Office what the government's financial priorities and overall level of government revenue and expenditure will be. New policy proposals and new spending initiatives must also be specifically approved at this level.

The whole budgetary process has been portrayed as a contest between "spenders" and "guardians."[24] The spenders are most of the ministers and departments in whose interest it is to increase their budgets. Spenders try to introduce new programs and expand existing ones in order to raise their prestige and enhance the support of their clientele. There are few incentives for spending ministers to restrain themselves. The guardians are essentially the minister of Finance and the president of the Treasury Board along with their respective departments. Ordinarily seen as villains by almost everyone else involved, they now receive at least some public praise if they manage to balance the budget.

Many government programs are automatically funded by the statutes that create them. The expenditures for these programs, called "statutory appropriations," cannot be changed without amending the relevant statutes; they are therefore more or less fixed and uncontrollable. Since these appropriations constitute about three-quarters of the total budget, they seriously limit the Cabinet's discretion in altering the level or pattern of government expenditure.

The preparation of the Estimates involves projections of the cost of new and existing programs at the departmental level within the limits and guidelines laid down by higher authorities. The preparation of the Estimates involves a great deal of interaction between the managerial personnel of each department and the Treasury Board Secretariat, as deputy ministers and ministers try to maximize their departmental allocations while Treasury Board personnel engage in cutting them back. At the end of the process, the Estimates are consolidated for Cabinet approval and introduced into Parliament by the president of the Treasury Board before the beginning of the next fiscal year. They now consist of a separate volume for each department and agency. Since the Estimates are prepared so far in advance of actual spending, several sets of supplementary Estimates are usually necessary to provide for unforeseen contingencies throughout the fiscal year.

Departmental Interaction with Provinces and Pressure Groups

Ministers and leading departmental officials do not only interact with other ministers and other officials within the federal government. Two other common forms of interaction are with the provinces and with pressure groups.

As noted in Chapter 17, much of the interaction between federal and provincial governments takes place at the bureaucratic level. Because the division of powers between federal and provincial governments is often vague and because both levels usually try to maximize their jurisdiction, the two levels end up operating programs in the same fields. Limitations on provincial finances have also prompted the provinces to request federal financial assistance to which Ottawa has usually attached conditions, making it even more intertwined with provincial governments.

At the height of cooperative federalism, federal and provincial program administrators would interact harmoniously in the design and operation of such integrated programs. An excellent example was the Canada Assistance Plan in which cooperation was facilitated by personal friendships, frequent informal contact, and shared professional norms.[25] It is still the case that in almost every federal department line officials interact regularly with their provincial counterparts, often by letter, fax, or telephone, and sometimes more formally in federal–provincial conferences at the bureaucratic level. Nowadays, however, with public funding in short supply, they are less likely to be engaged in developing new initiatives and more often aiming to disengage so as to reduce duplication.

In addition to such vertical department-to-department interaction, each level of government has set up bureaucratic agencies to supervise federal–provincial relations. While these central agencies are necessary to keep track of the maze of such interaction and while they may facilitate federal–provincial bureaucratic cooperation in some instances, they often complicate the friendly relations that individual federal departments have established with their provincial counterparts.

The close relationship between pressure groups and the bureaucracy has already been discussed in Chapter 15. Groups that wish to influence either the formulation or implementation of policies and programs are active in taking their message to the relevant government department. Sometimes public servants resist the approach of self-seeking groups, but at other times the department may actually welcome it, especially if the group has vital, reliable information that will lead to the development of a more effective program, if the group can help muster support for the departmental initiative among other key players in the policymaking process, or if it can serve as a channel of communication to that part of the public that is interested in the particular proposal.

These mutually advantageous contacts between a group and a department may become so close and congenial that a symbiotic, **clientele relationship** develops. The department gives official recognition to the group, regularly consults it on policy development and implementation, and gives it representation on advisory committees. It will generally be in the interest of both the department and the group to keep their relationship confidential so that they can present a united front in case central agencies and Cabinet committees become involved. It is in this connection that Chapters 15 and 19 spoke of "policy communities" and of the interest articulation function of government departments. Where such a congenial, supportive group does not already exist, it may even be necessary for the department to create it.[26]

CROWN CORPORATIONS

The second most important form of bureaucratic organization is the **Crown corporation**. These are government-owned operations that assume a structure similar to a private corporation. Crown corporations may be private firms that have been nationalized by the government by buying their shares (CN and Petro-Canada), they may be transformed from regular departments (Canada Post), or, most typically in Canada, they may be created from scratch (Canada Mortgage and Housing Corporation). Not counting other corporate holdings and subsidiaries, there are officially about 50 parent Crown corporations at the federal level, of which the largest are listed in Table 21.5, together with their number of employees in 1997–98.

The corporate structure referred to includes a board of directors, president, vice-presidents, and general manager. The Cabinet appoints the board of directors, which theoretically sets the general policy of the corporation. However, the directors often lack credibility, normally being part-time, patronage appointees. The Cabinet also appoints the president, but since this is a significant, full-time position whose performance reflects on the government, it is more often based on merit. Thus one major difference between a Crown corporation and a regular government department can be seen in terms of structure.

TABLE 21.5 **Major Federal Crown Corporations**

Canada Post Corporation	43 064
Canadian Broadcasting Corporation	6 728
Atomic Energy of Canada Ltd.	3 675
VIA Rail Canada Inc.	2 969
Canada Mortgage and Housing Corporation	2 366
Marine Atlantic Inc.	2 011
Cape Breton Development Corporation	1 894
Bank of Canada	1 500
Business Development Bank of Canada	1 066
Farm Credit Corporation	800
St. Lawrence Seaway Authority	711
Export Development Corporation	602
Royal Canadian Mint	510
Canadian Museum of Civilization	510

Source: Privy Council Office, Portfolio Management, *January 1999. Reproduced with the permission of the Minister of Public Works and Government Services Canada, 2000.*

A second distinguishing feature of the Crown corporation is that it is not subject to day-to-day political direction. The statute that creates the corporation sets out its objectives to some extent and the Cabinet may issue certain general policy guidelines, but the corporation otherwise operates more or less independently. The Cabinet minister to whom the Crown corporation is attached largely acts as a channel of communication between it and Parliament, passing on answers to parliamentary inquiries but not being held responsible for them in the same way as for a regular department. On the other hand, because the government created the Crown corporation, appoints its leading personnel, and usually provides some of its funds, the minister and Cabinet cannot totally avoid responsibility for its actions. Crown corporations must now submit a corporate plan to the minister as well as an annual year-end report to Parliament. In some cases the Cabinet can issue a directive to the corporation if informal persuasion to change its ways has not been effective, and a government obsessed with its deficit can make deep cuts in a Crown corporation's budget, as the CBC found throughout the Mulroney and Chrétien periods.

In the third place, because many of them compete with private-sector firms, Crown corporations are expected to function without undue interference from bureaucratic administrative policies. They are not usually subject to the same personnel supervision of the Public Service Commission, for example, or quite the same financial control of the Treasury Board. The Financial Administration Act contains different categories of Crown corporations, ranged in order of increasing independence from government control; as a general rule, the greater the financial self-sufficiency of the corporation, the greater its autonomy.

The reasons for government intervention at all are often related to national integration (Canada Post, VIA Rail, and Marine Atlantic), national identity and culture (CBC, Canada Museums, Canada Council of the Arts, Telefilm Canada, and the National Gallery), economic development of a particular region (Cape Breton Development Corporation), promotion of a particular industry (Farm Credit Corporation, Canadian Dairy Commission, Atomic Energy of Canada Ltd., Canadian Wheat Board, Freshwater Fish Marketing Corporation, and Canada Mortgage and Housing Corporation), promoting business in general (Export Development Corporation and Business Development Bank of Canada), and issuing and/or protecting currency (the Bank of Canada and the Royal Canadian Mint).

But why establish a Crown corporation rather than an ordinary department, or why convert a department into a Crown corporation, as in the case of Canada Post? The Crown corporation is a logical structure for a governmental operation of a commercial or industrial nature; it may also be used in politically sensitive areas such as broadcasting; and the case for a Crown corporation rather than a department is always stronger if the operation has private-sector competition. Canada once had a unique blend of public and private corporations in such areas as air and rail transportation, broadcasting, and petroleum that led one observer to refer to Canada's "public enterprise" political culture.[27]

Like other government operations, then, Crown corporations have a **public policy purpose**. They are created where, for one reason or another, the private sector has not met public needs, often because no profit would be feasible in serving the widely dispersed Canadian population. The basic objective of Crown corporations is to provide a public service, not to make a profit, but because most Crown corporations need annual public subsidies, they are often criticized for being inefficient. In fact, however, they are usually just as efficient as private companies; the subsidies are necessary to finance operations that are simply unprofitable by any standard.

The 1980s witnessed a worldwide trend toward the **privatization** of public enterprises, led by Margaret Thatcher in Britain, and the Mulroney government happily jumped on the privatization bandwagon. Such privatizations were made for largely ideological reasons:[28] Conservative governments in particular had an instinctive preference for the private sector, and the sale of Crown corporation shares often helped to reduce the national deficit. Sometimes privatizations were undertaken in order to create an "entrepreneurial climate," that is, to send a signal to corporations that a jurisdiction was "open for business" and was a place where profits could be made. Privatizers also argued that such Crown corporations no longer served a public policy purpose and that they would operate more efficiently as private companies. Moreover, the leading officials of Air Canada and Petro-Canada themselves urged the government to privatize them in order to allow them to compete more freely with other private companies. When shares are purchased by a broad cross-section of Canadians, the privatization has not been as controversial as when they are all sold to a single company (Teleglobe to Memotec) or when the corporation is sold to a foreign company (de Havilland to Boeing, before being resold to Bombardier). Table 21.6 lists some of the main privatizations at the federal level.

By 1993 the new Liberal government claimed, somewhat contentiously, that privatization was no longer an ideological issue, and Finance Minister Paul Martin (a "business liberal") said: "If the government doesn't need to run something, it shouldn't. And in future, it won't." He argued that privatization freed up scarce resources for deficit reduction or new initiatives, that government was rethinking its role in society, that privatization reduced the scope of

TABLE 21.6 Major Federal Privatizations, 1984–1999

Air Canada
Canada Development Corporation
Canadair
Canadian Arsenals Ltd.
Canadian Communications Group
Canadian National Railway and subsidiaries (CN Hotels, CPCN
    Telecommunications, etc.)
Co-Enerco Resources
de Havilland Aircraft
Eldorado Nuclear (Cameco)
Fishery Products International
Northern Canada Power Commission
Northern Transportation Company
Petro-Canada
Teleglobe Canada
Telesat

government to essentials, and that it improved service delivery, exposed government organizations to competitive business pressures, and broadened ownership of the Canadian economy. Against this background, the government announced that it would privatize the second-largest Crown corporation, the historic Canadian National Railway Company.

Other changes in the operation of Crown corporations are also afoot. In recent years, several have moved to shared-governance structures, especially local port corporations, and the Canada Ports Corporation will be closed. Subject to much controversy, the Canada Wheat Board will change from a parent Crown corporation to a shared-governance corporation with farmers electing 10 out of 15 members of the board of directors. In 1999, the government announced that it would abandon the Cape Breton Development Corporation and close or sell its coal mines, while at the same time a new Crown corporation was created, the Canada Pension Plan Investment Board.[29]

....

ADMINISTRATIVE AGENCIES AND REGULATORY TRIBUNALS

Administrative agencies and regulatory tribunals constitute a third form of bureaucratic organization. Important examples of those of a regulatory nature are listed in Table 21.7, together with their number of employees.

TABLE 21.7   **Leading Regulatory Tribunals**

Immigration and Refugee Board	1 026
Atomic Energy Control Board	430
Canadian Radio-television and Telecommunications Commission	404
National Parole Board	330
National Energy Board	286
Canadian Transportation Agency	249
Canadian Human Rights Commission	181
Veterans Review and Appeals Board	105
Canada Labour Relations Board	97

Source: Privy Council Office, Portfolio Management, *January 1999; calculations by author. Reproduced with the permission of the Minister of Public Works and Government Services Canada, 2000.*

In structure, **regulatory tribunals** bear considerable resemblance to Crown corporations. They are usually made up of a chair and board appointed by the Cabinet, and advised by a permanent, expert staff. Like Crown corporations, they are at least somewhat exempt from the Public Service Employment Act and Treasury Board human resource policies. The incidence of partisanship in appointments to the chair and board is unfortunately quite large; indeed, such agencies remain one of the last refuges of patronage in the political system. Regulatory tribunals typically receive policy guidelines from the Cabinet, but, as with Crown corporations, ministers are kept at arm's length from their day-to-day operations.

Regulatory tribunals may make **quasi-legislative** rules and regulations, such as in the case of the Canadian-content regulations of the Canadian Radio-television and Telecommunications Commission. A typical regulatory agency also makes **quasi-judicial** decisions based on the Cabinet's policy guidelines and its own regulations. They issue radio and television licences and approve long-distance telephone rates (CRTC), recognize unions (Canada Labour Relations Board), decide contentious immigration cases (Immigration and Refugee Board), review transportation rates (Canadian Transportation Agency), approve exports of natural gas and electricity (National Energy Board), allow prisoners out of jail (National Parole Board), and hear veterans' pension appeals (Veterans Review and Appeals Board).

These functions could presumably be performed by regular government departments, but they are given to semi-independent regulatory tribunals in order to divorce them from political and especially partisan considerations. Such functions are usually of an adjudicative nature and could also be performed by the courts. But these kinds of decisions demand a technical expertise not expected in judges, and, given the backlog in the court system, it is hoped that the decisions of regulatory agencies will be made more quickly and more cheaply than those of the courts.

At the same time, however, regulatory tribunals are expected to provide an impartial, court-like hearing, and in many cases lawyers are present in the same capacity as in court. Decisions of such agencies are normally appealable to the courts on procedural grounds but not on the substance of the case. Some are appealable to the Cabinet on the merits of the case (e.g., CRTC decisions on long-distance telephone rates), but the Cabinet usually declines to overturn the agency's decision. It was therefore of some significance when the Cabinet overturned a CRTC decision in 1995 with respect to direct-to-home satellite services, after Power Corporation of Montreal was unhappy with the regulatory body's ruling.

Two main criticisms of regulatory tribunals have been made in recent years. On the one hand, it is argued that there are too many regulatory agencies with too much power. Hence, **deregulation** was a companion ingredient to privatization in the Anglo-American neoconservatism of the 1980s. The Mulroney government issued a regulatory reform strategy in 1986 and proceeded to deregulate the transportation industry. On the other hand, an almost opposite criticism is that regulatory agencies become captives of the very industries they are supposed to be regulating. The agency and the industry operate as their own little policy community, divorced from other influences. In this connection it is often said that the consumer interest is overlooked as the regulatory tribunal falls victim to corporate pressure, with the CRTC being a good example. This problem is sometimes lessened by allowing consumer groups to intervene in the hearings of regulatory tribunals or in government funding of intervener groups.

There is a wide variety of other **administrative agencies**. Such "structural heretics"[30] include royal commissions, task forces, advisory councils like the National Council of Welfare, funding bodies, agents of Parliament, and other one-of-a-kind agencies. The largest such agencies are the RCMP, the Canadian Food Inspection Agency, Statistics Canada, and Correction Services of Canada. These agencies exhibit varying degrees of independence from the minister, and some are listed in Table 21.8.

TABLE 21.8   Leading Administrative Agenices

Agents of Parliament	Funding Agencies	Unique Agencies
Public Service Commission	Medical Research Council	RCMP
Auditor General	National Research Council	Canadian Security Intelligence Service (CSIS)
Commissioner of Official Languages	Social Science & Humanities Research Council	National Library
Privacy & Information Commissioners	National Science and Engineering Research Council	National Archives
		Canadian Food Inspection Agency
Elections Canada		Correctional Service
		Statistics Canada

Agents of Parliament are agencies that are attached to Parliament rather than to the executive branch of government. They are somewhat divorced from the government of the day, either because they are meant to be critical or because they are supposed to serve all members impartially. In contrast, the scholarly research funding agencies are loosely attached to a department and minister, but they are clearly intended to operate at arm's length, and ministers are occasionally embarrassed by the projects that have received government funding. Similarly, while such agencies as the RCMP, CSIS, and Statistics Canada are part of the executive rather than the legislative branch, they are expected to operate without ministerial interference.

Task forces are an informal means of quickly acquiring information and recommendations.[31] They may be composed of members of Parliament, ministers, public servants, outsiders, or some combination thereof. Task forces were used most extensively in the early Trudeau years when a new prime minister came to power with a desire to do things differently but without much knowledge of many issues and with typical suspicion of public-service resistance to change. The most prominent were probably Paul Hellyer's Task Force on Housing and Urban Development and Herb Gray's Task Force on Foreign Investment.

Royal commissions are a much older instrument, about 450 having been appointed since 1867. Generally speaking, royal commissions are very formal, in-depth inquiries set up by the Cabinet to investigate some difficult problem for which the resources of the regular public service are considered inadequate. Royal commissions may be made up of from one to ten commissioners, usually people of stature and expertise, and normally involve extensive public hearings and an elaborate research program. They are often regarded somewhat cynically because of the length of time it takes them to produce a report, and because they cost a great deal of money. The cynics also point out that governments have not had a good record of implementing Royal Commission recommendations, and that such commissions often appear to be appointed to take the heat off a particular issue.

Sometimes they are also seen as devices with which to educate the public to the government's way of thinking or of generating support for a policy the government already had in mind. Nevertheless, many royal commissions have served a useful purpose, and many public policies such as equalization payments, medicare, bilingualism, and free trade owe their existence, at least in part, to Royal Commission reports. The Royal Commission on Aboriginal Peoples (RCAP) is the most significant in recent times. Whatever their formal name, royal commissions are often referred to by the name of their chair, such as Rowell–Sirois (Federal–Provincial Relations, 1940), Hall (Health Services, 1964–65), and Macdonald (Economic Prospects, 1985).

CONTROLLING THE BUREAUCRACY

Given the enormous influence and considerable power of the bureaucracy in the modern state, democracies are understandably concerned about keeping the public service under control. A number of means of doing so can be identified.

Prime Minister, Ministers, and Cabinet

In the first place, the prime minister, individual ministers, and the Cabinet as a whole are supposed to provide political control of the bureaucracy. The minister both gives direction to the public service and has the power to veto any of its proposals, at least in theory. Real ministers have provided varied accounts of what actually happens in practice: some argue that ministers can control their departments, while others feel that they were often manipulated by their public servants. Even where the minister in charge is weak or manipulated, however, the prime minister or Cabinet as a whole are likely to step in from time to time to reject bureaucratic advice and opt for an alternate proposal whose political implications are more favourable.

Bureaucrats Controlling Bureaucrats

In the second place, the power of some bureaucrats is controlled by other bureaucrats, such as the financial control of the Treasury Board and the Finance Department, the personnel control of the Public Service Commission, and the policy control of the Privy Council Office. To some extent the central agencies operate on the orders of the prime minister, Cabinet, or Cabinet committees, so that these agencies supplement the political control mentioned above.

House of Commons

The third line of defence against bureaucratic power is the House of Commons. While its operations will be examined in more detail in Chapter 22, one principle of parliamentary government relevant here is that the executive (Cabinet or bureaucracy) is not allowed to either raise or spend money without parliamentary approval. In practice, proposals for tax changes as well as spending proposals all originate with the executive, they are rarely altered in the legislative process, and the taxing and spending usually begin before Parliament has given its consent. But ultimately Parliament must pass all such financial measures. The process of examining the Estimates gives the House of Commons an opportunity to question and criticize ministers and deputy ministers about all aspects of their departmental spending, programs, and policies. Furthermore, once the money has been spent, an official of Parliament, the **Auditor General**, inspects the Public Accounts and informs Parliament in an annual report of instances where funds were spent unlawfully or unwisely.[32] Considerable controversy raged in the 1980s over the size of the Auditor General's staff, their ability to gain access to Cabinet documents, and whether they should function narrowly as auditors or make broader policy recommendations to individual departments. The **Public Accounts Committee** of the House (chaired by an opposition member) goes through the Auditor General's report and calls onto the carpet those ministers or deputy ministers who have committed the worst financial faults.

Another principal means used by the House of Commons to control the bureaucracy is the daily, oral Question Period. In this case, the Commons must act through the intermediary minister who is theoretically responsible for everything the department does. While the minister is expected to take the blame for bureaucratic errors, public servants seek to avoid bringing such embarrassment or disrepute upon their minister and department. In addition, members of Parliament receive requests on a daily basis from their constituents to intervene on their behalf to speed up or correct bureaucratic decisions. MPs and their staff normally handle such problems with a telephone call or a letter to the public servant or minister concerned. Another kind of parliamentary control of the bureaucracy is exercised by the Standing Joint Committee on the Scrutiny of Regulations, which attempts to review the reams of regulations that the bureaucracy produces annually.

The Judiciary

A fourth kind of control of the bureaucracy is provided by the judiciary. The power of the courts to overturn decisions of bureaucrats in regular government departments is essentially restricted to breaches of the law or actions taken beyond the public servant's jurisdiction. Such cases are rare, but the Charter of Rights and Freedoms provides more scope for this kind of judicial review of bureaucratic action than in the past. In the *Singh* case, for example, the Supreme Court ruled that the Immigration Department had to provide an oral hearing for refugee claimants. The Charter's effect on the bureaucracy primarily relates to police officers, a special kind of public servant. Regulatory agencies are usually expected to operate in a court-like manner, and their decisions can be overturned by the courts for procedural abuses as well as for exceeding their jurisdiction. The Federal Court of Canada, to be discussed in Chapter 23, specializes in hearing appeals from such regulatory agencies.

Ombudsmen

Every Canadian province except Prince Edward Island has supplemented these four means of controlling the bureaucracy with the appointment of an ombudsman, an official of the legislature to whom people can complain about bureaucratic decisions, mistakes, abuse, discrimination, delays, or indecision. Ombudsmen try to correct such errors by persuasion, but if that fails, they can resort to the power of legislative and media publicity. Canada has no overall ombudsman at the federal level, but several ombudsman-like officials exist to deal with specialized complaints. The Correctional Investigator looks into complaints from inmates against prison authorities; the Commissioner of Official Languages investigates public or bureaucratic claims regarding infringement of the Official Languages Act; and the Privacy Commissioner investigates complaints from citizens who believe that their privacy rights have been invaded.

The Information Commissioner

Perhaps the most important of these watchdog agencies is the **Information Commissioner**. Canadian governments traditionally functioned under a thick cloak of secrecy at both the Cabinet and bureaucratic levels. This tradition prevented the opposition and the public from knowing what alternative policies were considered in the executive branch, what kind of public opinion polling was carried out, and what advice was actually offered by the bureaucracy to the Cabinet. The Canadian **Access to Information Act** was passed in 1983 and considerably improved the situation, although the many exemptions in the act mean that it is not entirely effective. When citizens, journalists, companies, or pressure groups apply to a department for a piece of government information, they are supposed to receive it within 30 days; if they are denied such government information, they can appeal to the Information Commissioner, who can overrule the department in the matter, with a final to appeal to the Federal Court. Former Information Commissioner John Grace repeatedly reprimanded the bureaucrats for the culture of secrecy that continued to flourish long after the passage of the act.

DYSFUNCTIONS AND REFORM OF THE BUREAUCRACY

Dysfunctions of the Bureaucracy

Apart from the problem of keeping the bureaucracy under some kind of democratic control, three other problems or dysfunctions are often identified. First, from the public's perspective, there is the constant accusation of "red tape." This generally includes a collection of sins that characterize the behaviour of all large organizations, including delays, a multitude of forms, excessive rules and regulations, difficulty of communicating with the official who could solve the problem, and lack of helpful, personal attention. If these dysfunctions are more characteristic of government than of large private firms, it is partly because governments are required to function according to the law and the rules and regulations issued under the law. Government must also treat everyone in exactly the same way, so, unlike private firms, which may be able to modify their rules, services, and prices, it cannot show favouritism or make individual deals. Delays are usually the result of public servants wanting to be certain that any decision is absolutely right, because mistakes may be criticized in Parliament or in the media. There is no excuse for public servants not to be prompt and courteous, but the public environment in which they work requires an equality of treatment that many people are not accustomed to in the private sector.

A second general criticism of bureaucracy is that it is inefficient because it lacks the profit motive of the private sector. Officials in private firms are said to move more quickly because they are in greater danger of losing their jobs and because minimizing costs is a higher priority. To some extent this is true. The essential difference between the public and private

By Denny Pritchard. Reproduced with permission.

sectors, however, is that the bureaucracy is charged with providing a public service, and it should be judged primarily on the adequacy of that service. Nevertheless, there was a widespread belief among the business community, politicians, and the public at large that a great deal of "fat" could be squeezed out of the bureaucracy, at least until the dramatic layoffs in the Mulroney and Chrétien regimes.

From a management point of view, the main dysfunction of the public service is that deputy ministers and other managerial personnel are too hemmed in by rules and regulations and their authority is too limited by central agencies. In consequence, in 1986 the Mulroney government introduced the Increased Ministerial Authority and Accountability (IMAA) process. The objective of IMAA was to provide more autonomy and managerial flexibility to deputy ministers by relaxing some of the detailed rules and reporting requirements if they signed a Memorandum of Understanding (MOU) with the Treasury Board. IMAA was followed up in 1989 by Public Service 2000, an initiative to "enable the Public Service to provide the best possible service to Canadians into the 21st century."[33] PS 2000 involved the creation of several task forces made up of senior public servants and dealing with such matters as classification, compensation, staffing, training and development, staff relations, budget controls, and service to the public. It also introduced the operating budget concept that allowed departments to use salary money for other operating costs and vice versa, rather than having each individual position controlled by the Treasury Board.

Reform of the Bureaucracy: The New Public Management

The issues mentioned above were merely parts of a major transformation of the Canadian federal public service over the past 10 or 15 years that has parallels around the world and that is often called the **New Public Management (NPM)**. General factors leading to such public-service reform included debts and deficits, changing public- and private-sector expectations, an altered international trading environment (globalization), new technologies, growing doubts about the capacity of state institutions to fulfill their mandates, and citizen demands for direct political participation.[34] It should be said, however, that not everyone thinks the reality of NPM matches its rhetoric, and, as will be noted, many observers do not believe it to be a good idea at all.

Apart from giving managers more autonomy, privatizing Crown corporations, and reducing the powers of regulatory agencies, the first major reform began with a dramatic restructuring of government departments in 1993, as discussed above. This idea had long been in the works, and the installation of the Kim Campbell government seemed to be a good time to implement it. The personnel implications were felt most heavily at the assistant deputy minister level, where 53 ADMs were laid off.

The second major reform, inaugurated by the 1994 and 1995 budgets, was generally labelled Program Review and involved rethinking what government did and how it did it— in essence, redefining the role of government—and consumed a great deal of ministerial and bureaucratic effort.[35] The Program Review process asked the following six questions of virtually every government activity:

- Is the program still in the public interest?
- Is its delivery a legitimate and necessary role for government?
- Is the current federal role appropriate or should the program be realigned with the provinces?

- Should it be delivered in partnership with the private or voluntary sector?
- How can it be redesigned for efficiency?
- Is it affordable, given fiscal constraints?[36]

Through this process, the federal government determined which activities it could continue to deliver or support within a much reduced budget. It also identified the activities it had to cease providing, scale back, devolve, or deliver or finance differently. It involved reducing subsidy programs, increasing user fees, and putting many government activities on a commercial basis.[37] In the 1995 budget the minister of Finance ensured that real Program Review would happen when he declared his intention to eliminate 45 000 public-service jobs by 1998 to help the government reduce its deficit. Some public servants were eligible for buyouts and early retirement packages, and some were able to swap jobs with those who wished to leave but whose job was secure. Eleven departments were targeted for the most drastic cuts—especially Transport, many of whose operations were privatized—but the policy was service-wide. The announcement aroused great opposition from public-sector unions, especially the PSAC, which had earlier suggested alternative ways of saving government money.

The third major reform was called **Alternative Service Delivery (ASD)**. While ASD reforms began during the Mulroney period, they reached new heights after the Liberals came to power in 1993 and were part and parcel of the Program Review process. ASD is a generic term covering a variety of innovative means of providing government services that arise from a congruence of circumstances and objectives: reducing the size and expense of government, making government more citizen-oriented, involving users in service delivery, providing more flexibility in service delivery, enhancing employee motivation, and incorporating new developments in information technology. ASD consists primarily of special operating agencies, service agencies, partnerships, and the commercialization of certain government services.

Special operating agencies (SOAs) are units that function with relative autonomy within government departments. In most cases they have the potential to become self-financing, and the basic objective is to deliver a service along private-sector lines, that is, in a manner that is more sensitive to client requirements, that promotes a more creative, entrepreneurial working environment, and that brings savings to government. These units have a minimal role in policy advice, and their autonomy is based on a framework agreement with the department and a departmentally approved business plan. The head of the unit reports to the deputy minister, and the departmental minister retains political responsibility. The Passport Office and the Translation Bureau are examples of the 19 SOAs created by 1997, but more are likely in the future. Even so, the Canadian effort pales in comparison to that in Britain, where 67 percent of the civil service were transferred to executive agencies by 1996 and where the head of the agency reports to the minister, not to the equivalent of the deputy minister.[38]

Service agencies are somewhat akin to SOAs, being defined as a mission-driven, client-oriented organization established under constituent legislation to manage the delivery of federal services. They remain within the federal government and under the direction of a minister but the intention is to provide more responsive and streamlined operations and to partner with the provinces to provide services to citizens in an efficient manner. Two of the first main initiatives in this category were the Canadian Food Inspection Agency (CFIA) and the Canada Customs and Revenue Agency (CCRA). The CFIA combines the food inspection services previously provided by three separate federal departments and opens the way for provincial government involvement. The CCRA is a transformation of the Revenue Canada department into an agency responsible for collecting most federal taxes, and with provincial representation on its board of directions, will provide better coordination with provincial tax collection efforts.[39]

Partnerships have already been mentioned in passing, and embrace a wide array of new administrative arrangements based on the principle that government does not need to "do it all" for the public interest to be well served.[40] Beyond interdepartmental partnerships, the federal government may enter such partnerships with private firms, other governments, or nonprofit, noncommercial or volunteer organizations. According to the Treasury Board, partnering arrangements can be consultative (sharing information), contributory (sharing financial support), operational (sharing work), or collaborative (sharing decision making). The government–private company relationship behind the construction and operation of the Confederation Bridge between Prince Edward Island and New Brunswick and the creation of local authorities to operate Canadian airports are prominent examples. Another example of collaborative partnerships are the Labour Market Development Agreements that Ottawa signed with the provinces between 1996 and 1998.[41]

Commercialization is essentially the same as privatization and can also be seen as a category of partnership. But beyond the sale of Crown corporations, commercialization can involve turning a government function over to a not-for-profit corporation. The leading example is the creation of Nav Canada to replace the government's air traffic control system. The Nav Canada board of directors includes representatives of the airlines, government, and employee unions, and sets its rates so that it breaks even.[42] Commercialization also includes contracting out government services or encouraging employees to deliver services from the private sector that they previously provided as public servants, as has been done with some Parks Canada functions.

ASD, especially in the form of partnerships, continued to be a priority while the government battled the deficit and even after it succeeded in 1999. Otherwise, at the dawn of the new century, public service reform centred primarily on making the public service a better place to work and on strengthening its policy capacity. La Relève was an initiative undertaken in 1997 by Jocelyn Bourgon, Secretary to the Cabinet and Clerk of the Privy Council, to focus on people issues within the public service of Canada. It sought to address "the quiet crisis of downsizing, pay freezes, criticism, insufficient recruitment, and premature departure of experienced public servants."[43] Besides improving the quality of the workplace for those already there, including accelerated executive development, it aimed to portray public employment as a rewarding career in order to recruit good new blood. La Relève basically evolved into the Leadership Network in 1998, a separate agency reporting to the Cabinet Secretary to ensure the effective management of ADMs as a valued corporate resource.

Meanwhile, in 1996, the government established a Policy Review Committee that brought together 30 federal departments and agencies to anticipate the policy issues of greatest importance to Canada in the year 2005. Now called the Policy Review Initiative (PRI), it seeks to strengthen the federal government's policy research capacity. By 1999, the PRI was ready to go beyond the federal government itself and forge "new knowledge partnerships" with other levels of government, nongovernment players, and researchers in other countries. These two priorities would be central to the new Cabinet Secretary, Mel Cappe, as well as to Bourgon as she left that position to head the Canadian Centre for Management Development.

··

CONCLUSION

This chapter illuminates the usually invisible world of the Canadian bureaucracy, an exceedingly complex operation that is charged to undertake an incredible number of tasks. It is a challenge to organize and coordinate the thousands of people performing such specialized functions, and as in any large organization, informal relationships based on individual personalities may deviate from formal lines of authority. The central question that arises in any discussion of the bureaucracy is whether it is out of control. This issue primarily relates to the delicate relationship between the public service and the politicians. Several means of control were discussed above, but the question remains. The other main issues that this subject raises are ensuring that the public service is well positioned to offer the best possible advice to the government and that it provides services to the public in the most satisfactory way. The Canadian bureaucracy continues to strive to improve its performance in both respects.

SC Bureaucratic power is central to the state-centred approach, which generally contends that the bureaucracy is a world unto itself. Ministers are so busy with Cabinet and Cabinet committee meetings, parliamentary responsibilities, public-speaking engagements, listening to pressure group and other demands, and looking after their constituencies, that they have little or no time left to spend in their department. They have only the most superficial idea of what their department is doing; for the most part, it is a self-governing operation, subject only to the authority of other bureaucratic central agencies. Even the prime minister and Cabinet as a whole can do little but take the advice of the secretary to the Cabinet, the deputy minister of Finance, the secretary of the Treasury Board, the governor of the Bank of Canada, and a handful of other key officials, as outlined in this chapter as well as in Chapter 20.

State-centred theorists do not necessarily argue that such officials act only in their own narrow self-interest, however; they may pursue the public interest as they see it. The period between 1935 and 1957, for example, is sometimes seen as the era of the powerful **mandarins**, who brought Keynesian economics to Canada and developed the government's whole postwar social and economic program.[44] While such a small group of mandarins may not have exercised the same kind of innovative influence during the past 30 years or so, the politicians have become even more dependent on the bureaucracy as a whole. In an example from the 1960s, federal welfare officials pushed the politicians for reforms that in their opinion would help the poor and working classes.[45]

P Pluralists are not alarmed at the extent of bureaucratic power because they see it limited by the power of the Cabinet, the House of Commons, the courts, and other agencies. Furthermore, pluralists emphasize the rivalry and competition within the bureaucracy, which make it difficult for any single bureaucrat, department, or agency to become authoritarian. They also see the widespread interest group interaction with departments as a way of influencing the outputs of government. The concept of government as a plethora of specialized policy communities, each with its own minister, department, associated agencies, pressure groups, and interested individuals, is particularly appealing to pluralists and brings this approach together with that of state-centred theorists.

PC The "bureaucratic game" is another aspect of bargaining that is central to public choice theory. In their rational, mutually self-seeking relationship with ministers, bureaucrats seek to increase their jurisdiction, their staff, their status, their budget, and their salary, and pursue or recommend policy options that are most convenient and congenial to themselves. Politicians are agreeable to these bureaucratic objectives as long as public servants help them stay in power by keeping them out of trouble and by pacifying electorally strategic special-interest groups. On the other hand, the uninformed, the unorganized, and "committed opponents in never-to-be-won constituencies"[46] can be ignored.

C Class analysts argue that the bureaucracy primarily serves the interests of the corporate elite.[47] This is historically related to the commonalities in socioeconomic characteristics of the senior public service and the business community, and the elite accommodation that goes on between the bureaucracy, Cabinet, and pressure groups.[48] In the modern "globalized" world, the bureaucracy joins all other agencies of government in being even more sensitive to the mobility of capital and the need to defer to the value of capital accumulation. Class analysts reject the argument that privatization and the various tenets of the New Public Management are nonideological issues, and make the basic point that it is the groups that speak for the corporate elite—the Business Council on National Issues and the C.D. Howe Institute—that have set the overall context for the reduction in the size and range of activities of the state.

It has also been noted that in its never-ending search for profitable investment outlets, capital is seeking to gain access to the public sector. In *The Unconscious Civilization*, John Ralston Saul observes that privatization involves corporations trying to get their hands on easy profits—profits from administering that which already exists—rather than seeking to make profits by being innovative in the development of new products and services.[49] Despite the conditions of the Canada Health Act, for example, public health care provides a major target for such privatization efforts. De-listing of services at the provincial level has created room for private health insurers, and the closing of hospitals has meant big opportunities for private profit-oriented home care companies.[50] Class analysts also note that a similar process is under way in public education and in Public-Private Partnerships (PPPs) at the municipal level.[51]

Increasingly, public servants are applying a class analysis to their own employment situation. After years of pay freezes and with new and drastic cuts to public-service jobs, they are beginning to feel exploited themselves. Many feel that public-sector restraint programs are simply designed "to advance business interests behind a facade of protecting the public." They point to "the frequent use of back-to-work legislation, the jailing of union leaders, and reducing the right to strike by designating an increasing number of public sector workers as essential."[52]

DISCUSSION QUESTIONS

1. What is the ideal relationship between the minister and the deputy minister?

2. Should deputy ministers be replaced with partisan appointees?

3. Do central agencies interfere excessively with the deputy minister's responsibility to manage the department?

4. To what extent should Canada establish a "representative bureaucracy"?

5. What limits, if any, should be put on the political activity of public servants? On their right to bargain collectively and to strike?

6. Given the necessity of the bureaucracy in the modern state, are the democratic controls on its power sufficient?

7. How do you feel about downsizing the public service, privatizing Crown corporations, deregulation, and other current reforms being undertaken?

8. How do each of the approaches outlined in Chapter 1 enhance our understanding of the material in this chapter?

NOTES

1. Kenneth Kernaghan and David Siegel, *Public Administration in Canada: A Text,* 2nd ed. (Scarborough: Nelson Canada, 1991), p. 137. A third edition was published in 1995, and a fourth in 1999; Barbara Wade Carroll and David Siegel, *Service in the Field* (Montreal: McGill–Queen's University Press, 1998).

2. Donald J. Savoie, *Governing from the Centre: The Concentration of Power in Canadian Politics* (Toronto: University of Toronto, 1999), pp. 7–8.

3. Jocelyne Bourgon, *Fourth Annual Report to the Prime Minister on the Public Service of Canada 1997,* p. 16.

4. S.L. Sutherland, "Responsible Government and Ministerial Responsibility: Every Reform Is Its Own Problem," *Canadian Journal of Political Science* (March 1991), pp. 91–120.

5. Kernaghan and Siegel, *Public Administration in Canada,* 2nd ed., pp. 379–85; and S.L. Sutherland, "The Al-Mashat Affair: Administrative Responsibility in Parliamentary Institutions," *Canadian Public Administration* (Winter 1991), pp. 573–603.

6. Savoie, *Governing from the Centre,* p. 248.

7. Gordon Osbaldeston, *Keeping Deputy Ministers Accountable* (Toronto: McGraw-Hill Ryerson, 1990).

8. See the exchange between Flora MacDonald and Mitchell Sharp in Paul Fox and Graham White, eds., *Politics: Canada,* 7th ed. (Toronto: McGraw-Hill Ryerson, 1991), and between Flora MacDonald and Don Page in Mark Charlton and Paul Barker, eds., *Crosscurrents: Contemporary Political Issues,* 2nd ed. (Scarborough: Nelson Canada, 1994).

9. Savoie, *Governing from the Centre,* pp. 241–42.

10. Ibid., p. 10.

11. Blair Williams, "The Para-Political Bureaucracy in Ottawa," in Harold D. Clarke et al., eds., *Parliament, Policy and Representation* (Toronto: Methuen, 1980); Gerald Lenoski, "Ministers' Staffs and Leadership Politics," in Thomas A. Hockin, ed., *Apex of Power,* 2nd ed. (Scarborough: Prentice-Hall Canada, 1977); and Kernaghan and Siegel, *Public Administration in Canada,* 2nd ed., pp. 370–72.

12. Savoie, *Governing from the Centre,* pp. 13, 56–57, and 62.

13. "According to the Financial Administration Act, the Treasury Board can deal with any question concerning financial management, giving it authority over departmental budgets, expenditure, financial commitments, revenue, accounts, personnel management, and all the principles governing the administration of the public service." Privy Council Office, *Decision-Making Processes and Central Agencies in Canada: Federal, Provincial and Territorial Practices* (Ottawa, 1998), p. 5. Program evaluation has been a continuing activity spearheaded by the Treasury Board Secretariat. Leslie A. Pal, *Beyond Policy Analysis: Public Issue Management in Turbulent Times* (Scarborough: ITP Nelson, 1997), ch. 7, and Savoie, *Governing from the Centre,* pp. 295–96.

14. On the question of patronage, see Jeffrey Simpson, *Spoils of Power* (Toronto: Collins, 1988); S.J.R. Noel, "Leadership and Clientelism," in David Bellamy et al., eds., *The Provincial Political Systems* (Toronto: Methuen, 1976).

15. J.L. Granatstein, *The Ottawa Men: The Civil Service Mandarins 1935–1957* (Toronto: Oxford University Press, 1982).

16. Bourgon, *Third Annual Report to the Prime Minister, 1995*, p. 23.

17. John Porter, *The Vertical Mosaic* (Toronto: University of Toronto Press, 1965); Dennis Olsen, *The State Elite* (Toronto: McClelland and Stewart, 1980); and Kernaghan and Siegel, *Public Administration in Canada*, 2nd ed., p. 329.

18. Treasury Board, *Official Languages in Federal Institutions, Annual Report, 1997–98*, pp. 11–12.

19. Kathleen Archibald, *Sex and the Public Service* (Ottawa: Queen's Printer, 1970); Task Force on Barriers to Women in the Public Service, *Beneath the Veneer*, vol. 1 (Ottawa: Supply and Services, 1990).

20. Robert Adie and Paul Thomas, *Canadian Public Administration*, 2nd ed. (Scarborough: Prentice-Hall Canada, 1987), pp. 121–26. For a critique of pay and employment equity, see Martin Loney, *The Pursuit of Division: Race, Gender and Preferential Hiring in Canada* (Montreal: McGill–Queen's University Press, 1998).

21. *Osborne v. Canada (Treasury Board)*, [1991] 2 S.C.R. 69. See also *OPSEU v. Ontario (Attorney General)*, [1987] 2 S.C.R. 2.

22. Peter Warrian, *Hard Bargain: Transforming Public Sector Labour–Management Relations* (Toronto: McGilligan Books, 1997); André Blais et al., *Governments, Parties, and Public Sector Employees* (Montreal: McGill–Queen's University Press, 1997); and Leo Panitch and Donald Swartz, *The Assault on Trade Union Freedoms: From Wage Controls to Social Contract*, rev. ed. (Toronto: Garamond Press, 1993).

23. Noel, "Leadership and Clientelism."

24. Donald J. Savoie, *The Politics of Public Spending in Canada* (Toronto: University of Toronto Press, 1990).

25. Rand Dyck, "The Canada Assistance Plan: The Ultimate in Cooperative Federalism," *Canadian Public Administration* (Winter 1976).

26. Paul Pross, *Group Politics and Public Policy* (Toronto: Oxford University Press, 1986); William D. Coleman and Grace Skogstad, eds., *Policy Communities and Public Policy in Canada* (Mississauga: Copp Clark Pitman, 1990).

27. Herschel Hardin, *A Nation Unaware: The Canadian Economic Culture* (Vancouver: J.S. Douglas, 1974).

28. Herschel Hardin, *The Privatization Putsch* (Halifax: Institute for Research on Public Policy, 1989).

29. President of the Treasury Board's *Annual Report to Parliament on Crown Corporations and Other Corporate Interests of Canada* (Ottawa: Public Works and Government Services, 1998).

30. J.E. Hodgetts, *The Canadian Public Service: A Physiology of Government, 1867–1970* (Toronto: University of Toronto Press, 1973).

31. Kernaghan and Siegel, *Public Administration in Canada*, 2nd ed., pp. 255–63.

32. S.L. Sutherland, "On the Audit Trail of the Auditor General: Parliament's Servant, 1973–80," *Canadian Public Administration* (Winter 1980), pp. 616–44; and S.L. Sutherland, "The Politics of Audit: The Federal Office of the Auditor General in Comparative Perspective," *Canadian Public Administration* (Spring 1986), pp. 118–48.

33. *Public Service 2000: The Renewal of the Public Service of Canada* (Ottawa: Supply and Services, 1990); David Zussman, "Managing the Federal Public Service as the Knot Tightens," in Katherine Graham, ed., *How Ottawa Spends 1990–91* (Ottawa: Carleton University Press, 1990); Kenneth Kernaghan, "Career Public Service 2000: Road to Renewal or Impractical Vision?" *Canadian Public Administration* (Winter 1991), pp. 551–72; F. Leslie Seidel, *Rethinking the Delivery of Public Services to Citizens* (Montreal: Institute for Research on Public Policy, 1995), ch. 4; and Savoie, *Governing from the Centre*, pp. 142–46.

34. Brian O'Neil, "Reorganizing Government: New Approaches to Public Service Reform" (Ottawa: Library of Parliament, 1994); Pal, *Beyond Policy Analysis: Public Issue Management in Turbulent Times*; O.P. Dwivedi, and James Iain Gow, *From Bureaucracy to Public Management: The Administrative Culture of the Government of Canada* (Peterborough: Broadview Press, 1999); B. Guy Peters and Donald J. Savoie, *Taking Stock* (Montreal: McGill–Queen's University Press, 1998).

35. Jocelyn Bourgon, *Third Annual Report to the Prime Minister of Canada, 1995*, pp. 19–21; Savoie, *Governing from the Centre*, pp. 172–81.

36. Treasury Board, *Getting Government Right: Governing for Canadians*, February 1997, p. 5.

37. Bourgon, *Third Annual Report to the Prime Minister of Canada, 1995*, p. 20.

38. Canadian Centre for Management Development, *Key Characteristics of Departments and Executive Agencies in the Westminster Democracies*. Ottawa, 1996; Seidel, *Rethinking the Delivery of Public Services to Citizens*, ch. 2; Savoie, *Governing from the Centre*, p. 216.

39. Kernaghan and Siegel, *Public Administration in Canada*, 4th ed., p. 302.

40. Bourgon, *Fourth Annual Report to the Prime Minister of Canada*, 1997, pp. 11–12; Treasury Board Secretariat, website, Alternative Service Delivery.

41. Jim Armstrong and Donald G. Lenihan, *From Controlling to Collaborating: When Governments Want to Be Partners* (Toronto: Institute of Public Administration of Canada, 1999).

42. Kernaghan and Siegel, *Public Administration in Canada*, 4th ed., p. 310.

43. Bourgon, *Fifth Annual Report to the Prime Minister, 1998*, p. 18; *Fourth Annual Report*, ch. 6; Savoie, *Governing from the Centre*, pp. 227–31; Leslie A. Pal, ed., *How Ottawa Spends 1999–2000: Shape Shifting: Canadian Governance Toward the 21st Century* (Toronto: Oxford University Press, 1999).

44. Granatstein, *The Ottawa Men*.

45. Richard Splane, "Social Policy-Making in the Government of Canada: Reflections of a Reformist Bureaucrat," in S.A. Yelaja, ed., *Canadian Social Policy* (Waterloo: Wilfrid Laurier University Press, 1978).

46. Douglas Hartle, *The Expenditure Process of the Government of Canada: A Public Choice–Rent-Seeking Perspective* (Toronto: Canadian Tax Foundation, 1988).

47. Ralph Miliband, *The State in Capitalist Society* (London: Weidenfeld and Nicolson, 1969).

48. Robert Presthus, *Elite Accommodation in Canadian Politics* (Toronto: Macmillan, 1973).

49. John Ralston Saul, *The Unconscious Civilization* (Concord, ON: House of Anansi Press, 1995).

50. Colleen Fuller, *Caring for Profit: How Corporations Are Taking Over Canada's Health Care System* (Vancouver: New Star Books, 1999).

51. Canadian Centre for Policy Alternatives, *The Education Monitor* and *Education, Limited* (both quarterly publications).

52. Kernaghan and Siegel, *Public Administration in Canada*, 2nd ed., p. 558; Panitch and Swartz, *The Assault on Trade Union Freedoms*.

FURTHER READING

Abele, Frances, ed. *How Ottawa Spends 1991–92: The Politics of Fragmentation*. Ottawa: Carleton University Press, 1991.

———. *How Ottawa Spends 1992–93: The Politics of Competitiveness*. Ottawa: Carleton University Press, 1992.

Blais, André, et al. *Governments, Parties, and Public Sector Employees*. Montreal: McGill–Queen's University Press, 1997.

Blakeney, Allan, and Sandford Borins. *Political Management in Canada: Conversations on Statecraft*, 2nd ed. Toronto: University of Toronto Press, 1998.

Carroll, Barbara Wade, and David Siegel. *Service in the Field*. Montreal: McGill–Queen's University Press, 1998.

Doern, G. Bruce. *The Road to Better Public Services: Progress & Constraints in Five Canadian Federal Agencies*. Montreal: Institute for Research on Public Policy, 1994.

Dwivedi, O.P., and James Iain Gow. *From Bureaucracy to Public Management: The Administrative Culture of the Government of Canada*. Peterborough: Broadview Press, 1999.

Ferguson, Mary, ed. *Federal Guidebook: A Guide to the Canadian Federal Government and Its Decision-Makers* (Perth, ON: J-K Carruthers, annual).

Graham, Katherine A., ed. *How Ottawa Spends 1990–91*. Ottawa: Carleton University Press, 1990.

Granatstein, J.L. *The Ottawa Men: The Civil Service Mandarins 1935–1957*. Toronto: Oxford University Press, 1982.

Hardin, Herschel. *The Privatization Putsch*. Halifax: Institute for Research on Public Policy, 1989.

Hodgetts, J.E. *The Canadian Public Service: A Physiology of Government, 1867–1970*. Toronto: University of Toronto Press, 1973.

Inwood, Gregory J. *Understanding Canadian Public Administration: An Introduction to Theory and Practice*. Scarborough: Prentice Hall Canada, 1999.

Johansen, David. *Federal and Provincial Access to Information Legislation: An Overview*. Ottawa: Parliamentary Research Bureau, BP-383E, 1997.

Kernaghan, Kenneth, and David Siegel. *Public Administration in Canada: A Text*, 2nd ed. Scarborough: Nelson Canada, 1991; 3rd ed., 1995; 4th ed., 1999.

Laux, Jeanne, and Maureen Molot. *State Capitalism: Public Enterprise in Canada*. Ithaca, NY: Cornell University Press, 1988.

Osbaldeston, Gordon. *Keeping Deputy Ministers Accountable*. Toronto: McGraw-Hill Ryerson, 1989.

Pal, Leslie A. *Beyond Policy Analysis: Public Issue Management in Turbulent Times*. Scarborough: ITP Nelson, 1997.

Pal, Leslie A., ed. *How Ottawa Spends 1998–99: Balancing Act: The Post-Deficit Mandate*. Toronto: Oxford University Press, 1998.

———. *How Ottawa Spends 1999–2000: Shape Shifting: Canadian Governance Toward the 21st Century*. Toronto: Oxford University Press, 1999.

Panitch, Leo, and Donald Swartz. *The Assault on Trade Union Freedoms: From Wage Controls to Social Contract*, rev. ed. Toronto: Garamond Press, 1993.

Peters, B. Guy, and Donald J. Savoie. *Taking Stock*. Montreal: McGill–Queen's University Press, 1998.

Phillips, Susan D., ed. *How Ottawa Spends 1993–94: A More Democratic Canada …?* Ottawa: Carleton University Press, 1993.

———. *How Ottawa Spends 1994–95: Making Change*. Ottawa: Carleton University Press, 1994.

———. *How Ottawa Spends 1995–96: Mid-Life Crises*. Ottawa: Carleton University Press, 1995.

Privy Council Office. *Decision-Making Processes and Central Agencies in Canada: Federal, Provincial and Territorial Practices* (Ottawa, 1998).

Savoie, Donald J. *The Politics of Public Spending in Canada*. Toronto: University of Toronto Press, 1990.

———. *Governing from the Centre: The Concentration of Power in Canadian Politics*. Toronto: University of Toronto Press, 1999.

Seidel, F. Leslie. *Rethinking the Delivery of Public Services to Citizens*. Montreal: Institute for Research on Public Policy, 1995.

Seidel, F. Leslie, ed. *Rethinking Government: Reform or Reinvention?* Montreal: Institute for Research on Public Policy, 1993.

Starnes, John. *Closely Guarded*. Toronto: University of Toronto Press, 1998.

Swimmer, Gene, ed. *How Ottawa Spends 1996–97: Life under the Knife*. Ottawa: Carleton University Press, 1996.

———. *How Ottawa Spends 1997–98: Seeing Red: A Liberal Report Card*. Ottawa: Carleton University Press, 1997.

Warrian, Peter. *Hard Bargain: Transforming Public Sector Labour–Management Relations*. Toronto: McGilligan Books, 1997.

Waterfall, Don. *Dismantling Leviathan: Cutting Government Down to Size*. Toronto: Dundurn Press, 1995.

Chapter 22

PARLIAMENT

Almost every day the elected representatives of the Canadian people meet in open, verbal combat in Question Period in the House of Commons. Members of Parliament on the opposition side of the House attack the prime minister and other ministers for acts of omission and commission, while the government responds with laudatory statements and statistics on its own performance. In these exchanges and other debates, politicians' reputations are often made and broken. The House of Commons is the central link between the public and the government in Canadian democracy, and, as such, it is the furnace of national politics. Most interests in society are represented there in one way or another, and they clash on a daily basis. The Commons is the primary battleground for the hearts and minds of Canadian voters, and House debate is a "lead-up" to the subsequent election campaign. The Senate, on the other hand, is normally a much more peaceful place, and is viewed by many Canadians as a group of unelected, elderly party hacks who collect generous remuneration for doing little work. When its majority belongs to a different party from that in the Commons, however, the work of the Senate becomes much more interesting.

Every four or five years, voters in each of 301 local constituencies elect their representative to the House of Commons. Partly because they have a direct part in electing its members and partly because it operates publicly and they often see it in action on television, the House of Commons is the political institution most familiar to Canadians. This familiarity has sometimes led such voters and viewers to think that the Commons has more power in the policy-making process than it actually does. While it is largely to enhance that power that the procedures of the House are regularly reformed, the institution has other functions and values that are probably not widely understood.

As well as the House of Commons, the **Parliament of Canada** includes the Queen and the Senate, and a law must be approved by all three parts. Indeed, every federal statute begins with the words, "Her Majesty, by and with the Advice and Consent of the Senate and House of Commons of Canada, enacts as follows. ..." In this respect Canada is sometimes said to employ the **Westminster model** of government because it is based on the British system. As noted in Chapter 2, this model begins with a bicameral legislature—an elected lower house with primary legislative powers answerable to the polity through elections, and an upper house with limited legislative powers, in law or in fact. The executive is part of the lower house and through the Cabinet drives or "energizes" the legislative process. The government or Cabinet is in charge of and responsible for the conduct of parliamentary business, while an institutionalized opposition has the right to criticize the government and the ability to make that criticism felt. The Westminister model, therefore, promises potent government and political stability through the prime minister and Cabinet, along with political accountability through open debate.

In popular parlance, however, the word "Parliament" is often used synonymously with the Commons, which is by far its most important part. Hence members of the House of Commons are called members of Parliament or MPs. MPs can be largely divided into three main groups: those who also serve as Cabinet ministers (the government), those who support the Cabinet (government **backbenchers**), and those who oppose the government (the **opposition**).

This chapter examines the House of Commons from a number of perspectives. These include its functions and powers, its composition, the parliamentary timetable, party discipline and the party caucus, stages and kinds of legislation, the organization and officers of the House, the committee system, members' services, the roles of MPs, the government–opposition balance, minority government, and reform of the institution. The chapter later explores the role of the Senate.

FUNCTIONS AND POWERS OF THE HOUSE OF COMMONS

Historically, a basic principle of Canadian government has been the sovereignty or **supremacy of Parliament**; that is, apart from interfering in provincial jurisdiction and with other minor exceptions, Parliament could pass laws of any kind that were virtually beyond review by any other organ of government, including the courts. This principle was considerably transformed in 1982, however, with the adoption of the Canadian Charter of Rights and Freedoms. The courts have now been given the power to review both federal and provincial legislation in terms of the Charter and to invalidate such legislation to the extent of any contradiction. On the other hand, the courts have often suggested that the legislation be redrafted to fit within the boundaries of the Charter, and the "notwithstanding" clause allows for the reassertion of parliamentary sovereignty on many points.

In terms of the seven functions performed in the political system (outlined in Chapter 1), the House of Commons (and Senate) fall best into the rule-making category, although as the previous two chapters have shown, the rules are actually formulated in the executive branch. MPs (and senators) articulate local and other interests, and party caucuses try to come up with compromises in which diverse interests are aggregated. The Commons also engages in political recruitment and political communication, and these four functions may actually be more important than its legislative role. Another way to address the functions of the House of Commons is in its relationship to the prime minister and Cabinet. The House of Commons does not make policy or govern, but in the first instance, through motions of confidence and nonconfidence, it decides who will form the government; second, it provides that government, on behalf of the people, with the authority, funds, and other resources necessary for governing the country; third, it makes the government behave by acting as a constant critic and watchdog; and fourth, it provides an alternative government by enabling the opposition to present its case to the public and become a credible choice for replacing the party in power.[1]

In discussing the functions of the House of Commons it is also instructive to examine its role in the chart of the policymaking process outlined in Chapter 19. In the first place, Parliament may be involved in the initiation phase by raising issues in the daily Question

Period and in general debates, in criticizing existing spending programs, or by means of private members' bills. It is then virtually nonexistent in the priority-setting and policy formulation phases. Where the Commons dominates the picture is in the legitimation stage. Whether or not bills are refined in the course of their passage through the House of Commons, what is most important is that they are legitimated. This means that Cabinet proposals embodied in bills are made legitimate by their passage through the formal, authorized, democratic channels of the Commons. It may not make many significant changes, but the House does subject bills to extended debate and publicizes their advantages and disadvantages before converting them into laws or statutes. C.E.S. Franks calls this process the "mobilization of consent."[2] The legislative stage serves to inform the public of the content of new policies, and out of this "prolonged warfare," consent or acceptance is eventually obtained. This debate essentially prepares the electorate for its decision on how to vote in the next election. The House then has little say in the fifth and sixth phases, the implementation and interpretation of laws, including scant supervision of regulations issued by the executive.

The various ways of looking at the functions of the House of Commons noted above emphasize the role of the institution as a whole. Individual members also have interest-articulation, representational, and ombudsman functions, as they speak out for their constituencies and generally take care of their constituents.

COMPOSITION OF THE HOUSE OF COMMONS

The basic principle in establishing the House of Commons is that each province is represented in proportion to its population. Chapter 12 outlined how the 301 seats in the Commons are distributed among the provinces, with the following results: Ontario, 103; Quebec, 75; BC, 34; Alberta, 26; Manitoba, 14; Saskatchewan, 14; Nova Scotia, 11; New Brunswick, 10; Newfoundland, 7; PEI, 4; NWT, 1; Nunavut, 1; and Yukon, 1.

Even if members of Parliament other than Cabinet ministers have only a limited role in the policymaking process, they are important enough to justify an inquiry into their social background characteristics.[3] Since they are elected to represent territorial units and usually live in or near their constituencies, MPs almost automatically become representative of the population in a geographic sense. Although it is not quite so inevitable that they will be representative in terms of ethnic background, this also turns out to be the case, at least for those of English and French origins. The Constitution Act, 1867, required from the beginning that all House documents be printed in English and French, but the absence of simultaneous interpretation until 1958 and the unilingualism of most MPs served to limit the interaction between the two linguistic groups within the institution.

On the other hand, members of Parliament do not reflect the population very well in terms of education, occupation, or class. Although not as exclusive in these respects as Cabinet ministers, MPs have higher educational levels and higher-status occupations than the general population. Historically the legal profession has furnished the largest single group in the Commons, but the number of MPs with a business background equalled or exceeded the number of lawyers in the 1984 and 1988 Conservative victories, and the number of lawyers declined throughout the 1990s. They were now also outnumbered by educators, administrators, and those in other professions. An indication of the occupational distribution of members of Parliament in 1998 is provided in Table 22.1.

TABLE 22.1	Occupational Distribution of MPs, 1998		
Business	60	Administration	35
Education	60	Farmer	18
Lawyer	35	Technician/Labour organizer	18
Other Professional	60	Political activist	15

Source: Compiled by author from John Bejermi, Canadian Parliamentary Handbook *(Ottawa: Borealis Press, 1999).*

Members are also unrepresentative of the population with respect to gender. Relatively few women have been elected to the House of Commons, although the number is on the increase, reaching 39 out of 295 in 1988, 54 in 1993, and 60 out of 301 in 1997. The increasing proportion of MPs without any previous service in elected office at the municipal or provincial levels should also be mentioned. A municipal or provincial political career in Canada is usually quite distinct from one in federal politics.

What is probably most striking about Canadian members of Parliament, especially compared with other legislatures around the world, is their rapid turnover in office. With such a small number of **safe seats**, the proportion of new members after each election averages 40 percent, and the average length of time in office is less than ten years.[4] This means that Canadian MPs are transient amateurs who engage in "avocational politics."[5] Few members remain in Parliament long enough to develop an understanding of the institution, to master their extra-parliamentary responsibilities, or to stand up to a long-serving prime minister. The 1993 turnover was over 75 percent, due to the decimation of the Conservatives and NDP, but even the relatively calm 1997 election produced a turnover of 30 percent.

....

THE PARLIAMENTARY TIMETABLE

Perhaps the best way to get an overview of the work of the House of Commons is by examining the parliamentary timetable—the agenda of a typical session and a typical week. The Constitution requires that Parliament meet at least once a year, but it now sits for about 27 weeks, or 135 days, per year, mid-September to mid-December, and February to mid-June, incorporating one weekly break per month. A session of Parliament is normally completed every 12 months, but it has often spilled over to two or even three years.

The Typical Session

A session begins with the **speech from the throne**, prepared by the prime minister (and advisers) and read by the governor general. Its function is to outline the government's legislative plans for the session, although the speech is often worded so vaguely that it is not a reliable guide. That speech introduces the throne speech debate, a six-day debate in which MPs can talk about anything under the sun. Party leaders and Cabinet ministers may use the occasion to articulate their priorities, while backbenchers often expound on the wonders or troubles of their constituency.

The second major event of the session is the **budget** and the budget debate. The budget itself is a statement delivered by the minister of Finance, chiefly concerned with tax changes (i.e., the revenue side of the government's books) but also dealing with government finances in general. Among other things, the budget usually fleshes out the vague promises of the speech from the throne. So that no one can take advantage of tax changes beforehand, the budget is shrouded in secrecy until its delivery, and real or apparent "budget leaks" always generate great controversy.[6] The budget sets the stage for a four-day freewheeling debate and provides the opposition with a second opportunity to try to defeat the government. Majority governments need not worry, but the Trudeau and Clark minority governments were defeated on their budgets in 1974 and 1979 respectively. Legislation incorporating the specific tax changes mentioned in the budget comes along later, although the changes usually take effect as of budget night.

The other side of the financial picture is the government's spending proposals for the next fiscal year, the **Estimates**. Their presentation is the third major item of business in the session. Once tabled, however, the Estimates are transmitted to standing committees of the House for scrutiny, so that they actually occupy little of the Commons time as a whole.

A fourth element of the session consists of the 21 days when the opposition parties choose the subject of debate and the government in turn responds, variously called "allotted," "supply," or **opposition days**. These are divided proportionately among the opposition parties (in the 36th Parliament, beginning in 1997: 9 Reform, 6 Bloc, 3 NDP, and 3 PC annually), and distributed throughout the session at the rate of approximately one per week.

Other than these four components, the time of the House of Commons is essentially taken up with the discussion of bills, and most of that time with bills introduced by the government. Indeed, it is partly because of the volume of government legislation that some sessions of Parliament exceed a year in length, but the cycle of events just outlined is ideally repeated annually.

When the government wishes to take a break within a session, it "adjourns" the House; when it wants to bring a session to an end, it "prorogues" the Commons; and an election call results in the **dissolution of Parliament**. It is partly because any bills not passed by prorogation die and must start again from scratch in the next session that governments are tempted to allow sessions to continue beyond one year until all current legislation is disposed of. A rule change in 1999 allowed private members' bills to be reintroduced at the same stage that they achieved in the previous session, however, and the government can actually do the same with its own bills by introducing a motion to this effect.

The Typical Week

The weekly House of Commons schedule can be seen in Figure 22.1. The 1982 reforms eliminated the traditional evening sittings in favour of meeting in the morning, now starting at 11 a.m. on Monday, 10 a.m. on Tuesday, Thursday, and Friday, and 2 p.m. on Wednesday. Wednesday mornings are reserved for party caucus meetings. The items on the daily agenda are

Members' Statements, Question Period, government orders (usually government bills), private members' business (usually private members' bills), and the adjournment proceedings. "Routine proceedings" include the tabling of documents, statements by ministers, presentation of petitions and committee reports, and introduction and first reading of bills.

The highlight of the day is the 45-minute **Question Period**. This period offers the opposition its best opportunity to criticize and embarrass the government as it grills the prime minister and Cabinet ministers about their deficiencies and faults. Ministers are not given notice of such questions, but before going into the chamber they are briefed by aides who try to anticipate what questions might be asked. Even greater daily effort goes into the preparation and

....

Figure 22.1 **Weekly Order of Business**

HOURS	MONDAY	TUESDAY	WEDNESDAY	THURSDAY	FRIDAY	HOURS
10:00–11:00		Routine Proceedings		Routine Proceedings	Government Orders	10:00–11:00
11:00–11:15	Private Members' Business (3)				Members' Statements	11:00–11:15
11:15–12:00					Oral Questions	11:15–12:00
12:00–1:00					Routine Proceedings (1)	12:00–1:00
1:00–1:30	Government Orders	Government Orders (2)	Review of Delegated Legislation (4)	Government Orders (2)	Government Orders (2)	1:00–1:30
1:30–2:00					Private Members' Business	1:30–2:00
2:00–2:15	Members' Statements	Members' Statements	Members' Statements	Members' Statements		2:00–2:15
2:15–2:30	Oral Questions	Oral Questions	Oral Questions	Oral Questions		2:15–2:30
2:30–3:00						2:30–3:00
3:00–5:30	Routine Proceedings (1) Government Orders (2)	(1) Government Orders (2)	Routine Proceedings (1) Notices of Motions for the Production of Papers Government Orders (2)	(1) Government Orders (2)		3:00–5:30
5:30–6:30		Private Members' Business (3)	Private Members' Business (3)	Private Members' Business (3)		5:30–6:30
6:30–7:00	Adjournment Proceedings (2)	Adjournment Proceedings (2)	Adjournment Proceedings (2)	Adjournment Proceedings (2)		6:30–7:00

(1) Possible extension of Routine Proceedings to complete Introduction of Government Bills pursuant to Standing Order 30(4).
(2) Possible extension or delay pursuant to Standing Order 33(2) respecting Ministerial Statements.
(3) Possible delay or rescheduling pursuant to Standing Order 30(7) to compensate for a delay or an interruption of more than 30 minutes, and pursuant to Standing Order 33(2) respecting Ministerial Statements.
(4) If required, House to sit at 1:00 p.m. for the review of Delegated Legislation pursuant to Standing Order 128(1).
Reproduced with permission.

rehearsal of questions by opposition party leaders and their staff. The **Leader of the Opposition** and the leader of any other recognized party begin the attack, and the Speaker of the House distributes questions to various opposition parties in a rough proportion to their numbers. Government backbenchers are also allowed to participate, but they usually ask "planted" questions to which ministers give prepared and self-serving replies. Since ministers often respond in a deliberately vague manner, several supplementary questions are allowed to those initially posed, but the objective of the opposition is not so much to elicit information as to portray the government in a negative light. Such exchanges, along with corridor interviews and hallway "scrums"—a melee of reporters, microphones, and cameras—based on Question Period, find their way onto the television news and form the backbone of all media reporting on the House. Exciting as it is, many observers regret that Question Period gets so much attention and other aspects of Commons activity receive so little. Provision is also made for written questions from MPs who are genuinely concerned with seeking detailed information.

The 15 minutes preceding Question Period each day are set aside for members' statements, during which MPs can get something off their chests in 60 seconds, such as reminding the House that this is cancer month or organ donor week. After Question Period, the regular business is the discussion of government orders, usually government bills, debates that are the basic routine of Commons life. At this point in the day most of the **parliamentary press gallery** and MPs leave the chamber in search of more pressing or more interesting activity, and the Deputy Speaker replaces the Speaker, completely changing the atmosphere of the House. The speeches in these debates, even with their 20-minute time limit, are often dull, although the ten-minute "question and comment" period after each sometimes adds a modicum of life to the proceedings. But the public and media can hardly be blamed for paying so little attention to them when MPs themselves rarely listen to each other. The few members assigned to make up quorum on any day are more likely to be answering their mail, reading the newspaper, or working on their laptop computer!

Only five hours a week are reserved for **private members' bills** and motions, at the normal rate of one hour per bill. These bills and motions, introduced either by government supporters not in the Cabinet or by opposition members, are usually even more uninteresting than government bills, and are virtually assured of being dropped to the bottom of the pile when their hour on the stage has elapsed. As mentioned below, however, they have attracted a little more attention in recent years.

Finally, the adjournment proceeding, or "late show," is a half-hour opportunity at the end of the daily sitting (6:30 to 7:00 p.m.) four times a week to pursue issues that MPs feel were inadequately answered in the Question Period. Five members have four minutes each to restate their question, and a parliamentary secretary representing the minister has two minutes to respond.

Given the sharply adversarial nature of Question Period and the relative dullness of the rest of the parliamentary day, television coverage of the House of Commons does little to enhance the public's support of the government or politicians in general. Television coverage may help to explain the high turnover rate of individual MPs and governments in Canada, as well as the public's attraction to parties and politicians yet unsullied by parliamentary exposure. On the other hand, "the all-consuming ritual of adversarial combat completely dominated by political parties" has its defenders. It serves the functions of keeping government conduct under constant surveillance and of providing an alternative,[7] and it presents a clearcut picture to the electorate of which party is responsible for everything that has been done.[8]

In the House of Commons during Question Period, June 1, 1999, Prime Minister Jean Chrétien responds to questions from the Opposition (with Deborah Grey and Preston Manning in the background) after they accused him of steering a big government contract to a man who bought land next to a golf course in which Chrétien had an interest. (Fred Chartrand/Canapress)

PARTY DISCIPLINE

Probably the most significant aspect of the operation of the House of Commons is that everything is organized along party lines and that **party discipline** is so rigid. Almost all members belong to one party or another, and, with rare exceptions, the MPs of each party vote together. Why is it that members of Parliament so consistently toe the party line? The most obvious reason for party discipline, at least on the government side of the House, is the system of **responsible government**. It is generally believed, both inside and outside Parliament, that if the Cabinet is defeated on a major measure, it must resign or call an election; therefore, its backbenchers must always ensure that Cabinet proposals are passed.[9] The principle of responsible government could be interpreted more flexibly—by regarding a limited number of non-confidence motions as really critical and then allowing the Cabinet to carry on in spite of the occasional defeat of a piece of legislation—but until it is, government supporters will always have to put party loyalty ahead of the consideration of their own views or those of their constituents.

Apart from the fact that some degree of party discipline is a corollary of the principle of responsible government, several reasons can be cited to explain why MPs of any party stick together in parliamentary votes. One is the tendency of people who belong to a political party to see things in a similar light—a natural cohesiveness common to most organized groups. Related to this cohesiveness is an equally natural deference to the leadership of the party and a desire to present an image of party unity to the public. In addition, MPs are encouraged to support the party line because of the prospects of promotion. Government backbenchers who are well behaved can become committee chairs, parliamentary secretaries, or Cabinet ministers, while even in opposition parties one can be moved up to more important responsibilities.[10] Members also want to participate in the distribution of perks available in parliamentary life, especially opportunities to travel at public expense, which are generally in the control of the party whips. Those who demonstrate greatest party loyalty can be rewarded with such favours as inclusion in the Canadian delegation to the United Nations or in many other parliamentary junkets. Another inducement is to receive full support of the party organization in the next election, including campaign funds and a visit by the party leader. Moreover, many MPs depend on the government to provide them with employment if they suffer defeat, and are not unmindful of this dependence while serving in the House. The ultimate sanctions for disloyal behaviour are expulsion from the party caucus, involving relegation to the unpleasant status of an independent, and denial of the party label in the next election. For all these reasons, parties vote as blocs, and a government with a majority of seats in the Commons has always felt confident that it could get parliamentary approval for almost anything it wanted.

The British House of Commons is the model for the Canadian House in many ways, but party discipline is looser there and government legislation is frequently defeated without entailing the resignation of the government.[11] C.E.S. Franks attributes this significant difference in the operation of the two chambers to several factors: the larger number of members in Britain means that discipline is harder to enforce; incumbent British MPs can be sure of renomination, regardless of their degree of party loyalty; and the large proportion of safe seats results in fewer members being dependent on party patronage for their post-parliamentary livelihood. Moreover, long-serving British MPs co-exist with short-term prime ministers (with the exception of Margaret Thatcher) and are not so obsessed with promotion to the Cabinet. They are more content than their Canadian counterparts to remain on the backbenches or act as committee chairs, combining outside interests with their parliamentary responsibilities.[12] Franks does not expect any dramatic change in the operation of the Canadian House of Commons to come from technical procedural reform; party discipline will predominate until such time as a sizable proportion of government backbenchers feel secure enough to act independently and force the Cabinet to change its attitude about giving them more flexibility. Less media alarm about such dissent would also help.

It is fashionable to advocate more **free votes** and greater opportunity for MPs to represent the interests of their constituencies rather than slavishly follow the dictates of the party. The "free vote" on capital punishment in 1987 was a rare event, and featured a dramatic split among Tory MPs. A series of free votes on alternative ways of dealing with abortion in 1988 failed to produce a consensus, and the Mulroney government's "compromise" abortion bill of 1990 was defeated in a free vote in the Senate. Few would argue against a little more autonomy and freedom for the individual MP, but free-vote advocates sometimes fail to appreciate the merits of an executive-centred system. Forcing MPs to toe the party line has allowed the executive to pursue a collectivist public interest beyond the narrow interests of constituencies, provinces, parties, pressure groups, and lobbyists, and has permitted Canadian governments to be more activist and welfare-oriented than legislature-centred systems such as in the United States.[13] Party discipline protects MPs individually and collectively from the blandishments and threats of single-interest pressure groups and lobbyists, whose presence is increasing, and promotes the accountability of the government party to the electorate. It also frees the prime minister from time-consuming negotiations with individual MPs.

In recent years, three Conservative MPs were expelled from the party caucus (Alex Kindy, David Kilgour, and Suzanne Blais-Grenier) and two (Leonard Jones and Sinclair Stevens) were denied the party's candidacy.[14] Then, in 1995, despite concessions made to Liberal dissenters and other opponents of the Chrétien government's gun control bill, many backbenchers absented themselves from the vote and three voted against it. The PM quickly retaliated by removing them from their committee assignments. When veteran MP and former minister Warren Allmand voted against the 1995 budget, because it dismantled historic Liberal social programs, the prime minister's attempt to remove him as a committee chair was delayed by Reformers, who disagreed with what he said but defended his right to dissent from the Liberal line. The prime minister even threatened not to sign the nomination papers of Liberal candidates in the next election if they voted against government measures. Such a fate befell John Nunziata, who was expelled from the Liberal caucus for his attack on the government for not removing the GST. Nevertheless, he ran successfully in 1997 as an Independent.

In his second term, Chrétien faced caucus divisions over Reform motions demanding compensation to a wider range of victims of Hepatitis C and use of the notwithstanding clause to override a lower BC court decision upholding child pornography; over constitutional amendments with respect to denominational schools in Newfoundland; and over several bills having to do with same-sex issues. In most of these cases, the prime minister imposed strict discipline on Liberal members or had the Liberal party whip send dissident MPs away on long trips. On the other hand, Liberal MPs were free to vote as they chose on private members' bills, unless a particular minister imposed discipline on the matter. But as talk circulated of Chrétien's intention to retire, his increasingly "lame-duck" status made it more tempting for Liberal MPs to vote against government measures with which they disagreed.

By *Andy Donato* (Toronto Sun). *Reproduced with permission.*

CAUCUS MEETINGS

The other side of this public display of party discipline is that MPs are allowed to speak their mind in the secrecy of the **party caucus**.[15] Chrétien encouraged such open debate in caucus, for example, but then expected party solidarity in public. The caucus consists of all the elected members of each party (and such senators who choose to attend) who meet separately behind closed doors on Wednesday mornings. As in the case of Cabinet secrecy, however, members occasionally "leak" caucus information for their own benefit. In the case of the government party, the prime minister and Cabinet ministers attend such meetings, unlike the practice in Britain. Provincial and regional caucus meetings of each party are held prior to the general caucus meeting, and caucus committees are often appointed. In the second term of the Chrétien government, for example, the Liberal caucus established committees on social policy, transportation, sustainable development, and women's issues, among others. MPs of like mind could also form informal task forces, such as the Ianno task force on Bank Mergers.

Some prime ministers and cabinets use caucus primarily to inform their backbenchers of government plans; others are reasonably receptive to backbench arguments and suggested alternatives; and some do both. Ministers may discuss the principles of a new policy with interested backbenchers in the course of its development, but it would breach the tradition of the House to show the caucus an actual bill before it is introduced in the Commons. Although no votes are taken, sufficient backbench dissatisfaction may occasionally carry the day. It is generally believed, for example, that backbench pressure had an influence on Cabinet policy on electronic eavesdropping, immigration, and unemployment insurance in the 1974–79 period; on two railway bills and the Canada Health Act between 1980 and 1984; and on amendments to the Official Languages Act, gun control legislation, and the hiring of homosexuals in the armed forces between 1984 and 1993. The aforementioned Mulroney compromise abortion bill was probably unique in actually being written by a committee of four ministers and eight backbenchers.[16] In the early years of the Chrétien government, the caucus was successful in amending gun control legislation and delaying the inclusion of sexual orientation in the Canadian Human Rights Act. In the second term, the social policy committee of caucus had considerable impact on the 1999 budget, the rural caucus had influence on agricultural policy, and caucus pressure was part of the equation in denying the bank mergers, along with ensuring that banks would not be allowed to sell insurance and lease cars.

STAGES AND KINDS OF LEGISLATION

The great bulk of legislation introduced takes the form of **public bills**. These are general bills that relate to matters of public policy and affect all Canadians, such as the Income Tax Act or the Canada Health Act. Most public bills (and virtually all that involve the raising or spending of money) are sponsored by the government and introduced by a Cabinet minister, thereby being titled **government bills**. They are numbered from C-1 to C-200 in each session. As noted earlier, most of the weekly and yearly agenda is taken up with such government business.

A certain amount of time, however, now normally five hours per week, is set aside for members who are not in the Cabinet to introduce legislation and motions of their own. Since these MPs (on whichever side of the House) are private members, their proposals are called private members' bills, and are numbered from C-201 upward in each session.[17] These bills are also of a general public policy nature, but until 1995 they could not involve the expenditure of public funds. Since then, private members' bills that entail spending can be introduced, but they require a "royal recommendation" before third reading, and they still cannot impose or increase taxes. Private members' bills almost never reach the statute books because the government arranges to have them "talked out"; that is, the Cabinet ensures that a government backbencher is still talking when the hour for their consideration expires, and they go back to the bottom of the order of precedence. Historically, the most that private members could hope for was that the Cabinet might incorporate their ideas into a government bill, and this still frequently happens. Since 1986, however, the situation has improved, and there is now provision for a more in-depth examination of 15 private members' bills and 15 private members' motions drawn from a hat.

The subcommittee on private members' business of the Standing Committee on Procedure and House Affairs chooses up to 10 of the 30 as "votable" and these get expanded debate (three hours as opposed to one) and come to a vote. If they pass, they go on to committee for further review. Lynn McDonald's 1988 private member's bill on nonsmokers' rights was a rare example of one that made it to the statute books; others included the bill to change the name of Trans-Canada Airlines to Air Canada, the bill that recognized the beaver as a symbol of Canadian sovereignty, the bills to create the Centennial Flame Research Award and the Canadian Peacekeeping Service medal, the bill to recognize hockey as Canada's national winter sport and lacrosse as our national summer sport, the one designating national organ donor week, and numerous bills to change the name of a member's constituency.[18] In 1999, the government allowed a private member's bill preventing judges from giving concurrent sentences to multiple rapists and murderers to pass in a diluted form. Changes adopted in 1998 also allowed one private members' item at a time to be put on the list by an alternate route—if it is supported by 100 MPs, including at least 10 from each of a majority of the recognized parties in the House. Another change required that private members' bills that get to committee be reported back to the House within 60 sitting days, rather than never being heard from again.

Private bills, on the other hand, refer to a specific person or corporation. They originate in a petition, and require the payment of a fee. Certain divorces used to be effected by Acts of Parliament and took the form of private bills, while today this category mostly consists of bills incorporating companies and religious denominations. Other recent examples included a bill for the City of Windsor to acquire the Canadian portion of the Windsor–Detroit Tunnel, and those that allowed certain couples to marry even though they were related to each other within prohibited degrees of consanguinity. Private bills now originate in the Senate and occupy very little of the Commons' time.

Turning to the stages of the legislative process, the first requirement is for three readings in each chamber. Most government bills originate in the Commons, although, with the exception of money bills, they may be first introduced in the Senate. First reading simply means that a bill has been introduced—it is tabled, printed, and made public—and may be briefly explained.

Some days later, the bill comes up for second reading. This stage involves a debate on the principle of the bill and may last several days, or even weeks if it is controversial. The clauses of the bill are not discussed in detail at this stage, and the opportunity for amendments is very limited. A favourable vote at the end of the second-reading debate therefore means that the bill has been approved in principle.

Even if the opposition has little hope of defeating a bill, it may expect that prolonged exposure of the flaws in the legislation will persuade the government to amend it. Failing that, public opinion can be aroused via television or other media coverage to the extent that the electorate will remember the incident when the next election occurs. Excessive opposition debate is called a **filibuster**, but government and opposition rarely agree on what is excessive. In 1913, during protracted opposition to the government's Naval Bill, the Borden government introduced **closure**, a rule allowing a majority government to cut off debate. This device was used with discretion until the **pipeline debate** of 1956, and it is widely believed that the abusive resort to closure helped to defeat the government a year later.[19] Although the closure rule is still on the books and is used more routinely in recent years, it is both more common and more civilized to negotiate with the opposition parties over the time to be allocated to debating various issues. Standing Order 78 provides for three kinds of time allocation motions depending on how much opposition consent can be acquired; even if none is forthcoming, which is usually the case, it is still considered less draconian than to use closure, as such.

It is partly because of the length of debates that government legislation deliberately leaves wide discretion to the executive to issue regulations so that acts will not have to come back to the House for frequent amendments. Similarly, the government often introduces omnibus bills that deal with several different issues simultaneously because a number of individual bills would take longer to pass.

Following second reading, a bill goes to committee, where it is examined in detail. In the small, informal confines of a Commons committee, ministers, public servants, interest groups, and other experts offer explanations or criticisms, after which the committee members scrutinize the bill clause by clause, voting on each, and occasionally amending them.

After being approved, sometimes with amendments, the bill is reported back to the House in what is called the Report stage. This phase gives all members of the House, especially those not on the committee, an opportunity to approve or reject amendments made in committee or to consider other amendments. Once the bill is concurred in here, it goes to third reading for a final, overall appraisal.

Assuming that the bill started in the Commons, it must then go through the same procedure in the Senate, but there it is usually disposed of in much faster order.[20] In the rare case that the Senate amends a bill already approved by the Commons, the bill will have to go back to that house to see if it is acceptable in its amended form. If the Senate and House of Commons continue to disagree, the bill is usually abandoned, although a rarely used provision exists for a conference between representatives of the two houses.

Once a bill is passed in identical form by both houses, it is given royal assent in a special ceremony held in the Senate. The governor general or more likely a Supreme Court judge acting as "deputy governor general" nods in approval, and the bill becomes a law or statute, although it may not be immediately proclaimed.

Although this may seem like an overly complicated process, each stage has a distinctive purpose and most bills must be debated for some time before the media and public begin to pay attention to them. Besides being necessary to engender eventual public knowledge of and consent to the law, reasonably lengthy consideration of the merits and faults of the bill is required in the formulation of public opinion. It serves to help the electorate gradually make up its mind about whether to re-elect the government that introduced such legislation or to opt for an opposition party that criticized it effectively.

In 1994, the House adopted rule changes that allowed a bill to go to committee after first reading, before it had been approved in principle. Such a procedure considerably widens the scope of committee influence, but it only applies to government legislation and can only be used with the minister's consent. According to another new procedure, a committee can be directed to study an issue and prepare a bill. This was done in the case of the post-1991 census redistribution process, but the Senate was not happy with the result and delayed the bill's adoption. These cases illustrate a slight loosening up of the Cabinet's dominance of the legislative process, but these devices are not often used.

ORGANIZATION AND OFFICERS OF THE COMMONS

The Speaker

The layout of the Commons chamber is illustrated in Figure 22.2. The leading official of the House of Commons is the presiding officer, the **Speaker**, for whom one deputy and two acting speakers can substitute in the chair. In addition to ceremonial and administrative functions, the Speaker interprets and enforces the written rules of the Commons, which are called the **Standing Orders**,[21] plus unwritten traditions, practices, conventions, and usages. It used to be that Speakers would look to British precedents to fill in gaps in Canadian rules, but since 1986, there is no reference to Great Britain at the beginning of the Standing Orders, only to "parliamentary tradition in Canada and other jurisdictions."[22] Given the powers of the Speakership—recognizing which member can speak, and ruling on whether motions are in order, whether debate is relevant, whether questions are urgent, and whether an unruly MP should be expelled—it is important for the person selected to be competent as well as totally impartial. In the past, many Speakers have lacked one or both of these qualities. Speakers were historically chosen by prime ministers from among their party's MPs and thus carried the suspicion of being biased in favour of the government. In seeking eventual reward beyond the Speakership such as promotion to the Cabinet, some also feared displeasing the prime minister, the dispenser of such rewards.

A major change was adopted in 1986 that allowed MPs to choose their own Speaker by secret ballot, rather than merely ratifying the nomination of the prime minister. The first elected Speaker, John Fraser, was re-elected when the procedure was repeated after the 1988 election. At the same time, the Speaker was given new authority to "name" (i.e., suspend) a member for the rest of the day and for a period of five days for a second breach of the rules. Gilbert Parent was elected Speaker in 1994, and re-elected in 1997. The prime minister nominates and the House elects a Deputy Speaker for the length of a whole Parliament, as well as a Deputy Chairman and Assistant Deputy Chairman of Committees of the Whole for each session, the latter also effectively functioning as deputy speakers.

Many Canadians are upset at the rowdy behaviour of members of Parliament, and it is true that the British chamber is more sedate. This contrast is partly explained by the fact that opposition members in Britain expect to be on the government side some day, whereas in Canada, with long periods of one-party dominance, many MPs serve their entire parliamentary career in opposition. Never given the chance to govern, and rarely having the opportunity to amend legislation, they see victory in catcalls and obstruction. On the other hand, the rules demand a certain amount of civility, such as prohibiting name-calling or accusations of

Figure 22.2 Layout of the House of Commons Chamber

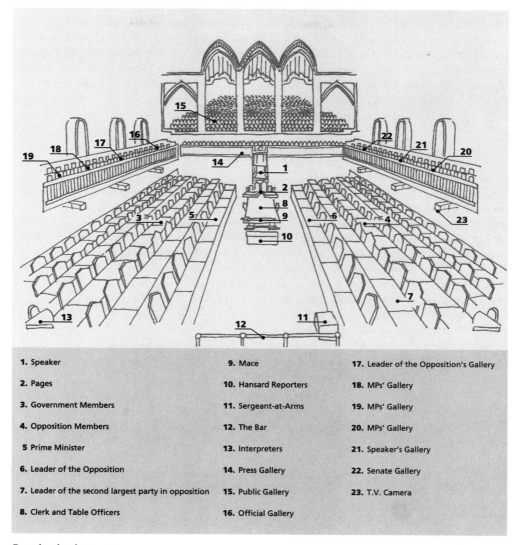

1. Speaker	9. Mace	17. Leader of the Opposition's Gallery
2. Pages	10. Hansard Reporters	18. MPs' Gallery
3. Government Members	11. Sergeant-at-Arms	19. MPs' Gallery
4. Opposition Members	12. The Bar	20. MPs' Gallery
5 Prime Minister	13. Interpreters	21. Speaker's Gallery
6. Leader of the Opposition	14. Press Gallery	22. Senate Gallery
7. Leader of the second largest party in opposition	15. Public Gallery	23. T.V. Camera
8. Clerk and Table Officers	16. Official Gallery	

Reproduced with permission.

lying, and require MPs to speak to each other through the Chair and to refer to each other by the name of their constituency, as the "Honourable Member for ..."

Speakers can only vote in the case of a tie and cannot articulate the needs of their constituency or constituents in the Commons as such. In compensation, ministers and bureaucrats are especially sensitive to the concerns that the Speaker discusses with them outside the chamber.

House Leaders, Party Whips, and Clerk

From within their ranks, each party selects a House leader and a party whip. The government **House leader** is a Cabinet minister who manages the government's business in the Commons. This minister seeks to work out an agenda for House business with the opposition House leaders, who function as procedural strategists for their parties and often speak for their parties if their leaders are absent. **Party whips**, on the other hand, are responsible for ensuring that their members are present for important votes and that their members vote the right way.[23] Whips must therefore know the whereabouts of all their members at all times. They also distribute members' offices, assign members to parliamentary committees, and line up the order of party speakers in Question Period and debates. It is largely through the whips, therefore, that party leaders impose discipline on their members. Members' opportunities to speak, to serve on the committee of their choice, and to travel as part of parliamentary delegations are largely influenced by their degree of party loyalty. In return, whips seek out backbench opinion on various matters and transmit it to the party leadership. Given the power of the party whips and party House leaders to organize its business, independent MPs find little opportunity to participate, even those who belong to a party with fewer than 12 members.

The chief permanent official of the Commons is the Clerk of the House. This position is analogous to a deputy minister in a government department. As chief procedural adviser to the Speaker and manager of the support staff attached to the Commons, the Clerk is also required to act in a totally nonpartisan manner. The Clerk is assisted at the table by the deputy clerk and several principal clerks.

Voting

Turning to the voting procedure in the Commons, decisions are in the first instance taken orally when the Speaker invites members to say "aye" or "nay." In declaring which side won, the Speaker is guided by the numbers rather than the volume on each side, and on a routine matter in a majority situation, this will probably suffice. When either side wants a formal recorded vote it will request a **division**. In this case the division bells ring until the government and official opposition party whips agree that all their available members have arrived, at which time a standing vote is conducted. It used to be that if either whip refused to give the go-ahead, the bells could ring indefinitely, but after the two-week "bell-ringing incident" of 1982, a 30-minute limit was adopted in 1986. A new procedure in 1994 allowed for deferred divisions with all-party consent, so that most votes are now held between late Monday and late Wednesday, when most members are there. In order to save time, if several votes are to take place in sequence, the result of one vote can be "applied" to subsequent votes with unanimous consent.

Until the early 1980s, MPs sometimes engaged in the practice of **pairing**, in which two members on opposite sides would make arrangements so that if one was legitimately absent for a vote, the other would not vote either. Indeed, in 1926, a "broken pair" resulted in the defeat of the government.[24] After being discontinued for about ten years, a more limited kind of pairing appeared again in the early 1990s and has been increasingly institutionalized. Party whips are involved in putting members' names in the registry of pairs, and paired members are listed at the end of the division list printed in Hansard. In general, pairing is only advantageous for the government, so that it will not be defeated on a crucial vote, and opposition parties are therefore not enthusiastic about the practice. Indeed, with the slim Liberal majority in Chrétien's second term, ministers sometimes had to cancel trips in order to be present for a vote, or else, to reduce the numbers on the other side, face the unappetizing alternative of taking an opposition member along with them!

Speeches

The length of speeches that MPs are allowed to make has been severely curtailed over the past 20 or so years. The 1982 reforms generally shortened them from 40 minutes to 20, but this depends on who is speaking, in what debate, and at what stage of the debate. In many cases, especially as a debate drags on, the maximum length is reduced to 10 minutes.

What is said in such speeches is also of interest here. Of all the **parliamentary privileges** and rights of MPs, individual and collective, the most important is the protection from libel action for anything said in the chamber. Occasionally MPs take advantage of their privileged position in this respect by declining to repeat outside the House certain remarks they have made within.

THE COMMITTEE SYSTEM

Much of the important legislative work of the House takes place outside the Commons chamber in a variety of committees. These include standing and special committees of the Commons itself, as well as joint standing and special committees of the Commons and Senate combined. Committees allow a small number of people to develop expertise in a particular field and to examine proposals in depth; moreover, if several committees operate simultaneously, a greater volume of business can be accomplished. In the parliamentary context, committees could allow private members to make constructive contributions to the governing of the country and to do so in a consensual rather than an adversarial atmosphere. Unfortunately, the Canadian Commons committee system did not function well during the first 100 years after Confederation. Committees were not used in a systematic way, and membership was so unstable that they failed to develop expertise. Repeated reforms of the Commons committee system since 1968 have made it more significant.

The 18 **standing committees** are set up more or less permanently in most of the substantive areas of government policy, such as Fisheries and Oceans or Transport. They have two principal functions: to examine the Estimates, that is, the government's spending proposals, and to examine legislation at the committee stage. The Estimates of the Department of Health, for example, are scrutinized by the Standing Committee on Health, and such an examination can now go beyond the spending plans of the current year. In examining bills, clause by clause, after second reading, committees question ministers, public servants, pressure groups, and other expert witnesses, who either try to convince committee members to approve the bill as introduced or else to effect changes. Sometimes a minister will ask a standing committee to study a problem in the absence of legislation, such as the Transport Committee's 1998 investigation of the future of passenger rail travel in Canada. The Standing Committee on Finance is perhaps most important, and now engages in wide-ranging pre-budget consultations, as mentioned in Figure 20.1, while the Liaison Committee, composed of other committee chairs, decides how to divide up funds allotted for committee work.

As a result of the 1986 changes, standing committees have new functions and resources. Since they largely parallel government departments, they are authorized to investigate any aspect of the department with which they are associated, including a review of nonjudicial government appointments (usually after they are made). Committee clerks are employees of the House of Commons and provide administrative and procedural support, but committees also have a budget to hire supporting staff and researchers, and thus to develop independent expertise. They can request the services of the staff of the Library of Parliament (Research Branch) or they can apply for funding to hire outside personnel.

Standing committees had 20 or 30 members in the past, but in 1984 their size was reduced to 10 or 15 members, and after 1997, increased to 16 to 18. Smaller, more stable, and more expert membership has served to increase the effectiveness of their deliberations. Because they often have a number of different issues on their agenda, they sometimes set up sub-committees. Representation on all committees is proportional to party standings in the House, so that in the "Pizza Parliament" after 1997, 16-member committees had 9 Liberal members, 3 Reformers, 2 from the Bloc, 1 New Democrat, and 1 PC. A recent innovation is that each committee has "associate members," a pool of loosely attached MPs who are eligible to sit as substitutes.

Committee chairs are elected by committee members, but they are usually pre-selected by the PMO, and are therefore members of the government party; since Reform was the official opposition in the Commons after 1997, a Reform MP was vice-chair of most committees. Thus, in a majority situation, the government will have a majority on each committee and its own designated choice as chair. In Britain, committees have always had a more autonomous position, including the choice of their own chair, and many members have found career satisfaction at this level rather than yearning for appointment to the Cabinet. The one exception to this government control in Canada is the **Public Accounts Committee**, which normally has a government majority but has been chaired by an opposition MP since 1958. It has the important function of examining the report of the **Auditor General**, the official of Parliament who audits the government's accounts.

Special committees are occasionally established for some specific, temporary purpose, especially if the government party has an excess of backbenchers and some issue arises that is beyond the normal jurisdiction of standing committees. They usually have an investigatory function—to examine an issue before the government has made up its mind on how to deal with it. Such committees may therefore be an important part of the initiation phase of the legislative process and have sometimes been called legislative task forces.

In addition to the standing and special committees of the House of Commons alone, the Commons and Senate sometimes work together in **joint committees**. Joint committees obviously avoid duplication and also give senators a chance to get involved at an earlier stage of the process than is usually the case. The most important joint standing committee is that on the **Scrutiny of Regulations**, which has the vital but unenviable responsibility of scrutinizing the mounds of regulations and other subordinate legislation issued by the executive branch each year, and which has been given the power to recommend rescission of offensive delegated legislation. The other two standing joint committees are on official languages and the parliamentary library. Special joint committees can also be established, such as the one that was involved in the development of the Constitution Act, 1982.

Finally, there is the committee of the whole. This is simply the entire Commons membership sitting in the chamber as a committee. In such a case, the Speaker is replaced in the chair by the deputy speaker, and the rules are somewhat relaxed. This committee is only used to debate appropriation bills (once the Estimates have been approved), urgent bills (such as back-to-work legislation), and certain noncontroversial bills. Otherwise, the House prefers to use smaller committees that can meet simultaneously in committee rooms outside the Commons chamber.

It is primarily the transformation of the committee system in recent years that has enhanced the position of ordinary MPs in the legislative process. As committees became smaller, more stable in their membership, and more expert in their field, and as their members developed greater collegiality, they sometimes shed some of their partisanship. Between 1986 and 1993, for example, many of these standing and legislative committees developed a consensus on the issues before them that cut across party lines. Examples include constitutional affairs and official languages, environmental legislation, the Public Accounts, and Scrutiny of Regulations committees, and the final stages of the PC gun control legislation. Such committees became newly independent sources of power in the legislative system, and this led to the acceptance of an unprecedented number of committee amendments to government bills. Since 1993, and especially in the five-party Parliament after 1997, committees found it more difficult to achieve such a cross-party consensus.

One advantage of all committees that meet outside the Commons chamber is that they can listen to representations from interest groups, bureaucrats, and other experts.[25] It was traditionally said that pressure groups and lobbyists did not make much use of the legislative branch of government because the crucial decisions had previously been made in the executive. Paul Pross argues, however, that it is a sign of the increasing autonomy and cross-party cohesiveness of Commons committees that pressure groups are giving them more attention than in the past.[26] One example of a committee that made substantial changes to government proposals as a result of group pressure was that reviewing the Constitution Act, 1982.

MEMBERS' SERVICES[27]

How much to pay members of Parliament is an intractable problem. To pay considerably more than the average industrial wage is to ensure public criticism, but as a general rule, the higher the level of remuneration, the better the quality of person that will be attracted to parliamentary life. The peculiar insecurity of political office in Canada must also be taken into account.

As of January 1, 2000, ordinary MPs received $68 200 in "sessional allowance" plus $22 500 in a tax-free expense allowance. Since the equivalent taxable value of the expense allowance would be about double, the total remuneration package is worth approximately $100 000. Because of the typical public uproar over increasing this amount, the government has appointed a succession of external, independent committees to review such levels of remuneration. On top of this basic income, a large number of MPs receive additional payments for supplementary responsibilities. These supplementary payments, as of 2000, are shown in Table 22.2.

In addition to this basic pay, backbench MPs received many other benefits and services at public expense or on a subsidized basis. MPs are given an annual office budget of approximately $190 000 from which to hire staff, at a maximum salary of $62 000 per person. They are provided with an office on Parliament Hill and in the constituency, and virtually unlimited telephone, mailing, and travel privileges. Parliamentary parties received ample funds for

TABLE 22.2   **Supplementary Allowances for Additional Responsibilities (Dollars)**

Prime minister	74 100
Speaker, opposition leader	52 000
Cabinet minister	49 300
Secretary of state	36 975
Other recognized party leader	31 200
Deputy speaker	27 200
Opposition house leader	25 000
Chief whip—government and opposition	13 800
Assistant deputy speaker and parliamentary secretary	11 100
Other party house leader	10 700
Deputy government and opposition party whip and other party chief whip	7 800

Source: House of Commons, Financial and Human Resources Services Directorate, "Miscellaneous Allowance and Rate Schedule."

research purposes, and additional funds were provided for the operation of the offices of opposition leaders, whips, House leaders, and caucus chairs. Such funding is only provided to recognized parties in the House—that is, groups of at least 12 members—a major blow to the Conservatives and NDP after the 1993 election.

More controversial is the MPs' pension plan. Although contributory, many observers felt that it was too generous because it was indexed to the cost of living and because, regardless of age, members became eligible for the pension immediately upon leaving the Commons after six years of service. Moreover, those subsequently appointed to a government position continued to receive the pension on top of their new salary. In 1995, the Liberals removed some of these provisions for newly elected MPs: they would have to wait to age 55 to collect, they could not "double-dip," and they could opt out entirely. Some Reform MPs who opted out later re-entered the plan.

The lot of backbench members of Parliament is obviously much improved over the situation in the pre-1960 period, in which they were not considered to occupy full-time positions, and their every need is now provided for. While their remuneration and services might seem excessive to many reporters[28] and members of the general public, the expenses of serving nearly 100 000 constituents and the insecurity of parliamentary life should not be underestimated. If their expenses were not completely covered, only wealthy individuals could seek federal political office.

ROLES OF MEMBERS OF PARLIAMENT

The roles that members of Parliament perform can be seen in two different lights. First, in terms of how they vote, MPs can be classified as trustees, constituency delegates, or party delegates. "Trustees" would be MPs who felt obliged to vote according to their own conscience, their own understanding of the issue in question, or their own conception of the national interest. Alternatively, "constituency delegates" would be MPs who voted the way they thought a majority of their constituents would want them to vote or in their conception of the best interests of their constituency. In other words, in situations where the two did not coincide, trustees would place their own views above those of their constituents, while constituency delegates would do the reverse. However much MPs may claim to fall into either of these categories, in practice they rarely deviate from the party line. In fact, then, they could all be labelled "party delegates." If the party caucus determines a position that conflicts with either their own views or those of their constituents, MPs are almost always obliged to put the party position first. The reasons for such rigid party discipline were discussed earlier in the chapter. Public pressure for more free votes seems to be increasing, however, and such discipline may also be in decline at the committee stage.

The other way to examine the roles of MPs is in terms of how they spend their time or what their priorities are.[29] The first role in this respect is the lawmaker, consisting of MPs who devote most of their attention to the legislative process, introducing, amending, and debating legislation. MPs are supported in these tasks by the Research Branch of the Library of Parliament, but since this role is almost completely irrelevant to their constituents, not many MPs fall into this category. Another group sees its role primarily as being a propagandist for one or more causes. These MPs use every opportunity available—Question Period, general debates, and even public speeches outside of Parliament—to press for certain reforms they believe in. Determined crusaders in favour of capital punishment would be good examples. Then there are MPs whose main goal is to promote their constituency and bring back public favours, a role that could be called representational. These members lobby ministers and public servants for new public buildings, roads, wharves, and other facilities so that they will have something "concrete" to show for themselves by the time of the next election. Finally, all MPs function frequently as ombudsmen or social workers for their individual constituents, intervening with ministers or public servants to hasten administrative decisions, to correct bureaucratic errors, and to repair governmental injustices. There will always be constituents with passport, immigration, Employment Insurance, pension, and many other kinds of problems, and some MPs specialize in trying to resolve them. This "caseload" of MPs is now so heavy that they are provided with considerable administrative assistance both in their Ottawa and constituency offices so that they will have some time available for their other duties. Figure 22.3 presents, in graphic form, a picture of how MPs spend their time.

The life of an MP is extremely busy; MPs are constantly engaged in meetings and talking with individual and groups of constituents, organized interest groups, the media, bureaucrats, party officials, staff, and other parliamentarians. Besides assuming heavy responsibilities in Ottawa, they are expected to be seen frequently in the constituency, both in their offices and at myriad social events, usually on weekends or when Parliament is recessed. All this activity interferes with a normal family life, whether those with spouses and/or children move their families to Ottawa or leave them at home to be visited when time permits.

Figure 22.3 **How an MP Spends the Day (Percentage of Working Time Devoted to Different Tasks)**

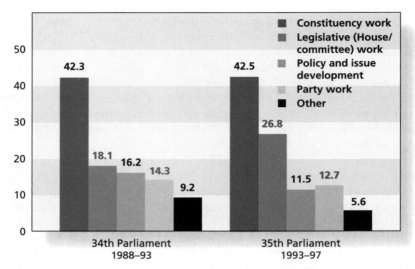

■ Constituency work
■ Legislative (House/ committee) work
■ Policy and issue development
■ Party work
■ Other

Source: David C. Docherty, Mr. Smith Goes to Ottawa, p. 129 (UBC Press, 1997). Reproduced with permission.

THE GOVERNMENT–OPPOSITION BALANCE

An objective look at Parliament reveals a basic dilemma: the government wants to get legislation passed expeditiously, but the opposition must have time to articulate constituency needs as well as a chance to criticize government proposals in order to make the public aware of their defects. One manner of addressing this conflict is to summarize the ways in which the Cabinet controls the Commons, especially in a **majority government** position, and then the ways in which the Commons controls the Cabinet.

The prime minister and Cabinet, through the governor general, summon, prorogue, and dissolve Parliament, and then basically determine the agenda of parliamentary business. The Cabinet has a monopoly on the introduction of financial legislation and a virtual monopoly on the legislation that actually gets passed. Through the whip, the prime minister and Cabinet control almost all parliamentary committee work and also have the power to introduce closure to cut off debate or time allocation motions to curtail it. Backing up all these specific devices of Cabinet dominance are two other general powers. The prime minister and Cabinet continually enforce party discipline on their MPs in order to achieve their ends and have at their disposal the vast informational resources of the public service. Thus it is sometimes said that the prime minister and Cabinet operate as a virtual dictatorship until they have to face the electorate again some four or five years down the road.

Parliamentary control over the Cabinet, on the other hand, refers mainly to opportunities to criticize and to delay, rather than any real power to alter the Cabinet's proposals or to throw the government out. MPs, especially on the opposition side, have the daily option to ask oral questions of ministers, in addition to the 15 minutes set aside for members' statements, and 30 minutes for adjournment proceedings four times per week. They can also submit written questions seeking detailed information. MPs have the throne speech and budget debates in which to criticize the government generally or raise their own alternatives, as well as 21 days per session to select the topic of debate. Limited research funds and the services of the Library of Parliament are made available in an attempt to begin to restore the balance in advisory and informational resources, and MPs can introduce legislation in the form of private members' bills. MPs can criticize specific Cabinet measures at the second-reading stage, introduce amendments at the committee and report stages, and have a chance to scrutinize the government's spending proposals. Opposition MPs may at least delay the adoption of government measures by prolonging debates and by raising procedural points. But when all is said and done, the prime minister and Cabinet almost always get their way.

MINORITY GOVERNMENT

The foregoing account assumes that the government is in a majority position in the Commons. A **minority government** situation—in which the government is outnumbered by opposition members—is slightly better balanced. The government may have to negotiate with opposition parties to some extent, such as to amend its proposals, abandon them, or even accept opposition initiatives. Many observers who deplore the normal arrogance of a majority government and who regret that so much opposition talent and so many opposition ideas ordinarily go to waste actually prefer the minority government situation.

Eugene Forsey has reminded us that minority government is not exceptional, is not necessarily weak and indecisive, and does not have to be short-lived.[30] Between 1867 and 2000 there were nine minority governments in Canada: 1921–25 (King); 1925–26 (King); 1926 (Meighen); 1957–58 (Diefenbaker); 1962–63 (Diefenbaker); 1963–65 (Pearson); 1965–68 (Pearson); 1972–74 (Trudeau); and 1979–80 (Clark). Few of these governments could have been called weak and indecisive because of their minority position; many, such as the 1957–58 Diefenbaker government, were more active and courageous than the majority governments that preceded or followed them. Some were exceptionally bold and decisive, especially the Pearson governments and the Trudeau minority, the latter being particularly sensitive to opposition demands. While minority governments admittedly did not last as long as majority governments, not all of them ended by being defeated. The first Diefenbaker government and the two Pearson governments, for example, ended when the prime minister himself decided to call an election.

In a minority government situation, much is made of one or more opposition parties holding the balance of power. On occasion, for example, this position has allowed the CCF or NDP to force a Liberal minority to adopt some of its policies. But holding the balance of power is not normally an enviable position, especially if the opposition cannot amend or defeat a government measure without throwing out the whole government. If any such defeat were taken as a vote of nonconfidence in the government, it would precipitate another election. Such an opposition party may not have the finances to engage in a quick succession of election campaigns, and is sometimes thought to suffer at the hands of an electorate that blames it for the inconvenience and expense of another vote.

This leads to a discussion of the principle of responsible government—that the Cabinet must have the confidence of the Commons or else call an election or resign. It is not always clear whether the Cabinet is required to take such drastic action. In a majority situation the problem is most unlikely to arise, but does a government in a minority position have to resign or call an election over any and every defeat? There is no question about the defeat of the government on a **nonconfidence motion**, including the speech from the throne and the budget; the uncertainty arises over the defeat of government bills. In 1968, the Pearson government was defeated on a piece of financial legislation, but Pearson argued that the defeat was a fluke and that his government should be allowed to carry on. In that case the matter was decided when the Cabinet subsequently survived an explicit nonconfidence motion.[31] Alternatively, in the 1985 Liberal–NDP accord in Ontario, the two parties agreed that the defeat of individual government measures would not entail a loss of confidence in the government as a whole.[32] If such an understanding were extended to majority situations as well, government backbenchers would have more freedom to vote according to the interests of their constituencies. Another alternative would be to adopt fixed election dates, subject to a government defeat on a motion of nonconfidence, as New Zealand has done.

REFORM OF THE HOUSE OF COMMONS

The imbalance between government and opposition is so great and the legislative role of ordinary MPs has been so ineffective that parliamentary reform is never far from the minds of political scientists and politicians alike. Reform proposals have primarily been designed to remedy excessive partisanship, Cabinet domination, and the lack of influence of the private member.

At the end of the 1960s, changes in the committee system, provision for timetabling the business of the House, and funding of parliamentary parties for research purposes "inaugurated the modern era of parliamentary government."[33] Then in the 1970s, MPs saw considerable improvement in their services, especially in parliamentary and constituency offices and staff. In addition, the proceedings of the Commons began to be televised in 1977, with later provision being made to televise some committee proceedings. One of the ways in which television changed members' behaviour was that they began to applaud instead of pounding on their desks to indicate approval.[34] In 1982, a severe altercation occurred between the Trudeau government and the Conservative opposition over the form and substance of the National Energy Program, such that the opposition left the division bells ringing for 15 days. This incident led all concerned to strive to improve Commons procedures, and the recommendations of the Lefebvre Committee on procedural reform were implemented promptly. This momentum for reform survived the 1984 election, and as a result of the McGrath Committee, further reforms were made in 1986.[35] All of these procedural changes had the general objective of improving the lot of the backbench MP and were based on a consensus of the House. In 1991, responding to the low esteem in which politicians were held by the public, the Mulroney government introduced further changes. While the changes were aimed to accomplish as much parliamentary work in less time, to give MPs more time in their constituencies, and to make the committee system more effective, they were not the result of all-party agreement and opposition parties were not completely satisfied. Several modest changes have been made since 1993, primarily related to the committee system and private members' bills. Some form of electronic voting and removal of Friday sittings are two issues that have not yet been resolved.

Despite the impressive changes made since the 1960s, several recommendations of the 1985–86 Special Committee on Reform of the House of Commons were not immediately implemented. Chief among them was any loosening of party discipline or alteration in the concept of "confidence" in the government on individual pieces of legislation. Such a change could take the form of relaxing party discipline somewhat, accepting more opposition amendments to government initiatives, or even allowing the occasional defeat of a government scheme without entailing the government's resignation. As mentioned earlier, a small start has been made in the last few years in giving more latitude to committees and private members' bills, but the Cabinet, perhaps not surprisingly, was unwilling to go so far as to reduce its crushing monopoly on the legislative process.[36]

Such changes would enhance the legislative role of backbenchers, but Franks argues that this would be at the expense of the advantages of an executive-centred system. He feels that reform should be advocated with caution and that "Parliament is more in need of understanding than change."[37] He recommends that salaries be raised to attract a better calibre of member (and therefore Cabinet minister), and that the Commons be enlarged so that more members are available to take care of legislative and constituency business.

Beyond changes in the existing operation of the Commons, some reformers advocate the adoption of such populist devices as the recall, the initiative, and the referendum. The **recall** would allow a certain proportion of the electorate to petition a sitting legislator to resign; the **initiative** would require the legislature to respond to a policy initiative endorsed by a certain proportion of the electorate; and the **referendum** would submit certain public policy proposals to the electorate. Such devices were widely advocated in the 1920s in Western Canada and have recently re-emerged on the political agenda, largely thanks to the Reform Party. More radical than the idea of loosening party discipline, these techniques are subject to even greater reservations in terms of an executive-centred system. As mentioned in Chapter 10, the recall has been established at the provincial level in British Columbia, and several wild and bitter recall campaigns have ensued.

PURPOSES AND POWERS OF THE SENATE

The ideal of democracy was still not enthusiastically accepted in the 1860s and the Fathers of Confederation felt it advisable to provide for an appointed body that would exercise "sober second thought" with respect to measures emanating from the popularly elected House of Commons. Thus the Senate was to be the equivalent of the British House of Lords, an older, conservative influence, with a minimum age of 30, appointment for life, and a relatively high property qualification ($4000 of equity in land in the province or territory of residence and $4000 over and above all debts). Sir John A. Macdonald argued that the Senate should protect minorities and the rich were always fewer in number than the poor![38]

In the second place, the smaller provinces would only agree to join Confederation and accept representation by population in the House of Commons if they were overrepresented in the Senate. The Fathers settled on a Senate that would be based on equal *regional* representation, a compromise between equal provincial representation (as in the United States and as since demanded by Triple-E advocates) and the principle of representation by population. Such a system gave the Maritimes and Quebec a limited amount of protection against the voting power of Ontario in the House of Commons. It followed that senators were supposed to represent their regions and provinces within the national policymaking system.

A third function of the Senate, not explicitly provided for in 1867 but that can also be seen as part of the concept of sober second thought, is to improve legislation from a technical point of view. This function—to act as a nonideological, routine revising chamber that picks up on flaws in legislation that have not been noticed during its passage through the busy Commons—has become one of the Senate's most important roles over the years.

As far as powers were concerned, the Senate was given a veto over all legislation, a power that was not restricted as in the case of the British House of Lords. The only point of Senate inferiority to the Commons was that "money bills," that is, legislation involving the raising or spending of money, had to be introduced in the lower chamber. Nothing in law prevented the Senate from delaying, amending, or vetoing any bills, whether or not they involved money, although in the latter case, amendments could not increase taxes or expenditures. It was only the Standing Orders of the House of Commons that claimed the Senate could not amend money bills, an assertion never accepted by the Senate.[39]

It was not until 1982 that the Senate's power was in any way reduced, and that had to do only with constitutional amendments, not ordinary legislation. According to the Constitution Act, 1982, the Senate can only delay a constitutional amendment for 180 days. If the Senate has not approved such an amendment by then, it can be repassed by the Commons, and bypasses the Senate in the process of ratification. If the 1992 Charlottetown Accord had been ratified, the range of ordinary legislation over which the Senate retained an absolute veto would have been severely restricted.

COMPOSITION OF THE SENATE

The basic structural principle of the Senate agreed to at the time of Confederation was equal regional representation. Thus Ontario, Quebec, and the Maritimes received 24 senators each. In the case of Quebec, the province was divided into 24 senatorial regions so that an appropriate balance of anglophone and francophone representatives would be chosen. Otherwise, senators do not officially represent a specific region of their province, although they may choose to do so on an individual, unofficial basis. When Prince Edward Island joined Confederation, it received 4 of the 24 Maritime senators, reducing Nova Scotia's and New Brunswick's share to 10 each. In a general reform in 1915 the West was designated as a senatorial region with 24 senators, preserving the principle of equal regional representation, with 6 allocated to each Western province. In 1949, Newfoundland was awarded 6 senators in addition to the 96 already allotted, so as to leave the Maritime contingent intact. Finally, in 1975, the Yukon and Northwest Territories were given 1 senator each, as was Nunavut in 1999, so that the total became 105 ($4 \times 24 + 6 + 3$), with only slight deviations from the principle of equal regional representation.

Section 24 of the 1867 Constitution Act gives the governor general the power to appoint senators, but by convention this is done on the advice of the prime minister. Prime ministers have almost always chosen partisan supporters such as MPs seeking a safe haven, defeated MPs or candidates, those who have served the party organization well, retired premiers or other former provincial politicians, and federal Cabinet ministers who have outlived their usefulness. Rewarding party services, regenerating the Cabinet, and maintaining party unity were the main considerations in the prime minister's mind. Hence, almost all of those appointed could be called "party hacks," and the image of the Senate was set: a home for the aged, a pension scheme for retired party warriors, and a reward for businessmen's contributions to the party war chest.[40]

In addition to rewarding faithful service to the party in the past, many appointments were made on the assumption that the new senator would continue to promote the party in the future. Such senators carried on as party fundraisers ("bagmen"), party presidents, party organizers, election campaign strategists or managers, or in other partisan capacities. Since Canadian parties are usually short of funds, it saved the party salary money if some of its officials could work out of the Senate at public expense. Most prime ministers have made the occasional nonpartisan or cross-party appointment, perhaps as a "cover" for yet more partisan nominees, and because the Senate was already overwhelmingly stacked with Liberals, Pierre Trudeau deliberately replaced a Tory with a Tory on six occasions.

Senators have traditionally been English or French male lawyers or businessmen and have maintained active business connections after their appointment.[41] Most saw nothing wrong with carrying on as directors of various corporations or even being appointed to new ones at the same time as they held public office. They always had spare time, they welcomed the supplementary income, and they could be useful links between the corporate and political worlds. Because of ideological opposition to the whole concept of an appointed chamber, left-wing groups have refused the occasional offer of appointment, leaving labour and working-class representation in the Senate virtually nonexistent.

The Constitution Act, 1867, speaks of "qualified persons" being eligible for appointment to the Senate, and this was originally understood to include only men. In one of the most famous court cases in Canadian history, however, an enterprising group of women challenged this interpretation, and in the 1929 **Persons case**, the Judicial Committee of the Privy Council decided that "persons" did indeed include women.[42] Henceforth women were eligible to sit in the Senate, although relatively few have been appointed (about 30 out of 105 in 1999). In addition, ethnic and religious considerations have often played a part in Senate appointments. From the Diefenbaker period onward, prime ministers sought to diversify Senate membership in ethnic terms, and senators have been appointed as representatives of the Aboriginal, Ukrainian, Italian, Greek, Icelandic, and Black communities, among others.

Senators originally served for life, and many lived to the ripe old age of 80, 90, or 100 before they died. Lester Pearson had a constitutional amendment passed in 1965 to the effect that incumbent senators could stay until death or retire at 75 with a pension, but all subsequent appointees would have to retire at 75. In normal circumstances only one senator sits in the Cabinet (the government leader in the Senate). But both Joe Clark (1979–80) and Pierre Trudeau (1980–84) had three or four senators in their cabinets to fill in gaps in their provincial representation.

OPERATION OF THE SENATE

In the light of its intended functions, what can be said about the actual operations of the Senate? First, as for acting as a conservative influence on legislation and representing the interests of property, two examples stand out. The Senate defeated the first Old Age Pensions bill in 1925, but after an election in which Mackenzie King was deemed to receive a mandate for the legislation, the Senate passed the bill a year later. The other was the Senate's repeated refusal to repeal the notorious section 98 of the Criminal Code that had been passed at the height of the Winnipeg General Strike in 1919; the Senate did not repeal it until 1936. It is not so much with reference to other social legislation that this conservative role is most obvious, but in relation to bills affecting the corporate community, discussed below.

Second, it must be concluded that the Senate has never effectively represented provincial and regional interests in the national policymaking process.[43] This is not particularly surprising when senators owe their appointment to the federal prime minister and not to any provincial or regional constituency. Moreover, many senators settle down in the comfortable environs of Ottawa and never go near the region they ostensibly represent. As a result, this function was soon undertaken by the Judicial Committee of the Privy Council, regional ministers in the federal Cabinet, and provincial premiers in federal–provincial conferences.

Of its original purposes, then, the first has been rendered archaic and the second has been assumed by other agencies. Today's senators therefore try to justify their existence primarily in terms of the third function mentioned, routine revision of bills. R.A. MacKay argues that the nonpartisan, noncontroversial revising function of the Senate is virtually indispensable, and F.A. Kunz calls it one of great usefulness.[44] In addition to routine revision of government bills, the Senate sometimes undertakes detailed and protracted examination of complex legislation, such as the Bankruptcy Act or the Criminal Code. Similarly, the rules allow a bill to be introduced simultaneously in both chambers so that the Senate can engage in an unhurried "pre-study" of the bill rather than wait until it has passed three readings in the Commons, but this provision is rarely used.

Senators also seek to emphasize other important aspects of their work. One is the Senate's consideration of private bills. These concern individuals, companies, churches, professional associations, and other institutions, and are a nuisance to the busy House of Commons, which is often backlogged with public bills. Since 1934, almost all private bills have been introduced in the Senate, where the background work can be done so that the Commons can approve them routinely at a later date. This practice does help the Commons, but private bills are not numerous and do not absorb much of anyone's time.

For a period the Senate functioned more or less as a divorce court for Quebec and Newfoundland, when religious opposition to divorce in those two provinces pre-empted turning this responsibility over to their courts. Divorces were a special kind of private bill, and between 1964 and 1968 (when they finally became a judicial matter in those two provinces) divorces were disposed of by the Senate without reference to the Commons.

Another kind of work not originally provided for is the study of various public problems by Senate committees in what Colin Campbell calls "social investigations."[45] Senators often have the expertise and certainly the time to conduct inquiries that relieve the pressure on the House of Commons and are cheaper than royal commissions. Among the issues investigated by the Senate over the years were poverty, aging, unemployment, the mass media, science policy, land use, national defence, Canadian–American relations, and the Canadian Security Intelligence Service. More recently, activity has centred on the Senate's Standing Committee on Fisheries, the Standing Committee on Legal and Constitutional Affairs, the Special Committee on the Pearson Airport Agreements, and the Special Joint Committees on Constitutional Amendments (regarding Newfoundland and Quebec school systems).

Finally, the Senate reviews regulations issued by various government departments. The Standing Joint Committee on the Scrutiny of Regulations has the responsibility of reviewing the great quantity of subordinate legislation issued every year. Although this is a joint

By Mike Graston (Windsor Star). *Reproduced with permission.*

Commons–Senate committee, the senators who sit on it have more time to devote to its tedious work and perhaps more independence of mind in approaching it.

Worthy as all these functions are, they do not even collectively justify the expense of the Senate, especially given its lack of a popular base. Some impressive people have been appointed over the years, and a small group of 15 or 20 take their work seriously, but few who accept appointment to the Senate expect to work very hard, and almost all who go there have other interests on the side. Lacking even minimal popular accountability, it is possible for some senators to do absolutely nothing and still collect their paycheques until the age of 75. Senator Andrew Thompson was eventually shamed into resigning from the Senate, after having been kicked out of the Liberal caucus, when it was revealed that he had hardly ever attended in over ten years, and instead, lived a rather carefree existence in Mexico. A senator has to be absent for two consecutive sessions before any action is taken. As of January 1999, senators were paid $66 900 plus a nontaxable expense account of $10 500, for an actual value of approximately $85 000.[46]

The Senate timetable is very lax, meeting three days a week for no more than 27 weeks a year. There being no shortage of time, the rules are quite relaxed; the Speaker is chosen by the prime minister and has a vote on all matters. There is a question period, but the one senator who normally sits in the Cabinet cannot be expected to answer for the whole range of government activity. Prime ministers and cabinets have often been disrespectful of the institution, leaving many vacancies for long periods of time, and expecting it to pass large quantities of legislation quickly at the end of a session.

The harshest criticism of the Senate is that it is sometimes accused of systemic corruption. This accusation is particularly levelled at the Senate Committee on Banking, Trade and Commerce, which reviews a great deal of legislation at the committee stage, regardless of its subject matter. Colin Campbell detailed and condemned these corporate connections in his book *The Canadian Senate: A Lobby from Within.* He writes of the Senate's adopted function of "business review," as its members "bargain and negotiate on business's behalf for amendments which are essential for a favourable financial and commercial climate." Campbell reveals the "one-sided review which takes place in a legislature created by a political system which bends over backwards to ensure that business has preferential access to the policy process."[47] Unrestrained by any conflict-of-interest legislation (except for the formal abstention from voting), members of the Senate's Banking Committee energetically engage in debating legislation dealing with companies on whose boards of directors they sit. Many senators also act as lobbyists for business beyond the confines of the Senate chamber. Thus, "senators' lobbying activities are paid for by the people of Canada and not by the business firms and groups whose interests they advance." Even worse, some senators (usually lawyers) have received payment for acting as business lobbyists even after the Lobbyists Registration Act purported to make this illegal.[48]

Over the years, the Senate consistently challenged, delayed, and amended legislative provisions that might endanger major business or financial concerns. Examples include protecting the existing commercial banks, on which many senators were directors, in both the 1960s and 1970s; delaying and gutting the Hazardous Products bill in 1968–69; delaying and diluting the Investment Companies bill in 1969; and amending the Income Tax Act in 1973.[49]

The Senate's exercise of its power to amend or veto legislation must be put into the context that an appointed legislative chamber lost much of its legitimacy with the spread of democratic sentiment shortly after Confederation. Thus, the Senate did not usually feel justified in defying the will of the popularly elected House of Commons.[50] Moreover, given the partisan nature of Senate appointments, the majority in that chamber usually corresponded to the partisan complexion of the Commons. Both had a Conservative majority for about the first 30 years and both usually had a Liberal majority since 1900.

As for amendments, Kunz calculates that between 1923 and 1963 the Senate made amendments to about 15 percent of the bills coming from the Commons, while MacKay finds about 20 percent between 1867 and 1960.[51] Andrew Heard shows, however, that between 1957 and 1986 this figure fell to about 4 percent.[52] It must be said that in many cases such amendments were introduced in the Senate by the Cabinet itself, reflecting its second thoughts on the matter after it had been approved by the Commons, and most of the others were of a technical nature. To reinforce this point, in accounting for the incidence of Senate amendments to Commons bills, it made little difference whether or not the majority in both chambers belonged to the same party.

On the other hand, partisanship is most striking when one considers the Senate's vetoing of Commons legislation. In almost all such cases, a Liberal majority in the Senate has obstructed a Conservative majority in the Commons, or vice versa. According to MacKay, of approximately 4200 public bills passed by the Commons between 1867 and 1960, about 100 failed to pass the Senate, although many of these were withdrawn voluntarily by the government. Kunz found 18 vetoes of 1918 bills between 1926 and 1963. Rather than concentrate on total numbers, Table 22.3 lists the 13 most controversial Senate vetoes up to 1961. That year also included the "Coyne affair," in which the Senate held up the government bill firing James Coyne as Governor of the Bank of Canada until he had had a chance to defend himself before it. MacKay argues that in these and other cases the Senate has never defeated the real will of the people when clearly expressed.[53]

Brian Mulroney had considerable difficulty with the Senate, when, between 1984 and 1991, a Liberal majority in that chamber coincided with a Conservative majority in the Commons. The Senate delayed a government borrowing bill in 1984; it tried to amend a gov-

TABLE 22.3   **The 13 Most Controversial Senate Vetoes (1867–1961)**

1. 1875—rejection of a bill for the construction of the Esquimalt–Nanaimo railway
2. 1899–1900—rejection of a bill to readjust representation in the House of Commons for Ontario
3. 1912—amendment of Highways bill that government rejected
4. 1912—amendment of Tariff Commission bill that government rejected
5. 1913—rejection of Borden's Naval bill
6. 1914—rejection of amendment of the BNA Act re provincial representation in the Senate
7. 1914—rejection of Farmers Bank Depositors' Relief bill
8. 1923—rejection of bill for construction of CNR branch lines
9. 1926—rejection of Old Age Pensions bill
10. 1926, 1927, 1928, 1929—rejection of repeal of s. 98 of Criminal Code
11. 1936—rejection of amendment of the BNA Act re allowing provinces to levy sales taxes
12. 1937—rejection of bill expanding jurisdiction of Board of Transport Commissioners
13. 1961—rejection of amendment to the Customs Act

ernment measure on mandatory supervision of parolees; it repeatedly passed amendments to the government's drug patent bill, only retreating at the last minute; and it delayed amendments to copyright, immigration, and income tax acts.[54] The Senate also tried to alter the Meech Lake Accord, and its amendments had to be overridden by the Commons after the expiry of the 180-day limit on constitutional amendments. Then, in mid-1988, at John Turner's direction, the Liberal majority in the Senate held up the Canada–U.S. Free Trade Agreement until the electorate had a chance to express its will on such an important measure. After the 1988 election, the Senate bowed to the popular will and passed the Free Trade Agreement, but later dug in its heels on unemployment insurance amendments, cutbacks to social programs, and especially the Goods and Services Tax (GST).

It is unlikely that the GST would have passed if Prime Minister Mulroney had not invoked an obscure clause in the 1867 Constitution Act, section 26, which allowed him to appoint eight additional senators (two for each of the four senatorial regions) to tip the balance in favour of the Conservatives.[55] After the GST passed in an atmosphere of great bitterness on both sides, the Senate went ahead and defeated the government's compromise abortion bill (on a tie vote). This became the first measure in 30 years that the Senate actually defeated, but it was a peculiar case in that the government allowed a "free vote" and some Cabinet ministers were probably secretly relieved that the Senate had exercised such a rare veto.

Besides the intense partisan confrontation between the two chambers, the Mulroney period was exceptional for two reasons: first, the government had embarked on a new, neoconservative ideological tangent; and second, the Liberal ex-ministers in the Senate had a difficult time accepting the fact that they were no longer in power. In most of these cases, ironically, the House of Commons was acting in a more conservative manner than the Senate, which suddenly saw itself protecting the little people!

By the time the Liberals came to power in 1993, the Conservatives had established a clear majority in the Senate, so positions were reversed, and the Liberals began to pay for their intransigence of a few years earlier. On a rather nonpartisan note, though, the Senate responded to demands from the academic community to veto a bill that would have merged the Social Sciences and Humanities Research Council with the Canada Council. The Conservative majority in the Senate was particularly incensed about the Liberal bill limiting the right to claim damages as a result of cancelling the privatization of the Toronto Pearson Airport. The Liberals felt justified because the privatization had been done amid charges of patronage and profiteering at public expense, but the bill was defeated on another tie vote. The PC-controlled Senate then stalled the Liberals' redistribution bill to the point of abandonment, which was also the fate of pro-labour amendments to the Canada Labour Code. The Senate defeated the Newfoundland constitutional amendment with respect to removing denominational schools, until it was overridden after 180 days. It also delayed passage of Canada Pension Plan amendments, the GST harmonization bill, and the Gun Control bill. Even after the Liberals regained a majority in the Senate, the second chamber remained a more active place than normal, as it amended the government's own Canada Wheat Board bill. But it then did the government a favour by defeating a private members' bill (dealing with profiteering from crime) that had slipped unnoticed through the Commons.

Andrew Heard argues that a modern convention has developed such that the Senate can make purely technical amendments or others that it knows will be acceptable to the Commons and to the government. While it should not act to frustrate the general thrust of Commons legislation put before it, the Senate can on rare occasions make substantive amendments "when the government has no clear support from the majority of Canadians to implement a policy that adversely affects some individuals or groups." If legislation is repassed by the Commons, however, the Senate should give way.[56]

· ·

SENATE REFORM

Given the limited value of the Senate as it currently operates, its reform is high on the political agenda. All sorts of proposals have been made, ranging from abolition to election, to having provinces choose some or all of its members. The CCF/NDP has always favoured abolition because of the undemocratic nature of the Senate and its close links to the business community. Campbell also recommended abolition because of the Senate's illegitimate defence of corporate interests and the impossibility of making the institution more effective and more democratic without interfering with the will of the House of Commons. A group of MPs spearheaded a new Senate abolition campaign after 1997.

Many reformers have advocated reactivating the Senate's role of representing regional and provincial interests at the federal level because the existing mechanisms of "intrastate federalism" have been flawed. The Trudeau government first attempted to make the Senate a

House of the Federation in 1978 with half its members selected by the provinces. However, the Supreme Court held that such changes to the structure of the Senate required provincial approval.[57] To legitimize its existence in a democratic age, there is an increasing consensus that the Senate should also be elected.

To ensure that provinces other than Quebec could get something out of the 1987 Meech Lake Accord, three points regarding the Senate were agreed on in that document.[58] First, no changes could be made to the Senate without unanimous provincial consent; second, Senate reform would be the next topic of constitutional change; and third, until such time as the selection process was officially changed, the prime minister would appoint senators from lists provided by the provinces. By the time the Meech Lake Accord died and these interim measures with it, Brian Mulroney had only appointed a handful of senators from provincial lists.

Meanwhile, Alberta began pushing its **Triple-E Senate** proposal: elected, effective, and equal.[59] Triple-E advocates were not entirely clear on what powers they saw as necessary to make the Senate "effective," but since they generally felt that laws currently emanating from the House of Commons were designed in the interests of central Canada, such proponents were not overly concerned about deadlock between their revamped Senate and the lower house.

The government of Alberta felt so strongly about an elected Senate that it held a "senatorial election" in 1989 when a vacancy occurred during the period in which Mulroney asked for a list of provincial nominees. The Reform Party candidate won the provincewide contest (coinciding with municipal elections), and Premier Don Getty forwarded his name to the prime minister. Although Mulroney preferred to choose from a *list* of provincial nominees, rather than being presented with a single name, and was certainly not happy to appoint a Reform Party senator, he eventually gave in. Senate reform was then a prominent part of the 1992 Charlottetown Accord.

That accord would have provided for a new 62-member Senate, with six representatives from each province and one from each territory. They would be popularly elected at the same time as MPs, except in Quebec where they would be chosen by the National Assembly. To reinforce their new role as independent, provincial representatives in Ottawa, they would not be eligible to sit in the Cabinet. Defeat of a government bill in the Senate would not be considered a vote of nonconfidence; instead, when the Senate rejected a Commons bill, a joint sitting of both houses would be held and a combined vote taken in which the Commons would outnumber the Senate 337 to 62. However, legislation dealing with the taxation of natural resources, as in the case of the National Energy Program, could be killed by a simple majority in the Senate. It could also veto government appointments to national institutions such as the governor of the Bank of Canada. Bills dealing with the French language and culture would have to be approved by a majority of francophone senators as well as by the Senate as a whole. Any kind of legislation except government money (supply) bills could be initiated in the Senate, but a Senate vote against a supply bill could be simply overridden by reintroducing it in the Commons.

Such a system was not exactly the Triple-E Senate, but it was close enough to satisfy Premier Getty and different enough not to offend other participants in the conference. Ontario and Quebec were willing to give up 18 senators each in return for 18 additional seats in the House of Commons, while Nova Scotia and New Brunswick surrendered four Senate seats each. Some provinces indicated an interest in guaranteeing gender equality among their six Senate members. However, when the accord went down to popular defeat, the Senate remained unreformed. Little on the subject has been heard since, except for Alberta's holding of another senatorial election in 1998. Chrétien slyly filled a vacancy from that province a month before the election, appointing a former Tory, who sits as an Independent, so the two Reform candidates "elected" became "senators in waiting," with little assurance of ever taking their place in the Red Chamber.

CONCLUSION

This chapter demonstrates that apart from MPs who double as Cabinet ministers, the role of the House of Commons in the policymaking process is not impressive, and that of the Senate even less so. On the other hand, the Commons at least does have significant functions—in debating public issues, in keeping the government honest, and in educating the electorate. The prime minister and Cabinet can win almost every "battle" with Parliament, but may still lose the next electoral "war" if the opposition has alerted the public to their faults via the media. There are advantages to concentrating the responsibility for public policy in the hands of the prime minister and Cabinet, but these could still be achieved if better use were made of the talent in the House of Commons.

P Pluralists note the diversity in the social background of MPs, such as the rising numbers of women and ethnic minorities, and emphasize the opportunities available to MPs to articulate a variety of interests. Pluralists also point to the participation of parliamentary committees and individual MPs in various policy communities, and see pressure groups interacting more regularly with MPs than in the past. On the other hand, pluralists question whether the rigid party discipline in the Canadian House of Commons is appropriate for such a pluralistic society. Such rigidity has forced various regional, ethnic, and class interests to form their own political parties when they felt unable to make themselves heard within traditional national parties. It has also led many people to look to provincial governments and premiers to articulate regional concerns. As for the Senate, pluralists emphasize its increasingly diversified membership and the wide range of its social investigations. While it was once the preserve of French and English males, the Senate now contains about 30 percent women and conventional representation of a variety of ethnic groups. Rather surprisingly, most of its recent committee inquiries have recommended changes that were at odds with the business sector, such as improving the lot of the poor and the aged and providing greater regulation of the mass media.

PC Public choice theory sees the House of Commons as the focal point of party conflict between elections in order to influence the electorate in its next trip to the polls. Much of the activity in the Commons is designed to manipulate public opinion, as all parties try to present themselves in the best possible light and have nothing but condemnation for their opponents. This chapter has shown the many opportunities available in the Commons to pursue this intensely adversarial activity. Since media coverage of the Commons is usually dominated by opposition criticism, however, the Cabinet does its best to ignore the House and to interact (and bargain) directly with the public.

C Class analysts find that the "Commons" is still an elitist institution. Very few of its members come from manual occupations, for example, and a high proportion have post-secondary education. Even more telling are the results of a survey that indicated MPs over-estimate the economic well-being of the other members of society.[60] At the very least, class analysts advocate more working-class representation in Parliament. But that in itself would be of limited value since MPs are largely impotent as representatives of the general public, and the prime minister and Cabinet generally act at the command of the corporate elite.

Class analysts find that the Senate performs one principal role: the systematic review of legislation from the standpoint of the interests of business.[61] As mentioned, many senators simultaneously sit on various corporate boards and lobby fellow senators, MPs, bureaucrats, and Cabinet ministers on behalf of individual corporations or the general capitalist cause. Campbell quotes one senator as follows: "without us the Cabinet and the bureaucracy would never get the type of cooperation out of the private sector which is needed to make the system run."[62] Class analysts argue that "technical review" is in reality "business review" and, at least until the Mulroney period, senatorial vetoes were usually in the corporate interest. The "social investigators" are a small minority within the Senate whose broader concerns mask the behind-the-scenes efforts of the majority, who unashamedly pursue corporate goals.

SC State-centred theorists also minimize the role of the House of Commons in the policy-making process and argue that MPs who do try to represent constituency and societal concerns are voices in the wilderness. The prime minister, Cabinet, and bureaucracy decide what they want to do and, via orders-in-council and regulations, avoid the House of Commons as much as possible. Only when absolutely necessary do they go to Parliament for legitimation of their initiatives; otherwise MPs are kept busy with constituency work and content with generous salaries and services. The advantage of such a state-centred system is that special interests are subordinated to the collective public interest. State-centred theorists find that rather than represent societal interests within the government, the Senate is a useful mechanism through which the authorities—prime minister, Cabinet, bureaucracy, and government party—can pursue their own objectives. Prime ministers make senatorial appointments primarily for partisan rather than policy purposes, but these usually guarantee that the institution will rubber-stamp government legislation, as carefully prepared by the bureaucracy. In 1990, Prime Minister Mulroney deliberately appointed senators and even "extra" senators who would support his highly unpopular GST bill. State-centred theorists argue that senators do not undertake studies because society demands them, but only to pre-empt public cries for abolition of the chamber. Moreover, Senators have virtually unrestricted access to the public trough, deciding almost unilaterally how much pay and what additional benefits to give themselves.

DISCUSSION QUESTIONS

1. If Parliament does not play a significant part in the policymaking process, what are its basic functions?

2. What are the advantages and disadvantages of rigid party discipline in the House of Commons?

3. Should the concept of "confidence" be limited to nonconfidence votes rather than be applied to every government bill?

4. What other aspects of the House of Commons, if any, should be reformed?

5. What are the advantages and disadvantages of the initiative, the referendum, and the recall?

6. Does the Senate do enough to justify its existence, or should it be abolished?

7. What are the pros and cons of the Triple-E Senate?

8. If elected, to what extent should the Senate be able to interfere with the will of the Cabinet and the House of Commons?

9. How is our understanding of Parliament enhanced by each of the approaches outlined in Chapter 1?

NOTES

1. C.E.S. Franks, *The Parliament of Canada* (Toronto: University of Toronto Press, 1987), p. 5. In his book *The Canadian House of Commons: Procedure and Reform* (Montreal: McGill–Queen's University Press, 1977), John Stewart lists essentially the same functions: "first, to support a government; second, to prevent clandestine governing; third, to test the government's administrative policies and legislative proposals; fourth, to constrain the ministers; and fifth, to educate the electorate," p. 30.

2. Franks, *The Parliament of Canada*, p. 216.

3. John Bejermi, *Canadian Parliamentary Handbook 1999* (Ottawa: Borealis Press, 1999).

4. Franks, *The Parliament of Canada*, p. 73; David C. Docherty, *Mr. Smith Goes to Ottawa: Life in the House of Commons* (Vancouver: UBC Press, 1997), ch. 2.

5. John Porter, *The Vertical Mosaic* (Toronto: University of Toronto Press, 1965), p. 402.

6. For example, the budgets of 1963 and 1990.

7. Franks, *The Parliament of Canada*, p. 142.

8. Stewart, *The Canadian House of Commons*, pp. 29–30.

9. Eugene Forsey and Graham Eglington, "Twenty-Five Fairy Tales about Parliamentary Government," in Paul Fox and Graham White, eds., *Politics: Canada*, 7th ed. (Toronto: McGraw-Hill Ryerson, 1991), argue that this is a mistaken belief; Docherty, *Mr. Smith Goes to Ottawa*, ch. 6; Mark Charlton and Paul Barker, eds., *Crosscurrents: Contemporary Political Issues*, 3rd ed. (Scarborough: ITP Nelson, 1998), ch. 13.

10. Sometimes the concept of a "shadow cabinet" is used by opposition leaders, but if the party becomes the government, there is no guarantee that "shadow critics" will be given the corresponding Cabinet post.

11. Andrew Heard, *Canadian Constitutional Conventions* (Toronto: Oxford University Press, 1991), p. 80.

12. Franks, *The Parliament of Canada*, pp. 110–14. Donald Savoie confirms my contention that in Canada, almost every MP wants to be a minister in *Governing from the Centre: The Concentration of Political Power in Canada* (Toronto: University of Toronto Press, 1999), p. 83.

13. Franks, *The Parliament of Canada*, pp. 6, 29, 96, 268.

14. Heard, *Canadian Constitutional Conventions*, p. 83.

15. Paul Thomas, "Parliamentary Reform through Political Parties," in John Courtney, ed., *The Canadian House of Commons: Essays in Honour of Norman Ward* (Calgary: University of Calgary Press, 1985); and Paul Thomas, "The Role of National Party Caucuses," in Peter Aucoin, ed., *Party Government and Regional Representation in Canada* (Toronto: University of Toronto Press, 1985). Savoie, *Governing from the Centre*, pp. 91–93, quotes MPs as referring to caucus as "bitching sessions."

16. Thomas, "The Role of the National Party Caucuses."

17. Bills introduced in the Senate have an *S* designation.

18. Heard, *Canadian Constitutional Conventions*, p. 78.
19. The government's resort to closure on every stage of the bill was seen as the work of Trade and Commerce Minister C.D. Howe, who was obsessed with getting the construction of the pipeline started.
20. The exceptional delays of the 1984–90 and 1994–96 periods are discussed below.
21. For compilation of and/or commentary on the rules, see the most recent edition of *Standing Orders of the House of Commons* or *House of Commons Précis of Procedure*, now on the Internet (http://www.parl.gc.ca), and Alistair Fraser, W.F. Dawson, and John Holtby, eds., *Beauchesne's Rules and Forms of the House of Commons of Canada*, 6th ed. (Toronto: Carswell, 1989).
22. James Robertson, *House of Commons Procedure: Its Reform* (Ottawa: Library of Parliament, Current Issue Review 82-15E, 1998).
23. Martin Westmacott, "Whips and Party Cohesion," *Canadian Parliamentary Review* (Autumn 1988). Conservative and Liberal whips are chosen by the party leader, but the NDP caucus elects its whip.
24. W.F. Dawson, *Procedure in the Canadian House of Commons*. Toronto: University of Toronto Press, 1962, pp. 188–90.
25. Grace Skogstad, "Interest Groups, Representation and Conflict Management in the Standing Committees of the House of Commons," *Canadian Journal of Political Science* (December 1985), pp. 739–72; David M. McInnes, *Taking It to the Hill: The Complete Guide to Appearing Before (and Surviving) Parliamentary Committees* (Ottawa: University of Ottawa Press, 1999).
26. Paul Pross, "Parliamentary Influence and the Diffusion of Power," *Canadian Journal of Political Science* (June 1985).
27. This subject has been well documented in the works of R.J. Fleming on Canadian legislatures, e.g., *Fleming's Canadian Legislatures*, 11th ed. (Toronto: University of Toronto Press, 1997).
28. Robert Fife and John Warren, *A Capital Scandal* (Toronto: Key Porter Books, 1991).
29. Docherty, *Mr. Smith Goes to Ottawa*, ch. 5.
30. Eugene Forsey, "The Problem of 'Minority Government' in Canada," *Canadian Journal of Economics and Political Science* (February 1964).
31. According to Franks, the Trudeau minority was actually defeated on 18 of 81 votes between 1972 and 1974 but chose to resign only on the defeat of the 1974 budget, while the Pearson government had suffered two other defeats without much fanfare. Franks, *The Parliament of Canada*, p. 139.
32. Bob Rae, "Changing the Confidence Convention in Ontario," *Canadian Parliamentary Review* (Winter 1985–86).
33. Franks, *The Parliament of Canada*, p. 132; and John Stewart, "Commons Procedure in the Trudeau Era," in John Courtney, ed., *The Canadian House of Commons: Essays in Honour of Norman Ward* (Calgary: University of Calgary Press, 1985).
34. One of the more controversial aspects of television was the rule that the camera could focus only on the person recognized by the Speaker, rather than show what was going on elsewhere in the chamber.
35. *Report of the Special Committee on Reform of the House of Commons* (Ottawa: House of Commons, 1985).
36. Paul Thomas argues that attitudinal change on the part of political parties in Parliament is just as important as technical procedural changes in enhancing its role in the policymaking process, in "Parliamentary Reform through Political Parties," in Courtney, *The Canadian House of Commons*.
37. Franks, *The Parliament of Canada*, pp. 9, 261.
38. Quoted in R.A. MacKay, *The Unreformed Senate of Canada*, rev. ed. (Toronto: McClelland and Stewart, 1967), pp. 47–48.
39. MacKay, *The Unreformed Senate*, pp. 91–95; and F.A. Kunz, *The Modern Senate of Canada 1925–1963: A Re-Appraisal* (Toronto: University of Toronto Press, 1965), pp. 337–47. Andrew Heard argues that a constitutional convention is emerging that the Senate may not insist on altering the financial provisions of money bills. *Canadian Constitutional Conventions*, p. 94.
40. MacKay, *The Unreformed Senate*, p. 9.
41. MacKay, *The Unreformed Senate* (ch. 9), and Kunz, *The Modern Senate of Canada* (ch. 2), both discuss socioeconomic backgrounds up to 1960 and 1963 respectively.
42. Kunz, *The Modern Senate of Canada*, discusses this issue on pp. 53–56. The case was officially referred to as *Edwards v. Att. Gen. of Can.*, [1930] AC 124.
43. Both MacKay and Kunz address this point. The former finds the record ambiguous (pp. 112–23), while the latter argues that the Senate was a supplementary line of defence of sectional interests (p. 336).

44. MacKay, *The Unreformed Senate*, p. 110; and Kunz, *The Modern Senate of Canada*, p. 186. The Senate has produced its own complimentary brochure, *The Senate Today* (1997).

45. Colin Campbell, *The Canadian Senate: A Lobby from Within* (Toronto: Macmillan, 1978).

46. Senators also receive free transportation to and from Parliament, of course, but unlike MPs they keep their "frequent flyer" points, even though these trips are paid for from the public purse.

47. Campbell, *The Canadian Senate*, pp. 10–11.

48. John McMenemy, "The Senate as an Instrument of Business and Party," in Paul Fox and Graham White, eds., *Politics: Canada*, 7th ed. (Toronto: McGraw-Hill Ryerson, 1991), p. 455.

49. Campbell, *The Canadian Senate*, pp. 12–19, 147.

50. MacKay, *The Unreformed Senate*, writes that it is an "institutional survival of a pre-democratic age" (p. 10) and that "in a democratic age an appointed upper house labours under the handicap that it has no political foundation" (p. 62).

51. MacKay, *The Unreformed Senate*, p. 87; and Kunz, *The Modern Senate of Canada*, pp. 116–17.

52. Heard, *Canadian Constitutional Conventions*, p. 89.

53. MacKay, *The Unreformed Senate*, pp. 96–112.

54. See the justification offered by Senator Lorna Marsden in "Doing Its Thing—Providing Sober Second Thought: The Canadian Senate, 1984–1990," in Fox and White, *Politics: Canada*, 7th ed. (1991).

55. In 1873 Alexander Mackenzie had asked the British government to summon additional senators but was refused on the ground that it was not necessary at the time.

56. Heard, *Canadian Constitutional Conventions*, p. 95.

57. *Reference Re Legislative Authority of Parliament to Alter or Replace the Senate*, [1980] 1 S.C.R. 54.

58. Gordon Robertson, *A House Divided: Meech Lake, Senate Reform, and the Canadian Union* (Halifax: Institute for Research on Public Policy, 1989).

59. See, for example, Peter McCormick, "Canada Needs a Triple E Senate," in Fox and White, eds., *Politics: Canada*, 7th ed. (1991); and H. McConnell, "The Case for a 'Triple E' Senate," *Queen's Quarterly* (Autumn 1988).

60. Franks, *The Parliament of Canada*, p. 69.

61. Campbell, *The Canadian Senate*, p. 9.

62. Ibid., p. 71.

....

FURTHER READING

Liberal Party

Bejermi, John. *Canadian Parliamentary Handbook 1999*. Ottawa: Borealis Press, 1999.

Courtney, John, ed. *The Canadian House of Commons: Essays in Honour of Norman Ward*. Calgary: University of Calgary Press, 1985.

Docherty, David C. *Mr. Smith Goes to Ottawa: Life in the House of Commons*. Vancouver: UBC Press, 1997.

Eagles, Munroe, et al. *The Almanac of Canadian Politics*, 2nd ed. Toronto: Oxford University Press, 1995.

Fleming, R.J. *Fleming's Canadian Legislatures*, 11th ed. Toronto: University of Toronto Press, 1997.

Forsey, Eugene. "The Problem of 'Minority Government' in Canada." *Canadian Journal of Economics and Political Science* (February 1964).

Franks, C.E.S. *The Parliament of Canada*. Toronto: University of Toronto Press, 1987.

Fraser, Alistair, W.F. Dawson, and John Holtby, eds. *Beauchesne's Rules and Forms of the House of Commons of Canada*, 6th ed. Toronto: Carswell, 1989.

Heard, Andrew. *Canadian Constitutional Conventions*. Toronto: Oxford University Press, 1991.

House of Commons. *A Glossary of Parliamentary Procedure*. Internet: http://www.parl.gc.ca.

———. *Précis of Procedure*. Internet: http://www.parl.gc.ca.

———. *Standing Orders of the House of Commons* (regularly revised).

McInnes, David M. *Taking It to the Hill: The Complete Guide to Appearing Before (and Surviving) Parliamentary Committees*. Ottawa: University of Ottawa Press, 1999.

Rae, Bob. "Changing the Confidence Convention in Ontario." *Canadian Parliamentary Review* (Winter 1985–86).

Robertson, James. *House of Commons Procedure: Its Reform*. Ottawa: Library of Parliament Current Issue Review 82-15E, 1998.

Stewart, John. *The Canadian House of Commons: Procedure and Reform*. Montreal: McGill–Queen's University Press, 1977.

Thomas, Paul. "Parliamentary Reform through Political Parties." In John Courtney, ed., *The Canadian House of Commons*. Calgary: University of Calgary Press, 1985.

————. "The Role of National Party Caucuses." In Peter Aucoin, ed., *Party Government and Regional Representation in Canada*. Toronto: University of Toronto Press, 1985.

Westmacott, Martin. "Whips and Party Cohesion." *Canadian Parliamentary Review* (Autumn 1988).

Senate

Campbell, Colin. *The Canadian Senate: A Lobby from Within*. Toronto: Macmillan, 1978.

Forsey, Eugene. "No—More Than a Triple E Senate Is Needed." In Robert J. Fleming, ed., *Canadian Legislatures 1987–1988*. Ottawa: Ampersand Communications, 1988.

Government of Canada. *Reform of the Senate: A Discussion Paper*. Ottawa: Supply and Services, 1983.

Kunz, F.A. *The Modern Senate of Canada 1925–1963: A Re-Appraisal*. Toronto: University of Toronto Press, 1965.

Mackay, R.A. *The Unreformed Senate of Canada*, rev. ed. Toronto: McClelland and Stewart, 1967.

Marsden, Lorna. "Doing Its Thing—Providing 'Sober Second Thought': The Canadian Senate, 1984–1990." In Paul Fox and Graham White, eds., *Politics: Canada*, 7th ed. Toronto: McGraw-Hill Ryerson, 1991.

McConnell, H. "The Case for a 'Triple E' Senate." *Queen's Quarterly* (Autumn 1988).

McCormick, Peter. "Canada Needs a Triple E Senate." In Paul Fox and Graham White, eds., *Politics: Canada*, 7th ed. Toronto: McGraw-Hill Ryerson, 1991.

McMenemy, John. "The Senate as an Instrument of Business and Party." In Paul Fox and Graham White, eds., *Politics: Canada*, 7th ed. Toronto: McGraw-Hill Ryerson, 1991.

Special Joint Committee on Senate Reform. *Report*. Ottawa: Supply and Services, 1984.

White, R. *Voice of Region: The Long Journey to Senate Reform in Canada*. Toronto: Dundurn Press, 1990.

Chapter 23

The JUDICIARY

Louise Arbour's appointment to the Supreme Court of Canada in 1999 was greeted with universal acclaim. The BC courts have ruled that freedom of expression allows the possession of child pornography, and the Alberta Court of Appeal has upheld the federal gun control act. The Supreme Court decided that jurors can be challenged for racial bias when an accused person is a member of a group subject to widespread prejudice, has told lower court judges to find alternatives to putting offenders in prison, and has also denied Quebec the right to make a unilateral declaration of independence. The Federal Court of Canada quashed a decision of the Immigration and Refugee Board and upheld public servants' pay equity claim. Women's and ethnic groups criticize the general dominance of white male judges across the country, and Natives demand a parallel Aboriginal justice system. The public is appalled at residual patronage appointments to the bench, and troubled by cutbacks to legal aid plans.

Canadian political science was traditionally interested in the judiciary or court system primarily in terms of its interpretation of the federal–provincial division of powers. Now that the Charter of Rights and Freedoms has catapulted the courts into the middle of many heated political issues, however, political scientists are giving this fourth branch of government much more attention.

This chapter examines the judiciary as an institution of government, discussing the function of adjudication, categories of laws, the structure of the courts, the Supreme Court of Canada, and the appointment, retirement, removal, and independence of judges. Chapter 18 considered the role of the courts in interpreting the Charter of Rights and Freedoms.

THE FUNCTION OF ADJUDICATION

The judiciary has always been associated with the rule adjudication function in the political system, although other institutions may perform part of this function, too. Adjudication can be defined as interpreting the law in cases of dispute, of settling disputes by applying the law to them, or making a judgment based on the law. Peter Russell defines the term as follows: "providing authoritative settlements in disputes about the law."[1]

Judges engage in the authoritative resolution of legal disputes, but many legal disputes are resolved without going to court or before going through the entire judicial process. Such an "out-of-court" settlement, especially that between individuals or between governments, is likely to be some sort of personal or political compromise. It is only when an accommodation satisfactory to both sides cannot be reached that the formal adjudicatory process is pursued to the bitter end.

The function of the judiciary therefore is to render formal, impartial, authoritative judgments in the case of legal disputes between two parties that cannot be settled otherwise. It is a process that generally relies on the adversarial system, with lawyers representing each side. The judge, clothed with the coercive powers of the state, acts as an independent referee and decides which of the disputants is legally right. As a result, the process usually culminates in the designation of a winner and a loser, rather than in the achievement of some acceptable middle ground.

Other governmental structures also engage in rule adjudication, especially a great variety of administrative tribunals, as discussed in Chapter 21, and the distinction between them and real courts is often very subtle. On the other hand, the judiciary also has certain nonadjudicative functions. Because of their prestige and impartiality, for example, judges have frequently been appointed to head royal commissions or other commissions of inquiry. The nature of many such commissions has unfortunately been more political than judicial, and most observers feel that this is an inappropriate use of judicial personnel, especially given increasing backlogs in their regular adjudicative work.

Apart from the civil law system in Quebec, Canadian federal and provincial legal systems operate in the tradition of the English **common law**. The basis of that system is the accumulation over the centuries of judicial precedents, both in England and more recently in Canada. Thus, in a typical court case, the two sides seek to find precedents—previous court decisions—favouring their respective points of view. The judge (and sometimes the jury) have to decide which precedents most closely resemble the case currently before the court. The principle that precedents are binding on successive decisions is called **stare decisis**.

If the law were always comprehensive and crystal clear, and if the situations to which it applied were always simple and straightforward, rule adjudication would be fairly routine and the judiciary would not have much discretion in performing this function. The real world is more complex, however, and the law may not be clear on all points or provide for every conceivable situation. Moreover, judges can usually avoid a precedent they dislike by "distinguishing" it, that is, deciding that the facts in the case before them are sufficiently different from the facts of the precedent case that to follow the latter would be inappropriate.[2] Russell refers to the "inescapable generality of the law" such that, while judges theoretically settle disputes according to pre-existing law, they actually shape and develop the law in the very process of settling disputes about it. They "put flesh on the bare skeleton of the law and shape its substance."[3]

The judiciary and the function of judicial interpretation were included in the chart of the policymaking process in Chapter 19. Rather than taking place subsequent to policymaking, where it once was placed, rule adjudication can now be considered as part of the policymaking process. Unlike Americans, Canadian observers did not give much recognition to the concept of judicial involvement in this process until recently. But Russell argues that this Canadian approach "wrongly assumes that all important public policies are expressed in statutes passed by legislatures ... and overlooks the extent to which [such] policies ... are shaped through the process of being applied in particular cases by judges and administrators."[4] He cites such examples as the large element of discretion left to judges in the sentencing process, the decision of the Canadian courts to give little weight to the Canadian Bill of Rights, and the increasing judicial supervision of the operation of administrative agencies. In

The Supreme Court of Canada. (Photographer unknown/Canapress)

addition, judicial interpretation of anti-monopoly laws "decisively shaped industrial policy by making it nearly impossible to convict corporations for monopolistic practices."[5] In the course of adjudicating disputes, therefore, the courts are inherently involved in policymaking.

One step beyond judicial interpretation is the explicit power of **judicial review**. Rather than merely interpret laws with discretion, judicial review is the power of the courts to declare them invalid. The original Constitution Act of 1867 did not contain any such provision, although the courts soon appropriated this power in one respect. Chapter 17 detailed the extent to which the courts invalidated federal and provincial legislation as violations of the division of powers between the two levels of government. In rendering federal or provincial legislation void if either encroached on the jurisdiction of the other level of government, the decisions of the courts had a significant effect on the shape of Canadian federalism. The court's power of judicial review was greatly enhanced with the adoption of the Canadian Charter of Rights and Freedoms in 1982, and the effects of the first 18 years of that review were discussed in Chapter 18. Peter McCormick writes in this connection: "we should recognize that judges have always had power, have always affected our society by the decisions they make.... The Charter has simply made a longstanding reality more immediately visible and directed us belatedly to an assessment of the implications of judicial power."[6]

Access to and Costs of Justice

Many people cannot afford to hire a lawyer to defend themselves in a criminal (or even civil) case, yet the objective of the court system must be the search for truth and the obtaining of justice, goals that have traditionally rested on the adversarial system. To ensure that those without the financial resources have a fairer chance to achieve justice, legal aid programs financed jointly by the federal and provincial governments have been established. Although these vary in detail from one province to another, do not cover every kind of legal work, and have been subject to severe funding cutbacks in recent years, they go some way to meet the fairness objective. Community legal clinics serve a similar function. The Supreme Court ruled in 1999 that legal aid plans must supply funding to indigent parents who risk losing their children to the state.

A related means of reducing the costs of the administration of justice as a whole are the practices of plea bargaining and pre-trial conferences. Plea bargaining involves discussions between defence and Crown attorneys with the aim of achieving agreement on charges to be pursued, typically by having the accused agree to plead guilty to one charge and the Crown agree to drop other charges. This practice is routine at the provincial court level and avoids a lengthy, costly trial. In the higher trial courts it is increasingly common for the judge to hold a pre-trial conference with the lawyers for each side. Such conferences can result in a negotiated settlement or at least a time-saving clarification of the issues involved. They have also proved to be useful at the level of family and small-claims courts. While plea bargaining and pre-trial conferences must not be allowed to subvert justice, they are valuable devices to cut costs for everyone involved (including the public), and to reduce the workload of the usually congested court system.

CATEGORIES OF LAWS

The law can be defined as "society's system of binding rules."[7] Laws are commonly divided into different categories, primarily "civil" and "criminal." A **civil law** regulates relationships between two private parties such as individuals or corporations, and if private agreement cannot be reached in the case of dispute, one party may take the other to court. Most aspects of civil law in Canada are within provincial jurisdiction, largely because of the provincial power over property and civil rights. Civil cases often involve disputes over commercial contracts or property, and such cases are normally resolved by the court's ordering one party to pay damages to the other. Civil cases are decided on the basis of the "balance of probabilities" of the merits of each side.

Criminal law, on the other hand, is primarily a federal responsibility; it is thus more or less uniform throughout the country and has been consolidated in the **Criminal Code**. In this case, the commission of a crime such as murder, sexual assault, or theft is considered to be a wrong against society as a whole, and the state takes the initiative to bring the suspect to justice by means of the police and Crown attorneys. In criminal cases, judges may impose fines or prison sentences if the accused is found guilty, such guilt having been proven "beyond a reasonable doubt."

One of the peculiarities of Canadian federalism is that while criminal law is within federal jurisdiction, it is usually the provincial attorneys general and their agents, the Crown attorneys, who are responsible for initiating proceedings against the person who is charged. This situation has come about because the provinces have jurisdiction over the administration of justice. Sometimes a case contains both civil and criminal elements, such as a drunken driver who does damage to another person's car. The state pursues the violation of the Criminal Code, but the victim's insurance company would have to take the initiative to sue for property damage.

Instead of this basic division between civil and criminal law, a distinction is sometimes made between public and private law.[8] Private law is essentially the same thing as civil law described above, that is, law that centres on private interests. Beyond the contracts and property mentioned, however, private law includes torts, wills, company law, and family law. Public law, primarily involving the public interest or the government, goes beyond criminal law to include constitutional law, administrative law, and taxation law. Constitutional law has traditionally involved questions about federal or provincial jurisdiction, and governments themselves have often been the parties to a constitutional case. With the adoption of the Charter of Rights and Freedoms, a whole new aspect of constitutional law in Canada has emerged. Administrative law concerns the operation of government departments and agencies, and as government activity has expanded over the years, this branch of law has also increased in significance.

By giving the provinces jurisdiction over property and civil rights, the Fathers of Confederation allowed the province of Quebec to retain its distinctive private or civil law system based on the French Napoleonic Code and called the **Code Civil du Québec**, a new edition of which came into force in January 1994. The private law system in the other provinces is based on the English common law tradition. The theoretical distinction between the two systems in terms of form is that while the common law consists of a hodge-podge of judicial precedents, the Code Civil is a single comprehensive document. As Gall puts it, "in a common law system, the courts extract existing principles of law from decisions of previous cases, while in the civil law system, the courts look to the civil code to determine a given principle and they then apply the facts of an instant case to that principle."[9] The state has far greater ability to assert its authority and power through the written code than in the common law tradition where the law is written in more general terms and is susceptible to interpretation and application by judges and juries. There are also certain differences in substance, but while much attention is given to this distinction in Canadian legal and political life, the actual difference between the two systems is probably not as great as is often assumed. Lawyers and judges in the civil law system cannot help but pay some attention to precedents within that system, and cannot help but be influenced by the common law system surrounding them.[10]

STRUCTURE OF THE COURTS

Because the provinces that formed Confederation in 1867 already possessed a court system, and because the Judicial Committee of the Privy Council continued to function as a court of appeal for the whole British Empire, it was not necessary to devote much attention to the judiciary in the Constitution Act, 1867. The new federal government was allowed to establish a general court of appeal and any additional courts, but the provinces were otherwise given responsibility for the administration of justice, which included the establishment of a provincial court system. McCormick describes the logic of the court structure as follows:

First: Identify the more routine cases and those that involve less serious possible outcomes and assign them to an accessible high-volume, low-delay court, preferably one that sits in many different centres.

Second: Assign the less routine and more serious cases to a lower-volume court that can devote more time and more focused attention to each individual case.

Third: Establish a court of appeal to correct simple errors and to promote uniformity in the application of the law within each province.

Fourth: Establish a "general court of appeal" to promote uniformity in the application of the law within the country as a whole and to provide judicial leadership.

Fifth: Create a system of federal courts for cases directly involving the federal government as a party or raising issues concerning the administrative law applied by federal departments.[11]

As seen in Figure 23.1, the court systems within each province developed into a reasonably uniform three-level hierarchy. At the top are two "superior" courts—the superior trial court and the court of appeal, although they go by different names from province to province. At the bottom are provincial courts. Most provinces set up district and/or county courts between these two levels, but over the 1975–95 period they abolished this intermediate tier and integrated it with their superior courts.[12]

Because of the assumption that provinces could not be trusted to make worthy appointments to superior, district, and county courts, the Fathers of Confederation provided that the judges of these courts would be appointed by the governor general, conventionally meaning the federal Cabinet or minister of Justice. Such judges were also paid by the federal government. Thus, in another peculiarity of Canadian federalism, each province determines how many superior court judges it needs, but they are appointed and paid by Ottawa.[13] Since these courts were provided for in section 96 of the 1867 document, they are often called "section 96 courts" and their judges, "section 96 judges." Below the level of section 96 courts, each province established various "provincial courts" to which provincial cabinets appointed the judges. A brief discussion of each level of the judicial hierarchy follows.

Figure 23.1 The Court Structure in Canada

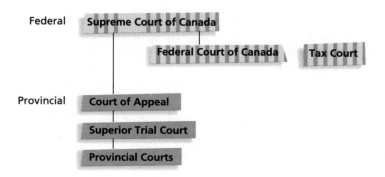

Provincial Courts

Whatever their structure or name, provincial courts generally have the following functions:

1. Summary offences including less serious crimes, provincial and municipal offences.
2. Most aspects of indictable offences, some mandatory and others optional.
3. Preliminary hearings for most serious crimes.
4. Bail hearings.
5. Young Offenders Act (Youth Criminal Justice Act) offences.
6. Family law, except divorce and proceedings flowing from divorce.
7. Small civil cases.

Provincial courts have a monopoly on summary (that is, less serious) offences except where even lower tribunals such as justices of the peace in some provinces have been given this responsibility. More serious crimes, called indictable offences, can be subdivided into three categories. Some, like murder, are reserved for superior courts; some, like theft, are assigned to provincial courts; and those in an intermediate category can be tried in either section 96 or provincial courts. The federal Young Offenders Act (to be renamed the Youth Criminal Justice Act) covers offences committed by those aged 12 to 18. This is a complex area of federal–provincial interaction, but as far as courts are concerned, the offences are tried in provincial courts or special youth courts established in some provinces.

Family law is another area of great federal–provincial complexity. Since divorce is a federal responsibility, divorces are dealt with in section 96 courts, and any proceedings flowing from the divorce must also be dealt with there. On the other hand, as long as divorce is not involved, such matters as custody, access, maintenance, alimony, adoption, guardianship, and protection of children are handled in provincial courts or family courts at that level. The fragmentation of family law presents one of the most serious problems of the Canadian court structure, not only because parts of it must be handled by section 96 courts and other aspects fall into the jurisdiction of provincial courts, but also because some problems, such as support payments, often involve both levels of courts.[14] Several provinces have tried to overcome the latter problem by experimenting with a "unified family court" presided over by a section 96 judge, but most authorities would prefer to unify family law jurisdiction at the provincial court level.[15]

Provincial courts, sometimes in a civil division, also have jurisdiction over disputes involving small amounts of money, although some provinces have established small-claims courts for this purpose. Each province determines the monetary limit for cases that can be considered at that level, with disputes involving larger sums being initiated at the section 96 court level. Some provinces have also tried to remove the adversarial nature of small-claims disputes by instituting mediation services, such as Alternative Dispute Resolution (ADR), by professional mediators.

The Superior Trial Court

The functions of the superior trial court in the province, whatever its name, are as follows:

1. Some mandatory and other elective indictable offences.
2. Civil matters over a given monetary amount.

3. Divorces and proceedings flowing therefrom.

4. Appeals from lower courts re summary convictions, juvenile, and family cases.

5. Administrative law cases.

In the superior trial court, the accused often has the option of trial by judge alone or trial by judge and jury. The former is increasingly the preferred option, and the latter has been curtailed to some extent by legislation. In the famous trials concerning Dr. Henry Morgentaler on charges of performing illegal abortions, juries repeatedly found him not guilty, although they were overruled on occasion by appeal courts. The jury had less trouble establishing the guilt of serial killer Paul Bernardo.

Provincial Courts of Appeal

Provincial courts of appeal hear criminal, civil, and other appeals, some of which have already been appealed from a lower court to a section 96 trial court. Although some of its judgments are appealed to the Supreme Court of Canada, in 98.5 percent of cases the decision of the provincial court of appeal is final, which adds to the significance of this level of court.[16] The basic function of an appeal court is to correct errors or injustices that one side claims were made in a lower court, but an appeal court is primarily interested in legal rather than factual issues. The second function of the appeal court is to render an opinion in a reference case, that is, on a constitutional issue referred to it by the provincial cabinet. Russell thus speaks of the "law-making" role of appeal courts because their legal interpretations have a "creative legislative dimension."[17] Decisions of the provincial court of appeal are binding on all courts below it in the same province and are "strongly persuasive" for trial courts in other provinces. Courts of appeal normally sit in banks of three judges, but the size of these panels can be increased to five for very important cases. Each side of a case submits a brief or "factum" in advance that summarizes its arguments, and lawyers then engage in oral argument.

Ian Greene and associates calculate that civil appeals outnumber criminal appeals, and in the latter category, the Crown appeals less frequently than the accused. One-third of appeals are successful: only about one-quarter of those launched by the accused, compared to two-thirds of those selected by the Crown.[18]

The Federal Court of Canada

The **Federal Court of Canada** was established in 1971 to replace the Exchequer Court created in 1875. Unlike its predecessor, the Federal Court has trial and appeal divisions. It was intended to relieve the Supreme Court of hearing routine appeals from certain federal administrative tribunals and to strengthen judicial review of federal administration by developing a more unified and cohesive body of federal administrative law.[19] Between its two divisions, the Federal Court has the following functions:

1. Cases involving admiralty law, and copyright, trademark, and patent disputes.

2. Citizenship and immigration appeals.

3. Appeals from other federal administrative tribunals.

4. Civil cases involving the federal government.

5. Cases involving bills of exchange, promissory notes, aeronautics, and interprovincial works and undertakings.

6. Appeals from boards of referees under the Employment Insurance Act.

7. Prerogative writs (e.g., injunctions) applying to agencies of the federal government.

8. Appeals re the Access to Information and Privacy acts.

9. Issuance of Canadian Security Intelligence Service warrants.

These functions reveal that while it is not well known to the public, the Federal Court has significant powers over the operation of the federal government. Federal administrative activities have been subject to much more frequent and consistent judicial review since the creation of the Federal Court. The court has wider authority to review decisions of judicial and quasi-judicial tribunals than of administrative agencies, but this distinction is difficult to draw in the field of administrative law. In the former case, the court may review a tribunal's decision on the basis that it breached the principles of natural justice, that it acted beyond its jurisdiction, or that it made errors in law, but purely administrative agencies must also act fairly. During its first 20 years, the jurisdiction of the Federal Court was restricted in several Supreme Court decisions, but amendments passed by Parliament in 1990 straightened out these problems.[20] In 1999, the Federal Court upheld the decision of the Canadian Human Rights Commission with respect to pay equity in the federal public service.

The work of the Federal Court is dominated by cases involving the Immigration Act and Immigration and Refugee Board, Employment Insurance, penitentiaries and the Parole Board, the Public Service Commission and Public Service Staff Relations Board, and the Revenue Canada. It has recently seen a growth in Aboriginal cases, dealing with monetary and constitutional issues, land entitlements, and natural resources. Of great interest to political science, the Federal Court also hears appeals regarding the Access to Information and Privacy Acts and decides on requests for warrants from the Canadian Security Intelligence Service in order to plant bugs, open mail, and engage in other surreptitious activities.

The Federal Court consists of a chief justice and 10 other judges on its appeal division and the associate chief justice and 19 other full-time and assorted part-time judges on its trial division. The appeal division judges sit in panels of at least three members.

The Tax Court of Canada is not so much a court as a judicialization of its predecessor, the Tax Review Board. It provides an easily accessible and independent tribunal for the disposition of tax disputes between citizens and the federal government. It deals primarily with matters arising under the Income Tax Act, the Employment Insurance Act, and the Excise Tax Act. Headed by a chief judge, it consists of 21 other full-time and assorted part-time judges, who hear cases across the country.

THE SUPREME COURT OF CANADA

The Supreme Court of Canada sits at the apex of the Canadian court system. About 85 percent of its work consists of hearing appeals from the provincial courts of appeal in civil and criminal cases,[21] but it also receives cases from the appeals division of the Federal Court of

Canada in administrative law matters. Besides hearing actual appeal cases from lower courts, the Supreme Court can be asked by the federal Cabinet to consider an important question of law, usually on a constitutional matter, in what are called **reference cases**. That part of its work of most interest to political science involves constitutional law, whether in terms of the division of powers between federal and provincial governments or of interpretations of the Charter of Rights and Freedoms. While the Supreme Court hears fewer cases per year than any lower court—approximately 120 annually—it is interested almost exclusively in questions of law. Thus, of all courts, it is the most heavily engaged in a "law-making" role, and its decisions are binding on all lower courts.

Until 1949, the Supreme Court was a seriously deficient institution. First, its decisions could be appealed to Canada's pre-1949 final court of appeal, the **Judicial Committee of the Privy Council (JCPC)** located in London, and it was bound by JCPC precedents. But even more humiliating, appeals could also go directly to that Empire court from provincial appeal courts, completely bypassing the Supreme Court of Canada. Until 1949, 253 cases went to the JCPC from the Supreme Court of Canada and 414 went there straight from provincial appeal courts.[22] This weakness in authority was enhanced by the relatively poor quality of judges appointed to it in that earlier period, apart from such individuals as Lyman Duff and Ivan Rand.[23]

Canada could have cut off appeals to the Judicial Committee after obtaining complete independence in 1931, and pressure mounted to do so after the unpopular "New Deal" decisions of 1935 that were mentioned in Chapter 17. But the Second World War intervened, and it was unclear whether the provinces would have to be involved in this decision since their appeals could already go directly to the JCPC. If so, there was some question of whether the provinces would agree to it, since they had been so well served by the Judicial Committee over the years. In 1947 it was determined that Ottawa could unilaterally curtail all such appeals, and it promptly did so. The Supreme Court of Canada has not been formally bound by Judicial Committee decisions since 1949 and has explicitly overruled them on occasion.

Until 1974, the Supreme Court had little discretion in deciding which cases it heard, but since then it has basically been in control of its own agenda. Today, only two categories of cases have an automatic right of appeal to the Supreme Court: provincial reference cases, and murder cases in which the provincial court of appeal was split on a question of law. Applications for leave (that is, permission) to appeal discretionary cases are normally handled in writing by a panel of three judges, but sometimes the panel hears them live, giving lawyers 15 minutes to make their case, via two-way satellite television if they choose. These panels annually hear some 550 to 650 applications for leave to appeal, accepting only about 1 in 5: those that involve a question of public importance or an important issue of law. Such discretion considerably enhances the stature of the institution. Public law cases, especially criminal and constitutional, now clearly predominate over private law disputes on the Supreme Court docket. Figure 23.2 outlines the Supreme Court appeal process.

Although an increasingly important institution of government, the Supreme Court rests primarily on the **Supreme Court Act** rather than being embedded in any constitution act as such.[24] The Supreme Court Act now provides for a nine-member court (six from 1875 to 1927 and seven from 1927 to 1949). Three of the nine must come from Quebec with its distinctive civil law system, while convention dictates that the other six be selected from a variety of locations, normally three from Ontario, two from the West, and one from Atlantic Canada. The act requires that at least five judges constitute a quorum, with the result that civil law cases from Quebec can be heard by a five-member panel including a majority (three) from the

Figure 23.2   Supreme Court Appeal Process

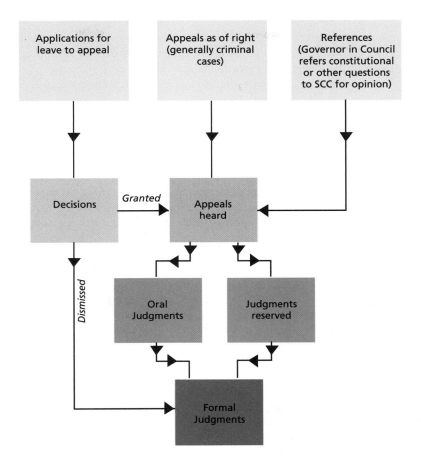

Source: *Public Works and Government Services Canada,* 1999–2000 Estimates.

civil law system. The position of Chief Justice normally alternates between francophone and anglophone members, simultaneous interpretation is available, and Supreme Court judges are now expected to be at least functionally bilingual. Among other provisions of the Supreme Court Act are those that lay out the grounds for appeal and reference cases and those that stipulate that judges hold office during good behaviour until the age of 75. One of the merits of the Meech Lake and Charlottetown accords would have been to "constitutionalize" the Supreme Court in order to give it a firmer foundation and to clarify how it could be changed.

The Court holds three sessions of about two months each per year and adjourns in between to write up its decisions. Justices usually wear black silk robes at sittings of the Court, but have ceremonial robes of bright scarlet trimmed with Canadian white mink for special occasions. As much as possible, the Court tries to hear cases with a full complement of nine. Judges study the lower court proceedings and judgments in advance, along with the written arguments of the lawyers for each side. In preparing for the case, as well as in writing the first draft of decisions, each Supreme Court judge is assisted by three outstanding new law school graduates called law clerks. They help the busy judges search for and sift through precedents and other relevant material including academic articles on the issues involved. The Court usually hears two cases per day, and oral arguments for each case normally last only two hours, during which time the judges often ask trenchant questions. In some instances the Court also grants "intervener status" to provincial governments and interest groups that are concerned about a case but not directly a party to it.

Once the arguments are completed, the judges usually "reserve judgment" and meet in private conference to discuss the case. Starting with the most recent appointee, each gives his or her tentative decision, and if there is a consensus, the Chief Justice will ask one member to draft the judgment. The Court tries to come to a unanimous decision, which it achieves in about 75 percent of cases,[25] but if this is not possible, one or more other judges will be asked to draft separate concurring decisions or dissenting opinions. Regardless, these drafts are later circulated among all the judges on the case, and evoke comments before being revised. So much effort is put into the process of preparing their opinions that a decision is typically not issued until about six months after the Court hears the case, and it has occasionally taken over a year for all members of the Court to make up their minds, write their opinion, or concur with a colleague. When it comes to citing other cases as a basis for their decisions, the Supreme Court of Canada most frequently mentions its own decisions, followed by those of the Ontario Court of Appeal; in the 1984–94 period, about 15 percent of its citations were to English courts and 7 percent, U.S. courts.[26] Decisions are usually released in written form by depositing them with the Registrar, but the Court can pronounce formal judgments in the courtroom. Recent membership in the Supreme Court can be seen in Table 23.1.

This discussion of the structure of Canadian courts reveals an essentially integrated, vertical court system rather than two parallel systems of federal and provincial courts. With the exception of some federal matters that must be initiated in the Federal Court of Canada, the provincial court systems and the Supreme Court of Canada hear cases dealing with both federal and provincial laws. The judicial system is further integrated with provincial governments prosecuting federal crimes and with the federal Cabinet appointing judges to section 96 courts within the provinces. Some aspects of the federal–provincial judicial integration could be improved, such as in the areas of Young Offenders and Family Law, the jurisdiction of the Federal Court, and the appointment of section 96 and Supreme Court of Canada judges. Some federal–provincial conflict has arisen over provincial attempts to enhance the powers of their provincial courts and administrative tribunals at the expense of section 96 courts.[27] However, most authorities argue strenuously in favour of maintaining such an integrated system.[28]

··

THE APPOINTMENT OF JUDGES

As has already been established, Supreme and Federal Court of Canada judges, as well as judges of provincial superior, district, and county courts are appointed by the federal Cabinet, while provincial court judges are appointed by provincial cabinets. There are approximately 1000 judges in each category. All of the first group must be qualified lawyers of at least ten years'

TABLE 23.1   Recent Membership in the Supreme Court of Canada

Appointment	Name	Retirement (Death)
1973	Brian Dickson CJ:* 1984–1990	1990
1974	Jean Beetz	1988
1977	William Estey	1988
1979	William McIntyre	1989
1979	Jean Chouinard	(1987)
1980	Antonio Lamer CJ:* 1990–2000	2000
1982	Bertha Wilson	1990
1984	Gerald Le Dain	1988
1985	Gerald La Forest	1997
1987	Claire L'Heureux-Dubé	
1988	John Sopinka	(1997)
1989	Peter Cory	1999
1989	Charles Gonthier	
1989	Beverley McLachlin CJ:* 2000–	
1990	William Stevenson	(1992)
1991	Frank Iacobucci	
1992	John C. Major	
1997	Michel Bastarache	
1998	Ian Binnie	
1999	Louise Arbour	
2000	Louis LeBel	

*CJ = Chief Justice

standing, as must provincial court judges in Ontario and Quebec. Elsewhere, provincial court judges have to be members of the bar for a minimum of five years.

In a high proportion of cases over the years Canadian cabinets at both federal and provincial levels have used judicial appointments to reward faithful party supporters, often defeated candidates.[29] Legal knowledge was also taken into account in some cases, but it was rarely the primary criterion. The prospect of a judgeship accounts in part for the active involvement of lawyers in many party organizations, while the promise of government legal business explains another part. Patronage raises three main problems in this area: unsuitable individuals are appointed because of their partisan connections; well-qualified candidates are overlooked because of their lack of service to the party in power; and partisan judges may favour their former political colleagues.[30] This patronage system of appointing judges is still alive, although it is not as blatant as it once was.

At the federal level, Pierre Trudeau as minister of Justice in 1967 instituted an informal practice of submitting names of potential judicial appointments to the National Committee on the Judiciary of the Canadian Bar Association. To his credit, the next Justice minister, John Turner, appointed several prominent judges of non-Liberal backgrounds. Trudeau sullied his own government's record in this field with the appointment of six high-profile Liberal partisans in 1984, including the minister of Justice himself and another minister who was not even assessed by the CBA committee. After an even more partisan record of judicial appointments during its first term,[31] the Mulroney government established a somewhat more satisfactory appointment system in 1988 for all "federal" judges except those on the Supreme Court of Canada, and modified it slightly in 1991. An independent **Commissioner for Federal Judicial Affairs** now maintains a record of those interested in federal judicial appointments. This official then submits such names to a seven-member committee set up in each province, which includes a section 96 judge; one nominee of each of the provincial law society, the provincial branch of the CBA, and the provincial attorney general; and three nominees of the federal minister of Justice. This committee ranks each candidate as "highly recommended," "recommended," or "not able to recommend," and the minister makes the final decision, still being entitled to choose from the list of nonqualified candidates.[32] The minister may also consult senior members of the judiciary and the bar and the provincial attorney general. Greene and cohorts found that even in the late 1990s a high proportion of appeal court judges had been candidates, party activists, or at least party members.[33] Moreover, most appellate court judges are recruited from the ranks of trial judges, but once appointed at the trial level, there is no subsequent evaluation system when it comes to the minister of Justice promoting them.

The prime minister chooses the chief justices in each province, almost always from the existing bench, as well as new members of the Supreme Court of Canada. Patronage has not been much of a problem on the Supreme Court since the appointment of Finance minister Douglas Abbott in 1954. Prime ministers consult widely before making such appointments, have managed to overcome their penchant for partisanship in this one area, and are pleased to be evaluated on the quality of their choices. Chief Justices Bora Laskin, Brian Dickson, and Antonio Lamer, and the first female appointee, Bertha Wilson, are outstanding examples. The Supreme Court of Canada is usually composed of seven judges with experience on provincial appeal courts, one from the Federal Court, and one without judicial experience, representing the "practising bar."[34]

At the provincial court level, it is now usually the case that the province's attorney general consults with the local judicial council or equivalent in making such appointments. For example, a central nonpartisan nominating commission, half of them non-lawyers, was established in Ontario in 1988, originally headed by political scientist Peter Russell. It advertises widely, encourages women and minority candidates, and screens judicial applicants on their merits. Through the Liberal and NDP regimes, the attorney general almost always appointed those so recommended, but one commission member resigned in 1997 because the new Tory attorney general sometimes bypassed the commission. On the other hand, party service or legislative experience should not automatically disqualify a worthy candidate from a judicial appointment.[35]

Another controversial aspect of judicial appointments concerns the Supreme Court of Canada alone. Because this Court must adjudicate federal–provincial disputes, concern has been expressed in some quarters that all of its members are federally appointed. In theory, once appointed, judges act with total impartiality, and their independence is protected in various ways. Nevertheless, it may not *appear* as if justice has been done. As early as 1971, federal–provincial agreement was achieved on provincial consultation in the appointment of Supreme Court judges, but such agreement was never implemented. Later, the Meech Lake and Charlottetown accords provided for Ottawa to make Supreme Court of Canada appointments from lists provided by the provinces, but this too was ultimately abandoned. The 1992 document went beyond that of 1987 to outline a procedure to be used in case of federal–provincial deadlock. It also proposed federal and provincial consultation with Aboriginal peoples in the appointment process. Some mechanism for federal–provincial consultation in this area is bound to be adopted in the future. On the other hand, to begin to regard Supreme Court judges as provincial representatives would do great disservice to the principle of judicial independence.

If a proper geographic balance is characteristic of Canadian judges, what can be said of their other socioeconomic characteristics? Partly as a consequence of geography, judicial appointments have also balanced francophone and anglophone origins at both federal and provincial court levels, especially in recent years as provinces have made more French-language court services available. Those of other origins have generally been excluded, but names such as Laskin (Jewish), Sopinka (Ukrainian), and Iacobuccci (Italian) are now appearing on the Supreme Court of Canada and increasingly on lower courts as well. Thus the most serious aspects of judicial underrepresentation relate to women and the working class.[36] In this connection, Paul Weiler writes:

> It is very natural that well-to-do families of the founding races and religions in Canada, especially those with a background of professional and/or public involvement, will produce the sons who will get the right kind of education, and thus the entrée into the kind of practice or position which produces a likely candidate for the Court.[37]

Just as in the case of "other ethnics," however, more female and working-class law school graduates are becoming available for judicial appointments, and governments have at least begun to recognize the necessity of appointing greater numbers of female judges. The Supreme Court finally saw its first woman member in 1982, and for the second time at the beginning of the new millennium had a total of three women out of nine. Such female judges have sometimes used their position to point out the male bias in legislatures, judiciaries, and laws.[38] In 1996, women made up one-half of the judges on the Alberta Court of Appeal.

As noted in Chapter 4, Aboriginal Canadians have even more serious misgivings about the Canadian judicial system, feeling that it discriminates against them at every turn. They argue that an increase in the number of Native judges would not substantially improve this situation, and therefore advocate the establishment of a parallel justice system (at least where they did no harm to non-Aboriginals) that would reflect their own distinctive concepts of guilt and punishment.

Given the significant law-making potential of higher-level judges, another dimension of the appointment process is a consideration of candidates' views on other issues. Chapter 18 noted that the decisions rendered by the Supreme Court of Canada depended to some extent on the makeup of the panel considering the case. That being so, those who appoint judges are able to take into account the predilections of candidates with respect to being hawks or doves on criminal matters or Charter enthusiasts as opposed to legislative deferentialists.[39] To some extent, such preferences are reflected in the success rate of different categories of litigants,

Louise Arbour, newly appointed Supreme Court Justice, speaks to reporters in Montreal, September 1999. (Ryan Remiorz/Canapress)

which for the Supreme Court of Canada in the 1982–93 period was as follows: Crown, 66 percent; provincial government, 57 percent; federal government, 56 percent; big business, 55 percent; smaller business, 46 percent; municipal government, 45 percent; unions, 42 percent; and individuals, 41 percent.[40] This issue prompts some authorities to recommend public hearings to fathom the views of judicial nominees.[41] Jacob Ziegel proposes an alternative to confirmation of appointments by a House of Commons committee: establishing a Supreme Court nominating commission whenever a vacancy arose. This nine-member body, representing a variety of constituencies, would present the prime minister with a shortlist of candidates from which the federal government would have to pick one.[42] Ironically, in the eyes of many observers, appointments to the Supreme Court that are made without consultation have been superior to those to other federal courts in which an elaborate consultation process is in place.

RETIREMENT, REMOVAL, AND INDEPENDENCE OF JUDGES

Whatever the process involved in making judicial appointments, and whatever biases exist in the composition of the courts, judges are expected to abide by the principle of **judicial independence** or impartiality once they are on the bench. They are supposed to adjudicate without fear or favour with respect to private or political interests, and especially without any incentive to give preference to the government side where it is involved.

The independence of judges is primarily based on security of tenure, and it is difficult for the government to remove them before their scheduled date of retirement. Judges on the Supreme and Federal Courts of Canada and provincial superior courts have a mandatory retirement age of 75 years, and provincial court judges of 65 or 70. The general rule for all federally appointed judges and most provincial court judges is that they serve on "good behaviour"—that is, they do not serve at the pleasure of the government and cannot be removed unless they have been guilty of misbehaviour. While the meaning of these terms has never been definitively established, judges are certainly removable for serious criminal acts and possibly for reasons of infirmity or incapacity, failure to execute their duties, or bringing the judicial system into disrepute. On the other hand, they cannot be removed merely because the government regards their decisions as erroneous or contrary to government policy, nor because they ruled against the Crown.

The process of removing a judge varies with the level of the position, and the degree of difficulty increases with the judge's rank in the hierarchy. Except in Ontario, where legislation is required, provincial court judges can be removed by an order-in-council of the provincial cabinet but only after an inquiry has been conducted by one of the judge's peers or by the provincial judicial council. It is even more difficult to remove judges of the provincial superior courts and the federal courts. In that situation, the Canadian Judicial Council conducts an inquiry and reports to the minister of Justice, after which the passage of a joint address of both houses of Parliament is required.

The **Canadian Judicial Council**, created in 1971, consists of all the chief justices and associate chief justices of courts staffed by federally appointed judges, and is chaired by the Chief Justice of the Canadian Supreme Court. Like the provincial judicial councils, its primary purpose is to deal with complaints raised against individual judges, but it also has a role in the continuing education of judges, provides a forum for developing consensus among its members, and makes representations to government with respect to judicial salaries and benefits.

While a number of judges have been reprimanded by judicial councils, the issue of judicial removal has rarely arisen. Several provincial court judges have been removed over the years, a practice that is increasingly common as the public becomes less tolerant of their faults.[43] For example, a New Brunswick provincial judge was recently removed by the provincial cabinet on the recommendation of the provincial Judicial Council for making disparaging remarks about the honesty of the people of her community, although she appealed her removal. But only four judges at the old intermediate county and district level met this fate since 1867, and not a single superior court judge has been removed from office. Such proceedings were initiated in five cases, but judges either died or resigned during the removal process. Jean Bienvenue of the Quebec Superior Court eventually resigned in 1997 after the Canadian Judicial Council asked the federal Parliament to remove him for having said on the bench that women can be more cruel than men and that even Nazis exterminated Jews painlessly.[44] Two years later, Robert Flahiff of the same court was sentenced to three years in jail after being found guilty of laundering $1.7 million in drug money when he was a practising lawyer.

Besides security of tenure, judicial independence involves financial, administrative, and political independence.[45] Salaries and pensions are fixed in such a way that neither individually nor collectively can judges be intimidated by government threats to reduce them, although some judges went to court to challenge freezes or reductions in their salaries as part of provincial government restraint programs.[46] In addition, judges are increasingly in control of the administration of the court system.

Judges must also be able to function without political pressure—from Cabinet ministers, legislators, bureaucrats, or other judges—whether in public or in private. At both federal and provincial levels, many cases have occurred of Cabinet ministers contacting judges, but however innocent their questions might seem, this must not be done.[47] Greene and cohorts report that judges increasingly feel their independence is threatened by special-interest groups, political correctness, media criticism, political criticism, and even demonstrations. On the other hand, individual judges have occasionally made outrageous sexist, racist, or other inappropriate comments from the bench.

It is sometimes thought that the prospect of promotion from one court to another might bias a judge's decisions, but no evidence has been found to justify this fear. Judges are rarely promoted from "provincial" to "federal" courts, but, as mentioned, 70 percent of appeal court judges have previous judicial experience.[48] In 1988 it was also felt (by fellow judges) that to deny judges a vote in federal elections was not necessary to guarantee their independence. On the other hand, judges are not supposed to make public speeches that could compromise their impartiality. For example, when Tom Berger of the BC Supreme Court publicly (and validly!)

criticized the 1982 Constitution Act for its omission of Quebec and virtual neglect of Aboriginals, his actions were investigated by the Canadian Judicial Council. Although its recommendation was not to dismiss him, he resigned to protest the process employed.[49]

CONCLUSION

Rule adjudication remains the basic function of the judiciary, one that is becoming increasingly important in the political system. Judges also engage in pre-trial mediation of one kind or another and are occasionally called on to head commissions of inquiry. Other branches of government, especially administrative tribunals, also exercise the rule adjudication function to some extent, but this function can be generally equated with the courts.

In looking at the judiciary, class analysts begin with the argument that entry into law school has traditionally been restricted to the middle and upper classes, and then note the powers of the legal profession to govern itself. Moreover, federal or provincial authorities who make judicial appointments are usually lawyers themselves, and consultation with the Canadian Bar Association or judicial councils on new appointments gives the legal profession yet another avenue of influence in the selection of judges. Indeed, a disproportionate number of judges have previously served on the CBA executive.[50] "Appointing judges is part of the process of recruiting a society's governing elite," and with cabinets looking "for someone very much like themselves," the result is a judiciary that bears little resemblance to the general population in socioeconomic background.[51] The elitist nature of the judiciary in terms of gender and ethnicity was noted above, while of the first 50 judges of the Supreme Court only two came from working-class origins, as did only one among senior judges between 1961 and 1973.[52] Although it does not concern him, even Russell admits that "as long as judges are recruited entirely from the ranks of successful lawyers ... the bourgeois orientation of the Canadian judiciary is unavoidable. This may very well mean that when class issues are clearly at stake in adjudication, the Canadian judiciary is not impartial."[53]

The elitist origins of judges, combined with the expense involved in going to court, leadsclass analysts to talk about a class system of justice. Michael Mandel notes that in a typical trial,"in terms of social class, the crown attorney, defence counsel, and judge have far more in common with each other than they have with either the victim or the criminal andvice versa."[54]

Class analysts dismiss notions of judicial impartiality and independence "as rhetorical facades behind which judges are free to exercise raw political power on behalf of themselves or their 'political masters,' or against their political or economic opponents."[55] Class analysts remember how often the courts, on the altar of section 92, responded to corporate claims in invalidating federal legislation that might have benefited the working class and point to the judicial emasculation of laws prohibiting corporate monopolies. Olsen mentions the high proportion of cases before the courts dealing with the protection of property, the high rate of incarceration of those accused who do not own property, the inadequacies of legal aid schemes, and the limited provision for "class action" suits in Canada in which small consumers can collectively take on giant corporations. He concludes that the judiciary provides legitimacy for the established social order, arguing that the chief function of the higher judiciary is to rationalize formal arrangements for the elites and the privileged classes and, by articulating these as principles and precedents, impose norms and values downward on the lower courts and hence on the behaviour of the lower classes. In this task they are most heartily joined by the various political elites who passed the controlling legislation in the first place.[56]

McCormick adds that "to make the courts more representative of women, of Canadians other than French and English, of visible minorities, and so on perhaps simply disguises, and may well reinforce, the extent to which they continue to be unrepresentative on a class basis."[57] Moreover, as mentioned earlier, big business had a significantly higher success rate in the Supreme Court of Canada from 1982 to 1993 than individuals and unions.

(SC) State-centred theorists argue that the judiciary is part of the state apparatus and is not as independent of other institutions of government as is commonly assumed. Judges are appointed, promoted, and occasionally dismissed by politicians; judges are called upon to assist politicians in conducting inquiries; judges are of the same elitist origins as politicians and bureaucrats and move in many of the same social and professional circles, even after their appointment. Many provincial authorities have felt, rightly or wrongly, that the Supreme Court of Canada was an agent of the federal government, rather than a totally impartial referee of federal–provincial disputes, and others could argue that the Canadian Judicial Council is too eager to reprimand a judge who has criticized government policy.[58] Then, although some judicial decisions can be modified or overturned by subsequent legislation, state-centred theorists point out that the judiciary is the branch of government most insulated from public opinion. However "objective" its decisions, it has sometimes aided and abetted government policy that was at odds with public sentiment, such as in the Supreme Court's series of decisions with respect to official bilingualism.

[P] Pluralists, on the other hand, argue that the judiciary adds a relatively independent point of authoritative decision making to the political system and counterbalances the other institutions of government. In Russell's words, "to liberals who are distrustful of an excessive concentration of power in the hands of any group or bureaucrats, the political pluralism fostered by a judiciary enjoying a high degree of independence is fundamental to maintaining political liberty."[59] Public opinion polls have repeatedly indicated greater confidence in judges than in politicians and a preference for courts rather than legislatures to have the final say in the interpretation of the Charter of Rights.[60] Pluralists also note the division of appointing power between federal and provincial governments, the different procedures involved, and the increasing proportion of female and other ethnic appointments. They are encouraged by the number of suits launched by interest groups and by the practice of allowing such groups to become interveners in constitutional cases. McCormick concludes that despite all the undemocratic aspects of the judiciary, "the law and the courts are nothing more than the continuation of politics by other means,"[61] and are likely to be an even more prominent part in the future.

DISCUSSION QUESTIONS

1. Why should the Supreme Court of Canada be constitutionalized?

2. Should all vestiges of patronage be removed from the appointment of judges, or have existing reforms in this area gone far enough?

3. Should the provinces be involved in the appointment of provincial superior court judges? Of judges of the Supreme Court of Canada? If so, how?

4. Apart from provincial involvement, if any, what kind of consultation process, if any, should be involved in the appointment of judges to the Supreme Court of Canada?

5. What should be the criteria for reprimanding or removing a judge? Should Mr. Justice Tom Berger have been able to engage in public criticism of the 1982 Constitution Act?

6. How can justice be ensured for women involved in the courts?

7. How can justice be ensured for the working class?

8. Should Canada establish a parallel Aboriginal justice system?

9. How do each of the critical approaches outlined in Chapter 1 enhance our understanding of the judiciary?

NOTES

1. Peter Russell, *The Judiciary in Canada: The Third Branch of Government* (Toronto: McGraw-Hill Ryerson, 1987), p. 5.
2. Ian Greene et al., *Final Appeal: Decision-Making in Canadian Courts of Appeal* (Toronto: James Lorimer & Co., 1998), p. 201.
3. Ibid., p. 14.
4. Peter Russell, "The Effect of a Charter of Rights on the Policy-Making Role of the Canadian Courts," *Canadian Public Administration* (Spring 1982), p. 2.
5. Ibid., p. 12.
6. Peter McCormick, *Canada's Courts* (Toronto: James Lorimer & Company Ltd., Publishers, 1994), p. 3.
7. Russell, *The Judiciary in Canada*, p. 6.
8. See, for example, Gerald L. Gall, *The Canadian Legal System*, 3rd ed. (Toronto: Carswell, 1990), pp. 23–28; 4th ed., 1995.
9. Ibid., p. 30.
10. Greene et al., *Final Appeal*, pp. 32 and 85.
11. McCormick, *Canada's Courts*, p. 23. Reproduced with permission.
12. Gall outlines this integration on pp. 157–59 of the third edition, *The Canadian Legal System*.
13. Occasional federal–provincial disputes have occurred over this point. See Russell, *The Judiciary in Canada*, pp. 122–23.
14. Russell says, for example, that the "judges who order the support have no role in overseeing its enforcement, and the judges responsible for enforcing the order play no role in either determining or modifying the level of support," *The Judiciary in Canada*, p. 228.
15. Ibid, pp. 229–35; Peter Hogg, *Constitutional Law of Canada*, 2nd ed. (Toronto: Carswell, 1985), pp. 546–49.
16. Greene et al., *Final Appeal: Decision-Making in Canadian Courts of Appeal*, p. x; McCormick, *Canada's Courts*, p. 56.

17. Russell, *The Judiciary in Canada*, p. 290.
18. Greene et al., *Final Appeal*, pp. 46, 55, 79–80, and 175.
19. Russell, *The Judiciary in Canada*, p. 313.
20. Ibid, pp. 319–27; and Hogg, *Constitutional Law of Canada*, 2nd ed., pp. 142–48.
21. Greene et al., *Final Appeal*, p. 149.
22. Ibid., p. 141.
23. James G. Snell and Frederick Vaughan, *The Supreme Court of Canada: History of the Institution* (Toronto: Osgoode Society, 1985), and Russell, *The Judiciary in Canada*, p. 337.
24. Peter Russell, "Constitutional Reform of the Judicial Branch: Symbolic vs. Operational Considerations," *Canadian Journal of Political Science* (June 1984).
25. Supreme Court of Canada, "Statistics 1988–1998," Supreme Court website—http://www.scc-csc.gc.ca), p. 10—but Greene et al., *Final Appeal*, p. 150, have different figures.
26. Greene et al., *Final Appeal*, pp. 151–56.
27. In 1981, for example, the Supreme Court ruled that Ontario legislation had given Residential Tenancy Commissions powers that could reside only in the courts.
28. Russell, *The Judiciary in Canada*, pp. 49–54, 327–29; and Hogg, *Constitutional Law in Canada*, ch. 7.
29. Carl Baar quotes an oft-repeated maxim that "to become a judge in the United States, you must be elected; to become a judge in Canada, you must be defeated," in "The Structure and Personnel of the Canadian Judiciary," in Paul Fox and Graham White, eds., *Politics: Canada*, 7th ed. (Toronto: McGraw-Hill Ryerson, 1991), p. 513.
30. Andrew Heard, *Canadian Constitutional Conventions* (Toronto: Oxford University Press, 1991), p. 135.
31. One study of the first-term record of the Mulroney government revealed that 48 percent of all judges appointed were known Conservative supporters compared with 7 percent who supported opposition parties. Peter Russell and Jacob Ziegel, "Federal Judicial Appointments: An Appraisal of the First Mulroney Government's Appointments and the New Judiciary Advisory Committees," *University of Toronto Law Journal* 41 (1991).
32. The new procedure is outlined in two documents published by the Commissioner for Federal Judicial Affairs: *Judicial Appointments: Information Guide* and *A New Judicial Appointments Process* (Ottawa: Supply and Services, 1988).
33. Greene et al., *Final Appeal*, p. 36.
34. Ibid., p. 101.
35. McCormick, *Canada's Courts*, p. 112.
36. Dennis Olsen, *The State Elite* (Toronto: McClelland and Stewart, 1980), ch. 3; Russell, *The Judiciary in Canada*, pp. 164–65; and Greene et al., *Final Appeal*, p. 42.
37. Quoted, with contempt, in Olsen, *The State Elite*, p. 47.
38. Bertha Wilson said that men didn't understand abortion in the *Morgentaler* case, but Peter McCormick, *Canada's Courts*, p. 115, discounts the distinctiveness of the judgments of women or visible minorities.
39. Ibid., p. 108.
40. Ibid., p. 165.
41. F.L. Morton and H. Patrick Glenn debate this subject in Mark Charlton and Paul Barker, eds., *Crosscurrents: Contemporary Political Issues*, 3rd ed. (Scarborough: ITP Nelson, 1998), ch. 15. See also note 42.
42. Joseph S. Ziegel, *Merit Selection and Democratization of Appointments to the Supreme Court of Canada* (Montreal: Institute for Research on Public Policy, 1999).
43. Greene et al., *Final Appeal*, p. 186.
44. The other most famous case concerned Leo Landreville of the Supreme Court of Ontario. See Gall, *The Canadian Legal System*, pp. 231, 238–39, and Russell, *The Judiciary in Canada*, pp. 176–79.
45. The classic statement on this question was made by Mr. Justice LeDain in *Valente v. the Queen*, [1985] 2 SCR 673; see also Perry S. Millar and Carl Baar, *Judicial Administration in Canada* (Montreal: McGill–Queen's University Press, 1981).
46. *Manitoba Provincial Judges Association v. Manitoba (Minister of Justice)*, [1997] 3 S.C.R. 3; *Reference re Remuneration of Judges of the Provincial Court of PEI*; *Reference re the Independence and Impartiality of Judges of the Provincial Court of PEI*, [1998] 1 S.C.R. 3.

47. See Heard, *Canadian Constitutional Conventions*, p. 128, and Russell, *The Judiciary in Canada*, pp. 78–81, especially regarding the "Judges Affair."
48. According to Russell and Ziegel, "Federal Judicial Appointments," former party ties count in promotions.
49. Heard, *Canadian Constitutional Conventions*, p. 131; Russell, *The Canadian Judiciary*, pp. 85–89; Gall, *The Canadian Legal System*, 3rd ed., pp. 236–38; and McCormick, *Canada's Courts*, pp. 130–31.
50. Russell, *The Judiciary in Canada*, p. 163; Olsen, *The State Elite*, p. 48; and Russell and Ziegel, "Federal Judicial Appointments."
51. Russell, *The Judiciary in Canada*, p. 107; and Olsen, *The State Elite*, p. 46.
52. Russell, *The Judiciary in Canada*, p. 164; and Olsen, *The State Elite*, p. 51.
53. Russell, *The Judiciary in Canada*, p. 165; Greene and cohorts, *Final Appeal*, p. 42, also admit that judges are elitist, but are not overly concerned either.
54. Michael Mandel, *The Charter of Rights and the Legalization of Politics in Canada* (Toronto: Wall and Thompson, 1989), p. 135.
55. Russell, *The Judiciary in Canada*, p. 4.
56. Olsen, *The State Elite*, p. 58.
57. McCormick, *Canada's Courts*, p. 115.
58. Despite all of his excellent work on the Supreme Court, there was some suggestion that Chief Justice Bora Laskin was too close to Prime Minister Trudeau in some of his judgments and in his eagerness to reprimand Tom Berger. Michael Mandel, *The Charter of Rights and the Legalization of Politics in Canada*, pp. 17, 20, 22, 111.
59. Russell, *The Judiciary in Canada*, p. 24.
60. Russell, *The Judiciary in Canada*, p. 35; Heard, *Canadian Constitutional Conventions*, p. 138; Maureen Mancuso et al., *A Question of Ethics: Canadians Speak Out* (Toronto: Oxford University Press, 1998), pp. 41–43.
61. McCormick, *Canada's Courts*, ch. 12.

• •

FURTHER READING

Baar, Carl. "The Structure and Personnel of the Canadian Judiciary." In Paul Fox and Graham White, eds., *Politics: Canada*, 7th ed. Toronto: McGraw-Hill Ryerson, 1991.

Canadian Bar Association. *The Independence of the Judiciary in Canada*. Ottawa: Canadian Bar Association, 1985.

Canadian Centre for Justice Studies. *The Juristat Reader: A Statistical Overview of the Canadian Justice System*. Toronto: Thompson Books, 1999.

Case, Roland. *Understanding Judicial Reasoning: Controversies, Concepts and Cases*. Toronto: Thompson Books, 1997.

Commissioner for Federal Judicial Affairs. *A New Judicial Appointments Process*. Ottawa: Supply and Services, 1988.

————. *Judicial Appointments: Information Guide*. Ottawa: Supply and Services, 1988.

Gall, Gerald. *The Canadian Legal System*, 3rd ed. Toronto: Carswell, 1990; 4th ed., 1995.

Greene, Ian, et al. *Final Appeal: Decision-Making in Canadian Courts of Appeal*. Toronto: James Lorimer & Co., 1998.

Heard, Andrew. *Canadian Constitutional Conventions*. Toronto: Oxford University Press, 1991.

Hogg, Peter. *Constitutional Law of Canada*, 2nd ed. Toronto: Carswell, 1985; Student ed., 1999.

Mandel, Michael. *The Charter of Rights and the Legalization of Politics in Canada*. Toronto: Wall and Thompson, 1989; rev. ed., 1994.

McCormick, Peter. *Canada's Courts*. Toronto: Lorimer, 1994.

McCormick, Peter, and Ian Greene. *Judges and Judging: Inside the Canadian Judicial System*. Toronto: Lorimer, 1990.

Morton, F.L., ed. *Law, Politics and the Judicial Process in Canada*. Calgary: University of Calgary Press, 1984.

Olsen, Dennis. *The State Elite*. Toronto: McClelland and Stewart, 1980.

Russell, Peter. "The Effect of a Charter of Rights on the Policymaking Role of the Canadian Courts." *Canadian Public Administration* (Spring 1982).

———. "Constitutional Reform of the Judicial Branch: Symbolic vs. Operational Considerations." *Canadian Journal of Political Science* (June 1984).

———. *The Judiciary in Canada: The Third Branch of Government*. Toronto: McGraw-Hill Ryerson, 1987.

Russell, Peter, and Jacob Ziegel. "Federal Judicial Appointments: An Appraisal of the First Mulroney Government's Appointments." *University of Toronto Law Journal* 41 (1991).

Snell, James G., and Frederick Vaughan. *The Supreme Court of Canada: History of the Institution*. Toronto: The Osgoode Society, 1985.

Ziegel, Jacob S. *Merit Selection and Democratization of Appointments to the Supreme Court of Canada*. Montreal: Institute for Research on Public Policy, 1999.

PART 6

Conclusion

This conclusion is composed of three parts. The first part is a brief chapter that highlights some of the main points made in the course of the other five parts of the book and presents several critical, realistic reforms. The second part is a Glossary of key terms used in previous chapters. The third, consisting of Appendix A and Appendix B, contains a selection of Canadian constitutional documents.

Chapter 24

CONCLUSION

However complacent the politicians, Canada faces a long list of political problems as it enters the new millennium. The first and perennial one is the role of Quebec and French Canada generally within the Canadian federation. The results of the 1995 referendum on Quebec sovereignty and the re-election of the PQ in 1998 did not make this problem any easier to resolve.

The second historic problem, involving fewer people but not necessarily less territory, is improving the condition of Aboriginal life in the country. Partly due to the Royal Commission on Aboriginal Peoples, this issue is finally on the political agenda, although that is only the starting point. It is an incredibly complex situation that will require huge amounts of money, imagination, intelligence, flexibility, and good will.

The third historic problem is the difficulty of maintaining a distinctive polity in the shadow of the United States. For better or worse, Canada has tied its economic future to that country in terms of wide-ranging free trade agreements, and the character of the global economy makes it hard for any state to pursue economic sovereignty in the future. The east–west economy is fragmenting into a series of north–south economies, and pressure for additional political integration is increasing, the latest being the idea of a common currency. "Advances" in telecommunications technology mean that even more streams of American culture will be flooding the Canadian market and the Canadian living room, and it will take a courageous government to do something to stop them. Severely weakening the Canadian Broadcasting Corporation and selling out the magazine industry hardly seem the way to begin.

Other ethnic/linguistic/cultural and regional issues also exist and are of intense concern to those involved. The problem of Western alienation having subsided to some extent, these other issues pale in comparison to the two domestic issues mentioned above, both in terms of longevity and overall significance.

The topic of minority rights has been in the forefront of political discourse in recent years—official-language minorities, ethnic and cultural minorities (apart from Aboriginal Canadians), the gay and lesbian community, and women—the majority that has been treated as a minority. These groups have all made substantial gains in public policy since 1970, although a backlash in public opinion was detectable in some respects in the 1990s. As has been pointed out throughout this book, however, regardless of any negative prospects in dealing with the regular political process, these groups have the Charter of Rights and Freedoms as a tool for further advancement. In the second decade of its existence, for example, the Charter seemed to be doing for the gay and lesbian community what it had accomplished for official-language minorities in its first.

The other main question on the political agenda at the start of the new millennium is that of public finance, relating in particular to taxation, poverty, health, and education. In order to balance their budgets in the late 1990s, federal and provincial governments cut expenditures rather than raise taxes or reduce the billions of dollars lost annually to tax credits and tax deductions. Some governments even cut taxes *before* they balanced their budgets, necessitating a starvation of social programs. Now that most governments are running an annual surplus, it is time to address the increased levels of poverty and homelessness that are a legacy of the 1990s, as well as to reinvest in education and health care, in order to regain the once-heralded universal and egalitarian nature of such programs.

CRITICAL, REALISTIC REFORMS

Although Canada is not an easy country to govern, political behaviour and institutions can be altered in a variety of ways to render its governance more satisfactory. In the preceding chapters many defects in the machinery of Canadian politics and government have been identified, and among these at least ten critical but fairly straightforward and realistic reforms can be reiterated here. In outlining such areas for reform, it will sometimes be useful to refer to the experience of other political systems.

Reducing the Incidence of Partisanship, Patronage, and Corruption

One of the main complaints about politicians is the excessive partisanship that characterizes their activities. An adversarial system has its merits, primarily in ensuring that issues are thor-

By *Steve Nease* (Oakville Beaver). *Reproduced with permission.*

oughly debated and that the public has a chance to see how different parties would deal with each problem. But no one can blame the public for its disgust at much of the partisan confrontation they see in the House of Commons and the Senate. The British House of Commons, by contrast, demonstrates that parliamentary behaviour can be civilized and adversarial at the same time.

Another practice that stems from excessive partisanship is the widespread incidence of party patronage. It is an inescapable reality that many people who join or volunteer to help political parties or agree to become candidates expect some tangible reward, especially if and when their party forms the government. The Senate, the judiciary, and especially the regulatory agencies have been filled with people who had few credentials other than past party service. Once again, the British system shows that patronage does not need to infiltrate every nook and cranny of the political system; indeed, in that country political patronage barely exists in the very areas where it is most predominant in Canada. Instead, political rewards take the form of a system of innocuous national honours, but even they are distributed on a multipartisan basis.

Canadians were led to believe that the Chrétien Liberals would be less patronage-oriented than the Mulroney Conservatives. But the Liberals made patronage appointments in all directions—to the Senate, courts, ambassadorships, Crown corporations, and regulatory agencies—rendering their record no better than that of their widely discredited predecessors.

A step beyond patronage is political corruption, and while this occurs in every political system to some extent, it became much too common during the Mulroney regime. The widespread incidence of corruption of individual Conservative ministers and MPs tended to reduce the image of all politicians in the eyes of Canadians. Chrétien appointed an impotent Ethics Commissioner, but refused to make public the code of ethics for ministers; moreover, the Canadian system continues to lack such rules for members of Parliament, senators, and public servants. Unfortunately, the century ended with the prime minister himself under attack for personal business deals and for giving government grants to shady business friends in his own constituency. Canadians are demanding a much higher standard of political ethics.[1]

Loosening Party Discipline in the House of Commons

One of the most disconcerting aspects of Canadian politics to the average voter is the rigidity of party discipline in the House of Commons. People generally believe that MPs should vote according to the wishes of their constituents rather than obey the edicts of the party leadership. Although this book sees the value in some degree of such discipline, loosening the constraints in the daily work of the Commons and instead making periodic confidence or nonconfidence votes crucial to a government's survival would give voters the feeling that their MPs were really representing them. It would also reduce the momentum for greater use of referendums, which sound reasonable in theory but raise many problems in practice.

Once again, the British system provides a useful model. During the Thatcher years, for example, some 120 legislative amendments were carried against the government's wishes and 17 government bills were defeated; sanctions against the dissidents were minimal, and such gaps in discipline no longer attract particular attention.

The famous first Liberal Red Book specifically promised some kind of relaxation of party discipline, but when the party line was threatened on gun control and other issues during his first term, Chrétien would not budge. He imposed what most observers felt were unnecessarily harsh sanctions on the dissenters, but did not make a strong case for the virtues of party discipline. Such discipline remained intact in the second term, although the incidence of dissent may have increased in spite of it.

Supplying the Need for Stronger Politicians

The problems of patronage and party discipline are related to the generally weak contingent of politicians who obtain office in Canada. Many only intend to stay for a short stint, practising "avocational politics," and others are cut off by electoral defeat. It often seems that the public prefers a fresh face over political experience. This is not the case in the United States, however, where incumbents are almost never defeated. Because the turnover in the Canadian House of Commons is very high, and because they are looking for an eventual patronage position when they leave, MPs are weak in relation to their own party leaders. (That is not to say that party leaders are particularly strong in Canada, either, many of them coming to the job with minimal political experience and/or understanding of the country). In addition, there is little "bench strength" when it comes to forming a Cabinet or choosing a party leader, and ministers are not strong in interacting with their bureaucrats or the prime minister. Canada needs politicians of higher quality and greater experience. In Britain, prospective party candidates are thoroughly screened for intelligence, aptitude, and literary ability, and then usually work themselves up through two or three elections to a safe seat. Once elected to the government side, MPs serve a few years as a backbencher, then as a parliamentary secretary, and then as a minister not in the cabinet, until they become a cabinet minister with an average of about 11 years of Commons' experience.

Reforming the Electoral System

Chapter 12 showed how the existing Canadian electoral system exacerbates regional/ethnic divisions because it awards seats to individual winning candidates with no concern about a party's popular vote within a province or at the national level. Once the obsession only of academics, more and more general observers of the political scene are concerned about the discrepancy between parties' popular vote and parliamentary representation. Parties have often attracted as much as 20 to 25 percent of the vote in a province without winning any seats. This becomes especially serious when a party forms the government and it has no MPs from a province or region to put into the Cabinet. Such provinces and regions feel left out of the policymaking process and start to think in separatist terms.

Chapter 12 also demonstrated how this problem—at both national and provincial levels—could be overcome by awarding some 50 supplementary seats on the basis of popular vote per party per province, drawing to some extent on the German system or even more so, on the Jenkins Report in Britain. If such a relatively minor innovation would help to strengthen Canada's fragile state, it deserves more consideration than it has so far received, especially when a growing academic consensus seems to support it.[2]

The 1993 election produced a Liberal majority government with seats in every province, and that party did almost as well in 1997, so that it was not particularly affected by the problem identified here. But this electoral system also rewards regionally concentrated third-party support, as in the case of Reform in the West and the Bloc Québécois in Quebec, parties that are either separatist or not conducive to national unity. At the same time, parties such as the Conservatives and NDP, still striving for nationwide support, are denied the seats that would be merited by their popular vote. After the 1993 and 1997 elections, the House of Commons had no national opposition party, which has proved to be almost as harmful as not having a pan-Canadian party on the government side.

Reforming the Senate

Assessments of the present Senate range from the view that it is harmless or useless to the opinion that it is positively corrupt. If the troubled Canadian political system is to have a second chamber, that institution must obviously play a more useful part than at present. Given that second chambers traditionally represent regions at the centre and that such representation is currently perceived to be lacking in Canada, the Senate must be reformed in order to perform this function. Being the site of the most blatant patronage in the whole system, it must also become an elected rather than an appointed body. On the other hand, to avoid paralyzing the operation of government, the Senate should be given only a suspensive veto over the House of Commons. Being popularly elected, senators would likely better represent provincial and regional interests than at present. Election would also likely change the character of Senate members, reducing their links to the corporate elite and the backrooms of political parties.

Restricting Corporate Funding of Political Parties

Even though they have made some strides to reduce their dependence on corporate contributions and to attract donations from individuals, the Liberal and Conservative parties continue to rely to a large extent on corporate funding. Small financial contributions to political parties usually have no strings attached, but no corporation makes a donation of $50 000 or $100 000 without expecting something in return. Is it any coincidence that the major banks, which give some of the largest contributions to the Liberal and Conservative parties, are allowed to accumulate the largest profits of any corporate sector? So used to getting their own way, four of them arrogantly expected their proposed mergers to be automatically approved! To enhance the democratic character of Canadian parties and elections, contributions should ideally be restricted to individuals; if corporations and unions are allowed to contribute on the grounds that Canadian parties should be strengthened rather than weakened, then a meaningful ceiling should be put on the size of such contributions. The Royal Commission on Electoral Reform was mistaken in not making such a recommendation.[3]

Strengthening Political Parties

Chapter 13 noted that, for one reason or another, many alternative institutions, especially pressure groups, are assuming the traditional functions of political parties. This is unfortunate because political parties are one of the few national institutions that try to bridge all the divisions within Canadian society. Perhaps too much is expected of parties in this connection, but the least that can be done is to strengthen them so that they can better perform such functions as interest aggregation. This can be done by enhanced public funding of political parties. It is inappropriate that many self-interested pressure groups have a budget and staff several times the size of a national political party. The activities of pressure groups should also be restricted to some extent, especially during election campaigns. Uninhibited advocacy advertising during elections not only makes a mockery of the concept of a fair election, but it also diverts attention from the real contestants in the race.

Strengthening the Lobbyists Registration and Access to Information Acts

Chapters 15 and 21 respectively noted that the Lobbyists Registration Act and the Access to Information Act were not particularly effective. The former act has not prevented unseemly acts of lobbying, often still based on partisan connections, provides only minimal information on the process, and is virtually unenforceable. In the interests of maintaining a degree of political equality in the Canadian political system, the use of paid, professional lobbyists must be kept under control, and with that objective, the act must be strengthened.

The Access to Information Act has opened up access to government documents to a considerable extent, but still contains many exceptions and is not taken seriously by many public servants. In order to promote an informed citizenry, the loopholes in this act should be narrowed, and bureaucratic attitudes toward it must be changed.

The first Liberal Red Book made promises in both of these directions. The Chrétien government did amend the Lobbyists Registration Act, but not to the extent promised. Moreover, as Information Commissioner John Grace pointed out in his 1997–98 report, Canada's Access to Information Act is being left in the dust by a new act in Britain, the "mother not only of parliaments but the culture of bureaucratic secrecy."[4]

Improving Mass Media Coverage of Politics

The importance of the mass media ensured their inclusion in almost every chapter of this book, and some of the principal faults of the media were catalogued in Chapter 11. At the governmental level, Donald Savoie writes that the media dominate the agenda of morning meetings between the prime minister and the clerk of the Privy Council and that relatively minor issues that receive a good deal of media attention come to dominate the government agenda.[5] At the level of voters, David Taras's central concern is "the extent to which citizens are increasingly deprived of the vital information they need to make decisions about their communities and their lives."[6] The main faults of television are that it is too superficial and too Americanized. These could be corrected to some extent by giving politicians longer sound bites, by covering political issues in greater depth, by strengthening the CBC, and by toughening CRTC Canadian-content requirements. As for newspapers, the right-wing slant on political issues has been exacerbated by Conrad Black's establishment of the *National Post*, along with his purchase of a majority of other Canadian dailies. A whole host of social issues such as poverty and homelessness get ignored or downplayed in such circumstances. James Winter writes that the media promote "a narrow, ideological perspective on the world around us, in the guise of a common sense consensus with which no right thinking person could disagree."[7]

Reversing Prime Ministerial Government

A tenth problem, reversing prime ministerial government, will probably be even more difficult to solve. It is all very well if, via central agencies in general and the clerk of the Privy Council in particular, government policies are well coordinated as prime ministerial government replaces cabinet government. Since prime ministers are as fallible as the rest of us, however, it is not beneficial to place so much power in the hands of one individual and his or her immediate advisers.[8] Democracy assumes that power will be more widely shared.

Canadian politicians have many faults. So do the media, the electoral system, political parties, pressure groups, the Constitution, and all the institutions of government. However, the Canadian electorate also has its faults, especially the fact that it does not put much effort into improving its knowledge of the country and its politics. This is not an easy country to govern, but the better Canadian citizens understand it, the less difficult that task will be.

NOTES

1. Ian Greene and David P. Shugarman, *Honest Politics: Seeking Integrity in Canadian Public Life* (Toronto: Lorimer, 1998); John Langford and Allan Tupper, *Corruption, Character, and Conduct: Essays on Canadian Government Ethics* (Toronto: Oxford University Press, 1994); and Maureen Mancuso et al., *A Question of Ethics: Canadians Speak Out* (Toronto: Oxford University Press, 1998).
2. Henry Milner et al., *Making Every Vote Count: Reassessing Canada's Electoral System* (Peterborough: Broadview Press, 1999).
3. The organization Democracy Watch also criticized the government's 1999 amended Canada Elections bill for not prohibiting corporate contributions.
4. Information Commissioner, *Annual Report 1997–98*, p. 9.
5. Donald J. Savoie, *Governing from the Centre: The Concentration of Power in Canadian Politics* (Toronto: University of Toronto Press, 1999), pp. 342 and 314.
6. David Taras, *Power and Betrayal in the Canadian Media* (Peterborough: Broadview Press, 1999), p. 219.
7. James Winter, *Democracy's Oxygen: How Corporations Control the News* (Montreal: Black Rose Books, 1997), p. 140.
8. Savoie, *Governing from the Centre*, p. 339.

Glossary[1]

(Numbers in parentheses refer to the chapter(s) containing the main discussion of the term).

Aboriginal self-government. A demand by Aboriginal groups that they be able to govern themselves. Aboriginals also want recognition that the right is inherent (in their having been here first), and not a gift of the current occupants of their land. (4, 16)

Aboriginal title. The Aboriginal claim to land on the basis of traditional occupancy and use rather than treaty, as recognized in the 1973 *Calder* case. (4)

Absent mandate. The notion that governments come to power without a clear-cut policy mandate. (14)

Access to Information Act. The 1983 act that gave citizens, journalists, and others the right to gain access to government documents, with certain exceptions, and established the office of Information Commissioner. (21)

Act of Union. The 1840 act that united the colonies of Upper and Lower Canada into the colony of Canada, partly designed to assimilate the French. (2)

Administrative agencies. Government agencies established to administer a politically sensitive area of public policy that operate at arm's length from the Cabinet. (21)

Advocacy advertising. Advertising that advocates a political point of view rather than trying to sell a good or service. (11)

Affirmative action. A law or program that gives preference to individuals with certain characteristics in the hiring or promotion process. (7, 18)

Agreement on Internal Trade. A federal–provincial agreement signed in 1995 in which provinces promised to remove preferences for local individuals and companies and other barriers to the free movement of goods, services, and people across provincial borders. (17)

Allaire Report. The 1991 Report of the Quebec Liberal Party in response to the rejection of the Meech Lake Accord that advocated a wholesale transfer of federal powers to Quebec. (5, 16)

Alliance of Manufacturers and Exporters Canada (AMEC). A large and powerful business interest group representing a wide range of Canadian manufacturers and exporters, a recent merger of the Canadian Manufacturers' Association and the Canadian Exporters' Association. (15)

---

[1] A fuller definition of many of these terms can be found in John McMenemy, *The Language of Canadian Politics: A Guide to Important Terms and Concepts*, rev. ed. (Waterloo: Wilfrid Laurier University Press, 1995).

Alternative Service Delivery (ASD). Part of the New Public Management movement, ASD embodies a variety of innovative means of providing government services distinct from the traditional departmental model. (21)

Assembly of First Nations. The largest interest group representing status Indians, who now prefer to be called First Nations peoples. (4, 15)

Atlantic Canada Opportunities Agency (ACOA). The federal agency that seeks to reduce regional economic disparities in the Atlantic region primarily through grants and loans to private firms. (3)

Auditor General. The official of Parliament whose staff audit the expenditures of government departments and who provides an annual report on instances of funds being unlawfully or unwisely spent. (21, 22)

Auto Pact. The 1965 bilateral Canada–U.S. agreement under which automobiles and auto parts flowed across the border duty-free as long as the value of purchases equalled that of production in each country. (9)

Backbenchers. Members of Parliament on the government side who sit on the backbenches and are not in the Cabinet, or those similarly distant from important posts in opposition parties. (22)

Bandwagon effect. The notion that, if and when they know which party or candidate is going to win the election, voters will move en masse in that direction. (11)

Bélanger–Campeau Committee. The all-party committee appointed in Quebec after the rejection of the Meech Lake Accord to consider the province's future options and that recommended a referendum on sovereignty. (5, 16)

Bill 22. The 1974 language law passed by Quebec that sought to enhance the status of the French language in that province and, among other things, required that immigrant children go to French schools unless they could already speak English. (5)

Bill 86. The 1993 language law, passed by Quebec when Bill 178 expired, that permitted bilingual signs outside as well as inside commercial establishments if French lettering was larger than English. (5)

Bill 101. The 1977 Quebec language law that sought to make French the official language of Quebec and put restrictions on the use of English in the courts, schools, and private sector. For example, all commercial signs had to be in French only. (5)

Bill 178. The 1988 language law, passed by Quebec under the notwithstanding clause, that continued to require unilingual French signs on the outside of commercial establishments but permitted bilingual signs inside if French lettering was larger than English. (5)

Block grant. A federal–provincial grant that is given for a specific purpose such as post-secondary education or health care but does not contain rigid conditions or standards. (17)

Bourgeoisie. A Marxist term referring to those who own the means of production, otherwise known as the corporate elite. (8)

British North America Act. The 1867 act of the British Parliament that created Canada by combining Ontario, Quebec, Nova Scotia, and New Brunswick and that also provided some of the essential elements of the new country's Constitution. Renamed the Constitution Act, 1867, in 1982. (2, 16)

Broker or brokerage. A kind of party system in which political parties try to appeal to many different interests and "broker" compromises among them, rather than having any distinct ideology. (13)

Budget. The annual financial statement of the government issued in the early spring by the minister of Finance that introduces tax changes and gives an overview of government spending for the next fiscal year. (20, 22)

Business Council on National Issues (BCNI). The most powerful peak business interest group in Canada, representing the 150 largest firms in the country. (8, 15)

Cabinet government. A system of government in which the major political decisions are made by the Cabinet as a whole, as opposed to one in which the prime minister acts with considerable autonomy. (2, 20)

Cabinet secrecy. A convention that Cabinet and Cabinet committee meetings are held behind closed doors and that all documents and discussions relating thereto are strictly confidential. Only final, official decisions are made public, while documents remain locked up for 30 years. (20)

Cabinet solidarity. A convention that all Cabinet ministers publicly support whatever decisions the Cabinet has taken, whatever their personal views. (20)

Cadre party. A kind of political party that is run by a small elite, a few national and local notables, who do not share power with a wider party membership. (13)

Calgary Declaration. A document drawn up by nine premiers (excluding Quebec) in 1997 that proposed to appeal to Quebec with a recognition of its distinct-society status but at the same time not offend those who believed in the equality of all the provinces. (5, 16)

Canada Act. The 1982 act passed by Britain that terminated all British authority over Canada and under which Canada passed the Constitution Act, 1982, with a domestic constitutional amending formula. (16)

Canada Assistance Plan (CAP). The 1966 act, the last of the major conditional grant programs, under which Ottawa shared the cost of provincial and municipal social assistance and welfare service programs; replaced by the Canada Health and Social Transfer. (8, 17)

Canada Clause. The clause in the 1992 Charlottetown Accord that attempted to define the fundamental characteristics of Canada. (10, 16)

Canada Council on the Arts. The government agency established in 1957 as the Canada Council to provide financial support to all aspects of the artistic community. (9)

Canada Elections Act. The act that governs all aspects of federal elections. (12)

Canada Health Act. The 1984 act that reimposed conditions on federal block grants to the provinces for health programs, especially to prevent extra-billing or other moves toward a two-tier health system. (17)

Canada Health and Social Transfer (CHST). The annual federal block grant to the provinces that replaced the Canada Assistance Plan and Established Program Funding (health insurance and postsecondary education) after 1996–97. (8, 17)

Canada–U.S. Free Trade Agreement. The agreement signed by Canada and the United States that came into effect in 1989 and that gradually eliminated tariffs between the two countries and otherwise prohibited governments from interfering in the private market-place. (9)

Canadian Bill of Rights. An act of the Canadian Parliament passed in 1960 that outlined the basic civil liberties of Canadians but whose defects caused judicial confusion and limited the bill's effectiveness. (18)

Canadian Broadcasting Corporation (CBC). The large, national Crown corporation (including its French equivalent, Radio-Canada) with radio and television arms whose mandate is to promote meaningful communication among all parts of the country. (3, 9, 11)

Canadian Chamber of Commerce (CCC). A large national peak business interest group with strong provincial and local bases. (15)

Canadian Federation of Independent Business (CFIB). A large interest group representing small business operations. (15)

Canadian Judicial Council. An agency composed of the federal and provincial chief justices that disciplines federally appointed judges and otherwise provides leadership and coordination among federal and provincial judicial systems. (23)

Canadian Labour Congress (CLC). The largest labour interest group in Canada; the political voice of over two million members. (8, 15)

Canadian Radio-television and Telecommunications Commission (CRTC). The regulatory agency established to police the communications industry, including radio, television, telephones, and telecommunications. (3, 9)

Canadian Wheat Board. A federal Crown corporation established to help grain farmers market their product in an aggressive way and to provide equitable returns to producers. (3)

Central agencies. Government agencies such as the PMO, the PCO, the Treasury Board, and the Finance Department that have certain coordinating functions across the whole federal public service and that prevent individual departments from acting with too much autonomy. (20)

Charlottetown Accord. The constitutional agreement of 1992 that responded to Quebec's demands for distinct-society status, Aboriginal demands for self-government, and the West's demand for a Triple-E Senate that was approved by federal, provincial, territorial, and Aboriginal leaders, but then turned down in a national referendum. (5, 16)

Charter of Rights and Freedoms. The 1982 document added to the Canadian Constitution that guaranteed fundamental freedoms and rights (legal, democratic, linguistic, mobility, egalitarian, and limited Aboriginal) to individual Canadian citizens. (2, 16, 18)

Chief electoral officer. The independent and impartial official who is in charge of the operation of the whole electoral system. (12)

Citizens' Forum. An operation headed by Keith Spicer in 1991–92 to hear what ordinary Canadians felt about constitutional issues after charges that they had not been able to contribute to the recently rejected Meech Lake Accord. (16)

Civil law. A branch of the law dealing with relations between private parties, such as individuals and corporations, that do not involve government. (23)

Civil liberties. Liberties or freedoms, including the fundamental freedoms of speech, press, religion, and assembly, that citizens enjoy and that cannot be infringed or encroached upon by government. (18)

Class-based parties. Political parties that appeal to a single socioeconomic class; when all parties do so, they constitute a class-based party system. (13)

Class-consciousness. An awareness of the social class to which one belongs, which is notoriously lacking in the case of most working-class Canadians. (8, 14)

Classical federalism. A variant of Canadian federalism in which the federal and provincial governments were not subordinate to each other and operated independently of each other. (17)

Clerk of the Privy Council and Secretary to the Cabinet. The head of the Privy Council Office and head of the federal public service; the chief nonpartisan adviser to the prime minister and Cabinet. (20)

Clientele relationship. The intimate and mutually advantageous relationship that sometimes develops between a government department or agency and the interest group with which it most frequently interacts. (15, 21)

Closure. A rule in the House of Commons in which a Cabinet minister introduces a motion to cut off debate. (22)

Code Civil du Québec. The unique system of civil law used in Quebec and based on the Napoleonic Code. (23)

Coercion. Power based on authorized physical force (including police, armed forces, jails, etc.) on which government has a near monopoly. Also used by class analysts as a term for what government does (at the behest of the corporate elite) when the state cannot otherwise get the public to accept its decisions. (1)

Collective responsibility. A convention holding that all Cabinet ministers are collectively responsible for government policy and under which the whole Cabinet must resign if defeated on a motion of nonconfidence. (20)

Collectivism. An ideology holding that the public interest is enhanced by substantial collective action, normally via government, as opposed to individualism, which minimizes the role of government. (10)

Commissioner for Federal Judicial Affairs. The official in charge of coordinating the process for the appointment of those judges who fall under the federal minister of Justice. (23)

Common law. The basis of the British and Canadian legal systems, apart from the civil law system in Quebec, that consists of the accumulation of judicial precedents and seeks out the previous decisions in cases most closely resembling the one at hand. (23)

Comprehensive claims. Aboriginal land claims based on Aboriginal title—that is, traditional use and occupancy—rather than on treaties or other legal documents. (4)

Concurrent powers. Powers officially shared by the federal and provincial governments, which in the Constitution Act, 1867, were agriculture, immigration, and, later, old age pensions. (17)

Conditional grant. A federal grant to the provinces, usually in support of a subject within provincial jurisdiction, to which Ottawa attaches conditions or standards before the province receives the money. (17)

Confederation Settlement. The deal made among the Fathers of Confederation that entailed setting up a new federal system of government with a division of powers, a division of financial powers, federal controls over the provinces, provincial representation in federal institutions, and certain cultural guarantees. (17)

Conflictual federalism. A variant of Canadian federalism, especially between 1970 and 1984 (during the Trudeau regime), characterized by provincial demands for increased decentralization, federal refusal, mutual recrimination, failed negotiations, and unilateral federal actions. (17)

Conscription crises. Two political crises in Canada, one in each world war, in which the population and government were divided, largely on ethnic lines, over the necessity of compulsory military service. (5)

Conservatism. A political ideology generally characterized by a belief in individualism and a minimum of government intervention in the economy and society, as well as by tradition, elitism, and opposition to change. (13)

Constitution. The whole body of rules and principles according to which the state is governed that, in the Canadian case, consists of a conglomeration of documents and conventions. (2, 16)

Constitution Act, 1867. The new name (changed in 1982) for the British North America Act, 1867. (2, 16)

Constitutional Act of 1791. The British law that divided Canada into two separate colonies, Upper and Lower Canada, each with a governor, executive and legislative councils, and an assembly. (2)

Constitutional amending formula. The process for amending the Constitution. (16)

Constitutional conventions. Unwritten rules of constitutional behaviour that are considered to be binding by and upon those who operate the Constitution, but that are not enforceable by the courts. (16)

Constitutional monarchy. The official designation of the Canadian form of government, characterized by a monarch who is head of state but who rules according to the Constitution, which confides almost all governmental power into other hands. (2, 20).

Cooperative federalism. A variant of Canadian federalism, in place in the post-1945 and especially post-1960 period, in which neither level of government is subordinate to the other and in which there is an extensive degree of interaction between them. (17)

Corporate elite. A synonym for "big business" or the bourgeoisie—that is, the collection of individuals who own or manage the largest corporations in the country. (8)

Corporatism. A notion that society can be divided into relatively few functional sectors, such as business, labour, farmers, and professions, that can either be self-governing or with whom the government can interact to make general policies. (15)

Court Challenges Program. A program established after the adoption of the Charter of Rights and Freedoms in which the federal government helped to finance those (especially francophone minorities and women) who challenged laws on the basis of the Charter, on the assumption that the costs involved would otherwise be prohibitive. (7)

Criminal Code. A federal document that codifies most of the criminal law in the country. (23)

Criminal law. That branch of the law dealing with wrongs committed against others that are considered to be offensive to society as a whole, for which the state takes the initiative to investigate, and for which perpetrators can be fined or jailed. (23)

Crow rate. A subsidized rail freight rate for Western goods, named after the Crow's Nest Pass, that was established in 1897, reduced in the 1970s, and eliminated in 1995. (3)

Crown. The collectivity of executive powers exercised by or in the name of the monarch. (20)

Crown corporation. A corporation owned by the government that assumes a structure similar to that of a private company and that operates semi-independently of the Cabinet. (21)

Declaratory power. The power in section 92(10)(c) of the Constitution Act, 1867, under which Ottawa can declare any local work or undertaking to be for the general advantage of Canada and thereby place it under federal jurisdiction. (17)

Deference to authority. A value considered to be part of the Canadian political culture in which citizens are respectful of government authority and accept its word and orders with little question. (10)

Democracy. A political system characterized by popular sovereignty, political equality, political freedom, and majority rule. (2, 10)

Democratic rights. A section of the Charter of Rights and Freedoms that, among other things, guarantees the vote to every Canadian citizen. (18)

Democratic socialism. A leftist political ideology that emphasizes the principle of equality and usually prescribes a large role for government to intervene in society and the economy via taxation, regulation, redistribution, and public ownership. (13)

Department. A kind of government organization headed by a minister who is politically accountable for its operations and a deputy minister who is in charge of its hierarchical administrative apparatus. (21)

Department of Finance. The government department that has overall responsibility for the government's finances and its role in the economy and that has a powerful influence on all government policy. (20)

Departmental Cabinet. A Cabinet characterized by ministers and departments that operate with substantial autonomy from other ministers, departments, and central agencies. (17, 20)

Deputy minister. The public servant who heads each government department, manages the department, and advises the minister. (21)

Deregulation. A government policy that removes previous regulations, especially those affecting the corporate sector. (19, 21)

Direct taxes. A category of taxation that can be used by either level of government to extract money from the very person or corporation that is intended to pay it. (17)

Disallowance. A power given to the federal government in the Constitution Act, 1867, but long since dormant, under which the prime minister and Cabinet can disallow any provincial law. (17)

Disengaging federalism. A variant of Canadian federalism, especially since about 1984, in which the federal government withdrew from some of its existing programs and policies, such as labour market training, that are constitutionally within provincial jurisdiction. (17)

Dispute-settlement mechanism. A clause in the Canada–U.S. Free Trade Agreement designed to settle such trade disputes as might arise under the treaty by means of binational panels. (9)

Dissolution of Parliament. The ending of a Parliament, usually after four or more years, by calling an election, an act normally in the hands of the prime minister but that formally requires the approval of the governor general. (20, 22)

Distinct-society clause. A controversial clause in the Meech Lake Accord, and slightly modified in the Charlottetown Accord, claiming that Quebec constituted, within Canada, a distinct society. (5, 16)

Division. A formal standing, roll-call vote in the House of Commons in which members' names are recorded in Hansard. (22)

Division of powers. The distribution of legislative powers between the federal and provincial governments, largely contained in sections 91 and 92 of the Constitution Act, 1867. (17)

Durham Report. The 1839 report by Lord Durham that recommended the union of Upper and Lower Canada and the granting of responsible government to the colony of Canada. (2)

Egalitarianism. As opposed to elitism, the philosophy or practice of providing everyone with an equal amount of power and/or of treating everyone more or less equally. (10)

Elite accommodation. The notion that public policies emerge from the interaction of various elites (small groups of people with a disproportionate amount of power) in society, who, sharing many socioeconomic characteristics and values, find it relatively easy to come to agreement. (1, 15)

Embedded state. The notion that the operations of the state are so extensive that they are connected to virtually every aspect of society, and that government therefore cannot act independently of societal forces. (1)

Emergency doctrine. A constitutional doctrine invented by the Judicial Committee of the Privy Council that in times of national emergency the Peace, Order and Good Government clause of the 1867 Constitution Act became an emergency clause. (17)

Emergency federalism. The highly centralized variant of Canadian federalism that characterized the period of the two world wars. (17)

Employment equity. A policy that seeks to guarantee fairness in hiring, promotion, or remuneration, regardless of gender, ethnicity, etc., and that may or may not incorporate affirmative action. (6, 7)

Enumerated powers. The powers of the federal and provincial governments explicitly listed in sections 91 and 92 of the Constitution Act, 1867. (17)

Equality rights. A section of the Charter of Rights and Freedoms that prohibits governments from discriminating against certain categories of people. (18)

Equalization payments. A large annual cash payment made by the federal government to have-not provinces to help them provide a satisfactory level of public services. (3, 17)

Established Programs Financing Act. An act passed in 1977 that altered the basis for federal–provincial grants, making health insurance a block grant rather than a conditional grant program, and superseded by the Canada Health and Social Transfer. (17)

Estimates. The annual spending plans of government departments and agencies for the following fiscal year, arrived at after gruelling negotiation with the Treasury Board Secretariat. (21, 22)

Executive federalism. A variant of cooperative federalism characterized by extensive federal–provincial interaction at the level of first ministers, departmental ministers, and deputy ministers, such as the process that produced the Meech Lake Accord. (17)

Expenditure Management System (EMS). The current process for determining government financial priorities and the annual distribution of funds. (20)

Extra-parliamentary party. That part of a political party beyond its members of Parliament, that is, party members, local and national executives, and party headquarters. (13)

Extraterritoriality. The ability of a state to pass laws having authority beyond its borders, especially related to the United States telling Canadian branches of U.S.-based transnational corporations with whom they can trade. (9)

Federal Court of Canada. A court established by the federal government dealing with cases involving that level of government and other specialized subjects within federal jurisdiction. (23)

Federalism (federation). A system of government characterized by two levels of authority (federal and provincial) and a division of powers such that neither is subordinate to the other. (2, 17)

Federal–provincial conferences. Periodic meetings of federal and provincial officials, especially first ministers or departmental ministers, characteristic of cooperative federalism, often making decisions that legislatures are not allowed to change. (17)

Feminists. People who believe in removing barriers to the full equality of men and women. (7)

Feminization of poverty. The notion that a high proportion of people living below the poverty line are women, usually sole-parent women with children. (7, 8)

Filibuster. An organized attempt by the opposition in the House of Commons to prolong debate and delay adoption of government measures. (22)

First ministers' conference. A federal–provincial conference consisting of the prime minister and provincial premiers (and sometimes territorial and Aboriginal leaders). (17)

First Nations. The new term preferred by Aboriginal Canadians to describe themselves, especially status Indians and those based on reserves. (4)

First-past-the-post. The kind of electoral system used in Canada in which the candidate with the most votes wins, regardless if it is over 50 percent. (12)

Foreign Investment Review Agency (FIRA). The agency established in the early 1970s to screen foreign investment in Canada and approve of foreign takeovers of Canadian firms; discontinued by the Mulroney government. (9)

Franchise. The right to vote. (12)

Francophonie. The international organization of French-speaking countries. (5)

Free vote. A rare vote in the House of Commons (or Senate) in which members are not required to abide by the party line. (22)

Front de Libération du Québec (FLQ). The terrorist wing of the Quebec separatist movement in the 1960s and 1970s. (5)

Fundamental freedoms. Political freedoms—of speech, religion, press, assembly, association, etc.—that governments are not supposed to encroach on and that are guaranteed by the Charter of Rights and Freedoms. (18)

Gerrymandering. An attempt to design constituency boundaries in the interests of the government party of the day in order to maximize the number of that party's seats and minimize the seats won by the opposition. (12)

Globalization. The modern phenomenon characterized by nation states declining in stature and power as they give way to the demands of transnational corporations via comprehensive free trade agreements, by massive diffusion of technological change, and by worldwide corporate competition or mega-mergers. (1, 9)

Government. The set of institutions that make and enforce collective, public decisions for a society (1); the group of people—the prime minister and Cabinet—and their supporters in Parliament who are currently charged to make such decisions. (20)

Government bills. Bills introduced by a Cabinet minister on behalf of the government (Cabinet), the kind of bills dominating discussion in the House of Commons. (22)

Gray Report. The government report authored by Herb Gray in 1972 expressing concern about the extent of foreign investment in Canada and recommending a screening agency. (9)

Horse-race effect. The notion that election campaigns have degenerated into a "horse race" where everyone, especially the media, are concerned with which party is ahead, not with how parties would tackle serious public issues. (11)

House leader. The person appointed by each party in the House of Commons to deal with counterparts in other parties with respect to scheduling Commons business. (22)

Immigration Act. The law that regulates the immigration process and determines the qualifications, categories, and, to some extent, the origins of immigrants. (6)

Implied bill of rights. The notion that even before the enactment of the Canadian Bill of Rights or the Charter of Rights and Freedoms, the Constitution, especially in its preamble, contained an implied bill that protected civil liberties to some extent. (18)

Incrementalism. The notion that, when confronted with a problem, governments—politicians and/or bureaucrats—prefer to make minor adjustments in existing policy rather than engage in a consideration of all possible alternative approaches. (21)

Indian Act. The act that governed almost all aspects of Indian life in Canada since the 1870s, giving extensive authority to government bureaucrats and minimal discretion to Indians themselves. (4)

Indirect taxes. A category of taxation, especially a tariff or customs duty, restricted to the federal government, in which the party that pays the tax is assumed to pass it along to some other customer. (17)

Individualism. An ideology that individuals should have maximum freedom or liberty to do as they please, especially in economic terms, and that governments should not get involved in taxation, regulation, redistribution, or ownership. (10, 13)

Information Commissioner. The official of Parliament who encourages government to operate on a more open and transparent basis and makes judgments in cases where departments withhold information under the Access to Information Act. (21)

Initiative. A populist device that would require the legislature to respond to a policy initiative endorsed by a certain proportion of the electorate signing a petition. (10, 22)

Institutionalized Cabinet. A Cabinet characterized by collective ministerial decision making and strong central agencies that support collective Cabinet operations. (17, 20)

Institutionalized pressure groups. A kind of pressure group characterized by permanence, resources, government acceptance, and well-developed links with the authorities. (15)

Iron law of oligarchy. An observation about political parties that they almost always come to be controlled by a small group of permanent professional politicians and officials who are in charge of policy, finance, and strategy. (13)

Issue-oriented groups. A kind of pressure group that springs up around an issue and disappears once that issue has been resolved. (15)

James Bay and Northern Quebec Agreement. The deal signed in 1975 by the government of Quebec and its northern Aboriginal residents that gave the latter land, cash, and hunting rights in return for surrendering land for the James Bay hydroelectric project. (4)

Japanese Redress Agreement. The deal signed by the Mulroney government in 1988 to compensate Japanese Canadians for their internment and the confiscation of their property during the Second World War. (6)

Joint committees. Parliamentary committees containing members from both the House of Commons and the Senate. (22)

Judicial Committee of the Privy Council (JCPC). A committee of the British Parliament that functioned as Canada's final court of appeal until 1949. (2, 16, 17, 23)

Judicial discretion. The leeway inevitably bestowed on the courts when they interpret laws, even when they do not, or have no power to, overturn them. (18)

Judicial independence. The constitutional principle that the courts should function independently of the rest of the government apparatus—that is, the politicians and bureaucrats—with implications for security of tenure and remuneration. (2, 23)

Judicial review. The power of the courts to overturn legislation. (2, 18, 23)

Kent Royal Commission on Newspapers. The Royal Commission established in 1980 to investigate the newspaper industry after a rash of takeovers and closures in the 1970s. (11)

Keynesian economics. An economic theory first enunciated by John Maynard Keynes that to promote general economic stability, government should counterbalance the private sector, spending (running deficit budgets) in periods of unemployment when the private sector doesn't spend, and taxing (running a budget surplus) in periods of inflation when the private sector is spending too much. (17)

King–Byng dispute. The dispute in 1926 between Prime Minister Mackenzie King and Governor General Lord Byng over King's request for a dissolution of Parliament, which Byng denied. (20)

Leader of the Opposition. The leader of the main opposition party in the House of Commons, normally the party with the second-largest number of seats. (22)

Leadership review. A clause in the constitutions of some political parties that allows party members to review the leader's performance and to vote on whether they want a leadership convention. (13)

Left. That part of the ideological spectrum that believes in equality in society and the intervention of government via such collectivist measures as taxation, regulation, redistribution, and public ownership to effect such equality. (13)

Legal rights. The rights of a person suspected or accused of committing a crime, now listed in the Charter of Rights and Freedoms. (18)

Liberalism. An ideology based on a belief in the rationality of the individual and on maximizing individual freedom, liberty, and self-fulfillment. Before 1900 this was assumed to entail a minimal role for government, but post-1900 liberalism usually advocated a larger role for the state and therefore was placed on the centre-left of the spectrum. (13)

Limited identities. The notion that while the overall Canadian national identity is elusive, Canadian society is made up of all sorts of more limited identities or subcultures—regional, ethnic, linguistic, etc. (10)

Lobbying. Any organized attempt to influence the authorities, now often performed by professional lobbyist firms. (15)

Lobbyists Registration Act. The law passed in 1989 that sought to have lobbyists register with a government agency and submit certain information about what they were doing to influence government. (15)

Majority government. A situation in which the party in power has over 50 percent of the seats in the House of Commons. (2, 22)

Majority rule. An element in the definition of democracy that in any decision-making setting involving a difference of opinion, the larger number should carry the day. (10)

Mandarins. A term applied to senior bureaucrats who are known to have great influence in government policymaking. (21)

Mass party. A kind of political party in which the membership plays a meaningful role in such operations as financing, choosing and reviewing the leadership, and determining party policy. (13)

Massey Royal Commission. A 1951 Royal Commission that expressed concern about the future prospects of Canadian culture and recommended ways to promote and protect it. (9)

Meech Lake Accord. The 1987 package of constitutional amendments intended to bring Quebec back into the constitutional fold. (5, 16)

Memorandum to Cabinet (MC). The formal written document that a minister submits to Cabinet seeking to initiate or change a government policy. (20)

Merit system. A system of hiring or promoting public servants on the basis of their merits (education, training, experience, etc.) rather than on party preference or other considerations. (21)

Ministerial responsibility. The principle that Cabinet ministers are individually responsible to the House of Commons for everything that happens in their department. (20, 21)

Minority government. A situation in which the government party has less than 50 percent of the seats in the House of Commons. (22)

Minority-language education rights. Rights established by the 1982 Charter of Rights and Freedoms whereby French-speaking Canadians have the right to send their children to French-language schools, wherever their numbers warrant, applying to English-speaking Canadians as well. (5, 18)

Mobility rights. A category of rights in the Charter of Rights and Freedoms guaranteeing the freedom to move from one province to another and seek employment there. (18)

Multiculturalism. A policy of encouraging ethnic and cultural groups to maintain their customs and traditions, often with public financial assistance. (6)

Multilateral Agreement on Investment (MAI). A proposed agreement discussed among highly industrialized countries that would have set the rules for the operation of the global economy, further restricting state regulation of transnational corporate behaviour. (9)

Multi-party system. Typically European in nature, a party system characterized by many parties, without any one having a majority in the legislature. (13)

National Action Committee on the Status of Women. The largest and most vocal women's interest group. (7)

National Citizens' Coalition (NCC). A right-wing pressure group that successfully challenged limitations on third-party advertising during election campaigns. (12)

National Energy Board. A regulatory agency that makes decisions relating to exports of electricity and petroleum. (9)

National Energy Program (NEP). A 1980 initiative associated with Pierre Trudeau and designed to skim off more petroleum tax revenue for Ottawa, keep the price of petroleum below world levels, encourage conservation, and Canadianize the industry, which met with great opposition in Western Canada. (3, 9)

National Policy. A broad nation-building policy of John A. Macdonald unveiled in 1879 that included tariff protection for central Canadian manufacturing, massive immigration, and the construction of a national transportation system. (3)

Neoconservative. An ideological term characterizing parties or politicians in the 1980s and after who not only advocated an end to government expansion, but believed in reducing its role via privatization, deregulation, deficit cutting, and elimination of social programs. (13)

New middle class. A term from class analysis describing salaried professionals such as teachers, public servants, nurses, and so on. (5, 8)

New Public Management (NPM). A movement within public administration since about 1990 that involved downsizing government, encouraging technological change, finding new ways to provide public services, and forming partnerships with private-sector agencies. (21)

News management. A variety of techniques used by politicians and governments to ensure positive media coverage. (11)

Nomination. The act of becoming a candidate in an election, normally entailing being selected to represent a party at a nomination meeting and then completing official nomination forms. (12, 14)

Nonconfidence motion. A periodic motion in the House of Commons, moved by the opposition, inviting the House to demonstrate its lack of confidence in the government; if successful, such a motion would require the Cabinet's resignation or the calling of an election. (22)

North American Free Trade Agreement (NAFTA). The 1994 extension of the Canada–U.S. Free Trade Agreement to Mexico, with provision for other Latin American countries to join. (9)

Notwithstanding clause. Section 33 of the Charter of Rights and Freedoms, which allows federal or provincial governments to pass laws that violate certain sections of the Charter. (18)

Nunavut. The eastern half of the Northwest Territories, which was established as a separate, Inuit territory in 1999. (3, 4)

Oakes test. The strategy outlined in the *Oakes* case for interpreting the reasonable limits clause of the Charter of Rights and Freedoms. (18)

Official Languages Act. A law passed in 1969 giving citizens the right to deal with head offices as well as certain local offices of the federal government in either official language, and necessitating the hiring and promotion of francophone public servants. (5, 21)

One-party dominance. A party system characterized by the dominance of a single party, usually related to Conservative Party dominance before 1900 and Liberal Party dominance since. (13)

Opposition. Those members of Parliament who do not support the government of the day. (22)

Opposition days. Twenty-one days per session set aside in the House of Commons for the opposition to determine the topic of debate and for the government to respond. (22)

Pacific scandal. A party finance scandal involving John A. Macdonald's Conservative Party and a group of businessmen who sought the contract to build the Canadian Pacific Railway. (12)

Padlock Law. An infamous law passed by Premier Maurice Duplessis in Quebec in the late 1930s that allowed him to place a padlock on any building that was being used for purposes of opposing the government. (18)

Pairing. A practice in the House of Commons whereby two MPs from opposite sides agree that if either is legitimately away for a vote the other will not vote either. (22)

Parliament of Canada. Theoretically, the Queen, the House of Commons, and the Senate functioning collectively, such as in the approval of legislation, but often used to refer to the Commons alone or sometimes the Commons and Senate. (22)

Parliamentary party. That wing of a political party made up of its elected members, that is, its MPs or its parliamentary caucus. (13)

Parliamentary press gallery. Those members of the media who are registered to sit in the press gallery in the House of Commons and who report on its proceedings or on government in general. (11, 22)

Parliamentary privileges. Historic privileges that adhere to a member of Parliament, the most important residual one being the freedom from prosecution for anything said in the Commons chamber. (22)

Parliamentary secretaries. Government MPs who have been given additional responsibilities to assist a Cabinet minister. (20)

Particularism. A value identified as part of the Canadian political culture that encourages diversity rather than uniformity, and most commonly taking the form of a mosaic of ethnic diversity and multiculturalism, in contrast to the U.S. melting pot. (10)

Party caucus. The whole body of MPs of any party, who hold a regular weekly closed meeting, together with such senators as choose to attend, to discuss parliamentary strategy, party policy, and so on. (13, 22)

Party discipline. The convention that all MPs within any party vote together on every occasion, as predetermined in the party caucus meeting and as enforced by the party whip. (22)

Party whip. An official of each party in the House of Commons whose function is to enforce party discipline, in part by drawing up speaking lists, committee assignments, office allocations, and official parliamentary travel plans. (22)

Pay equity. An element of employment equity programs designed to ensure that all employees are paid equally for work of equal value and are not discriminated against on the basis of gender or other factors. (7)

Peace, Order, and Good Government clause (POGG). The opening words of section 91 of the Constitution Act, 1867, describing the residual powers of the federal government (as well as the essence of the Canadian political culture), but often misinterpreted by the courts as an emergency power only. (17)

Persons case. The decision by the Judicial Committee of the Privy Council that determined that women were persons for the purposes of appointment to the Senate. (7, 22)

Petite bourgeoisie. A Marxist term to describe self-employed professionals, affluent farmers, and those operating small businesses. (8)

Pipeline debate. The heated House of Commons debate in the mid-1950s regarding the construction of the Trans-Canada Pipeline in which the Liberals treated Parliament in a particularly arrogant way. (13, 22)

Policy communities. The notion that government policy is made in a series of discrete and specialized clusters of government departments and agencies, interest groups, politicians, corporations, and interested individuals. (15, 19)

Policy instruments. The devices chosen by the government to effect public policy that are commonly arrayed in terms of degree of intrusion in society and the economy. (19)

Political culture. The sum total of the politically relevant values, attitudes, beliefs, and orientations in any political system. (10)

Political efficacy. The feeling that one has political influence and that one's political participation can make an impact. (10)

Political equality. An element in the definition of democracy that entails the principle of "one person–one vote"—every citizen has a vote and each counts equally. (10)

Political freedom. An element in the definition of democracy that entails freedom of speech, press, assembly, association, etc., such that people can organize and advocate in order to influence election results and public policy. (10)

Political party. An organized group that makes nominations and contests elections in the hope of influencing the personnel and policy of government. (13)

Political patronage. Making appointments to public offices or awarding government contracts on a partisan basis. (13, 21)

Political socialization. The process whereby individuals acquire their political values, attitudes, beliefs, and orientations. (11)

Politics. The activity in which conflicting interests struggle for advantage, whether in governmental or nongovernmental settings. (1)

Popular sovereignty. An element in the definition of democracy that entails periodically allowing the public at large to exert its will—to have the final say—normally through general elections. (10)

Popular vote. The percentage of all votes cast won by a candidate or party, regardless of who was elected. (12)

Poverty line. An amount of income such that anyone who received less would be living in poverty. (8)

Power. The ability of one actor to impose its will on another, usually considered to be the essence of politics and government. (1)

Prerogative powers. That small residual of powers of the Crown—the Queen or governor general—that remain from the era of an all-powerful monarch and that the Crown can still exercise at its own discretion. (20)

Pressure group or interest group. Any group seeking to influence government policy without contesting elections; organizations whose members act together to influence public policy in order to promote their common interest. (15)

Prime ministerial government. The notion that the prime minister is now so pre-eminent that the label "Cabinet government" no longer accurately describes how decisions are made in the political executive. (20)

Prime Minister's Office (PMO). The office that supports and advises the prime minister in partisan terms. (20)

Private bills. Bills introduced in Parliament that only affect a specific individual, company, organization, or group. (22)

Private members' bills. Public bills introduced in the House of Commons or Senate by members who are not in the Cabinet. (22)

Private sector. That part of the economy operated by individuals, corporations, and other non-governmental groups. (1)

Privatization. Transferring a government program, agency, or Crown corporation to the private sector, such as by selling shares in a Crown corporation to the public at large or to a private firm. (19, 21)

Privy Council Office (PCO). The office that supports and advises the prime minister, Cabinet, and Cabinet committees in nonpartisan terms on such matters as overall government policy, the machinery of government, and senior bureaucratic appointments. (20)

Proletariat. A Marxist term referring to those who sell their labour for an undervalued price to the bourgeoisie; the working class. (8)

Province-building. The converse of "nation-building," the notion of developing strong provincial governments, especially after 1960 or so, whether through provincial bureaucracies, Crown corporations, or central planning agencies, and their capacity to intervene in the process of industrial development. (17)

Public Accounts Committee. The House of Commons committee that examines the Public Accounts and the Auditor General's Report and criticizes government officials for illegal or unwise expenditures. (21, 22)

Public bills. Those bills introduced in Parliament that affect society in general. (22)

Public opinion. The sum total of opinions held by members of the public on any subject. (11)

Public ownership. A policy instrument involving government purchase ("nationalization") of a private corporation or the creation of a Crown corporation. (19)

Public policy. A course of action or inaction chosen by public authorities to address a given problem or interrelated set of problems. (19)

Public policy purpose. The point of creating a Crown corporation or other government program or agency—that is, to achieve the objectives of a public policy or to serve some public interest. (3, 21)

Public sector. That part of the economy operated or financed by government. (1)

Public Service Commission. The central personnel agency of government designed to police the merit system and ensure that partisanship is kept out of the regular public service. (21)

Quasi-federalism. That phase of Canadian federalism (1867–1896) in which the federal government was predominant over the provinces, just as John A. Macdonald intended. (17)

Quasi-judicial. Of court-like functions, powers, and procedures often possessed by regulatory tribunals (e.g., CRTC licence-issuing powers). (21)

Quasi-legislative. Of functions and powers of regulatory agencies to make law-like regulations (e.g., CRTC Canadian-content regulations). (21)

Quebec Act. The British law passed in 1774 that provided for a system of government for the colony of Quebec (Canada) and that provided certain privileges to the French-speaking, Roman Catholic majority. (2)

Question Period. The daily 45-minute period in the House of Commons in which opposition members spar with the prime minister and Cabinet ministers. (22)

Quiet Revolution. The dramatic change of values and attitudes—especially toward the state—the new collective self-confidence, and the new brand of nationalism that characterized Quebec in the 1960s. (5, 16)

Rational choice. A model of the public-policymaking process that prescribes consideration of the positive and negative implications of all policy alternatives until the most rational alternative is ultimately identified. (21)

Reasonable limits clause. Section 1 of the Charter of Rights and Freedoms, which allows the courts to find that even though a law violates a Charter right, it is a reasonable limit on such and is therefore allowed to stand. (18)

Recall. A populist device in which a certain proportion of the electorate signing a petition could cause an elected member of a legislature to resign. (10, 22)

Red tories. A minority faction within the Canadian Conservative Party that has collectivist leanings akin to many British and European conservatives, stressing order, tradition, stability, and a paternalistic concern for the condition of the working class. (13)

Redistribution. The process of reallocating seats in the House of Commons among the provinces after each decennial census and then redrawing constituency boundaries within each province. (12)

Reference cases. Cases referred to the courts by provincial or federal cabinets in order to obtain a ruling on their constitutionality. (23)

Referendum. A populist device in which certain public policy proposals are submitted directly to the electorate. (5, 10, 16, 22)

Regional economic development programs. Government programs designed to improve employment prospects in have-not parts of the country, usually by means of giving loans or grants to companies to establish or expand operations in such areas. (3)

Regulations. The detailed rules drafted by the bureaucracy under the authority of laws passed by Parliament that are too voluminous and technical to put into the legislation itself. (19, 21)

Regulatory tribunals. Government agencies established to regulate an area of public policy, such as transportation or communications, that operate at arm's length from the Cabinet and often have quasi-legislative and/or quasi-judicial powers. (21)

Representative bureaucracy. A public service that reflects the composition of the population, with the most usual concerns being gender, ethnicity, or region. (21)

Representative government. A form of government including an assembly elected by the citizens, but one that does not necessarily incorporate the principle of responsible government. (2)

Reservation. An obsolete power of the federally appointed lieutenant governor of each province to refrain from giving royal assent to provincial legislation and to send it instead to the federal Cabinet for its consideration. (17)

Residual powers. Those powers not explicitly given to the provinces in the Constitution Act, 1867, that were assigned to the federal government under the opening words of section 91. (17)

Responsible government. A form of government in which the political executive must retain the confidence of the elected legislature or assembly and must resign or call an election if and when it is defeated on a vote of nonconfidence. (2, 22)

Right. That part of the ideological spectrum that cherishes individualism and believes in leaving the private sector to operate with minimal government intervention. (13)

Rowell–Sirois Commission. The Royal Commission appointed in 1937 to examine federal–provincial relations and whose 1940 report eventually led to many changes in the federal–provincial financial relationship. (17)

Royal Commission. An elaborate investigation set up by the Cabinet to research significant policy problems, to listen to and educate the public, and to make recommendations to the government. (21)

Royal Commission on Aboriginal Peoples. The Royal Commission appointed in the wake of the defeat of the Meech Lake Accord and the Oka standoff to provide a blueprint for addressing the long-standing needs of the Aboriginal community. (4)

Royal Commission on Bilingualism and Biculturalism. The Royal Commission established in reaction to the Quiet Revolution in Quebec in the 1960s that recommended official bilingualism as a way of keeping the country together. (5)

Royal Commission on Electoral Reform and Party Financing. The Royal Commission established in the wake of the controversial 1988 federal election, with the objective of enhancing the democratic character of Canadian elections. (12)

Royal Commission on the Status of Women. The Royal Commission that reported in 1970 and helped to inspire the women's movement in its demands for policy changes over the following decades. (7)

Royal Proclamation of 1763. The British policy enunciated after Britain won Quebec from France that in a large area called Indian Territory the purchase or settlement of land was forbidden without a treaty between the Crown and the Indian people concerned. (2, 4)

Rule of law. The constitutional principle that all government action must be based on law and that governments and government officials must obey the law. (2, 18)

Safe seats. Constituencies that a single party can be assured of winning election after election, the small number of which in the Canadian House of Commons resulting in a high MP turnover rate. (14, 22)

Scrutiny of Regulations. The joint parliamentary committee that is appointed to wade through the voluminous regulations issued by government departments under the authority of legislation and that has the power to recommend rescinding such regulations. (22)

Sexual orientation. One's sexual preference, usually either heterosexual or homosexual, a ground on which governments and courts now prohibit discrimination. (7)

Shared-cost programs. Government programs whose cost is shared by the federal and provincial governments. (17)

Social movements. An informal network of organizations and individuals who on the basis of a collective identity and shared values engage in political struggle intended to expand the boundaries of the existing system, such as the women's and environmental movements. (15)

Social safety net. The conglomeration of social programs developed over the years by federal and provincial governments, individually and jointly, and designed to help those who could not otherwise care for their own basic needs or those of their family. (8)

Social Union Framework. An overall framework of federal–provincial relations, agreed to by the federal government and all provinces except Quebec in 1999, that sought to end longstanding irritants on both sides and clarify where and how either level of government could act unilaterally or engage in joint programs. (17)

Sovereignty. Ultimate control or independence, whether in terms of Canadian national sovereignty vis-à-vis other countries or of Quebec sovereignty vis-à-vis the federal government. (5, 9)

Sovereignty association. The Parti Québécois proposal in which Quebec would be sovereign while maintaining an economic association with the rest of Canada. (5, 16)

Speaker. The presiding officer of the House of Commons whose additional administrative responsibility includes the supervision of the staff of the chamber. (22)

Special committees. Committees of the House of Commons appointed for special, temporary purposes, such as to investigate a problem before the government has prepared legislation on the subject. (22)

Special operating agencies (SOAs). An aspect of the New Public Management movement, SOAs are units that function with relative autonomy within government departments and that aim to deliver a service along private-sector lines. (21)

Specific claims. Aboriginal land claims arising from the alleged nonfulfillment of Indian treaties and other lawful obligations, as opposed to those based on traditional occupancy and use. (4)

Speech from the throne. The document prepared by the prime minister and Cabinet and read by the governor general at the opening of each session of Parliament outlining the government's legislative proposals for the session to follow. (20, 22)

Spending power. The unofficial power of the federal government to spend money on any subject, including those within provincial jurisdiction, and even to attach conditions to such grants to the provinces. (17)

Spin doctors. Party officials and ministerial aides who talk to the media and try to influence media coverage by putting the best face on an event from their party's point of view. (11)

Split-run magazines. American magazines directed at Canadians by adding a minimal amount of Canadian editorial material and a maximum number of Canadian advertisements. (9)

Spoils system. Hiring public servants on the basis of political partisanship. (21)

Stakeholders. Those individuals, groups, corporations, or other organizations who have a stake in any issue; the principal players involved in any policy community. (19)

Standing committees. Those committees of the House of Commons that are set up semipermanently and parallel government departments. (22)

Standing Orders. The written rules of the House of Commons. (22)

Staples theory. The notion that Canadian economic development has gone through a series of stages based on the exploitation of one natural resource or another and the export of such resources without the development of a secondary or tertiary sector. (3)

Stare decisis. The legal principle that precedents are binding on similar subsequent cases, which forms the basis of the common law system. (23)

State of emergency. A policy instrument that involves the greatest degree of intrusion and coercion on the part of the state, now based on the Emergencies Act rather than the War Measures Act. (19)

Status Indians. Those Aboriginal Canadians registered with the federal government according to the terms of the Indian Act who have not had their status removed for any reason, or those who have regained it. (4)

Statute of Westminster. The 1931 British law that declared Canada and the other Dominions to be fully independent. (2, 16)

Subcultures. Clusters of people who share basic political values and attitudes based on common regional, ethnic, class, or other characteristics. (10)

Supremacy of Parliament. The principle that no other organ of government can overrule Parliament or its laws, a principle modified to some extent in 1982 with an expanded power of judicial review incorporated in the Canadian Charter of Rights. (2, 22)

Supreme Court Act. The 1875 law of the Canadian Parliament that provided for the Supreme Court of Canada and that serves as a legal base for the institution in the absence of further constitutional entrenchment. (16, 23)

Tariff. A federal tax placed on imports that raises revenue for Ottawa and protects domestic manufacturers by making imported goods more expensive to buy. (3)

Task forces. Informal devices set up by the Cabinet, made up of bureaucrats, MPs, outside experts, or some combination thereof, to study an issue and make recommendations quickly. (21)

Taxation agreements. Federal–provincial agreements, especially with respect to personal and corporate income taxes since 1945, under which Ottawa collects the taxes if provinces use a similar base for calculating their portion of the tax. (17)

Tax expenditures. A policy instrument that provides a tax credit or tax deduction if tax-payers spend money in a desired way. (19)

Third-party advertising. Advertising by advocacy groups, as opposed to political parties, during an election campaign. (12)

Three-party system. A party system characterized by three main parties, all with approximately similar levels of support, as in Canada during the 1980s. (13)

Trade and Commerce clause. Subsection 2 of section 91 of the Constitution Act, 1867, which was intended to provide a broad base for federal jurisdiction in this field but which was whittled away by judicial interpretation. (17)

Transnational corporations. Corporations operating simultaneously in many countries throughout the world that often take orders from company headquarters and that individual states find difficult to control. (9)

Treasury Board. A Cabinet committee whose primary responsibility is to restrain government spending. (20)

Treasury Board Secretariat. The government department that advises the Treasury Board in its deliberations and that functions as a restraining influence on departmental spending. (20, 21)

Treaty power. Section 132 of the Constitution Act, 1867, which speaks of Empire treaties and was intended to provide the federal government with a broad power to sign and implement treaties, but whose scope was limited by judicial interpretation. (17)

Triple-E Senate. A proposal for Senate reform in which each province would have an equal number of senators, who would be elected and who would be given effective powers. (16, 22)

Two-party system. A type of party system in which two main parties are of approximately equal strength and alternate in office, as in Canada between 1896 and 1921. (13)

Two-plus or two-and-a-half party system. A type of party system in which two main parties are of approximately equal strength and alternate in office, but which are accompanied by one or more minor parties of significant strength, as in Canada between 1921 and 1980. (13)

Union Government. The coalition government from 1917 to the end of the First World War made up of Conservatives and English-speaking Liberals whose aim was to enforce conscription and conduct the war in a vigorous manner. (5, 13)

Victoria Charter. The 1971 package of constitutional amendments including an amending formula, a charter of rights, and provisions designed to respond to demands emanating from the Quiet Revolution in Quebec. (16)

Visible minorities. Members of ethnic groups, other than Aboriginals, whose skin colour is not white. (6)

Voters' list. The list of eligible voters that used to be prepared from scratch via door-to-door enumeration once the election was called, but is now called the Register of Electors and is maintained on a permanent basis. (12)

Wage and price controls. A controversial proposal put forward by the Conservatives in the 1974 election campaign to put a cap on wage and price increases. (13)

War Measures Act. The law invoked during both world wars and during the 1970 FLQ crisis under which the federal Cabinet is given emergency powers to deal with a crisis; later replaced by the Emergencies Act. (5, 19)

Western alienation. The feeling shared by many Western Canadians that their interests are not taken seriously in the national policymaking process. (3, 10)

Westminster model. The model of government developed in Britain in which the political executive is given extensive power to provide effective leadership. (2, 22)

White Paper on Indians. The 1969 Trudeau–Chrétien policy proposal to do away with the Indian Act and fully integrate Aboriginals into Canadian society. (4)

Women's movement. The collection of women's groups that mushroomed across the country starting about 1970 demanding complete equality for women. (7)

World Trade Organization (WTO). Successor to the General Agreement on Tariffs and Trade, an organization to which Canada and most other countries belong and which has the power to disallow national policies and practices that it deems discriminates against companies from other states. (9)

Appendix A

Constitution Act, *1867 (excerpts)*

···

VI. DISTRIBUTION OF LEGISLATIVE POWERS

Powers of the Parliament

Legislative
Authority of
Parliament of
Canada

91. It shall be lawful for the Queen, by and with the Advice and Consent of the Senate and House of Commons, to make Laws for the Peace, Order, and good Government of Canada, in relation to all Matters not coming within the Classes of Subjects by this Act assigned exclusively to the Legislatures of the Provinces; and for greater Certainty, but not so as to restrict the Generality of the foregoing Terms of this Section, it is hereby declared that (notwithstanding anything in this Act) the exclusive Legislative Authority of the Parliament of Canada extends to all Matters coming within the Classes of Subjects next hereinafter enumerated; that is to say,—

1. *The amendment from time to time of the Constitution of Canada, except as regards matters coming within the classes of subjects by this Act assigned exclusively to the Legislatures of the provinces, or as regards rights or privileges by this or any other Constitutional Act granted or secured to the Legislature or the Government of a province, or to any class of persons with respect to schools or as regards the use of the English or the French language or as regards the requirements that there shall be a session of the Parliament of Canada at least once each year, and that no House of Commons shall continue for more than five years from the day of the return of the Writs for choosing the House: Provided, however, that a House of Commons may in time of real of apprehended war, invasion or insurrection be continued by the Parliament of Canada if such continuation is not opposed by the votes of more than one-third of the members of such House.*

[Note: Class 1 was added by the *British North America Act (No. 2), 1949* and repealed by the *Constitution Act, 1982.*]

1A. The Public Debt and Property.

   2. The Regulation of Trade and Commerce.

2A. Unemployment insurance.

3. The raising of Money by any Mode or System of Taxation.
4. The borrowing of Money on the Public Credit.
5. Postal Service.
6. The Census and Statistics.
7. Militia, Military and Naval Service, and Defence.
8. The fixing of and providing for the Salaries and Allowances of Civil and other Officers of the Government of Canada.
9. Beacons, Buoys, Lighthouses, and Sable Island.
10. Navigation and Shipping.
11. Quarantine and the Establishment and Maintenance of Marine Hospitals.
12. Sea Coast and Inland Fisheries.
13. Ferries between a Province and any British or Foreign Country or between Two Provinces.
14. Currency and Coinage.
15. Banking, Incorporation of Banks, and the Issue of Paper Money.
16. Savings Banks.
17. Weights and Measures.
18. Bills of Exchange and Promissory Notes.
19. Interest.
20. Legal Tender.
21. Bankruptcy and Insolvency.
22. Patents of Invention and Discovery.
23. Copyrights.
24. Indians, and Lands reserved for the Indians.
25. Naturalization and Aliens.
26. Marriage and Divorce.
27. The Criminal Law, except the Constitution of Courts of Criminal Jurisdiction, but including the Procedure in Criminal Matters.
28. The Establishment, Maintenance, and Management of Penitentiaries.
29. Such Classes of Subjects as are expressly excepted in the Enumeration of the Classes of Subjects by this Act assigned exclusively to the Legislatures of the Provinces.

And any Matter coming within any of the Classes of Subjects enumerated in this Section shall not be deemed to come within the Class of Matters of a local or private Nature comprised in the Enumeration of the Classes of Subjects by this Act assigned exclusively to the Legislatures of the Provinces.

Exclusive Powers of Provincial Legislatures

92. In each Province the Legislature may exclusively make Laws in relation to Matters coming within the Classes of Subjects next hereinafter enumerated; that is to say,— Subjects of exclusive Provincial Legislation

1. *The Amendment from Time to Time, notwithstanding anything in this Act, of the Constitution of the Province, except as regards the Office of the Lieutenant Governor.*

[Note: Class 1 was repealed by the *Constitution Act, 1982*. The subject is now provided for in section 45 of that Act, and see also sections 38 and 41 to 43 of the same Act.]

2. Direct Taxation within the Province in order to the raising of a Revenue for Provincial Purposes.
3. The borrowing of Money on the sole Credit of the Province.
4. The Establishment and Tenure of Provincial Offices and the Appointment and Payment of Provincial Officers.
5. The Management and Sale of the Public Lands belonging to the Province and of the Timber and Wood thereon.
6. The Establishment, Maintenance, and Management of Public and Reformatory Prisons in and for the Province.
7. The Establishment, Maintenance, and Management of Hospitals, Asylums, Charities, and Eleemosynary Institutions in and for the Province, other than Marine Hospitals.
8. Municipal Institutions in the Province.
9. Shop, Saloon, Tavern, Auctioneer, and other Licences in order to the raising of a Revenue for Provincial, Local, or Municipal Purposes.
10. Local Works and Undertakings other than such as are of the following Classes:—
    (a) Lines of Steam or other Ships, Railways, Canals, Telegraphs, and other Works and Undertakings connecting the Province with any other or others of the Provinces, or extending beyond the Limits of the Province;
    (b) Lines of Steam Ships between the Province and any British or Foreign Country;
    (c) Such Works as, although wholly situate within the Province, are before or after their Execution declared by the Parliament of Canada to be for the general Advantage of Canada or for the Advantage of Two or more of the Provinces.
11. The Incorporation of Companies with Provincial Objects.
12. The Solemnization of Marriage in the Province.
13. Property and Civil Rights in the Province.
14. The Administration of Justice in the Province, including the Constitution, Maintenance, and Organization of Provincial Courts, both of Civil and of Criminal Jurisdiction, and including Procedure in Civil Matters in those Courts.
15. The Imposition of Punishment by Fine, Penalty, or Imprisonment for enforcing any Law of the Province made in relation to any Matter coming within any of the Classes of Subjects enumerated in this Section.
16. Generally all Matters of a merely local or private Nature in the Province.

Non-Renewable Natural Resources, Forestry Resources and Electrical Energy

Laws respecting non-renewable natural resources, forestry resources and electrical energy

92A. (1) In each province, the legislature may exclusively make laws in relation to
   (a) exploration for non-renewable natural resources in the province;
   (b) development, conservation and management of non-renewable natural resources and forestry resources in the province, including laws in relation to the rate of primary production therefrom; and
   (v) development, conservation and management of sites and facilities in the province for the generation and production of electrical energy.

(2) In each province, the legislature may make laws in relation to the export from the province to another part of Canada of the primary production from non-renewable natural resources and forestry resources in the province and the production from facilities in the province for the generation of electrical energy, but such laws may not authorize or provide for discrimination in prices or in supplies exported to another part of Canada.

Export from province of resources

(3) Nothing in subsection (2) derogates from the authority of Parliament to enact laws in relation to the matters referred to in that subsection and, where such a law of Parliament and a law of a province conflict, the law of Parliament prevails to the extent of the conflict.

Authority of Parliament

(4) In each province, the legislature may make laws in relation to the raising of money by any mode or system of taxation in respect of

Taxation of resources

(a) non-renewable natural resources and forestry resources in the province and the primary production therefrom, and

(b) sites and facilities in the province for the generation of electrical energy and the production therefrom,

whether or not such production is exported in whole or in part from the province, but such laws may not authorize or provide for taxation that differentiates between production exported to another part of Canada and production not exported from the province.

(5) The expression "primary production" has the meaning assigned by the Sixth Schedule.

(6) Nothing in subsections (1) to (5) derogates from any powers or rights that a legislature or government of a province had immediately before the coming into force of this section.

"Primary production" Existing powers or rights

Education

93. In and for each Province the Legislature may exclusively make Laws in relation to Education, subject and according to the following Provisions:—

Legislation respecting Education

(1) Nothing in any such Law shall prejudicially affect any Right or Privilege with respect to Denominational Schools which any Class of Persons have by Law in the Province at the Union:

(2) All the Powers, Privileges, and Duties at the Union by Law conferred and imposed in Upper Canada on the Separate Schools and School Trustees of the Queen's Roman Catholic Subjects shall be and the same are hereby extended to the Dissentient Schools of the Queen's Protestant and Roman Catholic Subjects in Quebec:

(3) Where in any Province a System of Separate or Dissentient Schools exists by Law at the Union or is thereafter established by the Legislature of the Province, an Appeal shall lie to the Governor General in Council from any Act or Decision of any Provincial Authority affecting any Right or Privilege of the Protestant or Roman Catholic Minority of the Queen's Subjects in relation to Education:

(4) In case any such Provincial Law as from Time to Time seems to the Governor General in Council requisite for the due Execution of the Provisions of this Section is not made, or in case any Decision of the Governor General in Council on any appeal under this Section is not duly executed by the proper Provincial Authority in that Behalf, then and in every such Case, and as far only as the Circumstances of each Case

require, the Parliament of Canada may make remedial Laws for the due Execution of the Provisions of this Section and of any Decision of the Governor General in Council under this Section.

Uniformity of Laws in Ontario, Nova Scotia and New Brunswick

Legislation for Uniformity of Laws in Three Provinces

94. Notwithstanding anything in this Act, the Parliament of Canada may make Provision for the Uniformity of all or any of the Laws relative to Property and Civil Rights in Ontario, Nova Scotia, and New Brunswick, and of the Procedure of all or any of the Courts in Those Three Provinces, and from and after the passing of any Act in that Behalf the Power of the Parliament of Canada to make Laws in relation to any Matter comprised in any such Act shall, notwithstanding anything in this Act, be unrestricted; but any Act of the Parliament of Canada making Provision for such Uniformity shall not have effect in any Province unless and until it is adopted and enacted as Law by the Legislature thereof.

Old Age Pensions

Legislation respecting old age pensions and supplementary benefits

94A. The Parliament of Canada may make laws in relation to old age pensions and supplementary benefits, including survivors' and disability benefits irrespective of age, but no such law shall affect the operation of any law present or future of a provincial legislature in relation to any such matter.

Agriculture and Immigration

Concurrent Powers of Legislation respecting Agriculture, etc.

95. In each Province the Legislature may make Laws in relation to Agriculture in the Province, and to Immigration into the Province; and it is hereby declared that the Parliament of Canada may from Time to Time make Laws in relation to Agriculture in all or any of the Provinces, and to Immigration into all or any of the Provinces; and any Law of the Legislature of a Province relative to Agriculture or to Immigration shall have effect in and for the Province as long and as far only as it is not repugnant to any Act of the Parliament of Canada.

VII. JUDICATURE

Appointment of Judges

96. The Governor General shall appoint the Judges of the Superior, District, and County Courts in each Province, except those of the Courts of Probate in Nova Scotia and New Brunswick.

Selection of Judges in Ontario, etc.

97. Until the Laws relative to Property and Civil Rights in Ontario, Nova Scotia, and New Brunswick, and the Procedure of the Courts in those Provinces, are made uniform, the Judges of the Courts of those Provinces appointed by the Governor General shall be selected from the respective Bars of those Provinces.

98. The Judges of the Courts of Quebec shall be selected from the Bar of that Province.

99. The Judges of the Supreme Courts shall hold Office during good Behaviour, but shall be removable by the Governor General on Address of the Senate and the House of Commons.

99. (1) Subject to subsection two of this section, the Judges of the Superior Courts shall hold office during good behaviour, but shall be removable by the Governor General on Address of the Senate and House of Commons.

(2) A Judge of a Superior Court, whether appointed before or after the coming into force of this section, shall cease to hold office upon attaining the age of seventy-five years, or upon the coming into force of this section if at that time he has already attained that age.

[Note: Section 99 (in italics) was repealed and the new section substituted by the *Constitution Act, 1960.*]

100. The Salaries, Allowances, and Pensions of the Judges of the Superior, District, and County Courts (except the Courts of Probate in Nova Scotia and New Brunswick), and of the Admiralty Courts in Cases where the Judges thereof are for the Time being paid by Salary, shall be fixed and provided by the Parliament of Canada.

101. The Parliament of Canada may, notwithstanding anything in this Act, from Time to Time provide for the Constitution, Maintenance, and Organization of a General Court of Appeal for Canada, and for the Establishment of any additional Courts for the better Administration of the Laws of Canada.

Selection of Judges in Quebec

Tenure of office of Judges

Termination at age 75

Salaries, etc., of Judges

General Court of Appeal, etc.

IX. MISCELLANEOUS PROVISIONS
General

132. The Parliament and Government of Canada shall have all Powers necessary or proper for performing the Obligations of Canada or of any Province thereof, as Part of the British Empire, towards Foreign Countries, arising under Treaties between the Empire and such Foreign Countries.

133. Either the English or the French Language may be used by any Person in the Debates of the Houses of the Parliament of Canada and of the Houses of the Legislature of Quebec; and both those Languages shall be used in the respective Records and Journals of those Houses; and either of those Languages may be used by any Person or in any Pleading or Process in or issuing from any Court of Canada established under this Act, and in or from all or any of the Courts of Quebec.

The Acts of the Parliament of Canada and of the Legislature of Quebec shall be printed and published in both those Languages.

Treaty Obligations

Use of English and French Languages

Appendix B
Constitution Act, 1982
SCHEDULE B

PART I
CANADIAN CHARTER OF RIGHTS AND FREEDOMS

Whereas Canada is founded upon principles that recognize the supremacy of God and the rule of law:

Guarantee of Rights and Freedoms

Rights and free-
doms in Canada

1. The *Canadian Charter of Rights and Freedoms* guarantees the rights and freedoms set out in it subject only to such reasonable limits prescribed by law as can be demonstrably justified in a free and democratic society.

Fundamental Freedoms

Fundamental
freedoms

2. Everyone has the following fundamental freedoms:
(a) freedom of conscience and religion;
(b) freedom of thought, belief, opinion and expression, including freedom of the press and other media of communication;
(c) freedom of peaceful assembly; and
(d) freedom of association.

Democratic Rights

Democratic rights
of citizens

3. Every citizen of Canada has the right to vote in an election of members of the House of Commons or of a legislative assembly and to be qualified for membership therein.

4. (1) No House of Commons and no legislative assembly shall continue for longer than five years from the date fixed for the return of the writs at a general election of its members.

    (2) In time of real or apprehended war, invasion or insurrection, a House of Commons may be continued by Parliament and a legislative assembly may be continued by the legislature beyond five years if such continuation is not opposed by the votes of more than one-third of the members of the House of Commons or the legislative assembly, as the case may be.

5. There shall be a sitting of Parliament and of each legislature at least once every twelve months.

Maximum duration of legislative bodies

Continuation in special circumstances

Annual sitting of legislative bodies

Mobility Rights

6. (1) Every citizen of Canada has the right to enter, remain in and leave Canada.

    (2) Every citizen of Canada and every person who has the status of a permanent resident of Canada has the right

        (a) to move to and take up residence in any province; and

        (b) to pursue the gaining of a livelihood in any province

    (3) The rights specified in subsection (2) are subject to

        (a) any laws or practices of general application in force in a province other than those that discriminate among persons primarily on the basis of province of present or previous residence; and

        (b) any laws providing for reasonable residency requirements as a qualification for the receipt of publicly provided social services.

    (4) Subsections (2) and (3) do not preclude any law, program or activity that has as its object the amelioration in a province of conditions of individuals in that province who are socially or economically disadvantaged if the rate of employment in that province is below the rate of employment in Canada.

Mobility of citizens

Rights to move and gain livelihood

Limitation

Affirmative action programs

Legal Rights

7. Everyone has the right to life, liberty and security of the person and the right not to be deprived thereof except in accordance with the principles of fundamental justice.

8. Everyone has the right to be secure against unreasonable search or seizure.

9. Everyone has the right not to be arbitrarily detained or imprisoned.

10. Everyone has the right on arrest or detention

    (a) to be informed promptly of the reasons therefor;

    (b) to retain and instruct counsel without delay and to be informed of that right; and

    (c) to have the validity of the detention determined by way of *habeas corpus* and to be released if the detention is not lawful.

11. Any person charged with an offence has the right

    (a) to be informed without unreasonable delay of the specific offence;

    (b) to be tried within a reasonable time;

Life, liberty and security of person

Search or seizure

Detention or imprisonment

Arrest or detention

Proceedings in criminal and penal matters

(c) not to be compelled to be a witness in proceedings against that person in respect of the offence;

(d) to be presumed innocent until proven guilty according to law in a fair and public hearing by an independent and impartial tribunal;

(e) not to be denied reasonable bail without just cause;

(f) except in the case of an offence under military law tried before a military tribunal, to the benefit of trial by jury where the maximum punishment for the offence is imprisonment for five years or a more severe punishment;

(g) not to be found guilty on account of any act or omission unless, at the time of the act or omission, it constituted an offence under Canadian or international law or was criminal according to the general principles of law recognized by the community of nations;

(h) if finally acquitted of the offence, not to be tried for it again and, if finally found guilty and punished for the offence, not to be tried or punished for it again; and

(i) if found guilty of the offence and if the punishment for the offence has been varied between the time of commission and the time of sentencing, to the benefit of the lesser punishment.

Treatment or punishment   **12.** Everyone has the right not to be subjected to any cruel and unusual treatment or punishment.

Self-incrimination   **13.** A witness who testifies in any proceedings has the right not to have any incriminating evidence so given used to incriminate that witness in any other proceedings, except in a prosecution for perjury or for the giving of contradictory evidence.

Interpreter   **14.** A party or witness in any proceedings who does not understand or speak the language in which the proceedings are conducted or who is deaf has the right to the assistance of an interpreter.

Equality Rights

Equality before and under law and equal protection and benefit of law   **15.** (1) Every individual is equal before and under the law and has the right to the equal protection and equal benefit of the law without discrimination and, in particular, without discrimination based on race, national or ethnic origin, colour, religion, sex, age or mental or physical disability.

Affirmative action programs   (2) Subsection (1) does not preclude any law, program or activity that has as its object the amelioration of conditions of disadvantaged individuals or groups including those that are disadvantaged because of race, national or ethnic origin, colour, religion, sex, age or mental or physical disability.

Official Languages of Canada

Official languages of Canada   **16.** (1) English and French are the official languages of Canada and have equality of status and equal rights and privileges as to their use in all institutions of the Parliament and government of Canada.

(2) English and French are the official languages of New Brunswick and have equality of status and equal rights and privileges as to their use in all institutions of the legislature and government of New Brunswick.

Official languages of New Brunswick

(3) Nothing in this Charter limits the authority of Parliament or a legislature to advance the equality of status or use of English and French.

Advancement of status and use

17. (1) Everyone has the right to use English or French in any debates and other proceedings of Parliament.

Proceedings of Parliament

(2) Everyone has the right to use English or French in any debates and other proceedings of the legislature of New Brunswick.

Proceedings of New Brunswick legislature

18. (1) The statutes, records and journals of Parliament shall be printed and published in English and French and both language versions are equally authoritative.

Parliamentary statutes and records

(2) The statutes, records and journals of the legislature of New Brunswick shall be printed and published in English and French and both language versions are equally authoritative.

New Brunswick statutes and records

19. (1) Either English or French may be used by any person in, or in any pleading in or process issuing from, any court established by Parliament.

Proceedings in courts established by Parliament

(2) Either English or French may be used by any person in, or in any pleading in or process issuing from, any court of New Brunswick.

Proceedings in New Brunswick courts

20. (1) Any member of the public in Canada has the right to communicate with, and to receive available services from, any head or central office of an institution of the Parliament or government of Canada in English or French, and has the same right with respect to any other office of any such institution where

Communications by public with federal institutions

(a) there is a significant demand for communications with and services from that office in such language; or

(b) due to the nature of the office, it is reasonable that communications with and services from that office be available in both English and French.

(2) Any member of the public in New Brunswick has the right to communicate with, and to receive available services from, any office of an institution of the legislature or government of New Brunswick in English or French.

Communications by public with New Brunswick institutions

21. Nothing in sections 16 to 20 abrogates or derogates from any right, privilege or obligation with respect to the English and French languages, or either of them, that exists or is continued by virtue of any other provision of the Constitution of Canada.

Continuation of existing constitutional provisions

22. Nothing in sections 16 to 20 abrogates or derogates from any legal or customary right or privilege acquired or enjoyed either before or after the coming into force of this Charter with respect to any language that is not English or French.

Rights and privileges preserved

Minority Language Educational Rights

23. (1) Citizens of Canada

Language of instruction

(a) whose first language learned and still understood is that of the English or French linguistic minority population of the province in which they reside, or

(b) who have received their primary school instruction in Canada in English or French and reside in a province where the language in which they received that instruction is the language of the English or French linguistic minority population of the province, have the right to have their children receive primary and secondary school instruction in that language in that province.

Continuity of language instruction

(2) Citizens of Canada of whom any child has received or is receiving primary or secondary school instruction in English or French in Canada, have the right to have all their children receive primary and secondary school instruction in the same language.

Application where numbers warrant

(3) The right of citizens of Canada under subsections (1) and (2) to have their children receive primary and secondary school instruction in the language of the English or French linguistic minority population of a province

(a) applies wherever in the province the number of children of citizens who have such a right is sufficient to warrant the provision to them out of public funds of minority language instruction; and

(b) includes, where the number of those children so warrants, the right to have them receive that instruction in minority language educational facilities provided out of public funds.

Enforcement

Enforcement of guaranteed rights and freedoms

24. (1) Anyone whose rights or freedoms, as guaranteed by this Charter, have been infringed or denied may apply to a court of competent jurisdiction to obtain such remedy as the court considers appropriate and just in the circumstances.

Exclusion of evidence bringing administration of justice into disrepute

(2) Where, in proceedings under subsection (1), a court concludes that evidence was obtained in a manner that infringed or denied any rights or freedoms guaranteed by this Charter, the evidence shall be excluded if it is established that, having regard to all the circumstances, the admission of it in the proceedings would bring the administration of justice into disrepute.

General

Aboriginal rights and freedoms not affected by Charter

25. The guarantee in this Charter of certain rights and freedoms shall not be construed so as to abrogate or derogate from any aboriginal, treaty or other rights or freedoms that pertain to the aboriginal peoples of Canada including

(a) any rights or freedoms that have been recognized by the Royal Proclamation of October 7, 1763;

(b) *any rights or freedoms that may be acquired by the aboriginal peoples of Canada by way of land claims settlement;* and

(b) any rights or freedoms that now exist by way of land claims agreements or may be so acquired.

[Note: Paragraph 25(*b*) (in italics) was repealed and the new paragraph substituted by the *Constitution Amendment Proclamation, 1983.*]

Other rights and freedoms not affected by Charter

26. The guarantee in this Charter of certain rights and freedoms shall not be construed as denying the existence of any other rights or freedoms that exist in Canada.

Multicultural heritage

27. This Charter shall be interpreted in a manner consistent with the preservation and enhancement of the multicultural heritage of Canadians.

Rights guaranteed equally to both sexes

28. Notwithstanding anything in this Charter, the rights and freedoms referred to in it are guaranteed equally to male and female persons.

29. Nothing in this Charter abrogates or derogates from any rights or privileges guaranteed by or under the Constitution of Canada in respect of denominational, separate or dissentient schools.

30. A reference in this Charter to a Province or to the legislative assembly or legislature of a province shall be deemed to include a reference to the Yukon Territory and the Northwest Territories, or to the appropriate legislative authority thereof, as the case may be.

31. Nothing in this Charter extends the legislative powers of any body or authority.

Application of Charter

32. (1) This Charter applies
   (a) to the Parliament and government of Canada in respect of all matters within the authority of Parliament including all matters relating to the Yukon Territory and Northwest Territories; and
   (b) to the legislature and government of each province in respect of all matters within the authority of the legislature of each province.

   (2) Notwithstanding subsection (1), section 15 shall not have effect until three years after this section comes into force.

33. (1) Parliament or the legislature of a province may expressly declare in an Act of Parliament or of the legislature, as the case may be, that the Act or a provision thereof shall operate notwithstanding a provision included in section 2 or sections 7 to 15 of this Charter.

   (2) An Act or a provision of an Act in respect of which a declaration made under this section is in effect shall have such operation as it would have but for the provision of this Charter referred to in the declaration.

   (3) A declaration made under subsection (1) shall cease to have effect five years after it comes into force or on such earlier date as may be specified in the declaration.

   (4) Parliament or the legislature of a province may re-enact a declaration made under subsection (1).

   (5) Subsection (3) applies in respect of a re-enactment made under subsection (4).

Citation

34. This Part may be cited as the *Canadian Charter of Rights and Freedoms*.

PART II
RIGHTS OF THE ABORIGINAL PEOPLES OF CANADA

35. (1) The existing aboriginal and treaty rights of the aboriginal peoples of Canada are hereby recognized and affirmed.

Definition of "aboriginal peoples of Canada"

(2) In this Act, "aboriginal peoples of Canada" includes the Indian, Inuit and Métis peoples of Canada.

Land claims agreements

(3) For greater certainty, in subsection (1) "treaty rights" includes rights that now exist by way of land claims agreements or may be so acquired.

Aboriginal and treaty rights are guaranteed equally to both sexes

(4) Notwithstanding any other provision of this Act, the aboriginal and treaty rights referred to in subsection (1) are guaranteed equally to male and female persons.

35.1 The government of Canada and the provincial governments are committed to the principle that, before any amendment is made to Class 24 of section 91 of the "*Constitution Act, 1867*", to section 25 of this Act or to this Part,

(a) a constitutional conference that includes in its agenda an item relating to the proposed amendment, composed of the Prime Minister of Canada and the first ministers of the provinces, will be convened by the Prime Minister of Canada; and

(b) the Prime Minister of Canada will invite representative of the aboriginal peoples of Canada to participate in the discussions on that item.

PART III
EQUALIZATION AND REGIONAL DISPARITIES

Commitment to promote equal opportunities

36. (1) Without altering the legislative authority of Parliament or of the provincial legislatures, or the rights of any of them with respect to the exercise of their legislative authority, Parliament and the legislatures, together with the government of Canada and the provincial governments, are committed to

(a) promoting equal opportunities for the well-being of Canadians;

(b) furthering economic development to reduce disparity in opportunities; and

(c) providing essential public services of reasonable quality to all Canadians.

Commitment respecting public services

(2) Parliament and the government of Canada are committed to the principle of making equalization payments to ensure that provincial governments have sufficient revenues to provide reasonably comparable levels of public services at reasonably comparable levels of taxation.

PART IV
CONSTITUTIONAL CONFERENCE

Constitutional conference

37. (1) A constitutional conference composed of the Prime Minister of Canada and the first ministers of the provinces shall be convened by the Prime Minister of Canada within one year after this Part comes into force.

Participation of aboriginal peoples

(2) The conference convened under subsection (1) shall have included in its agenda an item respecting constitutional matters that directly affect the aboriginal peoples of Canada, including the identification and definition of the rights of those peoples to be included in the Constitution of Canada, and the Prime Minister of Canada shall invite representatives of those peoples to participate in the discussions on that item.

(3) The Prime Minister of Canada shall invite elected representatives of the governments of the Yukon Territory and the Northwest Territories to participate in the discussions on any item on the agenda of the conference convened under subsection (1) that, in the opinion of the Prime Minister, directly affects the Yukon Territory and the Northwest Territories.

Participation of territories

....

PART V
PROCEDURE FOR AMENDING CONSTITUTION OF CANADA

38. (1) An amendment to the Constitution of Canada may be made by proclamation issued by the Governor General under the Great Seal of Canada where so authorized by

General procedure for amending Constitution

    (a) resolutions of the Senate and House of Commons; and

    (b) resolutions of the legislative assemblies of at least two-thirds of the provinces that have, in the aggregate, according to the then latest general census, at least fifty per cent of the population of all the provinces.

Majority of members

(2) An amendment made under subsection (1) that derogates from the legislative powers, the proprietary rights or any other rights or privileges of the legislature or government of a province shall require a resolution supported by a majority of the members of each of the Senate, the House of Commons and the legislative assemblies required under subsection (1).

(3) An amendment referred to in subsection (2) shall not have effect in a province the legislative assembly of which has expressed its dissent thereto by resolution supported by a majority of its members prior to the issue of the proclamation to which the amendment relates unless that legislative assembly, subsequently, by resolution supported by a majority of its members, revokes its dissent and authorizes the amendment.

Expression of dissent

(4) A resolution of dissent made for the purposes of subsection (3) may be revoked at any time before or after the issue of the proclamation to which it relates.

Revocation of proclamation

39. (1) A proclamation shall not be issued under subsection 38(1) before the expiration of one year from the adoption of the resolution initiating the amendment procedure thereunder, unless the legislative assembly of each province has previously adopted a resolution of assent or dissent.

Restriction on proclamation

(2) A proclamation shall not be issued under subsection 38(1) after the expiration of three years from the adoption of the resolution initiating the amendment procedure thereunder.

Idem

40. Where an amendment is made under subsection 38(1) that transfers provincial legislative powers relating to education or other cultural matters from provincial legislatures to Parliament, Canada shall provide reasonable compensation to any province to which the amendment does not apply.

Compensation

41. An amendment to the Constitution of Canada in relation to the following matters may be made by proclamation issued by the Governor General under the Great Seal of Canada only where authorized by resolutions of the Senate and House of Commons and of the legislative assembly of each province:

Amendment by unanimous consent

(a) the office of the Queen, the Governor General and the Lieutenant Governor of a province;

(b) the right of a province to a number of members in the House of Commons not less than the number of Senators by which the province is entitled to be represented at the time this Part comes into force;

(c) subject to section 43, the use of the English or the French language;

(d) the composition of the Supreme Court of Canada; and

(e) an amendment to this Part.

Amendment by general procedure

42. (1) An amendment to the Constitution of Canada in relation to the following matters may be made only in accordance with subsection 38(1):

(a) the principle of proportionate representation of the provinces in the House of Commons prescribed by the Constitution of Canada;

(b) the powers of the Senate and the method of selecting Senators;

(c) the number of members by which a province is entitled to be represented in the Senate and the residence qualifications of Senators;

(d) subject to paragraph 41(d), the Supreme Court of Canada;

(e) the extension of existing provinces into the territories; and

(f) notwithstanding any other law or practice, the establishment of new provinces.

Exception

(2) Subsections 38(2) to (4) do not apply in respect of amendments in relation to matters referred to in subsection (1).

Amendment of provisions relating to some but not all provinces

43. An amendment to the Constitution of Canada in relation to any provision that applies to one or more, but not all, provinces, including

(a) any alteration to boundaries between provinces, and

(b) any amendment to any provision that relates to the use of the English or the French language within a province,

may be made by proclamation issued by the Governor General under the Great Seal of Canada only where so authorized by resolutions of the Senate and House of Commons and of the legislative assembly of each province to which the amendment applies.

Amendments by Parliament

44. Subject to sections 41 and 42, Parliament may exclusively make laws amending the Constitution of Canada in relation to the executive government of Canada or the Senate and House of Commons.

Amendments by provincial legislatures

45. Subject to section 41, the legislature of each province may exclusively make laws amending the constitution of the province.

Initiation of amendment procedures

46. (1) The procedures for amendment under sections 38, 41, 42 and 43 may be initiated either by the Senate or the House of Commons or by the legislative assembly of a province.

Revocation of authorization

(2) A resolution of assent made for the purposes of this Part may be revoked at any time before the issue of a proclamation authorized by it.

Amendments without Senate resolution

47. (1) An amendment to the Constitution of Canada made by proclamation under section 38, 41, 42 or 43 may be made without a resolution of the Senate authorizing the issue of the proclamation if, within one hundred and eighty days after the adoption by the House of Commons of a resolution authorizing its issue, the Senate has not adopted such a resolution and if, at any time after the expiration of that period, the House of Commons again adopts the resolution.

(2) Any period when Parliament is prorogued or dissolved shall not be counted in computing the one hundred and eighty day period referred to in subsection (1).

Computation of period

48. The Queen's Privy Council for Canada shall advise the Governor General to issue a proclamation under this Part forthwith on the adoption of the resolutions required for an amendment made by proclamation under this Part.

Advice to issue proclamation

49. A constitutional conference composed of the Prime Minister of Canada and the first ministers of the provinces shall be convened by the Prime Minister of Canada within fifteen years after this Part comes into force to review the provisions of this Part.

Constitutional conference

PART VI
AMENDMENT TO THE CONSTITUTION ACT, 1867

50. [See section 92A of the Constitution Act, 1867]

51. The said Act is further amended by adding thereto the following Schedule:

"THE SIXTH SCHEDULE"

Primary Production from Non-Renewable Natural Resources and Forestry Resources

1. For the purposes of Section 92A of this Act,
   (a) production from a non-renewable natural resource is primary production therefrom if
     (i) it is in the form in which it exists upon its recovery or severance from its natural state, or
     (ii) it is a product resulting from processing or refining the resource, and is not a manufactured product or a product resulting from refining crude oil, refining upgraded heavy crude oil, refining gases or liquids derived from coal or refining a synthetic equivalent of crude oil; and
   (b) production from a forestry resource is primary production therefrom if it consists of sawlogs, poles, lumber, wood chips, sawdust or any other primary wood product, or wood pulp, and is not a product manufactured from wood."

PART VII
GENERAL

52. (1) The Constitution of Canada is the supreme law of Canada, and any law that is inconsistent with the provisions of the Constitution is, to the extent of the inconsistency, of no force or effect.

Primacy of Constitution of Canada

(2) The Constitution of Canada includes
   (a) the *Canada Act 1982*, including this Act;
   (b) the Acts and orders referred to in the schedule; and

(c) any amendment to any Act or order referred to in paragraph (a) or (b).

Amendments to Constitution of Canada

(3) Amendments to the Constitution of Canada shall be made only in accordance with the authority contained in the Constitution of Canada.

Repeals and new names

53. (1) The enactments referred to in Column I of the schedule are hereby repealed or amended to the extent indicated in Column II thereof and, unless repealed, shall continue as law in Canada under the names set out in Column III thereof.

Consequential amendments

(2) Every enactment, except the *Canada Act 1982*, that refers to an enactment referred to in the schedule by the name in Column I thereof is hereby amended by substituting for that name the corresponding name in Column III thereof, and any British North America Act not referred to in the schedule may be cited as the *Constitution Act* followed by the year and number, if any, of its enactment.

Repeal and consequential amendments

54. Part IV is repealed on the day that is one year after this Part comes into force and this section may be repealed and this Act renumbered, consequentially upon the repeal of Part IV and this section, by proclamation issued by the Governor General under the Great Seal of Canada.

54. (1) *Part IV.1 and this section are repealed on April 18, 1987.*

[Note: Added by the *Constitution Amendment Proclamation, 1983.*]

French version of Constitution of Canada

55. A French version of the portions of the Constitution of Canada referred to in the schedule shall be prepared by the Minister of Justice of Canada as expeditiously as possible and, when any portion thereof sufficient to warrant action being taken has been so prepared, it shall be put forward for enactment by proclamation issued by the Governor General under the Great Seal of Canada pursuant to the procedure then applicable to an amendment of the same provisions of the Constitution of Canada.

English and French versions of certain constitutional texts

56. Where any portion of the Constitution of Canada has been or is enacted in English and French or where a French version of any portion of the Constitution is enacted pursuant to section 55, the English and French versions of that portion of the Constitution are equally authoritative.

English and French versions of this Act

57. The English and French versions of this Act are equally authoritative.

Commencement

58. Subject to section 59, this Act shall come into force on a day to be fixed by proclamation issued by the Queen or the Governor General under the Great Seal of Canada.

Commencement of paragraph 23(1)(a) in respect of Quebec

59. (1) Paragraph 23(1)(a) shall come into force in respect of Quebec on a day to be fixed by proclamation issued by the Queen or the Governor General under the Great Seal of Canada.

Authorization of Quebec

(2) A proclamation under subsection (1) shall be issued only where authorized by the legislative assembly or government of Quebec.

Repeal of this section

(3) This section may be repealed on the day paragraph 23(1)(a) comes into force in respect of Quebec and this Act amended and renumbered, consequentially upon the repeal of this section, by proclamation issued by the Queen or the Governor General under the Great Seal of Canada.

Short title and citations

60. This Act may be cited as the *Constitution Act, 1982*, and the Constitution Acts 1867 to 1975 (No. 2) and this Act may be cited together as the *Constitution Acts, 1867 to 1982*.

61. A reference to the "*Constitution Acts, 1867 to 1982*" shall be deemed to include a reference to the "*Constitutional Amendment Proclamation, 1983.*"

Index

A

Aberhart, William, 202, 287

Aboriginal Canadians, 6, 50, 63–80, 129, 169, 204, 215, 264, 278, 355, 390–91, 431, 480, 521–23, 571, 599, 611

Aboriginal land claims (including Aboriginal title), 50, 69–73, 442–43

Aboriginal self-government, 23, 63, 71, 73, 75–78, 389

Abortion, 129, 131, 233, 356, 359, 437, 447, 493, 553, 555, 575, 592

Access to Information Act, 243, 534, 593, 616

Accumulation, 14, 19, 145, 471

Act of Union, 25

Administrative agencies, 485, 513–15, 529, 531, 589, 592

Advocacy advertising, 233, 355, 616

Affirmative action, 112, 125, 440–41, 520–21

Agenda-setting, 160, 239, 247, 358, 366, 484, 503, 559, 566, 616

Agents of political socialization, 230–34, 248

Agreement on Internal Trade, 420

Agriculture, 49, 168–69, 345, 352, 403. *See also* Farmers

Air Canada, airlines, and airports, 42, 171, 364, 407, 470, 528–29, 538, 556, 572, 576

Alaska Boundary Dispute, 32

Alberta, 96, 132, 158, 215, 218, 287, 295, 311, 376, 390, 410, 412, 415, 424, 441, 444, 577–78. *See also* Prairie Provinces; West

Alberta Press Bill, 202, 381, 431

Allaire Report, 93, 382, 387

Alliance of Manufacturers and Exporters Canada, 343, 345

Alternative Dispute Resolution, 591

Alternative Service Delivery, 537–38

Anti-combines legislation, 145–46, 235, 439, 587, 602

Appointments and contracts, 4, 388, 478, 482, 485, 490, 496, 520, 561, 613

Armed forces and defence, 26, 72, 91, 120, 125, 173–74, 470, 513

Asia-Pacific Economic Cooperation (APEC), 16, 169, 243, 486

Assembly of First Nations (AFN), 68, 74, 79, 343, 346

Atlantic provinces, 25–26, 29, 41, 47–48, 54, 58–59, 214, 322, 335, 420, 569, 594. *See also individual provinces*

Atomic Energy of Canada Ltd. (AECL) and Atomic Energy Control Board (AECB), 178–79, 470, 527–28, 530

Auditor General and Public Accounts Committee, 533, 562

Authority and authorities, 4–7, 13, 16–19, 241, 247, 461, 465

Auto Pact, 181, 187

Axworthy, Lloyd, 175, 278, 490

B

Backbenchers, 546, 551–55, 560, 563, 568–69

Ballot, 262–63

Bank of Canada, 158, 178, 470, 527–28, 574, 577

Banks and banking, 47, 52, 143, 176, 179, 276, 343, 353, 358, 364, 424, 555, 574, 615

Bélanger–Campeau Report, 93, 382, 387

Bennett, R.B., 156, 270, 286–87, 298, 309, 485, 487–88, 494

Berger, Thomas, 68, 601

Bilingualism (including Official Languages Act), 6–7, 25, 84–90, 92, 95–98, 111, 202, 210, 375, 379–80, 383–84, 386, 404, 419, 441, 519, 521, 532, 547, 595, 603

Bill of Rights, 128, 377, 381, 430–32, 586

Bills, 463–64, 555–58
    government, 549–51, 555, 568
    money (supply), 374, 477, 482–83, 556, 570, 577
    private, 4, 556, 572
    private members', 547, 549–51, 554–56, 567–69, 576

Black, Conrad, 235–36, 616

Blacks, 106, 108, 110, 115, 431, 571

Bloc Québécois (BQ), 5, 93, 219, 266–68, 272–74, 289–90, 294–97, 305–7, 310, 321–24, 326–27, 332–35, 615

Bond-rating agencies, 183

Books, 185, 188–89

Borden, R.L., 32–33, 86, 120, 285–86, 487–88, 557

Bouchard, Lucien, 93–94, 298, 305–6, 391–93, 422

Bourassa, Robert, 91–93, 98, 384, 444

Bourgeoisie. *See* Corporate elite; Upper class; Business influence; Corporations

Bourgon, Jocelyn, 498, 538

Bowell, Mackenzie, 285, 487–89

British Columbia, 32, 41, 71, 182, 264, 287, 305, 375, 390, 415, 431, 436, 569

British North America Act (BNA Act). *See* Constitution Act, 1867

British parliamentary system. *See* Westminster model

Broadbent, Ed, 298

Brokerage, 11, 290–91, 306, 336

Bronfman family, 142–45, 244

Budget, 492, 495, 499, 501–2, 549, 561, 566, 568

Bureaucracy, 4, 17–19, 27–28, 73, 79, 124–25, 133, 153, 160–61, 207, 222, 293, 301, 306, 310, 342, 350–53, 359, 362, 401, 411, 418–19, 423, 435, 443, 460, 462–66, 471, 475, 483, 485–86, 493, 497, 503, 511–40, 557, 559, 561, 565–66, 614, 616

Business Council on National Issues (BCNI), 147, 181, 336, 358, 364, 366, 394, 471, 540

Business influence, 6, 11–12, 14–16, 18–19, 52–53, 59–60, 80, 88, 97, 116, 125, 141–47, 158–59, 171–73, 181, 187–88, 191, 343–45, 353–54, 358, 366, 424, 448–49, 492, 531, 571, 573–74, 576.

See also Corporations; Corporate elite

C

Cabinet, 4, 24, 27, 262, 269, 350, 353–54, 374, 378, 388, 401–4, 462–66, 475–504, 513, 524, 526–27, 531–33, 545–46, 552–53, 555–56, 562, 566, 568–69, 571, 573, 577–79, 590, 594, 596–97, 614

    Cabinet committees, 419, 465, 484–85, 492–502

    Departmental and institutionalized cabinets, 419, 493–95

    Secrecy, solidarity, and collective responsibility, 492–93

Caisse de Dépôt et Placement du Québec, 49

Calgary Declaration, 98, 382, 392, 394

Callbeck, Catherine, 124

Campbell, Kim, 124, 288, 298, 303, 327, 488, 496, 514, 536

Canada Act, 376

Canada Assistance Plan (CAP), 156, 158, 410–12, 420, 525

Canada Clause, 129, 210, 388

Canada Council on the Arts, 189, 478, 528

Canada Customs and Revenue Agency, 537–38

Canada Elections Act, 201, 247, 264, 271, 277–78, 377, 435–36

Canada Health Act, 412, 420–21, 540

Canada Health and Social Transfer, 158, 412, 414–15, 421

Canada Pension Plan (CPP), 88–89, 132, 156, 288, 576. *See also* Pensions

Canada–U.S. Free Trade Agreement, 52, 158, 170, 179, 181, 183, 234, 276–77, 289, 332–33, 345, 356, 366, 420, 532, 572, 575

Canada's Research-Based Pharmaceutical Companies, 343, 355, 361, 364

Canadian Auto Workers (CAW), 150, 184, 277

Canadian Bar Association (CBA), 343, 346, 353, 358, 598, 602

Canadian Broadcasting Corporation (CBC), including Radio-Canada, 43, 185–86, 236–39, 242–43, 308, 325, 470, 527–28, 611, 616

Canadian Centre for Policy Alternatives, 163, 234, 348

Canadian Chamber of Commerce, 5, 343, 345, 349, 354, 357–58

Canadian Conference of Catholic Bishops, 344, 346

Canadian Council on Social Development, 154, 156, 159, 344, 347, 353

Canadian culture, 43, 67, 110–11, 184–90, 215, 236–39, 528

Canadian Federation of Agriculture, 343, 345–46, 352–53, 359

Canadian Federation of Independent Business (CFIB), 343, 345

Canadian Federation of Students (CFS), 343, 348, 355–57, 359, 364. *See also* Students; Postsecondary education

Canadian Food Inspection Agency, 537–38

Canadian Human Rights Act and Commission, 112, 132, 377, 521, 530, 593

Canadian Labour Congress (CLC), 5, 152, 159, 192, 233, 275, 277, 288, 292, 343, 346, 348–49, 355–58

Canadian Manufacturers' Association. *See* Alliance of Manufacturers and Exporters Canada

Canadian Medical Association, 233, 343, 346, 349, 352–53, 355, 359

Canadian national identity, 199–213, 231, 528. *See also* National symbols

Canadian National Railway (CNR), 41, 276, 308, 470, 526, 529

Canadian nationalism, 178–79, 183–91

Canadian Pacific Railway (CPR). *See* Railways

Canadian Press (CP), 239, 241

Canadian Radio-television and Telecommunications Commission (CRTC), 43, 115, 145, 186, 236–39, 483, 530–31, 616

Canadian Security Intelligence Service (CSIS), 531–32, 572, 593

Canadian Television Network (CTV), 237

Canadian Union of Public Employees (CUPE), 150, 277

Canadian Wheat Board, 51, 528–29, 576

Candidates, 271–74, 283, 320–21, 329–32, 570, 597–98

Capital punishment, 248, 493, 553, 565

Caucus (Party), 295, 298, 306, 354, 462–64, 478, 487, 501, 549, 553, 555, 565, 573

C.D. Howe Institute, 181–82, 234, 336, 366, 394, 540

Central agencies, 401, 419, 465, 495–503

Charest, Jean, 94, 296–99, 300–1, 322, 328, 393

Charlottetown Accord, 74–75, 93, 115, 129, 382, 388–89, 415, 420, 570, 577–78, 595, 599

Charter groups, 128–29, 203, 385, 447, 611

Charter of Rights and Freedoms, 30, 112, 128, 190, 201–3, 208, 210, 212, 289, 294, 354, 377, 380–81, 383, 405, 429, 432–49, 464, 534, 546, 585, 587, 589, 594, 611

 section 1 (reasonable limits), 277–78, 433–34

 section 2 (fundamental freedoms), 92, 243, 247, 275, 429, 434–36, 443

 section 3 (democratic rights), 260, 264, 436–37, 444

 section 6 (mobility rights), 437, 444

 sections 7–14 (legal rights), 429, 437–40, 443

 section 15 (equality rights), 112, 128, 132, 429, 440–41, 444

 sections 16–23 (language rights), 92, 94, 441–42, 444

 sections 25 and 35 (Aboriginal rights), 73–75, 76, 377, 389, 442–43

 section 33 (notwithstanding clause), 92, 128, 202–3, 432–33, 443–44, 546, 554

Chief Electoral Officer, 262, 277

Chief Justice, 478, 595–96, 598, 601

Children and child care, 120, 122, 127–28, 130, 154, 156, 158, 421, 436

Chrétien, Jean, 41, 43, 52, 76, 92–93, 98, 114, 128, 131, 145, 152, 154, 158, 171, 174, 186, 191, 237, 263, 298–301, 306, 310–11, 320, 323, 326, 328, 362, 365–66, 384, 391–92, 418, 420–21, 470, 487–92, 495–99, 501, 503–4, 514, 516, 520, 527, 536, 554–55, 613–14, 616–17

Churches. *See* Religion; Roman Catholic Church in Quebec

Churchill Falls, 55

Cities, 45, 67, 78–79, 108, 115

Citizens' Forum, 382, 387

Civil law, 586, 588–59

Civil law (Quebec), 24, 84, 120, 210, 404, 589, 594–95

Civil liberties, 429–49, 470

Clark, Joe, 288–89, 298–301, 311, 332, 388, 488, 490, 496, 501, 517, 549, 567, 571

Class analysis, 9–10, 12, 14–16, 18–19, 35, 60, 80, 100, 116, 134, 160, 191–92, 222–23, 248–49, 279, 295, 312, 336, 366, 394, 424, 449, 471, 503–4, 540, 579, 602–3. *See also* Class and class consciousness; Middle class; Poverty; Upper class; Working class

Class and class consciousness, 38, 100, 134, 139, 150, 159–60, 206–7, 209, 215–16, 290–92, 294, 334, 357, 446, 522, 540, 547–48

Cleavages, 8, 38, 51–55, 85–87, 98, 139, 160, 311, 334

Clerk of the Privy Council (and Secretary to the Cabinet), 125, 478, 495, 497–99, 514–15, 538, 616–17

Clientele relationship, 352, 358, 526

Coalition government. *See* Union Government

Coercion, 3, 15, 19, 223, 470–71

Collective bargaining, 149–50, 519, 523–24

Collectivism, 64, 204–6, 212, 295, 307–10, 446, 470, 553

Common Law, 34, 430, 586, 589

Commonwealth, 33, 481, 486

Communications, 43–44, 48

Communist Party, 202, 278

Confederation, 25–26, 29–30, 35, 402–4, 569

Confederation of Regions Party (COR), 95–96, 294

Confederation of Tomorrow Conference, 381–82

Conscription, 86–87, 220, 286

Conservatism, 307–10

Conservative Party. *See* Progressive Conservative Party

Constitution, 31, 373–94, 475

Constitution Act, 1867, 26, 32, 64, 84–85, 257, 374–75, 402–4, 431, 441, 477, 482, 571, 575, 587, 590

Constitution Act, 1982, 73–74, 92, 94, 376–77, 379–80, 382–84, 420, 476, 520, 563, 570, 601. *See also* Charter of Rights and Freedoms

Constitutional Act (1791), 24, 84

Constitutional amending formula, 379–80, 383–85, 387, 391–92, 394

Constitutional amendments, 33, 375, 379, 393, 405, 570–72

Constitutional conventions, 378–79, 383, 418, 477, 482, 489–90, 594

Cooperation and cooperatives, 209, 292, 295

Cooperative Commonwealth Federation (CCF), 149, 156, 265, 270, 287–88, 292, 294, 295–96, 308, 410, 567, 576

Cooperative federalism, 418–22, 525

Copps, Sheila, 278, 299, 488

Core-periphery analysis, 44–45, 47, 51, 295

Corporate elite, 35, 97, 100, 139–47, 156, 159–60, 181, 248–49, 275, 424, 471, 503, 540, 573, 579, 615. *See also* Elites and elitism; Business influence; Corporations; Upper class

Corporations, 4–5, 12, 14–16, 29, 41, 43–44, 59, 70, 80, 116, 125, 143–47, 149, 158, 170, 233, 244, 270, 272–73, 275–77, 330, 344, 354–55, 359–66, 408, 434, 446, 448–49, 463, 465–66, 468, 524, 556, 571–72, 587, 602, 615. *See also* Transnational corporations

Corporatism, 79, 354

Council of Canadians, 234, 344, 348, 356

Courts and judges, 16, 124, 132–33, 201, 207, 264–65, 294, 353, 355, 374–75, 379, 402, 430–49, 530, 585–603. *See also* Judiciary and judicial system

Crime, criminal law and Criminal Code, 24, 78, 94, 202, 207, 402, 431, 435–39, 588

Crow Rate. *See* Freight rates

Crown, 26, 31, 475–82

Crown corporations, 41–43, 178, 185, 188, 206, 308, 364, 401, 465, 469–70, 476, 513–15, 520, 526–29, 536, 613

D

d'Aquino, Tom, 147, 345, 366,

Defence. *See* Armed forces and defence

Deference to authority, 202, 207–8, 212, 222

Deficit and debt reduction, 16, 145–47, 157–58, 212, 308, 310, 345, 366, 420, 460–61, 495, 528, 536

Delegated legislation. *See* Regulations

Demands, 3–11, 46–47, 59, 145–55, 293, 342, 400, 461, 467

Democracy, 12, 30–31, 200–3, 211, 215, 248, 446–47, 479, 482, 489, 617

Democratic socialism (including social democracy), 209, 307–10, 517

Department of Finance, 160, 352, 465, 488, 492–95, 499–502, 516, 520, 524–25, 533

Department of Indian Affairs and Northern Development, 76–77

Department of Justice, 466, 488, 492

Depression, 286–87, 292, 406, 409

Deputy Minister, 483, 485, 514–17, 519–20, 523–24, 533, 536–37

Desmarais, Paul, 142–45, 235, 276, 531

Diefenbaker, John, 42, 89, 122, 156, 173–74, 180, 287–88, 298–301, 303, 332, 334, 381, 419, 431–32, 485, 487–89, 494, 517, 567

Diffidence and caution, 209

Disallowance and reservation. *See* Reservation, disallowance and declaratory power

Discrimination, 67, 109–10, 128, 132, 159, 203, 381, 415, 429, 431, 440–41, 446

Dissolution of Parliament, 477–78, 482, 549, 566

Distinct society (Quebec), 89–93, 98, 111, 129, 214, 322, 384–85, 388, 391–92

Division of powers, 29–30, 149, 349, 355, 374, 377, 379, 381, 387, 389, 391–92, 399, 403–8, 418, 430–31, 464, 525, 585, 587, 594. *See also* Federalism

Divorce, 120, 123, 128, 347, 556, 572, 591

Douglas, T.C., 287–88, 298–99

Duceppe, Gilles, 198, 323

Duplessis, Maurice, 88, 202, 243, 287, 431

Durham Report, 25, 84

E

Economic union, 389

Education, 112, 230–31, 250, 401, 404, 434, 443, 612. *See also* Postsecondary education; Students

Egalitarianism, 208–9

Election campaign, 240, 247–48, 319–31, 435, 485, 553, 571, 616
Election platform, 301, 306, 323–24, 485
Elections and electoral system, 200–1, 257–80
Electoral behaviour, 331–35
Electoral reform, 265–70, 614
Electricity, 48–50, 183, 470
Elite accommodation, 20, 222, 353–54, 423, 492, 504, 540
Elites and elitism, 9–11, 14, 20, 237, 240–41, 249, 310, 312, 329, 353, 394, 423–24, 446, 471, 480, 602
Embedded state, 20
Emergency doctrine (and state of emergency), 405–8, 417–18, 470
Employment and pay equity, 112, 122, 125, 521–23, 593
Energy. *See* Electricity; Petroleum; National Energy Program
Environment, 51, 71–72, 141, 145, 150, 171, 182–83, 347, 356, 407, 471
Equality and inequality (in party ideology), 307–10
Equalization payments, 56–58, 377, 384, 412–15, 420, 532
Erasmus, Georges, 74
Established Program Funding (EPF), 411
Estimates, 499, 519, 524–25, 533, 549, 561
Ethnicity, 83–100, 105–16, 215, 264, 297, 334, 343, 346, 352, 431, 490, 571, 599, 611
Europe and European Union, 168, 181–83
Evidence (admissibility of), 207, 442
Executive, 4, 16–17, 19, 27, 210, 353–54, 374, 378, 475–504, 545–46, 553, 563, 569
Executive federalism, 418–19
Exhortation, 467–68
Expenditure Management System, 501–2, 524
Extraterritoriality, 33, 177

F

Fairclough, Ellen, 122
Family, 120, 122, 126–27, 132–33, 156, 230, 591,
Farmers, 52–53, 119, 139, 149, 182, 286, 292, 295, 334, 354. *See also* Agriculture
Federal controls. *See* Reservation, disallowance, and declaratory power
Federal Court of Canada, 377, 521, 534–35, 592–93, 596, 598, 600
Federalism, 26, 29, 46, 210, 304–5, 307, 349–50, 399–424, 430, 447, 587–91, 596, 598. *See also* Division of powers

Federal–provincial conferences and relations, 293, 381–84, 386, 394, 418–19, 423, 484, 495–96, 498–99, 526
Federal–provincial finance, 88–89, 158, 375, 384–85, 403, 408–15
Feminism, 119, 123, 128–29. *See also* Women
Film, 185, 187–88, 433
First Nations, 63, 67–68, 76–77, 364. *See also* Aboriginal Canadians
First World War, 32, 86, 109, 173, 286, 409, 470
First-past-the-post, 263, 265
Fishing and fishing rights, 48, 50, 55, 72, 168, 182–83, 572
Focus groups, 245, 248
Foreign investment, 52, 175–79, 181, 532
Foreign policy, 18, 113, 174–75, 182, 191, 207, 482
Forestry, 49–50, 168, 178, 421
Fragment theory, 204, 307–9
France, 23, 84, 89
Franchise, 67, 120, 149, 264–65, 436, 601
Francophonie, 92, 486
Free votes, 552, 576
Freight rates, 41, 52
Front de Libération du Québec (FLQ), 91, 202, 220, 243, 470
Fundamental freedoms. *See* Charter of Rights and Freedoms

G

G7, G8, 169, 486
General Agreement on Tariffs and Trade. *See* World Trade Organization
Gerrymandering, 258
Globalization, 8, 15, 150, 167, 172, 348
Globe and Mail, 233, 235, 241, 325
Goods and Services Tax (GST), 145, 158, 233–34, 333, 374, 420, 469, 575–76
Gordon, Walter, 191, 503
Government (including state), 3–6, 170, 172, 182, 199, 207, 234, 307–10, 366, 459, 476, 481–82, 536, 545, 552, 562, 565–8, 589
Government advertising, 17, 234, 243, 250, 337, 467–48, 501, 504, 513
Government department, 460, 463, 483, 485, 488, 490, 493–94, 500–2, 513–26, 536–37, 561
Governor General, 27, 33, 261, 374, 378–79, 462, 464, 475–82, 486, 548, 557, 566, 570
Governor in Council, 374, 477, 482

Gray Report and Herb Gray, 176, 178, 191, 488, 491, 496, 532

Great Britain, 23–26, 32–34, 84, 173–75, 180–81, 191, 218, 270, 291, 308–9, 375, 380, 430–31, 476, 480, 486, 489, 553, 555, 558, 562, 570, 586, 596, 613–14, 616

Green papers, 463, 494

Groups and group rights, 11, 206, 219, 233, 283, 311, 341–42, 424. See also Pressure groups

Gulf War, 174–75

Gun control, 207, 554–55, 563, 576

H

Harper, Elijah, 68, 74–75, 386

Harris, Mike, 125, 234, 310, 322–33. See also Ontario

Hatfield, Richard, 95

Health care, 67, 130, 156–59, 190, 206, 212, 288, 308, 349, 352, 401, 410, 412, 418, 420–21, 532, 612

Hill and Knowlton, 245–46, 363

Honours, 478, 480, 482

House of Commons, 26–27, 121–24, 267, 333, 374, 379, 388, 403, 462, 464, 482, 485, 489, 501–2, 533–34, 545–69, 572, 577, 600, 613

committees, 354, 465–66, 502, 549, 552, 554, 556–58, 561–63, 566–69

debates, 556–58, 560–61, 565–67

officials, 559–60

pairing, 560

privilege, 561

remuneration, 563–64, 569, 573

Speaker, 234, 259, 551, 558–60, 562, 564

standing orders, 558, 570

timetable, 548–51

Housing and homelessness, 158–59, 612, 616

Howe, C.D., 42, 191, 488

Human rights codes, 132, 441, 443. See also Canadian Human Rights Act and Commission

I

Ideology. See Party ideology

Immigration (and refugees), 50, 85, 91, 105–9, 112–14, 190, 334, 384–86, 403, 438, 449, 481, 514, 534, 592–93

Immigration and Refugee Board, 114, 530

Income, 56–57, 140, 143, 156, 159, 220, 468

Indian Act, 64, 67, 73–74, 129. See also Aboriginal Canadians

Indians. See Aboriginal Canadians; First Nations

Individualism, 204–6, 307–10, 446, 448

Information Commissioner, 534

Institutionalism, 17, 280

Interest aggregation, 8, 283, 290, 319, 342, 616

Interest articulation, 8, 319, 341–42

Interest groups. See Pressure groups

International Monetary Fund and World Bank, 169

Inuit, 63, 65–66, 77, 79

Iron Law of Oligarchy, 305–6

Irving family, 141–43, 235

Issues, 6, 239, 283, 347–48, 463, 471

J

James Bay Hydro-electric Project, 49, 70–71, 74

Japan, 182

Japanese-Canadians, 109, 112, 202, 381, 431

Jehovah's Witnesses (Quebec), 381, 431

Judicial appointments, 16, 124, 374, 402, 447, 482, 485, 520, 590, 594, 596–99, 613

Judicial Committee of the Privy Council, 33, 377, 405–8, 571–72, 589, 594

Judicial councils, 598, 601–2

Judicial discretion, judicial interpretation, and judicial review, 5, 28, 30, 405–8, 416–17, 430–49, 464, 586–87, 592, 594, 599

Judicial independence, 28, 599–602

Judiciary and judicial system, 4–5, 67, 78, 128, 145, 374, 377, 402, 429, 476, 534, 556, 585–603. See also Courts and judges

K

Kennedy, John, 173

Keynesian economics, 309, 419, 539

King, Mackenzie, 33, 39, 86–87, 121, 270, 286–87, 291, 298, 399, 479, 484, 487–88, 493, 503–4, 567

King–Byng Dispute, 261, 286, 478

Klein, Ralph, 158, 310, 412. See also Alberta

Korean War, 173

L

Labour force, labour movement, and labour legislation, 125–28, 145, 149, 169, 181, 286, 292, 297, 302, 346, 406, 435, 448, 471, 504, 571. See also Working class

Laurier, Wilfrid, 32–33, 86, 284–86, 488

Laws, categories of, 588–89

Leaders' debate, 131, 240, 321, 327–28
Leadership Network, 538
Leadership review, 300
Leaders' tour, 240, 321, 325
Le Devoir, 241–42
Left, 307–8, 571
Legal aid, 439, 587, 602
Legislature, 4, 68, 380, 401, 418, 435, 444, 446–47, 545–69
Legitimacy and legitimation, 4, 7, 15, 19, 213, 319, 342, 350, 464, 471, 547, 574
Lesage, Jean, 88–89, 379
Lévesque, René, 91, 289, 384
Lewis, David, 146, 288, 298–99
Libel, 242, 561
Liberalism, 159, 204, 307–10, 448
Liberal Party, 5, 110, 113, 147, 156, 219, 245–46, 266–76, 278, 285–93, 295–312, 319–23, 331–35, 449, 567, 576
Lieutenant Governor, 374, 379, 400, 403, 477, 520
Lobbying and lobbyists, 147, 190, 201, 246, 341, 353, 359–66, 461, 465, 501, 504, 516, 524, 553, 563, 574, 616
Lougheed, Peter, 181, 242

M

Macdonald, John A., 29–30, 32, 41, 52, 85, 149, 270, 284–85, 377, 402, 407, 416, 478, 488, 491, 569
MacEachen, Allan, 490
Mackenzie, Alexander, 285, 488
Macphail, Agnes, 120
Magazines, 169, 185, 187, 611
Majority government, 27, 265, 269, 566–67
Majority rule, 202–3, 214, 447
Mandate (including absent mandate), 200, 333
Mandate letters, 463, 484, 499, 520
Manitoba, 76, 78, 85, 96, 214, 320, 376, 386, 441, 470. *See also* Prairie provinces; West
Manning, E.C., 287
Manning, Preston, 212, 289, 297–300, 302, 305–6, 311, 322, 335
Manufacturing, 47, 49, 52, 172, 176
Maritime provinces. *See* Atlantic provinces
Marshall, Donald, 72, 78
Martin, Paul (Jr.), 145, 147, 158, 310, 488, 501, 503, 528
Marx, Karl, 14, 139, 148–49
Mass and cadre parties, 295–306

Mass media, 5, 16, 110, 159, 220, 229, 232–33, 234–44, 247–50, 293, 300, 325–27, 329, 347, 461–62, 481, 484, 486, 501, 535, 551, 553, 557, 572, 578, 616. *See also* Newspapers; Television and Radio
Massey, Vincent, and Massey Commission, 189, 476–77
Mazankowski, Don, 488, 490
McDonough, Alexa, 124, 298–99, 310, 322, 335
McLaughlin, Audrey, 124, 298–99
Meech Lake Accord, 68, 93, 98, 128, 289, 380, 382, 384–86, 420, 575, 577, 595, 599
Meighen, Arthur, 285–86, 479, 488, 567
Members of Parliament (MPs), 354, 446, 464, 466, 481, 524, 533, 545–70, 613
Members' statements, 550–51, 566
Memorandum to Cabinet, 243, 462–63, 496–97, 499–501, 520
Merit system, 519–20
Métis, 65–66, 72, 79, 85
Metropolis-Hinterland Analysis. *See* Core-Periphery Analysis
Mexico, 171, 182, 192
Middle class, 15, 89, 97, 100, 139–40, 147–49, 159, 207, 292, 303, 334
Mining, 48–50, 71, 421
Ministerial responsibility, 483, 514, 517
Ministers, 60, 120, 122, 147, 210, 353, 361–62, 366, 418–19, 443, 462–64, 466, 481–84, 492–96, 500–2, 511, 516–17, 519, 524, 527, 533, 540, 550, 557–59, 561, 564, 566, 570, 572
Minor parties, 294
Minority government, 265, 269, 271, 288, 567–68
Minority language education, 84, 86, 92, 94–96, 203, 348, 355, 432, 442, 447–48, 611
Minority rights, 84, 112, 132–33, 202–3, 248, 336, 447, 611
Missiles, 173–74, 437
Monarchy, 27, 31, 33, 207, 376, 379, 475–81, 486
Morgentaler, Henry, 129, 437, 447, 592
Mosaic and melting pot, 115, 206
Mulroney, Brian, 41–43, 53, 74, 92–93, 98, 112, 128–31, 143, 145, 147, 154, 158, 170, 174, 179, 181, 183, 185, 191, 212, 234, 237, 263, 277, 289, 298–301, 308–10, 312, 327, 332, 348, 358–59, 361, 366, 374, 384–87, 390, 412, 418, 420, 447, 449, 470, 477, 485–90, 495–97, 503–4, 516–17, 520, 527–28, 531, 536, 553, 568, 575, 577, 598, 613
Multiculturalism, 110–14, 206, 377, 443

Multilateral Agreement on Investment (MAI), 172, 192, 348, 366

Multinational corporations. *See* Transnational corporations

Municipal government, 29, 96, 349, 402, 443, 540

N

National Action Committee on the Status of Women (NAC), 128, 131, 344, 347–48, 357–58

National Anti-Poverty Organization (NAPO), 155, 159, 344, 348

National Citizens' Coalition (NCC), 275, 278–79, 356

National Council of Welfare, 155, 159, 344, 353, 531

National Energy Board, 179, 183, 308–9, 530

National Energy Program (NEP), 53, 179, 183, 289, 419, 424, 568, 577

National Film Board, 43, 188μ

National Policy (1879), 52, 106, 176

National Post, 233, 235, 242, 616

National symbols, 6, 33, 199, 209, 215, 231, 288, 432, 475–81. *See also* Canadian national identity

Natural resources, 47–51, 53, 70, 80, 143, 146–47, 149, 176, 180–81, 375, 377, 384, 388, 403, 405, 408, 413, 420, 577

Neoconservatism, 181, 212, 235, 244, 309–10, 469–70, 576

New Brunswick, 84, 92, 94–95, 97, 265, 374, 384, 386, 393, 441. *See also* Atlantic provinces

New Deal, 309, 406, 485, 594

New Democratic Party (NDP), 5, 149, 152, 156, 219, 232, 265–68, 270–75, 277, 288–90, 292–94, 296–300, 302–10, 319–23, 326–27, 329, 346, 355, 420, 424, 563, 567, 576, 615

New Public Management, 536–38

Newfoundland and Labrador, 41, 55, 71–72, 386, 393, 419, 554, 570, 572, 576. *See also* Atlantic provinces

News leaks and management, 243, 493

Newspapers, 143, 179, 189, 218, 232, 234–44, 325. *See also* Mass media

Nisga'a First Nation and Treaty, 69, 71

Nonconfidence motion, 479, 546, 552, 567–68, 613

Nongovernmental organizations (NGOs), 8, 16

North, 42–43, 50, 96, 570

North American Aerospace Defence Command (NORAD), 173–74

North American Free Trade Agreement (NAFTA), 170–71, 420

North Atlantic Treaty Organization (NATO), 68, 72, 173–74

Northwest Territories, 50, 69, 77, 375–76

Notwithstanding clause. *See* Charter of Rights

Nova Scotia, 24–25, 77–78, 374, 435. *See also* Atlantic provinces

Nunavut, 50, 69–70, 77, 377

O

Oakes test, 433, 440

Oka standoff, 68, 72, 74–75, 220

Ombudsman, 534, 565

One-party dominance, 285, 293, 295, 558

Ontario, 49, 51–53, 55, 60, 73, 86, 94–96, 112, 125, 133, 158, 181, 214, 268, 279, 311, 322, 334, 374, 568–69, 577, 594, 596, 598

Opposition (Official), 461–62, 476, 545–46, 549–51, 557–59, 565–69, 578

Organization of Petroleum Exporting Countries (OPEC), 53, 169

P

Pacific Scandal, 41, 270, 285

Padlock Law, 431

Parizeau, Jacques, 93, 323, 391–92

Parliament, 354–55, 377, 464, 483, 486, 514, 535, 545, 601. *See also* House of Commons; Senate

Parliamentary Secretary, 492, 552

Parliamentary sovereignty, 27, 430, 546

Parliamentary system. *See* Westminster model

Parti Québécois (PQ), 91–94, 98, 289, 299, 305, 310, 382–83, 391, 444

Particularism, 206–7

Partisanship, 4, 232, 242, 262, 359, 361, 365, 479, 497, 519–20, 530, 563, 568, 571, 574, 597–98, 612–13, 615

Partnerships, 350, 352, 465–66, 538

Party advertising, 240, 271, 278, 321, 325–27

Party conventions, 240, 297–302

Party discipline, 27, 211, 295, 486, 552–54, 560, 565–66, 568–69, 578, 613

Party finance, 201, 219, 270–78, 296, 304–5, 321, 336, 570–71, 615

Party headquarters, 303–4, 321–22

Party identification, 230, 233, 331–32

Party ideology, 145, 190, 204–6, 249, 291, 293, 306–11, 446, 489, 528

Party leaders and leadership selection, 190, 262, 275, 278, 291, 293, 295–302, 305–6, 332–33, 485, 489, 564, 614

Party membership, 219, 296–97, 301–2

Party nominations, 113, 262–63, 278, 297, 329

Party policy and policymaking, 296, 300–2, 306–7

Party structures, 296, 302–6

Party whips, 553–54, 560, 564, 566

Peace, order, and good government, 204, 207, 405–7, 416–17

Peacekeeping, 169, 174–75, 209

Pearson, Lester, 89, 109, 174, 181, 187, 209, 288, 298, 301, 312, 411, 418, 420, 488, 490, 493–94, 496, 521, 567–68, 571

Peers, 231, 239–40, 328

Pensions, 120, 132, 150, 156, 158, 375, 379, 405, 409, 564, 571. *See also* Canada Pension Plan

Petro-Canada, 178, 183, 526, 528–29

Petroleum, 48–50, 53–54, 183, 413

Pharmaceutical Manufacturers Association of Canada. *See* Canada's Research-Based Pharmaceutical Companies

Pipelines, 42–43, 183, 288, 557

Plebiscites. *See* Referendums

Pluralism and Pluralist analysis, 9–12, 18–19, 34, 59, 79, 99, 115, 133, 161, 206, 222, 250, 279, 311–12, 336, 350, 365, 394, 399, 408, 423, 448, 480, 504, 539, 578, 603

Police, 15, 72, 78, 91, 115, 139, 207, 223, 439, 443, 448, 470–71, 534, 588. *See also* RCMP

Policy and Expenditure Management System (PEMS). *See* Expenditure Management System

Policy communities, 17, 350–51, 365, 465–66, 526

Policy instruments, 16, 463, 467–70

Policy Review Initiative, 538

Policymaking process, 459, 461–64, 489, 512–13, 546, 586

Political communication, 8–9, 229, 319, 342

Political culture, 17, 199–216, 331, 400, 447, 470, 528

Political equality, 201, 260

Political freedom, 201–2

Political knowledge and information, 13, 218, 231, 234, 245, 248, 330–31, 617

Political participation, 199, 216–23, 241, 331, 394

Political parties, 5, 11, 13, 110, 121, 201, 233, 239–40, 283–312, 319–336, 342, 365, 400, 552. *See also specific parties*

Political patronage, 283, 305, 475, 490, 492, 526, 530, 553, 597, 612–13, 615

Political protest, 25, 51–52, 72–73, 91, 120, 139, 220–21, 223, 240, 347, 356

Political recruitment, 8, 283, 319, 329

Political socialization, 8, 229–34, 249, 331

Political system, 3–9, 400

Politicians, 9, 12–13, 17, 121, 131, 201, 212, 222, 240–43, 248, 258, 293, 352, 390, 423, 440, 444–47, 460, 465, 471, 520, 539, 568, 603, 611, 614

Politics, 6, 15, 445, 519

Popular sovereignty, 200

Popular vote–seats ratio, 265–70, 333, 614

Population, 44–45

Pornography, 129, 435–36, 444

Postsecondary education, 73, 158, 208, 410–12, 420. *See also* Students; CFS

Poverty, 67, 76, 78, 114, 130, 153–59, 215–16, 460, 572, 612, 616

Power, 3, 6, 9–11, 465, 513, 587, 602

Prairie provinces, 49–50, 51–54, 214–15. *See also* West *and individual provinces*

Premiers, 46, 60, 75, 92, 94, 184, 218, 383–84, 390, 392, 401, 404, 408, 418, 420, 444, 524, 570, 572, 578

Prerogative powers, 477

Press gallery, 239, 551

Pressure groups, 5, 11–12, 18, 79, 96, 112–13, 130–32, 147, 152, 154–55, 201, 220, 249, 291, 293, 336, 341–66, 400, 461–63, 465–66, 501, 516, 524, 526, 553, 557, 561, 563, 596, 615–16

Primary industry. *See* Natural resources

Prime minister, 27, 261, 294, 350, 353–54, 374, 378, 462–63, 465, 475–504, 511, 513–14, 516, 520, 533, 546, 548, 550, 553, 555, 558, 564, 566, 570, 572–73, 577, 579, 598, 616

Prime Minister's Office (PMO), 243, 303, 306, 322, 361, 486, 494–95, 497, 499–500, 520, 562

Prime ministerial government, 483–87, 617

Prince Edward Island, 42, 217, 375–76, 393, 437, 538, 570. *See also* Atlantic provinces

Priorities and Planning Committee (of Cabinet), 490, 494, 496

Private bills. *See* Bills

Private members' bills and motions. *See* Bills

Privatization, 41–43, 158, 212, 308, 310, 401, 470, 528–29, 536, 538, 576

Privy Council, 374, 482

Privy Council Office (PCO), 465, 484–86, 494–502, 516, 520, 524, 533

Program Review, 536–37

Progressive Conservative Party, 5, 85–86, 110, 147, 219, 245, 266–77, 279, 284–93, 296–312, 319–23, 326–27, 330–35, 478, 490, 563, 576, 578, 615
Progressive Party, 286, 295
Proletariat. *See* Working class
Property and civil rights, 404, 406–7, 588–89
Proportional representation, 269
Prostitution, 129, 436
Province-building, 402, 423
Provinces, 29–30, 41, 44, 46–47, 51, 56, 70, 95, 121–23, 154–56, 158, 207, 213–15, 217, 231, 258–59, 264, 267–69, 275, 295, 304–5, 349, 374, 379–80, 383–85, 390, 399–424, 431, 447, 461–63, 465–66, 470, 486, 489–90, 495, 516–17, 525–26, 538, 547, 569, 572, 577, 588–92, 594, 596, 598–99. *See also individual provinces*
Public choice analysis, 9–10, 12–13, 18–19, 60, 99, 116, 134, 160, 222, 250, 279, 311, 336, 424, 470, 504, 540, 578
Public expenditures, 146, 468
Public opinion and public opinion polls, 229, 235, 245–50, 261, 278, 291, 293, 301, 320, 330, 336, 355, 435, 501, 557, 578
Public ownership, 469–70
Public policy, 3, 248, 283, 301, 310–11, 333, 350, 461, 498, 500, 520, 578
Public policy purpose, 42, 469, 528
Public (and private) sector, 3, 89, 91, 148, 150, 204–8, 443, 459, 461, 467, 528, 535, 537
Public Service Alliance of Canada (PSAC), 150, 521, 524, 537
Public Service Commission, 519, 527, 530, 533, 593
Public Works and Government Services, 518

Q
Quebec, 29, 44, 49, 55–58, 70, 83–100, 112–3, 129–30, 132, 181, 202, 207, 210–11, 215, 267–69, 278, 304, 307, 311, 322, 324, 327, 334–35, 349–50, 374, 376, 379, 381–93, 404, 409, 411, 419–21, 431, 444, 447, 521, 569–70, 572, 577, 586, 589, 594, 601, 611, 615
Quebec Act, 1774, 24, 84
Quebec language legislation, 91–92, 169, 434, 441–42, 444
Quebec nationalism, 49, 88–91, 288, 310, 381
Quebec separatism, 46, 78, 91, 93–94, 98, 243, 432
Queen, 33–34, 379, 475–82, 545

Question Period, 239–40, 485, 514, 533, 546–47, 550–51, 560, 566
Quiet Revolution (Quebec), 88–91, 94, 378, 381–82, 419

R
Rae, Bob, 123, 389
Railways, 35, 41, 52, 64, 146, 276, 415, 561
Rational decision-making, 419, 495, 503, 512
Reagan, Ronald, 181, 188
Reasonable limits clause, 433–36, 439–41, 443, 446, 449
Recall, 211, 569
Red Book, 301, 323, 333, 361, 499, 613, 616
Red Tories, 308–9
Redistribution (of seats), 257–60, 436–37, 576
Reference cases, 402, 592, 594
Referendums, 86, 92–94, 98, 200, 211, 336, 382, 389–92, 394, 569, 613
Reform Party, 5, 54, 83, 98, 114, 132, 190, 211, 219, 266–68, 272–76, 289–90, 293–300, 302–11, 319–24, 326–27, 329, 332–35, 444, 554, 562, 564, 569, 577–78, 615
Regional economic development programs, 58–59, 146
Regional economic disparities, 56–57
Regionalism, 46–47, 55, 60, 213–15, 289, 294, 334–35, 408, 494, 569, 572, 577, 615
Regulation (and deregulation), 42–43, 145, 212, 307–10, 460, 468–70, 531
Regulations, 350, 358, 407, 464, 466, 483, 512, 534, 557, 562, 572
Regulatory tribunals, 178, 186, 465, 520, 529, 531, 534, 536, 586, 592, 613
Religion, 84–85, 131, 157, 207, 233, 240, 334, 344, 346, 404, 434, 443, 490–91, 571
Representation by population, 30, 201, 259–60, 279, 380, 403, 569
Representative bureaucracy, 520–23
Representative democracy, 200, 221, 336
Representative government, 24
Research and development (R & D), 47, 177
Reservation, disallowance, and declaratory power, 403, 415
Residential schools, 67, 77
Responsible government, 24–25, 27–28, 378, 552, 567–68
Returning officer, 262, 278
Riel, Louis, 65, 85, 220, 231, 285
Right, 307–11
Rodriguez, Sue, 429, 437

Rogers, Ted, 142, 237, 276

Roman Catholic Church in Quebec, 24, 57, 84, 88, 97, 215, 233

Royal Canadian Legion, 115, 344, 346, 352

Royal Canadian Mounted Police (RCMP), 115, 207–8, 308, 364, 476, 513, 523–24, 531–32

Royal commissions, 301, 355, 462–63, 467, 476, 482, 531–32, 586

    Aboriginal peoples, 76–77, 532, 611

    bilingualism and biculturalism, 68, 89, 110

    dominion–provincial relations, 409–10, 532

    economic union and development prospects, 181, 532

    electoral reform and party finance, 247, 260, 263, 277–78, 326–27, 615

    newspapers, 235, 249

    status of women, 123, 130

Royal Proclamation of 1763, 23, 64, 74, 442

Rule adjudication, 8, 373, 511–12, 530, 585

Rule application, 8, 373, 511

Rule making, 8, 342, 373, 481, 511, 546

Rule of Law, 31, 150, 430–31

S

Safe seats, 264, 333, 548, 553

St. Laurent, Louis, 286–87, 298–99, 487–88, 493–95

St. Lawrence Seaway, 40, 46

Saskatchewan, 85, 96, 156, 215, 287, 295, 308, 349, 376, 419, 424, 436, 444. *See also* Prairie provinces; West

Sauvé, Jeanne, 123–24

Scandals and corruption, 270, 613

Schreyer, Ed, 477, 479

Second World War, 34, 86–87, 109, 112, 173, 287, 409, 419, 470

Secondary industry. *See* Manufacturing

Self-regulation, 352, 354, 467

Senate (and Senate reform), 24, 26–28, 30, 60, 129, 145, 181, 214, 258, 260, 270, 275, 303, 355, 374–75, 379, 386, 390, 403–4, 462, 464, 477, 482, 484–85, 489–90, 520, 545, 553, 556–67, 561–62, 569–78, 613, 615. *See also* Triple-E Senate.

Separate schools. *See* Religion

Service agencies, 537–38

Service sector, 47–49, 150

Sexual harassment and sexual assault, 129, 130, 438

Sexual orientation, 131–33, 347, 355, 441, 444, 554–55, 611

Shared-cost programs, 89, 157, 389, 410–12, 418, 422

Sikhs, 115

Social Credit Party (including Créditistes), 53, 243, 287–88, 294–95, 415

Social movements, 190, 297, 347–48, 448

Social programs, 147, 155–59, 169, 206, 308–10, 410–12, 421–22, 424, 612

Social Union, 382, 393, 421–22

Socialism. *See* Democratic Socialism

Somalia, 175

Southam, 235, 247, 439, 449

Sovereignty association, 92, 382–83

Special Operating Agencies, 537

Speech from the Throne, 476, 479, 482, 499, 548–49, 566, 568

Spending power, 386, 411, 421–22, 468

Spin doctors, 243, 328

Sport, 190, 347, 556

Stanfield, Robert, 263, 288–89, 298–99, 301, 309

Staples theory, 47

State. *See* Government

State-centred analysis, 9–10, 16–19, 34, 60, 79, 94, 99, 112, 116, 133, 160, 191, 222, 250, 280, 312, 336–37, 365, 393–94, 424, 449, 471, 503, 539, 579, 603,

Statute of Westminster, 33, 375, 378–79

Strikes, 149, 202, 220, 431, 436, 471, 524, 571

Structural-functionalism, 8–9

Students, 157–59, 220, 349. *See also* CFS; Education; Postsecondary education

Subcultures and limited identities, 11, 213–16, 222

Subordinate legislation. *See* Regulations

Support, 6–7

Supreme Court of Canada, 5, 124, 374, 377, 380, 382–86, 392–93, 407, 433–49, 593–600, 603

Symbolic outputs, 467, 471

T

Tariffs, 32, 52, 170, 172, 176, 179–80, 307

Task Force on Canadian Unity, 46, 93, 269, 382–83

Task forces, 467, 494, 531–32, 562

Tax expenditures, 147, 468, 470

Taxation, 56, 78, 128, 140, 143, 145–48, 158, 179, 187–88, 205–6, 307–10, 366, 403, 408–10, 412–13, 418, 459, 469–71, 548, 593, 612

Taxation agreements (federal–provincial), 88, 409–10, 417–18

Teleglobe Canada, 42–43, 528–29

Telesat, 42–43, 529

Television and radio, 43, 184–86, 189, 236–44, 288, 291, 299, 325–29, 551, 568, 616

Territories, 46–47, 69, 77, 96, 380, 400

Tertiary industry. *See* Service sector

Think tanks, 181, 233–34, 244, 459

Third-party advertising, 275–78, 355, 435

Thomson, Ken, 141–43, 235, 247, 439

Tobacco, 341, 345, 352, 359, 434, 446, 449, 556

Toronto Star, 233, 235

Trade and trade agreements, 150, 170–71, 179–82, 212, 407, 469, 611

Trans-Canada Highway, 41

Trans-Canada Pipelines. *See* Pipelines

Transnational corporations, 8, 15–16, 150, 171–72, 176–77, 184, 293

Transportation, 41–43, 52

Treasury Board and Treasury Board Secretariat, 465, 488, 494–502, 519–21, 523–25, 527, 530, 533

Treaties, 32, 64–65, 69, 71–72, 403, 407, 477, 482

Triple-E Senate, 190, 388, 577

Trudeau, Pierre, 52–53, 68, 74, 89–94, 97–99, 110, 112, 116, 174, 181, 183, 187, 212, 287–89, 298–301, 305, 312, 332, 349, 382–86, 418–20, 432, 437, 442, 444, 447, 479, 485–90, 492, 494–95, 498, 503, 549, 567–68, 571, 577, 598

Tupper, Charles, 478, 488

Turner, John, 147, 261, 288, 298–300, 327, 487–89, 495, 504, 575, 598

U

Unemployment and unemployment insurance, 57, 67, 78, 114, 151–52, 154, 156, 158, 375, 379, 405–6, 409, 437, 441, 593

Union Government, 86, 286

Union Nationale. *See* Maurice Duplessis

Unions, 148–51, 156, 184, 207, 209, 270–73, 275, 277, 292, 330, 334, 357, 364, 410, 436, 446, 449, 524

United Alternative, 297, 311

United Empire Loyalists, 24, 64, 84, 204, 309

United Farmers. *See* Progressive Party

United Nations and League of Nations, 32, 157, 159, 168–69, 175, 209

United States, 16, 24–26, 28–30, 34, 39, 43–44, 167–90, 203–9, 218, 237–38, 244, 270, 308–9, 327, 360, 430, 446, 462–63, 481–82, 486, 489, 553, 596, 611, 614, 616

Universal Classification Standard, 517, 519, 524

Upper class, 14–16, 97, 139–47, 156, 292, 334, 602

V

Values (including U.S. influence on and differences from), 19, 190, 203–13, 230–31, 238, 249, 430

Victoria Charter, 381–82

Violence, 25, 34, 67, 72–73, 86, 91, 130, 147, 149, 209, 220, 356

Visible minorities, 108–10, 112, 320–21, 521–23

Voter turnout, 216–18, 247

Voters, 12–14, 141, 246, 330–36, 390

Voters' list, 262, 329–30

W

Wage and price controls, 289, 309, 333

War Measures Act and Emergencies Act, 91, 202, 377, 417, 432, 470

Welfare, 154, 158–59

Welfare state, 155–59, 287, 310, 410

Wells, Clyde, 80, 385–86

West, 45, 181, 208, 214–15, 267–69, 289, 292, 307, 310, 322, 334–35, 390–91, 419–20, 490, 570, 594, 615. *See also* Prairie Provinces *and individual provinces*

Western alienation, 51–55, 214

Westminster model, 26–28, 30, 210, 545–46

Weston, Galen, 142–44

White Paper on Indians, 68, 73

White papers, 463, 494

Wilson, Bertha, 124

Wilson, Michael, 145, 147

Women, 74, 119–34, 150, 154, 169, 181, 203, 206, 208, 264, 278, 303, 320–21, 329, 347–48, 354, 385–86, 438, 441, 443, 491, 521–23, 571, 599, 611

Women's movement, 120, 123, 128

Woodsworth, J.S., 287, 298

Working class, 14–16, 139–40, 148–51, 159, 291–92, 329, 334, 571, 599, 602

World Trade Organization (WTO), 169, 179, 187

Y

Yukon, 50, 69, 77, 79

To the owner of this book

We hope that you have enjoyed Rand Dyck's *Canadian Politics,* Third Edition (ISBN 0-17-616792-7), and we would like to know as much about your experiences with this text as you would care to offer. Only through your comments and those of others can we learn how to make this a better text for future readers.

School _____ Your instructor's name _____

Course _____ Was the text required? _____ Recommended? _____

1. What did you like the most about *Canadian Politics?*

_____

_____

_____

2. How useful was this text for your course?

_____

_____

_____

3. Do you have any recommendations for ways to improve the next edition of this text?

_____

_____

_____

4. In the space below or in a separate letter, please write any other comments you have about the book. (For example, please feel free to comment on reading level, writing style, terminology, design features, and learning aids.)

_____

_____

_____

_____

Optional

Your name _____ Date _____

May Nelson Thomson Learning quote you, either in promotion for *Canadian Politics* or in future publishing ventures?

Yes _____ No _____

Thanks!

You can also send your comments to us via e-mail at
college@nelson.com

PLEASE TAPE SHUT. DO NOT STAPLE.

TAPE SHUT

TAPE SHUT

- - - - FOLD HERE - - - -

MAIL▶POSTE
Canada Post Corporation
Société canadienne des postes
Postage paid   Port payé
if mailed in Canada   si posté au Canada
Business Reply   Réponse d'affaires

0066102399   01

Nelson

0066102399-M1K5G4-BR01

NELSON THOMSON LEARNING
HIGHER EDUCATION
PO BOX 60225 STN BRM B
TORONTO ON M7Y 2H1

TAPE SHUT

TAPE SHUT